ADVANCED TEXTS IN ECONC

General Editors

C. W. J. Granger G. E. Mizon

STOCHASTIC LIMIT THEORY

An Introduction for Econometricians

JAMES DAVIDSON

Oxford University Press
1994

Oxford University Press, Walton Street, Oxford OX2 6DP
Oxford New York
Athens Auckland Bangkok Bombay
Calcutta Cape Town Dar es Salaam Delhi
Florence Hong Kong Istanbul Karachi
Kuala Lumpur Madras Madrid Melbourne
Mexico City Nairobi Paris Singapore
Taipei Tokyo Toronto
and associated companies in
Berlin Ibadan

Oxford is a trade mark of Oxford University Press

Published in the United States
by Oxford University Press Inc., New York

British Library Cataloguing in Publication Data
Data available

Library of Congress Cataloging in Publication Data
Data available
ISBN 0–19–877402–8
ISBN 0–19–877403–6 (Pbk)

1 3 5 7 9 10 8 6 4 2

Printed in Great Britain
on acid-free paper by
Biddles Ltd., Guildford and King's Lynn

For
Lynette,
Julia, and Nicola.

'... what in me is dark
Illumine, what is low raise and support,
That, to the height of this great argument,
I may assert Eternal Providence,
And justify the ways of God to men.'

Paradise Lost, Book I, 16-20

Contents

Part III: Theory of Stochastic Processes

Preface

Recent years have seen a marked increase in the mathematical sophistication of econometric research. While the theory of linear parametric models which forms the backbone of the subject makes an extensive and clever use of matrix algebra, the statistical prerequisites of this theory are comparatively simple. But now that these models are pretty thoroughly understood, research is concentrated increasingly on the less tractable questions, such as nonlinear and nonparametric estimation and nonstationary data generation processes. The standard econometrics texts are no longer an adequate guide to this new technical literature, and a sound understanding of the probabilistic foundations of the subject is becoming less and less of a luxury.

The asymptotic theory traditionally taught to students of econometrics is founded on a small body of classical limit theorems, such as Khinchine's weak law of large numbers and the Lindeberg-Lévy central limit theorem, relevant to the stationary and independent data case. To deal with linear stochastic difference equations, appeal can be made to the results of Mann and Wald (1943a), but even these are rooted in the assumption of independent and identically distributed disturbances. This foundation has become increasingly inadequate to sustain the expanding edifice of econometric inference techniques, and recent years have seen a systematic attempt to construct a less restrictive limit theory. Hall and Heyde's *Martingale Limit Theory and its Application* (1980) is an important landmark, as are a series of papers by econometricians including among others Halbert White, Ronald Gallant, Donald Andrews, and Herman Bierens. This work introduced to the econometrics profession pioneering research into limit theory under dependence, done in the preceding decades by probabilists such as J. L. Doob, I. A. Ibragimov, Patrick Billingsley, Robert Serfling, Murray Rosenblatt, and Donald McLeish.

These latter authors devised various concepts of limited dependence for general nonstationary time series. The concept of a martingale has a long history in probability, but it was primarily Doob's *Stochastic Processes* (1953) that brought it to prominence as a tool of limit theory. Martingale processes behave like the wealth of a gambler who undertakes a succession of fair bets; the differences of a martingale (the net winnings at each step) are unpredictable from lagged information. Powerful limit theorems are available for martingale difference sequences involving no further restrictions on the dependence of the process. Ibragimov and Rosenblatt respectively defined *strong mixing* and *uniform mixing* as characterizations of 'limited memory', or independence at long range. McLeish defined the notion of a *mixingale*, the asymptotic counterpart of a martingale difference, becoming unpredictable m steps ahead as m becomes large. This is a weaker property than mixing because it involves only low-order moments of the distribution, but mixingales possess most of those attributes of mixing processes needed to make limit theorems work. Very important from the econometrician's point of view is the property dubbed by Gallant and White (1988) *near-epoch dependence* from a phrase in one of McLeish's papers, although the idea itself goes back to Billingsley (1968) and Ibragimov (1962). The mixing property may not be preserved by transformations of sequences involving an infinite number of lags, but near-epoch dependence is a condition under which the outputs of a dynamic econometric model can be shown, given some further conditions, to be mixingales when the inputs are mixing. Applications of these results are increasingly in evidence in the econometric literature; Gallant and White's monograph provides an excellent survey of the possibilities.

Limit theorems impose restrictions on the amount of dependence between sequence coordinates, and on their marginal distributions. Typically, the probability of outliers must be controlled by requiring the existence of higher-order moments, but there are almost always trade-offs between dependence and moment restrictions, allowing one to buy more of one at the price of less of the other. The fun of proving limit theorems has been to see how far out the envelope of sufficient conditions can be stretched, in one direction or another. To complicate matters, one can get results both by putting limits on the rate of approach to independence (the rate of mixing), and by limiting the *type* of dependence (the martingale approach), as well as by combining both types of constraint (the mixingale approach). The results now available are remarkably powerful, judged by the yardstick of the classical theory. Proofs of necessity are elusive and the limits to the envelope are not yet known with certainty, but they probably lie not too far beyond the currently charted points.

Perhaps the major development in time-series econometrics in the 1980s has been the theory of cointegration, and dealing with the distributions of estimators when time series are generated by unit root processes also requires a new type of limit theory. The essential extra ingredient of this theory is the *functional central limit theorem* (FCLT). The proof of these weak convergence results calls for a limit theory for the space of functions, which throws up some interesting problems which have no counterpart in ordinary probability. These ideas were pioneered by Russian probabilists in the 1950s, notably A. V. Skorokhod and Yu. V. Prokhorov. It turns out that FCLTs hold under properties generally similar to those for the ordinary CLT (though with a crucial difference), and they can be analysed with the same kind of tools, imposing limitations on dependence and outliers.

The probabilistic literature which deals with issues of this kind has been seen as accessible to practising econometricians only with difficulty. Few concessions are made to the nonspecialist, and the concerns of probabilists, statisticians, and econometricians are frequently different. Textbooks on stochastic processes (Cox and Miller 1965 is a distinguished example) often give prominence to topics that econometricians would regard as fairly specialized (e.g. Markov chains, processes in continuous time), while the treatment of important issues like nonstationarity gets tucked away under the heading of advanced or optional material if not omitted altogether. Probability texts are written for students of mathematics and assume a familiarity with the folklore of the subject that econometricians may lack. The intellectual investment required is one that students and practitioners are often, quite reasonably, disinclined to make.

It is with issues of this sort in mind that the present book has been written. The first objective has been to provide a coherent and unified account of modern asymptotic theory, which can function as both a course text, and as a work of reference. The second has been to provide a grounding in the requisite mathematics and probability theory, making the treatment sufficiently self-contained that even readers with limited mathematical training might make use of it. This is not to say that the material is elementary. Even when the mathematics is mastered, the reasoning can be intricate and demand a degree of patience to absorb. Proofs for nearly all the results are provided, but readers should never hesitate to pass over these when they impede progress. The book is also intended to be useful as a reference for students and researchers who only wish to know basic things, like the meaning of technical terms, and the variety of limit results available. But, that said, it will not have succeeded in its aim unless the reader is sometimes stimulated to gain a deeper understanding of the material—if for no better reason, because this is a theory abounding in mathematical elegance, and technical ingenuity which is often dazzling.

Outline of the Work

Part I covers almost all the mathematics used subsequently. Calculus and matrix algebra are not treated, but in any case there is little of either in the book. Most readers should probably begin by reading Chapters 1 and 2, and perhaps the first sections only of Chapters 3 and 4, noting the definitions and examples but skipping all but the briefest proofs initially. These chapters contain some difficult material, which does not all need to be mastered immediately. Chapters 5 and 6 are strictly required only for Chapter 21 and Part VI, and should be passed over on first reading. Nearly everything needed to read the probability literature is covered in these chapters, with perhaps one notable exception—the theory of normed spaces. Some treatments in probability use a Hilbert space framework, but it can be avoided. The number of applications exploiting this approach seemed currently too small to justify the added technical overhead, although future developments may require this judgement to be revised.

Part II covers what for many readers will be more familiar territory. Chapters 7, 8, and 9 contain essential background to be skimmed or studied in more depth, as appropriate. It is the collections of inequalities in §9.3 and §9.5 that we will have the most call to refer to subsequently. The content of Chapter 10 is probably less familiar, and is very important. Most readers will want to study this chapter carefully sooner or later. Chapter 11 can be passed over initially, but is needed in conjunction with Part V.

In Part III the main business of the work begins. Chapter 12 gives an introduction to the main concepts arising in the study of stochastic sequences. Chapters 13 and 14 continue the discussion by reviewing concepts of dependence, and Chapters 15, 16, and 17 deal with specialized classes of sequence whose properties make them amenable to the application of limit theorems. Nearly all readers will want to study Chapters 12, 13, and the earlier sections of 14 and 15 before going further, whereas Chapters 16 and 17 are rather technical and should probably be avoided until the context of these results is understood.

In Parts IV and V we arrive at the study of the limit theorems themselves. The aim has been to contrast alternative ways of approaching these problems, and to present a general collection of results ranging from the elementary to the very general. Chapter 18 is devoted to fundamentals, and everyone should read this before going further. Chapter 19 compares classical techniques for proving laws of large numbers, depending on the existence of second moments, with more modern methods. Although the concept of convergence in probability is adequate in many econometric applications, proofs of strong consistency of estimators are increasingly popular in the econometrics literature, and techniques for dependent processes are considered in Chapter 20. Uniform stochastic convergence is an essential concept in the study of econometric estimators, although it has only recently been systematically researched. Chapter 21 contains a synthesis of results that have appeared in print in the last year or two.

Part V contrasts the classical central limit theorems for independent processes with the modern results for martingale differences and general dependent processes. Chapter 22 contains the essentials of weak convergence theory for random variables. The treatment is reasonably complete, although one neglected topic, to which much space is devoted in the probability literature, is convergence to stable laws for sequences with infinite variance. This material has found few applications in econometrics to date, although its omission is another judgement that may need to be revised in the future. Chapter 23 describes the classic CLTs for independent processes, and Chapter 24 treats modern techniques for dependent, heterogeneous processes.

Part VI deals with the functional central limit theorem and related convergence results, including convergence to limits that can be identified with stochastic integrals. A number of new mathematical challenges are presented by this theory, and readers who wish to tackle it seriously will probably want to go back and apply themselves to Chapters 5 and 6 first. Chapter 26 is both the hardest going and the least essential to subsequent developments. It deals with the theory of weak convergence on metric spaces at a greater level of generality than we strictly need, and is the one section where topological arguments seriously intrude. Almost certainly one should go first to Chapter 27, referring back as needed for definitions and statements of the prerequisite theorems, and pursue the rationale for these results further only as interest dictates. Chapter 28 is likewise a technical prologue to Chapers 29 and 30, and might be skipped over at first reading. The meat of this part of the book is in these last two chapters. Results are given on the multivariate invariance principle for heterogeneous dependent processes, paralleling the central limit theorems of Chapter 24.

A number of the results in the text are, to the author's knowledge, new. These include **14.13/14**, **19.11**, **20.18/19**, **20.21**, **24.6/7/14**, **29.14/29.18**, and **30.13/14**, although some have now appeared in print elsewhere.

Further Reading

There is a huge range of texts in print covering the relevant mathematics and probability, but the following titles were, for one reason or another, the most frequently consulted in the course of writing this book. T. M. Apostol's *Mathematical Analysis* (2nd edition) hits just the right note for the basic bread-and-butter results. For more advanced material, Dieudonné's *Foundations of Modern Analysis* and Royden's *Real Analysis* are well-known references, the latter being the more user-friendly although the treatment is often fairly concise. Halmos's classic *Measure Theory* and Kingman and Taylor's *Introduction to Measure and Probability* are worth having access to. Willard's *General Topology* is a clear and well-organized text to put alongside Kelley's classic of the same name. Halmos's *Naive Set Theory* is a slim volume whose main content falls outside our sphere of interest, but is a good read in its own right. Strongly recommended is Borowski and Borwein's *Collins Reference Dictionary of Mathematics*; one can learn more about mathematics in less time by browsing in this little book, and following up the cross references, than by any other method I can think of. For a stimulating introduction to metric spaces see Michael Barnsley's popular *Fractals Everywhere*.

For further reading on probability, one might begin by browsing the slim volume that started the whole thing off, Kolmogorov's *Foundations of the Theory of Probability*. Then, Billingsley's *Probability and Measure* is an inspiration, both authoritative and highly readable. Breiman's *Probability* has a refreshingly informal style, and just the right emphasis. Chung's *A Course in Probability Theory* is idiosyncratic in parts, but strongly recommended. The value of the classic texts, Loève's *Probability Theory* (4th edition) and Feller's *An Introduction to Probability Theory and its Applications* (3rd edition) is self-evident, although these are dense and detailed books that can take a little time and patience to get into, and are chiefly for reference. Cramér's *Mathematical Methods of Statistics* is now old-fashioned, but still useful. Two more recent titles are Shiryayev's *Probability*, and R. M. Dudley's tough but stimulating *Real Analysis and Probability*.

Of the more specialized monographs on stochastic convergence, the following titles (in order of publication date) are all important: Doob, *Stochastic Processes*; Révész, *The Laws of Large Numbers*; Parthasarathy, *Probability Measures on Metric Spaces*; Billingsley, *Convergence of Probability Measures*; Iosifescu and Theodorescu, *Random Processes and Learning*; Ibragimov and Linnik, *Independent and Stationary Sequences of Random Variables*; Stout, *Almost Sure Convergence*; Lukacs, *Stochastic Convergence*; Hall and Heyde, *Martingale Limit Theory and its Application*; Pollard, *Convergence of Stochastic Processes*; Eberlein and Taqqu (eds.), *Dependence in Probability and Statistics*.

Doob is the founding father of the subject, and his book its Old Testament. Of the rest, Billingsley's is the most original and influential. Ibragimov and Linnik's essential monograph is now, alas, hard to obtain. The importance of Hall and Heyde was mentioned above. Pollard's book takes up the weak convergence story more or less where Billingsley leaves off, and much of the material complements the coverage of the present volume. The Eberlein-Taqqu collection contains up-to-date accounts of mixing theory, covering some related topics outside the range of the present work. The literature on Brownian motion and stochastic integration is extensive, but Karatzas and Shreve's *Brownian Motion and Stochastic Calculus* is a recent and comprehensive source for reference, and Kopp's *Martingales and Stochastic Integrals* was found useful at several points.

These items receive an individual mention by virtue of being between hard covers. References to the journal literature will be given in context, but it is worth mentioning that the four papers by Donald McLeish, appearing between 1974 and 1977, form possibly the most influential single contribution to our subject.

Finally, titles dealing with applications and related contributions include Serfling, *Approximation Theorems of Mathematical Statistics*; White, *Asymptotic Theory for Econometricians*; Gallant, *Nonlinear Statistical Methods*; Gallant and White, *A Unified Theory of Estimation and Inference for Nonlinear Dynamic Models*, Amemiya, *Advanced Econometrics*. All of these are highly recommended for forming a view of what stochastic limit theory is for, and why it matters.

Acknowledgements

The idea for this book originated in 1987, in the course of writing a chapter of mathematical and statistical prerequisites for a projected textbook of econometric theory. The initial, very tentative draft was completed during a stay at the University of California (San Diego) Department of Economics in 1988, whose hospitality is gratefully acknowledged. It has grown a great deal since then, and getting it finished has involved a struggle with competing academic commitments as well as the demands of family life. My family deserve special thanks for their forbearance.

My colleague Peter Robinson has been a great source of encouragement and help, and has commented on various drafts. Other people who have read portions of the manuscript and provided invaluable feedback, not least in pointing out my errors, include Getullio Silveira, Robert de Jong, and especially Elizabeth Boardman, who took immense trouble to help me lick the chapters on mathematics into shape. I am also most grateful to Don Andrews, Graham Brightwell, Søren Johansen, Donald McLeish, Peter Phillips, Hal White, and a number of anonymous referees for helpful conversations, comments and advice. None of these people is responsible for the various flaws that doubtless remain.

The book was written using the ChiWriter 4 technical word processor, and after conversion to Postscript format was produced as camera-ready copy on a Hewlett-Packard LaserJet 4M printer, direct from the original files. I must particularly thank Cay Horstmann, of Horstmann Software Design Corp., for his technical assistance with this task.

London, June 1994

Mathematical Symbols and Abbreviations

In the text, the symbol □ is used to terminate examples and definitions, and also theorems and lemmas unless the proof follows directly. The symbol ■ terminates proofs. References to numbered expressions are enclosed in parentheses. References to numbered theorems, examples etc. are given in bold face. References to chapter sections are preceded by §.

In statements of theorems, roman numbers (i), (ii), (iii),... are used to indicate the parts of a multi-part result. Lower case letters (a), (b), (c),... are used to itemize the assumptions or conditions specified in a theorem, and also the components of a definition.

The page numbers below refer to fuller definitions or examples of use, as appropriate.

$\lvert . \rvert$	absolute value	20
$\lVert . \rVert_p$	L_p-norm	132
$\lVert . \rVert$	Euclidean norm;	23
	also fineness (of a partition)	438
$\Rightarrow$	weak convergence (of measures);	347, 418
	also implication	19
$\uparrow, \downarrow$	monotone convergence	23
$\to$	convergence	23
$\xrightarrow{as}$	almost sure convergence	179
$\xrightarrow{D}$	convergence in distribution	347
$\xrightarrow{Lp}$	convergence in L_p norm	287
$\xrightarrow{pr}$	convergence in probability	284
$\mapsto$	mapping, function	6
$\circ$	composition of mappings	7
$\sim$	equivalence in order of magnitude (of sequences);	32
	also equivalence in distribution (of r.v.s)	123
$\dot{+}$	addition modulo 1	46
$-$, $/$	set difference	3
$\leq, \geq$	partial ordering, inequality	5
$<, >$	strict ordering, strict inequality	5
$\ll$	order of magnitude inequality (sequences);	32
	also absolutely continuous (measures)	69
$\perp$	mutually singular (of measures)	69
$1_A(.)$	indicator function	53
a.e.	almost everywhere	38
AR	autoregressive process	218
ARMA	autoregressive moving average process	215
a.s., a.s.[μ]	almost surely, (with resp. to p.m. μ)	113

A^c	complement of A	3
$\overline{A}$, $(A)^-$	closure of A	21, 77
A^o	interior of A	21, 77
α_m	strong mixing coefficient	209
$\aleph_0$	aleph-nought (cardinality of $\mathbb{N}$)	8
$\forall$	'for every'	12
$B(n,p)$	Binomial distribution with parameters n and p	122
$\mathcal{B}$	Borel field	16
CLT	central limit theorem	364
ch.f.	characteristic function	162
c.d.f.	cumulative distribution function	117
$C_{[0,1]}$	continuous functions on the unit interval	437
$\subseteq$, $\supseteq$	set containment	3
$\subset$, $\supset$	strict containment	3
$\chi^2(n)$	chi-squared distribution with n degrees of freedom	124
$d(x,y)$	distance between x and y	75
$D_{[0,1]}$	cadlag functions on the unit interval	456
$\mathbb{D}$	dyadic rationals	26
Δ	symmetric difference	3
∂A	boundary of A	21, 77
$\in$	set membership	3
ess sup	essential supremum	117
$E(.)$	expectation	128
$E(.\|x)$	conditional expectation (on variable x)	144
$E(.\|\mathcal{G})$	conditional expectation (on σ-field $\mathcal{G}$)	147
$\exists$	'there exists'	15
f^+, f^-	positive, negative parts of f	61
FCLT	functional central limit theorem	450
$F(.)$	cumulative distribution function	118
$\phi_X(.)$	characteristic function of X	162
ϕ_m	uniform mixing coefficient	209
iff	'if and only if'	5
inf	infimum	12
i.i.d.	independently and identically distributed	193
i.o.	infinitely often	281
in pr.	in probability	284
LIE	law of iterated expectations	149
LIL	law of the iterated logarithm	408
lim	limit (sets); *also* limit (numbers)	13, 23
limsup, $\overline{\lim}$	superior limit (sets); *also* superior limit (numbers)	13, 25
liminf, $\underline{\lim}$	inferior limit (sets); *also* inferior limit (numbers)	13, 25
$L(n)$	slowly varying function	32
L_p-NED	near-epoch dependent in L_p-norm	261
MA	moving average process	193
$m(.)$	Lebesgue measure	37

m.d.	martingale difference	230
m.g.f.	moment-generating function	162
m.s.	mean square	287
$\mathbb{M}$	space of measures	418
$N(\mu,\sigma^2)$	Gaussian distribution with mean μ and variance σ^2	123
$\mathbb{N}$	natural numbers	8
$\mathbb{N}_0$	$\mathbb{N} \cup \{0\}$	8
$\cap$, $\bigcap$	intersection	3
$m \wedge n$	minimum of m and n	258
$O(.)$	'Big Oh', order of magnitude relation	31
$o(.)$	'Little Oh', strict order of magnitude relation	31
$O_p(.)$	stochastic order relation	187
$o_p(.)$	strict stochastic order relation	187
$\varnothing$	null set	8
p.d.f.	probability density function	122
p.m.	probability measure	111
$P(.)$	probability	111
$P(.\|A)$	conditional probability (on event A)	113
$P(.\|\mathcal{G})$	conditional probability (on σ-field $\mathcal{G}$)	114
Π, $\prod$	product of numbers;	167
	also partition of an interval	58
π	product measure	64
$\pi_t(.)$	coordinate projection	434
$\mathbb{Q}$	rational numbers	9
r.v.	random variable	117
$R_{[0,1]}$	real valued functions on [0,1]	434
xRy	relation	5
$\mathbb{R}$	real line	10
$\mathbb{R}^+$	non-negative reals	11
$\overline{\mathbb{R}}$	extended real line, $\mathbb{R} \cup \{-\infty,+\infty\}$	12
$\overline{\mathbb{R}}^+$	$\mathbb{R}^+ \cup \{+\infty\}$	12
$\mathbb{R}^n$	n-dimensional Euclidean space	11
s.e.	stochastic equicontinuity	336
s.s.e.	strong stochastic equicontinuity	336
SLLN	strong law of large numbers	289
sup	supremum	12
$S(x,\varepsilon)$	ε-neighbourhood, sphere	20, 76
S_n	sum of random variables	290
s_n^2	variance of S_n	364
$\sigma(\mathcal{C})$	σ-field generated by collection $\mathcal{C}$	16
$\sigma(X)$	σ-field generated by r.v. X	146
$\int f dx$	Lebesgue integral	57
$\int f d\mu$, $\int f dF$	Lebesgue-Stieltjes integral	57
$\int f dP$	expected value (integral with resp. to p.m.)	128
Σ, $\sum$	sum	31

$T\omega$	shift transformation	191
$\cup$, $\bigcup$	union	3
$U[a,b]$	uniform distribution on interval $[a,b]$	123
$\vee$, $\bigvee$	union of σ-fields	17
$m \vee n$	maximum of m and n	257
WLLN	weak law of large numbers	289
w.p.1	with probability 1	113
$\bar{X}_n$	sample mean of sequence $\{X_t\}_1^n$	289
$\times$, X	Cartesian product	5
$\otimes$	σ-field of product sets	48
$\mathbb{Z}$	integers	9
$\{.\}$	set designation; *also* sequence, array	3, 23
$\{.\}_1^\infty$, $\{.\}_{-\infty}^\infty$	infinite sequences	23
$\{\{.\}\}$	array	34
$[x]$	largest integer $\leq x$	9
$[a,b]$	closed interval bounded by a,b	11
(a,b)	open interval bounded by a,b	11
$(\Omega,\mathcal{F})$	measurable space	36
$(\Omega,\mathcal{F},\mu)$	measure space	36
$(\Omega,\bar{\mathcal{F}},\bar{\mu})$	complete measure space	38
$(\Omega,\mathcal{F},P)$	probability space	111
$(\mathbb{S},d)$	metric space	75
$(\mathbb{X},\tau)$	topological space	93

Common usages

$A,B,C,D,\ldots$	sets
$X,Y,Z,\ldots$	random variables
$\boldsymbol{X},\boldsymbol{Y},\boldsymbol{Z},\ldots$	random vectors
$f,g,h,\ldots$	functions
ε,δ,η	positive constants
B,M	bounding constants
$\mathcal{A},\mathcal{C},\mathcal{D},\mathcal{V},\ldots$	collections of subsets
$\mathcal{F},\mathcal{G},\mathcal{H},\ldots$	σ-fields
$\mathbb{S},\mathbb{T},\mathbb{X},\ldots$	spaces
$\mu,\nu,\ldots$	measures
d,ρ	metrics
τ	topology

I

MATHEMATICS

1
Sets and Numbers

1.1 Basic Set Theory

A *set* is any specified collection of objects. In this book the objects in question are often numbers, but they may also be functions, or other sets, or indeed wholly arbitrary, to be determined by the context in which the theory is applied. In any analysis there is a set which defines the universe of discourse, containing all the objects under consideration, and in what follows, sets denoted A, B etc., are subsets of a set X, with generic element x.

Set membership is denoted by the symbol '$\in$', $x \in A$ meaning 'x belongs to the set A'. To show sets A and B have the same elements, one writes $A = B$. The usual way to define a set is by a descriptive statement enclosed in braces, so that for example $A = \{x: x \in B\}$ defines membership of A in terms of membership of B, and is an alternative way of writing $A = B$. Another way to denote set membership is by *labels*. If a set has n elements one can write $A = \{x_i,\ i = 1,\ldots,n\}$, but any set of labels will do. The statement $A = \{x_\alpha,\ \alpha \in C\}$ says that A is the set of elements bearing labels α contained in another set C, called the *index set* for A. The labels (indices) need not be numbers, and can be any convenient objects at all. Sets whose elements are sets (the word 'collection' tends to be preferred in this context) are denoted by upper-case script characters. $A \in \mathscr{C}$ denotes that the set A is in the collection $\mathscr{C}$, or using indices one could write $\mathscr{C} = \{A_\alpha: \alpha \in C\}$.

B is called a *subset* of A, written $B \subseteq A$, if all the elements of B are also elements of A. If B is a proper subset of A, ruling out $B = A$, the relation is written $B \subset A$. The *union* of A and B is the set whose elements belong to either or both sets, written $A \cup B$. The union of a collection $\mathscr{C}$, the set of elements belonging to one or more $A \in \mathscr{C}$, is denoted $\bigcup_{A \in \mathscr{C}} A$, or, alternatively, one can write $\bigcup_{\alpha \in C} A_\alpha$ for the union of the collection $\{A_\alpha: \alpha \in C\}$. The *intersection* of A and B is the set of elements belonging to both, written $A \cap B$. The intersection of a collection $\mathscr{C}$ is the set of elements common to all the sets in $\mathscr{C}$, written $\bigcap_{A \in \mathscr{C}} A$ or $\bigcap_{\alpha \in C} A_\alpha$. In particular, the union and intersection of $\{A_1, A_2, \ldots, A_n\}$ are written $\bigcup_{i=1}^n A_i$ and $\bigcap_{i=1}^n A_i$. When the index set is implicit or unspecified we may write just $\bigcup_\alpha A_\alpha$, $\bigcap_i A_i$ or similar.

The difference of sets A and B, written $A - B$ or by some authors $A \backslash B$, is the set of elements belonging to A but not to B. The *symmetric difference* of two sets is $A \Delta B = (A - B) \cup (B - A)$. $X - A$ is the *complement* of A in X, also denoted A^c when X is understood, and we have the general result that $A - B = A \cap B^c$. The *null set* (or *empty set*) is $\varnothing = X^c$, the set with no elements. Sets with no elements in common (having empty intersection) are called *disjoint*. A *partition* of a set is a collection of disjoint subsets whose union is the set, such that each of its elements belongs to one and only one member of the collection.

Here are the basic rules of set algebra. Unions and intersections obey commutative, associative and distributive laws:

$$A \cup B = B \cup A, \tag{1.1}$$

$$A \cap B = B \cap A, \tag{1.2}$$

$$(A \cup B) \cup C = A \cup (B \cup C), \tag{1.3}$$

$$(A \cap B) \cap C = A \cap (B \cap C), \tag{1.4}$$

$$A \cap (B \cup C) = (A \cap B) \cup (A \cap C), \tag{1.5}$$

$$A \cup (B \cap C) = (A \cup B) \cap (A \cup C). \tag{1.6}$$

There are also rules relating to complements known as de Morgan's laws:

$$(A \cup B)^c = A^c \cap B^c, \tag{1.7}$$

$$(A \cap B)^c = A^c \cup B^c. \tag{1.8}$$

Venn diagrams, illustrated in Fig. 1.1, are a useful device for clarifying relationships between subsets.

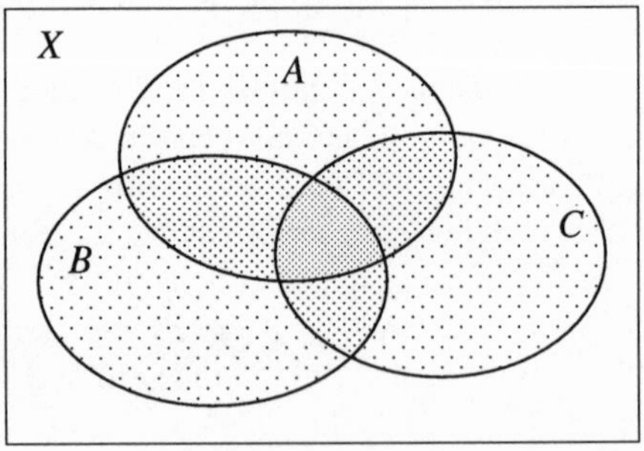

Fig. 1.1

The distributive and de Morgan laws extend to general collections, as follows.

1.1 Theorem Let $\mathscr{C}$ be a collection of sets, and B a set. Then

(i) $\left(\bigcup_{A\in\mathscr{C}} A\right) \cap B = \bigcup_{A\in\mathscr{C}} (A \cap B),$

(ii) $\left(\bigcap_{A\in\mathscr{C}} A\right) \cup B = \bigcap_{A\in\mathscr{C}} (A \cup B),$

(iii) $\left(\bigcap_{A\in\mathscr{C}} A\right)^c = \bigcup_{A\in\mathscr{C}} A^c,$

(iv) $\left(\bigcup_{A\in\mathscr{C}} A\right)^c = \bigcap_{A\in\mathscr{C}} A^c$. □

The *Cartesian product* of two sets A and B, written $A\times B$, is the set of all possible ordered pairs of elements, the first taken from A and the second from B; we write $A\times B = \{(x,y)\colon x \in A,\ y \in B\}$. For a collection of n sets the Cartesian product is the set of all the n-tuples (ordered sets of n elements, with the ith element drawn from A_i), and is written

$$\bigtimes_{i=1}^{n} A_i = \{(x_1, x_2, \ldots, x_n)\colon x_i \in A_i,\ i = 1,\ldots,n\}. \tag{1.9}$$

If one of the factor sets A_i is empty, $\bigtimes_{i=1}^{n} A_i$ is also empty.

Product sets are important in a variety of different contexts in mathematics. Some of these are readily appreciated; for example, sets whose elements are n-vectors of real numbers are products of copies of the real line (see §1.3). But product sets are also central to the mathematical formalization of the notion of relationship between set elements.

Thus: a *relation* R on a set A is any subset of $A\times A$. If $(x,y) \in R$, we usually write xRy. R is said to be

reflexive iff xRx,
symmetric iff xRy implies yRx,
antisymmetric iff xRy and yRx implies $x = y$,
transitive iff xRy and yRz implies xRz,

where in each case the indicated condition holds for every x, y, and $z \in A$, as the case may be. (Note: 'iff' means 'if and only if'.)

An *equivalence relation* is a relation that is reflexive, symmetric, and transitive. Given an equivalence relation R on A, the *equivalence class* of an element $x \in A$ is the set $E_x = \{y \in A\colon xRy\}$. If E_x and E_y are the equivalence classes of elements x and y, then either $E_x \cap E_y = \varnothing$, or $E_x = E_y$. The equality relation $x = y$ is the obvious example of an equivalence relation, but by no means the only one.

A *partial ordering* is any relation that is reflexive, antisymmetric, and transitive. Partial orderings are usually denoted by the symbols $\leq$ or $\geq$, with the understanding that $x \geq y$ is the same as $y \leq x$. To every partial ordering there corresponds a *strict ordering*, defined by the omission of the elements (x,x) for all $x \in A$. Strict orderings, usually denoted by $<$ or $>$, are not reflexive or antisymmetric, but they are transitive. A set A is said to be *linearly ordered* by a partial ordering $\leq$ if one of the relations $x < y$, $x > y$, and $x = y$ hold for every pair $(x,y) \in A\times A$. If there exist elements $a \in A$ and $b \in A$ such that $a \leq x$ for all $x \in A$, or $x \leq b$ for all $x \in A$, a and b are called respectively the *smallest* and *largest* elements of A. A linearly ordered set A is called *well-ordered* if every subset of A contains a smallest element. It is of course in sets whose elements are numbers that the ordering concept is most familiar.

Consider two sets X and Y, which can be thought of as representing the universal sets for a pair of related problems. The following bundle of definitions contains the basic ideas about relationships between the elements of such sets. A *mapping* (or *transformation* or *function*)

$$T: X \mapsto Y$$

is a rule that associates each element of X with a unique element of Y; in other words, for each $x \in X$ there exists a specified element $y \in Y$, denoted $T(x)$. X is called the *domain* of the mapping, and Y the *codomain.* The set

$$G_T = \{(x,y): x \in X,\ y = T(x)\} \subseteq X \times Y \tag{1.10}$$

is called the *graph* of T. For $A \subseteq X$, the set

$$T(A) = \{T(x): x \in A\} \subseteq Y \tag{1.11}$$

is called the *image* of A under T, and for $B \subseteq Y$, the set

$$T^{-1}(B) = \{x: T(x) \in B\} \subseteq X \tag{1.12}$$

is called the *inverse image* of B under T. The set $T(X)$ is called the *range* of T, and if $T(X) = Y$ the mapping is said to be from X *onto* Y, and otherwise, *into* Y. If each y is the image of one and only one $x \in X$, so that $T(x_1) = T(x_2)$ if and *only* if $x_1 = x_2$, the mapping is said to be *one-to-one*, or 1-1.

The notions of mapping and graph are really interchangeable, and it is permissable to say that the graph *is* the mapping, but it is convenient to keep a distinction in mind between the rule and the subset of $X \times Y$ which it generates. The term *function* is usually reserved for cases when the codomain is the set of real numbers (see §1.3). The term *correspondence* is used for a rule connecting elements of X to elements of Y where the latter are not necessarily unique. T^{-1} is a correspondence, but not a mapping unless T is one-to-one. However, the term *one-to-one correspondence* is often used specifically, in certain contexts that will arise below, to refer to a mapping that is both 1-1 and onto. If partial orderings are defined on both X and Y, a mapping is called *order-preserving* if $T(x_1) \le T(x_2)$ iff $x_1 \le x_2$. On the other hand, if X is partially ordered by $\le$, a 1-1 mapping *induces* a partial ordering on the codomain, defined by '$T(x_1) \le T(x_2)$ iff $x_1 \le x_2$'. And if the mapping is also onto, a linear ordering on X induces a linear ordering on Y.

The following is a miscellany of useful facts about mappings.

1.2 Theorem

(i) For a collection $\{A_\alpha \subseteq X\}$, $T\left(\bigcup_\alpha A_\alpha\right) = \bigcup_\alpha T(A_\alpha)$;

(ii) for a collection $\{B_\alpha \subseteq Y\}$, $T^{-1}\left(\bigcup_\alpha B_\alpha\right) = \bigcup_\alpha T^{-1}(B_\alpha)$;

(iii) for $B \subseteq Y$, $T^{-1}(B^c) = T^{-1}(B)^c$;

(iv) for $A \subseteq X$, $A \subseteq T^{-1}(T(A))$;

(v) for $B \subseteq Y$, $T(T^{-1}(B)) \subseteq B$. □

Here, $T^{-1}(B)^c$ means $X - T^{-1}(B)$. Using de Morgan's laws, properties (ii) and

(iii) are easily extended to the inverse images of intersections and differences; for example, we may show that the inverse images of disjoint sets are also disjoint. However, $Y - T(A) = T(A)^c \neq T(A^c)$, in general. Parts (iv) and (v) are illustrated in Fig. 1.2, where X and Y both correspond to the real line, A and B are intervals of the line, and T is a function of a real variable.

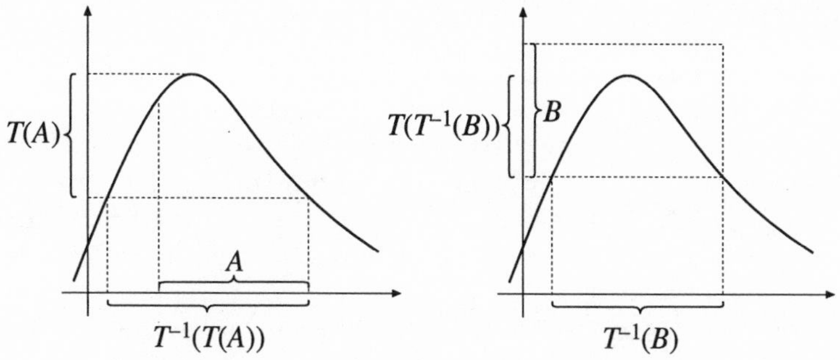

Fig. 1.2

When T is a 1-1 correspondence (1-1 and onto) so is T^{-1}. These properties then hold symmetrically, and the inclusion relations of parts (iv) and (v) also become equalities for all $A \subseteq X$ and $B \subseteq Y$. If Z is a third set, and

$$U \colon Y \mapsto Z$$

is a further mapping, the composite mapping

$$U \circ T \colon X \mapsto Z$$

takes each $x \in X$ to the element $U(T(x)) \in Z$. $U \circ T$ operates as a simple transformation from X to Z, and **1.2** applies to this case. For $C \subseteq Z$, $(U \circ T)^{-1}(C) = T^{-1}(U^{-1}(C))$.

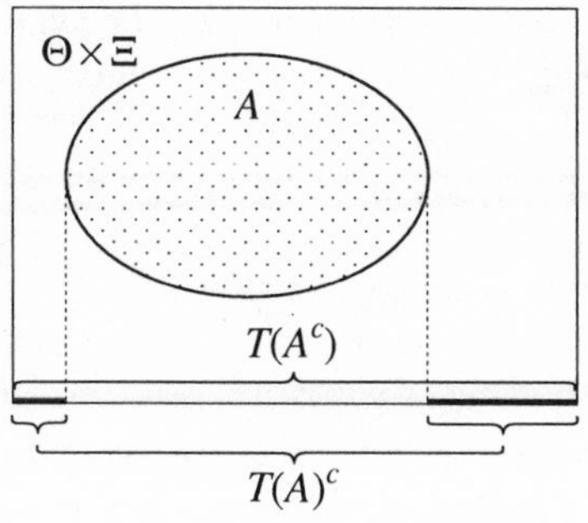

Fig. 1.3

1.3 Example If $X = \Theta \times \Xi$ is a product space, having as elements the ordered pairs $x = (\theta, \xi)$, the mapping

$$T \colon \Theta \times \Xi \mapsto \Xi,$$

defined by $T(\theta,\xi) = \xi$, is called the *projection mapping* onto Ξ. The projection of a set $A \subseteq \Theta\times\Xi$ onto Ξ (respectively, Θ) is the set consisting of the second (resp., first) members of each pair in A. On the other hand, for a set $B \in \Xi$, $T^{-1}(B) = \Theta\times B$. It is a useful exercise to verify **1.2** for this case, and also to check that $T(A)^c \neq T(A^c)$ in general. In Fig. 1.3, Θ and Ξ are line segments and $\Theta\times\Xi$ is a rectangle in the plane. Here, $T(A)^c$ is the union of the indicated line segments, whereas $T(A^c) = \Xi$. □

The number of elements contained in a set is called the *cardinality* or *cardinal number* of the set. The notion of 'number' in this context is not a primitive one, but can be reduced to fundamentals by what is called the 'pigeon-hole' principle. A set A is said to be *equipotent* with a set B if there exists a 1-1 correspondence connecting A and B. Think in terms of taking an element from each set and placing the pair in a pigeon-hole. Equipotency means that such a procedure can never exhaust one set before the other.

Now, think of the number 0 as being just a name for the null set, $\varnothing$. Let the number 1 be the name for the set that has a single element, the number 0. Let 2 denote the set whose elements are the numbers 0 and 1. And proceeding recursively, let n be the name for the set $\{0,\dots,n-1\}$. Then, the statement that a set A has n elements, or has cardinal number n, can be interpreted to mean that A is equipotent with the set n. The set of *natural numbers*, denoted $\mathbb{N}$, is the collection $\{n: n = 1,2,3,\dots\}$. This collection is well ordered by the relation usually denoted $\leq$, where $n \leq m$ actually means the same as $n \subseteq m$ under this definition of a number.

1.2 Countable Sets

Set theory is trivial when the number of elements in the set is finite, but formalization becomes indispensable for dealing with sets having an infinite number of elements. The set of natural numbers $\mathbb{N}$ is a case in point. If n is a member so is $n+1$, and this is true for every n. None the less, a cardinal number is formally assigned to $\mathbb{N}$, and is represented by the symbol $\aleph_0$ ('aleph-nought').

When the elements of an infinite set can be put into a one-to-one correspondence with the natural numbers, the set is said to have cardinal number $\aleph_0$, but, more commonly, to be *countable*, or equivalently, *denumerable*. Countability of a set requires that a scheme can be devised for labelling each element with a unique element of $\mathbb{N}$. This imposes a well-ordering on the elements, such that there is a 'first' element labelled 1, and so on, although this ordering may have significance or be arbitrary, depending on the circumstances. It is the pigeon-hole principle that matters here, that each element has its own unique label.

With infinite sets, everyday notions of size and quantity tend to break down. Augmenting the natural numbers by the number 0 defines the set $\mathbb{N}_0 = \{0,1,2,3,\dots\}$. The commonplace observation that $\mathbb{N}_0$ has 'one more' element than $\mathbb{N}$ is contradicted by the fact that $\mathbb{N}$ and $\mathbb{N}_0$ are equipotent (label $n-1 \in \mathbb{N}_0$ by $n \in \mathbb{N}$). Still more surprisingly, the set of even numbers, $\mathbb{E} = \{2n, n \in \mathbb{N}\}$, also has an obvious labelling scheme demonstrating equipotency with $\mathbb{N}$. The naïve idea that there are 'twice as many' elements in $\mathbb{N}$ as in $\mathbb{E}$ is without logical foundation. *Every* infinite subset A of $\mathbb{N}$ has a natural well-ordering and is equipotent with $\mathbb{N}$ itself, the label of an element $x \in A$ being the cardinal number of the set $\{y \in A: y \leq x\}$.

Turning to sets apparently 'larger' than $\mathbb{N}$, consider the *integers*, $\mathbb{Z} = \{...,-1,0,1,2,...\}$, the set containing the signed whole numbers and zero. These are linearly ordered although not well ordered. They can, however, be paired with the natural numbers using the 'zig-zag' scheme:

$$(1,0),\ (2,1),\ (3,-1),\ (4,2),...,\ (n,\ [n/2](-1)^n),...,$$

where $[x]$ denotes the largest whole number below x. Thus, $\mathbb{N}$ and $\mathbb{Z}$ are equipotent. Then there are the *rational numbers*,

$$\mathbb{Q} = \{x\colon x = a/b,\ a \in \mathbb{Z},\ b \in \mathbb{Z},\ b \neq 0\}. \tag{1.13}$$

We can also show the following.

1.4 Theorem $\mathbb{Q}$ is a countable set.

Proof We construct a 1-1 correspondence between $\mathbb{Z}\times\mathbb{Z}$ and $\mathbb{N}$. A 1-1 correspondence between $\mathbb{Z}\times\mathbb{Z}$ and $\mathbb{Z}\times\mathbb{N}$ is obtained by the method just used to show $\mathbb{Z}$ countable, and one between $\mathbb{Z}\times\mathbb{N}$ and $\mathbb{N}\times\mathbb{N}$ is got by the same method. Then note that the number $2^a3^b \in \mathbb{N}$ is *uniquely* associated with each pair $(a,b) \in \mathbb{N}\times\mathbb{N}$; the rule for recovering a and b from 2^a3^b is 'get a as the number of divisions by 2 required to get an odd number, and the number so obtained is 3^b'. The collection $\{2^a3^b\colon a \in \mathbb{N},\ b \in \mathbb{N}\} \subset \mathbb{N}$ is equipotent with $\mathbb{N}$ itself, as shown in the preceding paragraph. The composition of all these mappings is the desired correspondence. ■

Generalizing this type of argument leads to the following fundamental result.

1.5 Theorem The union of a countable collection of countable sets is a countable set. □

The concept of a *sequence* is fundamental to all the topics in this book. A sequence can be thought of as a mapping whose domain is a well-ordered countable set, the index set. Since there is always an order-preserving 1-1 mapping from $\mathbb{N}$ to the index set, there is usually no loss of generality in considering the composite mapping and thinking of $\mathbb{N}$ itself as the domain. Another way to characterize a sequence is as the graph of the mapping, that is, a countable collection of pairs having the ordering conferred on it by the elements of the domain. The ranges of the sequences we consider below typically contain either sets or real numbers; the associated theory for these cases is to be found respectively in §1.4 and §2.2.

The term sequence may also be applied to mappings having $\mathbb{Z}$ or another linearly ordered set as index set. This usage broadens the notion, since while such sets can be re-indexed by $\mathbb{N}$ (see above) this cannot be done while preserving the original ordering.

1.3 The Real Continuum

The real-number continuum $\mathbb{R}$ is such a complex object that no single statement of definition can do it justice. One can emphasize the ordinal and arithmetic properties of the reals, or their geometrical interpretation as the distances of points on a line from the origin (the point zero). But from a set-theoretic point of view, the essentials are captured by defining $\mathbb{R}$ as the set of countably infinite sequences of decimal digits, having a decimal point inserted at exactly one position in the sequence, and possibly preceded by a minus sign.

Thus, the real number x can be written in the form

$$x = m(x)10^{p(x)}\sum_{i=1}^{\infty} d_i(x)10^{-i}, \tag{1.14}$$

where the sequence $\{d_1(x), d_2(x),...\}$ consists of decimal digits (elements of the set $\{0,1,...,9\}$), $p(x) \in \mathbb{N}_0$ denotes the position of the decimal point in the string (the decimal exponent), and $m(x) = +1$ if $x \geq 0$, and -1 otherwise (the sign). When $d_i(x) = 0$ for all but a finite number of terms, the decimal expansion of x is said to terminate and the final 0s are conventionally omitted from the representation.

The representation of x by (1.14) is not always unique, and there exists a 1-1 correspondence between elements of $\mathbb{R}$ and sequences $\{m,p,d_1,d_2,d_3,...\}$ only after certain of the latter are excluded. To eliminate arbitrary leading zeros we must stipulate that $d_1 \neq 0$ unless $p = 0$. And since for example, 0.49999... (the sequence of 9s not terminating) is the same number as 0.5, we always take the terminating representation of a number and exclude sequences having $d_i = 9$ in all but a finite number of places. $\mathbb{R}$ is of course linearly ordered, and in terms of (1.14) the ordering corresponds to the lexicographic ordering of the sequences $\{m,mp,md_1,md_2,md_3...\}$.

The choice of base 10 in the definition is of course merely conventional, and of the alternative possibilities, the most important is the binary (base 2) representation,

$$x = m(x)2^{q(x)}\sum_{i=1}^{\infty} b_i(x)2^{-i}, \tag{1.15}$$

where the b_i are binary digits, either 0 or 1, and $q(x)$ is the binary exponent.

The integers have the representation in (1.14) with the strings terminating after $p(x)$ digits. The rationals are also elements of $\mathbb{R}$, being those which either terminate after a finite number of places, or else cycle repeatedly through a finite sequence of digits beyond a certain finite point. The real numbers that are not rational are called *irrational*. The irrational numbers are overwhelmingly more numerous than the rationals, representing a higher order of infinity. The following is the famous 'diagonal' argument of Cantor.

1.6 Theorem The set $\mathbb{R}$ is uncountable.

Proof Assume a 1-1 correspondence between $\mathbb{R}$ and $\mathbb{N}$ exists. Now construct a real number in the following way. Let the first digit be different from that of the real number labelled 1, the second digit be different from that of the real number labelled 2, and in general the *n*th digit be different from that of the real number labelled *n*, for every *n*. This number is different from every member of the labelled collection, and hence it has no label. Since this construction can be performed for any labelling scheme, the assumption is contradicted. ∎

We say that $\aleph_0 < c$, where c is the cardinal number of $\mathbb{R}$.

The linear ordering on $\mathbb{R}$ is of interest to us chiefly for providing the basis for constructing the fundamental subsets of $\mathbb{R}$, the *intervals*. The set $A = \{x\colon a < x < b\}$ is called an *open* interval, since it does not contain the end points, whereas the interval $B = \{x\colon a \le x \le b\}$ is said to be *closed*. Common notations are $[a,b]$, (a,b), $(a,b]$ and $[a,b)$ to denote closed, open and half-open intervals. A set containing just a single point a is called a *singleton*, written $\{a\}$. Unbounded intervals such as $C = \{x\colon a < x\}$, defined by a single boundary point, are written $(a,+\infty)$, $(-\infty,b)$, and $[a,+\infty)$, $(-\infty,b]$ for the open and closed cases respectively, where the infinities $+\infty$ and $-\infty$ are the fictional 'points' (not elements of $\mathbb{R}$) with the respective properties $x < +\infty$ and $x > -\infty$, for all $x \in \mathbb{R}$. An important example is the positive half-line $[0,+\infty)$, which we will denote subsequently by $\mathbb{R}^+$.

1.7 Theorem Every open interval is uncountable.

Proof Let the interval in question be (a,b). If $a < b$, there exists $n \ge 0$ such that the $(n+1)$th term of the sequence $(m,mp,md_1,md_2,\ldots)$ in the expansion of (1.14) defining b exceeds that in the corresponding sequence for a, whereas the first n digits of each sequence are the same. The elements of (a,b) are those reals whose expansions generate the same initial sequence, with the $(n+1)$th terms not exceeding that of b nor being exceeded by that of a. If a and b are distinct, n is finite. The result follows on applying the diagonal argument in **1.6** to these expansions, beginning at position $n+2$. ∎

Other useful results concerning $\mathbb{R}$ and its intervals include the following.

1.8 Theorem The points of any open interval are equipotent with $\mathbb{R}$.

Proof This might be proved by elaborating the argument of **1.7**, but it is simpler just to exhibit a 1-1 mapping from $\mathbb{R}$ onto (a,b). For example, the function

$$y = \frac{a+b}{2} + \frac{(b-a)x}{2(1+|x|)} \tag{1.16}$$

for $x \in \mathbb{R}$ fulfils the requirement. ∎

1.9 Theorem The real plane $\mathbb{R}^2 = \mathbb{R}\times\mathbb{R}$ is equipotent with $\mathbb{R}$.

Proof In view of the last theorem, it suffices to show that the unit interval $[0,1]$ is equipotent with the unit square $[0,1]^2$. Given points $x, y \in [0,1]$, define the point $z \in [0,1]$ according to the decimal expansion in (1.14), by the rule

$$d_i(z) = \begin{cases} d_{(i+1)/2}(x), & i \text{ odd} \\ d_{i/2}(y), & i \text{ even} \end{cases}, \quad i = 1,2,3,... \tag{1.17}$$

In words, construct z by taking a digit from x and y alternately. Such a z exists for every pair x and y, and, given z, x and y can be uniquely recovered by setting

$$d_i(x) = d_{2i-1}(z),\ d_i(y) = d_{2i}(z),\ i = 1,2,3,..., \tag{1.18}$$

This defines a 1-1 mapping from $[0,1]^2$ onto $[0,1]$, as required. ■

This argument can be extended from $\mathbb{R}^2$ to $\mathbb{R}^n$, for any $n \in \mathbb{N}$.

1.10 Theorem Every open interval contains a rational number.

Proof This is equivalent to the proposition that if $x < y$, there exists rational r with $x < r < y$. First suppose $x \geq 0$. Choose q as the smallest integer exceeding $1/(y - x)$, such that $qy > qx + 1$, and choose p as the smallest integer exceeding qy. Then $x < (p - 1)/q < y$. For the case $x < 0$ choose an integer $n > -x$, and then $x < r - n < y$, where r is the rational satisfying $n + x < r < n + y$, found as above. ■

1.11 Corollary Every collection of disjoint open intervals is countable.

Proof Since each open interval contains a rational appearing in no other interval disjoint with it, a set of disjoint open intervals can be placed in 1-1 correspondence with a subset of the rationals. ■

The *supremum* of a set $A \subset \mathbb{R}$, when it exists, is the smallest number y such that $x \leq y$ for every $x \in A$, written $\sup A$. The *infimum* of A, when it exists, is the largest number y such that $x \geq y$ for every $x \in A$, written $\inf A$. These may or may not be elements of A. In particular, $\inf[a,b] = \inf(a,b) = a$, and $\sup[a,b] = \sup(a,b) = b$. Open intervals do not possess largest or smallest elements. However, every subset of $\mathbb{R}$ which is bounded above (resp. below) has a supremum (resp. infimum). While unbounded sets in $\mathbb{R}$ lack suprema and/or infima, it is customary to define the set $\overline{\mathbb{R}} = \mathbb{R} \cup \{-\infty, +\infty\}$, called the *extended* real line. In $\overline{\mathbb{R}}$, every set has a supremum, either a finite real number or $+\infty$, and similarly, every set has an infimum. The notation $\overline{\mathbb{R}}^+$ will also be used subsequently to denote $\mathbb{R}^+ \cup \{+\infty\}$.

1.4 Sequences of Sets

Set sequences $\{A_1, A_2, A_3, ...\}$ will be written, variously, as $\{A_n : n \in \mathbb{N}\}$, $\{A_n\}_1^\infty$, or just $\{A_n\}$ when the context is clear.

A *monotone* sequence is one that is either *non-decreasing*, with each member of the sequence being contained in its successor ($A_n \subseteq A_{n+1}$, $\forall\, n$), or *non-increasing*, with each member containing its successor ($A_{n+1} \subseteq A_n$, $\forall\, n$). We also speak of increasing (resp. decreasing) sequences when the inclusion is strict, with $\subset$ (resp. $\supset$) replacing $\subseteq$ (resp. $\supseteq$). For a non-decreasing sequence, define the set $A = \bigcup_{n=1}^\infty A_n$ and for a non-increasing sequence the set $A = \bigcap_{n=1}^\infty A_n = (\bigcup_{n=1}^\infty A_n^c)^c$. These sets are called the *limits* of the respective sequences. We may write $A_n \uparrow A$ and $A_n \downarrow A$, and also, in general, $\lim_{n\to\infty} A_n = A$ and $A_n \to A$.

1.12 Example The sequence $\{[0, 1/n], n \in \mathbb{N}\}$ is decreasing and has as limit the singleton $\{0\}$. In fact, $\lim_{n\to\infty}[0,1/n) = \{0\}$ also, whereas $\lim_{n\to\infty}(0,1/n] = \emptyset$. The decreasing sequence of open intervals, $\{(a - 1/n,\ b + 1/n),\ n \in \mathbb{N}\}$, has as its limit the closed interval $[a, b]$. On the other hand, the sequence $\{[a + 1/n,\ b - 1/n],\ n \in \mathbb{N}\}$ is increasing, and its limit is (a, b). □

Consider an arbitrary sequence $\{A_n\}$. The sequence $B_n = \bigcup_{m=n}^{\infty} A_m$ is non-increasing, so that $B = \lim_{n\to\infty} B_n$ exists. This set is called the *superior limit* of the sequence $\{A_n\}$, written $\limsup_n A_n$, and also as $\overline{\lim}_n A_n$. Similarly, the limit of the non-decreasing sequence $C_n = \bigcap_{m=n}^{\infty} A_m$ is called the *inferior limit* of the sequence, written $\liminf_n A_n$, or $\underline{\lim}_n A_n$. Formally: for a sequence $\{A_n, n \in \mathbb{N}\}$,

$$\limsup_n A_n = \bigcap_{n=1}^{\infty}\left(\bigcup_{m=n}^{\infty} A_m\right) \tag{1.19}$$

$$\liminf_n A_n = \bigcup_{n=1}^{\infty}\left(\bigcap_{m=n}^{\infty} A_m\right). \tag{1.20}$$

De Morgan's laws imply that $\liminf_n A_n = (\limsup_n A_n^c)^c$. The limsup is the set of elements contained in *infinitely many* of the A_n, while the liminf is the set belonging to *all but a finite number* of the A_n, that is, to every member of the sequence from some point onwards.

These concepts provide us with a criterion for convergence of set sequences in general. $\text{Liminf}_n A_n \subseteq \limsup_n A_n$, and if these two sets differ, there are elements that belong to infinitely many of the A_n, but also do *not* belong to infinitely many of them. Such a sequence is not convergent. On the other hand, if $\liminf_n A_n = \limsup_n A_n = A$, the elements of A belong to infinitely many of the A_n and do not belong to at most a finite number of them. Then the sequence $\{A_n\}$ is said to converge to A, and A is called the limit of the sequence.

1.5 Classes of Subsets

The set of all the subsets of X is called the *power set* of X, denoted 2^X. The power set of a set with n elements has 2^n elements, which accounts for its name and representation. In the case of a countable set, the power set is thought of formally as having $2^{\aleph_0}$ elements. One of the fundamental facts of set theory is that the number of subsets of a given set strictly exceeds the number of its elements. For finite sets this is obvious, but when extended to countable sets it amounts to the claim that $2^{\aleph_0} > \aleph_0$.

1.13 Theorem $2^{\aleph_0} = c$.

Proof The proposition is proved if we can show that $2^{\mathbb{N}}$ is equipotent with $\mathbb{R}$ or, equivalently (in view of **1.8**), with the unit interval $[0,1]$. For a set $A \in 2^{\mathbb{N}}$, construct the sequence of binary digits $\{b_1, b_2, b_3, \ldots\}$ according to the rule, 'b_n

$= 1$ if $n \in A$, $b_n = 0$ otherwise'. Using formula (1.15) with $m = 1$ and $q = 0$, let this sequence define an element x_A of $[0,1]$ (the case where $b_n = 1$ for all n defines 1). On the other hand, for any element $x \in [0,1]$, construct the set $A_x \in 2^{\mathbb{N}}$ according to the rule, 'include n in A_x if and only if the nth digit in the binary expansion of x is a 1'. These constructions define a 1-1 correspondence between $2^{\mathbb{N}}$ and $[0,1]$. ∎

When studying the subsets of a given set, particularly their measure-theoretic properties, the power set is often too big for anything very interesting or useful to be said about it. The idea behind the following definitions is to specify subsets of 2^X that are large enough to be interesting, but whose characteristics may be more tractable. We typically do this by choosing a base collection of sets with known properties, and then specifying certain operations for creating new sets from existing ones. These operations permit an interesting diversity of class members to be generated, but important properties of the sets may be deduced from those of the base collection, as the following examples show.

1.14 Definition A *ring* $\mathcal{R}$ is a nonempty class of subsets of X satisfying

(a) $\varnothing \in \mathcal{R}$.

(b) If A and $B \in \mathcal{R}$ then $A \cup B \in \mathcal{R}$, $A \cap B \in \mathcal{R}$ and $A - B \in \mathcal{R}$. □

One generates a ring by specifying an arbitrary basic collection $\mathcal{C}$, which must include $\varnothing$, and then declaring that any sets that can be generated by the specified operations also belong to the class. A ring is said to be *closed* under the operations of union, intersection and difference.

Rings lack a crucial piece of structure, for there is no requirement for the set X itself to be a member. If X is included, a ring becomes a *field*, or synonymously an *algebra.* Since $X - A = A^c$, this amounts to including all complements, and, in view of the de Morgan laws, specifying the inclusion of intersections and differences becomes redundant.

1.15 Definition A field $\mathcal{F}$ is a class of subsets of X satisfying

(a) $X \in \mathcal{F}$.

(b) If $A \in \mathcal{F}$ then $A^c \in \mathcal{F}$.

(c) If A and $B \in \mathcal{F}$ then $A \cup B \in \mathcal{F}$. □

A field is said to be *closed* under complementation and finite union, and hence under intersections and differences too; none of these operations can take one outside the class.

These classes can be very complex, and also very trivial. The simplest case of a ring is $\{\varnothing\}$. The smallest possible field is $\{X,\varnothing\}$. Scarcely less trivial is the field $\{X, A, A^c, \varnothing\}$, where A is any subset of X. What makes any class of sets interesting, or not, is the collection $\mathcal{C}$ of sets it is declared to contain, which we can think of as the 'seed' for the class. We speak of the smallest field containing $\mathcal{C}$ as 'the field generated by $\mathcal{C}$'.

Rings and fields are natural classes in the sense of being defined in terms of the simple set operations, but their structure is rather restrictive for some of the applications in probability. More inclusive definitions, carefully tailored to include some important cases, are as follows.

1.16 Definition A *semi-ring* $\mathcal{S}$ is a non-empty class of subsets of X satisfying

(a) $\varnothing \in \mathcal{S}$.

(b) If $A, B \in \mathcal{S}$ then $A \cap B \in \mathcal{S}$.

(c) If $A, B \in \mathcal{S}$ and $A \subseteq B$, $\exists\, n < \infty$ such that $B - A = \bigcup_{j=1}^{n} C_j$, where $C_j \in \mathcal{S}$ and $C_j \cap C_{j'} = \varnothing$ for each j, j'. □

More succinctly, condition (c) says that the difference of two $\mathcal{S}$-sets has a finite partition into $\mathcal{S}$-sets.

1.17 Definition A *semi-algebra* $\mathcal{S}$ is a class of subsets of X satisfying

(a) $X \in \mathcal{S}$.

(b) If $A, B \in \mathcal{S}$ then $A \cap B \in \mathcal{S}$.

(c) If $A \in \mathcal{S}$, $\exists\, n < \infty$ such that $A^c = \bigcup_{j=1}^{n} C_j$, where $C_j \in \mathcal{S}$ and $C_j \cap C_{j'} = \varnothing$ for each j, j'. □

A semi-ring containing X is a semi-algebra.

1.18 Example Let $X = \mathbb{R}$, and consider the class of all the half-open intervals $I = (a,b]$ for $-\infty < a \le b < +\infty$, together with the empty set. If $I_1 = (a_1,b_1]$ and $I_2 = (a_2,b_2]$, then $I_1 \cap I_2$ is one of I_1, I_2, $(a_1,b_2]$, $(a_2,b_1]$, and $\varnothing$. And if $I_1 \subseteq I_2$ so that $a_2 \le a_1$ and $b_1 \le b_2$, then $I_2 - I_1$ is one of $\varnothing$, $(a_2,a_1]$, $(b_1,b_2]$, $(a_2,a_1] \cup (b_1,b_2]$, and I_2. The conditions defining a semi-ring are therefore satisfied, although not those defining a ring.

If we now let $\mathbb{R}$ be a member of the class and follow **1.17**, we find that the half-open intervals, plus the unbounded intervals of the form $(-\infty,b]$ and $(a,+\infty)$, plus $\varnothing$ and $\mathbb{R}$, constitute a semi-algebra. □

1.6 Sigma Fields

When we say that a field contains the complements and finite unions, the qualifier *finite* deserves explanation. It is clear that $A_1, \dots, A_n \in \mathcal{F}$ implies that $\bigcup_{j=1}^{n} A_j \in \mathcal{F}$ by a simple n-fold iteration of pairwise union. But, given the constructive nature of the definition, it is not legitimate without a further stipulation to assume that such an operation can be taken to the limit. By making this additional stipulation, we obtain the concept of a σ-field.

1.19 Definition A σ-field (σ-algebra) $\mathcal{F}$ is a class of subsets of X satisfying

(a) $X \in \mathcal{F}$.

(b) If $A \in \mathcal{F}$ then $A^c \in \mathcal{F}$.

(c) If $\{A_n,\, n \in \mathbb{N}\}$ is a sequence of $\mathcal{F}$-sets, then $\bigcup_{n=1}^{\infty} A_n \in \mathcal{F}$. □

A σ-field is closed under the operations of complementation and *countable* union, and hence, by the de Morgan laws, of countable intersection also. A σ-ring can be defined similarly, although this is not a concept we shall need in the sequel. Given a collection of sets $\mathcal{C}$, the intersection of all the σ-fields containing $\mathcal{C}$ is called the σ-field *generated by* $\mathcal{C}$, customarily denoted $\sigma(\mathcal{C})$.

The following theorem establishes a basic fact about σ-fields.

1.20 Theorem If $\mathcal{C}$ is a finite collection $\sigma(\mathcal{C})$ is finite, otherwise $\sigma(\mathcal{C})$ is always uncountable.

Proof Define the relation R between elements of X by 'xRy iff x and y are elements of the same sets of $\mathcal{C}$'. R is an equivalence relation, and hence defines an equivalence class $\mathcal{E}$ of disjoint subsets. Each set of $\mathcal{E}$ is the intersection of all the $\mathcal{C}$-sets containing its elements and the complements of the remainder. (For example, see Fig. 1.1. For this collection of regions of $\mathbb{R}^2$, $\mathcal{E}$ is the partition defined by the complete network of set boundaries.) If $\mathcal{C}$ contains n sets, $\mathcal{E}$ contains at most 2^n sets and $\sigma(\mathcal{C})$, in this case the collection of all unions of $\mathcal{E}$-sets, contains at most 2^{2^n} sets. This proves the first part of the theorem.

Let $\mathcal{C}$ be infinite. If it is uncountable then so is $\sigma(\mathcal{C})$ and there is nothing more to show, so assume $\mathcal{C}$ is countable. In this case every set in $\mathcal{E}$ is a countable intersection of $\mathcal{C}$-sets or the complements of $\mathcal{C}$-sets, hence $\mathcal{E} \subseteq \sigma(\mathcal{C})$, and hence also $\mathcal{U}(\mathcal{E}) \subseteq \sigma(\mathcal{C})$, where $\mathcal{U}(\mathcal{E})$ is the collection of all the countable unions of $\mathcal{E}$-sets. If we show $\mathcal{U}(\mathcal{E})$ is uncountable, the same will be true of $\sigma(\mathcal{C})$. We may assume that $\mathcal{E}$ is countable, since otherwise there is nothing more to show. So let the sets of $\mathcal{E}$ be indexed by $\mathbb{N}$. Then every union of $\mathcal{E}$-sets corresponds uniquely with a subset of $\mathbb{N}$, and every subset of $\mathbb{N}$ corresponds uniquely to a union of $\mathcal{E}$-sets. In other words, the elements of $\mathcal{U}(\mathcal{E})$ are equipotent with those of $2^{\mathbb{N}}$, which are uncountable by **1.13**. This completes the proof. ■

1.21 Example Let $X = \mathbb{R}$, and let $\mathcal{C} = \{(-\infty,r],\ r \in \mathbb{Q}\}$, the collection of *closed half-lines with rational endpoints*. $\sigma(\mathcal{C})$ is called the *Borel field* of $\mathbb{R}$, generally denoted $\mathcal{B}$. A number of different base collections generate $\mathcal{B}$. Since countable unions of open intervals can be closed intervals, and vice versa, (compare **1.12**), the set of open half-lines, $\{(-\infty,r),\ r \in \mathbb{Q}\}$, will also serve. Or, letting $\{r_n\}$ be a decreasing sequence of rational numbers with $r_n \downarrow x$,

$$(-\infty, x] = \bigcap_{n=1}^{\infty}(-\infty, r_n]. \tag{1.21}$$

Such a sequence exists for any $x \in \mathbb{R}$ (see **2.15**), and hence the same σ-field is generated by the (uncountable) collection of half-lines with real endpoints, $\{(-\infty,x],\ x \in \mathbb{R}\}$. It easily follows that various other collections generate $\mathcal{B}$, including the open intervals of $\mathbb{R}$, the closed intervals, and the half-open intervals. □

1.22 Example Let $X = \overline{\mathbb{R}}$, the extended real line. The Borel field of $\overline{\mathbb{R}}$ is easily given. It is

$$\overline{\mathcal{B}} = \{B,\ B\cup\{+\infty\},\ B\cup\{-\infty\},\ B\cup\{+\infty\}\cup\{-\infty\}\colon B \in \mathcal{B}\},$$

where $\mathcal{B}$ is the Borel field of $\mathbb{R}$. You can verify that $\overline{\mathcal{B}}$ is a σ-field, and is generated by the collection $\mathcal{C}$ of **1.21** augmented by the sets $\{-\infty\}$ and $\overline{\mathbb{R}}$. □

1.23 Example Given an interval I of the line, the class $\mathcal{B}_I = \{B\cap I\colon B \in \mathcal{B}\}$ is called the restriction of $\mathcal{B}$ to I, or the Borel field on I. In fact, $\mathcal{B}_I$ is the σ-field generated from the collection $\mathcal{C} = \{(-\infty,r]\cap I\colon r \in \mathbb{Q}\}$. □

Notice how $\sigma(\mathcal{C})$ has been defined 'from the outside'. It might be thought that $\sigma(\mathcal{C})$ could be defined 'from the inside', in terms of a specified sequence of the operations of complementation and countable union applied to the elements of $\mathcal{C}$. But, despite the constructive nature of the definitions, **1.20** suggests how this may be impossible. Suppose we define $\mathcal{A}_1$ as the set that contains $\mathcal{C}$, together with the complement of every set in $\mathcal{C}$ and all the finite and countable unions of the sets of $\mathcal{C}$. Of course, $\mathcal{A}_1$ is not $\sigma(\mathcal{C})$ because it does not contain the complements of the unions. So let $\mathcal{A}_2$ be the set containing $\mathcal{A}_1$ together with all the complements and finite and countable unions of the sets in $\mathcal{A}_1$. Defining $\mathcal{A}_3$, $\mathcal{A}_4$,... in the same manner, it might be thought that the monotone sequence $\{\mathcal{A}_n\}$ would approach $\sigma(\mathcal{C})$ as $n \to \infty$; but in fact this is not so. In the case of the class $\mathcal{B}_{[0,1]}$, for example, it can be shown that $\mathcal{A}_\infty$ is strictly smaller than $\sigma(\mathcal{C})$ (see Billingsley 1986: 26). On the other hand, $\sigma(\mathcal{C})$ may be smaller than 2^X. This fact is demonstrated, again for $\mathcal{B}_{[0,1]}$, in §3.4.

The union of two σ-fields (the set of elements contained in either or both of them) is not generally a σ-field, for the unions of the sets from one field with those from the other are not guaranteed to belong to it. The concept of union for σ-fields is therefore extended by adding in these sets. Given σ-fields $\mathcal{F}$ and $\mathcal{G}$, the smallest σ-field containing all the elements of $\mathcal{F}$ and all the elements of $\mathcal{G}$ is denoted $\mathcal{F} \vee \mathcal{G}$, called the union of $\mathcal{F}$ and $\mathcal{G}$. On the other hand, $\mathcal{F} \cap \mathcal{G} = \{A\colon A \in \mathcal{F}$ and $A \in \mathcal{G}\}$ *is* a σ-field, although for uniformity the notation $\mathcal{F} \wedge \mathcal{G}$ may be used for such intersections. Formally, $\mathcal{F} \wedge \mathcal{G}$ denotes the largest of the σ-fields whose elements belong to both $\mathcal{F}$ and $\mathcal{G}$. Both of these operations generalize to the countable case, so that for a sequence of σ-fields $\mathcal{F}_n$, $n = 1,2,3,...$ we may define $\bigvee_{n=1}^\infty \mathcal{F}_n$ and $\bigcap_{n=1}^\infty \mathcal{F}_n$.

Without going prematurely into too many details, it can be said that a large part of the intellectual labour in probability and measure theory is devoted to proving that particular classes of sets are σ-fields. Problems of this kind will arise throughout this book. It is usually not too hard to show that $A^c \in \mathcal{F}$ whenever $A \in \mathcal{F}$, but the requirement to show that a class contains the countable unions can be tough to fulfil. The following material can be helpful in this connection.

A *monotone class* $\mathcal{M}$ is a class of sets such that, if $\{A_n\}$ is a monotone sequence with limit A, and $A_n \in \mathcal{M}$ for all n, then $A \in \mathcal{M}$. If $\{A_n\}$ is non-decreasing, then $A = \bigcup_{n=1}^\infty A_n$. If it is non-increasing, then $A = \bigcap_{n=1}^\infty A_n$. The next theorem shows that, to determine whether or not we are dealing with a σ-field, it is sufficient to consider whether the limits of monotone sequences belong to it, which should often be easier to establish than the general case.

1.24 Theorem $\mathcal{F}$ is a σ-field iff it is both a field and a monotone class.

Proof The 'only if' part of the theorem is immediate. For the 'if' part, define $A_n = \bigcup_{m=1}^n E_m$, for any sequence $\{E_m \in \mathcal{F}, m \in \mathbb{N}\}$. Since $\mathcal{F}$ is a field, $A_n \in \mathcal{F}$ for any finite n. But $\{A_n, n \in \mathbb{N}\}$ is a monotone sequence with limit $\bigcup_{n=1}^\infty A_n \in \mathcal{F}$, by assumption. $\bigcup_{n=1}^{\infty} A_n = \bigcup_{m=1}^{\infty} E_m$, so the theorem follows. ■

Another useful trick is Dynkin's π-λ theorem.[1] To develop this result, we define two new classes of subsets of X.

1.25 Definition A class $\mathcal{P}$ is a *π-system* if A and $B \in \mathcal{P}$ implies $A \cap B \in \mathcal{P}$. A class $\mathcal{L}$ is a *λ-system* if

(a) $X \in \mathcal{L}$.

(b) If A and $B \in \mathcal{L}$ and $B \subseteq A$, then $A - B \in \mathcal{L}$.

(c) If $\{A_n \in \mathcal{L}\}$ is a non-decreasing sequence and $A_n \uparrow A$, then $A \in \mathcal{L}$. □

Conditions (a) and (b) imply that a λ-system is closed under complementation (put $A = X$). Moreover, since (b) implies that $B_n = A_{n+1} - A_n \in \mathcal{L}$ for each n, (c) implies that a countable union of *disjoint* $\mathcal{L}$-sets is in $\mathcal{L}$. In fact, these implications hold in both directions, and we have the following.

1.26 Theorem A class $\mathcal{L}$ is a λ-system if and only if

(a) $X \in \mathcal{L}$.

(b) If $B \in \mathcal{L}$ then $B^c \in \mathcal{L}$.

(c) If $\{A_n \in \mathcal{L}\}$ is a disjoint sequence, then $\bigcup_n A_n \in \mathcal{L}$. □

In particular, a σ-field is a λ-system, and moreover, a class that is both a π-system and a λ-system is a σ-field. This follows by **1.24**, because a λ-system is a monotone class by **1.25**(c), and by de Morgan's laws is closed under unions if closed under both intersections and complementation.

The following result makes these definitions useful.

1.27 Dynkin's π-λ theorem (Billingsley 1979, 1986: th. 3.2) If $\mathcal{P}$ is a π-system, $\mathcal{L}$ is a λ-system, and $\mathcal{P} \subseteq \mathcal{L}$, then $\sigma(\mathcal{P}) \subseteq \mathcal{L}$.

Proof Let $\lambda(\mathcal{P})$ denote the smallest λ-system containing $\mathcal{P}$ (the intersection of all the λ-systems containing $\mathcal{P}$), so that in particular, $\lambda(\mathcal{P}) \subseteq \mathcal{L}$. We show that $\lambda(\mathcal{P})$ is a π-system. By the remarks above, it will then follow that $\lambda(\mathcal{P})$ is a σ-field, and hence that $\sigma(\mathcal{P}) \subseteq \lambda(\mathcal{P}) \subseteq \mathcal{L}$, as required.

For a set $A \in \lambda(\mathcal{P})$, let $\mathcal{G}_A$ denote the class of sets B such that $A \cap B \in \lambda(\mathcal{P})$. We shall show that $\mathcal{G}_A$ is a λ-system. Clearly, $X \in \mathcal{G}_A$, so that condition **1.25**(a) is satisfied. Let $B_1, B_2 \in \mathcal{G}_A$, and $B_1 \subset B_2$; then $A \cap B_1 \in \lambda(\mathcal{P})$ and $A \cap B_2 \in \lambda(\mathcal{P})$, and $(A \cap B_1) \subset (A \cap B_2)$, which implies that

$$(A \cap B_2) - (A \cap B_1) = A \cap (B_2 - B_1) \in \lambda(\mathcal{P}). \tag{1.22}$$

But this means that $B_2 - B_1 \in \mathcal{G}_A$, and condition **1.25**(b) is satisfied. Lastly, suppose $A \cap B_i \in \lambda(\mathcal{P})$ for each $i = 1,2,...$ and $B_i \uparrow B$. Then $A \cap B \in \lambda(\mathcal{P})$ by **1.25**(c), which means that **1.25**(c) holds for $\mathcal{G}_A$, and $\mathcal{G}_A$ is a λ-system as asserted.

Suppose $A \in \mathcal{P}$. Then $B \in \mathcal{P}$ implies $A \cap B \in \mathcal{P}$ ($\mathcal{P}$ is a π-system) and since $\mathcal{P} \subseteq \lambda(\mathcal{P})$, this further implies $B \in \mathcal{G}_A$. Hence $\mathcal{P} \subseteq \mathcal{G}_A$. Since $\mathcal{G}_A$ is a λ-system, and $\lambda(\mathcal{P})$ is the smallest λ-system containing $\mathcal{P}$, we also have $\lambda(\mathcal{P}) \subseteq \mathcal{G}_A$ in this case. So, when $A \in \mathcal{P}$, $B \in \lambda(\mathcal{P})$ implies $B \in \mathcal{G}_A$ and hence $A \cap B \in \lambda(\mathcal{P})$.

We can summarize the last conclusion as:

$$\{A \in \mathcal{P},\ B \in \lambda(\mathcal{P})\} \Rightarrow \{A \cap B \in \lambda(\mathcal{P})\}. \tag{1.23}$$

Now defining $\mathcal{G}_B$ by analogy with $\mathcal{G}_A$, so that

$$\{B \in \lambda(\mathcal{P}),\ A \cap B \in \lambda(\mathcal{P})\} \Rightarrow \{A \in \mathcal{G}_B\}, \tag{1.24}$$

we see that (1.23) and (1.24) together yield $\mathcal{P} \subseteq \mathcal{G}_B$. Since $\mathcal{G}_B$ is also a λ-system by the same argument as held for $\mathcal{G}_A$, and contains $\mathcal{P}$, $\lambda(\mathcal{P}) \subseteq \mathcal{G}_B$ by definition of $\lambda(\mathcal{P})$.

Thus, suppose $B \in \lambda(\mathcal{P})$ and $C \in \lambda(\mathcal{P})$. Then $C \in \mathcal{G}_B$, which means that $B \cap C \in \lambda(\mathcal{P})$. So $\lambda(\mathcal{P})$ is a π-system as required. ■

2
Limits and Continuity

2.1 The Topology of the Real Line

The purpose of this section is to treat rigorously the idea of 'nearness', as it applies to points of the line. The key ingredient of the theory is the distance between a pair of points, x, $y \in \mathbb{R}$, defined as the non-negative real number $|x-y|$, what is formally called the *Euclidean* distance. In Chapters 5 and 6 we examine the generalization of this theory to non-Euclidean spaces, and find not only that most aspects of the theory have a natural generalization, but that the concept of distance itself can be dispensed with in their development. We are really studying a special case of a very powerful general theory. This fact may be helpful in making sense of certain ideas, the definition of compactness for example, which can otherwise appear a little puzzling at first sight.

An *ε-neighbourhood* of a point $x \in \mathbb{R}$ is a set $S(x,\varepsilon) = \{y\colon |x-y| < \varepsilon\}$, for some $\varepsilon > 0$. An *open set* is a set $A \subseteq \mathbb{R}$ such that for each $x \in A$, there exists for some $\varepsilon > 0$ an ε-neighbourhood which is a subset of A. The open intervals defined in §1.3 are open sets since if $a < x < b$, $\varepsilon = \min\{|b-x|,|a-x|\} > 0$ satisfies the definition. $\mathbb{R}$ and $\varnothing$ are also open sets on the definition.

The concept of an open set is subtle and often gives beginners some difficulty. Naive intuition strongly favours the notion that in any bounded set of points there ought to be one that is 'next to' a point outside the set. But open sets are sets that do not have this property, and there is no shortage of them in $\mathbb{R}$. For a complete understanding of the issues involved we need the additional concepts of *Cauchy sequence* and *limit*, to appear in §2.2 below. Doubters are invited to suspend their disbelief for the moment and just take the definition at face value.

The collection of all the open sets of $\mathbb{R}$ is known as the *topology* of $\mathbb{R}$. More precisely, we ought to call this the *usual topology on* $\mathbb{R}$, since other ways of defining open sets of $\mathbb{R}$ can be devised, although these will not concern us. (See Chapter 6 for more information on these matters.) More generally, we can discuss subsets of $\mathbb{R}$ from a topological standpoint, although we would tend to use the term *subspace* rather than subset in this context. If $A \subseteq \mathbb{S} \subseteq \mathbb{R}$, we say that A is *open in* $\mathbb{S}$ if for each $x \in A$ there exists $S(x,\varepsilon)$, $\varepsilon > 0$, such that $S(x,\varepsilon) \cap \mathbb{S}$ is a subset of A. Thus, the interval $[0,\frac{1}{2})$ is not open in $\mathbb{R}$, but it is open in $[0,1]$. These sets define the *relative topology* on $\mathbb{S}$, that is, the topology on $\mathbb{S}$ relative to $\mathbb{R}$. The following result is an immediate consequence of the definition.

2.1 Theorem If A is open in $\mathbb{R}$, $A \cap \mathbb{S}$ is open in the relative topology on $\mathbb{S}$. □

A *closure point* of a set A is a point $x \in \mathbb{R}$ such that, for every $\varepsilon > 0$, the set

$A \cap S(x,\varepsilon)$ is not empty. The closure points of A are not necessarily elements of A, open sets being a case in point. The set of closure points of A is called the closure of A, and will be denoted $\bar{A}$ or sometimes $(A)^-$ if the set is defined by an expression. On the other hand, an *accumulation point* of A is a point $x \in \mathbb{R}$ which is a closure point of the set $A - \{x\}$. An accumulation point has other points of A arbitrarily close to it, and if x is a closure point of A and $x \notin A$, it must also be an accumulation point. A closure point that is not an accumulation point (the former definition being satisfied because each ε-neighbourhood of x contains x itself) is an *isolated* point of A.

A *boundary point* of a set A is a point $x \in \bar{A}$ such that the set $A^c \cap S(x,\varepsilon)$ is not empty for any $\varepsilon > 0$. The set of boundary points of A is denoted ∂A, and $\bar{A} = A \cup \partial A$. The *interior* of A is the set $A^o = A - \partial A$. A *closed* set is one containing all its closure points, i.e. a set A such that $\bar{A} = A$. For an open interval $A = (a,b) \subset \mathbb{R}$, $\bar{A} = [a,b]$. Every point of (a,b) is a closure point, and a and b are also closure points, not belonging to (a,b). They are the boundary points of both (a,b) and $[a,b]$.

2.2 Theorem The complement of an open set in $\mathbb{R}$ is a closed set. □

This gives an alternative definition of a closed set. According to the definitions, $\varnothing$ (the empty set) and $\mathbb{R}$ are both open *and* closed. The half-line $(-\infty,x]$ is the complement of the open set $(x,+\infty)$ and is hence closed. Extending this result to relative topologies, we have the following.

2.3 Theorem If A is open in $\mathbb{S} \subset \mathbb{R}$, then $\mathbb{S} - A$ is closed in $\mathbb{S}$. □

In particular, a corollary to **2.1** is that if B is closed in $\mathbb{R}$ then $\mathbb{S} \cap B$ is closed in $\mathbb{S}$. But, for example, the interval $[\frac{1}{2},1)$ is not closed in $\mathbb{R}$, although it is closed in the set $(0,1)$, since its complement $(0,\frac{1}{2})$ is open in $(0,1)$.

Some additional properties of open sets are given in the following theorems.

2.4 Theorem (i) The union of a collection of open sets is open.
(ii) If A and B are open, then $A \cap B$ is open. □

This result is be proved in a more general context below, as **5.4**. Arbitrary intersections of open sets *need not* be open. See **1.12** for a counter-example.

2.5 Theorem Every open set $A \subseteq \mathbb{R}$ is the union of a countable collection of disjoint open intervals.

Proof Consider a collection $\{S(x,\varepsilon_x), x \in A\}$, where for each x, $\varepsilon_x > 0$ is chosen small enough that $S(x,\varepsilon_x) \subseteq A$. Then $\bigcup_{x \in A} S(x,\varepsilon_x) \subseteq A$, but, since necessarily $A \subseteq \bigcup_{x \in A} S(x,\varepsilon_x)$, it follows that $\bigcup_{x \in A} S(x,\varepsilon_x) = A$. This shows that A is a union of open intervals.

Now define a relation R for elements of A, such that xRy if there exists an open interval $I \subseteq A$ with $x \in I$ and $y \in I$. Every $x \in A$ is contained in some interval by the preceding argument, so that xRx for all $x \in A$. The symmetry of R is obvious. Lastly, if $x,y \in I \subseteq A$ and $y,z \in I' \subseteq A$, $I \cap I'$ is nonempty and hence $I \cup I'$ is also an open interval, so R is transitive. Hence R is an equivalence relation, and the intervals I are an equivalence class partitioning A. Thus, A is a union of disjoint open intervals. The theorem now follows from **1.11**. ∎

Recall from **1.21** that $\mathcal{B}$, the Borel field of $\mathbb{R}$, is the σ-field of sets generated by both the open and the closed half-lines. Since every interval is the intersection of a half-line (open or closed) with the complement of another half-line, **2.2** and **2.5** yield directly the following important fact.

2.6 Theorem $\mathcal{B}$ contains the open sets and the closed sets of $\mathbb{R}$. □

A collection $\mathcal{C}$ is called a *covering* for a set $A \subseteq \mathbb{R}$ if $A \subseteq \bigcup_{B \in \mathcal{C}} B$. If each B is an open set, it is called an *open covering.*

2.7 Lindelöf's covering theorem If $\mathcal{C}$ is any collection of open subsets of $\mathbb{R}$, there is a countable subcollection $\{B_i \in \mathcal{C},\ i \in \mathbb{N}\}$ such that

$$\bigcup_{B \in \mathcal{C}} B = \bigcup_{i=1}^{\infty} B_i. \tag{2.1}$$

Proof Consider the collection $\mathcal{S} = \{S_k = S(r_k,s_k),\ r_k \in \mathbb{Q},\ s_k \in \mathbb{Q}^+\}$; that is the collection of all neighbourhoods of rational points of $\mathbb{R}$, having rational radii. The set $\mathbb{Q}\times\mathbb{Q}^+$ is countable by **1.5**, and hence $\mathcal{S}$ is countable; in other words, indexing by $k \in \mathbb{N}$ exhausts the set. We show that, for any open set $B \subseteq \mathbb{R}$ and point $x \in B$, there is a set $S_k \in \mathcal{S}$ such that $x \in S_k \subseteq B$. Since x has a ε-neighbourhood inside B by definition, the desired S_k is found by setting s_k to any rational from the open interval $(0,\frac{1}{2}\varepsilon)$, for $\varepsilon > 0$ sufficiently small, and then choosing $r_k \in S(x,\frac{1}{4}\varepsilon)$ as is possible by **1.10**.

Now for each $x \in \bigcup_{B \in \mathcal{C}} B$ choose a member of $\mathcal{S}$, say $S_{k(x)}$, satisfying $x \in S_{k(x)} \subseteq B$ for any $B \in \mathcal{C}$. Letting $k(x)$ be the smallest index which satisfies the requirement gives an unambiguous choice. The distinct members of this collection form a set that covers $\bigcup_{B \in \mathcal{C}} B$, but is a subset of $\mathcal{S}$ and hence countable. Labelling the indices of this set as $k_1,k_2,\ldots$, choose B_i as any member of $\mathcal{C}$ containing S_{k_i}. Clearly, $\bigcup_{i=1}^{\infty} B_i$ is a countable covering for $\bigcup_{i=1}^{\infty} S_{k_i}$, and hence also for $\bigcup_{B \in \mathcal{C}} B$. ∎

It follows that, if $\mathcal{C}$ is a covering for a set in $\mathbb{R}$, it contains a countable *subcovering*. This is sometimes called the Lindelöf property.

The concept of a covering leads on to the crucial notion of *compactness*. A set A is said to be *compact* if every open covering of A contains a *finite* subcovering. The words that matter in this definition are 'every' and 'open'. Any open covering that has $\mathbb{R}$ as a member obviously contains a finite subcovering. But for a set to be compact, there must be no way to construct an irreducible, infinite open covering. Moreover, every interval has an irreducible infinite cover, consisting of the singleton sets of its individual points; but these sets are not open.

2.8 Example Consider the half-open interval $(0,1]$. An open covering is the countable collection $\{(1/n,1],\ n \in \mathbb{N}\}$. It is easy to see that there is no finite subcollection covering $(0,1]$ in this case, so $(0,1]$ is not compact. □

A set A is *bounded* if $A \subseteq S(x,\varepsilon)$ for some $x \in A$ and $\varepsilon > 0$. The idea here is that

ε is a possibly large but finite number. In other words, a bounded set must be containable within a finite interval.

2.9 Theorem A set in $\mathbb{R}$ is compact iff it is closed and bounded. □

This can be proved as a case of **5.12** below, and provides an alternative definition of compactness in $\mathbb{R}$. The sufficiency part is known as the Heine-Borel theorem.

A subset B of A is said to be *dense* in A if $B \subseteq A \subseteq \overline{B}$. Readers may think they know what is implied here after studying the following theorem, but denseness is a slightly tricky notion. See also **2.15** and the remarks following before coming to any premature conclusions.

2.10 Theorem Let A be an interval of $\mathbb{R}$, and $C \subseteq A$ be a countable set. Then $A - C$ is dense in A.

Proof By **1.7**, each neighbourhood of a point in A contains an uncountable number of points. Hence for each $x \in A$ (whether or not $x \in C$), the set $(A - C) \cap S(x,\varepsilon)$ is not empty for every $\varepsilon > 0$, so that x is a closure point of $A - C$. Thus, $A - C \subseteq (A - C) \cup C = A \subseteq \overline{(A - C)}$. ■

The k-fold Cartesian product of $\mathbb{R}$ with copies of itself generates what is called *Euclidean k-space*, $\mathbb{R}^k$. The points of $\mathbb{R}^k$ have the interpretation of k-vectors, or ordered k-tuples of real numbers, $\boldsymbol{x} = (x_1,x_2,\ldots,x_k)'$. All the concepts defined above for sets in $\mathbb{R}$ generalize directly to $\mathbb{R}^k$. The only modification required is to replace the scalars x and y by vectors $\boldsymbol{x}$ and $\boldsymbol{y}$, and define an ε-neighbourhood in a new way. Let $\|\boldsymbol{x} - \boldsymbol{y}\|$ be the Euclidean distance between $\boldsymbol{x}$ and $\boldsymbol{y}$, where $\|\boldsymbol{a}\| = [\sum_{i=1}^k a_i^2]^{1/2}$ is the length of the vector $\boldsymbol{a} = (a_1,\ldots,a_k)'$ and then define $S(\boldsymbol{x},\varepsilon) = \{\boldsymbol{y}\colon \|\boldsymbol{x} - \boldsymbol{y}\| < \varepsilon\}$, for some $\varepsilon > 0$. An open set A of $\mathbb{R}^2$ is one in which every point $\boldsymbol{x} \in A$ can be contained in an open disk with positive radius centred on $\boldsymbol{x}$. In $\mathbb{R}^3$ the open disk becomes an open sphere, and so on.

2.2 Sequences and Limits

A *real sequence* is a mapping from $\mathbb{N}$ into $\mathbb{R}$. The elements of the domain are called the *indices* and those of the range variously the *terms*, *members*, or *coordinates* of the sequence. We will denote a sequence either by $\{x_n, n \in \mathbb{N}\}$, or more briefly by $\{x_n\}_1^\infty$, or just by $\{x_n\}$ when the context is clear.

$\{x_n\}_1^\infty$ is said to *converge* to a limit x, if for every $\varepsilon > 0$ there is an integer N_ε for which

$$|x_n - x| < \varepsilon \text{ for all } n > N_\varepsilon. \tag{2.2}$$

Write $x_n \to x$, or $x = \lim_{n\to\infty} x_n$. When a sequence is tending to $+\infty$ or $-\infty$ it is often said to *diverge*, but it may also be said to converge in $\overline{\mathbb{R}}$, to distinguish those cases when it is does not approach *any* fixed value, but is always wandering.

A sequence is *monotone* (non-decreasing, increasing, non-increasing, or decreasing) if one of the inequalities $x_n \le x_{n+1}$, $x_n < x_{n+1}$, $x_n \ge x_{n+1}$, or $x_n > x_{n+1}$ holds for every n. To indicate that a monotone sequence is converging, one may write for emphasis either $x_n \uparrow x$ or $x_n \downarrow x$, as appropriate, although $x_n \to x$ will also do in both cases. The following result does not require elaboration.

2.11 Theorem Every monotone sequence in a compact set converges. □

A sequence that does not converge may none the less visit the same point an infinite number of times, so exhibiting a kind of convergent behaviour. If $\{x_n, n \in \mathbb{N}\}$ is a real sequence, a *subsequence* is $\{x_{n_k}, k \in \mathbb{N}\}$ where $\{n_k, k \in \mathbb{N}\}$ is any increasing sequence of positive integers. If there exists a subsequence $\{x_{n_k}, k \in \mathbb{N}\}$ and a constant c such that $x_{n_k} \to c$, c is called a *cluster point* of the sequence. For example, the sequence $\{(-1)^n, n = 1,2,3,...\}$ does not converge, but the subsequence obtained by taking only even values of n converges trivially. c is usually a finite constant, but $+\infty$ and $-\infty$ may be cluster points of a sequence if we allow the notion of convergence in $\overline{\mathbb{R}}$. If a subsequence is convergent, then so is any subsequence *of* the subsequence, defined as $\{x_{m_k}, k \in \mathbb{N}\}$ where $\{m_k\}$ is an increasing sequence whose members are also members of $\{n_k\}$.

The concept of a subsequence is often useful in arguments concerning convergence. A typical line of reasoning employs a two-pronged attack; first one identifies a convergent subsequence (a monotone sequence, perhaps); then one uses other characteristics of the sequence to show that the cluster point is actually a limit. Especially useful in this connection is the knowledge that the members of the sequence are points in a compact set. Such sequences cannot diverge to infinity, since the set is bounded; and because the set is closed, any limit points or cluster points that exist must be in the set. Specifically, we have two useful results.

2.12 Theorem Every sequence in a compact set of $\mathbb{R}$ has at least one cluster point.

Proof A monotone sequence converges in a compact set by **2.11**. We show that every sequence $\{x_n, n \in \mathbb{N}\}$ has a monotone subsequence. Define a subsequence $\{x_{n_k}\}$ as follows. Set $n_1 = 1$, and for $k = 1,2,3,...$ let $x_{n_{k+1}} = \sup_{n \geq n_k} x_n$ if there exists a finite n_{k+1} satisfying this condition; otherwise let the subsequence terminate at n_k. This subsequence is non-increasing. If it terminates, the subsequence $\{x_n, n \geq n_k\}$ must contain a non-decreasing subsequence. A monotone subsequence therefore exists in every case. ■

2.13 Theorem A sequence in a compact set either has two or more cluster points, or it converges.

Proof Suppose that c is the unique cluster point of the sequence $\{x_n\}$, but that $x_n \not\to c$. Then there is an infinite set of integers $\{n_k, k \in \mathbb{N}\}$ such that $|x_{n_k} - c| \geq \varepsilon$ for some $\varepsilon > 0$. Define a sequence $\{y_k\}$ by setting $y_k = x_{n_k}$. Since $\{y_k\}$ is also a sequence on a compact set, it has a cluster point c' which by construction is different from c. But c' is also a cluster point of $\{x_n\}$, of which $\{y_k\}$ is a subsequence, which is a contradiction. Hence, $x_n \to c$. ■

2.14 Example Consider the sequence $\{1, x, x^2, x^3, ..., x^n, ...\}$, or more formally $\{x^n, n \in \mathbb{N}_0\}$, where x is a real number. In the case $|x| < 1$, this sequence converges to zero, $\{|x^n|\}$ being monotone on the compact interval $[0,1]$. The condition specified in (2.2) is satisfied for $N_\varepsilon = \log(\varepsilon)/\log|x|$ in this case. If $x = 1$ it converges to 1, trivially. If $x > 1$ it diverges in $\mathbb{R}$, but converges in $\overline{\mathbb{R}}$ to $+\infty$. If $x = -1$ it neither converges nor diverges, but oscillates between cluster points +1 and −1. Finally, if $x < -1$ the sequence diverges in $\mathbb{R}$, but does not converge in $\overline{\mathbb{R}}$. Ultimately, it oscillates between the cluster points $+\infty$ and $-\infty$. □

We may discuss the asymptotic behaviour of a real sequence even when it has no limit. The *superior limit* of a sequence $\{x_n\}$ is

$$\limsup_n x_n = \inf_n \sup_{m\geq n} x_m. \tag{2.3}$$

(Alternative notation: $\overline{\lim}_n x_n$.) The limsup is the *eventual* upper bound of a sequence. Think of $\{\sup_{m\geq n} x_m,\ n = 1,2,...\}$ as the sequence of the largest values the sequence takes beyond the point n. This may be $+\infty$ for every n, but in all cases it must be a non-increasing sequence having a limit, either $+\infty$ or a finite real number; this limit is the limsup of the sequence. A link with the corresponding concept for set sequences is that if $x_n = \sup A_n$ for some sequence of sets $\{A_n \subseteq \mathbb{R}\}$, then $\limsup x_n = \sup A$, where $A = \limsup_n A_n$. The inferior limit is defined likewise, as the eventual lower bound:

$$\liminf_n x_n = -\left(\limsup_n(-x_n)\right) = \sup_n \inf_{m\geq n} x_m, \tag{2.4}$$

also written $\underline{\lim}_n x_n$. Necessarily, $\liminf_n x_n \leq \limsup_n x_n$. When the limsup and liminf of a sequence are equal the sequence is convergent, and the limit is equal to their common value. If both equal $+\infty$, or $-\infty$, the sequence converges in $\overline{\mathbb{R}}$.

The usual application of these concepts is in arguments to establish the value of a limit. It may not be permissible to *assume* the existence of the limit, but the limsup and liminf always exist. The trick is to derive these and show them to be equal. For this purpose, it is sufficient in view of the above inequality to show $\liminf_n x_n \geq \limsup_n x_n$. We often use this type of argument in the sequel.

To determine whether a sequence converges it is not necessary to know what the limit is; the relationship between sequence coordinates 'in the tail' (as n becomes large) is sufficient for this purpose. The *Cauchy criterion* for convergence of a real sequence states that $\{x_n\}$ converges iff for every $\varepsilon > 0\ \exists\ N_\varepsilon$ such that $|x_n - x_m| < \varepsilon$ whenever $n > N_\varepsilon$ and $m > N_\varepsilon$. A sequence satisfying this criterion is called a *Cauchy sequence*. Any sequence satisfying (2.2) is a Cauchy sequence, and conversely, a real Cauchy sequence must possess a limit in $\mathbb{R}$. The two definitions are therefore equivalent (in $\mathbb{R}$, at least), but the Cauchy condition may be easier to verify in practice.

The limit of a Cauchy sequence whose members all belong to a set A is by definition a closure point of A, though it need not itself belong to A. Conversely, for every accumulation point x of a set A there must exist a Cauchy sequence in the set whose limit is x. Construct such a sequence by taking one point from each of the sequence of sets,

$$\{A \cap S(x,1/n),\ n = 1,2,3,..\},$$

none of which are empty by definition. The term *limit point* is sometimes used synonymously with accumulation point.

The following is a fundamental property of the reals.

2.15 Theorem Every real number is the limit of a Cauchy sequence of rationals.

Proof For finite n let x_n be a number whose decimal expansion consists only of zeros beyond the nth place in the sequence. If the decimal point appears at position m, with $m > n$, then x_n is an integer. If $m \leq n$, removing the decimal point produces a finite integer a, and $x_n = a/10^{n-m}$, so x_n is rational. Given any real x, a sequence of rationals $\{x_n\}$ is obtained by replacing with a zero every digit in the decimal expansion of x beyond the nth, for $n = 1,2,...$ Since $|x_{n+1} - x_n| < 10^{-n}$, $\{x_n\}$ is a Cauchy sequence and $x_n \to x$ as $n \to \infty$. ■

The sequence exhibited is increasing, but a decreasing sequence can also be constructed, as $\{-y_n\}$ where $\{y_n\}$ is an increasing sequence tending to $-x$. If x is itself rational, this construction works by putting $x_n = x$ for every n, which trivially defines a Cauchy sequence, but certain arguments such as in **2.16** below depend on having $x_n \neq x$ for every n. To satisfy this requirement, choose the 'non-terminating' representation of the number; for example, instead of 1 take 0.9999999..., and consider the sequence $\{0.9, 0.99, 0.999, ...\}$. This does not work for the point 0, but then one can choose $\{0.1, 0.01, 0.001,...\}$.

One interesting corollary of **2.15** is that, since every ε-neighbourhood of a real number must contain a rational, $\mathbb{Q}$ is dense in $\mathbb{R}$. We also showed in **2.10** that $\mathbb{R} - \mathbb{Q}$ is dense in $\mathbb{R}$, since $\mathbb{Q}$ is countable. We must be careful not to jump to the conclusion that because a set is dense, its complement must be 'sparse'. Another version of this proof, at least for points of the interval [0,1], is got by using the binary expansion of a real number. The *dyadic rationals* are the set

$$\mathbb{D} = \{i/2^n,\ i = 1,...,2^n - 1,\ n \in \mathbb{N}\}. \tag{2.5}$$

The dyadic rationals corresponding to a finite n define a covering of [0,1] by intervals of width $1/2^n$, which are bisected each time n is incremented. For any $x \in [0,1]$, a point of the set $\{i/2^n, i = 1,...,2^n - 1\}$ is contained in $S(x,\varepsilon)$ for $\varepsilon < 2/2^n$, so the dyadic rationals are dense in [0,1]. $\mathbb{D}$ is a convenient analytic tool when we need to define a sequence of partitions of an interval that is becoming dense in the limit, and will often appear in the sequel.

Another set of useful applications concern set limits in $\mathbb{R}$.

2.16 Theorem Every open interval is the limit of a sequence of closed subintervals with rational endpoints.

Proof If (a,b) is the interval, with $a < b$, choose Cauchy sequences of rationals $a_n \downarrow a$ and $b_n \uparrow b$, with $a_1 < b_1$ (always possible by **1.10**). By definition, for every $x \in (a,b)$ there exists $N \geq 1$ such that $x \in [a_n,b_n]$ for all $n \geq N$, and hence $(a,b) \subseteq \liminf_n[a_n,b_n]$. On the other hand, since $a_n > a$ and $b > b_n$, $(a,b)^c \subseteq [a_n,b_n]^c$ for all $n \geq 1$, so that $(a,b)^c \subseteq \liminf_n[a_n,b_n]^c$. This is equivalent to $\limsup_n[a_n,b_n] \subseteq (a,b)$. Hence $\lim_n[a_n,b_n]$ exists and is equal to (a,b). ■

This shows that the limits of sequences of open sets need not be open, nor the limits of sequences of closed sets closed (take complements above). The only hard and fast rules we may lay down are the following corollaries of **2.4**(i): the limit of a non-decreasing sequence of open sets is open, and (by complements) the limit of a non-increasing sequence of closed sets is closed.

2.3 Functions and Continuity

A *function* of a real variable is a mapping $f: \mathbb{S} \mapsto \mathbb{T}$, where $\mathbb{S} \subseteq \mathbb{R}$, and $\mathbb{T} \subseteq \mathbb{R}$. By specifying a subset of $\mathbb{R}$ as the codomain, we imply without loss of generality that $f(\mathbb{S}) = \mathbb{T}$, such that the mapping is *onto* $\mathbb{T}$.

Consider the image in $\mathbb{T}$, under f, of a Cauchy sequence $\{x_n\}$ in $\mathbb{S}$ converging to x. If the image of every such sequence converging to $x \in \mathbb{S}$ is a Cauchy sequence in $\mathbb{T}$ converging to $f(x)$, the function is said to be *continuous* at x. Continuity is formally defined, without invoking sequences explicitly, using the $\varepsilon - \delta$ approach. f is continuous at the point $x \in \mathbb{S}$ if for any $\varepsilon > 0 \; \exists \; \delta > 0$ such that $|y - x| < \delta$ implies $|f(y) - f(x)| < \varepsilon$, whenever $y \in \mathbb{S}$. The choice of δ here may depend on x. If f is continuous at every point of $\mathbb{S}$, it is simply said to be continuous on $\mathbb{S}$.

Perhaps the chief reason why continuity matters is the following result.

2.17 Theorem If $f: \mathbb{S} \mapsto \mathbb{T}$ is continuous at all points of $\mathbb{S}$, $f^{-1}(A)$ is open in $\mathbb{S}$ whenever A is open in $\mathbb{T}$, and $f^{-1}(A)$ is closed in $\mathbb{S}$ whenever A is closed in $\mathbb{T}$. □

This important result has several generalizations, of which one, the extension to vector functions, is given in the next section. A proof will be given in a still more general context below; see **5.19**.

Continuity does *not* ensure that $f(A)$ is open when A is open. A mapping with this property is called an *open mapping*, although, since $f(A^c) \neq f(A)^c$ in general, we cannot assume that an open mapping is also a closed mapping, taking closed sets to closed sets. However, a *homeomorphism* is a function which is 1-1 onto, continuous, and has a continuous inverse. If f is a homeomorphism so is f^{-1}, and hence by **2.17** it is both an open mapping and a closed mapping. It therefore preserves the structure of neighbourhoods, so that, if two points are close in the domain, their images are always close in the range. Such a transformation amounts to a relabelling of axes.

If $f(x+h)$ has a limit as $h \downarrow 0$, this is denoted $f(x+)$. Likewise, $f(x-)$ denotes the limit of $f(x-h)$. It is not necessary to have $x \in \mathbb{S}$ for these limits to exist, but if $f(x)$ exists, there is a weaker notion of continuity at x. f is said to be *right-continuous* at the point $x \in \mathbb{S}$ if, for any $\varepsilon > 0$, $\exists \; \delta > 0$ such that whenever $0 \leq h < \delta$ and $x + h \in \mathbb{S}$,

$$|f(x+h) - f(x)| < \varepsilon. \tag{2.6}$$

It is said to be *left-continuous* at x if, for any $\varepsilon > 0$, $\exists \; \delta > 0$ such that whenever $0 \leq h < \delta$ and $x - h \in \mathbb{S}$,

$$|f(x) - f(x-h)| < \varepsilon. \tag{2.7}$$

Right continuity at x implies $f(x) = f(x+)$ and left continuity at x implies $f(x) = f(x-)$. If $f(x) = f(x+) = f(x-)$, the function is continuous at x.

Continuity is the property of a point x, not of the function f as a whole. Despite continuity holding pointwise on $\mathbb{S}$, the property may none the less break down as certain points are approached.

2.18 Example Consider $f(x) = 1/x$, with $\mathbb{S} = \mathbb{T} = (0, \infty)$. For $\varepsilon > 0$,

$$|f(x+\delta) - f(x)| = \frac{\delta}{x(x+\delta)} < \varepsilon \text{ iff } \delta < \frac{\varepsilon x^2}{1-\varepsilon x}$$

and hence the choice of δ depends on both ε and x. $f(x)$ is continuous for all $x > 0$, but not in the limit as $x \to 0$. □

The function $f: \mathbb{S} \mapsto \mathbb{T}$ is *uniformly* continuous if for every $\varepsilon > 0 \; \exists \; \delta > 0$ such that

$$|x - y| < \delta \Rightarrow |f(x) - f(y)| < \varepsilon \tag{2.8}$$

for every $x,y \in \mathbb{S}$. In **2.18** the function is not uniformly continuous, for whichever δ is chosen, we can pick x small enough to invalidate the definition. The problem arises because the set on which the function is defined is open and the boundary point is a discontinuity. Another class of cases that gives difficulty is the one where the domain is unbounded, and continuity at x is breaking down as $x \to \infty$. However, we have the following result.

2.19 Theorem If a function is continuous everywhere on a compact set $\mathbb{S}$, then it is bounded and uniformly continuous on $\mathbb{S}$. □

(For proof, see **5.20** and **5.21**.)

Continuity is the weakest concept of smoothness of a function. So-called *Lipschitz conditions* provide a whole class of smoothness properties. A function f is said to satisfy a Lipschitz condition at a point x if, for any $y \in S(x,\delta)$ for some $\delta > 0$, $\exists \; M > 0$ such that

$$|f(y) - f(x)| \leq Mh(|x - y|) \tag{2.9}$$

where h: $\mathbb{R}^+ \mapsto \mathbb{R}^+$ satisfies $h(d) \downarrow 0$ as $d \downarrow 0$. f is said to satisfy a *uniform Lipschitz condition* if condition (2.9) holds, with fixed M, for all $x,y \in \mathbb{S}$. The type of smoothness imposed depends on the function h. Continuity (resp. uniform continuity) follows from the Lipschitz (resp. uniform Lipschitz) property for any choice of h. Implicit in continuity is the idea that some function $\delta(.)$: $\mathbb{R}^+ \mapsto \mathbb{R}^+$ exists satisfying $\delta(\varepsilon) \downarrow 0$ as $\varepsilon \downarrow 0$. This is equivalent to the Lipschitz condition holding for *some* $h(.)$, the case $h = \delta^{-1}$. By imposing some degree of smoothness on h—making it a positive power of the argument for example—we impose a degree of smoothness on the function, forbidding sharp 'corners'.

The next smoothness concept is undoubtedly well known to the reader, although differential calculus will play a fairly minor role here. Let a function $f: \mathbb{S} \mapsto \mathbb{T}$ be continuous at $x \in \mathbb{S}$. If

$$f'_+(x) = \lim_{h \downarrow 0} \left\{ \frac{f(x+h) - f(x)}{h} \right\} \tag{2.10}$$

exists, $f'_+(x)$ is called the *left-hand derivative* of f at x. The *right-hand derivative*, $f'_-(x)$, is defined correspondingly for the case $h \uparrow 0$. If $f'_+(x) = f'_-(x)$, the common value is called the *derivative* of f at x, denoted $f'(x)$ or df/dx, and f is said to be *differentiable* at x. If $f'\colon \mathbb{S} \mapsto \mathbb{R}$ is a continuous function, f is said to be *continuously differentiable* on $\mathbb{S}$.

A function f is said to be non-decreasing (resp. increasing) if $f(y) \geq f(x)$ (resp. $f(y) > f(x)$) whenever $y > x$. It is non-increasing (resp. decreasing) if $-f$ is non-decreasing (resp. increasing). A *monotone* function is either non-decreasing or non-increasing.

When the domain is an interval we have yet another smoothness condition. A function $f\colon [a,b] \mapsto \mathbb{R}$ is *of bounded variation* if $\exists\ M < \infty$ such that for every partition of $[a,b]$ by finite collections of points $a = x_0 < x_1 < \ldots < x_n = b$,

$$\sum_{k=1}^{n} |f(x_i) - f(x_{i-1})| \leq M. \tag{2.11}$$

2.20 Theorem If and only if f is of bounded variation, there exist non-decreasing functions f_1 and f_2 such that $f = f_2 - f_1$. □

(For proof see Apostol 1974: Ch. 6.) A function that satisfies the uniform Lipschitz condition on $[a,b]$ with $h(|x-y|) = |x-y|$ is of bounded variation on $[a,b]$.

2.4 Vector Sequences and Functions

A sequence $\{\boldsymbol{x}_n\}$ of real k-vectors is said to converge to a limit $\boldsymbol{x}$ if for every $\varepsilon > 0$ there is an integer N_ε for which

$$\|\boldsymbol{x}_n - \boldsymbol{x}\| < \varepsilon \text{ for all } n > N_\varepsilon. \tag{2.12}$$

The sequence is called a Cauchy sequence in $\mathbb{R}^k$ iff $\|\boldsymbol{x}_n - \boldsymbol{x}_m\| < \varepsilon$ whenever $n > N_\varepsilon$ and $m > N_\varepsilon$.

A function

$$f\colon \mathbb{S} \mapsto \mathbb{T},$$

where $\mathbb{S} \subseteq \mathbb{R}^k$, and $\mathbb{T} \subseteq \mathbb{R}$, associates each point of $\mathbb{S}$ with a unique point of $\mathbb{T}$. Its graph is the subset of $\mathbb{S} \times \mathbb{T}$ consisting of the $(k+1)$-vectors $\{\boldsymbol{x}, f(\boldsymbol{x})\}$ for each $\boldsymbol{x} \in \mathbb{S}$. f is continuous at $\boldsymbol{x} \in \mathbb{S}$ if for any $\varepsilon > 0\ \exists\ \delta > 0$ such that

$$\|\boldsymbol{b}\| < \delta \Rightarrow |f(\boldsymbol{x}+\boldsymbol{b}) - f(\boldsymbol{x})| < \varepsilon \tag{2.13}$$

whenever $\boldsymbol{x}+\boldsymbol{b} \in \mathbb{S}$. The choice of δ may here depend on $\boldsymbol{x}$. On the other hand, f is uniformly continuous on $\mathbb{S}$ if for any $\varepsilon > 0$, $\exists\ \delta > 0$ such that

$$\|\boldsymbol{b}\| < \delta \Rightarrow \sup_{\boldsymbol{x} \in \mathbb{S}, \boldsymbol{x}+\boldsymbol{b} \in \mathbb{S}} |f(\boldsymbol{x}+\boldsymbol{b}) - f(\boldsymbol{x})| < \varepsilon. \tag{2.14}$$

A vector $\boldsymbol{f} = (f_1,\dots,f_m)'$ of functions of $\boldsymbol{x}$ is called, simply enough, a vector function.[2] Continuity concepts apply element-wise to $\boldsymbol{f}$ in the obvious way. The function

$$\boldsymbol{f}: \mathbb{S} \mapsto \mathbb{S},\ \mathbb{S} \subseteq \mathbb{R}^k$$

is said to be one-to-one if there exists a vector function $\boldsymbol{f}^{-1}: \mathbb{S} \mapsto \mathbb{S}$, such that $\boldsymbol{f}^{-1}(\boldsymbol{f}(\boldsymbol{x})) = \boldsymbol{x}$ for each $\boldsymbol{x} \in \mathbb{S}$. An example of a 1-1 continuous function is the affine transformation[3]

$$\boldsymbol{f}(\boldsymbol{x}) = \boldsymbol{A}\boldsymbol{x} + \boldsymbol{b}$$

for constants $\boldsymbol{b}$ $(k \times 1)$ and $\boldsymbol{A}$ $(k \times k)$ with $|\boldsymbol{A}| \neq 0$, having inverse $\boldsymbol{f}^{-1}(\boldsymbol{y}) = \boldsymbol{A}^{-1}(\boldsymbol{y} - \boldsymbol{b})$. In most other cases the function $\boldsymbol{f}^{-1}$ does not possess a closed form, but there is a generalization of **2.17**, as follows.

2.21 Theorem Iff $\boldsymbol{f}: \mathbb{S} \mapsto \mathbb{T}$ is continuous, where $\mathbb{S} \subseteq \mathbb{R}^k$ and $\mathbb{T} \subseteq \mathbb{R}^m$, $\boldsymbol{f}^{-1}(A)$ is open in $\mathbb{S}$ when A is open in $\mathbb{T}$, and $\boldsymbol{f}^{-1}(A)$ is closed in $\mathbb{S}$ when A is closed in $\mathbb{T}$. □

2.5 Sequences of Functions

Let $f_n: \Omega \mapsto \mathbb{T}$, $\mathbb{T} \subseteq \mathbb{R}$, be a function, where in this case Ω may be an arbitrary set, not necessarily a subset of $\mathbb{R}$. Let $\{f_n,\ n \in \mathbb{N}\}$ be a sequence of such functions. If there exists f such that, for each $\omega \in \Omega$, and $\varepsilon > 0$, $\exists\ N_{\varepsilon\omega}$ such that $|f_n(\omega) - f(\omega)| < \varepsilon$ when $n > N_{\varepsilon\omega}$, then f_n is said to converge to f, *pointwise* on Ω. As for real sequences, we use the notations $f_n \to f$, $f_n \uparrow f$, or $f_n \downarrow f$, as appropriate, for general or monotone convergence, where in the latter case the monotonicity must apply for every $\omega \in \Omega$. This is a relatively weak notion of convergence, for it does not rule out the possibility that the convergence is breaking down at certain points of Ω. The following example is related to **2.18** above.

2.22 Example Let $f_n(x) = n/(nx + 1)$, $x \in (0,\infty)$. The pointwise limit of $f_n(x)$ on $(0,\infty)$ is $1/x$. But

$$\left| f_n(x) - \frac{1}{x} \right| = \frac{1}{x(nx+1)},$$

and $1/(x(N_{\varepsilon x}x + 1)) < \varepsilon$ only for $N_{\varepsilon x} > (1/\varepsilon x - 1)(1/x)$. Thus for given ε, $N_{\varepsilon x} \to \infty$ as $x \to 0$ and it is not possible to put an upper bound on $N_{\varepsilon x}$ such that $|f_n(x) - 1/x| < \varepsilon$, $n \geq N_{\varepsilon x}$, for every $x > 0$. □

To rule out cases of this type, we define the stronger notion of *uniform convergence*. If there exists a function f such that, for each $\varepsilon > 0$, there exists N such that

$$\sup_{\omega \in \Omega} |f_n(\omega) - f(\omega)| < \varepsilon \text{ when } n > N,$$

f_n is said to converge to f uniformly on Ω.

2.6 Summability and Order Relations

The sum of the terms of a real sequence $\{x_n\}_1^\infty$ is called a *series*, written $\sum_{n=1}^\infty x_n$ (or just $\sum x_n$). The terms of the real sequence $\{\sum_{m=1}^n x_m,\ n \in \mathbb{N}\}$ are called the *partial sums* of the series. We say that the series converges if the partial sums converge to a finite limit. A series is said to *converge absolutely* if the monotone sequence $\{\sum_{m=1}^n |x_m|,\ n \in \mathbb{N}\}$ converges.

2.23 Example Consider the *geometric series*, $\sum_{j=1}^\infty x^j$. This converges to $1/(1-x)$ when $|x| < 1$, and also converges absolutely. It oscillates between cluster points 0 and 1 for $x = -1$, and for other values of x it diverges. □

2.24 Theorem If a series converges absolutely, then it converges.

Proof The sequence $\{\sum_{m=1}^n |x_m|,\ n \in \mathbb{N}\}$ is monotone, and either diverges to $+\infty$ or converges to a finite limit. In the latter case the Cauchy criterion implies that $|x_n| + \dots + |x_{n+m}| \to 0$ as m and n tend to infinity. Since $|x_n| + \dots + |x_{n+m}| \geq |x_n + \dots + x_{n+m}|$ by the triangle inequality,[4] convergence of $\{\sum_{m=1}^n x_m,\ n \in \mathbb{N}\}$ follows by the same criterion. ■

An alternative terminology speaks of *summability*. A real sequence $\{x_n\}_1^\infty$ is said to be summable if the series $\sum x_n$ converges, and absolutely summable if $\{|x_n|\}_1^\infty$ is summable. Any absolutely summable sequence is summable by **2.24**, and any summable sequence must be converging to zero. Convergence to zero does not imply summability (see **2.27** below, for example), but convergence of the *tail sums* to zero is necessary and sufficient.

2.25 Theorem Iff $\{x_n\}_1^\infty$ is summable, $\sum_{m=n}^\infty x_m \to 0$ as $n \to \infty$.

Proof For necessity, write $|\sum_{m=1}^\infty x_m| \leq |\sum_{m=1}^{n-1} x_m| + |\sum_{m=n}^\infty x_m|$. Since for any $\varepsilon > 0$ there exists N such that $|\sum_{m=n}^\infty x_m| < \varepsilon$ for $n \geq N$, it follows that $|\sum_{m=1}^\infty x_m| \leq |\sum_{m=1}^{N-1} x_m| + \varepsilon < \infty$. Conversely, assume summability and let $A = \sum_{n=1}^\infty x_n$. Then $\sum_{m=n}^\infty x_m = A - \sum_{m=1}^{n-1} x_m \to 0$ as $n \to \infty$. ■

A sequence $\{x_n\}_1^\infty$ is *Cesàro-summable* if the sequence $\{n^{-1}\sum_{m=1}^n x_m\}_1^\infty$ converges. This is weaker than ordinary convergence.

2.26 Theorem If $\{x_n\}_1^\infty$ converges to x, its Cesàro sum also converges to x. □

But a sequence can be Cesàro-summable in spite of not converging. The sequence $\{(-1)^n\}_0^\infty$ converges in Cesàro sum to zero, whereas the partial sum sequence $\{\sum_{m=0}^n (-1)^m\}_0^\infty$ converges in Cesàro sum to $\frac{1}{2}$ (compare **2.14**).

Various notations are used to indicate the relationships between rates of divergence or convergence of different sequences. If $\{x_n\}_1^\infty$ is any real sequence, $\{a_n\}_1^\infty$ is a sequence of positive real numbers, and there exists a constant $B < \infty$ such that $|x_n|/a_n \leq B$ for all n, we say that x_n is (at most) of the order of magnitude of a_n, and write $x_n = O(a_n)$. If $\{x_n/a_n\}$ converges to zero, we write $x_n = o(a_n)$, and say that x_n is of smaller order of magnitude than a_n. a_n can be increasing or decreasing, so this notation can be used to express an upper bound either on the rate of growth of a divergent sequence, or on the rate of convergence of a sequence to zero. Here are some rules for manipulation of $O(.)$, whose proof follows from the definition. If $x_n = O(n^\alpha)$ and $y_n = O(n^\beta)$, then

$$x_n + y_n = O(n^{\max\{\alpha,\beta\}}) \tag{2.15}$$

$$x_n y_n = O(n^{\alpha+\beta}), \tag{2.16}$$

$$x_n^\beta = O(n^{\alpha\beta}), \text{ whenever } x_n^\beta \text{ is defined.} \tag{2.17}$$

An alternative notation for the case $x_n \geq 0$ is $x_n \ll a_n$, which means that there is a constant, $0 < B < \infty$, such that $x_n \leq Ba_n$ for all n. This may be more convenient in algebraic manipulations.

The notation $x_n \sim a_n$ will be used to indicate that there exist $N \geq 0$, and finite constants $A > 0$ and $B \geq A$, such that $\inf_{n\geq N}(x_n/a_n) \geq A$ and $\sup_{n\geq N}(x_n/a_n) \leq B$. This says that $\{x_n\}$ and $\{a_n\}$ grow ultimately at the same rate, and is different from the relation $x_n = O(a_n)$, since the latter does not exclude $x_n/a_n \to 0$. Some authors use $x_n \sim a_n$ in the stronger sense of $x_n/a_n \to 1$.

2.27 Theorem If $\{x_n\}$ is a real positive sequence, and $x_n \sim n^\alpha$,
(i) if $\alpha > -1$ then $\sum_{m=1}^n x_m \sim n^{1+\alpha}$;
(ii) if $\alpha = -1$ then $\sum_{m=1}^n x_m \sim \log n$;
(iii) if $\alpha < -1$ then $\sum_{m=1}^\infty x_m < \infty$ and $\sum_{m=n}^\infty x_m = O(n^{1+\alpha})$.

Proof By assumption there exist $N \geq 1$ and constants $A > 0$ and $B \geq A$ such that $An^\alpha \leq x_n \leq Bn^\alpha$ for $n \geq N$, and hence $A\sum_{m=N}^n m^\alpha \leq \sum_{m=N}^n x_m \leq B\sum_{m=N}^n m^\alpha$. The limit of $\sum_{m=1}^n m^\alpha$ as $n \to \infty$ for different values of α defines the *Riemann zeta function* for $\alpha < -1$, and its rates of divergence for $\alpha \geq -1$ are standard results; see e.g. Apostol (1974: Sects. 8.12-8.13). Since the sum of terms from 1 to $N-1$ is finite, their omission cannot change the conclusions. ∎

It is common practice to express the rate of convergence to zero of a positive real sequence in terms of the summability of the coordinates raised to a given power. The following device allows some further refinement of summability conditions. Let $U(\nu)$ be a positive function of ν. If $U(\nu x)/U(\nu) \to x^\rho$ as $\nu \to \infty$ (0) for $x > 0$ and $-\infty < \rho < +\infty$, U is said to be *regularly varying at infinity* (*zero*). If a positive function $L(\nu)$ has the property $L(\nu x)/L(\nu) \to 1$ for $x > 0$ as $\nu \to \infty$ (0), it is said to be *slowly varying at infinity* (*zero*). Evidently, any regularly varying function can be expressed in the form $U(\nu) = \nu^\rho L(\nu)$, where $L(\nu)$ is slowly varying. While the definition allows ν to be a real variable, in the cases of interest we will have $\nu = n$ for $n \in \mathbb{N}$, with U and L having the interpretation of positive sequences.

2.28 Example $(\log \nu)^\alpha$ is slowly varying at infinity, for any α. □

On the theory of regular variation see Feller (1971), or Loève (1977). The important property is the following.

2.29 Theorem If L is slowly varying at infinity, then for any $\delta > 0$ there exists $N \geq 1$ such that

$$\nu^{-\delta} < L(\nu) < \nu^{\delta},\ \text{all } \nu > N. \ \square \tag{2.18}$$

Hence we have the following corollary of **2.27**, which shows how the notion of a convergent power series can be refined by allowing for the presence of a slowly varying function.

2.30 Corollary If $x_n = O(n^{\alpha}L(n))$ then $\sum_{n=1}^{\infty} x_n < \infty$ for all $\alpha < -1$ and all functions $L(n)$ which are slowly varying at infinity. □

On the other hand, the presence of a slowly varying component can affect the summability of a sequence. The following result can be proved using the integral test for series convergence (Apostol 1974: Sect. 8.12).

2.31 Theorem If $x_n \sim 1/[n(\log n)^{1+\delta}]$ with $\delta > 0$, then $\sum_{n=1}^{\infty} x_n < \infty$. If $\delta = 0$, then $\sum_{m=1}^{n} x_m \sim \log\log n$. □

2.32 Theorem (Feller 1971: 275) If a positive *monotone* function $U(\nu)$ satisfies

$$\frac{U(\nu x)}{U(\nu)} \to \psi(x),\ \text{all } x \in D, \tag{2.19}$$

where D is dense in $\mathbb{R}^+$, and $0 < \psi(x) < \infty$, then $\psi(x) = x^{\rho}$ for $-\infty < \rho < \infty$. □

To the extent that (2.19) is a fairly general property, we can conclude that monotone functions are as a rule regularly varying.

2.33 Theorem The derivative of a monotone regularly varying function is regularly varying at ∞.

Proof Given $U(\nu) = \nu^{\rho}L(\nu)$, write

$$U'(\nu) = \rho\nu^{\rho-1}L(\nu) + \nu^{\rho}L'(\nu) = \nu^{\rho-1}(\rho L(\nu) + \nu L'(\nu)). \tag{2.20}$$

If $L'(\nu) \to 0$ there is no more to show, so assume $\liminf_{\nu} L'(\nu) > 0$. Then

$$\frac{d}{d\nu}\left(\frac{L(\nu x)}{L(\nu)}\right) = \frac{L'(\nu)}{L(\nu)}\left(\frac{L'(\nu x)}{L'(\nu)} - \frac{L(\nu x)}{L(\nu)}\right) \to 0, \tag{2.21}$$

which implies $L'(\nu x)/L'(\nu) \to 1$. Thus,

$$\frac{U'(\nu x)}{U'(\nu)} = x^{\rho-1}\frac{\rho L(\nu x) + \nu x L'(\nu x)}{\rho L(\nu) + \nu L'(\nu)} \to x^{\rho}. \ \blacksquare \tag{2.22}$$

2.7 Arrays

Arguments concerning stochastic convergence often involve a double-indexing of elements. An *array* is a mapping whose domain is the Cartesian product of countable, linearly ordered sets, such as $\mathbb{N}\times\mathbb{N}$ or $\mathbb{Z}\times\mathbb{N}$, or a subset thereof. A real double array, in particular, is a double-indexed collection of numbers, or, alternatively, a sequence whose members are real sequences. We will use notation such as $\{\{x_{nt},\ t \in \mathbb{Z}\},\ n \in \mathbb{N}\}$, or just $\{x_{nt}\}$ when the context is clear.

A collection of finite sequences $\{\{x_{nt}, t = 1,...,k_n\}, n \in \mathbb{N}\}$, where $k_n \uparrow \infty$ as $n \to \infty$, is called a *triangular array*. As an example, consider array elements of the form $x_{nt} = y_t/n$, where $\{y_t, t = 1,...,n\}$ is a real sequence. The question of whether the series $\{\sum_{t=1}^n x_{nt}, n \in \mathbb{N}\}$ converges is equivalent to that of the Cesàro convergence of the original sequence; however, the array formulation is frequently the more convenient.

2.34 Toeplitz's lemma Suppose $\{y_n\}$ is a real sequence and $y_n \to y$. If $\{\{x_{nt}, t = 1,...,k_n\}, n \in \mathbb{N}\}$ is a triangular array such that

(a) $x_{nt} \to 0$ as $n \to \infty$ for each fixed t,

(b) $\displaystyle\lim_{n\to\infty} \sum_{t=1}^{k_n} |x_{nt}| \le C < \infty$,

(c) $\displaystyle\lim_{n\to\infty} \sum_{t=1}^{k_n} x_{nt} = 1$,

then $\sum_{t=1}^{k_n} x_{nt}y_t \to y$. For $y = 0$, (c) can be omitted.

Proof By assumption on $\{y_n\}$, for any $\varepsilon > 0$ $\exists$ $N_\varepsilon \ge 1$ such that for $n > N_\varepsilon$, $|y_n - y| < \varepsilon/C$. Hence by (c), and then (b) and the triangle inequality,

$$\lim_{n\to\infty} \left| \sum_{t=1}^{k_n} x_{nt}y_t - y \right| = \lim_{n\to\infty} \left| \sum_{t=1}^{k_n} x_{nt}(y_t - y) \right|$$

$$\le \lim_{n\to\infty} \left| \sum_{t=1}^{N_\varepsilon} x_{nt}(y_t - y) \right| + \varepsilon = \varepsilon, \tag{2.23}$$

in view of (a). This completes the proof, since ε is arbitrary. ■

A particular case of an array $\{x_{nt}\}$ satisfying the conditions of the lemma is $x_{nt} = (\sum_{s=1}^n y_s)^{-1} y_t$, where $\{y_t\}$ is a positive sequence and $\sum_{s=1}^n y_s \to \infty$.

A leading application of this result is to prove the following theorem, a fundamental tool of limit theory.

2.35 Kronecker's lemma Consider sequences $\{a_t\}_1^\infty$ and $\{x_t\}_1^\infty$ of positive real numbers, with $a_t \uparrow \infty$. If $\sum_{t=1}^n x_t/a_t \to C < \infty$ as $n \to \infty$,

$$\frac{1}{a_n}\sum_{t=1}^n x_t \to 0. \tag{2.24}$$

Proof Defining $c_0 = 0$ and $c_n = \sum_{t=1}^n x_t/a_t$ for $n \in \mathbb{N}$, note that $x_t = a_t(c_t - c_{t-1})$, $t = 1,...,n$. Also define $a_0 = 0$ and $b_t = a_t - a_{t-1}$ for $t = 1,...,n$, so that $a_n = \sum_{t=1}^n b_t$. Now apply the identity for arbitrary sequences $a_0,...,a_n$ and $c_0,...,c_n$,

$$\sum_{t=1}^n a_t(c_t - c_{t-1}) = \sum_{t=1}^n (a_{t-1} - a_t)c_{t-1} + a_nc_n - a_0c_0. \tag{2.25}$$

(This is known as Abel's partial summation formula.) We obtain

$$\frac{1}{a_n}\sum_{t=1}^{n}x_t = \frac{1}{a_n}\sum_{t=1}^{n}a_t(c_t - c_{t-1})$$

$$= c_n - \frac{1}{a_n}\sum_{t=1}^{n}b_t c_{t-1} \to C - C = 0 \tag{2.26}$$

where the convergence is by the Toeplitz lemma, setting $x_{nt} = b_t/a_n$. ■

The notion of array convergence extends the familiar sequence concept. Consider for full generality an array of subsequences, a collection $\{\{x_{mn_k}, k \in \mathbb{N}\}\ m \in \mathbb{N}\}$, where $\{n_k, k \in \mathbb{N}\}$ is an increasing sequence of positive integers. If the limit $x_m = \lim_{k\to\infty} x_{mn_k}$ exists for each $m \in \mathbb{N}$, we would say that the array is convergent; and its limit is the infinite sequence $\{x_m, m \in \mathbb{N}\}$. Whether *this* sequence converges is a separate question from whether it exists at all.

Suppose the array is bounded, in the sense that $\sup_{k,m}|x_{mn_k}| \le B < \infty$. We know by **2.12** that for each m there exists at least one cluster point, say x_m, of the inner sequence $\{x_{mn_k}, k \in \mathbb{N}\}$. An important question in several contexts is this: is it valid to say that the array as a whole has a cluster point?

2.36 Theorem Corresponding to any bounded array $\{\{x_{mn_k}, k \in \mathbb{N}\}, m \in \mathbb{N}\}$, there exists a sequence $\{x_m\}$, the limit of the array $\{\{x_{mn_k^*}, k \in \mathbb{N}\}, m \in \mathbb{N}\}$ as $k \to \infty$, where $\{n_k^*\}$ is the *same* subsequence of $\{n_k\}$ for each m.

Proof This is by construction of the required subsequence. Begin with a convergent subsequence for $m = 1$; let $\{n_k^1\}$ be a subsequence of $\{n_k\}$ such that $x_{1,n_k^1} \to x_1$. Next, consider the sequence $\{x_{2,n_k^1}\}$. Like $\{x_{2,n_k}\}$, this is on the bounded interval $(-B,B)$, and so contains a convergent subsequence. Let the indices of this latter subsequence, drawn from the members of $\{n_k^1\}$, be denoted $\{n_k^2\}$ and note that $x_{1,n_k^2} \to x_1$ as well as $x_{2,n_k^2} \to x_2$. Proceeding in the same way for each m generates an array $\{\{n_k^m, k \in \mathbb{N}\}, m \in \mathbb{N}\}$, having the property that $\{x_{i,n_k^m}, k \in \mathbb{N}\}$ is a convergent sequence for $1 \le i \le m$.

Now consider the sequence $\{n_k^k, k \in \mathbb{N}\}$; in other words, take the first member of $\{n_k^1\}$, the second member of $\{n_k^2\}$, and so on. For each m, this sequence is a subsequence of $\{n_k^m\}$ from the mth point of the sequence onwards, and hence the sequence $\{x_{m,n_k^k}, k \ge m\}$ is convergent. This means that the sequence $\{x_{m,n_k^k}, k \in \mathbb{N}\}$ is convergent, so setting $\{n_k^*\} = \{n_k^k\}$ satisfies the requirement of the theorem. ■

This is called the 'diagonal method'. The elements n_k^k may be thought of as the diagonal elements of the square matrix (of infinite order) whose rows contain the sequences $\{n_k^m\}$, each a subsequence of the row above it. This theorem holds independently of the nature of the elements $\{x_{mn}\}$. Any space of points on which convergent sequences are defined could be substituted for $\mathbb{R}$. We shall need a generalization on these lines in Chapter 26, for example.

3
Measure

3.1 Measure Spaces

A measure is a set function, a mapping which associates a (possibly extended) real number with a set. Commonplace examples of measures include the lengths, areas, and volumes of geometrical figures, but wholly abstract sets can be 'measured' in an analogous way. Formally, we have the following definition.

3.1 Definition Given a class $\mathcal{F}$ of subsets of a set Ω, a *measure*

$$\mu: \mathcal{F} \mapsto \overline{\mathbb{R}}$$

is a function having the following properties:

(a) $\mu(A) \geq 0$, all $A \in \mathcal{F}$.

(b) $\mu(\varnothing) = 0$.

(c) For a countable collection $\{A_j \in \mathcal{F}, j \in \mathbb{N}\}$ with $A_j \cap A_{j'} = \varnothing$ for $j \neq j'$ and $\bigcup_j A_j \in \mathcal{F}$,

$$\mu\left(\bigcup_j A_j\right) = \sum_j \mu(A_j). \quad \square \tag{3.1}$$

The particular cases at issue in this book are of course the probabilities of random events in a sample space Ω; more of this in Chapter 7. Condition (a) is optional and set functions taking either sign may be referred to as measures (see e.g. §4.4), but non-negativity is desirable for present purposes.

A *measurable space* is a pair $(\Omega,\mathcal{F})$ where Ω is any collection of objects, and $\mathcal{F}$ is a σ-field of subsets of Ω. When $(\Omega,\mathcal{F})$ is a measurable space, the triple $(\Omega,\mathcal{F},\mu)$ is called a *measure space*. More than one measure can be associated with the measurable space $(\Omega,\mathcal{F})$, hence the distinction between measure space and measurable space is important.

Condition **3.1**(c) is called *countable additivity*. If a set function has the property

$$\mu(A \cup B) = \mu(A) + \mu(B) \tag{3.2}$$

for each disjoint pair A,B, a property that extends by iteration to finite collections $A_1,\dots,A_n$, it is said to be *finitely additive*. In **3.1** $\mathcal{F}$ could be a field, but the possibility of extending the properties of μ to the corresponding σ-field, by allowing additivity over countable collections, is an essential feature of a measure.

If $\mu(\Omega) < \infty$ the measure is said to be *finite*. And if $\Omega = \bigcup_j \Omega_j$ where $\{\Omega_j\}$ is a countable collection of $\mathcal{F}$-sets, and $\mu(\Omega_j) < \infty$ for each j, μ is said to be *σ-finite*. In particular, if there is a collection $\mathcal{S}$ such that $\mathcal{F} = \sigma(\mathcal{S})$ and $\Omega_j \in \mathcal{S}$

for each j, μ is said to be σ-finite *on* $\mathcal{S}$ (rather than on $\mathcal{F}$). If $\mathcal{F}_A = \{A \cap B \colon B \in \mathcal{F}\}$ for some $A \in \mathcal{F}$, $(A, \mathcal{F}_A)$ is a measurable space and $(A, \mathcal{F}_A, \mu)$ is a measure space called the *restriction* of $(\Omega, \mathcal{F}, \mu)$ to A. If in this case $\mu(A^c) = 0$ (equivalent to $\mu(A) = \mu(\Omega)$ when $\mu(\Omega) < \infty$) A is called a *support* of the measure. When A supports Ω, the sets of $\mathcal{F}_A$ have the same measures as the corresponding ones of $\mathcal{F}$. A point $\omega \in \Omega$ with the property $\mu(\{\omega\}) > 0$ is called an *atom* of the measure.

3.2 Example The case closest to everyday intuition is *Lebesgue measure*, m, on the measurable space $(\mathbb{R}, \mathcal{B})$, where $\mathcal{B}$ is the Borel field on $\mathbb{R}$. Generalizing the notion of length in geometry, Lebesgue measure assigns $m((a,b]) = b - a$ to an interval $(a,b]$. Additivity is an intuitively plausible property if we think of measuring the total length of a collection of disjoint intervals.

Lebesgue measure is atomless (see **3.15** below), every point of the line taking measure 0, but $m(\mathbb{R}) = \infty$. Letting $((a,b], \mathcal{B}_{(a,b]}, m)$ denote the restriction of $(\mathbb{R}, \mathcal{B}, m)$ to a finite interval, m is a finite measure on $(a,b]$. Since $\mathbb{R}$ can be partitioned into a countable collection of finite intervals, m is σ-finite. □

Some additional properties may be deduced from the definition:

3.3 Theorem For arbitrary $\mathcal{F}$-sets A, B, and $\{A_j, j \in \mathbb{N}\}$,

(i) $A \subseteq B \Rightarrow \mu(A) \le \mu(B)$ (monotonicity).

(ii) $\mu(A \cup B) + \mu(A \cap B) = \mu(A) + \mu(B)$.

(iii) $\mu(\bigcup_j A_j) \le \sum_j \mu(A_j)$ (countable subadditivity).

Proof To show (i) note that A and $B - A$ are disjoint sets whose union is B, by hypothesis, and use **3.1**(a) and **3.1**(c). To show (ii), use $A \cup B = A \cup (B - A)$ and $B = (A \cap B) \cup (B - A)$, where again the sets in each union are disjoint. The result follows on application of **3.1**(c). To show (iii), define $B_1 = A_1$ and $B_n = A_n - \bigcup_{j=1}^{n-1} A_j$. Note that the sets B_n are disjoint, that $B_n \subseteq A_n$, and that $\bigcup_{j=1}^{\infty} B_j = \bigcup_{j=1}^{\infty} A_j$. Hence,

$$\mu\left(\bigcup_{j=1}^{\infty} A_j\right) = \mu\left(\bigcup_{j=1}^{\infty} B_j\right) = \sum_{j=1}^{\infty} \mu(B_j) \le \sum_{j=1}^{\infty} \mu(A_j). \quad \blacksquare \tag{3.3}$$

This proof illustrates a standard technique of measure theory, converting a sequence of sets into a disjoint sequence having the same union by taking differences. This trick will become familiar in numerous later applications.

The idea behind **3.3**(ii) can be extended to give an expression for the measure of any finite union. This is the *inclusion-exclusion formula*:

$$\mu\left(\bigcup_{j=1}^{n} A_j\right) = \sum_{j=1}^{n} \mu(A_j) - \sum_{k \ne j} \mu(A_j \cap A_k) + \sum_{k \ne j \ne l} \mu(A_j \cap A_k \cap A_l) - \ldots$$
$$\pm\, \mu(A_1 \cap A_2 \cap \ldots \cap A_n), \tag{3.4}$$

where the sign of the last term is negative if n is even and positive if n is odd, and there are $2^n - 1$ terms in the sum in total. The proof of (3.4) is by induction from **3.3**(ii), substituting for the second term on the right-hand side of

$$\mu\left(\bigcup_{j=1}^{n} A_j\right) = \mu(A_n) + \mu\left(\bigcup_{j=1}^{n-1} A_j\right) - \mu\left(\bigcup_{j=1}^{n-1} A_j \cap A_n\right) \tag{3.5}$$

repeatedly, for $n-1$, $n-2,\dots,1$.

Let $\{A_n, n \in \mathbb{N}\}$ be a monotone sequence of $\mathcal{F}$-sets with limit $A \in \mathcal{F}$. A set function on μ is said to be *continuous* if $\mu(A_n) \to \mu(A)$.

3.4 Theorem A finite measure is continuous.

Proof First let $\{A_n\}$ be increasing, with $A_{n-1} \subseteq A_n$, and $A = \bigcup_{n=1}^{\infty} A_n$. The sequence $\{B_j, j \in \mathbb{N}\}$, where $B_1 = A_1$, and $B_j = A_j - A_{j-1}$ for $j > 1$ is disjoint by construction, with $B_j \in \mathcal{F}$, $A_n = \bigcup_{j=1}^{n} B_j$, and

$$\mu(A_n) = \sum_{j=1}^{n} \mu(B_j). \tag{3.6}$$

The real sequence $\{\mu(A_n)\}$ is therefore monotone, and converges since it is bounded above by $\mu(\Omega) < \infty$. Countable additivity implies $\sum_{j=1}^{\infty} \mu(B_j) = \mu(\bigcup_{j=1}^{\infty} B_j) = \mu(A)$. Alternatively, let $\{A_n\}$ be decreasing, with $A_{n-1} \supseteq A_n$ and $A = \bigcap_{n=1}^{\infty} A_n$. Consider the increasing sequence $\{A_j^c\}$, determine $\mu(A^c)$ by the same argument, and use finite additivity to conclude that $\mu(A) = \mu(\Omega) - \mu(A^c)$ is the limit of $\mu(A_n) = \mu(\Omega) - \mu(A_n^c)$. ∎

The finiteness of the measure is needed for the second part of the argument, but the result that $\mu(A_n) \to \mu(A)$ when $A_n \uparrow A$ actually holds generally, not excluding the case $\mu(A) = \infty$. This theorem has a partial converse:

3.5 Theorem A non-negative set function μ which is finitely additive and continuous is countably additive.

Proof Let $\{B_n\}$ be a countable, disjoint sequence. If $A_n = \bigcup_{j=1}^{n} B_j$, the sequence $\{A_n\}$ is increasing, $B_n \cap A_{n-1} = \varnothing$, and so $\mu(A_n) = \mu(B_n) + \mu(A_{n-1})$ for every n, by finite additivity. Given non-negativity, it follows by induction that $\{\mu(A_n)\}$ is monotone. If $A = \bigcup_{j=1}^{\infty} B_j$, $\mu(A) = \sum_{j=1}^{\infty} \mu(B_j)$, whereas continuity implies that $\mu(A) = \mu(\bigcup_{j=1}^{\infty} B_j)$. ∎

Arguments in the theory of integration often turn on the notion of a 'negligible' set. In a measure space $(\Omega, \mathcal{F}, \mu)$, a *set of measure zero* is (simply enough) a set $M \in \mathcal{F}$ with $\mu(M) = 0$. A condition or restriction on the elements of Ω is said to occur *almost everywhere* (a.e.) if it holds on a set E and $\Omega - E$ has measure zero. If more than one measure is assigned to the same space, it may be necessary to indicate which measure the statement applies to, by writing a.e.[μ] or a.e.[ν] as the case may be.

3.6 Theorem

(i) If M and N are $\mathcal{F}$-sets, M has measure 0 and $N \subseteq M$, then N has measure 0.

(ii) If $\{M_j\}$ is a countable sequence with $\mu(M_j) = 0$, $\forall\, j$, then $\mu(\bigcup_j M_j) = 0$.

(iii) If $\{E_j\}$ is a countable sequence with $\mu(E_j^c) = 0$, $\forall\, j$, then $\mu((\bigcup_j E_j)^c) = 0$.

Proof (i) is an application of monotonicity; (ii) is a consequence of countable additivity; and (iii) follows likewise, using the second de Morgan law. ■

In §3.2 and §3.3 we will be concerned about the measurability of the sets in a given space. We show that, if the sets of a given collection are measurable, the sets of the σ-field generated by that collection are also measurable (the Extension Theorem). For many purposes this fact is sufficient, but there may be sets outside the σ-field which can be shown in other ways to be measurable, and it might be desirable to include these in the measure space. In particular, if $\mu(A) = \mu(B)$ it would seem reasonable to assign $\mu(E) = \mu(A)$ whenever $A \subset E \subset B$. This is equivalent to assigning measure 0 to any subset of a set of measure 0.

The measure space $(\Omega,\mathcal{F},\mu)$ is said to be *complete* if, for any set $E \in \mathcal{F}$ with $\mu(E) = 0$, all subsets of E are also in $\mathcal{F}$. According to the following result, every measure space can be completed without changing any of our conclusions except in respect of these negligible sets.

3.7 Theorem Given any measure space $(\Omega,\mathcal{F},\mu)$, there exists a complete measure space $(\Omega,\mathcal{F}^{\mu},\bar{\mu})$, called the *completion* of $(\Omega,\mathcal{F},\mu)$, such that $\mathcal{F} \subseteq \mathcal{F}^{\mu}$, and $\mu(E) = \bar{\mu}(E)$ for all $E \in \mathcal{F}$. □

Notice that the completion of a space is defined with respect to a particular measure. The measurable space $(\Omega,\mathcal{F})$ has a different completion for each measure that can be defined on it.

Proof Let $\mathcal{N}^{\mu}$ denote the collection of all subsets of $\mathcal{F}$-sets of μ-measure 0, and

$$\mathcal{F}^{\mu} = \{F \subseteq \Omega\colon E\Delta F \in \mathcal{N}^{\mu} \text{ for some } E \in \mathcal{F}\}. \tag{3.7}$$

If $\mu(E) = 0$, any set $F \subset E$ satisfies the criterion of (3.7) and so is in $\mathcal{F}^{\mu}$ as the definition requires. For $F \in \mathcal{F}^{\mu}$, let $\bar{\mu}(F) = \mu(E)$, where E is any $\mathcal{F}$-set satisfying $E\Delta F \in \mathcal{N}^{\mu}$. To show that the choice of E is immaterial, let E_1 and E_2 be two such sets, and note that

$$\mu(E_1 \Delta E_2) = \mu((F\Delta E_1)\Delta(F\Delta E_2)) = 0. \tag{3.8}$$

Since $\mu(E_1 \cup E_2) = \mu(E_1 \cap E_2) + \mu(E_1 \Delta E_2)$, we must conclude that

$$\mu(E_1 \cap E_2) \geq \mu(E_i) \geq \mu(E_1 \cap E_2) \tag{3.9}$$

for $i = 1$ and 2, or, $\mu(E_1) = \mu(E_2)$. Hence, the measure is unique. When $F \in \mathcal{F}$, we can choose $E = F$, since $F\Delta F = \varnothing \in \mathcal{N}^{\mu}$, confirming that the measures agree on $\mathcal{F}$.

It remains to show that $\mathcal{F}^{\mu}$ is a σ-field containing $\mathcal{F}$. Choosing $E = F$ in (3.7) for $F \in \mathcal{F}$ shows $\mathcal{F} \subseteq \mathcal{F}^{\mu}$. If $F \in \mathcal{F}^{\mu}$, then $E\Delta F \in \mathcal{N}^{\mu}$ for $E \in \mathcal{F}$ and hence $E^c \Delta F^c = E\Delta F \in \mathcal{N}^{\mu}$ where $E^c \in \mathcal{F}$, and so $F^c \in \mathcal{F}^{\mu}$. And finally if $F_j \in \mathcal{F}^{\mu}$ for $j \in \mathbb{N}$, there exist $E_j \in \mathcal{F}$ for $j \in \mathbb{N}$, such that $E_j \Delta F_j \in \mathcal{N}^{\mu}$. Hence

$$\Big(\bigcup_j E_j\Big) \Delta \Big(\bigcup_j F_j\Big) \subseteq \bigcup_j (E_j \Delta F_j) \in \mathcal{N}^{\mu}, \tag{3.10}$$

by **3.6**(ii). This means that $\bigcup_j F_j \in \mathcal{F}^{\mu}$, and completes the proof. ■

3.2 The Extension Theorem

You may wonder why, in the definition of a measurable space, $\mathcal{F}$ could not simply be the set of *all* subsets; the power set of Ω. The problem is to find a consistent method of assigning a measure to every set. This is straightforward when the space has a finite number of elements, but not in an infinite space where there is no way, even conceptually, to assign a specific measure to each set. It is necessary to specify a *rule* which generates a measure for any designated set. The problem of measurability is basically the problem of going beyond constructive methods without running into inconsistencies. We now show how this problem can be solved for σ-fields. These are a sufficiently general class of sets to cope with most situations arising in probability.

One must begin by assigning a measure, to be denoted μ_0, to the members of some basic collection $\mathcal{C}$ for which this can feasibly be done. For example, to construct Lebesgue measure we started by assigning to each interval $(a,b]$ the measure $b-a$. We then reason from the properties of μ_0 to extend it from this basic collection to all the sets of interest. $\mathcal{C}$ must be rich enough to allow μ_0 to be uniquely defined by it. A collection $\mathcal{C} \subseteq \mathcal{F}$ is called a *determining class* for $(\Omega,\mathcal{F})$ if, whenever μ and ν are measures on $\mathcal{F}$, $\mu(A) = \nu(A)$ for all $A \in \mathcal{C}$ implies that $\mu = \nu$.

Given $\mathcal{C}$, we must also know how to assign μ_0-values to any sets derived from $\mathcal{C}$ by operations such as union, intersection, complementation, and difference. For disjoint sets A and B we have $\mu_0(A \cup B) = \mu_0(A) + \mu_0(B)$ by finite additivity, and when $B \subseteq A$, $\mu_0(A - B) = \mu_0(A) - \mu_0(B)$. We also need to be able to determine $\mu_0(A \cap B)$, which will require specific knowledge of the relationship between the sets. When such assignments are possible for any pair of sets whose measures are themselves known, the measure is thereby extended to a wider class of sets, to be denoted $\mathcal{S}$. Often $\mathcal{S}$ and $\mathcal{C}$ are the same collection, but in any event $\mathcal{S}$ is closed under various finite set operations, and must at least be a semi-ring. In the applications $\mathcal{S}$ is typically either a field (algebra) or a semi-algebra. Example **1.18** is a good case to keep in mind.

However, $\mathcal{S}$ cannot be a σ-field since at most a finite number of operations are permitted to determine $\mu_0(A)$ for any $A \in \mathcal{S}$. At this point we might pose the opposite question to the one we started with, and ask why $\mathcal{S}$ might not be a rich enough collection for our needs. In fact, events of interest frequently arise which $\mathcal{S}$ cannot contain. **3.15** below illustrates the necessity of being able to go to the limit, and consider events that are expressible only as countably infinite unions or intersections of $\mathcal{C}$-sets. Extending to the events $\mathcal{F} = \sigma(\mathcal{S})$ proves indispensable. We have two results, establishing existence and uniqueness respectively.

3.8 Extension theorem (existence) Let $\mathcal{S}$ be a semi-ring, and let $\mu_0\colon \mathcal{S} \mapsto \overline{\mathbb{R}}^+$ be a measure on $\mathcal{S}$. If $\mathcal{F} = \sigma(\mathcal{S})$, there exists a measure μ on $(\Omega,\mathcal{F})$, such that $\mu(E) = \mu_0(E)$ for each $E \in \mathcal{S}$. □

Although the proof of the theorem is rather lengthy and some of the details are fiddly, the basic idea is simple. Take an event $A \subseteq \Omega$ to which we wish to assign a measure $\mu(A)$. If $A \in \mathcal{S}$, we have $\mu(A) = \mu_0(A)$. If $A \notin \mathcal{S}$, consider choosing a finite or countable covering for A from members of $\mathcal{S}$; that is, a selection of sets $E_j \in \mathcal{S}$, $j = 1,2,3,...$ such that $A \subseteq \bigcup_j E_j$. The object is to find as 'economical' a covering as possible, in the sense that $\sum_j \mu_0(E_j)$ is as small as possible. The *outer measure* of A is

$$\mu^*(A) = \inf \sum_j \mu_0(E_j), \tag{3.11}$$

where the infimum is taken over all finite and countable coverings of A by $\mathcal{S}$-sets. If no such covering exists, set $\mu^*(A) = \infty$. Clearly, $\mu^*(A) = \mu_0(A)$ for each $A \in \mathcal{S}$. μ^* is called the outer measure because, for any eligible definition of $\mu(A)$,

$$\mu^*(A) \geq \sum_j \mu(E_j) \geq \mu\left(\bigcup_j E_j\right) \geq \mu(A), \text{ for } E_j \in \mathcal{S}. \tag{3.12}$$

The first inequality here is by the stipulation that $\mu(E_j) = \mu_0(E_j)$ for $E_j \in \mathcal{S}$ in the case where a covering exists, or else the majorant side is infinite. The second and third follow by countable subadditivity and monotonicity respectively, because μ is a measure.

We could also construct a minimal covering for A^c and, at least if the relevant outer measures are finite, define the *inner measure* of A as $\mu_*(A) = \mu^*(\Omega) - \mu^*(A^c)$. Note that since $\mu(A) = \mu(\Omega) - \mu(A^c)$ and $\mu^*(A^c) \geq \mu(A^c)$ by (3.12),

$$\mu(A) \geq \mu_*(A). \tag{3.13}$$

If $\mu^*(A) = \mu_*(A)$, it would make sense to call this common value the measure of A, and say that A is measurable. In fact, we employ a more stringent criterion. A set $A \subseteq \Omega$ is said to be *measurable* if, for any $B \subseteq \Omega$,

$$\mu^*(A \cap B) + \mu^*(A^c \cap B) = \mu^*(B). \tag{3.14}$$

This yields $\mu^*(A) = \mu_*(A)$ as a special case on putting $B = \Omega$, but remains valid even if $\mu(\Omega) = \infty$.

Let $\mathcal{M}$ denote the collection of all measurable sets, those subsets of Ω satisfying (3.14). Since $\mu^*(A) = \mu_0(A)$ for $A \in \mathcal{S}$ and $\mu_0(\varnothing) = 0$, putting $A = \varnothing$ in (3.14) gives the trivial equality $\mu^*(B) = \mu^*(B)$. Hence $\varnothing \in \mathcal{M}$, and since the definition implies that $A^c \in \mathcal{M}$ if $A \in \mathcal{M}$, $\Omega \in \mathcal{M}$ too.

The next steps are to determine what properties the set function $\mu^*\colon \mathcal{M} \mapsto \overline{\mathbb{R}}$ shares with a measure. Clearly,

$$\mu^*(A) \geq 0 \text{ for all } A \subseteq \Omega. \tag{3.15}$$

Another property which follows directly from the definition of μ^* is monotonicity:

$$A_1 \subseteq A_2 \Rightarrow \mu^*(A_1) \leq \mu^*(A_2), \text{ for } A_1, A_2 \subseteq \Omega. \tag{3.16}$$

Our goal is to show that countable additivity also holds for μ^* in respect of $\mathcal{M}$-sets, but it proves convenient to begin by establishing countable *sub*additivity.

3.9 Lemma If $\{A_j, j \in \mathbb{N}\}$ is any sequence of subsets of Ω, then

$$\mu^*\left(\bigcup_j A_j\right) \le \sum_j \mu^*(A_j). \tag{3.17}$$

Proof Assume $\mu^*(A_j) < \infty$ for each j. (If not, the result is trivial.) For each j, let $\{E_{jk}\}$ denote a countable covering of A_j by $\mathcal{S}$-sets, which satisfies

$$\sum_k \mu_0(E_{jk}) < \mu^*(A_j) + 2^{-j}\varepsilon$$

for any $\varepsilon > 0$. Such a collection always exists, by the definition of μ^*. Since $\bigcup_j A_j \subseteq \bigcup_{j,k} E_{jk}$, it follows by definition that

$$\mu^*\left(\bigcup_j A_j\right) \le \sum_{j,k} \mu_0(E_{jk}) < \sum_j \mu^*(A_j) + \varepsilon, \tag{3.18}$$

noting $\sum_{j=1}^{\infty} 2^{-j} = 1$. (3.17) now follows since ε is arbitrary and the last inequality is strict. ■

The following is an immediate consequence of the theorem, since subadditivity supplies the reverse inequality to give (3.14).

3.10 Corollary A is measurable if, for any $B \subseteq \Omega$,

$$\mu^*(A \cap B) + \mu^*(A^c \cap B) \le \mu^*(B). \; \square \tag{3.19}$$

The following lemma is central to the proof of the extension theorem. It yields countable additivity as a corollary, but also has a wider purpose.

3.11 Lemma $\mathcal{M}$ is a monotone class.

Proof Letting $\{A_j, j \in \mathbb{N}\}$ be an increasing sequence of $\mathcal{M}$-sets converging to $A = \bigcup_j A_j$, we show $A \in \mathcal{M}$. For $n > 1$ and $E \in \Omega$, the definition of an $\mathcal{M}$-set gives

$$\begin{aligned} \mu^*(A_n \cap E) &= \mu^*(A_{n-1} \cap (A_n \cap E)) + \mu^*(A_{n-1}^c \cap (A_n \cap E)) \\ &= \mu^*(A_{n-1} \cap E) + \mu^*(B_n \cap E). \end{aligned} \tag{3.20}$$

where $B_n = A_n - A_{n-1}$, and the sequence $\{B_j\}$ is disjoint. Put $A_0 = \varnothing$ so that $\mu^*(A_0 \cap E) = 0$; then by induction,

$$\mu^*(A_n \cap E) = \sum_{j=1}^{n} \mu^*(B_j \cap E) \tag{3.21}$$

holds for every n. The right-hand side of (3.21) for $n \in \mathbb{N}$ is a monotone real sequence, and $\mu^*(A_n \cap E) \to \mu^*(A \cap E)$ as $n \to \infty$. Now, since $A_n \in \mathcal{M}$,

$$\begin{aligned} \mu^*(E) &= \mu^*(A_n \cap E) + \mu^*(A_n^c \cap E) \\ &\ge \mu^*(A_n \cap E) + \mu^*(A^c \cap E), \end{aligned} \tag{3.22}$$

using the monotonicity of μ^* and the fact that $A^c \subseteq A_n^c$. Taking the limit, we have from the foregoing argument that

$$\mu^*(E) \geq \mu^*(A \cap E) + \mu^*(A^c \cap E), \tag{3.23}$$

so that $A \in \mathcal{M}$ by **3.10**. For the case of a decreasing sequence, simply move to the complements and argue as above. ■

Since $\{B_j\}$ is a disjoint sequence, countable additivity emerges as a by-product of the lemma, as the following corollary shows.

3.12 Corollary If $\{B_j\}$ is a disjoint sequence of $\mathcal{M}$-sets,

$$\mu^*\left(\bigcup_j B_j\right) = \sum_j \mu^*(B_j). \tag{3.24}$$

Proof Immediate on putting $E = \Omega$ in (3.21) and letting $n \to \infty$, noting $\bigcup_j B_j = A$. ■

Notice how we needed **3.10** in the proof of **3.11**, which is why additivity has been derived from subadditivity rather than the other way about.

Proof of 3.8 We have established in (3.15) and (3.24) that μ^* is a measure for the elements of $\mathcal{M}$. If it can be shown that $\mathcal{F} \subseteq \mathcal{M}$, setting $\mu(A) = \mu^*(A)$ for all $A \in \mathcal{F}$ will satisfy the existence criteria of the theorem.

The first step is to show that $\mathcal{S} \subseteq \mathcal{M}$ or, by **3.10**, that $A \in \mathcal{S}$ implies

$$\mu^*(E \cap A) + \mu^*(E \cap A^c) \leq \mu^*(E) \tag{3.25}$$

for any $E \subseteq \Omega$. Let $\{A_j \in \mathcal{S}\}$ denote a finite or countable covering of E such that $\sum_j \mu_0(A_j) < \mu^*(E) + \varepsilon$, for $\varepsilon > 0$. If no such covering exists, $\mu^*(E) = \infty$ by definition and (3.25) holds trivially. Note that $E \cap A \subseteq \bigcup_j (A_j \cap A)$, and since $\mathcal{S}$ is a semi-ring the sets $A_j \cap A$ are in $\mathcal{S}$. Similarly, $E \cap A^c \subseteq \bigcup_j (A_j \cap A^c)$, and by simple set algebra and the definition of a semi-ring,

$$A_j \cap A^c = A_j - (A_j \cap A) = \bigcup_k C_{jk} \tag{3.26}$$

where the C_{jk} are a finite collection of $\mathcal{S}$-sets, disjoint with each other and also with $A_j \cap A$. Now, applying **3.9** and the fact that $\mu^*(B) = \mu_0(B)$ for $B \in \mathcal{S}$, we find

$$\begin{aligned} \mu^*(E \cap A) + \mu^*(E \cap A^c) &\leq \sum_j \mu_0(A_j \cap A) + \sum_j \sum_k \mu_0(C_{jk}) \\ &= \sum_j \mu_0(A_j) < \mu^*(E) + \varepsilon, \end{aligned} \tag{3.27}$$

where the equality follows from (3.26) because μ_0 is finitely additive, and $A_j \cap A$ and the C_{jk} are mutually disjoint. Since ε is arbitrary, (3.25) follows.

Next, we show that $\mathcal{M}$ is a σ-field. We have only to show that $\mathcal{M}$ is a field, because **3.11** implies it is also a σ-field, by **1.24**. We already know that $\Omega \in \mathcal{M}$ and $\mathcal{M}$ is closed under complementation, so it remains to show that unions of $\mathcal{M}$-sets are in $\mathcal{M}$. Suppose that A_1 and A_2 are $\mathcal{M}$-sets and $E \subseteq \Omega$. Then

$$\mu^*(E) = \mu^*(A_1 \cap E) + \mu^*(A_1^c \cap E)$$

$$= \mu^*(A_2 \cap A_1 \cap E) + \mu^*(A_2^c \cap A_1 \cap E)$$
$$+ \mu^*(A_2 \cap A_1^c \cap E) + \mu^*(A_2^c \cap A_1^c \cap E)$$
$$\geq \mu^*(A_2 \cap A_1 \cap E)$$
$$+ \mu^*((A_2^c \cap A_1 \cap E) \cup (A_2 \cap A_1^c \cap E) \cup (A_2^c \cap A_1^c \cap E))$$
$$= \mu^*((A_2 \cap A_1) \cap E) + \mu^*((A_2 \cap A_1)^c \cap E), \tag{3.28}$$

where the inequality is by subadditivity, and the rest is set algebra. By **3.10** this is sufficient for $A_1 \cap A_2 \in \mathcal{M}$, and hence also for $A_1 \cup A_2 \in \mathcal{M}$, using closure under complementation.

It follows that $\mathcal{M}$ is a σ-field containing $\mathcal{S}$, and since $\mathcal{F}$ is the smallest such σ-field, we have that $\mathcal{F} \subseteq \mathcal{M}$, as required. ∎

Notice that (3.28) was got by using (3.14) as the relation defining measurability. The proof does not go through using $\mu^*(A) = \mu_*(A)$ as the definition.

The style of this argument tells us some important things about the role of $\mathcal{S}$. Any set that has no covering by $\mathcal{S}$-sets is assigned the measure ∞, so for finite measures it is a requisite that $\Omega \subseteq \bigcup_j E_j$ for a finite or countable collection $\{E_j \in \mathcal{S}\}$. The measure of a union of $\mathcal{S}$-sets must be able to approximate the measure of any $\mathcal{F}$-set arbitrarily well, and the basic content of the theorem is to establish that a semi-ring has this property.

To complete the demonstration of the extension, there remains the question of uniqueness. To get this result we need to impose σ-finiteness, which was not needed for existence.

3.13 Extension theorem (uniqueness) Let μ and μ′ denote measures on a space $(\Omega, \mathcal{F})$, where $\mathcal{F} = \sigma(\mathcal{S})$, and $\mathcal{S}$ is a semi-ring. If the measures are σ-finite on $\mathcal{S}$ and $\mu(E) = \mu'(E)$ for all $E \in \mathcal{S}$, then $\mu(E) = \mu'(E)$ for all $E \in \mathcal{F}$.

Proof We first prove the theorem for the case of finite measures, by an application of the π-λ theorem. Define $\mathcal{A} = \{E \in \mathcal{F}: \mu(E) = \mu'(E)\}$. Then $\mathcal{S} \subseteq \mathcal{A}$ by hypothesis. If $\mathcal{S}$ is a semi-ring, it is also a π-system. By **1.27**, the proof is completed if we can show that $\mathcal{A}$ is a λ-system, and hence contains $\sigma(\mathcal{S})$.

When the measure is finite, $\Omega \in \mathcal{A}$ and condition **1.26**(a) holds. Additivity implies that, for $A \in \mathcal{A}$,

$$\mu(A^c) = \mu(\Omega) - \mu(A) = \mu'(\Omega) - \mu'(A) = \mu'(A^c), \tag{3.29}$$

so that **1.26**(b) holds. Lastly, let $\{A_j\}$ be a disjoint sequence in $\mathcal{A}$. By countable additivity,

$$\mu\left(\bigcup_{j=1}^{\infty} A_j\right) = \sum_{j=1}^{\infty} \mu(A_j) = \sum_{j=1}^{\infty} \mu'(A_j) = \mu'\left(\bigcup_{j=1}^{\infty} A_j\right), \tag{3.30}$$

and **1.26**(c) holds. It follows by **1.26** and the π-λ theorem that $\mathcal{F} = \sigma(\mathcal{S}) \subseteq \mathcal{A}$.

Now consider the σ-finite case. Let $\Omega = \bigcup_j B_j$ where $B_j \in \mathcal{S}$ and $\mu(B_j) = \mu'(B_j) < \infty$. $\mathcal{F}_j = \{B_j \cap A: A \in \mathcal{F}\}$ is a σ-field, so that the $(B_j, \mathcal{F}_j)$ are measurable spaces, on which μ and μ' are finite measures agreeing on $\mathcal{S} \cap B_j$. The preceding argument showed that, for $A \in \mathcal{F}$, $\mu(B_j \cap A) = \mu'(B_j \cap A)$ only if μ and μ' are the same measure.

Consider the following recursion. By **3.3**(ii) we have

$$\mu(A \cap (B_1 \cup B_2)) = \mu(A \cap B_1) + \mu(A \cap B_2) - \mu(A \cap B_1 \cap B_2). \tag{3.31}$$

Letting $C_n = \bigcup_{j=1}^n B_j$ the same relation yields

$$\mu(A \cap C_n) = \mu(A \cap B_n) + \mu(A \cap C_{n-1}) - \mu(A \cap B_n \cap C_{n-1}). \tag{3.32}$$

The terms involving C_{n-1} on the right-hand side can be solved backwards to yield an expression for $\mu(A \cap C_n)$, as a sum of terms having the general form

$$\mu(A \cap B_{j_1} \cap B_{j_2} \cap B_{j_3} \cap \dots) = \mu(D \cap B_j) < \infty \tag{3.33}$$

for *some* j, say $j = j_1$, in which case $D = A \cap B_{j_2} \cap B_{j_3} \cap \dots \in \mathcal{F}$. Since we know that $\mu(D \cap B_j) = \mu'(D \cap B_j)$ for all $D \in \mathcal{F}$ by the preceding argument, it follows that in (3.32)

$$\mu(A \cap C_n) = \mu'(A \cap C_n). \tag{3.34}$$

This holds for any n. Since $C_n \to \Omega$ as $n \to \infty$, we obtain in the limit

$$\mu(A) = \mu'(A), \tag{3.35}$$

the two sides of the equality being either finite and equal, or both equal to $+\infty$. This completes the proof, since A is arbitrary. ■

3.14 Example Let $\mathcal{M}$ denote the subsets of $\mathbb{R}$ which are measurable according to (3.14) when μ^* is the outer measure defined on the half-open intervals, whose measures μ_0 are taken equal to their lengths. This defines Lebesgue measure m. These sets form a semi-ring by **1.18**, a countable collection of them covers $\mathbb{R}$, and the extension theorem shows that, given m is a σ-finite measure, $\mathcal{M}$ contains the Borel field on $\mathbb{R}$ (see **1.21**), so $(\mathbb{R},\mathcal{B},m)$ is a measure space. It can be shown (we won't) that all the Lebesgue-measurable sets *not* in $\mathcal{B}$ are subsets of $\mathcal{B}$-sets of measure 0. For any measure μ on $(\mathbb{R},\mathcal{B})$, the complete space $(\mathbb{R},\mathcal{B}^{\mu},\bar{\mu})$ includes all of the Lebesgue-measurable sets. □

The following is a basic property of Lebesgue measure. Notice the need to deal with a countable intersection of intervals to determine so simple a thing as the measure of a point.

3.15 Theorem Any countable set from $\mathbb{R}$ has Lebesgue measure 0.

Proof The measure of a point $\{x\}$ is zero, since for $x \in \mathbb{R}$,

$$\{x\} = \bigcap_{n=1}^{\infty}(x - 1/n,\, x] \in \mathcal{B} \tag{3.36}$$

and $m(\{x\}) = \lim_{n\to\infty} 1/n = 0$. The result follows by **3.6**(ii). ■

3.3 Non-measurability

To give the ideas of the last section their true force, it needs to be shown that $\mathcal{M} \subset 2^\Omega$ is possible, in other words, that Ω can contain non-measurable subsets. In this section we construct such a set in the half-open unit interval $(0,1]$, a standard counter-example from Lebesgue theory.

For $x, y \in (0,1]$, define the operator

$$y \dot{+} x = \begin{cases} y+x, & y+x \leq 1 \\ y+x-1, & y+x > 1 \end{cases}. \tag{3.37}$$

This is *addition modulo 1*. Imagine the unit interval mapped onto a circle, like a clock face with 0 at the top. $y \dot{+} x$ is the point obtained by moving a hand clockwise through an angle of $2\pi x$ from an initial point y on the circumference. For each set $A \subseteq (0,1]$, and $x \in (0,1]$, define the set

$$A \dot{+} x = \{y \dot{+} x \colon y \in A\}. \tag{3.38}$$

3.16 Theorem If A is Lebesgue-measurable so is $A \dot{+} x$, and $m(A \dot{+} x) = m(A)$, for any x.

Proof For $(a,b] \subseteq (0,1]$, $m((a+x, b+x]) = b-a = m((a,b])$, for any real x such that $a+x > 0$ and $b+x \leq 1$. The property extends to finite unions of intervals translated by x. If A is any Lebesgue-measurable subset of $(0,1]$, and $A+x \subseteq (0,1]$ where $A+x = \{y+x\colon y \in A\}$, the construction of the extension similarly implies that $A+x$ is measurable and $m(A) = m(A+x)$.

Now let $A_1 = A \cap (0, 1-x)$, and $A_2 = A \cap (1-x, 1]$. Then $m(A_1+x) = m(A_1)$ and $m(A_2+x-1) = m(A_2)$, where the sets on the left-hand sides of these equalities are in each case contained in $(0,1]$. A_1+x and A_2+x-1 are disjoint sets whose union is $A \dot{+} x$, and hence

$$\begin{aligned} m(A \dot{+} x) &= m(A_1+x) + m(A_2+x-1) \\ &= m(A_1) + m(A_2) = m(A). \blacksquare \end{aligned} \tag{3.39}$$

Define a relation for points of $(0,1]$, letting xRy if $y = x \dot{+} r$ for $r \in \mathbb{Q}$. That is, xRy if y is separated from x by a rational distance along the circle. R is an equivalence relation. Defining the equivalence classes

$$E^x = \{y\colon y = x \dot{+} r,\ r \in \mathbb{Q}\}, \tag{3.40}$$

the sets of the collection $\{E^x,\ x \in (0,1]\}$ are either identical, or disjoint. Since every x is a rational distance from *some* other point of the interval, these sets cover $(0,1]$. A collection formed by choosing just one of each of the identical sets, and discarding the duplicates, is therefore a partition of $(0,1]$. Write this as $\{E^x,\ x \in C\}$, where C denotes the residual set of indices.

Another example may help the reader to visualize these sets. In the set of integers, the set of even integers is an equivalence class and can be defined as E^0, the set of integers which differ from 0 an even integer. Of course $E^0 = E^2 =$

$E^4 = \ldots = E^{2n}$, for any $n \in \mathbb{Z}$. The set of odd integers can be defined similarly as E^1, the set of integers differing by an even integer from 1. $E^1 = E^3 = \ldots = E^{2n+1}$ for any $n \in \mathbb{Z}$. Discarding the redundant members of the collection $\{E^x, x \in \mathbb{Z}\}$ leaves just the collection $\{E^0, E^1\}$ to define a partition of $\mathbb{Z}$.

Now construct a set H by taking an element from E^x for each $x \in C$.

3.17 Theorem H is not Lebesgue-measurable.

Proof Consider the countable collection $\{H \dotplus r, r \in \mathbb{Q}\}$. We show that this collection is a partition of (0,1]. To show disjointness, argue by contradiction. Suppose $z \in H \dotplus r_1$ and $z \in H \dotplus r_2$, for $r_1 \neq r_2$. This means there are points $h_1, h_2 \in H$, such that

$$h_1 \dotplus r_1 = z = h_2 \dotplus r_2. \tag{3.41}$$

If $r_1 \neq r_2$, we cannot have $h_1 = h_2$; but if $h_1 \neq h_2$ then h_1 and h_2 belong to different equivalence classes by construction of H, and cannot be a rational distance $|r_1 - r_2|$ apart; hence no z satisfying (3.41) exists. On the other hand, let $H^* = \bigcup_r (H \dotplus r)$, and consider any point $x \in (0,1]$. x belongs to one of the equivalence classes, and hence is within a rational distance of some element of H; but H^* contains all the points that are a rational distance r from a point of H, for some r, and hence $x \in H^*$, and it follows that $(0,1] \subseteq H^*$.

Suppose $m(H)$ exists. Then by **3.16**, $m(H \dotplus r) = m(H)$ for all r. Since $m(H^*) \geq m((0,1]) = 1$, we must have $m(H) > 0$ by **3.6**(ii), but countable additivity then gives $m(H^*) = \sum_r m(H \dotplus r) = \infty$, which is impossible. It follows that $m(H)$ does not exist. ■

The definition of H involves a slightly controversial area of mathematics, since the set of equivalence classes is uncountable. It is not possible to devise, *even in principle*, constructive rules for selecting the set C, and elements from E^x for each $x \in C$. The proposition that sets like H exist cannot be deduced from the axioms of set theory but must be asserted as an additional axiom, the so-called *axiom of choice*. If one chooses to reject the axiom of choice, this counter-example fails. We have made no attempt here to treat set theory from the axiomatic standpoint, and the theory in Chapter 1 has been what is technically called *naïve* (i.e. based on the intuitive notion of what a 'set' is). For us, the problem of the axiom of choice reduces to the question: should we admit the existence of a mathematical object that cannot be constructed, even in imagination? The decision is ultimately personal, but suffice it to say that most mathematicians are willing to do so.

Sets like H do not belong to $\mathcal{B}_{(0,1]} = \{B \cap (0,1], B \in \mathcal{B}\}$. It is not difficult to show that all the sets of $\mathcal{B}_{(0,1]}$ are Lebesgue-measurable; see **3.14** and restrict m to (0,1] as in **3.2**. By sticking with Borel sets we shall not run into measurability difficulties on the line, but this example should serve to make us careful. In less familiar situations (such as will arise in Part VI) measurability can fail in superficially plausible cases. However, if measurability is in doubt one might remember that outer measure μ^* is well defined for all subsets of Ω, and coincides with μ whenever the latter is defined. Sometimes measurability problems are dealt with by working explicitly with outer measure, and forgetting about them.

3.4 Product Spaces

If $(\Omega,\mathcal{F})$ and $(\Xi,\mathcal{G})$ are two measurable spaces, let

$$\Omega\times\Xi = \{(\omega,\xi)\colon \omega \in \Omega,\ \xi \in \Xi\} \tag{3.42}$$

be the Cartesian product of Ω and Ξ, and define $\mathcal{F}\otimes\mathcal{G} = \sigma(\mathcal{R}_{\mathcal{F}\mathcal{G}})$, where

$$\mathcal{R}_{\mathcal{F}\mathcal{G}} = \{(F\times G),\ F \in \mathcal{F},\ G \in \mathcal{G}\}. \tag{3.43}$$

The space $(\Omega\times\Xi,\ \mathcal{F}\otimes\mathcal{G})$ is called a *product space*, and $(\Omega,\mathcal{F})$ and $(\Xi,\mathcal{G})$ are the *factor spaces*, or *coordinate spaces*, of the product. The elements of the collection $\mathcal{R}_{\mathcal{F}\mathcal{G}}$ are called the *measurable rectangles*. The rectangles of the Euclidean plane $\mathbb{R}\times\mathbb{R} = \mathbb{R}^2$ (products of intervals) are a familiar case.

3.18 Example Rather trivially, consider the two-element sets $A = \{\omega_1,\omega_2\} \in \mathcal{F}$, and $B = \{\xi_1,\xi_2\} \in \mathcal{G}$. The corresponding rectangle is

$$A\times B = \{(\omega_1,\xi_1),\ (\omega_1,\xi_2),\ (\omega_2,\xi_1),\ (\omega_2,\xi_2)\}.$$

The sets $\{(\omega_1,\xi_1),\ (\omega_2,\xi_2)\}$ and $\{(\omega_1,\xi_2),\ (\omega_2,\xi_1)\}$ are not rectangles, but are unions of rectangles and so are elements of $\mathcal{F}\otimes\mathcal{G}$. □

Two important pieces of terminology. If $E \subseteq \Omega\times\Xi$, the set $\pi_\Omega(E) = \{\omega\colon (\omega,\xi) \in E\}$ is called the *projection* of E onto Ω. And if $A \subseteq \Omega$, the *inverse projection* of A is the set

$$\pi_\Omega^{-1}(A) = A\times\Xi = \{(\omega,\xi)\colon \omega \in A,\ \xi \in \Xi\}. \tag{3.44}$$

$A\times\Xi$ is also called a *cylinder set* in $\Omega\times\Xi$, with *base* A. The latter terminology is natural if you think about the case $\Omega = \mathbb{R}^2$ and $\Xi = \mathbb{R}$. Cylinder sets with bases in $\mathcal{F}$ and $\mathcal{G}$ are elements of $\mathcal{R}_{\mathcal{F}\mathcal{G}}$. One might think that if $E \in \mathcal{F}\otimes\mathcal{G}$, $\pi_\Omega(E)$ should be an $\mathcal{F}$-set, but this is *not* necessarily the case. $\pi_\Omega(E)^c \neq \pi_\Omega(E^c)$ in general (see **1.3**) so that the collection $\mathcal{C}$ of projections of $\mathcal{F}\otimes\mathcal{G}$-sets onto Ω is not closed under complementation. However, notice that $A = \pi_\Omega(A\times\Xi)$ so that $\mathcal{F} \subseteq \mathcal{C}$.

The main task of this section is to establish a pair of results required in the construction of measures on product spaces.

3.19 Theorem If $\mathcal{C}$ and $\mathcal{D}$ are semi-rings of subsets of Ω and Ξ, respectively, then

$$\mathcal{R}_{\mathcal{C}\mathcal{D}} = \{C\times D\colon C \in \mathcal{C},\ D \in \mathcal{D}\}$$

is a semi-ring of $\Omega\times\Xi$.

Proof There are three conditions from **1.16** to be established. First, $\mathcal{R}_{\mathcal{C}\mathcal{D}}$ clearly contains $\emptyset$. Second, consider $C_1, C_2 \in \mathcal{C}$, and $D_1, D_2 \in \mathcal{D}$. $C_1 \cap C_2 \in \mathcal{C}$ and $D_1 \cap D_2 \in \mathcal{D}$, and as a matter of definition,

$$(C_1\times D_1)\cap(C_2\times D_2) = \{\omega \in C_1,\ \xi \in D_1\}\cap\{\omega \in C_2,\ \xi \in D_2\}$$

$$= \{\omega \in C_1 \cap C_2,\ \xi \in D_1 \cap D_2\}$$
$$= (C_1 \cap C_2) \times (D_1 \cap D_2) \in \mathcal{R}_{\mathcal{C}\mathcal{D}}. \tag{3.45}$$

Third, assume that $C_1 \times D_1 \subseteq C_2 \times D_2$, and by a similar argument,

$$\begin{aligned}(C_2 \times D_2) - (C_1 \times D_1) &= \{(\omega \in C_2,\ \xi \in D_2)\text{: either } \omega \notin C_1 \text{ or } \xi \notin D_1\} \\ &= ((C_2 - C_1) \times D_1) \cup (C_1 \times (D_2 - D_1)) \\ &\qquad \cup ((C_2 - C_1) \times (D_2 - D_1)),\end{aligned} \tag{3.46}$$

where the sets in the union on the right-hand side are disjoint. By hypothesis, the sets $C_2 - C_1$ and $D_2 - D_1$ are finite disjoint unions of $\mathcal{C}$-sets and $\mathcal{D}$-sets respectively, say $(C_1',\ldots,C_n')$, and $(D_1',\ldots,D_m')$. The product of a finite disjoint union of sets is a disjoint union of products; for example,

$$\left(\bigcup_{j=1}^{n} C_j'\right) \times D_1 = \left\{(\omega,\xi)\text{: } \omega \in \left(\bigcup_{j=1}^{n} C_j'\right),\ \xi \in D_1\right\} = \bigcup_{j=1}^{n} (C_j' \times D_1). \tag{3.47}$$

Extending the same type of argument, we may also write

$$(C_2 - C_1) \times (D_2 - D_1) = \left(\bigcup_{j=1}^{n} (C_j' \times D_1)\right) \cup \left(\bigcup_{k=1}^{m} (C_1 \times D_k')\right) \cup \left(\bigcup_{j,k} (C_j' \times D_k')\right). \tag{3.48}$$

All of the product sets in this union are disjoint (i.e., a pair (ω,ξ) can appear in at most one of them) and all are in $\mathcal{R}_{\mathcal{C}\mathcal{D}}$. This completes the proof. ■

The second theorem leads to the useful result that, to extend a measure on a product space, it suffices to assign measures to the elements of $\mathcal{R}_{\mathcal{C}\mathcal{D}}$, where $\mathcal{C}$ and $\mathcal{D}$ are suitable classes of the factor spaces.

3.20 Theorem If $\mathcal{F} = \sigma(\mathcal{C})$ and $\mathcal{G} = \sigma(\mathcal{D})$ where $\mathcal{C}$ and $\mathcal{D}$ are semi-rings of subsets of Ω and Ξ respectively, then $\mathcal{F} \otimes \mathcal{G} = \mathcal{C} \otimes \mathcal{D}$.

Proof It is clear that $\mathcal{R}_{\mathcal{C}\mathcal{D}} \subseteq \mathcal{R}_{\mathcal{F}\mathcal{G}}$, and hence that $\mathcal{C} \otimes \mathcal{D} \subseteq \mathcal{F} \otimes \mathcal{G}$. To show the converse, consider the collection of inverse projections,

$$\mathcal{I}_{\mathcal{F}} = \{\pi_\Omega^{-1}(F),\ F \in \mathcal{F}\} \subseteq \mathcal{R}_{\mathcal{F}\mathcal{G}}.$$

It can easily be verified that $\mathcal{I}_{\mathcal{F}}$ is a σ-field of $\Omega \times \Xi$, and is in fact the smallest σ-field containing the collection $\mathcal{I}_{\mathcal{C}} = \{\pi_\Omega^{-1}(C),\ C \in \mathcal{C}\} \subseteq \mathcal{C} \otimes \mathcal{D}$. $\mathcal{I}_{\mathcal{C}}$ is a π-system, and since $\mathcal{C} \otimes \mathcal{D}$ is a σ-field and hence a λ-system, it follows by the π-λ theorem that $\mathcal{I}_{\mathcal{F}} = \sigma(\mathcal{I}_{\mathcal{C}}) \subseteq \mathcal{C} \otimes \mathcal{D}$. Exactly same conclusion holds for $\mathcal{I}_{\mathcal{G}}$, the corresponding collection for $\mathcal{G}$. Every element of $\mathcal{R}_{\mathcal{F}\mathcal{G}}$ is the intersection of an element from $\mathcal{I}_{\mathcal{F}}$ and one from $\mathcal{I}_{\mathcal{G}}$, and it follows that $\mathcal{R}_{\mathcal{F}\mathcal{G}} \subseteq \mathcal{C} \otimes \mathcal{D}$. But $\mathcal{R}_{\mathcal{F}\mathcal{G}}$ is a π-system by **3.19** and hence a further application of the π-λ theorem gives $\mathcal{F} \otimes \mathcal{G} \subseteq \mathcal{C} \otimes \mathcal{D}$. ■

The notion of a product extends beyond pairs to triples and general n-tuples, and in particular we shall be interested in the properties of Euclidean n-space ($\mathbb{R}^n$).

For finite n at least, a separate theory is not needed because results can be obtained by recursion. If $(\Psi,\mathcal{H})$ is a third measurable space, then trivially,

$$\begin{aligned}\Omega\times\Xi\times\Psi &= \{(\omega,\xi,\psi)\colon \omega\in\Omega,\ \xi\in\Xi,\ \psi\in\Psi\}\\ &= \{((\omega,\xi),\psi)\colon (\omega,\xi)\in\Omega\times\Xi,\ \psi\in\Psi\}\\ &= (\Omega\times\Xi)\times\Psi.\end{aligned} \tag{3.49}$$

Either or both of $(\Omega,\mathcal{F})$ and $(\Xi,\mathcal{G})$ can be product spaces, and the last two theorems extend to product spaces of any finite dimension.

3.5 Measurable Transformations

Consider measurable spaces $(\Omega,\mathcal{F})$ and $(\Xi,\mathcal{G})$ in a different context, as domain and codomain of a mapping

$$T\colon \Omega \mapsto \Xi.$$

T is said to be *$\mathcal{F}/\mathcal{G}$-measurable* if $T^{-1}(B)\in\mathcal{F}$ for all $B\in\mathcal{G}$. The idea is that a measure μ defined on $(\Omega,\mathcal{F})$ can be mapped into $(\Xi,\mathcal{G})$, every event $B\in\mathcal{G}$ being assigned a measure $\nu(B)=\mu(T^{-1}(B))$. We have just encountered one example, the projection mapping, whose inverse defined in (3.44) takes each $\mathcal{F}$-set A into a measurable rectangle.

Corresponding to a measurable transformation there is always a transformed measure, in the following sense.

3.21 Theorem Let μ be a measure on $(\Omega,\mathcal{F})$ and $T\colon\Omega\mapsto\Xi$ a measurable transformation. Then μT^{-1} is a measure on $(\Xi,\mathcal{G})$, where

$$\mu T^{-1}(B) = \mu(T^{-1}(B)),\ \text{each } B\in\mathcal{G}. \tag{3.50}$$

Proof We check conditions **3.1**(a)-(c). Clearly $\mu T^{-1}(A)\geq 0$, all $A\in\mathcal{B}_T$. Since $T^{-1}(\Xi)=\Omega$ holds by definition, $T^{-1}(\varnothing)=\varnothing$ by **1.2**(iii) and so $\mu T^{-1}(\varnothing) = \mu(T^{-1}(\varnothing)) = \mu(\varnothing) = 0$. For countable additivity we must show

$$\mu T^{-1}\left(\bigcup_j B_j\right) = \sum_j \mu T^{-1}(B_j) \tag{3.51}$$

for a disjoint collection $B_1,B_2,\ldots\in\Xi$. Letting $B_j' = T^{-1}(B_j)$, **1.2** shows both that the B_j' are disjoint and that $T^{-1}(\bigcup_j B_j) = \bigcup_j B_j'$. Equation (3.51) therefore becomes

$$\mu\left(\bigcup_j B_j'\right) = \sum_j \mu(B_j') \tag{3.52}$$

for disjoint sets B_j', which holds because μ is a measure. ■

The main result on general transformations is the following.

3.22 Theorem Suppose $T^{-1}(B)\in\mathcal{F}$ for each $B\in\mathcal{D}$, where $\mathcal{D}$ is an arbitrary class of sets, and $\mathcal{G}=\sigma(\mathcal{D})$. Then the transformation T is $\mathcal{F}/\mathcal{G}$-measurable.

Proof By **1.2**(ii) and (iii), if $T^{-1}(B_j) \in \mathcal{F}$, $j \in \mathbb{N}$, then $T^{-1}(\bigcup_j B_j) = \bigcup_j T^{-1}(B_j) \in \mathcal{F}$, and if $T^{-1}(B) \in \mathcal{F}$ then $T^{-1}(B^c) = T^{-1}(B)^c \in \mathcal{F}$. It follows that the class of sets

$$\mathcal{A} = \{B\colon T^{-1}(B) \in \mathcal{F}\}$$

is a σ-field. Since $\mathcal{D} \subseteq \mathcal{A}$, $\mathcal{G} \subseteq \mathcal{A}$ by definition. ■

This result is easily iterated. If $(\Psi,\mathcal{H})$ is another measurable space and $U\colon \Xi \mapsto \Psi$ is a $\mathcal{G}/\mathcal{H}$-measurable transformation, then

$$U \circ T\colon \Omega \mapsto \Psi$$

is $\mathcal{F}/\mathcal{H}$-measurable, since for $C \in \mathcal{H}$, $U^{-1}(C) \in \mathcal{G}$, and hence

$$(U \circ T)^{-1}(C) = T^{-1}(U^{-1}(C)) \in \mathcal{F}. \tag{3.53}$$

An important special case: $T\colon \Omega \leftrightarrow \Xi$ is called a *measurable isomorphism* if it is 1-1 onto, and both T and T^{-1} are measurable. The measurable spaces $(\Omega,\mathcal{F})$ and $(\Xi,\mathcal{G})$ are said to be *isomorphic* if such a mapping between them exists. The implication is that measure-theoretic discussions can be conducted equivalently in either $(\Omega,\mathcal{F})$ or $(\Xi,\mathcal{G})$. This might appear related to the homeomorphic property of real functions, and a homeomorphism is indeed measurably isomorphic. But there is no implication the other way.

3.23 Example Consider $g\colon [0,1] \mapsto [0,1]$, defined by

$$g(x) = \begin{cases} x + \frac{1}{2}, & 0 \le x \le \frac{1}{2} \\ x - \frac{1}{2}, & \frac{1}{2} < x \le 1 \end{cases}. \tag{3.54}$$

Note that g is discontinuous, but is 1-1 onto, of bounded variation, and hence $\mathcal{B}_{[0,1]}/\mathcal{B}_{[0,1]}$-measurable by **3.32** below, and $g^{-1} = g$. □

The class of measurable transformations most often encountered is where the codomain is $(\mathbb{R},\mathcal{B})$, $\mathcal{B}$ being the linear Borel field. In this case we speak of a function, and generally use the notation f instead of T. A function may also have the extended real line $(\overline{\mathbb{R}},\overline{\mathcal{B}})$ as codomain. The measurability criteria are as follows.

3.24 Theorem

(i) A function $f\colon \Omega \mapsto \mathbb{R}$ for which $\{\omega\colon f(\omega) \le x\} \in \mathcal{F}$ for each $x \in \mathbb{Q}$ is $\mathcal{F}/\mathcal{B}$-measurable. So is a function for which $\{\omega\colon f(\omega) < x\} \in \mathcal{F}$ for each $x \in \mathbb{Q}$.

(ii) A function $f\colon \Omega \mapsto \overline{\mathbb{R}}$ for which $\{\omega\colon f(\omega) \le x\} \in \mathcal{F}$ for each $x \in \mathbb{Q} \cup \{+\infty\} \cup \{-\infty\}$ is $\mathcal{F}/\overline{\mathcal{B}}$-measurable.

Proof For case (i), the sets $\{\omega\colon f(\omega) \le x\}$ are of the form $f^{-1}(B)$, $B \in \mathcal{C}$ where $\mathcal{C}$ is defined in **1.21**. Since $\mathcal{B} = \sigma(\mathcal{C})$, the theorem follows by **3.22**. The other collection indicated also generates $\mathcal{B}$, and the same argument applies. The extension to case (ii) is equally straightforward. ■

The basic properties of measurable functions follow directly.

3.25 Theorem

(i) If f is measurable, so are $c+f$ and cf, where c is any constant.
(ii) If f and g are measurable, so is $f+g$.

Proof If $f \le x$, then $f+c \le x+c$, so that $f+c$ is measurable by **3.24**. Also, for $x \in \mathbb{R}$,

$$\{\omega\colon cf(\omega) \le x\} = \begin{cases} \{\omega\colon f(\omega) \le x/c\}, & c > 0 \\ \{\omega\colon f(\omega) < x/c\}^c, & c < 0 \\ \Omega, & c = 0 \text{ and } x \ge 0 \\ \varnothing, & c = 0 \text{ and } x < 0 \end{cases} \tag{3.55}$$

where for each of the cases on the right-hand side and each $x/c \in \mathbb{R}$ the sets are in $\mathcal{F}$, proving part (i).

If and only if $f+g < x$, there exist $r \in \mathbb{Q}$ such that $f < r < x-g$ (see **1.10**). It follows that

$$\{\omega\colon f(\omega)+g(\omega) < x\} = \bigcup_{r\in\mathbb{Q}} \{\omega\colon f(\omega) < r\} \cap \{\omega\colon g(\omega) < x-r\}. \tag{3.56}$$

The countable union of $\mathcal{F}$-sets on the right-hand side is an $\mathcal{F}$-set, and since this holds for every x, part (ii) also follows by **3.24**(i), where in this case it is convenient to generate $\mathcal{B}$ from the open half-lines. ■

Combining parts (i) and (ii) shows that if $f_1,\dots,f_n$ are measurable functions so is $\sum_{j=1}^n c_j f_j$, where the c_j are constant coefficients.

The measurability of suprema, infima, and limits of sequences of measurable functions is important in many applications, especially the derivation of integrals in Chapter 4. These are the main cases involving the extended line, because of the possibility that sequences in $\mathbb{R}$ are diverging. Such limits lying in $\overline{\mathbb{R}}$ are called extended functions.

3.26 Theorem Let $\{f_n\}$ be a sequence of $\mathcal{F}/\mathcal{B}$-measurable functions. Then $\inf_n f_n$, $\sup_n f_n$, $\liminf_n f_n$, and $\limsup_n f_n$ are $\mathcal{F}/\overline{\mathcal{B}}$-measurable.

Proof For any $x \in \overline{\mathbb{R}}$, $\{\omega\colon f_n(\omega) \le x\} \in \mathcal{F}$ for each n by assumption. Hence

$$\{\omega\colon \sup_n f_n(\omega) \le x\} = \bigcap_{n=1}^{\infty} \{\omega\colon f_n(\omega) \le x\} \in \mathcal{F}, \tag{3.57}$$

so that $\sup_n f_n$ is measurable by **3.24**(ii). Since $\inf_n f_n = -\sup_n(-f_n)$, we also obtain

$$\begin{aligned}\{\omega\colon \inf_n f_n(\omega) < x\} &= \{\omega\colon \sup_n(-f_n(\omega)) > -x\} \\ &= \{\omega\colon \sup_n(-f_n(\omega)) \le -x\}^c\end{aligned}$$

$$= \left(\bigcap_{n=1}^{\infty} \{\omega\colon -f_n(\omega) \le -x\} \right)^c$$

$$= \bigcup_{n=1}^{\infty} \{\omega\colon f_n(\omega) < x\} \in \mathcal{F}. \tag{3.58}$$

To extend this result from strong to weak inequalities, write

$$\{\omega\colon \inf_n f_n(\omega) \le x\} = \bigcap_{m=1}^{\infty} \{\omega\colon \inf_n f_n(\omega) < x + 1/m\} \in \mathcal{F}. \tag{3.59}$$

Similarly to (3.57), we may show

$$\{\omega\colon \sup_{k\ge n} f_k(\omega) \le x\} = \bigcap_{k\ge n} \{\omega\colon f_n(\omega) \le x\} \in \mathcal{F}, \tag{3.60}$$

and applying (3.59) to the sequence of functions $g_n = \sup_{k\ge n} f_k$ yields

$$\{\omega\colon \limsup_n f_n(\omega) \le x\} \in \mathcal{F}. \tag{3.61}$$

In much the same way, we can also show

$$\{\omega\colon \liminf_n f_n(\omega) \le x\} \in \mathcal{F}. \tag{3.62}$$

The measurability condition of **3.24** is therefore satisfied in each case. ■

We could add that $\lim_n f_n(\omega)$ exists and is measurable whenever $\limsup_n f_n(\omega) = \liminf_n f_n(\omega)$. This equality may hold only on a subset of Ω, but we say f_n converges a.e. when the complement of this set has measure zero.

The *indicator function* $1_E(\omega)$ of a set $E \in \mathcal{F}$ takes the value $1_E(\omega) = 1$ when $\omega \in E$, and $1_E(\omega) = 0$ otherwise. Some authors call 1_E the *characteristic function* of E. It may also be written as I_E or as χ_E. We now give some useful facts about indicator functions.

3.27 Theorem

(i) $1_E(\omega)$ is $\mathcal{F}/\mathcal{B}$ measurable if and only if $E \in \mathcal{F}$.

(ii) $1_{E^c}(\omega) = 1 - 1_E(\omega)$.

(iii) $1_{\bigcup_i E_i}(\omega) = \sup_i 1_{E_i}(\omega)$.

(iv) $1_{\bigcap_i E_i}(\omega) = \inf_i 1_{E_i}(\omega) = \prod_i 1_{E_i}(\omega)$.

Proof To show (i) note that, for each $B \in \mathcal{B}$,

$$1_E^{-1}(B) = \begin{cases} \Omega \text{ if } 0 \in B \text{ and } 1 \in B \\ E \text{ if } 1 \in B,\ 0 \notin B \\ E^c \text{ if } 0 \in B,\ 1 \notin B \\ \varnothing, \text{ otherwise} \end{cases} \tag{3.63}$$

These sets are in $\mathcal{F}$ if and only if $E \in \mathcal{F}$. The other parts of the theorem are immediate from the definition. ■

Indicator functions are the building blocks for more elaborate functions, constructed so as to ensure measurability. A *simple function* is a $\mathcal{F}/\mathcal{B}$-measurable function $f\colon \Omega \mapsto \mathbb{R}$ having finite range; that is, it has the form

$$f(\omega) = \sum_{i=1}^{n} \alpha_i 1_{E_i}(\omega) = \alpha_i,\ \omega \in E_i, \tag{3.64}$$

where the $\alpha_1,\dots,\alpha_n$ are constants and the collection of $\mathcal{F}$-sets $E_1,\dots,E_n$ is a finite partition of Ω. $\mathcal{F}/\mathcal{B}$-measurability holds because, for any $B \in \mathcal{B}$,

$$f^{-1}(B) = \bigcup_{\alpha_i \in B} E_i \in \mathcal{F}. \tag{3.65}$$

Simple functions are ubiquitous devices in measure and probability theory, because many problems can be solved for such functions rather easily, and then generalized to arbitrary functions by a limiting approximation argument such as the following.

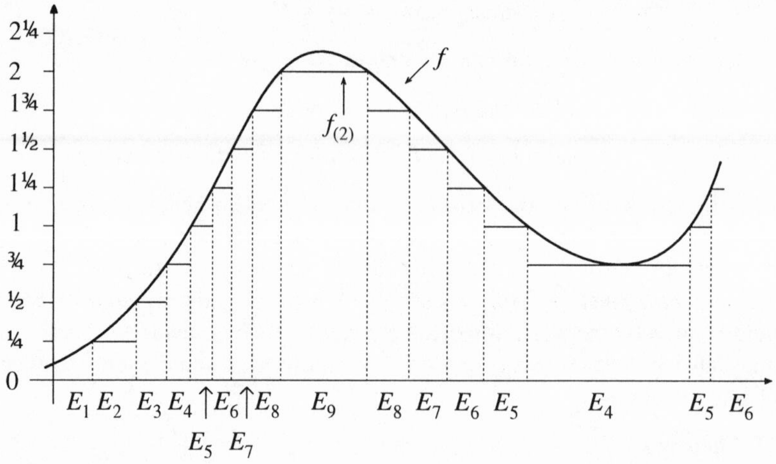

Fig. 3.1

3.28 Theorem If f is $\mathcal{F}/\mathcal{B}$-measurable and non-negative, there exists a monotone sequence of $\mathcal{F}/\mathcal{B}$-measurable simple functions $\{f_{(n)}, n \in \mathbb{N}\}$ such that $f_{(n)}(\omega) \uparrow f(\omega)$ for every $\omega \in \Omega$.

Proof For $i = 1,\dots,n2^n$, consider the sets $E_i = \{\omega\colon (i-1)/2^n \le f(\omega) < i/2^n\}$. Augment these with the set $E_{n2^n+1} = \{\omega\colon f(\omega) \ge n\}$. This collection corresponds to a $n2^n+1$-fold partition of $[0,\infty)$ into $\mathcal{B}$-sets, and since f is a function, each ω maps into one and only one $f(\omega)$, and hence belongs to one and only one E_i. The E_i therefore constitute a partition of Ω. Since f is measurable, $E_i \in \mathcal{F}$ for each i. Define a simple function $f_{(n)}$ on the E_i by letting $\alpha_i = (i-1)/2^n$, for $i = 1,\dots, n2^n+1$. Then $f_{(n)} \le f$, but $f_{n+1}(\omega) \ge f_n(\omega)$ for every ω; incrementing n bisects each interval, and if $f_{(n)}(\omega) = (i-1)/2^n$, $f_{(n+1)}(\omega)$ is equal to either $2(i-1)/2^{n+1} = f_{(n)}(\omega)$, or $(2i-1)/2^{n+1} > f_n(\omega)$. It follows that the sequence is monotone, and $\lim_{n\to\infty} f_{(n)}(\omega) = f(\omega)$. This holds for each $\omega \in \Omega$. To extend from non-negative to general functions, one takes the positive and negative parts. Define $f^+ = \max\{f,0\}$ and $f^- = f^+ - f$, so that both f^+ and f^- are non-negative functions. Then if $f^+_{(n)}$ and $f^-_{(n)}$ are the non-negative simple approximations to f^+ and f^- defined in **3.28**, and $f_{(n)} = f^+_{(n)} - f^-_{(n)}$, it is clear that

$$|f - f_{(n)}| \le |f^+ - f^+_{(n)}| + |f^- - f^-_{(n)}| \to 0. \ \blacksquare \tag{3.66}$$

Fig. 3.1 illustrates the construction for $n = 2$ and the case $\Omega = \mathbb{R}$, so that $f(\omega)$ is a function on the real line.

3.6 Borel Functions

If f is a measurable function, and

$$g\colon \mathbb{S} \mapsto \mathbb{T};\ \ \mathbb{S} \subseteq \mathbb{R}, \mathbb{T} \subseteq \mathbb{R}$$

is a function of a real variable, is the composite function $g \circ f$ measurable? The answer to this question is *yes* if and only if g is a *Borel function*. Let $\mathcal{B}_{\mathbb{S}} = \{B \cap \mathbb{S} \colon B \in \mathcal{B}\}$, where $\mathcal{B}$ is the Borel field of $\mathbb{R}$. $\mathcal{B}_{\mathbb{S}}$ is a σ-field of subsets of $\mathbb{S}$, and $B \cap \mathbb{S}$ is open (closed) in the relative topology on $\mathbb{S}$ whenever B is open (closed) in $\mathbb{R}$ (see **2.1** and **2.3**). $\mathcal{B}_{\mathbb{S}}$ is called the Borel field on $\mathbb{S}$. Define $\mathcal{B}_{\mathbb{T}}$ similarly with respect to $\mathbb{T}$. Then g is called a Borel function (i.e., is Borel-measurable) if $g^{-1}(B) \in \mathcal{B}_{\mathbb{S}}$ for all sets $B \in \mathcal{B}_{\mathbb{T}}$.

3.29 Example Consider $g(x) = |x|$. g^{-1} takes each point of $\mathbb{R}^+$ into the points x and $-x$. For any $B \in \mathcal{B}^+$ (the restriction of $\mathcal{B}$ to $\mathbb{R}^+$) the image under g^{-1} is the set containing the points x and $-x$ for each $x \in B$, which is an element of $\mathcal{B}$. □

3.30 Example Let $g(x) = 1$ if x is rational, 0 otherwise. Note that $\mathbb{Q} \in \mathcal{B}$ (see **3.15**), and g^{-1} is defined according to (3.63) with $E = \mathbb{Q}$, so g is Borel-measurable. □

In fact, to construct a 'plausible' non-measurable function is quite difficult, but the obvious case is the following.

3.31 Example Take a set $A \notin \mathcal{B}$; for example, let A be the set H defined in **3.17**. Now construct the indicator function $1_A(x)\colon \mathbb{R} \mapsto \{0,1\}$. Since $1_A^{-1}(\{1\}) = A \notin \mathcal{B}$, this function is not measurable. □

Necessary conditions for Borel measurability are hard to pin down, but the following sufficient conditions are convenient.

3.32 Theorem If $g\colon \mathbb{S} \mapsto \mathbb{T}$ is either (i) continuous or (ii) of bounded variation, it is Borel-measurable.

Proof (i) follows immediately from **3.22** and the definition of a Borel field, since continuity implies that $h^{-1}(B)$ is open (closed) in $\mathbb{S}$ whenever B is open (closed) in $\mathbb{T}$, by **2.17**.

To prove (ii), consider first a non-decreasing function $h\colon \mathbb{R} \mapsto \mathbb{R}$, having the property $h(y) \le h(x)$ when $y < x$; if $A = \{y\colon h(y) \le h(x)\}$, $\sup A = x$ and A is one of $(-\infty,x)$ and $(-\infty,x]$, so the condition of **3.24** is satisfied. So suppose g is non-decreasing on $\mathbb{S}$; applying the last result to any non-decreasing h with the property $h(x) = g(x)$, $x \in \mathbb{S}$, we have also shown that g is Borel-measurable because $g^{-1}(B \cap \mathbb{T}) = h^{-1}(B) \cap \mathbb{S} \in \mathcal{B}_{\mathbb{S}}$, for each $B \cap \mathbb{T} \in \mathcal{B}_{\mathbb{T}}$. Since a function of bounded variation is the difference of two non-decreasing functions by **2.20**, the theorem now follows easily by **3.25**. ∎

This result lets us add a further case to those of **3.25**.

3.33 Theorem If f and g are measurable, so is fg.

Proof $fg = \frac{1}{2}((f+g)^2 - f^2 - g^2)$, and the result follows on combining **3.32**(i) with **3.25**(ii). ∎

The concept of a Borel function extends naturally to Euclidean n-spaces, and indeed, to mappings between spaces of different dimension. A vector function

$$\boldsymbol{g}\colon \mathbb{S} \to \mathbb{T};\ \ \mathbb{S} \subseteq \mathbb{R}^k,\ \mathbb{T} \subseteq \mathbb{R}^m$$

is Borel-measurable if $\boldsymbol{g}^{-1}(B) \in \mathcal{B}_{\mathbb{S}}$ for all $B \in \mathcal{B}_{\mathbb{T}}$, where $\mathcal{B}_{\mathbb{S}} = \{B \cap \mathbb{S}\colon B \in \mathcal{B}^k\}$ and $\mathcal{B}_{\mathbb{T}} = \{B \cap \mathbb{T}\colon B \in \mathcal{B}^m\}$.

3.34 Theorem If $\boldsymbol{g}$ is continuous, it is Borel-measurable.

Proof By **2.21**. ∎

Finally, note the application of **3.21** to these cases.

3.35 Theorem If μ is a measure on $(\mathbb{R}^k,\mathcal{B}^k)$ and $\boldsymbol{g}\colon \mathbb{S} \mapsto \mathbb{T}$ is Borel-measurable where $\mathbb{S} \subseteq \mathbb{R}^k$ and $\mathbb{T} \subseteq \mathbb{R}^m$, $\mu\boldsymbol{g}^{-1}$ is a measure on $(\mathbb{T},\mathcal{B}_{\mathbb{T}})$ where

$$\mu\boldsymbol{g}^{-1}(B) = \mu(\boldsymbol{g}^{-1}(B)), \tag{3.67}$$

for each $B \in \mathcal{B}_{\mathbb{T}}$. □

A simple example is where $\boldsymbol{g}$ is the projection of $\mathbb{R}^k$ onto $\mathbb{R}^m$ for $m < k$. If $\boldsymbol{X}$ is $k \times 1$ with partition $\boldsymbol{X}' = (\boldsymbol{X}_*', \boldsymbol{X}_{**}')$, where $\boldsymbol{X}_*$ is $m \times 1$ and $\boldsymbol{X}_{**}$ is $(k-m) \times 1$, let $\boldsymbol{g}\colon \mathbb{R}^k \mapsto \mathbb{R}^m$ be defined by

$$\boldsymbol{g}(\boldsymbol{X}) = \boldsymbol{X}_*. \tag{3.68}$$

In this case, $\mu\boldsymbol{g}^{-1}(B) = \mu(\boldsymbol{g}^{-1}(B)) = \mu(B \times \mathbb{R}^{k-m})$ for $B \in \mathbb{R}^m$.

4
Integration

4.1 Construction of the Integral

The reader may be familiar with the Riemann integral of a bounded non-negative function f on a bounded interval of the line $[a,b]$, usually written $\int_a^b f dx$. The objects to be studied in this chapter represent a heroic generalization of the same idea. Instead of intervals of the line, the integral is defined on an arbitrary measure space.

Suppose $(\Omega,\mathcal{F},\mu)$ is a measure space and

$$f: \Omega \mapsto \overline{\mathbb{R}}^+$$

is a $\mathcal{F}/\overline{\mathcal{B}}$-measurable function into the non-negative, extended real line. The integral of f is defined to be the real valued functional

$$\int f d\mu = \sup\left\{\sum_i \left(\inf_{\omega\in E_i} f(\omega)\right)\mu(E_i)\right\} \tag{4.1}$$

where the supremum is taken over all finite partitions of Ω into sets $E_i \in \mathcal{F}$, and the supremum exists. If no supremum exists, the integral is assigned the value $+\infty$.[5] The integral of the function $1_A f$, where $1_A(\omega)$ is the indicator of the set $A \in \mathcal{F}$, is called the integral of f over A, and written $\int_A f d\mu$.

The expression in (4.1) is sometimes called the *lower integral*, and denoted $\int_* f d\mu$. Likewise defining the *upper integral* of f,

$$\int^* f d\mu = \inf\left\{\sum_i \left(\sup_{\omega\in E_i} f(\omega)\right)\mu(E_i)\right\}, \tag{4.2}$$

we should like these two constructions, approximating f from below and from above, to agree. And indeed, it is possible to show that $\int_* f d\mu = \int^* f d\mu$ whenever f is bounded and $\mu(\Omega) < \infty$. However, $\int^* f d\mu = \infty$ if either the set $\{\omega\colon f(\omega) > 0\}$ has infinite measure, or f is unbounded on sets of positive measure. Definition (4.1) is preferred because it can yield a finite value in these cases.

4.1 Example A familiar case is the measure space $(\mathbb{R},\mathcal{B},m)$, where m is Lebesgue measure. The integral $\int f dm$ where f is a Borel function is the *Lebesgue integral* of f. This is customarily written $\int f dx$, reflecting the fact that $m((x, x+dx]) = dx$, even though the sets $\{E_i\}$ in (4.1) need not be intervals. □

4.2 Example Consider a measure space $(\mathbb{R},\mathcal{B},\mu)$ where μ differs from m. The integral $\int f d\mu$, where f is a Borel function, is the *Lebesgue-Stieltjes integral*.

The monotone function

$$F(x) = \mu((-\infty, x]) \tag{4.3}$$

has the property $\mu((a,b]) = F(b) - F(a)$, and the measure of the interval $(x, x+dx]$ can be written $dF(x)$. The notation $\int f dF$ means exactly the same as $\int f d\mu$, the choice between the μ and F representations being a matter of taste. See §8.2 and §9.1 for details. □

For a contrast with these cases, consider the *Riemann-Stieltjes integral*. For an interval $[a,b]$, let a partition into subintervals be defined by a set of points $\Pi = \{x_1,\dots, x_n\}$, with $a = x_0 < x_1 < \dots < x_n = b$. Another set Π' is called a refinement of Π if $\Pi \subseteq \Pi'$. Given functions f and α: $\mathbb{R} \mapsto \mathbb{R}$, let

$$S(\Pi,\alpha,f) = \sum_{i=1}^{n} f(t_i)\big(\alpha(x_i) - \alpha(x_{i-1})\big), \tag{4.4}$$

where $t_i \in [x_{i-1}, x_i]$. If there exists a number $\int_a^b f d\alpha$, such that for every $\varepsilon > 0$ there is a partition Π_ε with

$$\left| S(\Pi,\alpha,f) - \int_a^b f d\alpha \right| < \varepsilon$$

for all $\Pi \supseteq \Pi_\varepsilon$ and every choice of $\{t_i\}$, this is called the Riemann-Stieltjes integral of f with respect to α. Recall in this connection the well-known formula for *integration by parts*, which states that when both integrals exist,

$$f(b)\alpha(b) = f(a)\alpha(a) + \int_a^b f d\alpha + \int_a^b \alpha df. \tag{4.5}$$

When $\alpha = x$ and f is bounded this definition yields the ordinary Riemann integral, and when it exists, this always agrees with the Lebesgue integral of f over $[a,b]$. Moreover, if α is an increasing function of the form in (4.3), this integral is equal to the Lebesgue-Stieltjes integral whenever it is defined. There do exist bounded, measurable functions which are not Riemann-integrable (consider **3.30** for example) so that even for bounded intervals the Lebesgue integral is the more inclusive concept.

However, the Riemann-Stieltjes integral is defined for more general classes of integrator function. In particular, if f is continuous it exists for α of bounded variation on $[a,b]$, not necessarily monotone. These integrals therefore fall outside the class defined by (4.1), although note that when α is of bounded variation, having a representation as the difference of two increasing functions, the Reimann-Stieltjes integral is the difference between a pair of Lebesgue-Stieltjes integrals on $[a,b]$.

The best way to understand the general integral is not to study a particular measure space, such as the line, but to restrict attention initially to particular classes of function. The simplest possible case is the indicator of a set. Then, every partition $\{E_i\}$ yields the same value for the sum of terms in (4.1), which is

$$\int_A d\mu = \int 1_A d\mu = \mu(A), \tag{4.6}$$

for any $A \in \mathcal{F}$. Note that if $A \notin \mathcal{F}$, the integral is undefined.

Another case of much importance is the following.

4.3 Theorem If $f = 0$ a.e.[μ], then $\int f d\mu = 0$.

Proof The theorem says there exists $C \subseteq \Omega$ with $\mu(C) = 1$, such that $f(\omega) = 0$ for $\omega \in C$. For any partition $\{E_1,...,E_n\}$ let $E_i' = E_i \cap C$, and $E_i'' = E_i - E_i'$. By additivity of μ,

$$\sum_i \left(\inf_{\omega \in E_i} f(\omega)\right)\mu(E_i) = \sum_i \left(\inf_{\omega \in E_i'} f(\omega)\right)\mu(E_i') + \sum_i \left(\inf_{\omega \in E_i''} f(\omega)\right)\mu(E_i'')$$
$$= 0, \tag{4.7}$$

the first sum of terms disappearing because $f(\omega) = 0$, and the second disappearing by **3.6**(i) since $\mu(E_i'') \le \mu(C^c) = 0$ for each i. ■

A class of functions for which evaluation of the integral is simple, as their name suggests, is the non-negative simple functions.

4.4 Theorem Let $\varphi(\omega) = \sum_{i=1}^n \alpha_i 1_{E_i}(\omega)$, where $\alpha_i \ge 0$ for $i = 1,...,n$, and $E_1,...,E_n \in \mathcal{F}$ is a partition of Ω. Then

$$\int \varphi d\mu = \sum_{i=1}^n \alpha_i \mu(E_i). \tag{4.8}$$

Proof Consider an arbitrary finite partition of Ω, $A_1,...,A_m$, and define $\beta_j = \inf_{\omega \in A_j} \varphi(\omega)$. Then, using additivity of μ,

$$\sum_{j=1}^m \beta_j \mu(A_j) = \sum_{j=1}^m \beta_j \sum_{i=1}^m \mu(A_j \cap E_i)$$
$$\le \sum_{i=1}^n \alpha_i \sum_{j=1}^m \mu(A_j \cap E_i)$$
$$= \sum_{i=1}^n \alpha_i \mu(E_i), \tag{4.9}$$

where the inequality uses the fact that β_j assumes the smallest value of α_i such that $A_j \cap E_i \ne \emptyset$, by definition. The theorem follows, given (4.1), since (4.9) holds as an equality for the case $m = n$ and $A_i = E_i$, $i = 1,...,n$. ■

So for functions with finite range, the integral is the sum of the possible values of f, weighted by the measures of the sets on which those values hold. Look at Fig. 3.1. The Lebesgue integral of the approximating function $f_{(2)}$ in the figure is the sum of the areas of the rectangular regions. To compute the Lebesgue-Stieltjes integral with respect to some measure μ, one replaces the width of the sets

E_i by their measures $\mu(E_i)$. The challenge is to find a way to construct the integrals of arbitrary non-negative functions, and then general functions. The next theorem is the cornerstone of integration theory, both providing the main step in the construction of the general integral and also spawning a range of useful corollaries.

4.5 Monotone convergence theorem If $\{f_n\}$ is a non-decreasing sequence of measurable non-negative functions, with $f_n(\omega) \uparrow f(\omega)$ for each $\omega \in \Omega$,

$$\lim_{n\to\infty} \int f_n d\mu = \int f d\mu, \tag{4.10}$$

where by implication the two sides of (4.10) are either both infinite, or finite and equal.

Proof If $0 \le f(\omega) \le g(\omega)$ for each $\omega \in \Omega$, it is immediate from (4.1) that $0 \le \int f d\mu \le \int g d\mu$. Hence, $\int f_n d\mu$ is a non-decreasing sequence bounded above by $\int f d\mu$, and has a limit, $\lim_{n\to\infty}\int f_n d\mu \le \int f d\mu$. To complete the proof, it suffices to show that $\lim_{n\to\infty}\int f_n d\mu \ge \int f d\mu$.

For a partition $\{A_i\}$ of Ω, let $\beta_i = \inf_{\omega\in A_i} f(\omega)$. For $k > 1$ define

$$b_i = \begin{cases} k, & \beta_i = \infty \\ (1 - 1/k)\beta_i, & 0 < \beta_i < \infty \\ 0, & \beta_i = 0 \end{cases} \tag{4.11}$$

so either $b_i = \beta_i = 0$ or $b_i < \beta_i$. Letting c denote a constant strictly less than $\sum_i \beta_i \mu(A_i)$, there exists k large enough that $c < \sum_i b_i \mu(A_i)$. By choice of $\{A_i\}$, $\int f d\mu - \sum_i \beta_i \mu(A_i) \ge 0$ can be made arbitrarily small, and hence c can be chosen such that $\int f d\mu - c > 0$ is arbitrarily small. The proof is therefore complete if we show that $\lim_{n\to\infty}\int f_n d\mu > c$.

Partition A_i into $A_{ni} = A_i \cap \{\omega\colon f_n(\omega) \ge b_i\}$ and $A_i - A_{ni}$, so that

$$\begin{aligned} \sum_i b_i \mu(A_{ni}) &\le \sum_i \Big(\inf_{\omega\in A_{ni}} f_n(\omega)\Big)\mu(A_{ni}) + \sum_i \Big(\inf_{\omega\in A_i - A_{ni}} f_n(\omega)\Big)\mu(A_i - A_{ni}) \\ &\le \int f_n d\mu, \end{aligned} \tag{4.12}$$

where the second inequality is by (4.1) since $A_{ni} \in \mathcal{F}$. For any $\omega \in A_i$, since $b_i < f(\omega)$ unless $f(\omega) = 0$, and $f_n \uparrow f$, there exists n large enough that $b_i \le f_n(\omega)$. Hence, $A_{ni} \uparrow A_i$ and $\mu(A_{ni}) \to \mu(A_i)$ as $n \to \infty$ (see the remark following **3.4**). Since for k large enough the minorant side of (4.12) strictly exceeds c in the limit, this completes the proof. ■

The leading application of this result may be apparent. For arbitrary non-negative f, a monotone sequence of simple functions converges to f from below, by **3.28**. The integral of f is the corresponding limit of the integrals of the simple functions defined in (4.8), whose existence is assured by **4.5.**

If **3.28** shows that a non-negative measurable function is the limit of a simple sequence, **3.26** shows that every convergent simple sequence has a measurable function as its limit. The next theorem teams these results with the monotone convergence theorem, and provides an alternative definition of the integral.

4.6 Theorem For any non-negative $\mathcal{F}/\mathcal{B}$-measurable function f,

$$\int f d\mu = \sup_{0\leq\varphi\leq f} \int \varphi d\mu, \tag{4.13}$$

where φ denotes the class of simple functions. □

For bounded f and finite μ, the equality also holds in respect of the infimum over simple functions $\varphi \geq f$, in parallel with (4.2).

The final extension is from non-negative functions to general functions, by taking positive and negative parts. If $f\colon \Omega \longrightarrow \overline{\mathbb{R}}$ is any measurable function, let $f^+ = \max\{f, 0\} \geq 0$ and $f^- = f^+ - f \geq 0$. The integral of f is defined as

$$\int f d\mu = \int f^+ d\mu - \int f^- d\mu \tag{4.14}$$

so long as at least one of the right-hand side integrals are finite. If both $\int f^+ d\mu = \infty$ and $\int f^- d\mu = \infty$, the integral is undefined; the difference of two infinities is undefined, and in particular, it is not zero. A function is said to be *integrable* only if its integral is both defined and finite. Noting that $|f| = f^+ + f^-$, f is integrable if and only if

$$\int |f| d\mu < \infty. \tag{4.15}$$

4.2 Properties of the Integral

A really useful feature of **4.6** is that it lets us prove easy results for the integrals of simple functions, and extend these to the general case by the limiting argument. The most important of the properties we establish in this way is linearity.

4.7 Theorem If f and g are $\mathcal{F}/\mathcal{B}$-measurable, integrable functions, and a and b are constants, $(af + bg)$ is integrable and

$$\int (af + bg) d\mu = a\int f d\mu + b\int g d\mu. \tag{4.16}$$

Proof First let f, g and a, b all be non-negative. If $\{A_i\}$ and $\{B_j\}$ are finite partitions of Ω, and $\varphi(\omega) = \sum_i \alpha_i 1_{A_i}(\omega)$ and $\gamma(\omega) = \sum_j \beta_j 1_{B_j}(\omega)$ are simple functions defined on these partitions, then

$$a\varphi(\omega) + b\gamma(\omega) = \sum_i \sum_j (a\alpha_i + b\beta_j) 1_{A_i \cap B_j}(\omega)$$

$$= b\alpha_i + a\beta_j,\ \omega \in A_i \cap B_j, \tag{4.17}$$

a simple function. Hence,

$$\begin{aligned}\int(a\varphi + b\gamma)d\mu &= \sum_i\sum_j(a\alpha_i + b\beta_j)\mu(A_i \cap B_j)\\ &= a\sum_i\alpha_i\sum_j\mu(A_i\cap B_j) + b\sum_j\beta_j\sum_i\mu(A_i\cap B_j)\\ &= a\sum_i\alpha_i\mu(A_i) + b\sum_j\beta_j\mu(B_j)\\ &= a\int\varphi d\mu + b\int\gamma d\mu,\end{aligned} \tag{4.18}$$

showing that linearity applies to simple functions. Now applying **4.6**,

$$\begin{aligned}\int(af + bg)d\mu &= \sup_{\varphi\le f,\gamma\le g}\int(a\varphi + b\gamma)d\mu\\ &= a\left(\sup_{\varphi\le f}\int\varphi d\mu\right) + b\left(\sup_{\gamma\le g}\int\gamma d\mu\right)\\ &= a\int f d\mu + b\int g d\mu.\end{aligned} \tag{4.19}$$

To extend the result to general functions, note that

$$|af + bg| \le |a|.|f| + |b|.|g|, \tag{4.20}$$

so (4.19) shows that $af + bg$ is integrable so long f and g are integrable, and a and b are finite. The identity

$$af + bg = (af)^+ - (af)^- + (bg)^+ - (bg)^- \tag{4.21}$$

implies, applying (4.19), that

$$\int(af + bg)d\mu = \int(af)^+d\mu - \int(af)^-d\mu + \int(bg)^+d\mu - \int(bg)^-d\mu. \tag{4.22}$$

If $a \ge 0$, then $\int(af)^+d\mu - \int(af)^-d\mu = a(\int f^+d\mu - \int f^-d\mu) = a\int fd\mu$, whereas if $a < 0$, $\int(af)^+d\mu - \int(af)^-d\mu = |a|(\int f^-d\mu - \int f^+d\mu) = |a|(-\int fd\mu) = a\int fd\mu$. The same argument applies to the terms in b and g. So (4.16) holds as required. ∎

Linearity is a very useful property. The first application is to show the invariance of the integral to the behaviour of functions on sets of measure 0, extending the basic result of **4.3**.

4.8 Lemma Let f and g be integrable functions.

(i) If $f \le g$ a.e.[μ], then $\int fd\mu \le \int gd\mu$.

(ii) If $f = g$ a.e.[μ], then $\int fd\mu = \int gd\mu$.

Proof For (i), consider first the case $f = 0$. If $g \ge 0$ everywhere, $\int gd\mu \ge 0$ directly from (4.1). So suppose $g \ge 0$ a.e.[μ] and define

$$h(\omega) = \begin{cases} 0, & g(\omega) \geq 0 \\ \infty, & g(\omega) < 0 \end{cases}.$$

Then $h = 0$ a.e.[μ] but $g + h \geq 0$ everywhere, and, applying **4.7**,

$$0 \leq \int (g+h)d\mu = \int g d\mu + \int h d\mu = \int g d\mu, \tag{4.23}$$

since $\int h d\mu = 0$ by **4.3**. Now replace g by $g - f$ in the last argument to show $\int (g-f)d\mu \geq 0$, and hence $\int g d\mu \geq \int f d\mu$ by **4.7**.

To prove (ii), let $h = f - g$ so that $h = 0$ a.e.[μ], and $\int h d\mu = 0$ by **4.3**. Then $\int f d\mu = \int (g+h)d\mu = \int g d\mu + \int h d\mu = \int g d\mu$, where the second equality is by **4.7**. ■

These results permit the extension to the more commonly quoted version of the monotone convergence theorem.

4.9 Corollary If $f_n \geq 0$ and $f_n \uparrow f$ a.e.[μ], $\lim_{n\to\infty} \int f_n d\mu = \int f d\mu$. □

Another implication of linearity is the following.

4.10 Modulus inequality $\int |f| d\mu \geq \left| \int f d\mu \right|$.

Proof

$$\int |f| d\mu = \int (f^+ + f^-) d\mu = \int f^+ d\mu + \int f^- d\mu$$

$$\geq \left| \int f^+ d\mu - \int f^- d\mu \right| = \left| \int f d\mu \right|. \ ■$$

In the form of **4.9**, the monotone convergence theorem has several other useful corollaries.

4.11 Fatou's lemma If $f_n \geq 0$ a.e.[μ], then

$$\liminf_{n\to\infty} \int f_n d\mu \geq \int \left(\liminf_{n\to\infty} f_n \right) d\mu.$$

Proof Let $g_n = \inf_{k \geq n} f_k$, so that $\{g_n\}$ is a non-decreasing sequence, and $g_n \uparrow g = \liminf_n f_n$. Since $f_n \geq g_n$, $\int f_n d\mu \geq \int g_n d\mu$. Letting $n \to \infty$ on both sides of the inequality gives

$$\liminf_{n\to\infty} \int f_n d\mu \geq \lim_{n\to\infty} \int g_n d\mu = \int g d\mu = \int \left(\liminf_{n\to\infty} f_n \right) d\mu. \ ■ \tag{4.24}$$

4.12 Dominated convergence theorem If $f_n \to f$ a.e.[μ], and there exists g such that $|f_n| \leq g$ a.e.[μ] for all n and $\int g d\mu < \infty$, then $\int f_n d\mu \to \int f d\mu$.

Proof According to **4.8**(i), $\int g d\mu < \infty$ implies $\int |f_n| d\mu < \infty$. Let $h_n = |f_n - f|$, such that $0 \leq h_n \leq 2g$ a.e.[μ] and $h_n \to 0$ a.e.[μ]. Applying **4.3** to $\liminf_n h_n$, linearity, and Fatou's lemma,

$$2\int g d\mu = \int \left(\liminf_{n\to\infty}(2g - h_n) \right) d\mu \le \liminf_{n\to\infty} \int \left((2g - h_n) d\mu \right)$$

$$= 2\int g d\mu - \limsup_{n\to\infty} \left(\int h_n d\mu \right), \tag{4.25}$$

where the last equality uses (2.4). Clearly, $\limsup_{n\to\infty}\int h_n d\mu = 0$, and since $\int h_n d\mu \ge 0$ the modulus inequality implies

$$\left| \lim_{n\to\infty} \int f_n d\mu - \int f d\mu \right| \le \lim_{n\to\infty} \int h_n d\mu = 0. \ \blacksquare \tag{4.26}$$

Taking the case where the g is replaced by a finite constant produces the following version, often more convenient:

4.13 Bounded convergence theorem If $f_n \to f$ a.e.[μ] and $|f_n| \le B < \infty$ for all n, then $\lim_{n\to\infty}\int f_n d\mu \to \int f d\mu < \infty$. □

Theorem **4.7** extends by recursion from pairs to arbitrary finite sums of functions, and in particular we may assert that $\int(\sum_{i=1}^n g_i)d\mu = \sum_{i=1}^n \int g_i d\mu$. Put $f_n = \sum_{i=1}^n g_i$ and $\int f_n d\mu = \sum_{i=1}^n \int g_i d\mu$, where the g_i are non-negative functions. Then, if $f_n \uparrow f = \sum_{i=1}^\infty g_i < \infty$ a.e., **4.9** also permits us to assert the following.

4.14 Corollary If $\{g_i\}$ is a sequence of non-negative functions,

$$\int \left(\sum_{i=1}^{\infty} g_i \right) d\mu = \sum_{i=1}^{\infty} \int g_i d\mu. \ \square \tag{4.27}$$

By implication, the two sides of this equation are either both infinite, or finite and equal. This has a particular application to results involving σ-finite measures. Suppose we wish to evaluate an integral $\int g d\mu$ using a method that works for finite measures. To extend to the σ-finite case, choose a countable partition $\{\Omega_i\}$ of Ω, such that $\mu(\Omega_i) < \infty$ for each i. Letting $g_i = 1_{\Omega_i} g$, note that $g = \sum_i g_i$, and $\int g d\mu = \sum_i \int g_i d\mu$ by (4.27).

4.3 Product Measure and Multiple Integrals

Let $(\Omega,\mathcal{F},\mu)$ and $(\Xi,\mathcal{G},\nu)$ be measure spaces. In general, $(\Omega\times\Xi, \mathcal{F}\otimes\mathcal{G}, \pi)$ might also be a measure space, with π a measure on the sets of $\mathcal{F}\otimes\mathcal{G}$. In this case measures μ and ν, defined by $\mu(F) = \pi(F\times\Xi)$ and $\nu(G) = \pi(\Omega\times G)$ respectively, are called the *marginal measures* corresponding to π.

Alternatively, suppose that μ and ν are given, and define the set function

$$\pi\colon \mathcal{R}_{\mathcal{F}\mathcal{G}} \mapsto \overline{\mathbb{R}}^+,$$

where $\mathcal{R}_{\mathcal{F}\mathcal{G}}$ denotes the measurable rectangles of the space $\Omega\times\Xi$, by

$$\pi(F\times G) = \mu(F)\nu(G). \tag{4.28}$$

We will show that π is a measure on $\mathcal{R}_{\mathcal{F}\mathcal{G}}$, called the *product measure*, and has an extension to $\mathcal{F}\otimes\mathcal{G}$, so that $(\Omega\times\Xi, \mathcal{F}\otimes\mathcal{G}, \pi)$ is indeed a measure space. The first step in this demonstration is to define the mapping

$$T_\omega\colon \Xi \mapsto \Omega\times\Xi$$

by $T_\omega(\xi) = (\omega,\xi)$, so that, for $G \in \mathcal{G}$, $T_\omega(G) = \{\omega\}\times G$. For $E \in \mathcal{F}\otimes\mathcal{G}$, let

$$E_\omega = T_\omega^{-1}(E) = \{\xi\colon (\omega,\xi) \in E\} \subseteq \Xi. \tag{4.29}$$

The set E_ω can be thought of as the cross-section through E at the element ω. For any countable collection of $\mathcal{F}\otimes\mathcal{G}$-sets $\{E_j,\, j \in \mathbb{N}\}$,

$$\left(\bigcup_j E_j\right)_\omega = \left\{\xi\colon (\omega,\xi) \in \bigcup_j E_j\right\} = \bigcup_j \{\xi\colon (\omega,\xi) \in E_j\} = \bigcup_j (E_j)_\omega. \tag{4.30}$$

For future reference, note the following.

4.15 Lemma T_ω is a $\mathcal{G}/(\mathcal{F}\otimes\mathcal{G})$-measurable mapping for each $\omega \in \Omega$.

Proof We must show that $E_\omega \in \mathcal{G}$ whenever $E \in \mathcal{F}\otimes\mathcal{G}$. If $E = F\times G$ for $F \in \mathcal{F}$ and $G \in \mathcal{G}$, it is obvious that

$$E_\omega = \begin{cases} G, & \omega \in F \\ \varnothing, & \omega \notin F \end{cases} \in \mathcal{G}. \tag{4.31}$$

Since $\mathcal{F}\otimes\mathcal{G} = \sigma(\mathcal{R}_{\mathcal{F}\mathcal{G}})$, the lemma follows by **3.22.** ∎

The second step is to show the following.

4.16 Theorem π is a measure on $\mathcal{R}_{\mathcal{F}\mathcal{G}}$.

Proof Clearly π is non-negative, and $\pi(\varnothing) = 0$, recalling that $F\times\varnothing = \varnothing\times G = \varnothing$ for any $F \in \mathcal{F}$ or $G \in \mathcal{G}$, and applying (4.28). It remains to show countable additivity. Let $\{E_j \in \mathcal{R}_{\mathcal{F}\mathcal{G}},\, j \in \mathbb{N}\}$ be a disjoint collection, such that there exist sets $F_j \in \mathcal{F}$ and $G_j \in \mathcal{G}$ with $E_j = F_j\times G_j$; and also suppose $E = \bigcup_j E_j \in \mathcal{R}_{\mathcal{F}\mathcal{G}}$, such that there exist sets F and G with $E = F\times G$. Any point $(\omega,\xi) \in F\times G$ belongs to one and only one of the sets $F_j\times G_j$, so that for any $\omega \in F$, the sets of the subcollection $\{G_j\}$ for which $\omega \in F_j$ must constitute a partition of G. Hence, applying (4.30) and (4.31),

$$\begin{aligned}\nu(E_\omega) &= \nu\left(\left(\bigcup_j E_j\right)_\omega\right) = \nu\left(\bigcup_j (E_j)_\omega\right) \\ &= \nu\left(\bigcup_j \begin{cases} G_j, & \omega \in F_j \\ \varnothing, & \omega \notin F_j \end{cases}\right) = \sum_j 1_{F_j}(\omega)\nu(G_j),\end{aligned} \tag{4.32}$$

where the additivity of ν can be applied since the sets G_j appearing in this decomposition are disjoint. Since we can also write $\nu(E_\omega) = \nu(G)1_F(\omega)$, we find

$$\pi(E) = \mu(F)\nu(G) = \int \nu(E_\omega)d\mu(\omega) = \int \left(\sum_j 1_{F_j}(\omega)\nu(G_j)\right) d\mu(\omega)$$

$$= \sum_j \mu(F_j)\nu(G_j) = \sum_j \pi(E_j) \tag{4.33}$$

as required, where the penultimate equality is by **4.14**. ■

It is now straightforward to extend the measure from $\mathcal{R}_{\mathcal{F}\mathcal{G}}$ to $\mathcal{F}\otimes\mathcal{G}$.

4.17 Theorem $(\Omega\times\Xi, \mathcal{F}\otimes\mathcal{G}, \pi)$ is a measure space.

Proof $\mathcal{F}$ and $\mathcal{G}$ are σ-fields and hence semi-rings; hence $\mathcal{R}_{\mathcal{F}\mathcal{G}}$ is a semi-ring by **3.19**. The theorem follows from **4.16** and **3.8**. ■

Iterating the preceding arguments (i.e. letting $(\Omega,\mathcal{F})$ and/or $(\Xi,\mathcal{G})$ be product spaces) allows the concept to be extended to products of higher order. In later chapters, product probability measures will embody the intuitive notion of statistical independence, although this is by no means the only application we shall meet. The following case has a familiar geometrical interpretation.

4.18 Example Lebesgue measure in the plane, $\mathbb{R}^2 = \mathbb{R}\times\mathbb{R}$, is defined for intervals by

$$m((a_1,b_1]\times(a_2,b_2]) = (b_1-a_1)(b_2-a_2). \tag{4.34}$$

Here the measurable rectangles include the actual geometrical rectangles (products of intervals), and $\mathcal{B}^2$, the Borel sets of the plane, is generated from these as a consequence of **3.20**. By the foregoing reasoning, $(\mathbb{R}^2,\mathcal{B}^2,m)$ is a measure space in which the measure of a set is given by its area. □

We now construct integrals of functions $f(\omega,\xi)$ on the product space. The following lemma is a natural extension of **4.15**, for it considers what we might think of as a cross-section through the mapping at a point $\omega\in\Omega$, yielding a function with domain Ξ.

4.19 Lemma Let $f:\Omega\times\Xi\mapsto\mathbb{R}$ be $\mathcal{F}\otimes\mathcal{G}/\mathcal{B}$-measurable. Define $f_\omega(\xi) = f(\omega,\xi)$ for fixed $\omega\in\Omega$. Then f_ω: $\Xi\mapsto\mathbb{R}$ is $\mathcal{G}/\mathcal{B}$-measurable.

Proof We can write

$$f_\omega(\xi) = f(\omega,\xi) = f(T_\omega(\xi)) = f\circ T_\omega(\xi). \tag{4.35}$$

By **4.15** and the remarks following **3.22**, the composite function $f\circ T_\omega$ is $\mathcal{G}/\mathcal{B}$-measurable. ■

Suppose we are able to integrate f_ω with respect to ν over Ξ. There are two questions of interest that arise here. First, is the resulting function $g(\omega) = \int_\Xi f_\omega d\nu$ $\mathcal{F}/\overline{\mathcal{B}}$-measurable? And second, if g is now integrated over Ω, what is the relationship between this integral and the integral $\int_{\Omega\times\Xi} fd\pi$ over $\Omega\times\Xi$? The affirmative answer to the first of these questions, and the fact that the 'iterated' integral is identical with the 'double' integral where these exist, are the most important results for product spaces, known jointly as the *Fubini theorem*. Since iterated integration is an operation we tend to take for granted with multiple Riemann integrals, perhaps the main point needing to be stressed here is that this convenient property of product measures (and multivariate Lebesgue measure in particular) does *not* generalize to arbitrary measures on product spaces.

The first step is to let f be the indicator of a set $E \in \mathcal{F} \otimes \mathcal{G}$. In this case f_ω is the indicator of the set E_ω defined in (4.29), and

$$\int f_\omega d\nu = \nu(E_\omega) = g_E(\omega), \tag{4.36}$$

say. In view of **4.15**, $E_\omega \in \mathcal{G}$ and the function g_E: $\Omega \mapsto \overline{\mathbb{R}}^+$ is well-defined, although, unless ν is a finite measure, it may take its values in the extended half line, as shown.

4.20 Lemma Let μ and ν be σ-finite. For all $E \in \mathcal{F} \otimes \mathcal{G}$, g_E is $\mathcal{F}/\overline{\mathcal{B}}$-measurable and

$$\int_\Omega g_E d\mu = \pi(E). \tag{4.37}$$

By implication, the two sides of the equality in (4.37) are either both infinite, or finite and equal.

Proof Assume first that the measures are finite. The theorem is proved for this case using the π-λ theorem. Let $\mathcal{A}$ denote the collection of sets E such that g_E satisfies (4.37). $\mathcal{R}_{\mathcal{F}\mathcal{G}} \subseteq \mathcal{A}$, since if $E = F \times G$ then, by (4.31),

$$g_E(\omega) = \nu(G)1_F(\omega), \quad F \in \mathcal{F}, \tag{4.38}$$

and $\int_\Omega g_E d\mu = \mu(F)\nu(G) = \pi(E)$ as required. We now show $\mathcal{A}$ is a λ-system. Clearly $\Omega \times \Xi \in \mathcal{A}$, so **1.25**(a) holds. If $E_1, E_2 \in \mathcal{A}$ and $E_1 \subset E_2$, then, since $1_{E_2 - E_1} = 1_{E_2} - 1_{E_1}$,

$$g_{E_2-E_1}(\omega) = \int_\Xi 1_{E_2}(\omega,\xi)d\nu(\xi) - \int_\Xi 1_{E_1}(\omega,\xi)d\nu(\xi)$$

$$= g_{E_2}(\omega) - g_{E_1}(\omega), \tag{4.39}$$

an $\mathcal{F}/\overline{\mathcal{B}}$ measurable function by **3.25**, and so, by additivity of π,

$$\int_\Omega g_{E_2-E_1} d\mu(\omega) = \pi(E_2) - \pi(E_1) = \pi(E_2 - E_1), \tag{4.40}$$

showing that $\mathcal{A}$ satisfies **1.25**(b). Finally, If A_1 and A_2 are disjoint so are $(A_1)_\omega$ and $(A_2)_\omega$, and $g_{A_1 \cup A_2}(\omega) = g_{A_1}(\omega) + g_{A_2}(\omega)$. To establish **1.25**(c), let $\{E_j \in \mathcal{A}, j \in \mathbb{N}\}$ be a monotone sequence, with $E_j \uparrow E$. Define the disjoint collection $\{A_j\}$ with $A_1 = E_1$ and $A_j = E_{j+1} - E_j$, $j > 1$, so that $E = \bigcup_{j=1}^\infty A_j$ and $A_j \in \mathcal{A}$ by (4.39). By countable additivity of ν,

$$g_E(\omega) = \sum_{j=1}^\infty g_{A_j}(\omega). \tag{4.41}$$

This is $\mathcal{F}/\mathcal{B}$-measurable by **3.26**, and

$$\int_\Omega \left(\sum_{j=1}^{\infty} g_{A_j}(\omega)\right) d\mu(\omega) = \sum_{j=1}^{\infty} \int_\Omega g_{A_j}(\omega) d\mu(\omega) = \sum_{j=1}^{\infty} \pi(A_j) = \pi(E), \tag{4.42}$$

where the first equality is by **4.14**. This shows that $\mathcal{A}$ is λ-system. Since $\mathcal{R}_{\mathcal{F}\mathcal{G}}$ is a semi-ring it is also a π-system, and $\mathcal{F} \otimes \mathcal{G} = \sigma(\mathcal{R}_{\mathcal{F}\mathcal{G}}) \subseteq \mathcal{A}$ by **1.27**. This completes the proof for finite measures.

To extend to the σ-finite case, let $\{\Omega_i\}$ and $\{\Xi_j\}$ be countable partitions of Ω and Ξ with finite μ-measure and ν-measure respectively; then the collection $\{\Omega_i \times \Xi_j \in \mathcal{R}_{\mathcal{F}\mathcal{G}}\}$ forms a countable partition of $\Omega \times \Xi$ having finite measures, $\pi(\Omega_i \times \Xi_j) = \mu(\Omega_i)\nu(\Xi_j)$. For a set $E \in \mathcal{F} \otimes \mathcal{G}$, write $E_{ij} = E \cap (\Omega_i \times \Xi_j)$. Then by the last argument,

$$\int_{\Omega_i} g_{E_{ij}} d\mu = \pi(E_{ij}), \tag{4.43}$$

where $g_{E_{ij}}\colon \Omega_i \mapsto \mathbb{R}^+$ is defined by $g_{E_{ij}}(\omega) = \nu((E_{ij})_\omega)$, $\omega \in \Omega_i$. The sets E_{ij} are disjoint and $g_E(\omega) = \nu((\bigcup_j E_{ij})_\omega)$ when $\omega \in \Omega_i$, or

$$g_E(\omega) = \sum_i 1_{\Omega_j}(\omega) \sum_j g_{E_{ij}}(\omega). \tag{4.44}$$

The sum on the right need not converge, and in that case $g_E(\omega) = +\infty$. However, $\mathcal{F}/\overline{\mathcal{B}}$-measurability holds by **3.25/3.26**, and

$$\int_\Omega g_E d\mu = \int_\Omega \left(\sum_i 1_{\Omega_j} \sum_j g_{E_{ij}}\right) d\mu$$

$$= \sum_i \sum_j \int_{\Omega_i} g_{E_{ij}} d\mu = \sum_i \sum_j \pi(E_{ij}) = \pi(E), \tag{4.45}$$

using **4.14** and countable additivity. This completes the proof. ■

Now extend from indicator functions to non-negative functions:

4.21 Tonelli's theorem Let π be a product measure with σ-finite marginal measures μ and ν, and let $f\colon \Omega \times \Xi \mapsto \mathbb{R}^+$ be $(\mathcal{F} \otimes \mathcal{G})/\mathcal{B}$-measurable. Define functions $f_\omega\colon \Xi \mapsto \mathbb{R}^+$ by $f_\omega(\xi) = f(\omega,\xi)$, and let $g(\omega) = \int_\Xi f_\omega d\nu$. Then

(i) g is $\mathcal{F}/\overline{\mathcal{B}}$-measurable,

(ii) $\int_{\Omega \times \Xi} f d\pi = \int_\Omega \left(\int_\Xi f_\omega d\nu\right) d\mu$. □

In part (ii) it is again understood that the two sides of the equation are either finite and equal, or both infinite. Like the other results of this section, the theorem is symmetric in $(\Omega,\mathcal{F},\mu)$ and $(\Xi,\mathcal{G},\nu)$, and the complementary results given by interchanging the roles of the marginal spaces do not require a separate statement. The theorem holds even for measures that are not σ-finite, but this further complicates the proof.

Proof This is on the lines of **4.6**. For a partition $\{E_1,...,E_n\}$ of $\mathcal{F} \otimes \mathcal{G}$ let $f = \sum_i \alpha_i 1_{E_i}$, and then $f_\omega = \sum_i \alpha_i 1_{(E_i)_\omega}$ and $g = \sum_i \alpha_i \nu((E_i)_\omega)$ by **4.4**. g is $\mathcal{F}/\overline{\mathcal{B}}$-measurable by **3.25**, and **4.20** gives

$$\int_{\Omega} g d\mu = \sum_i \alpha_i \int_{\Omega} \nu((E_i)_\omega) d\mu = \sum_i \alpha_i \pi(E_i) = \int_{\Omega\times\Xi} f d\pi, \tag{4.46}$$

so that the theorem holds for simple functions. For general non-negative f, choose a monotone sequence of simple functions converging to f as in **3.28**, show measurability of g in the limit using **3.26**, and apply the monotone convergence theorem. ∎

Extending to general f requires the additional assumption of integrability.

4.22 Fubini's theorem Let π be a product measure with σ-finite marginal measures μ and ν; let $f: \Omega\times\Xi \mapsto \mathbb{R}$ be $(\mathcal{F}\otimes\mathcal{G})/\mathcal{B}$-measurable with

$$\int_{\Omega\times\Xi} |f(\omega,\xi)| d\pi(\omega,\xi) < \infty; \tag{4.47}$$

define $f_\omega: \Xi \mapsto \mathbb{R}$ by $f_\omega(\xi) = f(\omega,\xi)$; and let $g(\omega) = \int_\Xi f_\omega d\nu$. Then

(i) f_ω is $\mathcal{G}/\mathcal{B}$-measurable and integrable for $\omega \in \Delta \subseteq \Omega$, with $\mu(\Omega - \Delta) = 0$;

(ii) g is $\mathcal{F}/\mathcal{B}$-measurable, and integrable on Δ;

(iii) $\int_{\Omega\times\Xi} f(\omega,\xi) d\pi(\omega,\xi) = \int_{\Omega}\left(\int_{\Xi} f(\omega,\xi) d\nu(\xi)\right) d\mu(\omega)$.

Proof Apart from the integrability, **4.19** shows (i) and Tonelli's Theorem shows (ii) and (iii) for the functions $f^+ = \max\{f,0\}$ and $f^- = f^+ - f$, where $|f| = f^+ + f^-$. But under (4.47), $|f(\omega,\xi)| < \infty$ on a set of π-measure 1. With Δ defined as the projection of this set onto Ω, (i), (ii) and (iii) hold for f^+ and f^-, with both sides of the equation finite in (iii). Since $f = f^+ - f^-$, (i) extends to f by **3.25**, and (ii) and (iii) extend to f by **4.7**. ∎

4.4 The Radon-Nikodym Theorem

Consider σ-finite measures μ and ν on a measurable space $(\Omega,\mathcal{F})$. μ is said to be *absolutely continuous* with respect to ν if $\nu(E) = 0$, for $E \in \mathcal{F}$, implies $\mu(E) = 0$. This relationship is written as $\mu \ll \nu$. If $\mu \ll \nu$ and $\nu \ll \mu$, the measures are said to be *equivalent*. If there exists a partition (A, A^c) of Ω, such that $\mu(A) = 0$ and $\nu(A^c) = 0$, then μ and ν are said to be *mutually singular*, written $\mu \perp \nu$. Mutual singularity is symmetric, such that $\mu \perp \nu$ means the same as $\nu \perp \mu$.

The following result defines the *Lebesgue decomposition* of μ with respect to ν.

4.23 Theorem If μ and ν are σ-finite measures, there exist measures μ_1 and μ_2 such that $\mu = \mu_1 + \mu_2$, $\mu_1 \perp \nu$, and $\mu_2 \ll \nu$. □

If there is a function

$$f: \Omega \mapsto \overline{\mathbb{R}}^+$$

such that $\mu(E) = \int_E f d\nu$, it follows fairly directly (choose E such that $\nu(E) = 0$) that $\mu \ll \nu$, and f might be thought of as the derivative of one measure with respect to the other; we could even write $f = d\mu/d\nu$. The result that absolute continuity of μ with respect to ν *implies* the existence of such a function is the Radon-Nikodym theorem.

4.24 Radon-Nikodym theorem Let ν and μ_2 be σ-finite measures and let $\mu_2 \ll \nu$. There exists a $\mathcal{F}/\overline{\mathcal{B}}$-measurable function $f: \Omega \mapsto \overline{\mathbb{R}}^+$ such that $\mu_2(E) = \int_E f d\nu$ for all $E \in \mathcal{F}$. □

f is called the Radon-Nikodym derivative of μ with respect to ν. If g is another such function and $\mu_2(E) = \int_E g d\nu$ for all $E \in \mathcal{F}$, then $\nu(f \neq g) = 0$, otherwise at least one of the sets $E_1 = \{\omega: f(\omega) > g(\omega)\}$ and $E_2 = \{\omega: f(\omega) < g(\omega)\}$ must contradict the definition.

Proof of these results requires the concept of a *signed measure.*

4.25 Definition A signed measure on $(\Omega,\mathcal{F})$ is a set function

$$\chi: \mathcal{F} \mapsto \overline{\mathbb{R}}$$

satisfying

(a) $\chi(\varnothing) = 0$.
(b) $\chi(\bigcup_j A_j) = \sum_j \chi(A_j)$ for any countable, disjoint collection $\{A_j \in \mathcal{F}\}$.
(c) Either $\chi < \infty$ or $\chi > -\infty$. □

For example, let μ and ν be non-negative measures on a space $(\Omega, \mathcal{F})$, with at least one of them finite. For a non-negative constant r, define

$$\chi(A) = \mu(A) - r\nu(A) \tag{4.48}$$

for any $A \in \mathcal{F}$. For disjoint $\{A_j\}$,

$$\chi\left(\bigcup_{j=1}^{\infty} A_j\right) = \mu\left(\bigcup_{j=1}^{\infty} A_j\right) - r\nu\left(\bigcup_{j=1}^{\infty} A_j\right) = \sum_{j=1}^{\infty}(\mu(A_j) - r\nu(A_j)), \tag{4.49}$$

so that countable additivity holds.

If A is a $\mathcal{F}$-set with the property that $\chi(B) \geq 0$ for every $B \in \mathcal{F}$ with $B \subseteq A$, A is called a *positive set*, a *negative set* being defined in the complementary manner. A set that is both positive and negative is called a *null set*. Be careful to distinguish between positive (negative, null) sets, and sets of positive measure (negative measure, measure zero). A set A has measure zero if $\mu(A) = r\nu(A)$ in (4.48), but it is not a null set. By the definition, any subset of a positive set is positive.

The following theorem defines the *Hahn decomposition.*

4.26 Theorem Let χ be a signed measure on a measurable space $(\Omega,\mathcal{F})$, having the property $\chi(A) < \infty$ for all $A \in \mathcal{F}$. There exists a partition of Ω into a positive set A^+ and a negative set A^-.

Proof Let $\lambda = \sup \chi(A)$, where the supremum is taken over the positive sets of χ. Choose a sequence of positive sets $\{A_n\}$ such that $\lim_{n\to\infty} \chi(A_n) = \lambda$, and let $A^+ = \bigcup_n A_n$. To show that A^+ is also a positive set, consider any measurable $E \subseteq A^+$. Letting $B_1 = A_1$ and $B_n = A_n - A_{n-1}$, $n > 1$, the sequence $\{B_n\}$ is disjoint, positive since $B_n \subseteq A_n$ for each n, and $\bigcup_n B_n = A^+$. Likewise, if $E_n = E \cap B_n$ the sequence $\{E_n\}$ is disjoint, positive since $E_n \subseteq B_n$, and $\bigcup_n E_n = E$. Hence $\chi(E) = \sum_n \chi(E_n) \geq 0$, and since E was arbitrary, A^+ is shown to be positive. $A^+ - A_n$ being therefore positive,

$$\chi(A^+) = \chi(A_n) + \chi(A^+ - A_n) \geq \chi(A_n), \text{ all } n, \tag{4.50}$$

and hence $\chi(A^+) \geq \lambda$, implying $\chi(A^+) = \lambda$.

Now let $A^- = \Omega - A^+$. We show, by contradiction, that A^- has no subset E with positive measure. Suppose there exists $E \subseteq A^-$ with $\chi(E) > 0$. By construction E and A^+ are disjoint. Every subset of $A^+ \cup E$ is the disjoint union of a subset of A^+ with a subset of E, so if E is a positive set, so is $A^+ \cup E$. By definition of λ,

$$\lambda \geq \chi(A^+ \cup E) = \lambda + \chi(E), \tag{4.51}$$

which requires $\chi(E) = 0$, so E cannot be a positive set. If F is a subset of E, it is also a subset of A^-, and if positive it must have zero measure, by the argument just applied to E. The desired contradiction is obtained by showing that if $\chi(E) > 0$, E must have a subset F which is both positive and has positive measure.

The technique is to successively remove subsets of negative measure from E until what is left has to be a positive set, and then to show that this remainder has positive measure. Let n_1 be the smallest integer such that there is a subset $E_1 \subseteq E$ with $\chi(E_1) < -1/n_1$, and define $F_1 = E - E_1$. Then let n_2 be the smallest integer such that there exists $E_2 \subseteq F_1$ with $\chi(E_2) < -1/n_2$. In general, for $k = 2,3,...$, let n_k be the smallest positive integer such that F_{k-1} has a subset E_k satisfying $\chi(E_k) < -1/n_k$, and let

$$F_k = E - \bigcup_{j=1}^{k} E_j. \tag{4.52}$$

If no such set exists for finite n_k, let $n_k = +\infty$ and $E_k = \varnothing$. The sequence $\{F_k\}$ is non-increasing and so must converge to a limit F as $k \to \infty$.

We may therefore write $E = F \cup (\bigcup_{k=1}^{\infty} E_k)$, where the sets on the right-hand side are mutually disjoint, and hence, by countable additivity,

$$\chi(E) = \chi(F) + \sum_{k=1}^{\infty} \chi(E_k) < \chi(F) - \sum_{k=1}^{\infty} 1/n_k. \tag{4.53}$$

Since $\chi(E) > 0$ it must be the case that $\chi(F) > 0$, but since $\chi(F) < \infty$ by assumption, it is also the case that $\sum_{k=1}^{\infty}(1/n_k) < \infty$, and hence $n_k \to \infty$ as $k \to \infty$. This means that F contains no subset with negative measure, and is therefore a positive set having positive measure. ■

For any set $B \in \mathcal{F}$, define $\chi^+(B) = \chi(A^+ \cap B)$ and $\chi^-(B) = -\chi(A^- \cap B)$, such that $\chi(B) = \chi^+(B) - \chi^-(B)$. It is easy to verify that χ^+ and χ^- are mutually singular, non-negative measures on $(\Omega, \mathcal{F})$. $\chi = \chi^+ - \chi^-$ is called the *Jordan decomposition* of a signed measure. χ^+ and χ^- are called the *upper variation* and *lower variation* of χ, and the measure $|\chi| = \chi^+ + \chi^-$ is called the *total variation* of χ. The Jordan decomposition shows that all signed measures can be represented in the form of (4.48). Signed measures therefore introduce no new technical difficulties. We can integrate with respect to χ by taking the difference of the integrals with respect to χ^+ and χ^-.

We are now able to prove the Radon-Nikodym theorem. It is actually most convenient to derive the Lebesgue decomposition (**4.23**) in such a way that the Radon-Nikodym theorem emerges as a fairly trivial corollary. It is also easiest to begin with finite measures, and then extend the results to the σ-finite case.

4.27 Theorem Finite, non-negative measures ν and μ have a Lebesgue decomposition $\mu = \mu_1 + \mu_2$ where $\mu_1 \perp \nu$ and $\mu_2 \ll \nu$, and there exists an $\mathcal{F}$-measurable function $f\colon \Omega \mapsto \mathbb{R}^+$ such that $\mu_2(E) = \int_E f d\nu$ for all $E \in \mathcal{F}$.

Proof[6] Let $\mathbb{G}$ denote the class of all $\mathcal{F}/\mathcal{B}$-measurable functions $g\colon \Omega \mapsto \mathbb{R}^+$ for which $\int_E g d\nu \leq \mu(E)$, all $E \in \mathcal{F}$. $\mathbb{G}$ is not empty since 0 is a member. Let $\alpha = \sup_{g\in\mathbb{G}} \int g d\nu$, so that $\alpha \leq \mu(\Omega) < \infty$. We show there is an element of $\mathbb{G}$ at which the supremum is attained. Either this element exists, and there is nothing further to show, or it is possible by definition of α to choose an element g_n of $\mathbb{G}$ satisfying $\alpha - 1/n \leq \int g_n d\nu \leq \alpha$, for each $n \in \mathbb{N}$. Generate a monotone sequence $\{f_n, n \in \mathbb{N}\}$ in $\mathbb{G}$ as follows. Put $f_1 = g_1$ and define f_n by $f_n(\omega) = \max\{f_{n-1}(\omega), g_n(\omega)\}$, so that $f_n \geq f_{n-1}$. Define the sets $A_n = \{\omega\colon f_{n-1}(\omega) > g_n(\omega)\}$ for $n = 2,3,\ldots$, and then if $f_{n-1} \in \mathbb{G}$,

$$\begin{aligned}\int_E f_n d\nu &= \int_{E\cap A_n} f_{n-1} d\nu + \int_{E\cap A_n^c} g_n d\nu \\ &\leq \mu(E\cap A_n) + \mu(E\cap A_n^c) = \mu(E) \end{aligned} \tag{4.54}$$

so that $f_n \in \mathbb{G}$. Since $f_n \uparrow f$, it follows by the monotone convergence theorem that $\int_E f_n d\nu \to \int_E f d\nu \leq \mu(E)$, and hence $f \in \mathbb{G}$. And since $f_n \geq g_n$ so that

$$\alpha - 1/n \leq \int g_n d\nu \leq \int f_n d\nu \leq \alpha,$$

we must conclude that $\int f d\nu = \alpha$, as was required. Now define μ_2 by

$$\mu_2(E) = \int_E f d\nu,\ E \in \mathcal{F}. \tag{4.55}$$

Evidently μ_2 is a non-negative measure (for countable additivity consider the functions $f_j = 1_{E_j} f$, and use **4.14**), and also $\mu_2 \ll \nu$. Define $\mu_1(E) = \mu(E) - \mu_2(E)$, which is non-negative by construction of f, and also a measure. It remains to show that $\mu_1 \perp \nu$.

Let (A_n^+, A_n^-) be a Hahn decomposition for the measure $\mu_1 - \nu/n$, for $n = 1,2,3,\ldots$. Then for $E \in \mathcal{F}$,

$$\begin{aligned}\mu(E\cap A_n^+) &= \mu_1(E\cap A_n^+) + \mu_2(E\cap A_n^+) \\ &\geq \frac{1}{n}\nu(E\cap A_n^+) + \int_{E\cap A_n^+} f d\nu = \int_{E\cap A_n^+}\left(f + \frac{1}{n}\right) d\nu,\end{aligned} \tag{4.56}$$

and hence

$$\mu(E) = \mu(E\cap A_n^+)+\mu(E\cap A_n^-) \geq \mu(E\cap A_n^+) + \mu_2(E\cap A_n^-)$$
$$\geq \int_{E\cap A_n^+}\left(f + \frac{1}{n}\right)d\nu + \int_{E\cap A_n^-} fd\nu = \int_E fd\nu + \frac{1}{n}\nu(E\cap A_n^+). \qquad (4.57)$$

Note from this inequality that $f + n^{-1}1_{A_n^+} \in \mathbb{G}$, so that

$$\alpha \geq \int fd\nu + \frac{1}{n}\nu(A_n^+) = \alpha + \frac{1}{n}\nu(A_n^+), \qquad (4.58)$$

implying $\nu(A_n^+)/n = 0$. This holds for each $n \in \mathbb{N}$, so if $A = \bigcup_{n=1}^\infty A_n^+$, $\nu(A) = 0$. Note that $A^c = \bigcap_{n=1}^\infty A_n^- \subseteq A_n^-$ for every n, and so $\mu_1(A^c) \leq \nu(A^c)/n$ for every n. Hence $\mu_1(A^c) = 0$, and so $\mu_1 \perp \nu$. ∎

It remains to extend this result to the σ-finite case.

Proof of 4.23 By σ-finiteness there exists a countable partition $\{\Omega_j\}$ of Ω, such that $\nu(\Omega_j)$ and $\mu(\Omega_j)$ are finite for each j. If $\{A_j\}$ is any collection with finite measures whose union is Ω, letting $\Omega_1 = A_1$ and $\Omega_j = A_j - A_{j-1}$ for $j > 1$ defines such a partition. If different collections with finite measures are known for ν and μ, say $\{A_{\mu j}\}$ and $\{A_{\nu j}\}$, the collection containing all the $A_{\mu j}\cap A_{\nu k}$ for $j,k \in \mathbb{N}$, is countable and of finite measure with respect to both ν and μ, and after re-indexing this collection can generate $\{\Omega_j\}$.

Consider the restrictions of μ and ν to the measurable spaces $(\Omega_j,\mathcal{F}_j)$, for $j \in \mathbb{N}$, where $\mathcal{F}_j = \{E\cap\Omega_j, E \in \mathcal{F}\}$. By countable additivity, $\mu(E) = \sum_j\mu(E\cap\Omega_j)$ with similar equalities for μ_1, μ_2, and ν; by implication, the two sides are in each case either finite and equal, or both $+\infty$. If $\nu(E\cap\Omega_j) = 0$ implies $\mu_2(E\cap\Omega_j) = 0$ for each j, then $\nu(E) = 0$ implies $\mu_2(E) = 0$ for $E \in \mathcal{F}$, and $\mu_2 \ll \nu$. Similarly, let (A_j, A_j^c) define partitions of the Ω_j such that $\mu_1(A_j) = \nu(A_j^c) = 0$; then $A = \bigcup_j A_j$, and $A^c = \bigcup_j A_j^c$ are disjoint unions, $\mu_1(A) = \sum_j\mu_1(A_j) = 0$, and $\nu(A^c) = \sum_j\nu(A_j^c) = 0$. Hence $\mu_1 \perp \nu$. ∎

The proof of the Radon-Nikodym theorem is now achieved by extending the other conclusion of **4.27** to the σ-finite case.

Proof of 4.24 In the countable partition of the last proof, **4.27** implies the existence of $\mathcal{F}_j/\mathcal{B}$-measurable non-negative f_j such that

$$\mu(E\cap\Omega_j) = \mu_1(E\cap\Omega_j) + \mu_2(E\cap\Omega_j)$$

where

$$\mu_2(E\cap\Omega_j) = \int_{E\cap\Omega_j} f_j d\nu, \text{ all } E \in \mathcal{F}. \qquad (4.59)$$

Define $f\colon \Omega \mapsto \mathbb{R}^+$ by

$$f(\omega) = \sum_j 1_{\Omega_j}(\omega)f_j(\omega). \qquad (4.60)$$

This is a function since the Ω_j are disjoint, and is $\mathcal{F}/\mathcal{B}$-measurable since $f^{-1}(B) = \bigcup_j f_j^{-1}(B) = \bigcup_j E_j \in \mathcal{F}$ where $E_j \in \mathcal{F}_j$, for each $B \in \mathcal{B}$. Apply **4.14** to give

$$\mu_2(E) = \sum_j \mu_2(E \cap \Omega_j) = \sum_j \left(\int_E 1_{\Omega_j} f_j d\nu \right)$$
$$= \int_E \sum_j 1_{\Omega_j} f_j d\nu = \int_E f d\nu. \blacksquare \tag{4.61}$$

Consider the case where μ is absolutely continuous with respect to another measure ν. If the Lebesgue decomposition with respect to ν is $\mu = \mu_1 + \mu_2$, $\nu(A) = 0$ implies $\mu(A) = 0$ which in turn implies $\mu_1(A) = 0$. But since $\mu_1 \perp \nu$, $\mu_1(A^c) = 0$ too. Thus, $\mu_1(\Omega) = 0$ and $\mu = \mu_2$. The absolute continuity of a measure implies the existence of a Radon-Nikodym derivative f as an equivalent representation of the measure, given ν, in the sense that $\mu(E) = \int_E f d\nu$ for any $E \in \mathcal{F}$. An important application of these results is to measures on the line.

4.28 Example Let ν in the last result be Lebesgue measure, m, and let μ be any other measure on the line. Clearly, $\mu_1 \perp m$ requires that $\mu_1(E) = 0$ except when E is of Lebesgue measure 0. On the other hand, absolute continuity of μ_2 with respect to m implies that any set of 'zero length', any countable collection of isolated points for example, must have zero measure under μ_2. If μ is absolutely continuous with respect to m, we may write the integral of a measurable function g as

$$\int_{-\infty}^{+\infty} g(x) d\mu(x) = \int_{-\infty}^{+\infty} g(x) f(x) dx, \tag{4.62}$$

so that all integrals reduce to Lebesgue integrals. Here, f is known as the *density function* of the measure μ and is an equivalent representation of μ, with the relation

$$\mu(E) = \int_E f(x) dx \tag{4.63}$$

(the Lebesgue integral of f over E) holding for each $E \in \mathcal{B}$. □

5
Metric Spaces

5.1 Distances and Metrics

Central to the properties of $\mathbb{R}$ studied in Chapter 2 was the concept of distance. For any real numbers x and y, the Euclidean distance between them is the number $d_E(x,y) = |x-y| \in \mathbb{R}^+$. Generalizing this idea, a set (otherwise arbitrary) having a distance measure, or metric, defined for each pair of elements is called a *metric space*. Let $\mathbb{S}$ denote such a set.

5.1 Definition A metric is a mapping d: $\mathbb{S}\times\mathbb{S} \mapsto \mathbb{R}^+$ having the properties

(a) $d(y,x) = d(x,y)$,

(b) $d(x,y) = 0$ iff if $x = y$,

(c) $d(x,y)+d(y,z) \geq d(x,z)$ (triangle inequality).

A metric space $(\mathbb{S},d)$ is a set $\mathbb{S}$ paired with metric d, such that conditions (a)-(c) hold for each pair of elements of $\mathbb{S}$. □

If **5.1**(a) and (c) hold, and $d(x,x) = 0$, but $d(x,y) = 0$ is possible when $x \neq y$, we would call d a *pseudo-metric.* A fundamental fact is that if (A,d) is a metric space and $B \subset A$, (B,d) is also a metric space. If $\mathbb{Q}$ is the set of rational numbers, $\mathbb{Q} \subset \mathbb{R}$ and $(\mathbb{Q},d_E)$ is a metric space; another example is $([0,1], d_E)$.

While the Euclidean metric on $\mathbb{R}$ is the familiar case, and the proof that d_E satisfies **5.1**(a)-(c) is elementary, d_E is not the only possible metric on $\mathbb{R}$.

5.2 Example For $x,y \in \mathbb{R}$ let

$$d_0(x,y) = \frac{|x-y|}{1 + |x-y|}. \tag{5.1}$$

It is immediate that **5.1**(a) and (b) hold. To show (c), note that $|x-y| = d_0(x,y)/(1-d_0(x,y))$. The inequality $a/(1-a)+b/(1-b) \geq c/(1-c)$ simplifies to $a+b \geq c+ab(2-c)$. We obtain **5.1**(c) on putting $a = d_0(x,y)$, $b = d_0(y,z)$, $c = d_0(x,z)$, and using the fact that $0 \leq d_0 \leq 1$. Unlike the Euclidean metric, d_0 is defined for x or $y = \pm\infty$. $(\overline{\mathbb{R}},d_0)$ is a metric space on the definition, while $\overline{\mathbb{R}}$ with the Euclidean metric is not. □

In the space $\mathbb{R}^2$ a larger variety of metrics is found.

5.3 Example The Euclidean distance on $\mathbb{R}^2$ is

$$d_E(x,y) = \|x-y\| = [(x_1-y_1)^2+(x_2-y_2)^2]^{1/2}, \tag{5.2}$$

and $(\mathbb{R}^2,d_E)$ is the Euclidean plane. An alternative is the 'taxicab' metric,

$$d_T(x,y) = |x_1 - y_1| + |x_2 - y_2|. \tag{5.3}$$

d_E is the shortest distance between two addresses in Manhattan as the crow flies, but d_T is the shortest distance by taxi (see Fig. 5.1). The reader will note that d_T and d_E are actually the cases for $p = 1$ and $p = 2$ of a sequence of metrics on $\mathbb{R}^2$. He/she is invited to supply the definition for the case $p = 3$, and so for any p. The limiting case as $p \to \infty$ is the maximum metric,

$$d_M(x,y) = \max\{|x_1 - y_1|, |x_2 - y_2|\}. \tag{5.4}$$

All these distance measures can be shown to satisfy **5.1**(a)-(c). Letting $\mathbb{R}^n = \mathbb{R} \times \mathbb{R} \times ... \times \mathbb{R}$ for any finite n, they can be generalized in the obvious fashion, to define metric spaces $(\mathbb{R}^n, d_E)$, $(\mathbb{R}^n, d_T)$, $(\mathbb{R}^n, d_M)$ and so forth. □

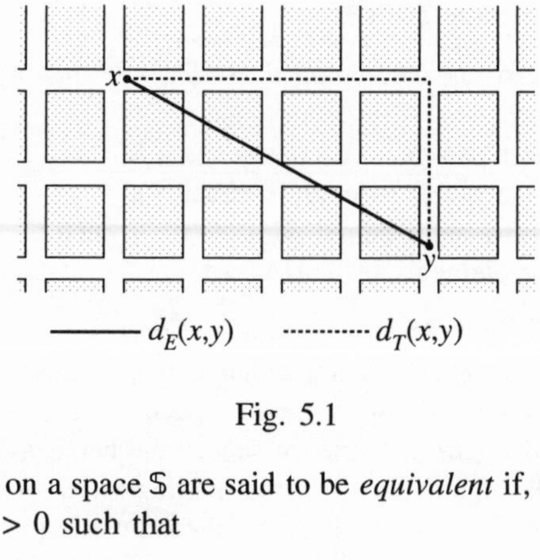

Fig. 5.1

Metrics d_1 and d_2 on a space $\mathbb{S}$ are said to be *equivalent* if, for each $x \in \mathbb{S}$ and $\varepsilon > 0$, there is a $\delta > 0$ such that

$$d_1(x,y) < \delta \;\Rightarrow\; d_2(x,y) < \varepsilon \tag{5.5}$$

$$d_2(x,y) < \delta \;\Rightarrow\; d_1(x,y) < \varepsilon \tag{5.6}$$

for each $y \in \mathbb{S}$. The idea here is that the two metrics confer essentially the same properties on the space, apart from a possible relabelling of points and axes. A metric that is a continuous, increasing function of another metric is equivalent to it; thus, if d is any metric on $\mathbb{S}$, it is equivalent to the bounded metric $d/(1+d)$. d_E and d_0 of **5.2** are equivalent in $\mathbb{R}$, as are are d_E and d_M in $\mathbb{R}^2$. On the other hand, consider for any $\mathbb{S}$ the *discrete* metric d_D, where for $x,y \in \mathbb{S}$, $d_D(x,y) = 0$ if $x = y$, and 1 otherwise. d_D is a metric, but d_D and d_E are not equivalent in $\mathbb{R}$.

In metric space theory, the properties of $\mathbb{R}$ outlined in §2.1 are revealed as a special case. Many definitions are the same, word for word, although other concepts are novel. In a metric space $(\mathbb{S},d)$ the concept of an open neighbourhood in $\mathbb{R}$ generalizes to the *sphere* or *ball*, a set $S_d(x,\varepsilon) = \{y\colon y \in \mathbb{S},\, d(x,y) < \varepsilon\}$, where $x \in \mathbb{S}$ and $\varepsilon > 0$. We write simply $S(x,\varepsilon)$ when the context makes clear which metric is being adopted. In $(\mathbb{R}^2,d_E)$, $S(x,\varepsilon)$ is a circle with centre at x and radius ε. In $(\mathbb{R}^2,d_T)$ it is a 'diamond' (rotated square) centred on x with ε the distance from x to the vertices. In $(\mathbb{R}^2,d_M)$ it is a regular square centred on x, with sides of 2ε. For $(\mathbb{R}^3,d_E)$ ... well, think about it!

An *open set* of $(\mathbb{S},d)$ is a set $A \subseteq \mathbb{S}$ such that, for each $x \in A$, $\exists\ \delta > 0$ such that $S(x,\delta)$ is a subset of A. If metrics d_1 and d_2 are equivalent, a set is open in $(\mathbb{S},d_1)$ iff it is open in $(\mathbb{S},d_2)$. The theory of open sets of $\mathbb{R}$ generalizes straightforwardly. For example, the Borel field of $\mathbb{S}$ is a well-defined notion, the smallest σ-field containing the open sets of $(\mathbb{S},d)$. Here is the general version of **2.4**.

5.4 Theorem

(i) If $\mathscr{C}$ is any collection of open sets of $(\mathbb{S},d)$, then

$$C = \bigcup_{A \in \mathscr{C}} A \tag{5.7}$$

is open.

(ii) If A and B are open in $(\mathbb{S},d)$, then $A \cap B$ is open.

Proof (i) If $S(x,\varepsilon) \subseteq A$ and $A \in \mathscr{C}$, then $S(x,\varepsilon) \subseteq C$. Since such a ball exists by definition for all $x \in A$, all $A \in \mathscr{C}$, it follows that one exists for all $x \in C$. (ii) If $S(x,\varepsilon_A)$ and $S(x,\varepsilon_B)$ are two spheres centred on x, then

$$S(x,\varepsilon_A) \cap S(x,\varepsilon_B) = S(x,\varepsilon), \tag{5.8}$$

where $\varepsilon = \min\{\varepsilon_A,\varepsilon_B\}$. If $x \in A$, $\exists\ S(x,\varepsilon_A) \subseteq A$ with $\varepsilon_A > 0$, and if $x \in B$, $\exists\ S(x,\varepsilon_B) \subseteq B$ similarly, with $\varepsilon_B > 0$. If $x \in A \cap B$, $S(x,\varepsilon) \subseteq A \cap B$, with $\varepsilon > 0$. ∎

The important thing to bear in mind is that openness is *not* preserved under arbitrary intersections.

A *closure point* of a set A is a point $x \in \mathbb{S}$ (not necessarily belonging to A) such that for all $\delta > 0\ \exists\ y \in A$ with $d(x,y) < \delta$. The set of closure points of A, denoted $\overline{A}$, is called the closure of A. Closure points are also called *adherent* points, 'sticking to' a set though not necessarily belonging to it. If for some $\delta > 0$ the definition of a closure point is satisfied only for $y = x$, so that $S(x,\delta) \cap A = \{x\}$, x is said to be an *isolated* point of A.

A *boundary point* of A is a point $x \in \overline{A}$, such that for all $\delta > 0\ \exists\ z \in A^c$ with $d(x,z) < \delta$. The set of boundary points of A is denoted ∂A, and $\overline{A} = A \cup \partial A$. The *interior* of A is $A^o = A - \partial A$. A *closed* set is one containing all its closure points, such that $\overline{A} = A$. An open set does not contain all of its closure points, since the boundary points do not belong to the set. The empty set $\varnothing$ and the space $\mathbb{S}$ are both open *and* closed. A subset B of A is said to be *dense* in A if $B \subseteq A \subseteq \overline{B}$.

A collection of sets $\mathscr{C}$ is called a *covering* for A if $A \subseteq \bigcup_{B \in \mathscr{C}} B$. If each B is open, it is called an *open covering*. A set A is called *compact* if every open covering of A contains a finite subcovering. A is said to be *relatively compact* if $\overline{A}$ is compact. If $\mathbb{S}$ is itself compact, $(\mathbb{S},d)$ is said to be a *compact space*. The remarks in §2.1 about compactness in $\mathbb{R}$ are equally relevant to the general case.

A is said to be *bounded* if $\exists\ x \in A$ and $0 < r < \infty$, such that $A \subseteq S(x,r)$; and also *totally bounded* (or *precompact*) if for every $\varepsilon > 0$ there exists a finite collection of points $x_1,...,x_m$ (called an *ε-net*) such that the spheres $S(x_i,\varepsilon)$, $i = 1,...,m$ form a covering for A. The $S(x_i,\varepsilon)$ can be replaced in this definition by their closures $\overline{S}(x_i,\varepsilon)$, noting that $\overline{S}(x_i,\varepsilon)$ is contained in $S(x_i, \varepsilon+\delta)$ for all $\delta > 0$. The points of the ε-net need not be elements of A. An attractive mental image is a region of $\mathbb{R}^2$ covered with little cocktail umbrellas of radius ε (Fig. 5.2). Any set that is totally bounded is also bounded. In certain cases such as $(\mathbb{R}^n,d_E)$ the converse is also true, but this is *not* true in general.

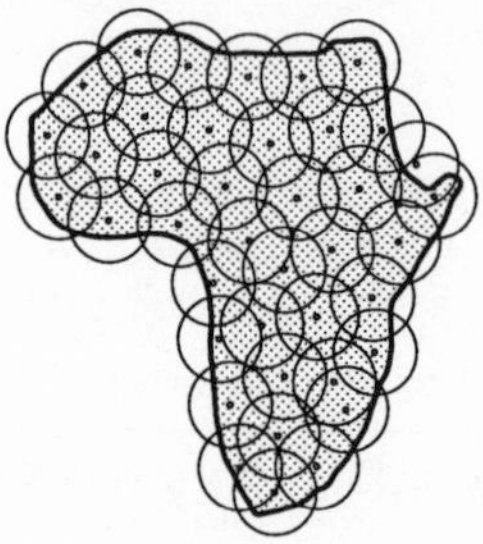

Fig. 5.2

5.5 Theorem If a set is relatively compact, it is totally bounded.

Proof Let A be relatively compact, and consider the covering of $\overline{A}$ consisting of the ε-balls $S(x,\varepsilon)$ for all $x \in \overline{A}$. By the definition this contains a finite subcover $S(x_i,\varepsilon)$, $i = 1,...,m$, which also covers A. Then $\{x_1,...,x_m\}$ is an ε-net for A, and the theorem follows since ε is arbitrary. ■

The converse is true only when the space is complete; see **5.13**.

5.2 Separability and Completeness

In thinking about metric spaces, it is sometimes helpful to visualize the analogue problem for $\mathbb{R}$, or at most for $\mathbb{R}^n$ with $n \leq 3$, and use one's intuitive knowledge of those cases. But this trick can be misleading if the space in question is too alien to geometrical intuition.

A metric space is said to be *separable* if it contains a countable, dense subset. Separability is one of the properties that might be considered to characterize an '$\mathbb{R}$-like' space. The rational numbers $\mathbb{Q}$ are countable and dense in $\mathbb{R}$, so $\mathbb{R}$ is separable, as is $\mathbb{R}^n$. An alternative definition of a separable metric space is a metric space for which the Lindelöf property holds (see **2.7**). This result can be given in the following form.

5.6 Theorem In a metric space $\mathbb{S}$ the following three properties are equivalent:

(a) $\mathbb{S}$ is separable.

(b) Every open set $A \subseteq \mathbb{S}$ has the representation

$$A = \bigcup_{i=1}^{\infty} B_i,\ B_i \in \mathcal{V}, \tag{5.9}$$

where $\mathcal{V}$ is a countable collection of open spheres in $\mathbb{S}$.

(c) Every open cover of a set in $\mathbb{S}$ has a countable subcover. □

A collection $\mathcal{V}$ with property (b) is called a *base* of $\mathbb{S}$, so that separability is equated in this theorem with the existence of a countable base for the space. In topology this property is called *second-countability* (see §6.2). (c) is the Lindelöf property.

Proof We first show that (a) implies (b). Let $\mathcal{V}$ be the countable collection of spheres $\{S(x,r): x \in D, r \in \mathbb{Q}^+\}$, where D is a countable, dense subset of $\mathbb{S}$, and $\mathbb{Q}^+$ is the set of positive rationals. If A is an open subset of $\mathbb{S}$, then for each $x \in A$, $\exists\ \delta > 0$ such that $S(x,\delta) \subseteq A$. For any such x, choose $x_i \in D$ such that $d(x_i,x) < \delta/2$ (possible since D is dense) and then choose rational r_i to satisfy $d(x_i,x) < r_i < \delta/2$. Define $B_i = S(x_i,r_i) \in \mathcal{V}$, and observe that

$$x \in B_i \subseteq S(x,\delta) \subseteq A. \tag{5.10}$$

Since $\mathcal{V}$ as a whole is countable, the subcollection $\{B_i\}$ of all the sets that satisfy this condition for at least one $x \in A$ is also countable, and clearly $A \subseteq \bigcup_i B_i \subseteq A$, so $A = \bigcup_i B_i$.

Next we show that (b) implies (c). Since $\mathcal{V}$ is countable we may index its elements as $\{V_j, j \in \mathbb{N}\}$. If $\mathcal{C}$ is any collection of open sets covering A, choose a subcollection $\{C_j, j \in \mathbb{N}\}$, where C_j is a set from $\mathcal{C}$ which contains V_j if such exists, otherwise let $C_j = \varnothing$. There exists a covering of A by $\mathcal{V}$-sets, as just shown, and each V_j can itself be covered by other elements of $\mathcal{V}$ with smaller radii, so that by taking small enough spheres we may always find an element of $\mathcal{C}$ to contain them. Thus $A \subseteq \bigcup_j C_j$, and the Lindelöf property holds.

Finally, to show that (c) implies (a), consider the open cover of $\mathbb{S}$ by the sets $\{S(x,1/n), x \in \mathbb{S}\}$. If there exists for each n a countable subcover $\{S(x_{nk},1/n), k \in \mathbb{N}\}$, for each k there must be one or more indices k' such that $d(x_{nk},x_{nk'}) < 2/n$. Since this must be true for every n, the countable set $\{x_{nk}, k \in \mathbb{N}, n \in \mathbb{N}\}$ must be dense in $\mathbb{S}$. This completes the proof. ■

The theorem has a useful corollary.

5.7 Corollary A totally bounded space is separable. □

Another important property is that subspaces of separable spaces are separable, which we show as follows.

5.8 Theorem If $(\mathbb{S},d)$ is a separable space and $A \subset \mathbb{S}$, then (A,d) is separable.

Proof Suppose D is countable and dense in $\mathbb{S}$. Construct the countable set E by taking one point from each non-empty set

$$A \cap S(y,r),\ y \in D,\ r \in \mathbb{Q}^+. \tag{5.11}$$

For any $x \in A$ and $\delta > 0$, we may choose $y \in D$ such that $d(x,y) < \delta/2$. For every such y, $\exists\ z \in E$ satisfying $z \in A \cap S(y,r)$ for $r < \delta/2$, so that $d(y,z) < \delta/2$. Thus

$$d(x,z) \le d(x,y) + d(y,z) < \delta, \tag{5.12}$$

and since x and δ are arbitrary it follows that E is dense in A. ■

This argument does not rule out the possibility that A and D are disjoint. The separability of the irrational numbers, $\mathbb{R} - \mathbb{Q}$, is a case in point.

On the other hand, certain conditions are incompatible with separability. A subset A of a metric space $(\mathbb{S},d)$ is *discrete* if for each $x \in A$, $\exists\ \delta > 0$ such that $(S(x,\delta) - \{x\}) \cap A$ is empty. In other words, each element is an isolated point. The integers $\mathbb{Z}$ are a discrete set of $(\mathbb{R},d_E)$, for example. If $\mathbb{S}$ is itself discrete, the discrete metric d_D is equivalent to d.

5.9 Theorem If a metric space contains an uncountable discrete subset, it is not separable.

Proof This is immediate from **5.6**. Let A be discrete, and consider the open set $\bigcup_{x \in A} S(x,\varepsilon_x)$, where ε_x is chosen small enough that the specified spheres form a disjoint collection. This is an open cover of A, and if A is uncountable it has no countable subcover. ■

The separability question arises when we come to define measures on metric spaces (see Chapter 26). Unless a space is separable, we cannot be sure that all of its Borel sets are measurable. The space $D_{[a,b]}$ discussed below (**5.27**) is an important example of this difficulty.

The concepts of sequence, limit, subsequence, and cluster point all extend from $\mathbb{R}$ to general metric spaces. A sequence $\{x_n\}$ of points in $(\mathbb{S},d)$ is said to *converge* to a limit x if for all $\varepsilon > 0$ there exists $N_\varepsilon \ge 1$ such that

$$d(x_n,x) < \varepsilon \text{ for all } n > N_\varepsilon. \tag{5.13}$$

Theorems **2.12** and **2.13** extend in an obvious way, as follows.

5.10 Theorem Every sequence on a compact subset of $\mathbb{S}$ has one or more cluster points. □

5.11 Theorem If a sequence on a compact subset of $\mathbb{S}$ has a unique cluster point, then it converges. □

The notion of a Cauchy sequence also remains fundamental. A sequence $\{x_n\}$ of points in a metric space $(\mathbb{S},d)$ is a Cauchy sequence if for all $\varepsilon > 0$, $\exists\ N_\varepsilon$ such that $d(x_n,x_m) < \varepsilon$ whenever $n > N_\varepsilon$ and $m > N_\varepsilon$. The novelty is that Cauchy sequences in a metric space do not always possess limits. It is possible that the point on which the sequence is converging lies outside the space. Consider the space $(\mathbb{Q},d_E)$. The sequence $\{x_n\}$, where $x_n = 1 + 1/2 + 1/6 + \ldots + 1/n! \in \mathbb{Q}$, is a Cauchy sequence since $|x_{n+1} - x_n| = 1/(n+1)! \to 0$; but of course, $x_n \to e$ (the base of the natural logarithms), an irrational number. A metric space $(\mathbb{S},d)$ is said to be *complete* if it contains the limits of all Cauchy sequences defined on it. $(\mathbb{R},d_E)$

is a complete space, while $(\mathbb{Q},d_E)$ is not.

Although compactness is a primitive notion which does not require the concept of a Cauchy sequence, we can nevertheless define it, following the idea in **2.12**, in terms of the properties of sequences. This is often convenient from a practical point of view.

5.12 Theorem The following statements about a metric space $(\mathbb{S},d)$ are equivalent:

(a) $\mathbb{S}$ is compact.

(b) Every sequence in $\mathbb{S}$ has a cluster point in $\mathbb{S}$.

(c) $\mathbb{S}$ is totally bounded and complete. □

Notice the distinction between completeness and compactness. In a complete space all Cauchy sequences converge, which says nothing about the behaviour of non-Cauchy sequences. But in a compact space, which is also totally bounded, *all* sequences contain Cauchy subsequences which converge in the space.

Proof We show in turn that (a) implies (b), (b) implies (c), and (c) implies (a).

Suppose $\mathbb{S}$ is compact. Let $\{x_n,\ n \in \mathbb{N}\}$ be a sequence in $\mathbb{S}$, and define a decreasing sequence of subsets of $\mathbb{S}$ by $B_n = \{x_k\colon k \geq n\}$. The sets $\overline{B}_n$ are closed, and the cluster points of the sequence, if any, compose the set $C = \bigcap_{n=1}^{\infty}\overline{B}_n = (\bigcup_{n=1}^{\infty}\overline{B}_n^c)^c$. If $C = \emptyset$, $\mathbb{S} = \bigcup_{n=1}^{\infty}\overline{B}_n^c$, so that the open sets $\overline{B}_n^c$ are a cover for $\mathbb{S}$, and by assumption these contain a finite subcover. This means that, for some $m < \infty$, $\mathbb{S} \subseteq \bigcup_{n=1}^{m}\overline{B}_n^c = (\bigcap_{n=1}^{m}\overline{B}_n)^c = \overline{B}_m^c$. This leads to the contradiction $\overline{B}_m = \emptyset$, so that C must be nonempty. Hence, (a) implies (b).

Now suppose that every sequence has a cluster point in $\mathbb{S}$. Considering the case of Cauchy sequences, it is clear that the space is complete; it remains to show that it is totally bounded. Suppose not: then there must exist an $\varepsilon > 0$ for which no ε-net exists; in other words, no finite n and points $\{x_1,\dots,x_n\}$ such that $d(x_j,x_k) \leq \varepsilon$ for all $j \neq k$. But letting $n \to \infty$ in this case, we have found a sequence with no cluster point, which is again a contradiction. Hence, (b) implies (c).

Finally, let $\mathscr{C}$ be an arbitrary open cover of $\mathbb{S}$. We assume that $\mathscr{C}$ contains no finite subcover of $\mathbb{S}$, and obtain a contradiction. Since $\mathbb{S}$ is totally bounded it must possess for each $n \geq 1$ a finite cover of the form

$$B_{ni} = S(x_{ni},\ 1/2^n),\ i = 1,\dots,k_n. \tag{5.14}$$

Fixing n, choose an i for which B_{ni} has no finite cover by $\mathscr{C}$-sets (at least one such exists by hypothesis) and call this set D_n. For $n > 1$, $\{B_{ni}\}_{i=1}^{k_n}$ is also a covering for D_{n-1} and we can choose D_n so that $D_n \cap D_{n-1}$ has no finite subcover by $\mathscr{C}$-sets, and accordingly is nonempty. Thus, choose a sequence of points $\{x_n \in D_n,\ n \in \mathbb{N}\}$. Since D_n is a ball of radius $1/2^n$, and contains x_n, and D_{n+1} is of radius $1/2^{n+1}$ and contains x_{n+1}, $d(x_n,x_{n+1}) < 3/2^n$. The triangle inequality implies that $d(x_n,x_{n+m}) < 3\sum_{i=0}^{m}2^{-n-i} \leq 6/2^n \to 0$ as $n \to \infty$. Thus, $\{x_n\}$ is a Cauchy sequence and converges to a limit $x \in \mathbb{S}$, by completeness.

Choose a set $A \in \mathscr{C}$ containing x, and since A is open, $S(x,\varepsilon) \subset A$ for some $\varepsilon > 0$. Since for any n $d(x_n,x) < 6/2^n$, and x_n is in D_n which has radius $1/2^n$, choosing ε

$< 9/2^n$ ensures that $D_n \subset S(x,\varepsilon)$. But this means $D_n \subset A$, which is a contradiction since D_n has no finite cover by $\mathscr{C}$-sets, Hence $\mathscr{C}$ contains a finite subcover, and (c) implies (a). ∎

In complete spaces, the set properties of relative compactness and precompactness are identical. The following is the converse of **5.5**.

5.13 Corollary In a complete metric space, a totally bounded set A is relatively compact.

Proof If $\mathbb{S}$ is complete, every Cauchy sequence in A has a limit in $\mathbb{S}$, and all such points are closure points of A. The subspace $(\bar{A},d)$ is therefore a complete space. It follows from **5.12** that if A is totally bounded, $\bar{A}$ is compact. ∎

5.3 Examples

The following cases are somewhat more remote from ordinary geometric intuition than the ones we looked at above.

5.14 Example In §12.3 and subsequently we shall encounter $\mathbb{R}^\infty$, that is, *infinite-dimensional Euclidean space.* If $x = (x_1,x_2,...) \in \mathbb{R}^\infty$, and $y = (y_1,y_2,...) \in \mathbb{R}^\infty$ similarly, a metric for $\mathbb{R}^\infty$ is given by

$$d_\infty(x,y) = \sum_{k=1}^{\infty} 2^{-k} d_0(x_k,y_k), \tag{5.15}$$

where d_0 is defined in (5.1). Like d_0, d_∞ is a bounded metric with $d_\infty(x,y) \le 1$ for all x and y. □

5.15 Theorem $(\mathbb{R}^\infty,d_\infty)$ is separable and complete.

Proof To show separability, consider the collection

$$A_m = \{x = (x_1,x_2,...)\colon x_k \text{ rational if } k \le m,\ x_k = 0 \text{ otherwise}\} \subseteq \mathbb{R}^\infty. \tag{5.16}$$

A_m is countable, and by **1.5** the collection $A = \{A_m,\ m = 1,2,...\}$ is also countable. For any $y \in \mathbb{R}^\infty$ and $\varepsilon > 0$, $\exists\ x \in A_m$ such that

$$d_\infty(x,y) \le \sum_{k=1}^{m} 2^{-k}\varepsilon + \sum_{k=m+1}^{\infty} 2^{-k} d_0(0,y_k) \le \varepsilon + 2^{-m}. \tag{5.17}$$

Since the right-hand side can be made as small as desired by choice of ε and m, y is a closure point of A. Hence, A is dense in $\mathbb{R}^\infty$.

To show completeness, suppose $\{x_n = (x_{1n},x_{2n},...),\ n \in \mathbb{N}\}$ is a Cauchy sequence in $\mathbb{R}^\infty$. Since $d_0(x_{kn},x_{km}) \le 2^k d_\infty(x_n,x_m)$ for any k, $\{x_{kn},\ n \in \mathbb{N}\}$ must be a Cauchy sequence in $\mathbb{R}$. Since

$$d_\infty(x,x_n) \le \sum_{k=1}^{m} 2^{-k} d(x_k,x_{kn}) + 2^{-m} \tag{5.18}$$

for all m, we can say that $x_n \to x = (x_1,x_2,...) \in \mathbb{R}^\infty$ iff $x_{kn} \to x_k$ for each $k = 1,2,...$; the completeness of $\mathbb{R}$ implies that $\{x_n\}$ has a limit in $\mathbb{R}^\infty$. ∎

5.16 Example Consider the 'infinite-dimensional cube', $[0,1]^\infty$; the Cartesian product of an infinite collection of unit intervals. The space $([0,1]^\infty, d_\infty)$ is separable by **5.8**. We can also endow $[0,1]^\infty$ with the equivalent and in this case bounded metric,

$$\rho_\infty(x,y) = \sum_{k=1}^{\infty} 2^{-k}|x_k - y_k|. \;\square \tag{5.19}$$

In a metric space $(\mathbb{S},d)$, where d can be assumed bounded without loss of generality, define the distance between a point $x \in \mathbb{S}$ and a subset $A \subseteq \mathbb{S}$ as $d(x,A) = \inf_{y\in A} d(x,y)$. Then for a pair of subsets A,B of $(\mathbb{S},d)$ define the function

$$d_H\colon 2^{\mathbb{S}} \times 2^{\mathbb{S}} \mapsto \mathbb{R}^+,$$

where $2^{\mathbb{S}}$ is the power set of $\mathbb{S}$, by

$$d_H(A,B) = \max\left\{\sup_{x\in B} d(x,A),\ \sup_{y\in A} d(y,B)\right\}. \tag{5.20}$$

$d_H(A,B)$ is called the *Hausdorff distance* between sets A and B.

5.17 Theorem Letting $\mathcal{H}_{\mathbb{S}}$ denote the compact, nonempty subsets of $\mathbb{S}$, $(\mathcal{H}_{\mathbb{S}}, d_H)$ is a metric space.

Proof Clearly d_H satisfies **5.1**(a). It satisfies **5.1**(b) since the sets of $\mathcal{H}_{\mathbb{S}}$ are closed, although note that $d_H(A,\bar{A}) = 0$, so that d_H is only a pseudo-metric for general subsets of $\mathbb{S}$. To show **5.1**(c), for any $x \in A$ and any $z \in C$ we have, by definition of $d(x,B)$ and the fact that d is a metric,

$$\sup_{x\in A} d(x,B) \le \sup_{x\in A}\{d(x,z) + d(z,B)\}. \tag{5.21}$$

Since C is compact, the infimum over C of the expression in braces on the right-hand side above is attained at a point $z \in C$. We can therefore write

$$\begin{aligned}\sup_{x\in A} d(x,B) &\le \sup_{x\in A}\left\{\inf_{z\in C}\big(d(x,z) + d(z,B)\big)\right\} \\ &\le \sup_{x\in A} d(x,C) + \sup_{z\in C} d(z,B).\end{aligned} \tag{5.22}$$

Similarly, $\sup_{y\in B} d(x,A) \le \sup_{z\in C} d(z,A) + \sup_{y\in B} d(y,C)$, and hence,

$$\begin{aligned}d_H(A,B) &\le \max\left\{\sup_{x\in A} d(x,C) + \sup_{z\in C} d(z,B),\ \sup_{z\in C} d(z,A) + \sup_{y\in B} d(y,C)\right\} \\ &\le d_H(B,C) + d_H(A,C). \;\blacksquare\end{aligned} \tag{5.23}$$

When $(\mathbb{S},d)$ is complete, it can be shown that $(\mathcal{H}_{\mathbb{S}}, d_H)$ is also complete.

5.18 Example Let $\mathbb{S} = \mathbb{R}$. The compact intervals with the Hausdorff metric define a complete metric space. Thus, $\{[0, 1 - 1/n], n \in \mathbb{N}\}$ is a Cauchy sequence which converges in the Hausdorff metric to $[0,1]$. This is the closure of the set $[0,1)$ which we usually regard as the limit of this sequence (compare **2.16**), but although $[0,1) \notin \mathcal{H}_{\mathbb{S}}$, $d_H([0,1),[0,1]) = 0$. □

Another case is where $\mathbb{S} = (\mathbb{R}^2, d_E)$ and $\mathcal{H}_{\mathbb{S}}$ contains the closed and bounded subsets of the Euclidean plane. To cultivate intuition about metric spaces, a useful exercise is to draw some figures on a sheet of paper and measure the Hausdorff distances between them, as in Fig. 5.3. For compact A and B, $d_H(A,B) = 0$ if and only if $A = B$; compare this with another intuitive concept of the 'distance between two sets', $\inf_{x \in A, y \in B} d_E(x,y)$, which is zero if the sets touch or intersect.

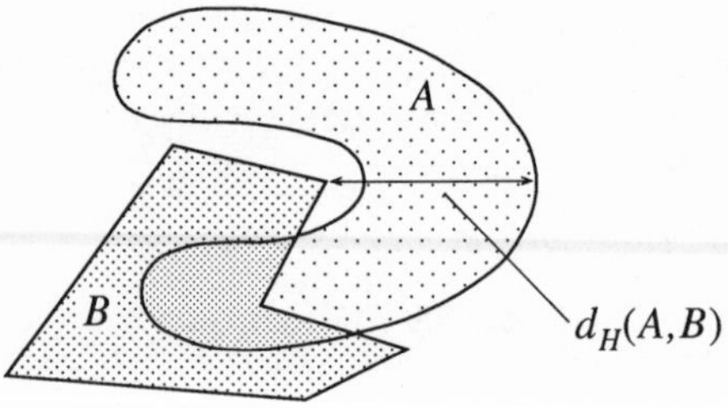

Fig. 5.3

5.4 Mappings on metric spaces

We have defined a function as a mapping which takes set elements to unique points of $\mathbb{R}$, but the term is also used where the codomain is a general metric space. Where the domain is another metric space, the results of §2.3 arise as special cases of the theory. Some of the following properties are generalizations of those given previously, while others are new. The terms mapping, transformation, etc., are again synonyms for function, but an extra usage is *functional*, which refers to the case where the domain is a space whose elements are themselves functions, with (usually) $\mathbb{R}$ as co-domain. An example is the integral defined in §4.1.

The function $f: (\mathbb{S},d) \mapsto (\mathbb{T},\rho)$ is said to be *continuous at* x if for all $\varepsilon > 0$ $\exists$ $\delta > 0$ such that

$$\sup_{y \in S_d(x,\delta)} \rho(f(y),f(x)) < \varepsilon. \tag{5.24}$$

Here, δ may depend on x. Another way to state the condition is that for $\varepsilon > 0$ $\exists$ $\delta > 0$ such that

$$f(S_d(x,\delta)) \subseteq S_\rho(f(x),\varepsilon), \tag{5.25}$$

where S_d and S_ρ are respectively balls in $(\mathbb{S},d)$ and $(\mathbb{T},\rho)$. Similarly, f is said to be *uniformly continuous* on a set $A \subseteq \mathbb{S}$ if for all $\varepsilon > 0$, $\exists\ \delta > 0$ such that

$$\sup_{x\in A}\ \sup_{y\in S_d(x,\delta)\cap A} \rho(f(y),f(x)) < \varepsilon. \tag{5.26}$$

Theorem **2.17** was a special case of the following important result.

5.19 Theorem For $A \subseteq \mathbb{T}$, $f^{-1}(A)$ is open (closed) in $\mathbb{S}$ whenever A is open (closed) in $\mathbb{T}$, iff f is continuous at all points of $\mathbb{S}$.

Proof Assume A is open, and let $f(x) \in A$ for $x \in f^{-1}(A)$. We have $S_\rho(f(x),\varepsilon) \subseteq A$ for some $\varepsilon > 0$. By **1.2**(iv) and continuity at x,

$$S_d(x,\delta) \subseteq f^{-1}(f(S_d(x,\delta))) \subseteq f^{-1}(S_\rho(f(x),\varepsilon)) \subseteq f^{-1}(A). \tag{5.27}$$

If A is open then $\mathbb{T} - A$ is closed and $f^{-1}(\mathbb{T} - A) = \mathbb{S} - f^{-1}(A)$ by **1.2**(iii), which is closed if $f^{-1}(A)$ is open. This proves sufficiency.

To prove necessity, suppose $f^{-1}(A)$ is open in $\mathbb{S}$ whenever A is open in $\mathbb{T}$, and in particular, $f^{-1}(S_\rho(f(x),\varepsilon))$ for $\varepsilon > 0$ is open in $\mathbb{S}$. Since $x \in f^{-1}(S_\rho(f(x),\varepsilon))$, there is a $\delta > 0$ such that (5.25) holds. Use complements again for the case of closed sets. ■

This property of inverse images under f provides an alternative characterization of continuity, and in topological spaces provides the primary definition of continuity. The notion of Borel measurability discussed in §3.6 extends naturally to mappings between pairs of metric spaces, and the theorem establishes that continuous transformations are Borel-measurable.

The properties of functions on compact sets are of interest in a number of contexts. The essential results are as follows.

5.20 Theorem The continuous image of a compact set is compact.

Proof We show that, if $A \subseteq \mathbb{S}$ is compact and f is continuous, then $f(A)$ is compact. Let $\mathscr{C}$ be an open covering of $f(A)$. Continuity of f means that the sets $f^{-1}(B)$, $B \in \mathscr{C}$ are open by **5.19**, and their union covers A by **1.2**(ii). Since A is compact, these sets contain a finite subcover, say, $f^{-1}(B_1),\dots,f^{-1}(B_m)$. It follows that

$$f(A) \subseteq f\left(\bigcup_{j=1}^{m} f^{-1}(B_j)\right) = \bigcup_{j=1}^{m} f(f^{-1}(B_j)) \subseteq \bigcup_{j=1}^{m} B_j, \tag{5.28}$$

where the equality is by **1.2**(i) and the second inclusion by **1.2**(v). Hence, $B_1,\dots,B_m$ is a finite subcover of $f(A)$ by $\mathscr{C}$-sets. Since $\mathscr{C}$ is arbitrary, it follows that $f(A)$ is compact. ■

5.21 Theorem If f is continuous on a compact set, it is uniformly continuous on the set.

Proof Let $A \subseteq \mathbb{S}$ be compact. Choose $\varepsilon > 0$, and for each $x \in A$, continuity at x means that there exists a sphere $S_d(x,r)$ (r may depend on x) such that $\rho(f(x),f(y)) < \frac{1}{2}\varepsilon$ for each $y \in S_d(x,2r) \cap A$. These balls cover A, and since A is compact they contain a finite subcover, say $S_d(x_k,r_k)$, $k = 1,...,m$. Let $\delta = \min_{1\le k\le m} r_k$, and consider a pair of points $x,y \in \mathbb{S}$ such that $d(x,y) < \delta$. Now, $y \in S_d(x_k,r_k)$ for some k, so that $\rho(f(x_k),f(y)) < \frac{1}{2}\varepsilon$, and also

$$d(x_k,x) \le d(x_k,y) + d(x,y) \le r_k + \delta \le 2r_k, \tag{5.29}$$

using the triangle inequality. Hence $\rho(f(x_k),f(x)) \le \frac{1}{2}\varepsilon$, and

$$\rho(f(x),f(y)) \le \rho(f(x),f(x_k)) + \rho(f(x_k),f(y)) < \varepsilon. \tag{5.30}$$

Since, δ independent of x and y, f is uniformly continuous on A. ■

If $f\colon \mathbb{S} \mapsto \mathbb{T}$ is 1-1 onto, and f and f^{-1} are continuous, f is called a *homeomorphism*, and $\mathbb{S}$ and $\mathbb{T}$ are said to be *homeomorphic* if such a function exists. If $\mathbb{S}$ is homeomorphic with a subset of $\mathbb{T}$, it is said to be *embedded* in $\mathbb{T}$ by f. If f also preserves distances so that $\rho(f(x),f(y)) = d(x,y)$ for each $x,y \in \mathbb{S}$, it is called an *isometry*. Metrics d_1 and d_2 in a space $\mathbb{S}$ are equivalent if and only if the identity mapping from $(\mathbb{S},d_1)$ to $(\mathbb{S},d_2)$ (the mapping which takes each point of $\mathbb{S}$ into itself) is an homeomorphism.

5.22 Example If d_∞ and ρ_∞ are the metrics defined in (5.15) and (5.19) respectively, the mapping $g\colon (\mathbb{R}^\infty,d_\infty) \to ([0,1]^\infty,\rho_\infty)$, where $g = (g_1,g_2,...)$ and

$$g_i(x) = \frac{1}{2} + \frac{x_i}{2(1+|x_i|)},\quad i = 1,2,... \tag{5.31}$$

is an homeomorphism. □

Right and left continuity are not well defined notions for general metric spaces, but there is a concept of continuity which is 'one-sided' with respect to the *range* of the function. A function $f\colon (\mathbb{S},d) \mapsto \mathbb{R}$ is said to be *upper semicontinuous* at x if for each $\varepsilon > 0\ \exists\ \delta > 0$ such that, for $y \in \mathbb{S}$,

$$d(x,y) < \delta \;\Rightarrow\; f(y) < f(x) + \varepsilon. \tag{5.32}$$

If $\{x_n\}$ is a sequence of points in $\mathbb{S}$ and $d(x_n,x) \to 0$, upper semicontinuity implies $\limsup_n f(x_n) \le f(x)$. The *level sets* of the form $\{x\colon f(x) < \alpha\}$ are open for all $\alpha \in \mathbb{R}$ iff f is upper semicontinuous everywhere on $\mathbb{S}$. f is *lower semicontinuous* iff $-f$ is upper semicontinuous, and f is continuous at x iff it is both upper and lower semicontinuous at x.

A function of a real variable is upper semicontinuous at x if it jumps at x with $f(x) \ge \max\{f(x-),f(x+)\}$; isolated discontinuities such as point A in Fig. 5.4 are not ruled out if this inequality is satisfied, On the other hand, upper semicontinuity fails at point B. Semicontinuity is not the same thing as right/left continuity except in the case of monotone functions; if f is increasing, right (left) continuity is equivalent to upper (lower) semicontinuity, and the reverse holds for decreasing functions.

The concept of a *Lipschitz condition* generalizes to metric spaces. A function f on $(\mathbb{S},d)$ satisfies a Lipschitz condition at $x \in \mathbb{S}$ if for $\delta > 0\ \exists\ M > 0$ such that, for any $y \in S_d(x,\delta)$,

$$\rho(f(y),f(x)) \le Mh(d(x,y)) \tag{5.33}$$

where $h(.)$: $\mathbb{R}^+ \mapsto \mathbb{R}^+$ satisfies $h(d) \downarrow 0$ as $d \downarrow 0$. It satisfies a *uniform Lipschitz condition* if condition (5.33) holds uniformly, with fixed M, for all $x \in \mathbb{S}$. The remarks following (2.9) apply equally here. Continuity is enforced by this condition with arbitrary h, and stronger smoothness conditions are obtained for special cases of h.

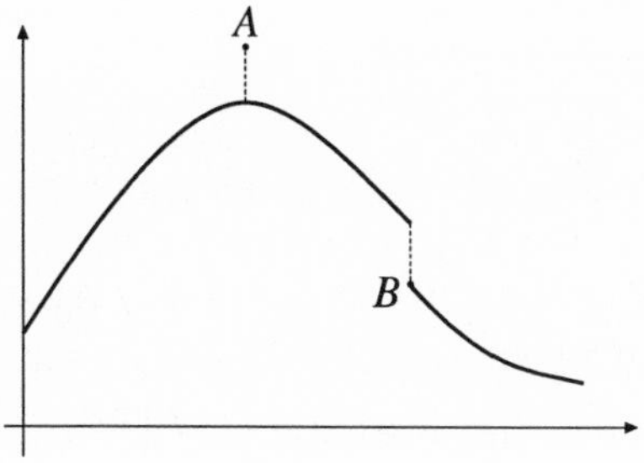

Fig. 5.4

5.5 Function Spaces

The non-Euclidean metric spaces met in later chapters are mostly spaces of real functions on an interval of $\mathbb{R}$. The elements of such spaces are graphs, subsets of $\mathbb{R}^2$. However, most of the relevant theory holds for functions whose domain is any metric space $(\mathbb{S},d)$, and accordingly, it is this more general case that we will study. Let $C_{\mathbb{S}}$ denote the set of all bounded continuous functions $f: \mathbb{S} \mapsto \mathbb{R}$, and define

$$d_U(f,g) = \sup_{x \in \mathbb{S}} |f(x) - g(x)|. \tag{5.34}$$

5.23 Theorem d_U is a metric.

Proof Conditions **5.1**(a) and (b) are immediate. To prove the triangle inequality write, given functions f, g and $h \in C_{\mathbb{S}}$,

$$\begin{aligned} d_U(f,h) &= \sup_{x \in \mathbb{S}} |f(x) - g(x) + g(x) - h(x)| \\ &\le \sup_{x \in \mathbb{S}} (|f(x) - g(x)| + |g(x) - h(x)|) \\ &\le d_U(f,g) + d_U(g,h). \quad \blacksquare \end{aligned} \tag{5.35}$$

d_U is called the *uniform* metric, and $(C_{\mathbb{S}},d_U)$ is a metric space.

An important subset of $C_{\mathbb{S}}$ is the space $U_{\mathbb{S}}$ of *uniformly* continuous functions. If $\mathbb{S}$ is compact, $C_{\mathbb{S}} = U_{\mathbb{S}}$ by **5.21**. Also, if $\mathbb{S}$ is relatively compact, every $f \in C_{\mathbb{S}}$ has a uniformly continuous restriction to $\mathbb{S}$, and every $f \in U_{\mathbb{S}}$ has a continuous extension to $\bar{\mathbb{S}}$, say $\bar{f}$, constructed by setting $\bar{f}(x) = f(x)$ for $x \in \mathbb{S}$ and $\bar{f}(x) = \lim_n f(x_n)$ for a sequence $\{x_n \in \mathbb{S}\}$ converging to x, for each $x \in \bar{\mathbb{S}} - \mathbb{S}$. Note that for any pair $f,f' \in \mathbb{S}$, $d_U(\bar{f},\bar{f}') = d_U(f,f')$, so that the spaces $C_{\bar{\mathbb{S}}}$ and $U_{\mathbb{S}}$ are isometric. There are functions that are continuous on $\mathbb{S}$ and not on $\bar{\mathbb{S}}$, but these cannot be uniformly continuous.

The following is a basic property of $C_{\mathbb{S}}$ which holds independently of the nature of the domain $\mathbb{S}$.

5.24 Theorem $(C_{\mathbb{S}},d_U)$ is complete.

Proof Let $\{f_n\}$ be a Cauchy sequence in $C_{\mathbb{S}}$; in other words, for $\varepsilon > 0$ $\exists$ $N_\varepsilon \geq 1$ such that $d_U(f_n,f_m) \leq \varepsilon$ for $n,m > N_\varepsilon$. Then for each $x \in \mathbb{S}$, the sequences $\{f_n(x)\}$ satisfy $|f_n(x) - f_m(x)| \leq d_U(f_n,f_m)$; these are Cauchy sequences in $\mathbb{R}$, and so have limits $f(x)$. In view of the definition of d_U, we may say that $f_n \to f$ uniformly in $\mathbb{S}$. For any $x,y \in \mathbb{S}$, the triangle inequality gives

$$|f(x)-f(y)| \leq |f(x)-f_n(x)| + |f_n(x)-f_n(y)| + |f_n(y)-f(y)|. \tag{5.36}$$

Fix $\varepsilon > 0$. Since $f_n \in C_{\mathbb{S}}$, $\exists$ $\delta > 0$ such that $|f_n(x) - f_n(y)| < \frac{1}{3}\varepsilon$ if $d(x,y) < \delta$. Also, by uniform convergence $\exists$ n large enough that

$$\max\{|f(x)-f_n(x)|,\ |f_n(y)-f(y)|\} < \tfrac{1}{3}\varepsilon, \tag{5.37}$$

so that $|f(x) - f(y)| < \varepsilon$. Hence $f \in C_{\mathbb{S}}$, which establishes that $C_{\mathbb{S}}$ is complete. ■

Notice how this property holds by virtue of the uniform metric. It is easy to devise sequences of continuous functions converging to discontinuous limits, but none of these are Cauchy sequences. It is not possible for a continuous function to be arbitrarily close to a discontinuous function at *every* point of the domain.

A number of the results to follow call for us to exhibit a continuous function which lies uniformly close to a function in $U_{\mathbb{S}}$, but is fully specified by a finite collection of numbers. This is possible when the domain is totally bounded.

5.25 Theorem Let $(\mathbb{S},d)$ be a totally bounded metric space. For any $f \in U_{\mathbb{S}}$, there exists for any $\varepsilon > 0$ a function $g \in U_{\mathbb{S}}$, completely specified by points of the domain $x_1,\ldots,x_m$ and rational numbers $a_1,\ldots,a_m$, such that $d_U(f,g) < \varepsilon$. □

We specify *rational* numbers here, because this will allow us to assert in applications that the set of all possible g is countable.

Proof[7] By total boundedness of $\mathbb{S}$, $\exists$ for $\delta > 0$ a finite δ-net $\{x_1,\ldots,x_m\}$. For each x_i, let $A_i = \{x\colon d(x,x_i) \geq 2\delta\}$ and $B_i = \{x\colon d(x,x_i) \leq \frac{1}{2}\delta\}$, and define functions $g_i\colon \mathbb{S} \mapsto [0,1]$ by

$$g_i(x) = \frac{d(x,A_i)}{d(x,A_i)+d(x,B_i)}, \tag{5.38}$$

where $d(x,A) = \inf_{y \in A} d(x,y)$. $d(x,A)$ is a uniformly continuous function of x by construction, and $g_i(x)$ is also uniformly continuous, for the denominator is never less than $\frac{3}{2}\delta$. Then define

$$g(x) = \frac{\sum_{i=1}^{m} g_i(x)a_i}{\sum_{i=1}^{m} g_i(x)}. \tag{5.39}$$

Being a weighted average of the numbers $\{a_i\}$, $g(x)$ is bounded. Also, since $\{x_i\}$ is a δ-net for $\mathbb{S}$, there exists for every $x \in \mathbb{S}$ *some* i such that $d(x,A_i) \geq \delta$, as well as $d(x,B_i) \leq d(x,x_i) \leq \delta$, and hence such that $g_i(x) \geq \frac{1}{2}$. Therefore, $\sum_{i=1}^{m} g_i(x) \geq \frac{1}{2}$ and uniform continuity extends from the g_i to g.

For arbitrary $f \in U_{\mathbb{S}}$, fix $\varepsilon > 0$ and choose δ small enough that $|f(x) - f(y)| < \frac{1}{2}\varepsilon$ when $d(x,y) < 2\delta$, for any $x,y \in \mathbb{S}$. Then fix m large enough and choose x_i and a_i for $i = 1,\dots,m$, so that the $S(x_i,\delta)$ cover $\mathbb{S}$, and $|f(x_i) - a_i| < \frac{1}{2}\varepsilon$ for each i. Note that if $d(x,x_i) \geq 2\delta$ then $x \in A_i$ and $g_i(x) = 0$, so that in all cases

$$g_i(x)|f(x) - f(x_i)| \leq \tfrac{1}{2}g_i(x)\varepsilon. \tag{5.40}$$

Hence

$$\begin{aligned} g_i(x)|f(x) - a_i| &\leq g_i(x)|f(x) - f(x_i)| + g_i(x)|f(x_i) - a_i| \\ &< g_i(x)\varepsilon \end{aligned} \tag{5.41}$$

for each $x \in \mathbb{S}$ and each i. We may conclude that

$$\begin{aligned} d_U(f,g) &= \sup_{x\in\mathbb{S}} |f(x) - g(x)| \\ &\leq \sup_{x\in\mathbb{S}} \left\{ \frac{\sum_{i=1}^{m} g_i(x)|f(x) - a_i|}{\sum_{i=1}^{m} g_i(x)} \right\} < \varepsilon. \ \blacksquare \end{aligned} \tag{5.42}$$

The next result makes use of this approximation theorem, and is fundamental. It tells us (recalling the earlier discussion of separability) that spaces of continuous functions are not such alien objects from an analytic point of view as they might at first appear, at least when the domain is totally bounded.

5.26 Theorem

(i) If $(\mathbb{S},d)$ is totally bounded then $(U_{\mathbb{S}},d_U)$ is separable.

(ii) If $(\mathbb{S},d)$ is compact then $(C_{\mathbb{S}},d_U)$ is separable.

Proof We need only prove part (i), since for part (ii), $C_{\mathbb{S}} = U_{\mathbb{S}}$ by **5.21** and the same conclusion follows.

Fix m and suitable points $\{x_1,\dots,x_m\}$ of $\mathbb{S}$ so as to define a countable family of functions $A_m = \{g_{mk}, k \in \mathbb{N}\}$, where the g_{mk} are defined as in **5.25**, and the index k enumerates the countable collection of m-vectors $(a_1,\dots,a_m)$ of rationals. For each $\varepsilon > 0$, there exists m large enough that, for each $f \in U_{\mathbb{S}}$, $d_U(f, g_{mk}) < \varepsilon$ for some k. By **1.5**, $A = \lim_{m\to\infty} A_m$ is countable, and there exists $g_k \in A$ such that $d_U(f, g_k) < \varepsilon$ for every $\varepsilon > 0$. This means that A is dense in $U_{\mathbb{S}}$. $\blacksquare$

To show that we cannot rely on these properties holding under more general circumstances, we exhibit a nonseparable function space.

5.27 Example For $\mathbb{S} = [a,b]$, an interval of the real line, consider the metric space $(D_{[a,b]},d_U)$ of real, bounded *cadlag* functions of a real variable. Cadlag is a colourful French acronym (*continue à droite, limites à gauche*) to describe functions of a real variable which may have discontinuities, but are right continuous at every point, with the image of every decreasing sequence in $[a,b]$ containing its limit point; in other words, there is a limit point to the left of every point. Of course, $C_{[a,b]} \subseteq D_{[a,b]}$. Functions with completely arbitrary discontinuities form a larger class still, but one that for most purposes is too unstructured to permit a useful theory.

To show that $(D_{[a,b]},d_U)$ is not separable, consider the subset with elements

$$f_\theta(t) = \begin{cases} 0, & t < \theta \\ 1, & t \geq \theta \end{cases}, \quad \theta \in [a,b]. \tag{5.43}$$

This set is uncountable, containing as many elements as there are points in $[a,b]$. But $d_U(f_\theta,f_{\theta'}) = 1$ for $\theta \neq \theta'$, so it is also discrete. Hence $(D_{[a,b]},d_U)$ is not separable by **5.9**. □

Let A denote a collection of functions $f\colon (\mathbb{S},d) \mapsto (\mathbb{T},\rho)$. A is said to be *equicontinuous* at $x \in \mathbb{S}$ if $\forall\ \varepsilon > 0\ \exists\ \delta > 0$ such that

$$\sup_{f\in A}\ \sup_{y\in S_d(x,\delta)} \rho(f(y),f(x)) < \varepsilon. \tag{5.44}$$

A is also said to be *uniformly equicontinuous* if $\forall\ \varepsilon > 0\ \exists\ \delta > 0$ such that

$$\sup_{f\in A}\ \sup_{x\in \mathbb{S}}\ \sup_{y\in S_d(x,\delta)} \rho(f(y),f(x)) < \varepsilon. \tag{5.45}$$

Equicontinuity is the property of a set of continuous functions (or uniformly continuous functions, as the case may be) which forbids limit points of the set to be not (uniformly) continuous. In the case when $A \subseteq C_\mathbb{S}$ $(U_\mathbb{S})$ but A is not (uniformly) equicontinuous, we cannot rule out the possibility that $\bar{A} \nsubseteq C_\mathbb{S}$ $(U_\mathbb{S})$.

An important class of applications is to countable A, and if we restrict attention to the case $A = \{f_n,\ n \in \mathbb{N}\}$, $A \subseteq C_\mathbb{S}$ (or $U_\mathbb{S}$) may not be essential. If we are willing to tolerate discontinuity in at most a finite number of the cases, the following concept is the relevant one. A sequence of functions $\{f_n,\ n \in \mathbb{N}\}$ will be said to be *asymptotically equicontinuous* at x if $\forall\ \varepsilon > 0\ \exists\ \delta > 0$ such that

$$\limsup_{n\to\infty} \left\{ \sup_{y\in S_d(x,\delta)} \rho\big(f_n(y),f_n(x)\big) \right\} < \varepsilon, \tag{5.46}$$

and *asymptotically uniformly equicontinuous* if $\forall\ \varepsilon > 0\ \exists\ \delta > 0$ such that

$$\limsup_{n\to\infty}\left\{\sup_{x\in\mathbb{S}}\ \sup_{y\in S_d(x,\delta)}\ \rho(f_n(y),f_n(x))\right\} < \varepsilon. \tag{5.47}$$

If the functions f_n are continuous for all n, $\limsup_{n\to\infty}$ can be replaced by $\sup_n$ in (5.46) and similarly for (5.47) when all the f_n are uniformly continuous. In these circumstances, the qualifier *asymptotic* can be dropped.

The main result on equicontinuous sets is the Arzelà-Ascoli theorem. This designation covers a number of closely related results, but the following version, which is the one appropriate to our subsequent needs, identifies equicontinuity as the property of a set of bounded real-valued functions on a totally bounded domain which converts boundedness into *total* boundedness.

5.28 Arzelà-Ascoli theorem Let $(\mathbb{S},d)$ be a totally bounded metric space. A set $A \subseteq C_{\mathbb{S}}$ is relatively compact under d_U iff it is bounded and uniformly equicontinuous.

Proof Since $C_{\mathbb{S}}$ is complete, total boundedness of A is equivalent to relative compactness by **5.13**. So to prove 'if', we assume boundedness and equicontinuity, and construct a finite ε-net for A.

It is convenient to define the *modulus of continuity* of f, that is, the function $w\colon C_{\mathbb{S}}\times\mathbb{R}^+ \mapsto \mathbb{R}^+$ where

$$w(f,\delta) = \sup_{x\in\mathbb{S}}\ \sup_{y\in S_d(x,\delta)}\ |f(y)-f(x)|. \tag{5.48}$$

Fix $\varepsilon > 0$, and choose δ (as is possible by uniform equicontinuity) such that

$$\sup_{f\in A} w(f,\delta) < \varepsilon. \tag{5.49}$$

Boundedness of A under the uniform metric means that there exist finite real numbers U and L such that

$$L \le \inf_{f\in A, x\in\mathbb{S}} f(x) \le \sup_{f\in A, x\in\mathbb{S}} f(x) \le U. \tag{5.50}$$

Let $\{x_1,...,x_m\}$ be a δ-net for $\mathbb{S}$, and construct the finite family

$$D_m = \{g_k \in A,\ k = 1,...,(v+1)^m\} \tag{5.51}$$

according to the recipe of **5.25**, with the constants a_i taken from the finite set $\{L+(U-L)u/v\}$, where u and v are integers with v exceeding $(U-L)/\varepsilon$ and $u = 0,...,v$. This set contains $v+1$ real values between U and L which are less than ε apart, so that D_m has $(v+1)^m$ members, as indicated. Since the assumptions imply $A \subseteq U_{\mathbb{S}}$, it follows by **5.25** that for every $f \in A$ there exists $g_k \in D_m$ with $d_U(f,g_k) < \varepsilon$. This shows that D_m is a ε-net for A, and A is totally bounded.

To prove 'only if', suppose A is relatively compact, and hence totally bounded. Trivially, total boundedness implies boundedness, and it remains to show uniform equicontinuity. Consider for $\varepsilon > 0$ the set

$$B_k(\varepsilon) = \{f\colon w(f,1/k) < \varepsilon\}. \tag{5.52}$$

Uniform equicontinuity of A is the condition that, for any $\varepsilon > 0$, there exists k large enough that $\bar{A} \subseteq B_k(\varepsilon)$. It is easily verified that

$$|w(f,\delta) - w(g,\delta)| \leq 2d_U(f,g), \tag{5.53}$$

so that the function $w(.,\delta)\colon (C_{\mathbb{S}},d_U) \mapsto (\mathbb{R}^+,d_E)$ is continuous. $B_k(\varepsilon)$ is the inverse image under $w(.,\delta)$ of the half-line $[0,\varepsilon)$ which is open in $\mathbb{R}^+$, and hence $B_k(\varepsilon)$ is open by **5.19**. By definition of $C_{\mathbb{S}}$, $w(f,1/k) \to 0$ as $k \to \infty$ for each $f \in C_{\mathbb{S}}$. In other words, w converges to 0 pointwise on $C_{\mathbb{S}}$, which implies that the collection $\{B_k(\varepsilon), k \in \mathbb{N}\}$ must be an open covering for $C_{\mathbb{S}}$, and hence for $\bar{A}$. But by hypothesis $\bar{A}$ is compact, every such covering of $\bar{A}$ has a finite subcover, and so $\bar{A} \subseteq B_k(\varepsilon)$ for finite k, as required. ∎

6
Topology

6.1 Topological Spaces

Metric spaces form a subclass of a larger class of mathematical objects called topological spaces. These do not have a distance defined upon them, but the concepts of open set, neighbourhood, and continuous mapping are still well defined. Even though only metric spaces are encountered in the sequel (Part VI), much of the reasoning is essentially topological in character. An appreciation of the topological underpinnings is essential for getting to grips with the theory of weak convergence.

6.1 Definition A *topological space* $(\mathbb{X},\tau)$ is a set $\mathbb{X}$ on which is defined a *topology*, a class of subsets τ called *open sets* having the following properties:

(a) $\mathbb{X} \in \tau$, $\varnothing \in \tau$.

(b) If $\mathscr{C} \subseteq \tau$, then $\bigcup_{O\in\mathscr{C}} O \in \tau$.

(c) If $O_1 \in \tau$, $O_2 \in \tau$, then $O_1 \cap O_2 \in \tau$. □

These three conditions *define* an open set, so that openness becomes a primitive concept of which the notion of ε-spheres around points is only one characterization. A metric induces a topology on a space because it is one way (though not the only way) of defining what an open set is, and all metric spaces are also topological spaces. On the other hand, some topological spaces may be made into metric spaces by defining a metric on them under which sets of τ are open in the sense defined in §5.1. Such spaces are called *metrizable*.

A subset of a topological space $(\mathbb{X},\tau)$ has a topology naturally induced on it by the parent space. If $A \subset \mathbb{X}$, the collection $\tau_A = \{A \cap O\colon O \in \tau\}$ is called the *relative topology* for A. (A,τ_A) would normally be referred to as a *subspace* of $\mathbb{X}$. If two topologies τ_1 and τ_2 are defined on a space and $\tau_1 \subset \tau_2$, then τ_1 is said to be *coarser*, or *weaker*, than τ_2, whereas τ_2 is *finer* (*stronger*) than τ_1. In particular, the power set of $\mathbb{X}$ is a topology, called the *discrete* topology, whereas $\{\varnothing,\mathbb{X}\}$ is called the *trivial* topology. Two metrics define the same topology on a space if and only if they are equivalent. If two points are close in one space, their images in the other space must be correspondingly close.

If a set O is open, its complement O^c on $\mathbb{X}$ is said to be closed. The *closure* $\overline{A}$ of an arbitrary set $A \subseteq \mathbb{X}$ is the intersection of all the closed sets containing A. As for metric spaces, a set $A \subseteq B$, for $B \subseteq \mathbb{X}$, is said to be dense in B if $B \subseteq \overline{A}$.

6.2 Theorem The intersection of any collection of closed sets is closed. $\mathbb{X}$ and $\varnothing$ are both open and closed. □

However, an arbitrary union of closed sets need not be closed, just as an arbitrary intersection of open sets need not be open.

For given $x \in \mathbb{X}$, a collection $\mathcal{V}_x$ of open sets is called a *base* for the point x if for every open O containing x there is a set $B \in \mathcal{V}_x$ such that $x \in B$ and $B \subset O$. This is the generalization to topological spaces of the idea of a system of neighbourhoods or spheres in a metric space. A *base for the topology* τ on $\mathbb{X}$ is a collection $\mathcal{V}$ of sets such that, for every $O \in \tau$, and every $x \in O$, there exists $B \in \mathcal{V}$ such that $x \in B \subset O$. The definition implies that any open set can be expressed as the union of sets from the base of the topology; a topology may be defined for a space by specifying a base collection, and letting the open sets be defined as the unions and finite intersections of the base sets. In the case of $\mathbb{R}$, for example, the open intervals form a base.

6.3 Theorem A collection $\mathcal{V}$ is a base for a topology τ on $\mathbb{X}$ iff

(a) $\bigcup_{B \in \mathcal{V}} B = \mathbb{X}$.

(b) $\forall\ B_1, B_2 \in \mathcal{V}$ and $x \in B_1 \cap B_2$, $\exists\ B_3 \in \mathcal{V}$ such that $x \in B_3 \subset B_1 \cap B_2$.

Proof Necessity of these conditions follows from the definitions of base and open set. For sufficiency, define a collection τ in terms of the base $\mathcal{V}$, as follows:

$$O \in \tau \text{ iff, for each } x \in O,\ \exists\ B \in \mathcal{V} \text{ such that } x \in B \subset O. \tag{6.1}$$

$\varnothing$ satisfies the condition in (6.1), and $\mathbb{X}$ satisfies it given condition (a) of the theorem. If $\mathcal{C}$ is a collection of τ-sets, $\bigcup_{O \in \mathcal{C}} O \in \tau$ since (6.1) holds in this case in respect of a base set B corresponding to any set in $\mathcal{C}$ which contains x. And if $O_1, O_2 \in \tau$, and $x \in O_1 \cap O_2$, then, letting B_1 and B_2 be the base sets specified in (6.1) in respect of x and O_1 and O_2 respectively, condition (b) implies that $x \in B_3 \subset O_1 \cap O_2$, which shows that τ is closed under finite intersections. Hence, τ is a topology for $\mathbb{X}$. ∎

The concept of base sets allows us to generalize two further notions familiar from metric spaces. The *closure points* (*accumulation points*) of a set A in a topological space $(\mathbb{X},\tau)$ are the points $x \in \mathbb{X}$ such that every set in the base of x contains a point of A (a point of A other than x). An important exercise is to show that x is a closure point of A if and only if x is in the closure of A.

We have generalizations of two other familiar concepts. A sequence $\{x_n\}$ of points in a topological space is said to *converge* to x if, for every open set O containing x, $\exists\ N \geq 1$ such that $x_n \in O$ for all $n \geq N$. And x is called a *cluster point* of $\{x_n\}$ if, for every open O containing x and every $N \geq 1$, $x_n \in O$ for some $n \geq N$. In general topological spaces the notion of a convergent sequence is inadequate for characterizing basic properties such as the continuity of mappings, and is augmented by the concepts of *net* and *filter*. Because we deal mainly with metric spaces, we do not require these extensions (see e.g. Willard 1970: Ch. 4).

6.2 Countability and Compactness

The *countability axioms* provide one classification of topological spaces according, roughly speaking, to their degree of structure and amenability to the methods of analysis. A topological space is said to satisfy the first axiom of countability (to be *first-countable*) if every point of the space has a countable base. It satisfies the second axiom of countability (is *second-countable*) if the space as a whole has a countable base. Every metric space is first-countable in view of the existence of the countable base composed of open spheres, $S(x,1/n)$ for each x. More generally, sequences in first-countable spaces tend to behave in a similar manner to those in metric spaces, as the following theorem illustrates.

6.4 Theorem In a first-countable space, x is a cluster point of a sequence $\{x_n, n \in \mathbb{N}\}$ iff there is a subsequence $\{x_{n_k}, k \in \mathbb{N}\}$ converging to x.

Proof Sufficiency is immediate. For necessity, the definition of a cluster point implies that $\exists\ n \geq N$ such that $x_n \in O$, for every open O containing x and every $N \geq 1$. Let the countable base of x be the collection $\mathcal{V}_x = \{B_i, i \in \mathbb{N}\}$, and choose a monotone sequence of base sets $\{A_k, k \in \mathbb{N}\}$ containing x (and hence nonempty) with $A_1 = B_1$, and $A_k \subset A_{k-1} \cap B_k$ for $k = 2,3,\ldots$; this is always possible by **6.3**. Since x is a cluster point, we may construct an infinite subsequence by taking x_{n_k} as the next member of the sequence contained in A_k, for $k = 1,2,\ldots$ For every open set O containing x, $\exists\ N \geq 1$ such that $x_{n_k} \in A_k \subseteq O$, for all $k \geq N$, and hence $x_{n_k} \to x$ as $k \to \infty$, as required. ■

The point of quoting a result such as this has less to do with demonstrating a new property than with reminding us of the need for caution in assuming properties we take for granted in metric spaces. While the intuition derived from $\mathbb{R}$-like situations might lead us to suppose that the existence of a cluster point and a convergent subsequence amount to the same thing, this need not be true unless we can establish first-countability.

A topological space is said to be *separable* if it contains a countable dense subset. Second-countable spaces are separable. This fact follows directly on taking a point from each set in a countable base, and verifying that these points are dense in the space. The converse is not generally true, but it is true for metric spaces, where separability, second countability and the Lindelöf property (that every open cover of $\mathbb{X}$ has a countable subcover) are all equivalent to one another. This is just what we showed in **5.6**. More generally, we can say the following.

6.5 Theorem A second-countable space is both separable and Lindelöf.

Proof The proof of separability is in the text above. To prove the Lindelöf property, let $\mathcal{C}$ be an open cover of $\mathbb{X}$, such that $\bigcup_{A \in \mathcal{C}} A = \mathbb{X}$. For each $A \in \mathcal{C}$ and $x \in A$, we can find a base set B_i such that $x \in B_i \subset A$. Since $\bigcup_{i=1}^{\infty} B_i = \mathbb{X}$, we may choose a countable subcollection A_i, $i = 1,2,\ldots$ such that $B_i \subset A_i$ for each i, and hence $\bigcup_{i=1}^{\infty} A_i = \mathbb{X}$. ■

A topological space is said to be *compact* if every covering of the space by open sets has a finite subcover. It is said to be *countably compact* if each countable covering has a finite subcovering. And it is said to be *sequentially compact* if each sequence on the space has a convergent subsequence. Sometimes, compactness is more conveniently characterized in terms of the complements. The complements of an open cover of $\mathbb{X}$ are a collection of closed sets whose intersection is empty; if and only if $\mathbb{X}$ is compact, every such collection must have a finite subcollection with empty intersection. An equivalent way to state this proposition is in terms of the converse implication. A collection of closed sets is said to have the *finite intersection property* if *no* finite subcollection has an empty intersection. Thus:

6.6 Theorem $\mathbb{X}$ is compact (countably compact) if and only if no collection (countable collection) of closed sets having the finite intersection property has an empty intersection. □

The following pair of theorems summarize important relationships between the different varieties of compactness.

6.7 Theorem A first-countable space $\mathbb{X}$ is countably compact iff it is sequentially compact.

Proof Let the space be countably compact. Let $\{x_n, n \in \mathbb{N}\}$ be a sequence in $\mathbb{X}$, and define the sets $B_n = \{x_n, x_{n+1}, \dots\}$, $n = 1,2,\dots$ The collection of closed sets $\{\overline{B}_n, n \in \mathbb{N}\}$ clearly possesses the finite intersection property, and hence $\bigcap_n \overline{B}_n$ is nonempty by **6.6**, which is another way of saying that $\{x_n\}$ has a cluster point. Since the sequence is arbitrary, sequential compactness follows by **6.4**. This proves necessity.

For sufficiency, **6.4** implies that under sequential compactness, all sequences in $\mathbb{X}$ have a cluster point. Let $\{C_i, i \in \mathbb{N}\}$ be a countable collection of closed sets having the finite intersection property such that $A_n = \bigcap_{i=1}^n C_i \neq \varnothing$, for every finite n. Consider a sequence $\{x_n\}$ chosen such that $x_n \in A_n$, and note since $\{A_n\}$ is monotone that $x_n \in A_m$ for all $n \geq m$; or in other words, A_m contains the sequence $\{x_n, n \geq m\}$. Since $\{x_n\}$ has a cluster point x and A_m is closed, $x \in A_m$. This is true for every $m \in \mathbb{N}$, so that $\bigcap_{i=1}^\infty C_i$ is nonempty, and $\mathbb{X}$ is countably compact by **6.6**. ■

6.8 Theorem A metric space $(\mathbb{S},d)$ is countably compact iff it is compact.

Proof Sufficiency is immediate. For necessity, we show first that if $\mathbb{S}$ is countably compact, it is separable. A metric space is first-countable, hence countable compactness implies sequential compactness (**6.7**), which in turn implies that every sequence in $\mathbb{S}$ has a cluster point (**6.4**). This must mean that for any $\varepsilon > 0$ there exists a finite ε-net $\{x_1,\dots,x_m\}$ such that, for all $x \in \mathbb{S}$, $d(x,x_k) < \varepsilon$ for some $k \in \{1,\dots,m\}$; for otherwise, we can construct an infinite sequence $\{x_n\}$ with $d(x_n,x_{n'}) \geq \varepsilon$ for $n \neq n'$, contradicting the existence of a cluster point. Thus, for each $n \in \mathbb{N}$ there is a finite collection of points A_n such that, for every $x \in \mathbb{S}$, $d(x,y) < 2^{-n}$ for some $y \in A_n$. The set $D = \bigcup_{n=1}^\infty A_n$ is countable and dense in $\mathbb{S}$, and $\mathbb{S}$ is separable.

Separability in a metric space is equivalent by **5.6** to the Lindelöf property, that every open cover of $\mathbb{S}$ has a countable subcover; but countable compactness implies that this countable subcover has a finite subcover in its turn, so that compactness is proved. ■

Like separability and compactness, the notion of a continuous mapping may be defined in terms of a distance measure, but is really topological in character. In a pair of topological spaces $\mathbb{X}$ and $\mathbb{Y}$, the mapping $f: \mathbb{X} \mapsto \mathbb{Y}$ is said to be *continuous* if $f^{-1}(B)$ is open in $\mathbb{X}$ when B is open in $\mathbb{Y}$, and closed in $\mathbb{X}$ when B is closed in $\mathbb{Y}$. That in metric spaces this definition is equivalent to the more familiar one in terms of ε- and δ-neighbourhoods follows from **5.19**. The concepts of homeomorphism and embedding, as mappings that are respectively onto or into, and 1-1 continuous with continuous inverse, remain well defined. The following theorem gives two important properties of continuous maps.

6.9 Theorem Suppose there exists a continuous mapping f from a topological space $\mathbb{X}$ *onto* another space $\mathbb{Y}$.

(i) If $\mathbb{X}$ is separable, $\mathbb{Y}$ is separable.

(ii) If $\mathbb{X}$ is compact, $\mathbb{Y}$ is compact.

Proof (i) The problem is to exhibit a countable, dense subset of $\mathbb{Y}$. Consider $f(D)$ where D is dense in $\mathbb{X}$. If $\overline{f(D)}$ is the closure of $f(D)$, the inverse image $f^{-1}(\overline{f(D)})$ is closed by continuity of f, and contains $f^{-1}(f(D))$, and hence also contains D by **1.2**(iv). Since $\overline{D}$ is the smallest closed set containing D, and $\mathbb{X} \subseteq \overline{D}$, it follows that $\mathbb{X} \subseteq f^{-1}(\overline{f(D)})$. But since the mapping is onto, $\mathbb{Y} = f(\mathbb{X}) \subseteq f(f^{-1}(\overline{f(D)})) \subseteq \overline{f(D)}$, where the last inclusion is by **1.2**(v). $f(D)$ is therefore dense in $\mathbb{Y}$ as required. $f(D)$ is countable if D is countable, and the conclusion follows directly.

(ii) Let $\mathscr{C}$ be an open cover of $\mathbb{Y}$. Then $\{f^{-1}(B): B \in \mathscr{C}\}$ must be an open cover of $\mathbb{X}$ by the definition. The compactness of $\mathbb{X}$ means that it contains a finite subcover, say $f^{-1}(B_1),\dots,f^{-1}(B_n)$ such that

$$\mathbb{Y} = f(\mathbb{X}) = f\left(\bigcup_{j=1}^{n} f^{-1}(B_j)\right) = f\left(f^{-1}\left(\bigcup_{j=1}^{n} B_j\right)\right) \subseteq \bigcup_{j=1}^{n} B_j, \tag{6.2}$$

where the third equality uses **1.2**(ii) and the inclusion, **1.2**(v). Hence $\mathscr{C}$ contains a finite subcover. ■

Note the importance of the stipulation 'onto' in both these results. The extension of (ii) to the case of compact subsets of $\mathbb{X}$ and $\mathbb{Y}$ is obvious, and can be supplied by the reader.

Completeness, unlike separability, compactness, and continuity, is *not* a topological property. To define a Cauchy sequence it is necessary to have the concept of a distance between points. One of the advantages of defining a metric on a space is that the relatively weak notion of completeness provides some of the essential features of compactness in a wider class than the compact spaces.

6.3 Separation Properties

Another classification of topological spaces is provided by the *separation axioms*, which in one sense are more primitive than the countability axioms. They are indicators of the richness of a topology, in the sense of our ability to distinguish between different points of the space. From one point of view, they could be said to define a hierarchy of resemblances between topological spaces and metric spaces. Don't confuse separation with separability, which is a different concept altogether. A topological space $\mathbb{X}$ is said to be:

- a T_1-space, iff $\forall\ x,y \in \mathbb{X}$ with $x \neq y\ \exists$ an open set containing x but not y and also an open set containing y but not x;
- a *Hausdorff* (or T_2-) space, iff $\forall\ x,y \in \mathbb{X}$ with $x \neq y\ \exists$ disjoint open sets O_1 and O_2 in $\mathbb{X}$ with $x \in O_1$ and $y \in O_2$;
- a *regular* space iff for each closed set C and $x \notin C\ \exists$ disjoint open sets O_1 and O_2 with $x \in O_1$ and $C \subset O_2$;
- a *normal* space iff, given disjoint closed sets C_1 and C_2, $\exists$ disjoint open sets O_1 and O_2 such that $C_1 \subset O_1$ and $C_2 \subset O_2$.

A regular T_1-space is called a T_3-space, and a normal T_1-space is called a T_4-space.

In a T_1-space, the singleton sets $\{x\}$ are always closed. In this case $y \in \{x\}^c$ whenever $y \neq x$, where $\{x\}^c$ is the complement of a closed set, and hence open. Conversely, if the T_1 property holds, every $y \neq x$ is contained in an open set not containing x, and the union of all these sets, also open by **6.1**(b), is $\{x\}^c$. It is easy to see that T_4 implies T_3 implies T_2 implies T_1, although the reverse implications do not hold, and without the T_1 property, normality need not imply regularity. Metric spaces are always T_4, for there is no difficulty in constructing the sets specified in the definition out of unions of ε-spheres.

We have the following important links between separation, compactness, countability, and metrizability. The first two results are of general interest but will not be exploited directly in this book, so we forgo the proofs. The proof of **6.12** needs some as yet undefined concepts, and is postponed to §6.6 below.

6.10 Theorem A regular Lindelöf space is normal. □

6.11 Theorem A compact Hausdorff space is T_4. □

6.12 Urysohn's metrization theorem A second-countable T_4-space is metrizable. □

In fact, the conditions of the last theorem can be weakened, with T_4 replaced by T_3 in view of **6.10**, since we have already shown that a second-countable space is Lindelöf (**6.5**).

The properties of functions from $\mathbb{X}$ to the real line play an important role in defining the separation properties of a space. The key to these results is the remarkable Urysohn's lemma.

6.13 Urysohn's lemma A topological space $\mathbb{X}$ is normal iff for any pair A and B of disjoint closed subsets there exists a continuous function $f: \mathbb{X} \to [0,1]$ such that $f(A) = 0$ and $f(B) = 1$. □

The function f is called a *separating function*.

Proof This is by construction of the required function. Recall that the dyadic rationals $\mathbb{D}$ are dense in [0,1]. We demonstrate the existence of a system of open sets $\{U_r,\ r \in \mathbb{D}\}$ with the properties

$$A \subset U_r; \tag{6.3}$$

$$\overline{U}_r \cap B = \varnothing; \tag{6.4}$$

$$\overline{U}_s \subseteq U_r \text{ for } r > s. \tag{6.5}$$

Normality implies the existence of an open set $U_{1/2}$ (say) such that $U_{1/2}$ contains A and $(\overline{U_{1/2}})^c$ contains B. The same story can be told with $U_{1/2}^c$ replacing B in the role of C_2 to define $U_{1/4}$, and then again with $\overline{U_{1/2}}$ replacing A in the role of C_1 to define $U_{3/4}$. The argument extends by induction to generate sets $\{U_{m/2^n},\ m = 1,\ldots,2^n - 1\}$ for any $n \in \mathbb{N}$, and the collection $\{U_r,\ r \in \mathbb{D}\}$ is obtained on letting $n \to \infty$. It is easy to verify conditions (6.3)-(6.5) for this collection. Fig. 6.1 illustrates the construction for $n = 3$ when A and B are regions of the plane. One must imagine countably many more 'layers of the onion' in the limiting case.

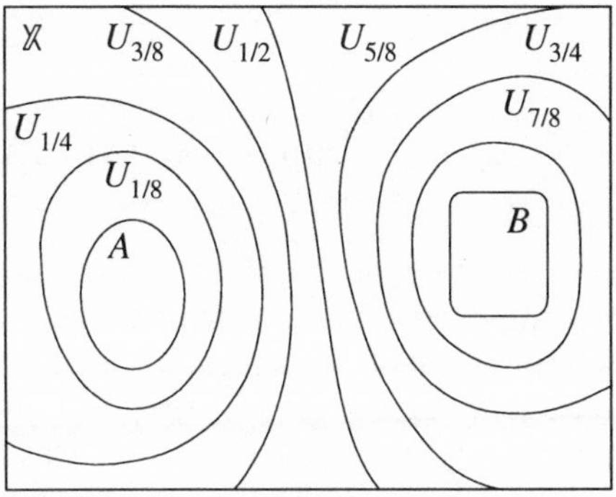

Fig. 6.1

Now define $f\colon \mathbb{X} \to [0,1]$ by

$$f(x) = \begin{cases} \inf\{r \in \mathbb{D}\colon x \in U_r\}, & x \in \bigcup_{r\in\mathbb{D}} U_r \\ 1, & x \in \mathbb{X} - \bigcup_{r\in\mathbb{D}} U_r \end{cases} \tag{6.6}$$

where, in particular, $f(x) = 1$ for $x \in B$. Because of the monotone property (6.5), we have for any $\alpha \in (0,1]$

$$\begin{aligned} \{x\colon f(x) < \alpha\} &= \{x\colon \inf\{r \in \mathbb{D}\colon x \in U_r\} < \alpha\} \\ &= \{x\colon \exists\ r < \alpha \text{ such that } x \in U_r\} \\ &= \bigcup_{r<\alpha} U_r, \end{aligned} \tag{6.7}$$

which is open. On the other hand, because $\mathbb{D}$ is dense in [0,1] we can deduce that, for any $\beta \in [0,1)$,

$$\begin{aligned}\{x\colon f(x) \le \beta\} &= \{x\colon \inf\{r \in \mathbb{D}\colon x \in U_r\} \le \beta\} \\ &= \{x\colon x \in U_r\ \forall\ r > \beta\} \\ &= \bigcap_{r>\beta} U_r \\ &= \bigcap_{r>\beta} \overline{U}_r \end{aligned} \tag{6.8}$$

which is closed. Here, the final equality must hold to reconcile the following two facts: first that $U_r \subseteq \overline{U}_r$, and second that, for all $r > \beta$, there exists (since $\mathbb{D}$ is dense) $s \in \mathbb{D}$ with $r > s > \beta$ and $\overline{U}_s \subseteq U_r$ by (6.5). We have therefore shown that, for $0 \le \beta < \alpha \le 1$,

$$\{x\colon \beta < f(x) < \alpha\} = \{x\colon f(x) < \alpha\} \cap \{x\colon f(x) \le \beta\}^c \tag{6.9}$$

is open, being the intersection of open sets. Since every open set of [0,1] is a union of open intervals (see **2.5**), it follows that $f^{-1}(A)$ is open in $\mathbb{X}$ whenever A is open in [0,1], and accordingly f is continuous. It is immediate that $f(A) = 0$ and $f(B) = 1$ as required, and necessity is proved.

Sufficiency is simply a matter, given the existence of f with the indicated properties, of citing the two sets $f^{-1}([0,\frac{1}{2}))$ and $f^{-1}((\frac{1}{2},1])$, whose images are open in $\mathbb{X}$, disjoint, and contain A and B respectively, so that $\mathbb{X}$ is normal. ■

It is delightful the way this theorem conjures a continuous function out of thin air! It shows that the properties of real-valued functions provide a legitimate means of classifying the separation properties of the space.

In metric spaces, separating functions are obtained by a simple direct construction. If A and B are closed and disjoint subsets of a metric space $(\mathbb{S},d)$, the normality property implies the existence of $\delta > 0$ such that $\inf_{x\in A, y\in B} d(x,y) \ge \delta$. The required function is

$$f(x) = \frac{d(x,A)}{d(x,A) + d(x,B)} \tag{6.10}$$

where $d(x,A) = \inf_{y\in A} d(x,y)$, and $d(x,B)$ is defined similarly. The continuity of f follows since $d(x,A)$ and $d(x,B)$ are continuous in x, and the denominator in (6.10) is bounded below by δ. A similar construction was used in the proof of **5.25**.

The regularity property can be strengthened by requiring the existence of separating functions for closed sets C and points x. A topological space $\mathbb{X}$ is said to be *completely regular* if, for all closed $C \subseteq \mathbb{X}$ and points $x \notin C$, $\exists$ a continuous function $f\colon \mathbb{X} \mapsto [0,1]$ with $f(C) = 0$ and $f(x) = 1$. A completely regular T_1-space is called a *Tychonoff space* or $T_{3\frac{1}{2}}$-space. As the tongue-in-cheek terminology suggests, a T_4-space is $T_{3\frac{1}{2}}$ (this is immediate from Urysohn's lemma) and a $T_{3\frac{1}{2}}$-space is clearly T_3, although the reverse implications do not hold. Being T_4, metric spaces are always $T_{3\frac{1}{2}}$.

6.4 Weak Topologies

Now let's go the other way and, instead of using a topology to define a class of real functions, use a class of functions to define a topology. Let $\mathbb{X}$ be a space and $\mathbb{F}$ a class of functions $f: \mathbb{X} \mapsto \mathbb{Y}_f$, where the codomains $\mathbb{Y}_f$ are topological spaces. The *weak topology* induced by $\mathbb{F}$ on $\mathbb{X}$ is the weakest topology under which every $f \in \mathbb{F}$ is continuous. Recall, continuity means that $f^{-1}(A)$ is open in $\mathbb{X}$ whenever A is open in $\mathbb{Y}_f$. We can also call the weak topology the topology generated by the base of sets $\mathcal{V}$ consisting of the inverse images of the open sets of the $\mathbb{Y}_f$, under $f \in \mathbb{F}$, together with the finite intersections of these sets. The inverse images themselves are called a *sub-base* for the topology, meaning that the sets of the topology can be generated from them by operations of union *and* finite intersection.

If we enlarge $\mathbb{F}$ we (potentially) increase the number of sets in this base and get a stronger topology, and if we contract $\mathbb{F}$ we likewise get a weaker topology. With a given $\mathbb{F}$, any topology stronger than the weak topology contains a richer collection of open sets, so the elements of $\mathbb{F}$ must retain their continuity in this case, but weakening the topology further must by definition force some $f \in \mathbb{F}$ to be discontinuous.

The class of cases in which $\mathbb{Y}_f = \mathbb{R}$ for each f suggests using the concept of a weak topology to investigate the structure of a space. One way to represent the richness of a given topology τ on $\mathbb{X}$ is to ask whether τ contains, or is contained in, the weak topology generated by a particular collection of bounded real-valued functions on $\mathbb{X}$. For example, complete regularity is the minimal condition which makes the sort of construction in **6.13** feasible. According to the next result, this is sufficient to allow the topology to be completely characterized in terms of bounded, continuous real-valued functions on the space.

6.14 Theorem If a topological space $(\mathbb{X},\tau)$ is completely regular, the topology τ is the weak topology induced by the set $\mathbb{F}$ of the separating functions.

Proof Let $\mathcal{V}$ denote the collection of inverse images of open sets under the functions of $\mathbb{F}$. And let T denote the weak topology induced by $\mathbb{F}$, such that the $\mathcal{V}$-sets, *together with* their finite intersections, form a base for T. We show that $T = \tau$.

For any $x \in \mathbb{X}$, let $O \in \tau$ be an open set containing x. Then O^c is closed, and by complete regularity there exists $f \in \mathbb{F}$ taking values in $[0,1]$ with $f(x) = 1$ and $f(O^c) = 0$. The set $(\frac{1}{2},1]$ is open in $[0,1]$, and $B = f^{-1}((\frac{1}{2},1])$ is therefore an open set, containing x and disjoint with O^c so that $B \subset O$. Since this holds for every such O, x has a base $\mathcal{V}_x$ consisting of inverse images of open sets under functions from $\mathbb{F}$. Since x is arbitrary the collection $\mathcal{V} = \{\mathcal{V}_x, x \in \mathbb{X}\}$ forms a base for τ. It follows that $\tau \subseteq T$.

On the other hand, T is by definition the weakest topology under which every $f \in \mathbb{F}$ is continuous. Since $f \in \mathbb{F}$ is a separating function and continuous under τ, it also follows that $T \subseteq \tau$. ■

6.5 The Topology of Product Spaces

Let $\mathbb{X}$ and $\mathbb{Y}$ be a pair of topological spaces, and consider the product space $\mathbb{X}\times\mathbb{Y}$. The plane $\mathbb{R}\times\mathbb{R}$ and subsets thereof are the natural examples for appreciating the properties of product spaces, although it is a useful exercise to think up more exotic cases. An example always given in textbooks of topology is $\mathbb{C}\times\mathbb{C}$ where $\mathbb{C}$ is the unit circle; this space has the topology of the torus (doughnut).

Let the ordered pair (x,y) be the generic element of $\mathbb{X}\times\mathbb{Y}$. The *coordinate projections* are the mappings $\pi_{\mathbb{X}}\colon \mathbb{X}\times\mathbb{Y} \mapsto \mathbb{X}$ and $\pi_{\mathbb{Y}}\colon \mathbb{X}\times\mathbb{Y} \mapsto \mathbb{Y}$, defined by

$$\pi_{\mathbb{X}}(x,y) = x \tag{6.11}$$

$$\pi_{\mathbb{Y}}(x,y) = y. \tag{6.12}$$

If $\mathbb{X}$ and $\mathbb{Y}$ are topological spaces, the coordinate projections can be used to generate a new topology on the product space. The *product topology* on $\mathbb{X}\times\mathbb{Y}$ is the weak topology induced by the coordinate projections.

The underlying idea here is very simple. If $A\subseteq\mathbb{X}$ and $B\subseteq\mathbb{Y}$ are open sets, the set $A\times B = (A\times\mathbb{Y})\cap(\mathbb{X}\times B)$, where $A\times\mathbb{Y} = \pi_{\mathbb{X}}^{-1}(A)$ and $\mathbb{X}\times B = \pi_{\mathbb{Y}}^{-1}(B)$, will be regarded as open in $\mathbb{X}\times\mathbb{Y}$, and is called an *open rectangle* of $\mathbb{X}\times\mathbb{Y}$. The *product topology* on $\mathbb{X}\times\mathbb{Y}$ is the one having the open rectangles as a base. This means that two points (x_1,y_1) and (x_2,y_2) are close in $\mathbb{X}\times\mathbb{Y}$ provided x_1 is close to x_2 in $\mathbb{X}$, and y_1 to y_2 in $\mathbb{Y}$. Equivalently, it is the weakest topology under which the coordinate projections are continuous.

If the factors are metric spaces $(\mathbb{X},d_{\mathbb{X}})$ and $(\mathbb{Y},d_{\mathbb{Y}})$, several metrics can be constructed to induce the product topology on $\mathbb{X}\times\mathbb{Y}$, including

$$\rho((x_1,y_1),(x_2,y_2)) = \max\{d_{\mathbb{X}}(x_1,x_2), d_{\mathbb{Y}}(y_1,y_2)\} \tag{6.13}$$

and

$$\rho'((x_1,y_1),(x_2,y_2)) = d_{\mathbb{X}}(x_1,x_2)+d_{\mathbb{Y}}(y_1,y_2). \tag{6.14}$$

An open sphere in the space $(\mathbb{X}\times\mathbb{Y},\rho)$, where ρ is the metric in (6.13), also happens to be an open rectangle, for

$$S_\rho((x,y),\delta) = S_{d_{\mathbb{X}}}(x,\delta)\times S_{d_{\mathbb{Y}}}(y,\delta); \tag{6.15}$$

but of course, this is not true for every metric.

Since either $\mathbb{X}$ or $\mathbb{Y}$ may be a product space, the generalization of these results from two to any finite number of factors is straightforward. The generic element of the space $\times_{i=1}^{n}\mathbb{X}_i$ is the n-tuple $(x_1,\dots,x_n\colon x_i \in \mathbb{X}_i)$, and so on. But to deal with infinite collections of factor spaces, as we shall wish to do below, it is necessary to approach the product from a slightly different viewpoint. Let A denote an arbitrary index set, and $\{\mathbb{X}_\alpha, \alpha\in A\}$ a collection of spaces indexed by A. The *Cartesian product* $\mathbb{X}^A = \times_{\alpha\in A}\mathbb{X}_\alpha$ is the collection of all the mappings $x\colon A \mapsto \bigcup_{\alpha\in A}\mathbb{X}_\alpha$ such that $x(\alpha)\in\mathbb{X}_\alpha$ for each $\alpha\in A$. This definition contains that given in §1.1 as a special case, but is fundamentally more general in character. The coordinate projections are the mappings $\pi_\alpha\colon \mathbb{X}^A \mapsto \mathbb{X}_\alpha$ with

$$\pi_\alpha(x) = x(\alpha), \tag{6.16}$$

but can also be defined as the images under x of the points $\alpha \in A$.

Thus, a *point* in the product space is a *mapping*, the one which generates the coordinate projections when it is evaluated at points of the domain A. In the case of a finite product, A can be the integers $1,\dots,n$. In a countable case $A = \mathbb{N}$, or a set equipotent with $\mathbb{N}$, and we should call x an infinite sequence, an element of $\mathbb{X}^\infty$ (say). A familiar uncountable example is provided by a class of real-valued functions $x: \mathbb{R} \mapsto \mathbb{R}$, so that $A = \mathbb{R}$. In this case, x associates each point $\alpha \in \mathbb{R}$ with a real number $x(\alpha)$, and defines an element of the product $\mathbb{R}^{\mathbb{R}}$.

The product topology is now generalized as follows. Let $\{\mathbb{X}_\alpha, \alpha \in A\}$ be an arbitrary collection of topological spaces. The *Tychonoff topology* (product topology) on the space $\mathbb{X}^A$ has as base the finite-dimensional open rectangles, sets of the form $\times_{\alpha \in A} O_\alpha$, where the $O_\alpha \subseteq \mathbb{X}_\alpha$ are open sets and $O_\alpha = \mathbb{X}_\alpha$ except for at most a finite number of coordinates. These basic sets can be written as the intersections of finite collections of cylinders, say

$$B = \pi_{\alpha_1}^{-1}(O_{\alpha_1}) \cap \dots \cap \pi_{\alpha_m}^{-1}(O_{\alpha_m}), \tag{6.17}$$

for indices $\alpha_1,\dots,\alpha_m \in A$.

Let τ be a topology under which the coordinate projections are continuous. If O_α is open in $\mathbb{X}_\alpha$, $\pi_\alpha^{-1}(O_\alpha) \in \tau$, and hence τ contains the Tychonoff topology. Since this is true for any such τ, we can characterize the Tychonoff topology as the weak topology generated by the coordinate projections. The sets $\pi_\alpha^{-1}(O_\alpha)$ form the sub-base for the topology, whose *finite* intersections yield the base sets.

Something to keep in mind in these infinite product spaces is that, if any of the sets $\mathbb{X}_\alpha$ are empty, $\mathbb{X}^A$ is empty. Some of our results are true only for non-empty spaces, so for full rigour the stipulation that elements exist is desirable.

6.15 Example The space (C,d_U) examined in §5.5 is an uncountable product space having the Tychonoff topology; the uniform metric is the generalization of the maximum metric ρ of (6.13). Continuous functions are regarded as close to one another under d_U only if they are close at every point of the domain. The subsequent usefulness of this characterization of (C,d_U) stems mainly from the fact that the coordinate projections are known to be continuous. □

The two essential theorems on product spaces extend separability and compactness from the factor spaces to the product. The following theorem has a generalization to uncountable products, which we shall not pursue since this is harder to prove, and the countable case is sufficient for our purposes.

6.16 Theorem Finite or countable product spaces are separable under the product topology iff the factor spaces are separable.

Proof The proof for finite products is an easy implication of the countable case, hence consider $\mathbb{X}^\infty = \times_{i=1}^\infty \mathbb{X}_i$. Let $D_i = \{d_{i1},d_{i2},\dots\} \subseteq \mathbb{X}_i$ be a countable dense set for each i, and construct a set $D \subseteq \mathbb{X}^\infty$ by defining

$$F_m = \bigtimes_{i=1}^{m} D_i \times \bigtimes_{i=m+1}^{\infty} \{d_{i1}\} \tag{6.18}$$

for $m = 1,2,...,$ and then letting $D = \bigcup_{m=1}^{\infty} F_m$. F_m is equipotent with the set of m-tuples formed from the elements of the countable $D_1,...,D_m$, and is countable by induction from **1.4**. Hence D is countable, as a countable union of countable sets.

We will show that D is dense in $\mathbb{X}^\infty$. Let $B = \bigtimes_{i=1}^{\infty} O_i$ be a non-empty basic set, with O_i open in $\mathbb{X}_i$ and $O_i = \mathbb{X}_i$ except for a finite number of coordinates. Choose m such that $O_i = \mathbb{X}_i$ for $i > m$, and then

$$B \cap F_m = \bigtimes_{i=1}^{m} (O_i \cap D_i) \times \bigtimes_{i=m+1}^{\infty} \{d_{i1}\} \neq \emptyset, \tag{6.19}$$

recalling that the dense property implies $O_i \cap D_i \neq \emptyset$, for $i = 1,...,m$. Since $B \cap F_m \subseteq B \cap D$, it follows that B contains a point of D; and since B is an arbitrary basic set, D is dense in $\mathbb{X}^\infty$, as required. ■

One of the most powerful and important results in topology is *Tychonoff's theorem*, which states that arbitrary products of compact topological spaces are also compact, under the product topology. It will suffice here to prove the result for countable products of metric spaces, and this case can be dealt with using a more elementary and familiar line of argument. It is not necessary to specify the metrics involved, for we need the spaces to be metric solely to exploit the equivalence of compactness and sequential compactness.

6.17 Theorem A finite or countable product of separable metric spaces $(\mathbb{X}_i, d_i)$ is compact under the product topology iff the factor spaces are compact.

Proof As before, the finite case follows easily from the countable case, so assume $\mathbb{X}^\infty = \bigtimes_{i=1}^{\infty} \mathbb{X}_i$, where the $\mathbb{X}_i$ are separable spaces. In a metric space, which is first countable, compactness implies separability and is equivalent to sequential compactness by **6.8** and **6.7**. Since $\mathbb{X}_i$ is sequentially compact and first-countable, every sequence $\{x_{in}, n \in \mathbb{N}\}$ on $\mathbb{X}_i$ has a cluster point x_i on the space (**6.4**). Applying the diagonal argument of **2.36**, there exists a single subsequence of integers, $\{n_k, k \in \mathbb{N}\}$, such that $x_{in_k} \to x_i$, for every i. Consider the subsequence in $\mathbb{X}^\infty$, $\{x_{n_k}, k \in \mathbb{N}\}$ where $x_{n_k} = (x_{1n_k}, x_{2n_k},...)$. In the product topology, $x_{n_k} \to x = (x_1, x_2,...)$ iff $x_{in_k} \to x_i$ for every i, which proves that $\mathbb{X}^\infty$ is sequentially compact. $\mathbb{X}^\infty$ can be endowed with the metric $\rho_\infty = \sum_{i=1}^{\infty} d_i/2^i$, which induces the product topology. $\mathbb{X}^\infty$ is separable by **6.16**, and sequential compactness is equivalent to compactness by **6.8** and **6.7**, as above. This proves sufficiency.

Necessity follows from **6.9**(ii), by continuity of the projections as before. ■

6.18 Example The space $\mathbb{R}^\infty$ (see **5.14**) is endowed with the Tychonoff topology if we take as the base sets of a point x the collection

$$N(x;k,\varepsilon) = \{y\colon |x_i - y_i| < \varepsilon,\ i = 1,...,k\};\ k \in \mathbb{N},\ \varepsilon > 0. \tag{6.20}$$

A point in $\mathbb{R}^\infty$ is close to x in this topology if many of its coordinates are close to those of x; another point is closer if either more coordinates are within ε of each other, or the same coordinates are closer than ε, or both. The metric d_∞ defined in (5.15) induces the topology of (6.20). If $\{x_n\}$ is a sequence in $\mathbb{X}$, $d_\infty(x_n,x) \to 0$ iff $\forall\ \varepsilon,k\ \exists\ N \geq 1$ such that $x_n \in N(x;k,\varepsilon)$ for all $n \geq N$. We already know that $\mathbb{R}^\infty$ is separable under d_∞ (**5.15**), but now we can deduce this as a purely topological property, since $\mathbb{R}^\infty$ inherits separability from $\mathbb{R}$ by **6.16**. □

The infinite cube $[0,1]^\infty$ shares the topology (6.20) with $\mathbb{R}^\infty$ and is a compact space by **6.17**; to show this we can assign the Euclidean metric to the factor spaces $[0,1]$. The trick of metrizing a space to establish a topological property is frequently useful, and is one we shall exploit again below.

6.6 Embedding and Metrization

Let $\mathbb{X}$ be a topological space, and $\mathbb{F}$ a class of functions $f\colon \mathbb{X} \mapsto \mathbb{Y}_f$. The *evaluation map* $e\colon \mathbb{X} \mapsto \times_{f\in\mathbb{F}}\mathbb{Y}_f$ is the mapping defined by

$$e(x)_f = f(x). \tag{6.21}$$

The class $\mathbb{F}$ may be quite general, but if it were finite we would think of $e(x)$ as the vector whose elements are the $f(x)$, $f \in \mathbb{F}$. (6.21) could also be written $\pi_f \circ e = f$ where π_f is the coordinate projection. A minor complication arises because f need not be *onto* $\mathbb{Y}_f$, and $e(\mathbb{X}) \subset \times_{f\in\mathbb{F}}\mathbb{Y}_f$ is possible. If A is a set of points in $\mathbb{Y}_f$, the inverse projection $\pi_f^{-1}(A)$ may contain points not in $e(\mathbb{X})$. We therefore need to express the inverse image of A under f, in terms of e, as

$$f^{-1}(A) = (\pi_f \circ e)^{-1}(A) = e^{-1}(\pi_f^{-1}(A) \cap e(\mathbb{X})) \subseteq \mathbb{X}. \tag{6.22}$$

The importance of this concept stems from the fact that, under the right conditions, the evaluation map embeds $\mathbb{X}$ in the product space generated by it. It would be homeomorphic to it in the case $e(\mathbb{X}) = \times_{f\in\mathbb{F}}\mathbb{Y}_f$.

6.19 Theorem Suppose the class $\mathbb{F}$ separates points of $\mathbb{X}$, meaning that $f(x) \neq f(y)$ for some $f \in \mathbb{F}$ whenever x and y are distinct points of $\mathbb{X}$. If $\mathbb{X}$ is endowed with the weak topology induced by $\mathbb{F}$, the evaluation map defines an embedding of $\mathbb{X}$ into $\times_f\mathbb{Y}_f$.

Proof It has to be shown that e is a 1-1 mapping from $\mathbb{X}$ onto a subset of $\times_f\mathbb{Y}_f$, which is continuous with continuous inverse. Since $\mathbb{F}$ separates points of $\mathbb{X}$, e is 1-1, since $e(x) \neq e(y)$ whenever $f(x) \neq f(y)$ for *some* $f \in \mathbb{F}$. To show continuity of e, note first that $f^{-1}(A)$ is open in $\mathbb{X}$ whenever A is open in $\mathbb{Y}_f$ under the weak topology, and sets of the form $\pi_f^{-1}(A)$ are likewise open in $\times_f\mathbb{Y}_f$ with the product topology, since the projections are continuous. But $e^{-1}(\pi_f^{-1}(A)) = (\pi_f \circ e)^{-1}(A) = f^{-1}(A)$, so we can conclude that the inverse images under e of sets of the form $\pi_f^{-1}(A)$, $A \subseteq \mathbb{Y}_f$, are open. Since inverse images preserve unions and intersections (see **1.2**) the same property extends, first to the base sets of $\times_f\mathbb{Y}_f$, which are finite intersections of these inverse projections under the product topology, and thence to all the open sets of $\times_f\mathbb{Y}_f$. So e is continuous.

e^{-1} is continuous if $e(B)$ is open in $e(\mathbb{X})$ whenever B is open in $\mathbb{X}$. Let B be a set of the form $f^{-1}(A)$, where A is open in $\mathbb{Y}_f$. Since $\mathbb{F}$ defines the topology on $\mathbb{X}$ we know this set to be open, and the finite intersections of such sets form a base for $\mathbb{X}$ by assumption. Since e is 1-1 and e^{-1} a mapping, it will suffice to verify that their images under e are open in $e(\mathbb{X})$. Noting that B is a set of the type shown in (6.22), $e(B) = \pi_f^{-1}(A) \cap e(\mathbb{X})$, but since $\pi_f^{-1}(A)$ is open, $e(B)$ is open in $e(\mathbb{X})$ as required. ■

The following is the (for us) most important case of *Urysohn's embedding theorem.*

6.20 Theorem A second-countable T_4-space $(\mathbb{X},\tau)$ can be embedded in $[0,1]^\infty$. □

The proof requires the sufficiency part of the following lemma.

6.21 Lemma Let $x \in \mathbb{X}$, and let $O \subseteq \mathbb{X}$ be any open set containing x. Iff $\mathbb{X}$ is a regular space, there exists an open set U with $x \in \overline{U} \subset O$.

Proof Let $\mathbb{X}$ be regular. If O is open and $x \in O$, there exist disjoint open sets U and C such that $x \in U$ and $O^c \subset C$, and hence $C^c \subseteq O$. Since $U \subseteq C^c$ by the disjointness and C^c is closed, we have $\overline{U} \subseteq C^c \subseteq O$, and sufficiency is proved. To prove necessity, suppose $x \in U$ and $\overline{U} \subset O$. O^c is a closed set not containing x, and $O^c \subset \overline{U}^c$, where U and $\overline{U}^c$ are disjoint open sets. Hence $\mathbb{X}$ is regular. ■

Proof of 6.20 Let $\mathcal{V}$ be a countable base for τ. Since the space is T_4 it is T_3 and hence regular. For any $x \in \mathbb{X}$ and $B \in \mathcal{V}$ containing x, we have by **6.21** a $U \in \tau$ such that $x \in \overline{U} \subset B$, and also by definition of a base $\exists\, A \in \mathcal{V}$ with $x \in A \subset U \subset \overline{U}$, and hence $x \in \overline{A} \subset \overline{U} \subset B$. ($\overline{A}$ is the smallest closed set containing A, note.) Since $\mathcal{V}$ is countable, the collection of all such pairs, say

$$\mathcal{A} = \{(A,B)\colon A \in \mathcal{V},\, B \in \mathcal{V};\, \overline{A} \subset B\}, \tag{6.23}$$

is countable, and so we can label its elements $(A,B)_i = (A_i,B_i)$, $i = 1,2,\ldots$ Every $x \in \mathbb{X}$ lies in A_i for some $i \in \mathbb{N}$.

Since the space is normal, we have by Urysohn's lemma a separating function f_i: $\mathbb{X} \mapsto [0,1]$ for each element of $\mathcal{A}$, such that $f_i(\overline{A}_i) = 1$ and $f_i(B_i^c) = 0$. For each $x \in \mathbb{X}$ and closed set C such that $x \neq C$, choose (A_i,B_i) such that $x \in \overline{A}_i \subset B_i \subset C^c$, and then $f_i(x) = 1$ and $f_i(C) = 0$. These separating functions form a countable class $\mathbb{F}$, a subset of $U(\mathbb{X})$. Since the space is T_1, C can be a point $\{y\}$ so that $\mathbb{F}$ separates points. And since the space is $T_{3\frac{1}{2}}$ and hence completely regular, τ is the weak topology induced by $\mathbb{F}$, by **6.14**. It follows by **6.19** that the evaluation map for $\mathbb{F}$ embeds $\mathbb{X}$ into $[0,1]^\infty$. ■

Recall that $[0,1]^\infty$ endowed with the metric ρ_∞ defined in (5.19) is a compact metric space. It follows that $e(\mathbb{X})$, which is homeomorphic to $\mathbb{X}$ under the evaluation mapping by $\mathbb{F}$, is a totally bounded metric space. It further follows that $(\mathbb{X},\tau)$ is metrizable, since, among other possibilities, it can be endowed with the metric under which the distance between points x and y of $\mathbb{X}$ is taken to be $\rho_\infty(e(x),e(y))$. We have therefore proved the Urysohn metrization theorem, **6.12**.

The topology induced by this metric on $[0,1]^\infty$ is the Tychonoff topology. A base for a point $p = (p_1,p_2,\ldots) \in [0,1]^\infty$ in this topology is provided by sets of the form

$$N(p;k,\varepsilon) = \{q \in [0,1]^\infty: |p_i - q_i| < \varepsilon,\ i = 1,...,k\}, \tag{6.24}$$

for some finite k, and $0 < \varepsilon < 1$, which is the same as (6.20). The topology induced on $\mathbb{X}$ by the embedding is accordingly generated by the base sets

$$N(x;k,\varepsilon) = \{y \in \mathbb{X}: |f_i(x) - f_i(y)| < \varepsilon,\ i = 1,...,k\}, \tag{6.25}$$

which can be recognized as finite intersections of the inverse images, under functions from $\mathbb{F}$, of ε-neighbourhoods of $\mathbb{R}$; this is indeed the weak topology induced by $\mathbb{F}$. This further serves to remind us of the close link between product topologies and weak topologies.

Since metric spaces are T_4, separable metric spaces can be embedded in $[0,1]^\infty$ by **6.20**. In this case the motivation is not metrization, but usually compactification—that is, to show that separable spaces can be topologized as totally bounded spaces. Both metrization and compactification are techniques with important applications in the theory of weak convergence, which we study in Chapter 26. Although the following theorem is a straightforward corollary of **6.20**, the result is of sufficient interest to deserve its own proof; the main interest is to see how in metric spaces there always exists a ready-made collection of functions to define the weak topology.

6.22 Theorem A separable metric space $(\mathbb{S},d)$ is homeomorphic to a subset of $[0,1]^\infty$.

Proof Let $d_0 = d/(1+d)$, which satisfies $0 \le d_0 \le 1$ and is equivalent to d, so that $(\mathbb{X},d_0)$ is homeomorphic to $(\mathbb{X},d)$. By separability there exists a countable set of points $\{z_i,\ i \in \mathbb{N}\}$ which is dense in $\mathbb{X}$. Let a countable family of functions be defined by $f_i(x) = d_0(x,z_i)$, $i = 1,2,...$, and define an evaluation map $h: \mathbb{X} \mapsto [0,1]^\infty$ by

$$h(x) = (d_0(x,z_1),\ d_0(x,z_2),...). \tag{6.26}$$

We show that h is an embedding in $([0,1]^\infty,\rho_\infty)$ where $\rho_\infty(h,g) = \sum_{k=1}^\infty |h_k - g_k|/2^k$. If $\{x_n\}$ is a sequence in $\mathbb{X}$ converging to x, then for each k, $d_0(x_n,z_k) \to d_0(x,z_k)$. Accordingly, $\forall\ k,\varepsilon\ \exists\ N \ge 1$ such that $x_n \in N(x;k,\varepsilon)$ for all $n \ge N$, $\rho_\infty(h(x_n),h(x)) \to 0$, and h is continuous at x. On the other hand, if $x_n \not\to x$, there exists $\varepsilon > 0$ such that $\forall\ N \ge 1$, $d_0(x_n,x) \ge \varepsilon$ for some $n \ge N$. Since $\{z_k\}$ is dense in $\mathbb{X}$, there is a k for which $d_0(x_n,z_k) \ge \frac{3}{4}\varepsilon$ and $d_0(x,z_k) < \frac{1}{4}\varepsilon$, so that $|d_0(x_n,z_k) - d_0(x,z_k)| \ge \frac{1}{2}\varepsilon$ and hence

$$\rho_\infty(h(x_n),h(x)) \ge \varepsilon/2^{k+1}. \tag{6.27}$$

Since this holds for some $n \ge N$ for *every* $N \ge 1$, it holds for infinitely many n, and $h(x_n) \not\to h(x)$. We have therefore shown that $h(x_n) \to h(x)$ if and *only if* $x_n \to x$. This is the property of a 1-1 continuous function with continuous inverse. ∎

But note too the alternative approach of transforming the distance functions into separating functions as in (6.10), and applying **6.20**.

II

PROBABILITY

7
Probability Spaces

7.1 Probability Measures

A *random experiment* is an action or observation whose outcome is uncertain in advance of its occurrence. Tosses of a coin, spins of a roulette wheel, and observations of the price of a stock are familiar examples. A *probability space*, the triple $(\Omega,\mathcal{F},P)$, is to be thought of as a mathematical model of a random experiment. Ω is the *sample space*, the set of all the possible outcomes of the experiment, called the *random elements*, individually denoted ω. The collection $\mathcal{F}$ of *random events* is a σ-field of subsets of Ω, the event $A \in \mathcal{F}$ being said to have occurred if the outcome of the experiment is an element of A. A measure P is assigned to the elements of $\mathcal{F}$, $P(A)$ being the *probability* of A. Formally, we have the following.

7.1 Definition A probability measure (p.m.) on a measurable space $(\Omega,\mathcal{F})$ is a set function $P\colon \mathcal{F} \mapsto [0,1]$ satisfying the *axioms of probability*:

(a) $P(A) \geq 0$, for all $A \in \mathcal{F}$.

(b) $P(\Omega) = 1$.

(c) Countable additivity: for a disjoint collection $\{A_j \in \mathcal{F},\ j \in \mathbb{N}\}$,

$$P\left(\bigcup_j A_j\right) = \sum_j P(A_j). \ \square \tag{7.1}$$

Under the frequentist interpretation of probability, $P(A)$ is the limiting case of the proportion of a long run of repeated experiments in which the outcome is in A. Alternatively, probability may be viewed as a subjective notion with $P(A)$ said to represent an observer's degree of belief that A will occur. For present purposes, the interpretation given to the probabilities has no relevance. The theory stands or falls by its mathematical consistency alone, although it is then up to us to decide whether the results accord with our intuition and are useful in the analysis of real-world problems.

Additional properties of P follow from the axioms.

7.2 Theorem If A, B, and $\{A_j,\ j \in \mathbb{N}\}$ are arbitrary $\mathcal{F}$-sets, then

(i) $P(A) \leq 1$.

(ii) $P(A^c) = 1 - P(A)$.

(iii) $P(\varnothing) = 0$.

(iv) $A \subseteq B \ \Rightarrow\ P(A) \leq P(B)$ (monotonicity).

(v) $(A \cup B) = P(A) + P(B) - P(A \cap B)$.

(vi) $P(\bigcup_j A_j) \leq \sum_j P(A_j)$ (countable subadditivity).

(vii) $A_j \uparrow A$ or $A_j \downarrow A \;\Rightarrow\; P(A_j) \to P(A)$ (continuity). □

Most of these are properties of measures in general. The complementation property (ii) is special to P, although an analogous condition holds for any finite measure, with $P(\Omega)$ replacing 1 in the formula. (iii) confirms P *is* a measure, on the definition.

Proof Applying **7.1**(a), (b), and (c),

$$P(A) + P(A^c) = P(A \cup A^c) = P(\Omega) = 1, \tag{7.2}$$

from which follow (i) and (ii), and also (iii) on setting $A = \Omega$. (iv)-(vi) follow by **3.3**, and (vii) by **3.4**. ■

To create a probability space, probabilities are assigned to a basic class of events $\mathcal{C}$, according to a hypothesis about the mechanisms underlying the random outcome. For example, in coin or die tossing experiments we have the usual hypothesis of a fair coin or die, and hence of equally likely outcomes. Then, provided $\mathcal{C}$ is rich enough to be a determining class for the space, $(\Omega,\mathcal{F},P)$ exists by **3.8** (extension theorem) where $\mathcal{F} = \sigma(\mathcal{C})$.

7.3 Example Let $\mathcal{B}_{[0,1]} = \{B \cap [0,1],\, B \in \mathcal{B}\}$, where $\mathcal{B}$ is the Borel field on $\mathbb{R}$. Then $([0,1], \mathcal{B}_{[0,1]}, m)$, where m is Lebesgue measure, is a probability space, since $m([0,1]) = 1$. The random elements of this space are real numbers between 0 and 1, and a drawing from the distribution is called a *random variable*. It is said to be *distributed uniformly* on the unit interval. The inclusion or exclusion of the endpoints is optional, remembering that $m([0,1]) = m((0,1)) = 1$. □

The *atoms* of a p.m. are the outcomes (singleton sets of Ω) that have positive probability. The following is true for finite measures generally but has special importance in the theory of distributions.

7.4 Theorem The atoms of a p.m. are at most countable.

Proof Let ω_1 be an atom satisfying $P(\{\omega_1\}) \geq P(\{\omega\})$ for all $\omega \in \Omega$, let ω_2 satisfy $P(\{\omega_2\}) \geq P(\{\omega\})$ for all $\omega \in \Omega - \{\omega_1\}$, and so forth, to generate a sequence with

$$P(\{\omega_1\}) \geq P(\{\omega_2\}) \geq P(\{\omega_3\}) \geq \ldots \tag{7.3}$$

The partial sums $\sum_{i=1}^{n} P(\{\omega_i\})$ form a monotone sequence which cannot exceed $P(\Omega) = 1$, and therefore converges by **2.11**, implying by **2.25** that $\lim_{n\to\infty} P(\{\omega_n\}) = 0$. All points with positive probability are therefore in the countable set $\{\omega_i,\, i \in \mathbb{N}\}$. ■

Suppose a random experiment represented by the space $(\Omega,\mathcal{F},P)$ is modified so as to confine the possible outcomes to a subset of the sample space, say $\Lambda \subset \Omega$. For example, suppose we switch from playing roulette with a wheel having a zero slot to one without. The restricted probability space is derived as follows. Let $\mathcal{F}_\Lambda$ denote the collection $\{E \cap \Lambda, E \in \mathcal{F}\}$. $\mathcal{F}_\Lambda$ is a σ-field (compare **1.23**) called $\mathcal{F}_\Lambda$ and is called the *trace* of $\mathcal{F}$ on Λ. Defining $P_\Lambda(E) = P(E)/P(\Lambda)$ for $E \in \mathcal{F}_\Lambda$, P_Λ can be verified to be a p.m. The triple $(\Lambda,\mathcal{F}_\Lambda,P_\Lambda)$ is called the trace of $(\Omega,\mathcal{F},P)$ on Λ.

This is similar to the restriction of a measure space to a subspace, except that the measure is renormalized so that it remains a p.m.

In everyday language, we are inclined to say that events may be 'impossible' or 'certain'. If such events are none the less elements of $\mathcal{F}$, and hence technically random, we convey the idea that they will occur or not occur with 'certainty' by assigning them probabilities of zero or one. The usage of the term 'certain' here is deliberately loose, as the quotation marks suggest. To say an event cannot occur because it has probability zero is different from saying it cannot occur because the outcomes it contains are not elements of Ω. Similarly, to say an event has probability 1 is different from saying it is the event Ω. In technical discussion we therefore make the nice distinction between *sure*, which means the latter, and *almost sure*, which means the former. An event E is said to occur *almost surely* (a.s.), or equivalently, *with probability one* (w.p.1) if $M = \Omega - E$ has probability measure zero. This terminology is synonymous with *almost everywhere* (a.e.) in the measure-theoretic context. When there is ambiguity about the p.m. being considered, the notation 'a.s.[P]' may be used.

7.2 Conditional Probability

A central issue of probability is the treatment of relationships. When random experiments generate a multi-dimensioned outcome (e.g. a poker deal generates several different hands) questions always arise about relationships between the different aspects of the experiment. The natural way to pose such questions is: 'if I observe only one facet of the outcome, does this change the probabilities I should assign to what is unobserved?' (Skilled poker players know the answer to this question, of course.)

The idea underlying conditional probability is that some but not all aspects of a random experiment have been observed. By eliminating some of the possible outcomes (those incompatible with our partial knowledge), we have to consider only a part of the sample space. In $(\Omega,\mathcal{F},P)$, suppose we have partial information about the outcome to the effect that 'the event A has occurred', where $A \in \mathcal{F}$. How should this knowledge change the probabilities we attach to other events? Since the outcomes in A^c are ruled out, the sample space is reduced from Ω to A. To generate probabilities on this restricted space, define the *conditional probability* of an event B as $P(B|A) = P(A \cap B)/P(A)$, for $A,B \in \mathcal{F}$, $P(A) > 0$. $P(.|A)$ satisfies the probability axioms as long as P does and $P(A) > 0$. In particular, $P(A|A) = 1$, and $P(B^c|A) = 1 - P(B|A)$, since $B \cap A$ and $B^c \cap A$ are disjoint, and their union is A. The space $(A,\mathcal{F}_A,P_A)$, the trace of the set A on $(\Omega,\mathcal{F},P)$, models the random experiment from the point of view of an observer who knows that $\omega \in A$. Events A and B are said to be *dependent* when $P(B|A) \neq P(B)$.

In certain respects the conditioning concept seems a little improper. A context in which the components of the random outcome are revealed sequentially to an observer might appear relevant only to a subjective interpretation of probability, and lead a sceptical reader to call the neutrality of the mathematical theory into question. We might also protest that a random event is random, and has no business defining a probability space. In practice, the applications of conditional probability in limit theory are usually quite remote from any considerations of subjectivity, but there is a serious point here, which is the difficulty of constructing a rigorous theory once we depart from the restricted goal of predicting random outcomes a priori.

The way we can overcome improprieties of this kind, and obtain a much more powerful theory into the bargain, is to condition on a *class* of events, a σ-subfield of $\mathcal{F}$. Given an event $B \in \mathcal{F}$, let the set function

$$P(B|\mathcal{G}): \mathcal{G} \mapsto [0,1]$$

represent the *contingent* probability to be assigned to B after drawing an event A from $\mathcal{G}$, where $\mathcal{G} \subseteq \mathcal{F}$. We can think of $\mathcal{G}$ as an information set in the sense that, for each $A \in \mathcal{G}$, an observer knows whether or not the outcome is in A. Since the elements of the domain are random events, we must think of $P(B|\mathcal{G})$ as itself a random outcome (a random variable, in the terminology of Chapter 8) derived from the restricted probability space $(\Omega,\mathcal{G},P)$. We may think of this space as a model of the action of an observer possessing information $\mathcal{G}$, who assigns the conditional probability $P(B|A)$ to B when be observes the occurrence of A, viewed from the standpoint of *another* observer who has no prior information. $\mathcal{G}$ is a σ-field, because if we know an outcome is in A we also know it is not in A^c, and if we know whether or not it is in A_j for each $j = 1,2,3,\ldots$, we know whether or not it is in $\bigcup_j A_j$. The more sets there are in $\mathcal{G}$ the larger the volume of information, all the way from the trivial set $\mathcal{T} = (\Omega,\varnothing)$ (complete ignorance, with $P(B|\mathcal{T}) = P(B)$ a.s.) to the set $\mathcal{F}$ itself, which corresponds to almost sure knowledge of the outcome. In the latter case, $P(B|\mathcal{F}) = 1$ a.s. if $\omega \in B$, and 0 otherwise. If you know whether or not $\omega \in A$ for every $A \in \mathcal{F}$, you *effectively* know ω.[8]

7.3 Independence

A pair of events $A, B \in \mathcal{F}$ is said to be independent if $P(A \cap B) = P(A)P(B)$, or, equivalently, if

$$P(B|A) = P(B). \tag{7.4}$$

If, in a collection of events $\mathcal{C}$, (7.4) holds for every pair of distinct sets A and B from the collection, $\mathcal{C}$ is said to be *pairwise* independent. In addition, $\mathcal{C}$ is said to be *totally* independent if

$$P\left(\bigcap_{A \in \mathcal{J}} A\right) = \prod_{A \in \mathcal{J}} P(A) \tag{7.5}$$

for every subset $\mathcal{J} \subseteq \mathcal{C}$ containing two or more events. This is a stronger condition than pairwise independence. Suppose $\mathcal{C}$ consists of sets A, B, and C. Knowing that B has occurred may not influence the probability we attach to A, and similarly for C; but the joint occurrence of B and C may none the less imply something about A. Pairwise independence implies that $P(A \cap B) = P(A)P(B)$, $P(A \cap C) = P(A)P(C)$, and $P(B \cap C) = P(B)P(C)$, but total independence would also require $P(A \cap B \cap C) = P(A)P(B)P(C)$.

Here are two useful facts about independent events. In each theorem let $\mathscr{C}$ be a totally independent collection, satisfying $P(\bigcap_{A\in\mathscr{J}}A) = \prod_{A\in\mathscr{J}}P(A)$ for each subset $\mathscr{J} \subseteq \mathscr{C}$.

7.5 Theorem The collection $\mathscr{C}'$ which contains A and A^c for each $A \in \mathscr{C}$ is totally independent.

Proof It is sufficient to prove that the independence of A and B implies that of A^c and B, for B can denote any arbitrary intersection of sets from the collection and (7.5) will be satisfied, for either A or A^c. This is certainly true, since if $P(A \cap B) = P(A)P(B)$, then

$$\begin{aligned} P(A^c \cap B) &= P(A^c \cap B) + P(A \cap B) - P(A)P(B) \\ &= P(B) - P(A)P(B) = P(A^c)P(B). \quad \blacksquare \end{aligned} \tag{7.6}$$

7.6 Theorem Let $\{B_j\}$ be a countable disjoint collection, and let the collections consisting of B_j and the sets of $\mathscr{C}$ be totally independent for each j. Then, if $B = \bigcup_j B_j$, the collection consisting of B and $\mathscr{C}$ is also independent.

Proof Let $\mathscr{J}$ be any subset of $\mathscr{C}$. Using the disjointness of the sets of B, and countable additivity,

$$\begin{aligned} P\left(B \cap \bigcap_{A\in\mathscr{J}} A\right) &= P\left(\bigcup_j B_j \cap \bigcap_{A\in\mathscr{J}} A\right) = \sum_j P\left(B_j \cap \bigcap_{A\in\mathscr{J}} A\right) \\ &= \sum_j P(B_j)P\left(\bigcap_{A\in\mathscr{J}} A\right) = P(B)\prod_{A\in\mathscr{J}} P(A). \quad \blacksquare \end{aligned} \tag{7.7}$$

7.4 Product Spaces

Questions of dependence and independence arise when multiple random experiments run in parallel, and product spaces play a natural role in the analysis of these issues. Let $(\Omega\times\Xi, \mathscr{F}\otimes\mathscr{G}, P)$ be a probability space where $\mathscr{F}\otimes\mathscr{G}$ is the σ-field generated by the measurable rectangles of $\Omega\times\Xi$, and $P(\Omega\times\Xi) = 1$. The random outcome is a pair (ω,ξ). This is no more than a case of the general theory of §7.1 (where the nature of ω is unspecified) except that it becomes possible to ask questions about the part of the outcome represented by ω or ξ alone. $P_\Omega(F) = P(F\times\Xi)$ for $F \in \mathscr{F}$, and $P_\Xi(G) = P(\Omega\times G)$ for $G \in \mathscr{G}$, are called the *marginal probabilities*. $(\Omega,\mathscr{F},P_\Omega)$ and $(\Xi,\mathscr{G},P_\Xi)$ are probability spaces representing an incompletely observed random experiment, with ω or ξ, respectively, being the only things observed in an experiment generating (ω,ξ).

On the other hand, suppose we observe ξ and subsequently consider the 'experiment' of observing ω. Knowing ξ means that for each $\Omega\times G$ we know whether or not (ω,ξ) is in it. The conditional probabilities generated by this two-stage experiment can be written by a slight abuse of notation as $P(F|\mathscr{G})$, although strictly speaking the relevant events are the cylinders $F\times\Xi$, and the elements of the conditioning σ-field are $\Omega\times G$ for $G \in \mathscr{G}$, so we ought to write something like

$P(F \times \Xi | \Omega \times \mathcal{G})$. In this context, product measure assumes a special role as the model of independence. In $(\Omega \times \Xi, \mathcal{F} \otimes \mathcal{G}, P)$, the coordinate spaces are said to be independent when

$$P(F \times G) = P_\Omega(F) P_\Xi(G) \tag{7.8}$$

for each $F \in \mathcal{F}$ and $G \in \mathcal{G}$.

Unity of the notation is preserved since $F \times G = (F \times \Xi) \cap (\Omega \times G)$. We can also write $P(F \times \Xi | \Omega \times G) = P_\Omega(F)$, or with a further slight abuse of notation $P(F | G) = P_\Omega(F)$, for any pair $F \in \mathcal{F}$ and $G \in \mathcal{G}$. Independence means that knowing ξ does not affect the probabilities assigned to sets of $\mathcal{F}$. Since the measurable rectangles are a determining class for the space, the p.m. P is entirely determined by the marginal measures.

8
Random Variables

8.1 Measures on the Line

Let $(\Omega,\mathcal{F},P)$ be a probability space. A real *random variable* (r.v.) is an $\mathcal{F}/\mathcal{B}$-measurable function $X: \Omega \mapsto \mathbb{R}$.[9] That is to say, $X(\omega)$ induces an inverse mapping from $\mathcal{B}$ to $\mathcal{F}$ such that $X^{-1}(B) \in \mathcal{F}$ for every $B \in \mathcal{B}$, where $\mathcal{B}$ is the linear Borel field. The term '$\mathcal{F}$-measurable r.v.' may be used when the role of $\mathcal{B}$ is understood. The symbol μ will be generally used to denote a p.m. on the line, reserving P for the p.m. on the underlying space.

Random variables therefore live in the space $(\mathbb{R},\mathcal{B},\mu)$, where μ is the derived measure such that $\mu(B) = P(X^{-1}(B)) = P(X \in B)$. The term *distribution* is synonymous with measure in this context. The properties of r.v.s are special cases of the results in Chapter 3; in particular, the contents of §3.6 should be reviewed in conjunction with this chapter. If $g: \mathbb{R} \mapsto \mathbb{R}$ is a Borel function, then $g\circ X(\omega) = g(X(\omega))$ is also a r.v., having derived p.m. μg^{-1} according to **3.21**.

If there is a set $S \in \mathcal{B}$ having the property $\mu(S) = 1$, the trace of $(\mathbb{R},\mathcal{B},\mu)$ on S is equivalent to the original space in the sense that the same measure is assigned to B and to $B \cap S$, for each $B \in \mathcal{B}$. Which space to work with is basically a matter of technical convenience. If X is a r.v., it may be more satisfactory to say that the Borel function X^2 is a r.v. distributed on $\mathbb{R}^+$, than that it is distributed on $\mathbb{R}$ but takes values in $\mathbb{R}^+$ almost surely. One could substitute for $(\mathbb{R},\mathcal{B},\mu)$ the extended space $(\overline{\mathbb{R}},\overline{\mathcal{B}},\mu)$ (see **1.22**), but note that assigning a positive probability to infinity does not lead to meaningful results. Random variables must be finite with probability 1. Thus $(\mathbb{R},\mathcal{B},\mu)$, the trace of $(\overline{\mathbb{R}},\overline{\mathcal{B}},\mu)$ on $\mathbb{R}$, is equivalent to it for nearly all purposes. However, while it is always finite a.s., a r.v. is not necessarily *bounded* a.s.; there may exist no constant B such that $|X(\omega)| \le B$ for all $\omega \in C$, with $P(\Omega - C) = 0$. The *essential supremum* of X is

$$\text{ess sup } X = \inf\{x: P(|X| > x) = 0\}, \tag{8.1}$$

and this may be either a finite number, or $+\infty$.

8.2 Distribution Functions

The *cumulative distribution function* (c.d.f.) of X is the function $F: \overline{\mathbb{R}} \mapsto [0,1]$, where

$$F(x) = \mu((-\infty, x]) = P(X \le x), \quad x \in \overline{\mathbb{R}}. \tag{8.2}$$

We take the domain to be $\overline{\mathbb{R}}$ since it is natural to assign the values 0 and 1 to

$F(-\infty)$ and $F(+\infty)$ respectively. No other values are possible so there is no contradiction in confining attention to just the points of $\mathbb{R}$. To specify a distribution for X it is sufficient to assign a functional form for F; μ and F are equivalent representations of the distribution, each useful for different purposes. To represent $\mu(A)$ in terms of F for a set A much more complicated than an interval would be cumbersome, but on the other hand, the graph of F is an appealing way to display the characteristics of the distribution.

To see how probabilities are assigned to sets using F, start with the half-open interval $(x,y]$ for $x < y$. This is the intersection of the half-lines $(\infty,y]$ and $(-\infty,x]^c = (x,+\infty)$. Let $A = (-\infty,x]$ and $B = (-\infty,y]$, so that $\mu(A) = F(x)$ and $\mu(B) = F(y)$; then

$$\begin{aligned}\mu((x,y]) &= \mu(A^c \cap B) = 1 - \mu(A \cup B^c) \\ &= 1 - (\mu(A) + 1 - \mu(B)) = \mu(B) - \mu(A) = F(y) - F(x), \qquad (8.3)\end{aligned}$$

A and B^c being disjoint. The half-open intervals form a semi-ring (see **1.18**), and from the results of §3.2 the measure extends uniquely to the sets of $\mathcal{B}$.

As an example of the extension, we determine $\mu(\{x\}) = P(X = x)$ for $x \in \mathbb{R}$ (compare **3.15**). Putting $x = y$ in (8.3) will not yield this result, since $A \cap A^c = \varnothing$, *not* $\{x\}$. We could obtain $\{x\}$ as the intersection of $(-\infty,x]$ and $[x,+\infty) = (-\infty,x)^c$, but then there is no obvious way to find the probability for the open interval $(-\infty,x) = (-\infty,x] - \{x\}$. The solution to the problem is to consider the monotone sequence of half-lines $(-\infty, x-1/n]$ for $n \in \mathbb{N}$. Since $(x-1/n,x] = (-\infty, x-1/n] \cap (-\infty,x]$, we have $\mu((x-1/n,x]) = F(x) - F(x-1/n)$, according to (8.3). Since $\{x\} = \bigcap_{n=1}^{\infty}(x-1/n,x]$, $\{x\} \in \mathcal{B}$ and $\mu(\{x\}) = F(x) - F(x-)$, where $F(x-)$ is the left limit of F at x. $F(x)$ exceeds $F(x-)$ (i.e. F jumps) at the atoms of the distribution, points x with $\mu(\{x\}) > 0$. We can deduce by the same kind of reasoning that $\mu((x,y)) = F(y-) - F(x)$, $\mu([x,y)) = F(y-) - F(x-)$, and that, generally, measures of open intervals are the same as those of closed intervals unless the endpoints are atoms of the distribution.

Certain characteristics imposed on the c.d.f. by its definition in terms of a measure were implicit in the above conclusions. The next three theorems establish these properties.

8.1 Theorem F is non-negative and non-decreasing, with $F(-\infty) = 0$ and $F(+\infty) = 1$, and is increasing at $x \in \mathbb{R}$ iff every open neighbourhood of x has positive measure.

Proof These are all direct consequences of the definition. Non-negativity is from (8.2), and monotonicity from **7.2**(iv). F is increasing at x if $F(x+\varepsilon) > F(x-\varepsilon)$ for each $\varepsilon > 0$. To show the asserted sufficiency, we have for each such ε,

$$F(x+\varepsilon) - F(x-\varepsilon) \geq F((x+\varepsilon)-) - F(x-\varepsilon) = \mu(S(x,\varepsilon)). \qquad (8.4)$$

For the necessity, suppose $\mu(S(x,\varepsilon)) = 0$ and note that, by monotonicity of F,

$$\mu(S(x,\varepsilon)) = F((x+\varepsilon)-) - F(x-\varepsilon) \geq F(x+\varepsilon/2) - F(x-\varepsilon/2). \ \blacksquare \qquad (8.5)$$

The collection of points on which F increases is known as the *support* of μ. Its complement in $\mathbb{R}$, the largest set of zero measure, consists of points that must all lie in open neighbourhoods of zero measure, and hence must be open. The support of μ is accordingly a closed set.

8.2 Theorem F is right-continuous everywhere.

Proof For $x \in \mathbb{R}$ and $n \geq 1$, additivity of the p.m. implies

$$\mu((-\infty, x+1/n]) = \mu((-\infty, x]) + \mu((x, x+1/n]). \tag{8.6}$$

As $n \to \infty$, $\mu((-\infty, x+1/n]) \downarrow \mu((-\infty, x])$ by continuity of the measure, and hence $\lim_{n\to\infty}\mu((x, x+1/n]) = 0$. It follows that for $\varepsilon > 0$ there exists N_ε such that $\mu((x, x+1/n]) < \varepsilon$, and, accordingly,

$$\mu((-\infty, x]) \leq \mu((-\infty, x+1/n]) < \mu((-\infty, x]) + \varepsilon, \tag{8.7}$$

for $n \geq N_\varepsilon$. Hence $F(x+) = F(x)$, proving the theorem since x was arbitrary. ∎

If $F(x)$ had been defined as $\mu((-\infty, x))$, similar arguments would show that it was left continuous in that case.

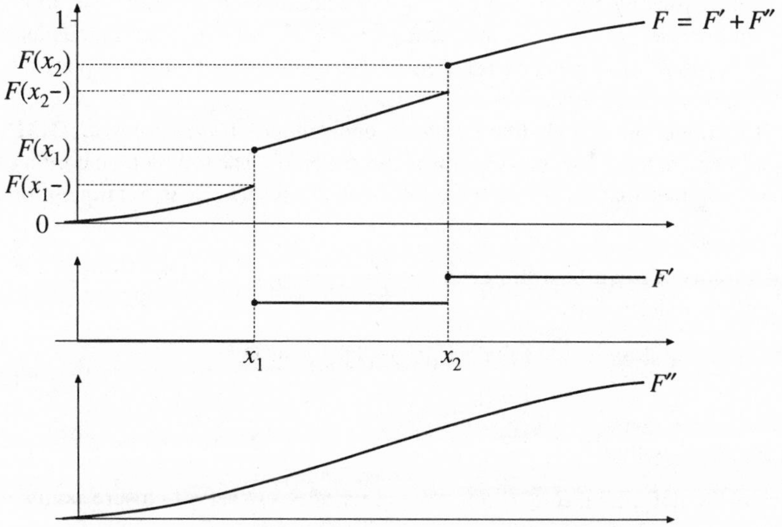

Fig. 8.1

8.3 Theorem F has the decomposition

$$F(x) = F'(x) + F''(x) \tag{8.8}$$

where $F'(x)$ is a right-continuous step function with at most a countable number of jumps, and $F''(x)$ is everywhere continuous.

Proof By **7.4**, the jump points of F are at most countable. Letting $\{x_1, x_2, ...\}$ denote these points,

$$F'(x) = \sum_{x_i \le x} (F(x_i) - F(x_i-)) \tag{8.9}$$

is a step function with jumps at the points x_i, and $F''(x) = F(x) - F'(x)$ has $F(x_i-) = F(x_i)$ at each x_i and is continuous everywhere. ■

Fig. 8.1 illustrates the decomposition.

This is not the only decomposition of F. The Lebesgue decomposition of μ with respect to Lebesgue measure on $\mathbb{R}$ (see **4.28**) is $\mu = \mu_1 + \mu_2$ where μ_1 is singular with respect to m (is positive only on a set of Lebesgue measure 0) and μ_2 is absolutely continuous with respect to Lebesgue measure. Recall that $\mu_2(A) = \int_A f(x)dx$ for $A \in \mathcal{B}$, where f is the associated Radon-Nikodym derivative (density function). If we decompose F in the same way, such that $F_i(x) = \mu_i((-\infty, x])$ for $i = 1$ and 2, we may write $F_2(x) = \int_{-\infty}^{x} f(\xi)d\xi$, implying that $f(x) = dF_2/d\xi|_{\xi=x}$. This must hold for almost all x (Lebesgue measure), and we call F_2 an absolutely continuous function, meaning it is differentiable almost everywhere on its domain. $F' \le F_1$ since F_1 may increase on a set of Lebesgue measure 0, and such sets can be uncountable, and hence larger than the set of atoms. It is customary to summarize these relations by decomposing F'' into two additive components, the absolutely continuous part F_2, and a component $F_3 = F'' - F_2$ which is continuous and also singular, constant except on a set of zero Lebesgue measure. This component can in most cases be neglected.

The collection of half-lines with rational endpoints generates $\mathcal{B}$ (**1.21**) and should be a determining class for measures on $(\mathbb{R},\mathcal{B})$. The following theorem establishes the fact that a c.d.f. defined on a dense subset of $\mathbb{R}$ is a unique representation of μ.

8.4 Theorem Let μ be a finite measure on $(\mathbb{R},\mathcal{B})$ and D a dense subset of $\mathbb{R}$. The function G defined by

$$G(x) = \begin{cases} F(x) = \mu((-\infty, x]), & x \in D \\ F(x+), & x \in \mathbb{R} - D \end{cases} \tag{8.10}$$

is identical with F.

Proof By definition, $\mathbb{R} \subseteq \overline{D}$ and the points of $\mathbb{R} - D$ are all closure points of D. For each $x \in \mathbb{R}$, not excluding points in $\mathbb{R} - D$, there is a sequence of points in D converging to x (e.g. choose a point from $S(x,1/n) \cap D$ for $n \in \mathbb{N}$). Since F is right-continuous everywhere on $\mathbb{R}$, $\mu((-\infty, x]) = F(x+)$ for each $x \in \mathbb{R} - D$. ■

Finally, we show that every F corresponds to some μ, as well as every μ to an F.

8.5 Theorem Let F: $\overline{\mathbb{R}} \to [0,1]$ be a non-negative, non-decreasing, right-continuous function, with $F(-\infty) = 0$ and $F(+\infty) = 1$. There exists a unique p.m. μ on $(\mathbb{R},\mathcal{B})$ such that $F(x) = \mu((-\infty, x])$ for all $x \in \mathbb{R}$. □

Right continuity, as noted above, corresponds to the convention of defining F by (8.2). If instead we defined $F(x) = \mu((-\infty, x))$, a left-continuous non-decreasing F

would represent a p.m.

Proof Consider the function ϕ: $[0,1] \mapsto \overline{\mathbb{R}}$, defined by

$$\phi(u) = \inf\{x \colon u \le F(x)\}. \tag{8.11}$$

ϕ can be thought of as the inverse of F; $\phi(0) = -\infty$, $\phi(1) = +\infty$, and since F is non-decreasing and right-continuous, ϕ is non-decreasing and left-continuous; ϕ is therefore Borel-measurable by **3.32**(ii). According to **3.21**, we may define a measure on $(\mathbb{R},\mathcal{B})$ by $m\phi^{-1}(B)$ for each $B \in \mathcal{B}$, where m is Lebesgue measure on the Borel sets of $[0,1]$.

In particular, consider the class $\mathcal{C}$ of the half-open intervals $(a,b]$ for all $a,b \in \mathbb{R}$ with $a < b$. This is a semi-ring by **1.18**, and $\sigma(\mathcal{C}) = \mathcal{B}$ by **1.21**. Note that

$$\phi^{-1}((a,b]) = \{u \colon \inf\{x \colon u \le F(x)\} \in (a,b]\} = (F(a), F(b)]. \tag{8.12}$$

For each of these sets define the measure

$$\mu((a,b]) = m\phi^{-1}((a,b])) = F(b) - F(a). \tag{8.13}$$

The fact that this is a measure follows from the argument of the preceding paragraph. $\mathcal{C}$ is a determining class for $(\mathbb{R},\mathcal{B})$, and the measure has an extension by **3.8**. It is a p.m. since $\mu(\mathbb{R}) = 1$, and is unique by **3.13**. ∎

The neat construction used in this proof has other applications in the theory of random variables, and will reappear in more elaborate form in §22.2. The graph of ϕ is found by rotating and reflecting the graph of F, sketched in Fig. 8.2; to see the former with the usual coordinates, turn the page on its side and view in a mirror.

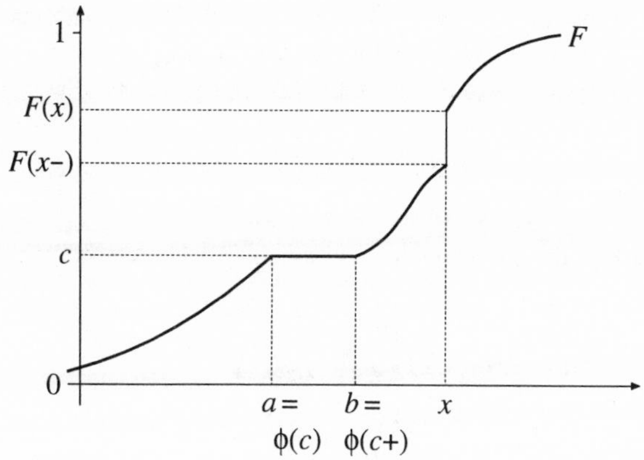

Fig. 8.2

If F has a discontinuity at x, then $\phi = x$ on the interval $(F(x-), F(x)]$, and $\phi^{-1}(\{x\}) = (F(x-), F(x)]$. Thus, $\mu(\{x\}) = m((F(x-), F(x)]) = F(x) - F(x-)$, as required. On the other hand, if an interval $(a,b]$ has measure 0 under F, F is constant on this interval and ϕ has a discontinuity at $F(a) = F(b) = c$ (say). ϕ takes the value a at this point, by left continuity. Note that $\phi^{-1}(c) = (a,b]$, so that $\mu((a,b]) = m(c) = 0$, as required.

8.3 Examples

Most of the distributions met with in practice are either *discrete* or *continuous*. A discrete distribution assigns zero probability to all but a countable set of points, with $F'' = 0$ in the decomposition of **8.3**.

8.6 Example The *Bernoulli* (or binary) r.v. takes values 1 and 0 with fixed probabilities p and $1-p$. Think of it as a mapping from any probability space containing two elements, such as 'Success' and 'Failure', 'Yes' and 'No', etc. □

8.7 Example The *binomial* distribution with parameters n and p (denoted $B(n,p)$) is the distribution of the number of 1s obtained in n independent drawings from the Bernoulli distribution, having the probability function

$$P(X = x) = \binom{n}{x} p^x (1-p)^{n-x},\ x = 0,\dots,n. \quad \square \tag{8.14}$$

8.8 Example The limiting case of (8.14) with $p = \lambda/n$, as $n \to \infty$, is the *Poisson* distribution, having probability function

$$P(X = x) = \frac{1}{x!} e^{-\lambda} \lambda^x,\ x = 0,1,2,\dots \tag{8.15}$$

This is a discrete distribution with a countably infinite set of outcomes. □

In a continuous distribution, F is absolutely continuous with $F_1 = 0$ in the Lebesgue decomposition of the c.d.f. The derivative $f = dF/dx$ exists a.e.$[m]$ on $\mathbb{R}$, and is called the *probability density function* (p.d.f.) of the p.m. According to the Radon-Nikodym theorem, the p.d.f. has the property that for each $E \in \mathcal{B}$,

$$\mu(E) = \int_E f(x)dx. \tag{8.16}$$

8.9 Example For the *uniform* distribution on [0,1] (see **7.3**),

$$F(x) = \begin{cases} 0, & x < 0 \\ x, & 0 \le x \le 1. \\ 1, & x > 1 \end{cases} \tag{8.17}$$

The p.d.f is constant at 1 on the interval, but is undefined at 0 and 1. □

8.10 Example The standard *normal* or *Gaussian* distribution has p.d.f.

$$f(x) = \frac{1}{\sqrt{2\pi}} e^{-x^2/2},\ -\infty < x < +\infty\ , \tag{8.18}$$

whose graph is the well-known bell-shaped curve with mode at zero. □

8.11 Example The *Cauchy* distribution has p.d.f.

$$f(x) = \frac{1}{\pi(1+x^2)},\ -\infty < x < +\infty, \tag{8.19}$$

which, like the Gaussian, is symmetric with mode at 0. □

When it exists, the p.d.f. is the usual means of characterizing a distribution. A particularly useful trick is to be able to derive the distribution of $g(X)$ from that of X, when g is a function of a suitable type.

8.12 Theorem Let $g\colon \mathbb{S} \mapsto \mathbb{T}$ be a 1-1 function onto $\mathbb{T}$, where $\mathbb{S}$ and $\mathbb{T}$ are open subsets of $\mathbb{R}$, and let $h = g^{-1}$ be continuously differentiable with $dh/dy \neq 0$ for all $y \in \mathbb{T}$. If X is continuously distributed with p.d.f. f_X, and $Y = g(X)$, then Y is continuously distributed with p.d.f.

$$f_Y(y) = f_X(g^{-1}(y))\left|\frac{dx}{dy}\right|. \ \square \tag{8.20}$$

The proof is an easy exercise in differential calculus. This result illustrates **3.21**, but in most other cases it is a great deal harder than this to derive a closed form for a transformed distribution.

8.13 Example Generalize the uniform distribution (**8.9**) from [0,1] to an arbitrary interval $[a,b]$. The transformation is linear,

$$y = a+(b-a)x, \tag{8.21}$$

so that $f_Y(y) = (b-a)^{-1}$ on (a,b), by (8.20). The c.d.f. is defined on $[a,b]$ by

$$F(y) = (y-a)/(b-a). \tag{8.22}$$

Membership of the uniform family is denoted by $X \sim U[a,b]$. □

8.14 Example Linear transformations of the standard Gaussian r.v.,

$$X = \mu+\sigma Z,\ \ \sigma > 0, \tag{8.23}$$

generate the Gaussian family of distributions, with p.d.f.s

$$f(x;\mu,\sigma) = \frac{1}{\sqrt{2\pi}\sigma}e^{-(x-\mu)^2/2\sigma^2},\ -\infty < x < +\infty\ .\ \square \tag{8.24}$$

The location parameter μ and scale parameter σ^2 have better-known designations as *moments* of the distribution; see **9.4** and **9.7** below. Membership of the Gaussian family is denoted by $X \sim N(\mu,\sigma^2)$.

8.15 Example A family of Cauchy distributions is generated from the standard Cauchy by linear transformations $X = \nu+\delta Z$, $\delta > 0$. The family of p.d.f.s with location parameter ν and scale parameter δ take the form

$$f(x;\,\nu,\delta) = \frac{1}{\pi\delta}\left(\frac{1}{1+[(x-\nu)/\delta]^2}\right), \quad -\infty < x < +\infty. \;\square \tag{8.25}$$

8.16 Example Consider the square of a standard Gaussian r.v. with $\mu = 0$ and $\sigma = 1$. Since the transformation is not monotone we cannot use **8.12** to determine the density, strictly speaking. But consider the 'half-normal' density,

$$f_{|Z|}(u) = \begin{cases} 2f(u), & u \geq 0 \\ 0, & u < 0 \end{cases} \tag{8.26}$$

where f is given by (8.18). This is the p.d.f. of the absolute value of a Gaussian variable. The transformation $g(|u|) = u^2$ is 1-1, so the p.d.f. of Z^2 is

$$f_{Z^2}(u) = \frac{1}{\sqrt{2\pi}}\,e^{-u/2}u^{-1/2}, \quad 0 < u < \infty, \tag{8.27}$$

applying (8.20). This is the *chi-squared* distribution with one degree of freedom, or $\chi^2(1)$. It is a member (with $p = \alpha = \frac{1}{2}$) of the gamma family,

$$G(u;\alpha,p) = \frac{\alpha}{\Gamma(p)}e^{-\alpha u}(\alpha u)^{p-1},\ 0 < u < \infty;\ \ \alpha > 0,\ p > 0, \tag{8.28}$$

where $\Gamma(p) = \int_0^\infty \xi^{p-1}e^{-\xi}d\xi$ is the gamma function, having the properties $\Gamma(\frac{1}{2}) = \sqrt{2\pi}$, and $\Gamma(n) = (n-1)\Gamma(n-1)$. □

8.4 Multivariate Distributions

In Euclidean k-space $\mathbb{R}^k$, the k-dimensional Borel field $\mathcal{B}^k$ is $\sigma(\mathcal{R}^k)$, where $\mathcal{R}^k$ denotes the measurable rectangles of $\mathbb{R}^k$, the sets of the form $B_1 \times B_2 \times \ldots \times B_k$ where $B_i \in \mathcal{B}$ for $i = 1,\ldots,k$. In a space $(\Omega,\mathcal{F},P)$, a random vector $(X_1,X_2,\ldots,X_k)'$ $= \boldsymbol{X}$ is a measurable mapping

$$\boldsymbol{X}\colon \Omega \to \mathbb{R}^k.$$

If μ is the derived measure such that $\mu(A) = P(E)$ for $A \in \mathcal{B}^k$ and $E \in \mathcal{F}$, the multivariate c.d.f., $F\colon \overline{\mathbb{R}}^k \to [0,1]$, is defined for $(x_1,\ldots,x_k)' = \boldsymbol{x}$ by

$$F(\boldsymbol{x}) = \mu((-\infty,x_1]\times\ldots\times(-\infty,x_k]). \tag{8.29}$$

The extension proceeds much like the scalar case.

8.17 Example Consider the random pair (X,Y). Let $F(x,y) = \mu((-\infty,x]\times(-\infty,y])$. The measure of the half-open rectangle $(x,x+\Delta x]\times(y,y+\Delta y]$ is

$$\Delta F(x,y) = F(x+\Delta x,y+\Delta y) - F(x+\Delta x,y) - F(x,y+\Delta y) + F(x,y). \tag{8.30}$$

To show this, consider the four disjoint sets of $\mathbb{R}^2$ illustrated in Fig. 8.3:

$$A = (x, x+\Delta x]\times(y, y+\Delta y], \quad B = (-\infty, x]\times(y, y+\Delta y],$$
$$C = (x, x+\Delta x]\times(-\infty, y], \quad D = (-\infty, x]\times(-\infty, y].$$

A is the set whose probability is sought. Since $P(A\cup B\cup C\cup D) = F(x+\Delta x, y+\Delta y)$, $P(B\cup D) = F(x, y+\Delta y)$, $P(C\cup D) = F(x+\Delta x, y)$, and $P(D) = F(x, y)$, the result is immediate from the probability axioms. □

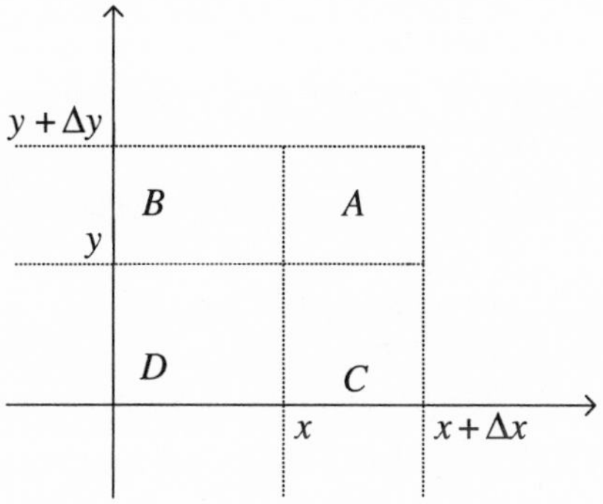

Fig. 8.3

Extending the approach of **8.17** inductively, the measure of the k-dimensional rectangle $\times_{i=1}^{k}(x_i, x_i+\Delta x_i]$ can be shown to be

$$\Delta F(x_1,\ldots, x_k) = \sum_j (\pm F_j), \tag{8.31}$$

where the sum on the right has 2^k terms, and the F_j are the values of F at each of the vertices of the k-dimensional rectangle extending from $(x_1,\ldots x_k)'$ with sides of length Δx_i, $i = 1,\ldots,k$. The sign pattern depends on k; if k is odd, the F_j having as arguments even numbers of upper vertices (points of the form $x_i+\Delta x_i$) take negative signs, and the others positive; while if k is even, the F_j with odd numbers of upper vertices as arguments are negative. Generalizing the monotonicity of the univariate c.d.f., F must satisfy the condition that $\Delta F(x_1,\ldots, x_k)$ be non-negative for every choice of $(x_1,\ldots, x_k)' \in \mathbb{R}^k$ and $(\Delta x_1,\ldots,\Delta x_k)' \in (\mathbb{R}^k)^+$. Applying **3.19** inductively shows that the class of k-dimensional half-open rectangles is a semi-ring, so that the measure defined by F extends to the sets of $\mathcal{B}^k$; hence $(\mathbb{R}^k,\mathcal{B}^k,\mu)$ is a probability space derived from $(\Omega,\mathcal{F},P)$.

If the distribution is continuous with p.d.f. $f(\boldsymbol{x})$, Fubini's theorem gives

$$F(\boldsymbol{x}) = \int_{(-\infty,x_1]\times\ldots\times(-\infty,x_k]} f(\xi_1,\ldots,\xi_k)d\xi_1\ldots d\xi_k$$
$$= \int_{-\infty}^{x_1}\cdots\int_{-\infty}^{x_k} f(\xi_1,\ldots,\xi_k)d\xi_1\ldots d\xi_k. \tag{8.32}$$

Theorem **8.12** has the following generalization. A *diffeomorphism* (also, *coor-*

dinate transformation) is a function $\boldsymbol{g}: \mathbb{S} \mapsto \mathbb{T}$ ($\mathbb{S}$ and $\mathbb{T}$ open subsets of $\mathbb{R}^k$) which is 1-1 onto and continuously differentiable with $\det(\partial \boldsymbol{g}/\partial \boldsymbol{x}') \neq 0$ for all $\boldsymbol{x} \in \mathbb{S}$, where $\partial \boldsymbol{g}/\partial \boldsymbol{x}'$ is the Jacobian matrix whose (i,j)th element is $\partial g_j/\partial x_i$ for $i,j = 1,\dots,k$. The inverse of a diffeomorphism is also continuously differentiable.

8.18 Theorem If $\boldsymbol{Y} = \boldsymbol{g}(\boldsymbol{X})$ where $\boldsymbol{g}$ is a diffeomorphism, the p.d.f. of $\boldsymbol{Y}$ is

$$h(\boldsymbol{y}) = f(\boldsymbol{g}^{-1}(\boldsymbol{y}))|J| \tag{8.33}$$

where $J = \det[\partial(\boldsymbol{g}^{-1})/\partial \boldsymbol{y}']$. □

This is a standard result in the theory of multiple Lebesgue integrals (see e.g. Apostol 1974: 15.10-15.12).

8.19 Example Letting f denote the standard Gaussian p.d.f. (see **8.10**), consider

$$\phi(\boldsymbol{z}) = \prod_{i=1}^{k} f(z_i) = (2\pi)^{-k/2}\exp\{-\tfrac{1}{2}(\boldsymbol{z}'\boldsymbol{z})\}. \tag{8.34}$$

This is a k-dimensional p.d.f., and the corresponding random vector $\boldsymbol{Z} = (Z_1,\dots,Z_k)'$, is the *standard Gaussian vector.* The affine transformation

$$\boldsymbol{X} = \boldsymbol{A}\boldsymbol{Z} + \boldsymbol{\mu}, \tag{8.35}$$

where $\boldsymbol{A}$ ($k \times k$ nonsingular) and $\boldsymbol{\mu}$ ($k \times 1$) are constants, is 1-1 continuous with inverse $\boldsymbol{Z} = \boldsymbol{A}^{-1}(\boldsymbol{X} - \boldsymbol{\mu})$, having $J = |\boldsymbol{A}^{-1}| = 1/|\boldsymbol{A}|$. Define $\boldsymbol{\Sigma} = \boldsymbol{A}\boldsymbol{A}'$ such that $(\boldsymbol{A}^{-1})'\boldsymbol{A}^{-1} = (\boldsymbol{A}\boldsymbol{A}')^{-1} = \boldsymbol{\Sigma}^{-1}$, and $||\boldsymbol{A}|^{-1}| = |\boldsymbol{\Sigma}|^{-1/2}$, the positive square root being understood. Applying **8.18** produces

$$\begin{aligned} f(\boldsymbol{x}) &= \phi(\boldsymbol{A}^{-1}(\boldsymbol{x} - \boldsymbol{\mu}))\left|\frac{1}{|\boldsymbol{A}|}\right| \\ &= (2\pi)^{-k/2}\left||\boldsymbol{A}^{-1}|\right|\exp\{-\tfrac{1}{2}(\boldsymbol{x} - \boldsymbol{\mu})'(\boldsymbol{A}^{-1})'\boldsymbol{A}^{-1}(\boldsymbol{x} - \boldsymbol{\mu})\}. \\ &= (2\pi)^{-k/2}|\boldsymbol{\Sigma}|^{-1/2}\exp\{-\tfrac{1}{2}(\boldsymbol{x} - \boldsymbol{\mu})'\boldsymbol{\Sigma}^{-1}(\boldsymbol{x} - \boldsymbol{\mu})\}. \end{aligned} \tag{8.36}$$

This is the multinormal p.d.f., depending on parameters $\boldsymbol{\mu}$ and $\boldsymbol{\Sigma}$. Every such distribution is generated by an affine transform applied to $\boldsymbol{Z}$. Membership of the multinormal family is denoted $\boldsymbol{X} \sim N(\boldsymbol{\mu},\boldsymbol{\Sigma})$. □

8.5 Independent Random Variables

Suppose that, out of a pair of r.v.s (X,Y) on $(\mathbb{R}^2,\mathcal{B}^2,\mu)$, we are interested only in predicting X. In this situation the events of interest are the cylinder sets in $\mathbb{R}^2$, having the form $B \times \mathbb{R}$, $B \in \mathcal{B}$. The marginal distribution of X is defined by $(\mathbb{R},\mathcal{B},\mu_X)$ where

$$\mu_X(A) = \mu(A \times \mathbb{R}) \tag{8.37}$$

for $A \in \mathcal{B}$. The associated marginal c.d.f. is $F_X = F(x, +\infty)$.
The notion of independence defined in §7.4 specializes in the following way. X and

Y are called independent r.v.s iff

$$\mu(A \times B) = \mu_X(A)\mu_Y(B) \tag{8.38}$$

for all pairs of events $A,B \in \mathcal{B}$, where μ_X is defined by (8.37) and μ_Y is analogous. Equivalently, μ is the product measure generated by μ_X and μ_Y.

8.20 Theorem X and Y are independent iff for each $x,y \in \mathbb{R}$

$$F(x,y) = F_X(x)F_Y(y). \tag{8.39}$$

If the distribution is continuous the p.d.f. factorizes as

$$f(x,y) = f_X(x)f_Y(y). \tag{8.40}$$

Proof Obviously, (8.39) is true only if μ satisfies (8.38). The problem is to show that the former condition is also sufficient. Consider the half-open rectangles,

$$\mathcal{C} = \{(a,b] \times (c,d],\ a,c \in \overline{\mathbb{R}},\ b,d \in \mathbb{R}\}.$$

If and only if (8.39) holds,

$$\begin{aligned}\mu((a,b] \times (c,d]) &= F(b,d) - F(b,c) - F(a,d) + F(a,c)\\ &= (F_X(b) - F_X(a))(F_Y(d) - F_Y(c))\\ &= \mu_X((a,b])\mu_Y((c,d]),\end{aligned} \tag{8.41}$$

where the first equality is by **8.17**. $\mathcal{C}$ is a determining class for $(\mathbb{R}^2,\mathcal{B}^2)$, and μ is defined by the extension of the measure satisfying (8.41) for ordinary rectangles or, equivalently, satisfying (8.39). The Extension Theorem (uniqueness part) shows that this is identical with the product measure satisfying (8.38). The extension to p.d.f.s follows directly from the definition. ■

With more than two variables there are alternative independence concepts (compare §7.3). Variables $X_1,\ldots,X_k$ distributed on the space $(\mathbb{R}^k,\mathcal{B}^k,\mu)$ are said to be *totally independent* if

$$\mu\left(\bigtimes_{i=1}^{k} A_i\right) = \prod_{i=1}^{k} \mu_{X_i}(A_i) \tag{8.42}$$

for all k-tuples of events $A_1,\ldots,A_k \in \mathcal{B}$. By contrast, pairwise independence can hold between each pair X_i,X_j without implying total independence of the set. Another way to think of total independence is in terms of a partitioning of a vector $\boldsymbol{X} = (X_1,\ldots,X_k)'$ into subvectors $\boldsymbol{X}_1$ $(j \times 1)$ and $\boldsymbol{X}_2$ $((k-j) \times 1)$ for $0 < j < k$. Under total independence, the measure of $\boldsymbol{X}$ is always expressible as the product measure of the two subvectors, under all orderings and partitionings of the elements.

9
Expectations

9.1 Averages and Integrals

When it exists, the *expectation*, or *mean*, of a r.v. $X(\omega)$ in a probability space $(\Omega,\mathcal{F},P)$ is the integral

$$E(X) = \int_\Omega X(\omega)dP(\omega). \tag{9.1}$$

$E(X)$ measures the central tendency of the distribution of X. It is sometimes identified with the limiting value of the sample average of realized values x_t drawn in n identical random experiments,

$$\bar{x}_n = \frac{1}{n}\sum_{t=1}^{n} x_t, \tag{9.2}$$

as n becomes large. However, the validity of this hypothesis depends on the method of repeating the experiment. See Part IV for the details, but suffice it to say at this point that the equivalence certainly holds if $E(X)$ exists and the random experiments are independent of one another.

The connection is most evident for simple random variables. If $X = \sum_j x_j 1_{E_j}$ where the $\{E_j\}$ are a partition of Ω, then by **4.4**,

$$E(X) = \sum_j x_j P(E_j). \tag{9.3}$$

When the probabilities are interpreted as relative frequencies of the events $E_j = \{\omega: X(\omega) = x_j\}$ in a large number of drawings from the distribution, (9.2) with large n should approximate (9.3). The values x_j will appear in the sum in a proportion roughly equal to their probability of occurrence.

$E(X)$ has a dual characterization, as an abstract integral on the parent probability space and as a Lebesgue-Stieltjes integral on the line, under the derived distribution. It is equally correct to write either (9.1) or

$$E(X) = \int_{-\infty}^{+\infty} x dF_X(x). \tag{9.4}$$

Which of these representations is adopted is mainly a matter of convenience. If $1_A(\omega)$ is the indicator function of a set $A \in \mathcal{F}$, then

$$E(1_A X) = \int_A X(\omega)dP(\omega) = \int_{X(A)} x dF(x), \tag{9.5}$$

where $X(A) \in \mathcal{B}$ is the image of A under X. Here the abstract integral is obviously the more direct and simple representation, but by the same token, the Stieltjes form is the natural way to represent integration over a set in $\mathcal{B}$.

If the distribution is discrete, X is a simple function and the formula in (9.3) applies directly. Under the derived distribution,

$$E(X) = \sum_j x_j \mu(\{x_j\}), \tag{9.6}$$

where x_j, $j = 1,2,...,$ are the atoms of the distribution.

9.1 Example If X is a Bernoulli variable (**8.6**), $E(X) = 1.p + 0.(1-p) = p$. □

9.2 Example If X is Poisson (**8.8**),

$$E(X) = e^{-\lambda}\sum_{x=1}^{\infty} x\frac{\lambda^x}{x!} = e^{-\lambda}\lambda\sum_{x=1}^{\infty}\frac{\lambda^{x-1}}{(x-1)!} = \lambda. \ \square \tag{9.7}$$

For a continuous distribution, the Lebesgue-Stieltjes integral of x coincides with the integral in ordinary Lebesgue measure of the function $xf(x)$.

9.3 Example For the uniform distribution on the interval $[a,b]$ (**8.13**),

$$E(X) = \frac{1}{b-a}\int_a^b x dx = \tfrac{1}{2}(a+b). \ \square \tag{9.8}$$

9.4 Example For the Gaussian family (**8.19**),

$$E(X) = \frac{1}{\sqrt{2\pi}\sigma}\int x e^{-(x-\mu)^2/2\sigma^2} dx = \mu. \tag{9.9}$$

This can be shown by integration by parts, but for a neater proof see **11.8**. □

In a mixed continuous-discrete distribution with atoms $x_1, x_2, ...,$ we can use the decomposition $F = F_1 + F_2$ where $F_1(x) = \sum_{x_j \le x}\mu_1(\{x_j\})$ and $F_2(x)$ is absolutely continuous with derivative $f_2(x)$. Then

$$E(X) = \sum_j x_j \mu_1(\{x_j\}) + \int x f_2(x) dx. \tag{9.10}$$

The set of atoms has Lebesgue measure zero in $\mathbb{R}$, so there is no need to exclude these from the integral on the right-hand side of (9.10).

Some random variables do not have an expectation.

9.5 Example Recall the condition for integrability in (4.15), and note that for the Cauchy distribution (**8.11**),

$$\frac{1}{\pi}\int_{-a}^{+a}\frac{|x|}{(1+x)^2} dx \to \infty \text{ as } a \to \infty. \ \square \tag{9.11}$$

9.2 Expectations of Functions of X

If X is a r.v. on the probability space $(\mathbb{R},\mathcal{B},\mu)$, and $g: \mathbb{R} \mapsto \mathbb{R}$ is a Borel function, $g\circ X = g(X)$ is a r.v. on the space $(\mathbb{R},\mathcal{B},\mu g^{-1})$, as noted in §8.1. This leads to the following dual characterization of the expectation of a function.

9.6 Theorem If g is a Borel function,

$$E(g(X)) = \int g(x)d\mu(x) = \int y d\mu g^{-1}(y). \tag{9.12}$$

Proof Define a sequence of simple functions $Z_{(n)}: \mathbb{R}^+ \mapsto \mathbb{R}^+$ by

$$Z_{(n)}(x) = \sum_{i=1}^{m}\left(\frac{i-1}{2^n}\right)1_{B_i}(x), \tag{9.13}$$

where $m = n2^n+1$ and $B_i = [2^{-n}(i-1), 2^{-n}i)$ for $i = 1,\ldots,m$. Then, $Z_{(n)}(x) \uparrow x$ for $x \geq 0$, by arguments paralleling **3.28**. According to **3.21**, $(\mathbb{R},\mathcal{B},\mu g^{-1})$ is a measure space where $\mu g^{-1}(B) = \mu(g^{-1}(B))$ for $B \in \mathcal{B}$, and so by the monotone convergence theorem,

$$\int Z_{(n)}(y)d\mu g^{-1}(y) = \sum_{i=1}^{m}\left(\frac{i-1}{2^n}\right)\mu g^{-1}(B_i) \to \int y d\mu g^{-1}(y). \tag{9.14}$$

Consider first the case of non-negative g. Let $1_B(x)$ be the indicator of the set $B \in \mathcal{B}$, and then if g is Borel, so is the composite function

$$(1_B\circ g)(x) = \begin{cases} 1, & g(x) \in B \\ 0, & g(x) \notin B \end{cases} = 1_{g^{-1}(B)}(x). \tag{9.15}$$

Hence, consider the simple function

$$(Z_{(n)}\circ g)(x) = \sum_{i=1}^{m}\left(\frac{i-1}{2^n}\right)(1_{B_i}\circ g)(x) = \sum_{i=1}^{m}\left(\frac{i-1}{2^n}\right)1_{g^{-1}(B_i)}(x). \tag{9.16}$$

By the same arguments as before, $Z_{(n)}\circ g \uparrow g$, and $E(Z_{(n)}\circ g) \to E(g) = \int g d\mu$. However,

$$E(Z_{(n)}\circ g) = \sum_{i=1}^{m}\left(\frac{i-1}{2^n}\right)\mu(g^{-1}(B_i))$$

$$= \sum_{i=1}^{m}\left(\frac{i-1}{2^n}\right)\mu g^{-1}(B_i) = \int Z_{(n)}(y)d\mu g^{-1}(y), \tag{9.17}$$

and (9.12) follows from (9.14).

To extend the result to general g, consider the non-negative functions $g^+ = \max\{g,0\}$ and $g^- = g^+ - g$ separately. It is immediate that

$$E(Z_{(n)}\circ g^+) - E(Z_{(n)}\circ g^-) \to E(g^+) - E(g^-) = E(g), \tag{9.18}$$

so consider each component of this limit separately.

$$E(Z_{(n)}\circ g^+) = \sum_{i=1}^{m}\left(\frac{i-1}{2^n}\right)\mu((g^+)^{-1}(B_i))$$

$$= \sum_{i=1}^{m}\left(\frac{i-1}{2^n}\right)\mu(g^{-1}(B_i)) \to \int_0^\infty y d\mu g^{-1}(y), \tag{9.19}$$

where the second equality holds because $(g^+)^{-1}(B_i) = g^{-1}(B_i)$ for $i \geq 2$ since the elements of B_i are all positive for these cases, whereas for $i = 1$ the term disappears. Similarly, $-Z_n(x) \downarrow x$ for $x < 0$, and

$$-E(Z_{(n)}\circ g^-) = -\sum_{i=1}^{m}\left(\frac{i-1}{2^n}\right)\mu((g^-)^{-1}(B_i))$$

$$= -\sum_{i=1}^{m}\left(\frac{i-1}{2^n}\right)\mu(g^{-1}(B_i^-)) \to \int_{-\infty}^0 y d\mu g^{-1}(y), \tag{9.20}$$

where $B_i^- = (-2^{-n}i, -2^{-n}(i-1)]$, and in this case the second equality holds because $(g^-)^{-1}(B_i) = g^{-1}(-B_i)$ for $i \geq 2$. Hence

$$E(Z_{(n)}\circ g^+) - E(Z_{(n)}\circ g^-) \to \int_{-\infty}^{\infty} y d\mu g^{-1}(y), \tag{9.21}$$

and the theorem follows in view of (9.18). ■

The quantities $E(X^k)$, for integer $k \geq 1$, are called the *moments* of the distribution of X, and for $k > 1$ the *central moments* are defined by

$$E(X - E(X))^k = \sum_{j=0}^{k}\binom{k}{j}E(X^j)(-E(X))^{k-j}. \tag{9.22}$$

A familiar case is the *variance*, $\mathrm{Var}(X) = E(X - E(X))^2 = E(X^2) - E(X)^2$, the usual measure of dispersion about the mean. When the distribution is symmetric, with $P(X - E(X) \in A) = P(E(X) - X \in A)$ for each $A \in \mathcal{B}$, the odd-order central moments are all zero.

9.7 Example. For the Gaussian case (**8.14**), the central moments are

$$E(X-\mu)^k = \begin{cases} \dfrac{k!\sigma^k}{2^{k/2}(k/2)!}, & k \text{ even}, \\ 0, & k \text{ odd}. \end{cases} \tag{9.23}$$

This formula may be derived after some manipulation from equation (11.22) below. $\mathrm{Var}(X) = \sigma^2$, and all the finite-order moments exist although the sequence increases monotonically. □

The existence of a moment of given order requires the existence of the corresponding *absolute moment*. If $E|X|^p < \infty$, for any real $p > 0$, X is sometimes said to belong to the set L_p (of functions Lebesgue-integrable to order p), or otherwise, to be *L_p-bounded*.

9.8 Example For $X \sim N(0,\sigma^2)$, we have, by (8.26),

$$E|X| = 2(2\pi\sigma^2)^{-1/2}\int_0^\infty x e^{-x^2/2\sigma^2}dx \tag{9.24}$$
$$= (2/\pi)^{1/2}\sigma. \ \square$$

Taking the corresponding root of the absolute moment is convenient for purposes of comparison (see **9.23**) and for $X \in L_p$, the *L_p-norm* of X is defined as

$$\|X\|_p = (E|X|^p)^{1/p}. \tag{9.25}$$

The Gaussian distribution possesses all finite-order moments according to (9.23), but its support is none the less the whole of $\mathbb{R}$, and its p-norms are not *uniformly* bounded. If $\|X\|_p$ has a finite limit as $p \to \infty$, it coincides with the essential supremum of X, so that a random variable belonging to L_∞ is bounded almost surely.

9.3 Theorems for the Probabilist's Toolbox

The following inequalities for expected values are exploited in the proof of innumerable theorems in probability. The first is better known as *Chebyshev's inequality* for the special case $p = 2$.

9.9 Markov's inequality For $\varepsilon > 0$ and $p > 0$,

$$P(|X| \geq \varepsilon) \leq \frac{E|X|^p}{\varepsilon^p}. \tag{9.26}$$

Proof $\varepsilon^p(P(|X| \geq \varepsilon) = \varepsilon^p\int_{|x|\geq\varepsilon} dF(x) \leq \int_{|x|\geq\varepsilon} |x|^p dF(x) \leq E(|X|^p)$. ■

This inequality does not bind unless $E|X|^p/\varepsilon^p < 1$, but it shows that if $E|X|^p < \infty$, the tail probabilities converge to zero at the rate ε^{-p} as $\varepsilon \to \infty$. The order of L_p-boundedness measures the tendency of a distribution to generate outliers. The Markov inequality is a special case of (at least) two more general inequalities.

9.10 Corollary For any event $A \in \mathcal{F}$,

$$\varepsilon^p\int_{A\cap\{|X|\geq\varepsilon\}} dP \leq \int_A |X|^p dP. \tag{9.27}$$

Equivalently, $P(\{\omega: |X(\omega)| \geq \varepsilon\} \cap A) \leq E(1_A|X|^p)/\varepsilon^p$.

Proof Obvious from **9.9.** ■

9.11 Corollary Let $g: \mathbb{R} \mapsto \mathbb{R}$ be a function with the property that $x \geq a$ implies $g(x) \geq g(a) > 0$, for a given constant a. Then

$$P(X \geq a) \leq \frac{E(g(X))}{g(a)}. \tag{9.28}$$

Proof $g(a)(P(X \geq a) = g(a)\int_{x \geq a} dF(x) \leq \int_{x \geq a} g(x)dF(x) \leq E(g(X))$. ∎

An increasing function has the requisite property for all $a > 0$.

Let $I \subseteq \mathbb{R}$ be any interval. A function $\phi: I \mapsto \mathbb{R}$ is said to be *convex* on I if

$$\phi((1-\lambda)x + \lambda y) \leq (1-\lambda)\phi(x) + \lambda\phi(y) \tag{9.29}$$

for all $x, y \in I$ and $\lambda \in [0,1]$. If $-\phi$ is convex on I, ϕ is *concave* on I.

9.12 Jensen's inequality If a Borel function ϕ is convex on an interval I containing the support of an integrable r.v. X, where $\phi(X)$ is also integrable,

$$\phi(E(X)) \leq E(\phi(X)). \tag{9.30}$$

For a concave function the reverse inequality holds. □

The intuition here is easily grasped by thinking about a binary r.v. taking values x_1 with probability p and x_2 with probability $1-p$. A convex ϕ is illustrated in Fig. 9.1. $E(X) = px_1 + (1-p)x_2$, whereas $E(\phi(X)) = p\phi(x_1) + (1-p)\phi(x_2)$. This point is mapped from $E(X)$ onto the vertical axis by the chord joining x_1 and x_2 on ϕ, while $\phi(E(X))$ is mapped from the same point by ϕ itself.

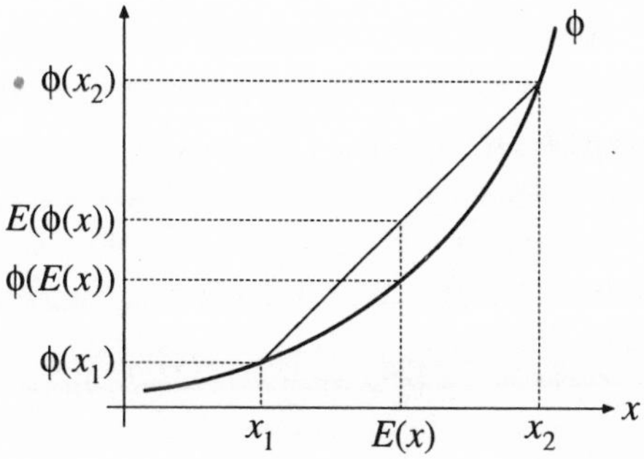

Fig. 9.1

A proof of the inequality is obtained from the following lemma. Let I^o denote the interior of I.

9.13 Lemma If ϕ is convex there exists a function $A(x)$ such that, for all $x \in I^o$ and $y \in I$,

$$A(x)(y-x) \leq \phi(y) - \phi(x). \tag{9.31}$$

Proof A convex function possesses right and left derivatives at all points of I^o.

This follows because (9.29) implies for $h > 0$ that

$$\frac{\phi(x+\lambda h)-\phi(x)}{\lambda h} \le \frac{\phi(x+h)-\phi(x)}{h}, \quad \lambda \in (0,1]. \tag{9.32}$$

The sequence $\{n(\phi(x+1/n)-\phi(x)), n \in \mathbb{N}\}$ is decreasing, and has a limit $\phi'_+(x)$. In the case $h < 0$ the inequality in (9.32) is reversed, showing the existence of $\phi'_-(x)$ as the limit of an increasing sequence. Note that $\phi'_-(x) \le \phi'_+(x)$. Taking the limit as $\lambda \downarrow 0$ with $h > 0$ fixed in (9.32) and $y = x+h$ gives

$$\phi'_-(x)(y-x) \le \phi'_+(x)(y-x) \le \phi(y)-\phi(x) \tag{9.33}$$

whereas the parallel argument with $h < 0$ gives, for $y < x$,

$$\phi'_+(x)(y-x) \le \phi'_-(x)(y-x) \le \phi(y)-\phi(x) \tag{9.34}$$

Inequality (9.31) is therefore satisfied with (say) $A(x) = \phi'_+(x)$. ∎

Proof of 9.12 Set $x = E(X)$, $y = X$ in (9.31) to give

$$A(E(X))(X-E(X)) \le \phi(X)-\phi(E(X)). \tag{9.35}$$

Taking expectations of both sides gives inequality (9.30), since the left-hand side has expectation zero. ∎

Next, we have an alternative approach to bounding tail probabilities which yields the Markov inequality as a corollary.

9.14 Theorem If X is a non-negative r.v. and r > 0,

$$E(X^r) = r\int_0^\infty x^{r-1}P(X > x)dx. \tag{9.36}$$

Proof Integration by parts gives, for some $b > 0$,

$$\begin{aligned}\int_0^b x^r dF(x) &= b^r F(b) - r\int_0^b x^{r-1}F(x)dx \\ &= r\int_0^b x^{r-1}(F(b)-F(x))dx \\ &= r\int_0^b x^{r-1}P(x < X \le b)dx.\end{aligned} \tag{9.37}$$

The theorem follows on letting b tend to infinity. ∎

If the left-hand side of (9.37) diverges, so does the right, and in this sense the theorem is true whether or not $E(X)$ is finite.

9.15 Corollary If X is non-negative and integrable,

$$\int_\varepsilon^\infty xdF = \varepsilon P(X \ge \varepsilon) + \int_\varepsilon^\infty P(X > x)dx. \tag{9.38}$$

Proof Apply **9.14** with $r = 1$ to the r.v. $1_{\{X\geq\varepsilon\}}X$. This gives

$$\begin{aligned}\int_{\varepsilon}^{\infty} xdF &= \int_0^{\infty} P(1_{\{X\geq\varepsilon\}}X > x)dx \\ &= \int_0^{\varepsilon} P(1_{\{X\geq\varepsilon\}}X > x)dx + \int_{\varepsilon}^{\infty} P(X > x)dx \\ &= P(X \geq \varepsilon)\int_0^{\varepsilon} dx + \int_{\varepsilon}^{\infty} P(X > x)dx. \;\blacksquare \end{aligned} \tag{9.39}$$

Not only does (9.38) give the Markov inequality on replacing non-negative X by $|X|^p$ for $p > 0$ and arbitrary X, but the error in the Markov estimate of the tail probability is neatly quantified. Noting that $P(|X| \geq \varepsilon) = P(|X|^p \geq \varepsilon^p)$,

$$\begin{aligned}\varepsilon^p P(|X| \geq \varepsilon) &= \int_{\varepsilon^p}^{\infty} |x|^p dF - \int_{\varepsilon^p}^{\infty} P(|X|^p > x)dx \\ &= E|X|^p - \int_0^{\varepsilon^p} |x|^p dF - \int_{\varepsilon^p}^{\infty} P(|X|^p > x)dx, \end{aligned} \tag{9.40}$$

where both the subtracted terms on the right-hand side are non-negative.

9.4 Multivariate Distributions

From one point of view, the integral of a function of two or more random variables presents no special problems. For example, if

$$g\colon \mathbb{R}^2 \mapsto \mathbb{R}$$

is Borel-measurable, meaning in this case that $g^{-1}(B) \in \mathcal{B}^2$ for every $B \in \mathcal{B}$, then $h(\omega) = g(X(\omega), Y(\omega))$ is just a $\mathcal{F}/\mathcal{B}$-measurable r.v., and

$$E(g(X,Y)) = \int_{\Omega} h(\omega)dP(\omega) \tag{9.41}$$

is its expectation, which involves no new ideas apart from the particular way in which the r.v. $h(\omega)$ happens to be defined.

Alternatively, the Lebesgue-Stieltjes form is

$$E(g(X,Y)) = \int_{\mathbb{R}^2} g(x,y)dF(x,y), \tag{9.42}$$

where $dF(x,y)$ is to be thought of as the limiting case of $\Delta F(x,y)$ defined in (8.30) as the rectangle tends the differential of area. When the distribution is continuous, the integral is the ordinary integral of $g(x,y)f(x,y)$ with respect to Lebesgue product measure. According to Fubini's theorem, it is equivalent to an iterated integral, and may be written

$$E(g(X,Y)) = \int_{-\infty}^{+\infty}\int_{-\infty}^{+\infty} g(x,y)f(x,y)dydx. \tag{9.43}$$

But caution must be exercised with formula (9.42) because this is *not* a double integral in general. It might seem more appropriate to write $d^2F(x,y)$ instead of $dF(x,y)$, but except in the continuous case this would *not* be correct. The abstract notation of (9.41) is often preferable, because it avoids these ambiguities.

In spite of these caveats, the expectation of a function of (say) X alone can in every case be constructed with respect to either the marginal distribution or the joint distribution.

9.16 Theorem $E(g(X)) = \int_{\mathbb{R}^2} g(x)dF(x,y) = \int_{\mathbb{R}} g(x)dF_X(x).$

Proof Define a function

$$g^*\colon \mathbb{R}^2 \mapsto \mathbb{R}$$

by setting $g^*(x,y) = g(x)$, all $y \in \mathbb{R}$. $g^{*-1}(B)$ is a cylinder in $\mathbb{R}^2$ with base $g^{-1}(B) \in \mathcal{B}$ for $B \in \mathcal{B}$, and g^* is $\mathcal{B}^2/\mathcal{B}$-measurable. For non-negative g, let

$$g^*_{(n)} = \sum_{i=1}^{m} \left(\frac{i-1}{2^n}\right) 1_{E_i} \tag{9.44}$$

where $m = n2^n+1$ and $E_i = \{(x,y)\colon 2^{-n}(i-1) \le g^*(x,y) < 2^{-n}i\} \in \mathcal{B}^2$. Since $E_i = A_i \times \mathbb{R}$ where $A_i = \{x\colon 2^{-n}(i-1) \le g(x) < 2^{-n}i\}$, and $\mu_X(A_i) = \mu(E_i)$,

$$E(g^*_{(n)}) = \sum_{i=1}^{m} \left(\frac{i-1}{2^n}\right) \mu(E_i) = \sum_{i=1}^{m} \left(\frac{i-1}{2^n}\right) \mu_X(A_i) = E(g_{(n)}). \tag{9.45}$$

By the monotone convergence theorem the left and right-hand members of (9.45) converge to $E(g^*) = \int g^*(x,y)dF(x,y)$ and $E(g) = \int g(x)dF_X(x)$ respectively. Extend from non-negative to general g to complete the proof. ∎

The means and variances of X and Y are the leading cases of this result. We also have cross moments, and in particular, the *covariance* of X and Y is

$$\mathrm{Cov}(X,Y) = E[(X-E(X))(Y-E(Y))] = E(XY) - E(X)E(Y). \tag{9.46}$$

Fubini's theorem suggests a characterization of pairwise independence:

9.17 Theorem If X and Y are independent r.v.s, $\mathrm{Cov}(\phi(X),\psi(Y)) = 0$ for all pairs of integrable Borel functions ϕ and ψ.

Proof Fubini's theorem gives

$$\begin{aligned} E(\phi(X)\psi(Y)) &= \int_{\mathbb{R}^2} \phi(x)\psi(y)dF(x,y) \\ &= \int_{\mathbb{R}} \phi(x)dF_X(x) \int_{\mathbb{R}} \psi(y)dF_Y(y) \\ &= E(\phi(X))E(\psi(Y)). \;\blacksquare \end{aligned} \tag{9.47}$$

The condition is actually sufficient as well as necessary for independence, although this cannot be shown using the present approach; see **10.25** below.

Extending from the bivariate to the general k-dimensional case adds nothing of substance to the above, and is mainly a matter of appropriate notation. If $\boldsymbol{X}$ is a random k-vector,

$$E(\boldsymbol{X}) = \int \boldsymbol{x}dF(\boldsymbol{x}) \tag{9.48}$$

denotes the k-vector of expectations, $E(X_i)$ for $i = 1,...,k$. The variance of a scalar r.v. generalizes to the covariance matrix of a random vector. The $k\times k$ matrix,

$$\boldsymbol{XX}' = \begin{bmatrix} X_1^2 & X_1X_2 & \dots & X_1X_k \\ X_2X_1 & X_2^2 & & \vdots \\ \vdots & & \ddots & \vdots \\ X_kX_1 & \dots & \dots & X_k^2 \end{bmatrix}, \tag{9.49}$$

is called the outer product of $\boldsymbol{X}$, and $E(\boldsymbol{XX}')$ is the $k\times k$ positive semi-definite matrix whose elements are the expectations of the elements of $\boldsymbol{XX}'$. The *covariance matrix* of $\boldsymbol{X}$ is

$$\mathrm{Var}(\boldsymbol{X}) = E[(\boldsymbol{X}-E(\boldsymbol{X}))(\boldsymbol{X}-E(\boldsymbol{X}))'] = E(\boldsymbol{XX}')-E(\boldsymbol{X})E(\boldsymbol{X})'. \tag{9.50}$$

$\mathrm{Var}(\boldsymbol{X})$ is positive semi-definite, generalizing the non-negative property of a scalar variance. It is of full rank (notwithstanding that $\boldsymbol{XX}'$ has rank 1) unless an element of $\boldsymbol{X}$ is an exact linear function of the remainder. The following generalizes **4.7**, the proof being essentially an exercise in interpreting the matrix formulae.

9.18 Theorem If $\boldsymbol{Y} = \boldsymbol{BX}+\boldsymbol{c}$ where $\boldsymbol{X}$ is an k-vector with $E(\boldsymbol{X}) = \boldsymbol{\mu}$ and $\mathrm{Var}(\boldsymbol{X}) = \boldsymbol{\Sigma}$, and $\boldsymbol{B}$ and $\boldsymbol{c}$ are respectively an $m\times k$ constant matrix and a constant m-vector, then

(i) $E(\boldsymbol{Y}) = \boldsymbol{B\mu}+\boldsymbol{c}$.
(ii) $\mathrm{Var}(\boldsymbol{Y}) = \boldsymbol{B\Sigma B}'$. □

Note that if $m > k$ $\mathrm{Var}(\boldsymbol{Y})$ is singular, having rank k.

9.19 Example If a random vector $\boldsymbol{Z} = (Z_1,...,Z_k)'$ is standard Gaussian (**8.19**), it is easy to verify, applying **9.17**, that $E(\boldsymbol{Z}) = \boldsymbol{0}$ and $E(\boldsymbol{ZZ}') = \boldsymbol{I}_k$. Applying **9.18** to the transformation in (8.35) produces $E(\boldsymbol{X}) = \boldsymbol{\mu}$ and

$$\mathrm{Var}(\boldsymbol{X}) = E(\boldsymbol{X}-\boldsymbol{\mu})(\boldsymbol{X}-\boldsymbol{\mu})' = E(\boldsymbol{AZZ}'\boldsymbol{A}') = \boldsymbol{A}E(\boldsymbol{ZZ}')\boldsymbol{A}' = \boldsymbol{AA}' = \boldsymbol{\Sigma}. \ \square$$

9.5 More Theorems for the Toolbox

The following collection of theorems, together with the Jensen and Markov inequalities of §9.3, constitute the basic toolbox for the proof of results in probability. The student will find that it will suffice to have his/her thumb in these pages to be able to follow a gratifyingly large number of the arguments to be encountered in subsequent chapters.

9.20 Cauchy-Schwartz inequality

$$E(XY)^2 \le E(X^2)E(Y^2), \tag{9.51}$$

with equality attained when $Y = cX$, c a constant.

Proof By linearity of the integral,

$$E[(aX+Y)^2] = a^2E(X^2) + 2aE(XY) + E(Y^2) \ge 0$$

for any constant a. (9.51) follows on setting $a = -E(XY)/E(X^2)$, and holds as an equality if and only if $aX+Y = 0$. ■

The *correlation coefficient*, $r_{XY} = \text{Cov}(X,Y)/(\text{Var}(X)\text{Var}(Y))^{1/2}$, accordingly lies in the interval $[-1,+1]$.

The Cauchy-Schwartz inequality is a special case (for $p = 2$) of the following.

9.21 Hölder's inequality For any $p \ge 1$,

$$E|XY| \le \|X\|_p\|Y\|_q. \tag{9.52}$$

where $q = p/(p-1)$ if $p > 1$, and $q = \infty$ if $p = 1$.

Proof The proof for the case $p > 1$ requires a small lemma.

9.22 Lemma For any pair of non-negative numbers a,b,

$$ab \le \frac{a^p}{p} + \frac{b^q}{q}. \tag{9.53}$$

Proof If either a or b are zero this is trivial. If both are positive, let $s = p\log a$ and $t = q\log b$. Inverting these relations gives $a = e^{s/p}$, $b = e^{t/q}$, $ab = e^{s/p+t/q}$, and (9.53) follows from the fact that e^x is a convex function of x, noting $1/q = 1 - 1/p$ and applying (9.29). ■

Choose $a = |X|/\|X\|_p$, $b = |Y|/\|Y\|_q$. For these choices, $E(a^p) = E(b^q) = 1$, and

$$\frac{E|XY|}{\|X\|_p\|Y\|_q} = E(ab) \le 1/p + 1/q = 1. \tag{9.54}$$

For the case $p = 1$, the inequality reduces to $E|XY| \le E|X|\text{ess sup } Y$, which holds since $Y \le \text{ess sup } Y$ a.s., by definition. ■

The Hölder inequality spawns a range of useful corollaries and special cases, including the following.

9.23 Liapunov's inequality (norm inequality) If $r > p > 0$, then $\|X\|_r \ge \|X\|_p$.

Proof Let $Z = |X|^p$, $Y = 1$, $s = r/p$. Then, (9.52) gives $E|ZY| \le \|Z\|_s\|Y\|_{s/(s-1)}$, or

$$E(|X|^p) \le E(|X|^{ps})^{1/s} = E(|X|^r)^{p/r}. \blacksquare \tag{9.55}$$

This result is also obtainable as a corollary of the Jensen inequality.

9.24 Corollary For each $A \in \mathcal{F}$ and $1/p + 1/q = 1$,

$$\int_A |XY| dP \le \left(\int_A |X|^p dP\right)^{1/p} \left(\int_A |Y|^q dP\right)^{1/q}.$$

Proof In (9.52), replace X by $X1_A$ and Y by $Y1_A$. ■

Alternative variants of the result are not explicitly probabilistic in character.

9.25 Corollary Let $x_1,...,x_n$ and $y_1,...,y_n$ be any sequences of numbers. Then

$$\sum_{i=1}^n |x_i y_i| \le \left(\sum_{i=1}^n |x_i|^p\right)^{1/p} \left(\sum_{i=1}^n |y_i|^q\right)^{1/q} \text{ for } 1/p + 1/q = 1. \ \square$$

9.26 Corollary Let $f(t)$ and $g(t)$ be Lebesgue-integrable functions of a real variable. Then

$$\int_{-\infty}^{\infty} |f(t)g(t)| dt \le \left(\int_{-\infty}^{\infty} |f(t)|^p dt\right)^{1/p} \left(\int_{-\infty}^{\infty} |g(t)|^q dt\right)^{1/q} \text{ for } 1/p + 1/q = 1. \ \square$$

Proofs are left as an exercise. The sequences in **9.25** and the functions in **9.26** can be either real or complex-valued (see §11.2).

9.27 Minkowski's inequality For $r \ge 1$, $\|X+Y\|_r \le \|X\|_r + \|Y\|_r$.

Proof For $r = 1$ this follows direct from the triangle inequality,

$$|X+Y| \le |X| + |Y|, \tag{9.56}$$

on taking expectations. For $r > 1$, note that

$$\begin{aligned} E|X+Y|^r &= E(|X+Y|\,|X+Y|^{r-1}) \\ &\le E((|X| + |Y|)|X+Y|^{r-1}) \\ &= E(|X|\,|X+Y|^{r-1}) + E(|Y|\,|X+Y|^{r-1}). \end{aligned} \tag{9.57}$$

Applying the Hölder inequality to the two right-hand-side terms yields

$$E|X+Y|^r \le (\|X\|_r + \|Y\|_r)(E|X+Y|^r)^{1-1/r}. \tag{9.58}$$

Cancelling $E|X+Y|^r$ and rearranging gives the result. ■

By recursive application to the sum of m variables, the Minkowski inequality generalizes directly to

$$\left\|\sum_{i=1}^m X_i\right\|_r \le \sum_{i=1}^m \|X_i\|_r \tag{9.59}$$

for $r \ge 1$. For an infinite series one can write

$$\left\| \sum_{i=1}^{\infty} X_i \right\|_r \le \sum_{i=1}^{m} \|X_i\|_r + \left\| \sum_{i=m+1}^{\infty} X_i \right\|_r . \tag{9.60}$$

If $\|\sum_{i=m+1}^{\infty} X_i\|_r \to 0$ as $m \to \infty$ it is permissable to conclude that

$$\left\| \sum_{i=1}^{\infty} X_i \right\|_r \le \sum_{i=1}^{\infty} \|X_i\|_r, \tag{9.61}$$

not ruling out the possibility that the right-hand side is infinite.

9.28 Loève's c_r inequality For $r > 0$,

$$E\left| \sum_{i=1}^{m} X_i \right|^r \le c_r \sum_{i=1}^{m} E|X_i|^r, \tag{9.62}$$

where $c_r = 1$ when $r \le 1$, and $c_r = m^{r-1}$ when $r \ge 1$.

Proof This goes by proving the inequality

$$\left| \sum_{i=1}^{m} a_i \right|^r \le c_r \sum_{i=1}^{m} |a_i|^r \tag{9.63}$$

for real numbers $a_1,\ldots,a_n$, then substituting random variables and taking expectations. Since $|\sum_{i=1}^{m} a_i|^r \le (\sum_{i=1}^{m} |a_i|)^r$, it will suffice to let the a_i be non-negative. For the case $0 < r \le 1$, $0 \le z_i \le 1$ implies $z_i^r \ge z_i$ and hence if $\sum_{i=1}^{m} z_i = 1$, $\sum_{i=1}^{m} z_i^r \ge 1$. (9.63) follows on putting $z_i = a_i/(\sum_{j=1}^{m} a_j)$. For $r \ge 1$, on the other hand, convexity implies directly that

$$\left(\frac{1}{m} \sum_{i=1}^{m} a_i \right)^r \le \frac{1}{m} \sum_{i=1}^{m} a_i^r. \ \blacksquare$$

9.29 Theorem If X, Y, and Z are non-negative r.v.s satisfying $X \le a(Y+Z)$ a.s. for a constant $a > 0$, then, for any constant $M > 0$,

$$E(1_{\{X>M\}}X) \le 2a\big(E(1_{\{Y>M/2a\}}Y) + E(1_{\{Z>M/2a\}}Z)\big). \tag{9.64}$$

Proof If we can prove the almost sure inequality

$$1_{\{X>M\}}X \le 2a\big(1_{\{Y>M/2a\}}Y + 1_{\{Z>M/2a\}}Z\big), \text{ a.s.,} \tag{9.65}$$

the theorem will follow on taking expectations. $1_{\{X>M\}}X$ is the r.v. that is equal to X if $X > M$ and 0 otherwise. If $X \le M$ (9.65) is immediate. At least one of the inequalities $Y \ge X/2a$, $Z \ge X/2a$ must hold, and if $X > M$, (9.65) is no less obviously true. ■

9.6 Random Variables Depending on a Parameter

Let $G(\omega,\theta)$: $\Omega \times \Theta \mapsto \mathbb{R}$, $\Theta \subseteq \mathbb{R}$, denote a random function of a real variable θ, or in other words, a family of random variables indexed on points of the real line.

The following results, due to Cramér (1946), are easy consequences of the dominated convergence theorem.

9.30 Theorem Suppose that for each $\omega \in C$, with $P(C) = 1$, $G(\omega,\theta)$ is continuous at a point θ_0, and $|G(\omega,\theta)| < Y(\omega)$ for each θ in an open neighbourhood N_0 of θ_0 where $E(Y) < \infty$. Then

$$\lim_{\theta\to\theta_0} E(G(\theta)) = E(G(\theta_0)). \tag{9.66}$$

Proof Passage to a limit θ_0 through a continuum of points in Θ, as indicated in (9.66), is implied by the convergence of a countable sequence in Θ. Let $\{\theta_\nu, \nu \in \mathbb{N}\}$ be such a sequence, in N_0, converging to θ_0. Putting $G_\nu(\omega) = G(\omega,\theta_\nu)$ defines a countable sequence of r.v.s. and $\limsup_\nu G_\nu(\omega)$ and $\liminf_\nu G_\nu(\omega)$ are r.v.s by **3.26**. By continuity, they are equal to each other and to $G(\omega,\theta_0)$ for $\omega \in C$; in other words, $G(\theta_\nu) \to G(\theta_0)$ a.s. The result follows from the dominated convergence theorem. ∎

9.31 Theorem If, for each $\omega \in C$ with $P(C) = 1$, $(dG/d\theta)(\omega)$ exists at a point θ_0 and

$$\left|\frac{G(\omega,\theta_0+h) - G(\omega,\theta_0)}{h}\right| < Y_1(\omega)$$

for $0 \le h \le h_1$, where $E(Y_1) < \infty$ and h_1 is independent of ω, then

$$\frac{d}{d\theta}E(G)\bigg|_{\theta=\theta_0} = E\left(\frac{dG}{d\theta}\bigg|_{\theta=\theta_0}\right). \tag{9.67}$$

Proof The argument goes like the preceding one, by considering a real sequence $\{h_\nu\}$ tending to zero through positive values and hence the sequence of r.v.s $\{H_\nu\}$ where $H_\nu = [G(\theta_0+h_\nu) - G(\theta_0)]/h_\nu$, whose limit $H = H(\theta_0)$ exists by assumption. ∎

The same sort of results hold for integrals. Fubini's Theorem provides the extension to general double integrals. The following result for Riemann integrals on intervals of the line is no more than a special case of Fubini, but it is useful to note the requisite assumptions in common notation with the above.

9.32 Theorem Suppose that for each $\omega \in C$, with $P(C) = 1$, $G(\omega,\theta)$ is continuous on a finite open interval (a,b), and $|G(\omega,\theta)| < Y_2(\omega)$ for $a < \theta < b$, where $E(Y_2) < \infty$. Then

$$\int_a^b E(G(\theta))d\theta = E\left(\int_a^b G(\theta)d\theta\right). \tag{9.68}$$

If $\int_0^\infty |G(\omega,\theta)|d\theta < Y_3(\omega)$ for $\omega \in C$ and $E(Y_3) < \infty$, (9.68) holds for either or both of $a = -\infty$ and $b = +\infty$.

Proof For the case of finite a and b, consider $H(\omega,t) = \int_a^t G(\omega,\theta)d\theta$. This has the properties $|H(\omega,t)| < (b-a)Y_2(\omega)$, and $|(dH/dt)(\omega)| = |G(\omega,t)| < Y_2(\omega)$, for each $t \in (a,b)$. Hence, $E(H(t))$ exists for each t, and by **9.31**,

$$\frac{d}{dt}E(H(t)) = E\left(\frac{dH}{dt}\right) = E(G(t)). \tag{9.69}$$

$E(G(t))$ is continuous on (a,b) by the a.s continuity of G and **9.30**, and hence

$$\Delta(t) = \int_a^t E(G(\theta))d\theta - E(H(t)) \tag{9.70}$$

is differentiable on (a,b), and $d\Delta/dt = 0$ at each point by (9.69). But by definition, $H(\omega,a) = 0$ for $\omega \in C$, so that $\Delta(a) = 0$, and hence $\Delta(b) = 0$ which is equivalent to (9.68).

Under the stated integrability condition on $G(\omega,\theta)$, $\int_{-\infty}^{\infty} G(\omega,\theta)d\theta$ exists and is finite on C. Hence $H(\omega,t) = \int_{-\infty}^{t} G(\omega,\theta)d\theta$ is well defined and has an expectation for all $t \in \mathbb{R}$, and the argument above goes through with $a = -\infty$ and/or $b = \infty$. ■

10
Conditioning

10.1 Conditioning in Product Measures

It is difficult to do justice to conditioning at an elementary level. Without resort to some measure-theoretic insights, one can get only so far with the theory before running into problems. There are none the less some relatively simple results which apply to a restricted (albeit important) class of distributions. We introduce the topic by way of this 'naive' approach, and so demonstrate the difficulties that arise, before going on to see how they can be resolved.

In the bivariate context, the natural question to pose is usually: 'if we know $X = x$, what is the best predictor of Y?' For a random real pair $\{X,Y\}$ on $(\Omega,\mathcal{F},P)$ we can evidently define (see §7.2) a class of conditional distribution functions for Y. For any $A \in \mathcal{B}$ such that $P(X \in A) > 0$, let

$$F(y|X \in A) = \frac{P(X \in A,\ Y \le y)}{P(X \in A)}. \tag{10.1}$$

This corresponds to the idea of working in the trace of $(\Omega,\mathcal{F},P)$ with respect to A, once A is known to have occurred. Proceeding in this way, we can attempt to construct a theory of conditioning for random variables based on the c.d.f. We may tentatively define the *conditional distribution function*, $F(y|x)$, when it exists, as a mapping from $\mathbb{R}^2$ to $\mathbb{R}$ which for fixed $x \in \mathbb{R}$ is a non-decreasing, right-continuous function of y with $F(-\infty|x) = 0$ and $F(+\infty|x) = 1$, and which for fixed $y \in \mathbb{R}$ satisfies the equation

$$P(X \in A,\ Y \le y) = \int_A F(y|x)dF_X(x) \tag{10.2}$$

for any $A \in \mathcal{B}$ (compare Rao 1965: §2a.8). Think of the graph of $F(y|x)$ in y-space as the profile of a 'slice' through the surface of the joint distribution function, parallel to the y-axis, at the point x.

However, much care is needed in interpreting this construction. Unlike the ordinary c.d.f., it does not represent a probability in general. If we try to interpret it as $P(Y \le y|X = x)$, we face the possibility that $P(X = x) = 0$, as in a continuous distribution. Since the integral of $F(y|x)$ over a set in the marginal distribution of X yields a probability, as in (10.2), it might even be treated as a type of density function. Taking $A = \{X \le x\}$ shows that we would need

$$F(x,y) = \int_{-\infty}^{x} F(y|\xi)dF_X(\xi) = \int_{-\infty}^{x}\int_{-\infty}^{y} dF(\upsilon|\xi)dF_X(\xi) \tag{10.3}$$

to hold. Since $F(x,y)$ is an integral over $\mathbb{R}^2$, Fubini's theorem implies that $F(y|x)$ is well defined *only* when the integrals in (10.3) are with respect to a product measure.

If X and Y are independent we can say unambiguously (but not very usefully) that $F(y|x) = F_Y(y)$. $F(y|x)$ is also well defined for continuous distributions. Let S_X denote the support of X (the set on which $f_X > 0$); the conditional p.d.f. is

$$f(y|x) = \frac{f(x,y)}{f_X(x)}, \quad x \in S_X, \tag{10.4}$$

where $f_X(x)$ is the marginal density of X. We may validly write, for $A \in \mathcal{B} \cap S_X$,

$$P(X \in A,\ Y \leq y) = \int_A \int_{-\infty}^{y} f(\upsilon|x) f_X(x) dx d\upsilon = \int_A F(y|x) f_X(x) dx \tag{10.5}$$

where

$$F(y|x) = \int_{-\infty}^{y} f(\upsilon|x) d\upsilon. \tag{10.6}$$

The second equality of (10.5) follows by Fubini's theorem, since the function $f(x,y)$ is integrated with respect to Lebesgue product measure. However, (10.6) appears to exist by a trick, rather than to have a firm relationship with our intuition. The problem is that we cannot work with the trace $(\Lambda, \mathcal{F}_\Lambda, P_\Lambda)$ when $\Lambda = \{\omega\colon X(\omega) = x\}$ and $P(\Lambda) = 0$, because then $P_\Lambda = P/P(\Lambda)$ is undefined. It is not clear what it means to 'consider the case when $\{X = x\}$ has occurred' when this event fails to occur almost surely.

Except in special cases such as the above, the factorization $dF(y,x) = dF(y|x)dF_X(x)$ is not legitimate, but with this very important caveat we can define the mean and other moments of the conditional distribution. The *conditional expectation* of a measurable function $g(X,Y)$, given $X = x$, can be defined as

$$E\big(g(X,Y)|x\big) = \int_{-\infty}^{+\infty} g(x,y) dF(y|x), \tag{10.7}$$

also written as $E\big(g(X,Y)|X = x\big)$. The simplest case is where $g(X,Y)$ is just Y. $E(Y|x)$ is to be understood in terms of the attempt of an observer to predict Y after the realization of X has been observed. When X and Y are independent, $E(Y|x) = E(Y)$, where $E(Y)$ is the ordinary expectation of Y, also called the marginal or unconditional expectation. In this case, the knowledge that $X = x$ is no help in predicting Y.

10.1 Example These concepts apply to the bivariate Gaussian distribution. From (8.36), the density is

$$f(x,y) = \frac{1}{2\pi \begin{vmatrix} \sigma_{11} & \sigma_{12} \\ \sigma_{12} & \sigma_{22} \end{vmatrix}^{1/2}} \exp\left\{ -\tfrac{1}{2}[x-\mu_1,\ y-\mu_2] \begin{bmatrix} \sigma_{11} & \sigma_{12} \\ \sigma_{12} & \sigma_{22} \end{bmatrix}^{-1} \begin{bmatrix} x-\mu_1 \\ y-\mu_2 \end{bmatrix} \right\}$$

$$= \frac{1}{2\pi(\sigma_{11}\sigma_{22} - \sigma_{12}^2)^{1/2}} \exp\left\{ -\frac{\left((y-\mu_2) - \frac{\sigma_{12}}{\sigma_{11}}(x-\mu_1) \right)^2}{2\left(\sigma_{22} - \frac{\sigma_{12}^2}{\sigma_{11}}\right)} - \frac{(x-\mu_1)^2}{2\sigma_{11}} \right\}, \quad (10.8)$$

where the last equality is got by completing the square in the exponent. Evidently, $f(x,y) = f(y|x)f_X(x)$ where

$$f(y|x) = \frac{1}{\sqrt{2\pi}\left(\sigma_{22} - \frac{\sigma_{12}^2}{\sigma_{11}}\right)^{1/2}} \exp\left\{ -\frac{\left((y-\mu_2) - \frac{\sigma_{12}}{\sigma_{11}}(x-\mu_1) \right)^2}{2\left(\sigma_{22} - \frac{\sigma_{12}^2}{\sigma_{11}}\right)} \right\} \quad (10.9)$$

and

$$f_X(x) = \frac{1}{\sqrt{2\pi\sigma_{11}}} \exp\left\{ -\frac{(x-\mu_1)^2}{2\sigma_{11}} \right\}. \quad (10.10)$$

Thus,

$$E(Y|x) = \mu_2 + \frac{\sigma_{12}}{\sigma_{22}}(x-\mu_1), \quad (10.11)$$

and

$$\mathrm{Var}(Y|x) = \sigma_{22} - \frac{\sigma_{12}^2}{\sigma_{11}}. \quad (10.12)$$

If $\sigma_{12} = 0$, $f(y|x)$ reduces to $f_Y(y)$, so that the joint density is the product of the marginals, and x and y are independent. □

10.2 Conditioning on a Sigma Field

In view of the limitations of working directly with the distribution of (X,Y), we pursue the approach introduced in §7.2, to represent partial knowledge of the distribution of Y by specifying a σ-field of events $\mathcal{G} \subseteq \mathcal{F}$ such that, for each $G \in \mathcal{G}$, an observer knows whether or not the realized outcome belongs to G.

The idea of knowing the value of a random variable is captured by the concept of subfield measurability. A random variable $X(\omega)$: $\Omega \mapsto \mathbb{R}$ is said to be measurable with respect to a σ-field $\mathcal{G} \subset \mathcal{F}$ if

$$X^{-1}(B) = \{\omega: X(\omega) \in B\} \in \mathcal{G}, \text{ for all } B \in \mathcal{B}. \quad (10.13)$$

The implication of the condition $\mathcal{G} \subset \mathcal{F}$ is that the r.v. X is not a complete representation of the random outcome ω. We denote by $\sigma(X)$ the intersection of all σ-fields with respect to which X is measurable, called the σ-field generated by X. If, on being confronted with the distribution of a random pair $(X(\omega),Y(\omega))$, we learn that $X = x$, we shall know whether or not each of the events $G \in \sigma(X)$ has occurred by determining whether $X(G)$ contains x. The image of each $G \in \sigma(X)$ under the mapping

$$(X(\omega),Y(\omega))\colon \Omega \mapsto \mathbb{R}^2$$

is a cylinder set in $\mathbb{R}^2$, and the p.m. defined on $\sigma(X)$ is the marginal distribution of X.

10.2 Example The knowledge that $x_1 \le X \le x_2$ can be represented by

$$\mathcal{H} = \sigma(\{(-\infty, x]\colon x < x_1\}, \{[x, \infty)\colon x > x_2\}, \mathbb{R}).$$

Satisfy yourself that for every element of this σ-field we know whether or not X belongs to the set; also that it contains all sets about which we possess this knowledge. The closer together x_1 and x_2 are, the more sets there are in $\mathcal{H}$. When $x_1 = x_2$, $\mathcal{H} = \sigma(X)$, and when $x_1 = -\infty$, $x_2 = +\infty$, $\mathcal{H} = \mathcal{T} = \{\emptyset,\mathbb{R}\}$. □

The relationships between transformations and subfield measurability are summarized in the next theorem, of which the first part is an easy consequence of the definitions but the second is trickier. If two random variables are measurable with respect to the same subfield, the implication is that they contain the same information; knowledge of one is equivalent to knowledge of the other. This means that *every* Borel set is the image of a Borel set under g^{-1}. This is a stronger condition than measurability, and requires that g is an isomorphism. It suffices for g to be a homeomorphism, although this is not necessary as was shown in **3.23**.

10.3 Theorem Let X be a r.v. on the space $(\mathbb{S},\mathcal{B}_{\mathbb{S}},\mu)$, and let $Y = g(X)$ where $g\colon \mathbb{S} \mapsto \mathbb{T}$ is a Borel function, with $\mathbb{S} \subseteq \mathbb{R}$ and $\mathbb{T} \subseteq \mathbb{R}$.

(i) $\sigma(Y) \subseteq \sigma(X)$.

(ii) $\sigma(Y) = \sigma(X)$ iff g is a Borel-measurable isomorphism.

Proof Each $B \in \mathcal{B}_{\mathbb{T}}$ has an image in $\mathcal{B}_{\mathbb{S}}$ under g^{-1}, which in turn has an image in $\sigma(X)$ under X^{-1}. This proves (i).

To prove (ii), define a class of subsets of $\mathbb{S}$, $\mathcal{C} = \{g^{-1}(B)\colon B \in \mathcal{B}_{\mathbb{T}}\}$. To every $A \subseteq \mathbb{S}$ there corresponds (since g is a mapping) a set $B \subseteq \mathbb{T}$ such that $A = g^{-1}(B)$, and making this substitution gives

$$\mathcal{B}_{\mathbb{S}} \subseteq \{A\colon g(A) \in \mathcal{B}_{\mathbb{T}}\} = \{g^{-1}(B)\colon g(g^{-1}(B)) \in \mathcal{B}_{\mathbb{T}}\} = \mathcal{C}, \qquad (10.14)$$

where the inclusion is by measurability of g^{-1}, and the second equality is because $g(g^{-1}(B)) = B$ for any $B \subseteq \mathbb{T}$, since g is 1-1 onto. It follows from (10.14) that

$$\{X^{-1}(A) \subseteq \Omega\colon A \in \mathcal{B}_{\mathbb{S}}\} \subseteq \{X^{-1}(g^{-1}(B)) \subseteq \Omega\colon B \in \mathcal{B}_{\mathbb{T}}\}. \qquad (10.15)$$

If Y is $\mathcal{G}$-measurable for some σ-field $\mathcal{G} \subseteq \mathcal{F}$ (such that $\mathcal{G}$ contains the sets of the right-hand member of (10.15)), then X is also $\mathcal{G}$-measurable. In particular, $\sigma(X) \subseteq \sigma(Y)$. Part (i) then implies $\sigma(X) = \sigma(Y)$, proving sufficiency of the conditions.

To show the necessity, suppose first that g is not 1-1 and $g(x_1) = g(x_2) = y$

(say) for $x_1 \neq x_2$. The sets $\{x_1\}$ and $\{x_2\}$ are elements of $\mathcal{B}_{\mathbb{S}}$ but not of $\mathcal{C}$, which contains only $g^{-1}(\{y\}) = \{x_1\} \cup \{x_2\}$. Hence, $\mathcal{B}_{\mathbb{S}} \not\subseteq \mathcal{C}$, and $\exists$ a $\mathcal{B}_{\mathbb{S}}$-set A for which there is no $\mathcal{B}_{\mathbb{T}}$-set B having the property $g^{-1}(B) = A$. This implies that $X^{-1}(A) \in \sigma(X)$ but $\notin \sigma(Y)$, so that $\sigma(Y) \subset \sigma(X)$.

We may therefore assume that g is 1-1. If g^{-1} is not Borel-measurable, then by definition $\exists\, A = g^{-1}(B) \in \mathcal{B}_{\mathbb{S}}$ such that $g(A) = B \notin \mathcal{B}_{\mathbb{T}}$, and hence $A \notin \mathcal{C}$; and again, $\mathcal{B}_{\mathbb{S}} \not\subseteq \mathcal{C}$, so that $\sigma(Y) \subset \sigma(X)$ by the same argument. This completes the proof of necessity. ■

We should briefly note the generalization of these results to the vector case. A random vector $\boldsymbol{X}(\omega)$: $\Omega \mapsto \mathbb{R}^k$ is measurable with respect to $\mathcal{G} \subseteq \mathcal{F}$ if

$$\boldsymbol{X}^{-1}(B) = \{\omega: \boldsymbol{X}(\omega) \in B\} \in \mathcal{G},\ \forall\ B \in \mathcal{B}^k. \tag{10.16}$$

If $\sigma(\boldsymbol{X})$ is the σ-field generated by $\boldsymbol{X}$, we have the following result.

10.4 Theorem Let $\boldsymbol{X}$ be a random vector on the probability space $(\mathbb{S},\mathcal{B}^k_{\mathbb{S}},\mu)$ where $\mathbb{S} \subseteq \mathbb{R}^k$ and $\mathcal{B}^k_{\mathbb{S}} = \{B \cap \mathbb{S}: B \in \mathcal{B}^k\}$, and consider a Borel function

$$\boldsymbol{Y} = \boldsymbol{g}(\boldsymbol{X}): \mathbb{S} \mapsto \mathbb{T},\ \ \mathbb{T} \subseteq \mathbb{R}^m. \tag{10.17}$$

(i) $\sigma(\boldsymbol{Y}) \subseteq \sigma(\boldsymbol{X})$.
(ii) If $m = k$ and $\boldsymbol{g}$ is 1-1 with Borel inverse, then $\sigma(\boldsymbol{Y}) = \sigma(\boldsymbol{X})$.

Proof This follows the proof of **10.3** almost word for word, with the substitutions of $\mathcal{B}^k_{\mathbb{S}}$ and $\mathcal{B}^k_{\mathbb{T}}$ for $\mathcal{B}_{\mathbb{S}}$ and $\mathcal{B}_{\mathbb{T}}$, $\boldsymbol{X}$ and $\boldsymbol{Y}$ for X and Y, and so forth. ■

10.3 Conditional Expectations

Let Y be an integrable r.v. on $(\Omega,\mathcal{F},P)$ and $\mathcal{G}$ a σ-field contained in $\mathcal{F}$. The term *conditional expectation*, and symbol $E(Y|\mathcal{G})$, can be used to refer to any integrable, $\mathcal{G}$-measurable r.v. having the property

$$\int_G E(Y|\mathcal{G})dP = \int_G YdP = E(Y|G)P(G),\ \text{all}\ G \in \mathcal{G}. \tag{10.18}$$

Intuitively, $E(Y|\mathcal{G})(\omega)$ represents the prediction of $Y(\omega)$ made by an observer having information $\mathcal{G}$, when the outcome ω is realized. The second equality of (10.18) supplies the definition of the constant $E(Y|G)$, although this need not exist unless $P(G) > 0$. The two extreme cases are $E(Y|\mathcal{F}) = Y$ a.s., and $E(Y|\mathcal{T}) = E(Y)$ a.s., where $\mathcal{T}$ denotes the trivial σ-field with elements $\{\Omega,\varnothing\}$. Note that $\Omega \in \mathcal{G}$, so integrability of Y is necessary for the existence of $E(Y|\mathcal{G})$.

The conditional expectation is a slightly bizarre construction, not only a r.v., but evidently not even an integral. To demonstrate that an object satisfying (10.18) actually does exist, consider initially the case $Y \geq 0$, and define

$$\nu(G) = \int_G YdP. \tag{10.19}$$

10.5 Theorem ν is a measure, and is absolutely continuous with respect to P.

Proof Clearly, $\nu(G) \geq 0$, and $P(G) = 0$ implies $\nu(G) = 0$. It remains to show countable additivity. If $\{G_j\}$ is a disjoint sequence, then

$$\nu\Big(\bigcup_j G_j\Big) = \int_{\bigcup_j G_j} YdP = \sum_j \int_{G_j} YdP = \sum_j \nu(G_j), \tag{10.20}$$

where the second equality holds under disjointness. ∎

So the implication of (10.18) for non-negative Y turns out to be that $E(Y|\mathcal{G})$ is the Radon-Nikodym derivative of ν with respect to P. The extension from non-negative to general Y is easy, since we can write $Y = Y^+ - Y^-$ where Y^+ and Y^- are non-negative, and from (10.18), $E(Y|\mathcal{G}) = E(Y^+|\mathcal{G}) - E(Y^-|\mathcal{G})$, where both of the right-hand r.v.s are Radon-Nikodym derivatives.

The Radon-Nikodym theorem therefore establishes the existence of $E(Y|\mathcal{G})$; at any rate, it establishes the existence of at least one r.v. satisfying (10.18). It does not guarantee that there is only one such r.v., and in the event of non-uniqueness, we speak of the different *versions* of $E(Y|\mathcal{G})$. The possibility of multiple versions is rarely of practical concern since **10.5** assures us that they are all equal to one another a.s.$[P]$, but it does make it necessary to qualify any statement we make about conditional expectations with the tag 'a.s.', to indicate that there may be sets of measure zero on which our assertions do not apply.

In the bivariate context, $E(Y|\sigma(X))$, which we can write as $E(Y|X)$ when the context is clear, is interpreted as the prediction of Y made by observers who observe X. This notion is related to (10.7) by thinking of $E(Y|x)$ as a drawing from the distribution of $E(Y|X)$.

10.6 Example In place of (10.11) we write

$$E(Y|X)(\omega) = \mu_2 + \frac{\sigma_{12}}{\sigma_{11}}(X(\omega) - \mu_1), \tag{10.21}$$

which is a function of $X(\omega)$, and hence a r.v. defined on the marginal distribution of X. $E(Y|X)$ is Gaussian with mean μ_2 and variance of $\sigma_{12}^2/\sigma_{11}$. □

Making $E(Y|x)$ a point in a probability space on $\mathbb{R}$ circumvents the difficulty encountered previously with conditioning on events of probability 0, and our construction is valid for all distributions. It *is* possible to define $E(Y|G)$ when $P(G) = 0$. What is required is to exhibit a decreasing sequence $\{G_n \in \mathcal{G}\}$ with $P(G_n) > 0$ for every n, and $G_n \downarrow G$, such that the real sequence $\{E(Y|G_n)\}$ converges. This is why (10.7) works for continuous distributions. Take $G_n = [x, x+1/n] \times \mathbb{R} \in \sigma(X)$, so that $G = \{x\} \times \mathbb{R}$. Using (10.4) in (10.18),

$$E(Y|G_n) = \frac{\int_{-\infty}^{+\infty}\int_x^{x+1/n} yf(\xi,y)d\xi dy}{\int_{-\infty}^{+\infty}\int_x^{x+1/n} f(\xi,y)d\xi dy} \to \int_{-\infty}^{+\infty} yf(y|x)dy = E(Y|x), \tag{10.22}$$

as $n \to \infty$. Fubini's theorem allows us to evaluate these double integrals one dimension at a time, and to take the limits with respect to n inside the integrals with respect to y.

Conditional probability can sometimes generate paradoxical results, as the following case demonstrates.

10.7 Example Let X be a drawing from the space $([0,1], \mathcal{B}_{[0,1]}, m)$, where m is Lebesgue measure. Let $\mathcal{G} \subset \mathcal{B}_{[0,1]}$ denote the σ-field generated from the singletons $\{x\}$, $x \in [0,1]$. All countable unions of singletons have measure 0, while all complements have measure 1. Since either $P(G) = 0$ or $P(G) = 1$ for each $G \in \mathcal{G}$, it is clear from (10.18) that $E(X|\mathcal{G}) = E(X) = \frac{1}{2}$, a.s. However, consider the following argument. 'Since $\{x\} \in \mathcal{G}$, if we know whether or not $x \in G$ for each $G \in \mathcal{G}$, we know x. In particular, $\mathcal{G}$ contains knowledge of the outcome. It ought to be the case that $E(X|\mathcal{G}) = X$ a.s.' □

The mathematics are unambiguous, but there is evidently some difficulty with the idea that $\mathcal{G}$ should always represent partial knowledge. It must be accepted that the mathematical model may sometimes part company with intuition, and generate paradoxical results. Whether it is the model or the intuition that fails is a nice point for debate.

10.4 Some Theorems on Conditional Expectations

10.8 Law of iterated expectations (LIE)

$$E[E(Y|\mathcal{G})] = E(Y). \tag{10.23}$$

Proof Immediate from (10.18), setting $G = \Omega$. ■

The intuitive idea that conditioning variables can be held 'as if constant' under the conditional distribution is confirmed by the following pair of results.

10.9 Theorem If X is integrable and $\mathcal{G}$-measurable, then $E(X|\mathcal{G}) = X$, a.s.

Proof Since X is $\mathcal{G}$-measurable, $E^+ = \{\omega: X(\omega) > E(X|\mathcal{G})(\omega)\} \in \mathcal{G}$. If $P(E^+) > 0$, then

$$\int_{E^+} XdP - \int_{E^+} E(X|\mathcal{G})dP = \int_{E^+} (X - E(X|\mathcal{G}))dP > 0. \tag{10.24}$$

This contradicts (10.18), so $P(E^+) = 0$. By the same argument, $P(E^-) = 0$ where $E^- = \{\omega: X(\omega) < E(X|\mathcal{G})(\omega)\} \in \mathcal{G}$. ■

10.10 Theorem If Y is $\mathcal{F}$-measurable and integrable, X is $\mathcal{G}$-measurable for $\mathcal{G} \subseteq \mathcal{F}$, and $E|XY| < \infty$, then $E(YX|\mathcal{G}) = XE(Y|\mathcal{G})$ a.s.

Proof By definition, the theorem follows if

$$\int_G XE(Y|\mathcal{G})dP = \int_G XYdP \text{ a.s., for all } G \in \mathcal{G}. \tag{10.25}$$

Let $X_{(n)} = \sum_{i=1}^n \alpha_i 1_{E_i}$ be a $\mathcal{G}$-measurable simple r.v., with $E_1,\dots,E_n$ a partition of

Ω and $E_i \in \mathcal{G}$ for each i. (10.25) holds for $X = X_{(n)}$ since, for all $G \in \mathcal{G}$,

$$\int_G X_{(n)} E(Y|\mathcal{G})dP = \sum_{i=1}^{n} \alpha_i \int_{G \cap E_i} E(Y|\mathcal{G})dP$$

$$= \sum_{i=1}^{n} \alpha_i \int_{G \cap E_i} YdP = \int_G X_{(n)} YdP, \qquad (10.26)$$

noting $G \cap E_i \in \mathcal{G}$ when $G \in \mathcal{G}$ and $E_i \in \mathcal{G}$.

Let $X \geq 0$ a.s., and let $\{X_{(n)}\}$ be a monotone sequence of simple $\mathcal{G}$-measurable functions converging to X as in **3.28**. Then $X_{(n)} Y \to XY$ a.s. and $|X_{(n)} Y| \leq |XY|$, where $E|XY| < \infty$ by assumption. Similarly, $X_{(n)} E(Y|\mathcal{G}) \to XE(Y|\mathcal{G})$ a.s., and

$$E|X_{(n)} E(Y|\mathcal{G})| = E|E(X_{(n)} Y|\mathcal{G})| \leq E(E(|X_{(n)} Y||\mathcal{G}))$$

$$= E|X_{(n)} Y| \leq E|XY| < \infty, \qquad (10.27)$$

where the first inequality is the conditional modulus inequality, shown in **10.14** below, and the second equality is the LIE. It follows by the dominated convergence theorem that $\int_G X_{(n)} E(Y|\mathcal{G})dP \to \int_G XE(Y|\mathcal{G})dP$, and so (10.25) holds for non-negative X. The extension to general $\mathcal{G}$-measurable X is got by putting

$$X = X^+ - X^-, \qquad (10.28)$$

where $X^+ = \max\{X,0\} \geq 0$ and $X^- \geq 0$, and noting

$$E(YX|\mathcal{G}) = E(YX^+ - YX^-|\mathcal{G}) = E(YX^+|\mathcal{G}) - E(YX^-|\mathcal{G})$$

$$= (X^+ - X^-)E(Y|\mathcal{G}) = XE(Y|\mathcal{G}) \text{ a.s.}, \qquad (10.29)$$

using (10.33) below and the result for non-negative X. ■

X does not need to be integrable for this result, but the following is an important application to integrable X.

10.11 Theorem If Y is $\mathcal{F}$-measurable and integrable and $E(Y|\mathcal{G}) = E(Y)$ for $\mathcal{G} \subseteq \mathcal{F}$, then $\mathrm{Cov}(X,Y) = 0$ for integrable, $\mathcal{G}$-measurable X.

Proof From **10.8** and **10.10**,

$$E(XY) = E[E(XY|\mathcal{G})] = E[XE(Y|\mathcal{G})]. \qquad (10.30)$$

If $E(Y|\mathcal{G}) = E(Y)$ a.s. (a constant), then $E(XY) = E(X)E(Y)$. ■

Note that in general $\mathrm{Cov}(X,Y)$ is defined only for *square* integrable r.v.s X and Y. But $\mathrm{Cov}(X,Y) = 0$, or $E(XY) = E(X)E(Y)$, is a property which an integrable pair can satisfy.

The following is the result that justifies the characterization of the conditional mean as the optimal predictor of Y given partial information. 'Optimal' is seen to have the specific connotation of minimizing the mean of the squared prediction errors.

10.12 Theorem Let $\hat{Y}$ denote any $\mathcal{G}$-measurable approximation to Y. Then

$$\|Y - E(Y|\mathcal{G})\|_2 \leq \|Y - \hat{Y}\|_2. \tag{10.31}$$

Proof $(Y-\hat{Y})^2 = [Y - E(Y|\mathcal{G})]^2 + 2[Y - E(Y|\mathcal{G})][E(Y|\mathcal{G}) - \hat{Y}] + [E(Y|\mathcal{G}) - \hat{Y}]^2$, and hence

$$E[(Y-\hat{Y})^2|\mathcal{G}] = E[(Y - E(Y|\mathcal{G}))^2|\mathcal{G}] + [E(Y|\mathcal{G}) - \hat{Y}]^2 \text{ a.s.,} \tag{10.32}$$

noting that the conditional expectation of the cross-product disappears by definition of $E(Y|\mathcal{G})$, and **10.10**. The proof is completed by taking unconditional expectations through (10.32) and using the LIE. ■

The foregoing are results that have no counterpart in ordinary integration theory, but we can often exploit the fact that the conditional expectation behaves like a 'real' expectation, apart from the standard caveat we are dealing with r.v.s so that different behaviour is possible on sets of measure zero. Linearity holds, for example, since

$$E(aX + bY|\mathcal{G}) = aE(X|\mathcal{G}) + bE(Y|\mathcal{G}), \text{ a.s.,} \tag{10.33}$$

is a direct consequence of the definition in (10.18). The following are conditional versions of various results in Chapters 4 and 9. The first extends **4.5** and **4.12**.

10.13 Lemma

(i) If $X = 0$ a.s., then $E(X|\mathcal{G}) = 0$ a.s.

(ii) If $X \leq Y$ a.s., then $E(X|\mathcal{G}) \leq E(Y|\mathcal{G})$ a.s.

(iii) If $X = Y$ a.s., then $E(X|\mathcal{G}) = E(Y|\mathcal{G})$ a.s.

Proof (i) follows directly from (10.18). To prove (ii), note that the hypothesis, (10.18) and **4.8**(i) together imply

$$\int_G E(X|\mathcal{G})dP = \int_G XdP \leq \int_G YdP = \int_G E(Y|\mathcal{G})dP$$

for all $G \in \mathcal{G}$. Since $A = \{\omega: E(X|\mathcal{G})(\omega) > E(Y|\mathcal{G})(\omega)\} \in \mathcal{G}$, it follows that $P(A) = 0$. The proof of (iii) uses **4.8**(ii), and is otherwise identical to that of (ii). ■

10.14 Conditional modulus inequality $|E(Y|\mathcal{G})| \leq E(|Y||\mathcal{G})$ a.s.

Proof Note that $|Y| = Y^+ + Y^-$, where Y^+ and Y^- are defined in (10.28). These are non-negative r.v.s so that $E(Y^+|\mathcal{G}) \geq 0$ a.s. and $E(Y^-|\mathcal{G}) \geq 0$ a.s. by **10.13**(i) and (ii). For $\omega \in C$ with $P(C) = 1$,

$$\begin{aligned} |E(Y^+ - Y^-|\mathcal{G})(\omega)| &= |E(Y^+|\mathcal{G})(\omega) - E(Y^-|\mathcal{G})(\omega)| \\ &\leq E(Y^+|\mathcal{G})(\omega) + E(Y^-|\mathcal{G})(\omega) \\ &= E(Y^+ + Y^-|\mathcal{G})(\omega), \end{aligned} \tag{10.34}$$

where both the equalities are by linearity. ■

10.15 Conditional monotone convergence theorem If $Y_n \le Y$ and $Y_n \uparrow Y$ a.s., then $E(Y_n|\mathcal{G}) \uparrow E(Y|\mathcal{G})$ a.s.

Proof Consider the monotone sequence $Z_n = Y_n - Y$. Since $Z_n \le 0$ and $Z_n \le Z_{n+1}$, **10.13** implies that the sequence $\{E(Z_n|\mathcal{G})\}$ is negative and non-decreasing a.s., and hence converges a.s. By Fatou's Lemma,

$$\int_G \left(\limsup_{n\to\infty} E(Z_n|\mathcal{G})\right) dP \ge \limsup_{n\to\infty} \int_G E(Z_n|\mathcal{G})dP$$

$$= \limsup_{n\to\infty} \int_G Z_n dP = 0 \tag{10.35}$$

for $G \in \mathcal{G}$, the first equality being by (10.18), and the second by regular monotone convergence. Choose $G = \{\omega: \limsup_n E(Z_n|\mathcal{G})(\omega) < 0\}$, which is in $\mathcal{G}$ by **3.26**, and (10.35) implies that $P(G) = 0$. It follows that

$$\lim_{n\to\infty} E(Z_n|\mathcal{G}) = 0, \text{ a.s. } \blacksquare \tag{10.36}$$

10.16 Conditional Fatou's lemma If $Y_n \ge 0$ a.s. then

$$\liminf_{n\to\infty} E(Y_n|\mathcal{G}) \ge E\left(\liminf_{n\to\infty} Y_n|\mathcal{G}\right) \text{ a.s.} \tag{10.37}$$

Proof Put $Y_n' = \inf_{k\ge n} Y_k$ so that Y_n' is non-decreasing, and converges to $Y' = \liminf_n Y_n$. Then $E(Y_n'|\mathcal{G}) \to E(Y'|\mathcal{G})$ by **10.15**. $Y_n \ge Y_n'$, and hence $E(Y_n|\mathcal{G}) \ge E(Y_n'|\mathcal{G})$ a.s. by **10.13**(ii). The theorem follows on letting $n \to \infty$. ■

Extending the various other corollaries, such as the dominated convergence theorem, follows the pattern of the last results, and is left to the reader.

10.17 Conditional Markov inequality

$$P(\{|Y| \ge \varepsilon\}|\mathcal{G}) \le \frac{E(|Y|^p|\mathcal{G})}{\varepsilon^p}, \text{ a.s.}$$

Proof By Corollary **9.10** we have

$$\varepsilon^p \int_G 1_{\{|Y|\ge\varepsilon\}} dP \le \int_G |Y|^p dP, \; G \in \mathcal{F}. \tag{10.38}$$

By definition, for $G \in \mathcal{G}$,

$$\int_G P(\{|Y| \ge \varepsilon\}|\mathcal{G})dP = \int_G 1_{\{|Y|\ge\varepsilon\}} dP, \tag{10.39}$$

and

$$\int_G E(|Y|^p|\mathcal{G})dP = \int_G |Y|^p dP. \tag{10.40}$$

Substituting (10.39) and (10.40) into (10.38), it follows that

$$\int_G [\varepsilon^p P(\{|Y| \geq \varepsilon\}|\mathcal{G}) - E(|Y|^p|\mathcal{G})]dP \leq 0. \tag{10.41}$$

The contents of the square brackets in (10.41) is a $\mathcal{G}$-measurable r.v. Let $G \in \mathcal{G}$ denote the set on which it is positive, and it is clear that $P(G) = 0$. ∎

10.18 Conditional Jensen's inequality Let a Borel function ϕ be convex on an interval I containing the support of a $\mathcal{F}$-measurable r.v. Y where Y and $\phi(Y)$ are integrable. Then

$$\phi(E(Y|\mathcal{G})) \leq E(\phi(Y)|\mathcal{G}), \text{ a.s.} \tag{10.42}$$

Proof The proof applies **9.13**. Setting $x = E(Y|\mathcal{G})$ and $y = Y$ in (9.31),

$$A(E(Y|\mathcal{G}))(Y - E(Y|\mathcal{G})) \leq \phi(Y) - \phi(E(Y|\mathcal{G})). \tag{10.43}$$

However, unlike $A(E(Y))$, $A(E(Y|\mathcal{G}))$ is a random variable. It is not certain that the left-hand side of (10.43) is integrable, so the proof cannot proceed exactly like that of **9.12**. The extra trick is to replace Y by $1_E Y$, where $E = \{\omega: E(Y|\mathcal{G})(\omega) \leq B\}$ for $B < \infty$. $E(Y|\mathcal{G})$ and hence also 1_E are $\mathcal{G}$-measurable random variables, so $E(1_E Y|\mathcal{G}) = 1_E E(Y|\mathcal{G})$ by **10.10**, and

$$\begin{aligned} E(\phi(1_E Y)|\mathcal{G}) &= E(\phi(Y)1_E + \phi(0)1_{E^c}|\mathcal{G}) \\ &= 1_E E(\phi(Y)|\mathcal{G}) + (1 - 1_E)\phi(0). \end{aligned} \tag{10.44}$$

Thus, instead of (10.43), consider

$$A(E(1_E Y|\mathcal{G}))(1_E Y - 1_E E(Y|\mathcal{G})) \leq \phi(1_E Y) - \phi(1_E E(Y|\mathcal{G})). \tag{10.45}$$

The majorant side of (10.45) is integrable given that $\phi(Y)$ is integrable, and hence so is the minorant side. Application of **10.9** and **10.10** establishes that the conditional expectation of the latter term is zero almost surely, so with (10.44) we get

$$\phi(1_E E(Y|\mathcal{G})) \leq 1_E E(\phi(Y)|\mathcal{G}) + (1 - 1_E)\phi(0), \text{ a.s.} \tag{10.46}$$

Finally, let $B \to \infty$ so that $1_E \to 1$ to complete the proof. ∎

The following is a simple application of the last result which will have use subsequently.

10.19 Theorem Let X be $\mathcal{G}$-measurable and L_r-bounded for $r \geq 1$. If Y is $\mathcal{F}$-measurable, $X + Y$ is also L_r-bounded, and $E(Y|\mathcal{G}) = 0$ a.s., then

$$E|X + Y|^r \geq E|X|^r. \tag{10.47}$$

Proof Take expectations and apply the LIE to the inequality

$$E(|X + Y|^r|\mathcal{G}) \geq |E(X + Y|\mathcal{G})|^r = |X|^r \text{ a.s. ∎} \tag{10.48}$$

Finally, we can generalize the results of §9.6. It will suffice to illustrate with the case of differentiation under the conditional expectation.

10.20 Theorem Let a function $G(\omega,\theta)$ satisfy the conditions of **9.31**. Then

$$E\left(\frac{dG}{d\theta}\bigg|_{\theta=\theta_0}\bigg|\mathcal{G}\right) = \frac{dE(G|\mathcal{G})}{d\theta}\bigg|_{\theta=\theta_0}, \text{ a.s.} \tag{10.49}$$

Proof Take a countable sequence $\{h_\nu, \nu \in \mathbb{N}\}$ with $h_\nu \to 0$ as $\nu \to \infty$. By linearity of the conditional expectation,

$$E\left(\frac{G(\theta_0+h_\nu) - G(\theta_0)}{h_\nu}\bigg|\mathcal{G}\right) = \frac{E(G(\theta_0+h_\nu)|\mathcal{G}) - (G(\theta_0)|\mathcal{G})}{h_\nu} \text{ a.s.} \tag{10.50}$$

If $C_\nu \in \mathcal{G}$ is the set on which the equality in (10.50) holds, with $P(C_\nu) = 1$, the two sequences agree in the limit on the set $\bigcap_\nu C_\nu$, and $P(\bigcap_\nu C_\nu) = 1$ by **3.6**. The left-hand side of (10.50) converges a.s. to the left-hand side of (10.49) by assumption, applying the conditional version of the dominated convergence theorem. Since whenever it exists the a.s. limit of the right-hand side of (10.50) is the right-hand side of (10.49) by definition, the theorem follows. ■

10.5 Relationships between Subfields

$\mathcal{G}_1 \subseteq \mathcal{F}$ and $\mathcal{G}_2 \subseteq \mathcal{F}$ are *independent* subfields if, for every pair of events $G_1 \in \mathcal{G}_1$ and $G_2 \in \mathcal{G}_2$,

$$P(G_1 \cap G_2) = P(G_1)P(G_2). \tag{10.51}$$

Note that if Y is measurable on $\mathcal{G}_1$ it is also measurable on any collection containing $\mathcal{G}_1$, and on $\mathcal{F}$ in particular. Theorems **10.10** and **10.11** cover cases where Y as well as X is measurable on a subfield.

10.21 Theorem Random variables X and Y are independent iff $\sigma(X)$ and $\sigma(Y)$ are independent.

Proof Under the inverse mapping in (10.13), $G_1 \in \sigma(X)$ if and only if $B_1 = X(G_1) \in \mathcal{B}$ with a corresponding condition for $\sigma(Y)$. It follows that (10.51) holds for each $G_1 \in \sigma(X)$, $G_2 \in \sigma(Y)$ iff $P(X \in B_1, Y \in B_2) = P(X \in B_1)P(Y \in B_2)$ for each $B_1 = X(G_1)$, $B_2 = Y(G_2)$. The 'only if' of the theorem then follows directly from the definition of $\sigma(X)$. The 'if' follows, given (8.38), from the fact that every $B_i \in \mathcal{B}$ has an inverse image in any subfield on which a r.v. is measurable. ■

The 'only if' in the first line of this proof is essential. Independence of the subfields always implies independence of X and Y, but the converse holds only for the infimal cases, $\sigma(X)$ and $\sigma(Y)$.

10.22 Theorem Let Y be integrable and measurable on $\mathcal{G}_1$. Then $E(Y|\mathcal{G}) = E(Y)$ a.s. for all $\mathcal{G}$ independent of $\mathcal{G}_1$.

Proof Define the simple $\mathcal{G}_1$-measurable r.v.s $Y_{(n)} = \sum_{i=1}^n \gamma_i 1_{G_{1i}}$ on a partition $G_{11},\dots,G_{1n}$ of Ω where $G_{1i} \in \mathcal{G}_1$, each i, with $Y_{(n)} \uparrow Y$ as in **3.28**. Then

$$\int_G E(Y_{(n)}|\mathcal{G})dP = \sum_{i=1}^{n}\gamma_i\int_G E(1_{G_{1i}}|\mathcal{G})dP = \sum_{i=1}^{n}\gamma_i P(G_{1i} \cap G)$$

$$= P(G)\sum_{i=1}^{n}\gamma_i P(G_{1i}) = P(G)E(Y_{(n)}) \text{ for all } G \in \mathcal{G}, \qquad (10.52)$$

$E(Y_{(n)}) \to E(Y)$ by the monotone convergence theorem. $E(Y_{(n)}|\mathcal{G})$ is not a simple function, but $E(Y_{(n)}|\mathcal{G}) \uparrow E(Y|\mathcal{G})$ a.s. by **10.15**, and

$$\int_G E(Y_{(n)}|\mathcal{G})dP \to \int_G E(Y|\mathcal{G})dP, \qquad (10.53)$$

by regular monotone convergence. Hence for $\mathcal{G}_1$-measurable Y,

$$\int_G E(Y|\mathcal{G})dP = P(G)E(Y) \text{ for all } G \in \mathcal{G}. \qquad (10.54)$$

From the second equality of (10.18) it follows that $E(Y|G) = E(Y)$ for all $G \in \mathcal{G}$, which proves the theorem. ∎

10.23 Corollary If X and Y are independent, then $E(Y|X) = E(Y)$.

Proof Direct from **10.21** and **10.22**, putting $\mathcal{G} = \sigma(X)$ and $\mathcal{G}_1 = \sigma(Y)$. ∎

10.24 Theorem A pair of σ-fields $\mathcal{G}_1 \subset \mathcal{F}$ and $\mathcal{G}_2 \subset \mathcal{F}$ are independent iff $\text{Cov}(X,Y) = 0$ for every pair of integrable r.v.s X and Y such that X is measurable on $\mathcal{G}_1$ and Y is measurable on $\mathcal{G}_2$.

Proof By **10.22**, independence implies the condition of **10.11** is satisfied for $\mathcal{G} = \mathcal{G}_1$, proving 'only if'. To prove 'if', consider $X = 1_{G_1}$, $G_1 \in \mathcal{G}_1$, and $Y = 1_{G_2}$ for $G_2 \in \mathcal{G}_2$. X is $\mathcal{G}_1$-measurable and Y is $\mathcal{G}_2$-measurable. For this case,

$$\text{Cov}(X,Y) = P(G_1 \cap G_2) - P(G_1)P(G_2). \qquad (10.55)$$

$\text{Cov}(X,Y) = 0$ for every such pair implies $\mathcal{G}_1$ and $\mathcal{G}_2$ are independent by (10.51). ∎

10.25 Corollary Random variables X and Y are independent iff $\text{Cov}(\phi(X),\psi(Y)) = 0$ for every pair of integrable Borel functions ϕ and ψ.

Proof By **10.3**(i), $\phi(X)$ is measurable with respect to $\sigma(X)$ for all ϕ, and $\psi(Y)$ is $\sigma(Y)$-measurable for all ψ. If and only if all these pairs are uncorrelated, it follows by **10.24** that $\sigma(X)$ and $\sigma(Y)$ are independent subfields. The result then follows by **10.21**. ∎

An alternative proof of the necessity part is given in **9.17**.

The next result generalizes the law of iterated expectations to subfields. We say that σ-fields $\mathcal{G}_1$ and $\mathcal{G}_2$ are *nested* if $\mathcal{G}_1 \subseteq \mathcal{G}_2$.

10.26 Theorem If $\mathcal{G}_1 \subseteq \mathcal{G}_2 \subseteq \mathcal{F}$, then for $\mathcal{F}$-measurable Y,

(i) $\mathrm{E}[E(Y|\mathcal{G}_2)|\mathcal{G}_1] = E(Y|\mathcal{G}_1)$ a.s.

(ii) $E[E(Y|\mathcal{G}_1)|\mathcal{G}_2] = E(Y|\mathcal{G}_1)$ a.s.

Proof By definition,

$$\int_G E[E(Y|\mathcal{G}_2)|\mathcal{G}_1]dP = \int_G E(Y|\mathcal{G}_2)dP \text{ for all } G \in \mathcal{G}_1. \quad (10.56)$$

But, since $G \in \mathcal{G}_1$ implies $G \in \mathcal{G}_2$, (10.18) and (10.56) imply that

$$\int_G E[E(Y|\mathcal{G}_2)|\mathcal{G}_1]dP = \int_G YdP \text{ for all } G \in \mathcal{G}_1, \quad (10.57)$$

so that $E[E(Y|\mathcal{G}_2)|\mathcal{G}_1]$ is a version of $E(Y|\mathcal{G}_1)$, proving (i). Part (ii) is by **10.9**, since $E(Y|\mathcal{G}_1)$ is a $\mathcal{G}_2$-measurable r.v. ∎

A simple application of the theorem is to a three-variable distribution. If $(X(\omega),Y(\omega),Z(\omega))$ is a random point in $\mathbb{R}^3$, measurable on $\mathcal{F}$, let $\sigma(Z)$ and $\sigma(Y,Z)$ be the infimal σ-fields on which Z and (Y,Z) respectively are measurable, and $\sigma(Z) \subseteq \sigma(Y,Z) \subseteq \mathcal{F}$. Unifying notation by writing $E(Y|Z) = E(Y|\sigma(Z))$ and $E(Y|X,Z) = E(Y|\sigma(X,Z))$, **10.26** implies that

$$E[E(Y|X,Z)|Z] = E[E(Y|Z)|X,Z)] = E(Y|Z). \quad (10.58)$$

Our final results derive from the conditional Jensen inequality.

10.27 Theorem Let Y be a $\mathcal{F}$-measurable r.v. and $\mathcal{G}_1 \subseteq \mathcal{G}_2 \subseteq \mathcal{F}$. If $\phi(.)$ is convex,

$$E(\phi(E(Y|\mathcal{G}_2))) \geq E(\phi(E(Y|\mathcal{G}_1))). \quad (10.59)$$

Proof Applying **10.18** to the $\mathcal{G}_2$-measurable r.v. $E(Y|\mathcal{G}_2)$ gives

$$E(\phi(E(Y|\mathcal{G}_2))|\mathcal{G}_1) \geq \phi(E(E(Y|\mathcal{G}_2)|\mathcal{G}_1)) = \phi(E(Y|\mathcal{G}_1)) \text{ a.s.} \quad (10.60)$$

where the a.s. equality is by **10.26**(i). The theorem follows on taking unconditional expectations and using the LIE. ∎

The application of interest here is the comparison of absolute moments. Since $|x|^p$ is convex for $p \geq 1$, the absolute moments of $E(Y|\mathcal{G}_2)$ exceed those of $E(Y|\mathcal{G}_1)$ when $\mathcal{G}_1 \subseteq \mathcal{G}_2$. In particular,

$$E[E(Y|\mathcal{G}_2)^2] \geq E[E(Y|\mathcal{G}_1)^2]. \quad (10.61)$$

Since $E(Y|\mathcal{G}_1)$ and $E(Y|\mathcal{G}_2)$ both have mean of $E(Y)$, (10.61) implies $\text{Var}(E(Y|\mathcal{G}_2)) \geq \text{Var}(E(Y|\mathcal{G}_1))$. Also, $E(E(Y|\mathcal{G}_i)^2) + E((Y - E(Y|\mathcal{G}_i))^2) = E(Y^2)$ for $i = 1$ or 2, (the expected cross-product vanishes by **10.10**), so that an equivalent inequality is

$$E[(Y - E(Y|\mathcal{G}_2))^2] \leq E[(Y - E(Y|\mathcal{G}_1))^2]. \quad (10.62)$$

The interpretation is simple. $\mathcal{G}_1$ represents a smaller information set than $\mathcal{G}_2$, and if one predictor is based on more information than another, it exhibits more variation and the prediction error accordingly less variation. The extreme cases are $E(Y|\mathcal{F}) = Y$ and $E(Y|\mathcal{T}) = E(Y)$, with variances of $\text{Var}(Y)$ and zero respectively. This generalizes a fundamental inequality, that a variance is non-negative, to the partial information case.

While (10.61) generalizes from the square to any convex function, (10.62) does not. However, there is the following norm inequality for prediction errors.

10.28 Theorem If Y is $\mathcal{F}$-measurable and $\mathcal{G}_1 \subseteq \mathcal{G}_2 \subseteq \mathcal{F}$,

$$\|Y - E(Y|\mathcal{G}_2)\|_p \le 2\|Y - E(Y|\mathcal{G}_1)\|_p,\ p \ge 1. \tag{10.63}$$

Proof Let $\eta = Y - E(Y|\mathcal{G}_1)$. Then by **10.26**(ii),

$$\begin{aligned}\eta - E(\eta|\mathcal{G}_2) &= Y - E(Y|\mathcal{G}_1) - E(Y|\mathcal{G}_2) + E(E(Y|\mathcal{G}_1)|\mathcal{G}_2) \\ &= Y - E(Y|\mathcal{G}_2).\end{aligned} \tag{10.64}$$

The theorem now follows, since

$$\|\eta - E(\eta|\mathcal{G}_2)\|_p \le \|\eta\|_p + \|E(\eta|\mathcal{G}_2)\|_p \le 2\|\eta\|_p \tag{10.65}$$

by, respectively, the Minkowski and conditional Jensen inequalities, and the LIE. ■

10.6 Conditional Distributions

The conditional probability of an event $A \in \mathcal{F}$ can evidently be defined as $P(A|\mathcal{G}) = E(1_A|\mathcal{G})$, where $1_A(\omega)$ is the indicator function of A. But is it therefore meaningful to speak of a conditional distribution on $(\Omega,\mathcal{F})$, which assigns probabilities $P(A|\mathcal{G})$ to each $A \in \mathcal{F}$? There are two ways to approach this question.

First, we can observe straightforwardly that conditional probabilities satisfy the axioms of probability except on sets of probability 0 and, in this sense, satisfactorily mimic the properties of true probabilities, just as was found for the expectations. Thus, we have the following.

10.29 Theorem

(i) $P(A|\mathcal{G}) \ge 0$, all $A \in \mathcal{F}$.
(ii) $P(\Omega|\mathcal{G}) = 1$ a.s.
(iii) For a countable collection of disjoint sets $A_j \in \mathcal{F}$,

$$P\left(\bigcup_j A_j|\mathcal{G}\right) = \sum_j P(A_j|\mathcal{G}) \text{ a.s.} \tag{10.66}$$

Proof To prove (i), suppose $\exists\, G \in \mathcal{G}$ with $P(A|\mathcal{G})(\omega) < 0$ for all $\omega \in G$. Then, by (10.18),

$$\int_{G\cap A} dP = \int_G P(A|\mathcal{G})dP < 0, \tag{10.67}$$

which is a contradiction, since the left-hand member is a probability. To prove (ii), note that $P(\Omega|\mathcal{G})$ is $\mathcal{G}$-measurable and let $G^+ \in \mathcal{G}$ denote the set of ω such that $P(\Omega|\mathcal{G})(\omega) > 1$. Suppose $P(G^+) > 0$. Then since $G^+ \cap \Omega = G^+$,

$$P(G^+) = \int_{G^+} dP < \int_{G^+} P(\Omega|\mathcal{G})dP = \int_{G^+\cap\Omega} dP = P(G^+), \tag{10.68}$$

which is a contradiction. Hence, $P(G^+) = 0$. Repeating the argument for a set G^- on which $P(\Omega|\mathcal{G})(\omega) < 1$ shows that $P(G^-) = 0$. For (iii), (10.18) gives, for any $G \in \mathcal{G}$,

$$\int_G P(\bigcup_j A_j|\mathcal{G})dP = \int_{G\cap(\bigcup_j A_j)} dP = \int_{\bigcup_j(G\cap A_j)} dP = \sum_j \int_{G\cap A_j} dP, \quad (10.69)$$

since the sets $G \cap A_j$ are disjoint if this is true of the A_j. By definition there exists a version of $P(A_j|\mathcal{G})$ such that $\forall\ G \in \mathcal{G}$,

$$\int_{G\cap A_j} dP = \int_G P(A_j|\mathcal{G})\, dP, \quad (10.70)$$

and hence

$$\int_G P(\bigcup_j A_j|\mathcal{G})dP = \sum_j \int_G P(A_j|\mathcal{G})dP = \int_G \left(\sum_j P(A_j|\mathcal{G})\right) dP. \quad (10.71)$$

The left- and right-hand members of (10.71) define the same measure on $\mathcal{G}$ (see **10.5**) and hence $P(\bigcup_j A_j|\mathcal{G}) = \sum_j P(A_j|\mathcal{G})$ a.s. by the Radon-Nikodym theorem. ∎

But there is also a more exacting criterion which we should consider. That is, does there exist, for fixed ω, a p.m. μ_ω on $(\Omega,\mathcal{F})$ which satisfies

$$\mu_\omega(A) = P(A|\mathcal{G})(\omega), \text{ each } A \in \mathcal{F} \quad (10.72)$$

for all $\omega \in C$, where $P(C) = 1$? If this condition holds, the fact that conditional expectations and probabilities behave like regular expectations and probabilities requires no separate proof, since the properties hold for μ_ω. If a family of p.m.s $\{\mu_\omega, \omega \in \Omega\}$ satisfying (10.72) does exist, it is said to define a *regular* conditional probability on $\mathcal{G}$.

However, the existence of regular conditioning is *not* guaranteed in every case, and counter-examples have been constructed (see e.g. Doob 1953: 623–4). The problem is this. In (10.66), there is allowed to exist for a given collection $\mathcal{A} = \{A_j \in \mathcal{F}\}$ an exceptional set, say $C_{\mathcal{A}}$ with $P(C_{\mathcal{A}}) = 0$, on which the equality fails. This in itself does not violate (10.72), but the set $C_{\mathcal{A}}$ is specific to $\mathcal{A}$, and since there are typically an uncountable number of countable subsets $\mathcal{A} \subseteq \mathcal{F}$, we cannot guarantee that $P(\bigcup_{\mathcal{A}} C_{\mathcal{A}}) = 0$, as would be required for μ_ω both to be a p.m. and to satisfy (10.72).

This is not a particularly serious problem because the existence of the family $\{\mu_\omega\}$ has not been critical to our development of conditioning theory, but for certain purposes it is useful to know, as the next theorem shows, that p.m.s on the line *do* admit regular conditional distributions.

10.30 Theorem Given a space $(\Omega,\mathcal{F},P)$ and a subfield $\mathcal{G} \subset \mathcal{F}$, a random variable Y has a regular conditional distribution defined by

$$F_Y(y|\mathcal{G})(\omega) = P((-\infty,y]|\mathcal{G})(\omega),\ y \in \mathbb{R}, \quad (10.73)$$

for $\omega \in C$ with $P(C) = 1$, where $F_Y(.|\mathcal{G})(\omega)$ is a c.d.f. for all $\omega \in \Omega$.

Proof Write $F^*_\omega(y)$ to denote a version of $P((-\infty,y]|\mathcal{G})(\omega)$. Let M_{ij} denote the set of ω such that $F^*_\omega(r_i) > F^*_\omega(r_j)$ for r_i, $r_j \in \mathbb{Q}$ with $r_i < r_j$. Similarly, let R_i denote the set of ω on which $\lim_{n\to\infty} F^*_\omega(r_i + 1/n) \neq F^*_\omega(r_i)$, $r_i \in \mathbb{Q}$. And finally, let L denote the set of those ω for which $F^*_\omega(+\infty) \neq 1$ and $F^*_\omega(-\infty) \neq 0$. Then $C = (\bigcup_{i,j} M_{ij})^c \cap (\bigcup_i R_i)^c \cap L^c$ is the set of ω on which $F^*_\omega(y)$ is monotone and right-continuous at all rational points of the line, with $F^*_\omega(+\infty) = 1$ and $F^*_\omega(-\infty) = 0$. For $y \in \mathbb{R}$ let

$$F_Y(.|\mathcal{G})(\omega) = \begin{cases} \left\{ \begin{array}{ll} F^*_\omega(y), & y \in \mathbb{Q} \\ F^*_\omega(y+), & y \in \mathbb{R} - \mathbb{Q} \end{array} \right\}, & \omega \in C, \\ G(y), & \text{otherwise}, \end{cases} \tag{10.74}$$

where G is an arbitrary c.d.f. In view of **10.29**, $P(M_{ij}) = 0$ for each pair i,j, $P(R_i) = 0$ for each i and $P(L) = 0$. (If need be, work in the completion of the space to define these probabilities.) Since this collection is countable, $P(C) = 1$, and in view of **8.4**, $F_Y(.|\mathcal{G})(\omega)$ is a c.d.f. which satisfies (10.73), as it was required to show. ■

It is straightforward, at least in principle, to generalize this argument to multivariate distributions.

For $B \in \mathcal{B}$ it is possible to write

$$E(1_B|\mathcal{G})(\omega) = \int_B dF_Y(y|\mathcal{G})(\omega) \text{ a.s.,} \tag{10.75}$$

and the standard argument by way of simple functions and monotone convergence leads us full circle, to the representation

$$E(Y|\mathcal{G})(\omega) = \int_{-\infty}^{+\infty} y dF_Y(y|\mathcal{G})(\omega), \text{ a.s.} \tag{10.76}$$

If $\mathcal{G} = \sigma(X)$, we have constructions to parallel those of §10.1. Since no restriction had to be placed on the distribution to obtain this result, we have evidently found a way around the difficulties associated with the earlier definitions.

However, $F_Y(.|\mathcal{G})(\omega)$ is something of a novelty, a c.d.f. that is a random element from a probability space. Intuitively, we must attempt to understand this as representing the subjective distribution of $Y(\omega)$ in the mind of the observer who knows whether or not $\omega \in G$ for each $G \in \mathcal{G}$. The particular case $F_Y(.|\mathcal{G})(\omega)$ is the one of interest to the statistical modeller when the outcome ω is realized. Many random variables may be generated from the elements of $(\Omega,\mathcal{F},P)$, not only the outcome itself—in the bivariate case the pair $Y(\omega),X(\omega)$—but also variables such as $E(Y|X)(\omega)$, and the quantiles of $F_Y(y|X)(\omega)$. All these have to be thought of as different aspects of the same random experiment.

Let X and Y be r.v.s, and $\mathcal{G}$ a subfield with $\mathcal{G} \subseteq \mathcal{H}_X = \sigma(X)$ and $\mathcal{G} \subseteq \mathcal{H}_Y = \sigma(Y)$. We say that X and Y are *independent conditional on* $\mathcal{G}$ if

$$F_{XY}(x,y|\mathcal{G}) = F_X(x|\mathcal{G})F_Y(y|\mathcal{G}) \text{ a.s.} \tag{10.77}$$

This condition implies, for example, that $E(XY|\mathcal{G}) = E(X|\mathcal{G})E(Y|\mathcal{G})$ a.s. Let $\mu_\omega = \mu(.,\omega)$ be the conditional measure such that

$$\mu_\omega(\{X \in (-\infty,x],\ Y \in (-\infty,y]\}) = F_{XY}(x,y|\mathcal{G})(\omega).$$

With ω fixed this is a regular p.m. by (the bivariate generalization of) **10.30**, and $\mu_\omega(A \cap B) = \mu_\omega(A)\mu_\omega(B)$ for each $A \in \mathcal{H}_X$ and $B \in \mathcal{H}_Y$, by **10.21**. In this sense, the subfields $\mathcal{H}_X$ and $\mathcal{H}_Y$ can be called conditionally independent.

10.31 Theorem. If X and Y are independent conditional on $\mathcal{G}$, then

$$E(Y|\mathcal{H}_X) = E(Y|\mathcal{G}) \text{ a.s.} \tag{10.78}$$

Proof By independence of $\mathcal{H}_X$ and $\mathcal{H}_Y$ under μ_ω we can write

$$\int_A E(Y|\mathcal{H}_X)d\mu_\omega = \int_A Yd\mu_\omega = \mu_\omega(A)\int Yd\mu_\omega,\ A \in \mathcal{H}_X. \tag{10.79}$$

This is equivalent to

$$\begin{aligned} E(1_A E(Y|\mathcal{H}_X)|\mathcal{G})(\omega) &= E(1_A Y|\mathcal{G})(\omega) \\ &= E(1_A E(Y|\mathcal{G})|\mathcal{G})(\omega) \text{ a.s.}[P], \end{aligned} \tag{10.80}$$

where the first equality also follows from **10.26**(i) and **10.10**. Integrating over Ω with respect to P, noting $\Omega \in \mathcal{G}$, using **4.8**(ii) and the LIE, we arrive at

$$\int_A E(Y|\mathcal{H}_X)dP = \int_A YdP = \int_A E(Y|\mathcal{G})dP,\ A \in \mathcal{H}_X. \tag{10.81}$$

This shows $E(Y|\mathcal{H}_X)$ is a version of $E(Y|\mathcal{G})$, competing the proof. ∎

Thus, while $E(Y|\mathcal{H}_X)$ is in principle $\mathcal{H}_X$-measurable, it is in fact almost surely $[P]$ equal to a $\mathcal{G}$-measurable r.v. Needless to say, the whole argument is symmetric in X and $\mathcal{H}_Y$.

The idea we are capturing here is that, to an observer who possesses the information in $\mathcal{G}$ (knows whether $\omega \in G$ for each $G \in \mathcal{G}$), observing X does not yield any additional information that improves his prediction of Y, and vice versa. This need not be true for an observer who does not possess prior information. Equation (10.77) shows that the predictors of Y based on the smaller and larger information sets are the same a.s.$[P]$, although this does not imply $E(Y|\mathcal{H}_X) = E(Y)$ a.s., so that X and Y are not independent in the ordinary sense.

11
Characteristic Functions

11.1 The Distribution of Sums of Random Variables

Let a pair of independent r.v.s X and Y have marginal c.d.f.s $F_X(x)$ and $F_Y(y)$. The c.d.f. of the sum $W = X+Y$ is given by the *convolution* of F_X and F_Y, the function

$$F_X{*}F_Y(w) = \int_{-\infty}^{+\infty} F_X(w-y)dF_Y(y). \tag{11.1}$$

11.1 Theorem If r.v.s X and Y are independent, then

$$F_X{*}F_Y(w) = P(X+Y \le w) = F_Y{*}F_X(w). \tag{11.2}$$

Proof Let $1_w(x,y)$ be the indicator function of the set $\{x,y\colon x \le w-y\}$, so that $P(X+Y \le w) = E(1_w(X,Y))$. By independence $F(x,y) = F_X(x)F_Y(y)$, so this is

$$\begin{aligned}\int_{\mathbb{R}^2} 1_w(x,y)F(x,y) &= \int_{-\infty}^{+\infty}\left(\int_{-\infty}^{+\infty} 1_w(x,y)dF_X(x)\right)dF_Y(y)\\ &= \int_{-\infty}^{+\infty}\left(\int_{-\infty}^{w-y} dF_X(x)\right)dF_Y(y)\\ &= \int_{-\infty}^{+\infty} F_X(w-y)dF_Y(y), \qquad (11.3)\end{aligned}$$

where the first equality is by Fubini's theorem. This establishes the first equality in (11.2). Reversing the roles of X and Y in (11.3) establishes the second. ■

For continuous distributions, the convolution $f = f_X{*}f_Y$ of p.d.f.s f_X and f_Y is

$$f(w) = \int_{-\infty}^{+\infty} f_X(w-y)f_Y(y)dy, \tag{11.4}$$

such that $\int_{-\infty}^{w} f(\xi)d\xi = F(w)$.

11.2 Example Let X and Y be independent drawings from the uniform distribution on [0,1], so that $f_X(x) = 1_{[0,1]}(x)$. Applying (11.4) gives

$$f_{X+Y}(w) = \int_0^1 1_{[w-1,w]}dy. \tag{11.5}$$

It is easily verified that the graph of this function forms an isosceles triangle with base [0,2] and height 1. □

This is the most direct result on the distribution of sums, but the formulae generated by applying the rule recursively are not easy to handle, and other approaches are preferred. The *moment generating function* (m.g.f.) of X, when it exists, is

$$M_X(t) = E(e^{tX}) = \int e^{tX} dF(x),\ t \in \mathbb{R}, \tag{11.6}$$

where e denotes the base of natural logarithms. (Integrals are taken over $(-\infty,+\infty)$ unless otherwise indicated.) If X and Y are independent,

$$\begin{aligned} M_{X+Y}(t) &= \iint e^{t(x+y)} dF_X(x) dF_Y(y) \\ &= \int e^{tx} dF_X(x) \int e^{ty} dF_Y(y) \\ &= M_X(t) M_Y(t). \end{aligned} \tag{11.7}$$

This suggests a simple approach to analysing the distribution of independent sums. The difficulty is that the method is not universal, since the m.g.f. is not defined for every distribution. Considering the series expansion of e^{tX}, all the moments of X must evidently exist. The solution to this problem is to replace the variable t by it, where i is the imaginary number, $\sqrt{-1}$. The *characteristic function* (ch.f.) of X is defined as

$$\phi_X(t) = E(e^{itX}) = \int e^{itx} dF(x). \tag{11.8}$$

11.2 Complex Numbers

A *complex number* is $z = a + ib$, where a and b are real numbers and $i = \sqrt{-1}$. a and b are called the real and imaginary parts of the number, denoted $a = \mathrm{Re}(z)$ and $b = \mathrm{Im}(z)$. The *complex conjugate* of z is the number $\bar{z} = a - ib$. Complex arithmetic is mainly a matter of carrying i as an algebraic unknown, and replacing i^2 by -1, i^3 by $-i$, i^4 by 1, etc., wherever these appear in an expression.

One can represent z as a point in the plane with Cartesian coordinates a and b. The *modulus* or absolute value of z is its Euclidean distance from the origin,

$$|z| = (z\bar{z})^{1/2} = (a^2 + b^2)^{1/2}. \tag{11.9}$$

Polar coordinates can also be used. Let the complex exponential be defined by

$$e^{i\theta} = \cos\theta + i\sin\theta \tag{11.10}$$

for real θ. All the usual properties of the exponential function, such as multiplication by summing exponents (according to the rules of complex arithmetic) go through under this definition, and

$$|e^{i\theta}| = (\cos^2\theta + \sin^2\theta)^{1/2} = 1 \tag{11.11}$$

for any θ, by a standard trigonometric identity. We may therefore write $z = |z|e^{i\theta}$, where Re(z) = $|z|\cos\theta$ and Im(z) = $|z|\sin\theta$. Also note, by (11.11), that

$$|e^z| = |e^{\mathrm{Re}(z)+i\mathrm{Im}(z)}| = e^{\mathrm{Re}(z)}|e^{i\mathrm{Im}(z)}| = e^{\mathrm{Re}(z)}. \tag{11.12}$$

If X and Y are real random variables, $Z = X+iY$ is a complex-valued random variable. Its distribution is defined in the obvious way, in terms of a bivariate c.d.f., $F(x,y)$. In particular,

$$E(Z) = E(X)+iE(Y). \tag{11.13}$$

Whereas $E(Z)$ is a complex variable, $E|Z|$ is of course real, and since $|Z| \le |X|+|Y|$ by the triangle inequality, integrability of X and Y is sufficient for the integrability of Z. Many of the standard properties of expectations extend to the complex case in a straightforward way. One result needing proof, however, is the generalization of the modulus inequality.

11.3 Theorem If Z is a complex random variable, $|E(Z)| \le E|Z|$.

Proof Consider a complex-valued simple r.v.

$$Z_{(n)} = \sum_{j=1}^{n}(\alpha_j+i\beta_j)1_{E_j}, \tag{11.14}$$

where the α_j and β_j are real non-negative constants and the $E_j \in \mathcal{F}$ for $j = 1,\dots,n$ constitute a partition of Ω. Write $P_j = E(1_{E_j})$. Then

$$|E(Z_{(n)})|^2 = \Big(\sum_j \alpha_j P_j\Big)^2 + \Big(\sum_j \beta_j P_j\Big)^2$$

$$= \sum_j(\alpha_j^2+\beta_j^2)P_j^2 + \sum_{j\neq k}\sum(\alpha_j\alpha_k+\beta_j\beta_k)P_jP_k, \tag{11.15}$$

whereas

$$(E|Z_{(n)}|)^2 = \Big(\sum_j(\alpha_j^2+\beta_j^2)^{1/2}P_j\Big)^2$$

$$= \sum_j(\alpha_j^2+\beta_j^2)P_j^2 + \sum_{j\neq k}\sum(\alpha_j^2+\beta_j^2)^{1/2}(\alpha_k^2+\beta_k^2)^{1/2}P_jP_k. \tag{11.16}$$

The modulus inequality holds for $Z_{(n)}$ if

$$0 \le (E|Z_{(n)}|)^2 - |E(Z_{(n)})|^2$$

$$= \sum_{j\neq k}\sum[(\alpha_j^2+\beta_j^2)^{1/2}(\alpha_k^2+\beta_k^2)^{1/2} - (\alpha_j\alpha_k+\beta_j\beta_k)]P_jP_k. \tag{11.17}$$

The coefficients of P_jP_k in this expression are the differences of pairs of non-negative terms, and these differences are non-negative if and only if the differences of the squares are non-negative. But as required,

$$(\alpha_j^2+\beta_j^2)(\alpha_k^2+\beta_k^2) - (\alpha_j\alpha_k+\beta_j\beta_k)^2 = \alpha_j^2\beta_k^2 + \alpha_k^2\beta_j^2 - 2\alpha_j\alpha_k\beta_j\beta_k$$
$$= (\alpha_j\beta_k - \alpha_k\beta_j)^2 \geq 0. \tag{11.18}$$

This result extends to any complex r.v. having non-negative real and imaginary parts by letting $Z_{(n)} = X_{(n)} + iY_{(n)} \uparrow Z = X + iY$, using **3.28**, and invoking the monotone convergence theorem. To extend to general integrable r.v.s, split X and Y into positive and negative parts, so that $Z = Z^+ - Z^-$, where $Z^+ = X^+ + iY^+$ with $X^+ \geq 0$ and $Y^+ \geq 0$, and $Z^- = X^- + iY^-$, with $X^- \geq 0$ and $Y^- \geq 0$. Noting that

$$|E(Z)| \leq |E(Z^+ + Z^-)| \leq E|Z^+ + Z^-| = E|Z| \tag{11.19}$$

completes the proof. ∎

11.3 The Theory of Characteristic Functions

We are now equipped to study some of the properties of the characteristic function $\phi_X(t)$. The fact that it is defined for *any* distribution follows from the fact that $|e^{itx}| = 1$ for all x; $E(|e^{itx}|) = 1$ and $E(e^{itx})$ is finite regardless of the distribution of X. The real and imaginary parts of $\phi_X(t)$ are respectively $E(\cos tX)$ and $E(\sin tX)$.

11.4 Theorem If $E|X|^k < \infty$, then

$$\frac{d^k\phi_X(t)}{dt^k} = E((iX)^k e^{itX}). \tag{11.20}$$

Proof

$$\frac{\phi_X(t+h) - \phi_X(t)}{h} = \int_{-\infty}^{+\infty} \frac{e^{ix(t+h)} - e^{itx}}{h} dF(x), \tag{11.21}$$

where, using (11.10),

$$\frac{e^{ix(t+h)} - e^{itx}}{h} = \frac{\cos x(t+h) - \cos tx}{h} + i\frac{\sin x(t+h) - \sin tx}{h}.$$

The limits of the real and imaginary terms in this expression as $h \to 0$ are respectively $-x\sin tx$ and $i(x\cos tx)$, so the limit if the integrand in (11.21) is

$$x(i\cos tx - \sin tx) = ix(\cos tx + i\sin tx) = (ix)e^{itx}.$$

Since $|(ix)e^{itx}| = |x|$, the integral exists if $E|X| < \infty$. This proves (11.20) for the case $k = 1$. To complete the proof, the same argument can be applied inductively to the integrands $(ix)^{k-1}e^{itx}$ for $k = 2,3,...$ ∎

It follows that the integer moments of the distribution can be obtained by repeated differentiation with respect to t.

11.5 Corollary If $E|X|^k < \infty$, then

$$\left.\frac{d^k\phi_X(t)}{dt^k}\right|_{t=0} = i^k E(X^k). \quad \square \tag{11.22}$$

An alternative way to approach the last result is to construct a series expansion of the ch.f. with remainder, using Taylor's theorem. This gives rise to a very useful approximation theorem.

11.6 Theorem If $E|X|^k < \infty$, then

$$\left|\phi_X(t) - \sum_{j=0}^{k}\frac{(it)^j E(X^j)}{j!}\right| \le E\left[\min\left\{\frac{2|tX|^k}{k!}, \frac{|tX|^{k+1}}{(k+1)!}\right\}\right]. \tag{11.23}$$

Proof A function f which is differentiable k times has the expansion

$$f(t) = f(0) + f'(0)t + \frac{f''(0)}{2}t^2 + \frac{f'''(0)}{6}t^3 + \ldots + \frac{f^{(k)}(\alpha t)}{k!}t^k,$$

where $0 \le \alpha \le 1$. The expansion of $f(t) = e^{itx}$ gives

$$e^{itx} = \sum_{j=0}^{k}\frac{(itx)^j}{j!} + \frac{|tx|^k}{k!}y_k, \tag{11.24}$$

where $y_k = i^k\mathrm{sgn}(tx)^k(e^{i\alpha tx} - 1)$ and

$$\mathrm{sgn}(tx) = \begin{cases} 1, & tx \ge 0 \\ -1, & tx < 0 \end{cases}.$$

Applying (11.10) and (11.11), we can show that $|y_k| = (2 - 2\cos\alpha tx)^{1/2} \le 2$. However, by extending the expansion to term $k+1$, we also have

$$e^{itx} = \sum_{j=0}^{k}\frac{(itx)^j}{j!} + \frac{|tx|^{k+1}}{(k+1)!}z_k, \tag{11.25}$$

where $z_k = i^{k+1}\mathrm{sgn}(tx)^{k+1}e^{i\alpha' tx}$ for $0 \le \alpha' \le 1$, and $|z_k| = 1$. Given that both of (11.24) and (11.25) hold, we may conclude that

$$\left|e^{itx} - \sum_{j=0}^{k}\frac{(itx)^j}{j!}\right| \le \min\left\{\frac{2|tx|^k}{k!}, \frac{|tx|^{k+1}}{(k+1)!}\right\}. \tag{11.26}$$

The theorem now follows on replacing x with the r.v. X in (11.26), taking expectations and using the modulus inequality:

$$\left| \phi_X(t) - \sum_{j=0}^{k} \frac{(it)^j E(X^j)}{j!} \right| \leq E \left| e^{itX} - \sum_{j=0}^{k} \frac{(itX)^j}{j!} \right|$$

$$\leq E\left[\min\left\{ \frac{2|tX|^k}{k!}, \frac{|tX|^{k+1}}{(k+1)!} \right\} \right]. \blacksquare \qquad (11.27)$$

There is no need for $E|X|^{k+1}$ to exist for this theorem to hold, and we can think of it as giving the best approximation regardless of whether $|tX|$ is large or small. To interpret the expectation on the right-hand side of (11.27), note that, for any pair of non-negative, measurable functions g and h,

$$E(\min\{g(X),h(X)\}) = \inf_{A \in \mathcal{B}} E(g(X)1_A + h(X)1_{A^c}), \qquad (11.28)$$

the infimal set being the one containing those points x on which $g(x) \leq h(x)$. In particular, for any $\varepsilon \geq 0$, the set $A = \{|X| > \varepsilon\}$ belongs to the class over which the infimum in (11.28) is taken, and we get the further inequality,

$$E\left[\min\left\{ \frac{2|tX|^k}{k!}, \frac{|tX|^{k+1}}{(k+1)!} \right\} \right] \leq E\left(\frac{2|tX|^k}{k!} 1_{\{|X|>\varepsilon\}} \right) + E\left(\frac{|tX|^{k+1}}{(k+1)!} 1_{\{|X|\leq\varepsilon\}} \right)$$

$$\leq \begin{cases} \dfrac{2t^k}{k!} E(|X|^k 1_{\{|X|>\varepsilon\}}) + \dfrac{|t|^{k+1}\varepsilon^{k+1}}{(k+1)!} \\[2ex] \dfrac{2t^k}{k!} E(|X|^k 1_{\{|X|>\varepsilon\}}) + \dfrac{|t|^{k+1}}{(k+1)!} E|X|^k \varepsilon \end{cases}. \qquad (11.29)$$

The second alternative on the right is obtained in view of the fact that $E(|X|^{k+1} 1_{\{|X|\leq\varepsilon\}}) = E(|X|^k |X| 1_{\{|X|\leq\varepsilon\}}) \leq E|X|^k \varepsilon$. Both of these versions of the bound on the truncation error prove useful subsequently.

Two other properties of the characteristic function will be much exploited. First, for a pair of constants a and b,

$$\phi_{aX+b}(t) = E(e^{it(aX+b)}) = e^{ibt}\phi_X(at). \qquad (11.30)$$

The second is the counterpart of (11.7). For a pair of independent random variables X and Y,

$$\phi_{X+Y}(t) = \int\int e^{it(x+y)} dF_X(x) dF_Y(y)$$

$$= \int e^{itx} dF_X(x) \int e^{ity} dF_Y(y)$$

$$= \phi_X(t)\phi_Y(t). \qquad (11.31)$$

An interesting case of the last result is $Y = -X'$ where X' is an independent drawing from the distribution of X. The distribution of $X - X'$ is the same as that of

$X'-X$, and hence this r.v. is symmetric about 0. The ch.f. of $X-X'$ is real, since

$$\phi_X(t)\phi_X(-t) = |\phi_X(t)|^2, \tag{11.32}$$

in view of the fact that $\phi_X(-t) = E(e^{-itX}) = \overline{\phi_X(t)}$. It can be verified from the expansion in (11.23) that with a real ch. f., all the existing odd-order moments must be zero, the trademark of a symmetric distribution.

Considering more generally a sum $S = \sum_{i=1}^n X_i$ where $\{X_1,\dots,X_n\}$ are a totally independent collection, recursive application of (11.31) yields

$$\phi_S(t) = \prod_{i=1}^n \phi_{X_i}(t). \tag{11.33}$$

To investigate the distribution of S, one need only establish the formulae linking the ch.f.s with the relevant c.d.f.s (or where appropriate p.d.f.s) which are known for the standard sampling distributions.

11.7 Example For the Poisson distribution (**8.8**),

$$\phi_X(t;\lambda) = E(e^{itX}) = e^{-\lambda}\sum_{x=0}^{\infty}\frac{1}{x!}\lambda^x e^{itx} = e^{\lambda(e^{it}-1)}. \ \square \tag{11.34}$$

11.8 Example In the standard Gaussian case, (**8.10**),

$$\phi_Z(t) = E(e^{itZ}) = \frac{1}{\sqrt{2\pi}}\int_{-\infty}^{+\infty} e^{itz-z^2/2}dz. \tag{11.35}$$

Completing the square yields $itz - z^2/2 = -(z-it)^2/2 - t^2/2$ and hence

$$\phi_Z(t) = e^{-t^2/2}\frac{1}{\sqrt{2\pi}}\int_{-\infty}^{+\infty} e^{-(z+it)^2}dz = e^{-t^2/2}. \tag{11.36}$$

(The integral in the middle member has the value $\sqrt{2\pi}$ for any choice of t, note.)

Accordingly, consider $X = \sigma Z+\mu$, whose p.d.f. is given by (8.24). Using (11.30), we obtain

$$\phi_X(t;\ \mu,\sigma) = e^{i\mu t-\sigma^2t^2/2}. \tag{11.37}$$

Equation (11.22) can be used to verify the moment formulae given in **9.4** and **9.7**. With $\mu = 0$ the ch.f. is real, reflecting the symmetry of the distribution. □

11.9 Example The Cauchy distribution (**8.11**) has no integer moments. The ch.f. turns out to be $e^{-|t|}$ which is not differentiable at $t = 0$, as (11.22) would lead us to expect. The ch.f. for the Cauchy family (**8.15**) is

$$\phi_X(t;\ \nu,\delta) = e^{it\nu-\delta|t|}. \ \square \tag{11.38}$$

The ch.f. is also defined for multivariate distributions. For a random vector $\boldsymbol{X}$ $(m\times 1)$ the ch.f. is

$$\phi(\boldsymbol{t}) = E(\exp\{i\boldsymbol{t}'\boldsymbol{X}\}), \tag{11.39}$$

where $\boldsymbol{t}$ is a m-vector of arguments. This case will be especially important, not least because of the ease with which, by the generalization of (11.30), the ch.f. can be derived for an affine transformation of the vector. Let $\boldsymbol{Y} = \boldsymbol{BX}+\boldsymbol{d}$ $(k\times 1)$, where $\boldsymbol{B}$ $(k\times m)$ and $\boldsymbol{d}$ $(k\times 1)$ are constants, and then we have

$$\phi_Y(\boldsymbol{t}) = E(\exp\{i\boldsymbol{t}'\boldsymbol{Y}\}) = \exp\{i\boldsymbol{t}'\boldsymbol{d}\}E(\exp\{i\boldsymbol{t}'\boldsymbol{BX}\}) = \exp\{i\boldsymbol{t}'\boldsymbol{d}\}\phi_X(\boldsymbol{B}'\boldsymbol{t}). \tag{11.40}$$

11.10 Example Let $\boldsymbol{X}$ $(m\times 1)$ be multinormal with p.d.f. as in (8.36). The ch.f. is

$$\phi_X(\boldsymbol{t};\boldsymbol{\mu},\boldsymbol{\Sigma}) = \frac{1}{(2\pi)^{m/2}|\boldsymbol{\Sigma}|^{1/2}}\int_{-\infty}^{+\infty}\cdots\int_{-\infty}^{+\infty}\exp\{i\boldsymbol{t}'\boldsymbol{x} - \tfrac{1}{2}(\boldsymbol{x}-\boldsymbol{\mu})'\boldsymbol{\Sigma}^{-1}(\boldsymbol{x}-\boldsymbol{\mu})\}d\boldsymbol{x}$$

$$= \exp\{i\boldsymbol{t}'\boldsymbol{\mu} - \tfrac{1}{2}\boldsymbol{t}'\boldsymbol{\Sigma}\boldsymbol{t}\}. \tag{11.41}$$

The second equality is obtained as before by completing the square:

$$i\boldsymbol{t}'\boldsymbol{x} - \tfrac{1}{2}(\boldsymbol{x}-\boldsymbol{\mu})'\boldsymbol{\Sigma}^{-1}(\boldsymbol{x}-\boldsymbol{\mu}) = i\boldsymbol{t}'\boldsymbol{\mu} - \tfrac{1}{2}\boldsymbol{t}'\boldsymbol{\Sigma}\boldsymbol{t} - \tfrac{1}{2}(\boldsymbol{x}-\boldsymbol{\mu}-i\boldsymbol{\Sigma}\boldsymbol{t})'\boldsymbol{\Sigma}^{-1}(\boldsymbol{x}-\boldsymbol{\mu}-i\boldsymbol{\Sigma}\boldsymbol{t}),$$

where it can be shown that the exponential of the last term integrates over $\mathbb{R}$ to $(2\pi)^{m/2}|\boldsymbol{\Sigma}|^{1/2}$. □

11.4 The Inversion Theorem

Paired with (11.8) is a unique inverse transformation from $\phi(t)$ to $F(x)$, so that the ch.f. and c.d.f. are fully equivalent representations of the distribution. The chief step in the proof of this proposition is the construction of the inverse transformation, as follows.

11.11 Lemma If $\phi(t)$ is defined by (11.8), then

$$F(b)-F(a) = \frac{1}{2\pi}\lim_{T\to\infty}\int_{-T}^{T}\frac{e^{-ita} - e^{-itb}}{it}\phi(t)dt \tag{11.42}$$

for any pair a and b of continuity points of F, with $a < b$. The multivariate generalization of this formula is

$$\Delta F(x_1,\dots,x_k) = \left(\frac{1}{2\pi}\right)^m\lim_{T\to\infty}\int_{-T}^{T}\cdots\int_{-T}^{T}\left[\prod_{j=1}^{k}\frac{e^{-it_jx_j} - e^{-it_j(x_j+\Delta x_j)}}{it_j}\right]$$

$$\times\phi_{X_1\dots X_k}(t_1,\dots,t_k)dt_1\dots dt_k. \tag{11.43}$$

where $\Delta F(x_1,\dots,x_k)$ is defined in (8.31) and the vertices of the rectangle based at the point $x_1,\dots,x_k$, with sides $\Delta x_j > 0$, are all continuity points of F. □

Here, $\phi_{X_1\dots X_k}$ is equivalent to (11.39). It can be verified using (11.10) that

$$\frac{e^{-ita}-e^{-itb}}{it} \to b-a \text{ as } t \to 0.$$

The integrals in (11.42) and (11.43) are therefore well defined in spite of including the point $t = 0$. Despite this, it is necessary to avoid writing (11.42) as

$$F(b)-F(a) = \int_{-\infty}^{+\infty} \frac{e^{-ita}-e^{-itb}}{2\pi it}\phi(t)dt, \tag{11.44}$$

because the Lebesgue integral on the right may not exist. For example, suppose the random variable is degenerate at the point 0; this means that $\phi(t) = e^{it.0} = 1$, and

$$\frac{1}{2\pi}\int_{-T}^{T}\left|\frac{e^{-ita}-e^{-itb}}{it}\right|dt \geq \frac{1}{\pi}\int_{1}^{T}\frac{1}{t}dt \sim \log T, \tag{11.45}$$

so that the criterion for Lebesgue integrability over $(-\infty,+\infty)$ fails. However, the limits in (11.42) and (11.43) do exist, as the proof reveals.

Proof of 11.11 Only the univariate case will be proved, the multivariate extension being identical in principle. After substituting for ϕ in (11.43) we can interchange the order of integration by **9.32**, whose continuity and a.s. boundedness requirements are certainly satisfied here:

$$\int_{-T}^{T} \frac{e^{-ita}-e^{-itb}}{2\pi it}\phi(t)dt = \int_{-T}^{T} \frac{e^{-ita}-e^{-itb}}{2\pi it}\left(\int_{-\infty}^{\infty} e^{itx}dF(x)\right)dt$$

$$= \int_{-\infty}^{+\infty}\left(\int_{-T}^{T} \frac{e^{it(x-a)}-e^{it(x-b)}}{2\pi it}dt\right)dF(x). \tag{11.46}$$

Using (11.10),

$$\int_{-T}^{T} \frac{e^{it(x-a)}-e^{it(x-b)}}{2\pi it}dt = \int_{0}^{T}\frac{\sin t(x-a)}{\pi t}dt - \int_{0}^{T}\frac{\sin t(x-b)}{\pi t}dt, \tag{11.47}$$

noting that the cosine is an even function, so that the terms containing cosines (which are also the imaginary terms) vanish in the integral. The limit as $T \to \infty$ of this expression is obtained from the standard formula

$$\int_{0}^{\infty}\frac{\sin \alpha t}{t}dt = \begin{cases} \pi/2, & \alpha > 0 \\ 0, & \alpha = 0 \\ -\pi/2, & \alpha < 0. \end{cases} \tag{11.48}$$

Substituting into (11.46) yields the result

$$\int_{-\infty}^{+\infty}\frac{e^{it(x-a)}-e^{it(x-b)}}{2\pi it}dt=\begin{cases}0, & x<a \text{ or } x>b\\ \tfrac{1}{2}, & x=a \text{ or } x=b\\ 1, & a<x<b.\end{cases} \tag{11.49}$$

Letting $T\to\infty$ in (11.46) and applying the bounded convergence theorem now gives

$$\lim_{T\to\infty}\int_{-T}^{T}\frac{e^{-ita}-e^{-itb}}{2\pi it}\phi(t)dt=\int_{-\infty}^{+\infty}(\tfrac{1}{2}1_{\{a\}}+\tfrac{1}{2}1_{\{b\}}+1_{(a,b)})dF(x)$$

$$=\tfrac{1}{2}(F(b)+F(b-)-F(a)-F(a-)), \tag{11.50}$$

which reduces to $F(b)-F(a)$ when a and b are continuity points of F. ■

Lemma **11.11** is the basic ingredient of the following key result, the one that primarily justifies our interest in characteristic functions.

11.12 Inversion theorem Distributions having the same ch.f. are the same.

Proof We give the proof for the unvariate case only. By (11.42), the c.d.f.s of the two distributions are the same at every point which is a continuity point of both c.d.f.s. Since the set of jump points of each c.d.f. is countable by **8.3** their union is countable, and it follows by **2.10** that the set of continuity points is dense in $\mathbb{R}$. It then follows by **8.4** that the c.d.f.s are the same everywhere. ■

A simple application of the inversion theorem is to provide a proof of a well known result, that affine functions of Gaussian vectors are also Gaussian.

11.13 Example Let $\boldsymbol{X}\sim N(\boldsymbol{\mu},\boldsymbol{\Sigma})$ $(m\times 1)$ and $\boldsymbol{Y}=\boldsymbol{BX}+\boldsymbol{d}$ $(n\times 1)$ where $\boldsymbol{B}$ $(n\times m)$ and $\boldsymbol{d}$ $(n\times 1)$ are constants. Then by (11.42),

$$\phi_Y(\boldsymbol{t})=\exp\{i\boldsymbol{t}'\boldsymbol{d}\}E(\exp\{i\boldsymbol{t}'\boldsymbol{BX}\})$$

$$=\exp\{i\boldsymbol{t}'(\boldsymbol{B\mu}+\boldsymbol{d})-\tfrac{1}{2}\boldsymbol{t}'\boldsymbol{B}'\boldsymbol{\Sigma}\boldsymbol{Bt}\}. \tag{11.51}$$

If $\text{rank}(\boldsymbol{B}'\boldsymbol{\Sigma}\boldsymbol{B})=n$, (implying $n\le m$), **11.12** implies that $\boldsymbol{Y}$ has p.d.f.

$$f(y)=\frac{\exp\{-\tfrac{1}{2}(y-\boldsymbol{B\mu}-\boldsymbol{d})'(\boldsymbol{B\Sigma B}')^{-1}(y-\boldsymbol{B\mu}-\boldsymbol{d})\}}{(2\pi)^{n/2}|\boldsymbol{B\Sigma B}'|^{1/2}}. \tag{11.52}$$

If $\text{rank}(\boldsymbol{B\Sigma B}')<n$, (11.51) remains valid although (11.52) is not. But by the same arguments, every linear combination $\boldsymbol{c}'\boldsymbol{Y}$, where $\boldsymbol{c}$ is $p\times 1$, is either scalar Gaussian with variance $\boldsymbol{c}'\boldsymbol{B\Sigma B}'\boldsymbol{c}$, or identically zero, corresponding to the cases $\boldsymbol{B}'\boldsymbol{c}\neq 0$ and $\boldsymbol{B}'\boldsymbol{c}=0$ respectively. In this case $\boldsymbol{Y}$ is said to have a singular Gaussian distribution. □

11.5 The Conditional Characteristic Function

Let Y be a $\mathcal{F}$-measurable r.v., and let $\mathcal{G} \subset \mathcal{F}$. The conditional ch.f. of $Y|\mathcal{G}$, $\phi_{Y|\mathcal{G}}(t)$, is for each t a random variable having the property

$$\int_G \phi_{Y|\mathcal{G}}(t)dP = \int_G e^{itY}dP, \text{ all } G \in \mathcal{G}. \tag{11.53}$$

The conditional ch.f. shares the properties of the regular ch.f. whenever the theory of conditional expectations parallels that of ordinary expectations according to the results of Chapter 10. Its real and imaginary parts are, respectively, the $\mathcal{G}$-measurable random variables $E(\cos tY|\mathcal{G})$ and $E(\sin tY|\mathcal{G})$. It can be expanded as in **11.6**, in terms of the existing conditional moments. If X is $\mathcal{G}$-measurable, the conditional ch.f. of $X+Y$ is $\phi_{X+Y|\mathcal{G}}(t) = e^{itX}E(e^{itY}|\mathcal{G})$ by **10.10**. And if Y is $\mathcal{G}_1$-measurable and $\mathcal{G}$ and $\mathcal{G}_1$ are independent subfields, then $\phi_{Y|\mathcal{G}}(t) = \phi_Y(t)$ a.s.

The conditional ch.f. is used to prove a useful inequality due to von Bahr and Esséen (1965). We start with a technical lemma which appears obscure at first sight, but turns out to have useful applications.

11.14 Lemma Suppose $E|Z|^r < \infty$, $0 < r < 2$. Then

$$E|Z|^r = K(r)\int_{-\infty}^{+\infty} \frac{1-\mathrm{Re}(\phi_Z(t))}{|t|^{1+r}}dt \tag{11.54}$$

where $K(r) = \left(\int_{-\infty}^{+\infty}(1-\cos u)/|u|^{1+r}du\right)^{-1} = \pi^{-1}\Gamma(r+1)\sin r\pi/2$. □

The last equality, with $\Gamma(.)$ denoting the gamma function, is a standard integral formula for $0 < r < 2$.

Proof The identity for real z,

$$|z|^r = K(r)\int_{-\infty}^{+\infty} \frac{1-\cos zt}{|t|^{1+r}}\, dt, \tag{11.55}$$

is easily obtained by a change of variable in the integral on the right. The lemma follows on applying **9.32** and noting that $\mathrm{Re}(\phi_Z(t)) = E(\cos tZ)$. ■

This equality also holds, for $\omega \in C$ with $P(C) = 1$, if $E(|Z|^r|\mathcal{G})(\omega)$ and $\phi_{Z|\mathcal{G}}(t)(\omega)$ are substituted for $E|Z|^r$ and $\phi_Z(t)$. In other words, the conditional rth moment and conditional ch.f are almost surely related by the same formula.

So consider L_r-bounded r.v.s Z and X, where Z is $\mathcal{F}$-measurable, and X is $\mathcal{G}$-measurable for $\mathcal{G} \subset \mathcal{F}$. Suppose that $\phi_{Z|\mathcal{G}}(t)$ is a real r.v. almost surely. Then for each $\omega \in \Omega$,

$$\begin{aligned} 1-\mathrm{Re}(\phi_{X+Z|\mathcal{G}}(t))(\omega) &= 1-\mathrm{Re}(e^{itX}\phi_{Z|\mathcal{G}}(t))(\omega) \\ &= 1-(\cos tX(\omega))\phi_{Z|\mathcal{G}}(t)(\omega) \\ &\le (1-\cos tX(\omega)) + (1-\phi_{Z|\mathcal{G}}(t)(\omega)), \end{aligned} \tag{11.56}$$

the difference between the last two members being $(1-\cos tX(\omega))(1-\phi_{Z|\mathcal{G}}(t)(\omega))$ which is non-negative for all ω. Hence, for $0 < r < 2$,

$$E(|X+Z|^r|\mathcal{G}) = K(r)\int_{-\infty}^{+\infty}\frac{1-\text{Re}(\phi_{X+Z|\mathcal{G}}(t))}{|t|^{1+r}}dt$$

$$\leq K(r)\int_{-\infty}^{+\infty}\frac{1-\cos tX}{|t|^{1+r}}dt + K(r)\int_{-\infty}^{+\infty}\frac{1-\phi_{Z|\mathcal{G}}(t)}{|t|^{1+r}}dt$$

$$= |X|^r + E(|Z|^r|\mathcal{G}), \text{ a.s.} \tag{11.57}$$

and taking expectations through yields

$$E|X+Z|^r \leq E|X|^r + E|Z|^r. \tag{11.58}$$

For the case $0 < r \leq 1$ this inequality holds by the c_r inequality for general Z and X, so it is the case $1 < r < 2$ that is of special interest here.

Generalizing from the remarks following (11.31), the condition that $\phi_{Z|\mathcal{G}}(t)$ be real a.s. can be fulfilled by letting $Z = Y - Y'$, where Y and Y' are identically distributed and independent, conditional on $\mathcal{G}$. Note that if $\mathcal{H} = \sigma(Y)$, then

$$E(Y'|\mathcal{H}) = E(Y'|\mathcal{G}), \text{ a.s.,} \tag{11.59}$$

by **10.31**. Identical conditional distributions means simply that $F_Y(.|\mathcal{G}) = F_{Y'}(.|\mathcal{G})$ a.s., and equivalently that $\phi_{Y|\mathcal{G}}(t) = \phi_{Y'|\mathcal{G}}(t)$ a.s. Hence

$$\begin{aligned}\phi_{Y-Y'|\mathcal{G}}(t) &= E(e^{itY}e^{-itY'}|\mathcal{G}) \\ &= E(e^{itY}|\mathcal{G})E(e^{-itY'}|\mathcal{G}) \\ &= |\phi_{Y|\mathcal{G}}(t)|^2, \text{ a.s.,}\end{aligned} \tag{11.60}$$

where the right-hand side is a real r.v. Now, for each $\omega \in \Omega$, the following identity can be verified:

$$2(1-\text{Re}(\phi_{Y|\mathcal{G}}(t)(\omega)) = 1 - \phi_{Y|\mathcal{G}}(t)(\omega)|^2 + |1-\phi_{Y|\mathcal{G}}(t)(\omega)|^2. \tag{11.61}$$

Applying (11.60) and **11.14**, and taking expectations, this yields the inequality

$$2E|Y|^r \geq E|Y-Y'|^r, \; 0 < r < 2, \tag{11.62}$$

noting that the difference between the two sides here is the non-negative function of r, $K(r)\int_{-\infty}^{+\infty}E|1-\phi_{Y|\mathcal{G}}(t)|^2/|t|^{1+r}dt$.

These arguments lead us to the following conclusion.

11.15 Theorem Suppose $E(Y|\mathcal{G}) = 0$ a.s. and X is $\mathcal{G}$-measurable where $\mathcal{G} \subseteq \mathcal{H} = \sigma(Y)$, and both variables are L_r-bounded. Then

$$E|X+Y|^r \leq E|X|^r + 2E|Y|^r, \; 0 \leq r \leq 2. \tag{11.63}$$

Proof Let Y' be independent and identical with Y, conditional on $\mathcal{G}$. Applying (11.59), these conditions jointly imply $E(Y'|\mathcal{H}) = E(Y'|\mathcal{G}) = E(Y|\mathcal{G}) = 0$. Noting that $X+Y$ is $\mathcal{H}$-measurable, it follows by **10.19** (in applying this result be careful to note that $\mathcal{H}$ plays the role of the subfield here) that

$$E|X+Y|^r \le E|X+(Y-Y')|^r. \tag{11.64}$$

The conclusion for $1 < r < 2$ now follows on applying (11.58) for the case $Z = Y-Y'$, and then (11.62). The inequality holds for $0 < r \le 1$ by the c_r inequality, and for $r = 2$ from elementary considerations since $E(YX) = 0$. In these latter cases the factor 2 in (11.63) can be omitted. ∎

This result can be iterated, given a sequence of r.v.s measurable on an increasing sequence of σ-fields. An easy application is to independent r.v.s $X_1,\dots,X_n$, for which the condition $E(X_t|\sigma(X_1,\dots,X_{t-1})) = 0$ certainly holds for $t = 2,\dots,n$. Letting $S_n = \sum_{t=1}^n X_t$, $\sigma(S_n) = \sigma(X_1,\dots,X_n)$ and **11.15** yields

$$\begin{aligned} E|S_n|^r &\le E|S_{n-1}|^r + 2E|X_n|^r \\ &\le \dots \\ &\le 2\sum_{t=1}^n E|X_t|^r,\ 0 \le r \le 2. \end{aligned} \tag{11.65}$$

If the series on the majorant side converges, this inequality remains valid as $n \to \infty$. It may be contrasted for tightness with the c_r inequality for general X_t, (9.62). In this case, 2 must be replaced by n^{r-1} for $1 < r \le 2$, which is of no use for large n.

III

THEORY OF STOCHASTIC PROCESSES

12
Stochastic Processes

12.1 Basic Ideas and Terminology

Let $(\Omega,\mathcal{F},P)$ be a probability space, let $\mathbb{T}$ be any set, and let $\mathbb{R}^{\mathbb{T}}$ be the product space generated by taking a copy of $\mathbb{R}$ for each element of $\mathbb{T}$. Then, a *stochastic process* is a measurable mapping $x\colon \Omega \mapsto \mathbb{R}^{\mathbb{T}}$, where

$$x(\omega) = \{X_\tau(\omega),\ \tau \in \mathbb{T}\}. \tag{12.1}$$

$\mathbb{T}$ is called the *index set*, and the r.v. $X_\tau(\omega)$ is called a *coordinate* of the process. A stochastic process can also be characterized as a mapping from $\Omega\times\mathbb{T}$ to $\mathbb{R}$. However, the significant feature of the definition given is the requirement of *joint* measurability of the coordinates. Something more is implied than having $X_\tau(\omega)$ a measurable r.v. for each τ.

Here, $\mathbb{T}$ is an arbitrary set which in principle need not even be ordered, although linear ordering characterizes the important cases. A familiar example is $\mathbb{T} = \{1,\dots,k\}$, where x is a random k-vector. Another important case of $\mathbb{T}$ is an interval of $\mathbb{R}$, such that $x(\omega)$ is a function of a real variable and $\mathbb{R}^{\mathbb{T}}$ the space of random functions. And when $\mathbb{T}$ is a countable subset of $\mathbb{R}$, $x = \{X_\tau(\omega),\ \tau \in \mathbb{T}\}$ defines a *stochastic sequence*. Thus, a stochastic sequence is a stochastic process whose index set is countable and linearly ordered. When the X_τ represent random observations equally spaced in time, no relevant information is lost by assigning a linear ordering through $\mathbb{N}$ or $\mathbb{Z}$, indicated by the notations $\{X_\tau(\omega)\}_1^\infty$ and $\{X_\tau(\omega)\}_{-\infty}^{\infty}$. The definition does not rule out $\mathbb{T}$ containing information about distances between the sequence coordinates, as when the observations are irregularly spaced in time with τ a real number representing elapsed time from a chosen origin, but cases of this kind will not be considered explicitly.

Familiarly, a *time series* is a time-ordered sequence of observations of (say) economic variables, although the term may extend to unobserved or hypothetical variables, such as the errors in a regression model. Time-series coordinates are labelled t. If a *sample* is defined as a time series of finite length n (or more generally, a collection of such series for different variables) it is convenient to assume that samples are embedded in infinite sequences of 'potential' observations. Various mathematical functions of sample observations, *statistics* or *estimators*, will also be well known to the reader, characteristically involving a summation of terms over the coordinates. The sample moments of a time series, regression coefficients, log-likelihood functions and their derivatives, are standard examples. By letting n take the values 1,2,3,..., these functions of n observations generate what we may call *derived* sequences. The notion of a sequence in this case comes from the idea of analysing samples of progressively increasing size. The mathematical theory often does not distinguish between the types of sequence under consideration, and some of our definitions and results apply generally, but a clue to the usual application will be given by the choice of index symbol, t or n as the case may be.

A leading case which does not fall under the definition of a sequence is where $\mathbb{T}$ is partially ordered. When there are two dimensions to the observations, as in a panel data set having both a time dimension and a dimension over agents, x may be called a *random field*. Such cases are not treated explicitly here, although in many applications one dimension is regarded as fixed and the sequence notion is adequate for asymptotic analysis. However, cases where $\mathbb{T}$ is either the product set $\mathbb{Z}\times\mathbb{N}$, or a subset thereof, are often met below in a different context. A *triangular stochastic array* is a doubly-indexed collection of random variables,

$$\begin{pmatrix} X_{11} & X_{21} & X_{31} & \cdots \\ X_{12} & X_{22} & X_{32} & \cdots \\ \vdots & \vdots & \vdots & \\ X_{1k_1} & \vdots & \vdots & \\ & X_{1k_2} & \vdots & \\ & & X_{3k_3} & \\ & & & \ddots \end{pmatrix}, \tag{12.2}$$

compactly written as $\{\{X_{nm}\}_{m=1}^{k_n}\}_{n=1}^{\infty}$, where $\{k_n\}_{n=1}^{\infty}$ is some increasing integer sequence. Array notation is called for when the points of a sample are subjected to scale transformations or the like, depending on the complete sample. A standard example is $\{\{X_{nt}\}_{t=1}^{n}\}_{n=1}^{\infty}$, where $X_{nt} = X_t/s_n$, and $s_n = \sum_{t=1}^{n}\text{Var}(X_t)$, or some similar function of the sample moments from 1 to n.

12.2 Convergence of Stochastic Sequences

Consider the functional expression $\{X_n(\omega)\}_1^{\infty}$ for a random sequence on the space $(\Omega,\mathcal{F},P)$. When evaluated at a point $\omega \in \Omega$ this denotes a *realization* of the sequence, the actual collection of real numbers generated when the outcome ω is drawn. It is natural to consider in the spirit of ordinary analysis whether this sequence converges to a limit, say $X(\omega)$. If this is the case for every $\omega \in \Omega$, we would say that $X_n \to X$ *surely* (or elementwise) where, if X_n is an $\mathcal{F}/\mathcal{B}$-measurable r.v. for each n, then so is X, by **3.26**.

But, except by direct construction, it is usually difficult to establish in terms of a given collection of distributional properties that a stochastic sequence converges surely to a limit. A much more useful notion (because more easily shown) is *almost sure convergence*. Let $C \subseteq \Omega$ be the set of outcomes such that, for every $\omega \in C$, $X_n(\omega) \to X(\omega)$ as $n \to \infty$. If $P(C) = 1$, the sequence is said to converge almost surely, or equivalently, *with probability one*. The notations $X_n \xrightarrow{as} X$, or $X_n \to X$ a.s., and $\text{a.s.}\lim X_n = X$ are all used to denote almost sure convergence. A similar concept, of convergence almost everywhere (a.e.), was invoked in connection with the properties of integrals in §4.2. For many purposes, almost sure convergence can be thought of as yielding the same implications as sure convergence in probabilistic arguments.

However, attaching probabilities to the convergent set is not the only way in which stochastic convergence can be understood. Associated with any stochastic sequence are various non-stochastic sequences of variables and functions describing aspects of its behaviour, moments being the obvious case. Convergence of the stochastic sequence may be defined in terms of the ordinary convergence of an associated sequence. If the sequence $\{E(X_n - X)^2\}_1^\infty$ converges to zero, there is a clearly a sense in which $X_n \to X$; this is called *convergence in mean square*. Or suppose that for any $\varepsilon > 0$, the probabilities of the events $\{\omega\colon |X_n(\omega) - X(\omega)| < \varepsilon\} \in \mathcal{F}$ form a real sequence converging to 1. This is another distinct convergence concept, so-called *convergence in probability*. In neither case is there any obvious way to attach a probability to the convergent set; this can even be zero! These issues are studied in Part IV.

Another convergence concept relates to the sequence of marginal p.m.s of the coordinates, $\{\mu_n\}_1^\infty$, or equivalently the marginal c.d.f.s, $\{F_n\}_1^\infty$. Here we can consider conditions for convergence of the real sequences $\{\mu_n(A)\}_1^\infty$ for various sets $A \in \mathcal{B}$, or alternatively, of $\{F_n(x)\}_1^\infty$ for various $x \in \mathbb{R}$. In the latter case, uniform or pointwise convergence on $\mathbb{R}$ is a possibility, but these are relatively strong notions. It is sufficient for a theory of the limiting distribution if convergence is confined just to the continuity points of the limiting function F, or equivalently (as we shall show in Chapter 22) of $\mu_n(A)$, to sets A having $\mu(\delta A) = 0$. This condition is referred to as the *weak convergence* of the distributions, and forms the subject of Part V.

12.3 The Probability Model

Some very important ideas are implicit in the notion of a stochastic sequence. Given the equipotency of $\mathbb{N}$ and $\mathbb{Z}$, it will suffice to consider the random element $\{X_t(\omega)\}_1^\infty$, $\omega \in \Omega$, mapping from a point of Ω to a point in infinite-dimensional Euclidean space, $\mathbb{R}^\infty$. From a probabilistic point of view, the entire infinite sequence corresponds to a *single* outcome ω of the underlying abstract probability space. In principle, a sampling exercise in this framework is the random drawing of a point in $\mathbb{R}^\infty$, called a realization or *sample path* of the random sequence; we may actually observe only a finite segment of this sequence, but the key idea is that a random experiment consists of drawing a complete realization. *Repeated sampling* means observing the same finite segment (relative to the origin of the index set) of different realizations, *not* different segments of the same realization.

The reason for this characterization of the random experiment will become clear in the sequel; for the moment we will just concentrate on placing this slightly outlandish notion of an infinite-dimensioned random element into perspective. To show that there is no difficulty in establishing a correspondence between a probability space of a familiar type and a random sequence, we discuss a simple example in some detail.

12.1 Example Consider a repeated game of coin tossing, generating a random sequence of heads and tails; if the game continues for ever, it will generate a sequence of infinite length. Let 1 represent a head and 0 a tail, and we have a random sequence of 1s and 0s. Such a sequence corresponds to the binary (base 2) representation of a real number; according to equation (1.15) there is a one-to-one correspondence between infinite sequences of coin tosses and points on the unit interval. On this basis, the fundamental space $(\Omega,\mathcal{F})$ for the coin tossing experiment can be chosen as $([0,1),\mathcal{B}_{[0,1)})$. The form of P can be deduced in an elementary way from the stipulation that $P(\text{heads}) = P(\text{tails}) = 0.5$ (i.e. the coin is fair) and successive tosses are independent. For example, the events {tails on first toss} and {heads on first toss} are the images of the sets $[0,0.5)$ and $[0.5,1)$ respectively, whose measures must accordingly be 0.5 each. More generally, the probability that the first n tosses in a sequence yields a given configuration of heads and tails out of the 2^n possible ones is equal in every case to $1/2^n$, so that each sequence is (in an appropriate limiting sense) 'equally likely'. The corresponding sets in $[0,1)$ of the binary expansions with the identical pattern of 0s and 1s in the first n positions occupy intervals all of width precisely $1/2^n$ in the unit interval. The conclusion is that the probability measure of any interval is equal to its width. This is nothing but Lebesgue measure on the half-open interval $[0,1)$. □

This example can be elaborated from binary sequences to sequences of real variables without too much difficulty. There is an intimate connection between infinite random sequences and continuous probability distributions on the line, and understanding one class of problem is frequently an aid to understanding the other. The question often posed about the probability of some sequence predicted in advance being realized, say an infinite run of heads or a perpetual alternation of heads and tails, is precisely answered. In either the decimal or binary expansions, all the numbers whose digit sequences either terminate or, beyond some point, are found to cycle perpetually through a finite sequence belong to the set of rational numbers. Since the rationals have Lebesgue measure zero in the space of the reals, we have a proof that the probability of *any* such sequence occurring is zero.

Another well-known conundrum concerns the troupe of monkeys equipped with typewriters who, it is claimed, will eventually type out the complete works of Shakespeare. We can show that this event will occur with probability 1. For the sake of argument, assume that a single monkey types into a word processor, and his ASCII-encoded output takes the form of a string of bits (binary digits). Suppose Shakespeare's encoded complete works occupy k bits, equivalent to $k/5$ characters allowing for a 32-character keyboard (upper-case only, but including some punctuation marks). This string is one of the 2^k possible strings of k bits. Assuming that each such string is equally likely to arise in $k/5$ random key presses, the probability that the monkey will type Shakespeare without an error *from scratch* is exactly 2^{-k}. However, the probability that the second string of 2^k bits it produces is the right one, given that the first one is wrong, is $(1-2^{-k})2^{-k}$ when the strings are independent. In general, the probability that the monkey will type Shakespeare correctly on the $(m+1)$th independent attempt, given that the first m attempts were failures, is $(1-2^{-k})^m 2^{-k}$. All these events are disjoint, and summing their probabilities over all $m \ge 0$ yields

$$P(\text{monkey types Shakespeare eventually}) = 1.$$

In the meantime, of course, the industrious primate has produced much of the rest of world literature, not to mention a good many telephone books. It is also advisable to estimate the length of time we are likely to wait for the desired text to appear, which requires a further calculation. The average waiting time, expressed in units of the time taken to type k bits, is $2^{-k}\sum_{m=1}^{\infty} m(1-2^{-k})^m = 2^k - 1$. If we scale down our ambitions and decide to be content with just 'TO BE OR NOT TO BE' ($5 \times 18 = 90$ bits), and the monkey takes 1 minute over each attempt, we shall wait on average 2.3×10^{21} years. So the Complete Works don't really bear thinking about.

What we have shown is that almost every infinite string of bits contains every finite string somewhere in its length; but also, that the mathematical concept of 'almost surely' has no difficulty in coinciding with an everyday notion indistinguishable from 'never'. The example is frivolous, but it is useful to be reminded occasionally that limit theory deals in large numbers. A sense of perspective is always desirable in evaluating the claims of the theory.

The first technical challenge we face in the theory of stochastic processes is to handle distributions on $\mathbb{R}^\infty$. To construct the Borel field $\mathcal{B}^\infty$ of events on $\mathbb{R}^\infty$, we implicitly endow $\mathbb{R}^\infty$ with the Tychonoff, or product, topology. It is not essential to have absorbed the theory of §6.5 to make sense of the discussion that follows, but it may help to glance at Example **6.18** to see what this assumption implies.

Given a process $x = \{X_t\}_1^\infty$ we shall write

$$\pi_k(x) = (X_1,\dots,X_k)\colon \mathbb{R}^\infty \mapsto \mathbb{R}^k \tag{12.3}$$

for each $k \in \mathbb{N}$, to denote the k-dimensional coordinate projection. Let $\mathcal{C}$ denote the collection of *finite-dimensional cylinder sets* of $\mathbb{R}^\infty$, the sets

$$C = \{x \in \mathbb{R}^\infty\colon \pi_k(x) \in E,\ E \in \mathcal{B}^k,\ k \in \mathbb{N}\} \tag{12.4}$$

In other words, elements of $\mathcal{C}$ have the form

$$C = \pi_k^{-1}(E) \tag{12.5}$$

for some $E \in \mathcal{B}^k$, and some finite k. Although we may wish to consider arbitrary finite dimensional cylinders, there is no loss of generality in considering the projections onto just the first k coordinates. Any finite dimensional cylinder can be embedded in a cylinder of the form $\pi_k^{-1}(E)$, $E \in \mathcal{B}^k$, where k is just the largest of the restricted coordinates. The distinguishing feature of an element of $\mathcal{C}$ is that at most a finite number of its coordinates are restricted.

12.2 Theorem $\mathcal{C}$ is a field.

Proof First, the complement in $\mathbb{R}^\infty$ of a set C defined by (12.4) is

$$C^c = \{x \in \mathbb{R}^\infty\colon (\pi_k(x) \in E^c,\ E \in \mathcal{B}^k\} = \pi_k^{-1}(E^c), \tag{12.6}$$

which is another element of $\mathcal{C}$, i.e. $C^c \in \mathcal{C}$. Second, consider the union of sets $C = \pi_k^{-1}(E) \in \mathcal{C}$ and $C' = \pi_k^{-1}(E') \in \mathcal{C}$, for $E, E' \in \mathcal{B}^k$. $C \cup C'$ is given by (12.4) with E replaced by $E \cup E'$, and hence $C \cup C' \in \mathcal{C}$. Third, if $E \in \mathcal{B}^k$ and $E' \in \mathcal{B}^m$ for $m > k$, then $E \times \mathbb{R}^{m-k} \in \mathcal{B}^m$, and so the argument of the second case applies. ■

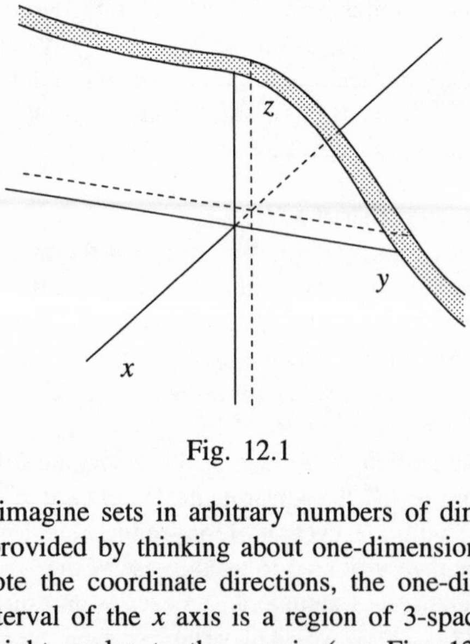

Fig. 12.1

It is not easy to imagine sets in arbitrary numbers of dimensions, but good visual intuition is provided by thinking about one-dimensional cylinders in $\mathbb{R}^3$. Letting (x,y,z) denote the coordinate directions, the one-dimensional cylinder generated by an interval of the x axis is a region of 3-space bounded by two infinite planes at right angles to the x axis (see Fig. 12.1 for a cut-away representation). A union of x-cylinders is another x-cylinder, a collection of parallel 'walls'. But the union and intersection of an x-cylinder with a y-cylinder are two-dimensional cylinder sets, a 'cross' and a 'column' respectively (see Fig. 12.2).

These examples show that the collection of cylinder sets in $\mathbb{R}^k$ for fixed k is *not* a field; the intersection of three mutually orthogonal 'walls' in $\mathbb{R}^3$ is a bounded 'cube', not a cylinder set. The set of finite-dimensional cylinders is not closed under the operations of union and complementation (and hence intersection) *except* in an infinite-dimensional space. This fact is critical in considering $\sigma(\mathcal{C})$, the class obtained by adding the countable unions to $\mathcal{C}$. By the last-mentioned property of unions, $\sigma(\mathcal{C})$ includes sets of the form (12.4) with k tending to infinity. Thus, we have the following theorem.

12.3 Theorem $\sigma(\mathscr{C}) = \mathscr{B}^\infty$, the Borel field of sets in $\mathbb{R}^\infty$ with the Tychonoff topology. □

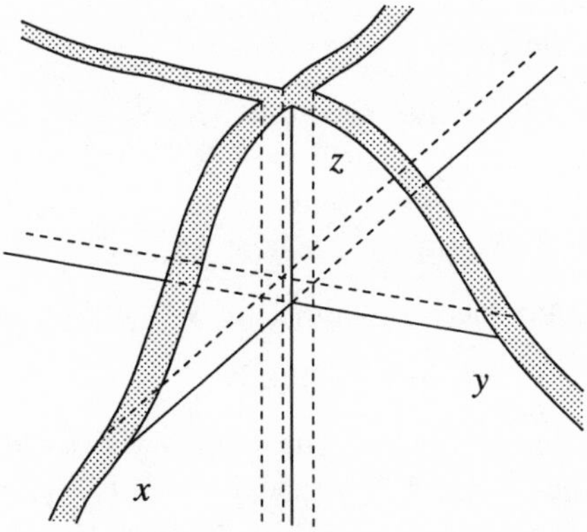

Fig. 12.2

The condition of this result is something we can take for granted in the usual applications. Recalling that the Borel field of a space is the smallest σ-field containing the open sets, **12.3** is true by definition, since $\mathscr{C}$ is a sub-base for the product topology (see §6.5) and all the open sets of $\mathbb{R}^\infty$ are generated by unions and finite intersections of $\mathscr{C}$-sets. To avoid explicit topological considerations, the reader may like to think of **12.3** as providing the definition of $\mathscr{B}^\infty$.

One straightforward implication, since the coordinate projections are continuous mappings and hence measurable, is that, given a distribution on $(\mathbb{R}^\infty,\mathscr{B}^\infty)$, finite collections of sequence coordinates can always be treated as random vectors. But, while this is obviously a condition that will need to be satisfied, the real problem runs the other way. The only *practical* method we have of defining distributions for infinite sequences is to assign probabilities to finite collections of coordinates, after the manner of §8.4. The serious question is whether this can be done in a consistent manner, so that in particular, there is one and only one p.m. on $(\mathbb{R}^\infty,\mathscr{B}^\infty)$ that corresponds to a given set of the finite-dimensional distributions. The affirmative answer to this question is the famous Kolmogorov consistency theorem.

12.4 The Consistency Theorem

The goal is to construct a p.m. on $(\mathbb{R}^\infty,\mathscr{B}^\infty)$, and, following the approach of §3.2, the plausible first step in this direction is to assign probabilities to elements of $\mathscr{C}$. Let μ_k denote a p.m. on the space $(\mathbb{R}^k,\mathscr{B}^k)$, for $k = 1,2,3,\ldots$. We will say that this family of measures satisfies the *consistency property* if

$$\mu_k(E) = \mu_m(E\times\mathbb{R}^{m-k}) \tag{12.7}$$

for $E \in \mathcal{B}_k$ and all $m > k > 0$. In other words, any k-dimensional distribution can be obtained from an m-dimensional distribution with $m > k$, by the usual operation of marginalization.

The consistency theorem actually generalizes to stochastic processes with uncountable index sets $\mathbb{T}$ (see **27.1**) but it is sufficient for present purposes to consider the countable case.

12.4 Kolmogorov's consistency theorem Suppose there exists a family of p.m.s $\{\mu_k\}$ which satisfy consistency condition (12.7). Then there exists a stochastic sequence $x = \{X_t, t \in \mathbb{N}\}$ on a probability space $(\mathbb{R}^\infty, \mathcal{B}^\infty, \mu)$ such that μ_k is the p.m. of the finite vector of coordinate functions $(X_1,\ldots,X_k)'$. □

The candidate measure for x is defined for sets in $\mathcal{C}$ by

$$\mu(C) = \mu_k(E), \tag{12.8}$$

where C and E are related by (12.4). The problem is to show that μ is a p.m. on $\mathcal{C}$. If this is the case, then, since $\mathcal{C}$ is a field and $\mathcal{B}^\infty = \sigma(\mathcal{C})$, we may appeal to the extension theorem (**3.8+3.13**) to establish the existence of a unique measure on $(\mathbb{R}^\infty, \mathcal{B}^\infty)$ which agrees with μ for all $C \in \mathcal{C}$. The theorem has a simple but important corollary.

12.5 Corollary $\mathcal{C}$ is a determining class for $(\mathbb{R}^\infty, \mathcal{B}^\infty)$. □

In other words, if μ and ν are two measures on $(\mathbb{R}^\infty, \mathcal{B}^\infty)$ and $\mu_k = \nu_k$ for every finite k, then $\mu = \nu$.

To prove the consistency theorem we require a technical lemma whose proof is beyond us at this stage. It is quite intuitive, however, and will be proved in a more general context as **26.23**.

12.6 Lemma For every $E \in \mathcal{B}^k$ and $\delta > 0$ there exists K, a compact subset of E, such that $\mu_k(E - K) < \delta$. □

In other words, a p.m. on the space $(\mathbb{R}^k, \mathcal{B}^k)$ has nearly all of its mass confined to a compact set; this implies in particular the proposition asserted in §8.1, that random variables are finite almost surely.

Proof of 12.4 We will verify that μ of (12.8) satisfies the probability axioms with respect to elements of $\mathcal{C}$. When $E = \mathbb{R}^k$, $C = \mathbb{R}^\infty$ so that the first two probability axioms, **7.1**(a) and (b), are certainly satisfied. To establish finite additivity, suppose we have $\mathcal{C}$-sets $C = \pi_k^{-1}(E)$, and $C' = \pi_m^{-1}(E')$ for $E \in \mathcal{B}^k$, $E' \in \mathcal{B}^m$ and $m \geq k$. If C and C' are disjoint,

$$\begin{aligned}\mu(C) + \mu(C') &= \mu_k(E) + \mu_m(E') = \mu_m(E \times \mathbb{R}^{m-k}) + \mu_m(E') \\ &= \mu_m(E \times \mathbb{R}^{m-k} \cup E') = \mu(C \cup C'),\end{aligned} \tag{12.9}$$

where the second equality applies the consistency condition (12.7), and the third one uses the fact that $E \times \mathbb{R}^{m-k}$ and E' are disjoint if C and C' are.

The remaining, relatively tricky, step is to extend finite additivity to countable additivity. This is done by proving continuity, which is an equivalent property according to **3.5**. If and only if the measure is continuous, a monotone sequence $\{C_j \in \mathcal{C}\}$ such that $C_j \downarrow C$ or $C_j \uparrow C$ has the property, $\mu(C_j) \to \mu(C)$. Since $C_j \uparrow C$ implies $C_j^c \downarrow C^c$ where $\mu(C^c) = 1 - \mu(C)$, it is sufficient to consider the decreasing case. And by considering the sequence $C_j - C$ there also is no loss of generality in setting $C = \emptyset$, so that continuity implies $\mu(C_j) \to 0$. To prove continuity, it is sufficient to show that if $\mu(C_j) \geq \varepsilon$ for some $\varepsilon > 0$, for every j, then C is nonempty.

If $C_j \in \mathcal{C}$ for some $j \geq 1$, then $\mu(C_j) = \mu_{k(j)}(E_j)$ for some set $E_j \in \mathcal{B}^{k(j)}$ where $k(j)$ is the dimension of the cylinder C_j. By consistency, $\mu_{k(j)}(E_j) = \mu_m(E_j \times \mathbb{R}^{m-k(j)})$ for any $m > k(j)$, so there is no loss of generality in assuming that $k(1) < k(2) < \dots < k(j) < \dots$. We may therefore define sets $E_i^* \in \mathcal{B}^{k(j)}$, $i = 1,\dots,j$, by setting $E_j^* = E_j$ and

$$E_i^* = E_i \times \mathbb{R}^{k(j)-k(i)},\ i = 1,\dots,j-1. \tag{12.10}$$

Since $\{C_i\}_{i=1}^j$ is a decreasing sequence, so is the sequence of $\mathcal{B}^{k(j)}$-sets $\{E_i^*\}_{i=1}^j$, for each $j \geq 1$.

Consider any fixed j. There exists, by **12.6**, a compact set $K_j \subseteq E_j$ such that

$$\mu_{k(j)}(E_j - K_j) < \varepsilon/2^{j+1}. \tag{12.11}$$

Define the sets $K_i^* = K_i \times \mathbb{R}^{k(j)-k(i)} \in \mathcal{B}^{k(j)}$ by analogy with the E_i^*, and so define

$$F_j = \bigcap_{i=1}^{j} K_i^* \in \mathcal{B}^{k(j)}. \tag{12.12}$$

$F_j \subseteq E_j$, and hence $D_j \subseteq C_j$ where

$$D_j = \pi_{k(j)}^{-1}(F_j) \in \mathcal{C}. \tag{12.13}$$

Applying **1.1**(iii) and then **1.1**(i), observe that

$$E_j - F_j = E_j \cap \left(\bigcup_{i=1}^{j} K_i^{*c}\right) = \bigcup_{i=1}^{j}(E_j - K_i^*) \subseteq \bigcup_{i=1}^{j}(E_i^* - K_i^*), \tag{12.14}$$

where the inclusion is because the sequence $\{E_i^*\}_{i=1}^j$ is decreasing. Hence

$$\begin{aligned}\mu_{k(j)}(E_j - F_j) &\leq \sum_{i=1}^{j} \mu_{k(j)}(E_i^* - K_i^*) \\ &= \sum_{i=1}^{j} \mu_{k(i)}(E_i - K_i) < \varepsilon/2.\end{aligned} \tag{12.15}$$

The first inequality here is from (12.14) by finite subadditivity, which follows from finite additivity as a case of **3.3**(iii). The equality applies consistency, and the second inequality applies the summation of 2^{-i-1}. Since $E_j - F_j$ and F_j are disjoint and $\mu_{k(j)}(E_j) = \mu(C_j) > \varepsilon$ by assumption, it follows from (12.15) that $\mu(D_j) = \mu_{k(j)}(F_j) > \varepsilon/2$, and accordingly that D_j is nonempty.

Now, we construct a point of C. Let $\{x(j), j \in \mathbb{N}\}$ denote a sequence of points of $\mathbb{R}^\infty$ with $x(j) \in D_j$ for each j, so that

$$(X_1(j),...,X_{k(j)}(j)) = \pi_{k(j)}(x(j)) \in F_j. \tag{12.16}$$

Note that for $m = 1,...,j$,

$$(X_1(j),...,X_{k(m)}(j)) = \pi_{k(m)}(x(j)) \in K_m, \tag{12.17}$$

by (12.12), where K_m is compact. Now let m be fixed. Our reasoning ensures that (12.17) holds for each $j \geq m$. A set in $\mathbb{R}^{k(m)}$ is compact if and only if each of the coordinate sets in $\mathbb{R}$ is compact, so consider the bounded scalar sequences, $\{X_i(j),\ j \geq m\}$ for $i = 1,...,k(m)$. Each of these has a cluster point X_i^*, and we can use the diagonal method (**2.36**) to construct a single subsequence $\{j_n\}$ with the property that $X_i(j_n) \to X_i^*$ for each $i = 1,...,k(m)$. By the compactness, $(X_1^*,...,X_{k(m)}^*) \in K_m \subseteq E_m$. This is true for every $m \in \mathbb{N}$.

Consider the point $x^* \in \mathbb{R}^\infty$ defined by $\pi_{k(m)}(x^*) = (X_1^*,...,X_{k(m)}^*)$ for each $m \in \mathbb{N}$. Since $x^* \in C_m$ for each m, we have $x^* \in \bigcap_{m=1}^\infty C_m = C$, as required. ■

This theorem shows that, if a p.m. satisfying (12.7) can be assigned to the finite-dimensional distributions of a sequence x, x is a random element of a probability space $(\mathbb{R}^\infty,\mathcal{B}^\infty,\mu)$. We shall often wish to think of $(\mathbb{R}^\infty,\mathcal{B}^\infty,\mu)$ as derived from an abstract probability space $(\Omega,\mathcal{F},P)$, and then we shall say that x is $\mathcal{F}/\mathcal{B}^\infty$-measurable if $x^{-1}(E) \in \mathcal{F}$ for each event $E \in \mathcal{B}^\infty$. This statement implies the coordinates X_t are $\mathcal{F}/\mathcal{B}$-measurable r.v.s for each t, but it also implies a great deal more than this, since it is possible to assign measures to events involving countably many sequence coordinates.

12.5 Uniform and Limiting Properties

Much the largest part of stochastic process theory has to do with the joint distributions of sets of coordinates, under the general heading of *dependence*. Before getting into these topics, we shall deal in the rest of this chapter with the various issues relating exclusively to the marginal distributions of the coordinates. Of special interest are conditions that limit the random behaviour of a sequence as the index tends to infinity. The concept of a *uniform* condition on the marginal distributions often plays a key role. Thus, a collection of r.v.s $\{X_\tau,\ \tau \in \mathbb{T}\}$ is said to be *uniformly bounded in probability* if, for any $\varepsilon > 0$, there exists $B_\varepsilon < \infty$ such that

$$\sup_\tau P(|X_\tau| \geq B_\varepsilon) < \varepsilon. \tag{12.18}$$

It is also said to be *uniformly L_p-bounded* for $p > 0$, if

$$\sup_\tau \|X_\tau\|_p \leq B < \infty. \tag{12.19}$$

For the case $p = \infty$, (12.19) reduces to the condition, $\sup_\tau|X_\tau| < \infty$ a.s. In this case we just say that the sequence is uniformly bounded a.s. For the case $p = 1$, we have $\sup_\tau E|X_\tau| < \infty$, and one might think it correct to refer to this property as 'uniform integrability', Unfortunately, this term is already in use for a different concept (see the next section) and so must be avoided here. Speak of 'uniform L_1-boundedness' in this context.

To interpret these conditions, recall that in mathematics a property is said to hold uniformly if holds for all members of a class of objects, *including* the limits of any convergent sequences in the class. Consider the case where the collection in question is itself a sequence, with $\mathbb{T} = \mathbb{N}$ and $\tau = t$. Random variables are finite with probability 1, and for each finite $t \in \mathbb{N}$, $P(|X_t| \geq B_{\varepsilon t}) < \varepsilon$ *always* holds for some $B_{\varepsilon t} < \infty$, for any $\varepsilon > 0$. The point of a uniform bound is to ensure that the constants $B_{\varepsilon t}$ are not having to get larger as t increases. 'Bounded uniformly in t' is a different and stronger notion than 'bounded for all $t \in \mathbb{N}$', because, for example, the supremum of the set $\{\|X_t\|_p\}_1^\infty$ may lie outside the set. If $\|X_t\|_p \leq B_t < \infty$ for every t, we would say that the sequence was L_p-bounded, but not uniformly L_p-bounded unless we also ruled out the possibility that $B_t \to \infty$ as $t \to \infty$ (or $-\infty$). Note that the statement '$\|X_t\|_p \leq B$, $t \in \mathbb{N}$', where B is the same finite constant for all t, *is* equivalent to '$\sup_t\|X_t\|_p \leq B$', because the former condition must extend to any limit of $\{\|X_t\|_p\}$. But the 'sup' notation is less ambiguous, and a good habit to adopt.

The relationships between integrability conditions studied in §9.3 and §9.5 can be used here to establish a hierarchy of boundedness conditions. Uniform L_r-boundedness implies uniform L_p-boundedness for $r > p > 0$, by Liapunov's inequality. Also, uniform L_p-boundedness for any $p > 0$ implies uniform boundedness in probability; the Markov inequality gives

$$P(|X_t| \geq B) \leq \|X_t\|_p^p/B^p, \tag{12.20}$$

so that, for given $\varepsilon > 0$, (12.18) holds for $B_\varepsilon > \|X_t\|_p/\varepsilon^{1/p}$. By a mild abuse of terminology we sometimes speak of L_0-boundedness in the case of (12.18).

A standard shorthand (due to Mann and Wald 1943b) for the maximum rate of (positive or negative) increase of a stochastic sequence uses the notion of uniform boundedness in probability to extend the 'Big Oh' and 'Little Oh' notation for ordinary real sequences (see §2.6). If, for $\varepsilon > 0$, there exists $B_\varepsilon < \infty$ such that the stochastic sequence $\{X_n\}_1^\infty$ satisfies $\sup_n P(|X_n| > B_\varepsilon) < \varepsilon$, we write $X_n = O_p(1)$. If $\{Y_n\}_1^\infty$ is another sequence, either stochastic or nonstochastic, and $X_n/Y_n = O_p(1)$ we say that $X_n = O_p(Y_n)$, or in words, 'X_n is at most of order Y_n in probability'. If $P(|X_n| > \varepsilon) \to 0$ as $n \to \infty$, we say that $X_n = o_p(1)$; more generally $X_n = o_p(Y_n)$ when $X_n/Y_n = o_p(1)$, or in words, 'X_n is of order less than Y_n in probability'.

The main use of these notations is in manipulating small-order terms in an expression, without specifying them explicitly. Usually, Y_n is a positive or negative power of n. To say that $X_n = o_p(1)$ is equivalent to saying that X_n converges in probability to zero, following the terminology of §12.2. Sometimes $X_n = O_p(1)$ is defined by the condition that for each $\varepsilon > 0$ there exists $B_\varepsilon < \infty$ and an integer $N_\varepsilon \geq 1$ such that $P(|X_n| > B_\varepsilon) < \varepsilon$ for all $n \geq N_\varepsilon$. But X_n is finite almost surely, and there necessarily exists (this is by **12.6**) a constant $B'_\varepsilon < \infty$, possibly larger than B_ε, such that $P(|X_n| > B'_\varepsilon) < \varepsilon$ for $1 \leq n < N_\varepsilon$. For all practical purposes, the formulations are equivalent.

12.6 Uniform Integrability

If a r.v. X is integrable, the contributions to the integral of extreme X values must be negligible. In other words, if $E|X| < \infty$,

$$E(|X|1_{\{|X|\geq M\}}) \to 0 \text{ as } M \to \infty. \tag{12.21}$$

However, it is possible to construct uniformly L_1-bounded sequences $\{X_n\}$ which fail to satisfy (12.21) in the limit.

12.7 Example Define a stochastic sequence as follows: for $n = 1,2,3,...$ let $X_n = 0$ with probability $1 - 1/n$, and $X_n = n$ with probability $1/n$. Note that $E(|X_n|) = n/n = 1$ for every n, and hence the sequence is uniformly L_1-bounded. But to have

$$\lim_{M\to\infty} E(|X_n|1_{\{|X_n|\geq M\}}) = 0 \tag{12.22}$$

uniformly in n requires that for each $\varepsilon > 0$ there exists M_ε such that $E(|X_n|1_{\{|X_n|\geq M\}}) < \varepsilon$ for all $M > M_\varepsilon$, uniformly in n. Clearly, this condition fails, for $\varepsilon < 1$, in view of the cases $n > M_\varepsilon$. □

Something very strange is going on in this example. Although $E(X_n) = 1$ for any n, $X_n = 0$ with probability approaching 1 as $n \to \infty$. To be precise, we may show that $X_n \xrightarrow{as} 0$ (see **18.15**). The intuitive concept of expectation appears to fail when faced with r.v.s taking values approaching infinity with probabilities approaching zero.

The *uniform integrability* condition rules out this type of perverse behaviour in a sequence. The collection $\{X_\tau, \tau \in \mathbb{T}\}$ is said to be uniformly integrable if

$$\sup_{\tau\in\mathbb{T}}\left\{\lim_{M\to\infty} E(|X_\tau|1_{\{|X_\tau|\geq M\}})\right\} = 0. \tag{12.23}$$

In our applications the collection in question is usually either a sequence or an array. In the latter case, uniform integrability of $\{X_{nt}\}$ (say) is defined by taking the supremum with respect to both t and n.

The following is a collection of theorems on uniform integrability which will find frequent application later on; **12.8** in particular provides insight into why this concept is so important, since the last example shows that the conclusion does not generally hold without uniform integrability.

12.8 Theorem Let $\{X_n\}_1^\infty$ be a uniformly integrable sequence. If $X_n \xrightarrow{as} X$, then $E(X_n) \to E(X)$.

Proof Note that

$$\begin{aligned} E(|X_n|) &= E(|X_n|1_{\{|X_n|<M\}}) + E(|X_n|1_{\{|X_n|\geq M\}}) \\ &\leq M + E(|X_n|1_{\{|X_n|\geq M\}}). \end{aligned} \tag{12.24}$$

By choosing M large enough the second term on the right can be made uniformly small by assumption, and it follows that $E|X_n|$ is uniformly bounded. Fatou's lemma implies that $E|X| < \infty$, and $E(X)$ exists. Define $Y_n = |X_n - X|$, so that $Y_n \to 0$ a.s. Since $Y_n \le |X_n| + |X|$ by the triangle inequality, **9.29** gives

$$E(Y_n 1_{\{Y_n > M\}}) \le 2E(|X_n| 1_{\{|X_n| > M/2\}}) + 2E(|X| 1_{\{|X| > M/2\}}). \tag{12.25}$$

The second right-hand-side term goes to zero as $M \to \infty$, so $\{Y_n\}$ is uniformly integrable if $\{X_n\}$ is. We may write

$$E(Y_n) = E(Y_n 1_{\{Y_n \le M\}}) + E(Y_n 1_{\{Y_n > M\}}), \tag{12.26}$$

and by the bounded convergence theorem there exists, for any $\varepsilon > 0$, N_ε such that $E(Y_n 1_{\{Y_n \le M\}}) < \varepsilon/2$ for $n > N_\varepsilon$, for $M < \infty$. M can be chosen large enough that $E(Y_n 1_{\{Y_n > M\}}) < \varepsilon/2$ uniformly in n, so that $E(Y_n) < \varepsilon$ for $n > N_\varepsilon$, or, since ε is arbitrary, $E(Y_n) \to 0$. But

$$E(Y_n) = E(|X_n - X|) \ge |E(X_n) - E(X)| \tag{12.27}$$

by the modulus inequality, and the theorem follows. ■

The next theorem gives an alternative form for the condition in (12.23) which is often more convenient for establishing uniform integrability.

12.9 Theorem A collection $\{X_\tau, \tau \in \mathbb{T}\}$ of r.v.s on a probability space $(\Omega, \mathcal{F}, P)$ is uniformly integrable iff it is uniformly L_1-bounded and satisfies the following condition: $\forall\ \varepsilon > 0$, $\exists\ \delta > 0$ such that, for $E \in \mathcal{F}$,

$$P(E) \le \delta \ \Rightarrow\ \sup_{\tau \in \mathbb{T}} \{E(|X_\tau| 1_E)\} < \varepsilon. \tag{12.28}$$

Proof To show sufficiency, fix $\varepsilon > 0$ and $\tau \in \mathbb{T}$. By L_1-boundedness and the Markov inequality for $p = 1$,

$$P(|X_\tau| \ge M) \le \frac{E|X_\tau|}{M} < \infty, \tag{12.29}$$

and for M large enough, $P(|X_\tau| \ge M) \le \delta$, for any $\delta > 0$. Choosing δ to satisfy (12.28), it follows since τ is arbitrary that

$$\sup_{\tau \in \mathbb{T}} \{E(|X_\tau| 1_{\{|X_\tau| \ge M\}})\} < \varepsilon, \tag{12.30}$$

and (12.23) follows since ε is arbitrary.

To show necessity, note that, for any $E \in \mathcal{F}$ and $\tau \in \mathbb{T}$,

$$\begin{aligned} E(|X_\tau| 1_E) &= E(|X_\tau| 1_E 1_{\{|X_\tau| < M\}}) + E(|X_\tau| 1_E 1_{\{|X_\tau| \ge M\}}) \\ &\le MP(E) + E(|X_\tau| 1_{\{|X_\tau| \ge M\}}). \end{aligned} \tag{12.31}$$

Consider the suprema with respect to τ of each side of this inequality. For $\varepsilon > 0$, (12.23) implies there exists $M < \infty$ such that

$$\sup_\tau \{E(|X_\tau| 1_E)\} < MP(E) + \tfrac{1}{2}\varepsilon. \tag{12.32}$$

Uniform L_1-boundedness now follows on setting $E = \Omega$, and (12.28) also follows with $\delta < \varepsilon/2M$. ■

Another way to express condition (12.28) is to say that the measures $\nu_\tau(E) = \int_E |X_\tau| dP$ must be absolutely continuous with respect to P, uniformly in τ.

Finally, we prove a result which shows why the uniform boundedness of moments of a given order may be important.

12.10 Theorem If

$$E|X_\tau|^{1+\theta} < \infty \tag{12.33}$$

for $\theta > 0$, then $\lim_{M\to\infty} E(|X_\tau| 1_{\{|X_\tau|\geq M\}}) = 0$.

Proof Note that

$$\begin{aligned} E|X_\tau|^{1+\theta} &\geq E(|X_\tau|^{1+\theta} 1_{\{|X_\tau|\geq M\}}) \\ &\geq M^\theta E(|X_\tau| 1_{\{|X_\tau|\geq M\}}) \end{aligned} \tag{12.34}$$

for any $\theta > 0$. The result follows on letting $M \to \infty$, since the majorant side of (12.34) is finite by (12.33). ■

Example **12.7** illustrated the fact that uniform L_1-boundedness is not sufficient for uniform integrability, but **12.10** shows that uniform $L_{1+\theta}$-boundedness *is* sufficient, for any $\theta > 0$. Adding this result to those of §12.5, we have established the hierarchy of uniform conditions summarized in the following theorem.

12.11 Theorem

Uniform boundedness a.s. $\Rightarrow$ uniform L_p-boundedness, p > 1
$\Rightarrow$ uniform integrability
$\Rightarrow$ uniform L_p-boundedness, $0 < p \leq 1$
$\Rightarrow$ uniform boundedness in probability. □

None of the reverse implications hold.

13
Dependence

13.1 Shift Transformations

We now consider relationships between the different members of a sequence. In what ways, for example, might the joint distribution of X_t and X_{t-k} depend upon k, and upon t? To answer questions such as these it is sometimes helpful to think about the sequence in a new way. Having introduced the notion of a random sequence as a point in a probability space, there is a useful analogy between studying the relationships within a sequence and comparing different sequences, that is, different sample outcomes $\omega \in \Omega$.

In a probability space $(\Omega,\mathcal{F},P)$, consider a 1-1 measurable mapping, T: $\Omega \mapsto \Omega$ (onto). This is a rule for pairing each outcome with another outcome of the space, but if each $\omega \in \Omega$ maps into an infinite sequence, T induces a mapping from one sequence to another. T is called *measure-preserving* if $P(TE) = P(E)$ for all $E \in \mathcal{F}$.

The *shift transformation* for a sequence $\{X_t(\omega)\}_1^\infty$ is defined by[10]

$$X_t(T\omega) = X_{t+1}(\omega). \tag{13.1}$$

T takes each outcome ω into the outcome under which the realized value of X occurring in period t now occurs in period $t+1$, for every t. In effect, each coordinate of the sequence from $t = 2$ onwards is relabelled with the previous period's index. More generally we can write $X_t(T^k\omega) = X_{t+k}(\omega)$, the relationship between points in the sequence k periods apart becoming a characteristic of the transformation T^k. Since X_t is a r.v. for all t, both the shift transformation and its inverse T^{-1}, the *backshift* transformation, must be measurable.

Taken together, the single r.v. $X_1(\omega)$: $\Omega \mapsto \mathbb{R}$ and the shift transformation T, can be thought of as generating a complete description of the sequence $\{X_t(\omega)\}_1^\infty$. This can be seen as follows. Given $X_1(\omega)$, apply the transformation T to ω, and obtain $X_2 = X_1(T\omega)$. Doing this for each $\omega \in \Omega$ defines the mapping $X_2(\omega)$: $\Omega \mapsto \mathbb{R}$, and we are ready to get $X_3 = X_2(T\omega)$. Iterating the procedure generates as many points in the sequence as we require.

13.1 Example Consider **12.1**. Let $\{X_t(\omega)\}_1^\infty$ be a sequence of coin tosses (with 1 for heads, 0 for tails) beginning 110100100011... (say). Somewhere on the interval [0,1] of real numbers (in binary representation), there is also a sequence $\{X_t(\omega')\}_1^\infty$ beginning 10100100011..., identical to the sequence indexed by ω apart from the dropping of the initial digit and the backshift of the remainder by one position. Likewise there is another sequence $\{X_t(\omega'')\}_1^\infty$, a backshifted version of $\{X_t(\omega')\}_1^\infty$ beginning 0100100011...; and so forth. If we define the transformation

T by $T^{-1}\omega = \omega'$, $T^{-1}\omega' = \omega''$, etc., the sequence $\{X_t(\omega)\}_1^\infty$ can be constructed as the sequence $\{X_1(T^{1-t}\omega)\}_1^\infty$; that is, the sequence of first members of the sequences found by iterating the transformation, in this case beginning 1,1,0,... □

This device reveals, among other things, the complex structure of the probability space we are postulating. To each point $\omega \in \Omega$ there must correspond a countably infinite set of points $T^k\omega \in \Omega$, which reproduce the same sequence apart from the absolute date associated with X_1. The intertemporal properties of a sequence can then be treated as a comparison of two sequences, the original and the sequence lagged k periods.

Econometricians attempt to make inferences about economic behaviour from recorded economic data. In time-series analysis, the sample available is usually a *single* realization of a random sequence, economic history as it actually occurred. Because we observe only one world, it is easy to make the mistake of looking on it as the whole sample space, whereas it is really only one of the many possible realizations the workings of historical chance might have generated. Indeed, in our probability model the whole economic universe is the counterpart of a single random outcome ω; there is an important sense in which the time series analyst is a statistician who draws inferences from single data points! But although a single realization of the sequence can be treated as a mapping from a single ω, it is linked to a countably infinite set of ωs corresponding to the leads and lags of the sequence. A large part of our subsequent enquiry can be summarized as posing the question: is this set really rich enough to allow us to make inferences about P from a single realization?

13.2 Independence and Stationarity

Independence and stationarity are the best-known restrictions on the behaviour of a sequence, but also the most stringent, from the point of view of describing economic time series. But while the emphasis in this book will mainly be on finding ways to relax these conditions, they remain important because of the many classic theorems in probability and limit theory which are founded on them.

The degree to which random variations of sequence coordinates are related to those of their neighbours in the time ordering is sometimes called the *memory* of a sequence; in the context of time-ordered observations, one may think in terms of the amount of information contained in the current state of the sequence about its previous states. A sequence with no memory is a rather special kind of object, because the ordering ceases to have significance. It is like the outcome of a collection of independent random experiments conducted in parallel, and indexed arbitrarily.

When a time ordering does nominally exist, we call such a sequence *serially independent*. Generalizing the theory of §8.6, a pair of sequences $[\{X_t(\omega)\}_1^\infty, \{Y_t(\omega)\}_1^\infty] \in \mathbb{R}^\infty \times \mathbb{R}^\infty$, is independent if, for all $E_1, E_2 \in \mathcal{B}^\infty$,

$$P(\{X_t\}_1^\infty \in E_1,\ \{Y_t\}_1^\infty \in E_2) = P(\{X_t\}_1^\infty \in E_1)P(\{Y_t\}_1^\infty \in E_2). \qquad (13.2)$$

Accordingly, a sequence $\{X_t(\omega)\}_1^\infty$ is serially independent if it is independent of

$\{X_t(T^k\omega)\}_1^\infty$ for all $k > 0$. This is equivalent to saying that every finite collection of sequence coordinates is totally independent.

Serial independence is the simplest possible assumption about memory. Similarly, looking at the distribution of the sequence as a whole, the simplest treatment is to assume that the joint distribution of the coordinates is invariant with respect to the time index. A random sequence is called *strictly stationary* if the shift transformation is measure-preserving. This implies that the sequences $\{X_t\}_{t=1}^\infty$ and $\{X_{t+k}\}_{t=1}^\infty$ have the same joint distribution, for every $k > 0$.

Subject to the existence of particular moments, less restrictive versions of the condition are also commonly employed. Letting $\mu_t = E(X_t)$, and $\gamma_{kt} = \text{Cov}(X_t, X_{t+k})$, consider those cases in which the sequence $\{\mu_t\}_{t=1}^\infty$, and also the array $\{\{\gamma_{mt}\}_{m=0}^\infty\}_{t=1}^\infty$, are well defined. If $\mu_t = \mu$, all t, we say the sequence is *mean stationary*. If a mean stationary sequence has $\gamma_{mt} = \gamma_m$ where $\{\gamma_m\}_0^\infty$ is a sequence of constants, it is called *covariance stationary*, or *wide sense* stationary.

If the marginal distribution of X_t is the same for any t, the sequence $\{X_t\}$ is said to be *identically distributed*. This concept is different from stationarity, which also restricts the joint distribution of neighbours in the sequence. However, when a stochastic sequence is both serially independent and identically distributed (or *i.i.d.*), this suffices for stationarity. An i.i.d. sequence is like an arbitrarily indexed random sample drawn from some a underlying population.

The following clutch of examples include both stationary and nonstationary cases.

13.2 Example Let the sequence $\{\varepsilon_t\}_{-\infty}^\infty$ be i.i.d. with mean 0 and variance $\sigma^2 < \infty$, and let $\{\theta_j\}_0^\infty$ be a square-summable sequence of constants. Then $\{X_t\}_1^\infty$, where

$$X_t = \sum_{j=0}^{\infty} \theta_j \varepsilon_{t-j}, \tag{13.3}$$

is a covariance stationary sequence, with $E(X_t) = 0$ and $E(X_t^2) = \sigma^2 \sum_{j=0}^\infty \theta_j^2$ for every t. This is the *infinite-order moving average* (MA(∞)) process. See §14.3 for additional details. □

13.3 Example If ε_t is i.i.d. with mean 0, and

$$X_t = \cos at + \varepsilon_t \tag{13.4}$$

for a constant a, then $E(X_t) = \cos at$, depending systematically on t. □

13.4 Example Let $\{X_t\}$ be any stationary sequence with autocovariance sequence $\{\gamma_m, m \geq 0\}$. The sequence $\{X_t + X_0\}$ has autocovariances given by the array

$$\{\gamma_0 + \gamma_m + \gamma_t + \gamma_{t+m},\ m \geq 0,\ t \geq 1\},$$

and hence it is nonstationary. □

13.5 Example Let X be a r.v. which is symmetrically distributed about 0, with variance σ^2. If $X_t = (-1)^t X$, then $\{X_t\}_1^\infty$ is a stationary sequence. In particular, $E(X_t) = 0$, and $\text{Cov}(X_t, X_{t+k}) = \sigma^2$ when k is even and $-\sigma^2$ when k is odd, independent of t. □

These examples show that, contrary to a common misconception, stationarity does not imply homogeneity in the appearance of a sequence, or the absence of periodic patterns. The essential feature is that any patterns in the sequence do not depend systematically on the time index. It is also important to distinguish between stationarity and limited dependence, although these notions are often closely linked. Example **13.4** is nonstationary in view of dependence on initial conditions. The square-summability condition in **13.2** allows us to show covariance stationarity, but is actually a limitation on the long-range dependence of the process. Treatments of time series modelling which focus exclusively on models in the linear MA class often fail to distinguish between these properties, but examples **13.3** and **13.5** demonstrate that there is no necessary connection between them.

Stationarity is a strong assumption, particularly for the description of empirical time series, where features like seasonal patterns are commonly found. It is useful to distinguish between 'local' nonstationarity, something we might think of as capable of elimination by local averaging of the coordinates, and 'global' nonstationarity, involving features such as persistent trends in the moments. If sequences $\{X_t\}_{t=1}^{\infty}$ and $\{X_{t+k}\}_{t=1}^{\infty}$ have the same distribution for *some* (not necessarily every) $k > 0$, it follows that $\{X_{t+2k}\}_{t=1}^{\infty}$ has the same distribution as $\{X_{t+k}\}_{t=1}^{\infty}$, and the same property extends to every integer multiple of k. Such a sequence accordingly has certain stationary characteristics, if we think in terms of the distributions of successive blocks of k coordinates. This idea retains force even as $k \to \infty$. Consider the limit of a finite sequence of length n, divided into $[n^{\alpha}]$ blocks of length $[n^{1-\alpha}]$, plus any remainder, for some α between 0 and 1. (Note, $[x]$ here denotes the largest integer below x.) The number of blocks as well as their extent is going to infinity, and the stationarity (or otherwise) of the sequence of blocks in the limit is clearly an issue. Important applications of these ideas arise in Parts V and VI below.

It is convenient to formulate a definition embodying this concept in terms of moments. Thus, a zero-mean sequence will be said to be *globally covariance stationary* if the autocovariance sequences $\{\gamma_{mt}\}_{t=1}^{\infty}$ are Cesàro-summable for each $m \geq 0$, where the Cesàro sum is strictly positive in the case of the variances ($m = 0$). The following are a pair of contrasting counter-examples.

13.6 Example A sequence with $\gamma_{0t} \sim t^{\beta}$ is globally nonstationary for any $\beta \neq 0$. □

13.7 Example Consider the integer sequence beginning

$$1,2,1,1,2,2,2,2,1,1,1,1,1,1,1,1,\ldots;$$

i.e. the value changes at points $t = 2^k$, $k = 1,2,3,\ldots$ The Cesàro sum of this sequence fails to converge as $n \to \infty$. It fluctuates eventually between the points 5/3 at $n = 2^k$, k odd, and 4/3 at $n = 2^k$, k even. A stochastic sequence having a variance sequence of this form is globally nonstationary. □

13.3 Invariant Events

The amount of dependence in a sequence is the chief factor determining how informative a realization of given length can be about the distribution that generated it. At one extreme, the i.i.d. sequence is equivalent to a true random sample. The classical theorems of statistics can be applied to this type of distribution. At the other extreme, it is easy to specify sequences for which a single realization can never reveal the parameters of the distribution to us, even in the limit as its length tends to infinity. This last possibility is what concerns us most, since we want to know whether averaging operations applied to sequences have useful limiting properties; whether, for example, parameters of the generation process can be consistently estimated in this way.

To clarify these issues, imagine repeated sampling of random sequences $\{X_t(\omega)\}_1^\infty$; in other words, imagine being given a function $X_1(.)$ and transformation T, making repeated random drawings of ω from Ω and constructing the corresponding random sequences; **13.1** illustrates the procedure. Let the sample drawings be denoted ω_i, $i = 1,\ldots,N$, and imagine constructing the average of the realizations at some fixed time t_0. The average $\bar{X}_{N,t_0} = N^{-1}\sum_{i=1}^N X_{t_0}(\omega_i)$ is called an *ensemble average*, which may be contrasted with the *time average* of a realization of length n for some given $\omega_i \in \Omega$, $\bar{X}_n(\omega_i) = n^{-1}\sum_{t=1}^n X_t(\omega_i)$. Fig. 13.1 illustrates this procedure, showing a sample of three realizations of the sequence. The ensemble average is the average of the points falling on the vertical line labelled t_0. It is clear that the limits of the time average and the ensemble average as n and N respectively go to infinity are not in general the same; we might expect the ensemble average to tend to the marginal expectation $E(X_{t_0})$, but the time average will not do so except in special cases. If the sequence is nonstationary $E(X_{t_0})$ depends upon t_0, but even assuming stationarity, it is still possible that different realizations of the sequence depend upon random effects which are common to all t.

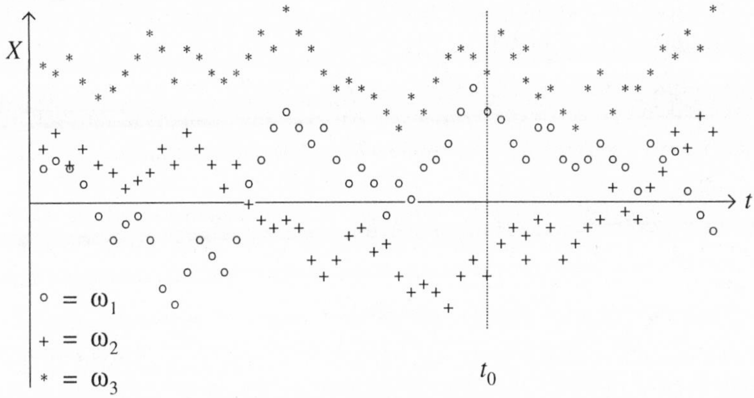

Fig. 13.1

In a probability space $(\Omega,\mathcal{F},P)$ the event $E \in \mathcal{F}$ is said to be *invariant* under a transformation T if $P(TE\,\Delta\, E) = 0$. The criterion for invariance is sometimes given as $TE = E$, but allowing the two events to differ by a set of measure zero does not change anything important in the theory. The set of events in $\mathcal{F}$ that are invariant under the shift transformation is denoted $\mathcal{I}$.

13.8 Theorem $\mathcal{I}$ is a σ-field.

Proof Since T is onto, Ω is clearly invariant. Since T is also 1-1,

$$TE^c\,\Delta\, E^c = (TE)^c\,\Delta\, E^c = TE\,\Delta\, E \tag{13.5}$$

by definition. And, given $\{E_n \in \mathcal{I},\ n \in \mathbb{N}\}$,

$$P(TE_n\,\Delta\, E_n) = P(TE_n - E_n) + P(E_n - TE_n) = 0 \tag{13.6}$$

for each n, and also

$$T\Big(\bigcup_n E_n\Big)\,\Delta\, \bigcup_n E_n = \bigcup_n TE_n\,\Delta\, \bigcup_n E_n, \tag{13.7}$$

using **1.2**(i). By **1.1**(i) and then **1.1**(iii),

$$\bigcup_n TE_n - \bigcup_n E_n = \bigcup_n\Big(TE_n \cap \bigcap_n E_n^c\Big) \subseteq \bigcup_n (TE_n - E_n), \tag{13.8}$$

and similarly,

$$\bigcup_n E_n - \bigcup_n TE_n \subseteq \bigcup_n (E_n - TE_n). \tag{13.9}$$

The conclusion $P[T(\bigcup_n E_n)\,\Delta\,(\bigcup_n E_n)] = 0$ now follows by (13.6) and **3.6**(ii), completing the proof. ■

An *invariant random variable* is one that is $\mathcal{I}/\mathcal{B}$-measurable. An invariant r.v. $Z(\omega)$ has the property that $Z(T\omega) = Z(\omega)$, and an $\mathcal{I}/\mathcal{B}$-measurable sequence $\{Z_t(\omega)\}_1^\infty$ is trivial in the sense that $Z_t(\omega) = Z_1(\omega)$ a.s. for every t. The invariant events and associated r.v.s constitute those aspects of the probability model that do not alter with the passage of time.

13.9 Example Consider the sequence $\{X_t(\omega)\}$ where $X_t(\omega) = Y_t(\omega) + Z(\omega)$, $\{Y_t(\omega)\}$ being a random sequence and $Z(\omega)$ a r.v. An example of an invariant event is $E = \{\omega\colon Z(\omega) \le z,\ Y_t(\omega) \in \mathbb{R}\}$. Clearly E and TE are the same event, since Z is the only thing subject to a condition.

Fig. 13.1 illustrates this case. If $\{Y_t(\omega)\}$ is a zero-mean stationary sequence, the figure illustrates the cases $Z(\omega_1) = Z(\omega_2) = 0$, and $Z(\omega_3) > 0$. Even if $E(Z) = 0$, the influence of $Z(\omega)$ in the time average is not 'averaged out' in the limit, as it will be from the ensemble average. □

The behaviour of the time average as $n \to \infty$ is summarized by the following fundamental result.

13.10 Theorem (Doob 1953: th. X.2.1) Let a stationary sequence $\{X_t(\omega)\}_1^\infty$ be defined by a measurable mapping $X_1(\omega)$ and measure-preserving shift transformation T, such that $X_t(\omega) = X_1(T^{t-1}\omega)$, and let $S_n(\omega) = \sum_{t=1}^{n} X_t(\omega)$. If $E|X_1| < \infty$,

$$\lim_{n\to\infty} S_n(\omega)/n = E(X_1 | \mathcal{I})(\omega), \text{ a.s. } \square \tag{13.10}$$

In words, the limiting case of the time average can be identified with the mean of the distribution conditional on the σ-field of invariant events.

The proof of **13.10** requires a technical lemma.

13.11 Lemma Let $\Lambda(\beta) = \{\omega: \sup_n(S_n(\omega) - n\beta) > 0\}$. Then for any set $M \in \mathcal{I}$,

$$\int_{M\cap\Lambda(\beta)} X_1(\omega)dP(\omega) \geq \beta P(M \cap \Lambda(\beta)). \tag{13.11}$$

Proof We establish this for the case $\beta = 0$. To generalize to any real β, consider the sequence $\{X_t - \beta\}$, which is stationary if $\{X_t\}$ is stationary.

Write Λ for $\Lambda(0)$, and let $\Lambda_j = \{\omega: \max_{1\leq k\leq j} S_k(\omega) > 0\}$, the set of outcomes for which the partial sum is positive at least once by time j. Note, the sequence $\{\Lambda_j\}$ is monotone and $\Lambda_j \uparrow \Lambda$ as $j \to \infty$. Also let

$$N_{nj} = T^{-j}\Lambda_{n-j} = \left\{\omega: \max_{1\leq k\leq n-j} S_k(T^j\omega) > 0\right\}. \tag{13.12}$$

Since

$$S_k(T^j\omega) = \sum_{t=1}^{k} X_t(T^j\omega) = \sum_{t=j+1}^{j+k} X_t(\omega) = S_{j+k}(\omega) - S_j(\omega), \tag{13.13}$$

by defining $S_0 = 0$ we may also write

$$N_{nj} = \left\{\omega: \max_{j+1\leq k\leq n} (S_k(\omega) - S_j(\omega)) > 0\right\}, \; 0 \leq j \leq n-1. \tag{13.14}$$

This is the set of outcomes for which the partial sums of the coordinates from $j+1$ to n are positive at least once, and we have the inequality (explained below)

$$\sum_{j=0}^{n-1} X_{j+1}(\omega) 1_{N_{nj}}(\omega) \geq 0, \text{ all } \omega \in \Omega. \tag{13.15}$$

Integrating this sum over the invariant set M gives

$$0 \leq \sum_{j=0}^{n-1} \int_{M\cap N_{nj}} X_{j+1}(\omega)dP(\omega) = \sum_{j=0}^{n-1} \int_{M\cap\Lambda_{n-j}} X_{j+1}(T^{-j}\omega)dP(\omega)$$

$$= \sum_{j=0}^{n-1} \int_{M\cap\Lambda_{n-j}} X_1(\omega)dP(\omega) = \sum_{j=1}^{n} \int_{M\cap\Lambda_j} X_1(\omega)dP(\omega), \tag{13.16}$$

where the first equality uses the fact that $\Lambda_{n-j} = \{\omega: T^{-j}\omega \in N_{nj}\}$ and the measure-preserving property of T, and the third is by reversing the order of summation. The dominated convergence theorem applied to $\{X_1 1_{M\cap\Lambda_j}\}$, with $|X_1|$ as the dominating function, yields

$$\int_{M\cap\Lambda_j} X_1(\omega)dP(\omega) \to \int_{M\cap\Lambda} X_1(\omega)dP(\omega). \tag{13.17}$$

This limit is equal to the Cesàro limit by **2.26**, so that, as required,

$$\int_{M\cap\Lambda} X_1(\omega)dP(\omega) = \lim_{n\to\infty} \frac{1}{n}\sum_{j=1}^{n} \int_{M\cap\Lambda_j} X_1(\omega)dP(\omega) \geq 0. \blacksquare \tag{13.18}$$

The inequality in (13.15) is not self-evident, but is justified as follows. The expression on the left is the sum containing only those $X_t(\omega)$ having the property that in realization ω, the partial sums from the point t onwards are positive at least once, otherwise the tth contribution to the sum is 0. The sum includes only X_t lying in segments of the sequence over which S_k increases, so that their net contribution must be positive. It would be zero only in the case $X_t \leq 0$ for $1 \leq t \leq n$. Fig. 13.2 depicts a realization. '∘' shows values of $S_k(\omega)$ for $k = 1,\ldots,n$, so the $X_t(\omega)$ are the vertical separations between successive '∘'. '+' shows the running sum of the terms of (13.15). The coordinates where the X_t are to be omitted from (13.15) are arrowed, the criterion being that there is no '∘' to the right which exceeds the current '∘'.

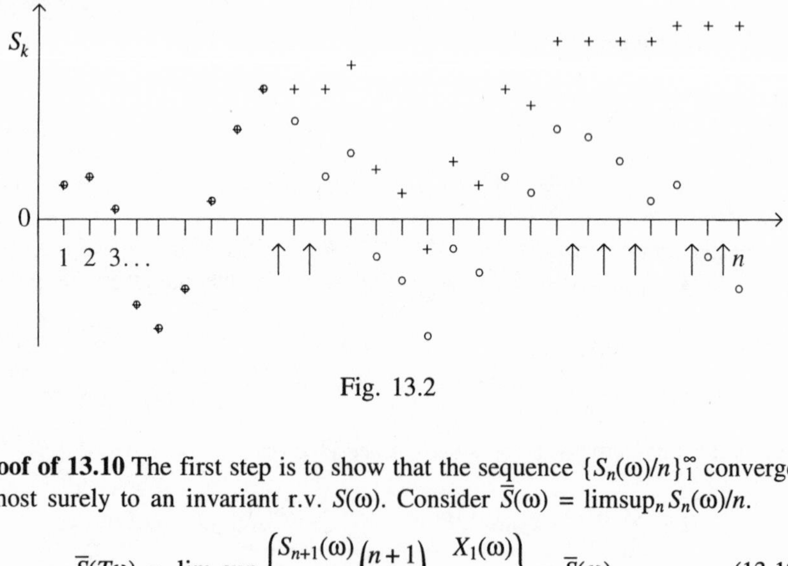

Fig. 13.2

Proof of 13.10 The first step is to show that the sequence $\{S_n(\omega)/n\}_1^\infty$ converges almost surely to an invariant r.v. $S(\omega)$. Consider $\overline{S}(\omega) = \limsup_n S_n(\omega)/n$.

$$\overline{S}(T\omega) = \lim_{m\to\infty}\sup_{n\geq m}\left\{\frac{S_{n+1}(\omega)}{n+1}\left(\frac{n+1}{n}\right) - \frac{X_1(\omega)}{n}\right\} = \overline{S}(\omega), \tag{13.19}$$

so that $\overline{S}(\omega)$ is invariant, the same being true for $\underline{S}(\omega) = \liminf_n S_n(\omega)/n$. Hence, the event $M(\alpha,\beta) = \{\omega\colon \underline{S}(\omega) < \alpha < \beta < \overline{S}(\omega)\}$ is invariant. Since $\sup_n S_n(\omega)/n \geq \overline{S}(\omega)$, $M(\alpha,\beta) \subseteq \Lambda(\beta)$ where $\Lambda(\beta)$ is defined in the statement of **13.11**. Hence, putting $M = M(\alpha,\beta)$ in the lemma gives

$$\int_{M(\alpha,\beta)} X_1(\omega)dP(\omega) \geq \beta P(M(\alpha,\beta)). \tag{13.20}$$

But now replace $X_t(\omega)$ in **13.11** by $-X_t(\omega)$, and observe that $M(\alpha,\beta) \subseteq \Lambda(-\alpha) = \{\omega\colon \sup_n(-S_n(\omega)/n) > -\alpha\}$. Hence we get

$$\int_{M(\alpha,\beta)} X_1(\omega)dP(\omega) \leq \alpha P(M(\alpha,\beta)). \tag{13.21}$$

Since the left-hand sides of (13.21) and (13.20) are equal and $\alpha < \beta$, it follows that $P(M(\alpha,\beta)) = 0$; that is, $\overline{S}(\omega) = \underline{S}(\omega) = S(\omega)$ with probability 1.

This completes the first stage of the proof. It is now required to show that $S = E(X_1|\mathcal{I})$ a.s., that is, according to equation (10.18), that

$$\int_M X_1(\omega)dP(\omega) = \int_M S(\omega)dP(\omega), \text{ each } M \in \mathcal{I}. \tag{13.22}$$

Since M is invariant,

$$\int_M X_1(\omega)dP(\omega) = \frac{1}{n}\sum_{t=1}^{n}\int_{T^{-t}M} X_t(\omega)dP(\omega) = \int_M \left(\frac{1}{n}S_n(\omega)\right)dP(\omega) \tag{13.23}$$

and the issue hinges on the convergence of the right-hand member of (13.24) to $E(S1_M)$. Since the sequence $\{X_t\}$ is stationary and integrable, it is also uniformly integrable, and the same is true of the sequence $\{Y_t\}$, where $Y_t = X_t 1_M$ and $M \in \mathcal{I}$. For $\varepsilon > 0$, it is possible by **12.9** to choose an event $E \in \mathcal{F}$ with $P(E) < \delta$, such that $\sup_t E(|Y_t|1_E) < \varepsilon$. For the same E, the triangle inequality gives

$$\int_E \left|\frac{1}{n}\sum_{t=1}^{n} Y_t\right| dP \leq \frac{1}{n}\sum_{t=1}^{n}\left(\int_E |Y_t|dP\right) < \varepsilon. \tag{13.24}$$

By the same argument, also using stationarity and integrability of Y_t,

$$\int \left|\frac{1}{n}\sum_{t=1}^{n} Y_t\right| dP \leq \frac{1}{n}\sum_{t=1}^{n}\int |Y_t|dP = E|Y_1| < \infty. \tag{13.25}$$

Hence by **12.9** the sequence $\{n^{-1}\sum_{t=1}^{n} Y_t\}$ is also uniformly integrable, where $n^{-1}\sum_{t=1}^{n} Y_t = n^{-1}S_n 1_M$. If $n^{-1}S_n \to S$ a.s., it is clear that $n^{-1}S_n 1_M \to S1_M$ a.s., so by **12.8**,

$$\int_M \left(\frac{1}{n}S_n(\omega)\right)dP(\omega) \to \int_M S(\omega)dP(\omega). \tag{13.26}$$

Since n is arbitrary, (13.26) and (13.23) together give (13.22), and the proof is complete. ■

13.4 Ergodicity and Mixing

The property of a stationary sequence which ensures that the time average and the ensemble average have the same limit is *ergodicity*, which is defined in terms of the probability of invariant events. A measure-preserving transformation T is ergodic if either $P(E) = 1$ or $P(E) = 0$ for all $E \in \mathcal{I}$, where $\mathcal{I}$ is the σ-field of invariant events under T. A stationary sequence $\{X_t(\omega)\}_{-\infty}^{+\infty}$ is said to be ergodic if $X_t(\omega) = X_1(T^{t-1}\omega)$ for every t where T is measure-preserving and ergodic. Some authors, such as Doob, use the term *metrically transitive* for ergodic. Events that are invariant under ergodic transformations either occur almost surely, or do not occur almost surely. In the case of **13.9**, Z must be a constant almost surely.

Intuitively, stationarity and ergodicity together are seen to be sufficient conditions for time averages and ensemble averages to converge to the same limit. Stationarity implies that, for example, $\mu = E(X_1(\omega))$ is the mean not just of X_1 but of any member of the sequence. The existence of events that are invariant under the shift transformation means that there are regions of the sample space which a particular realization of the sequence will never visit. If $P(TE \Delta E) = 1$, then the event E^c occurs with probability 0 in a realization where E occurs. However, if invariant events other than the trivial ones are ruled out, we ensure that a sequence will eventually visit all parts of the space, with probability 1. In this case time averaging and ensemble averaging are effectively equivalent operations.

The following corollary is the main reason for our interest in Theorem **13.10**.

13.12 Ergodic theorem Let $\{X_t(\omega)\}_1^\infty$ be a stationary, ergodic, integrable sequence. Then

$$\lim_{n\to\infty} S_n(\omega)/n = E(X_1), \text{ a.s.} \tag{13.27}$$

Proof This is immediate from **13.10**, since by ergodicity, $E(X_1 | \mathcal{I}) = E(X_1)$ a.s. ■

In an ergodic sequence, conditioning on events of probability zero or one is a trivial operation almost surely, in that the information contained in $\mathcal{I}$ is trivial. The ergodic theorem is an example of a law of large numbers, the first of several such theorems to be studied in later chapters. Unlike most of the subsequent examples this one is for stationary sequences. Its practical applications in econometrics are limited by the fact that the stationarity assumption is often inappropriate, but it is of much theoretical interest, because ergodicity is a very mild constraint on the dependence, as we now show.

A transformation that is measure-preserving eventually mixes up the outcomes in a non-invariant event A with those in A^c. The measure-preserving property rules out mapping sets into proper subsets of themselves, so we can be sure that $TA \cap A^c$ is nonempty. Repeated iterations of the transformation generate a sequence of sets $\{T^k A\}$ containing different mixtures of the elements of A and A^c. A positive dependence of B on A implies a negative dependence of B on A^c; that is, if $P(A \cap B) > P(A)P(B)$ then $P(A^c \cap B) = P(B) - P(A \cap B) < P(B) - P(A)P(B) = P(A^c)P(B)$. Intuition suggests that the average dependence of B on mixtures of A and A^c should tend to zero as the mixing-up proceeds. In fact, ergodicity can be characterized in just this kind of way, as the following theorem shows.

13.13 Theorem A measure-preserving shift transformation T is ergodic if and only if, for any pair of events $A, B \in \mathcal{F}$,

$$\lim_{n\to\infty} \frac{1}{n}\sum_{k=1}^{n} P(T^k A \cap B) = P(A)P(B). \tag{13.28}$$

Proof To show 'only if', let A be an invariant event and $B = A$. Then $P(T^k A \cap B) = P(A)$ for all k, and hence the left-hand side of (13.27) is equal to $P(A)$ for all k. This gives $P(A) = P(A)^2$, implying $P(A) = 0$ or 1.

To show 'if', apply the ergodic theorem to the indicator function of the sets $T^k A$, where T is measure-preserving and ergodic, to give

$$\lim_{n\to\infty} \frac{1}{n}\sum_{k=1}^{n} 1_{T^k A}(\omega) = P(A), \text{ a.s.} \tag{13.29}$$

But for any $B \in \mathcal{F}$,

$$\begin{aligned} \int \left| \frac{1}{n}\sum_{k=1}^{n} 1_{T^k A}(\omega) - P(A) \right| dP(\omega) &\geq \int_B \left| \frac{1}{n}\sum_{k=1}^{n} 1_{T^k A}(\omega) - P(A) \right| dP(\omega) \\ &\geq \left| \int_B \left(\frac{1}{n}\sum_{k=1}^{n} 1_{T^k A}(\omega) - P(A) \right) dP(\omega) \right| \\ &= \left| \frac{1}{n}\sum_{k=1}^{n} P(T^k A \cap B) - P(A)P(B) \right|. \end{aligned} \tag{13.30}$$

The sequence whose absolute value is the integrand in the left-hand member of (13.30) converges almost surely to zero as $n \to \infty$ by (13.29); it is bounded absolutely by $1 + P(A)$ uniformly in n, so is clearly uniformly integrable. Hence, the left-hand member of (13.30) converges to zero by **12.8**, and the theorem follows. ∎

Following from this result, ergodicity of a stationary sequence is often associated with convergence to zero in Cesàro-sum of the autocovariances, and indeed, in a Gaussian sequence the conditions are equivalent.

13.14 Corollary If $\{X_t(\omega)\}_1^\infty$ is a stationary, ergodic, square-integrable sequence, then

$$\frac{1}{n}\sum_{k=1}^{n} \mathrm{Cov}(X_1, X_k) \to 0 \text{ as } n \to \infty. \tag{13.31}$$

Proof Setting $B = A$ and defining a real sequence by the indicators of $T^k A$, $X_k(\omega) = 1_{T^k A}(\omega)$, (13.28) is equivalent to (13.31). First extend this result to sequences of simple r.v.s. Let $X_1(\omega) = \sum_i \alpha_i 1_{A_i}(\omega)$, so that $X_2(\omega) = X_1(T\omega) = \sum_i \alpha_i 1_{T^{-1}A_i}(\omega)$. The main point to be established is that the difference between X_2 and a simple r.v. can be ignored in integration. In other words, the sets $T^{-1}A_i$ must form a partition of Ω, apart possibly from sets of measure 0. Since T is measure-preserving, $P(\bigcup_i T^{-1}A_i) = P(T^{-1}(\bigcup_i A_i)) = P(\bigcup_i A_i) = 1$, using **1.2**(ii), and hence $P(\Omega - \bigcup_i T^{-1}A_i) = 0$. And since $\sum_i P(T^{-1}A_i) = \sum_i P(A_i) = 1$, additivity of the measure implies that the collection $\{T^{-1}A_i\}$ is also disjoint apart from possible sets of measure 0, verifying the required property.

This argument extends by induction to X_k for any $k \in \mathbb{N}$. Hence,

$$E(X_1X_k) = E\left(\sum_i\sum_j \alpha_i\alpha_j 1_{A_i\cap T^{-k}A_j}(\omega)\right)$$
$$= \sum_i\sum_j \alpha_i\alpha_j P(A_i \cap T^{-k}A_j), \tag{13.32}$$

(the sum being absolutely convergent by assumption), and by **13.13**,

$$\lim_{n\to\infty}\frac{1}{n}\sum_{k=1}^{n}E(X_1X_k) = \sum_i\sum_j \alpha_i\alpha_j\left(\lim_{n\to\infty}\frac{1}{n}\sum_{k=1}^{n}P(A_i\cap T^kA_j)\right)$$
$$= \sum_i\sum_j \alpha_i\alpha_j P(A_i)P(A_j) = E(X_1)^2, \tag{13.33}$$

where $E(X_1)^2 = E(X_1)E(X_k)$ for any k, by stationarity. The theorem extends to general sequences by the usual application of **3.28** and the monotone convergence theorem. ■

This result might appear to mean that ergodicity implies some form of asymptotic independence of the sequence, since one condition under which (13.31) certainly holds is where $\mathrm{Cov}(X_1,X_k) \to 0$ as $k \to \infty$. But this is not so. The following example illustrates nicely what ergodicity implies and does not imply.

13.15 Example Let the probability space $(\Omega,\mathcal{F},P)$ be defined by $\Omega = \{0,1\}$, so that $\mathcal{F} = (\{\varnothing\},\{0\},\{1\},\{0,1\})$ and $P(\omega) = 0.5$ for $\omega = 0$ and $\omega = 1$. Let T be the transformation that sets $T0 = 1$ and $T1 = 0$. In this setup a random sequence $\{X_t(\omega)\}$ may be defined by letting $X_1(\omega) = \omega$, and generating the sequence by iterating T. These sequences always consist of alternating 0s and 1s, but the initial value is randomly chosen with equal probabilities. Now, T is measure-preserving; the invariant events are Ω and $\varnothing$, both trivial, so the sequence is ergodic. And it is easily verified that $\lim_{n\to\infty}n^{-1}\sum_{k=1}^{n}P(T^kA\cap B) = P(A)P(B)$ for every pair $A,B \in \mathcal{F}$. For instance, let $B = \{1\}$, and then $P(T^kA \cap B) = 0.5$ for k even and 0 for k odd, so that the limit is indeed 0.25 as required. You can verify, equivalently, that the ergodic theorem holds, since the time average of the sequence will always converge to 0.5, which is the same as the ensemble mean of $X_1(\omega)$. □

In this example, X_t is perfectly predictable once we know X_1, for any t. This shows that ergodicity does *not* imply independence between different parts of the sequence, even as the time separation increases. By contrast, a *mixing* sequence has this property. A measure-preserving, ergodic shift transformation T is said to be mixing if, for each A, $B \in \mathcal{F}$,

$$\lim_{k \to \infty} P(T^k A \cap B) = P(A)P(B). \tag{13.34}$$

The stationary sequence $\{X_t\}_1^\infty$ is said to be mixing if $X_t(\omega) = X_1(T^{t-1}\omega)$ for each t where T is a mixing transformation.

Compare this condition with (13.28); Cesàro convergence of the sequence $\{P(T^k A \cap B), k \in \mathbb{N}\}$ has been replaced by actual convergence. To obtain a sound intuition about mixing transformations, one cannot do better than reflect on the following oft-quoted example, originally due to Halmos (1956).

13.16 Example Consider a dry martini initially poured as a layer of vermouth (10% of the volume) on top of the gin (90%). Let G denote the gin, and F an arbitrary small region of the fluid, so that $F \cap G$ is the gin contained in F. If $P(.)$ denotes the volume of a set as a proportion of the whole, $P(G) = 0.9$ and $P(F \cap G)/P(F)$, the proportion of gin in F, is initially either 0 or 1. Let T denote the operation of stirring the martini with a swizzle stick, so that $P(T^k F \cap G)/P(F)$ is the proportion of gin in F after k stirs. Assuming the fluid is incompressible, stirring is a measure-preserving transformation in that $P(T^k F) = P(F)$ for all k. If the stirring mixes the martini we would expect the proportion of gin in $T^k F$, which is $P(T^k F \cap G)/P(F)$, to tend to $P(G)$, so that each region F of the martini eventually contains 90% gin. □

This is precisely condition (13.34). Repeated applications of a mixing transformation to an event A should eventually mix outcomes in A and A^c so thoroughly that for large enough k the composition of $T^k A$ gives no clues about the original A. Mixing in a real sequence implies that events such as $A = \{\omega: X_t(\omega) \le a\}$ and $T^k A = \{\omega: X_{t+k}(\omega) \le a\}$ are becoming independent as k increases. It is immediate, or virtually so, that for stationary mixing sequences the result of **13.14** can be strengthened to $\mathrm{Cov}(X_1, X_k) \to 0$ as $n \to \infty$.

13.5 Subfields and Regularity

We now introduce an alternative approach to studying dependence which considers the collection of σ-subfields of events generated by a stochastic sequence. This theory is fundamental to nearly everything we do subsequently, particularly because, unlike the ergodic theory of the preceding sections, it generalizes beyond the measure-preserving (stationary) case.

Consider a doubly infinite sequence $\{X_t, t \in \mathbb{Z}\}$ (not necessarily stationary) and define the family of subfields $\{\mathcal{F}_s^t, s \le t\}$, where $\mathcal{F}_s^t = \sigma(X_s,\dots,X_t)$ is the smallest σ-field on which the sequence coordinates from dates s to t are measurable. The sets of $\mathcal{F}_s^t$ can be visualized as the inverse images of $(t-s)$-dimensional cylinder sets in $\mathcal{B}^\infty$; compare the discussion of §12.3, recalling that $\mathbb{N}$ and $\mathbb{Z}$ are equipotent. We can let one or other of the bounds tend to infinity, and a particularly important sub-family is the increasing sequence $\{\mathcal{F}_{-\infty}^t, t \in \mathbb{Z}\}$, which can be thought of as, in effect, 'the information contained in the sequence up to date t'. The σ-field on which the sequence as a whole is measurable is the limiting case $\mathcal{F}_{-\infty}^{+\infty} = \bigvee_t \mathcal{F}_{-\infty}^t$. In cases where the underlying probability model concerns just the sequence $\{X_t\}$ we shall identify $\mathcal{F}_{-\infty}^{+\infty}$ with $\mathcal{F}$.

Another interesting object is the *remote σ-field* (or tail σ-field), $\mathcal{F}_{-\infty} = \bigcap_t \mathcal{F}_{-\infty}^t$. This σ-field contains events about which we can learn something by observing *any* coordinate of the sequence, and it might plausibly be supposed that these events occurred at time $-\infty$, the 'remote' past when the initial conditions for the sequence were set. However, note that the set may be generated in other ways, such as $\bigcap_t \mathcal{F}_t^{+\infty}$, or $\bigcap_t \mathcal{F}_{-t}^t$.

One of the ways to characterize independence in a sequence is to say that any pair of non-overlapping subfields, of the form $\mathcal{F}_{t_2}^{t_1}$ and $\mathcal{F}_{t_4}^{t_3}$ where $t_1 \ge t_2 > t_3 \ge t_4$, are independent (see §10.5). One of the most famous early results in the theory of stochastic processes is Kolmogorov's 'zero-one law' for independent sequences. This theorem is usually given for the case of a sequence $\{X_t\}_1^\infty$, and the remote σ-field is defined in this case as $\bigcap_{t=1}^\infty \mathcal{F}_t^\infty$.

13.17 Zero-one law If the sequence $\{X_t\}_1^\infty$ is independent, every remote event is trivial, having either probability 0 or probability 1.

Proof Let A be a remote event, so that $A \in \mathcal{F}^\infty = \bigcap_{t=1}^\infty \mathcal{F}_t^\infty$, and let $\mathcal{G}$ be the collection of events having the property $P(A \cap B) = P(A)P(B)$ if $B \in \mathcal{G}$. By independence, $\mathcal{F}^\infty$ and $\mathcal{F}_1^t$ are independent subfields, so that $\mathcal{F}_1^t \subseteq \mathcal{G}$, for every t. We may therefore say that $\bigcup_{t=1}^\infty \mathcal{F}_1^t \subseteq \mathcal{G}$.

If $B, B' \in \bigcup_{t=1}^\infty \mathcal{F}_1^t$, then $B \in \mathcal{F}_1^t$ for some t, and $B' \in \mathcal{F}_1^{t'}$ for some t', and if $t' \ge t$ (say) then $B \in \mathcal{F}_1^{t'}$ so $B \cap B' \in \mathcal{F}_1^{t'} \subseteq \bigcup_{t=1}^\infty \mathcal{F}_1^t$, and accordingly $\bigcup_{t=1}^\infty \mathcal{F}_1^t$ is a field. Moreover, if $\{B_j \in \mathcal{G}\}$ is a monotone sequence and $B_j \to B$, then $A \cap B_j$ is also monotone and converges to $A \cap B$ for any $A \in \mathcal{F}^\infty$, and $B \in \mathcal{G}$ by continuity of P, so $\mathcal{G}$ is a monotone class. By the argument of **1.24**, $\mathcal{G}$ therefore contains the union of any countable collection of sets from $\bigcup_{t=1}^\infty \mathcal{F}_1^t$, and so $\mathcal{G} \supseteq \sigma(\bigcup_{t=1}^\infty \mathcal{F}_1^t) = \bigvee_{t=1}^\infty \mathcal{F}_1^t = \mathcal{F}$. However, $A \in \mathcal{F}$, so $A \in \mathcal{G}$ and we may set $B = A$, giving $P(A) = P(A)^2$. Hence $P(A) = 0$ or 1. ∎

The zero-one law shows us that for an independent sequence there are no events, other than trivial ones, that can be relevant to all sequence coordinates. But clearly, not only independent sequences have the zero-one property, and from our point of view the interesting problem is to identify the wider class of sequences that possess it.

A sequence $\{X_t\}_{-\infty}^{+\infty}$ is said to be *regular* or *mixing* if every remote event has probability 0 or 1. Regularity is the term adopted by Ibragimov and Linnik (1971), to whom the basics of this theory are due. In a suitably unified framework, this is essentially equivalent to the mixing concept defined in §13.4. The following theorem says that in a regular sequence, remote events must be independent of all events in $\mathcal{F}$. Note that trivial events are independent of themselves, on the definition.

13.18 Theorem (Ibragimov and Linnik 1971: th. 17.1.1) $\{X_t\}_{-\infty}^{+\infty}$ is regular if and only if, for every $B \in \mathcal{F}$,

$$\sup_{A \in \mathcal{F}_{-\infty}^{t}} |P(A \cap B) - P(A)P(B)| \to 0 \text{ as } t \to -\infty. \tag{13.35}$$

Proof To prove 'if', suppose $\exists\, E \in \mathcal{F}_{-\infty}$ with $0 < P(E) < 1$, so that $\{X_t\}_{-\infty}^{+\infty}$ is not regular. Then for every t, $E \in \mathcal{F}_{-\infty}^{t}$ and so

$$\sup_{A \in \mathcal{F}_{-\infty}^{t}} |P(A \cap E) - P(A)P(E)| \geq P(E) - P(E)^2 > 0, \tag{13.36}$$

which contradicts (13.35).

To prove 'only if', assume regularity and define random variables $\xi = 1_A - P(A)$ ($\mathcal{F}_{-\infty}^{t}/\mathcal{B}$-measurable) and $\eta = 1_B - P(B)$ ($\mathcal{F}/\mathcal{B}$-measurable), such that $P(A \cap B) - P(A)P(B) = E(\xi\eta)$. Then, by the Cauchy-Schwartz inequality,

$$|E(\xi\eta)| = |E(\xi E(\eta | \mathcal{F}_{-\infty}^{t}))| \leq \|\xi\|_2 \|E(\eta | \mathcal{F}_{-\infty}^{t})\|_2, \tag{13.37}$$

where the equality is by the law of iterated expectations because $A \in \mathcal{F}_{-\infty}^{t}$. Note that $\|\xi\|_2 \leq 1$. We show $\|E(\eta | \mathcal{F}_{-\infty}^{t})\|_2 \to 0$ as $t \to -\infty$, which will complete the proof, since A is an arbitrary element of $\mathcal{F}_{-\infty}^{t}$.

Consider the sequence $\{E(1_B | \mathcal{F}_{-\infty}^{t})(\omega)\}_{-\infty}^{+\infty}$. For any $\omega \in \Omega$,

$$E(1_B | \mathcal{F}_{-\infty}^{t})(\omega) \to E(1_B | \mathcal{F}_{-\infty})(\omega) \text{ as } t \to -\infty, \tag{13.38}$$

where by equation (10.18) and the zero-one property,

$$\int_E E(1_B | \mathcal{F}_{-\infty})(\omega)dP(\omega) = P(E \cap B)$$
$$= \begin{cases} P(B), & P(E) = 1 \\ 0, & P(E) = 0 \end{cases}, \quad E \in \mathcal{F}_{-\infty}. \tag{13.39}$$

It is clear that setting $E(1_B | \mathcal{F}_{-\infty})(\omega) = P(B)$ a.s. agrees with the definition, so we may say that $E(1_B | \mathcal{F}_{-\infty}^{t}) \to P(B)$ a.s., or, equivalently, that

$$(E(1_B | \mathcal{F}_{-\infty}^{t}) - P(B))^2 \to 0, \text{ a.s.} \tag{13.40}$$

Since $|1_B(\omega) - P(B)| < 1$ for all $\omega \in \Omega$, $(E(1_B | \mathcal{F}_{-\infty}^{t})(\omega) - P(B))^2$ is similarly bounded, uniformly in t. Uniform integrability of the sequence can therefore be assumed, and it follows from **12.8** that

$$\|E(\eta | \mathcal{F}_{-\infty}^{t})\|_2 = \|E(1_B | \mathcal{F}_{-\infty}^{t})(\omega) - P(B)\|_2 \to 0 \text{ as t} \to -\infty, \tag{13.41}$$

as required. ∎

In this theorem, it is less the existence of the limit than the passage to the limit, the fact that the supremum in (13.35) can be made small by choosing $-t$ large, that gives the result practical significance. When the only remote events are trivial, the dependence of X_{t+k} on events in $\mathcal{F}_{-\infty}^{k}$, for fixed k, must eventually decline as t increases. The zero-one law is an instant corollary of the necessity part of the theorem, since an independent sequence would certainly satisfy (13.35).

There is an obvious connection between the properties of invariance and remoteness. If T is a measure-preserving shift transformation we have the following simple implication.

13.19 Theorem If $TA = A$, then $A \in \mathcal{F}_{-\infty}$.

Proof If $A \in \mathcal{F}_{-\infty}^{t}$, then $TA \in \mathcal{F}_{-\infty}^{t+1}$ and $T^{-1}A \in \mathcal{F}_{-\infty}^{t-1}$. If $TA = A$, $T^{-1}A = A$ and it follows immediately that $A \in \left(\bigcap_{s=t}^{\infty}\mathcal{F}_{-\infty}^{s}\right)\cap\left(\bigcap_{s=-\infty}^{t}\mathcal{F}_{-\infty}^{s}\right) = \mathcal{F}_{-\infty}$. ■

The last result of this section establishes formally the relationship between regularity and ergodicity which has been implicit in the foregoing discussion.

13.20 Theorem (Ibragimov and Linnik 1971: cor. 17.1.1) If a stationary sequence $x(\omega) = \{X_t(\omega)\}_{-\infty}^{+\infty}$ is regular, it is also ergodic.

Proof Every set $A \in \mathcal{F}_{-\infty}^{+\infty}$ is contained in a set $A_t \in \mathcal{F}_{-t}^{t}$, with the sequence $\{A_t\}$ non-increasing and $A_t \downarrow A$. Thus, A_t may be constructed as the inverse image under x of the $(2t+1)$-dimensional cylinder set whose base is the product of the coordinate $\mathcal{B}$-sets for coordinates $-t,\dots,t$ of $x(A) \in \mathcal{B}^{\infty}$. The inclusion follows by **1.2**(iv). By continuity of P, we can assume that $P(A_t) \to P(A)$.

Let A be invariant. Using the measure-preserving property of T, we find

$$P(A_t\cap A) = P(A_t\cap T^{-k}A) = P(T^{k}A_t\cap A). \tag{13.42}$$

Since k is arbitrary, regularity implies by (13.34) that $P(A_t\cap A) = P(A_t)P(A)$. Letting $t \to \infty$ yields $P(A) = P(A)^2$, so that $P(A) = 0$ or 1, as required. ■

13.6 Strong and Uniform Mixing

The defect of mixing (regularity) as an operational concept is that remote events are of less interest than arbitrary events which happen to be widely separated in time. The extra ingredient we need for a workable theory is the concept of dependence between pairs of σ-subfields of events. There are several ways to characterize such dependence, but the following are the concepts that have been most commonly exploited in limit theory.

Let $(\Omega,\mathcal{F},P)$ be a probability space, and let $\mathcal{G}$ and $\mathcal{H}$ be σ-subfields of $\mathcal{F}$; then

$$\alpha(\mathcal{G},\mathcal{H}) = \sup_{G\in\mathcal{G},H\in\mathcal{H}} |P(G\cap H)-P(G)P(H)| \tag{13.43}$$

is known as the strong mixing coefficient, and

$$\phi(\mathcal{G},\mathcal{H}) = \sup_{G\in\mathcal{G},H\in\mathcal{H};P(G)>0} |P(H|G)-P(H)| \tag{13.44}$$

as the uniform mixing coefficient. These are alternative measures of the dependence between the subfields $\mathcal{G}$ and $\mathcal{H}$.

If the subfields $\mathcal{G}$ and $\mathcal{H}$ are independent, then $\alpha(\mathcal{G},\mathcal{H}) = 0$ and $\phi(\mathcal{G},\mathcal{H}) = 0$, and the converse is also true in the case of uniform mixing, although *not* for strong mixing. At first sight there may appear not much to choose between the definitions, but since they are set up in terms of suprema of the dependence measures over the sets of events in question, it is the extreme (and possibly anomalous) cases which define the characteristics of the mixing coefficients. The strong mixing concept is weaker than the uniform concept. Since

$$|P(G\cap H)-P(G)P(H)| \leq |P(H|G)-P(H)| \leq \phi(\mathcal{G},\mathcal{H}) \tag{13.45}$$

for all $G \in \mathcal{G}$ and $H \in \mathcal{H}$, it is clear that $\alpha(\mathcal{G},\mathcal{H}) \leq \phi(\mathcal{G},\mathcal{H})$. However, the following example shows how the two concepts differ more crucially.

13.21 Example Suppose that, for a sequence of subfields $\{\mathcal{G}_m\}_1^\infty$, and a subfield $\mathcal{H}$, $\alpha(\mathcal{G}_m,\mathcal{H}) \to 0$ as $m \to \infty$. This condition is compatible with the existence of sets $G_m \in \mathcal{G}_m$ and $H \in \mathcal{H}$ with the properties $P(G_m) = 1/m$, and $P(G_m \cap H) = a/m$ for $a \neq P(H)$. But $\phi(\mathcal{G}_m,\mathcal{H}) \geq |P(H|G_m) - P(H)| = |a - P(H)|$ for every $m \geq 1$, showing that subfields $\mathcal{G}_m$ and $\mathcal{H}$ are not independent in the limit. □

Evidently, the strong mixing characterization of 'independence' does not rule out the possibility of dependence between negligible sets.

α and ϕ are not the only mixing coefficients that can be defined, although they have proved the most popular in applications. Others that have appeared in the literature include

$$\beta(\mathcal{G},\mathcal{H}) = \sup_{H\in\mathcal{H}} E\left|P(H|\mathcal{G})-P(H)\right| \tag{13.46}$$

and

$$\rho(\mathcal{G},\mathcal{H}) = \sup\frac{|E(\xi\eta)|}{\|\xi\|_2\|\eta\|_2}, \tag{13.47}$$

where the latter supremum is taken with respect to all square integrable, zero mean, $\mathcal{G}$-measurable r.v.s ξ, and $\mathcal{H}$-measurable r.v.s η. To compare these alternatives, first let $\zeta(\omega) = P(H|\mathcal{G})(\omega) - P(H)$, so that

$$\begin{aligned}\beta(\mathcal{G},\mathcal{H}) &= \sup_{H\in\mathcal{H}} \int|\zeta|dP \\ &\geq \sup_{G\in\mathcal{G},H\in\mathcal{H}} \int_G|\zeta|dP \\ &\geq \sup_{G\in\mathcal{G},H\in\mathcal{H}} \left|\int_G\zeta dP\right| = \alpha(\mathcal{G},\mathcal{H}).\end{aligned} \tag{13.48}$$

Moreover, since for any sets $G \in \mathcal{G}$ and $H \in \mathcal{H}$, $\xi(\omega) = 1_G(\omega) - P(G)$ and $\eta(\omega) = 1_H(\omega) - P(H)$ are members of the set over which $\rho(\mathcal{G},\mathcal{H})$ is defined, and $E(\xi\eta) = P(G\cap H) - P(G)P(H)$ while $|\xi| \leq 1$ and $|\eta| \leq 1$ for these cases, it is also clear that $\rho \geq \alpha$. Thus, α mixing, notwithstanding its designation, is the weakest of these four 'strong' variants, although it is of course stronger than ordinary regularity characterized by trivial remote events. We also have $\beta \leq \phi$, by an immediate corollary of the following result.

13.22 Theorem $|P(H|\mathcal{G}) - P(H)| \le \phi(\mathcal{G},\mathcal{H})$ a.s., for all $H \in \mathcal{H}$. □

The main step in the proof of **13.22** is the following lemma.

13.23 Lemma Let X be an almost surely bounded, $\mathcal{G}$-measurable r.v. Then

$$\sup_{G\in\mathcal{G}, P(G)>0} \frac{1}{P(G)}\left|\int_G XdP\right| = \text{ess sup } X. \tag{13.49}$$

Proof $P(G)^{-1}|\int_G XdP| \le$ ess sup X, for any set G in the designated class. For any $\varepsilon > 0$, consider the sets

$$G^+ = \{\omega: X(\omega) \ge (\text{ess sup } X) - \varepsilon\},$$
$$G^- = \{\omega: -X(\omega) \ge (\text{ess sup } X) - \varepsilon\}.$$

By definition of ess sup X, both these sets belong to $\mathcal{G}$ and at least one of them is nonempty and has positive probability. Define the set

$$G^* = \begin{cases} G^+, & P(G^+) \ge P(G^-) \\ G^-, & \text{otherwise} \end{cases}$$

and we may conclude that

$$\frac{1}{P(G^*)}\left|\int_{G^*} XdP\right| \ge (\text{ess sup } X) - \varepsilon. \tag{13.50}$$

(13.49) now follows on letting ε approach 0. ■

Proof of 13.22 Put $X = P(H|\mathcal{G}) - P(H)$ in the lemma, noting that this is a $\mathcal{G}$-measurable r.v. lying between +1 and −1. Observe that, for any $G \in \mathcal{G}$, $P(G)^{-1}|\int_G XdP| = |P(H|G) - P(H)|$. Hence the lemma together with (13.44) implies that, for any $H \in \mathcal{H}$,

$$\begin{aligned}\phi(\mathcal{G},\mathcal{H}) &\ge \text{ess sup}\{P(H|\mathcal{G}) - P(H)\} \\ &\ge |P(H|\mathcal{G}) - P(H)|,\end{aligned} \tag{13.51}$$

with probability 1. ■

14
Mixing

14.1 Mixing Sequences of Random Variables

For a sequence $\{X_t(\omega)\}_{-\infty}^{\infty}$, let $\mathcal{F}_{-\infty}^{t} = \sigma(\ldots,X_{t-2},X_{t-1},X_t)$ as in §13.5, and similarly define $\mathcal{F}_{t+m}^{\infty} = \sigma(X_{t+m},X_{t+m+1},X_{t+m+2},\ldots)$. The sequence is said to be α-*mixing* (or strong mixing) if $\lim_{m\to\infty}\alpha_m = 0$ where

$$\alpha_m = \sup_t \alpha(\mathcal{F}_{-\infty}^{t},\mathcal{F}_{t+m}^{\infty}), \tag{14.1}$$

and α is defined in (13.43). It is said to be ϕ-*mixing* (or uniform mixing) if $\lim_{m\to\infty}\phi_m = 0$, where

$$\phi_m = \sup_t \phi(\mathcal{F}_{-\infty}^{t},\mathcal{F}_{t+m}^{\infty}), \tag{14.2}$$

and ϕ is defined in (13.44). ϕ-mixing implies α-mixing as noted in §13.6, while the converse does not hold. Another difference is that ϕ-mixing is not time-reversible; in other words, it is not necessarily the case that $\sup_t\phi(\mathcal{F}_{t+m}^{\infty},\mathcal{F}_{-\infty}^{t}) = \sup_t\phi(\mathcal{F}_{-\infty}^{t},\mathcal{F}_{t+m}^{\infty})$. By contrast, α-mixing *is* time-reversible. If the sequence $\{X_t\}_{-\infty}^{+\infty}$ is α-mixing, so is the sequence $\{Y_t\}_{-\infty}^{+\infty}$ where $Y_t = X_{-t}$.

$\{X_t(\omega)\}_{-\infty}^{\infty}$ is also said to be *absolutely regular* if $\lim_{m\to\infty}\beta_m = 0$ where

$$\beta_m = \sup_t \beta(\mathcal{F}_{-\infty}^{t},\mathcal{F}_{t+m}^{\infty}) \tag{14.3}$$

and β is defined in (13.46). According to the results in §13.6, absolute regularity is a condition intermediate between strong mixing and uniform mixing. On the other hand, if $\{X_t\}_{-\infty}^{+\infty}$ is a stationary, L_2-bounded sequence, and $\mathcal{F}_{-\infty}^{0} = \sigma(\ldots,X_{-1},X_0)$ and $\mathcal{F}_{m}^{+\infty} = \sigma(X_m,X_{m+1},\ldots)$, the sequence is said to be *completely regular* if $\rho_m = \rho(\mathcal{F}_{-\infty}^{0}, \mathcal{F}_{m}^{+\infty}) \to 0$, where ρ is defined in (13.47). In stationary Gaussian sequences, complete regularity is equivalent to strong mixing. Kolmogorov and Rozanov (1960) show that in this case

$$\alpha_m \le \rho_m \le 2\pi\alpha_m. \tag{14.4}$$

In a completely regular sequence, the autocovariances $\gamma_j = E(X_tX_{t-j})$ must tend to 0 as $j \to \infty$. A sufficient condition for complete regularity can be expressed in terms of the *spectral density function*. When it exists, the spectral density $f(\lambda)$ is the Fourier transform of the autocovariance function, that is to say,

$$f(\lambda) = \frac{1}{2\pi}\sum_{j=-\infty}^{\infty}\gamma_j e^{i\lambda j},\ \lambda \in [-\pi,\pi]. \tag{14.5}$$

The theorem of Kolmogorov and Rozanov leads to the result proved by Ibragimov and Linnik (1971: th. 17.3.3), that a stationary Gaussian sequence is strong mixing when $f(\lambda)$ exists and is continuous and strictly positive, everywhere on $[-\pi,\pi]$.

This topic is something of a terminological minefield. 'Regularity' is an undescriptive term, and there does not seem to be unanimity among authors with regard to usage, complete regularity and absolute regularity sometimes being used synonymously. Nor is the list of mixing concepts given here by any means exhaustive. Fortunately, we shall be able to avoid this confusion by sticking with the strong and uniform cases. While there are some applications in which absolute regularity provides just the right condition, we shall not encounter any of these. Incidentally, the term 'weak mixing' might be thought appropriate as a synonym for regularity, but should be avoided as there is a risk of confusion with *weak dependence*, a term used, often somewhat imprecisely, to refer to sequences having summable covariances. *Strongly dependent* sequences may be stationary and mixing, but their covariances are non-summable. ('Weak' implies *less* dependence than 'strong' in this instance, not more!)

Confining our attention now to the strong and uniform mixing definitions, measures of the dependence in a sequence can be based in various ways on the rate at which the mixing coefficients α_m or ϕ_m tend to zero. To avoid repetition we will discuss just strong mixing, but the following remarks apply equally to the uniform mixing case, on substituting ϕ for α throughout. Since the collections $\mathcal{F}_{-\infty}^{t}$ and $\mathcal{F}_{t+m}^{\infty}$ are respectively non-decreasing in t and non-increasing in t and m, the sequence $\{\alpha_m\}$ is monotone. The rate of convergence is often quantified by a summability criterion, that for some number $\varphi > 0$, $\alpha_m \to 0$ sufficiently fast that

$$\sum_{m=1}^{\infty} \alpha_m^{1/\varphi} < \infty. \tag{14.6}$$

The term *size* has been coined to describe the rate of convergence of the mixing numbers, although different definitions have been used by different authors, and the terminology should be used with caution. One possibility is to say that the sequence is of size $-\varphi$ if the mixing numbers satisfy (14.6). However, the commonest usage (see for example White 1984) is to say that a sequence is α-mixing of size $-\varphi_0$ if $\alpha_m = O(m^{-\varphi})$ for some $\varphi > \varphi_0$.[11] It is clear that such sequences are summable when raised to the power of $1/\varphi_0$, so that this concept of size is stronger than the summability concept. One temptation to be avoided is to define the size as '$-\varphi$, where φ is the largest constant such that the $\alpha_m^{1/\varphi}$ are summable'; for no such number may exist.

Since mixing is not so much a property of the sequence $\{X_t\}$ as of the sequences of σ-fields generated by $\{X_t\}$, it holds for any random variables measurable on those σ-fields, such as measurable transformations of X_t. More generally, we have the following implication:

14.1 Theorem Let $Y_t = g(X_t, X_{t-1}, \ldots, X_{t-\tau})$ be a measurable function, for finite τ. If X_t is α-mixing (ϕ-mixing) of size $-\varphi$, then Y_t is also.

Proof Let $\mathcal{G}_{-\infty}^{t} = \sigma(\ldots,Y_{t-1},Y_t)$, and $\mathcal{G}_{t+m}^{\infty} = \sigma(Y_{t+m},Y_{t+m+1},\ldots)$. Since Y_t is measurable on any σ-field on which each of $X_t,X_{t-1},\ldots,X_{t-\tau}$ are measurable, $\mathcal{G}_{-\infty}^{t} \subseteq \mathcal{F}_{-\infty}^{t}$ and $\mathcal{G}_{t+m}^{\infty} \subseteq \mathcal{F}_{t+m-\tau}^{\infty}$. Let $\alpha_{Y,m} = \sup_t (\mathcal{G}_{-\infty}^{t},\mathcal{G}_{t+m}^{\infty})$ and it follows that $\alpha_{Y,m} \le \alpha_{m-\tau}$ for $m \ge \tau$. With τ finite, $\alpha_{m-\tau} = O(m^{-\varphi})$ if $\alpha_m = O(m^{-\varphi})$ and the conclusion follows. The same argument follows word for word with 'ϕ' replacing 'α'. ■

14.2 Mixing Inequalities

Strong and uniform mixing are restrictions on the complete joint distribution of the sequence, and to make practical use of the concepts we must know what they imply about particular measures of dependence. This section establishes a set of fundamental moment inequalities for mixing processes. The main results bound the m-step-ahead predictions, $E(X_{t+m}|\mathcal{F}_{-\infty}^{t})$. Mixing implies that, as we try to forecast the future path of a sequence from knowledge of its history to date, looking further and further forward, we will eventually be unable to improve on the predictor based solely on the distribution of the sequence as a whole, $E(X_{t+m})$. The r.v. $E(X_{t+m}|\mathcal{F}_{-\infty}^{t}) - E(X_{t+m})$ is tending to zero as m increases. We prove convergence of the L_p-norm.

14.2 Theorem (Ibragimov 1962) For $r \ge p \ge 1$ and with α_m defined in (14.1),

$$\|E(X_{t+m}|\mathcal{F}_{-\infty}^{t}) - E(X_{t+m})\|_p \le 2(2^{1/p}+1)\alpha_m^{1/p-1/r}\|X_{t+m}\|_r. \tag{14.7}$$

Proof To simplify notation, substitute X for X_{t+m}, $\mathcal{G}$ for $\mathcal{F}_{-\infty}^{t}$, $\mathcal{H}$ for $\mathcal{F}_{t+m}^{\infty}$, and α for α_m. It will be understood that X is an $\mathcal{H}$-measurable random variable where $\mathcal{G}, \mathcal{H} \subseteq \mathcal{F}$. The proof is in two stages, first to establish the result for $|X| \le M_X < \infty$ a.s., and then to extend it to the case where X is L_r-bounded for finite r. Define the $\mathcal{G}$-measurable r.v.

$$\eta = \operatorname{sgn}(E(X|\mathcal{G}) - E(X)) = \begin{cases} 1, & E(X|\mathcal{G}) \ge E(X), \\ -1, & \text{otherwise.} \end{cases} \tag{14.8}$$

Using **10.8** and **10.10**,

$$\begin{aligned} E|E(X|\mathcal{G}) - E(X)| &= E[\eta(E(X|\mathcal{G}) - E(X))] \\ &= E[(E(\eta X|\mathcal{G}) - \eta E(X)] \\ &= \operatorname{Cov}(\eta,X) = |\operatorname{Cov}(\eta,X)|. \end{aligned} \tag{14.9}$$

Let Y be any $\mathcal{G}$-measurable r.v., such as η for example. Noting that $\xi = \operatorname{sgn}(E(Y|\mathcal{H}) - E(Y))$ is $\mathcal{H}$-measurable, similar arguments give

$$\begin{aligned} |\operatorname{Cov}(X,Y)| &= |E(X(E(Y|\mathcal{H}) - E(Y)))| \\ &\le E(|X||(E(Y|\mathcal{H}) - E(Y))|) \\ &\le M_X E|E(Y|\mathcal{H}) - E(Y)| \end{aligned}$$

$$\leq M_X|\text{Cov}(\xi,Y)|, \tag{14.10}$$

where the first inequality is the modulus inequality. ξ and η are simple random variables taking only two distinct values each, so define the sets $A^+ = \{\eta = 1\}$, $A^- = \{\eta = -1\}$, $B^+ = \{\xi = 1\}$, and $B^- = \{\xi = -1\}$. Putting (14.9) and (14.10) together gives

$$\begin{aligned}E|E(X|\mathcal{G}) - E(X)| &\leq M_X|\text{Cov}(\eta,\xi)| = M_X|E(\xi\eta) - E(\xi)E(\eta)| \\ &= M_X\Big|[P(A^+\cap B^+) + P(A^-\cap B^-) - P(A^+\cap B^-) - P(A^-\cap B^+)] \\ &\quad - [P(A^+)P(B^+) + P(A^-)P(B^-) - P(A^+)P(B^-) - P(A^-)P(B^+)]\Big| \\ &\leq 4M_X\alpha. \end{aligned} \tag{14.11}$$

Since $|E(X|\mathcal{G}) - E(X)| \leq |E(X|\mathcal{G})| + |E(X)| \leq 2M_X$, it follows that, for $p \geq 1$,

$$\|E(X|\mathcal{G}) - E(X)\|_p \leq 2M_X(2\alpha)^{1/p}. \tag{14.12}$$

This completes the first part of the proof. The next step is to let X be L_r-bounded. Choose a finite positive M_X, and define $X_1 = 1_{\{|X|\leq M_X\}}X$ and $X_2 = X - X_1$. By the Minkowski inequality and (14.11),

$$\begin{aligned}\|E(X|\mathcal{G}) - E(X)\|_p &\leq \|E(X_1|\mathcal{G}) - E(X_1)\|_p + \|(X_2|\mathcal{G}) - E(X_2)\|_p \\ &\leq 2M_X(2\alpha)^{1/p} + 2\|X_2\|_p,\end{aligned} \tag{14.13}$$

and the problem is to bound the second right-hand-side member. But

$$\|X_2\|_p \leq M_X^{1-r/p}\|X\|_r^{r/p} \tag{14.14}$$

for $r \geq p$, so we arrive at

$$\|E(X|\mathcal{G}) - E(X)\|_p \leq 2M_X(2\alpha)^{1/p} + 2M_X^{1-r/p}\|X\|_r^{r/p}. \tag{14.15}$$

Finally, choosing $M_X = \|X\|_r\alpha^{-1/r}$ and simplifying yields

$$\|E(X|\mathcal{G}) - E(X)\|_p \leq 2(2^{1/p} + 1)\alpha^{1/p-1/r}\|X\|_r,$$

which is the required result. ■

There is an easy corollary bounding the autocovariances of the sequence.

14.3 Corollary For $p > 1$ and $r \geq p/(p-1)$,

$$|\text{Cov}(X_t,X_{t+m})| \leq 2(2^{1-1/p} + 1)\alpha_m^{1-1/p-1/r}\|X_t\|_p\|X_{t+m}\|_r. \tag{14.16}$$

Proof

$$\begin{aligned}|\text{Cov}(X_t,X_{t+m})| &= |E(X_tX_{t+m}) - E(X_t)E(X_{t+m})| \\ &= \Big|E[X_t(E(X_{t+m}|\mathcal{F}_t) - E(X_{t+m}))]\Big| \\ &\leq \|X_t\|_p\|E(X_{t+m}|\mathcal{F}_t) - E(X_{t+m})\|_{p/(p-1)} \\ &\leq 2(2^{1-1/p} + 1)\|X_t\|_p\|X_{t+m}\|_r\alpha_m^{1-1/p-1/r},\end{aligned} \tag{14.17}$$

where the second equality is by **10.8** and **10.10**, noting that X_t is $\mathcal{F}_t$-measurable, the first inequality is the Hölder inequality, and the second inequality is by **14.2**. ■

14.4 Theorem (Serfling 1968: th. 2.2) For $r \geq p \geq 1$,

$$\|E(X_{t+m}|\mathcal{F}_{-\infty}^t) - E(X_{t+m})\|_p \leq 2\phi_m^{1-1/r}\|X_{t+m}\|_r. \tag{14.18}$$

where ϕ_m is defined in (14.2).

Proof The result is trivial for $r = p = 1$, so assume $r > 1$. The strategy is to prove the result initially for a sequence of simple r.v.s. Let $X_{t+m} = \sum_{i=1}^k x_i 1_{A_i}$, $A_i \in \mathcal{F}_{t+m}^\infty$, where $\mathcal{F}_{t+m}^\infty = \sigma(X_{t+m}, X_{t+m+1}, \ldots)$. For some $\omega \in \Omega$ consider the random element $E(X_{t+m}|\mathcal{F}_{-\infty}^t)(\omega)$, although for clarity of notation the dependence on ω is not indicated. For $r > 1$ and $q = r/(r-1)$, we have

$$\begin{aligned}
|E(X_{t+m}|\mathcal{F}_{-\infty}^t) - E(X_{t+m})|^r &= \Big|\sum_i x_i(P(A_i|\mathcal{F}_{-\infty}^t) - P(A_i))\Big|^r \\
&\leq \Big(\sum_i |x_i|\,|P(A_i|\mathcal{F}_{-\infty}^t) - P(A_i)|\Big)^r \\
&= \Big(\sum_i |x_i|\,|P(A_i|\mathcal{F}_{-\infty}^t) - P(A_i)|^{1/r}|P(A_i|\mathcal{F}_{-\infty}^t) - P(A_i)|^{1/q}\Big)^r \\
&\leq \Big(\sum_i |x_i|^r|P(A_i|\mathcal{F}_{-\infty}^t) - P(A_i)|\Big)\Big(\sum_i |P(A_i|\mathcal{F}_{-\infty}^t) - P(A_i)|\Big)^{r/q} \\
&\leq (E(|X_{t+m}|^r|\mathcal{F}_{-\infty}^t) + E|X_{t+m}|^r)\Big(\sum_i |P(A_i|\mathcal{F}_{-\infty}^t) - P(A_i)|\Big)^{r/q}.
\end{aligned} \tag{14.19}$$

The second inequality here is by **9.25**. The sets A_i partition Ω, and $P(A_i \cup A_{i'}|\mathcal{F}_{-\infty}^t) = P(A_i|\mathcal{F}_{-\infty}^t) + P(A_{i'}|\mathcal{F}_{-\infty}^t)$ a.s. and $P(A_i \cup A_{i'}) = P(A_i) + P(A_{i'})$ for $i \neq i'$. Letting A_j^+ denote the union of all those A_i for which $P(A_i|\mathcal{F}_{-\infty}^t) - P(A_i) \geq 0$, and A_j^- the complement of A_j^+ on Ω,

$$\sum_i |P(A_i|\mathcal{F}_{-\infty}^t) - P(A_i)| = |P(A_j^+|\mathcal{F}_{-\infty}^t) - P(A_i^+)| + |P(A_i^-|\mathcal{F}_{-\infty}^t) - P(A_i^-)|. \tag{14.20}$$

By **13.22**, the inequalities

$$|P(A_j^+|\mathcal{F}_{-\infty}^t) - P(A_i^+)| \leq \phi_m$$

$$|P(A_i^-|\mathcal{F}_{-\infty}^t) - P(A_i^-)| \leq \phi_m$$

hold with probability 1. Substituting into (14.19) gives

$$|E(X_{t+m}|\mathcal{F}_{-\infty}^t) - E(X_{t+m})|^r \geq [E(|X_{t+m}|^r|\mathcal{F}_{-\infty}^t) + E|X_{t+m}|^r](2\phi_m)^{r/q}, \text{ a.s.} \tag{14.21}$$

Taking expectations and using the law of iterated expectations then gives

$$E|E(X_{t+m}|\mathcal{F}_{-\infty}^t) - E(X_{t+m})|^r \leq 2E|X_{t+m}|^r(2\phi_m)^{r/q}, \tag{14.22}$$

and, raising both sides to the power $1/r$,

$$\|E(X_{t+m}|\mathcal{F}_{-\infty}^{t}) - E(X_{t+m})\|_r \le 2\|X_{t+m}\|_r\phi_m^{1-1/r}. \tag{14.23}$$

Inequality (14.18) follows by Liapunov's inequality.

The result extends from simple to general r.v.s using the construction of **3.28**. For any r.v. X_{t+m} there exists a monotone sequence of simple r.v.s $\{X_{(k)t+m}, k \in \mathbb{N}\}$ such that $|X_{(k)t+m}(\omega) - X_{t+m}(\omega)| \to 0$ as $k \to \infty$, for all $\omega \in \Omega$. This convergence transfers a.s. to the sequences $\{E(X_{(k)t+m}|\mathcal{F}_{-\infty}^{t}) - E(X_{(k)t+m}), k \in \mathbb{N}\}$ by **10.15.** Then, assuming X_{t+m} is L_r-bounded, the inequality in (14.22) holds as $k \to \infty$ by the dominated convergence theorem applied to each side, with $|X_{t+m}|^r$ as the dominating function, thanks to **10.13**(ii). This completes the proof. ∎

The counterpart of **14.3** is obtained similarly.

14.5 Corollary For $r \ge 1$,

$$|\text{Cov}(X_{t+m},X_t)| \le 2\phi_m^{1/r}\|X_t\|_r\|X_{t+m}\|_{r/(r-1)}, \tag{14.24}$$

where, if $r = 1$, replace $\|X_{t+m}\|_{r/(r-1)}$ by $\|X_{t+m}\|_\infty = \text{ess sup } X_{t+m}$.

Proof

$$\begin{aligned}|\text{Cov}(X_{t+m},X_t)| &\le \|X_t\|_r\|E(X_{t+m}|\mathcal{F}_{-\infty}^{t}) - E(X_{t+m})\|_{r/(r-1)} \\ &\le 2\phi_m^{1/r}\|X_t\|_r\|X_{t+m}\|_{r/(r-1)},\end{aligned} \tag{14.25}$$

where the first inequality corresponds to the one in (14.17), and the second one is by **14.4.** ∎

These results tell us a good deal about the behaviour of mixing sequences. A fundamental property is *mean reversion*. The mean deviation sequence $\{X_t - E(X_t)\}$ must change sign frequently when the rate of mixing is high. If the sequence exhibits persistent behaviour with $X_t - E(X_t)$ tending to have the same sign for a large number of successive periods, then $|E(X_{t+m}|\mathcal{F}_{-\infty}^{t}) - E(X_{t+m})|$ would likewise tend to be large for large m. If this quantity is small the sign of the mean deviation m periods hence is unpredictable, indicating that it changes frequently.

But while mixing implies mean reversion, mean reversion need not imply mixing. Theorems **14.2** and **14.4** isolate the properties of greatest importance, but not the only ones. A sequence having the property that $\|\text{Var}(X_{t+m}|\mathcal{F}_{-\infty}^{t}) - \text{Var}(X_{t+m})\|_p > 0$ is called *conditionally heteroscedastic*. Mixing also requires this sequence of norms to converge as $m \to \infty$, and similarly for other integrable functions of X_{t+m}.

Comparison of **14.2** and **14.4** also shows that being able to assert uniform mixing can give us considerably greater flexibility in applications with respect to the existence of moments. In (14.18), the rate of convergence of the left-hand side to zero with m does not depend upon p, and in particular, $E|E(X_{t+m}|\mathcal{F}_{-\infty}^{t}) - E(X_{t+m})|$ converges whenever $\|X_{t+m}\|_{1+\delta}$ exists for $\delta > 0$, a condition infinitesimally stronger than uniform integrability. In the corresponding inequality for α_m in **14.2**, $p < r$ is required for the restriction to 'bite'. Likewise, **14.5** for the case $p = 2$ yields

$$|\mathrm{Cov}(X_{t+m},X_t)| \le 2\phi_m^{1/2}\|X_t\|_2\|X_{t+m}\|_2, \tag{14.26}$$

but to be useful **14.3** requires that either X_t or X_{t+m} be $L_{2+\delta}$-bounded, for $\delta > 0$. Mere existence of the variances will not suffice.

14.3 Mixing in Linear Processes

A type of stochastic sequence $\{X_t\}_{-\infty}^{\infty}$ which arises very frequently in econometric modelling applications has the representation

$$X_t = \sum_{j=0}^{q} \theta_j Z_{t-j},\ 0 \le q \le \infty, \tag{14.27}$$

where $\{Z_t\}_{-\infty}^{+\infty}$ (called the *innovations* or *shocks*) is an independent stochastic sequence, and $\{\theta_j\}_{j=0}^{q}$ is a sequence of fixed coefficients. Assume without loss of generality that the Z_t have zero means and that $\theta_0 = 1$. (14.27) is called a *moving average* process of order q (MA(q)). Into this class fall the finite-order autoregressive and autoregressive-moving average (ARMA) processes commonly used to model economic time series. We would clearly like to know when such sequences are mixing, by reference to the properties of the innovations and of the sequence $\{\theta_j\}$. Several authors have investigated this question, including Ibragimov and Linnik (1971), Chanda (1974), Gorodetskii (1977), Withers (1981a), Pham and Tran (1985), and Athreya and Pantula (1986a, 1986b).

Mixing is an asymptotic property, and when $q < \infty$ the sequence is mixing infinitely fast. This case is called *q-dependence*. The difficulties arise with the cases with $q = \infty$. Formally, we should think of the MA(∞) as the weak limit of a sequence of MA(q) processes; the characteristic function of X_t has the form

$$\phi_{qt}(\lambda) = \prod_{j=1}^{q} \phi_{Z_{t-j}}(\theta_j\lambda), \tag{14.28}$$

and if $\phi_{qt}(\lambda) \to \phi_t(\lambda)$ (pointwise in $\mathbb{R}$) as $q \to \infty$ where $\phi_t(\lambda)$ is a ch.f. and continuous at $\lambda = 0$, we may invert the latter according to **11.12**, and identify the corresponding distribution as that of $X_t = \sum_{j=0}^{\infty}\theta_j Z_{t-j}$.[12] The existence of the limit imposes certain conditions on the coefficient sequence $\{\theta_j\}_{j=0}^{\infty}$. We clearly need $|\theta_j| \to 0$ as $j \to \infty$, and for the variance of X_t to exist, it is further necessary that the sequence be square-summable. Note that the solutions of finite-order ARMA processes are characterized by the approach of $|\theta_j|$ to 0 at an exponential rate, beyond a finite point in the sequence.

If $\{Z_t\}$ is i.i.d. with mean 0 and variance σ^2, X_t is stationary and has spectral density function

$$f(\lambda) = \frac{\sigma^2}{2\pi}\left|\sum_{j=0}^{\infty}\theta_j e^{i\lambda j}\right|^2. \tag{14.29}$$

The theorem of Ibragimov and Linnik cited in §14.1 yields the condition $\sum_{j=0}^{\infty}|\theta_j| < \infty$ as sufficient for strong-mixing in the Gaussian case. However, another standard result (see Doob 1953: ch. X.8, or Ibragimov and Linnik 1971: ch. 16.7) states that every wide-sense stationary sequence admitting a spectral density has a (doubly-infinite) moving average representation with orthogonal increments and *square* summable coefficients.

But allowing more general distributions for the innovations yields surprising results. Contrary to what might be supposed, having the θ_j tend to zero even at an exponential rate is not sufficient by itself for strong mixing. Here is a simple illustration. Recall that the first-order autoregressive process $X_t = \rho X_{t-1} + Z_t$, $|\rho| < 1$, has the MA(∞) form with $\theta_j = \rho^j$, $j = 0,1,2,...$

14.6 Example Let $\{Z_t\}_0^\infty$ be an independent sequence of Bernoulli r.v.s, with $P(Z_t = 1) = P(Z_t = 0) = \frac{1}{2}$. Let $X_0 = Z_0$ and

$$X_t = \tfrac{1}{2}X_{t-1} + Z_t = \sum_{j=0}^{t} 2^{-j} Z_{t-j},\ t = 1,2,3,... \tag{14.30}$$

It is not difficult to see that the term

$$\sum_{j=0}^{t} 2^{-j} Z_{t-j} = 2^{-t} \sum_{k=0}^{t} 2^k Z_k \tag{14.31}$$

belongs for each t to the set of dyadic rationals $W_t = \{k/2^t,\ k = 0,1,2,...,2^{t+1} - 1\}$. Each element of W_t corresponds to one of the 2^{t+1} possible drawings $\{Z_0,...,Z_t\}$, and has equal probability of 2^{-t-1}. Iff $Z_0 = 0$,

$$X_t \in B_t = \{k/2^t,\ k = 0,2,4,...,2(2^t - 1)\},$$

whereas iff $Z_0 = 1$,

$$X_t \in W_t - B_t = \{k/2^t,\ k = 1,3,5,...,2^{t+1} - 1\}.$$

It follows that $\{X_0 = 1\} \cap \{X_t \in B_t\} = \emptyset$, for every finite t. But it is clear that $P(X_t \in B_t) = P(X_0 = 0) = \frac{1}{2}$. Hence for every finite m,

$$\begin{aligned} \alpha_m &\geq \left| P(\{X_0 = 1\} \cap \{X_m \in B_m\}) - P(X_0 = 1)P(X_m \in B_m) \right| \\ &= \tfrac{1}{4}, \end{aligned} \tag{14.32}$$

which contradicts $\alpha_m \to 0$. □

Since the process starts at $t = 0$ in this case it is not stationary, but the example is easily generalized to a wider class of processes, as follows.

14.7 Theorem (Andrews 1984) Let $\{Z_t\}_{-\infty}^{\infty}$ be an independent sequence of Bernoulli r.v.s, taking values 1 and 0 with fixed probabilities p and $1-p$. If $X_t = \rho X_{t-1} + Z_t$ for $\rho \in (0,\frac{1}{2}]$, $\{X_t\}_{-\infty}^{\infty}$ is not strong mixing. □

Note, the condition on ρ is purely to expedite the argument. The theorem surely holds for other values of ρ, although this cannot be proved by the present approach.

Proof Write $X_{t+s} = \rho^s X_t + X_{t,s}$ where

$$X_{t,s} = \sum_{j=0}^{s-1} \rho^j Z_{t+s-j}. \tag{14.33}$$

The support of $X_{t,s}$ is finite for finite p, having at most 2^s distinct members. Call this set W_s, so that $W_1 = (0,1)$, $W_2 = (0, 1, \rho, 1+\rho)$, and so on. In general, W_{s+1} is obtained from W_s by adding ρ^s to each of its elements and forming the union of these elements with those of W_s; formally,

$$W_{s+1} = W_s \cup \{w+\rho^s\colon w \in W_s\},\ s = 2,3,... \tag{14.34}$$

For given s denote the distinct elements of W_s by w_j, ordered by magnitude with $w_1 < ... < w_J$, for $J \le 2^s$.

Now suppose that $X_t \in (0,\rho)$, so that $\rho^s X_t \in (0,\rho^{s+1})$. This means that X_{t+s} assumes a value between w_j and $w_j+\rho^{s+1}$, for some j. Defining events $A = \{X_t \in (0,\rho)\}$ and $B_s = \{X_{t+s} \in \bigcup_{j=1}^J (w_j,\ w+r^{s+1})\}$, we have $P(B_s|A) = 1$ for any s, however large. To see that $P(A) > 0$, consider the case $Z_t = Z_{t-1} = Z_{t-2} = 0$ and $Z_{t-3} = 1$ and note that

$$\sum_{j=3}^{\infty} \rho^j Z_{t-j} \le \sum_{j=3}^{\infty} \rho^j = \frac{\rho^3}{1-\rho} < \rho \tag{14.35}$$

for $\rho \in (0,\frac{1}{2}]$. So, unless $P(B_s) = 1$, strong mixing is contradicted.

The proof is completed by showing that the set $D = \{X_t \in [\rho,1]\}$ has positive probability, and is disjoint with B_s. D occurs when $Z_t = 0$ and $Z_{t-1} = 1$, since then, for $\rho \in (0,\frac{1}{2}]$,

$$\rho \le \sum_{j=1}^{\infty} \rho^j Z_{t-j} \le \sum_{j=1}^{\infty} \rho^j = \frac{\rho}{1-\rho} \le 1, \tag{14.36}$$

and hence $P(D) > 0$. Suppose that

$$\min_{j\ge 1}\{w_{j+1}-w_j\} \ge \rho^{s-1}. \tag{14.37}$$

Then, if D occurs,

$$w_j+\rho^{s+1} \le w_j+\rho^s X_t < w_j+\rho^{s-1} \le w_{j+1}, \tag{14.38}$$

hence, $X_{t+s} = w_j+\rho^s X_t \notin \bigcup_{j=1}^J (w_j,\ w_j+\rho^{s+1})$, or in other words, $B_s \cap D = \emptyset$.

The assertion in (14.37) is certainly true when $s = 1$, so consider the following inductive argument. Suppose the distance between two points in W_s is at least ρ^{s-1}. Then by (14.34), the smallest distance between two points of W_{s+1} cannot be less than the smaller of ρ^s and $\rho^{s-1}-\rho^s$. But when $\rho \in (0,\frac{1}{2})$, $\rho^s \le \frac{1}{2}\rho^{s-1}$, which implies $\rho^{s-1}-\rho^s \ge \rho^s$. It follows that (14.37) holds for every s. ■

These results may appear surprising when one thinks of the rate at which ρ^s approaches 0 with s; but if so, this is because we are unconsciously thinking about the problem of predicting gross features of the distribution of X_{t+s} from time t, things like $P(X_{t+s} \le x|A)$ for fixed x, for example. The notable feature of the sets B_s is their irrelevance to such concerns, at least for large s. What we have shown is that from a practical viewpoint the mixing concept has some undesirable features. The requirement of a decline of dependence is imposed over *all* events, whereas in practice it might serve our purposes adequately to tolerate certain uninteresting events, such as the B_s defined above, remaining dependent on the initial conditions even at long range.

In the next section we will derive some sufficient conditions for strong mixing, and it turns out that certain smoothness conditions on the marginal distributions of the increments will be enough to rule out this kind of counter-example. But now consider uniform mixing.

14.8 Example[13] Consider an AR(1) process with i.i.d. increments,

$$X_t = \rho X_{t-1} + Z_t,\ 0 < \rho < 1,$$

in which the marginal distribution of Z_t has unbounded support. We show that $\{X_t\}$ is not uniform mixing. For $\delta > 0$ choose a positive constant M to satisfy

$$P\left(\sum_{j=0}^{m-1} \rho^j Z_{m-j} \le -M\right) < \delta. \tag{14.39}$$

Then consider the events

$$A = \{X_0 \ge \rho^{-m}(L+M)\} \in \mathcal{F}_{-\infty}^{0}$$

$$B = \{X_m \le L\} \in \mathcal{F}_{m}^{+\infty},$$

where L is large enough that $P(B) \ge 1-\delta$. We show $P(A) > 0$ for every m. Let $p_K = P(Z_0 < K)$, for any constant K. Since Z_0 has unbounded support, either $p_K < 1$ for every $K > 0$ or, at worst, this holds after substituting $\{-Z_t\}$ for $\{Z_t\}$ and hence $\{-X_t\}$ for $\{X_t\}$. $p_k < 1$ for all K implies, by stationarity, $P(X_{-1} < 0) = P(X_0 < 0) < 1$. Since $\{X_0 < K\} \subseteq \{Z_0 < K\} \cup (\{Z_0 \ge K\} \cap \{X_{-1} < 0\})$, independence of the $\{Z_t\}$ implies that

$$P(X_0 < K) \le p_K + (1-p_K)P(X_{-1} < 0) < 1. \tag{14.40}$$

So $P(A) > 0$, since K is arbitrary. Since $X_m = \rho^m X_0 + \sum_{j=0}^{m-1} \rho^j Z_{m-j}$, it is clear that

$$P(B|A) = P\left(\rho^m X_0 + \sum_{j=0}^{m-1} \rho^j Z_{m-j} \le L \,\middle|\, \rho^m X_0 \ge L+M\right) < \delta \tag{14.41}$$

by (14.39). Hence $\phi_m \ge |P(B|A) - P(B)| > 1 - 2\delta$, and since δ is arbitrary, this means $\phi_m = 1$ for every m. □

Processes with Gaussian increments fall into the category covered by this example, and if ϕ-mixing fails in the first-order AR case it is pretty clear that counter-examples exist for more general MA(∞) cases too. The conditions for uniform mixing in linear processes are evidently extremely tough, perhaps too tough for this mixing condition to be very useful. In the applications to be studied in later chapters, most of the results are found to hold in some form for strong mixing processes, but the ability to assert uniform mixing usually allows a relaxation of conditions elsewhere in the problem, so it is still desirable to develop the parallel results for the uniform case.

The strong restrictions needed to ensure processes are mixing, which these examples point to (to be explored further in the next section), threaten to limit the usefulness of the mixing concept. However, technical infringements like the ones demonstrated are often innocuous in practice. Only certain aspects of mixing, encapsulated in the concept of a *mixingale*, are required for many important limit results to hold. These are shared with so-called *near-epoch dependent functions* of mixing sequences, which include cases like **14.7**. The theory of these dependence concepts is treated in Chapters 16 and 17. While Chapter 15 contains some necessary background material for those chapters, the interested reader might choose to skip ahead at this point to find out how, in essence, the difficulty will be resolved.

14.4 Sufficient Conditions for Strong and Uniform Mixing

The problems in the counter-examples above are with the form of the marginal shock distributions—discrete or unbounded, as the case may be. For strong mixing, a degree of smoothness of the distributions appears necessary in addition to summability conditions on the coefficients of linear processes. Several sufficient conditions have been derived, both for general MA(∞) processes and for autoregressive and ARMA processes. The sufficiency result for strong mixing proved below is based on the theorems of Chanda (1974) and Gorodetskii (1977). These conditions are not the weakest possible in all circumstances, but they have the virtues of generality and comparative ease of verification.

14.9 Theorem Let $X_t = \sum_{j=0}^{\infty}\theta_j Z_{t-j}$ define a random sequence $\{X_t\}_{-\infty}^{\infty}$, where, for either $0 < r \le 2$ or r an even positive integer,

(a) Z_t is uniformly L_r-bounded, independent, continuous with p.d.f. f_{Z_t}, and

$$\sup_t \int_{-\infty}^{+\infty} \left| f_{Z_t}(z_t + a) - f_{Z_t}(z)\right| dz \le M|a|,\ M < \infty, \tag{14.42}$$

whenever $|a| \le \delta$, for some $\delta > 0$;

(b) $\sum_{t=0}^{\infty} G_t(r)^{1/(1+r)} < \infty$, where

$$G_t(r) = \begin{cases} 2\sum_{j=t}^{\infty} |\theta_j|^r, & r \le 2, \\ 2^{r-1}\left(\sum_{j=t}^{\infty}\theta_j^2\right)^{r/2}, & r \ge 2; \end{cases} \tag{14.43}$$

(c) $\theta(x) = \sum_{j=1}^{\infty}\theta_j x^j \ne 0$ for all complex numbers x with $|x| \le 1$.

Then $\{X_t\}$ is strong mixing with $\alpha_m = O(\sum_{t=m+1}^{\infty} G_t(r)^{1/(1+r)})$. □

Before proceeding to the proof, we must discuss the implications of these three conditions in a bit more detail. Condition **14.9**(a) may be relaxed somewhat, as we show below, but we begin with this case for simplicity. The following lemma extends the condition to the joint distributions under independence.

14.10 Lemma Inequality (14.42) implies that for $|a_t| \le \delta$, $t = 1,\dots,k$,

$$\int_{\mathbb{R}^k} \left| \prod_{t=1}^{k} f_{Z_t}(z_t + a_t) - \prod_{t=1}^{k} f_{Z_t}(z_t) \right| dz_1 \dots dz_k \le M \sum_{t=1}^{k} |a_t|. \tag{14.44}$$

Proof Using Fubini's theorem,

$$\int_{\mathbb{R}^k} \left| \prod_{t=1}^{k} f_{Z_t}(z_t + a_t) - \prod_{t=1}^{k} f_{Z_t}(z_t) \right| dz_1 \dots dz_k$$

$$\le \int_{\mathbb{R}^k} \left| [f_{Z_1}(z_1 + a_1) - f_{Z_1}(z_1)] \prod_{t=2}^{k} f_{Z_t}(z_t + a_t) \right| dz_1 \dots dz_k$$

$$+ \int_{\mathbb{R}^k} \left| f_{Z_1}(z_1) \left(\prod_{t=2}^{k} f_{Z_t}(z_t + a_t) - \prod_{t=2}^{k} f_{Z_t}(z_t) \right) \right| dz_1 \dots dz_k$$

$$\le M|a_1| + \int_{\mathbb{R}^{k-1}} \left| \prod_{t=2}^{k} f_{Z_t}(z_t + a_t) - \prod_{t=2}^{k} f_{Z_t}(z_t) \right| dz_2 \dots dz_k.$$

The lemma follows on applying the same inequality to the second term on the right, iteratively for $t = 2,\dots,k$. ■

Condition **14.9**(b) is satisfied when $|\theta_j| \ll j^{-\mu}$ for $\mu > 1 + 2/r$ when $r \le 2$ and $\mu > 3/2 + 1/r$ when $r \ge 2$. The double definition of $G_t(r)$ is motivated by the fact that for cases with $r \le 2$ we use the von Bahr-Esseen inequality (**11.15**) to bound a certain sequence in the proof, whereas with $r > 2$ we rely on Lemma **14.11** below. Since the latter result requires r to be an even integer, the conditions in the theorem are to be applied in practice by taking r as the nearest even integer below the highest existing absolute moment. Gorodetskii (1977) achieves a further weakening of these summability conditions for $r > 2$ by the use of an inequality due to Nagaev and Fuk (1971). We will forgo this extension, both because proof of the Nagaev-Fuk inequalities represents a rather complicated detour, and because the present version of the theorem permits a generalization (Corollary **14.13**) which would otherwise be awkward to implement.

Define $W_t = \sum_{j=0}^{t-1} \theta_j Z_{t-j}$ and $V_t = \sum_{j=t}^{\infty} \theta_j Z_{t-j}$, so that $X_t = W_t + V_t$, and W_t and V_t are independent. Think of V_t as the $\mathcal{F}_{-\infty}^{0}$-measurable 'tail' of X_t, whose contribution to the sum should become negligible as $t \to \infty$.

14.11 Lemma If the sequence $\{Z_s\}$ is independent with zero mean, then

$$E(V_t^{2m}) \le 2^{2m-1} \left(\sum_{j=t}^{\infty} \theta_j^2 \right)^m \sup_{s \le 0} E(Z_s^{2m}) \tag{14.45}$$

for each positive integer m such that $\sup_{s \le 0} E(Z_s^{2m}) < \infty$.

Proof First consider the case where the r.v.s Z_{t-j} are symmetrically distributed, meaning that $-Z_{t-j}$ and Z_{t-j} have the same distributions. In this case all existing odd-order integer moments about 0 are zero, and

$$E\left(\sum_{j=t}^{t+k}\theta_j Z_{t-j}\right)^{2m} = \sum_{j_1=t}^{t+k}\dots\sum_{j_{2m}=t}^{t+k}\theta_{j_1}\dots\theta_{j_{2m}}E(Z_{t-j_1}\dots Z_{t-j_{2m}})$$

$$= \sum_{j_1=t}^{t+k}\dots\sum_{j_m=t}^{t+k}\theta_{j_1}^2\dots\theta_{j_m}^2 E(Z_{t-j_1}^2\dots Z_{t-j_m}^2)$$

$$\leq \left(\sum_{j=0}^{t+k}\theta_j^2\right)^m \sup_{s\leq 0} E(Z_s^{2m}). \tag{14.46}$$

The second equality holds since $E(Z_{t-j_1}\dots Z_{t-j_{2m}})$ vanishes unless the factors form matching pairs, and the inequality follows since, for any r.v. Y possessing the requisite moments, $E(Y^{j+k}) \geq E(Y^j)E(Y^k)$ (i.e., $\mathrm{Cov}(Y^j,Y^k) \geq 0$) for $j,k > 0$. The result for symmetrically distributed Z_s follows on letting $k \to \infty$.

For general Z_s, let Z_s' be distributed identically as, and independent of, Z_s, for each $s \leq 0$. Then $V_t' = \sum_{j=t}^{\infty}\theta_j Z_{t-j}'$ is independent of V_t, and $V_t - V_t'$ has symmetrically distributed independent increments $Z_{t-j} - Z_{t-j}'$. Hence

$$E(V_t^{2m}) \leq E(V_t - V_t')^{2m} \leq \left(\sum_{j=t}^{\infty}\theta_j^2\right)^m \sup_j E(Z_{t-j} - Z_{t-j}')^{2m}$$

$$\leq 2^{2m-1}\left(\sum_{j=0}^{\infty}\theta_j^2\right)^m \sup_j E(Z_{t-j}^{2m}), \tag{14.47}$$

where the first inequality is by **10.19**, the second by (14.45), and the third is the c_r inequality. ■

Lastly, consider condition **14.9**(c). This is designed to pin down the properties of the inverse transformation, taking us from the coordinates of $\{X_t\}$ to those of $\{Z_t\}$. It ensures that the function of a complex variable $\theta(x)$ possesses an analytic[14] inverse $\tau(x) = \sum_{j=0}^{\infty}\tau_j x^j$ for $|x| \leq 1$. The particular property needed and implied by the condition is that the coefficient sequence $\{\tau_j\}$ is absolutely summable. If $X_t = \sum_{j=0}^{\infty}\theta_j Z_{t-j}$, under **14.9**(c) the inverse representation is also defined, as $Z_t = \sum_{j=0}^{\infty}\tau_j X_{t-j}$. Note that $\tau_0 = 1$ if $\theta_0 = 1$. An effect of **14.9**(c) is to rule out 'over-differenced' cases, as for example where $\theta(x) = \theta_1(x)(1-x)$ with $\theta_1(.)$ a summable polynomial. The differencing transformation does *not* yield a mixing process in general, the exception being where it reverses the previous integration of a mixing process.

For a finite number of terms the transformation is conveniently expressed using matrix notation. Let

$$A_n = \begin{bmatrix} 1 & & & & \\ \theta_1 & 1 & & 0 & \\ \vdots & \theta_1 & 1 & & \\ \theta_{n-2} & \vdots & & \ddots & \\ \theta_{n-1} & \theta_{n-2} & \cdots & \theta_1 & 1 \end{bmatrix} (n\times n), \quad (14.48)$$

so that the equations $x_t = \sum_{j=0}^{t-1}\theta_j z_{t-j}$, $t = 1,\dots,n$ can be written $\boldsymbol{x} = \boldsymbol{A}_n\boldsymbol{z}$ where $\boldsymbol{x} = (x_1,\dots,x_n)'$ and $\mathbf{z} = (z_1,\dots,z_n)'$. $\boldsymbol{A}_n^{-1}$ is also lower triangular, with elements τ_j replacing θ_j for $j = 0,\dots,n-1$. If $\boldsymbol{v} = (v_1,\dots,v_n)'$ the vector $\hat{\boldsymbol{v}} = \boldsymbol{A}_n^{-1}\boldsymbol{v}$ has elements $\sum_{j=0}^{t-1}\tau_j v_{t-j}$, for $t = 1,\dots,n$. These operations can in principle be taken to the limit as $n \to \infty$, subject to **14.9**(c).

Proof of 14.9 Without loss of generality, the object is to show that the σ-fields $\mathcal{F}_{-\infty}^0 = \sigma(\dots,X_{-1},X_0)$ and $\mathcal{F}_{m+1}^\infty = \sigma(X_{m+1},X_{m+2},\dots,)$ are independent as $m \to \infty$. The result does not depend on the choice of origin for the indices. This is shown for a sequence $\{X_t\}_{t=1-p}^{m+k}$ for finite p and k, and since k and p are arbitrary, it then follows by the consistency theorem (**12.4**) that there exists a sequence $\{X_t\}_{-\infty}^{\infty}$ whose finite-dimensional distributions possess the property for every k and p. This sequence is strong mixing on the definition.

Define a $p+m+k$-vector $\boldsymbol{X} = (\boldsymbol{X}_0',\boldsymbol{X}_1',\boldsymbol{X}_2')'$ where $\boldsymbol{X}_0 = (X_{1-p},\dots,X_0)'$ $(p\times 1)$, $\boldsymbol{X}_1 = (X_1,\dots,X_m)'$ $(m\times 1)$, and $\boldsymbol{X}_2 = (X_{m+1},\dots,X_{m+k})'$ $(k\times 1)$, and also vectors $\boldsymbol{W} = (\boldsymbol{W}_1',\boldsymbol{W}_2')'$ and $\boldsymbol{V} = (\boldsymbol{V}_1',\boldsymbol{V}_2')'$ such that $\boldsymbol{X}_1 = \boldsymbol{W}_1 + \boldsymbol{V}_1$ and $\boldsymbol{X}_2 = \boldsymbol{W}_2 + \boldsymbol{V}_2$. (The elements of $\boldsymbol{W}$ and $\boldsymbol{V}$ are defined above **14.11**.) The vectors $\boldsymbol{X}_0$ and $\boldsymbol{V}$ are independent of $\boldsymbol{W}$. Now, use the notation $\mathcal{F}_s^t = \sigma(X_s,\dots,X_t)$ and define the following sets:

$$G = \{\omega\colon \boldsymbol{X}_0(\omega) \in C\} \in \mathcal{F}_{1-p}^0, \text{ for some } C \in \mathcal{B}^p,$$

$$H = \{\omega\colon \boldsymbol{X}_2(\omega) \in D\} \in \mathcal{F}_{m+1}^{m+k}, \text{ for some } D \in \mathcal{B}^k,$$

$$E = \{\omega\colon \boldsymbol{V}_2(\omega) \in B\} \in \mathcal{F}_{-\infty}^0,$$

where $B = \{\boldsymbol{v}_2\colon |\boldsymbol{v}_2| \le \boldsymbol{\eta}\} \in \mathcal{B}^k$, $|\boldsymbol{v}_2|$ denotes the vector whose elements are the absolute values of $\boldsymbol{v}_2$, and $\boldsymbol{\eta} = (\eta_{m+1},\dots,\eta_{m+k})'$ is a vector of positive constants. Also define

$$D - \boldsymbol{v}_2 = \{\boldsymbol{w}_2\colon \boldsymbol{w}_2 + \boldsymbol{v}_2 \in D\} \in \mathcal{B}^k.$$

H may be thought of as the random event that has occurred when, first $\boldsymbol{V}_2 = \boldsymbol{v}_2$ is realized, and then $\boldsymbol{W}_2 \in D - \boldsymbol{v}_2$. By independence, the joint c.d.f. of the variables $(\boldsymbol{W}_2,\boldsymbol{V}_2,\boldsymbol{X}_0)$ factorizes as $F = F_{W_2}F_{V_2,X_0}$ (say) and we can write

$$P(H) = P(\boldsymbol{X}_2 \in D) = \int_{\mathbb{R}^p}\int_{\mathbb{R}^k}\int_{D-\boldsymbol{v}_2} dF(\boldsymbol{w}_2,\boldsymbol{v}_2,\boldsymbol{x}_0)$$

$$= \int_{\mathbb{R}^p}\int_{\mathbb{R}^k}\chi(\boldsymbol{v}_2)dF_{V_2,X_0}(\boldsymbol{v}_2,\boldsymbol{x}_0), \quad (14.49)$$

where

$$\chi(\boldsymbol{v}_2) = P(\boldsymbol{W}_2 \in D - \boldsymbol{v}_2) = \int_{D-\boldsymbol{v}_2} dF_{\boldsymbol{W}_2}(\boldsymbol{w}_2). \tag{14.50}$$

These definitions set the scene for the main business of the proof, which is to show that events G and H are tending to independence as m becomes large. Given $\mathcal{F}/\mathcal{B}^{p+m+k}$-measurability of $\boldsymbol{X}$, this is sufficient for the result, since C and D are arbitrary. By the same reasoning that gave (14.49), we have

$$P(G \cap H \cap E) = \int_C \int_B \chi(\boldsymbol{v}_2) dF_{\boldsymbol{V}_2, \boldsymbol{X}_0}(\boldsymbol{v}_2, \boldsymbol{x}_0). \tag{14.51}$$

Define $\chi^* = \sup_{\boldsymbol{v}_2 \in B} \chi(\boldsymbol{v}_2)$ and $\chi_* = \inf_{\boldsymbol{v}_2 \in B} \chi(\boldsymbol{v}_2)$, and (14.51) implies

$$\chi_* P(G \cap E) \le P(G \cap H \cap E) \le \chi^* P(G \cap E). \tag{14.52}$$

Hence we have the bounds

$$\begin{aligned} P(G \cap H) &= P(G \cap H \cap E) + P(G \cap H \cap E^c) \\ &\le \chi^* P(G) + P(E^c), \end{aligned} \tag{14.53}$$

and similarly, since $\chi_* \le 1$,

$$\begin{aligned} P(G \cap H) &\ge \chi_* P(G \cap E) + P(G \cap H \cap E^c) \\ &= \chi_* P(G) - \chi_* P(G \cap E^c) + P(G \cap H \cap E^c) \\ &\ge \chi_* P(G) - P(E^c). \end{aligned} \tag{14.54}$$

Choosing $G = \Omega$ (i.e., $C = \mathbb{R}^p$) in (14.53) and (14.54) gives in particular

$$\chi_* - P(E^c) \le P(H) \le \chi^* + P(E^c), \tag{14.55}$$

and combining all these inequalities yields

$$|P(G \cap H) - P(G)P(H)| \le \chi^* - \chi_* + 2P(E^c). \tag{14.56}$$

Write $\boldsymbol{W} = \boldsymbol{A}_{m+k}\boldsymbol{Z}$, where $\mathbf{Z} = (Z_1, \ldots, Z_{m+k})'$ and $\boldsymbol{A}_{m+k}$ is defined by (14.48). Since $|\boldsymbol{A}_{m+k}| = 1$ and the $\{Z_1, \ldots, Z_{m+k}\}$ are independent, the change of variable formula from **8.18** yields the result that $\boldsymbol{W}$ is continuously distributed with

$$f_{\boldsymbol{W}}(\boldsymbol{w}) = f_{\mathbf{Z}}(\mathbf{z}) = \prod_{t=1}^{m+k} f_{Z_t}(z_t). \tag{14.57}$$

Define $B' = \{\boldsymbol{v}: \boldsymbol{v}_1 = \mathbf{0}, \boldsymbol{v}_2 \in B\} \in \mathcal{B}^{m+k}$. Then the following relations hold:

$$\begin{aligned} \chi^* - \chi_* &\le 2 \sup_{\boldsymbol{v}_2 \in B} \left| \chi(\boldsymbol{v}_2) - \chi(\mathbf{0}) \right| \\ &\le 2 \sup_{\boldsymbol{v}_2 \in B} \int_D \left| f_{\boldsymbol{W}_2}(\boldsymbol{w}_2 + \boldsymbol{v}_2) - f_{\boldsymbol{W}_2}(\boldsymbol{w}_2) \right| d\boldsymbol{w}_2 \end{aligned}$$

$$\leq 2\sup_{\boldsymbol{v}\in B'}\left\{\int_{\mathbb{R}^{m+k}}\left|f_W(\boldsymbol{w}+\boldsymbol{v})-f_W(\boldsymbol{w})\right|d\boldsymbol{w}\right\}$$

$$= 2\sup_{\boldsymbol{v}\in B'}\left\{\int_{\mathbb{R}^{m+k}}\left|\prod_{t=1}^{m+k}f_{Z_t}(z_t+\hat{v}_t)-\prod_{t=1}^{m+k}f_{Z_t}(z_t)\right|dz\right\}$$

$$\leq 2M\sup_{\boldsymbol{v}\in B'}\left\{\sum_{t=m+1}^{m+k}|\hat{v}_t|\right\}, \tag{14.58}$$

where it is understood in the final inequality (which is by **14.10**) that $|\hat{v}_t| \leq \delta$ where δ is defined in condition **14.9**(a). The third equality substitutes $\hat{\boldsymbol{v}} = \boldsymbol{A}_{m+k}^{-1}\boldsymbol{v}$ and uses the fact that $\hat{\boldsymbol{v}}_1 = \boldsymbol{0}$ if $\boldsymbol{v}_1 = \boldsymbol{0}$ by lower triangularity of $\boldsymbol{A}_{m+k}$. For $\boldsymbol{v} \in B'$, note that

$$\sum_{t=m+1}^{m+k}|\hat{v}_t| = \sum_{t=m+1}^{m+k}\left|\sum_{j=0}^{t-m-1}\tau_j v_{t-j}\right|$$

$$\leq \sum_{t=m+1}^{m+k}\left(\sum_{j=0}^{t-m-1}|\tau_j|\eta_{t-j}\right) \leq \left(\sum_{j=0}^{\infty}|\tau_j|\right)\sum_{t=m}^{m+k}\eta_t, \tag{14.59}$$

assuming $\boldsymbol{\eta}$ has been chosen with elements small enough that the terms in parentheses in the penultimate member do not exceed δ. This is possible by condition **14.9**(c).

For the final step, choose r to be the largest order of absolute moment if this is does not exceed 2, and the largest even integer moment, otherwise. Then

$$P(E^c) = P(|\boldsymbol{V}_2| > \boldsymbol{\eta})$$

$$= P\left(\bigcup_{t=m+1}^{m+k}\{|V_t| > \eta_t\}\right)$$

$$\leq \sum_{t=m+1}^{m+k}P(|V_t| > \eta_t) \leq \sum_{t=m+1}^{m+k}E|V_t|^r\eta_t^{-r}, \tag{14.60}$$

by the Markov inequality, and

$$E|V_t|^r \leq \sup_s E|Z_s|^r G_t(r), \tag{14.61}$$

where $G_t(r)$ is given by (14.43), applying **11.15** for $r \leq 2$ (see (11.65) for the required extension) and Lemma **14.11** for $r > 2$. Substituting inequalities (14.58), (14.59), (14.60), and (14.61) into (14.56) yields

$$|P(G\cap H)-P(G)P(H)| \ll \sum_{t=m+1}^{m+k}(\eta_t + G_t(r)\eta_t^{-r}). \tag{14.62}$$

Since $G_t(r) \downarrow 0$ by **14.9**(b), it is possible to choose m large enough that (14.59) and hence (14.62) hold with $\eta_t = G_t(r)^{1/(1+r)} = G_t(r)\eta_t^{-r}$ for each $t > m$. We obtain

$$|P(G \cap H) - P(G)P(H)| \ll \sum_{t=m+1}^{m+k} G_t(r)^{1/(1+r)}$$

$$\leq \sum_{t=m+1}^{\infty} G_t(r)^{1/(1+r)}, \tag{14.63}$$

where the right-hand sum is finite by **14.9**(b), and goes to zero as $m \to \infty$. This completes the proof. ∎

It is worth examining this argument with care to see how violation of the conditions can lead to trouble. According to (14.56), mixing will follow from two conditions: the obvious one is that the tail component V_2, the $\mathcal{F}_{-\infty}^0$-measurable part of X_2, becomes negligible, such that is, $P(E)$ gets close to 1 when m is large, even when η is allowed to approach $\mathbf{0}$. But in addition, to have $\chi^* - \chi_*$ disappear, $P(W_2 \in D - v_2)$ must approach a unique limit as $v_2 \to \mathbf{0}$, for any D, and whatever the path of convergence. When the distribution has atoms, it is easy to devise examples where this requirement fails. In **14.6**, the set B_t becomes $W_t - B_t$ on being translated a distance of 2^{-t}. For such a case these probabilities evidently do not converge, in the limiting case as $t \to \infty$.

However, this is a sufficiency result, and it remains unclear just how much more than the absence of atoms is strictly necessary. Consider an example where the distribution is continuous, having differentiable p.d.f., but condition (14.42) none the less fails.

14.12 Example Let $f(z) = C_0 z^{-2}\sin^2(z^4)$, $z \in \mathbb{R}$. This is non-negative, continuous everywhere, and bounded by $C_0 z^{-2}$ and hence integrable. By choice of C_0 we can have $\int_{-\infty}^{+\infty} f(z)dz = 1$, so f is a p.d.f. By the mean value theorem,

$$|f(z+a) - f(z)| = |a||f'(z+\alpha(z)a)|, \ \alpha(z) \in [0,1], \tag{14.64}$$

where $f'(z) = 8C_0\sin(z^4)\cos(z^4)z - 2C_0\sin^2(z^4)z^{-3}$. But note that $\int_{-\infty}^{+\infty}|f'(z)|dz = \infty$, and hence,

$$\frac{1}{|a|}\int_{-\infty}^{+\infty}|f(z+a) - f(z)|dz \to \infty \text{ as } |a| \to 0, \tag{14.65}$$

which contradicts (14.42). The problem is that the density is varying too rapidly in the tails of the distribution, and $|f(z+a) - f(z)|$ does not diminish rapidly enough in these regions as $a \to 0$.

The rate of divergence in (14.65) can be estimated.[15] For fixed (small) a, $|f(z+a) - f(z)|$ is at a local maximum at points at which $\sin(z+a)^4 = 1$ (or 0) and $\sin z^4 = 0$ (or 1), or in other words where $(z+a)^4 - z^4 = 4az^3 + O(a^2) = \pm\pi/2$. The solutions to these approximate relations can be written as $z = \pm C_1|a|^{-1/3}$ for $C_1 > 0$. At these points we can write, again approximately (orders of magnitude are all we need here),

$$|f(z+a)-f(z)| \leq 2f(z) \leq 2C_0C_1^{-2}|a|^{2/3}.$$

The integral is bounded within the interval $[-C_1|a|^{-1/3},\ C_1|a|^{-1/3}]$ by $4C_0C_1^{-1}|a|^{1/3}$, the area of the rectangle having height $2C_0C_1^{-2}|a|^{2/3}$. Outside the interval, f is bounded by C_0z^{-2}, and the integral over this region is bounded by

$$2C_0\int_{C_1|a|^{-1/3}}^{+\infty} z^{-2}dz = 2C_0C_1^{-1}|a|^{1/3}.$$

Adding up the approximations yields

$$\int_{-\infty}^{+\infty}|f(z+a)-f(z)|dz \leq M|a|^{1/3} \tag{14.66}$$

for $M < \infty$. □

The rate of divergence is critical for relaxing the conditions. Suppose instead of (14.42) that

$$\int_{-\infty}^{+\infty}|f(z+a)-f(z)|dz \leq Mh(|a|),\ |a| \leq \delta,\ \delta > 0 \tag{14.67}$$

could be shown sufficient, where $h(.)$ is an arbitrary increasing function with $h(|a|) \downarrow 0$ as $|a| \downarrow 0$. Since

$$\int_{-\infty}^{+\infty}|f(z+a)-f(z)|dz \leq 2\int_{-\infty}^{+\infty}f(z)dz = 2 \tag{14.68}$$

for any a, (14.67) effectively holds for *any* p.d.f., by the dominated convergence theorem. Simple continuity of the distributions would suffice.[16]

This particular result does not seem to be available, but it is possible to relax **14.9**(a) substantially, at the cost of an additional restriction on the moving average coefficients.

14.13 Corollary Modify the conditions of **14.9** as follows: for $0 < \beta \leq 1$, assume that

(a′) Z_t is uniformly L_r-bounded, independent, and continuously distributed with p.d.f. f_{Z_t}, and

$$\sup_t \int_{-\infty}^{+\infty}\left|f_{Z_t}(z+a)-f_{Z_t}(z)\right|dz \leq M|a|^{\beta},\ M < \infty; \tag{14.69}$$

whenever $|a| \leq \delta$, for some $\delta > 0$;

(b′) $\sum_{t=0}^{\infty}G_t(r)^{\beta/(\beta+r)} < \infty$, where $G_t(r)$ is defined in (14.43);

(c′) $1/\theta(x) = \tau(x) = \sum_{j=1}^{\infty}\tau_j x^j$ for $|x| \leq 1$, and $\sum_{j=1}^{\infty}|\tau_j|^{\beta} < \infty$.

Then X_t is strong mixing with $\alpha_m = O(\sum_{t=m+1}^{\infty}G_t(r)^{\beta/(\beta+r)})$.

Proof This follows the proof of **14.9** until (14.58), which becomes

$$\chi^* - \chi_* \le 2M \sup_{\nu \in B'} \left\{ \sum_{t=m+1}^{m+k} |\hat{\nu}_t|^\beta \right\}, \tag{14.70}$$

applying the obvious extension of Lemma **14.10**. Note that

$$\sum_{t=m+1}^{m+k} |\hat{\nu}_t|^\beta = \sum_{t=m+1}^{m+k} \left| \sum_{j=0}^{t-m-1} \tau_j \nu_{t-j} \right|^\beta \le \sum_{j=0}^{\infty} |\tau_j|^\beta \sum_{t=m+1}^{m+k} \eta_t^\beta \tag{14.71}$$

using (9.63), since $0 < \beta \le 1$. Applying assumption **14.13**(c′),

$$|P(G \cap H) - P(G)P(H)| \ll \sum_{t=m+1}^{m+k} (\eta_t^\beta + G_t(r)\eta_t^{-r}), \tag{14.72}$$

and the result is obtained as before, but in this case setting $\eta_t = G_t^{1/(\beta+r)}$. ■

Condition **14.13**(b′) is satisfied when $|\theta_j| \ll j^{-\mu}$ for $\mu > 1/\beta + 2/r$ when $r \le 2$, and $\mu > 1/2 + 1/r + 1/\beta$ when $r \ge 2$, which shows how the summability restrictions have to be strengthened when β is close to 0. This is none the less a useful extension because there are important cases where **14.13**(b′) and **14.13**(c′) are easily satisfied. In particular, if the process is finite-order ARMA, both $|\theta_j|$ and $|\tau_j|$ either decline geometrically or vanish beyond some finite j, and (b′) and (c′) both hold.

Condition **14.13**(a′) is a strengthening of continuity since there exist functions $h(.)$ which are slowly varying at 0, that is, which approach 0 more slowly than any positive power of the argument. Look again at **14.12**, and note that setting $\beta = \frac{1}{3}$ will satisfy condition **14.13**(a′) according to (14.65). It is easy to generalize the example. Putting $f(z) = C\sin^2(z^k)z^{-2}$ for $k \ge 4$, the earlier argument is easily modified to show that the integral converges at the rate $|a|^{1/(k-1)}$, and this choice of β is appropriate. But for $f(z) = C\sin^2(e^z)z^{-2}$ the integral converges more slowly than $|a|^\beta$ for all $\beta > 0$, and condition **14.13**(a′) fails.

To conclude this chapter, we look at the case of uniform mixing. Manipulating inequalities (14.52)–(14.55) yields

$$|P(H|G) - P(H)| \le \chi^* - \chi_* + P(E^c)\left(1 + \frac{1}{P(G)}\right), \tag{14.73}$$

which shows that uniform mixing can fail unless $P(E) = 1$ for all m exceeding a finite value. Otherwise, we can always construct a sequence of events G whose probability is positive but approaching 0 no slower than $P(E^c)$. When the support of $(X_{-p},\dots,X_0)$ is unbounded this kind of thing can occur, as illustrated by **14.8**. The essence of this example does not depend on the AR(1) model, and similar cases could be constructed in the general MA(∞) framework. Sufficient conditions must include a.s. boundedness of the distributions, and the summability conditions are also modified. We will adapt the extended version of the strong mixing condition in **14.13**, although it is easy to deduce the relationship between these conditions and **14.9** by setting $\beta = 1$ below.

14.14 Theorem Modify the conditions of **14.13** as follows. Let (a′) and (c′) hold as before, but replace (b′) by

(b″) $\sum_{t=0}^{\infty}(\sum_{j=t}^{\infty}|\theta_j|)^{\beta} < \infty$,

and add

(d) $\{Z_t\}$ is uniformly bounded a.s.

Then $\{X_t\}$ is uniform mixing with $\phi_m = O(\sum_{t=m+1}^{\infty}(\sum_{j=t}^{\infty}|\theta_j|)^{\beta})$.

Proof Follow the proof of **14.9** up to (14.55), but replace (14.56) by (14.73). By condition **14.14**(d), there exists $K < \infty$ such that $\sup_t|Z_t| < K$ a.s., and hence $|X_t| < K\sum_{j=0}^{\infty}|\theta_j|$ a.s. It further follows, recalling the definition of V_2, that $P(E) = 1$ when $\eta_t < K\sum_{j=t}^{\infty}|\theta_j|$ for $t = m+1,\dots,m+k$. Substituting directly into (14.73) from (14.70) and (14.71), and making this choice of η, gives (for any G with $P(G) > 0$)

$$|P(H|G) - P(H)| \ll \sum_{t=m+1}^{m+k}\left(\sum_{j=t}^{\infty}|\theta_j|\right)^{\beta}. \tag{14.74}$$

The result now follows by the same considerations as before. ∎

These summability conditions are tougher than in **14.13**. Letting $r \to \infty$ in the latter case for comparability, **14.13**(b′) is satisfied when $|\theta_j| = O(j^{-\mu})$ for $\mu > 1/2 + 1/\beta$, while the corresponding implication of **14.14**(b″) is $\mu > 1 + 1/\beta$.

15
Martingales

15.1 Sequential Conditioning

It is trivial to observe that the arrow of time is unidirectional. Even though we can study a sample realization *ex post*, we know that, when a random sequence is generated, the 'current' member X_t is determined in an environment in which the previous members, X_{t-k} for $k > 0$, are given and conditionally fixed, whereas the members following remain contingent. The past is known, but the future is unknown. The operation of conditioning sequentially on past events is therefore of central importance in time-series modelling. We characterize partial knowledge by specifying a σ-subfield of events from $\mathcal{F}$, for which it is known whether each of the events belonging to it has occurred or not. The accumulation of information by an observer as time passes is represented by an increasing sequence of σ-fields, $\{\mathcal{F}_t\}_{-\infty}^{\infty}$, such that $\ldots \subseteq \mathcal{F}_{-1} \subseteq \mathcal{F}_0 \subseteq \mathcal{F}_1 \subseteq \mathcal{F}_2 \subseteq \ldots \subseteq \mathcal{F}$.[17]

If X_t is a random variable that is $\mathcal{F}_t$-measurable for each t, $\{\mathcal{F}_t\}_{-\infty}^{\infty}$ is said to be *adapted* to the sequence $\{X_t\}_{-\infty}^{\infty}$. The pairs $\{X_t,\mathcal{F}_t\}_{-\infty}^{\infty}$ are called an adapted sequence. Setting $\mathcal{F}_t = \sigma(X_s, -\infty < s \leq t)$ defines the minimal adapted sequence, but $\mathcal{F}_t$ typically has the interpretation of an observer's information set, and can contain more information than the history of a single variable. When X_t is integrable, the conditional expectations $E(X_t|\mathcal{F}_{t-1})$ are defined, and can be thought of as the optimal predictors of X_t from the point of view of observers looking one period ahead (compare **10.12**).

Consider an adapted sequence $\{S_n,\mathcal{F}_n\}_{-\infty}^{\infty}$ on a probability space $(\Omega,\mathcal{F},P)$, where $\{\mathcal{F}_n\}$ is an increasing sequence. If the properties

$$E|S_n| < \infty, \tag{15.1}$$

$$E(S_n|\mathcal{F}_{n-1}) = S_{n-1}, \text{ a.s.}, \tag{15.2}$$

hold for every n, the sequence is called a *martingale*. In old-fashioned gambling parlance, a martingale was a policy of attempting to recoup a loss by doubling one's stake on the next bet, but the modern usage of the term in probability theory is closer to describing a gambler's worth in the course of a sequence of fair bets. In view of (10.18), an alternative version of condition (15.2) is

$$\int_A S_n dP = \int_A S_{n-1} dP, \text{ each } A \in \mathcal{F}_{n-1}. \tag{15.3}$$

Sometimes the sequence has a finite initial index, and may be written $\{S_n,\mathcal{F}_n\}_1^{\infty}$ where S_1 is an arbitrary integrable r.v.

15.1 Example Let $\{X_t\}_1^\infty$ be an i.i.d. integrable sequence with zero mean. If $S_n = \sum_{t=1}^n X_t$ and $\mathcal{F}_n = \sigma(X_n,X_{n-1},\dots,X_1)$, $\{S_n,\mathcal{F}_n\}_1^\infty$ is a martingale, also known as a *random walk* sequence. Note that $E|S_n| \le \sum_{t=1}^n E|X_t| < \infty$. □

15.2 Example Let Z be an integrable, $\mathcal{F}/\mathcal{B}$-measurable, zero-mean r.v., $\{\mathcal{F}_n\}_{-\infty}^\infty$ an increasing sequence of σ-fields with $\lim_{n\to\infty}\mathcal{F}_n = \mathcal{F}$, and $S_n = E(Z|\mathcal{F}_n)$. Then

$$E(S_n|\mathcal{F}_{n-1}) = E(E(Z|\mathcal{F}_n)|\mathcal{F}_{n-1}) = E(Z|\mathcal{F}_{n-1}) = S_{n-1}, \tag{15.4}$$

where the second equality is by **10.26**(i). $E|S_n| \le E|Z| < \infty$ by **10.27**, so S_n is a martingale. □

Following on the last definition, a *martingale difference* (m.d.) sequence $\{X_t,\mathcal{F}_t\}_{-\infty}^\infty$ is an adapted sequence on $(\Omega,\mathcal{F},P)$ satisfying the properties

$$E|X_t| < \infty, \tag{15.5}$$

$$E(X_t|\mathcal{F}_{t-1}) = 0, \text{ a.s.}, \tag{15.6}$$

for every t. Evidently, if $\{S_n\}$ is a martingale and $X_t = S_t - S_{t-1}$, then $\{X_t\}$ is a m.d. Conversely, we may define a martingale as the partial sum of a sequence of m.d.s, as in **15.1** (an independent integrable sequence is clearly a m.d.). However, if X_t has positive variance uniformly in t, condition (15.1) holds for all finite n but *not* uniformly in n. To define a martingale by $S_n = \sum_{t=-\infty}^n X_t$ can therefore lead to difficulties. Example **15.2** shows how a martingale can arise without reference to summation of a difference sequence.

It is important not to misunderstand the force of the integrability requirement in (15.1). After all, if we observe S_{n-1}, predicting S_n might seem to be just a matter of knowing something about the distribution of the increment. The problem is that we cannot treat $E(S_n|S_{n-1},\dots)$ *as a random variable* without integrability of S_n. Conditioning on S_{n-1} is not the same proposition as treating it as a constant, which entails restricting the probability space entirely to the set of repeated random drawings of X_n. The latter problem has no connection with the theory of random sequences.

A fundamental result is that a m.d. is uncorrelated with any measurable function of its lagged values.

15.3 Theorem If $\{X_t,\mathcal{F}_t\}$ is a m.d., then

$$\text{Cov}(X_t,\phi(X_{t-1},X_{t-2},\dots)) = 0,$$

where ϕ is any Borel-measurable, integrable function of the arguments.

Proof By **10.11** (see also the remarks following) noting that $\phi(X_{t-1},X_{t-2},\dots)$, is $\mathcal{F}_{t-1}$-measurable. ■

15.4 Corollary If $\{X_t,\mathcal{F}_t\}$ is a m.d., then $E(X_tX_{t-k}) = 0$, for all t and all $k \ne 0$.

Proof Put $\phi = X_{t-k}$ in **15.3**. For $k < 0$, redefine the subscripts, putting $t' = t-k$ and $t' - |k| = t$, so as to make the two cases equivalent. ■

One might think of the m.d. property as intermediate between uncorrelatedness and independence in the hierarchy of constraints on dependence. However, note the asymmetry with respect to time. Reversing the time ordering of an independent sequence yields another independent sequence, and likewise a reversed uncorrelated sequence is uncorrelated; but a reversed m.d. is not a m.d. in general.

The *Doob decomposition* of an integrable sequence $\{S_n,\mathcal{F}_n\}_0^\infty$ is

$$S_n = M_n + A_n, \tag{15.7}$$

where $A_0 = 0$, $M_0 = S_0$, and

$$M_n = M_{n-1} + S_n - E(S_n|\mathcal{F}_{n-1}), \tag{15.8}$$

$$A_n = A_{n-1} + E(S_n|\mathcal{F}_{n-1}) - S_{n-1}. \tag{15.9}$$

A_n is an $\mathcal{F}_{n-1}$-measurable sequence called the *predictable component* of S_n. Writing $\Delta S_n = Y_n$ and $\Delta M_n = X_n$, we find $\Delta A_n = E(Y_n|\mathcal{F}_{t-1})$, and

$$X_n = Y_n - E(Y_n|\mathcal{F}_{t-1}). \tag{15.10}$$

X_n is known as a *centred sequence*, and also as the *innovation sequence* of S_n. It is adapted if $\{Y_n,\mathcal{F}_n\}_0^\infty$ is, and since $E|Y_n| < \infty$ by assumption,

$$\begin{aligned} E|X_n| &\le E|Y_n| + E|E(Y_n|\mathcal{F}_{n-1})| \\ &\le E|Y_n| + E\big(E(|Y_n|\,|\mathcal{F}_{n-1})\big) \\ &= 2E|Y_n| < \infty, \end{aligned} \tag{15.11}$$

by (respectively) Minkowski's inequality, the conditional modulus inequality, and the LIE. Since it is evident that $E(X_t|\mathcal{F}_{t-1}) = 0$, $\{X_n,\mathcal{F}_n\}_0^\infty$ is a m.d. and so $\{M_n,\mathcal{F}_n\}_0^\infty$ is a martingale.

Martingales play an indispensable role in modern probability theory, because m.d.s behave in many important respects like independent sequences. Independence is the simplifying property which permitted the 'classical' limit results, laws of large numbers and central limit theorems, to be proved. But independence is a constraint on the entire joint distribution of the sequence. The m.d. property is a much milder restriction on the memory and yet, as we shall see in later chapters, most limit theorems which hold for independent sequences can also be proved for m.d.s, with few if any additional restrictions on the marginal distributions. For time series applications, it makes sense to go directly to the martingale version of any result of interest, unless of course a still weaker assumption will suffice. We will rarely need a stronger one.

Should we prefer to avoid the use of a definition involving σ-fields on an abstract probability space, it is possible to represent a martingale difference as, for example, a sequence with the property

$$E(X_t|X_{t-1},X_{t-2},\ldots) = 0 \text{ a.s.} \tag{15.12}$$

When a random variable appears in a conditioning set it is to be understood as representing the corresponding minimal σ-subfield, in this case $\sigma(X_{t-1},X_{t-2},\ldots)$.

This is appealing at an elementary level since it captures the notion of information available to an observer, in this case the sequence realization to date. But since, as we have seen, the conditioning information can extend more widely than the history of the sequence itself, this type of notation is relatively clumsy. Suppose we have a vector sequence $\{(X_t,Z_t)\}$, and X_t—though not necessarily Z_t—is a m.d. with respect to $\mathcal{F}_t = \sigma(X_t,Z_t,X_{t-1},Z_{t-1},...)$ in the sense of (15.6). This case is distinct from (15.12), and shows that that definition is inadequate, although (15.16) implies (15.12). More important, the representation of conditioning information is not unique, and we have seen (**10.3**(ii)) that any measurably isomorphic transformation of the conditioning variables contains the same information as the original variables. Indeed, the information need not even be represented by a variable, but is merely knowledge of the occurrence/non-occurrence of certain abstract events.

15.2 Extensions of the Martingale Concept

An adapted triangular array $\{\{X_{nt},\mathcal{F}_{nt}\}_{t=1}^{k_n}\}_{n=1}^{\infty}$, where $\{k_n\}_{n=1}^{\infty}$ is some increasing sequence of integers, for which

$$E|X_{nt}| < \infty, \tag{15.13}$$

$$E(X_{nt}|\mathcal{F}_{n,t-1}) = 0 \text{ a.s.} \tag{15.14}$$

for each $t = 1,...,k_n$ and $n \ge 1$, is called a *martingale difference array*. In many applications we would have just $k_n = n$. The double subscripting of the subfield $\mathcal{F}_{nt}$ may be superfluous if the information content of the array does not depend on n, with $\mathcal{F}_{nt} = \mathcal{F}_t$ for each n, but the additional generality given by the definition is harmless and could be useful. The sequence $\{S_n,\mathcal{F}_n\}_1^{\infty}$ where $S_n = \sum_{t=1}^{k_n}X_{nt}$ and $\mathcal{F}_n = \mathcal{F}_{n,k_n}$ is not a martingale, but the properties of martingales can be profitably used to analyse its behaviour. Consider the case $S_n = n^{-1/2}\sum_{t=1}^{n}X_t$ where $\{X_t,\mathcal{F}_t\}$ is a m.d. Such scaling by sample size may ensure that the distribution of S_n has a non-degenerate limit. S_n is not a martingale since

$$E(S_n|\mathcal{F}_{n-1}) = [(n-1)/n]^{1/2}S_{n-1}, \tag{15.15}$$

but each column of the m.d. array

$$\begin{bmatrix} X_1 & 2^{-1/2}X_1 & 3^{-1/2}X_1 & 4^{-1/2}X_1 & \dots \\ & 2^{-1/2}X_2 & 3^{-1/2}X_2 & 4^{-1/2}X_2 & \dots \\ & & 3^{-1/2}X_3 & 4^{-1/2}X_3 & \dots \\ & & & 4^{-1/2}X_4 & \dots \\ & & & & \ddots \end{bmatrix} \tag{15.16}$$

is a m.d. sequence, and S_n is the sum of column n. It is a term in a martingale sequence even though this is not the sequence $\{S_n\}$.

An adapted sequence $\{S_n,\mathcal{F}_n\}_{-\infty}^{\infty}$ of L_1-bounded variables satisfying

$$E(S_{n+1}|\mathcal{F}_n) \geq S_n \text{ a.s.} \tag{15.17}$$

is called a *submartingale*, in which case $X_n = S_n - S_{n-1}$ is a submartingale difference, having the property $E(X_{n+1}|\mathcal{F}_n) \geq 0$ a.s. In the Doob decomposition of a submartingale, the predictable sequence A_n is non-decreasing. Reversing the inequality defines a *supermartingale*, although, since $-S_n$ is a supermartingale whenever S_n is a submartingale, this is a minor extension. A supermartingale might represent a gambler's worth when a sequence of bets is unfair because of a house percentage. The generic term *semimartingale* covers all the possibilities.

15.5 Theorem Let $\phi(.)$: $\mathbb{R} \mapsto \mathbb{R}$ be continuous and convex. If $\{S_n,\mathcal{F}_n\}$ is a martingale and $E|\phi(S_n)| < \infty$, then $\{\phi(S_n),\mathcal{F}_n\}$ is a submartingale. If ϕ is also non-decreasing, $\{\phi(S_n),\mathcal{F}_n\}$ is a submartingale if $\{S_n,\mathcal{F}_n\}$ a submartingale.

Proof For the martingale case,

$$E(\phi(S_{n+1})|\mathcal{F}_n) \geq \phi(E(S_{n+1}|\mathcal{F}_n)) = \phi(S_n) \text{ a.s.} \tag{15.18}$$

by the conditional Jensen inequality (**10.18**). For the submartingale case, '=' becomes '≥' in (15.18) when $x_1 \leq x_2 \Rightarrow \phi(x_1) \leq \phi(x_2)$. ■

If $\{X_t,\mathcal{F}_t\}_1^\infty$ is a (sub)martingale difference, $\{Z_t,\mathcal{F}_t\}_0^\infty$ any adapted sequence, and

$$S_n = \sum_{t=1}^{n} X_t Z_{t-1}, \tag{15.19}$$

then $\{S_n,\mathcal{F}_n\}_1^\infty$ is a (sub)martingale since

$$E(S_{n+1}|\mathcal{F}_n) = \sum_{t=1}^{n} X_t Z_{t-1} + Z_n E(X_{n+1}|\mathcal{F}_n) = S_n \;(\geq S_n). \tag{15.20}$$

We might think of X_t as the random return on a stake of 1 unit in a sequence of bets, and the sequence $\{Z_t\}$ as representing a betting system, a rule based on information available at time $t-1$ for deciding how many units to bet in the next game. The implication of (15.20) is that, if the basic game (in which the same stake is bet every time) is fair, there is no betting system (based on no more than information about past play) that can turn it into a game favouring the player—or for that matter, a game favouring the house into a fair game.

For an increasing sequence $\{\mathcal{F}_t\}$ of σ-subfields of $(\Omega,\mathcal{F},P)$, a *stopping time* $\tau(\omega)$ is a random integer having the property $\{\omega: t = \tau(\omega)\} \in \mathcal{F}_t$. The classic example is a gambling policy which entails withdrawing from the game whenever a certain condition depending only on the outcomes to date (such as one's losses exceeding some limit, or a certain number of successive wins) is realized. If τ is the random variable defined as the first time the said condition is met in a sequence of bets, it is a stopping time.

Let τ be a stopping time of $\{\mathcal{F}_n\}$, and consider

$$S_{n\wedge\tau} = \begin{cases} S_n, & n \leq \tau \\ S_\tau, & n > \tau \end{cases} \tag{15.21}$$

where $n \wedge \tau$ stands for $\min\{n,\tau\}$. $\{S_{n\wedge\tau},\mathcal{F}_n\}_{n=1}^{\infty}$ is called a *stopped process.*

15.6 Theorem If $\{S_n,\mathcal{F}_n\}_1^{\infty}$ is a martingale (submartingale), then $\{S_{n\wedge\tau},\mathcal{F}_n\}_1^{\infty}$ is a martingale (submartingale).

Proof Since $\{\mathcal{F}_n\}_1^{\infty}$ is increasing, $\{\omega: k = \tau(\omega)\} \in \mathcal{F}_n$ for $k < n$, and hence also $\{\omega: n \le \tau(\omega)\} \in \mathcal{F}_n$, by complementation. Write $S_{n\wedge\tau} = \sum_{k=1}^{n-1} S_k 1_{\{k=\tau\}} + S_n 1_{\{n\le\tau\}}$, where the indicator functions are all $\mathcal{F}_n$-measurable. It follows by **3.25** and **3.33** that $S_{n\wedge\tau}$ is $\mathcal{F}_n$-measurable, and

$$E|S_{n\wedge\tau}| \le \sum_{k=1}^{n-1} E|S_k 1_{\{k=\tau\}}| + E|S_n 1_{\{n\le\tau\}}|$$

$$\le \sum_{k=1}^{n-1} E|S_k| + E|S_n| < \infty,\ n \ge 1. \tag{15.22}$$

If $\{S_n,\mathcal{F}_n\}_1^{\infty}$ is a martingale then for $A \in \mathcal{F}_n$, applying (15.3),

$$\int_A S_{(n+1)\wedge\tau}dP = \int_{A\cap\{n\le\tau\}} S_{n+1}dP + \int_{A\cap\{n>\tau\}} S_\tau dP$$

$$= \int_{A\cap\{n\le\tau\}} S_n dP + \int_{A\cap\{n>\tau\}} S_\tau dP = \int_A S_{n\wedge\tau}dP, \tag{15.23}$$

showing that $\{S_{n+1\wedge\tau},\mathcal{F}_n\}_1^{\infty}$ is a martingale. The submartingale case follows easily on replacing the second equality by the required inequality in (15.23). ∎

The general conclusion is that a gambler cannot alter the basic fairness characteristics of a game, *whatever* gambling policy (betting system plus stopping rule) he or she selects.

All these concepts have a natural extension to random vectors. An adapted sequence $\{\boldsymbol{X}_t,\mathcal{F}_t\}_{-\infty}^{\infty}$ is defined to be a *vector martingale difference* if and only if $\{\boldsymbol{\lambda}'\boldsymbol{X}_t, \mathcal{F}_t\}_{-\infty}^{\infty}$ is a scalar m.d. sequence for all conformable fixed vectors $\boldsymbol{\lambda} \ne \boldsymbol{0}$. It has the property

$$E(\boldsymbol{X}_{t+1}|\mathcal{F}_t) = \boldsymbol{0}. \tag{15.24}$$

The one thing to remember is that a vector martingale difference is not the same thing as a vector of martingale differences. A simple counter-example is the two-element vector $\boldsymbol{X}_t = (X_t,X_{t-1})'$, where X_t is a m.d.; $\{\lambda_1 X_t + \lambda_2 X_{t-1},\mathcal{F}_t\}$ is an adapted sequence, but

$$E(\lambda_1 X_t + \lambda_2 X_{t-1}|\mathcal{F}_{t-1}) = \lambda_2 X_{t-1} \ne 0,$$

so it is not a m.d.. On the other hand,

$$E(\lambda_1 X_{t+1} + \lambda_2 X_t|\mathcal{F}_{t-1}) = 0,$$

but $\{\lambda_1 X_{t+1} + \lambda_2 X_t, \mathcal{F}_t\}$ is not adapted, since X_{t+1} is not $\mathcal{F}_t$-measurable.

15.3 Martingale Convergence

Applying **15.5** to the case $\phi(.) = |.|^p$ and taking unconditional expectations shows that every martingale or submartingale has the property

$$E|S_{n+1}|^p \geq E|S_n|^p,\ p \geq 1. \tag{15.25}$$

By **2.11** the sequence of pth absolute moments converges as $n \to \infty$, either to a finite limit or to $+\infty$. In the case where the L_1-norms are uniformly bounded, (sub)martingales also exhibit a substantially stronger property; they converge, almost surely, to some point which is random in the sense of having a distribution over realizations, but does not change from one time period t to the next.

The intuition is reasonably transparent. $\{\mathcal{F}_n\}$ is an increasing sequence of σ-fields which converges to a limit $\mathcal{F}_\infty \subseteq \mathcal{F}$, the σ-field that contains $\mathcal{F}_n$ for every n. Since $E(S_n|\mathcal{F}_n) = S_n$, the convergence of the sequence $\{\mathcal{F}_n\}$ implies that of a uniformly bounded sequence with the property $E(S_{n+1}|\mathcal{F}_n) \geq S_n$, so long as these expectations remain well-defined in the limit. Thus, we have the following.

15.7 Theorem If $\{S_n,\mathcal{F}_n\}_1^\infty$ is a submartingale sequence and $\sup_n E|S_n| \leq M < \infty$, then $S_n \to S$ a.s. where S is a $\mathcal{F}$-measurable random variable with $E|S| \leq M$. □

The proof of **15.7**, due to Doob, makes use of a result called the *upcrossing inequality*, which is proved as a preliminary lemma. Considering the path of a submartingale through time, an *upcrossing* of an interval $[\alpha,\beta]$ is a succession of steps starting at or below α and terminating at or above β. To complete more than one upcrossing, there must be one and only one intervening downcrossing, so downcrossings do not require separate consideration. Fig. 15.1 shows two upcrossings of $[\alpha,\beta]$, spanning the periods marked by dots on the abscissa.

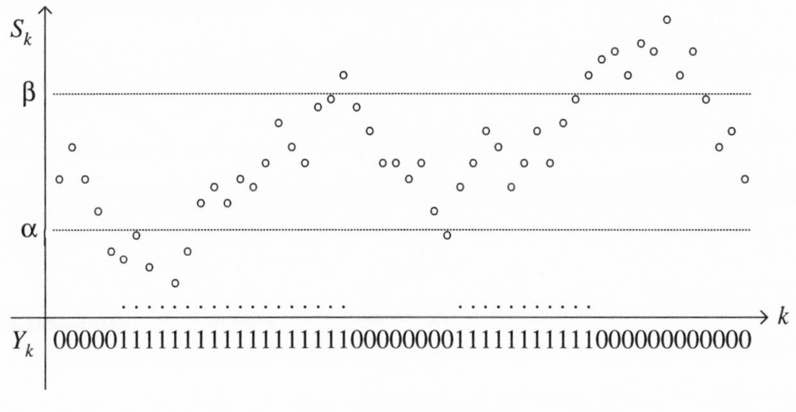

Fig. 15.1

Let the r.v. Y_k be the indicator of an upcrossing. To be precise, set $Y_1 = 0$, and then, for $k = 2,3,\ldots,n$,

$$Y_k = \begin{cases} 0 \text{ if either } Y_{k-1} = 0,\ S_{k-1} > \alpha, \text{ or } Y_{k-1} = 1,\ S_{k-1} \geq \beta, \\ 1 \text{ if either } Y_{k-1} = 0,\ S_{k-1} \leq \alpha, \text{ or } Y_{k-1} = 1,\ S_{k-1} < \beta. \end{cases} \tag{15.26}$$

The values of Y_k appear at the bottom of Fig. 15.1. Observe that an upcrossing begins the period after S_k falls to or below α, and ends at the first step thereafter where β is reached or exceeded. Y_k is a function of S_{k-1} and an $\mathcal{F}_{k-1}$-measurable random variable.

The number of upcrossings of $[\alpha,\beta]$ up to time n of the sequence $\{S_n(\omega)\}_1^\infty$, to be denoted $U_n(\omega)$, is an $\mathcal{F}_n$-measurable random variable. The sequence $\{U_n(\omega)\}_1^\infty$ is monotone, but it satisfies the following condition.

15.8 Upcrossing inequality The number of upcrossings of $[\alpha,\beta]$ by a submartingale $\{S_n,\mathcal{F}_n\}_1^\infty$ satisfies

$$E(U_n) \leq \frac{E|S_n| + |\alpha|}{\beta - \alpha}. \tag{15.27}$$

Proof Define $S_n' = \max\{S_n,\alpha\}$, a continuous, convex, non-decreasing function of S_n, such that $\{S_n',\mathcal{F}_n\}$ is an adapted sequence and also a submartingale. U_n is the set of upcrossings up to n for $\{S_n'\}$ as well as for $\{S_n\}$. Write

$$S_n' - S_1' = \sum_{k=2}^n X_k' = \sum_{k=2}^n Y_k X_k' + \sum_{k=2}^n (1 - Y_k)X_k', \tag{15.28}$$

where Y_k is from (15.26), and X_k' is a submartingale difference. Then

$$E\left(\sum_{k=2}^n (1 - Y_k)X_k'\right) = \sum_{k=2}^n \int_{\{Y_k=0\}} X_k' dP$$

$$= \sum_{k=2}^n \int_{\{Y_k=0\}} E(X_k'|\mathcal{F}_{k-1})dP \geq 0, \tag{15.29}$$

using the definition of a conditional expectation in the second equality (recalling that Y_k is $\mathcal{F}_{k-1}$-measurable), and the submartingale property, to give the inequality. We have therefore shown that

$$E(S_n' - S_1') \geq E\left(\sum_{k=2}^n Y_k X_k'\right). \tag{15.30}$$

$\sum_{k=2}^n Y_k X_k'$ is the sum of the steps made during upcrossings, by definition of Y_k. Since the sum of the X_k' over an upcrossing equals at least $\beta - \alpha$ by definition, we must have

$$\sum_{k=2}^n Y_k X_k' \geq (\beta - \alpha)U_n, \tag{15.31}$$

where U_n is the number of upcrossings completed by time n. Taking the expectation of (15.31) and substituting (15.30), we obtain, as required,

$$(\beta - \alpha)E(U_n) \leq E(S'_n - S'_1) \leq E(S'_n - \alpha)$$
$$= \int_{\{S_n > \alpha\}} (S_n - \alpha)dP \tag{15.32}$$
$$\leq E|S_n - \alpha| \leq E|S_n| + |\alpha|. \blacksquare$$

The upcrossing inequality contains the implication that, if the sequence is uniformly bounded in L_1, the expected number of upcrossings is finite, even as $n \to \infty$. This is the heart of the convergence proof, for it means that the sequence has to be settling down somewhere beyond a certain point.

Proof of 15.7 Fix α and $\beta > \alpha$. By **15.8**,

$$E(U_n) \leq \frac{E|S_n| + |\alpha|}{\beta - \alpha} \leq \frac{M + |\alpha|}{\beta - \alpha} < \infty. \tag{15.33}$$

For $\omega \in \Omega$, $\{U_n(\omega)\}_1^\infty$ is a positive, non-decreasing sequence and either diverges to $+\infty$ or converges to a finite limit $U(\omega)$ as $n \to \infty$. Divergence for $\omega \in C$ with $P(C) > 0$ would imply $E(U_n) \to \infty$, which contradicts (15.33), so $U_n \to U$ a.s., where $E(U) < \infty$.

Define $\overline{S}(\omega) = \limsup_{n\to\infty} S_n$ and $\underline{S}(\omega) = \liminf_{n\to\infty} S_n$. If $\underline{S}(\omega) < \alpha < \beta < \overline{S}(\omega)$, the interval $[\alpha,\beta]$ is crossed an infinite number of times as $n \to \infty$, so it must be the case that $P(\underline{S} < \alpha < \beta < \overline{S}) = 0$. This is true for any pair α,β. Hence consider

$$\{\omega: \underline{S}(\omega) < \overline{S}(\omega)\} = \bigcup_{\alpha,\beta} \{\underline{S} \leq \alpha < \beta \leq \overline{S}\}, \tag{15.34}$$

where the union on the right is taken over rational values of α and β. Evidently, $P(\underline{S} < \overline{S}) = 0$ by **3.6**(ii), which is the same as $\underline{S} = \overline{S} = S$ a.s., where S is the limit of $\{S_n\}$. Finally, note that

$$E|S| \leq \liminf_{n\to\infty} E|S_n| \leq \sup_n E|S_n| \leq M, \tag{15.35}$$

where the first inequality is from Fatou's lemma and the last is by assumption. This completes the proof. ■

Of the examples quoted earlier, **15.1** does not satisfy the conditions of **15.7**. A random walk does not converge, but wanders forever with a variance that is an increasing function of time. But in **15.2**, X_t is of course converging to Z.

15.9 Corollary Let $\{S_n,\mathcal{F}_n\}_{-\infty}^{\infty}$ be a doubly infinite martingale. Then $S_n \to S_{-\infty}$ a.s. as $n \to -\infty$, where $S_{-\infty}$ is an L_1-bounded r.v.

Proof Let U_{-n} denote the number of upcrossings of $[\alpha,\beta]$ performed by the sequence $\{S_j, -1 \geq j \geq -n\}$. The argument of **15.8** shows that

$$E(U_{-n}) \leq \frac{E|S_1| + |\alpha|}{\beta - \alpha}, \text{ all } n \geq 1. \tag{15.36}$$

Arguments precisely analogous to those of **15.7** show that

$$P\left(\liminf_{n\to-\infty} S_n < \limsup_{n\to-\infty} S_n\right) = 0, \tag{15.37}$$

so that the limit $S_{-\infty}$ exists a.s. The sequence $\{E|S_n|\}_{-\infty}^{-1}$ is non-negative, non-increasing as n decreases by (15.25), and $E|S_{-1}| < \infty$ by definition of a martingale. Hence $E|S_{-\infty}| < \infty$. ∎

If a martingale does not converge, it must not be thought of as converging in $\overline{\mathbb{R}}$, of heading off to $+\infty$ or $-\infty$, never to return. This is an event that occurs only with probability 0. Subject to the increments having a suitably bounded distribution, a nonconvergent martingale eventually visits all regions of the real line, almost surely.

15.10 Theorem Let $\{X_t,\mathcal{F}_t\}$ be a m.d. sequence with $E(\sup_t|X_t|) < \infty$, and let $S_n = \sum_{t=1}^{n}X_t$. If $C = \{\omega\colon S_n(\omega) \text{ converges}\}$, and

$$E = \{\omega\colon \text{either } \inf_n S_n(\omega) > -\infty \text{ or } \sup_n S_n(\omega) < \infty\},$$

then $P(E - C) = 0$.

Proof For a constant $M > 0$, define the stopping time $\tau_M(\omega)$ as the smallest integer n such that $S_n(\omega) > M$, if one exists, and $\tau_M(\omega) = \infty$ otherwise. The stopped process $\{S_{n\wedge\tau_M}, \mathcal{F}_{n\wedge\tau_M}\}_{n=1}^{\infty}$ is a martingale (**15.6**), and $S_{(n-1)\wedge\tau_M} \le M$ for all n. Letting $S^+_{n\wedge\tau_M} = \max\{S_{n\wedge\tau_M}, 0\}$,

$$S^+_{n\wedge\tau_M} \le S^+_{(n-1)\wedge\tau_M} + X^+_{n\wedge\tau_M} \le M + \sup_n |X_n|. \tag{15.38}$$

Since $E(S_{n\wedge\tau_M}) = 0$, $E|S_{n\wedge\tau_M}| = 2E(S^+_{n\wedge\tau_M})$, and hence $\sup_n E|S_{n\wedge\tau_M}| < \infty$, and $S_{n\wedge\tau_M}$ converges a.s., by **15.7**. And since $S_{n\wedge\tau_M}(\omega) = S_n(\omega)$ on the set $\{\omega\colon \sup_n S_n(\omega) \le M\}$, $S_n(\omega)$ converges a.s. on the same set. Letting $M \to \infty$, and then applying the same argument to $-S_n$, we obtain the conclusion that $S_n(\omega)$ converges a.s. on the set E; that is, $P(C \cap E) = P(E)$, from which the theorem follows. ∎

Note that $E^c = \{\omega\colon \sup_n S_n(\omega) = +\infty, \inf_n S_n(\omega) = -\infty\}$. Since $P(E^c) = P((C\cap E)^c) = P(C^c \cup E^c)$, a direct consequence of the theorem is that $C^c \subseteq E^c \cup N$ where $P(N) = 0$, which is the claim made above.

15.4 Convergence and the Conditional Variances

If $\{S_n\}$ is a square-integrable martingale with differences $\{X_n\}$,

$$E(S_n^2|\mathcal{F}_{n-1}) = E(S_{n-1}^2 + X_n^2 + 2X_nS_{n-1}|\mathcal{F}_{n-1}) \ge S_{n-1}^2,$$

and S_n^2 is a submartingale. The Doob decomposition of the sequence of squares has the form $S_n^2 = M_n + A_n$ where $\Delta M_n = X_n^2 - E(X_n^2|\mathcal{F}_{n-1})$, and $\Delta A_n = E(X_n^2|\mathcal{F}_{n-1})$. The sequence $\{A_n\}$ is called the *quadratic variation* of $\{S_n\}$. The following theorem reveals an intimate link between martingale convergence and the summability of the conditional variances; the latter property implies the former almost surely, and in particular, if $\sum_{t=1}^{\infty}E(X_t^2|\mathcal{F}_{t-1}) < \infty$ a.s. then $S_n \to S$ a.s.

15.11 Theorem Let $\{X_t,\mathcal{F}_t\}_1^\infty$ be a m.d. sequence, and $S_n = \sum_{t=1}^n X_t$. If

$$D = \{\omega: \textstyle\sum_{t=1}^\infty E(X_t^2|\mathcal{F}_{t-1})(\omega) < \infty\} \in \mathcal{F},$$

$$C = \{\omega: S_n(\omega) \text{ converges}\} \in \mathcal{F},$$

then $P(D-C) = 0$.

Proof Fix $M > 0$, and define the stopping time $\tau_M(\omega)$ as the smallest value of n having the property

$$\sum_{t=1}^n E(X_t^2|\mathcal{F}_{t-1})(\omega) \geq M. \tag{15.39}$$

If there is no finite integer with this property then $\tau_M(\omega) = \infty$. If $D_M = \{\omega: \tau_M(\omega) = \infty\}$, $D = \lim_{M\to\infty} D_M$. The r.v. $1_{\{\tau_M \geq n\}}(\omega)$ is $\mathcal{F}_{n-1}$-measurable, since it is known at time $n-1$ whether the inequality in (15.39) is true. Define the stopped process

$$\sum_{t=1}^n X_t 1_{\{\tau_M \geq t\}} = S_{n\wedge\tau_M}. \tag{15.40}$$

$S_{n\wedge\tau_M}$ is a martingale by **15.6**. The increments are orthogonal, and

$$\sup_n E(S_{n\wedge\tau_M}^2) = \sup_n E\left(\sum_{t=1}^n X_t^2 1_{\{\tau_M\geq n\}}\right)$$

$$= \sup_n E\left(\sum_{t=1}^n 1_{\{\tau_M\geq n\}} E(X_t^2|\mathcal{F}_{t-1})\right) < M, \tag{15.41}$$

where the final inequality holds for the expectation since it holds for each $\omega \in \Omega$ by definition of $\tau_M(\omega)$. By Liapunov's inequality,

$$\sup_n E|S_{n\wedge\tau_M}| \leq \sup_n \|S_{n\wedge\tau_M}\|_2 < M^{1/2},$$

and hence $S_{n\wedge\tau_M}$ converges a.s., by **15.7**. If $\omega \in D_M$, $S_{n\wedge\tau_M}(\omega) = S_n(\omega)$ for every $n \in \mathbb{N}$, and hence $S_n(\omega)$ converges, except for ω in a set of zero measure. That is, $P(D_M \cap C) = P(D_M)$. The theorem follows on taking complements, and then letting $M \to \infty$. ∎

15.12 Example To get an idea of what convergence entails, consider the case of $\{X_t\}$ an i.i.d. sequence (compare **15.1**). Then $\{X_t/a_t\}$ is a m.d. sequence for any sequence $\{a_t\}$ of positive constants. Since $E(X_t^2|\mathcal{F}_{t-1}) = E(X_t^2) = \sigma^2$, a constant which we assume finite, $S_n = \sum_{t=1}^n X_t/a_t$ is an a.s. convergent martingale whenever $\sum_{t=1}^\infty 1/a_t^2 < \infty$. For example, $a_t = t$ would satisfy the requirement. □

In the almost sure case of Theorem **15.11** (when $P(C) = P(D) = 1$), the summability of the conditional variances transfers to that of the ordinary variances, $\sigma_t^2 = E(X_t^2)$. Also when $E(\sup_t X_t^2) < \infty$, the summability of the conditional variances is almost equivalent to the summability of the X_t^2 themselves. These are consequences of the following pair of useful results.

15.13 Theorem Let $\{Z_t\}$ be a any non-negative stochastic sequence.

(i) $\sum_{t=1}^{\infty} E(Z_t) < \infty$ if and only if $\sum_{t=1}^{\infty} E(Z_t|\mathcal{F}_{t-1}) < \infty$ a.s.

(ii) If $E(\sup_t Z_t) < \infty$ then $P(D \,\Delta\, E) = 0$, where

$$D = \left\{\omega: \sum_{t=1}^{\infty} E(Z_t|\mathcal{F}_{t-1})(\omega) < \infty\right\},$$

$$E = \left\{\omega: \sum_{t=1}^{\infty} Z_t(\omega) < \infty\right\}.$$

Proof (i) The first of the sums is the expected value of the second, so the 'only if' part is immediate. Since $E(Z_t|\mathcal{F}_{t-1})$ is undefined unless $E(Z_t) < \infty$, we may assume $\sum_{t=1}^{n} E(Z_t) < \infty$ for each finite n. These partial sums form a monotone series which either converges to a finite limit or diverges to $+\infty$. Suppose $\sum_{t=1}^{n} E(Z_t|\mathcal{F}_{t-1})$ converges a.s, implying (by the Cauchy criterion) that $\sum_{t=n+1}^{n+m} E(Z_t|\mathcal{F}_{t-1}) \to 0$ a.s. as $m \wedge n \to \infty$. Then $\sum_{t=n+1}^{n+m} E(Z_t) \to 0$ by the monotone convergence theorem, so that by the same criterion $\sum_{t=1}^{n} E(Z_t) \to \sum_{t=1}^{\infty} E(Z_t) < \infty$, as required.

(ii) Define the m.d. sequence $X_t = Z_t - E(Z_t|\mathcal{F}_{t-1})$, and let $S_n = \sum_{t=1}^{n} X_t$. Clearly $\sup_n S_n(\omega) \le \sum_{t=1}^{\infty} Z_t(\omega)$, and if the majorant side of this inequality is finite, $S_n(\omega)$ converges in almost every case, by **15.10**. Given the definition of X_t, this implies in turn that $\sum_{t=1}^{\infty} E(Z_t|\mathcal{F}_{t-1})(\omega) < \infty$. In other words, $P(E - D) = 0$. Now apply the same argument to $-X_t = E(Z_t|\mathcal{F}_{t-1}) - Z_t$ to show that the reverse implication holds almost surely, and $P(D - E) = 0$ also. ∎

15.5 Martingale Inequalities

Of the many interesting results that can be proved for martingales, certain inequalities are essential tools of limit theory. Of particular importance are *maximal inequalities*, which place bounds on the extreme behaviour a sequence is capable of over a succession of steps. We prove two related results of this type. The first, a sophisticated cousin of the Markov inequality, was originally proved by Kolmogorov for the case where $\{X_t\}$ is an independent sequence rather than a m.d., and in this form is known as Kolmogorov's inequality.

15.14 Theorem Let $\{S_n, \mathcal{F}_n\}_1^{\infty}$ be a martingale. For any $p \ge 1$,

$$P\left(\max_{1 \le k \le n} |S_k| > \varepsilon\right) \le \frac{E|S_n|^p}{\varepsilon^p}. \tag{15.42}$$

Proof Define the events $A_1 = \{\omega: |S_1(\omega)| > \varepsilon\}$, and for $k = 2,\dots,n$,

$$A_k = \left\{\omega: \max_{1 \le j < k} |S_j(\omega)| \le \varepsilon,\ |S_k(\omega)| > \varepsilon\right\} \in \mathcal{F}_k.$$

The collection $A_1,\dots,A_n$ is disjoint, and

$$\bigcup_{k=1}^{n} A_k = \left\{\max_{1 \le k \le n} |S_k| > \varepsilon\right\}. \tag{15.43}$$

Since $A_k \subseteq \{|S_k| > \varepsilon\}$, the Markov inequality (**9.10**) gives

$$P(A_k) \leq \varepsilon^{-p} E(|S_k|^p 1_{A_k}). \tag{15.44}$$

By **15.5**, $|S_n|^p$ for $p \geq 1$ is a submartingale, so $|S_k|^p \leq E(|S_n|^p|\mathcal{F}_k)$ a.s., for $1 \leq k \leq n$. Since $A_k \in \mathcal{F}_k$, it follows that

$$E(|S_k|^p 1_{A_k}) \leq E(E(|S_n|^p|\mathcal{F}_k)1_{A_k}) = E(|S_n|^p 1_{A_k}), \tag{15.45}$$

where the equality applies (10.18). Noting $\sum_{k=1}^n 1_{A_k} = 1_{\bigcup_{k=1}^n A_k}$, we obtain from (15.43)–(15.45), as required,

$$P\left(\max_{1\leq k\leq n} |S_k| > \varepsilon\right) = \sum_{k=1}^n P(A_k) \leq \varepsilon^{-p}\sum_{k=1}^n E(|S_n|^p 1_{A_k})$$

$$= \varepsilon^{-p} E\left(|S_n|^p \sum_{k=1}^n 1_{A_k}\right) \leq \varepsilon^{-p} E(|S_n|^p). \ \blacksquare \tag{15.46}$$

The second result converts the probability bound of **15.14** into a moment inequality.

15.15 Doob's inequality Let $\{S_n, \mathcal{F}_n\}_1^\infty$ be a martingale. For $p > 1$,

$$E\left(\max_{1\leq k\leq n} |S_k|^p\right) \leq \left(\frac{p}{p-1}\right)^p E|S_n|^p. \tag{15.47}$$

Proof Consider the penultimate member of (15.46) for the case $p = 1$, that is,

$$P\left(\max_{1\leq k\leq n} |S_k| > \varepsilon\right) \leq \varepsilon^{-1} E(|S_n| 1_{\{\max_{1\leq k\leq n}|S_k|>\varepsilon\}}), \tag{15.48}$$

and apply the following ingenious lemma involving integration by parts.

15.16 Lemma Let X and Y be non-negative r.v.s. If $P(X > \varepsilon) \leq \varepsilon^{-1}E(Y1_{\{X>\varepsilon\}})$ for all $\varepsilon > 0$, then $E(X^p) \leq [p/(p-1)]^p E(Y^p)$, for $p > 1$.

Proof Letting F_X denote the marginal c.d.f. of X, and integrating by parts, using $d(1 - F_X) = -dF_X$ and $[x^p(1 - F_X(x))]_0^\infty = 0$,

$$E(X_p) = \int_0^\infty \xi^p dF_X(\xi) = -\int_0^\infty \xi^p d(1 - F_X(\xi))$$

$$= \int_0^\infty p\xi^{p-1}(1 - F_X(\xi))d\xi = \int_0^\infty p\xi^{p-1}P(X > \xi)d\xi. \tag{15.49}$$

Define the function $1_{\{x>\xi\}}(x) = 1$ when $x > \xi$, and 0 otherwise. Letting $F_{X,Y}$ denote the joint c.d.f. of X and Y and substituting the assumption of the lemma into (15.49), we have

$$E(X^p) \leq p\int_0^\infty \xi^{p-2}E(Y1_{\{X>\xi\}})d\xi$$

$$= p\int_0^\infty \xi^{p-2}\left(\int_{(\mathbb{R}^2)^+} y1_{\{x>\xi\}}(x)dF_{X,Y}(x,y)\right)d\xi$$

$$= p\int_{(\mathbb{R}^2)^+} y\left(\int_0^x \xi^{p-2}d\xi\right)dF_{X,Y}(x,y)$$

$$= \left(\frac{p}{p-1}\right)\int_{(\mathbb{R}^2)^+} yx^{p-1}dF_{X,Y}(x,y)$$

$$= \left(\frac{p}{p-1}\right)E(YX^{p-1}). \tag{15.50}$$

Here $(\mathbb{R}^2)^+$ denotes the non-negative orthant of $\mathbb{R}^2$, or $[0,\infty)\times[0,\infty)$. The second equality is permitted by Tonelli's theorem, noting that the function $F_{XY}\xi$ defines a σ-finite product measure on $(\mathbb{R}^3)^+$. By Hölder's inequality,

$$E(YX^{p-1}) \le E^{1/p}(Y^p)E^{1-1/p}(X^p).$$

Substituting into the majorant side of (15.50) and simplifying gives the result. ∎

To complete the proof of **15.15**, apply the lemma to (15.48) to yield (15.47), putting $X = \max_{1\le k\le n}|S_k|$ and $Y = |S_n|$. ∎

Because of the orthogonality of the differences, we have the interesting property of a martingale $\{S_n\}_1^\infty$ that

$$E(S_n^2) = E\left(\sum_{t=1}^n X_t^2\right), \tag{15.51}$$

where, with $S_0 = 0$, $X_t = S_t - S_{t-1}$. This lets us extend the last two inequalities for the case $p = 2$, to link $P(\max_{1\le k\le n}|S_n| > \varepsilon)$ and $E(\max_{1\le k\le n}S_k^2)$ directly with the variance of the increments. It would be most useful if this type of property extended to other values of p, in particular for $p \in (0,2)$.

One approach to this problem is the von Bahr-Esséen inequality of §11.5. Obviously, **11.15** has a direct application to martingales.

15.17 Theorem If $\{X_t,\mathcal{F}_t\}_1^\infty$ is a m.d. sequence and $S_n = \sum_{t=1}^n X_t$,

$$E|S_n|^p \le 2\sum_{t=1}^n E|X_t|^p \tag{15.52}$$

for $0 < p \le 2$.

Proof This is by iterating **11.15** with $Y = X_n$, $\mathcal{G} = \mathcal{F}_{n-1}$, and $X = S_{n-1}$, as in the argument leading to (11.65); note that the latter holds for m.d. sequences just as for independent sequences. ∎

Another route to this type of result is *Burkholder's inequality* (Burkholder 1973).

15.18 Theorem Let $\{S_n,\mathcal{F}_n\}_1^\infty$ be a martingale with increments $X_t = S_t - S_{t-1}$, and

$S_0 = 0$. For $0 < p \le 1$ there exist positive constants c_p and C_p, depending only on p, such that

$$c_pE\left(\sum_{t=1}^{n} X_t^2\right)^p \le E|S_n|^{2p} \le C_pE\left(\sum_{t=1}^{n} X_t^2\right)^p. \; \square \tag{15.53}$$

On the majorant side, this extends by the c_r inequality to

$$E|S_n|^{2p} \le C_pE\left|\sum_{t=1}^{n} X_t^2\right|^p \le C_p\sum_{t=1}^{n} E|X_t|^{2p},\; 0 < p \le 1, \tag{15.54}$$

which differs from (15.52) only in the specified constant.[18] In fact, the Burkholder inequality holds for $p > 1$ also, although we shall not need to use this result and extending the proof is fairly laborious. Concavity of $(.)^p$ becomes convexity, so that the arguments have to be applied in reverse. Readers may like to attempt this as an exercise.

The proof employs the following non-probabilistic lemma.

15.19 Lemma Let $\{y_t\}_1^n$ be a sequence of non-negative numbers with $y_1 > 0$, and let $Y_n = \sum_{t=1}^n y_t$ for $t \ge 1$ and $Y_0 = 0$. Then, for $0 < p \le 1$,

$$Y_n^p \le y_1^p + p\sum_{t=2}^{n} Y_{t-1}^{p-1}y_t \le (1+B_p)Y_n^p, \tag{15.55}$$

where $B_p \ge 0$ is a finite constant depending only on p.

Proof For $p = 1$ this is trivial, with $B_p = 0$. Otherwise, expand $Y_n^p = (Y_{n-1} + y_n)^p$ in a Taylor series of first order to get

$$Y_n^p = Y_{n-1}^p + p(Y_{n-1} + \theta_n y_n)^{p-1}y_n, \tag{15.56}$$

where $\theta_n \in [0,1]$. Solving the difference equation in (15.56) yields

$$Y_n^p = y_1^p + p\sum_{t=2}^{n}(Y_{t-1} + \theta_t y_t)^{p-1}y_t. \tag{15.57}$$

Defining

$$K_t = Y_{t-1}^{p-1} - (Y_{t-1} + \theta_t y_t)^{p-1}, \tag{15.58}$$

we obtain the result by showing that

$$0 \le p\sum_{t=2}^{n} K_t y_t \le B_pY_n^p. \tag{15.59}$$

The left-hand inequality is immediate. For the right-hand one, note that $y^r - x^r \le (y-x)^r$, for $y > x > 0$ and $0 < r \le 1$ (see (9.63)). Hence, (15.58) implies that

$$K_t \le \left(\frac{1}{Y_{t-1}} - \frac{1}{Y_{t-1} + \theta_t y_t}\right)^{1-p} = (Y_{t-1}(Y_{t-1} + \theta_t y_t))^{p-1}\theta_t^{1-p}y_t^{1-p}. \tag{15.60}$$

It follows that

$$0 \le K_t y_t \le Y_{t-1}^{2p-2} y_t^{2-p}, \tag{15.61}$$

and hence

$$\begin{aligned} Y_n^{-p} p \sum_{t=2}^{n} K_t y_t &\le p \sum_{t=2}^{n} (y_t/Y_{t-1})^{2(1-p)} (y_t/Y_n)^p \\ &= p \sum_{t=2}^{n} (y_t'/Y_{t-1}')^{2(1-p)} y_t'^p \\ &\le B_p(n), \end{aligned} \tag{15.62}$$

where $y_t' = y_t/Y_n$ for $t = 1,...,n$ is a collection of non-negative numbers summing to 1, $Y_t' = \sum_{s=1}^{t} y_s'$, and $B_p(n)$ denotes the supremum of the indicated sum over all such collections, given p and n.

The terms $y_t'/Y_{t-1}' = y_t/Y_{t-1}$ for $t \ge 2$ are finite since $y_1 > 0$. If at most a finite number of the y_t are positive the majorant side of (15.62) is certainly finite, so assume otherwise. Without loss of generality, by reinterpreting n if necessary as the number of nonzero terms, we can also assume $y_t > 0$ for every t. Then, $y_t'/Y_{t-1}' = O(t^{-1})$ and $y_t' = O(n^{-1})$, and applying **2.27** yields the result $B_p(n) = o(1)$ for all $p \in (0,1)$. Putting $B_p = \sup_n B_p(n) < \infty$ completes the proof. ■

Proof of 15.18 Put $A_n = \sum_{t=1}^{n} X_t^2$, and for $\varepsilon > 0$ and $\delta > 0$, set

$$Y_n = \varepsilon + S_n^2 + \delta(\varepsilon + A_n) = (1+\delta)(\varepsilon + A_n) + 2\sum_{t=1}^{n} S_{t-1} X_t, \tag{15.63}$$

so that in the notation of **15.19**, $y_t = Y_t - Y_{t-1} = (1+\delta)X_t^2 + 2S_{t-1}X_t$ for $t \ge 2$, with $y_1 = (1+\delta)(\varepsilon + X_1^2) > 0$. Then by the left-hand inequality of (15.55),

$$Y_n^p \le (1+\delta)^p(\varepsilon + X_1^2)^p + (1+\delta)p\sum_{t=2}^{n} Y_{t-1}^{p-1} X_t^2 + 2p\sum_{t=2}^{n} Y_{t-1}^{p-1} S_{t-1} X_t. \tag{15.64}$$

However, ε is arbitrary in (15.64), and we may allow it to approach 0. Taking expectations through, using the law of iterated expectations, and the facts that $E(X_t|\mathcal{F}_{t-1}) = 0$ and that $(.)^{p-1}$ is decreasing in its argument, we obtain

$$\begin{aligned} E(S_n^2 + \delta A_n)^p &\le E\left((1+\delta)^p X_1^{2p} + (1+\delta)p\sum_{t=2}^{n} (S_{t-1}^2 + \delta A_{t-1})^{p-1} X_t^2\right) \\ &\le E\left((1+\delta)^p X_1^{2p} + (1+\delta)\delta^{p-1} p\sum_{t=2}^{n} A_{t-1}^{p-1} X_t^2\right). \end{aligned} \tag{15.65}$$

But if we put now $Y_n = \varepsilon + A_n$, with $y_1 = \varepsilon + X_1^2$ and $y_t = X_t^2$ for $t \ge 2$, the right-hand inequality of (15.55) yields (again, as the limiting case as $\varepsilon \downarrow 0$)

$$X_1^{2p} + p\sum_{t=2}^{n} A_{t-1}^{p-1} X_t^2 \le (1+B_p)E(A_n^p). \tag{15.66}$$

and since $(1+\delta)^p \le (1+\delta)\delta^{p-1}$, this combines with (15.65) to give

$$(1+\delta)\delta^{p-1}(1+B_p)E(A_n^p) \ge E(S_n^2+\delta A_n)^p$$
$$\ge 2^{p-1}[E|S_n|^{2p}+\delta^p E(A_n^p)], \tag{15.67}$$

where the second inequality is by the concavity of the function $(.)^p$ for $p \le 1$. Rearrangement yields

$$E|S_n|^{2p} \le \delta^p[2^{1-p}(1+B_p)(1+\delta)/\delta - 1]E(A_n^p). \tag{15.68}$$

which is the right-hand inequality in (15.54), where C_p is given by choosing δ to minimize the expression on the majorant side of (15.68).

In a similar manner, combining the right-hand inequality of (15.55) with $Y_n = \varepsilon + S_n^2$ with (15.65) and (15.67), and using concavity, yields

$$(1+\delta)(1+B_p)E|S_n|^{2p} \ge (1+\delta)E\left(X_1^{2p} + p\sum_{t=2}^{n} S_{t-1}^{2(p-1)}X_t^2\right)$$
$$\ge E\left((1+\delta)^p X_1^{2p} + (1+\delta)p\sum_{t=2}^{n}(S_{t-1}^2+\delta A_{t-1})^{p-1}X_t^2\right)$$
$$\ge E(S_n^2+\delta A_n)^p$$
$$\ge 2^{p-1}(E|S_n|^{2p}+\delta^p E(A_n^p)) \tag{15.69}$$

which rearranges as

$$E|S_n|^{2p} \ge \delta^p[2^{1-p}(1+\delta)(1+B_p) - 1]^{-1}E(A_n^p), \tag{15.70}$$

which is the left hand inequality of (15.54), with c_p given by choosing δ to maximize the expression on the majorant side . ∎

For the case $p = 1$, $B_p = 0$ identically in (15.55) and $c_1 = C_1 = 1$ for any δ, reproducing the known orthogonality property.

Our final result is a so-called *exponential inequality*. This gives a probability bound for martingale processes whose increments are a.s. bounded, which is accordingly related directly to the bounding constants, rather than to absolute moments.

15.20 Theorem If $\{X_t,\mathcal{F}_t\}_1^\infty$ is a m.d. sequence with $|X_t| \le B_t$ a.s., where $\{B_t\}$ is a sequence of positive constants, and $S_n = \sum_{t=1}^n X_t$,

$$P(|S_n| > \varepsilon) \le 2\exp\{-\varepsilon^2/2(\textstyle\sum_{t=1}^n B_t^2)\}. \;\square \tag{15.71}$$

This is due, in a slightly different form, to Azuma (1967), although the corresponding result for independent sequences is Hoeffding's inequality, (Hoeffding 1963). The chief interest of these results is the fact that the tail probabilities decline *exponentially* as ε increases. To fix ideas, consider the case $B_t = B$ for all t, so that the probability bound becomes $P(|S_n| > \varepsilon) \le 2\exp\{-\varepsilon^2/2nB^2\}$. This inequality is trivial when n is small, since of course $P(|S_n| > nB) = 0$ by construction. However, choosing $\varepsilon = O(n^{1/2})$ allows us to estimate the tail probabilities associated with the quantity $n^{-1/2}S_n$. The fact that these are becoming exponential suggests an interesting connection with the central limit results to be studied in Chapter 24.

Proof of 15.20 By convexity, every $x \in [-B_t, B_t]$ satisfies

$$e^{\alpha x} \le \frac{(B_t + x)e^{\alpha B_t} + (B_t - x)e^{-\alpha B_t}}{2B_t} \tag{15.72}$$

for any $\alpha > 0$. Hence by the m.d. property,

$$E(e^{\alpha X_t}|\mathcal{F}_{t-1}) \le \tfrac{1}{2}(e^{\alpha B_t} + e^{-\alpha B_t}) \le \exp\{\tfrac{1}{2}\alpha^2 B_t^2\} \text{ a.s.,} \tag{15.73}$$

where the second inequality can be verified using the series expansion of the exponential function. Now employ a neat recursion of **10.10**:

$$\begin{aligned} E(e^{\alpha S_n}|\mathcal{F}_{n-1}) &= E(e^{\alpha S_{n-1} + \alpha X_n}|\mathcal{F}_{n-1}) \\ &= e^{\alpha S_{n-1}} E(e^{\alpha X_n}|\mathcal{F}_{n-1}) \\ &\le e^{\alpha S_{n-1}} \exp\{\tfrac{1}{2}\alpha^2 B_n^2\} \text{ a.s.} \end{aligned} \tag{15.74}$$

Generalizing this idea yields

$$\begin{aligned} E(e^{\alpha S_n}) &= E(E(\ldots E(E(e^{\alpha S_n}|\mathcal{F}_{n-1})|\mathcal{F}_{n-2})\ldots|\mathcal{F}_1)) \\ &\le \exp\{\tfrac{1}{2}\alpha^2 B_n^2\} E(E(\ldots E(e^{\alpha S_{n-1}}|\mathcal{F}_{n-2})\ldots|\mathcal{F}_1)) \\ &\le \ldots \\ &\le \exp\{\tfrac{1}{2}\alpha^2 \textstyle\sum_{t=1}^n B_t^2\}. \end{aligned} \tag{15.75}$$

Combining (15.75) with the generalized Markov inequality **9.11** gives

$$P(S_n > \varepsilon) \le \exp\{-\alpha\varepsilon + \tfrac{1}{2}\alpha^2 \textstyle\sum_{t=1}^n B_t^2\} \tag{15.76}$$

for $\varepsilon > 0$, which for the choice $\alpha = \varepsilon/(\sum_{t=1}^n B_t^2)$ becomes

$$P(S_n > \varepsilon) \le 2\exp\{-\varepsilon^2/2(\textstyle\sum_{t=1}^n B_t^2)\}. \tag{15.77}$$

The result follows on repeating the argument of (15.75)–(15.76) in respect of $-S_n$ and summing the two inequalities. ■

A practical application of this sort of result is to team it with a truncation or uniform integrability argument, under which the probabilities of the bound B being exceeded can also be suitably controlled.

16
Mixingales

16.1 Definition and Examples

Martingale differences are sequences of a rather special kind. One-step-ahead unpredictability is not a feature we can always expect to encounter in observed time series. In this chapter we generalize to a concept of *asymptotic* unpredictability.

16.1 Definition On a probability space $(\Omega,\mathcal{F},P)$, the sequence of pairs $\{X_t,\mathcal{F}_t\}_{-\infty}^{\infty}$, where $\{\mathcal{F}_t\}$ is an increasing sequence of σ-subfields of $\mathcal{F}$ and the X_t are integrable r.v.s, is called an L_p-*mixingale* if, for $p \geq 1$, there exist sequences of non-negative constants $\{c_t\}_{-\infty}^{\infty}$ and $\{\zeta_m\}_0^{\infty}$ such that $\zeta_m \to 0$ as $m \to \infty$, and

$$\|E(X_t|\mathcal{F}_{t-m})\|_p \leq c_t\zeta_m \tag{16.1}$$

$$\|X_t - E(X_t|\mathcal{F}_{t+m})\|_p \leq c_t\zeta_{m+1} \tag{16.2}$$

hold for all t, and $m \geq 0$. □

A martingale difference is a mixingale having $\zeta_m = 0$ for all $m > 0$. Indeed, 'mixingale differences' might appear the more logical terminology, but for the fact that the counterpart of the martingale (i.e. the cumulation of a mixingale sequence) does not play any direct role in this theory. The present terminology, due to Donald McLeish who invented the concept, is standard. Many of the results of this chapter are basically due to McLeish, although his theorems are for the case $p = 2$.

Unlike martingales, mixingales form a very general class of stochastic processes; many of the processes for which limit theorems are known to hold can be characterized as mixingales, although supplementary conditions are generally needed. Note that mixingales are not adapted sequences, in general. X_t is not assumed to be $\mathcal{F}_t$-measurable, although if it is, (16.2) holds trivially for every $m \geq 0$. The mixingale property captures the idea that the sequence $\{\mathcal{F}_s\}$ contains progressively more information about X_t as s increases; in the remote past nothing is known according to (16.1), whereas in the remote future everything will eventually be known according to (16.2).

The constants c_t are scaling factors to make the choice of ζ_m scale-independent, and multiples of $\|X_t\|_p$ will often fulfil this role. As for mixing processes (see §14.1), we usually say that the sequence is of *size* $-\varphi_0$ if $\zeta_m = O(m^{-\varphi})$ for $\varphi > \varphi_0$. However, the discussion following (14.6) also applies to this case.

16.2 Example Consider a linear process

$$X_t = \sum_{j=-\infty}^{\infty} \theta_j U_{t-j}, \tag{16.3}$$

where $\{U_s\}_{-\infty}^{+\infty}$ is a L_p-bounded martingale difference sequence, with $p \geq 1$. Also let $\mathcal{F}_t = \sigma(U_s,\ s \leq t)$. Then

$$E(X_t|\mathcal{F}_{t-m}) = \sum_{j=m}^{\infty} \theta_j U_{t-j}, \text{ a.s.} \tag{16.4}$$

$$X_t - E(X_t|\mathcal{F}_{t+m}) = \sum_{j=m+1}^{\infty} \theta_{-j} U_{t+j}, \text{ a.s.} \tag{16.5}$$

Assuming $\{U_s\}_{-\infty}^{\infty}$ to be *uniformly* L_p-bounded, the Minkowski inequality shows that (16.1) and (16.2) are satisfied with $c_t = \sup_s\|U_s\|_p$ for every t, and $\zeta_m = \sum_{j=m}^{\infty}(|\theta_j| + |\theta_{-j}|)$. $\{X_t,\mathcal{F}_t\}$ is therefore a L_p-mixingale if $\sum_{j=m}^{\infty}(|\theta_j| + |\theta_{-j}|) \to 0$ as $m \to \infty$, and hence if the coefficients $\{\theta_j\}_{-\infty}^{\infty}$ are absolutely summable. The 'one-sided' process in which $\theta_j = 0$ for $j < 0$ arises more commonly in the econometric modelling context. In this case X_t is $\mathcal{F}_t$-measurable and $X_t - E(X_t|\mathcal{F}_{t+m}) = 0$ a.s., but we may set $c_t = \sup_{s\leq t}\|U_s\|_p$ which may increase with t, and does not have to be bounded in the limit to satisfy the definition. To prove X_t integrable, given integrability of the U_s, requires the absolute summability of the coefficients, and in this sense, integrability is effectively sufficient for a linear process to be an L_1-mixingale □

We could say that mixingales are to mixing processes as martingale differences are to independent processes; in each case, a restriction on arbitrary dependence is replaced by a restriction on a simple type of dependence, predictability of the level of the process. Just as martingale differences need not be independent, so mixingales need not be mixing. However, application of **14.2** shows that a mixing zero-mean process is an adapted L_p-mixingale for some $p \geq 1$ with respect to the subfields $\mathcal{F}_t = \sigma(X_t, X_{t-1},\ldots)$, provided it is bounded in the relevant norm.

To be precise, the mean deviations of any L_r-bounded sequence which is α-mixing of size $-\varphi$, for $r > 1$, form an L_p-mixingale of size $-\varphi(1/p - 1/r)$ for p satisfying $1 \leq p < r$. If the process is also ϕ-mixing of size $-\varphi$, application of **14.4** tightens up the mixingale size. The mean deviations of a ϕ-mixing L_r-bounded sequence of size $-\varphi$ is an L_p-mixingale of size $-\varphi(1 - 1/r)$ for $1 \leq p \leq r$. The reader can supply suitable definitions of c_t in each case. It is interesting that the indicated mixingale size is lower (absolutely) than the mixing size, except only in the ϕ-mixing sequence having finite sup-norm (L_r-bounded for all r). Although these relative sizes could be an artefact of the inequalities which can be proved, rather than the sharpest available, this is not an unreasonable result. If a sequence has so many outliers that it fails to possess higher-order moments, it would not be surprising to find that it can be predicted further into the future than a sequence with the same dependence structure but more restricted variations.

The next examples show the type of case arising in the sequel.

16.3 Example An L_r-bounded, zero-mean adapted sequence is an L_2-mixingale of size $-\frac{1}{2}$ if either $r > 2$ and the sequence is α-mixing of size $-r/(r-2)$, or $r \geq 2$ and it is ϕ-mixing of size $-r/2(r-1)$. □

16.4 Example Consider for any $j \geq 0$ the adapted zero-mean sequence

$$\{X_tX_{t+j} - \sigma_{t,t+j}, \mathcal{F}_{t+j}\},$$

where $\sigma_{t,t+j} = E(X_tX_{t+j})$, and $\{X_t\}$ is defined as in **16.3**. By **14.1** this is α-mixing (ϕ-mixing) of the same size as X_t for finite j, and is $L_{r/2}$-bounded, since

$$\|X_tX_{t+j}\|_{r/2} \leq \|X_t\|_r\|X_{t+j}\|_r.$$

by the Cauchy-Schwartz inequality. Assuming $r > 2$ and applying **14.2**, this is an L_1-mixingale of size -1 in the α-mixing case. To get this result under ϕ-mixing also requires a size of $-r/(r-2)$, by **14.4**, but such a sequence is also α-mixing of size $-r/(r-2)$ so there is no separate result for the ϕ-mixing case. □

Mixingales generalize naturally from sequences to arrays.

16.5 Definition The integrable array $\{\{X_{nt}, \mathcal{F}_{nt}\}_{t=-\infty}^{\infty}\}_{n=1}^{\infty}$ is an L_p-mixingale if, for $p \geq 1$, there exists an array of non-negative constants $\{c_{nt}\}_{-\infty}^{\infty}$, and a non-negative sequence $\{\zeta_m\}_0^{\infty}$ such that $\zeta_m \to 0$ as $m \to \infty$, and

$$\|E(X_{nt}|\mathcal{F}_{n,t-m})\|_p \leq c_{nt}\zeta_m \tag{16.6}$$

$$\|X_{nt} - E(X_{nt}|\mathcal{F}_{n,t+m})\|_p \leq c_{nt}\zeta_{m+1} \tag{16.7}$$

hold for all t, n, and $m \geq 0$. □

The other details of the definition are as in **16.1**. All the relevant results for mixingales can be proved for either the sequence or the array case, and the proofs generally differ by no more than the inclusion or exclusion of the extra subscript. Unless the changes are more fundamental than this, we generally discuss the sequence case, and leave the details of the array case to the reader.

One word of caution. This is a low-level property adapted to the easy proof of convergence theorems, but it is not a useful construct at the level of time-series modelling. Although examples such as **16.4** can be exhibited, the mixingale property is not generally preserved under transformations, in the manner of **14.1** for example. Mixingales have too little structure to permit results of that sort. The mixingale concept is mainly useful in conjunction with either mixing assumptions, or approximation results of the kind to be studied in Chapter 17. There we will find that the mixingale property holds for processes for which quite general results on transformations are available.

16.2 Telescoping Sum Representations

Mixingale theory is useful mainly because of an ingenious approximation method. A sum of mixingales is 'nearly' a martingale process, involving a remainder which can be neglected asymptotically under various assumptions limiting the dependence. For the sake of brevity, let E_sX_t stand for $E(X_t|\mathcal{F}_s)$. Then note the simple identity, for any integrable random variable X_t and any $m \geq 1$,

$$X_t = \sum_{k=-m}^{m} (E_{t+k}X_t - E_{t+k-1}X_t) + E_{t-m-1}X_t + (X_t - E_{t+m}X_t). \tag{16.8}$$

Verify that each term on the right-hand side of (16.8) appears twice with opposite signs, except for X_t. For any k, the sequence

$$\{E_{t+k}X_t - E_{t+k-1}X_t,\ \mathcal{F}_{t+k}\}_{t=1}^{\infty}$$

is a martingale difference, since $E_{t+k-1}(E_{t+k}X_t - E_{t+k-1}X_t) = 0$ by the LIE. When $\{X_t,\mathcal{F}_t\}$ is a mixingale, the remainder terms can be made negligible by taking m large enough. Observe that $\{E_{t+m}X_t, \mathcal{F}_{t+m}\}_{m=-\infty}^{\infty}$ is a martingale, and since $\sup_m E|E_{t+m}X_t| \leq E|X_t| < \infty$ by **10.14**, it converges a.s. both as $m \to \infty$ and as $m \to -\infty$, by **15.7** and **15.9**, respectively. In view of the fact that $\|E_{t-m}X_t\|_p \to 0$ and $\|X_t - E_{t+m}X_t\|_p \to 0$, the respective a.s. limits must be 0 and X_t, and hence we are able to assert that

$$X_t = \sum_{k=-\infty}^{\infty} (E_{t+k}X_t - E_{t+k-1}X_t), \text{ a.s.} \tag{16.9}$$

Letting $S_n = \sum_{t=1}^{n} X_t$, we similarly have the decomposition

$$S_n = \sum_{k=-m}^{m} Y_{nk} + \sum_{t=1}^{n} E_{t-m-1}X_t + \sum_{t=1}^{n} (X_t - E_{t+m}X_t) \tag{16.10}$$

where

$$Y_{nk} = \sum_{t=1}^{n} (E_{t+k}X_t - E_{t+k-1}X_t), \tag{16.11}$$

and the processes $\{Y_{nk}, \mathcal{F}_{n+k}\}$ are martingales for each k. By taking m large enough, for fixed n, the remainders can again be made as small as desired. The advantage of this approach is that martingale properties can be exploited in studying the convergence characteristics of sequences of the type S_n. Results of this type are elaborated in §16.3 and §16.4.

If the sequence $\{X_t\}$ is stationary, the constants $\{c_t\}$ can be set to 1 with no loss of generality. In this case, a modified form of telescoping sum actually yields a representation of a partial sum of mixingales as a *single* martingale process, plus a remainder whose behaviour can be suitably controlled by limiting the dependence.

16.6 Theorem (after Hall and Heyde 1980: th. 5.4) Let $\{X_t,\mathcal{F}_t\}$ be a stationary L_1-mixingale of size -1. There exists the decomposition

$$X_t = W_t + Z_t - Z_{t+1}, \tag{16.12}$$

where $E|Z_t| < \infty$ and $\{W_t,\mathcal{F}_t\}$ is a stationary m.d. sequence. □

There is the immediate corollary that

$$S_n = Y_n + Z_1 - Z_{n+1} \tag{16.13}$$

where $\{Y_n, \mathcal{F}_n\}$ is a martingale.

Proof Start with the identity

$$X_t = W_{mt} + Z_{mt} - Z_{m,t+1}, \tag{16.14}$$

where, for $m \geq 1$,

$$W_{mt} = \sum_{s=-m}^{m} (E_t X_{t+s} - E_{t-1} X_{t+s}) + E_t X_{t+m+1} + X_{t-m-1} - E_{t-1} X_{t-m-1} \tag{16.15}$$

$$Z_{mt} = \sum_{s=0}^{m} (E_{t-1} X_{t+s} - X_{t-s-1} + E_{t-1} X_{t-s-1}). \tag{16.16}$$

As in (16.8), every term appears twice with different sign in (16.14), except for X_t. Consider the limiting cases of these random variables as $m \to \infty$, to be designated W_t and Z_t respectively. By stationarity,

$$E|E_{t-1}X_{t+s}| = E|E_{t-s-1}X_t|$$

and

$$E|X_{t-s-1} - E_{t-1}X_{t-s-1}| = E|X_t - E_{t+s}X_t|;$$

hence, applying the triangle inequality,

$$E|Z_t| \leq \sum_{s=0}^{\infty} E|E_{t-s-1}X_t| + \sum_{s=0}^{\infty} E|X_t - E_{t+s}X_t|$$

$$\leq 2\sum_{s=0}^{\infty} \zeta_s < \infty. \tag{16.17}$$

Writing $W_t = X_t - Z_t + Z_{t+1}$, note that

$$E|W_t| \leq E|X_t| + 2E|Z_t| < \infty, \tag{16.18}$$

and it remains to show that W_t is a m.d. sequence. Applying **10.26**(i) to (16.15),

$$E_{t-1} W_{mt} = E_{t-1} X_{t+m+1} \text{ a.s.}, \tag{16.19}$$

and stationarity and (16.1) imply that

$$E|E_{t-1}X_{t+m+1}| = E|E_{t-m-2}X_t| \to 0 \tag{16.20}$$

as $m \to \infty$, so that $E|E_{t-1}W_{mt}| \to 0$ also. Anticipating a result from the theory of stochastic convergence (**18.6**), this means that every subsequence $\{m_k, k \in \mathbb{N}\}$ contains a further subsequence $\{m_{k(j)}, j \in \mathbb{N}\}$ such that $|E_{t-1}W_{m_{k(j)},t}| \to 0$ a.s. as $j \to \infty$. Since $W_{m_{k(j)},t} \to W_t$ for every such subsequence, it is possible to conclude that $E(W_t|\mathcal{F}_{t-1}) = 0$ a.s. This completes the proof. ■

The technical argument in the final paragraph of this proof can be better appreciated after studying Chapter 18. It is neither possible nor necessary in this approach to assert that $E(W_{mt}|\mathcal{F}_{t-1}) \to 0$ a.s.

Note how taking conditional expectations of (16.12) yields

$$E(X_t|\mathcal{F}_{t-1}) = Z_t - Z_{t+1} \text{ a.s.} \tag{16.21}$$

It follows that W_t is almost surely equal to the centred r.v. $X_t - E(X_t|\mathcal{F}_{t-1})$.

16.7 Example Consider the linear process from **16.2**, with $\{U_t\}$ a stationary integrable sequence. Then X_t is stationary, and

$$E|X_1| \leq E|U_1|\sum_{j=-\infty}^{\infty}|\theta_j| < \infty.$$

If the coefficients satisfy a stronger summability condition, i.e.

$$\sum_{m=1}^{\infty}\sum_{j=m}^{\infty}(|\theta_j| + |\theta_{-j}|) = \sum_{m=1}^{\infty}m|\theta_m| + \sum_{m=1}^{\infty}m|\theta_{-m}| < \infty, \tag{16.22}$$

then X_t is an L_1-mixingale of size -1. By a rearrangement of terms we obtain the decomposition of (16.12) with

$$W_t = \left(\sum_{j=-\infty}^{\infty}\theta_j\right)U_t \tag{16.23}$$

and

$$Z_t = \sum_{m=1}^{\infty}\left(\left(\sum_{j=m}^{\infty}\theta_j\right)U_{t-m} - \left(\sum_{j=m}^{\infty}\theta_{-j}\right)U_{t+m-1}\right), \tag{16.24}$$

where $E|Z_t| < \infty$ by (16.22). □

16.3 Maximal Inequalities

As with martingales, maximal inequalities are central to applications of the mixingale concept in limit theory. The basic idea of these results is to extend Doob's inequality (**15.15**) by exploiting the representation as a telescoping sum of martingale differences. MacLeish's idea is to let m go to ∞ in (16.10), and accordingly write

$$S_n = \sum_{k=-\infty}^{\infty}Y_{nk}, \text{ a.s.} \tag{16.25}$$

16.8 Lemma Suppose $\{S_n\}_1^n$ has the representation in (16.25). Let $\{a_k\}_{-\infty}^{\infty}$ be a summable collection of non-negative real numbers, with $a_k = 0$ if $Y_{nk} = 0$ a.s., and $a_k > 0$ otherwise. For any $p > 1$,

$$E\left(\max_{1\leq j\leq n}|S_j|^p\right) \leq \left(\frac{p}{p-1}\right)^p\left(\sum_{k=-\infty}^{\infty}a_k\right)^{p-1}\sum_{a_k>0}a_k^{p-1}E|Y_{nk}|^p. \tag{16.26}$$

Proof For a real sequence $\{x_k\}_{-\infty}^{\infty}$ and *positive* real sequence $\{a_k\}_{-\infty}^{\infty}$, let $K = \sum_{k=-\infty}^{\infty} a_k$ and note that

$$\left|\sum_{k=-\infty}^{\infty} x_k\right|^p = K^p \left|\sum_{k=-\infty}^{\infty} (x_k/a_k)(a_k/K)\right|^p \leq K^{p-1} \sum_{k=-\infty}^{\infty} a_k^{1-p} |x_k|^p, \tag{16.27}$$

where the weights a_k/K sum to unity, and the inequality follows by the convexity of the power transformation (Jensen's inequality). Clearly, (16.27) remains true if the terms corresponding to zero x_k are omitted from the sums, and for these cases set $a_k = 0$ without loss of generality. Put $x_k = Y_{nk}$, take the max over $1 \leq j \leq n$, and then take expectations, to give

$$E\left(\max_{1\leq j\leq n} |S_j|^p\right) \leq \left(\sum_{k=-\infty}^{\infty} a_k\right)^{p-1} \sum_{a_k\neq 0} a_k^{1-p} E\left(\max_{1\leq j\leq n} |Y_{jk}|^p\right). \tag{16.28}$$

To get (16.26), apply Doob's inequality on the right-hand side. ∎

This lemma yields the key step in the proof of the next theorem, a maximal inequality for L_2-mixingales. This may not appear a very appealing result at first sight, but of course the interesting applications arise by judicious choice of the sequence $\{a_k\}$.

16.9 Theorem (Macleish 1975a: th. 1.6) Let $\{X_t, \mathcal{F}_t\}_{-\infty}^{\infty}$ be an L_2-mixingale, let $S_n = \sum_{t=1}^{n} X_t$, and let $\{a_k\}_0^{\infty}$ be any summable sequence of positive reals. Then

$$E\left(\max_{1\leq j\leq n} S_j^2\right) \leq 8\left(\sum_{k=0}^{\infty} a_k\right)\left((\zeta_0^2 + \zeta_1^2)a_0^{-1} + 2\sum_{k=1}^{\infty} \zeta_k^2(a_k^{-1} - a_{k-1}^{-1})\right)\left(\sum_{t=1}^{n} c_t^2\right). \tag{16.29}$$

Proof To get a doubly infinite sequence $\{a_k\}_{-\infty}^{\infty}$, put $a_{-k} = a_k$ for $k > 0$. Then, applying **16.8** for the case $p = 2$,

$$E\left(\max_{1\leq j\leq n} S_j^2\right) \leq 4\left(\sum_{k=-\infty}^{\infty} a_k\right)\left(\sum_{k=-\infty}^{\infty} a_k^{-1} E(Y_{nk}^2)\right). \tag{16.30}$$

Since the terms making up Y_{nk} are martingale differences and pairwise uncorrelated, we have

$$E(Y_{nk}^2) = \sum_{t=1}^{n} E(E_{t+k}X_t - E_{t+k-1}X_t)^2. \tag{16.31}$$

Now, $E(E_{t+k}X_t E_{t+k-1}X_t) = E(E_{t+k-1}(E_{t+k}X_t E_{t+k-1}X_t)) = E(E_{t+k-1}^2 X_t)$ by the LIE, from which it follows that

$$E(E_{t+k}X_t - E_{t+k-1}X_t)^2 = E(E_{t+k}^2 X_t - E_{t+k-1}^2 X_t). \tag{16.32}$$

Also let $Z_{tk} = X_t - E_{t+k}X_t$, and it is similarly easy to verify that

$$\begin{aligned} E(E_{t+k}X_t - E_{t+k-1}X_t)^2 &= E(Z_{t,k-1} - Z_{tk})^2 \\ &= E(Z_{t,k-1}^2 - Z_{tk}^2). \end{aligned} \tag{16.33}$$

Now apply Abel's partial summation formula (2.25), to get

$$\sum_{k=-\infty}^{\infty} a_k^{-1}E(Y_{nk}^2) = \sum_{t=1}^{n}\sum_{k=-\infty}^{\infty} a_k^{-1}E(E_{t+k}X_t - E_{t+k-1}X_t)^2$$

$$= \sum_{t=1}^{n}\left(\sum_{k=0}^{\infty} a_k^{-1}E(E_{t-k}^2X_t - E_{t-k-1}^2X_t) + \sum_{k=1}^{\infty} a_k^{-1}E(Z_{t,k-1}^2 - Z_{tk}^2)\right)$$

$$= \sum_{t=1}^{n}\left(a_0^{-1}E(E_t^2X_t) + \sum_{k=1}^{\infty} E(E_{t-k}^2X_t)(a_k^{-1} - a_{k-1}^{-1})\right.$$

$$\left. + \, a_1^{-1}E(Z_{t0}^2) + \sum_{k=1}^{\infty} E(Z_{tk}^2)(a_{k+1}^{-1} - a_k^{-1})\right) \tag{16.34}$$

where the second equality follows by substituting (16.32) for the cases $k \le 0$, and (16.33) for the cases $k > 0$. (16.29) now follows, noting from (16.1) that $E(E_{t-k}^2X_t) \le c_t^2\zeta_k^2$ and from (16.2) that $E(Z_{tk}^2) \le c_t^2\zeta_{k+1}^2$. ∎

Putting

$$K = 8\left(\sum_{k=0}^{\infty} a_k\right)\left(a_0^{-1}(\zeta_0^2 + \zeta_1^2) + 2\sum_{k=1}^{\infty}\zeta_k^2(a_k^{-1} - a_{k-1}^{-1})\right), \tag{16.35}$$

this result poses the question, whether there exists a summable sequence $\{a_k\}_0^\infty$ such that $K < \infty$. There is no loss of generality in letting the sequence $\{\zeta_k\}_0^\infty$ be monotone. If $\zeta_m = 0$ for $m < \infty$, then $\zeta_{m+j} = 0$ for all $j > 0$, and in this case one may choose $a_k = 1$, $k = 0,\dots,m+1$, and K reduces to $(m+1)(\zeta_0^2 + \zeta_1^2)$. Alternatively, consider the case where $\zeta_k > 0$ for every k. If we put $a_0 = \zeta_0$, and then define the recursion

$$a_k = \frac{\zeta_k}{2a_{k-1}}\left[(\zeta_k^2 + 4a_{k-1}^2)^{1/2} - \zeta_k\right], \tag{16.36}$$

a_k is real and positive if this is true of a_{k-1} and the relation

$$a_k^{-1} - a_{k-1}^{-1} = \zeta_k^{-2}a_k \tag{16.37}$$

is satisfied for each k. Since $a_0^{-1}(\zeta_0^2 + \zeta_1^2) \le 2a_0$, we have

$$K = 8\left(\sum_{k=0}^{\infty} a_k\right)\left(a_0^{-1}(\zeta_0^2 + \zeta_1^2) + 2\sum_{k=1}^{\infty} a_k\right) \le 16\left(\sum_{k=0}^{\infty} a_k\right)^2. \tag{16.38}$$

In this case, for $k > 0$ we find

$$\zeta_k^{-2} = (a_k^{-1} - a_{k-1}^{-1})a_k^{-1} \le a_k^{-2} - a_{k-1}^{-2} \tag{16.39}$$

so that

$$\sum_{k=0}^{m}\zeta_k^{-2} \le \zeta_0^{-2} + \sum_{k=1}^{m}(a_k^{-2} - a_{k-1}^{-2}) = a_m^{-2}. \tag{16.40}$$

Substituting into (16.38), we get

$$K \le 16\left\{\sum_{m=0}^{\infty}\left(\sum_{k=0}^{m}\zeta_k^{-2}\right)^{-1/2}\right\}^2. \tag{16.41}$$

This result links the maximal inequality directly with the issue of the summability of the mixingale coefficients. In particular, we have the following corollary.

16.10 Corollary Let $\{X_t,\mathcal{F}_t\}$ be an L_2-mixingale of size $-\frac{1}{2}$. Then

$$E\left(\max_{1\le j\le n} S_j^2\right) \le K\sum_{t=1}^{n} c_t^2, \tag{16.42}$$

where $K < \infty$.

Proof If $\zeta_k = O(k^{-1/2-\delta})$ for $\delta > 0$, as the theorem imposes, then $\Sigma_{k=1}^m\zeta_k^{-2} = O(m^{2+2\delta})$ by **2.27**, and $(\Sigma_{k=1}^m\zeta_k^{-2})^{-1/2} = O(m^{-1-\delta})$ and hence is summable over m. The theorem follows by (16.41). ∎

However, it should be noted that the condition

$$\sum_{m=0}^{\infty}\left(\sum_{k=0}^{m}\zeta_k^{-2}\right)^{-1/2} < \infty \tag{16.43}$$

is weaker than $\zeta_k = O(k^{-1/2-\delta})$. Consider the case $\zeta_k = (k+2)^{-1/2}(\log k+2)^{-1-\varepsilon}$ for $\varepsilon > 0$, so that $k^{1/2+\delta}\zeta_k \to \infty$ for every $\delta > 0$. Then

$$\sum_{k=0}^{m}\zeta_k^{-2} = \sum_{k=0}^{m}(k+2)(\log k+2)^{2+2\varepsilon} \le (m+2)^2(\log m+2)^{2+2\varepsilon}, \tag{16.44}$$

and (16.43) follows by **2.31**. One may therefore prefer to define the notion of 'size $= -\frac{1}{2}$' in terms of the summability condition (16.43), rather than by orders of magnitude in m. However, in a practical context assigning an order of magnitude to ζ_m is a convenient way to bound the dependence, and we shall find in the sequel that these summability arguments are greatly simplified when the order-of-magnitude calculus can be routinely applied.

Theorem **16.9** has no obvious generalization from the L_2-mixingale case to general L_p for $p > 1$, as in **15.15**, because (16.31) hinges on the uncorrelatedness of the terms. But because second moments may not exist in the cases under consideration, a comparable result for $1 < p < 2$ would be valuable. This is attainable by a slightly different approach, although at the cost of raising the mixingale size from $-\frac{1}{2}$ to -1; in other words, the mixingale numbers will need to be summable.

16.11 Theorem Let $\{X_t,\mathcal{F}_t\}_{-\infty}^{\infty}$ be an L_p-mixingale, $1 < p < 2$, of size -1, and let $S_n = \Sigma_{t=1}^n X_t$; then

$$E\left(\max_{1\le j\le n}|S_j|^p\right) \le 4^pC_p\left(\frac{p}{p-1}\right)^p\left(\sum_{k=0}^{\infty}\zeta_k\right)^p\sum_{t=1}^{n}c_t^p, \tag{16.45}$$

where C_p is a positive constant.

Proof Let Y_{nk} be defined as in (16.11), and apply Burkholder's inequality (**15.18**) and then Loève's c_r inequality with $r = p/2 \in (\frac{1}{2}, 1)$ to obtain

$$E|Y_{nk}|^p \le C_pE\left|\sum_{t=1}^{n}(E_{t+k}X_t - E_{t+k-1}X_t)^2\right|^{p/2}$$

$$\le C_p\sum_{t=1}^{n}E|(E_{t+k}X_t - E_{t+k-1}X_t|^p. \tag{16.46}$$

Now we have the mixingale inequalities,

$$\|E_{t+k}X_t - E_{t+k-1}X_t\|_p \le \|E_{t+k}X_t\|_p + \|E_{t+k-1}X_t\|_p \le 2c_t\zeta_k \tag{16.47}$$

for $k < 0$ and

$$\begin{aligned}\|E_{t+k}X_t - E_{t+k-1}X_t\|_p &= \|Z_{t,k-1} - Z_{tk}\|_p\\ &\le \|Z_{t,k-1}\|_p + \|Z_{tk}\|_p \le 2c_t\zeta_k\end{aligned} \tag{16.48}$$

for $k > 0$, where Z_{tk} is defined above (16.33). Hence,

$$E|Y_{nk}|^p \le 2^pC_p\zeta_k^p\sum_{t=1}^{n}c_t^p \tag{16.49}$$

(put $\zeta_0 = 1$), and substitution in (16.26), with $\{a_k\}_0^\infty$ a positive sequence and $-a_k = a_k$, gives

$$E\left(\max_{1\le j\le n}|S_j|^p\right) \le 2^{p+1}C_p\left(\frac{p}{p-1}\right)^p\left(\sum_{k=0}^{\infty}a_k\right)^{p-1}\left(\sum_{k=0}^{\infty}a_k^{1-p}\zeta_k^p\right)\sum_{t=1}^{n}c_t^p. \tag{16.50}$$

Both a_k and $a_k^{1-p}\zeta_k^p$ can be summable for $p > 1$ only in the case $\zeta_k = O(a_k)$, and the conclusion follows. ■

A case of special importance is the linear process of **16.2**. Here we can specialize **16.11** as follows:

16.12 Corollary For $1 < p \le 2$,

(i) if $X_t = \sum_{j=-\infty}^{\infty}\theta_jU_{t-j}$, then

$$E\left(\max_{1\le j\le n}|S_j|^p\right) \le C_p\left(\frac{p}{p-1}\right)^p\left(|\theta_0| + \sum_{k=1}^{\infty}(|\theta_k| + |\theta_{-k}|)\right)^p n\sup_s E|U_s|^p;$$

(ii) if $X_t = \sum_{j=0}^{\infty}\theta_jU_{t-j}$, then

$$E\left(\max_{1\le j\le n}|S_j|^p\right) \le C_p\left(\frac{p}{p-1}\right)^p\left(\sum_{k=0}^{\infty}|\theta_k|\right)^p\sum_{t=1}^{n}\sup_{s\le t}E|U_s|^p.$$

Proof In this case, $E_{t-k}X_t - E_{t-k-1}X_t = \theta_k U_{t-k}$. Letting $\{a_k\}_0^\infty$ be any non-negative constant sequence and $a_{-k} = a_k$,

$$\sum_{a_k \neq 0} a_k^{1-p} E|Y_{nk}|^p \leq C_p \sum_{a_k \neq 0} a_k^{1-p} |\theta_k|^p \sum_{t=1}^n c_t^p, \tag{16.51}$$

where $c_t = \sup_s \|U_s\|_p$ in case (i), and $c_t = \sup_{s \leq t} \|U_s\|_p$ in case (ii). Choosing $a_k = |\theta_k|$ and substituting in (16.26) yields the results. ∎

Recall that the mixingale coefficients in this case are $\zeta_m = \sum_{j=m}^\infty (|\theta_j| + |\theta_{-j}|)$, so linearity yields a dramatic relaxation of the conditions for the inequalities to be satisfied. Absolute summability of the θ_j is sufficient. This corresponds simply to $\zeta_m \to 0$. A mixingale size of zero suffices. Moreover, there is no separate result for L_2-bounded linear processes. Putting $p = 2$ yields a result that is correspondingly superior in terms of mixingale size restrictions to **16.11**.

16.4 Uniform Square-integrability

One of the most important of McLeish's mixingale theorems is a further consequence of **16.9**. It is not a maximal inequality, but belongs to the same family of results and has a related application. The question at issue is the uniform integrability of the sequence of squared partial sums.

16.13 Theorem (from MacLeish 1975b: lemma 6.5; 1977: lemma 3.5) Let $\{X_t, \mathcal{F}_t\}$ be an L_2-mixingale of size $-\frac{1}{2}$, $S_n = \sum_{t=1}^n X_t$, and $v_n^2 = \sum_{t=1}^n c_t^2$ where c_t is defined in (16.1)–(16.2). If the sequence $\{X_t^2/c_t^2\}_{t=1}^\infty$ is uniformly integrable, then so is the sequence $\{\max_{1 \leq j \leq n} S_j^2/v_n^2\}_{n=1}^\infty$.

Proof A preliminary step is to decompose X_t into three components. Choose positive numbers B and m (to be specified below), let $1_t^B = 1_{\{|X_t| \leq Bc_t\}}$, and then define

$$U_t = X_t - E_{t+m}X_t + E_{t-m}X_t \tag{16.52}$$

$$Y_t = E_{t+m}X_t 1_t^B - E_{t-m}X_t 1_t^B \tag{16.53}$$

$$Z_t = E_{t+m}X_t(1 - 1_t^B) - E_{t-m}X_t(1 - 1_t^B), \tag{16.54}$$

such that $X_t = U_t + Y_t + Z_t$. This decomposition allows us to exploit the following collection of properties. (To verify these, use various results from Chapter 10 on conditional expectations, and consider the cases $k \geq m$ and $k < m$ separately.) First,

$$E^2 E_{t-k} U_t = E^2 E_{t-(k \vee m)} X_t \leq c_t^2 \zeta_{k \vee m}^2, \tag{16.55}$$

$$E(U_t - E_{t+k}U_t)^2 = E(X_t - E_{t+(k \vee m)}X_t)^2 \leq c_t^2 \zeta_{(k \vee m)+1}^2, \tag{16.56}$$

for $k \geq 0$, where $k \vee m = \max\{k, m\}$. Second,

$$EE_{t-k}^2 Y_t = E(E_{t-(k \wedge m)}^2 X_t 1_t^B - E_{t-m}^2 X_t 1_t^B), \tag{16.57}$$

$$E(Y_t - E_{t+k}Y_t)^2 = E(E_{t+m}^2 X_t 1_t^B - E_{t+(k\wedge m)}^2 X_t 1_t^B), \tag{16.58}$$

where $k \wedge m = \min\{k,m\}$. The terms are both zero if $k \geq m$ and are otherwise bounded by $E(X_t^2 1_t^B) \leq Bc_t$. Third,

$$EE_{t-k}^2 Z_t = E(E_{t-(k\wedge m)}^2 X_t(1 - 1_t^B) - E_{t-m}^2 X_t(1 - 1_t^B)), \tag{16.59}$$

$$E(Z_t - E_{t+k}Z_t)^2 = E(E_{t+m}^2 X_t(1 - 1_t^B) - E_{t+(k\wedge m)}^2 X_t(1 - 1_t^B)), \tag{16.60}$$

where the terms are zero for $k \geq m$ and bounded by $E(X_t^2(1 - 1_t^B))$ otherwise. Note that $E(X_t^2(1 - 1_t^B))/c_t^2 = E((X_t/c_t)^2 1_{\{|X_t/c_t| > B\}}) \to 0$ as $B \to \infty$ uniformly in t, by the assumption of uniform integrability.

The inequality

$$\left(\sum_{t=1}^{j} X_t\right)^2 \leq 3\left[\left(\sum_{t=1}^{j} U_t\right)^2 + \left(\sum_{t=1}^{j} Y_t\right)^2 + \left(\sum_{t=1}^{j} Z_t\right)^2\right] \tag{16.61}$$

for $1 \leq j \leq n$ follows from substituting $X_t = U_t + Y_t + Z_t$, multiplying out, and applying the Cauchy-Schwartz inequality. For brevity, write

$$x_j = S_j^2/v_n^2,$$

$$u_j = (\textstyle\sum_{t=1}^{j} U_t)^2/v_n^2,$$

$$y_j = (\textstyle\sum_{t=1}^{j} Y_t)^2/v_n^2,$$

$$z_j = (\textstyle\sum_{t=1}^{j} Z_t)^2/v_n^2.$$

Then (16.61) is equivalent to $x_j \leq 3(u_j + y_j + z_j)$, for each $j = 1,\ldots,n$. Also let $\hat{x}_n = \max_{1\leq j\leq n} x_j$, and define $\hat{u}_n$, $\hat{y}_n$, and $\hat{z}_n$ similarly; then clearly,

$$\hat{x}_n \leq 3(\hat{u}_n + \hat{y}_n + \hat{z}_n). \tag{16.62}$$

For any r.v. $X \geq 0$ and constant $M > 0$, introduce the notation $\mathcal{E}_M(X) = E(1_{\{X>M\}}X)$, so that the object of the proof is to show that $\sup_n \mathcal{E}_M(\hat{x}_n) \to 0$ as $M \to \infty$. As a consequence of (16.62) and **9.29**,

$$\begin{aligned}\mathcal{E}_M(\hat{x}_n) &\leq 3\mathcal{E}_{M/3}(\hat{u}_n + \hat{y}_n + \hat{z}_n) \\ &\leq 6(E(\hat{u}_n) + \mathcal{E}_{M/6}(\hat{y}_n) + E(\hat{z}_n)).\end{aligned} \tag{16.63}$$

We now show that for any $\varepsilon > 0$, each of the expectations on the right-hand side of (16.63) can be bounded by ε by choosing M large enough. First consider $E(\hat{u}_n)$; given (16.55) and (16.56), and assuming $\zeta_m = O(m^{-1/2-\delta})$, we can apply **16.9** to this case, setting $a_k = m^{-1-\delta}$ for $k \leq m$, and $a_k = k^{-1-\delta}$ for $k > m$. Applying (16.29) with $\sum_{t=1}^{j} U_t$ substituted for S_j in that expression produces

$$\begin{aligned}E(\hat{u}_n) &\leq 8\left((m+1)m^{-1-\delta} + \sum_{k=m+1}^{\infty} k^{-1-\delta}\right)\left(\zeta_m^2 m^{1+\delta} + 2\sum_{k=m+1}^{\infty} \zeta_k^2 k^{\delta}\right) \\ &= O(m^{-\delta}),\end{aligned} \tag{16.64}$$

where the order of magnitude in m follows from **2.27**(iii). Evidently we can choose m large enough that $E(\hat{u}_n) < \varepsilon$. Henceforth, let m be fixed at this value.

A similar argument is applied to $E(\hat{z}_n)$, but in view of (16.59) and (16.60) we may choose $a_k = 1$, $k = 0,\dots,m$, and $a_k = 0$ otherwise. Write, formally, $EE_{t-k}^2 Z_t \leq c_t^2\zeta_k^2$ and $E(Z_t - E_{t+k}Z_t)^2 \leq c_t^2\zeta_k^2$, where

$$\zeta_k^2 = \begin{cases} \max_{1\leq t\leq n} E\big((X_t/c_t)^2 1_{\{|X_t/c_t|>B\}}\big), & k < m, \\ 0, & k \geq m, \end{cases} \tag{16.65}$$

and then application of (16.29) leads to

$$E(\hat{z}_n) \leq 16(m+1)\max_{1\leq t\leq n} E\big((X_t/c_t)^2 1_{\{|X_t/c_t|>B\}}\big). \tag{16.66}$$

This term goes to zero as $B \to \infty$, so let B be fixed at a value large enough that $E(\hat{z}_n) < \varepsilon$.

For the remaining term, notice that $Y_t = \sum_{k=-m+1}^{m} \xi_{tk}$ where

$$\xi_{tk} = E_{t+k}X_t 1_t^B - E_{t+k-1}X_t 1_t^B. \tag{16.67}$$

For each k, $\{\xi_{tk}, \mathcal{F}_{t+k}\}$ is a m.d. sequence. If **16.8** is applied for the case $p = 4$ and $a_k = 1$ for $|k| \leq m$, 0 otherwise, we obtain (not forgetting that for $y_j > 0$, $(\max_j y_j)^2 = \max_j\{y_j^2\}$)

$$E(\hat{y}_n^2) = \frac{1}{\nu_n^4} E\left(\max_{1\leq j\leq n}\left|\sum_{t=1}^{j} Y_t\right|^4\right) \leq \frac{1}{\nu_n^4}\left(\frac{4}{3}\right)^4 (2m+1)^3 \sum_{k=-m}^{m} E(Y_{nk}^4), \tag{16.68}$$

where $Y_{nk} = \sum_{t=1}^{n} \xi_{tk}$. Now, given $Y_{nk} = Y_{n-1,k} + \xi_{nk}$, we have the recursion

$$E(Y_{nk}^4) = E(Y_{n-1,k}^4) + 4E(Y_{n-1,k}^3\xi_{nk}) + 6E(Y_{n-1,k}^2\xi_{nk}^2) + 4E(Y_{n-1,k}\xi_{nk}^3) + E(\xi_{nk}^4). \tag{16.69}$$

The ξ_{tk} are bounded absolutely by $2Bc_t$; hence consider the terms on the right-hand side of (16.69). The second one vanishes, by the m.d. property. For the third one, we have

$$E(Y_{n-1,k}^2\xi_{nk}^2) \leq E(Y_{n-1,k}^2)(2Bc_n)^2 \leq (2B)^4\nu_{n-1}^2 c_n^2, \tag{16.70}$$

and for the fourth one, note that by the Cauchy-Schwartz inequality,

$$E|Y_{n-1,k}\xi_{nk}^3| \leq (2B)^4\nu_{n-1}c_n^3. \tag{16.71}$$

Making these substitutions into (16.69) and solving the implied inequality recursively yields

$$\begin{aligned} E(Y_{nk}^4) &\leq (2B)^4\left(6\sum_{t=1}^{n}\nu_{t-1}^2 c_t^2 + 4\sum_{t=2}^{n}\nu_{t-1}c_t^3 + \sum_{t=1}^{n} c_t^4\right) \\ &\leq 11(2B)^4\nu_n^4. \end{aligned} \tag{16.72}$$

Plugging this bound into (16.68), and applying the inequality $a\mathcal{E}_a(X) \le E(X^2)$ for $X \ge 0$ and $a > 0$, yields finally

$$\mathcal{E}_{M/6}(\hat{y}_n) \le \frac{6}{M}E(\hat{y}_n^2) \le \left(\frac{4}{3}\right)^4 \frac{6(2m+1)^4 11(2B)^4}{M}. \tag{16.73}$$

By choice of M, this quantity can be made smaller than ε.

Thus, according to (16.63) we have shown that $\mathcal{E}_M(\hat{x}_n) < 18\varepsilon$ for large enough M, or, equivalently,

$$\mathcal{E}_M(\hat{x}_n) \to 0 \text{ as } M \to \infty. \tag{16.74}$$

By assumption, the foregoing argument applies uniformly in n, so the proof is complete. ■

The array version of this result, which is effectively identical, is quoted for the record.

16.14 Corollary Let $\{X_{nt},\mathcal{F}_{nt}\}$ be an L_2-mixingale array of size $-\frac{1}{2}$, and let $S_n = \sum_{t=1}^n X_{nt}$ and $\nu_n^2 = \sum_{t=1}^n c_{nt}^2$, where c_{nt} is given by (16.6)–(16.7); if $\{X_{nt}^2/c_{nt}^2\}$ is uniformly integrable, $\{\max_{1\le j\le n} S_j^2/\nu_n^2\}_{n=1}^\infty$ is uniformly integrable.

Proof As for **16.13**, after inserting the subscript n as required. ■

17
Near-Epoch Dependence

17.1 Definitions and Examples

As noted in §14.3, the mixing concept has a serious drawback from the viewpoint of applications in time-series modelling, in that a function of a mixing sequence (even an independent sequence) that depends on an infinite number of lags and/or leads of the sequence is not generally mixing. Let

$$X_t = g_t(\ldots,V_{t-1},V_t,V_{t+1},\ldots), \tag{17.1}$$

where V_t is a vector of mixing processes. The idea to be developed in this chapter is that although X_t may not be mixing, if it depends almost entirely on the 'near epoch' of $\{V_t\}$ it will often have properties permitting the application of limit theorems, of which the mixingale property is the most important.

This idea goes back to Ibragimov (1962), and had been formalized in different ways by Billingsley (1968), McLeish (1975a), Bierens (1983), Gallant and White (1988), Andrews (1988), and Pötscher and Prucha (1991a), among others. The following definitions encompass and extend most existing ones. Consider first a definition for sequences.

17.1 Definition For a stochastic sequence $\{V_t\}_{-\infty}^{+\infty}$, possibly vector-valued, on a probability space $(\Omega,\mathcal{F},P)$, let $\mathcal{F}_{t-m}^{t+m} = \sigma(V_{t-m},\ldots,V_{t+m})$, such that $\{\mathcal{F}_{t-m}^{t+m}\}_{m=0}^{\infty}$ is an increasing sequence of σ-fields. If, for $p > 0$, a sequence of integrable r.v.s $\{X_t\}_{-\infty}^{+\infty}$ satisfies

$$\|X_t - E(X_t|\mathcal{F}_{t-m}^{t+m})\|_p \le d_t\nu_m, \tag{17.2}$$

where $\nu_m \to 0$, and $\{d_t\}_{-\infty}^{+\infty}$ is a sequence of positive constants, X_t will be said to be *near-epoch dependent in L_p-norm* (L_p-NED) on $\{V_t\}_{-\infty}^{+\infty}$. □

Many results in this literature are proved for the case $p = 2$ (Gallant and White, 1988, for example) and the term near-epoch dependence, without qualification, may be used in this case. As for mixingales, there is an extension to the array case.

17.2 Definition For a stochastic array $\{\{V_{nt}\}_{t=-\infty}^{+\infty}\}_{n=1}^{\infty}$, possibly vector-valued, on a probability space $(\Omega,\mathcal{F},P)$, let $\mathcal{F}_{n,t-m}^{t+m} = \sigma(V_{n,t-m},\ldots,V_{n,t+m})$. If an integrable array $\{\{X_{nt}\}_{t=-\infty}^{+\infty}\}_{n=1}^{\infty}$, satisfies

$$\|X_{nt} - E(X_{nt}|\mathcal{F}_{n,t-m}^{t+m})\|_p \le d_{nt}\nu_m, \tag{17.3}$$

where $\nu_m \to 0$, and $\{d_{nt}\}$ is an array of positive constants, it is said to be L_p-NED on $\{V_{nt}\}$. □

We discuss the sequence case below with the extensions to the array case being easily supplied when needed. The size terminology which has been defined for mixing processes and mixingales is also applicable here. We will say that the sequence or array is L_p-NED of size $-\varphi_0$ when $\nu_m = O(m^{-\varphi})$ for $\varphi > \varphi_0$.

According to the Minkowski and conditional modulus inequalities,

$$\begin{aligned}\|X_t - E(X_t|\mathcal{F}_{t-m}^{t+m})\|_p &\leq \|X_t - \mu_t\|_p + \|E(X_t - \mu_t|\mathcal{F}_{t-m}^{t+m})\|_p \\ &\leq 2\|X_t - \mu_t\|_p, \end{aligned} \tag{17.4}$$

where $\mu_t = E(X_t)$. The role of the sequence $\{d_t\}$ in (17.2) is usually to account for the possibility of trending moments, and when $\|X_t - \mu_t\|_p$ is uniformly bounded, we should expect to set d_t equal to a finite constant for all t. However, a drawback with the definition is that $\{d_t\}$ can always be chosen in such a way that

$$\inf_t \left\{ \frac{\|X_t - E(X_t|\mathcal{F}_{t-m}^{t+m})\|_p}{d_t} \right\} = 0,$$

for every m, so that the near-epoch dependence property can break down in the limit without violating (17.2). Indeed, (17.2) might not hold except with such a choice of constants. In many applications this would represent an undesirable weakening of the condition, which can be avoided by imposing the requirement $d_t \leq 2\|X_t - \mu_t\|_p$, or for the array case, $d_{nt} \leq 2\|X_{nt} - \mu_{nt}\|_p$. Under this restriction we can set $\nu_m \leq 1$ with no loss of generality.

Near-epoch dependence is not an alternative to a mixing assumption; it is a property of the *mapping* from $\{\boldsymbol{V}_t\}$ to $\{X_t\}$, not of the random variables themselves. The concept acquires importance when $\{\boldsymbol{V}_t\}$ is a mixing process, because then $\{X_t\}$ inherits certain useful characteristics. Note that $E(X_t|\mathcal{F}_{t-m}^{t+m})$ is a finite-lag, $\mathcal{F}_{t-m}^{t+m}/\mathcal{B}$-measurable function of a mixing process and hence is also mixing, by **14.1**. Near-epoch dependence implies that $\{X_t\}$ is 'approximately' mixing in the sense of being well approximated by a mixing process. And as we show below, a near-epoch-dependent function of a mixing process, subject to suitable restrictions on the moments, can be a mixingale, so that the various inequalities of §16.2 can be exploited in this case.

From the point of view of applications, near-epoch dependence captures nicely the characteristics of a stable dynamic econometric model in which a dependent variable X_t depends mainly on the recent histories of a collection of explanatory variables or shock processes $\boldsymbol{V}_t$, which might be assumed to be mixing. The symmetric dependence on past and future embodied in the definition of a L_p-NED function has no obvious relevance to this case, but it is at worst a harmless generalization. In fact, such cases do arise in various practical contexts, such as the application of two-sided seasonal adjustment procedures, or similar smoothing filters; since most published seasonally adjusted time series are the output of a two-sided filter, none of these variables is strictly measurable without reference to future events.

17.3 Example Let $\{V_t\}_{-\infty}^{+\infty}$ be a zero-mean, L_p-bounded scalar sequence, and define

$$X_t = \sum_{j=-\infty}^{\infty} \theta_j V_{t-j}. \tag{17.5}$$

Then, by the Minkowski inequality,

$$\|X_t - E(X_t|\mathcal{F}_{t-m}^{t+m})\|_p = \left\| \sum_{j=m+1}^{\infty} (\theta_j(V_{t-j} - E_{t-m}^{t+m}V_{t-j}) + \theta_{-j}(V_{t+j} - E_{t-m}^{t+m}V_{t+j})) \right\|_p$$

$$\leq d_t \nu_m, \tag{17.6}$$

where $\nu_m = \sum_{j=m+1}^{\infty}(|\theta_j| + |\theta_{-j}|)$, and $d_t = 2\sup_s\|V_s\|_p$, all t. Clearly, $\nu_m \to 0$ if the sequence $\{\theta_j\}$ is absolutely summable, and ν_m is of size $-\varphi_0$ if $|\theta_j| + |\theta_{-j}| = O(^{-1-\varphi})$ for $\varphi > \varphi_0$. In the one-sided case with $\theta_j = 0$ for $j < 0$, we may put $d_t = \sup_{s\leq t}\|V_s\|_p$, which may be an increasing function of t; compare **16.2**. □

The second example, suggested by Gallant and White (1988), illustrates how near-epoch dependence generalizes to a wide class of lag functions subject to a dynamic stability condition, analogous to the summability condition in the linear example.

17.4 Example Let $\{V_t\}$ be a L_p-bounded stochastic sequence for $p \geq 2$ and let a sequence $\{X_t\}$ be generated by the nonlinear difference equation

$$X_t = f_t(V_t, X_{t-1}), \tag{17.7}$$

where $\{f_t(.,.)\}$ is a sequence of differentiable functions satisfying

$$\sup_{v,x} \left| \frac{\partial f_t(v,x)}{\partial x} \right| \leq b < 1. \tag{17.8}$$

As a function of x, f_t is called a *contraction mapping*. Abstracting from the stochastic aspect of the problem, write v_t as the dummy first argument of f_t. By repeated substitution, we have

$$f_t = f_t(v_t, f_{t-1}(v_{t-1}, f_{t-2}(v_{t-2},\ldots)))$$

$$= g_t(v_t, v_{t-1}, v_{t-2},\ldots), \tag{17.9}$$

and, by the chain rule for differentiation of composite functions,

$$\left| \frac{\partial g_t}{\partial v_{t-j}} \right| \leq b^{j-1} \left| \frac{\partial f_{t-j}}{\partial v_{t-j}} \right|. \tag{17.10}$$

Define a $\mathcal{F}_{t-m}^{t}/\mathcal{B}$-measurable approximation to g_t by replacing the arguments with lag exceeding m by zeros:

$$g_t^m(v_t,\ldots,v_{t-m}) = g_t(v_t,\ldots,v_{t-m},0,0,\ldots). \tag{17.11}$$

By a Taylor expansion about 0 with respect to v_{t-j} for $j > m$,

$$g_t - g_t^m = \sum_{j=m+1}^{\infty} \left(\frac{\partial g_t}{\partial v_{t-j}} \right)^* v_{t-j}, \tag{17.12}$$

where * denotes evaluation of the derivatives at points in the intervals $[0,v_{t-j}]$.
Now define the stochastic sequence $\{X_t\}$ by evaluating g_t at $(V_t,V_{t-1},...)$. Note that

$$\|X_t - E(X_t|\mathcal{F}_{t-m}^{t+m})\|_2 \le \|X_t - g_t^m(V_t,...,V_{t-m})\|_2 \tag{17.13}$$

by **10.12**. The Minkowski inequality, (17.12), and then (17.10) further imply that

$$\begin{aligned}\|X_t - g_t^m\|_2 &= \left\|\sum_{j=m+1}^{\infty} G_{t-j}V_{t-j}\right\|_2 \\ &\le \sum_{j=m+1}^{\infty} \|G_{t-j}V_{t-j}\|_2 \\ &\le \sum_{j=m+1}^{\infty} b^{j-1}\|F_{t-j}V_{t-j}\|_2 \\ &\le \left(\frac{1}{1-b}\right) b^m \sup_{j>m} \|F_{t-j}V_{t-j}\|_2,\end{aligned} \tag{17.14}$$

where G_{t-j} is the random variable defined by evaluating $[(\partial/\partial v_{t-j})g_t]^*$ with respect to the random point $(V_{t-j},V_{t-j-1},...)$, and F_{t-j} bears the corresponding relationship with $(\partial/\partial v_{t-j})f_{t-j}$. X_t is therefore L_2-NED of size $-\infty$, with constants $d_t \ll \sup_{s\le t}\|F_sV_s\|_2$, if this norm exists. In particular, Hölder's inequality allows us to make this derivation whenever $\|V_t\|_{2r}$ and $\|F_t\|_{2r/r-1)}$ exist for $r > 1$, and also if $\|V_t\|_2 < \infty$ and F_t is a.s. bounded. □

17.2 Near-Epoch Dependence and Mixingales

The usefulness of the near-epoch depencence concept is due largely to the next theorem.

17.5 Theorem Let $\{X_t\}_{-\infty}^{\infty}$ be an L_r-bounded zero-mean sequence, for $r > 1$.

(i) Let $\{V_t\}$ be α-mixing of size $-a$. If X_t is L_p-NED of size $-b$ on $\{V_t\}$ for $1 \le p < r$ with constants $\{d_t\}$, $\{X_t,\mathcal{F}_{-\infty}^t\}$ is an L_p-mixingale of size $-\min\{b, a(1/p - 1/r)\}$ with constants $c_t \ll \max\{\|X_t\|_r, d_t\}$.

(ii) Let $\{V_t\}$ be ϕ-mixing, of size $-a$. If X_t is L_p-NED of size $-b$ on $\{V_t\}$ for $1 \le p \le r$ with constants $\{d_t\}$, $\{X_t,\mathcal{F}_{-\infty}^t\}$ is an L_p-mixingale of size $-\min\{b, a(1 - 1/r)\}$, with constants $c_t \ll \max\{\|X_t\|_r, d_t\}$.

Proof For brevity we write $E_s^t(.) = E(.|\mathcal{F}_s^t)$ where $\mathcal{F}_s^t = \sigma(V_s,...,V_t)$. Also, for $m \le 1$, let $k = [m/2]$, the largest integer not exceeding $m/2$. By the Minkowski inequality,

$$\|E_{-\infty}^{t-m}X_t\|_p \le \|E_{-\infty}^{t-m}(X_t - E_{t-k}^{t+k}X_t)\|_p + \|E_{-\infty}^{t-m}(E_{t-k}^{t+k}X_t)\|_p, \tag{17.15}$$

and we bound each of the right-hand-side terms. First,

$$\|E_{-\infty}^{t-m}(X_t - E_{t-k}^{t+k}X_t)\|_p \le [E(E_{-\infty}^{t-m}|X_t - E_{t-k}^{t+k}X_t|^p)]^{1/p}$$

$$= \|X_t - E_{t-k}^{t+k}X_t\|_p$$
$$\leq d_t \nu_k, \tag{17.16}$$

using the conditional Jensen inequality and law of iterated expectations. Second, $E_{t-k}^{t+k}X_t$ is a finite-lag measurable function of $V_{t-k},...,V_{t+k}$, and hence mixing of the same size as $\{V_t\}$ for finite k. Hence for part (i), we have, from **14.2**,

$$\|E_{-\infty}^{t-m}(E_{t-k}^{t+k}X_t)\|_p \leq 6\alpha_k^{1/p-1/r}\|E_{t-k}^{t+k}X_t\|_r \leq 6\alpha_k^{1/p-1/r}\|X_t\|_r. \tag{17.17}$$

Combining (17.16) and (17.17) into (17.15) yields

$$\|E_{-\infty}^{t-m}X_t\|_p \leq \max\{\|X_t\|_r, d_t\}\zeta_m, \tag{17.18}$$

where $\zeta_m = 6\alpha_k^{1/p-1/r} + \nu_k$. Also, applying **10.28** gives

$$\|X_t - E_{-\infty}^{t+m}X_t\|_p \leq 2\|X_t - E_{t-m}^{t+m}X_t\|_p \leq 2d_t\nu_m \leq 2d_t\zeta_m. \tag{17.19}$$

Since ζ_m is of size $-\min\{b, a(1/p - 1/r)\}$, part (i) of the theorem holds with $c_t \ll \max\{\|X_t\|_r, d_t\}$. The proof of part (ii) is identical except that in place of (17.17) we must substitute, by **14.4**,

$$\|E_{-\infty}^{t-m}(E_{t-k}^{t+k}X_t)\|_p \leq 2\phi_k^{1-1/r}\|E_{t-k}^{t+k}X_t\|_r \leq 2\phi_k^{1-1/r}\|X_t\|_r. \blacksquare \tag{17.20}$$

Let us also state the following corollary for future reference.

17.6 Corollary Let $\{\{X_{nt}\}_{t=-\infty}^{+\infty}\}_{n=1}^{\infty}$ be an L_r-bounded zero-mean array, $r > 1$.

(i) If X_{nt} is L_p-NED of size $-b$ for $1 \leq p < r$ with constants $\{d_{nt}\}$ on an array $\{V_{nt}\}$ which is α-mixing of size $-a$, then $\{X_{nt}, \mathcal{F}_{n,-\infty}^t\}$ is an L_p-mixingale of size $-\min\{b, a(1/p - 1/r)\}$, with respect to constants $c_{nt} \ll \max\{\|X_{nt}\|_r, d_{nt}\}$.

(ii) If X_{nt} is L_p-NED of size $-b$ for $1 \leq p \leq r$ with constants $\{d_{nt}\}$ on an array $\{V_{nt}\}$ which is ϕ-mixing of size $-a$, then $\{X_{nt}, \mathcal{F}_{n,-\infty}^t\}$ is an L_p-mixingale of size $-\min\{b, a(1 - 1/r)\}$, with respect to constants $c_{nt} \ll \max\{\|X_{nt}\|_r, d_{nt}\}$.

Proof Immediate on inserting n before the t subscript wherever required in the last proof. ∎

The replacement of V_t by V_{nt} and $\mathcal{F}_s^t$ by $\mathcal{F}_{ns}^t$ is basically a formality here, since none of our applications will make use of it. The role of the array notation will always be to indicate a transformation by a function of sample size, typically the normalization of the partial sums to zero mean and unit variance, and in these cases $\mathcal{F}_{ns}^t = \mathcal{F}_s^t$ for all n.

Reconsider the AR process of **14.7**. As a special case of **17.3**, it is clear that in that example X_t is L_p-NED of size $-\infty$ on Z_t, an independent process, and hence is a L_p-mixingale of size $-\infty$, for every $p > 0$. There is no need to impose smoothness assumptions on the marginal distributions to obtain these properties, which will usually be all we need to apply limit theory to the process.

These results allow us to fine-tune assumptions on the rates of mixing and near-epoch dependence to ensure specific low-level properties which are needed to prove convergence theorems. Among the most important of these is summability of the sequences of autocovariances. If for example we have a sum of terms, $S_n = \sum_{t=1}^n X_t$, we should often like to know at what rate the variance of this sum grows with n. Assuming $E(X_t) = 0$ with no loss of generality,

$$E(S_n^2) = \sum_{t=1}^{n} E(X_t^2) + 2\sum_{t=1}^{n-1}\left(\sum_{m=1}^{n-t} E(X_t X_{t+m})\right),$$

a sum of n^2 terms. If the sequence $\{X_t\}$ is uncorrelated only the n variances appear and, assuming uniformly bounded moments, $E(S_n^2) = O(n)$. For general dependent processes, summability of the sequences of autocovariances $\{E(X_t X_{t-j}), j \in \mathbb{N}\}$ implies that on a global scale the sequence behaves like an uncorrelated sequence, in the sense that, again, $E(S_n^2) = O(n)$.

For future reference, here is the basic result on absolute summability. To fulfil subsequent requirements, this incorporates two easy generalizations. First we consider a pair (X_t, Y_t), which effectively permits a generalization to random vectors since any element of an autocovariance matrix can be considered. To deal with the leading case discussed above we simply set $Y_t = X_t$. Second, we frame the result in such a way as to accommodate trending moments, imposing L_r-boundedness but not uniform L_r-boundedness. It is also noted that, like previous results, this extends trivially to the array case.

17.7 Theorem Let $\{X_t, Y_t\}$ be a pair of sequences, each $L_{r/(r-1)}$-NED of size -1, with respect to constants $\{d_t^X, d_t^Y\}$ for $r > 2$, on either (i) an α-mixing process of size $-r/(r-2)$, or (ii) a ϕ-mixing process of size $-r/(r-1)$, where $d_t^X \ll \|X_t\|_r$ and $d_t^Y \ll \|Y_t\|_r$. Then the sequences

$$\left\{\frac{|E(X_t Y_{t+m})|}{\|X_t\|_r \|Y_{t+m}\|_r},\ m \in \mathbb{N}\right\} \tag{17.21}$$

are summable for each t. Also, if arrays $\{X_{nt}, Y_{nt}\}$ are similarly $L_{r/(r-1)}$-NED of size -1 with respect to constants $\{d_{nt}^X, d_{nt}^Y\}$ with $d_{nt}^X \ll \|X_{nt}\|_r$ and $d_{nt}^Y \ll \|Y_{nt}\|_r$, the sequences

$$\left\{\frac{|E(X_{nt} Y_{n,t+m})|}{\|X_{nt}\|_r \|Y_{n,t+m}\|_r},\ m \in \mathbb{N}\right\} \tag{17.22}$$

are summable for each n and t. □

Since $r > 2$, the constants appearing in (17.21) and (17.22) are smaller (absolutely) than the autocorrelations, and the latter need not converge at the same rate. But notice too that $r/(r-1) < 2$, so it is always sufficient for the result if the functions are L_2-NED.

Proof As before, let $E_s^t(.) = E(.|\mathcal{F}_s^t)$, and let $k = [m/2]$. By the triangle inequality,

$$|E(Y_{t+m}X_t)| \le |E(Y_{t+m}(X_t - E_{t-k}^{t+k}X_t))| + |E(Y_{t+m}E_{t-k}^{t+k}X_t)|. \tag{17.23}$$

The modulus and Hölder inequalities give

$$|E(Y_{t+m}(X_t - E_{t-k}^{t+k}X_t))| \le \|Y_{t+m}\|_r\|X_t - E_{t-k}^{t+k}X_t\|_{r/(r-1)} \tag{17.24}$$
$$\le \|Y_{t+m}\|_r d_t^X \nu_k^X,$$

where ν_m^X is of size -1. Also, applying **17.5**(i) with $p = r/(r-1)$, $a = r/(r-2)$, and $b = 1$,

$$|E(Y_{t+m}E_{t-k}^{t+k}X_t)| = |E(E_{t-k}^{t+k}Y_{t+m}E_{t-k}^{t+k}X_t)|$$
$$\le \|E_{t-k}^{t+k}Y_{t+m}\|_{r/(r-1)}\|E_{t-k}^{t+k}X_t)\|_r$$
$$\le \|E_{-\infty}^{t+k}Y_{t+m}\|_{r/(r-1)}\|X_t\|_r$$
$$\le \|X_t\|_r c_{t+m}^Y \zeta_k^Y, \tag{17.25}$$

where $c_t^Y \ll \max\{\|Y_t\|_r, d_t^Y\}$ and ζ_m^Y is of size -1. Combining the inequalities in (17.24) and (17.25) in (17.23) gives

$$|E(X_tY_{t+m})| \le \max\{\|Y_{t+m}\|_r d_t^X, \|X_t\|_r c_{t+m}^Y\}(\nu_k^X + \zeta_k^Y)$$
$$\ll \|X_t\|_r\|Y_{t+m}\|_r\xi_m, \tag{17.26}$$

where $\xi_m = (\nu_k^X + \zeta_k^Y)$ is of size -1. This completes the proof of (i). The proof of (ii) is similar using **17.5**(ii) with $p = a = r/(r-1)$ and $b = 1$.

For the array generalization, simply insert the n subscript after every random variable and scaling constant. The argument is identical except that **17.6** is applied in place of **17.5**. ■

17.3 Near-Epoch Dependence and Transformations

Suppose that $(X_{1t},\dots,X_{vt})' = \boldsymbol{X}_t = \boldsymbol{g}(\dots,V_{t-1},V_t,V_{t+1},\dots)$ is a v-vector of L_p-NED functions, and interest focuses on the scalar sequence $\{\phi_t(\boldsymbol{X}_t)\}$, where $\phi_t\colon \mathbb{T} \mapsto \mathbb{R}$, $\mathbb{T} \subseteq \mathbb{R}^v$, is a $\mathcal{B}^v/\mathcal{B}$-measurable function. We may presume that, under certain conditions on the function, $\phi_t(\boldsymbol{X}_t)$ will be near-epoch dependent on $\{V_t\}$ if the elements of $\boldsymbol{X}_t$ are. This setup subsumes the important case $v = 1$, in which the question at issue is the effect of nonlinear transformations on the NED property. The dependence of the functional form $\phi_t(.)$ on t is only occasionally needed, but is worth making explicit.

The first cases we look at are the sums and products of pairs of sequences, for which specialized results exist.

17.8 Theorem Let X_t and Y_t be L_p-NED on $\{V_t\}$ of respective sizes $-\varphi_X$ and $-\varphi_Y$. Then $X_t + Y_t$ is L_p-NED of size $-\min\{\varphi_X,\varphi_Y\}$.

Proof Minkowski's inequality gives

$$\|(X_t + Y_t) - E_{t-m}^{t+m}(X_t + Y_t)\|_p \le \|X_t - E_{t-m}^{t+m}X_t\|_p + \|Y_t - E_{t-m}^{t+m}Y_t\|_p$$
$$\le d_t^X\nu_m^X + d_t^Y\nu_m^Y \le d_t\nu_m, \tag{17.27}$$

where $d_t = \max\{d_t^X, d_t^Y\}$ and $\nu_m = \nu_m^X + \nu_m^Y = O(m^{-\min\{\varphi_X,\varphi_Y\}})$. ■

A variable that is L_q-NED is L_p-NED for $1 \le p \le q$, by the Liapunov inequality, so there is no loss of generality in equating the orders of norm in this result. The same consideration applies to the next theorem.

17.9 Theorem Let X_t and Y_t be L_2-NED on $\{V_t\}$ of respective sizes $-\varphi_X$ and $-\varphi_Y$. Then, X_tY_t is L_1-NED of size $-\min\{\varphi_Y,\varphi_X\}$.

Proof By rearrangement, and applications of the triangle and Cauchy-Schwartz inequalities, we have

$$\begin{aligned}
&E|X_tY_t - E_{t-m}^{t+m}(X_tY_t)| \\
&\quad = E\Big|(X_tY_t - X_tE_{t-m}^{t+m}Y_t) + (X_tE_{t-m}^{t+m}Y_t - (E_{t-m}^{t+m}X_t)(E_{t-m}^{t+m}Y_t)) \\
&\qquad\qquad - E_{t-m}^{t+m}((X_t - E_{t-m}^{t+m}X_t)(Y_t - E_{t-m}^{t+m}Y_t))\Big| \\
&\quad \le \|X_t\|_2\|Y_t - E_{t-m}^{t+m}Y_t\|_2 + \|E_{t-m}^{t+m}Y_t\|_2\|X_t - E_{t-m}^{t+m}X_t\|_2 \\
&\qquad\qquad + \|X_t - E_{t-m}^{t+m}X_t\|_2\|Y_t - E_{t-m}^{t+m}Y_t\|_2 \\
&\quad \le \|X_t\|_2 d_t^Y\nu_m^Y + \|Y_t\|_2 d_t^X\nu_m^X + d_t^Y\nu_m^Y d_t^X\nu_m^X \\
&\quad \le d_t\nu_m,
\end{aligned} \tag{17.28}$$

where $d_t = \max\{\|X_t\|_2 d_t^Y,\ \|Y_t\|_2 d_t^X,\ d_t^Y d_t^X\}$ and

$$\nu_m = \nu_m^Y + \nu_m^X + \nu_m^Y\nu_m^X = O(m^{-\min\{\varphi_X,\varphi_Y\}}). \ ■$$

In both of the last results we would like to be able to set $Y_t = X_{t+j}$ for some finite j. A slight modification of the argument is required here.

17.10 Theorem If X_t is L_p-NED on $\{V_t\}$, so is X_{t+j} for $0 < j < \infty$.

Proof If X_t is L_p-NED, then

$$\begin{aligned}
\|X_{t+j} - E(X_{t+j}|\mathcal{F}_{t-j-m}^{t+j+m})\|_p &\le 2\|X_{t+j} - E(X_{t+j}|\mathcal{F}_{t+j-m}^{t+j+m})\|_p \\
&\le d_t'^X\nu_m,
\end{aligned} \tag{17.29}$$

using **10.28**, where $d_t'^X = 2d_{t+j}^X$. We can write

$$\|X_{t+j} - E(X_{t+j}|\mathcal{F}_{t-m}^{t+m})\|_p \le d_t'^X\nu_m', \tag{17.30}$$

where

$$\nu_m' = \begin{cases} \nu_0, & m \le j \\ \nu_{m-j}, & m > j \end{cases}$$

and ν_m' is of size $-\varphi$ if ν_m is of size $-\varphi$. ■

Putting the last two results together gives the following corollary.

17.11 Corollary If X_t and Y_t are L_2-NED of size $-\varphi_X$ and $-\varphi_Y$, X_tY_{t+k} is L_1-NED of size $-\min\{\varphi_Y,\varphi_X\}$. □

By considering $Z_t = X_{t-[k/2]}Y_{t+k-[k/2]}$, the L_1-NED numbers can be given here as

$$\nu'_m = \begin{cases} \nu_0, & m \le [k/2]+1 \\ \nu_{m-[k/2]-1}, & m > [k/2]+1 \end{cases}$$

where $\nu_m = \nu^Y_m + \nu^X_m + \nu^Y_m\nu^X_m$, and the constants are $4d^X_{t-[k/2]}d^Y_{t+k-[k/2]}$, assuming that d^X_t and d^Y_t are not smaller than the corresponding L_2 norms.

All these results extend to the array case as before, by simply including the extra subscript throughout. Corollary **17.11** should be compared with **17.7**, and care taken not to confuse the two. In the former we have k fixed and finite, whereas the latter result deals with the case as $m \to \infty$. The two theorems naturally complement each other in applying truncation arguments to infinite sums of products. Applications will arise in subsequent chapters.

More general classes of function can be treated under an assumption of continuity, but in this case we can deal only with cases where $\phi_t(X_t)$ is L_2-NED. Let

$$\phi(x)\colon \mathbb{T} \mapsto \mathbb{R},\ \mathbb{T} \subseteq \mathbb{R}^\nu$$

be a function of ν real variables, and use the taxicab metric on $\mathbb{R}^\nu$,

$$\rho(x^1,x^2) = \sum_{i=1}^{\nu} |x^1_i - x^2_i|, \tag{17.31}$$

to measure the distance between points x^1 and x^2. We consider a set of results that impose restrictions of differing severity on the types of function allowed, but offer a trade-off with the severity of the moment restrictions. To begin with, impose the uniform Lipschitz condition,

$$|\phi_t(X^1) - \phi_t(X^2)| \le B_t\rho(X^1,X^2) \text{ a.s.}, \tag{17.32}$$

where B_t is a finite constant.

17.12 Theorem Let X_{it} be L_2-NED of size $-a$ on $\{V_t\}$ for $i = 1,\dots,\nu$, with constants d_{it}. If (17.32) holds, $\{\phi_t(X_t)\}$ is also L_2-NED on $\{V_t\}$ of size $-a$, with constants a finite multiple of $\max_i\{d_{it}\}$.

Proof Let $\hat{\phi}_t$ denote a $\mathcal{F}^{t+m}_{t-m}$-measurable approximation to $\phi_t(X_t)$. Then

$$\|\phi_t(X_t) - E^{t+m}_{t-m}\phi_t(X_t)\|_2 \le \|\phi_t(X_t) - \hat{\phi}_t\|_2 \tag{17.33}$$

by **10.12**. Since $\phi_t(E^{t+m}_{t-m}X_t)$ is an $\mathcal{F}^{t+m}_{t-m}$-measurable random variable, (17.33) holds for this choice of $\hat{\phi}_t$, and by Minkowski's inequality,

$$\begin{aligned}\|\phi_t(X_t) - E^{t+m}_{t-m}\phi_t(X_t)\|_2 &\le B_t\|\rho(X_t,E^{t+m}_{t-m}X_t)\|_2 \\ &\le B_t\sum_{i=1}^{\nu}\|X_{it} - E^{t+m}_{t-m}X_{it}\|_2 \\ &\le B_t\sum_{i=1}^{\nu} d_{it}\nu_{im}\end{aligned}$$

$$\leq d_t \nu_m, \tag{17.34}$$

where $d_t = vB_t\max_i\{d_{it}\}$ and $\nu_m = v^{-1}\sum_{i=1}^{v}\nu_{im}$, the latter sequence being of size $-a$ by assumption. ■

If we can assume only that the X_{it} are L_p-NED on V_t for some $p \in [1,2)$, this argument fails. There is a way to get the result, however, if the functions ϕ_t are bounded almost surely.

17.13 Theorem Let X_{it} be L_p-NED of size $-a$ on $\{V_t\}$, for $1 \leq p \leq 2$, with constants d_{it}, $i = 1,\dots,v$. Suppose that, for each t, $|\phi_t(X_t)| \leq M < \infty$ a.s., and also that

$$|\phi_t(X^1) - \phi_t(X^2)| \leq \min\{B_t\rho(X^1, X^2),\ 2M\} \text{ a.s.}, \tag{17.35}$$

where $B_t < \infty$. Then $\{\phi_t(X_t)\}$ is L_2-NED on $\{V_t\}$ of size $-ap/2$, with constants a finite multiple of $\max_i\{d_{it}^{p/2}\}$.

Proof For brevity, write $\phi_t^i = \phi_t(X^i)$, and let $Z = B_t\rho(X^1, X^2)/2M$, so that $|\phi_t^1 - \phi_t^2| \leq 2M\min\{Z,1\}$. Then

$$
\begin{aligned}
E(\phi_t^1 - \phi_t^2)^2 &= \int_{\{Z\leq 1\}}(\phi_t^1 - \phi_t^2)^2 dP + \int_{\{Z>1\}}(\phi_t^1 - \phi_t^2)^2 dP \\
&\leq (2M)^2\left(\int_{\{Z\leq 1\}} Z^2 dP + \int_{\{Z>1\}} dP\right) \\
&\leq (2M)^2 E(Z^p) \\
&= B_{1t}^2 E(\rho(X^1, X^2)^p),
\end{aligned} \tag{17.36}
$$

where $B_{1t} = B_t^{p/2}(2M)^{1-p/2}$. Combining (17.33) with (17.36), we can write

$$
\begin{aligned}
\|\phi_t(X_t) - E_{t-m}^{t+m}\phi_t(X_t)\|_2 &\leq B_{1t}\|\rho(X_t, E_{t-m}^{t+m}X_t)\|_p^{p/2} \\
&\leq B_{1t}\left(\sum_{i=1}^{v}\|X_{it} - E_{t-m}^{t+m}X_{it}\|_p\right)^{p/2} \\
&\leq B_{1t}\left(\sum_{i=1}^{v} d_{it}\nu_{im}\right)^{p/2} \\
&\leq d_t\nu_m,
\end{aligned} \tag{17.37}
$$

where $d_t = B_{1t}v^{p/2}\max_i\{d_{it}^{p/2}\}$ and $\nu_m = (v^{-1}\sum_{i=1}^{v}\nu_{im})^{p/2}$, which is of size $-ap/2$ by assumption. ■

An important example of this case (with $v = 1$) is the truncation of X_t, although this must be defined as a continuous transformation.

17.14 Example For $M > 0$ let

$$\phi(x) = \begin{cases} x, & |x| \le M \\ M, & x > M \\ -M, & x < -M \end{cases} \tag{17.38}$$

or, equivalently, $\phi(x) = x1_{\{|x|\le M\}} + M(x/|x|)1_{\{|x|>M\}}$. In this case

$$|\phi(X^1) - \phi(X^2)| \le |X^1 - X^2|,$$

so set $B = 1$, and **17.13** can be used to show that $\{\phi(X_t)\}$ is L_2-NED if $\{X_t\}$ is L_p-NED. The more conventional truncation,

$$X_t 1_{\{|x|\le M\}} = \begin{cases} X_t, & |X_t| \le M \\ 0, & \text{otherwise,} \end{cases} \tag{17.39}$$

cannot be shown to be near-epoch dependent by this approach, because of the lack of continuity. □

A further variation on **17.12** is to relax the Lipschitz condition (17.32) by letting the scale factor B be a possibly unbounded function of the random variables. Assume

$$|\phi_t(X^1) - \phi_t(X^2)| \le B_t(X^1, X^2)\rho(X^1, X^2) \text{ a.s.,} \tag{17.40}$$

where, for each t,

$$B_t(X^1, X^2)\colon \mathbb{T}\times\mathbb{T} \mapsto \mathbb{R}^+ \tag{17.41}$$

is a non-negative, $\mathcal{B}^{2\nu}/\mathcal{B}$-measurable function. To deal with this case requires a lemma due to Gallant and White (1988).

17.15 Lemma Let B and ρ be non-negative r.v.s and assume $\|\rho\|_q < \infty$, $\|B\|_{q/(q-1)} < \infty$, and $\|B\rho\|_r < \infty$, for $q \ge 1$, and $r > 2$. Then

$$\|B\rho\|_2 \le 2(\|\rho\|_q^{r-2}\|B\|_{q/(q-1)}^{r-2}\|B\rho\|_r^r)^{1/2(r-1)}. \tag{17.42}$$

Proof Define

$$C = (\|\rho\|_q\|B\|_{q/(q-1)}\|B\rho\|_r^{-r})^{1/(1-r)}, \tag{17.43}$$

and let $B_1 = 1_{\{B\rho\le C\}}B$. Then by the Minkowski inequality,

$$\|B\rho\|_2 \le \|B_1\rho\|_2 + \|(B - B_1)\rho\|_2. \tag{17.44}$$

The right-hand-side terms are bounded by the same quantity. First,

$$\begin{aligned} \|B_1\rho\|_2 &= \left(\int_{B\rho\le C}(B\rho)^2 dP\right)^{1/2} \\ &\le C^{1/2}\left(\int B\rho\, dP\right)^{1/2} \\ &\le C^{1/2}(\|\rho\|_q\|B\|_{q/(q-1)})^{1/2}, \end{aligned} \tag{17.45}$$

applying the Hölder inequality. Second,

$$\|(B-B_1)\rho\|_2 = \left(\int_{B\rho>C}(B\rho)^2dP\right)^{1/2}$$

$$\leq C^{1-r/2}\left(\int_{B\rho>C}(B\rho)^r dP\right)^{1/2}$$

$$\leq C^{1-r/2}\|B\rho\|_r^{r/2} \tag{17.46}$$

where the first inequality follows from $r > 2$ and $B\rho/C > 1$. Substituting for C in (17.45) and (17.46) and applying (17.44) yields the result. ∎

The general result is then as follows.

17.16 Theorem Let $\{X_t\}$ be a ν-dimensioned random sequence, of which each element is L_2-NED of size $-a$ on $\{V_t\}$, and suppose that $\phi_t(X_t)$ is L_2-bounded. Suppose further that for $1 \leq q \leq 2$,

$$\|\rho(X_t,E_{t-m}^{t+m}X_t)\|_q < \infty,$$

$$\|B_t(X_t,E_{t-m}^{t+m}X_t)\|_{q/(q-1)} < \infty,$$

and for $r > 2$,

$$\|B_t(X_t,E_{t-m}^{t+m}X_t)\rho(X_t,E_{t-m}^{t+m}X_t)\|_r < \infty.$$

Then $\{\phi_t(X_t)\}$ is L_2-NED on $\{V_t\}$ of size $-a(r-2)/2(r-1)$.

Proof For ease of notation, write ρ for $\rho(X_t,E_{t-m}^{t+m}X_t)$ and B for $B_t(X_t,E_{t-m}^{t+m}X_t)$. As in the previous two theorems, the basic inequality (17.33) is applied, but now we have

$$\|\phi(X_t)-E_{t-m}^{t+m}\phi(X_t)\|_2 \leq \|\phi(X_t)-\phi(E_{t-m}^{t+m}X_t)\|_2$$

$$\leq \|B\rho\|_2$$

$$\leq 2\|\rho\|_q^{(r-2)/2(r-1)}\|B\|_{q/(q-1)}^{(r-2)/2(r-1)}\|B\rho\|_r^{r/2(r-1)}, \tag{17.47}$$

where the last step is by **17.15**. For $q \leq 2$,

$$\|\rho\|_q \leq \|\rho\|_2 \leq \sum_{i=1}^{\nu}\|X_{it}-E_{t-m}^{t+m}X_{it}\|_2 \leq \sum_{i=1}^{\nu}d_{it}\nu_{im} = d_t\nu_m, \tag{17.48}$$

where $d_t = \nu\max_i\{d_{it}\}$ and $\nu_m = \nu^{-1}\sum_{i=1}^{\nu}\nu_{im}$, which is of size $-a$ by assumption. Hence, under the stated assumptions,

$$\|\phi_t(X_t)-E_{t-m}^{t+m}\phi_t(X_t)\|_2 \leq d_t'\nu_m^{(r-2)/2(r-1)}, \tag{17.49}$$

where $d_t' = \|B\|_{q/(q-1)}^{(r-2)/2(r-1)}\|B\rho\|_r^{r/2(r-1)}d_t$. ∎

Observe the important role of **17.15** in tightening this result. Without it, the best we could do in (17.47) would be to apply Hölder's inequality directly, to obtain

$$\|B\rho\|_2 \le \|\rho\|_{2q}\|B\|_{2q/(q-1)},\ q \ge 1. \tag{17.50}$$

The minimum requirement for this inequality to be useful is that B is bounded almost surely permitting the choice $q = 1$, which is merely the case covered by **17.12** with the constant scale factors set to ess sup $B_t(X^1, X^2)$.

The following application of this theorem may be contrasted with **17.9**. The moment conditions have to be strengthened by a factor of at least 2 to ensure that the product of L_2-NED functions is also L_2-NED, rather than just L_1-NED. There is also a penalty in terms of the L_2-NED size which does not occur in the other case.

17.17 Example Let $\boldsymbol{X}_t = (X_t, Y_t)$ and $\phi(\boldsymbol{X}_t) = X_tY_t$. Assume that $\|X_t\|_{2r} < \infty$ and $\|Y_t\|_{2r} < \infty$ for $r > 2$, and that X_t and Y_t are L_2-NED on $\{\boldsymbol{V}_t\}$ of size $-a$. Then

$$\begin{aligned} |X_t^1Y_t^1 - X_t^2Y_t^2| &\le |X_t^1|\,|Y_t^1 - Y_t^2| + |X_t^1 - X_t^2|\,|Y_t^2| \\ &\le (|X_t^1| + |Y_t^2|)(|Y_t^1 - Y_t^2| + |X_t^1 - X_t^2|) \\ &= B(\boldsymbol{X}_t^1, \boldsymbol{X}_t^2)\rho(\boldsymbol{X}_t^1, \boldsymbol{X}_t^2), \end{aligned} \tag{17.51}$$

defining B and ρ. For any q in the range [4/3,4], the assumptions imply

$$\|B(\boldsymbol{X}_t^1, \boldsymbol{X}_t^2)\|_{q/(q-1)} \le \|X_t^1\|_{q/(q-1)} + \|Y_t^2\|_{q/(q-1)} < \infty, \tag{17.52}$$

$$\|\rho(\boldsymbol{X}_t^1, \boldsymbol{X}_t^2)\|_q \le \|Y_t^1\|_q + \|Y_t^2\|_q + \|X_t^1\|_q + \|X_t^2\|_q < \infty, \tag{17.53}$$

and

$$\begin{aligned} \|B(\boldsymbol{X}_t^1, \boldsymbol{X}_t^2)\rho(\boldsymbol{X}_t^1, \boldsymbol{X}_t^2)\|_r \le\ & \|X_t^1\|_{2r}\|Y_t^1\|_{2r} + \|X_t^1\|_{2r}\|Y_t^2\|_{2r} + \|X_t^1\|_{2r}^2 \\ & + \|X_t^1\|_{2r}\|X_t^2\|_{2r} + \|Y_t^2\|_{2r}\|Y_t^1\|_{2r} + \|Y_t^2\|_{2r}^2 \\ & + \|Y_t^2\|_{2r}\|X_t^1\|_{2r} + \|Y_t^2\|_{2r}\|X_t^2\|_{2r} \\ <\ & \infty. \end{aligned} \tag{17.54}$$

Putting $\boldsymbol{X}_t^1 = \boldsymbol{X}_t$ and $\boldsymbol{X}_t^2 = E_{t-m}^{t+m}\boldsymbol{X}_t$, the conditions of **17.16** are satisfied for q in the range [4/3,2] and X_tY_t is L_2-NED of size $-a(r-2)/2(r-1)$. □

17.4 Approximability

In §17.2 we showed that L_p-NED functions of mixing processes were mixingales, and most of the subsequent applications will exploit this fact. Another way to look at the L_p-NED property is in terms of the existence of a finite lag approximation to the process. The conditional mean $E(X_t|\mathcal{F}_{t-m}^{t+m})$ can be thought of as a function of the variables $\boldsymbol{V}_{t-m},\dots,\boldsymbol{V}_{t+m}$, and if $\{\boldsymbol{V}_t\}$ is a mixing sequence so is $\{E(X_t|\mathcal{F}_{t-m}^{t+m})\}$, by **14.1**. One approach to proving limit theorems is to team a limit theorem for mixing processes with a proof that the difference between the actual sequence and its approximating sequence can be neglected. This is an alternative way to overcome the problem that lag functions of mixing processes need not be mixing.

But once this idea occurs to us, it is clear that the conditional mean might not be the only function to possess the desired approximability property. More generally, we might introduce a definition of the following sort. Letting $\boldsymbol{V}_t$ be $l\times 1$, we shall think of h_t^m: $\mathbb{R}^{l(2m+1)} \mapsto \mathbb{R}$ as a $\mathcal{F}_{t-m}^{t+m}/\mathcal{B}$-measurable function, where $\mathcal{F}_{t-m}^{t+m} = \sigma(\boldsymbol{V}_{t-m},\dots,\boldsymbol{V}_{t+m})$.

17.18 Definition The sequence $\{X_t\}$ will be called *L_p-approximable* ($p > 0$) on the sequence $\{\boldsymbol{V}_t\}$ if for each $m \in \mathbb{N}$ there exists a sequence $\{h_t^m\}$ of $\mathcal{F}_{t-m}^{t+m}$-measurable random variables, and

$$\|X_t - h_t^m\|_p \le d_t\nu_m, \tag{17.55}$$

where $\{d_t\}$ is a non-negative constant sequence, and $\nu_m \to 0$ as $m \to \infty$. $\{X_t\}$ will also be said to be *approximable in probability* (or L_0-approximable) on $\{\boldsymbol{V}_t\}$ if there exist $\{h_t^m\}$, $\{d_t\}$, and $\{\nu_m\}$ as above such that, for every $\delta > 0$,

$$P(|X_t - h_t^m| > d_t\delta) \le \nu_m. \ \square \tag{17.56}$$

The usual size terminology can be applied here. There is also the usual extension to arrays, by inclusion of the additional subscript wherever appropriate.

If a sequence is L_p-approximable for $p > 0$, then by the Markov inequality

$$P(|X_t - h_t^m| > d_t\delta) \le (d_t\delta)^{-p}\|X_t - h_t^m\|_p^p \le \nu_m', \tag{17.57}$$

where $\nu_m' = \delta^{-p}\nu_m^p$; hence an L_p-approximable process is also L_0-approximable. An L_p-NED sequence is L_p-approximable, although only in the case $p = 2$ are we able to claim (from **10.12**) that $E(X_t|\mathcal{F}_{t-m}^{t+m})$ is the best L_p-approximator in the sense that the p-norms in (17.55) are smaller than for any alternative choice of h_t^m.

17.19 Example Consider the linear process of **17.3**. The function

$$h_t^m = \sum_{j=-m}^{m} \theta_j V_{t-j} \tag{17.58}$$

is different from $E(X_t|\mathcal{F}_{t-m}^{t+m})$ unless $\{V_t\}$ is an independent process, but is also an L_p-approximator for X_t since

$$\|X_t - h_t^m\|_p = \left\| \sum_{j=m+1}^{\infty} (\theta_j V_{t-j} + \theta_{-j}V_{t+j}) \right\|_p \le d_t\nu_m, \tag{17.59}$$

where $\nu_m = \sum_{j=m+1}^{\infty}(|\theta_j| + |\theta_{-j}|)$ and $d_t = \sup_t\|V_t\|_p$. $\square$

17.20 Example In **17.4**, the functions g_t^m are L_p-approximators for X_t, of infinite size, whenever $\sup_{s\le t}\|F_sV_s\|_p < \infty$. $\square$

One reason why approximability might have advantages over the L_p-NED property is the ease of handling transformations. As we found above, transferring the L_p-NED property to transformations of the original functions can present difficulties, and impose undesirable moment restrictions. With approximability, these difficulties can be largely overcome. The first step is to show that, subject to L_r-boundedness, a sequence that is approximable in probability is also L_p-approximable for $p < r$, and moreover, that the approximator functions can be bounded for each finite m. The following is adapted from Pötscher and Prucha (1991a).

17.21 Theorem Suppose $\{X_t\}$ is L_r-bounded, $r > 1$, and L_0-approximable by h_t^m. Then for $0 < p < r$ it is L_p-approximable by $\tilde{h}_t^m = h_t^m 1_{\{|h_t^m| \le d_t M_m\}}$, where $M_m < \infty$ for each $m \in \mathbb{N}$.

Proof Since h_t^m is an L_0-approximator of X_t, we may choose a positive sequence $\{\delta_m\}$ such that $\delta_m \to 0$ and yet $P(|X_t - h_t^m| > d_t\delta_m) \le \nu_m \to 0$ as $m \to \infty$. Also choose a sequence of numbers $\{M_m\}$ having the properties $M_m \to \infty$, but $M_m\nu_m \to 0$. For example, $M_m = \nu_m^{-1/2}$ would serve. There is no loss of generality in assuming $\sup_m M_m^{-1} \le 1$. By Minkowski's inequality we are able to write

$$\|X_t - \tilde{h}_t^m\|_p \le A_{tm}^1 + A_{tm}^2 + A_{tm}^3, \tag{17.60}$$

where

$$A_{tm}^1 = \|(X_t - \tilde{h}_t^m)1_{\{|X_t - \tilde{h}_t^m| > d_t\delta_m\}}\|_p,$$
$$A_{tm}^2 = \|(X_t - \tilde{h}_t^m)1_{\{|X_t - \tilde{h}_t^m| \le d_t\delta_m, |h_t| > d_tM_m\}}\|_p,$$
$$A_{tm}^3 = \|(X_t - \tilde{h}_t^m)1_{\{|X_t - \tilde{h}_t^m| \le d_t\delta_m, |h_t^m| \le d_tM_m\}}\|_p.$$

Hölder's inequality implies that

$$\|XY\|_p \le \|X\|_{pq}\|Y\|_{pq/(q-1)},\ q > 1. \tag{17.61}$$

Choose $q = r/p$ and apply (17.61) to A_{mt}^i for $i = 1,2,3$. Noting that $\|X_t - \tilde{h}_t^m\|_r \le \|X_t\|_r + d_tM_m$, again by Minkowski's inequality, and that $\|1_E\|_s^s = P(E)$, we obtain the following inequalities. First,

$$\begin{aligned} A_{tm}^1 &\le \|X_t - \tilde{h}_t^m\|_r P(|X_t - \tilde{h}_t^m| > d_t\delta_m) \\ &\le d_t(\|X_t/d_t\|_r M_m^{-1} + 1)M_m\nu_m. \end{aligned} \tag{17.62}$$

Second, observe that

$$\{|X_t - \tilde{h}_t^m| \le d_t\delta_m,\ |\tilde{h}_t^m| > d_tM_m\} \subseteq \{|X_t| > d_t(M_m - \delta_m)\}$$

and hence, when $M_m > \delta_m$,

$$\begin{aligned} P(|X_t - \tilde{h}_t^m| \le d_t\delta_m,\ |\tilde{h}_t^m| > d_tM_m) &\le P(|X_t| > d_t(M_m - \delta_m)) \\ &\le \|X_t\|_r^r d_t^{-r}(M_m - \delta_m)^{-r} \end{aligned} \tag{17.63}$$

by the Markov inequality, so that

$$\begin{aligned} A_{tm}^2 &\le \|X_t - \tilde{h}_t^m\|_r P(|X_t - \tilde{h}_t^m| \le d_t\delta_m,\ |\tilde{h}_t^m| > d_tM_m) \\ &\le (\|X_t\|_r + d_tM_m)\|X_t\|_r^r d_t^{-r}(M_m - \delta_m)^{-r} \\ &\le d_t(\|X_t/d_t\|_r^{r+1} + \|X_t/d_t\|_r^r)M_m(M_m - \delta_m)^{-r}. \end{aligned} \tag{17.64}$$

(The final inequality is from replacing M_m^{-1} by 1.) And lastly,

$$A_{tm}^3 \le d_t\delta_m \tag{17.65}$$

in view of the fact that $\tilde{h}_t^m = h_t^m$ on the set $\{|\tilde{h}_t^m| \le d_tM_m\}$. We have therefore established that

$$\|X_t - \tilde{h}_t^m\|_p \le d_t'\nu_m', \tag{17.66}$$

where

$$\nu_m' = M_m\nu_m + M_m(M_m - \delta_m)^{-r} + \delta_m \tag{17.67}$$

and $\nu_m' \to 0$ by assumption, since $r > 1$, and

$$d_t' = 2d_t\max\{\|X_t/d_t\|_r,\ \|X_t/d_t\|_r^{r+1},\ \|X_t/d_t\|_r^r,\ 1\}. \ \blacksquare \tag{17.68}$$

If L_0-approximability is satisfied with $d_t \ll \|X_t\|_r$, then $d_t' = 2d_t$.

The value of this result is that we have only to show that the transformation of an L_0-approximable variable is also L_0-approximable, and establish the existence of the requisite moments, to preserve L_p-approximability under the transformation. Consider the Lipschitz condition specified in (17.40). The conditions that need to be imposed on $B(.,.)$ are notably weaker than those in **17.16** for the L_p-NED case.

17.22 Theorem Let $\boldsymbol{h}_t^m = (h_{1t}^m,\dots,h_{\nu t}^m)$ be the L_0-approximator of $\boldsymbol{X}_t = (X_{1t},\dots,X_{\nu t})'$ of size $-\varphi$. If $\phi_t\colon \mathbb{R}^\nu \mapsto \mathbb{R}$ satisfies (17.40), and $E(B_t(\boldsymbol{X}_t,\boldsymbol{h}_t^m)^\varepsilon) < \infty$ for $\varepsilon > 0$, then $\phi_t(\boldsymbol{X}_t)$ is L_0-approximable of size $-\varphi$.

Proof Fix $\delta > 0$ and $M > 0$, and define $d_t = \sum_{i=1}^\nu d_{it}$. The Markov inequality gives

$$\begin{aligned} P(|\phi_t(\boldsymbol{X}_t) - \phi_t(\boldsymbol{h}_t^m)| > d_t\delta) &\le P(B_t(\boldsymbol{X}_t,\boldsymbol{h}_t^m)\rho(\boldsymbol{X}_t,\boldsymbol{h}_t^m) > d_t\delta,\ B_t(\boldsymbol{X}_t,\boldsymbol{h}_t^m) > M) \\ &\quad + P(B_t(\boldsymbol{X}_t,\boldsymbol{h}_t^m)\rho(\boldsymbol{X}_t,\boldsymbol{h}_t^m) > d_t\delta,\ B_t(\boldsymbol{X}_t,\boldsymbol{h}_t^m) \le M) \\ &\le E(B_t(\boldsymbol{X}_t,\boldsymbol{h}_t^m)^\varepsilon)/M^\varepsilon + P(\rho(\boldsymbol{X}_t,\boldsymbol{h}_t^m) > d_t\delta/M). \end{aligned} \tag{17.69}$$

Since M is arbitrary the first term on the majorant side can be made as small as desired. The proof is completed by noting that

$$\begin{aligned} P(\rho(\boldsymbol{X}_t,\boldsymbol{h}_t^m) > d_t\delta/M) &= P\left(\sum_{i=1}^\nu |X_{it} - h_{it}^m| > d_t\delta/M\right) \\ &\le P\left(\bigcup_{i=1}^\nu \{|X_{it} - h_{it}^m| > d_{it}\delta/M\}\right) \\ &\le \sum_{i=1}^\nu P(|X_{it} - h_{it}^m| > d_{it}\delta/M) \\ &\le \sum_{i=1}^\nu \nu_{im} \to 0 \text{ as } m \to \infty. \ \blacksquare \end{aligned} \tag{17.70}$$

It might seem as if teaming **17.22** with **17.21** would allow us to show that, given an L_r-bounded, L_2-NED sequence, $r > 2$, which is accordingly L_2-approximable and hence L_0-approximable, any transformation satisfying the conditions of **17.22** is L_2-approximable, and therefore also L_2-NED, by **10.12**. The catch with circumventing the moment restrictions of **17.16** in this manner is that it is not possible to specify the L_2-NED size of the transformed sequence. In (17.67), one cannot put a bound on the rate at which the sequence $\{\delta_m\}$ may converge without specifying the distributions of the X_{it} in greater detail. However, if it *is* possible to do this in a given application, we have here an alternative route to dealing with transformations.

Pötscher and Prucha (1991a), to whom the concepts of this section are due, define approximability in a slightly different way, in terms of the convergence of the Cesàro-sums of the p-norms or probabilities. These authors say that X_t is L_p-approximable ($p > 0$) if

$$\limsup_{n\to\infty} \frac{1}{n}\sum_{t=1}^{n} \|X_t - h_t^m\|_p \to 0 \text{ as } m \to \infty, \tag{17.71}$$

and is L_0-approximable if, for every $\delta > 0$,

$$\limsup_{n\to\infty} \frac{1}{n}\sum_{t=1}^{n} P(|X_t - h_t^m| > \delta) \to 0 \text{ as } m \to \infty. \tag{17.72}$$

It is clear that we might choose to define near-epoch dependence and the mixingale property in an analogous manner, leading to a whole class of alternative convergence results. Comparing these alternatives, it turns out that neither definition dominates, each permitting a form of behaviour by the sequences which is ruled out by the other. If (17.55) holds, we may write

$$\limsup_{n\to\infty} \frac{1}{n}\sum_{t=1}^{n} \|X_t - h_t^m\|_p \le \limsup_{n\to\infty}\left(\frac{1}{n}\sum_{t=1}^{n} d_t\right)\nu_m \to 0 \tag{17.73}$$

so long as the limsup on the majorant side is bounded. On the other hand, if (17.71) holds we may define

$$\nu_m = \limsup_{n\to\infty} \frac{1}{n}\sum_{t=1}^{n} \|X_t - h_t^m\|_p, \tag{17.74}$$

and then $d_t = \sup_m\{\|X_t - h_t^m\|_p/\nu_m\}$ will satisfy **17.18** *so long as* it is finite for finite t. Evidently, (17.71) permits the existence of a set of sequence coordinates for which the p-norms fail to converge to 0 with m, so long as these are ultimately negligible, accumulating at a rate strictly less than n as n increases. On the other hand, (17.55) permits trending moments, with for example $d_t = O(t^\lambda)$, $\lambda > 0$, which would contradict (17.71).

Similarly, for $\delta_m > 0$, and $\nu_m > 0$, define d_{tm} by the relation

$$P(|X_t - h_t^m| > d_{tm}\delta_m) = \nu_m, \tag{17.75}$$

and then, allowing $\nu_m \to 0$ and $\delta_m \to 0$, define $d_t = \sup_m d_{tm}$. (17.56) is satisfied if $d_t < \infty$ for each finite t; this latter condition need not hold under (17.72). On the other hand, (17.72) could fail in cases where, for *fixed* δ and every m, $P(|X_t - h_t^m| > \delta)$ is tending to unity as $t \to \infty$.

IV

THE LAW OF LARGE NUMBERS

18
Stochastic Convergence

18.1 Almost Sure Convergence

Almost sure convergence was defined formally in §12.2. Sometimes the condition is stated in the form

$$P\left(\limsup_{n\to\infty}|X_n - X| > \varepsilon\right) = 0, \text{ for all } \varepsilon > 0. \tag{18.1}$$

Yet another way to express the same idea is to say that $P(C) = 1$ where, for each $\omega \in C$ and any $\varepsilon > 0$, $|X_n(\omega) - X(\omega)| > \varepsilon$ at most a finite number of times as we pass down the sequence. This is also written as

$$P(|X_n - X| > \varepsilon, \text{ i.o.}) = 0, \text{ all } \varepsilon > 0, \tag{18.2}$$

where i.o. stands for 'infinitely often'.

Note that the probability in (18.2) is assigned to an attribute of the whole sequence, not to a particular n. One way to grasp the 'infinitely often' idea is to consider the event $\bigcup_{n=m}^{\infty}\{|X_n - X| > \varepsilon\}$; in words, 'the event that has occurred whenever $\{|X_n - X| > \varepsilon\}$ occurs for at least one n beyond a given point m in the sequence'. If this event occurs for every m, no matter how large, $\{|X_n - X| > \varepsilon\}$ occurs infinitely often. In other words,

$$\begin{aligned}\{|X_n - X| > \varepsilon, \text{ i.o.}\} &= \bigcap_{m=1}^{\infty}\bigcup_{n=m}^{\infty}\{|X_n - X| > \varepsilon\} \\ &= \limsup_{n\to\infty}\{|X_n - X| > \varepsilon\}.\end{aligned} \tag{18.3}$$

Useful facts about this set and its complement are contained in the following lemma.

18.1 Lemma Let $\{E_n \in \mathcal{F}\}_1^{\infty}$ be an arbitrary sequence. Then

(i) $P\left(\limsup\limits_{n\to\infty} E_n\right) = \lim\limits_{n\to\infty} P\left(\bigcup\limits_{m=n}^{\infty} E_m\right)$.

(ii) $P\left(\liminf\limits_{n\to\infty} E_n\right) = \lim\limits_{n\to\infty} P\left(\bigcap\limits_{m=n}^{\infty} E_m\right)$.

Proof The sequence $\{\bigcup_{n=m}^{\infty} E_n\}_{m=1}^{\infty}$ is decreasing monotonically to $\limsup_n E_n$. Part (i) therefore follows by **3.4**. Part (ii) follows in exactly the same way, since the sequence $\{\bigcap_{n=m}^{\infty}E_n\}_{m=1}^{\infty}$ increases monotonically to liminf E_n. ∎

A fundamental tool in proofs of a.s. convergence is the *Borel-Cantelli lemma*. This has two parts, the 'convergence' part and the 'divergence' part. The former is the most useful, since it yields a very general sufficient condition for convergence, whereas the second part, which generates a necessary condition for convergence, requires independence of the sequence.

18.2 Borel-Cantelli lemma

(i) For an arbitrary sequence of events $\{E_n \in \mathcal{F}\}_1^{\infty}$,

$$\sum_{n=1}^{\infty} P(E_n) < \infty \;\Rightarrow\; P(E_n, \text{ i.o.}) = 0. \tag{18.4}$$

(ii) For a sequence $\{E_n \in \mathcal{F}\}_1^{\infty}$ of *independent* events,

$$\sum_{n=1}^{\infty} P(E_n) = \infty \;\Rightarrow\; P(E_n \text{ i.o.}) = 1. \tag{18.5}$$

Proof By countable subadditivity,

$$P\left(\bigcup_{n=m}^{\infty} E_n\right) \le \sum_{n=m}^{\infty} P(E_n). \tag{18.6}$$

The premise in (18.4) is that the majorant side of (18.6) is finite for $m = 1$. This implies $\sum_{n=m}^{\infty} P(E_n) \to 0$ as $m \to \infty$ (by **2.25**), which further implies

$$\lim_{m\to\infty} P\left(\bigcup_{n=m}^{\infty} E_n\right) = 0. \tag{18.7}$$

Part (i) now follows by part (i) of **18.1**.

To prove (ii), note by **7.5** that the collection $\{E_n^c \in \mathcal{F}\}_1^{\infty}$ is independent; hence for any $m > 0$, and $m' > m$,

$$P\left(\bigcap_{n=m}^{m'} E_n^c\right) = \prod_{n=m}^{m'} P(E_n^c) = \prod_{n=m}^{m'} (1 - P(E_n))$$

$$\le \exp\left\{-\sum_{n=m}^{m'} P(E_n)\right\} \to 0 \text{ as } m' \to \infty \tag{18.8}$$

by hypothesis, since $e^{-x} \ge 1 - x$. (18.8) holds for all m, so

$$P(\liminf E_n^c) = \lim_{m\to\infty} P\left(\bigcap_{n=m}^{\infty} E_n^c\right) = 0, \tag{18.9}$$

by **18.1**(ii). Hence,

$$P(E_n \text{ i.o.}) = P(\limsup E_n) = 1 - P(\liminf E_n^c) = 1. \;\blacksquare \tag{18.10}$$

To appreciate the role of this result (the convergence part) in showing a.s. convergence, consider the particular case

$$E_n = \{\omega\colon\ |X_n(\omega) - X(\omega)| > \varepsilon\}.$$

If $\sum_{n=1}^{\infty} P(E_n) < \infty$, the condition $P(E_n) > 0$ can hold for at most a finite number of n. The lemma shows that $P(E_n \text{ i.o.})$ has to be zero to avoid a contradiction.

Yet another way to characterize a.s. convergence is suggested by the following theorem.

18.3 Theorem $\{X_n\}$ converges a.s. to X if and only if for all $\varepsilon > 0$

$$\lim_{m\to\infty} P\left(\sup_{n\geq m}|X_n - X| \leq \varepsilon\right) = 1. \tag{18.11}$$

Proof Let

$$A_m(\varepsilon) = \bigcap_{n=m}^{\infty}\{\omega\colon\ |X_n(\omega) - X(\omega)| \leq \varepsilon\} \in \mathcal{F}, \tag{18.12}$$

and then (18.11) can be written in the form $\lim_{m\to\infty} P(A_m(\varepsilon)) = 1$. The sequence $\{A_m(\varepsilon)\}_1^{\infty}$ is non-decreasing, so $A_m(\varepsilon) = \bigcup_{j=1}^{m} A_j(\varepsilon)$; letting $A(\varepsilon) = \bigcup_{m=1}^{\infty} A_m(\varepsilon)$, (18.11) can be stated as $P(A(\varepsilon)) = 1$.

Define the set C by the property that, for each $\omega \in C$, $\{X_n(\omega)\}_1^{\infty}$ converges. That is, for $\omega \in C$,

$$\exists\ m(\omega) \text{ such that } \sup_{n\geq m(\omega)} |X_n(\omega) - X(\omega)| \leq \varepsilon, \text{ for all } \varepsilon > 0. \tag{18.13}$$

Evidently, $\omega \in C \Rightarrow \omega \in A_m(\varepsilon)$ for some m, so that $C \subseteq A(\varepsilon)$. Hence $P(C) = 1$ implies $P(A(\varepsilon)) = 1$, proving 'only if'.

To show 'if', assume $P(A(\varepsilon)) = 1$ for all $\varepsilon > 0$. Set $\varepsilon = 1/k$ for positive integer k, and define

$$A^* = \bigcap_{k=1}^{\infty} A(1/k) = \left(\bigcup_{k=1}^{\infty} A(1/k)^c\right)^c. \tag{18.14}$$

The second equality here is **1.1**(iv). By **3.6**(ii), $P(A^*) = 1 - P(\bigcup_{k=1}^{\infty} A(1/k)^c) = 1$. But every element of A^* is a convergent outcome in the sense of (18.13), hence $A^* \subseteq C$, and the conclusion follows. ∎

The last theorem characterizes a.s. convergence in terms of the *uniform* proximity of the tail sequences $\{|X_n(\omega) - X(\omega)|\}_{n=m}^{\infty}$ to zero, on a set A_m whose measure approaches 1 as $m \to \infty$. A related, but distinct, result establishes a direct link between a.s. convergence and uniform convergence on subsets of Ω.

18.4 Egoroff's Theorem If and only if $X_n \xrightarrow{as} X$, there exists for every $\delta > 0$ a set $C(\delta)$ with $P(C(\delta)) \geq 1 - \delta$, such that $X_n(\omega) \to X(\omega)$ uniformly on $C(\delta)$.

Proof To show 'only if', suppose $X_n(\omega)$ converges uniformly on sets $C(1/k)$, $k = 1,2,3,\ldots$ The sequence $\{C(1/k), k \in \mathbb{N}\}$ can be chosen as non-decreasing by monotonicity of P, and $P(\bigcup_{k=1}^{\infty} C(1/k)) = 1$ by continuity of P. To show 'if', let

$$A_m(\delta) = \bigcap_{n=k(m)}^{\infty} \{\omega\colon |X_n(\omega) - X(\omega)| < 1/m\}, \tag{18.15}$$

$k(m)$ being chosen to satisfy the condition $P(A_m(\delta)) \ge 1 - 2^{-m}\delta$. In view of a.s. convergence and **18.3**, the existence of finite $k(m)$ is assured for each m. Then if

$$C(\delta) = \bigcap_{m=1}^{\infty} A_m(\delta), \tag{18.16}$$

convergence is uniform on $C(\delta)$ by construction; that is, for *every* $\omega \in C(\delta)$, $|X_n(\omega) - X(\omega)| < 1/m$ for $n \ge k(m)$, for each $m > 0$. Applying **1.1**(iii) and subadditivity, we find, as required,

$$\begin{aligned} P(C(\delta)) &= 1 - P\left(\bigcup_{m=1}^{\infty} A_m(\delta)^c\right) \\ &\ge 1 - \sum_{m=1}^{\infty} (1 - P(A_m(\delta))) \\ &\ge 1 - \delta. \ \blacksquare \end{aligned} \tag{18.17}$$

18.2 Convergence in Probability

In spite of its conceptual simplicity, the theory of almost sure convergence cannot easily be appreciated without a grasp of probability fundamentals, and traditionally, an alternative convergence concept has been preferred in econometric theory. If, for any $\varepsilon > 0$,

$$\lim_{n\to\infty} P(|X_n - X| > \varepsilon) = 0, \tag{18.18}$$

X_n is said to *converge in probability* (in pr.) to X. Here the convergent sequences are specified to be, not random elements $\{X_n(\omega)\}_1^\infty$, but the nonstochastic sequences $\{P(|X_n - X| > \varepsilon)\}_1^\infty$. The probability of the convergent subset of Ω is left unspecified. However, the following relation is immediate from **18.3**, since (18.11) implies (18.18).

18.5 Theorem If $X_n \xrightarrow{as} X$ then $X_n \xrightarrow{pr} X$. □

The converse does not hold. Convergence in probability imposes a limiting condition on the marginal distribution of the nth member of the sequence as $n \to \infty$. The probability that the deviation of X_n from X is negligible approaches 1 as we move down the sequence. Almost sure convergence, on the other hand, requires that beyond a certain point in the sequence the probability that deviations are negligible *from there on* approaches 1. While it may not be intuitively obvious that a sequence can converge in pr. but not a.s., in **18.16** below we show that convergence in pr. is compatible with a.s. *non*convergence.

However, convergence in probability is equivalent to a.s. convergence *on a subsequence*; given a sequence that converges in pr., it is always possible, by throwing away some of the members of the sequence, to be left with an a.s. convergent sequence.

18.6 Theorem $X_n \xrightarrow{pr} X$ if and only if every subsequence $\{X_{n_k}, k \in \mathbb{N}\}$ contains a further subsequence $\{X_{n_{k(j)}}, j \in \mathbb{N}\}$ which converges a.s. to X.

Proof To prove 'only if': suppose $P(|X_n - X| > \varepsilon) \to 0$ for any $\varepsilon > 0$. This means that, for any sequence of integers $\{n_k, k \in \mathbb{N}\}$, $P(|X_{n_k} - X| > \varepsilon) \to 0$. Hence for each $j \in \mathbb{N}$ there exists an integer $k(j)$ such that

$$P(|X_{n_k} - X| > 1/j) < 2^{-j}, \text{ all } k \geq k(j). \tag{18.19}$$

Since this sequence of probabilities is summable over j, we conclude from the first Borel-Cantelli lemma that

$$P(|X_{n_{k(j)}} - X| > 1/j \text{ i.o.}) = 0. \tag{18.20}$$

It follows, by consideration of the infinite subsequences $\{j \geq J\}$ for $J > 1/\varepsilon$, that $P(|X_{n_{k(j)}} - X| > \varepsilon \text{ i.o.}) = 0$ for every $\varepsilon > 0$, and hence the subsequence $\{X_{n_{k(j)}}\}$ converges a.s. as required.

To prove 'if': if $\{X_n\}$ does not convergence in probability, there must exist a subsequence $\{n_k\}$ such that $\inf_k\{P(|X_{n_k} - X| > \varepsilon)\} \geq \varepsilon$, for some $\varepsilon > 0$. This rules out convergence in pr. on any subsequence of $\{n_k\}$, which rules out convergence a.s. on the same subsequence, by **18.5**. ∎

18.3 Transformations and Convergence

The following set of results on convergence, a.s. and in pr., are fundamental tools of asymptotic theory. For completeness they are given for the vector case, even though most of our own applications are to scalar sequences. A random k-vector $\boldsymbol{X}_n$ is said to converge a.s. (in pr.) to a vector $\boldsymbol{X}$ if each element of $\boldsymbol{X}_n$ converges a.s. (in pr.) to the corresponding element of $\boldsymbol{X}$.

18.7 Lemma $\boldsymbol{X}_n \to \boldsymbol{X}$ a.s. (in pr.) if and only if $\|\boldsymbol{X}_n - \boldsymbol{X}\| \to 0$ a.s. (in pr.).[19]

Proof Take first the case of a.s. convergence. The relation $\|\boldsymbol{X}_n - \boldsymbol{X}\| \xrightarrow{as} 0$ may be expressed as

$$P\left(\lim_{n\to\infty} \sum_{i=1}^{k} (X_{ni} - X_i)^2 < \varepsilon^2\right) = 1 \tag{18.21}$$

for any $\varepsilon > 0$. But (18.21) implies that

$$P\left(\lim_{n\to\infty} |X_{ni} - X_i| < \varepsilon,\ i = 1,\dots,k\right) = 1, \tag{18.22}$$

proving 'if'. To prove 'only if', observe that if (18.22) holds, $P(\lim_{n\to\infty}\|\boldsymbol{X}_n - \boldsymbol{X}\| < k^{1/2}\varepsilon) = 1$, for any $\varepsilon > 0$. To get the proof for convergence in pr., replace $P(\lim_{n\to\infty}\dots)$ everywhere by $\lim_{n\to\infty}P(\dots)$, and the arguments are identical. ∎

There are three different approaches, established in the following theorems, to the problem of preserving convergence (a.s. or in pr.) under transformations.

18.8 Theorem Let $g: \mathbb{R}^k \to \mathbb{R}$ be a Borel function, let $C_g \subseteq \mathbb{R}^k$ be the set of continuity points of g, and assume $P(X \in C_g) = 1$.

(i) If $X_n \xrightarrow{as} X$ then $g(X_n) \xrightarrow{as} g(X)$.

(ii) If $X_n \xrightarrow{pr} X$ then $g(X_n) \xrightarrow{pr} g(X)$.

Proof For case (i), there is by hypothesis a set $D \in \mathcal{F}$, with $P(D) = 1$, such that $X_n(\omega) \to X(\omega)$, each $\omega \in D$. Continuity and **18.7** together imply that $g(X_n(\omega)) \to g(X(\omega))$ for each $\omega \in X^{-1}(C_g) \cap D$. This set has probability 1 by **3.6**(iii).

To prove (ii), analogous reasoning shows that, for each $\varepsilon > 0$, $\exists\ \delta > 0$ such that

$$\{\omega: \|X_n(\omega) - X(\omega)\| < \delta\} \cap X^{-1}(C_g) \subseteq \{\omega: |g(X_n(\omega)) - g(X(\omega))| < \varepsilon\}. \quad (18.23)$$

Note that if $P(B) = 1$ then for any $A \in \mathcal{F}$,

$$P(A \cap B) = 1 - P(A^c \cup B^c) \geq P(A) - P(B^c) = P(A) \quad (18.24)$$

by de Morgan's law and subadditivity of P. In particular, when $P(X \in C_g) = 1$, (18.23) and monotonicity imply

$$P(\|X_n - X\| < \delta) \leq P(|g(X_n) - g(X)| < \varepsilon). \quad (18.25)$$

Taking the limit of each side of the inequality, the minorant side tends to 1 by hypothesis. ■

We may also have cases where only the difference of two sequences is convergent.

18.9 Theorem Let $\{X_n\}$ and $\{Z_n\}$ be sequences of random k-vectors (not necessarily converging) and g the function defined in **18.8**, and let $P(X_n \in C_g) = P(Z_n \in C_g) = 1$ for every n.

(i) If $\|X_n - Z_n\| \xrightarrow{as} 0$ then $|g(X_n) - g(Z_n)| \xrightarrow{as} 0$.

(ii) If $\|X_n - Z_n\| \xrightarrow{pr} 0$ then $|g(X_n) - g(Z_n)| \xrightarrow{pr} 0$.

Proof Put $E_n^X = X_n^{-1}(C_g)$, $E_n^Z = Z_n^{-1}(C_g)$, $E^X = \bigcap_{n=1}^{\infty} E_n^X$, and $E^Z = \bigcap_{n=1}^{\infty} E_n^Z$. $P(E^X) = P(E^Z) = 1$, by assumption and **3.6**(iii). Also let D be the set on which $\|X_n - Z_n\|$ converges. The proof is now a straightforward variant of the preceding one, with the set $E^X \cap E^Z$ playing the role of $X^{-1}(C_g)$. ■

The third result specifies convergence to a constant limit, but relaxes the continuity requirements.

18.10 Theorem Let $g: \mathbb{R}^k \to \mathbb{R}$ be a Borel function, continuous at $\boldsymbol{a}$.

(i) If $X_n \xrightarrow{as} \boldsymbol{a}$ then $g(X_n) \xrightarrow{as} g(\boldsymbol{a})$.

(ii) If $X_n \xrightarrow{pr} \boldsymbol{a}$ then $g(X_n) \xrightarrow{pr} g(\boldsymbol{a})$.

Proof By hypothesis there is a set $D \in \mathcal{F}$, with $P(D) = 1$, such that $X_n(\omega) \to \boldsymbol{a}$, each $\omega \in D$. Continuity implies $g(X_n(\omega)) \to g(\boldsymbol{a})$ for $\omega \in D$, proving (i). Likewise,

$$\{\omega: \|X_n(\omega) - \boldsymbol{a}\| < \delta\} \subseteq \{\omega: |g(X_n(\omega)) - g(\boldsymbol{a})| < \varepsilon\}, \quad (18.26)$$

and (ii) follows much as in the preceding theorems. ■

Theorem **18.10**(ii) is commonly known as Slutsky's theorem (Slutsky 1925). These results have a vast range of applications, and represent one of the chief reasons why limit theory is useful. Having established the convergence of one set of statistics, such as the first few empirical moments of a distribution, one can then deduce the convergence of any continuous function of these. Many commonly used estimators fall into this category.

18.11 Example Let $\boldsymbol{A}_n$ be a random matrix whose elements converge a.s. (in pr.) to a limit $\boldsymbol{A}$. Since the matrix inversion mapping is continuous everywhere, the results a.s.lim $\boldsymbol{A}_n^{-1} = \boldsymbol{A}^{-1}$ (plim$\boldsymbol{A}_n^{-1} = \boldsymbol{A}^{-1}$) follow on applying **18.8** element by element. □

The following is a useful supplementary result, for a case not covered by the Slutsky theorem because Y_n is not required to converge in any sense.

18.12 Theorem Let a sequence $\{Y_n\}_1^\infty$ be bounded in probability (i.e., $O_p(1)$ as $n \to \infty$); if $X_n \xrightarrow{pr} 0$, then $X_nY_n \xrightarrow{pr} 0$.

Proof For a constant $B > 0$, define $Y_n^B = Y_n 1_{\{|Y_n| \le B\}}$. The event $\{|X_nY_n| \ge \varepsilon\}$ for $\varepsilon > 0$ is expressible as a disjoint union:

$$\{|X_nY_n| \ge \varepsilon\} = \{|X_n||Y_n^B| \ge \varepsilon\} \cup \{|X_n||Y_n - Y_n^B| \ge \varepsilon\}. \tag{18.27}$$

For any $\varepsilon > 0$, $\{|X_n||Y_n^B| \ge \varepsilon\} \subseteq \{|X_n| \ge \varepsilon/B\}$, and

$$P(|X_n||Y_n^B| \ge \varepsilon) \le P(|X_n| \ge \varepsilon/B) \to 0. \tag{18.28}$$

By the $O_p(1)$ assumption there exists, for each $\delta > 0$, $B_\delta < \infty$ such that $P(|Y_n - Y_n^{B_\delta}| > 0) < \delta$ for $n \in \mathbb{N}$. Since $\{|X_n||Y_n - Y_n^B| \ge \varepsilon\} \subseteq \{|Y_n - Y_n^B| > 0\}$, (18.27) and additivity imply, putting $B = B_\delta$ in (8.28), that

$$\lim_{n\to\infty} P(|X_nY_n| \ge \varepsilon) < \delta. \tag{18.29}$$

The theorem follows since both ε and δ are arbitrary. ■

18.4 Convergence in L_p Norm

Recall that when $E(|X_n|^p) < \infty$, we have said that X_n is L_p-bounded. Consider, for $p > 0$, the sequence $\{\|X_n - X\|_p\}_1^\infty$. If $E(\|X_n\|_p) < \infty$, all n, and $\lim_{n\to\infty}\|X_n - X\|_p = 0$, X_n is said to *converge in L_p norm* to X (write $X_n \xrightarrow{L_p} X$). When $p = 2$ we speak of *convergence in mean square* (m.s.).

Convergence in probability is sometimes called L_0-convergence, terminology which can be explained by the fact that L_p-convergence implies L_q-convergence for $0 < q < p$ by Liapunov's inequality, together with the following relationship, which is immediate from the Markov inequality.

18.13 Theorem If $X_n \xrightarrow{L_p} X$ for any $p > 0$, then $X_n \xrightarrow{pr} X$. □

The converse does not follow in general, but see the following theorem.

18.14 Theorem If $X_n \xrightarrow{pr} X$, and $\{|X_n|^p\}_1^\infty$ is uniformly integrable, then $X_n \xrightarrow{L_p} X$.

Proof For $\varepsilon > 0$,

$$E|X_n - X|^p = E(1_{\{|X_n-X|^p>\varepsilon\}}|X_n - X|^p) + E(1_{\{|X_n-X|^p\le\varepsilon\}}|X_n - X|^p)$$
$$\le E(1_{\{|X_n-X|^p>\varepsilon\}}|X_n - X|^p) + \varepsilon. \tag{18.30}$$

Convergence in pr. means that $P(|X_n - X| > \varepsilon) \to 0$ as $n \to \infty$. Uniform integrability therefore implies, by **12.9**, that the expectation on the majorant side of (18.30) converges to zero. The theorem follows since ε is arbitrary. ∎

We proved the a.s. counterpart of this result, in effect, as **12.8**, whose conclusion can be written as: $|X_n - X| \xrightarrow{as} 0$ implies $E|X_n - X| \to 0$. The extension from the L_1 case to the L_p case is easily obtained by applying **18.8**(i) to the case $g(.) = |.|^p$.

One of the useful features of L_p convergence is that the L_p norms of $X_n - X$ define a sequence of constants whose order of magnitude in n may be determined, providing a measure of the rate of approach to the limit. We will say for example that X_n converges to X in mean square at the rate n^k if $\|X_t - X\|_2 = O(n^{-k})$, but not $o(n^{-k})$. This is useful in that the scaled random variable $n^k(X_t - X)$ may be non-degenerate in the limit, in the sense of having positive but finite limiting variance. Determining this rate of convergence is often the first step in the analysis of limiting distributions, as discussed in Part V below.

18.5 Examples

Convergence in pr. is a weak mode of convergence in that without side conditions it does not imply, yet is implied by, a.s. convergence and L_p convergence. However, there is no implication from a.s. convergence to L_p convergence, or *vice versa.* A good way to appreciate the distinctions is to consider 'pathological' cases where one or other mode of convergence fails to hold.

18.15 Example Look again at **12.7**, in which $X_n = 0$ with probability $1 - 1/n$, and $X_n = n$ with probability $1/n$, for $n = 1,2,3,\ldots$. A convenient model for this sequence is to let ω be a drawing from the space $([0,1],\mathcal{B}_{[0,1]},m)$ where m is Lebesgue measure, and define the random variable

$$X_n(\omega) = \begin{cases} n, & \omega \in [0,1/n), \\ 0, & \text{otherwise.} \end{cases} \tag{18.31}$$

The set $\{\omega: \lim_n X_n(\omega) \ne 0\}$ consists of the point $\{0\}$, and has p.m. zero, so that $X_n \xrightarrow{as} 0$ according to (18.1). But $E|X_n|^p = 0.(1 - 1/n) + n^p/n = n^{p-1}$. It will be recalled that this sequence is not uniformly integrable. It fails to converge in L_p for any $p > 1$, but for the case $p = 1$ we obtain $E(X_n) = 1$ for every n. The limiting expectation of X_n is therefore different from its almost sure limit. □

The same device can be used to define a.s. convergent sequences which do not converge in L_p for any $p > 0$. It is left to the reader to construct examples.

18.16 Example Let a sequence be generated as follows: $X_1 = 1$ with probability 1; (X_2,X_3) are either (0,1) or (1,0) with equal probability; (X_4,X_5,X_6) are chosen from (1,0,0), (0,1,0), (0,0,1) with equal probability; and so forth. For $k = 1,2,3,...$ the next k members of the sequence are randomly selected such that one of them is unity, the others zero. Hence, for n in the range $[\frac{1}{2}k(k-1)+1, \frac{1}{2}k(k+1)]$, $P(X_n = 1) = 1/k$, as well as $E|X_n|^p = 1/k$ for $p > 0$. Since $k \to \infty$ as $n \to \infty$, it is clear that X_n converges to zero both in pr. and in L_p norm. But since, for any n, $X_{n+j} = 1$ a.s. for infinitely many j,

$$P(|X_n| < \varepsilon, \text{ i.o.}) = 0 \tag{18.32}$$

for $0 \le \varepsilon \le 1$. The sequence not only fails to converge a.s., but actually converges with probability 0.

Consider also the sequence $\{k^{1/r}X_n\}$, whose members are either 0 or $k^{1/r}$ in the range $[\frac{1}{2}k(k-1)+1, \frac{1}{2}k(k+1)]$. Note that $E(|k^{1/r}X_n|^p) = k^{p/r-1}$, and by suitable choice of r we can produce a sequence that does not converge in L_p for $p > r$. With $r = 1$ we have $E(kX_n) = 1$ for all n, but as in **18.15**, the sequence is not uniformly integrable. The limiting expectation of the sequence exists, but is different from the probability limit. □

In these non-uniformly integrable cases in which the sequence converges in L_1 but not in $L_{1+\theta}$ for any $\theta > 0$, one can see the expectation remaining formally well-defined in the limit, but breaking down in the sense of losing its intuitive interpretation as the limit of a sample average. Example **18.15** is a version of the well-known St Petersburg Paradox. Consider a game of chance in which the player announces a number $n \in \mathbb{N}$, and bets that a succession of coin tosses will produce n heads before tails comes up, the pay-off for a correct prediction being £2^{n+1}. The probability of winning is 2^{-n-1}, so the expected winnings are £1; that is to say, it is a 'fair game' if the stake is fixed at £1. The sequence of random winnings X_n generated by choosing $n = 1,2,3,...$ is exactly the process specified in **18.15**.[20] If n is chosen to be a very large number, a moment's reflection shows that the probability limit is a much better guide to one's prospective winnings in a finite number of plays than the expectation. The paradox that with large n no one would be willing to bet on this apparently fair game has been explained by appeal to psychological notions such as risk aversion, but it would appear to be an adequate explanation that, for large enough n, the expectation is simply not a practical predictor of the outcome.

18.6 Laws of Large Numbers

Let $\{X_t\}_1^\infty$ be a stochastic sequence and define $\bar{X}_n = n^{-1}\sum_{t=1}^n X_t$. Suppose that $E(X_t) = \mu_t$ and $n^{-1}\sum_{t=1}^n \mu_t \to \mu$ with $|\mu| < \infty$; this is trivial in the mean-stationary case in which $\mu_t = \mu$ for all t. In this simple setting, the sequence is said to obey the weak law of large numbers (WLLN) when $\bar{X}_n \xrightarrow{pr} \mu$, and the strong law of large numbers (SLLN) when $\bar{X}_n \xrightarrow{as} \mu$.

These statements of the LLNs are standard and familiar, but as characterizations of a class of convergence results they are rather restrictive. We can set $\mu = 0$ with no loss of generality, by simply considering the centred sequence $\{X_t - \mu_t\}_1^\infty$; centring is generally a good idea, because then it is no longer necessary for the time average of the means to converge in the manner specified. We can quite easily have $n^{-1}\sum_{t=1}^n \mu_t \to \infty$ at the same time that $n^{-1}\sum_{t=1}^n (X_t(\omega) - \mu_t) \to 0$. In such cases the law of large numbers requires a modified interpretation, since it ceases to make sense to speak of convergence of the sequence of sample means.

More general modes of convergence also exist. It is possible that $\bar{X}_n$ does not converge in the manner specified, even after centring, but that there exists a sequence of positive constants $\{a_n\}_1^\infty$ such that $a_n \uparrow \infty$ and $a_n^{-1}\sum_{t=1}^n X_t \to 0$. Results below will subsume these possibilities, and others too, in a fully general array formulation of the problem. If $\{\{X_{nt}\}_{t=1}^{k_n}\}_{n=1}^\infty$ is a triangular stochastic array with $\{k_n\}_{n=1}^\infty$ an increasing integer sequence, we will discuss conditions for

$$S_n = \sum_{t=1}^{k_n} X_{nt} \xrightarrow{pr} 0. \tag{18.33}$$

A result in this form can be specialized to the familiar case with $X_{nt} = a_n^{-1}(X_t - \mu_t)$ and $a_n = k_n = n$, but there are important applications where the greater generality is essential.

We have already encountered two cases where the strong law of large numbers applies. According to **13.12**, $\bar{X}_n \xrightarrow{as} \mu = E(X_1)$ when $\{X_t\}$ is a stationary ergodic sequence and $E|X_1| < \infty$. We can illustrate the application of this type of result by an example in which the sequence is independent, which is sufficient for ergodicity.

18.17 Example Consider a sequence of independent Bernoulli variables X_t with $P(X_t = 1) = P(X_t = 0) = \frac{1}{2}$; that is, of coin tosses expressed in binary form (see **12.1**). The conditions of the ergodic theorem are clearly satisfied, and we can conclude that $n^{-1}\sum_{t=1}^n X_t \xrightarrow{as} E(X_t) = \frac{1}{2}$. This is called *Borel's normal number theorem*, a normal number being defined as one in which 0s and 1s occur in its binary expansion with equal frequency, in the limit. The normal number theorem therefore states that almost every point of the unit interval is a normal number; that is, the set of normal numbers has Lebesgue measure 1.

Any number with a terminating expansion is clearly non-normal and we know that all such numbers are rationals; however, rationals can be normal, as for example $\frac{1}{3}$, which has the binary expansion 0.01010101010101... This is a different result from the well-known zero measure of the rationals, and is much stronger, because the non-normal numbers include irrationals, and form an uncountable set. For example, any number with a binary expansion of the form $0.11b_111b_211b_311...$ where the b_i are arbitrary digits is non-normal; yet this set can be put into 1-1 correspondence with the expansions $0.b_1b_2b_3,...$, in other words, with the points of the whole interval. The set of non-normal numbers is equipotent with the reals, but it none the less has Lebesgue measure 0. □

A useful fact to remember is that the stationary ergodic propery is preserved under measurable transformations; that is, if $\{X_t\}$ is stationary and ergodic, so is the sequence $\{g(X_t)\}$ whenever $g: \mathbb{R} \mapsto \mathbb{R}$ is a measurable function. For example, we only need to know that $E(X_1^2) < \infty$ to be able to assert that $n^{-1}\sum_{t=1}^n X_t^2 \xrightarrow{as} E(X_1^2)$. The ergodic theorem serves to establish the strong law for most stationary sequences we are likely to encounter; recall from §13.5 that ergodicity is a weaker property than regularity or mixing. The interesting problems in stochastic convergence arise when the distributions of sequence coordinates are heterogeneous, so that it is not trivial to assume that averaging of coordinates is a stable procedure in the limit.

Another result we know of which yields a strong law is the martingale convergence theorem (**15.7**), which has the interpretation that $a_n^{-1}\sum_{t=1}^n X_t \xrightarrow{as} 0$ whenever $\{\sum_{t=1}^n X_t\}$ is a submartingale with $E|\sum_{t=1}^n X_t| < \infty$ uniformly in n, and $a_n \to \infty$. This particular strong law needs to be combined with additional results to give it a broad application, but this is readily done, as we shall show in §20.3.

But, lest the law of large numbers appear an altogether trivial problem, it might also be a good idea to exhibit some cases where convergence fails to occur.

18.18 Example Let $\{X_t\}$ denote a sequence of independent Cauchy random variables with characteristic function $\phi_{X_t}(\lambda) = e^{-|\lambda|}$ for each t (**11.9**). It is easy to verify using formulae (11.30) and (11.33) that $\phi_{\bar{X}_n}(\lambda) = e^{-n|\lambda|/n} = e^{-|\lambda|}$. According to the inversion theorem, the average of n independent Cauchy variables is also a Cauchy variable. This result holds for any n, contradicting the possibility that $\bar{X}_n$ could converge to a constant. □

18.19 Example Consider a process

$$X_t = \sum_{s=1}^{t} \psi_s Z_s = X_{t-1} + \psi_t Z_t,\ t = 1,2,3,... \tag{18.34}$$

with $X_0 = 0$, where $\{Z_t\}_1^\infty$ is an independent stationary sequence with mean 0 and variance σ^2, and $\{\psi_s\}_1^\infty$ is a sequence of constant coefficients. Notice, these are indexed with the absolute date rather than the lag relative to time t, as in the linear processes considered in §14.3. For $m > 0$,

$$\mathrm{Cov}(X_t, X_{t+m}) = \mathrm{Var}(X_t) = \sigma^2 \sum_{s=1}^{t} \psi_s^2. \tag{18.35}$$

For $\{X_t\}_1^\infty$ to be uniformly L_2-bounded requires $\sum_{s=1}^\infty \psi_s^2 < \infty$; in this case the effect of the innovations declines to zero with t and X_t approaches a limiting random variable X, say. Without the square-summability assumption, $\mathrm{Var}(X_t) \to \infty$. An example of the latter case is the *random walk* process, in which $\psi_s = 1$, all s. Since $\mathrm{Cov}(X_1, X_t) = \psi_1^2\sigma^2$ for every t, these processes are not mixing. $\bar{X}_n$ has zero mean, but

$$\mathrm{Var}(\bar{X}_n) = \frac{1}{n^2}\left(\sum_{t=1}^{n} \mathrm{Var}(X_t) + 2\sum_{t=2}^{n}\sum_{j=1}^{t-1} \mathrm{Var}(X_j)\right). \tag{18.36}$$

If $\sum_{s=1}^\infty \psi_j^2 < \infty$, then $\lim_{n\to\infty} \mathrm{Var}(\bar{X}_n) = \sigma^2 \sum_{s=1}^\infty \psi_j^2$; otherwise $\mathrm{Var}(\bar{X}_n) \to \infty$. In either case the sequence $\{\bar{X}_n\}$ fails to converge to a fixed limit, being either stochastic asymptotically, or divergent. □

These counter-examples illustrate the fact that, to obey the law of large numbers, a sequence must satisfy regularity conditions relating to two distinct factors: the probability of outliers (limited by bounding absolute moments) and the degree of dependence between coordinates. In **18.18** we have a case where the mean fails to exist, and in **18.19** an example of long-range dependence. In neither case can $\bar{X}_n$ be thought of as a sample statistic which is estimating a parameter of the underlying distribution in any meaningful fashion. In Chapters 19 and 20 we devise sets of regularity conditions sufficient for weak and strong laws to operate, constraining both characteristics in different configurations. The *necessity* of a set of regularity conditions is usually hard to prove (the exception is when the sequences are independent), but various configurations of mixing and L_p-boundedness conditions can be shown to be sufficient. These results usually exhibit a trade-off between the two dimensions of regularity; the stronger the moment restrictions are, the weaker dependence restrictions can be, and vice versa.

One word of caution before we proceed to the theorems. In §9.1 we sought to motivate the idea of an expectation by viewing it as the limit of the empirical average. There is a temptation to attempt to *define* an expectation as such a limit; but to do so would inevitably involve us in circular reasoning, since the arguments establishing convergence are couched in the language of probability. The aim of the theory is to establish convergence in particular sampling schemes. It cannot, for example, be used to validate the frequentist interpretation of probability. However, it *does* show that axiomatic probability yields predictions that accord with the frequentist model, and in this sense the laws of large numbers are among the most fundamental results in probability theory.

19
Convergence in L_p Norm

19.1 Weak Laws by Mean-Square Convergence

This chapter surveys a range of techniques for proving (mainly) weak laws of large numbers, ranging from classical results to recent additions to the literature. The common theme in these results is that they depend on showing convergence in L_p-norm, where in general p lies in the interval [1,2]. Initially we consider the case $p = 2$. The regularity conditions for these results relate directly to the variances and covariances of the process. While for subsequent results these moments will not need to exist, the L_2 case is of interest both because the conditions are familiar and intuitive, and because in certain respects the results available are more powerful.

Consider a stochastic sequence $\{X_t\}_1^\infty$, with sequence of means $\{\mu_t\}_1^\infty$, and variances $\{\sigma_t^2\}_1^\infty$. There is no loss of generality in setting $\mu_t = 0$ by simply considering the case of $\{X_t - \mu_t\}_1^\infty$, but to focus the discussion on a familiar case, let us initially assume $\bar{\mu}_n = n^{-1}\sum_{t=1}^n \mu_t \to \mu$ (finite), and so consider the question, what are sufficient conditions for $E(\bar{X}_n - \mu)^2 \to 0$? An elementary relation is

$$E(\bar{X}_n - \mu)^2 = \mathrm{Var}(\bar{X}_n) + (E(\bar{X}_n) - \mu)^2; \tag{19.1}$$

where the second term on the right-hand side converges to zero by definition of μ. Thus the question becomes: when does $\mathrm{Var}(\bar{X}_n) \to 0$? We have

$$\mathrm{Var}(\bar{X}_n) = E\left(n^{-1}\sum_{t=1}^n (X_t - \mu_t)\right)^2 = n^{-2}\left(\sum_{t=1}^n \sigma_t^2 + 2\sum_{t=2}^n \sum_{s=1}^{t-1} \sigma_{ts}\right), \tag{19.2}$$

where $\sigma_t^2 = \mathrm{Var}(X_t)$ and $\sigma_{ts} = \mathrm{Cov}(X_t, X_s)$. Suppose, to make life simple, we assume that the sequence is uncorrelated, with $\sigma_{ts} = 0$ for $t \neq s$ in (19.2). Then we have the following well-known result.

19.1 Theorem If $\{X_t\}_1^\infty$ is uncorrelated sequence and

$$\sum_{t=1}^\infty t^{-2}\sigma_t^2 < \infty, \tag{19.3}$$

then $\bar{X}_n \xrightarrow{L_2} \mu$.

Proof This is an application of Kronecker's lemma (**2.35**), by which (19.3) implies $\mathrm{Var}(\bar{X}_n) = n^{-2}\sum_t \sigma_t^2 \to 0$. ∎

This result yields a weak law of large numbers by application of **18.13**, known as Chebyshev's theorem. An (amply) sufficient condition for (19.3) is that the variances are uniformly bounded with, say, $\sup_t\sigma_t^2 \le B < \infty$. Wide-sense stationary sequences fall into this class. In such cases we have $\mathrm{Var}(\bar{X}_n) = O(n^{-1})$. But since all we need is $\mathrm{Var}(\bar{X}_n) = o(1)$, $\sigma_t^2 \to \infty$ is evidently permissable. If $\sigma_t^2 \sim t^{1-\delta}$ for $\delta > 0$, $\sum_{t=1}^n t^{-2}\sigma_t^2$ has terms of $O(t^{-1-\delta})$, and therefore converges by **2.27**.

Looking at (19.2) again, it is also clear that uncorrelatedness is an unnecessarily tough condition. It will suffice if the magnitude of the covariances can be suitably controlled. Imposing uniform L_2-boundedness to allow the maximum relaxation of constraints on dependence, the Cauchy-Schwartz inequality tells us that $|\sigma_{ts}| \le B$ for all t and s. Rearranging the formula in (19.2),

$$\mathrm{Var}(\bar{X}_n) = \frac{1}{n^2}\left(\sum_{t=1}^n \sigma_t^2 + 2\sum_{t=2}^n \sigma_{t,t-1} + 2\sum_{t=3}^n \sigma_{t,t-2} + \ldots + 2\sigma_{n1}\right)$$

$$\le \frac{1}{n^2}\sum_{t=1}^n \sigma_t^2 + \frac{2}{n^2}\sum_{m=1}^{n-1}\sum_{t=m+1}^n \left|\sigma_{t,t-m}\right|$$

$$\le \frac{B}{n} + \frac{2}{n^2}\sum_{m=1}^{n-1}(n-m)B_m, \tag{19.4}$$

where $B_m = \sup_t|\sigma_{t,t-m}|$, and $B_m \le B$, all $m \ge 1$. This suggests the following variant on **19.1**.

19.2 Theorem If $\{X_t\}_1^\infty$ is a uniformly L_2-bounded sequence, and $\sum_{m=1}^\infty m^{-1}B_m < \infty$ where $B_m = \sup_t|\sigma_{t,t-m}|$, then $\bar{X}_n \xrightarrow{L_2} \mu$.

Proof Since $(n-m)/n < 1$, it is sufficient by (19.4) to show the convergence of $(2/n)\sum_{m=1}^{n-1}B_m$ to zero. This follows immediately from the stated condition and Kronecker's lemma. ∎

A sufficient condition, in view of **2.30**, is $B_m = O((\log m)^{-1-\delta})$, $\delta > 0$; a very mild restriction on the autocovariances.

There are two observations that we might make about these results. The first is to point to the trade-off between the dimensions of dependence and the growth of the variances. Theorems **19.1** and **19.2** are easily combined, and it is found that by tightening the rate at which the covariances diminish the variances can grow faster, and vice versa. The reader can explore these possibilities using the rather simple techniques of the above proofs, although remember that the $|\sigma_{t,t-m}|$ will need to be treated as growing with t as well as diminishing with m. Analogous trade-offs are derived in a different context below.

The order of magnitude in n of $\mathrm{Var}(\bar{X}_n)$, which depends on these factors, can be thought of as a measure of the *rate* of convergence. With no correlation and bounded variances, convergence is at the rate $n^{-1/2}$ in the sense that $\mathrm{Var}(\bar{X}_n) = O(n^{-1})$; but from (19.4), $B_m = O(m^{-\delta})$ implies that $\mathrm{Var}(\bar{X}_n) = O(n^{-\delta})$. If convergence rates are thought of as indicating the number of sample observations required to get $\bar{X}_n$ close to μ with high confidence, the weakest sufficient conditions evidently yield convergence only in a notional sense. It is less easy in some of the more general results below to link explicitly the rate of convergence with the degree of dependence and/or nonstationarity; this is always an issue to keep in mind.

Mixing sequences have the property that the covariances tend to zero, and the mixing inequalities of §14.2 gives the following corollary to **19.2**.

19.3 Corollary If $\{X_t\}_1^\infty$ is either (i) uniformly L_2-bounded and uniform mixing with

$$\sum_{m=1}^{\infty} m^{-1}\phi_m^{1/2} < \infty, \tag{19.5}$$

or (ii) uniformly $L_{2+\delta}$-bounded for $\delta > 0$, and strong mixing with

$$\sum_{m=1}^{\infty} m^{-1}\alpha_m^{\delta/(2+\delta)} < \infty, \tag{19.6}$$

then $\bar{X}_n \xrightarrow{L_2} \mu$.

Proof For part (i), **14.5** for the case $r = 2$ yields the inequality $B_m \le 2B\phi_m^{1/2}$. For part (ii), **14.3** for the case $p = r = 2+\delta$ yields $B_m \le 6\|X_t\|_{2+\delta}^2\alpha_m^{\delta/(2+\delta)}$. Noting that $B \le \|X_t\|_{2+\delta}^2$, the conditions of **19.2** are satisfied in either case. ■

A sufficient condition for **19.3**(i) is $\phi_m = O((\log m)^{-2-\varepsilon})$ for any $\varepsilon > 0$. For **19.3**(ii), $\alpha_m = O((\log m)^{-(1+2/\delta)(1+\varepsilon)})$ for $\varepsilon > 0$ is sufficient. In the size terminology of §14.1, mixing of any size will ensure these conditions. The most significant cost of using the strong mixing condition is that simple existence of the variances is not sufficient. This is not of course to say that no weak law exists for L_2-bounded strong mixing processes, but more subtle arguments, such as those of §19.4, are needed for the proof.

19.2 Almost Sure Convergence by the Method of Subsequences

Almost sure convergence does not follow from convergence in mean square (a counter-example is **18.16**), but a clever adaptation of the above techniques yields a result. The proof of the following theorems makes use of the *method of subsequences*, exploiting the relation between convergence in pr. and convergence a.s. demonstrated in **18.6**.

Mainly for the sake of clarity, we first prove the result for the uncorrelated case. Notice how the conditions have to be strengthened, relative to **19.1**.

19.4 Theorem If $\{X_t\}_1^\infty$ is uniformly L_2-bounded and uncorrelated, $\bar{X}_n \xrightarrow{as} \mu$. □

A natural place to start in a sufficiency proof of the strong law is with the convergence part of the Borel-Cantelli lemma. The Chebyshev inequality yields, under the stated conditions,

$$P(|\bar{X}_n - \bar{\mu}_n| > \varepsilon) \le \frac{\mathrm{Var}(\bar{X}_n)}{\varepsilon^2} \le \frac{B}{n\varepsilon^2} \tag{19.7}$$

for $B < \infty$, with the probability on the left-hand side going to zero with the right-hand side as $n \to \infty$. One approach to the problem of bounding the quantity

$P(|\bar{X}_n - \bar{\mu}_n| > \varepsilon, \text{i.o.})$ would be to add up the inequalities in (19.7) over n. Since the partial sums of $1/n$ form a divergent sequence, a direct attack on these lines does not succeed. However, $\sum_{n=1}^{\infty} n^{-2} \approx 1.64$, and we can add up the *sub*sequence of the probabilities in (19.7), for $n = 1,4,9,16,\ldots$, as follows.

Proof of 19.4 By (19.7),

$$\sum_{n^2} P(|\bar{X}_{n^2} - \bar{\mu}_{n^2}| > \varepsilon) \le \frac{1.64B}{\varepsilon^2} < \infty. \tag{19.8}$$

Now **18.2**(i) yields the result that the subsequence $\{\bar{X}_{n^2}, n \in \mathbb{N}\}$ converges a.s. The proof is completed by showing that the maximum deviation of the omitted terms from the nearest member of $\{\bar{X}_{n^2}\}$ also converges in mean square. For each n define

$$D_{n^2} = \max_{n^2 \le k < (n+1)^2} |\bar{X}_k - \bar{X}_{n^2}| \tag{19.9}$$

and consider the variance of D_{n^2}. Given the assumptions, the sequence of the $\mathrm{Var}(\bar{X}_n) = (1/n^2)\sum_{t=1}^{n}\sigma_t^2$ tends monotonically to zero. For $n^2 < k < (n+1)^2$, re-arrangement of the terms produces

$$\bar{X}_k - \bar{X}_{n^2} = \left(\frac{n^2}{k} - 1\right)\bar{X}_{n^2} + \left(\frac{1}{k}\right)\sum_{t=n^2+1}^{k} X_t, \tag{19.10}$$

and when the sequence is uncorrelated the two terms on the right are also uncorrelated. Hence

$$\begin{aligned}\mathrm{Var}(\bar{X}_k - \bar{X}_{n^2}) &= \left(1 - \frac{n^2}{k}\right)^2 \mathrm{Var}(\bar{X}_{n^2}) + \left(\frac{1}{k}\right)^2 \sum_{t=n^2+1}^{k} \sigma_t^2 \\ &\le \left(1 - \frac{n^2}{k}\right)^2 \frac{B}{n^2} + (k - n^2)\frac{B}{k^2} \\ &= B\left(\frac{1}{n^2} - \frac{1}{k}\right) \le B\left(\frac{1}{n^2} - \frac{1}{(n+1)^2}\right).\end{aligned} \tag{19.11}$$

$\mathrm{Var}(D_{n^2})$ cannot exceed the last term in (19.11), and

$$\sum_{n^2}(n^{-2} - (n+1)^{-2}) < \sum_{n}(n^{-2} - (n+1)^{-2}) = 1, \tag{19.12}$$

so the Chebyshev inequality gives

$$\sum_{n^2} P(D_{n^2} > \varepsilon) \le \frac{B}{\varepsilon^2} < \infty, \tag{19.13}$$

and the subsequence $\{D_{n^2}, n \in \mathbb{N}\}$ also converges a.s. $D_{n^2} \ge |\bar{X}_k - \bar{X}_{n^2}|$ for any k between n^2 and $(n+1)^2$, and hence, by the triangle inequality,

$$|\bar{X}_k - \bar{\mu}_k| \le |\bar{X}_{n^2} - \bar{\mu}_{n^2}| + |\bar{X}_k - \bar{X}_{n^2}| + |\bar{\mu}_k - \bar{\mu}_{n^2}|$$

$$\leq |\bar{X}_{n^2} - \bar{\mu}_{n^2}| + D_{n^2} + |\bar{\mu}_k - \bar{\mu}_{n^2}|. \tag{19.14}$$

The sequences on the majorant side are positive and converge a.s. to zero, hence so does their sum. But (19.14) holds for $n^2 \leq k < (n+1)^2$ for $\{n^2, n \in \mathbb{N}\}$, so that k ranges over every integer value. We must conclude that $\bar{X}_n \xrightarrow{as} \mu$. ■

We can generalize the same technique to allow autocorrelation.

19.5 Corollary If $\{X_t\}_1^\infty$ is uniformly L_2-bounded, and

$$B^* = \sum_{m=1}^{\infty} B_m < \infty, \tag{19.15}$$

where $B_m = \sup_t |\sigma_{t,t-m}|$, then $\bar{X}_n \xrightarrow{as} \mu$. □

Note how much tougher these conditions are than those of **19.2**. It will suffice here for $B_m = O(m^{-1}(\log m)^{-1-\delta})$ for $\delta > 0$. Instead of, in effect, having the autocovariances merely decline to zero, we now require their summability.

Proof of 19.5 By (19.4), $\text{Var}(\bar{X}_n) \leq (B + 2B^*)/n$ and hence equation (19.7) holds in the modified form,

$$\sum_{n^2} P(|\bar{X}_{n^2} - \bar{\mu}_{n^2}| > \varepsilon) \leq \frac{1.64(B + 2B^*)}{\varepsilon^2} < \infty. \tag{19.16}$$

Instead of (19.11) we have, on multiplying out and taking expectations,

$$\text{Var}(\bar{X}_k - \bar{X}_{n^2}) = \text{Var}\left[\frac{1}{k}\sum_{t=n^2+1}^{k} X_t - \left(1 - \frac{n^2}{k}\right)\bar{X}_{n^2}\right]$$

$$= \left(1 - \frac{n^2}{k}\right)^2 \text{Var}(\bar{X}_{n^2}) + \frac{1}{k^2}\left(\sum_{t=n^2+1}^{k} \sigma_t^2 + 2\sum_{t=n^2+2}^{k}\sum_{m=1}^{t-n^2-1} \sigma_{t,t-m}\right)$$

$$- \frac{2}{k}\left(1 - \frac{n^2}{k}\right)\left(\sum_{t=n^2+1}^{k}\sum_{m=t-n^2}^{t-1} \sigma_{t,t-m}\right). \tag{19.17}$$

The first term on the right-hand side is bounded by $(1 - n^2/k)^2(B + 2B^*)/n^2$, the second by $(k - n^2)(B + 2B^*)/k^2$, and the third (absolutely) by $2(1 - n^2/k)^2 B^*$. Adding together these latter terms and simplifying yields

$$\text{Var}(\bar{X}_k - \bar{X}_{n^2}) \leq \left(\frac{1}{n^2} - \frac{1}{k}\right)B + 2\left[\frac{1}{n^2} - \frac{1}{k} + \left(1 - \frac{n^2}{k}\right)^2\right]B^*$$

$$\leq \left(\frac{1}{n^2} - \frac{1}{(n+1)^2}\right)B + 2\left[\frac{1}{n^2} - \frac{1}{(n+1)^2} + \left(1 - \frac{n^2}{(n+1)^2}\right)^2\right]B^*. \tag{19.18}$$

Note, $(1 - n^2/(n+1)^2)^2 = O(n^{-2})$, so the term in B^* is summable. In place of (19.13) we can write

$$\sum_{n^2} P(D_{n^2} > \varepsilon) \le \frac{B + K_1 B^*}{\varepsilon^2} < \infty, \tag{19.19}$$

where K_1 is a finite constant. From here on the proof follows that of **19.4.** ■

Again there is a straightforward extension to mixing sequences by direct analogy with **19.3**.

19.6 Corollary If $\{X_t\}_1^\infty$ is either (i) uniformly L_2-bounded and uniform mixing with

$$\sum_{m=1}^{\infty} \phi_m^{1/2} < \infty, \tag{19.20}$$

or (ii) uniformly $L_{2+\delta}$-bounded for $\delta > 0$, and strong mixing with

$$\sum_{m=1}^{\infty} \alpha_m^{\delta/(2+\delta)} < \infty, \tag{19.21}$$

then $\bar{X}_n \xrightarrow{as} 0$. □

Let it be emphasized that these results have no pretensions to being sharp! They are given here as an illustration of technique, and also to define the limits of this approach to strong convergence. In Chapter 20 we will see how they can be improved upon.

19.3 A Martingale Weak Law

We now want to relax the requirement of finite variances, and prove L_p-convergence for $p < 2$. The basic idea underlying these results is a truncation argument. Given a sequence $\{X_t\}_1^\infty$ which we assume to have mean 0, define $Y_t = 1_{\{|X_t| \le B\}} X_t$, which equals X_t when $|X_t| \le B < \infty$, and 0 otherwise. Letting $Z_t = X_t - Y_t$, the 'tail component' of X_t, notice that $E(Z_t) = -E(Y_t)$ by construction, and $\bar{X}_n = \bar{Y}_n + \bar{Z}_n$. Since Y_t is a.s. bounded and possesses all its moments, arguments of the type used in §19.1 might be brought to bear to show that $\bar{Y}_n \xrightarrow{L_2} \mu_Y$ (say). Some other approach must then be used to show that $\bar{Z}_n \xrightarrow{pr} \mu_Z = -\mu_Y$. An obvious technique is to assume uniform integrability of $\{|X_t|^p\}$. In this case, $\sup_t E|Z_t|^p$ can be made as small as desired by choosing B large enough, leading (*via* the Minkowski inequality, for example) to an L_p-convergence result for $\bar{Z}_n$.

A different approach to limiting dependence is called for here. We cannot assume that Y_t is serially uncorrelated just because X_t is. The serial independence assumption would serve, but is rather strong. However, if we let X_t be a martingale difference, a mild strengthening of uncorrelatedness, *this* property can also be passed on to Y_t, after a centring adjustment. This is the clever idea behind the next result, based on a theorem of Y. S. Chow (1971). Subsequently (see §19.4) the m.d. assumption can be relaxed to a mixingale assumption.

We will take this opportunity to switch to an array formulation. The theorems are easily specialized to the case of ordinary sample averages (see §18.6), but in subsequent chapters, array results will be indispensable.

19.7 Theorem Let $\{X_{nt},\mathcal{F}_{nt}\}$ be a m.d. array, $\{c_{nt}\}$ a positive constant array, and $\{k_n\}$ an increasing integer sequence with $k_n \uparrow \infty$. If, for $1 \le p \le 2$,

(a) $\{|X_{nt}/c_{nt}|^p\}$ is uniformly integrable,

(b) $\limsup_{n\to\infty} \sum_{t=1}^{k_n} c_{nt} < \infty$, and

(c) $\lim_{n\to\infty} \sum_{t=1}^{k_n} c_{nt}^2 = 0$,

then $\sum_{t=1}^{k_n} X_{nt} \xrightarrow{L_p} 0$. □

The leading specialization of this result is where $X_{nt} = X_t/a_n$, where $\{X_t,\mathcal{F}_t\}$ is a m.d. sequence with $\mathcal{F}_{nt} = \mathcal{F}_t$ and $\{a_n\}$ is a positive constant sequence. This deserves stating as a corollary, since the formulation can be made slightly more transparent.

19.8 Corollary Suppose $\{X_t,\mathcal{F}_t\}_0^\infty$ is a m.d. sequence, and $\{b_t\}$, $\{a_n\}$, and $\{k_n\}$ are constant positive sequences with $a_n \uparrow \infty$ and $k_n \uparrow \infty$, and satisfying

(a) $\{|X_t/b_t|^p\}$ is uniformly integrable, $1 \le p \le 2$,

(b) $\sum_{t=1}^{k_n} b_t = O(a_n)$, and

(c) $\sum_{t=1}^{k_n} b_t^2 = o(a_n^2)$;

then $a_n^{-1}\sum_{t=1}^{k_n} X_t \xrightarrow{L_p} 0$.

Proof Immediate from **19.7**, defining $X_{nt} = X_t/a_n$ and $c_{nt} = b_t/a_n$. ■

Be careful to distinguish the constants a_n and k_n. Although both are equal to n in the sample-average case, more generally their roles are quite different. The case with k_n different from n typically arises in 'blocking' arguments, where the array coordinates are generated from successive blocks of underlying sequence coordinates. We might have $k_n = [n^\alpha]$ for $\alpha \in (0,1)$ ($[x]$ denoting the largest integer below x) where the length of a block does not exceed $[n^{1-\alpha}]$. For an application of this sort see §24.4.

Conditions **19.8**(b) and (c) together imply $a_n \uparrow \infty$, so this does not need to be separately asserted. To form a clear idea of the role of the assumptions, it is helpful to suppose that b_t and a_n are regularly varying functions of their arguments. It is easily verified by **2.27** that the conditions are observed if $b_t \sim t^\beta$ for any $\beta \ge -1$, by choosing $a_n \sim n^{1+\beta}$ for $\beta > -1$, and $a_n \sim \log n$ for $\beta = -1$. In particular, setting $b_t = 1$ for all t, $a_n = k_n = n$ yields

$$\|\bar{X}_n\|_p \to 0. \tag{19.22}$$

Choosing $a_n = \sum_{t=1}^{k_n} b_t$ will automatically satisfy condition (a), and condition (b) will also hold when $b_t = O(t^\beta)$. On the other hand, a case where the conditions fail is where $b_1 = 1$ and, for $t > 1$, $b_t = \sum_{s=1}^{t-1} b_s = 2^t$. In this case condition (a) imposes the requirement $b_n = O(a_n)$, so that $b_n^2 = O(a_n^2)$, contradicting condition (b). The growth rate of b_t exceeds that of t^β for every $\beta > 0$.

Proof of 19.7 Uniform integrability implies that

$$\sup_{n,t} E(|X_{nt}/c_{nt}|^p 1_{\{|X_{nt}/c_{nt}|>M\}}) \to 0 \text{ as } M \to \infty.$$

One may therefore find, for $\varepsilon > 0$, a constant $B_\varepsilon < \infty$ such that

$$\sup_{n,t}\left\{\|X_{nt}1_{\{|X_{nt}|>B_\varepsilon c_{nt}\}}\|_p / c_{nt}\right\} \le \varepsilon. \tag{19.23}$$

Define $Y_{nt} = X_{nt}1_{\{|X_{nt}|\le B_\varepsilon c_{nt}\}}$, and $Z_{nt} = X_{nt} - Y_{nt}$. Then since $E(X_{nt}|\mathcal{F}_{n,t-1}) = 0$,

$$X_{nt} = Y_{nt} - E(Y_{nt}|\mathcal{F}_{n,t-1}) + Z_{nt} - E(Z_{nt}|\mathcal{F}_{n,t-1}).$$

By the Minkowski inequality,

$$\left\|\sum_{t=1}^{k_n} X_{nt}\right\|_p \le \left\|\sum_{t=1}^{k_n}(Y_{nt} - E(Y_{nt}|\mathcal{F}_{n,t-1}))\right\|_p + \left\|\sum_{t=1}^{k_n}(Z_{nt} - E(Z_{nt}|\mathcal{F}_{n,t-1}))\right\|_p. \tag{19.24}$$

Consider each of these right-hand-side terms. First,

$$\begin{aligned}\left\|\sum_{t=1}^{k_n}(Y_{nt} - E(Y_{nt}|\mathcal{F}_{n,t-1}))\right\|_p &\le \left\|\sum_{t=1}^{k_n}(Y_{nt} - E(Y_{nt}|\mathcal{F}_{n,t-1}))\right\|_2 \\ &= \left(\sum_{t=1}^{k_n} E(Y_{nt} - E(Y_{nt}|\mathcal{F}_{n,t-1}))^2\right)^{1/2} \\ &\le \left(\sum_{t=1}^{k_n} EY_{nt}^2\right)^{1/2} \le B_\varepsilon\left(\sum_{t=1}^{k_n} c_{nt}^2\right)^{1/2}.\end{aligned} \tag{19.25}$$

The first inequality in (19.25) is Liapunov's inequality, and the equality follows because $\{Y_{nt} - E(Y_{nt}|\mathcal{F}_{n,t-1})\}$ is a m.d., and hence orthogonal. Second,

$$\begin{aligned}\left\|\sum_{t=1}^{k_n}(Z_{nt} - E(Z_{nt}|\mathcal{F}_{n,t-1}))\right\|_p &\le \sum_{t=1}^{k_n}\|Z_{nt}\|_p + \sum_{t=1}^{k_n}\|E(Z_{nt}|\mathcal{F}_{n,t-1})\|_p \\ &\le 2\sum_{t=1}^{k_n}\|Z_{nt}\|_p \le 2\varepsilon\sum_{t=1}^{k_n} c_{nt}.\end{aligned} \tag{19.26}$$

The second inequality here follows because

$$E|E(Z_{nt}|\mathcal{F}_{n,t-1})|^p \le E(E(|Z_{nt}|^p|\mathcal{F}_{n,t-1})) = E|Z_{nt}|^p,$$

from, respectively, the conditional Jensen inequality and the law of iterated expectations. The last is by (19.23).

It follows by (c) that for $\varepsilon > 0$ there exists $N_\varepsilon \ge 1$ such that, for $n \ge N_\varepsilon$,

$$\sum_{t=1}^{k_n} c_{nt}^2 \leq B_\varepsilon^{-2}\varepsilon^2. \tag{19.27}$$

Putting together (19.24) with (19.25) and (19.23) shows that

$$\left\| \sum_{t=1}^{k_n} X_{nt} \right\|_p \leq B\varepsilon \tag{19.28}$$

for $n \geq N_\varepsilon$, where $B = 1 + 2\sum_{t=1}^{k_n} c_{nt} < \infty$, by condition (b). Since ε is arbitrary, this completes the proof. ■

The weak law for martingale differences follows directly, on applying **18.13**.

19.9 Corollary Under the conditions of **19.7** or **19.8**, $\sum_{t=1}^{k_n} X_{nt} \xrightarrow{pr} 0$. □

If we take the case $p = 1$ and set $c_{nt} = 1/n$ and $k_n = n$ as above, we get the result that uniform integrability of $\{X_t\}$ is sufficient for convergence in probability of the sample mean $\bar{X}_n$. This cannot be significantly weakened even if the martingale difference assumption is replaced by independence. If we assume identically distributed coordinates, the explicit requirement of uniform integrability can be dropped and L_1-boundedness is enough; but of course, this is only because the uniform property is subsumed under the stationarity.

You may have observed that (b) in **19.7** can be replaced by

$$\text{(b}'\text{)}\ \limsup_{n\to\infty} k_n^{p-1}\sum_{t=1}^{k_n} c_{nt}^p < \infty.$$

It suffices for the two terms on the majorant side of (19.24) to converge in L_p, and the c_r inequality can be used instead of the Minkowski inequality in (19.26) to obtain

$$E\left|\sum_{t=1}^{k_n}(Z_{nt} - E(Z_{nt}|\mathcal{F}_{n,t-1})\right|^p \leq \varepsilon(2k_n)^{p-1}\sum_{t=1}^{k_n} c_{nt}^p. \tag{19.29}$$

However, the gain in generality here is notional. Condition (b′) requires that $\limsup_{t,n\to\infty} k_n^p c_{nt}^p < \infty$, and if this is true the same property obviously extends to $\{k_n c_{nt}\}$. For concreteness, put $c_{nt} = b_t/a_n$ as in **19.8** with $b_t \sim t^\beta$ and $a_n \sim n^\gamma$, where β and γ can be any real constants. With $k_n \sim n^\alpha$ for $\alpha > 0$, note that the majorant side of (19.29) is bounded if $\alpha(1+\beta) - \gamma \leq 0$, *independent* of the value of p. This condition is automatically satisfied as an equality by setting $a_n = \sum_{t=1}^{k_n} b_t$, but note how the choice of a_n can accommodate different choices of k_n.

None the less, in some situations condition (b) is stronger than what we know to be sufficient. For the case $p = 2$ it can be omitted, in addition to weakening the martingale difference assumption to uncorrelatedness, and uniform integrability to simple L_2-boundedness. Here is the array version of **19.1**, with the conditions cast in the framework of **19.7** for comparability, although all they do is to ensure that the variance of the partial sums goes to zero.

19.10 Corollary If $\{X_{nt}\}$ is a zero-mean stochastic array with $E(X_{nt}X_{ns}) = 0$ for $t \neq s$, and

(a) $\{X_{nt}/c_{nt}\}$ is uniformly L_2-bounded, and

(b) $\lim_{n\to\infty} \sum_{t=1}^{k_n} c_{nt}^2 = 0$,

then $\sum_{t=1}^{k_n} X_{nt} \xrightarrow{L_2} 0$. □

19.4 A Mixingale Weak Law

To generalize the last results from martingale differences to mixingales is not too difficult. The basic tool is the 'telescoping series' argument developed in §16.2. The array element X_{nt} can be decomposed into a finite sum of martingale differences, to which **19.7** can be applied, and two residual components which can be treated as negligible. The following result, from Davidson (1993a), is an extension to the heterogeneous case of a theorem due to Andrews (1988).

19.11 Theorem Let the array $\{X_{nt},\mathcal{F}_{nt}\}_{-\infty}^{\infty}$ be a L_1-mixingale with respect to a constant array $\{c_{nt}\}$. If

(a) $\{X_{nt}/c_{nt}\}$ is uniformly integrable,

(b) $\limsup_{n\to\infty} \sum_{t=1}^{k_n} c_{nt} < \infty$, and

(c) $\lim_{n\to\infty} \sum_{t=1}^{k_n} c_{nt}^2 = 0$,

where k_n is an increasing integer-valued function of n and $k_n \uparrow \infty$, then $\sum_{t=1}^{k_n} X_{nt} \xrightarrow{L_1} 0$. □

There is no restriction on the size here. It suffices simply for the mixingale coefficients to tend to zero. The remarks following **19.7** apply here in just the same way. In particular, if X_t is a L_1-mixingale sequence and $\{X_t/b_t\}$ is uniformly integrable for positive constants $\{b_t\}$, the theorem holds for $X_{nt} = X_t/a_n$ and $c_{nt} = b_t/a_n$ where $a_n = \sum_{t=1}^{n} b_t$. Theorems **14.2** and **14.4** give us the corresponding results for mixing sequences, and **17.5** and **17.6** for NED processes. It is sufficient for, say, X_{nt} to be L_r-bounded for $r > 1$, and L_p-NED, for $p \geq 1$, on a α-mixing process. Again, no size restrictions need to be specified. Uniform integrability of $\{X_{nt}/c_{nt}\}$ will obtain in those cases where $\|X_{nt}\|_r$ is finite for $r > 1$ and each t, and the NED constants likewise satisfy $d_{nt} \gg \|X_{nt}\|_r$.

A simple lemma is required for the proof:

19.12 Lemma If the array $\{X_{nt}/c_{nt}\}$ is uniformly integrable for $p \geq 1$, so is the array $\{E_{t-j}X_{nt}/c_{nt}\}$ for $j > 0$.

Proof By the necessity part of **12.9**, for any $\varepsilon > 0$ $\exists$ $\delta > 0$ such that

$$\sup_{n,t}\left\{\sup\int_E |X_{nt}/c_{nt}|dP\right\} < \varepsilon, \tag{19.30}$$

where the inner supremum is taken over all $E \in \mathcal{F}$ satisfying $P(E) < \delta$. Since $\mathcal{F}_{n,t-j} \subseteq \mathcal{F}$, (19.30) also holds when the supremum is taken over $E \in \mathcal{F}_{n,t-j}$ satisfying $P(E) < \delta$. For any such E,

$$\int_E |X_{nt}/c_{nt}|dP = \int_E E_{t-j}|X_{nt}/c_{nt}|dP \geq \int_E |E_{t-j}X_{nt}/c_{nt}|dP, \tag{19.31}$$

by definition of $E_{t-j}(.)$, and the conditional Jensen inequality (**10.18**). We may accordingly say that, for $\varepsilon > 0$ $\exists$ $\delta > 0$ such that

$$\sup_{n,t}\left\{\sup\int_E |E_{t-j}X_{nt}/c_{nt}|dP\right\} < \varepsilon, \tag{19.32}$$

taking the inner supremum over $E \in \mathcal{F}_{n,t-j}$ satisfying $P(E) < \delta$. Since $E_{t-j}X_{nt}$ is $\mathcal{F}_{n,t-j}$-measurable, uniform integrability holds by the sufficiency part of **12.9**. ∎

Proof of 19.11 Fix an integer j and let

$$Y_{nj} = \sum_{t=1}^{k_n}(E_{t+j}X_{nt} - E_{t+j-1}X_{nt}).$$

The sequence $\{Y_{nj}, \mathcal{F}_{n,n+j}\}_{n=1}^{\infty}$ is a martingale, for each j. Since the array

$$\{(E_{t+j}X_{nt} - E_{t+j-1}X_{nt})/c_{nt}\}$$

is uniformly integrable by (a) and **19.12**, it follows by (b) and (c) and **19.7** that

$$Y_{nj} \xrightarrow{L_1} 0. \tag{19.33}$$

We now express $\sum_{t=1}^{k_n}X_{nt}$ as a telescoping sum. For any $M \geq 1$,

$$\sum_{j=1-M}^{M-1} Y_{nj} = \sum_{t=1}^{k_n} E_{t+M-1}X_{nt} - \sum_{t=1}^{k_n} E_{t-M}X_{nt}, \tag{19.34}$$

and hence

$$\sum_{t=1}^{k_n}X_{nt} = \sum_{j=1-M}^{M-1} Y_{nj} + \sum_{t=1}^{k_n}(X_{nt} - E_{t+M-1}X_{nt}) + \sum_{t=1}^{k_n}E_{t-M}X_{nt}. \tag{19.35}$$

The triangle inequality and the L_1-mixingale property now give

$$\begin{aligned} E\left|\sum_{t=1}^{k_n}X_{nt}\right| &\leq \sum_{j=1-M}^{M-1} E|Y_{nj}| + \sum_{t=1}^{k_n}E|X_{nt} - E_{t+M-1}X_{nt}| + \sum_{t=1}^{k_n}E|E_{t-M}X_{nt}| \\ &\leq \sum_{j=1-M}^{M-1} E|Y_{nj}| + 2\zeta_M\sum_{t=1}^{k_n} c_{nt}. \end{aligned} \tag{19.36}$$

According to the assumptions, the second member on the right-hand side of (19.36) is $O(M^{-\delta})$ for some $\delta > 0$, and given $\varepsilon > 0$ there exists M_ε such that $\zeta_M\sum_{t=1}^{k_n}c_{nt} <$

$\frac{1}{2}\varepsilon$ for $M \geq M_\varepsilon$. By choosing n large enough, the sum of $2M - 1$ terms on the right-hand side of (19.36) can be made smaller than $\frac{1}{2}\varepsilon$ for any finite M, by (19.33). So, by choosing $M \geq M_\varepsilon$ we have $E|\sum_{t=1}^{k_n} X_{nt}| < \varepsilon$ when n is large enough. The theorem is now proved since ε is arbitrary. ■

A comparison with the results of §19.1 is instructive. In an L_2-bounded process, the L_2-mixingale property would be a stronger form of dependence restriction than the limiting uncorrelatedness specified in **19.2**, just as the martingale property is stronger than simple uncorrelatedness. The value of the present result is the substantial weakening of the moment conditions.

19.5 Approximable Processes

There remains the possibility of cases in which the mixingale property is not easily established—perhaps because of a nonlinear transformation of a L_p-NED process which cannot be shown to preserve the requisite moments for application of the results in §17.3. In such cases the theory of §17.4 may yield a result. On the assumption that the approximator sequence is mixing, so that its mean deviations converge in probability by **19.11**, it will be sufficient to show that this implies the convergence of the approximable sequence. This is the object of the following theorem.

19.13 Theorem Suppose that, for each $m \in \mathbb{N}$, $\{h_{nt}^m\}$ is a stochastic array and the centred array $\{h_{nt}^m - E(h_{nt}^m)\}$ satisfies the conditions of **19.11**. If the array $\{X_{nt}\}$ is L_1-approximable by $\{h_{nt}^m\}$ with respect to a constant array $\{d_{nt}\}$, and $\limsup_{n\to\infty} \sum_{t=1}^{k_n} d_{nt} \leq B < \infty$, then $\sum_{t=1}^{k_n} X_{nt} \xrightarrow{pr} 0$. □

Establishing the conditions of the theorem will typically be achieved using **17.21**, by showing that X_{nt} is L_r-bounded for $r > 1$, and approximable in probability on h_{nt}^m for each m, the latter being m-order lag functions of a mixing array of any size.

Proof Since

$$\left|\sum_{t=1}^{k_n} X_{nt}\right| \leq \left|\sum_{t=1}^{k_n}(X_{nt} - h_{nt}^m)\right| + \left|\sum_{t=1}^{k_n}(h_{nt}^m - E(h_{nt}^m))\right| + \left|\sum_{t=1}^{k_n} E(h_{nt}^m)\right| \tag{19.37}$$

by the triangle inequality, we have for $\delta > 0$

$$P\left(\left|\sum_{t=1}^{k_n} X_{nt}\right| > \delta\right) \leq P\left(\left|\sum_{t=1}^{k_n}(X_{nt} - h_{nt}^m)\right| > \frac{\delta}{3}\right)$$

$$+ P\left(\left|\sum_{t=1}^{k_n}(h_{nt}^m - E(h_{nt}^m))\right| > \frac{\delta}{3}\right) + P\left(\left|\sum_{t=1}^{k_n} E(h_{nt}^m)\right| > \frac{\delta}{3}\right) \tag{19.38}$$

by subadditivity, since the event whose probability is on the minorant side implies at least one of those on the majorant. By the Markov inequality,

$$P\left(\left|\sum_{t=1}^{k_n}(X_{nt}-h_{nt}^m)\right| > \frac{\delta}{3}\right) \le \frac{3}{\delta}E\left|\sum_{t=1}^{k_n}(X_{nt}-h_{nt}^m)\right|$$

$$\le \frac{3}{\delta}\sum_{t=1}^{k_n}E|X_{nt}-h_{nt}^m|$$

$$\le \frac{3}{\delta}\left(\sum_{t=1}^{k_n}d_{nt}\right)\nu_m. \tag{19.39}$$

$P(|\sum_{t=1}^{k_n}E(h_{nt}^m)| > \delta/3)$ is equal to either 0 or 1, according to whether the non-stochastic inequality holds or does not hold. By the fact that $E(X_{nt}) = 0$ and L_1-approximability,

$$|E(h_{nt}^m)| = |E(X_{nt}) - E(h_{nt}^m)| \le E|X_{nt}-h_{nt}^m| \le d_{nt}\nu_m, \tag{19.40}$$

and hence

$$\left|\sum_{t=1}^{k_n}E(h_{nt}^m)\right| \le \sum_{t=1}^{k_n}|E(h_{nt}^m)| \le \sum_{t=1}^{k_n}d_{nt}\nu_m \le B\nu_m. \tag{19.41}$$

We therefore find that for each $m \in \mathbb{N}$

$$\limsup_{n\to\infty} P\left(\left|\sum_{t=1}^{k_n}X_{nt}\right| > \delta\right)$$

$$\le \frac{3B}{\delta}\nu_m + \limsup_{n\to\infty} P\left(\left|\sum_{t=1}^{k_n}(h_{nt}^m - E(h_{nt}^m))\right| > \frac{\delta}{3}\right) + 1_{\{B\nu_m > \delta/3\}}$$

$$= \frac{3B}{\delta}\nu_m + 1_{\{B\nu_m > \delta/3\}}, \tag{19.42}$$

by the assumption that h_{nt}^m satisfies the WLLN for each $m \in \mathbb{N}$. The proof is completed by letting $m \to \infty$. ■

20
The Strong Law of Large Numbers

20.1 Technical Tricks for Proving LLNs

In this chapter we explore the strong law under a range of different assumptions, from independent sequences to near-epoch dependent functions of mixing processes. Many of the proofs are based on one or more of a collection of ingenious technical lemmas, and we begin by studying these results. The reader has the option of skipping ahead to §20.2, and referring back as necessary, but there is something to be said for forming an impression of the method of attack at the outset. These theorems are found in several different versions in the literature, usually in a form adapted to the particular problem in hand. Here we will take note of the minimal conditions needed to make each trick work.

We start with the basic convergence result that shows why maximal inequalities (for example, **15.14**, **15.15**, **16.9**, and **16.11**) are important.

20.1 Convergence lemma Let $\{X_t\}_1^\infty$ be a stochastic sequence on a probability space $(\Omega,\mathcal{F},P)$, and let $S_n = \sum_{t=1}^n X_t$ and $S_0 = 0$. For $\omega \in \Omega$, let

$$M(\omega) = \inf_m \left(\sup_{j>m} |S_j(\omega) - S_m(\omega)| \right). \tag{20.1}$$

If $P(M > \varepsilon) = 0$ for all $\varepsilon > 0$, then $S_n \xrightarrow{as} S$.

Proof By the Cauchy criterion for convergence, the realization $\{S_n(\omega)\}$ converges if we can find an m such that $|S_j - S_m| \le \varepsilon$ for all $j > m$, for all $\varepsilon > 0$; in other words, it converges if $M(\omega) \le \varepsilon$ for all $\varepsilon > 0$. ■

This result is usually applied in the following way.

20.2 Corollary Let $\{c_t\}_1^\infty$ be a sequence of constants, and suppose there exists $p > 0$ such that, for every $m \ge 0$ and $n > m$, and every $\varepsilon > 0$,

$$P\left(\max_{m<j\le n} |S_j - S_m| > \varepsilon \right) \le \frac{K}{\varepsilon^p} \sum_{t=m+1}^n c_t^p, \tag{20.2}$$

where K is a finite constant. If $\sum_{t=1}^\infty c_t^p < \infty$, then $S_n \xrightarrow{as} S$.

Proof Since $\{c_t^p\}$ is summable it follows by **2.25** that $\lim_{m\to\infty}\sum_{t=m+1}^\infty c_t^p = 0$. Let M be the r.v. in (20.1). By definition, $M \le \sup_{j>m}|S_j - S_m|$ for any $m > 0$, and hence

$$P(M > \varepsilon) \le \lim_{m\to\infty} \left(\sup_{j>m} |S_j - S_m| > \varepsilon \right)$$

$$\leq \frac{K}{\varepsilon^p} \lim_{m\to\infty} \sum_{t=m+1}^{\infty} c_t^p = 0, \tag{20.3}$$

where the final inequality is the limiting case of (20.2). **20.1** completes the proof. ∎

Notice how this proof does not make a direct appeal to the Borel-Cantelli lemma to get a.s. convergence. The method is closer to that of **18.3**. The essential trick with a maximal inequality is to put a bound on the probability of *all* occurrences of a certain type of event as we move down the sequence, by specifying a probability for the most extreme of them.

Since S is finite almost surely, $\bar{X}_n \xrightarrow{as} 0$ is an instant corollary of **20.2**. However, the result can be also used in a more subtle way in conjunction with Kronecker's lemma. If $\sum_{t=1}^n Y_t$ converges a.s., where $\{Y_t\} = \{X_t/a_t\}$ and $\{a_t\}$ is a sequence of positive constants with $a_n \uparrow \infty$, it follows that $a_n^{-1}\sum_{t=1}^n X_t \xrightarrow{as} 0$. This is of course a much weaker condition than the convergence of $\sum_{t=1}^n X_t$ itself. Most applications feature $a_t = t$, but the more general formulation also has uses.

There is a standard device for extending a.s. convergence to a wider class of sequences, once it has been proved for a given class: the method of *equivalent sequences*. Sequences $\{X_t\}_1^\infty$ and $\{Y_t\}_1^\infty$ are said to be equivalent if

$$\sum_{t=1}^{\infty} P(X_t \neq Y_t) < \infty. \tag{20.4}$$

By the first Borel-Cantelli lemma (**18.2**(i)), (20.4) implies $P(X_t \neq Y_t, \text{ i.o.}) = 0$. In other words, only on a set of probability measure zero are there more than a finite number of t for which $X_t(\omega) \neq Y_t(\omega)$.

20.3 Theorem If X_t and Y_t are equivalent, $\sum_{t=1}^n (X_t - Y_t)$ converges a.s.

Proof By definition of equivalence and **18.2**(i) there exists a subset C of Ω, with $P(\Omega - C) = 0$, and with the following property: for all $\omega \in C$, there is a finite $n_0(\omega)$ such that $X_t(\omega) = Y_t(\omega)$ for $t > n_0(\omega)$. Hence

$$\sum_{t=1}^{n} (X_t(\omega) - Y_t(\omega)) = \sum_{t=1}^{n_0(\omega)} (X_t(\omega) - Y_t(\omega)),\ \forall\ n \geq n_0(\omega),$$

and the sum converges, for all $\omega \in C$. ∎

The equivalent sequences concept is often put to use by means of the following theorem.

20.4 Theorem Let $\{X_t\}_1^\infty$ be a zero-mean random sequence satisfying

$$\sum_{t=1}^{\infty} E|X_t|^p / a_t^p < \infty \tag{20.5}$$

for some $p \geq 1$, and a sequence of positive constants $\{a_t\}$. Then, putting 1_t^a for the indicator function $1_{\{|X_t| \leq a_t\}}(\omega)$,

$$\sum_{t=1}^{\infty} P(|X_t| > a_t) < \infty, \tag{20.6}$$

$$\sum_{t=1}^{\infty} |E(X_t 1_t^a)|/a_t < \infty, \tag{20.7}$$

and for any $r \geq p$,

$$\sum_{t=1}^{\infty} E(|X_t|^r 1_t^a)/a_t^r < \infty. \ \square \tag{20.8}$$

The idea behind this result may be apparent. The indicator function is used to truncate a sequence, replacing a member by 0 if it exceeds a given absolute bound. The ratio of the truncated sequence to the bound cannot exceed 1 and possesses all its absolute moments, while inequality (20.6) tells us that the truncated sequence is equivalent to the original under condition (20.5). Proving a strong law under (20.5) can therefore be accomplished by proving a strong law for a truncated sequence, subject to (20.7) and (20.8).

Proof of Theorem 20.4 We prove the following three inequalities:

$$\begin{aligned} P(|X_t| > a_t) &= E(1 - 1_t^a) \\ &\leq E(|X_t|^p(1 - 1_t^a))/a_t^p \\ &\leq E(|X_t|^p)/a_t^p. \end{aligned} \tag{20.9}$$

Here the inequalities are because $|X_t(\omega)|^p/a_t^p > 1$ for $\omega \in \{|X_t| > a_t\}$, and because $E(|X_t|^p 1_t^a)$ is non-negative, respectively.

$$\begin{aligned} |E(X_t 1_t^a)|/a_t &= |E(X_t(1 - 1_t^a))|/a_t \\ &\leq E(|X_t|(1 - 1_t^a))/a_t \\ &\leq E(|X_t|^p(1 - 1_t^a))/a_t^p \\ &\leq E(|X_t|^p)/a_t^p. \end{aligned} \tag{20.10}$$

The equality in (20.10) is because $E(X_t) = 0$, hence $E(X_t 1_t^a) = -E(X_t(1 - 1_t^a))$. The first inequality is the modulus inequality, and the second is because on the event $\{|X_t| > a_t\}$, $(|X_t|/a_t)^p \geq |X_t|/a_t$ for $p \geq 1$. Finally, by similar arguments to the above,

$$\begin{aligned} E(|X_t|^r 1_t^a)/a_t^r &\leq E(|X_t|^p 1_t^a)/a_t^p \text{ for } p \leq r \\ &\leq E(|X_t|^p)/a_t^p. \end{aligned} \tag{20.11}$$

The theorem follows on summing over t. ■

There are a number of variations on this basic result. The first is a version for martingale differences in terms of the one-step-ahead conditional moments, where the weight sequence is also allowed to be stochastic. The style of this result is appropriate to the class of martingale limit theorems we shall examine in §20.4, in which we establish almost-sure equivalence between sets on which certain conditions obtain and on which sequences converge.

20.5 Corollary Let $\{X_t,\mathcal{F}_t\}$ be a m.d. sequence, let $\{W_t\}$ be a sequence of positive $\mathcal{F}_{t-1}$-measurable r.v.s, and for some $p \geq 1$ let

$$D = \left\{\omega\colon \sum_{t=1}^{\infty} E(|X_t|^p|\mathcal{F}_{t-1})(\omega)/W_t^p(\omega) < \infty\right\} \in \mathcal{F}. \tag{20.12}$$

Also define

$$D_1 = \left\{\omega\colon \sum_{t=1}^{\infty} P(|X_t| > W_t|\mathcal{F}_{t-1})(\omega) < \infty\right\} \in \mathcal{F} \tag{20.13}$$

$$D_2 = \left\{\omega\colon \sum_{t=1}^{\infty} |E(X_t 1_t^W|\mathcal{F}_{t-1})(\omega)|/W_t(\omega) < \infty\right\} \in \mathcal{F} \tag{20.14}$$

$$D_3 = \left\{\omega\colon \sum_{t=1}^{\infty} E(|X_t|^r 1_t^W|\mathcal{F}_{t-1})(\omega)/W_t^r(\omega) < \infty\right\} \in \mathcal{F}, \tag{20.15}$$

and let $D' = D_1 \cap D_2 \cap D_3$. Then $P(D - D') = 0$. In particular, If $P(D) = 1$ then $P(D') = 1$.

Proof It suffices to prove the three inequalities (20.9), (20.10), and (20.11) for the case of conditional expectations. Noting that $E(X_t|\mathcal{F}_{t-1}) = 0$ a.s. and using the fact that W_t is $\mathcal{F}_{t-1}$-measurable, all of these go through unchanged, except that the conditional modulus inequality **10.14** is used to get (20.14). It follows that almost every $\omega \in D$ is in D'. ∎

Another version of this theorem uses a different truncation, with the truncated variable chosen to be a continuous function of X_t; see **17.13** to appreciate why this variation might be useful.

20.6 Corollary Let $\{X_t\}_1^\infty$ be a zero-mean random sequence satisfying (20.5) for $p \geq 1$. Define

$$Y_t = X_t 1_t^a/a_t + (X_t/|X_t|)(1 - 1_t^a) = \begin{cases} X_t/a_t, & |X_t| \leq a_t \\ 1, & X_t > a_t \\ -1, & X_t < -a_t. \end{cases} \tag{20.16}$$

Then,

$$\sum_{t=1}^{\infty} |E(Y_t)| < \infty, \tag{20.17}$$

$$\sum_{t=1}^{\infty} E|Y_t|^r < \infty, \; r \geq p. \tag{20.18}$$

Proof Write $\pm a_t$ to denote $a_tX_t/|X_t|$. Inequalities (20.10) and (20.11) of **20.4** are adapted as follows.

$$\begin{aligned} |E(Y_t)| &= |E(X_t1_t^a + (1 - 1_t^a)(\pm a_t))|/a_t \\ &= |E(X_t - (\pm a_t))(1 - 1_t^a)|/a_t \\ &\leq E|X_t|(1 - 1_t^a)/a_t + E|1 - 1_t^a| \\ &\leq E(|X_t|^p(1 - 1_t^a))/a_t^p + P(|X_t| > a_t) \\ &\leq 2E(|X_t|^p)/a_t^p. \end{aligned} \tag{20.19}$$

The second equality in (20.19) is again because $E(X_t) = 0$. The first inequality is an application of the modulus inequality and triangle inequalities in succession, and the last one uses (20.9). By similar arguments, except that here the c_r inequality is used in the second line, we have

$$\begin{aligned} E(|Y_t|^r) &\leq E|X_t1_t^a + (1 - 1_t^a)(\pm a_t)|^r/a_t^r \\ &\leq 2^{r-1}(E|X_t1_t^a|^r/a_t^r + E|(1 - 1_t^a)|^r) \\ &\leq 2^{r-1}(E(|X_t|^p1_t^a)/a_t^p + P(|X_t| > a_t)) \text{ for } p \leq r \\ &\leq 2^rE(|X_t|^p)/a_t^p. \end{aligned} \tag{20.20}$$

The theorem follows on summing over t as before. ∎

Clearly, **20.5** could be adapted to this case if desired, but that extension will not be needed for our results.

The last extension is relatively modest, but permits summability conditions for norms to be applied.

20.7 Corollary (20.6), (20.7), (20.8), (20.17), and (20.18) all continue to hold if (20.5) is replaced by

$$\sum_{t=1}^{\infty} E(|X_t|^p)^{1/q}/a_t^{p/q} < \infty \tag{20.21}$$

for any $q \geq 1$.

Proof The modified forms of (20.9), and of (20.19) and (20.20) (say) are

$$P(|X_t| > a_t) \leq P(|X_t| > a_t)^{1/q} \leq (E(|X_t|^p)/a_t^p)^{1/q}, \tag{20.22}$$

$$|E(Y_t)| \leq |E(Y_t)|^{1/q} \leq 2^{1/q}(E(|X_t|^p)/a_t^p)^{1/q}, \tag{20.23}$$

$$E|Y_t|^r \leq (E|Y_t|^r)^{1/q} \leq 2^{r/q}(E(|X_t|^p)/a_t^p)^{1/q}, \tag{20.24}$$

where in each case the first inequality is because the left-hand-side member does not exceed 1. ■

For example, by choosing $p = q$ the condition that the sequence $\{\|X_t/a_t\|_p\}$ is summable is seen to be sufficient for **20.4** and **20.6**.

20.2 The Case of Independence

The classic results on strong convergence are for the case of independent sequences. The following is the 'three series theorem' of Kolmogorov:

20.8 Three series theorem Let $\{X_t\}$ be an independent sequence, and $S_n = \sum_{t=1}^n X_t$. $S_n \xrightarrow{as} S$ if and only if the following conditions hold for some fixed $a > 0$:

$$\sum_{t=1}^{\infty} P(|X_t| > a) < \infty, \tag{20.25}$$

$$\sum_{t=1}^{\infty} E(1_{\{|X_t| \leq a\}} X_t) < \infty, \tag{20.26}$$

$$\sum_{t=1}^{\infty} \mathrm{Var}(1_{\{|X_t| \leq a\}} X_t) < \infty. \ \square \tag{20.27}$$

Since the event $\{S_n \to S\}$ is the same as the event $\{S_{n+1} \to S\}$, convergence is invariant to shift transformations. It is a remote event by **13.19** and hence in independent sequences occurs with probability either 0 or 1, according to **13.17**. **20.8** gives the conditions under which the probability is 1, rather than 0. The theorem has the immediate corollary that $S_n/a_n \to 0$, whenever $a_n \uparrow \infty$.

The basic idea of these proofs is to prove the convergence result for the truncated variables $1_{\{|X_t| \leq a\}} X_t$, and then use the equivalent sequences theorem to extend it to X_t itself. In view of **20.4**, the condition

$$\sum_{t=1}^{\infty} E|X_t|^p < \infty, \ 1 \leq p \leq 2, \tag{20.28}$$

is sufficient for convergence, although not necessary. Another point to notice about the proof is that the necessity part does not assign a value to a. Convergence implies that (20.25)–(20.27) hold for *every* $a > 0$.

Proof of 20.8 Write $Y_t = 1_{\{|X_t| \leq a\}} X_t$, so that the summands in (20.26) and (20.27) are respectively the means and variances of Y_t. The sequence $\{Y_t - E(Y_t)\}$ is independent and hence a martingale difference, so that $S_n' - S_m' = \sum_{t=m+1}^n (Y_t - E(Y_t))$ is a martingale for fixed $m \geq 0$, and $\sum_{t=m+1}^n \mathrm{Var}(Y_t) = \mathrm{Var}(S_n' - S_m')$. Theorem **15.14** combined with **20.2**, setting $p = 2$ in each case and putting $c_t^2 = \mathrm{Var}(Y_t)$ and $K = 1$, together yield the result that $S_n' \xrightarrow{as} S'$ when (20.27) holds. If (20.26) holds, this further implies that $\sum_{t=1}^n Y_t$ converges. And then if (20.25) holds the sequences $\{X_t\}$ and $\{Y_t\}$ are equivalent, and so $S_n \xrightarrow{as} S$, by **20.3**. This proves sufficiency of the three conditions.

Conversely, suppose $S_n \xrightarrow{as} S$. By **2.25** applied to $S_n(\omega)$ for each $\omega \in \Omega$, it follows that $\lim_{m\to\infty}\sum_{t=m}^{\infty}X_t = 0$ a.s. This means that $P(|X_t| > a, \text{i.o.}) = 0$, for any $a > 0$, and so (20.25) must follow by the divergence part of the Borel-Cantelli lemma (**18.2**(ii)). **20.3** then assures us that $\sum_{t=1}^{n}Y_t$ also converges a.s.

Write $s_n^2 = \sum_{t=1}^{n}\text{Var}(Y_t)$. If $s_n^2 \to \infty$ as $n \to \infty$, $\sum_{t=1}^{n}(Y_t - E(Y_t))/s_n$ fails to converge, but is asymptotically distributed as a standard Gaussian r.v. (This is the central limit theorem - see **23.6**.) This fact contradicts the possibility of $\sum_{t=1}^{n}Y_t$ converging, so we conclude that s_n^2 is bounded in the limit, which is equivalent to (20.27).

Finally, consider the sequence $\{Y_t - E(Y_t)\}$. This has mean zero, the same variance as Y_t, and $P(|Y_t - E(Y_t)| > 2a) = 0$ for all t. Hence, it satisfies the conditions (20.25)-(20.27) (in respect of the constant $2a$) and the sufficiency part of the theorem implies that $\sum_{t=1}^{n}(Y_t - E(Y_t))$ converges. And since $\sum_{t=1}^{n}Y_t$ converges, (20.26) must hold. This completes the proof of necessity. ∎

The sufficiency part of this result is subsumed under the weaker conditions of **20.10** below, and is now mainly of historical interest; it is the necessity proof that is interesting, since it has no counterpart in the LLNs for dependent sequences. In these cases we cannot use the divergence part of the Borel-Cantelli lemma, and it appears difficult to rule out special cases in which convergence is achieved with arbitrary moment conditions. Incidentally, Kolmogorov originally proved the maximal inequality of **15.14**, cited in the proof, for the independent case; but again, his result can now be subsumed under the case of martingale differences, and does not need to be quoted separately.

Another reason why the independent case is of interest is because of the following very elegant result due to Lévy. This shows that, when we are dealing with partial sums of independent sequences, the concepts of weak and strong convergence coincide.

20.9 Theorem When $\{X_t\}$ is an independent sequence and $S_n = \sum_{t=1}^{n}X_t$, $S_n \xrightarrow{pr} S$ if and only if $S_n \xrightarrow{as} S$.

Proof Sufficiency is by **18.5**. It is the necessity that is unique to the particular case cited. Let $S_{mn} = \sum_{t=m+1}^{n}X_t$, and for some $\varepsilon > 0$ consider the various ways in which the event $\{|S_{mn}| > \varepsilon\}$ can occur. In particular, consider the disjoint collection

$$\left\{\max_{m\le j\le k-1}|S_{mj}| \le 2\varepsilon,\ |S_{mk}| > 2\varepsilon\right\},\ k = m+1,\ldots,n.$$

For each k, this is the event that the sum from m onwards exceeds 2ε absolutely for the *first* time at time k, and thus

$$\bigcup_{k=m+1}^{n}\left\{\max_{m\le j\le k-1}|S_{mj}| \le 2\varepsilon,\ |S_{mk}| > 2\varepsilon\right\} = \left\{\max_{m\le j\le n}|S_{mj}| > 2\varepsilon\right\}, \tag{20.29}$$

where the sets of the union are disjoint. It is also the case that

$$\bigcup_{k=m+1}^{n}\left\{\max_{m\le j\le k-1}|S_{mj}|\le 2\varepsilon,\ |S_{mk}|>2\varepsilon\right\}\cap\{|S_{kn}|\le\varepsilon\}\subseteq\{|S_{mn}|>\varepsilon\},\tag{20.30}$$

where the inclusion is ensured by imposing the extra condition for each k. The events in this union are still disjoint, and by the assumption of an independent sequence they are the intersections of independent pairs of events. On applying (20.29), we can conclude from (20.30) that

$$P\Big(\max_{m\le j\le n}|S_{mj}| > 2\varepsilon\Big)\min_{m<k\le n}P(|S_{kn}|\le\varepsilon)$$

$$\le\sum_{k=m+1}^{n}P\Big(\max_{m\le j\le k-1}|S_{mj}|\le 2\varepsilon,\ |S_{mk}|>2\varepsilon\Big)P(|S_{kn}|\le\varepsilon)$$

$$\le P(|S_{mn}|>\varepsilon).\tag{20.31}$$

If $S_n \xrightarrow{pr} S$, there exists by definition $m \ge 1$ such that

$$P(|S_{mn}| > \varepsilon) < \varepsilon \tag{20.32}$$

for all $n > m$. According to (20.32), the second factor on the minorant side of (20.31) is at least as great as $1-\varepsilon$, so for $0 < \varepsilon < 1$,

$$P\Big(\max_{m\le j\le n}|S_{mj}| > 2\varepsilon\Big) < \frac{\varepsilon}{1-\varepsilon}.\tag{20.33}$$

Letting $n \to \infty$ and then $m \to \infty$, the theorem now follows by **18.3**. ∎

This equivalence of weak and strong results is one of the chief benefits stemming from the independence assumption. Since the three-series theorem is equivalent to a weak law according to **20.9**, we also have necessary conditions for convergence in probability. As far as sufficiency results go, however, practically nothing is lost by passing from the independent to the martingale case, and since showing convergence is usually of disproportionately greater importance than showing nonconvergence, the absence of necessary conditions may be regarded a small price to pay.

However, a feature of the three series theorem that is common to all the strong law results of this chapter is that it is not an array result. Being based on the convergence lemma, all these proofs depend on teaming a convergent stochastic sequence with an increasing constant sequence, such that their ratio goes to zero. Although the results can be written down in array form, there is no counterpart of the weak law of **19.7**, more general than its specialization in **19.8**.

20.3 Martingale Strong Laws

Martingale limit results are remarkably powerful. So long as a sequence is a martingale difference, no further restrictions on its dependence are required and the moment assumptions called for are scarcely tougher than those imposed in the independent case. Moreover, while the m.d. property is stronger than the uncorrelatedness assumed in §19.2, the distinction is very largely technical. Given the nature of econometric time-series models, we are usually able to assert that a sequence is uncorrelated *because* it is a m.d., basically a sequence which is not forecastable in mean one step ahead. The case when it is uncorrelated with its own past values but not with some other function of lagged information could arise, but would be in the nature of a special case.

The results in this section and the next one are drawn or adapted chiefly from Stout (1974) and Hall and Heyde (1980), although many of the ideas go back to Doob (1953). We begin with a standard SLLN for L_2-bounded sequences.

20.10 Theorem Let $\{X_t,\mathcal{F}_t\}_0^\infty$ be a m.d. sequence with variance sequence $\{\sigma_t^2\}$, and $\{a_t\}$ a positive constant sequence with $a_t \uparrow \infty$. $S_n/a_n \xrightarrow{as} 0$ if

$$\sum_{t=1}^{\infty} \sigma_t^2/a_t^2 < \infty. \; \square \tag{20.34}$$

There are (at least) two ways to prove this result. The first is to use the martingale convergence theorem (**15.7**) directly, and the second is to combine the maximal inequality of **15.14** with the convergence lemma **20.2**. In effect, the second line of argument provides an alternative proof of martingale convergence for the square-integrable case, providing an interesting comparison of techniques.

First proof Define $T_n = \sum_{t=1}^n X_t/a_t$, so that $\{T_n,\mathcal{F}_n\}$ is a square-integrable martingale. We can say, using the norm inequality and orthogonality of $\{X_t\}$,

$$\sup_n E|T_n| \le \sup_n E(T_n^2)^{1/2} = \left(\sum_{t=1}^{\infty} \sigma_t^2/a_t^2\right)^{1/2} < \infty, \tag{20.35}$$

leading directly to the conclusion $T_n \to T$ a.s., by **15.7**. Now apply the Kronecker lemma to the sequences $\{T_n(\omega)\}$ for $\omega \in \Omega$, to show that $S_n/a_n \xrightarrow{as} 0$. ∎

Second proof For $m \ge 0$, $\{T_n - T_m, \mathcal{F}_n\}$ is a martingale with

$$E(T_n - T_m)^2 = \sum_{t=m+1}^n \sigma_t^2/a_t^2. \tag{20.36}$$

Apply **15.14** for $p = 2$, and then **20.2** with $c_t^2 = \sigma_t^2/a_t^2$. Finally, apply the Kronecker lemma as before. ∎

Compare this result with **19.4**. If $\mathrm{Var}(X_t) = \sigma_t^2 \le B < \infty$, say, then setting $a_t = t$, we have $\sum_{t=1}^\infty \sigma_t^2/t^2 \le B\sum_{t=1}^\infty 1/t^2 \approx 1.64B < \infty$, and the condition of the theorem is satisfied, hence $\bar{X}_n = S_n/n \xrightarrow{as} 0$, the same conclusion as before. But the conditions on the variances are now a lot weaker, and in effect we have converted the weak law of **19.1** into a strong law, at the small cost of substituting the m.d. assumption for orthogonality. As an example of the general formulation, suppose the sequence satisfies

$$\sum_{t=1}^{\infty} E(X_t^2)/t^4 < \infty. \tag{20.37}$$

We cannot then rely upon $\bar{X}_n$ converging to zero, but (putting $a_t = t^2$) we can show that $n^{-2}\sum_{t=1}^n X_t = \bar{X}_n/n$ will do so.

The limitation of **20.10** is that it calls for square integrability. The next step is to use **20.4** to extend it to the class of cases that satisfy

$$\sum_{t=1}^{\infty} E|X_t|^p/a_t^p < \infty \tag{20.38}$$

for $1 \le p \le 2$, and some $\{a_t\} \uparrow \infty$. It is important to appreciate that (20.38) for $p < 2$ is not a *weaker* condition than for $p = 2$, and the latter does not imply the former. For contrast, consider $p = 1$. The Kronecker lemma applied to (20.38) implies that

$$a_n^{-1}\sum_{t=1}^{n} E|X_t| \to 0. \tag{20.39}$$

For $a_n \sim n$, such a sequence has got to be zero or very close to it most of the time. In fact, there is a trivially direct proof of convergence. Applying the monotone convergence theorem (**4.9**),

$$E\left(\lim_{n\to\infty} a_n^{-1}|S_n|\right) \le E\left(\lim_{n\to\infty} a_n^{-1}\sum_{t=1}^{n}|X_t|\right)$$

$$= \lim_{n\to\infty} a_n^{-1}\sum_{t=1}^{n} E|X_t|. \tag{20.40}$$

For any random variable X, $E|X| = 0$ if and only if $X = 0$ a.s.. Nothing more is needed to show that S_n/a_n converges, regardless of other conditions.

Thus, having latitude in the value of p for which the theorem may hold is really a matter of being able to trade off the existence of absolute moments against the rate of damping necessary to make them summable. We may meet interesting cases in which (20.38) holds for $p < 2$ only rarely, but since this extension is available at small extra cost in complexity, it makes sense to take advantage of it.

20.11 Theorem If $\{X_t,\mathcal{F}_t\}_1^\infty$ is a m.d. sequence satisfying (20.38) for $1 \le p \le 2$, $S_n/a_n \xrightarrow{as} 0$.

Proof Let $Y_t = 1_{\{|X_t| \le a_t\}}X_t$, and note that $\{X_t\}$ and $\{Y_t\}$ are equivalent under (20.38), by **20.4**. Y_t is also $\mathcal{F}_t$-measurable, and hence the centred sequence $\{Z_t,\mathcal{F}_t\}$, where $Z_t = Y_t - E(Y_t|\mathcal{F}_{t-1})$, is a m.d. Now,

$$E(Z_t^2) = E(E(Z_t^2|\mathcal{F}_{t-1}))$$

$$= E(E(Y_t^2|\mathcal{F}_{t-1}) - E(Y_t|\mathcal{F}_{t-1})^2)$$

$$= E(Y_t^2) - E(E(Y_t|\mathcal{F}_{t-1})^2). \tag{20.41}$$

According to **20.4** with $r = 2$, (20.38) implies that $\sum_{t=1}^{\infty} E(Y_t^2)/a_t^2 < \infty$, and so, since $E(Z_t^2) \le E(Y_t^2)$ by (20.41),

$$\sum_{t=1}^{\infty} E(Z_t^2)/a_t^2 < \infty. \tag{20.42}$$

By **20.10**, this is sufficient for $\sum_{t=1}^{n} Z_t/a_t \xrightarrow{as} S_1$, where S_1 is some random variable. But

$$\sum_{t=1}^{n} Z_t/a_t = \sum_{t=1}^{n} Y_t/a_t - \sum_{t=1}^{n} E(Y_t|\mathcal{F}_{t-1})/a_t. \tag{20.43}$$

By **15.13**(i), (20.38) is equivalent to

$$\sum_{t=1}^{\infty} E(|X_t|^p|\mathcal{F}_{t-1})/a_t^p < \infty, \text{ a.s.} \tag{20.44}$$

According to **20.5**, (20.44) implies that $\sum_{t=1}^{\infty} |E(Y_t|\mathcal{F}_{t-1})|/a_t < \infty$, a.s. Absolute convergence of a series implies convergence by **2.24**, so we may say that $\sum_{t=1}^{n} E(Y_t|\mathcal{F}_{t-1})/a_t \xrightarrow{as} S_2$. Hence, $\sum_{t=1}^{n} Y_t/a_t \xrightarrow{as} S_1 + S_2$ and so $a_n^{-1}\sum_{t=1}^{n} Y_t \xrightarrow{as} 0$ by the Kronecker lemma. It follows by **20.3** and the equivalence of X_t and Y_t implied by (20.38) that $S_n/a_n \xrightarrow{as} 0$. ∎

Notice that in this proof there are no short cuts through the martingale convergence theorem. While we know that $\sum_{t=1}^{n} X_t/a_t$ is a martingale, the problem is to establish that it is uniformly L_1-bounded, given only information about the joint distribution of $\{X_t\}$, in the form of (20.38). We have to go by way of a result for $p = 2$ to exploit orthogonality, which is where the truncation arguments come in handy.

20.4 Conditional Variances and Random Weighting

A feature of martingale theory exploited in the last theorem is the possibility of relating convergence to the behaviour of the sequences of one-step-ahead conditional moments; we now extend this principle to the conditional variances $E(X_t^2|\mathcal{F}_{t-1})$. The elegant results of this section contain those such as **20.10** and **20.11**.

The conditional variance of a centred coordinate is the variance of the innovation, that is, of $X_t - E(X_t|\mathcal{F}_{t-1})$, and in some circumstances it may be more natural to place restrictions on the behaviour of the innovations than on the original sequence. In regression models, for example, the innovations may correspond to the regression disturbances. Moreover, the fact that the conditional moments are $\mathcal{F}_{t-1}$-measurable random variables, so that any constraint upon them is probabilistic, permits a generalization of the concept of convergence, following the results of §15.4; our confidence in the summability of the weighted conditional variances translates into a probability that the sequence converges, in the manner of the following theorem. A nice refinement is that the constant weight sequence $\{a_t\}$ can be replaced by a sequence of $\mathcal{F}_{t-1}$-measurable random weights.

20.12 Theorem Let $\{X_t,\mathcal{F}_t\}_0^\infty$ be a m.d. sequence, $\{W_t\}$ a non-decreasing sequence of positive, $\mathcal{F}_{t-1}$-measurable r.v.s, and $S_n = \sum_{t=1}^n X_t$. Then

$$P\left(\left\{\sum_{t=1}^{\infty} E(X_t^2|\mathcal{F}_{t-1})/W_t^2 < \infty\right\}\cap\left\{W_t \uparrow \infty\right\}-\left\{S_n/W_n \to 0\right\}\right) = 0. \; \square \qquad (20.45)$$

The last statement is perhaps a little opaque, but roughly translated it says that the probability of convergence, of the event $\{S_n/W_n \to 0\}$, is not less than that of the intersection of the two other events in (20.45). In particular, when one probability is 1, so is the other.

Proof If $\{X_t\}$ is a m.d. sequence so is $\{X_t/W_t\}$, since W_t is $\mathcal{F}_{t-1}$-measurable, and $T_n = \sum_{t=1}^n X_t/W_t$ is a martingale. For $\omega \in \Omega$, if $T_n(\omega) \to T(\omega)$ and $W_n(\omega) \uparrow \infty$ then $S_n(\omega)/W_n(\omega) \to 0$ by Kronecker's lemma. Applying **15.11** completes the proof. ∎

See how this result contains **20.10**, corresponding to the case of a fixed, divergent weight sequence and a.s. summability. As before, we now weaken the summability conditions from conditional variances to pth absolute moments for $1 \le p \le 2$. However, to exploit **20.5** outside the almost sure case requires a modification to the equivalent sequences argument (**20.3**), as follows.

20.13 Theorem If $\{X_t\}$ and $\{Y_t\}$ are sequences of $\mathcal{F}_t$-measurable r.v.s,

$$P\left(\left\{\sum_{t=1}^{n} P(X_t \ne Y_t|\mathcal{F}_{t-1}) < \infty\right\}\Delta\left\{\sum_{t=1}^{n}(X_t - Y_t) \text{ converges}\right\}\right) = 0. \qquad (20.46)$$

Proof Let $E_t = \{X_t \ne Y_t\} \in \mathcal{F}_t$, so that $P(X_t \ne Y_t|\mathcal{F}_{t-1}) = E(1_{E_t}|\mathcal{F}_{t-1})$. According to **15.13**(ii),

$$P\left(\left\{\omega: \sum_{t=1}^{\infty} E(1_{E_t}|\mathcal{F}_{t-1})(\omega) < \infty\right\}\Delta\left\{\omega: \sum_{t=1}^{\infty} 1_{E_t}(\omega) < \infty\right\}\right) = 0. \qquad (20.47)$$

But $\sum_{t=1}^\infty 1_{E_t}(\omega) < \infty$ means that the number of coordinates for which $X_t(\omega) \ne Y_t(\omega)$ is finite, and hence $\sum_{t=1}^\infty (X_t(\omega) - Y_t(\omega)) < \infty$. (20.47) therefore implies (20.46). ∎

Now we are able to prove the following extension of **20.11**.

20.14 Theorem For $1 \le p \le 2$, let $E_1 = \{\sum_{t=1}^\infty E(|X_t|^p|\mathcal{F}_{t-1})/W_t^p < \infty\}$ and $E_2 = \{W_t \uparrow \infty\}$. Under the conditions of **20.12**,

$$P((E_1 \cap E_2) - \{S_n/W_n \to 0\}) = 0. \qquad (20.48)$$

Proof The basic line of argument follows closely that of **20.11**. As before, let $Y_t = 1_{\{|X_t| \le a_t\}}X_t$, so that $Z_t = Y_t - E(Y_t|\mathcal{F}_{t-1})$ is a m.d. and

$$E(Z_t^2|\mathcal{F}_{t-1}) = E(Y_t^2|\mathcal{F}_{t-1}) - (E(Y_t|\mathcal{F}_{t-1}))^2$$

$$\leq E(Y_t^2|\mathcal{F}_{t-1}), \text{ a.s.} \tag{20.49}$$

Applying **20.5** and the last inequality,

$$P\left(E_1 - \left\{\sum_{t=1}^{\infty} E(Z_t^2|\mathcal{F}_{t-1})/W_t^2 < \infty\right\}\right) = 0. \tag{20.50}$$

It follows by **15.11** and the fact that $E_1 - C \subseteq (E_1 - D) \cup (D - C)$ that

$$P\left(E_1 - \left\{\sum_{t=1}^{n} Z_t/W_t \to S_1\right\}\right) = 0, \tag{20.51}$$

where S_1 is some a.s. finite random variable. A second application of **20.5** gives

$$P\left(E_1 - \left\{\sum_{t=1}^{\infty} |E(Y_t|\mathcal{F}_{t-1})|/W_t < \infty\right\}\right) = 0, \tag{20.52}$$

which is equivalent (by **2.24**) to

$$P\left(E_1 - \left\{\sum_{t=1}^{\infty} E(Y_t|\mathcal{F}_{t-1})/W_t \to S_2\right\}\right) = 0, \tag{20.53}$$

where S_2 is another a.s. finite r.v. And a third application of **20.5** together with **20.13** gives

$$P\left(E_1 - \left\{\sum_{t=1}^{\infty} X_t - \sum_{t=1}^{\infty} Y_t \to S_3\right\}\right) = 0, \tag{20.54}$$

for some a.s. finite r.v. S_3. Now (20.51), (20.53), (20.54), the definition of Z_t, the Kronecker lemma and some more set algebra yield, as required,

$$\begin{aligned} 0 &= P\left[\left(E_1 - \left\{\sum_{t=1}^{\infty} Y_t/W_t \to S_1 + S_2\right\}\right) \cap E_2\right] \\ &= P\left((E_1 \cap E_2) - \left\{W_n^{-1}\sum_{t=1}^{\infty} Y_t \to 0\right\}\right) \\ &= P((E_1 \cap E_2) - \{S_n/W_n \to 0\}). \ \blacksquare \end{aligned} \tag{20.55}$$

20.5 Two Strong Laws for Mixingales

The martingale difference assumption is specialized, and the last results are not sufficient to support a general treatment of dependent processes, although they are the central prop. The key to extending them, as in the weak law case, is the mixingale concept. In this section we contrast two approaches to proving mixingale strong convergence. The first applies a straightforward generalization of the methods introduced by McLeish (1975a); see also Hansen (1991, 1992a) for related results. We have two versions of the theorem to choose from, a milder constraint on the dependence being available in return for the existence of second moments.

20.15 Theorem Let the sequence $\{X_t,\mathcal{F}_t\}_{-\infty}^{\infty}$ be a L_p-mixingale with respect to constants $\{c_t\}$, for either

(i) $p = 2$, with mixingale size $-\frac{1}{2}$, or

(ii) $1 < p < 2$, with mixingale size -1.

If $\sum_{t=1}^{\infty} c_t^p < \infty$ then $S_n \xrightarrow{as} S$.

Proof We have the maximal inequality,

$$E\left(\max_{1\le j\le n} |S_j|^p\right) \le K\sum_{t=1}^{n} c_t^p, \tag{20.56}$$

where K is a finite constant. This is by **16.10** in the case of (i) and **16.11** in case (ii). By relabelling coordinates it can be expressed in the form

$$E\left(\max_{1\le j\le n} |S_j - S_m|^p\right) \le K\sum_{t=m+1}^{n} c_t^p \tag{20.57}$$

for any choice of m and n. Moreover,

$$P\left(\max_{m<j\le n} |S_j - S_m| > \varepsilon\right) = P\left(\max_{m<j\le n} |S_j - S_m|^p > \varepsilon^p\right)$$

$$\le \frac{1}{\varepsilon^p} E\left(\max_{m<j\le n} |S_j - S_m|^p\right) \tag{20.58}$$

by the Markov inequality. Inequalities (20.57) and (20.58) combine to yield (20.2), and the convergence lemma **20.2** now yields the result. ■

We can add the usual corollary from Kronecker's lemma.

20.16 Corollary Let $\{X_t/a_t,\mathcal{F}_t\}_{-\infty}^{\infty}$ satisfy either (i) or (ii) of **20.15** with respect to constants $\{c_t/a_t\}$, for a positive sequence $\{a_t\}$ with $a_t \uparrow \infty$. If

$$\sum_{t=1}^{\infty} c_t^p/a_t^p < \infty, \tag{20.59}$$

then $S_n/a_n \xrightarrow{as} 0$. □

The second result exploits a novel and remarkably powerful argument due to R. M. de Jong (1992).

20.17 Theorem Let $\{X_t,\mathcal{F}_t\}$ be an L_r-bounded, L_1-mixingale with respect to constants $\{c_t\}$ for $r \ge 1$, and let $\{a_t\}$, $\{B_t\}$ be positive constant sequences, and $\{M_t\}$ a positive integer sequence, with $a_n \uparrow \infty$. If

$$\sum_{n=1}^{\infty} M_n \exp\left\{-\varepsilon^2 a_n^2 \Big/ \left(32 M_n^2 \sum_{t=1}^{n} B_t^2\right)\right\} < \infty, \tag{20.60}$$

$$\sum_{t=1}^{\infty} B_t^{1-r} E|X_t|^r / a_t < \infty, \tag{20.61}$$

$$\sum_{t=1}^{\infty} \zeta_{M_t} c_t / a_t < \infty, \tag{20.62}$$

where $\{\zeta_m\}_{m=0}^{\infty}$ are the mixingale coefficients, then $S_n/a_n \xrightarrow{as} 0$. □

Here $\{B_t\}$ and $\{M_t\}$ are chosen freely to satisfy the conditions, given $\{a_t\}$ and $\{c_t\}$, which suggests a considerable amount of flexibility in application. The sequence $\{B_t\}$ will be used to define a truncation of $\{X_t\}$, the role which was played by $\{a_t\}$ in **20.11**. The most interesting of the conditions is (20.62), which explicitly trades off the rate of decrease of the mixingale numbers with that of the sequence $\{c_t/a_t\}$. This approach is in contrast with the McLeish method of defining separate summability conditions for the moments and mixingale numbers, as detailed in §16.3.

Proof Writing 1_t^B for $1_{\{|X_t| \le B_t\}}$, start by noting that

$$E_{t+j}X_t = E_{t+j}1_t^B X_t + E_{t+j}(1 - 1_t^B)X_t.$$

Hence, we have the identity

$$X_t = (E_{t+M_t-1}1_t^B X_t - E_{t-M_t}1_t^B X_t) + (E_{t+M_t-1}(1 - 1_t^B)X_t - E_{t-M_t}(1 - 1_t^B)X_t) + (X_t - E_{t+M_t-1}X_t) + E_{t-M_t}X_t, \tag{20.63}$$

and, by the usual 'telescoping sum' argument,

$$E_{t+M_t-1}1_t^B X_t - E_{t-M_t}1_t^B X_t = \sum_{j=1-M_t}^{M_t-1} Z_{jt}, \tag{20.64}$$

where $Z_{jt} = E_{t+j}1_t^B X_t - E_{t+j-1}1_t^B X_t$, and $\{Z_{jt}, \mathcal{F}_{t+j}\}$ is a m.d. sequence. Note that $|Z_{jt}| \le 2B_t$ a.s., by a double application of **10.13**(ii). Summing yields

$$\sum_{t=1}^{n} X_t = \sum_{t=1}^{n}\sum_{j=1-M_t}^{M_t-1} Z_{jt} + \sum_{t=1}^{n} E_{t+M_t-1}(1 - 1_t^B)X_t - \sum_{t=1}^{n} E_{t-M_t}(1 - 1_t^B)X_t + \sum_{t=1}^{n}(X_t - E_{t+M_t-1}X_t) + \sum_{t=1}^{n} E_{t-M_t}X_t$$

$$= S_{1n} + S_{2n} - S_{3n} + S_{4n} + S_{5n}. \tag{20.65}$$

The object will be to show that $S_{kn}/a_n \xrightarrow{as} 0$ for $k = 1,\dots,5$.

Starting with S_{1n}, the main task is to reorganize the double sum. It can be verified by inspection that

$$\sum_{t=1}^{n}\sum_{j=1-M_t}^{M_t-1} Z_{jt} = \sum_{j=1-M_n}^{M_n-1}\sum_{t=q_j}^{n} Z_{jt}$$

$$= \sum_{j=1-M_n}^{M_n-1}\sum_{t=1}^{n} Z_{jt} - \left(\sum_{j=1-M_n}^{-M_2} + \sum_{j=M_2}^{M_n-1}\right)\sum_{t=1}^{q_j-1} Z_{jt}, \tag{20.66}$$

where $q_j = 1$ for $-M_1 < j < M_1$, and $q_j = t$ for $-M_t < j \le -M_{t-1}$ and $M_{t-1} \le j < M_t$, for $t = 2,\dots,n$. Note that, for arbitrary numbers $x_1,\dots,x_k$, $\{|\sum_{i=1}^{k}x_i| > \varepsilon\} \subseteq \bigcup_{i=1}^{k}\{|x_i| > \varepsilon/k\}$. Hence by subadditivity, and Azuma's inequality (**15.20**),

$$P(|S_{1n}| > a_n\varepsilon) \le \sum_{j=1-M_n}^{M_n-1} P\left(\left|\sum_{t=1}^{n} Z_{jt}\right| > a_n\varepsilon/4M_n\right)$$

$$+ \left(\sum_{j=1-M_n}^{-M_2} + \sum_{j=M_2}^{M_n-1}\right) P\left(\left|\sum_{t=1}^{q_j-1} Z_{jt}\right| > a_n\varepsilon/4M_n\right)$$

$$\le 2M_n\exp\left\{-\varepsilon^2 a_n^2/\left(32M_n^2\sum_{t=1}^{n}B_t^2\right)\right\}$$

$$+ \left(\sum_{j=1-M_n}^{-M_2} + \sum_{j=M_2}^{M_n-1}\right)\exp\left\{-\varepsilon^2 a_n^2/\left(32M_n^2\sum_{t=1}^{q_j-1}B_t^2\right)\right\}$$

$$\le 4M_n\exp\left\{-\varepsilon^2 a_n^2/\left(32M_n^2\sum_{t=1}^{n}B_t^2\right)\right\}. \tag{20.67}$$

Under (20.60), these probabilities are summable over n and so $S_{1n}/a_n \xrightarrow{as} 0$ by the first Borel-Cantelli lemma.

Now let $\{Y_t\}$ be any integrable sequence and define

$$S_n^a = \sum_{t=1}^{n} Y_t/a_t. \tag{20.68}$$

By the Markov inequality,

$$P\left(\max_{m<j\le n}|S_j^a - S_m^a| > \varepsilon\right) \le \frac{1}{\varepsilon}E\left(\max_{m<j\le n}|S_j^a - S_m^a|\right) \tag{20.69}$$

$$\le \frac{1}{\varepsilon}\sum_{t=m+1}^{n} E|Y_t|/a_t.$$

If

$$\sum_{t=1}^{\infty} E|Y_t|/a_t < \infty, \tag{20.70}$$

then $S_n^a \xrightarrow{as} S^a$ by an application of **20.2**, and hence $S_n^a/a_n \xrightarrow{as} 0$ by Kronecker's lemma. We apply this result to each of the remaining terms. For S_{2n}, put $Y_t = E_{t+M_t-1}X_t(1 - 1_t^B)$, and note that

$$\sum_{t=1}^{n} E|Y_t|/a_t \le \sum_{t=1}^{n} E|(1-1_t^B)X_t|/a_t \le \sum_{t=1}^{n} B_t^{1-r}E|X_t|^r/a_t, \tag{20.71}$$

using the fact that $|X_t(1-1_t^B)/B_t| \le |X_t(1-1_t^B)/B_t|^r$. S_{3n} is dealt with in exactly the same way. For S_{4n} and S_{5n}, put successively $Y_t = X_t - E_{t+M_t-1}X_t$ and $Y_t = E_{t-M_t}X_t$, and by the mixingale assumption,

$$\sum_{t=1}^{n} E|Y_t|/a_t \le \sum_{t=1}^{n} (c_t/a_t)\zeta_{M_t}. \tag{20.72}$$

The proof is completed by noting that the majorant terms of (20.71) and (20.72) are bounded in the limit by assumption. ■

The conditions of **20.17** are rather difficult to apply and interpret. We will restrict them very slightly, to derive a simple summability condition which can be compared directly with **20.15**.

20.18 Corollary Let $\{X_t,\mathcal{F}_t\}$ be an L_r-bounded, L_1-mixingale of size $-\varphi_0$ with respect to constants $\{c_t\}$. If $\{c_t\}$ and $\{a_t\}$ are positive, regularly varying sequences of constants with $\|X_t\|_r \ll c_t$ and $a_n \uparrow \infty$, and

$$\sum_{t=1}^{n} (c_t/a_t)^{\xi_0} < \infty \tag{20.73}$$

where

$$\xi_0 = \frac{2r\varphi_0 + 2(r-1)}{(1+r)\varphi_0 + 2(r-1)}, \tag{20.74}$$

then $S_n/a_n \xrightarrow{as} 0$.

Proof Define $o_t = (\log t)^{-1-\delta}$ for $\delta > 0$. This is slowly varying at infinity by **2.28**, and the sequence $\{o_t/t\}$ is summable by **2.31**. Apply the conditions of **20.17** with the added stipulation that $\{B_t\}$ and $\{M_t\}$ are regularly varying, increasing sequences, and so consider the conditions for summability of a series of the form $\sum_n U_1(n)\exp\{-\eta U_2(n)\}$, for $\eta > 0$. Since $\sum_n (o_n/n)$ converges, summability follows from $(n/o_n)U_1(n)\exp\{-\eta U_2(n)\} \to 0$. Taking logarithms, this is equivalent to

$$\log n - \log(o_n) + \log U_1(n) - \eta U_2(n) \to -\infty. \tag{20.75}$$

Since $U(n) = n^{\rho}L(n)$ where $L(n)$ is slowly varying, this condition has the form

$$\log n - \log(o_n) + \rho_1 \log n + \log(L_1(n)) - \eta n^{\rho_2}L_2(n) \to -\infty, \tag{20.76}$$

where ρ_1 and ρ_2 are non-negative constants and $L_1(n)$ and $L_2(n)$ are slowly varying. The terms $\log(o_n)$ and $\log(L_1(n))$ can be neglected here. Put $\rho_2 = 0$ and $L_2(n) = 1/o_n = (\log n)^{1+\delta}$, and the condition reduces to

$$(1+\rho_1-\eta(\log n)^{\delta})\log n \to -\infty, \tag{20.77}$$

which holds for all ρ_1, for any $\eta > 0$ and $\delta > 0$. Condition (20.60) is therefore satisfied (recalling that $\{B_t\}$ is monotone) if

$$nM_n^2B_n^2/a_n^2 \ll o_n. \tag{20.78}$$

Similarly, conditions (2.61) and (2.62) are satisfied if, respectively,

$$B_t^{1-r}E|X_t|^r/a_t \ll B_t^{1-r}c_t^r/a_t \ll o_t/t, \tag{20.79}$$

and

$$M_t^{-\varphi}c_t/a_t \ll o_t/t,\ \varphi > \varphi_0. \tag{20.80}$$

We can identify the bounding cases of B_t and M_t by replacing the second order-of-magnitude inequality sign in (20.79), and that in (20.80), by equalities, leaving the required scaling constants implicit. Solving for M_t and B_t in this way, substituting into (20.78), and simplifying yields the condition

$$(c_t/a_t)^{\xi} \ll o_t/t, \tag{20.81}$$

where $\xi = [2r\varphi+2(r-1)]/[(1+r)\varphi+2(r-1)]$. This is sufficient for (20.60), (20.61), and (20.62) to hold.

Since c_t and a_t are specified to be regularly varying, there exist non-negative constants ρ_3, ρ_4, and slowly varying functions L_3 and L_4 such that $c_t = t^{\rho_3}L_3(t)$ and $a_t = t^{\rho_4}L_4(t)$. The assumption that $\{(c_t/a_t)^{\xi_0}\}$ is summable implies that $(\rho_3-\rho_4)\xi_0 \le -1$. But $\varphi > \varphi_0$ implies $\xi > \xi_0$, so that $(\rho_3-\rho_4)\xi < -1$, which in turn implies (20.81). This completes the proof. ∎

Noting that $1 \le \xi_0 \le 2$, the condition in (20.73) may be compared with (20.59). Put $\varphi_0 = \frac{1}{2}$ and $r = 2$ and we obtain $\xi_0 = \frac{8}{7}$, whereas with $\varphi_0 = 1$, we get $\xi_0 = 2(2r-1)/(3r-1)$ which does not exceed r in the relevant range, taking values between 1 when $r = 1$ and $\frac{6}{5}$ when $r = 2$. Square-summability of c_t/a_t is sufficient only in the limit as both $\varphi_0 \to \infty$ and $r \to \infty$. Thus, this theorem does not contain **20.16**. On the other hand, in the cases where $\{c_t\}$ is uniformly bounded and $a_t = t$, we need only $\xi_0 > 1$, so that *any* $r > 1$ and $\varphi_0 > 0$ will serve. These dependence restrictions are on a par with those of the L_1 convergence law of **19.10**, and a striking improvement on **20.16**. The case $r = 1$ is not permitted for sample averages, but is compatible with $a_t = t(\log t)^{1+\delta}$ for $\delta > 0$. In other words, the theorem shows that

$$(n(\log n)^{1+\delta})^{-1}\sum_{t=1}^{n} X_t \to 0 \text{ a.s.} \tag{20.82}$$

This amounts to saying that the sequence of sample means is almost surely slowly varying as $n \to \infty$; it could diverge, but no faster than a power of $\log n$.

20.6 Near-Epoch Dependent and Mixing Processes

In view of the last results, there are two possible approaches to the NED case. It turns out that neither approach dominates the other in terms of permissable conditions. We begin with the simplest of the arguments, the straightforward extension of **20.18**.

20.19 Theorem Let a sequence $\{X_t\}_{-\infty}^{\infty}$ with means $\{\mu_t\}_{-\infty}^{\infty}$ be L_p-NED of size $-b$, for $1 \le p \le 2$, with constants $d_t \ll \|X_t - \mu_t\|_p$, on a (possibly vector-valued) sequence $\{V_t\}_{-\infty}^{\infty}$ which is α-mixing (ϕ-mixing) of size $-a$. If

$$\sum_{t=1}^{\infty} \|(X_t - \mu_t)/a_t\|_q^{\xi} < \infty \tag{20.83}$$

for $q > p$ in the α-mixing case ($q \ge p$ in the ϕ-mixing case) where

$$\xi = \min\left\{\frac{2qb + 2(q-1)}{(1+q)b + 2(q-1)}, \frac{2q(a+1)}{(1+q)a + 2q}\right\}, \tag{20.84}$$

then $a_n^{-1}\sum_{t=1}^n (X_t - \mu_t) \xrightarrow{as} 0$.

Proof By **17.5**, $\{X_t - \mu_t\}$ is a L_1-mixingale of size $-\min\{b, a(1-1/q)\}$ with respect to constants $\{c_t\}$, with $c_t \ll \|X_t - \mu_t\|_q$. This is by **17.5**(i) in the α-mixing case and by **17.5**(ii) in the ϕ-mixing case. The theorem follows by **20.18**, after substituting for φ_0 in (20.74) and simplifying. ■

This permits arbitrary mixing and NED sizes and arbitrary moment restrictions, so long as (20.83) holds with ξ arbitrarily close to 1. By letting $b \to \infty$ one obtains a result for mixing sequences, and by letting $a \to \infty$ a result for sequences that are L_p-NED on an independent underlying process. Interestingly, in each of these special cases ξ ranges over the interval $(1, 2q/(q+1))$ as the mixing/L_p-NED size is allowed to range from zero to $-\infty$.

By contrast, a result based on **20.15** would be needed if we could claim only square-summability of the sequence $\{\|(X_t - \mu_t)/a_t\|_p\}$ for finite p; this rules out (20.83) for any choices of a and b. The first of these results comes directly by applying **17.5**.

20.20 Theorem For real numbers b, p and r, let a sequence $\{X_t\}_{-\infty}^{\infty}$ with means $\{\mu_t\}_{-\infty}^{\infty}$ be L_p-NED of size $-b$ on a sequence $\{V_t\}_{-\infty}^{\infty}$, with constants $d_t \ll \|X_t - \mu_t\|_p$. For a positive constant sequence $\{a_t\} \uparrow \infty$, let $\{(X_t - \mu_t)/a_t\}_1^{\infty}$ be uniformly L_r-bounded, and let

$$\sum_{t=1}^{\infty} \|(X_t - \mu_t)/a_t\|_p^p < \infty. \tag{20.85}$$

Then $a_n^{-1}\sum_{t=1}^n (X_t - \mu_t) \xrightarrow{as} 0$ in each of the following cases:

(i) $b = \frac{1}{2}$, $p = 2$, $r > 2$, $\{V_t\}$ is α-mixing of size $-r/(r-2)$;

(ii) $b = 1$, $1 < p < 2$, $r > p$, $\{V_t\}$ is α-mixing of size $-pr/(r-p)$;

(iii) $b = \frac{1}{2}$, $p = 2$, $r \ge 2$, $\{V_t\}$ is ϕ-mixing of size $-r/2(r-1)$;

(iv) $b = 1$, $1 < p < 2$, $r \ge p$, $\{V_t\}$ is ϕ-mixing of size $-r/(r-1)$.

Proof By **17.5**, conditions (i)–(iv) are all sufficient for $\{(X_t - \mu_t)/a_t, \mathcal{F}_t\}$ to be an L_p-mixingale of size $-b$, where $\mathcal{F}_t = \sigma(V_s, s \le t)$. The mixingale constants are $c_t/a_t \ll \max\{d_t, \|X_t - \mu_t\|_r\}/a_t = \|X_t - \mu_t\|_r/a_t$. The theorem follows by **20.16**. ∎

As an example, let X_t possess moments of all orders and be L_2-NED of size $-\frac{1}{2}$, on an α-mixing process of size close to -1 (letting $r \to \infty$). Summability of the terms $\mathrm{Var}(X_t/a_t)$ is sufficient by (20.85). The same numbers yield $\xi = \frac{8}{7}$ on putting $q = 2$ and $a = 1$ in (20.84), which is not far from requiring summability of the L_2-norms.

However, this theorem requires L_r-boundedness, which if r is small constrains the permitted mixing size, as well as offering poor NED size characteristics for cases with $p < 2$. It can be improved upon in these situations by introducing a truncation argument. The third of our strong laws is the following.

20.21 Theorem Let a sequence $\{X_t\}_{-\infty}^{\infty}$ with means $\{\mu_t\}_{-\infty}^{\infty}$ be L_p-NED of size $-1/p$ for $1 \le p \le 2$, with constants $d_t \ll \|X_t - \mu_t\|_p$, on a sequence $\{V_t\}_{-\infty}^{\infty}$ which is either

(i) α-mixing of size $-r/(r-2)$ for $r > 2$ or

(ii) φ-mixing of size $-r/2(r-1)$ for $r > 1$, and $r \ge p$;

and for q with $p \le q \le r$ and a constant positive sequence $\{a_t\} \uparrow \infty$, let

$$\sum_{t=1}^{\infty} \|(X_t - \mu_t)/a_t\|_q^{\min\{p,2q/r\}} < \infty; \tag{20.86}$$

then $a_n^{-1}\sum_{t=1}^{n}(X_t - \mu_t) \xrightarrow{as} 0$. □

Note the different roles of the three constants specified in the conditions. p controls the size of the NED numbers, q is the minimum order of moment required to exist, and r controls the mixing of $\{V_t\}$. The distribution of X_t does not otherwise depend on r.

Proof The strategy is to show that there is a sequence equivalent to $\{(X_t - \mu_t)/a_t\}$, and satisfying the conditions of **20.15**(i). As in **20.6**, let

$$Y_t = (X_t - \mu_t)1_t^a/a_t \pm (1 - 1_t^a), \tag{20.87}$$

where $1_t^a = 1_{\{|X_t| \le a_t\}}$ and '±' denotes '+' if $X_t > \mu_t$, '−' otherwise. Note that $\{(X_t - \mu_t)/a_t\}$ is L_p-NED with constants d_t/a_t, and Y_t is a continuous function of $(X_t - \mu_t)/a_t$ with $|Y_t| \le 1$ a.s. Applying **17.13** shows that Y_t is L_2-NED on $\{V_t\}$ of size $-\frac{1}{2}$ with constants $2^{1-p/2}(d_t/a_t)^{p/2}$. Since $\|Y_t\|_r < \infty$ for every finite r, it further follows by **17.5** that if $\mathcal{F}_t = \sigma(V_{t-s},\ s \ge 0)$, $\{Y_t - E(Y_t), \mathcal{F}_t\}_0^{\infty}$ is an L_2-mixingale of size $-\frac{1}{2}$ with constants

$$c_t \ll \max\{(d_t/a_t)^{p/2},\ \|Y_t\|_r\}. \tag{20.88}$$

Here, $d_t \le 2\|X_t - \mu_t\|_q$ for any $q \ge p$, and $\|Y_t\|_r \le 2(\|X_t - \mu_t\|_q/a_t)^{q/r}$ for any $q \le r$ by the second inequality of (20.24). Condition (20.86) is therefore sufficient for the sequence $\{c_t^2\}$ to be summable, and $\{Y_t - E(Y_t)\}$ satisfies the conditions of **20.15**(i). We can conclude that $\sum_{t=1}^{n}(Y_t - E(Y_t)) \xrightarrow{as} S_1$, where S_1 is some random variable.

According to **20.6**, condition (20.86) is sufficient for $\sum_{t=1}^{\infty}|E(Y_t)| < \infty$. The series $\sum_{t=1}^{n}E(Y_t)$ therefore converges to a finite limit by **2.24**, say $\sum_{t=1}^{\infty}E(Y_t) =$

C_1, and

$$\sum_{t=1}^{n} Y_t \xrightarrow{as} S_1 + C_1. \tag{20.89}$$

Inequalities (20.22) and (20.6) further imply that Y_t and $(X_t - \mu_t)/a_t$ are equivalent sequences, and hence

$$\sum_{t=1}^{n} ((X_t - \mu_t)/a_t - Y_t) \xrightarrow{as} S_2, \tag{20.90}$$

where S_2 is another random variable, by **20.3**. We conclude that

$$\sum_{t=1}^{n} (X_t - \mu_t)/a_t \xrightarrow{as} S_1 + S_2 + C_1 = S_3, \tag{20.91}$$

say. It follows by Kronecker's lemma that $a_n^{-1}\sum_{t=1}^{n}(X_t - \mu_t) \xrightarrow{as} 0$, the required conclusion. ■

Here is a final, more specialized, result. The linear function of martingale differences with summable coefficients is a case of particular interest since it unifies our two approaches to the strong law.

20.22 Theorem Let $X_t = \sum_{j=-\infty}^{\infty}\theta_j U_{t-j}$ where $\{U_t\}$ is a uniformly L_p-bounded m.d. sequence with $p > 1$, and $\sum_{j=-\infty}^{\infty}|\theta_j| < \infty$. Then

$$\frac{1}{n}\sum_{t=1}^{n} X_t \xrightarrow{as} 0. \tag{20.92}$$

Proof $Y_t = X_t/t$ is a L_p-mixingale with $c_t \ll 1/t$ and arbitrary size. It was shown in **16.12** that the maximal inequality (20.56) holds for this case. Application of the convergence lemma and Kronecker's lemma lead directly to the result. Alternatively, apply **20.18** to X_t with $a_t = t$. ■

In these results, four features summarize the relevant characteristics of the stochastic process: the order of existing moments, the summability characteristics of the moments, and the sizes of the mixing and near-epoch dependence numbers. The way in which the currently available theorems trade off these features suggests that some unification should be possible. The McLeish-style argument is revealed by de Jong's approach to be excessively restrictive with respect to the dependence conditions it imposes, whereas the tough summability conditions the latter's theorem requires may also be an artefact of the method adopted. The repertoire of dependent strong laws is currently being extended (de Jong, 1994) in work as yet too recent for incorporation in this book.

21
Uniform Stochastic Convergence

21.1 Stochastic Functions on a Parameter Space

The setting for this chapter is the class of functions

$$f: \Omega\times\Theta \to \overline{\mathbb{R}},$$

where $(\Omega,\mathcal{F},\mu)$ is a measure space, and (Θ,ρ) is a metric space. We write $f(\omega,\theta)$ to denote the real value assumed by f at the point (ω,θ), which is a random variable for fixed θ. But $f(\omega,.)$, alternatively written just $f(\omega)$, is *not* a random variable, but a random element of a space of functions.

Econometric analysis is very frequently concerned with this type of object. Log-likelihoods, sums of squares, and other criterion functions for the estimation of econometric models, and also the first and second derivatives of these criterion functions, are all the subject of important convergence theorems on which proofs of consistency and the derivation of limiting distributions are based. Except in a restricted class of linear models, all of these are typically functions both of the model parameters and of random data.

To deal with convergence on a function space, it is necessary to have a criterion by which to judge when two functions are close to one another. In this chapter we examine the questions posed by stochastic convergence (almost sure or in probability) when the relevant space of functions is endowed with the uniform metric. A class of set functions that are therefore going to be central to our discussion have the form $f^*: \Omega \to \overline{\mathbb{R}}$, where

$$f^*(\omega) = \sup_{\theta\in\Theta} f(\omega,\theta). \tag{21.1}$$

For example, if g and h are two stochastic functions whose uniform proximity is at issue, we would be interested in the supremum of

$$f(\omega,\theta) = |g(\omega,\theta) - h(\omega,\theta)|.$$

An important technical problem arises here which ought to be confronted at the outset. We have not so far given any results that would justify treating f^* as a random variable, when (Θ,ρ) may be an arbitrary metric space. We can write

$$\{\omega: f^*(\omega) > x\} = \bigcup_{\theta\in\Theta} \{\omega: f(\theta,\omega) > x\}, \tag{21.2}$$

and the results of **3.26** show that $\{\omega: f^*(\omega) > x\} \in \mathcal{F}$ when $\{\omega: f(\theta,\omega) > x\} \in \mathcal{F}$ for each θ, when Θ is a *countable* set. But typically Θ is a subset of $(\mathbb{R}^k, d_E)$ or something of the kind, and is uncountable.

This is one of a class of measurability problems having ramifications far beyond the uniform convergence issue, and to handle it properly requires a mathematical apparatus going beyond what is covered in Chapter 3. We shall not attempt to deal with this question in depth, and will offer no proofs in this instance. We will merely outline the main features of the theory required for its solution. The essential step is to recognize that the set on the left-hand side of (21.2) can be expressed as a projection.

Let $\mathcal{B}_\Theta$ denote the Borel field of subsets of Θ, that is, the smallest σ-field containing the sets of Θ that are open with respect to ρ. Then let $(\Omega\times\Theta, \mathcal{F}\otimes\mathcal{B}_\Theta)$ denote the product space endowed with the product σ-field (the σ-field generated from the measurable rectangles of $\mathcal{F}$ and $\mathcal{B}_\Theta$), and suppose that $f(.,.)$ is $\mathcal{F}\otimes\mathcal{B}_\Theta/\overline{\mathcal{B}}$-measurable. Observe that, if

$$A_x = \{(\omega,\theta)\colon f(\omega,\theta) > x\} \in \mathcal{F}\otimes\mathcal{B}_\Theta, \tag{21.3}$$

the projection of A_x into Ω is

$$E_x = \{\omega\colon f(\omega,\theta) > x,\ \theta \in \Theta\}$$
$$= \{\omega\colon f^*(\omega) > x\}. \tag{21.4}$$

In view of **3.24**, measurability of f^* is equivalent to the condition that $E_x \in \mathcal{F}$ for rational x. Projections are *not* as a rule measurable transformations,[21] but under certain conditions it can be shown that $E_x \in \mathcal{F}^P$, where $(\Omega,\mathcal{F}^P,\overline{P})$ is the completion of the probability space.

The key notion is that of an *analytic* set. A standard reference on this topic is Dellacherie and Meyer (1978); see also Dudley (1989: ch. 13), and Stinchcombe and White (1992). The latter authors provide the following definition. Letting $(\Omega,\mathcal{F})$ be a measurable space, a set $E\subset\Omega$ is called $\mathcal{F}$-analytic if there exists a compact metric space (Θ,ρ) such that E is the projection onto Ω of a set $A \in \mathcal{F}\otimes\mathcal{B}_\Theta$. The collection of $\mathcal{F}$-analytic sets is written $\mathcal{A}(\mathcal{F})$. Also, a function $f\colon \Omega \mapsto \overline{\mathbb{R}}$ is called $\mathcal{F}$-analytic if $\{\omega\colon f(\omega) \le x\} \in \mathcal{A}(\mathcal{F})$ for each $x \in \overline{\mathbb{R}}$.

Since every $E\in\mathcal{F}$ is the projection of $E\times\Theta\in\mathcal{F}\otimes\mathcal{B}_\Theta$, $\mathcal{F}\subseteq\mathcal{A}(\mathcal{F})$. A measurable set (or function) is therefore also analytic. $\mathcal{A}(\mathcal{F})$ is not in general a σ-field, although it can be shown to be closed under countable unions and countable intersections. The conditions under which an image under projection is known to be analytic are somewhat weaker than the definition might suggest, and it will actually suffice to let $(\Theta,\mathcal{B}_\Theta)$ be a *Souslin space*, that is, a space that is measurably isomorphic to an analytic subset of a compact metric space. A sufficient condition, whose proof can be extracted from the results in Stinchcombe and White (1992), is the following:

21.1 Theorem Let $(\Omega,\mathcal{F})$ be a measurable space and $(\Theta,\mathcal{B}_\Theta)$ a Souslin space. If $B \in \mathcal{A}(\mathcal{F}\otimes\mathcal{B}_\Theta)$, the projection of B onto Ω is in $\mathcal{A}(\mathcal{F})$. □

Now, given the measurable space $(\Omega,\mathcal{F})$, define $\mathcal{F}^U=\bigcap_\mu\mathcal{F}^\mu$, where $(\Omega,\mathcal{F}^\mu,\overline{\mu})$ is the completion of the probability space $(\Omega,\mathcal{F},\mu)$ (see **3.7**) and the intersection is taken over all p.m.s μ defined on the space. The elements of $\mathcal{F}^U$ are called *univer-*

sally measurable sets. The key conclusion, from Dellacherie and Mayer (1978: III.33(a)), is the following.

21.2 Theorem For a measurable space $(\Omega,\mathcal{F})$,

$$\mathcal{A}(\mathcal{F}) \subseteq \mathcal{F}^U. \ \Box \tag{21.5}$$

Since by definition $\mathcal{F}^U \subset \mathcal{F}^\mu$ for any choice of μ, it follows that the analytic sets of $\mathcal{F}$ are measurable under the completion of $(\Omega,\mathcal{F},\mu)$ for any choice of μ. In other words, if E is analytic there exist $A, B \in \mathcal{F}$ such that $A \subseteq E \subseteq B$ and $\mu(A) = \mu(B)$. In this sense we say that analytic sets are 'nearly' measurable. All the standard probabilistic arguments, and in particular the values of integrals, will be unaffected by this technical non-measurability, and we can ignore it. We can legitimately treat $f^*(\omega)$ as a random variable, *provided* the conditions on Θ are observed and we can assume $f(.,.)$ to be (near-) $\mathcal{F}\otimes\mathcal{B}_\Theta/\overline{\mathcal{B}}$-measurable.

An analytic subset of a compact space need not be compact but must be totally bounded. It is convenient that we do not have to insist on compactness of the parameter space, since the latter is often required to be open, thanks to strict inequality constraints (think of variances, stable roots of polynomials and the like). In the convergence results below, we find that Θ will in any case have to be totally bounded for completely different reasons: to ensure equicontinuity; to ensure that the stochastic functions have bounded moments; and that when a stochastic criterion function is being optimized with respect to θ, the optimum is usually required to lie almost surely in the interior of a compact set. Hence, total boundedness is not an extra restriction in practice.

The measurability condition on $f(\omega,\theta)$ might be verifiable using an argument from simple functions. It is certainly necessary by **4.19** that the cross-section functions $f(.,\theta)\colon \Omega \mapsto \overline{\mathbb{R}}$ and $f(\omega,.)\colon \Theta \mapsto \overline{\mathbb{R}}$ be, respectively, $\mathcal{F}/\overline{\mathcal{B}}$-measurable for each $\theta \in \Theta$ and $\mathcal{B}_\Theta/\overline{\mathcal{B}}$-measurable for each $\omega \in \Omega$. For a finite partition $\{\Theta_1,\ldots,\Theta_m\}$ of Θ by $\mathcal{B}_\Theta$-sets, consider the functions

$$f_{(m)}(\omega,\theta) = f(\omega,\theta_j),\ \theta \in \Theta_j,\ j = 1,\ldots,m, \tag{21.6}$$

where θ_j is a point of Θ_j. If $E_j^x = \{\omega\colon f(\omega,\theta_j) \le x\} \in \mathcal{F}$ for each j, then

$$A_x = \{(\omega,\theta)\colon f_{(m)}(\omega,\theta) \le x\} = \bigcup_j E_j^x \times \Theta_j \in \mathcal{F}\otimes\mathcal{B}_\Theta, \tag{21.7}$$

being a finite union of measurable rectangles. Since this is true for any x, $f_{(m)}$ is $\mathcal{F}\otimes\mathcal{B}_\Theta/\overline{\mathcal{B}}$-measurable. The question to be addressed in any particular case is whether a sequence of such partitions can be constructed such that $f_{(m)} \to f$ as $m \to \infty$.

Henceforth we shall assume without further comment that suprema of stochastic functions are random variables. The following result should be carefully noted, not least because of its deceptive similarity to the monotone convergence theorem, although this inequality goes the opposite way. The monotone convergence theorem concerns the expectation of the supremum of a class of functions $\{f_n(\omega)\}$, whereas the present one is more precisely concerned with the *envelope* of a class of functions, the function $f^*(\omega)$ which assumes the value $\sup_{\theta\in\Theta} f(\omega,\theta)$ at each point of Ω.

21.3 Theorem $\sup_{\theta\in\Theta} E(f(\theta)) \leq E\left(\sup_{\theta\in\Theta} f(\theta)\right)$.

Proof Appealing to **3.28**, it will suffice to prove this inequality for simple functions. A simple function depending on θ has the form

$$\varphi(\omega,\theta) = \sum_{i=1}^{m} \alpha_i(\theta) 1_{E_i}(\omega) = \alpha_i(\theta),\ \omega \in E_i. \tag{21.8}$$

Defining $\alpha_i^* = \sup_{\theta\in\Theta}\alpha_i(\theta)$,

$$\sup_{\theta\in\Theta} \varphi(\omega,\theta) = \alpha_i^*,\ \omega \in E_i. \tag{21.9}$$

Hence

$$\sup_{\theta\in\Theta} E(\varphi(\theta)) - E\left(\sup_{\theta\in\Theta} \varphi(\theta)\right) = \sup_{\theta\in\Theta} \sum_{i=1}^{m} (\alpha_i(\theta) - \alpha_i^*) P(E_i) \leq 0, \tag{21.10}$$

where the final inequality is by definition of α_i^*. ■

21.2 Pointwise and Uniform Stochastic Convergence

Consider the convergence (a.s., in pr., in L_p, etc.) of the sequence $\{Q_n(\theta)\}$ to a limit function $Q(\theta)$, Typically this is a law-of-large-numbers-type problem, with

$$Q_n(\theta) = \sum_{t=1}^{n} q_{nt}(\theta) \tag{21.11}$$

(we use array notation for generality, but the case $q_{nt} = q_t/n$ may usually be assumed), and $Q(\theta) = \lim_{n\to\infty} E(Q_n(\theta))$. Alternatively, we may want to consider the case $G_n(\theta) \to 0$ where

$$G_n(\theta) = \sum_{t=1}^{n} (q_{nt}(\theta) - E(q_{nt}(\theta))). \tag{21.12}$$

By considering (21.12) we divide the problem into two parts, the stochastic convergence of the sum of the mean deviations to zero, and the nonstochastic convergence assumed in the definition of $Q(\theta)$. This raises the separate question of whether the latter convergence is uniform, which is a matter for the problem at hand and will not concern us here.

As we have seen in previous chapters, obedience to a law of large numbers calls for both the boundedness and the dependence of the sequence to be controlled. In the case of a function on Θ, the dependence question presents no extra difficulty; for example, if $q_{nt}(\theta_1)$ is a mixing or near-epoch dependent array of a given class, the property will generally be shared by $q_{nt}(\theta_2)$, for any $\theta_1, \theta_2 \in \Theta$. But the existence of particular moments is clearly not independent of θ. If there exists a positive array $\{D_{nt}\}$ such that $|q_{nt}(\theta)| \le D_{nt}$ for all $\theta \in \Theta$, and $\|D_{nt}\|_r < \infty$, uniformly in t and n, $q_{nt}(\theta)$ is said to be L_r*-dominated.* To ensure pointwise convergence on Θ, we need to postulate the existence of a dominating array. There is no problem if the $q_{nt}(\theta)$ are bounded functions of θ. More generally it is necessary to bound Θ, but since Θ will often have to be bounded for a different set of reasons, this does not necessarily present an additional restriction.

Given restrictions on the dependence plus suitable domination conditions, pointwise stochastic convergence follows by considering $\{G_n(\theta)\}$ as an ordinary stochastic sequence, for each $\theta \in \Theta$. However, this line of argument does not guarantee that there is a minimum rate of convergence which applies for all θ, the condition of uniform convergence. If pointwise convergence of $\{G_n(\theta)\}$ to the limit $G(\theta)$ is defined by

$$G_n(\theta) \to 0 \text{ (a.s., in } L_p\text{, or in pr.), each } \theta \in \Theta, \tag{21.13}$$

a sequence of stochastic functions $\{G_n(\theta)\}$ is said to *converge uniformly* (a.s., in L_p, or in pr.) on Θ if

$$\sup_{\theta\in\Theta}|G_n(\theta)| \to 0 \text{ (a.s., in } L_p\text{, or in pr.).} \tag{21.14}$$

To appreciate the difference, consider the following example.

21.4 Example Let $\Theta = [0,\infty)$, and define a zero-mean array $\{g_{nt}(\theta)\}$ where

$$g_{nt}(\theta) = \frac{h_t}{n} + \begin{cases} Z\theta, & 0 \le \theta \le 1/2n \\ Z(1/n - \theta), & 1/2n < \theta \le 1/n \\ 0, & 1/n < \theta < \infty \end{cases} \tag{21.15}$$

where $\{h_t\}$ is a zero-mean stochastic sequence, and Z is a binary r.v. with $P(Z = 1) = P(Z = -1) = \frac{1}{2}$. Then $G_n(\theta) = \sum_{t=1}^n g_{nt}(\theta) = H_n + K_n(\theta)$, where $H_n = n^{-1}\sum_{t=1}^n h_t$, and

$$K_n(\theta) = \begin{cases} Zn\theta, & 0 \le \theta \le 1/2n \\ Z(1 - n\theta), & 1/2n < \theta \le 1/n. \\ 0, & 1/n < \theta < \infty \end{cases} \tag{21.16}$$

We assume $H_n \xrightarrow{as} 0$. Since $G_n(\theta) = H_n$ for $\theta > 1/n$ as well as for $\theta = 0$, $G_n(\theta) \xrightarrow{as} 0$ for each fixed $\theta \in \Theta$. In other words, $G_n(\theta)$ converges pointwise to zero, a.s.

However, $\sup_{\theta\in\Theta}|K_n(\theta)| = |\frac{1}{2}Z| = \frac{1}{2}$ for every $n \ge 1$. Because H_n converges a.s. there will exist N such that $|H_n| < \frac{1}{4}$ for all $n \ge N$, with probability 1. You can verify that when $|H_n| < \frac{1}{4}$ the supremum on Θ of $|H_n + K_n(\theta)|$ is always attained at the point $\theta = 1/2n$. Hence, with probability 1,

$$\sup_{\theta\in\Theta}|G_n(\theta)| = |H_n + \tfrac{1}{2}Z| \text{ for } n \ge N,$$

$$\to \tfrac{1}{2} \text{ as } n \to \infty. \tag{21.17}$$

It follows that the uniform a.s. limit of $G_n(\theta)$ is not zero.

Similarly, for $n \geq N$,

$$P\left(\sup_{\theta \in \Theta} |G_n(\theta)| \geq \varepsilon\right) = P(|H_n + \tfrac{1}{2}Z| \geq \varepsilon)$$

$$\to P(|\tfrac{1}{2}Z| \geq \varepsilon) = 1, \tag{21.18}$$

so that the uniform probability limit is not zero either, although the pointwise probability limit must equal the pointwise a.s. limit. □

Our first result on uniform a.s. convergence is a classic of the probability literature, the *Glivenko-Cantelli theorem.* This is also of interest as being a case outside the class of functions we shall subsequently consider. For a collection of identically distributed r.v.s $\{X_1(\omega),\dots,X_n(\omega)\}$ on the probability space $(\Omega,\mathcal{F},P)$, the *empirical distribution function* is defined as

$$F_n(x,\omega) = \frac{1}{n}\sum_{t=1}^{n} 1_{(-\infty,x]}(X_t(\omega)). \tag{21.19}$$

In other words, the random variable $F_n(x,\omega)$ is the relative frequency of the variables in the set not exceeding x. A natural question to pose is whether (and in what sense) F_n converges to F, the true marginal c.d.f. for the distribution.

For fixed x, $\{F_n(x,\omega)\}_1^\infty$ is a stochastic sequence, the sample mean of n Bernoulli-distributed random variables which take the value 1 with probability $F(x)$ and 0 otherwise. If these form a stationary ergodic sequence, for example, we know that $F_n(x,\omega) \to F(x)$ a.s. for each $x \in \mathbb{R}$. We may say that the strong law of large numbers holds pointwise on $\mathbb{R}$ in such a case. Convergence is achieved at x for all $\omega \in C_x$, where $P(C_x) = 1$. The problem is that to say that the *functions* F_n converge a.s. requires that a.s. convergence is achieved at each of an uncountable set of points. We cannot appeal to **3.6**(iii) to claim that $P(\bigcap_{x \in \mathbb{R}} C_x) = 1$, and hence the assertion that $F_n(x,\omega) \to F(x)$ with probability 1 *at a point x not specified beforehand* cannot be proved in this manner. This is a problem for a.s. convergence *additional* to the possibility of convergence breaking down at certain points of the parameter space, illustrated by **21.4**. However, uniform convergence is the condition that suffices to rule out either difficulty.

In this case, thanks to the special form of the c.d.f. which as we know is bounded, monotone, and right-continuous, uniform continuity can be proved by establishing a.s. convergence just at a countable collection of points of $\mathbb{R}$.

21.5 Glivenko-Cantelli theorem If $F_n(x,\omega) \to F(x)$ a.s. pointwise, for $x \in \mathbb{R}$, then

$$\sup_x |F_n(x,\omega) - F(x)| \to 0 \text{ a.s. } \square \tag{21.20}$$

Proof First define, in parallel with F_n,

$$F'_n(x,\omega) = \frac{1}{n}\sum_{t=1}^{n} 1_{(-\infty,x)}(X_t(\omega)), \tag{21.21}$$

and note that $F'_n(x,\omega) \to F(x-)$ for all ω in a set C'_x, where $P(C'_x) = 1$. For an integer $m > 1$ let

$$x_{jm} = \inf\{x \in \mathbb{R}: F(x) \geq j/m\},\ j = 1,\dots,m-1, \tag{21.22}$$

and also let $x_{0m} = -\infty$ and $x_{mm} = +\infty$, so that, by construction,

$$F(x_{jm}-) - F(x_{j-1,m}) \leq 1/m,\ j = 1,\dots,m. \tag{21.23}$$

Lastly let

$$\mathrm{M}_{mn}(\omega) = \max_{1\leq j\leq m}\left\{\max\{|F_n(x_{jm},\omega) - F(x_{jm})|, |F'_n(x_{jm},\omega) - F(x_{jm}-)|\}\right\}. \tag{21.24}$$

Then, for $j = 1,\dots,m$ and $x \in [x_{j-1,m}, x_{jm})$,

$$\begin{aligned} F(x) - \frac{1}{m} - M_{mn}(\omega) &\leq F(x_{j-1,m}) - M_{mn}(\omega) \\ &\leq F_n(x_{j-1,m},\omega) \leq F_n(x,\omega) \leq F'_n(x_{jm},\omega) \\ &\leq F(x_{jm}-) + M_{mn}(\omega) \leq F(x) + \frac{1}{m} + M_{mn}(\omega). \end{aligned} \tag{21.25}$$

That is to say, $|F_n(x,\omega) - F(x)| \leq 1/m + M_{mn}(\omega)$ for every $x \in \mathbb{R}$.

By pointwise strong convergence we may say that $\lim_{n\to\infty} M_{mn}(\omega) = 0$ for finite m, and hence that $\lim_{n\to\infty}\sup_x|F_n(x,\omega) - F(x)| \leq 1/m$, for all $\omega \notin C^*_m$, where

$$C^*_m = \bigcap_{j=1}^{m}(C_{x_{mj}} \cap C'_{x_{mj}}). \tag{21.26}$$

But $P(\lim_{m\to\infty} C^*_m) = 1$ by **3.6**(iii), and this completes the proof. ■

Another, quite separate problem calling for uniform convergence is when a sample statistic is not merely a stochastic function of parameters, but is to be evaluated at a random point in the parameter space. Estimates of covariance matrices of estimators generally have this character, for example. One way such estimates are obtained is as the inverted negative Hessian matrix of the associated sample log-likelihood function, evaluated at estimated parameter values. The problem of proving consistency involves two distinct stochastic convergence phenomena, and it does not suffice to appeal to an ordinary law of large numbers to establish convergence to the true function evaluated at the true point. The following theorem gives sufficient conditions for the double convergence to hold.

21.6 Theorem Let $(\Omega,\mathcal{F},P)$ be a probability space and (Θ,ρ) a metric space, and let Q_n: $\Theta\times\Omega \mapsto \mathbb{R}$ be $\mathcal{F}/\mathcal{B}$-measurable for each $\theta \in \Theta$. If

(a) $\theta^*_n \xrightarrow{pr} \theta_0$, and

(b) $Q_n(\theta) \xrightarrow{pr} Q(\theta)$ uniformly on an open set B_0 containing θ_0, where $Q(\theta)$ is a nonstochastic function continuous at θ_0, then $Q_n(\theta_n^*) \xrightarrow{pr} Q(\theta_0)$.

Proof Uniform convergence in probability of Q_n on B_0 implies that, for any $\varepsilon > 0$ and $\delta > 0$, there exists $N_1 \geq 1$ large enough that, for $n \geq N_1$,

$$P\left(\sup_{\theta \in B_0} |Q_n(\theta) - Q(\theta)| < \tfrac{1}{2}\varepsilon\right) \geq 1 - \tfrac{1}{4}\delta. \tag{21.27}$$

Also, since $\theta_n^* \xrightarrow{pr} \theta_0$, there exists N_2 such that, for $n \geq N_2$,

$$P(\theta_n^* \in B_0) \geq 1 - \tfrac{1}{4}\delta. \tag{21.28}$$

To consider the joint occurrence of these two events, use the elementary relation

$$P(A \cap B) \geq P(A) + P(B) - 1. \tag{21.29}$$

Since

$$\{\theta_n^* \in B_0\} \cap \left\{\sup_{\theta \in B_0} |Q_n(\theta) - Q(\theta)| < \tfrac{1}{2}\varepsilon\right\} \subseteq \{|Q_n(\theta_n^*) - Q(\theta_n^*)| < \tfrac{1}{2}\varepsilon\}, \tag{21.30}$$

for $n \geq \max(N_1, N_2)$,

$$P\{|Q_n(\theta_n^*) - Q(\theta_n^*)| < \tfrac{1}{2}\varepsilon\} \geq 2(1 - \tfrac{1}{4}\delta) - 1 = 1 - \tfrac{1}{2}\delta. \tag{21.31}$$

Using continuity at θ_0 and **18.10**(ii), there exists N_3 large enough that, for $n \geq N_3$,

$$P(|Q(\theta_n^*) - Q(\theta_0)| < \tfrac{1}{2}\varepsilon) \geq 1 - \tfrac{1}{2}\delta. \tag{21.32}$$

By the triangle inequality,

$$|Q_n(\theta_n^*) - Q(\theta_n^*)| + |Q(\theta_n^*) - Q(\theta_0)| \geq |Q_n(\theta_n^*) - Q(\theta_0)| \tag{21.33}$$

and hence

$$\{|Q_n(\theta_n^*) - Q(\theta_n^*)| < \tfrac{1}{2}\varepsilon\} \cap \{|Q(\theta_n^*) - Q(\theta_0)| < \tfrac{1}{2}\varepsilon\} \subseteq \{|Q_n(\theta_n^*) - Q(\theta_0)| < \varepsilon\}. \tag{21.34}$$

Applying (21.29) again gives, for $n \geq \max(N_1, N_2, N_3)$,

$$P(|Q_n(\theta_n^*) - Q(\theta_0)| < \varepsilon) \geq 1 - \delta. \tag{21.35}$$

The theorem follows since δ and ε are arbitrary. ∎

Notice why we need uniform convergence here. Pointwise convergence would not allow us to assert (21.27) for a *single* N_1 which works for all $\theta \in B_0$. There would be the risk of a sequence of points existing in B_0 on which N_1 is diverging. Suppose $\theta_0 = 0$ and $G_n(\theta) = Q_n(\theta) - Q(\theta)$ in **21.4**. A sequence approaching θ_0, say $\{1/m, m \in \mathbb{N}\}$, has this property; we should have

$$P(|Q_n(1/m) - Q(1/m)| < \tfrac{1}{2}\varepsilon) \geq 1 - \tfrac{1}{4}\delta \tag{21.36}$$

for arbitrary $\varepsilon > 0$ and $\delta > 0$, *only* for $n > m$. Therefore we would not be able to claim the existence of a finite n for which (21.31) holds, and the proof collapses.

In this example, the sequence of functions $\{G_n(\theta)\}$ is continuous for each n, but the continuity breaks down in the limit. This points to a link between uniform convergence and continuity. We had no need of continuity to prove the Glivenko-Cantelli theorem, but the c.d.f. is rather a special type of function, with its behaviour at discontinuities (and elsewhere) subject to tight limitations. In the wider class of functions, not necessarily bounded and monotone, continuity is the condition that has generally been exploited to get uniform convergence results.

21.3 Stochastic Equicontinuity

Example **21.4** is characterized by the breakdown of continuity in the limit of the sequence of continuous functions. We may conjecture that to impose continuity uniformly over the sequence would suffice to eliminate failures of uniform convergence. A natural comparison to draw is with the uniform integrability property of sequences, but we have to be careful with our terminology because, of course, uniform continuity is a well-established term for something completely different.

The concept we require is *equicontinuity*, or, to be more precise, *asymptotic uniform equicontinuity*; see (5.47). Our results will be based on the following version of the Arzelà-Ascoli theorem (**5.28**).

21.7 Theorem Let $\{f_n(\theta),\, n \in \mathbb{N}\}$ be sequence of (nonstochastic) functions on a totally bounded parameter space (Θ,ρ). Then, $\sup_{\theta\in\Theta}|f_n(\theta)| \to 0$ if and only if $f_n(\theta) \to 0$ for all $\theta \in \Theta_0$, where Θ_0 is a dense subset of Θ, and $\{f_n\}$ is asymptotically uniformly equicontinuous. □

The set $\mathbb{F} = \{f_n,\, n \in \mathbb{N}\} \cup \{0\}$, endowed with the uniform metric, is a subspace of (C_Θ, d_U), and by definition, convergence of f_n to 0 in the uniform metric is the same thing as uniform convergence on Θ. According to **5.12**, compactness of $\mathbb{F}$ is equivalent to the property that every sequence in $\mathbb{F}$ has a cluster point. In view of the pointwise convergence, the cluster point must be unique and equal to 0, so that the conclusion of this theorem is really identical with the Arzelà-Ascoli theorem, although the method of proof will be adapted to the present case.

Where convenient, we shall use the notation

$$w(f_n,\delta) = \sup_{\theta\in\Theta}\ \sup_{\theta'\in S(\theta,\delta)} |f_n(\theta') - f_n(\theta)|. \tag{21.37}$$

The function $w(f_n,.)$: $\mathbb{R}^+ \mapsto \mathbb{R}^+$ is called the *modulus of continuity* of f_n. Asymptotic uniform equicontinuity of the sequence $\{f_n\}$ is the property that $\limsup_n w(f_n,\delta) \downarrow 0$ as $\delta \downarrow 0$.

Proof of 21.7 To prove 'if': given $\varepsilon > 0$, there exists by assumption $\delta > 0$ to satisfy

$$\limsup_{n\to\infty} w(f_n,\delta) < \varepsilon. \tag{21.38}$$

Since Θ is totally bounded, it has a cover $\{S(\theta_i,\delta/2),\ i = 1,\dots,m\}$. For each i, choose $\tilde{\theta}_i \in \Theta_0$ such that $\rho(\theta_i,\tilde{\theta}_i) < \delta/2$ (possible because Θ_0 is dense in Θ) and note that $\{S(\tilde{\theta}_i,\delta),\ i = 1,\dots,m\}$ is also a cover for Θ. Every $\theta \in \Theta$ is contained in $S(\tilde{\theta}_i,\delta)$ for some i, and for this i,

$$\begin{aligned} |f_n(\theta)| &\le \sup_{\theta' \in S(\tilde{\theta}_i,\delta)} |f_n(\theta')| \\ &\le \sup_{\theta' \in S(\tilde{\theta}_i,\delta)} |f_n(\theta') - f(\tilde{\theta}_i)| + |f(\tilde{\theta}_i)|. \end{aligned} \tag{21.39}$$

We can therefore write

$$\begin{aligned} \sup_{\theta\in\Theta} |f_n(\theta)| &\le \max_{1\le i\le m} \sup_{\theta' \in S(\tilde{\theta}_i,\delta)} |f_n(\theta') - f(\tilde{\theta}_i)| + \max_{1\le i\le m} |f(\tilde{\theta}_i)| \\ &\le w(f_n,\delta) + \max_{1\le i\le m} |f(\tilde{\theta}_i)|. \end{aligned} \tag{21.40}$$

Sufficiency follows on taking the limsup of both sides of this inequality.

'Only if' follows simply from the facts that uniform convergence entails pointwise convergence, and that

$$w(f_n,\delta) \le 2\sup_{\theta\in\Theta} |f_n(\theta)|. \blacksquare \tag{21.41}$$

To apply this result to the stochastic convergence problem, we must define concepts of stochastic equicontinuity. Several such definitions can be devised, of which we shall give only two: respectively, a weak convergence (in pr.) and a strong convergence (a.s.) variant. Let (Θ,ρ) be a metric space and $(\Omega,\mathcal{F},P)$ a probability space, and let $\{G_n(\theta,\omega)),\ n \in \mathbb{N}\}$ be a sequence of stochastic functions $G_n\colon \Theta\times\Omega \mapsto \mathbb{R}$, $\mathcal{F}/\mathcal{B}$-measurable for each $\theta \in \Theta$. The sequence is said to be *asymptotically uniformly stochastically equicontinuous* (in pr.) if for all $\varepsilon > 0\ \exists\ \delta > 0$ such that

$$\limsup_{n\to\infty} P\big(w(G_n,\delta) \ge \varepsilon\big) < \varepsilon. \tag{21.42}$$

And it is said to be *strongly asymptotically uniformly stochastically equicontinuous* if for all $\varepsilon > 0\ \exists\ \delta > 0$ such that

$$P\left(\limsup_{n\to\infty} w(G_n,\delta) \ge \varepsilon\right) = 0. \tag{21.43}$$

Clearly, there is a bit of a terminology problem here! The qualifiers 'asymptotic' and 'uniform' will be adopted in all the applications in this chapter, so let these be understood, and let us speak simply of stochastic equicontinuity and strong stochastic equicontinuity. The abbreviations s.e. and s.s.e. will sometimes be used.

21.4 Generic Uniform Convergence

Uniform convergence results and their application in econometrics have been researched by several authors including Hoadley (1971), Bierens (1989), Andrews (1987a, 1992), Newey (1991), and Pötscher and Prucha (1989, 1994). The material in the remainder of this chapter is drawn mainly from the work of Andrews and Pötscher and Prucha, who have pioneered alternative approaches to deriving 'generic' uniform convergence theorems, applicable in a variety of modelling situations.

These methods rely on establishing a stochastic equicontinuity condition. Thus, once we have **21.7**, the proof of uniform almost sure convergence is direct.

21.8 Theorem Let $\{G_n(\theta), n \in \mathbb{N}\}$ be a sequence of stochastic real-valued functions on a totally bounded metric space (Θ,ρ). Then

$$\sup_{\theta\in\Theta} |G_n(\theta)| \xrightarrow{as} 0 \tag{21.44}$$

if and only if

(a) $G_n(\theta) \xrightarrow{as} 0$ for each $\theta \in \Theta_0$, where Θ_0 is a dense subset of Θ,

(b) $\{G_n\}$ is strongly stochastically equicontinuous.

Proof Because (Θ,ρ) is totally bounded it is separable (**5.7**) and Θ_0 can be chosen to be a countable set, say $\Theta_0 = \{\theta_k, k \in \mathbb{N}\}$. Condition (a) means that for $k = 1,2,...$ there is a set C_k with $P(C_k) = 1$ such that $G_n(\theta_k,\omega) \to 0$ for $\omega \in C_k$. Condition (b) means that the sequences $\{G_n(\omega)\}$ are asymptotically equicontinuous for all $\omega \in C'$, with $P(C') = 1$. By the sufficiency part of **21.7**, $\sup_{\theta\in\Theta}|G_n(\theta,\omega)| \to 0$ for $\omega \in C^* = \bigcap_{k=1}^{\infty} C_k \cap C'$. $P(C^*) = 1$ by **3.6**(iii), proving 'if'.

'Only if' follows from the necessity part of **21.7** applied to $\{G_n(\omega)\}$ for each $\omega \in C^*$. ■

The corresponding 'in probability' result follows very similar lines. The proof cannot exploit **21.7** quite so directly, but the family resemblance in the arguments will be noted.

21.9 Theorem Let $\{G_n(\theta), n \in \mathbb{N}\}$ be a sequence of stochastic real-valued functions on a totally bounded metric space (Θ,ρ). Then

$$\sup_{\theta\in\Theta} |G_n(\theta)| \xrightarrow{pr} 0 \tag{21.45}$$

if and only if

(a) $G_n(\theta) \xrightarrow{pr} 0$ for each $\theta \in \Theta_0$, where Θ_0 is a dense subset of Θ,

(b) $\{G_n\}$ is stochastically equicontinuous.

Proof To show 'if', let $\{S(\tilde{\theta}_i,\delta), i = 1,...,m\}$ with $\tilde{\theta}_i \in \Theta_0$ be a finite cover for θ. This exists by the assumption of total boundedness and the argument used in the proof of **21.7**. Then,

$$P\Big(\sup_{\theta\in\Theta}|G_n(\theta)| \geq 2\varepsilon\Big)$$

$$\leq P\Big(\max_{1\leq i\leq m}\ \sup_{\theta'\in S(\tilde{\theta}_i,\delta)}(|G_n(\theta')-G_n(\theta_i)|+|G_n(\theta_i)|) \geq 2\varepsilon\Big)$$

$$\leq P(w(G_n,\delta)\geq\varepsilon)+P\Big(\max_{1\leq i\leq m}|G_n(\theta_i)|\geq\varepsilon\Big)$$

$$\leq P(w(G_n,\delta)\geq\varepsilon)+P\Big(\bigcup_{i=1}^{m}\{|G_n(\tilde{\theta}_i)|\geq\varepsilon\}\Big)$$

$$\leq P(w(G_n,\delta)\geq\varepsilon)+\sum_{i=1}^{m}P(|G_n(\tilde{\theta}_i)|\geq\varepsilon), \tag{21.46}$$

where we used the fact that

$$\{x+y\geq 2\varepsilon\}\subseteq\{x\geq\varepsilon\}\cup\{y\geq\varepsilon\} \tag{21.47}$$

for real numbers x and y, to get the third inequality. Taking the limsup of both sides of (21.46), (a) and (b) imply that

$$\limsup_{n\to\infty} P\Big(\sup_{\theta\in\Theta}|G_n(\theta)|\geq 2\varepsilon\Big) < \varepsilon. \tag{21.48}$$

To prove 'only if', pointwise convergence follows immediately from uniform convergence, so it remains to show that s.e. holds; but this follows easily in view of the fact (see (21.41)) that

$$P(w(G_n,\delta)\geq\varepsilon) \leq P\Big(\sup_{\theta\in\Theta}|G_n(\theta)|\geq\varepsilon/2\Big). \ \blacksquare \tag{21.49}$$

There is no loss of generality in considering the case $G_n \to 0$ in these theorems. We can just as easily apply them to the case where $G_n(\theta) = Q_n(\theta) - \overline{Q}_n(\theta)$ and $\overline{Q}_n$ is a nonstochastic function which may really depend on n, or just be a limit function, so that $\overline{Q}_n = \overline{Q}$. In the former case there is no need for Q_n to converge, as long as $Q_n - \overline{Q}_n$ does. Applying the triangle inequality and taking complements in (21.47), we obtain

$$\{w(Q_n,\delta)<\varepsilon\}\cap\{w(\overline{Q}_n,\delta)<\varepsilon\}\subseteq\{w(Q_n-\overline{Q}_n,\ \delta)<2\varepsilon\}. \tag{21.50}$$

This means that $\{Q_n-\overline{Q}_n\}$ is s.e., or s.s.e. as the case may be, provided that $\{Q_n\}$ is s.e., or s.s.e., and $\{\overline{Q}_n\}$ is asymptotically equicontinuous in the ordinary sense of §5.5. This extension of **21.8** is obvious, and in **21.9** we can insert the step

$$P(w(Q_n-\overline{Q}_n,\delta)\geq 2\varepsilon) \leq P(w(Q_n,\delta)\geq\varepsilon)+1_{\{w(\overline{Q}_n,\delta)\geq\varepsilon\}} \tag{21.51}$$

into (21.46), where the second term on the right is 0 or 1 depending on whether the indicated nonstochastic condition holds, and this term will vanish when $n \geq N$

for some $N \geq 1$, by assumption.

The s.e. and s.s.e. conditions may not be particularly easy to verify directly, and the existence of Lipschitz-type sufficient conditions could then be very convenient. Andrews (1992) suggests conditions of the following sort.

21.10 Theorem Suppose there exists $N \geq 1$ such that

$$|Q_n(\theta') - Q_n(\theta)| \leq B_n h(\rho(\theta,\theta')), \text{ a.s.} \tag{21.52}$$

holds for all $\theta,\theta' \in \Theta$ and $n \geq N$, where h is nonstochastic and $h(x) \downarrow 0$ as $x \downarrow 0$, and $\{B_n\}$ is a stochastic sequence not depending on θ. Then

(i) $\{Q_n\}$ is s.e. if $B_n = O_p(1)$.

(ii) $\{Q_n\}$ is s.s.e. if $\limsup_n B_n < \infty$, a.s.

Proof The definitions imply that $w(Q_n,\delta) \leq B_n h(\delta)$ a.s. for $n \geq N$. To prove (i), note that, for any $\varepsilon > 0$ and $\delta > 0$,

$$\limsup_{n\to\infty} P(w(Q_n,\delta) \geq \varepsilon) \leq \limsup_{n\to\infty} P(B_n \geq \varepsilon/h(\delta)). \tag{21.53}$$

By definition of $O_p(1)$, the right-hand side can be made arbitrarily small by choosing $\varepsilon/h(\delta)$ large enough. In particular, fix $\varepsilon > 0$, and then by definition of h we may take δ small enough that $\limsup_{n\to\infty} P(B_n \geq \varepsilon/h(\delta)) < \varepsilon$.

For (ii), we have in the same way that, for small enough δ,

$$P\left(\limsup_{n\to\infty} w(Q_n,\delta) \geq \varepsilon\right) \leq P\left(\limsup_{n\to\infty} B_n \geq \varepsilon/h(\delta)\right) < \varepsilon. \;\blacksquare \tag{21.54}$$

A sufficient condition for $B_n = O_p(1)$ is to have B_n uniformly bounded in L_1 norm, i.e., $\sup_n E(B_n) < \infty$ (see **12.11**), and it is sufficient for $\limsup_n B_n$ to be a.s. bounded if, in addition to this, $B_n - E(B_n) \xrightarrow{as} 0$.

The conditions of **21.10** offer a striking contrast in restrictiveness. Think of (21.52) as a continuity condition, which says that $Q_n(\theta')$ must be close to $Q_n(\theta)$ when θ' is close to θ. When Q_n is stochastic these conditions are very hard to satisfy for *fixed* B_n, because random changes of scale may lead the condition to be violated from time to time even if $Q_n(\theta,\omega)$ is a continuous function for all ω and n. The purpose of the factor B_n is to allow for such random scale variations.

Under s.e., we require that the probability of large variations declines as their magnitude increases; this is what $O_p(1)$ means. But in the s.s.e. case, the requirement that $\{B_n\}$ be bounded a.s. except for at most a finite number of terms implies that $\{Q_n\}$ must satisfy the same condition. This is very restrictive. It means for example that $Q_n(\theta)$ cannot be Gaussian, nor have any other distribution with infinite support. In such a case, no matter what $\{B_n\}$ and h were chosen, the condition in (21.52) would be violated eventually. It does not matter that the probability of large deviations might be extremely small, because over an *infinite* number of sequence coordinates they will still arise with probability 1.

Thus, strong uniform convergence is a phenomenon confined, as far as we are able to show, to a.s. bounded sequences. Although (21.52) is only a sufficient condition, it can be verified that this feature of s.s.e. is implicit in the definition. This fact puts the relative merits of working with strong and weak laws of large numbers in a new light. The former are simply not available in many important cases. Fortunately, 'in probability' results are often sufficient for the purpose at hand, for example, determining the limits in distribution of estimators and sample statistics; see §25.1 for more details.

Supposing $(\Theta,\rho) \subset (\mathbb{R}^k, d_E)$, suppose further that $Q_n(\theta)$ is differentiable a.s. at each point of Θ; to be precise, we must specify differentiability a.s. at each point of an open convex set Θ^* containing Θ. (A set $B \subset \mathbb{R}^k$ is said to be convex if $\boldsymbol{x} \in B$ and $\boldsymbol{y} \in B$ imply $\lambda\boldsymbol{x} + (1-\lambda)\boldsymbol{y} \in B$ for $\lambda \in [0,1]$.) The mean value theorem yields the result that, at a pair of points $\boldsymbol{\theta}, \boldsymbol{\theta}' \in \Theta^*$,[22]

$$Q_n(\boldsymbol{\theta}) - Q_n(\boldsymbol{\theta}') = \sum_{i=1}^{k} \frac{\partial Q_n}{\partial \theta_i}\bigg|_{\theta=\theta^*}(\theta_i - \theta_i') \text{ a.s.,} \tag{21.55}$$

where $\boldsymbol{\theta}^* \in \Theta^*$ is a point on the line segment joining $\boldsymbol{\theta}$ and $\boldsymbol{\theta}'$, which exists by convexity of Θ^*. Applying the Cauchy-Schwartz inequality, we get

$$|Q_n(\boldsymbol{\theta}) - Q_n(\boldsymbol{\theta}')| \le \sum_{i=1}^{k} \left| \frac{\partial Q_n}{\partial \theta_i}\bigg|_{\theta=\theta^*} \right| |\theta_i - \theta_i'|$$

$$\le B_n \|\boldsymbol{\theta} - \boldsymbol{\theta}'\| \text{ a.s.,} \tag{21.56}$$

where

$$B_n = \sup_{\theta^* \in \Theta^*} \left\| \frac{\partial Q_n}{\partial \boldsymbol{\theta}}\bigg|_{\theta=\theta^*} \right\|. \tag{21.57}$$

Here $\|.\|$ denotes the Euclidean length, and $\partial Q_n/\partial\boldsymbol{\theta}$ is the gradient vector whose elements are the partials of Q_n with respect to the θ_i. Clearly, (21.52) is satisfied by taking h as the identity function, and B_n defined in (21.57) is a random variable for all n. Subject to this condition, and B_n satisfying the conditions specified in **21.10**, a.s. differentiability emerges as a sufficient condition for s.e..

21.5 Uniform Laws of Large Numbers

In the last section it was shown that stochastic equicontinuity (strong or in pr.) is a necessary and sufficient condition to go from pointwise to uniform convergence (strong or in pr.). The next task is to find sufficient conditions for stochastic equicontinuity when $\{Q_n(\theta)\}$ is a sequence of partial sums, and hence to derive uniform laws of large numbers. There are several possible approaches to this problem, of which perhaps the simplest is to establish the Lipschitz condition of **21.10**.

21.11 Theorem Let $\{\{q_{nt}(\omega,\theta)\}_{t=1}^{n}\}_{n=1}^{\infty}$ denote a triangular array of real stochastic functions with domain (Θ,ρ), satisfying, for $N \ge 1$,

$$|q_{nt}(\theta') - q_{nt}(\theta)| \le B_{nt}h(\rho(\theta,\theta')), \text{ a.s.,} \tag{21.58}$$

for all $\theta,\theta' \in \Theta$ and $n \ge N$, where h is nonstochastic and $h(x) \downarrow 0$ as $x \downarrow 0$, and $\{B_{nt}\}$ is a stochastic array not depending on θ with $\sum_{t=1}^n E(B_{nt}) = O(1)$. If $Q_n(\theta) = \sum_{t=1}^n q_{nt}(\theta)$, then

(i) Q_n is s.e.;

(ii) Q_n is s.s.e. if $\sum_{t=1}^n (B_{nt} - E(B_{nt})) \xrightarrow{as} 0$.

Proof For (i) it is only necessary by **21.10**(i) and the triangle inequality to establish that $\sum_{t=1}^n B_{nt} = O_p(1)$. This follows from the stated condition by the Markov inequality. Likewise, (ii) follows directly from **21.10**(ii). ■

A second class of conditions is obtained by applying a form of s.e. to the summands. For these results we need to specify G_n to be an unweighted average of n functions, since the conditions to be imposed take the form of Cesàro summability of certain related sequences. It is convenient to confine attention to the case

$$G_n(\omega,\theta) = \frac{1}{n}\sum_{t=1}^n (q_t(X_t(\omega),\theta) - E(q_t(X_t,\theta))), \tag{21.59}$$

where $X_t \in \mathbb{X}$ is a random element drawn from the probability space $(\mathbb{X},\mathcal{X},\mu_t)$. Typically, though *not* necessarily, X_t is a vector of real r.v.s with $\mathbb{X}$ a subset of $\mathbb{R}^m$, $m \ge 1$, $\mathcal{X}$ being the restriction of $\mathcal{B}^m$ to $\mathbb{X}$. The point here is not to restrict the form of the functional relation between q_t and ω, but to specify the existence of marginal derived measures μ_t, with $\mu_t(A) = P(X_t \in A)$ for $A \in \mathcal{X}$. The usual context will have G_n the sample average of functions that are stochastic through their dependence on some kind of data set, indexed on t. The functions themselves, not just their arguments, can be different for different t.

We must find conditions on both the functions $q_t(.,.)$ and the p.m.s μ_t which yield the s.e. condition on G_n. The first stage of the argument is to establish conditions on the stochastic functions $q_t(\theta)$ which have to be satisfied for s.e. to hold. Andrews (1992) gives the following result.

21.12 Theorem If

(a) there exists a positive stochastic sequence $\{d_t\}$ satisfying

$$\sup_{\theta\in\Theta}|q_t(\theta)| \le d_t, \text{ all } t \tag{21.60}$$

and

$$\limsup_{n\to\infty} \frac{1}{n}\sum_{t=1}^n E(d_t 1_{\{d_t > M\}}) \to 0 \text{ as } M \to \infty; \tag{21.61}$$

(b) for every $\varepsilon > 0$, there exists $\delta > 0$ such that

$$\limsup_{n\to\infty} \frac{1}{n}\sum_{t=1}^n P(w(q_t,\delta) > \varepsilon) < \varepsilon; \tag{21.62}$$

then G_n is s.e. □

Condition (21.61) is an interesting Cesàro-sum variation on uniform integrability, and actual uniform integrability of $\{d_t\}$ is sufficient, although not necessary. Condition (a) is a domination condition, while condition (b) is called by Andrews *termwise stochastic equicontinuity.*

Proof Given $\varepsilon > 0$, choose M such that $\limsup_{n\to\infty} n^{-1}\sum_{t=1}^n E(2d_t 1_{\{2d_t > M\}}) < \frac{1}{6}\varepsilon^2$, and then δ such that

$$\limsup_{n\to\infty} \frac{1}{n}\sum_{t=1}^n P(w(q_t,\delta) > \tfrac{1}{6}\varepsilon^2) < \tfrac{1}{6}M^{-1}\varepsilon^2. \tag{21.63}$$

The first thing to note is that

$$\begin{aligned} w((q_t - E(q_t)),\delta) &\le w(q_t,\omega) + w(E(q_t),\delta) \\ &\le w(q_t,\omega) + E(w(q_t,\delta)), \end{aligned} \tag{21.64}$$

where the last inequality is an application of **21.3**. Applying (21.64) and using Markov's inequality,

$$\begin{aligned} P(w(G_n,\delta) > \varepsilon) &\le P\left(\frac{1}{n}\sum_{t=1}^n w(q_t - E(q_t),\delta) > \varepsilon\right) \\ &\le P\left(\frac{1}{n}\sum_{t=1}^n (w(q_t,\delta) + E(w(q_t,\delta))) > \varepsilon\right) \\ &\le \frac{2}{n\varepsilon}\sum_{t=1}^n E(w(q_t,\delta)) \\ &= \frac{2}{n\varepsilon}\sum_{t=1}^n E\big[w(q_t,\delta)\big(1_{\{w(q_t,\delta)\le\varepsilon^2/6\}} \\ &\qquad + 1_{\{\varepsilon^2/6 < w(q_t,\delta)\le M\}} + 1_{\{w(q_t,\delta)>M\}}\big)\big], \end{aligned} \tag{21.65}$$

where the indicator functions in the last member add up to 1. Using the fact that $w(q_t,\delta) \le 2d_t$, and hence $\{w(q_t,\delta) > M\} \subseteq \{2d_t > M\}$, and taking the limsup, we now obtain

$$\begin{aligned} \limsup_{n\to\infty} P(w(G_n,\delta) > \varepsilon) &\le \frac{2}{\varepsilon}\left[\frac{\varepsilon^2}{6} + M\limsup_{n\to\infty}\frac{1}{n}\sum_{t=1}^n P\left(w(q_t,\delta) > \frac{\varepsilon^2}{6}\right)\right. \\ &\qquad \left. + \limsup_{n\to\infty}\frac{1}{n}\sum_{t=1}^n E(2d_t 1_{\{2d_t>M\}})\right] \\ &\le \varepsilon, \end{aligned} \tag{21.66}$$

in view of the values chosen for M and δ. ■

Clearly, whether condition **21.12**(a) is satisfied depends on both the distribution of X_t and functional form of $q_t(.)$. But something relatively general can be said about termwise s.e. (condition **21.12**(b)). Assume, following Pötscher and Prucha (1989), that

$$q_t(x,\theta) = \sum_{k=1}^{p} r_{kt}(x)s_{kt}(x,\theta), \tag{21.67}$$

where r_{kt}: $\mathbb{X} \to \mathbb{R}$, and $s_{kt}(.,\theta)$: $\mathbb{X} \to \mathbb{R}$ for fixed θ, are $\mathcal{X}/\mathcal{B}$-measurable functions. The idea here is that we can be more liberal in the behaviour allowed to the factors r_{kt} as functions of X_t than to the factors s_{kt}; discontinuities are permitted, for example. To be exact, we shall be content to have the r_{kt} uniformly L_1-bounded in Cesàro mean:

$$\sup_n \frac{1}{n}\sum_{t=1}^{n} E|r_{kt}(X_t)| \leq B < \infty,\ k = 1,\ldots,p. \tag{21.68}$$

As to the factors $s_{kt}(x,\theta)$, we need these to be asymptotically equicontinuous for a sufficiently large set of x values. Assume there is a sequence of sets $\{K_m \in \mathcal{X},\ m = 1,2,\ldots\}$, such that

$$\limsup_{n\to\infty} \frac{1}{n}\sum_{t=1}^{n} \mu_t(K_m^c) \to 0 \text{ as } m \to \infty, \tag{21.69}$$

and that for each $m \geq 1$ and $\varepsilon > 0$, there exists $\delta > 0$ such that

$$\limsup_{n\to\infty} \sup_{x\in K_m} w(s_{kt}(x,.),\delta) < \varepsilon,\ k = 1,\ldots,p. \tag{21.70}$$

Notice that (21.70) is a *non*stochastic equicontinuity condition, but under condition (21.69) it holds (as one might say) 'almost surely, on average' when the r.v. X_t is substituted into the formula.

These conditions suffice to give termwise s.e., and hence can be used to prove s.e. of G_n by application of **21.12**.

21.13 Theorem If $q_t(X_t,\theta)$ is defined by (21.67), and (21.68), (21.69), and (21.70) hold, then for every $\varepsilon > 0$ there exists $\delta > 0$ such that

$$\limsup_{n\to\infty} \frac{1}{n}\sum_{t=1}^{n} P(w(q_t,\delta) > \varepsilon) < \varepsilon. \tag{21.71}$$

Proof Fix $\varepsilon > 0$, and first note that

$$P(w(q_t,\delta) > \varepsilon) \leq P\left(\sum_{k=1}^{p} |r_{kt}|w(s_{kt},\delta) > \varepsilon\right)$$

$$\leq P\left(\bigcup_{k=1}^{p}\{|r_{kt}|w(s_{kt},\delta) > \varepsilon/p\}\right)$$

$$\leq \sum_{k=1}^{p} P(|r_{kt}|w(s_{kt},\delta) > \varepsilon/p)$$

$$\leq \sum_{k=1}^{p} \left[P\left(|r_{kt}|w(s_{kt},\delta)1_{K_m} > \frac{\varepsilon}{2p} \right) + P\left(|r_{kt}|w(s_{kt},\delta)1_{K_m^c} > \frac{\varepsilon}{2p} \right) \right]. \quad (21.72)$$

Consider any one of these p terms. Choose m large enough that

$$\limsup_{n\to\infty} \frac{1}{n} \sum_{t=1}^{n} \mu_t(K_m^c) < \frac{\varepsilon}{2p}, \quad (21.73)$$

and for this m choose δ small enough that

$$\limsup_{n\to\infty} \sup_{x\in K_m} w(s_{kt}(x,.),\delta) < \frac{\varepsilon^2}{4Bp^2}. \quad (21.74)$$

Then, by the Markov inequality,

$$\limsup_{n\to\infty} \frac{1}{n} \sum_{t=1}^{n} P\left(|r_{kt}|w(s_{kt},\delta)1_{K_m} > \frac{\varepsilon}{2p} \right) \leq \limsup_{n\to\infty} \frac{1}{n} \sum_{t=1}^{n} P\left(|r_{kt}| \frac{\varepsilon^2}{4Bp^2} > \frac{\varepsilon}{2p} \right)$$

$$\leq \limsup_{n\to\infty} \frac{1}{n} \sum_{t=1}^{n} E|r_{kt}| \frac{\varepsilon}{2Bp}$$

$$\leq \frac{\varepsilon}{2p}, \quad (21.75)$$

and by (21.73),

$$\limsup_{n\to\infty} \frac{1}{n} \sum_{t=1}^{n} P\left(|r_{kt}|w(s_{kt},\delta)1_{K_m^c} > \frac{\varepsilon}{2p} \right) \leq \limsup_{n\to\infty} \frac{1}{n} \sum_{t=1}^{n} P(X_t \notin K_m)$$

$$\leq \frac{\varepsilon}{2p}. \quad (21.76)$$

Substituting these bounds into (21.72) yields the result. ■

V

THE CENTRAL LIMIT THEOREM

22
Weak Convergence of Distributions

22.1 Basic Concepts

The objects we examine in this part of the book are not sequences of random variables, but sequences of marginal distribution functions. There will of course be associated sequences of r.v.s generated from these distributions, but the concept of convergence arising here is quite distinct. Formally, if $\{F_n\}_1^\infty$ is a sequence of c.d.f.s, we say that the sequence *converges weakly* to a limit F if $F_n(x) \to F(x)$ pointwise for each $x \in C$, where $C \subseteq \mathbb{R}$ is the set of points at which F is continuous. Then, if X_n has c.d.f. F_n and X has c.d.f. F, we say that X_n *converges in distribution* to X. These terms are in practice used more or less interchangeably for the distributions and associated r.v.s.

Equivalent notations for weak convergence are $F_n \Rightarrow F$, and $X_n \xrightarrow{D} X$. Although the latter notation is customary, it is also slightly irregular, since to say a sequence of r.v.s converges in distribution means only that the limiting r.v. has the given distribution. If both X and Y have the distribution specified by F, then $X_n \xrightarrow{D} X$ and $X_n \xrightarrow{D} Y$ are equivalent statements. Moreover, we write things like $X_n \xrightarrow{D} N(0,1)$ to indicate that the limiting distribution is standard Gaussian, although '$N(0,1)$' is shorthand for 'a r.v. having the standard Gaussian distribution'; it does not denote a particular r.v.. Also used by some authors is the notation '$\xrightarrow{L}$' standing for 'convergence in probability law', but we avoid this form because of possible confusion with convergence in L_p-norm.

Pointwise convergence of the distribution functions is all that is needed, remembering that F is non-decreasing, bounded by 0 and 1, and that every point is either a continuity point or a jump point. It is possible that F could possess a jump at a point x_0 which is a continuity point of F_n for all finite n, and in these cases $F_n(x_0)$ does not have a unique limit since any point between $F(x_0-)$ and $F(x_0)$ is a candidate. But the jump points of F are at most countable in number, and according to **8.4** the true F can be constructed by assigning the value $F(x_0)$ at every jump point x_0; hence, the above definition is adequate.

If μ represents the corresponding probability measure such that $F(x) = \mu((-\infty, x])$ for each $x \in \mathbb{R}$, we know (see §8.2) that μ and F are equivalent representations of the same measure, and similarly for μ_n and F_n. Hence, the statement $\mu_n \Rightarrow \mu$ is equivalent to $F_n \Rightarrow F$. The corresponding notion of weak convergence for the sequence of measures $\{\mu_n\}$ is given by the following theorem.

22.1 Theorem $\mu_n \Rightarrow \mu$ iff $\mu_n(A) \to \mu(A)$ for every $A \in \mathcal{B}$ for which $\mu(\partial A) = 0$. □

The proof of this theorem is postponed to a later point in the development. Note meanwhile that the exclusion of events whose boundary points have positive probability corresponds to the exclusion of jump points of F, where the events in question have the form $\{(-\infty,x]\}$.

Just as the theory of the expectation is an application of the general theory of integrals, so the theory of weak convergence is a general theory for sequences of finite measures. The results below do not generally depend upon the condition $\mu_n(\mathbb{R}) = 1$ for their validity, provided definitions are adjusted appropriately. However, a serious concern of the theory is whether a sequence of distribution functions has a distribution function as its limit; more specifically, should it follow because $\mu_n(\mathbb{R}) = 1$ for every n that $\mu(\mathbb{R}) = 1$? This is a question that is taken up in §22.5. Meanwhile, the reader should not be distracted by the use of the convenient notations $E(.)$ and $P(.)$ from appreciating the generality of the theory.

22.2 Example Consider the sequence of binomial distributions $\{B(n,\lambda/n),\ n = 1,2,3,\ldots\}$, where the probability of x successes in n Bernoulli trials is given by

$$P(X_n = x) = \binom{n}{x}(\lambda/n)^x(1-\lambda/n)^{n-x},\ x = 0,\ldots,n \tag{22.1}$$

(see **8.7**). Here, λ is a constant parameter, so that the probability of a success falls linearly as the number of trials increases. Note that $E(X_n) = \lambda$ for every n. For fixed x, $\binom{n}{x}n^{-x} \to 1/x!$ as $n \to \infty$, and taking the binomial expansion of $(1-\lambda/n)^n$ shows that $(1-\lambda/n)^n \to e^{-\lambda}$ as $n \to \infty$, whereas $(1-\lambda/n)^{-x} \to 1$. We may therefore conclude that

$$P(X_n = x) \to \frac{\lambda^x}{x!}e^{-\lambda},\ x = 0,1,2,\ldots, \tag{22.2}$$

and accordingly,

$$F_n(a) = \sum_{0\le x\le a} P(X_n = x) \to e^{-\lambda}\sum_{0\le x\le a}\frac{\lambda^x}{x!} \tag{22.3}$$

at all points $a < \infty$. Thus the limit (and hence the weak limit) of the sequence $\{B(n,\lambda/n)\}$ is the Poisson distribution with parameter λ. □

22.3 Example A sequence of discrete distributions on $[0,1]$ is defined by

$$P(X_n = x) = \begin{cases} 1/n, & x = i/n \\ 0, & \text{otherwise} \end{cases},\ i = 1,\ldots,n. \tag{22.4}$$

This sequence actually converges weakly to Lebesgue measure m on $[0,1]$, although this fact may be less than obvious; it will be demonstrated below. For any $x \in [0,1]$, $\mu_n([0,x]) = [nx]/n \to x = m([0,x])$, where $[nx]$ denotes the largest integer less than nx. There are sets for which convergence fails, notably the set $\mathbb{Q}_{[0,1]}$ of all rationals in $[0,1]$, in view of the fact that $\mu_n(\mathbb{Q}_{[0,1]}) = 1$ for every n, and $m(\mathbb{Q}_{[0,1]}) = 0$. But $\overline{\mathbb{Q}_{[0,1]}} = [0,1]$ and $m(\partial(\mathbb{Q}_{[0,1]})) = 1$, thus the definition of weak convergence in **22.1** is not violated. □

Although convergence in distribution is fundamentally different from convergence a.s. and in pr., the latter imply the former. In the next result, '$\xrightarrow{as}$' can be substituted for '$\xrightarrow{pr}$', by **18.5**.

22.4 Theorem If $X_n \xrightarrow{pr} X$, then $X_n \xrightarrow{D} X$.

Proof For $\varepsilon > 0$, we have

$$\begin{aligned} P(X_n \leq x) &= P(\{X_n \leq x\} \cap \{|X_n - X| \leq \varepsilon\}) \\ &\qquad + P(\{X_n \leq x\} \cap \{|X_n - X| > \varepsilon\}) \\ &\leq P(X \leq x + \varepsilon) + P(|X_n - X| > \varepsilon), \end{aligned} \tag{22.5}$$

where the events whose probabilities appear on the right-hand side of the inequality contain (and hence are at least as probable as) the corresponding events on the left. $P(|X_n - X| > \varepsilon) \to 0$ by hypothesis, and hence

$$\limsup_{n\to\infty} P(X_n \leq x) \leq P(X \leq x + \varepsilon). \tag{22.6}$$

Similarly,

$$\begin{aligned} P(X \leq x - \varepsilon) &= P(\{X \leq x - \varepsilon\} \cap \{|X_n - X| \leq \varepsilon\}) \\ &\qquad + P(\{X \leq x - \varepsilon\} \cap \{|X_n - X| > \varepsilon\}) \\ &\leq P(X_n \leq x) + P(|X_n - X| > \varepsilon), \end{aligned} \tag{22.7}$$

and so

$$P(X \leq x - \varepsilon) \leq \liminf_{n\to\infty} P(X_n \leq x). \tag{22.8}$$

Since ε is arbitrary, it follows that $\lim_{n\to\infty} P(X_n \leq x) = P(X \leq x)$ at every point x for which $P(X = x) = 0$, such that $\lim_{\varepsilon\downarrow 0} P(X \leq x - \varepsilon) = P(X \leq x)$. This condition is equivalent to weak convergence. ∎

The converse of **22.4** is not true in general, but the two conditions are equivalent when the probability limit in question is a constant. A *degenerate distribution* has the form

$$F(x) = \begin{cases} 0, & x < a \\ 1, & x \geq a \end{cases} \tag{22.9}$$

If a random variable is converging to a constant, its c.d.f. converges to the step function (22.9), through a sequence of the sort illustrated in Fig. 22.1.

22.5 Theorem X_n converges in probability to a constant a iff its c.d.f. converges to a step function with jump at a.

Proof For any $\varepsilon > 0$

$$P(|X_n - a| < \varepsilon) = P(a - \varepsilon \leq X_n \leq a + \varepsilon)$$

$$= F_n(a+\varepsilon) - F_n((a-\varepsilon)-). \tag{22.10}$$

Convergence to a step function with jump at a implies $\lim_{n\to\infty} F_n(a+\varepsilon) = F(a+\varepsilon) = 1$, and similarly $\lim_{n\to\infty} F_n((a-\varepsilon)-) = F((a-\varepsilon)-) = 0$ for all $\varepsilon > 0$. The sufficiency part follows from (22.10) and the definition of convergence in probability. For the necessity, let the left-hand side of (22.10) have a limit of 1 as $n \to \infty$, for all $\varepsilon > 0$. This implies

$$\lim_{n\to\infty} \left[F_n(a+\varepsilon) - F_n((a-\varepsilon)-)\right] = 1. \tag{22.11}$$

Since $0 \le F \le 1$, (22.11) will be satisfied for all $\varepsilon > 0$ only if $F(a) = 1$ and $F(a-) = 0$, which defines the function in (22.9). ■

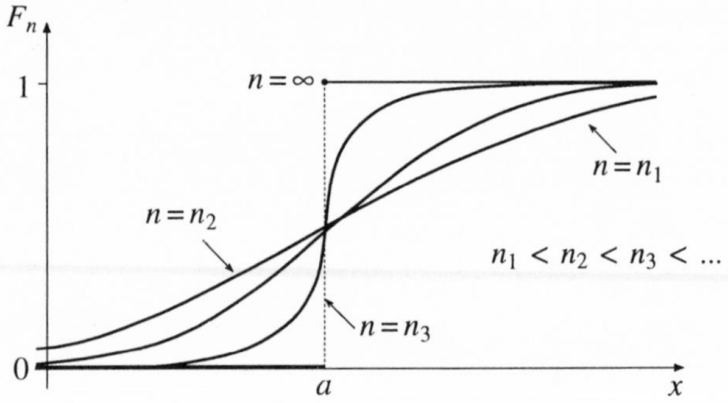

Fig. 22.1.

22.2 The Skorokhod Representation Theorem

Notwithstanding the fact that $X_n \xrightarrow{D} X$ does not imply $X_n \xrightarrow{as} X$, whenever a sequence of distributions $\{F_n\}$ converges weakly to F one can construct a sequence of r.v.s with distributions F_n, which converges almost surely to a limit having distribution F. Shown by Skorokhod (1956) in a more general context (see §26.6), this is an immensely useful fact for proving results about weak convergence.

Consider the sequence $\{F_n\}$ converging to F. Each of these functions is a monotone mapping from $\bar{\mathbb{R}}$ to the interval [0,1]. The idea is to invert this mapping. Let a random variable ω be defined on the probability space $([0,1],\mathcal{B}_{[0,1]},m)$, where $\mathcal{B}_{[0,1]}$ is the Borel field on the unit interval and m is the Lebesgue measure. Define for $\omega \in [0,1]$

$$Y_n(\omega) = \inf\{x\colon \omega \le F_n(x)\}. \tag{22.12}$$

In words, Y_n is the random variable obtained by using the inverse distribution function to map from the uniform distribution on [0,1] onto $\bar{\mathbb{R}}$, taking care of any discontinuities in $F_n^{-1}(\omega)$ (corresponding to intervals with zero probability mass under F_n) by taking the infimum of the eligible values. Y_n is therefore a non-decreasing, left-continuous function. Fig. 22.2 illustrates the construction, essentially the same as used in the proof of **8.5** (compare Fig. 8.2). When F_n has discontinuities it is only possible to assert (by right-continuity) that $F_n(Y_n(\omega)) \geq \omega$, whereas $Y_n(F_n(x)) \leq x$, by left-continuity of Y_n.

The first important feature of the Skorokhod construction is that, for any constant $a \in \mathbb{R}$,

$$P(Y_n(\omega) \leq a) = P(\omega \leq F_n(a)) = F_n(a), \tag{22.13}$$

where the last equality follows from the fact that ω is uniformly distributed on [0,1]. Thus, F_n is the c.d.f. of Y_n.[23] Letting F be a c.d.f. and Y the r.v. corresponding to F according to (22.12), the second important feature of the construction is contained in the following result.

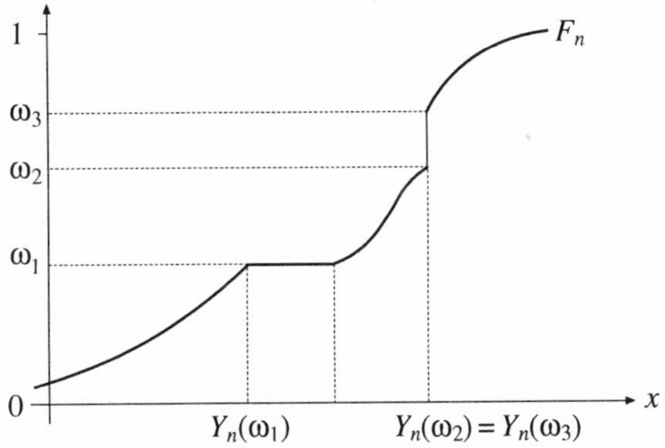

Fig. 22.2

22.6 Theorem If $F_n \Rightarrow F$ then $Y_n \to Y$ a.s.[m] as $n \to \infty$. □

In working through the proof, it may be helpful to check each assertion about the functions F and Y against the example in Fig. 22.3. This represents the extreme case where F, and hence also Y, is a step function; of course, if F is everywhere continuous and increasing, the mappings are 1-1 and the problem becomes trivial.

Proof Let ω be any continuity point of Y, excluding the end points 0 and 1. For any $\varepsilon > 0$, choose x as a continuity point of F satisfying $Y(\omega) - \varepsilon < x < Y(\omega)$. Given the countability of the discontinuities of F, such a point will always exist, and according to the definition of Y, it must have the property $F(x) < \omega$. If $F_n(x) \to F(x)$, there will be n large enough that $F_n(x) < \omega$, and hence $x < Y_n(\omega)$, by definition. We therefore have

$$Y(\omega) - \varepsilon < x < Y_n(\omega). \tag{22.14}$$

Without presuming that $\lim_{n\to\infty} Y_n(\omega)$ exists, since ε is arbitrary (22.14) allows us to conclude that $\liminf_{n\to\infty} Y_n(\omega) \geq Y(\omega)$.

Next, choose y as a continuity point of F satisfying $Y(\omega) < y < Y(\omega) + \varepsilon$. The properties of F give $\omega \leq F(Y(\omega)) \leq F(y)$. For large enough n we must also have $\omega \leq$

$F_n(y)$, and hence, again by definition of Y_n,

$$Y_n(\omega) \leq y < Y(\omega) + \varepsilon. \tag{22.15}$$

In the same way as before, we may conclude that $\limsup_{n\to\infty} Y_n(\omega) \leq Y(\omega)$. The superior and inferior limits are therefore equal, and $\lim_{n\to\infty} Y_n(\omega) = Y(\omega)$.

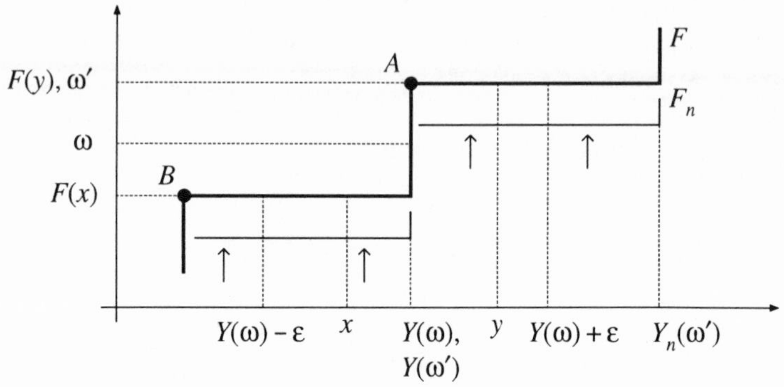

Fig. 22.3

This result only holds for continuity points of Y. However, there is a 1-1 correspondence between the discontinuity points of Y and intervals having zero probability under μ in $\mathbb{R}$. A collection of disjoint intervals on the line is at most countable (**1.11**), and hence the discontinuities of Y (plus the points 0 and 1) are countable, and have Lebesgue measure zero. Hence, $Y_n \to Y$ w.p.1 $[m]$, as asserted. ■

In Fig. 22.3, notice how both functions take their values at the discontinuities at the points marked A and B. Thus, $F(Y(\omega)) = \omega' > \omega$. Inequality (22.15) holds for ω, but need not hold for ω', a discontinuity point. A counter-example is the sequence of functions F_n obtained by vertical translations of the fixed graph from below, as illustrated. In this case $Y_n(\omega') > Y(\omega') + \varepsilon$ for every n.

22.7 Corollary Define random variables Y_n', so that $Y_n'(\omega) = Y_n(\omega)$ at each ω where the function is continuous, and $Y_n'(\omega) = 0$ at discontinuity points and at $\omega = 0$ and 1. Define Y' similarly. If $F_n \Rightarrow F$ then $Y_n'(\omega) \to Y'(\omega)$ for every $\omega \in [0,1]$, and F_n and F are the distribution functions of Y_n' and Y'.

Proof The convergence for every ω is immediate. The equivalence of the distributions follows from **8.4**, since the discontinuity points are countable and their complement is dense in [0,1], by **2.10**. ■

In the form given, **22.6** does not generalize very easily to distributions in $\mathbb{R}^k$ for $k > 1$, although a generalization does exist. This can be deduced as a special case of **26.25**, which derives the Skorokhod representation for distributions on general metric spaces of suitable type.

A final point to observe about Skorokhod's representation is its generalization to any finite measure. If F_n is a non-decreasing right-continuous function with codomain $[a,b]$, (22.12) defines a function $Y_n(\omega)$ on a measure space $([a,b], \mathcal{B}_{[a,b]}, m)$, where m is Lebesgue measure as before. With appropriate modifications, all the foregoing remarks continue to apply in this case.

The following application of the Skorokhod representation yields a different, but equivalent, characterization of weak convergence.

22.8 Theorem $X_n \xrightarrow{D} X$ iff

$$\lim_{n\to\infty} E(f(X_n)) = E(f(X)) \tag{22.16}$$

for every bounded, continuous real function f. □

The necessity half of this result is known as the Helly-Bray theorem.

Proof To prove sufficiency, construct an example. For $a \in \mathbb{R}$ and $\delta > 0$, let

$$f(x) = \begin{cases} 1, & x \le a - \delta \\ (a-x)/\delta, & a - \delta < x \le a \\ 0, & x > a \end{cases} \tag{22.17}$$

We call this the 'smoothed indicator' of the set $(-\infty,a]$. (See Fig. 22.4.) It is a continuous function with the properties

$$F_n(a-\delta) \le \int f dF_n \le F_n(a), \text{ all } n, \tag{22.18}$$

$$F(a-\delta) \le \int f dF \le F(a). \tag{22.19}$$

By hypothesis, $\int f dF_n \to \int f dF$, and hence

$$\limsup_{n\to\infty} F_n(a-\delta) \le \int f dF \le \liminf_{n\to\infty} F_n(a). \tag{22.20}$$

Letting $\delta \to 0$, combining (22.19) and (22.20) yields

$$\limsup_{n\to\infty} F_n(a-) \le F(a), \tag{22.21}$$

$$F(a-) \le \liminf_{n\to\infty} F_n(a). \tag{22.22}$$

These inequalities show that $\lim_n F_n(a)$ exists and is equal to $F(a)$ whenever $F(a-) = F(a)$, that is, $F_n \Rightarrow F$.

To prove necessity, let f be a bounded function whose points of discontinuity are contained in a set D_f, where $\mu(D_f) = 0$, μ being the p.m. such that $F(x) = \mu((-\infty,x])$. When $F_n \Rightarrow F$ (F_n being the c.d.f. of X_n and F that of X) $Y_n'(\omega) \to Y'(\omega)$ for every $\omega \in [0,1]$, where $Y_n'(\omega)$ and $Y'(\omega)$ are the Skorokhod variables defined in **22.7**. Since $m(\omega\colon Y'(\omega) \in D_f) = \mu(D_f) = 0$, $f(Y_n') \to f(Y')$ a.s.[μ] by **18.8**(i). The bounded convergence theorem then implies $E(f(Y_n')) \to E(f(Y'))$, or

$$\int f(y)d\mu_n(y) \to \int f(y)d\mu(y), \tag{22.23}$$

where μ_n is the p.m. corresponding to F_n. But **9.6** allows us to write

$$\int f(y)d\mu_n(y) = \int yd\mu_n f^{-1}(y) = \int xd\mu_n f^{-1}(x) = E(f(X_n)), \tag{22.24}$$

with a similar equality for $E(f(X))$. (The trivial change of dummy argument from y to x is just to emphasize the equivalence of the two formulations.) Hence we have $E(f(X_n)) \to E(f(X))$. The result certainly holds for the case $D_f = \varnothing$, so 'only if' is proved. ■

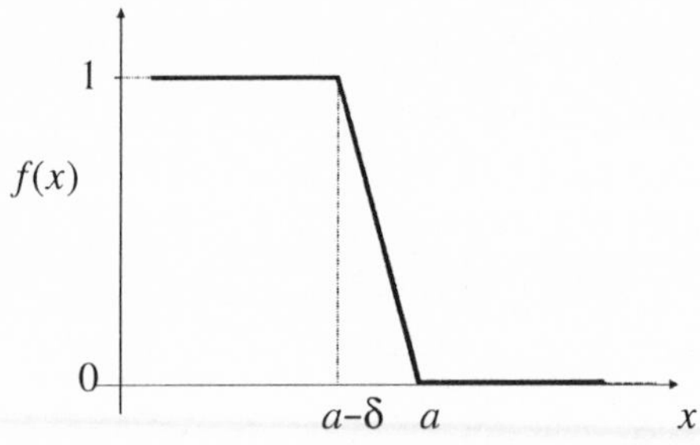

Fig. 22.4

Notice how the proof cleverly substitutes $([0,1],\mathcal{B}_{[0,1]},m)$ for the fundamental probability space $(\Omega,\mathcal{F},P)$ generating $\{X_n\}$, exploiting the fact that the derived distributions are the same. This result does not say that the expectations converge *only* for bounded continuous functions; it is simply that convergence is implied at least for all members of this large class of functions. The theorem also holds if we substitute any subclass of the class of bounded continuous functions which contains at least the smoothed indicator functions of half-lines, for example the bounded uniformly continuous functions.

22.9 Example We now give the promised proof of weak convergence for **22.3**. Clearly, in that example,

$$\int fd\mu_n = \frac{1}{n}\sum_{i=1}^{n} f(i/n). \tag{22.25}$$

The limit of the expression on the right of (22.25) as $n \to \infty$ is by definition the Riemann integral of f on the unit interval. Since this agrees with the Lebesgue integral, we have a proof of weak convergence in this case. □

We shall subsequently require the generalization of Theorem **22.8** to general finite measures. This will be stated as a corollary, the modifications to the proof being left to the reader to supply; it is mainly a matter of modifying the notation to suit.

22.10 Corollary Let $\{F_n\}$ be a sequence of bounded, non-decreasing, right-continuous functions. $F_n \Rightarrow F$ if and only if

$$\int f dF_n \to \int f dF \tag{22.26}$$

for every bounded, continuous real function f. □

Another proof which was deferred earlier can now be given.

Proof of 22.1 To show sufficiency, consider $A = (-\infty, x]$, for which $\partial A = \{x\}$. Weak convergence is defined by the condition $\mu_n(\{(-\infty, x]\}) \to \mu(\{(-\infty, x]\})$ whenever $\mu(\{x\}) = 0$. To show necessity, consider in the necessity part of **22.8** the case $f(x) = 1_A(x)$ for any $A \in \mathcal{B}$. The discontinuity points of this function are contained in the set ∂A, and if $\mu(\partial A) = 0$, we have $\mu_n(A) \to \mu(A)$ as a case of (22.16), when $F_n \Rightarrow F$. ■

22.3 Weak Convergence and Transformations

The next result might be thought of as the weak convergence counterpart of **18.8**.

22.11 Continuous mapping theorem Let $h: \mathbb{R} \mapsto \mathbb{R}$ be Borel-measurable with discontinuity points confined to a set D_h, where $\mu(D_h) = 0$. If $\mu_n \Rightarrow \mu$, then $\mu_n h^{-1} \Rightarrow \mu h^{-1}$.

Proof By the argument used to prove the Helly-Bray theorem, $h(Y_n') \to h(Y')$ a.s.[μ]. It follows from **22.4** that $h(Y_n') \xrightarrow{D} h(Y')$. Since $m(\omega: Y_n'(\omega) \in A) = \mu_n(A)$,

$$m(\omega: h(Y_n'(\omega)) \in A) = m(\omega: Y_n'(\omega) \in h^{-1}(A)) = \mu_n h^{-1}(A) \tag{22.27}$$

for each $A \in \mathcal{B}$, using **3.21**. Similarly, $m(h(Y') \in A) = \mu h^{-1}(A)$. According to the definition of weak convergence, $h(Y_n') \xrightarrow{D} h(Y')$ is equivalent to $\mu_n h^{-1} \Rightarrow \mu h^{-1}$. ■

22.12 Corollary If h is the function of **22.11** and $X_n \xrightarrow{D} X$, then $h(X_n) \xrightarrow{D} h(X)$.

Proof Immediate from the theorem, given that $X_n \sim F_n$ and $X \sim F$. ■

22.13 Example If $X_n \xrightarrow{D} N(0,1)$, then $X_n^2 \xrightarrow{D} \chi^2(1)$. □

Our second result on transformations is from Cramér (1946), and is sometimes called Cramér's theorem:

22.14 Cramér's theorem If $X_n \xrightarrow{D} X$ and $Y_n \xrightarrow{pr} a$ (constant), then

(i) $(X_n + Y_n) \xrightarrow{D} (X + a)$.
(ii) $Y_n X_n \xrightarrow{D} aX$.
(iii) $X_n / Y_n \xrightarrow{D} X/a$, for $a \neq 0$.

Proof This is by an extension of the type of argument used in **22.4**.

$$P(X_n + Y_n \le x) = P(X_n + Y_n \le x,\ |Y_n - a| < \varepsilon)$$

$$+ P(X_n + Y_n \le x,\ |Y_n - a| \ge \varepsilon)$$

$$\le P(X_n \le x - a + \varepsilon) + P(|Y_n - a| \ge \varepsilon). \quad (22.28)$$

Similarly,

$$P(X_n \le x - a - \varepsilon) \le P(X_n + Y_n \le x) + P(|Y_n - a| \ge \varepsilon), \quad (22.29)$$

and putting these inequalities together, we have

$$P(X_n \le x - a - \varepsilon) - P(|Y_n - a| \ge \varepsilon) \le P(X_n + Y_n \le x)$$
$$\le P(X_n \le x - a + \varepsilon) + P(|Y_n - a| \ge \varepsilon). \quad (22.30)$$

Let F_{X_n} and $F_{X_n+Y_n}$ denote the c.d.f.s of X_n and $X_n + Y_n$ respectively, and let F_X be the c.d.f. of X, such that $F_X = \lim_{n\to\infty} F_{X_n}(x)$ at all continuity points of F_X. Since $\lim_{n\to\infty} P(|Y_n - a| \ge \varepsilon) = 0$ for all $\varepsilon > 0$ by assumption, (22.30) implies

$$F_X(x - a - \varepsilon) \le \liminf_{n\to\infty} F_{X_n+Y_n}(x)$$
$$\le \limsup_{n\to\infty} F_{X_n+Y_n}(x) \le F_X(x - a + \varepsilon). \quad (22.31)$$

Taking ε arbitrarily close to zero shows that

$$\lim_{n\to\infty} F_{X_n+Y_n}(x) = F_X(x - a) = F_{X+a}(x) \quad (22.32)$$

whenever $x - a$ is a continuity point of F_X. This proves (i).

To prove (ii), suppose first that $a > 0$. By taking $\varepsilon > 0$ small enough we can ensure $a - \varepsilon > 0$, and applying the type of argument used in (i) with obvious variations, we obtain the inequalities

$$P(X_n(a + \varepsilon) \le x) - P(|Y_n - a| \ge \varepsilon) \le P(X_n Y_n \le x)$$
$$\le P(X_n(a - \varepsilon) \le x) + P(|Y_n - a| \ge \varepsilon). \quad (22.33)$$

Taking limits gives

$$F_X(x/(a + \varepsilon)) \le \liminf_{n\to\infty} F_{X_n Y_n}(x)$$
$$\le \limsup_{n\to\infty} F_{X_n Y_n}(x) \le F_X(x/(a - \varepsilon)), \quad (22.34)$$

and thus

$$\lim_{n\to\infty} F_{X_n Y_n}(x) = F_X(x/a) = F_{aX}(x). \quad (22.35)$$

If $a < 0$, replace Y_n by $-Y_n$ and a by $-a$, repeat the preceding argument, and then apply **22.12.** And if $a = 0$, (22.33) becomes

$$P(X_n \varepsilon \le x) - P(|Y_n| \ge \varepsilon) \le P(X_n Y_n \le x)$$

$$\leq P(-X_n\varepsilon \leq x) + P(|Y_n| \geq \varepsilon). \tag{22.36}$$

For $x > 0$, this yields in the limit $F_{X_nY_n}(x) = 1$, and for $x < 0$, $F_{X_nY_n}(x) = 0$, which defines the degenerate distribution with the mass concentrated at 0. In this case $X_nY_n \xrightarrow{pr} 0$ in view of **22.5**. (Alternatively, see **18.12**.)

To prove (iii) it suffices to note by **18.10**(ii) that plim $1/Y_n = 1/a$ if $a \neq 0$. Replacing Y_n by $1/Y_n$ in (ii) yields the result directly. ∎

22.4 Convergence of Moments and Characteristic Functions

Paralleling the sequence of distribution functions, there may be sequences of moments. If $X_n \xrightarrow{D} X$ where the c.d.f. of X is F, then $E(X) = \int x dF(x)$, where it exists, is sometimes called the *asymptotic expectation* of X_n. There is a temptation to write $E(X) = \lim_{n\to\infty} E(X_n)$, but there are cases where $E(X_n)$ does not exist for any finite n while $E(X)$ exists, and also cases where $E(X_n)$ exists for every n but $E(X)$ does not. This usage is therefore best avoided except in specific circumstances when the convergence is known to obtain.

Theorem **22.8** assures us that expectations of bounded random variables converge under weak convergence of the corresponding measures. The following theorems indicate how far this result can be extended to more general cases. Recall that $E|X|$ is defined for every X, although it may take the value $+\infty$.

22.15 Theorem If $X_n \xrightarrow{D} X$ then $E|X| \leq \liminf_{n\to\infty} E|X_n|$.

Proof The function $h_\alpha(x) = |x| 1_{\{|x|\leq\alpha\}}$ is real and bounded. If $P(|X| = \alpha) = 0$, it follows by **22.11** that $h_\alpha(X_n) \xrightarrow{D} h_\alpha(X)$, and from **22.8** (letting f be the identity function which is bounded in this case) that

$$E(h_\alpha(X)) = \lim_{n\to\infty} E(h_\alpha(X_n)) \leq \liminf_{n\to\infty} E|X_n|. \tag{22.37}$$

The result follows on letting α approach $+\infty$ through continuity points of the distribution. ∎

The following theorem gives a sufficient condition for $E(X)$ to exist, given that $E(X_n)$ exists for each n.

22.16 Theorem If $X_n \xrightarrow{D} X$ and $\{X_n\}$ is uniformly integrable, then $E|X| < \infty$ and $E(X_n) \to E(X)$.

Proof Let Y_n and Y be the Skorokhod variables of (22.12), so that $Y_n \xrightarrow{as} Y$. Since X_n and Y_n have the same distribution, uniform integrability of $\{X_n\}$ implies that of $\{Y_n\}$. Hence we can invoke **12.8** to show that $E(Y_n) \to E(Y)$, Y being integrable. Reversing the argument then gives $E|X| < \infty$ and $E(X_n) \to E(X)$ as required. ∎

Uniform integrability is a sufficient condition, and although where it fails the existence of $E(X)$ may not be ruled out, **12.7** showed that its interpretation is questionable in these circumstances.

A sequence of complex r.v.s which is always uniformly integrable is $\{e^{itX_n}\}$, for any sequence $\{X_n\}$, since $|e^{itX_n}| = 1$. Given the sequence of characteristic functions $\{\phi_{X_n}(t)\}$, we therefore know that if $F_n \Rightarrow F$, then

$$\phi_{X_n}(t) \to \phi_X(t) \tag{22.38}$$

(pointwise on $\mathbb{R}$), where the indicated limit should be the characteristic function associated with F. In view of the inversion theorem (**11.12**), we could then say that $X_n \xrightarrow{D} X$ only if (22.38) holds, where $\phi_X(t)$ is the ch.f. of X. However, it is the 'if' rather than the 'only if' that is the point of interest here. If a sequence of characteristic functions converges pointwise to a limit, under what circumstances can we be sure that the limit is a ch.f., in the sense that inverting yields a c.d.f.? A sufficient condition for this is provided by the so-called Lévy continuity theorem:

22.17 Lévy continuity theorem Suppose that $\{F_n\}$ is a sequence of c.d.f.s and $F_n \Rightarrow F$, where F is any non-negative, bounded, non-decreasing, right-continuous function. If

$$\phi_n(t) = \int_{-\infty}^{+\infty} e^{itx} dF_n \to \phi(t), \tag{22.39}$$

and $\phi(t)$ is continuous at the point $t = 0$, then F is a c.d.f. (i.e., $\int dF = 1$) and ϕ is its ch.f. □

The fact that the conditions imposed on the limit F in this theorem are not unreasonable will be established by the Helly selection theorem, to be discussed in the next section.

Proof Note that $\phi_n(0) = \int dF_n = 1$ for any n, by (22.39) and the fact that F_n is a c.d.f. For $\nu > 0$,

$$\frac{1}{\nu}\int_0^{\nu} \phi_n(t)dt = \int_{-\infty}^{+\infty} \left(\frac{1}{\nu}\int_0^{\nu} e^{itx}dt\right) dF_n = \int_{-\infty}^{+\infty} \left(\frac{e^{i\nu x} - 1}{i\nu x}\right) dF_n, \tag{22.40}$$

the change in order of integration being permitted by **9.32**. By **22.10**, which extends to complex-valued functions by linearity of the integral, we have, as $n \to \infty$,

$$\int_{-\infty}^{+\infty} \left(\frac{e^{i\nu x} - 1}{i\nu x}\right) dF_n \to \int_{-\infty}^{+\infty} \left(\frac{e^{i\nu x} - 1}{i\nu x}\right) dF = \frac{1}{\nu}\int_0^{\nu} \phi(t)dt, \tag{22.41}$$

where the equality is by (22.40) and the definition of ϕ. Since ϕ is continuous at $t = 0$, $\lim_{\nu\to\infty}\nu^{-1}\int_0^{\nu}\phi(t)dt = \phi(0)$ and since $\phi_n \to \phi$ we must have $\phi(0) = 1$. It follows from (22.41) that

$$1 = \int_{-\infty}^{+\infty} \lim_{\nu\to 0} \left(\frac{e^{i\nu x} - 1}{i\nu x}\right) dF = \int_{-\infty}^{+\infty} dF. \tag{22.42}$$

In view of the other conditions imposed, this means F is a c.d.f. It follows by **22.8** that $\phi(t) = E(e^{itX})$ where X is a random variable having c.d.f. F. This completes the proof. ■

The continuity theorem provides the basic justification for investigating limiting distributions by evaluating the limits of sequences of ch.f.s, and then using the inversion theorem of §11.5. The next two chapters are devoted to developing these methods. Here we will take the opportunity to mention one useful application, a result similar to **22.4** which may also be proved as a corollary.

22.18 Theorem If $|X_n - Z_n| \xrightarrow{pr} 0$ and $\{X_n\}$ converges in distribution, then $\{Z_n\}$ converges in distribution to the same limit.

Proof $|e^{itX_n} - e^{itZ_n}| \xrightarrow{pr} 0$ by **18.9**(ii). Since $|e^{itX}| = 1$ these functions are L_∞-bounded, and the sequence $\{|e^{itX_n} - e^{itZ_n}|\}$ is uniformly integrable. So by **18.14**, $|e^{itX_n} - e^{itZ_n}| \xrightarrow{L_1} 0$. However, the complex modulus inequality **(11.3)** gives

$$E|e^{itX_n} - e^{itZ_n}| \geq |E(e^{itX_n}) - E(e^{itZ_n})|, \tag{22.43}$$

so that a further consequence is $|\phi_{X_n}(t) - \phi_{Z_n}(t)| \to 0$ as $n \to \infty$, pointwise on $\mathbb{R}$. Given the assumption of weak convergence, the conclusion now follows from the inversion theorem. ■

To get the alternative proof of **22.4**, set $Z_n = X$ for each n.

22.5 Criteria for Weak Convergence

Not every sequence of c.d.f.s has a c.d.f. as its limit. Counter-examples are easy to construct.

22.19 Example Consider the uniform distribution on the interval $[-n,n]$, such that $F_n(a) = \frac{1}{2}(1 + a/n)$, $-n \leq a \leq n$. Then $F_n(a) \to \frac{1}{2}$ for all $a \in \mathbb{R}$. □

22.20 Example Consider the degenerate r.v., $X_n = n$ w.p.1. The c.d.f. is a step function with jump at n. $F_n(a) \to 0$, all $a \in \mathbb{R}$. □

Although F_n is a c.d.f. for all n, in neither of these cases is the limit F a c.d.f., in the sense that $F(a) \to 1$ (0) as $a \to \infty$ ($-\infty$). Nor does intuition suggest to us that the limiting distributions are well defined. The difficulty in the first example is that the probability mass is getting smeared out evenly over an infinite support, so that the density is tending everywhere to zero. It does not make sense to define a random variable which can take any value in $\mathbb{R}$ with equal probability, any more than it does to make a random variable infinite almost surely, which is the limiting case of the second example.

In view of these pathological cases, it is important to establish the conditions under which a sequence of measures can be expected to converge weakly. The condition that ensures the limit is well-defined is called *uniform tightness*. A sequence $\{\mu_n\}$ of p.m.s on $\mathbb{R}$ is uniformly tight if there exists a finite interval $(a,b]$ such that, for any $\varepsilon > 0$, $\sup_n \mu_n((a,b]) > 1 - \varepsilon$. Equivalently, if $\{F_n\}$ is the sequence of c.d.f.s corresponding to $\{\mu_n\}$, uniform tightness is the condition that for $\varepsilon > 0$ $\exists$ a,b with $b - a < \infty$ and

$$\sup_n \{F_n(b) - F_n(a)\} > 1 - \varepsilon. \tag{22.44}$$

It is easy to see that examples **22.19** and **22.20** both fail to satisfy the uniform tightness condition. However, we can show that, provided a sequence of p.m.s $\{\mu_n\}$ is uniformly tight, it does converge to a limit μ which is a p.m. This terminology derives from the designation *tight* for a measure with the property that for every $\varepsilon > 0$ there is a compact set K_ε such that $\mu(K_\varepsilon^c) \le \varepsilon$. Every p.m. on $(\mathbb{R},\mathcal{B})$ is tight, although this is not necessarily the case in more general probability spaces. See §26.5 for details on this.

An essential ingredient in this argument is a classic result in analysis, Helly's selection theorem.

22.21 Helly's selection theorem If $\{F_n\}$ is any sequence of c.d.f.s, there exists a subsequence $\{n_k, k = 1,2,...\}$ such that $F_{n_k} \Rightarrow F$, where F is bounded, non-decreasing and right-continuous, and $0 \le F \le 1$.

Proof Consider the bounded array $\{\{F_n(x_i), n \in \mathbb{N}\}, i \in \mathbb{N}\}$, where $\{x_i, i \in \mathbb{N}\}$ is an enumeration of the rationals. By **2.36**, this array converges on a subsequence, so that $\lim_{k\to\infty}F_{n_k}(x_i) = F^*(x_i)$ for every i. Note that $F^*(x_{i_1}) \le F^*(x_{i_2})$ whenever $x_{i_1} < x_{i_2}$, since this property is satisfied by F_n for every n. Hence consider the non-decreasing function on $\mathbb{R}$,

$$F(x) = \inf_{x_i > x} F^*(x_i). \tag{22.45}$$

Clearly $0 \le F^*(x_i) \le 1$ for all i, since the $F_{n_k}(x_i)$ have this property for every k. By definition of F, for $x \in \mathbb{R}\ \exists\ x_i > x$ such that $F(x) \le F^*(x_i) < F(x) + \varepsilon$ for any $\varepsilon > 0$, showing that F is right-continuous since $F^*(x_i) = F(x_i)$. Further, for continuity points x of F, there exist $x_{i_1} < x$ and $x_{i_2} > x$ such that

$$F(x) - \varepsilon < F^*(x_{i_1}) \le F^*(x_{i_2}) < F(x) + \varepsilon. \tag{22.46}$$

The following inequalities hold in respect of these points for every k:

$$\begin{aligned} F^*(x_{i_1}) &= \lim_{k\to\infty} F_{n_k}(x_{i_1}) \le \liminf_{k\to\infty} F_{n_k}(x) \\ &\le \limsup_{k\to\infty} F_{n_k}(x) \le \lim_{k\to\infty} F_{n_k}(x_{i_2}) = F^*(x_{i_2}). \end{aligned} \tag{22.47}$$

Combining (22.46) with (22.47),

$$F(x) - \varepsilon < \liminf_{k\to\infty} F_{n_k}(x) \le \limsup_{k\to\infty} F_{n_k}(x) < F(x) + \varepsilon. \tag{22.48}$$

Since ε is arbitrary, $\lim_{k\to\infty}F_{n_k}(x) = F(x)$ at all continuity points of F. ∎

The only problem here is that F need not be a c.d.f., as in **22.19** and **22.20**. We need to ensure that $F(x) \to 1$ (0) as $x \to \infty$ $(-\infty)$, and tightness is the required property.

22.22 Theorem Let $\{F_n\}$ be a sequence of c.d.f.s. If

(a) $F_{n_k} \Rightarrow F$ for every convergent subsequence $\{n_k\}$, and
(b) the sequence is uniformly tight,
then $F_n \Rightarrow F$, where F is a c.d.f. Condition (b) is also necessary. □

Helly's theorem tells us that $\{F_n\}$ has a cluster point F. Condition (a) requires that this F be the *unique* cluster point, regardless of the subsequence chosen, and the argument of **2.13** applied pointwise to $\{F_n\}$ implies that F is the actual limit of the sequence. Uniform tightness is necessary and sufficient for this limit F to be a c.d.f.

Proof of 22.22 Let x be a continuity point of F, and suppose $F_n(x) \not\to F(x)$. Then $|F_n(x) - F(x)| \geq \varepsilon > 0$ for an infinite subsequence of integers, say $\{n_k, k \in \mathbb{N}\}$. Define a sequence of c.d.f.s by $F'_k = F_{n_k}$, $k = 1,2,...$ According to Helly's theorem, this sequence contains a convergent subsequence, $\{k_i, i \in \mathbb{N}\}$, say, such that $F'_{k_i} \Rightarrow F'$. But by (a), $F' = F$, and we have a contradiction, given how the subsequence $\{k_i\}$ was constructed. Hence, $F_n \Rightarrow F$.

Since F_n is a c.d.f. for every n, $F_n(b) - F_n(a) > 1 - \varepsilon$ for some $b - a < \infty$, for any $\varepsilon > 0$. Since $F_n \to F$ at continuity points, increase b and reduce a as necessary to make them continuity points of F. Assuming uniform tightness, we have by (22.44) that $F(b) - F(a) > 1 - \varepsilon$, as required. It follows that $\lim_{x\to\infty}F(x) = 1$ and $\lim_{x\to-\infty}F(x) = 0$. Given the monotonicity and right continuity of F established by Helly's theorem, this means that F is a c.d.f.

On the other hand, if the sequence is not uniformly tight, $F(b) - F(a) \leq 1 - \varepsilon$ for some $\varepsilon > 0$, and every $b > a$. Letting $b \to +\infty$ and $a \to -\infty$, we have $F(+\infty) - F(-\infty) \leq 1 - \varepsilon < 1$. Hence, either $F(+\infty) < 1$ or $F(-\infty) > 0$ or both, and F is not a c.d.f. ■

The role of the continuity theorem (**22.17**) should now be apparent. Helly's theorem ensures that the limit F of a sequence of c.d.f.s has all the properties of a c.d.f. except possibly that of $\int dF = 1$. Uniform tightness ensures this property, and the continuity of the limiting ch.f. at the origin can now be interpreted as a sufficient condition for tightness of the sequence. It is of interest to note what happens in the case of our counter-examples. The ch.f. corresponding to example **22.19** is

$$\phi_n(\nu) = (2n)^{-1}\int_{-n}^{n}(\cos \nu x + i \sin \nu x)dx = \frac{\sin \nu n}{\nu n}. \tag{22.49}$$

We may show (use l'Hôpital's rule) that $\phi_n(0) = 1$ for every n, whereas $\phi_n(\nu) \to 0$ for all $\nu \neq 0$. In the case of **22.20** we get

$$\phi_n(\nu) = \cos \nu n + i \sin \nu n, \tag{22.50}$$

which fails to converge except at the point $\nu = 0$.

22.6 Convergence of Random Sums

Most of the important weak convergence results concern sequences of partial sums of a random array $\{X_{nt}, t = 1,...,n, n \in \mathbb{N}\}$. Let

$$S_n = \sum_{t=1}^{n} X_{nt}, \tag{22.51}$$

and consider the distributions of the sequence $\{S_n\}$ as $n \to \infty$. The array notation (double indexing) permits a normalization depending on n to be introduced. Central limit theorems, the cases in which typically $X_{nt} = n^{-1/2}X_t$, and S_n converges to the Gaussian distribution, are to be examined in detail in the following chapters, but these are not the only possibility.

22.23 Example The $B(n,\lambda/n)$ distribution is the distribution of the sum of n independent Bernoulli random variables X_{nt}, where $P(X_{nt} = 1) = \lambda/n$ and $P(X_{nt} = 0) = 1 - \lambda/n$. From **22.2** we know that in this case

$$S_n = \sum_{t=1}^{n} X_{nt} \xrightarrow{D} \text{Poisson with mean } \lambda. \ \square \tag{22.52}$$

From **11.1** we know that the distribution of a sum of independent r.v.s is given by the convolution of the distributions of the summands. The weak limits of independent sum distributions therefore have to be expressible as infinite convolutions. The class of distributions that have such a representation is necessarily fairly limited. A distribution F is called *infinitely divisible* if for every $n \in \mathbb{N}$ there exists a distribution F_n such that F has a representation as the n-fold convolution

$$F = F_n * F_n * \ldots * F_n. \tag{22.53}$$

In view of (11.33), infinite divisibility implies a corresponding multiplicative rule for the ch.f.s.

22.24 Example For the Poisson distribution, $\phi_X(t;\lambda) = \exp\{\lambda e^{it} - 1\}$, from (11.34), and

$$\phi_X(t;\lambda) = \left(\exp\{(\lambda/n)(e^{it} - 1)\}\right)^n = (\phi_X(t;\ \lambda/n))^n. \tag{22.54}$$

The sum of n independent Poisson variates having parameter λ/n is therefore a Poisson variate with parameter λ. □

In certain infinitely divisible distributions, F_n and F have a special relationship, expressed through their characteristic functions. A distribution with ch.f. ϕ_X is called *stable*, with index p, if for each n,

$$(\phi_X(t))^n = e^{itb(n)}\phi_X(n^{1/p}t),\ 0 < p \leq 2, \tag{22.55}$$

where $b(n)$ is some function of n. According to (11.30), the right-hand side of (22.55) is the ch.f. of the r.v. $b(n) + n^{1/p}X$; that is, the sum of n independent drawings from the distribution is a drawing from the same distribution apart from a change of scale and origin. If a stable distribution is also symmetric about zero, it can be shown that the ch.f. must belong to the family of real-valued functions having the form

$$\phi_X(t) = \exp\{-a|t|^p\},\ a \geq 0. \tag{22.56}$$

22.25 Example The Cauchy distribution is stable with $p = 1$ and $b(n) = 0$, having ch.f. $\phi_X(t;\ \nu,\delta) = \exp\{it\nu - \delta|t|\}$, from (11.38). If $X_t \sim C(\nu,\delta)$ for $t = 1,\dots,n$, then $\bar{X}_n \sim C(\nu,\delta)$. This result reflects the fact already noted (see **18.18**) that Cauchy variates fail to observe the law of large numbers. □

22.26 Example For Gaussian X, $\phi_X(t;\ \mu,\sigma^2) = \exp\{i\mu t - \frac{1}{2}\sigma^2 t^2\}$ by (11.37). This is stable with index $p = 2$ and $b_n = (n - n^{1/2})\mu$. With $\mu = 0$ we have symmetry about 0, and obtain the formula in (22.56) with $a = \frac{1}{2}\sigma^2$. Thus, if $X_t \sim N(0,\sigma^2)$ for $t = 1,\dots,n$, then $n^{-1/2}\sum_{t=1}^n X_t \sim N(0,\ \sigma^2)$. □

It turns out that a stable distribution with index $p < 2$ possesses absolute moments of order at most $r < p$. Thus, the Gaussian is the *only* stable law for which a variance exists.

This last fact is most important in motivating the central limit theorem. Each of the foregoing examples illustrates the possibility of a limit law for sums. A stable distribution naturally has the potential to act as an attractor for arbitrarily distributed sums. While stable convergence laws do operate in cases where the summands possess absolute moments only up to order $r < 2$, the key result, to be studied in detail in the following chapters, is that the Gaussian acts as the unique attractor for the distributions of scaled sums of arbitrary r.v.s having zero mean and finite variances.

23
The Classical Central Limit Theorem

23.1 The i.i.d. Case

The 'normal law of error' is justly the most famous result in statistics, and to the susceptible mind has an almost mystical fascination. If a sequence of random variables $\{X_t\}_1^\infty$ have means of zero, and the partial sums $\sum_{t=1}^n X_t$, $n = 1,2,3,...$ have variances s_n^2 tending to infinity with n although finite for each finite n, then, subject to rather mild additional conditions on the distributions and the sampling process,

$$S_n = \frac{1}{s_n}\sum_{t=1}^n X_t \xrightarrow{D} N(0,1). \tag{23.1}$$

This is the central limit theorem (CLT). Establishing sets of sufficient conditions is the main business of this chapter and the next, but before getting into the formal results it might be of interest to illustrate the operation of the CLT as an approximation theorem. Particularly if the distribution of the X_t is symmetric, the approach to the limit can be very rapid.

23.1 Example In **11.2** we derived the distribution of the sum of two independent $U[0,1]$ drawings. Similarly, the sum of three such drawings has density

$$f_{X+Y+Z}(w) = \int_0^1\int_0^1 1_{\{w-z-1,w-z\}}dydz, \tag{23.2}$$

which is plotted in Fig. 23.1. This function is actually piecewise quadratic (the three segments are on [0,1], [1,2] and [2,3] respectively), but lies remarkably close to the density of the Gaussian r.v. having the same mean and variance as $X+Y+Z$ (also plotted). The sum of 10 or 12 independent uniform r.v.s is almost indistinguishable from a Gaussian variate; indeed, the formula $S = \sum_{i=1}^{12}X_i - 6$, which has mean 0 and variance 1 when $X_i \sim U[0,1]$ and independent, provides a simple and perfectly adequate device for simulating a standard Gaussian variate in computer modelling exercises. □

23.2 Example For a contrast in the *manner* of convergence consider the $B(n,p)$ distribution, the sum of n Bernoulli(p) variates for fixed $p \in (0,1)$. The probabilities for $p = \frac{1}{2}$ and $n = 20$ are plotted in Fig. 23.2, together with the Gaussian density with matching mean and variance. These distributions are of course discrete for every finite n, and continuous only in the limit. The correspondence of the ordinates is remarkably close, although remember that for $p \neq \frac{1}{2}$ the binomial distribution is not symmetric and the convergence is correspondingly slower. This example should be compared with **22.2**, the non-Gaussian limit in the latter case being obtained by having p decline as a function of n. □

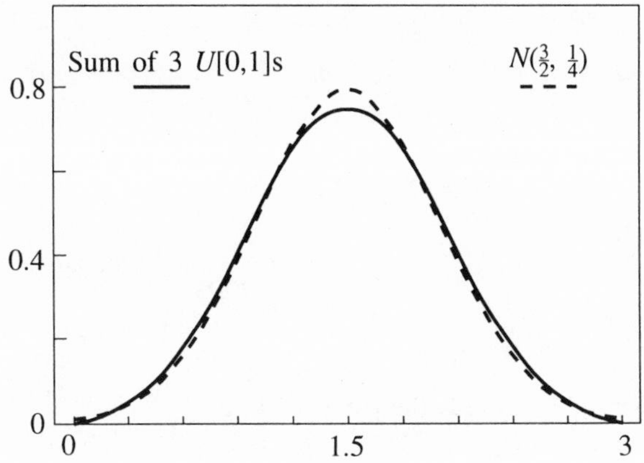

Fig. 23.1

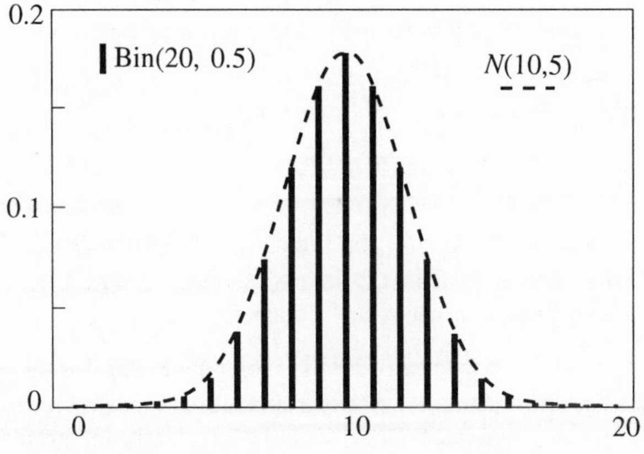

Fig. 23.2

Proofs of the CLT, like proofs of stochastic convergence, depend on establishing properties for certain *non*stochastic sequences. Previously we considered sample points $|X_n(\omega) - X(\omega)|$ for $\omega \in C$ with $P(C) = 1$, probabilities $P(|X_n - X| > \varepsilon)$, and moments $E|X_n - X|^p$, as different sequences to be shown to converge to 0 to establish the convergence of X_n to X, respectively a.s., in pr., or in L_p. In the present case we consider the expectations of certain functions of the S_n; the key result is Theorem **22.8**. The practical trick is to find functions that will fingerprint the limiting distribution conclusively. The characteristic function is by common consent the convenient choice, since we can exploit the multiplicative property for independent sums. This is not the only possible method though, and the reader can find an alternative approach in Pollard (1984: III.4), for example.

The simplest case is where the sequence $\{X_t\}$ is both stationary and independently drawn.

23.3 Lindeberg-Lévy theorem If $\{X_t\}_1^\infty$ is an i.i.d. sequence having zero mean and variance σ^2,

$$S_n = n^{-1/2}\sum_{t=1}^{n} X_t/\sigma \xrightarrow{D} N(0,1). \ \square \tag{23.3}$$

Proof The ch.f.s $\phi_X(\lambda)$ of X_t are identical for all t,[24] so from (11.30) and (11.33),

$$\phi_{S_n}(\lambda) = (\phi_X(\lambda\sigma^{-1}n^{-1/2}))^n. \tag{23.4}$$

Applying **11.6** with $k = 2$ yields the expansion

$$|\phi_X(\lambda\sigma^{-1}n^{-1/2}) - 1 - \lambda^2/2n| \le E\min\left\{\frac{(\lambda X_t)^2}{\sigma^2 n}, \frac{|\lambda X_t|^3}{6\sigma^3 n^{3/2}}\right\}, \tag{23.5}$$

which makes it possible to write, for fixed λ,

$$\phi_X(\lambda\sigma^{-1}n^{-1/2}) = 1 - \lambda^2/2n + O(n^{-3/2}). \tag{23.6}$$

Applying the binomial expansion, $(1 + a/n)^n = \sum_{j=0}^{n}\binom{n}{j}(a/n)^j \to \sum_{j=0}^{\infty}a^j/j! = e^a$ as $n \to \infty$, and setting $a = -\frac{1}{2}\lambda^2 + O(n^{-1/2})$, we find

$$\lim_{n\to\infty} \phi_{S_n}(\lambda) = e^{-\lambda^2/2}. \tag{23.7}$$

Comparing this formula with (11.36), the limiting ch.f. is revealed as that of the $N(0,1)$ variable. We then appeal to the inversion theorem (**11.12**) to establish that the limiting distribution is necessarily Gaussian. ■

Be careful to note how the existence of $E|X|^3$ is not necessary for the expansion in (23.6) to hold. The 'min' function whose expectation appears on the majorant side of (23.5) is unquestionably of $O(n^{-3/2})$, but also clearly integrable for each n on the assumption of finite variance.

The Lindeberg-Lévy theorem imposes strong assumptions, but offers the benefit of a simple and transparent proof. All the key features of the central limit property are discernible. In (23.6), the expansion of the ch.f. of $n^{-1/2}X_t$ consists either of terms common to every centred distribution with finite variance, or of terms that can be neglected asymptotically, a fact that ensures that the limiting sum distribution is invariant to the component distributions. The imaginary part of $\phi_X(\lambda\sigma^{-1}n^{-1/2})$ is of smaller order than the real part, which would appear to require a symmetric limit by the remarks following (11.31). The coincidence of these facts with the fact that the centred Gaussian is the only stable symmetric distribution having a second moment appears to rule out any alternative to the central limit property under the specified conditions, that is, zero mean and finite variance. The earlier remark that symmetry of the distribution of $n^{-1/2}X_t$ improves the rate of convergence to the limit can be also appreciated here. If we can assume $E(X_t^3) = 0$, the expansion in (23.5) can be taken to third order, and the remainder in (23.6) is of $O(n^{-2})$.

On the other hand, if the variance does not exist the expansion of (23.6) fails. Indeed, in the specific case we know of, in which the X_t are centred Cauchy, $n^{1/2}\bar{X}_n = O(n^{1/2})$; the sequence of distributions of $\{n^{1/2}\bar{X}_n\}$ is not tight, and there is no weak convergence. The limit law for the sum would itself be Cauchy under the appropriate scaling of n^{-1}.

The distinction between convergence in distribution and convergence in probability, and in particular the fact that the former does not imply the latter, can be demonstrated here by means of a counter-example. Consider the sequence $\{X_t\}_1^\infty$ defined in the statement of the Lindeberg-Lévy theorem, and the corresponding S_n in (23.3).

23.4 Theorem S_n does not converge in probability.

Proof If it was true that $\text{plim}_{n\to\infty}S_n = Z$, it would also be the case that $\text{plim}_{n\to\infty}S_{2n} = Z$, implying

$$\text{plim}_{n\to\infty} (S_{2n} - S_n) = 0. \tag{23.8}$$

We will show that (23.8) is false. We have

$$S_{2n} = (2n)^{-1/2}\left(\sum_{t=1}^{n} X_t/\sigma + \sum_{t=n+1}^{2n} X_t/\sigma\right) = (S_n + S_n')/\sqrt{2}, \tag{23.9}$$

where $S_n' = n^{-1/2}\sum_{t=n+1}^{2n}X_t/\sigma$, hence

$$S_{2n} - S_n = S_n(1/\sqrt{2} - 1) + S_n'/\sqrt{2}. \tag{23.10}$$

According to the Lindeberg-Lévy theorem, $\phi_{S_n}(\lambda) \to \exp\{-\frac{1}{2}\lambda^2\sigma^2\}$ and $\phi_{S_n'}(\lambda) \to \exp\{-\frac{1}{2}\lambda^2\sigma^2\}$. Since no X_t is contained in both sums, S_n and S_n' are independent, each with mean zero and variance σ^2. Noting $[1/\sqrt{2} - 1)]^2 + (1/\sqrt{2})^2 = 2 - \sqrt{2}$ and applying the properties of ch.f.s,

$$\phi_{S_{2n}-S_n}(\lambda) \to \exp\{-\tfrac{1}{2}\lambda^2(2 - \sqrt{2})\sigma^2\}. \tag{23.11}$$

In other words,

$$S_{2n} - S_n \xrightarrow{D} N(0, \sigma^2(2 - \sqrt{2})), \tag{23.12}$$

which is the required contradiction of (23.8). ■

Compare the sequence $\{S_n(\omega)\}_1^\infty$ with, say, $\{X(\omega) + Y(\omega)/n\}_1^\infty$, $\omega \in \Omega$, where X and Y are random variables. For given ω, the latter sequence converges to a fixed limit, $X(\omega)$. On the other hand, each new contribution to S_n has *equal* weight with the others, ensured by re-scaling the sum as the sample size increases. For given ω, $S_n(\omega) = n^{-1/2}\sum_{t=1}^{n}X_t(\omega)$ is *not* a convergent sequence, for as **23.4** shows $S_{2n}(\omega)$ is not necessarily close to $S_n(\omega)$ no matter how large n becomes. Weak convergence of the distribution functions does not imply convergence of the random sequence.

Characteristic function-based arguments can also be used to show convergence in distribution to a degenerate limit. The following is a well-known proof of the weak law of large numbers for i.i.d. sequences, which circumvents the need to show L_1 convergence.

23.5 Khinchine's theorem If $\{X_t\}_1^\infty$ is an identically and independently distributed sequence with finite mean μ, then $\bar{X}_n = n^{-1}\sum_{t=1}^n X_t \xrightarrow{pr} \mu$.

Proof The characteristic function of $\bar{X}_n$ has the form

$$\phi_{\bar{X}_n}(\lambda) = (\phi_X(\lambda/n))^n, \tag{23.13}$$

where, by application of the argument used for **23.3**, $\phi_X(\lambda/n) = 1 + i\lambda\mu/n + O(\lambda^2/n^2)$. Letting $n \to \infty$ we find, by analogy with (23.7),

$$\lim_{n\to\infty} \phi_{\bar{X}_n}(\lambda) = e^{i\lambda\mu}. \tag{23.14}$$

But $E(e^{i\lambda x}) = e^{i\lambda\mu}$ only for the case where $X = \mu$ with probability 1. The distribution is degenerate, and convergence in probability follows from **22.5**. ∎

23.2 Independent Heterogeneous Sequences

The Lindeberg-Lévy theorem imposes conditions which are too strong for the result to have wide practical applications in econometrics. In the remainder of this chapter we retain the assumption of independence (to be relaxed in Chapter 24), but allow the summands to have different distributions.

In this theory it is convenient to work with normalized variables, such that the partial sums always have unit variance. This entails a double indexing scheme. Define the triangular array

$$\{X_{nt},\ t = 1,\ldots,n,\ n \in \mathbb{N}\},$$

the elements having zero mean and variances σ_{nt}^2, such that if

$$S_n = \sum_{t=1}^n X_{nt}, \tag{23.15}$$

then (under independence)

$$E(S_n^2) = \sum_{t=1}^n \sigma_{nt}^2 = 1. \tag{23.16}$$

Typically we would have $X_{nt} = (Y_t - \mu_t)/s_n$ where $\{Y_t\}$ is the 'raw' sequence under study, with means $\{\mu_t\}$, and $s_n^2 = \sum_{t=1}^n E(Y_t - \mu_t)^2$. In this case $\sigma_{nt}^2 = E(Y_t - \mu_t)^2/s_n^2$, so that these variances sum to unity by construction. It is also possible to have $X_{nt} = (Y_{nt} - \mu_{nt})/s_n$, the double indexing of the mean arising in situations where the sequence depends on a parameter whose value in turn depends on n. This case arises, for example, in the study of the limiting distributions of test statistics under a sequence of 'local' deviations from the null hypothesis, the device known as Pitman drift.

The existence of each variance σ_{nt}^2 is going to be a necessary baseline condition in all the theorems, just as the existence of the common variance σ^2 was required in the Lindeberg-Lévy theorem. However, with heterogeneity, not even uniformly bounded variances are sufficient to get a central limit result. If the Y_t are identically distributed, we do not have to worry about a small (i.e. finite) number of members of the sequence exhibiting such extreme behaviour as to influence the distribution of the sum as a whole, even in the limit. But in a heterogeneous sequence this is possible, and could interfere with convergence to the normal, which usually depends on the contribution of each individual member of the sequence being negligible.

The standard result for independent, non-identically distributed sequences is the Lindeberg-Feller theorem, which establishes that a certain condition on the distributions of the summands is sufficient, and in some circumstances also necessary. Lindeberg is credited with the sufficiency part, and Feller the necessity; we look at the latter in the next section.

23.6 Lindeberg theorem Let the array $\{X_{nt}\}$ be independent with zero mean and variance sequence $\{\sigma_{nt}^2\}$ satisfying (23.16). Then, $S_n \xrightarrow{D} N(0,1)$ if

$$\lim_{n\to\infty} \sum_{t=1}^{n} \int_{\{|X_{nt}|>\varepsilon\}} X_{nt}^2 dP = 0, \text{ for all } \varepsilon > 0. \quad \square \tag{23.17}$$

Equation (23.17) is known as the *Lindeberg condition.*

The proof of the Lindeberg theorem requires a couple of purely mechanical lemmas.

23.7 Lemma If $x_1,\dots,x_n$ and $y_1,\dots,y_n$ are collections of complex numbers with $|x_t| \le 1$ and $|y_t| \le 1$ for $t = 1,\dots,n$, then

$$\left| \prod_{t=1}^{n} x_t - \prod_{t=1}^{n} y_t \right| \le \sum_{t=1}^{n} |x_t - y_t|. \tag{23.18}$$

Proof For $n = 2$,

$$\begin{aligned} |x_1x_2 - y_1y_2| &= |(x_1-y_1)x_2 + (x_2-y_2)y_1| \\ &\le |x_1-y_1||x_2| + |x_2-y_2||y_1| \\ &\le |x_1-y_1| + |x_2-y_2|. \end{aligned} \tag{23.19}$$

The general case follows easily by induction. ∎

23.8 Lemma If z is a complex number and $|z| \le \frac{1}{2}$, then $|e^z - 1 - z| \le |z|^2$.

Proof Using the triangle inequality,

$$|e^z - 1 - z| = \left| \sum_{j=2}^{\infty} \frac{z^j}{j!} \right| = \left| z^2 \sum_{j=0}^{\infty} \frac{z^j}{(j+2)!} \right| \le |z|^2 \sum_{j=0}^{\infty} \frac{|z|^j}{(j+2)!}. \tag{23.20}$$

Since $\sum_{j=0}^{\infty} 2^{-j} = 2$, the infinite series on the right-hand side cannot exceed 1. ■

Proof of 23.6 We have to show that $\phi_{S_n}(\lambda) \to e^{-\lambda^2/2}$ as $n \to \infty$. The difference is bounded by

$$\left| \phi_{S_n}(\lambda) - e^{-\lambda^2/2} \right| = \left| \prod_{t=1}^{n} \phi_{X_{nt}}(\lambda) - \prod_{t=1}^{n} e^{-\lambda^2\sigma_{nt}^2/2} \right|$$

$$\leq \left| \prod_{t=1}^{n} \phi_{X_{nt}}(\lambda) - \prod_{t=1}^{n} (1 - \tfrac{1}{2}\lambda^2\sigma_{nt}^2) \right|$$

$$+ \left| \prod_{t=1}^{n} e^{-\lambda^2\sigma_{nt}^2/2} - \prod_{t=1}^{n} (1 - \tfrac{1}{2}\lambda^2\sigma_{nt}^2) \right|, \tag{23.21}$$

where the equality is by definition, using the fact that $\sum_{t=1}^{n}\sigma_{nt}^2 = 1$, and the inequality is the triangle inequality. The proof will be complete if we can show that each of the right-hand side terms converges to zero.

The integrals in (23.17) may be expressed in the form $E(1_{\{|X_{nt}|>\varepsilon\}}X_{nt}^2)$, and

$$\begin{aligned} \sigma_{nt}^2 &= E(1_{\{|X_{nt}|\leq\varepsilon\}}X_{nt}^2) + E(1_{\{|X_{nt}|>\varepsilon\}}X_{nt}^2) \\ &\leq \varepsilon^2 + E(1_{\{|X_{nt}|>\varepsilon\}}X_{nt}^2) \\ &\to \varepsilon^2 \text{ as } n \to \infty, \text{ all } 1 \leq t \leq n, \end{aligned} \tag{23.22}$$

since the Lindeberg condition implies that the second term on the right-hand side of the inequality (which is positive) goes to zero; since ε can be chosen arbitrarily small, this shows that

$$\max_{1\leq t\leq n} \sigma_{nt}^2 \to 0. \tag{23.23}$$

In the first of the two terms on the majorant side of (23.21), the ch.f.s are all less than 1 in modulus, and by taking n large enough we can make $|1 - \frac{1}{2}\lambda^2\sigma_{nt}^2| \leq 1$ for any fixed value of λ. Hence by **23.7**,

$$\left| \prod_{t=1}^{n} \phi_{X_{nt}}(\lambda) - \prod_{t=1}^{n} (1 - \tfrac{1}{2}\lambda^2\sigma_{nt}^2) \right| \leq \sum_{t=1}^{n} \left| \phi_{X_{nt}}(\lambda) - (1 - \tfrac{1}{2}\lambda^2\sigma_{nt}^2) \right|. \tag{23.24}$$

To break down the terms on the majorant side of (23.24), note that **11.6** for the case $k = 2$, combined with (11.29), yields

$$\begin{aligned} \left| \phi_{X_{nt}}(\lambda) - (1 - \tfrac{1}{2}\lambda^2\sigma_{nt}^2) \right| &\leq E(\min\{(\lambda X_{nt})^2, \tfrac{1}{6}|\lambda X_{nt}|^3\}) \\ &\leq \lambda^2 E(1_{\{|X_{nt}|>\varepsilon\}}X_{nt}^2) + \tfrac{1}{6}|\lambda|^3\varepsilon\sigma_{nt}^2. \end{aligned} \tag{23.25}$$

Hence, recalling $\sum_{t=1}^{n}\sigma_{nt}^2 = 1$,

$$\sum_{t=1}^{n} \left| \phi_{X_{nt}}(\lambda) - (1 - \tfrac{1}{2}\lambda^2\sigma_{nt}^2) \right| \leq \lambda^2 \sum_{t=1}^{n} E(1_{\{|X_{nt}|>\varepsilon\}}X_{nt}^2) + \tfrac{1}{6}|\lambda|^3\varepsilon$$

$$\to \tfrac{1}{6}|\lambda|^3\varepsilon \text{ as } n \to \infty, \tag{23.26}$$

since the first majorant-side term vanishes by the Lindeberg condition. Since ε is arbitrary, this limit can be made as small as desired.

Similarly, for the second term of (23.21), take n large enough so that

$$\left|\prod_{t=1}^{n} e^{-\lambda^2\sigma_{nt}^2/2} - \prod_{t=1}^{n}(1 - \tfrac{1}{2}\lambda^2\sigma_{nt}^2)\right| \le \sum_{t=1}^{n}\left|e^{-\lambda^2\sigma_{nt}^2/2} - 1 - \tfrac{1}{2}\lambda^2\sigma_{nt}^2\right|. \tag{23.27}$$

Setting $z = -\frac{1}{2}\lambda^2\sigma_{nt}^2$ (a real number, actually) in **23.8** and applying the result to the majorant side of (23.27) gives

$$\left|\prod_{t=1}^{n} e^{-\lambda^2\sigma_{nt}^2/2} - \prod_{t=1}^{n}(1 - \tfrac{1}{2}\lambda^2\sigma_{nt}^2)\right| \le \tfrac{1}{4}\lambda^4\sum_{t=1}^{n}\sigma_{nt}^4. \tag{23.28}$$

But,

$$\sum_{t=1}^{n}\sigma_{nt}^4 \le (\max \sigma_{nt}^2)\sum_{t=1}^{n}\sigma_{nt}^2 = \max \sigma_{nt}^2 \to 0 \text{ as } n \to \infty, \tag{23.29}$$

by (23.23). The proof is therefore complete. ■

The Lindeberg condition is subtle, and its implications for the behaviour of random sequences call for careful interpretation. This will be easier if we look at the case $X_{nt} = X_t/s_n$, where X_t has mean 0 and variance σ_t^2 and $s_n^2 = \sum_{t=1}^n \sigma_t^2$. Then the Lindeberg condition becomes

$$\lim_{n\to\infty} \frac{1}{s_n^2}\sum_{t=1}^{n}\int_{\{|X_t|>s_n\varepsilon\}} X_t^2 dP = 0, \text{ for all } \varepsilon > 0. \tag{23.30}$$

One point easily verified is that, when the summands are identically distributed, $s_n = \sqrt{n}\sigma$, and (23.30) reduces to $\lim_{n\to\infty} s_n^{-2}E(X_1^2 1_{\{|X_1|>\sigma\sqrt{n}\varepsilon\}}) = 0$. The Lindeberg condition then holds if and only if X_1 has finite variance, so that the Lindeberg theorem contains the Lindeberg-Lévy as a special case.

The problematical cases the Lindeberg condition is designed to exclude are those where the behaviour of a finite subset of sequence elements dominates all the others, even in the limit. This can occur either by the sequence becoming excessively disorderly in the limit, or (the other side of the same coin, really) by its being not disorderly enough, beyond a certain point.

Thus, the condition clearly fails if the variance sequence $\{\sigma_t^2\}$ is tending to zero in such a way that $s_n^2 = \sum_{t=1}^n \sigma_t^2$ is bounded in n. On the other hand, if $s_n^2 \to \infty$, then $s_n\varepsilon \to \infty$ for any fixed positive ε, and the Lindeberg condition resembles a condition of 'average' uniform integrability of $\{X_t^2\}$. The sum of the terms $E(1_{\{|X_t|>s_n\varepsilon\}}X_t^2)$ must grow less fast than s_n^2, no matter how close ε is to zero. The following is a counter-example (compare **12.7**).

23.9 Example Let $X_t = Y_t - E(Y_t)$ where $Y_t = 0$ with probability $1 - t^{-2}$, and t with probability t^{-2}. Thus $E(Y_t) = t^{-1}$ and X_t is converging to a degenerate r.v., equal to 0 with probability 1, although $\mathrm{Var}(Y_t) = 1 - t^{-2}$ for every t. The Lindeberg condition fails here. $s_n^2 = n - \sum_{t=1}^n t^{-2}$, and for $0 < \varepsilon \le 1$ we certainly have $t > s_n\varepsilon$ whenever $t > n^{1/2}$. Therefore,

$$\frac{1}{s_n^2}\sum_{t=1}^n \int_{\{|X_t|>s_n\varepsilon\}} X_t^2 dP \ge \sum_{t=[\sqrt{n}]+1}^n \frac{(t-t^{-1})^2 t^{-2}}{n - \sum_{t=1}^n t^{-2}} \to 1 \tag{23.31}$$

as $n \to \infty$. And indeed, we can show rather easily that the CLT fails here. For any $n_0 \ge 1$, if we put $B_0 = \sum_{t=1}^{n_0} t$, then

$$\sup_n P\left(\left|\sum_{t=1}^n Y_t\right| > B_0\right) \le P\left(\bigcup_{t=n_0+1}^\infty \{|Y_t| > 0\}\right) \le \sum_{t=n_0+1}^\infty t^{-2}, \tag{23.32}$$

where the majorant side can be made as small as desired by choosing n_0 large enough. It follows that $\sum_{t=1}^n Y_t = O_p(1)$ and hence, since we also have $\sum_{t=1}^n E(Y_t) = O(\log n)$, that $\sum_{t=1}^n X_t/s_n \xrightarrow{pr} 0$, confirming that the CLT does not operate in this case. □

Uniform square-integrability is neither sufficient nor necessary for the Lindeberg condition, so parallels must be drawn with caution. However, the following theorem gives a simple sufficient condition.

23.10 Theorem If $\{X_t^2\}$ is uniformly integrable, and $s_n^2/n \ge B > 0$ for all n, then (23.30) holds.

Proof For any n and $\varepsilon > 0$, the latter assumption implies

$$\frac{1}{s_n^2}\sum_{t=1}^n E(1_{\{|X_t|>s_n\varepsilon\}}X_t^2) \le \frac{1}{B}\max_{1\le t\le n}\left\{E(1_{\{|X_t|>s_n\varepsilon\}}X_t^2)\right\}. \tag{23.33}$$

Hence

$$\begin{aligned}\lim_{n\to\infty}\frac{1}{s_n^2}\sum_{t=1}^n E(1_{\{|X_t|>s_n\varepsilon\}}X_t^2) &\le \frac{1}{B}\limsup_{n\to\infty}\max_{1\le t\le n}\left\{E(1_{\{|X_t|>s_n\varepsilon\}}X_t^2)\right\}\\ &\le \frac{1}{B}\sup_t \lim_{n\to\infty} E(1_{\{|X_t|>s_n\varepsilon\}}X_t^2)\\ &= 0,\end{aligned} \tag{23.34}$$

where the last equality follows by uniform integrability. ■

There is no assumption here that the sequence is independent. The conditions involve only the sequence of marginal distributions of the variables. None the less, the conditions are stronger than necessary, and a counter-example as well as further discussion of the conditions appears in §23.4.

The following is a popular version of the CLT for independent processes.

23.11 Liapunov's theorem A sufficient condition for (23.17) is

$$\lim_{n\to\infty}\sum_{t=1}^{n}E|X_{nt}|^{2+\delta} = 0, \text{ for some } \delta > 0. \tag{23.35}$$

Proof For $\delta > 0$ and $\varepsilon > 0$,

$$\begin{aligned} E|X_{nt}|^{2+\delta} &\geq E(1_{\{|X_{nt}|>\varepsilon\}}|X_{nt}|^{2+\delta}) \\ &\geq \varepsilon^{\delta}E(1_{\{|X_{nt}|>\varepsilon\}}X_{nt}^2). \end{aligned} \tag{23.36}$$

The theorem follows since, if $\varepsilon^{\delta}\lim_{n\to\infty}\sum_{t=1}^{n}E(1_{\{|X_{nt}|>\varepsilon\}}X_{nt}^2) = 0$ for fixed $\varepsilon > 0$, then the same holds with ε^{δ} replaced by 1. ■

Condition (23.35) is called the *Liapunov condition*, although this term is also used to refer to Liapunov's original result, in which the condition was cast in terms of integer moments, i.e.

$$\lim_{n\to\infty}\sum_{t=1}^{n}E|X_{nt}|^{3} = 0. \tag{23.37}$$

Although stronger than necessary, the Liapunov condition has the advantage of being more easily checkable, at least in principle, than the Lindeberg condition, as the following example illustrates.

23.12 Theorem Liapunov's condition holds if $s_n^2/n > 0$ uniformly in n and $E|X_t|^{2+\delta} < \infty$ uniformly in t, $\delta > 0$.

Proof Under the stated conditions,

$$\frac{1}{s_n^2}\sum_{t=1}^{n}E|X_t|^{2+\delta} \leq \frac{nB_2}{s_n^2} \leq \frac{B_1}{B_2} < \infty \tag{23.38}$$

for all n, where $B_1 \geq \sup_t E|X_t|^{2+\delta}$ and $B_2 \leq \inf_n s_n^2/n$. Then

$$\lim_{n\to\infty}\frac{1}{s_n^{2+\delta}}\sum_{t=1}^{n}E|X_t|^{2+\delta} = 0 \tag{23.39}$$

follows immediately. ■

Note that these conditions imply those of **23.10**, by **12.10**. It is sufficient to avoid the 'knife-edge' condition in which variances exist but no moments even fractionally higher, provided the sum of those variances is also $O(n)$.

23.3 Feller's Theorem and Asymptotic Negligibility

We said above that the Lindeberg condition is sufficient and sometimes also necessary. The following result specifies the side condition which implies necessity.

23.13 Feller's theorem Let $\{X_{nt}\}$ be an independent sequence with zero mean and variance sequence $\{\sigma_{nt}^2\}$. If $S_n \xrightarrow{D} N(0,1)$ and

$$\max_{1 \le t \le n} P(|X_{nt}| > \varepsilon) \to 0 \text{ as } n \to \infty, \text{ any } \varepsilon > 0, \tag{23.40}$$

the Lindeberg condition must hold. □

The proof of Feller's theorem is rather fiddly and mechanical, but necessary conditions are rare and difficult to obtain in this theory, and it is worth a little study for that reason alone. Several of the arguments are of the type used already in the sufficiency part.

Proof Since $\sigma_{nt}^2 \to 0$ for every t, the series expansion of the ch.f. suggests that $|\phi_{X_{nt}}(\lambda) - 1|$ converges to zero for each t. In fact, we can show that the sum of the squares of these terms converges, and this is the first step in the proof. Applying **11.6** for $k = 0$ and $k = 1$ respectively, we can assert that

$$|\phi_{X_{nt}}(\lambda) - 1| \le E(\min\{2, |\lambda X_{nt}|\}) \le 2P(|X_{nt}| > \varepsilon) + \varepsilon|\lambda| \tag{23.41}$$

and

$$|\phi_{X_{nt}}(\lambda) - 1| \le E(\min\{2|\lambda X_{nt}|, \lambda^2 X_{nt}^2\}) \le \lambda^2\sigma_{nt}^2. \tag{23.42}$$

In each case the second inequality is by (11.29), setting $\varepsilon = 0$ for (23.42). Squaring $|\phi_{X_{nt}}(\lambda) - 1|$, adding up over t, and substituting from the inequalities remembering $\sum_{t=1}^n \sigma_{nt}^2 = 1$, we obtain

$$\begin{aligned}\sum_{t=1}^n |\phi_{X_{nt}}(\lambda) - 1|^2 &\le \max_{1 \le t \le n} \left|\phi_{X_{nt}}(\lambda) - 1\right| \left(\sum_{t=1}^n |\phi_{X_{nt}}(\lambda) - 1|\right) \\ &\le \left(2\max_{1 \le t \le n} P(|X_{nt}| > \varepsilon) + \varepsilon|\lambda|\right)\lambda^2 \\ &\to |\lambda|^3\varepsilon \text{ as } n \to \infty, \end{aligned} \tag{23.43}$$

using (23.40) and (23.41).

This result is used to show that $\phi_{S_n}(\lambda) = \prod_{t=1}^n \phi_{X_{nt}}(\lambda)$ can be approximated by $\exp\{\sum_{t=1}^n \phi_{X_{nt}}(\lambda) - 1\}$. Note that if $z = re^{i\theta}$ and $r \le 1$, then $|e^{z-1}| = e^{r\cos\theta - 1} \le 1$ using (11.12). Lemma **23.7** can therefore be applied, and for some n large enough,

$$\begin{aligned}\left|\exp\left\{\sum_{t=1}^n (\phi_{X_{nt}}(\lambda) - 1)\right\} - \prod_{t=1}^n \phi_{X_{nt}}(\lambda)\right| &\le \sum_{t=1}^n |\exp\{\phi_{X_{nt}}(\lambda) - 1\} - \phi_{X_{nt}}(\lambda)| \\ &\le \sum_{t=1}^n |\phi_{X_{nt}}(\lambda) - 1|^2, \end{aligned} \tag{23.44}$$

where the second inequality is an application of **23.8** with $z = \phi_{X_{nt}}(\lambda) - 1$. The condition of the lemma can be satisfied for large enough n according to (23.42) and (23.23). By hypothesis $\phi_{S_n}(\lambda) \to e^{-\lambda^2/2}$, so by choosing ε arbitrarily small in (23.43), (23.44) implies that $\exp\{\sum_{t=1}^n (\phi_{X_{nt}}(\lambda) - 1)\} \to e^{-\lambda^2/2}$. The limit being a positive real number, this is equivalent to

$$\log \left| \exp\left\{ \sum_{t=1}^{n} (\phi_{X_{nt}}(\lambda) - 1) \right\} \right| = \sum_{t=1}^{n} E(\cos \lambda X_{nt} - 1) \to -\tfrac{1}{2}\lambda^2, \tag{23.45}$$

using (11.12) and (11.13) to get the equality.

Taking the real part of the expansion in (11.24) up to $k = 2$ gives $\cos x = 1 - \frac{1}{2}x^2 \cos \alpha x$ for $0 \leq \alpha \leq 1$, so that $\frac{1}{2}x^2 - 1 + \cos x \geq 0$ for any x. Fix $\varepsilon > 0$ and choose $\lambda > 2/\varepsilon$, so that the contents of the parentheses on the minorant side below is positive. Then we have

$$\begin{aligned} \left(\frac{\lambda^2}{2} - \frac{2}{\varepsilon^2}\right) \sum_{t=1}^{n} \int_{\{|X_{nt}|>\varepsilon\}} X_{nt}^2 \, dP &\leq \sum_{t=1}^{n} \int_{\{|X_{nt}|>\varepsilon\}} \left(\tfrac{1}{2}\lambda^2 X_{nt}^2 - 2\right) dP \\ &\leq \sum_{t=1}^{n} \int_{\{|X_{nt}|>\varepsilon\}} \left(\tfrac{1}{2}\lambda^2 X_{nt}^2 - 1 + \cos \lambda X_{nt}\right) dP \\ &\leq \sum_{t=1}^{n} E(\tfrac{1}{2}\lambda^2 X_{nt}^2 - 1 + \cos \lambda X_{nt}) \to 0, \end{aligned} \tag{23.46}$$

where the last inequality holds since the integrand is positive by construction for every X_{nt}, and the convergence is from (23.45) after substituting $\sum_t \sigma_{nt}^2 = 1$. Since ε is arbitrary, the Lindeberg condition must hold according to (23.46). ■

Condition (23.40) is a condition of 'asymptotic negligibility', under which no single summand may be so influential as to dominate the sum as a whole. The chief reason why we could have $\phi_{S_n}(\lambda) \to e^{-\lambda^2/2}$ without the Lindeberg condition, unless (23.40) holds, is that a finite number of summands dominating all the others could happen to be individually Gaussian. The following example illustrates.

23.14 Example Let $X_t \sim N(0,\sigma_t^2)$ where $\sigma_t^2 = 2^t$. Note that $s_n^2 = \sum_{t=1}^{n} 2^t = 2^n \sum_{t=0}^{n-1} 2^{-t} = 2^{n+1} - 2$, and $X_{nn} = X_n/s_n \sim N(0,\, 2^n/(2^{n+1} - 2))$. Clearly $S_n \sim N(0,1)$ for every n, by the linearity property of the Gaussian, but condition (23.40) fails. The Lindeberg condition also fails, since

$$\begin{aligned} \sum_{t=1}^{n} \int_{\{|X_{nt}|>\varepsilon\}} X_{nt}^2 \, dP &\geq \int_{\{|X_{nn}|>\varepsilon\}} X_{nn}^2 \, dP \\ &\to \tfrac{1}{2} E(1_{\{|Z|>\sqrt{2}\varepsilon\}} Z^2) > 0 \end{aligned} \tag{23.47}$$

where Z is a standard Gaussian variate. □

A condition related to (23.40) is

$$P\left(\max_{1 \leq t \leq n} |X_{nt}| > \varepsilon \right) \to 0 \text{ as } n \to \infty, \text{ any } \varepsilon > 0, \tag{23.48}$$

which says that the largest X_{nt} converges in probability to zero.

23.15 Theorem (23.48) implies (23.40).

Proof (23.48) is the same as $P(\max_{1\le t\le n}|X_{nt}| \le \varepsilon) \to 1$. But

$$P\left(\max_{1\le t\le n}|X_{nt}| \le \varepsilon\right) = P\left(\bigcap_{t=1}^{n}\{|X_{nt}| \le \varepsilon\}\right)$$

$$\le \min_{1\le t\le n} P(|X_{nt}| \le \varepsilon)$$

$$= 1 - \max_{1\le t\le n} P(|X_{nt}| > \varepsilon), \tag{23.49}$$

where the inequality is by monotonicity of P. If the first member of (23.49) converges to 1, so does the last. ∎

Also, interestingly enough, we have the following.

23.16 Theorem The Lindeberg condition implies (23.48).

Proof Another way to write (23.17) (interchanging the order of summation and integration) is

$$\sum_{t=1}^{n} 1_{\{|X_{nt}|>\varepsilon\}}X_{nt}^2 \xrightarrow{L_1} 0,\ \text{all } \varepsilon > 0. \tag{23.50}$$

According to **18.13** this implies $\sum_{t=1}^{n} 1_{\{|X_{nt}|>\varepsilon\}}X_{nt}^2 \xrightarrow{pr} 0$, or, equivalently,

$$P\left(\sum_{t=1}^{n} 1_{\{|X_{nt}|>\varepsilon\}}X_{nt}^2 > \varepsilon^2\right) \to 0 \text{ as } n \to \infty, \tag{23.51}$$

for any $\varepsilon > 0$. But notice that

$$\left\{\omega\colon \sum_{t=1}^{n} 1_{\{|X_{nt}|>\varepsilon\}}(\omega)X_{nt}^2(\omega) > \varepsilon^2\right\} = \left\{\omega\colon \max_{1\le t\le n}|X_{nt}(\omega)| > \varepsilon\right\}, \tag{23.52}$$

so (23.51) is equivalent to (23.48). ∎

Note that the last two results hold generally, and do not impose independence on the sequence.

The foregoing theorems establish a network of implications which it may be helpful to summarize symbolically. Let

L = the Lindeberg condition;
I = independence of the sequence;
AG = asymptotic Gaussianity ($\phi_{S_n}(\lambda) \to e^{-\lambda^2/2}$);
AN = asymptotic negligibility (condition (23.40)); and
PM = $\max|X_{nt}| \xrightarrow{pr} 0$ (condition (23.48)).

Then we have the implications

$$\text{L}+\text{I} \Rightarrow \text{AG}+\text{PM}+\text{I} \Rightarrow \text{AG}+\text{AN}+\text{I} \Rightarrow \text{L}+\text{I}, \tag{23.53}$$

where the first implication is the Lindeberg theorem and **23.16**, the second is by **23.15**, and the third is by the Feller theorem. Under independence, conditions L, AG+PM, and AG+AN are therefore equivalent to one another.

However, this is not quite the end of the story. The following example shows the possibility of a true CLT operating under asymptotic negligibility, *without* the Lindeberg condition.

23.17 Example Let $X_t = \frac{1}{2}$ and $-\frac{1}{2}$ with probabilities $\frac{1}{2}(1-t^{-2})$ each, and t and $-t$ with probabilities $\frac{1}{2}t^{-2}$ each, so that $E(X_t) = 0$ and $\text{Var}(X_t) = \frac{5}{4} - \frac{1}{4}t^2$, and $s_n^2 = \frac{5}{4}n + O(1)$. This case has similar characteristics to **23.9**. Since $|X_{nt}| = ts_n^{-1}$ with probability t^{-2} and $\frac{1}{2}s_n^{-1}$ otherwise, we have for any $\varepsilon > 0$ that, whenever n is large enough that $\varepsilon s_n > \frac{1}{2}$,

$$P(|X_{nt}| > \varepsilon) \leq n_\varepsilon^{-2} \tag{23.54}$$

where n_ε is the smallest integer such that $n_\varepsilon s_n^{-1} > \varepsilon$. Since $n_\varepsilon = O(n^{1/2})$, (23.40) holds in this case. However, the argument used in **23.9** shows that the Lindeberg condition is *not* satisfied. $E(1_{\{|X_{nt}|>\varepsilon\}}X_{nt}^2) \geq s_n^{-2}$ for $t \geq n_\varepsilon$, and hence

$$\sum_{t=1}^{n} \int_{\{|X_{nt}|>\varepsilon\}} X_{nt}^2 dP \geq (n - n_\varepsilon)s_n^{-2} \to \tfrac{4}{5} > 0. \tag{23.55}$$

However, consider the random sequence $\{W_t\}$, where $W_t = X_t$ when $|X_t| = \frac{1}{2}$ and $W_t = 0$ otherwise. As t increases, W_t tends to a centred Bernoulli variate with $p = \frac{1}{2}$, and defining $W_{nt} = W_t/s_n$, it is certainly the case that

$$\sum_{t=1}^{n} W_{nt} \xrightarrow{D} N(0, \tfrac{1}{5}). \tag{23.56}$$

However, $|X_t - W_t|$ is distributed like Y_t in **23.9**, and applying (23.32) shows that $\sum_{t=1}^{n}|X_t - W_t| = O_p(1)$, and hence $|\sum_{t=1}^{n}X_{nt} - \sum_{t=1}^{n}W_{nt}| \leq \sum_{t=1}^{n}|X_{nt} - W_{nt}| = O_p(n^{-1/2})$. It follows that $\sum_{t=1}^{n}X_{nt} \xrightarrow{D} N(0,\frac{1}{5})$, according to **22.18**. □

A CLT therefore does operate in this case. Feller's theorem is not contradicted because the limit is not the *standard* Gaussian. The clue to this apparent paradox is that the sequence is not uniformly square-integrable, having a component which contributes to the variance asymptotically in spite of vanishing in probability. In these circumstances S_n can have a 'variance' of 1 for every n despite the fact that its limiting distribution has a variance of $\frac{1}{5}$!

23.4 The Case of Trending Variances

The Lindeberg-Feller theorems do not impose uniform integrability or L_r-boundedness conditions, for any r. A trending variance sequence, with no uniform bound, is compatible with the Lindeberg condition. It would be sufficient if, for example, $\sigma_t^2 < \infty$ for each finite t and the unit-variance sequence $\{X_t/\sigma_t\}$ is uniformly square-integrable, provided that the variances do not grow so fast that the largest of them dominates the Cesàro sum of the sequence. The following is an extension of the sufficient condition of **23.10**.

23.18 Theorem Suppose $\{X_t^2/c_t^2\}$ is uniformly integrable, where $\{c_t\}$ is a sequence of positive constants. Then $\{X_t\}$ satisfies the Lindeberg condition, (23.30), if

$$\sup_n nM_n^2/s_n^2 = C < \infty, \tag{23.57}$$

where $M_n = \max_{1\le t\le n} c_t$. □

One way to construct the c_t might be as $\max\{1,\sigma_t\}$. The variances of the transformed sequence are then bounded by 1, but $\sigma_t^2 = 0$ is not ruled out for some t.

Proof of 23.18 The inequality of (23.33) extends to

$$\frac{1}{s_n^2}\sum_{t=1}^n E(1_{\{|X_t|>s_n\varepsilon\}}X_t^2) \le \frac{n}{s_n^2}\max_{1\le t\le n}\left\{c_t^2 E(1_{\{|X_t/c_t|>s_n\varepsilon/c_t\}}(X_t/c_t)^2)\right\}$$

$$\le C\max_{1\le t\le n}\left\{E(1_{\{|X_t/c_t|>s_n\varepsilon/c_t\}}(X_t/c_t)^2)\right\}. \tag{23.58}$$

The analogous modification of (23.34) then gives

$$\sup_t \lim_{n\to\infty} E(1_{\{|X_t/c_t|>s_n\varepsilon/c_t\}}(X_t/c_t)^2) = 0. \blacksquare \tag{23.59}$$

Notice how (23.57) restricts the growth of the variances whether this be positive or negative. Regardless of the choice of $\{c_t\}$, it requires that $s_n^2/n > 0$ uniformly in n. It permits the c_t to grow without limit so long as they are finite for all t, so the variances can do the same; but the rate of increase must not be so rapid as to have a single coordinate dominate the whole sequence. If we let $c_t = \max\{1,\sigma_t\}$ as above, (23.57) is satisfied (according to **2.27**) when $\sigma_t^2 \sim t^\alpha$ for any $\alpha \ge 0$, but not when $\sigma_t^2 \sim 2^t$.

In fact, the conditions of **23.18** are stronger than necessary in the case of *decreasing* variances. The variance sequence may actually decline to zero without violating the Lindeberg condition, but in this case it is not possible to state a general sufficient condition on the sequence. If $\sigma_t^2 \sim t^\alpha$ with $-1 < \alpha < 0$, we would have to replace (23.33) by the condition

$$\frac{1}{s_n^2}\sum_{t=1}^n E(1_{\{|X_t|>s_n\varepsilon\}}X_t^2) \le \frac{1}{Bn^\alpha}\max_{1\le t\le n}\left\{E(1_{\{|X_t|>s_n\varepsilon\}}X_t^2)\right\}, \tag{23.60}$$

where $B = \inf_n(s_n^2/n^{1+\alpha}) > 0$ by assumption (note, $s_n^2 \sim n^{1+\alpha}$ under independence). Convergence of the majorant side of (23.60) to zero as $n \to \infty$ is not ruled out, but depends on the distribution of the X_t.

The following example illustrates both possibilities.

23.19 Example Let $\{X_t\}$ be a zero-mean independent sequence with $X_t \sim U[-t^\alpha,t^\alpha]$ for some real α, such that $\sigma_t^2 = \frac{1}{3}t^{2\alpha}$, either growing with t ($\alpha > 0$) or declining with t ($\alpha < 0$). However, X_t is L_∞-bounded for finite t (see **8.13**). The integrals in (23.30) each take the form

$$\frac{1}{2t^\alpha}\int_{-t^\alpha}^{t^\alpha} 1_{\{|\xi|>s_n\varepsilon\}}\xi^2 d\xi, \tag{23.61}$$

where $s_n^2 = \frac{1}{3}\sum_{\tau=1}^n \tau^{2\alpha}$. Now, $\sum_{\tau=1}^n \tau^{2\alpha} = O(n^{2\alpha+1})$ for $\alpha > -\frac{1}{2}$ and $O(\log n)$ for $\alpha = -\frac{1}{2}$ (**2.27**). Condition (23.57) is satisfied when $\alpha \geq 0$. Note that (23.61) is zero if $(\frac{1}{3}\sum_{\tau=1}^n \tau^{2\alpha})^{1/2}\varepsilon > t^\alpha$; $(\sum_{\tau=1}^n \tau^{2\alpha})^{1/2}$ grows faster than n^α for all $\alpha \geq 0$, and hence (23.61) vanishes in the limit for every t in these cases, and the Lindeberg condition is satisfied. But if $X_t \sim U[-2^t, 2^t]$, 2^n grows at the same rate as $(\sum_{\tau=1}^n 2^{2\tau})^{1/2}$, the above argument does not apply, and the Lindeberg condition fails. Note how condition (23.57) is violated in this case.

However, the fact that condition (23.57) is not necessary is evident from the fact that the variance sum diverges at a positive rate when $X_t \sim U[-t^\alpha, t^\alpha]$ for any $\alpha \geq -\frac{1}{2}$ even though the variance sequence itself goes to zero. It can be verified that (23.61) vanishes in the limit, and accordingly the Lindeberg condition holds, for these cases too. On the other hand, if $\alpha < -\frac{1}{2}$, s_n^2 is bounded in the limit and (23.17) becomes

$$\frac{3}{B}\lim_{n\to\infty}\sum_{t=1}^{n}\frac{1}{2t^\alpha}\int_{-t^\alpha}^{t^\alpha} 1_{\{|\xi|>\sqrt{B/3}\varepsilon\}}\xi^2 d\xi, \tag{23.62}$$

where $B = \lim_{n\to\infty}\sum_{t=1}^n t^{2\alpha} < \infty$, and by choice of small enough ε, (23.62) can be made arbitrarily close to 1. This is the other extreme at which the Lindeberg condition fails. □

24
CLTs for Dependent Processes

24.1 A General Convergence Theorem

The results of this chapter are derived from the following fundamental theorem, due to McLeish (1974).

24.1 Theorem Let $\{Z_{ni}, i = 1,...,r_n, n \in \mathbb{N}\}$ denote a zero-mean stochastic array, where r_n is a positive, increasing integer-valued function of n, and let[25]

$$T_{r_n} = \prod_{i=1}^{r_n}(1 + i\lambda Z_{ni}), \quad \lambda > 0. \tag{24.1}$$

Then, $S_{r_n} = \sum_{i=1}^{r_n} Z_{ni} \xrightarrow{D} N(0, 1)$ if the following conditions hold:

(a) T_{r_n} is uniformly integrable,

(b) $E(T_{r_n}) \to 1$ as $n \to \infty$,

(c) $\sum_{i=1}^{r_n} Z_{ni}^2 \xrightarrow{pr} 1$ as $n \to \infty$,

(d) $\max_{1 \le i \le r_n}|Z_{ni}| \xrightarrow{pr} 0$ as $n \to \infty$. □

There are a number of features requiring explanation here, regarding both the theorem and the way it has been expressed. This is a generic result in which the elements of the array need not be data points in the conventional way, so that their number r_n does not always correspond with the number of sample observations, n. $r_n = n$ is a leading case, but see **24.6** for another possibility.

It is interesting to note that the Lindeberg condition is not imposed in **24.1**, nor is anything specific assumed about the dependence of the sequence. Condition **24.1**(d) is condition PM defined in (23.48), and by **23.16** it follows from the Lindeberg condition. We noted in (23.53) that under independence the condition is equivalent to the Lindeberg condition in cases where (as we shall prove here) the central limit theorem holds. But without independence, conditions **24.1**(a)–(d) need not imply the Lindeberg condition.

Proof of 24.1 Consider the series expansion of the logarithmic function, defined for $|x| < 1$,

$$\log(1 + x) = x - \tfrac{1}{2}x^2 + \tfrac{1}{3}x^3 - ...$$

Although a complex number does not possess a unique logarithm, the arithmetic identity obtained by taking the exponential of both sides of this equation is well-defined when x is complex. The formula yields

$$1 + i\lambda Z_{ni} = \exp\{i\lambda Z_{ni}\}\exp\{\tfrac{1}{2}\lambda^2 Z_{ni}^2 + r(i\lambda Z_{ni})\},\tag{24.2}$$

where the remainder satisfies $|r(x)| \le |x|^3$ for $|x| < 1$. Multiplying up the terms for $i = 1,\ldots,r_n$ yields

$$\exp\{i\lambda S_{r_n}\} = T_{r_n}U_{r_n},$$

where T_{r_n} is defined in (24.1) and

$$U_{r_n} = \exp\left\{-\tfrac{1}{2}\lambda^2\sum_{i=1}^{r_n} Z_{ni}^2 - \sum_{i=1}^{r_n} r(i\lambda Z_{ni})\right\}.\tag{24.3}$$

Taking expectations produces

$$\phi_{S_{r_n}}(\lambda) = E(T_{r_n}U_{r_n}) = e^{-\lambda^2/2}E(T_{r_n}) + E(T_{r_n}(U_{r_n} - e^{-\lambda^2/2})),\tag{24.4}$$

so given condition (b) of the theorem, $\phi_{S_{r_n}}(\lambda) \to e^{-\lambda^2/2}$ if

$$\lim_{n\to\infty} E\left|T_{r_n}(U_{r_n} - e^{-\lambda^2/2})\right| = 0.\tag{24.5}$$

The sequence

$$T_{r_n}(U_{r_n} - e^{-\lambda^2/2}) = \exp\{i\lambda S_{r_n}\} - T_{r_n}e^{-\lambda^2/2}\tag{24.6}$$

is uniformly integrable in view of condition (a), the first term on the right-hand side having unit modulus. So in view of **18.14**, it suffices to show that

$$\operatorname*{plim}_{n\to\infty} T_{r_n}(U_{r_n} - e^{-\lambda^2/2}) = 0.\tag{24.7}$$

Since T_{r_n} is clearly $O_p(1)$, the problem reduces, by **18.12**, to showing that $\text{plim}_{n\to\infty}U_{r_n} = e^{-\lambda^2/2}$, and for this in turn it suffices, by condition (c), if

$$\operatorname*{plim}_{n\to\infty}\sum_{i=1}^{r_n} r(i\lambda Z_{ni}) = 0.\tag{24.8}$$

To show that this convergence obtains, we have by the triangle inequality

$$\left|\sum_{i=1}^{r_n} r(i\lambda Z_{ni})\right| \le |\lambda|^3\sum_{i=1}^{r_n}|Z_{ni}|^3 \le |\lambda|^3\left(\max_{1\le i\le n}|Z_{ni}|\right)\sum_{i=1}^{r_n} Z_{ni}^2.\tag{24.9}$$

The result now follows from conditions (c) and (d), and **18.12**. ■

It is instructive to compare this proof with that of the Lindeberg theorem. A different series approximation of the ch.f. is used, and the assumption from independence, that

$$\phi_{S_{r_n}} = \Pi_i\phi_{Z_{ni}},$$

is avoided. Of course, we have yet to show that conditions **24.1**(a) and **24.1**(b) hold under convenient and plausible assumptions about the sequence. The rest of this chapter is devoted to this question. **24.1**(b) will turn out to result from suitable restrictions on the dependence. **24.1**(a) can be shown to follow from a more primitive moment condition by an argument based on the 'equivalent sequences' idea.

24.2 Theorem For an array $\{Z_{ni}\}$, let

$$\tilde{Z}_{ni} = Z_{ni}1(\textstyle\sum_{k=1}^{i-1}Z_{nk}^2 \le 2). \tag{24.10}$$

(i) The sequence $\tilde{T}_{r_n} = \prod_{i=1}^{r_n}(1+i\lambda\tilde{Z}_{ni})$ is uniformly integrable if

$$\sup_n E\left(\max_{1\le i\le r_n} Z_{ni}^2\right) < \infty. \tag{24.11}$$

And if $\sum_{i=1}^{r_n}Z_{ni}^2 \xrightarrow{pr} 1$, then

(ii) $\displaystyle\sum_{i=1}^{r_n}\tilde{Z}_{ni}^2 \xrightarrow{pr} 1$;

(iii) $\tilde{S}_{r_n} = \displaystyle\sum_{i=1}^{r_n}\tilde{Z}_{ni}$ has the same limiting distribution as S_{r_n}.

Proof Let

$$J_n = \begin{cases} \min\{j: \sum_{i=1}^{j}Z_{ni}^2 > 2\}, & \text{if } \sum_{i=1}^{r_n}Z_{ni}^2 > 2 \\ r_n, & \text{otherwise} \end{cases} \tag{24.12}$$

such that $\tilde{Z}_{ni} = 0$, if at all, from the point $i = J_n+1$ onwards. Note that

$$|\tilde{T}_{r_n}|^2 = \prod_{i=1}^{r_n}(1+\lambda^2\tilde{Z}_{ni}^2) = \prod_{i=1}^{J_n}(1+\lambda^2Z_{ni}^2). \tag{24.13}$$

The terms $\lambda^2Z_{ni}^2$ are real and positive. The inequality $1+x < e^x$ for $x > 0$ implies that $\prod_i(1+x_i) \le \prod_i e^{x_i}$ for $x_i > 0$. Hence,

$$\begin{aligned} |\tilde{T}_{r_n}|^2 &= \prod_{i=1}^{J_n-1}(1+\lambda^2Z_{ni}^2)(1+\lambda^2Z_{nJ_n}^2) \\ &\le \exp\{\lambda^2\textstyle\sum_{i=1}^{J_n-1}Z_{ni}^2)\}(1+\lambda^2Z_{nJ_n}^2) \\ &\le e^{2\lambda^2}(1+\lambda^2Z_{nJ_n}^2), \end{aligned} \tag{24.14}$$

where the last inequality is by definition of J_n. Then by (24.11),

$$\sup_n E|\tilde{T}_{r_n}|^2 \le e^{2\lambda^2}(1+\lambda^2\sup_n E(Z_{nJ_n}^2)) < \infty. \tag{24.15}$$

Uniform boundedness of $E|\tilde{T}_{r_n}|^2$ is sufficient for uniform integrability of $\tilde{T}_{r_n}$, proving (i). Since by construction $\sum_{i=1}^{r_n}\tilde{Z}_{ni}^2 \le 2$,

$$P\Big(\sum_i \tilde{Z}_{ni}^2 \neq \sum_i Z_{ni}^2\Big) = P\Big(\sum_i Z_{ni}^2 > 2\Big)$$

$$\leq P\Big(\Big|\sum_i Z_{ni}^2 - 1\Big| > \varepsilon\Big), \text{ for } 0 < \varepsilon < 1,$$

$$\to 0 \text{ as } n \to \infty, \tag{24.16}$$

by assumption, which proves (ii). In addition,

$$P(Z_{ni} \neq \tilde{Z}_{ni}, \text{ some } 1 \leq i \leq r_n) = P(\textstyle\sum_{k=1}^{r_n} Z_{nk}^2 > 2) \to 0 \text{ as } n \to \infty,$$

so $|\tilde{S}_n - S_n| \xrightarrow{pr} 0$, and by **22.18**, $\tilde{S}_n$ and S_n have the same limiting distribution, proving (iii). ■

24.2 The Martingale Case

Although it permits a law of large numbers, uncorrelatedness is not a strong enough assumption to yield a central limit result. But the martingale difference assumption is similar to uncorrelatedness for practical purposes, and is attractive in other ways too. The next theorem shows how **24.1** applies to this case.

24.3 Theorem Let $\{X_{nt},\mathcal{F}_{nt}\}$ be a martingale difference array with finite unconditional variances $\{\sigma_{nt}^2\}$, and $\sum_{t=1}^n \sigma_{nt}^2 = 1$. If

(a) $\displaystyle\sum_{t=1}^n X_{nt}^2 \xrightarrow{pr} 1$, and

(b) $\max_{1\leq t\leq n}|X_{nt}| \xrightarrow{pr} 0$,

then $S_n = \displaystyle\sum_{t=1}^n X_{nt} \xrightarrow{D} N(0,1)$.

Proof We use **24.1** and **24.2**, setting $r_n = n$, $i = t$, and $Z_{ni} = X_{nt}$. Conditions (a) and (b) are the same as (c) and (d) of **24.1**, so it remains to show that the other conditions of **24.1** are satisfied; not actually by X_{nt}, but by an equivalent sequence in the sense of **24.2**(iii).

If $T_n = \prod_{t=1}^n (1 + i\lambda X_{nt})$, we show that $\lim_{n\to\infty} E(T_n) = 1$ when $\{X_{nt}\}$ is a m.d. array. By repeated multiplying out,

$$T_n = \prod_{t=1}^n (1 + i\lambda X_{nt}) = T_{n-1} + i\lambda T_{n-1}X_{nn}$$

$$= \dots$$

$$= 1 + i\lambda \sum_{t=1}^n T_{t-1}X_{nt}. \tag{24.17}$$

$T_{t-1} = \prod_{s=1}^{t-1}(1 + i\lambda X_{ns})$ is an $\mathcal{F}_{t-1}$-measurable r.v., so by the LIE,

$$E(T_n) = 1 + i\lambda\sum_{t=1}^{n} E(T_{t-1}X_{nt})$$

$$= 1 + i\lambda\sum_{t=1}^{n} E(T_{t-1}E(X_{nt}|\mathcal{F}_{n,t-1})) = 1. \qquad (24.18)$$

This is an exact result for any n, so certainly holds in the limit.

If X_{nt} is a m.d., so is $\tilde{X}_{nt} = X_{nt}1(\sum_{k=1}^{t-1}X_{nk}^2 \le 2)$, and this satisfies **24.1**(b) as above, and certainly also **24.1**(d) according to condition (b) of the theorem. Since $\sum_{t=1}^{n}E(X_{nt}^2) = 1$, condition (24.11) holds for X_{nt}. Hence, $\tilde{X}_{nt}$ satisfies **24.1**(a) and **24.1**(c) according to **24.2**(i) and (ii), and so obeys the CLT. The theorem now follows by **24.2**(iii). ∎

This theorem holds for independent sequences as a special case of m.d. sequences, but the conditions are slightly stronger than those of the Lindeberg theorem. Under independence, we know by (23.53) that **24.3**(b) is equivalent to the Lindeberg condition when the CLT holds. However, **24.3**(a) is not a consequence of the Lindeberg condition. For the purpose of discussion, assume that $X_{nt} = X_t/s_n$, where $s_n^2 = \sum_{t=1}^{n}\sigma_t^2$ and $\sigma_t^2 = E(X_t^2)$. Under independence, a sufficient extra condition for **24.3**(a) is that the sequence $\{X_t^2/\sigma_t^2\}$ be uniformly integrable. In this case, independence of $\{X_t\}$ implies independence of $\{X_t^2\}$, $\{X_t^2 - \sigma_t^2, \mathcal{F}_t\}$ is a m.d., and **19.8** (put $a_n = s_n^2$ and $b_t = \sigma_t^2$) gives sufficient conditions for $s_n^{-2}\sum_{t=1}^{n}(X_t^2 - \sigma_t^2) \xrightarrow{pr} 0$. This is equivalent to **24.3**(a). But of course, it is not the case that $\{X_t^2 - \sigma_t^2, \mathcal{F}_t\}$ is a m.d. merely because $\{X_t, \mathcal{F}_t\}$ is a m.d. If **24.3**(a) cannot be imposed in any other manner, we should have to require $E(X_t^2|\mathcal{F}_{t-1}\} = \sigma_t^2$, a significant strengthening of the assumptions.

On the other hand, the theorem does not rule out trending variances. Following the approach of §23.5, we can obtain such a case as follows.

24.4 Theorem If $\{X_t, \mathcal{F}_t\}$ is a square-integrable m.d. sequence and $E(X_t^2|\mathcal{F}_{t-1}) = \sigma_t^2$ a.s., and there exists a sequence of positive constants $\{c_t\}$ such that $\{X_t^2/c_t^2\}$ is uniformly integrable and

$$\sup_n nM_n^2/s_n^2 < \infty \qquad (24.19)$$

where $M_n^2 = \max_{1\le t\le n}c_t^2$, conditions **24.3**(a) and **24.3**(b) hold for $X_{nt} = X_t/s_n$.

Proof By **23.18** the sequence $\{X_{nt}\}$ satisfies the Lindeberg condition, and hence, **24.3**(b) holds by **23.16**. Note that neither of these results imposes restrictions on the dependence of the sequence. To get **24.3**(a), apply **19.8** to the m.d. sequence $(X_t^2 - \sigma_t^2)$, putting $p = 1$, $b_t = c_t^2$, and $a_n = s_n^2$. The sequence $\{(X_t^2 - \sigma_t^2)/c_t^2\}$ is uniformly integrable on the assumptions, and note that $\sum_{t=1}^{n}b_t \le nM_n^2 = O(s_n^2)$ and that $\sum_{t=1}^{n}b_t^2 \le nM_n^4 = o(s_n^4)$, both as consequences of (24.19). The conditions of **19.8** are therefore satisfied, and the required result follows by **19.9**. ∎

24.3 Stationary Ergodic Sequences

It is easy to see that any stationary ergodic martingale difference having finite variance satisfies the conditions of **24.3**. Under stationarity, finite variance is sufficient for the Lindeberg condition, which ensures **24.3**(b) by **23.16**, and **24.3**(a) follows from the ergodicity by **13.12**.

The interest of this case stems from the following result, attributed by Hall and Heyde (1980: 137) to unpublished work of M. I. Gordin.

24.5 Theorem Let $\{X_t,\mathcal{F}_t\}$ be a stationary ergodic L_1-mixingale of size -1, and if $S_n = \sum_{t=1}^n X_t$ assume that

$$\limsup_{n\to\infty} n^{-1/2}E|S_n| < \infty. \tag{24.20}$$

Then $n^{-1/2}E|S_n| \to \lambda$, $0 \le \lambda < \infty$. If $\lambda > 0$, $n^{-1/2}S_n \xrightarrow{D} N(0,\frac{1}{2}\pi\lambda^2)$. □

Notice that the assumptions for this CLT do not include $E(X_1^2) < \infty$.

Proof Let $X_t^B = X_t 1_{\{|X_t|\le B\}}$. The centred sequence $Y_t^B = X_t^B - E(X_t^B|\mathcal{F}_{t-1})$ is a stationary ergodic m.d. with bounded variance $\sigma_B^2 \le 2B^2$, and hence $n^{-1/2}\sum_{t=1}^n Y_t^B \xrightarrow{D} N(0,\sigma_B^2)$, by **24.3**. Further, the m.d. orthogonality property implies

$$E\left(n^{-1/2}\sum_{t=1}^n Y_t^B\right)^2 = \sigma_B^2. \tag{24.21}$$

The sequence $\{n^{-1/2}|\sum_{t=1}^n Y_t^B|\}$ is therefore uniformly integrable (**12.11**), and by the continuous mapping theorem it converges in distribution to the half-Gaussian limit (see **8.16**); hence, by **9.8**,

$$n^{-1/2}E\left|\sum_{t=1}^n Y_t^B\right| \to \sigma_B(2/\pi)^{1/2}. \tag{24.22}$$

Now define $Y_t = X_t - E(X_t|\mathcal{F}_{t-1})$, corresponding to Y_t^B for $B = \infty$, and apply the decomposition of **16.6** to write $X_t = Y_t + Z_t - Z_{t+1}$, where Y_t is a stationary ergodic m.d. and Z_t is stationary with $E|Z_1| < \infty$. Hence $S_n = \sum_{t=1}^n Y_t + Z_1 - Z_{n+1}$, and by (24.20) there exists $A < \infty$ such that

$$\limsup_{n\to\infty} n^{-1/2}E\left|\sum_{t=1}^n Y_t\right| = \limsup_{n\to\infty} n^{1/2}E|S_n - Z_1 + Z_{n+1}|$$

$$\le \limsup_{n\to\infty} n^{-1/2}(E|S_n| + 2E|Z_1|) \le A. \tag{24.23}$$

Noting that $\sigma_B^2 = \int_{\{|X_1|\le B\}} X_1^2 dP$, $\{\sigma_B^2, B = 1,2,...\}$ is a monotone sequence converging either to a finite limit σ^2 (say) or to $+\infty$. In the latter case, in view of (24.22) there would exist N such that $n^{-1/2}E|\sum_{t=1}^n Y_t| > A$ for $N \ge n$, which contradicts (24.23), so we can conclude that $\sigma^2 < \infty$. Taking $B = \infty$ in (24.22) yields, in view of the fact that $n^{-1/2}E|Z_1 - Z_{n+1}| \to 0$,

$$n^{-1/2}E|S_n| = n^{-1/2}E\left|\sum_{t=1}^{n} Y_t + Z_1 - Z_{n+1}\right| \to \sigma(2/\pi)^{1/2}. \tag{24.24}$$

Hence, $\lambda = \sigma(2/\pi)^{1/2}$. Since Y_t is now known to be a stationary ergodic m.d. with finite variance σ^2, and $\sigma^2 > 0$, **24.3** and **22.18** imply that $n^{-1/2}S_n \xrightarrow{D} N(0,\sigma^2)$, which completes the proof. ∎

This result can be thought of as the counterpart for dependent sequences of the Lindeberg-Levy theorem, but unlike that case, we do not have to assume explicitly that $E(X_1^2) < \infty$. Independence of $\{X_t\}$ enforces the condition $Z_t = 0$ for all t, and then the conditions of the theorem imply $E(X_1^2) = \sigma^2$. It might appear that the existence of dependence weakens the moment restrictions required for the CLT, but this gain is more technical than real, for it is not obvious how to construct a stationary sequence such that X_1 is not square-integrable but Y_1 *is*. The most useful implication is that the independence assumption can be replaced by arbitrary local dependence (controlled by the mixingale assumption) without weakening any of the conclusions of the Lindeberg-Levy theorem.

24.4 The CLT for NED Functions of Strong Mixing Processes

The traditional approach to the problem of general dependence is the so-called method of 'Bernstein sums' (Bernstein 1927). That is, break up S_n into blocks (partial sums), and consider the sequence of blocks. Each block must be so large, relative to the rate at which the memory of the sequence decays, that the degree to which the next block can be predicted from current information is negligible; but at the same time, the number of blocks must increase with n so that a CLT argument can be applied to this derived sequence. It would suffice to require the sequence of blocks to approach independence in the limit, but a result can also be obtained if it behaves asymptotically like a martingale difference. This is the approach we adopt.

The theorem we prove (from Davidson 1992, 1993b) is given in two versions. The first, **24.6**, is fully general but the conditions are complicated and not very intuitive. The second, **24.7**, is a special case, whose conditions are simpler but cover almost all the possibilities. The exceptional cases for which **24.6** is essential are those in which the variances of the process tend to 0 as t increases.

24.6 Theorem Let $\{X_{nt},\ t = 1,\dots,n,\ n \ge 1\}$ be a triangular stochastic array, let $\{V_{nt},\ -\infty < t < \infty,\ n \ge 1\}$ be a (possibly vector-valued) stochastic array, and let $\mathcal{F}_{n,t-m}^{t+m} = \sigma(V_{ns},\ t-m \le s \le t+m)$. Also, let $S_n = \sum_{t=1}^n X_{nt}$. Suppose the following assumptions hold:

(a) X_{nt} is $\mathcal{F}_{n,-\infty}^{t}/\mathcal{B}$-measurable, with $E(X_{nt}) = 0$ and $E(S_n^2) = 1$.

(b) There exists a positive constant array $\{c_{nt}\}$ such that $\sup_{n,t}\|X_{nt}/c_{nt}\|_r < \infty$ for $r > 2$.

(c) X_{nt} is L_2-NED of size -1 on $\{V_{nt}\}$ with respect to the constants $\{c_{nt}\}$ specified in (b), and $\{V_{nt}\}$ is α-mixing of size $-(1+2\theta)r/(r-2)$, $0 \le \theta < \frac{1}{2}$.

(d) Letting $b_n = [n^{1-\alpha}]$ and $r_n = [n/b_n]$ for some $\alpha \in (0,1]$, and defining $M_{ni} = \max_{(i-1)b_n < t \leq ib_n}\{c_{nt}\}$ for $i = 1,\dots,r_n$ and $M_{n,r_n+1} = \max_{r_nb_n < t \leq n}\{c_{nt}\}$, the following conditions hold:

$$\max_{1 \leq i \leq r_n+1} M_{ni} = o(b_n^{-1/2}), \tag{24.25}$$

$$\sum_{i=1}^{r_n+1} M_{ni} = O(b_n^{\theta-1/2}), \tag{24.26}$$

where θ is given in (c), and

$$\sum_{i=1}^{r_n+1} M_{ni}^2 = O(b_n^{-1}). \tag{24.27}$$

Then, $S_n \xrightarrow{D} N(0,1)$. □

24.7 Corollary The conclusion of **24.6** holds if assumptions (c) and (d) are replaced by

(c′) X_{nt} is L_2-NED of size -1 on $\{V_{nt}\}$, which is α-mixing of size $-r/(r-2)$.

(d′) Letting $M_n = \max_{1 \leq t \leq n}\{c_{nt}\}$,

$$\sup_n nM_n^2 < \infty. \ □ \tag{24.28}$$

Note that (c′) is just **24.6**(c) with $\theta = 0$. If (24.28) holds, $M_{ni} = O(n^{-1/2})$ for each i. Since $r_nb_n \sim n$, (24.25) and (24.27) hold in this case for any α in (0,1]. While (24.26) holds only for a strictly positive choice of θ, with $0 < \alpha \leq 2\theta/(2\theta+1)$, **24.7**(c′) entails satisfaction of **24.6**(c) for *some* $\theta > 0$. Hence, **24.6** contains **24.7** as a special case.

The adaptation assumption in **24.6**(a) will be needed because of the asymptotic m.d. property the Bernstein blocks must possess; see **24.19** below for the application. This assumption says that X_{nt} must not depend on *future* values of the underlying mixing process, V_{ns} for $s > t$. In econometric applications at least, such an assumption would typically be innocuous. The remaining parts of condition (a) specify the assumed normalization.

The roles of the remaining conditions are not particularly transparent in either version of the result, and in reviewing these it will be helpful to keep in mind the leading case with $X_{nt} = (Y_t - \mu_t)/s_n$ where $s_n^2 = E(\sum_{t=1}^n (Y_t - \mu_t))^2$, although more general interpretations are possible, as noted in §23.2. In this case it would often be legitimate to choose

$$c_{nt} = \max\{\sigma_t, 1\}/s_n, \tag{24.29}$$

where σ_t^2 is the variance of Y_t. The c_{nt} have to be thought of as tending to zero with n, although possibly growing or shrinking with t also, subject to **24.6**(d) or **24.7**(d′). Because autocorrelation of the sequence is not ruled out, s_n^2 is no longer just the partial sum of the variances, but is defined as

$$s_n^2 = \sum_{t=1}^{n} \sigma_t^2 + 2\sum_{t=2}^{n}\sum_{k=1}^{t-1} \sigma_{t,t-k}, \tag{24.30}$$

where $\sigma_{t,t-k} = \mathrm{Cov}(Y_t, Y_{t-k})$.

Assumptions **24.6**(c) or **24.7**(c′) imply, by the norm inequality, that

$$\|X_{nt} - E(X_{nt}|\mathcal{F}_{n,\,t-m}^{t+m})\|_p \le c_{nt}\nu_m, \tag{24.31}$$

for $0 < p \le 2$, where ν_m is of size -1. The following lemma is an immediate consequence of **17.6**.

24.8 Lemma Under assumptions **24.6**(a), (b), and (c), $\{X_{nt}, \mathcal{F}_{n,-\infty}^t\}$ is an L_p-mixingale of size $-\min\{1, (1+2\theta)(r-p)/p(r-2)\}$ for $1 \le p \le 2$, with constants $\{c_{nt}\}$. □

In particular, when $p = 2$ the size is $-(\frac{1}{2}+\theta)$, and when $p = r/(r-1)$ the size is -1. Under the assumptions of **24.7** the same conclusions apply, except that $\theta = 0$.

There is also a more subtle implication which happens to be very convenient for the present result. This is the following.

24.9 Lemma Under **24.6**(a) and (b), plus either **24.6**(c) or **24.7**(c′),

$$E|E(X_{nt}X_{n,t+k}|\mathcal{F}_{-\infty}^{t-m}) - \sigma_{nt,t+k}| \le c_{nt}c_{n,t+k}\xi_m \tag{24.32}$$

and

$$E|X_{nt}X_{n,t+k} - E(X_{nt}X_{nt+k}|\mathcal{F}_{-\infty}^{t+k+m})| \le c_{nt}c_{n,t+k}\xi_{m+1} \tag{24.33}$$

for each $k \in \mathbb{N}$, where $\sigma_{nts} = E(X_{nt}X_{ns})$, and $\xi_m = O(m^{-1-\delta})$ for $\delta > 0$. □

These inequalities are convenient for the subsequent analysis, but in effect the lemma asserts that for each fixed k the products $X_{nt}X_{n,t+k}$, after centring, form L_1-mixingales of size -1 with constants given by $\max\{c_{nt}^2, c_{n,t+k}^2\}$. One of these might be written as, say, $\{U_{nt}, \mathcal{F}_{n,-\infty}^t\}$, where

$$U_{nt} = X_{n,t-[k/2]}X_{n,t+k-[k/2]} - \sigma_{n,t-[k/2],t+k-[k/2]}.$$

The mixingale coefficients here are $\xi'_m = \xi_0$ for $m = 0,\ldots,[k/2]$, and $\xi'_m = \xi_{m-[k/2]}$ for $m > [k/2]$.

Proof of 24.9 The array $\{X_{nt}X_{n,t+k}\}$ is L_1-NED on $\{V_{nt}\}$ of size -1 by **17.11**. The conclusion then follows by **17.6**(i), noting that any constant factors generated in forming the inequalities have been absorbed into ξ_m in (24.32) and (24.33). ■

Now consider **24.6**(d) and **24.7**(d′). These assumptions permit global nonstationarity (see §13.2). This is a fact worthy of emphasis, because in the functional CLT (see Chapters 27 and 29 for details) global stationarity is a requirement. In this respect the ordinary CLT is notably unrestrictive, provided we normalize by s_n as we do here. The following cases illustrate what is allowed.

24.10 Example Let $\{Y_t\}$ be an independent sequence with variances $\sigma_t^2 \sim t^\beta$ for any $\beta \ge 0$ (compare **13.6**). It is straightforward to verify that assumption **24.7**(d′) is satisfied for $X_{nt} = Y_t/s_n$ where $c_{nt} = \sigma_t/s_n$, and in this case $s_n^2 = \sum_{t=1}^n \sigma_t^2$. It is however violated when $\sigma_t^2 \sim 2^t$, a case that is incompatible with the asymptotic negligibility of individual summands (compare **23.19**). It is also violated when $\beta < 0$ (see below). □

24.11 Example Let $\{Y_t\}$ be an independent sequence with variance sequence generated by the scheme described in **13.7**. Putting $X_{nt} = Y_t/s_n$, **24.7**(d′) is satisfied with $c_{nt} = 1/s_n$ for all t. □

Among the cases that **24.7**(d′) rules out are asymptotically degenerate sequences, having $\sigma_t^2 \to 0$ as $t \to \infty$. In these cases, $\max_{1\le t\le n}\sigma_t^2 = O(1)$ as $n \to \infty$, but given **24.7**(c′), it will usually be the case that $s_n^2/n \to 0$. It is certain of these cases that assumption **24.6**(d) is designed to allow. To see what is going on here, it is easiest to think in terms of the array $\{c_{nt}\}$ as varying regularly with n and t, within certain limits to be determined. We have the following lemma, whose conditions are somewhat more general than we require, but are easily specialized.

24.12 Lemma Suppose $c_{nt}^2 \sim t^\beta n^{-\gamma-1}$ for $\beta,\gamma \in \mathbb{R}$. Then, **24.6**(d) holds iff

$$\beta \le \gamma \tag{24.34}$$

and

$$\beta < 2[\theta + \gamma(1+\theta)]. \; \square \tag{24.35}$$

Notice that β and γ can be of either sign, subject to the indicated constraints.

Proof We establish that an $\alpha \in (0, 1]$ exists such that each of conditions (24.25)–(24.27) are satisfied. We have either $M_{ni}^2 \sim (ib_n)^\beta n^{-\gamma-1}$ for $\beta \ge 0$, or $M_{ni}^2 \sim ((i-1)b_n)^\beta n^{-\gamma-1}$ for $\beta < 0$, but in both cases

$$\sum_{i=1}^{r_n} M_{ni}^2 \sim r_n^{1+\beta} b_n^\beta n^{-\gamma-1} \sim n^{\alpha(1+\beta)+(1-\alpha)\beta-\gamma-1}. \tag{24.36}$$

Simplifying shows that condition (24.34) is necessary and sufficient for (24.27), independently of the value of α, note. Next, (24.25) is equivalent to

$$\max_{1\le t\le n} c_{nt}^2 = o(n^{\alpha-1}), \tag{24.37}$$

which (since the maximum is at $t = n$ for $\beta \ge 0$, and $t = 1$ otherwise) imposes the requirement

$$\max\{\beta,0\} - \gamma < \alpha. \tag{24.38}$$

In view of (24.34) this constraint only binds if $\gamma < 0$, and is equivalent to just

$$-\gamma < \alpha. \tag{24.39}$$

Also,

$$\sum_{i=1}^{r_n} M_{ni} \sim r_n^{1+\beta/2} b_n^{\beta/2} n^{-(\gamma+1)/2}$$

$$\sim n^{\alpha(1+\beta/2)+((1-\alpha)\beta-\gamma-1)/2}, \tag{24.40}$$

and (24.26) reduces to

$$\alpha \leq \frac{2\theta+\gamma-\beta}{1+2\theta}. \tag{24.41}$$

The existence of α satisfying (24.41) and (24.39) requires two strict inequalities to be satisfied by β, γ, and θ, but since θ is positive the first of these, which is $\theta > \frac{1}{2}(\beta-\gamma)$, holds by (24.34). The second is $-\gamma(1+2\theta) < 2\theta+\gamma-\beta$, which is the same as (24.35). It follows that (24.34) and (24.36) are equivalent to **24.6**(d), as asserted. ■

In terms of the leading case with $X_{nt} = (Y_t - \mu_t)/s_n$, with s_n^2 given by (24.30), consider first the case $\sigma_t^2 \sim t^\beta$, $\beta \geq 0$. To have c_{nt} monotone in t (not essential, but analytically convenient), we could often set

$$c_{nt} = \max_{1\leq s\leq t}\{\sigma_s\}/s_n. \tag{24.42}$$

In this case, under **24.6**(b) and **24.7**(c′), the conditions of **17.7** are satisfied. Note however that $\|Y_t - \mu_t\|_r \sim \sigma_t$ is required by **24.6**(b). Since $\{\zeta_k\}$ is of size -1 we have, substituting into (24.30),

$$s_n^2 \ll \sum_{t=1}^{n} t^\beta + 2\sum_{t=1}^{n} t^{\beta/2}\sum_{k=1}^{t-1}(t-k)^{\beta/2}\zeta_k = O(n^{1+\beta}). \tag{24.43}$$

This only provides an upper bound, and condition **24.7**(c′) alone does not exclude the possibility that $s_n^2 \sim n^{1+\gamma}$ for some $\gamma < \beta$. However, compliance with condition (24.34), which follows in turn from **24.7**(d′) (note, $M_n^2 = c_{nn}^2$ in this case), enforces $\gamma = \beta$. This condition says that the variance of the sum must grow no more slowly than the sum of the variances.

Now consider the case $\sigma_t^2 \sim t^\beta$ with $\beta < 0$. Here, we might be able to set

$$c_{nt} = \sup_{s\geq t}\{\sigma_s\}/s_n. \tag{24.44}$$

Under **24.7**(c′) and (24.34) we would again have $c_{nt}^2 \sim t^\beta n^{-\beta-1}$, but here $M_n^2 = \sigma_{t^*}^2/s_n^2$ for some $t^* < \infty$; hence $M_n^2 \sim n^{-\beta-1}$, and **24.7**(d′) ceases to hold. However, with $\beta = \gamma$, condition (24.35) reduces to

$$\beta > \frac{-2\theta}{1+2\theta}, \tag{24.45}$$

and it is possible for the conditions of **24.12** to be satisfied, although only with $\theta > 0$. As θ is increased, limiting the dependence, α can be increased according to (24.36) and this allows smaller β, increasing the permitted rate of degeneration. As θ approaches $\frac{1}{2}$, so that the mixing size approaches $-2r/(r-2)$, β may approach $-\frac{1}{2}$, with α also approaching $\frac{1}{2}$.

These conclusions are summarized in the following corollary. Part (i) is a case of **24.7**, and part (ii) a case of **24.6**.

24.13 Corollary Let $X_{nt} = (Y_t - \mu_t)/s_n$ where $\sigma_t^2 \sim t^{\beta}$ and $s_n^2 \sim n^{1+\beta}$. If either
(i) $0 \le \beta < \infty$, and **24.6**(b) and **24.7**(c′) hold with c_{nt} defined in (24.42); or
(ii) there exists θ such that (24.45), **24.6**(b) and **24.6**(c) hold with c_{nt} defined by (24.44);
then $S_n \xrightarrow{D} N(0,1)$. □

By an apparent artefact of the proof, $t^{-1/2}$ represents a limit on the permitted rate of degeneration of the variances. We may conjecture that with mixing sizes exceeding $2r/(r-2)$, the CLT can hold with $\beta \le -\frac{1}{2}$, but a different method of attack would be necessary to obtain this result. Also, both the above cases appear to require that $\alpha \in (0,\frac{1}{2})$, and it is not clear whether larger values of α might be possible generally. The plausibility of both these conjectures is strengthened by the existence of the following special case.

24.14 Corollary If conditions **24.6**(a) and (b) hold, and also
(c″) $\{X_{nt}, \mathcal{F}_{n,-\infty}^{t}\}$ is a martingale difference array, and
(d″) conditions (24.25) and (24.27) hold with $b_n = 1$,
then $S_n \xrightarrow{D} N(0,1)$. □

In the case $X_{nt} = (Y_t - \mu_t)/s_n$, where by the m.d. assumption $s_n^2 = \sum_{t=1}^{n}\sigma_t^2$, note that (24.27) is satisfied with $b_n = 1$ by construction, and (24.25) requires only that $s_n^2 \uparrow \infty$, so that $\sigma_t^2 \sim t^{\beta}$ is permitted for any $\beta \ge -1$ under **2.14**(d″). This result may be compared with **24.4**, whose conditions it extends rather as **24.6** extends **24.7**. The proof will be given below after the intermediate results for the proof of **24.6** have been established. As an example, let $Y_t - \mu_t$ be a m.d. with $\sigma_t^2 = \sigma^2/t$ where σ^2 is constant, so that $s_n^2 \sim \log n$. Corollary **24.14** establishes that

$$(\log n)^{-1/2}\sum_{t=1}^{n}(Y_t - \mu_t) \xrightarrow{D} N(0,\sigma^2).$$

The limit on the permissable rate of degeneration here is set by the requirement $s_n^2 \to \infty$ as $n \to \infty$. If the variances are summable, the central limit theorem surely fails. Here is a well-known case where the non-summability condition is violated.

24.15 Example Consider the sequence $\{Y_t\}$ of first differences, with $Y_1 = Z_1$ and

$$Y_t = Z_t - Z_{t-1},\ t = 2,3,\dots,$$

where $\{Z_t\}$ is a zero-mean, uniformly L_r-bounded, independent sequence, with $r>2$. Here $\{Y_t\}$ satisfies **24.6**(a)–(c), but $\sum_{t=1}^{n}Y_t = Z_n$ and $s_n^2 = \mathrm{Var}(Z_n) = O(1)$. □

24.5 Proving the CLT by the Bernstein Blocking Method

We shall prove only **24.6**, the arguments being at worst a mild extension of those required for **24.7**. We show that with a suitable Bernstein-type blocking scheme the blocks will satisfy the conditions of **24.1**. In effect, we show that the blocks behave like martingale differences. In most applications of the Bernstein approach alternating big and small blocks are defined, with the small blocks containing of the order of $[n^{\beta(1-\alpha)}]$ summands for some $\beta \in (0,1)$, small enough that their omission is negligible in the limit but increasing with n so that the big blocks are asymptotically independent. Our martingale difference approximation method has the advantage that the small blocks can be dispensed with.

Define b_n and r_n as in condition **24.6**(d) for some $\alpha \in (0,1)$, and let

$$Z_{ni} = \sum_{t=(i-1)b_n+1}^{ib_n} X_{nt},\ i = 1,\ldots,r_n, \tag{24.46}$$

such that

$$S_n = \sum_{t=1}^{n} X_{nt} = \sum_{i=1}^{r_n} Z_{ni} + (X_{n,r_nb_n+1} + \ldots + X_{nn}). \tag{24.47}$$

The final fragment has fewer than b_n terms, and is asymptotically negligible in the sense that $b_nr_n/n \longrightarrow 1$.

Our method is to show the existence of $\alpha > 0$ for which an array $\{Z_{ni}\}$ can be constructed according to (24.46), such that **24.1**(c) is satisfied, and such that the truncated sequence $\{\tilde{Z}_{ni}\}$ defined in (24.10) satisfies the other conditions of **24.1**. This will be sufficient to prove the theorem, since then $\sum_{i=1}^{r_n}\tilde{Z}_{ni} \xrightarrow{pr} 1$ according to **24.2**(ii), and Z_{ni} and $\tilde{Z}_{ni}$ are equivalent sequences when **24.1**(c) holds, by **24.2**(iii).

Since $\{X_{nt}\}$ is a L_2-mixingale array of size $-\frac{1}{2}$ according to **24.8**, we may apply **16.14** to establish that the sequences

$$\{\max_{j\le ib_n}(\textstyle\sum_{t=(i-1)b_n+1}^{j}X_{nt})^2/\nu_{ni}^2,\ n \in \mathbb{N}\} \tag{24.48}$$

are uniformly integrable, where $\nu_{ni}^2 = \sum_{t=(i-1)b_n+1}^{ib_n}c_{nt}^2$. At least, this follows directly in the case $i = 1$, and it is also clear that the result generalizes to any i, for, although the starting point $(i-1)b_n+1$ is increasing with n, the nth coordinate of the sequence in (24.48) can be embedded in a sequence with fixed starting point which is uniformly integrable by **16.14**. This holds uniformly in n and i, and it follows in particular that the array $\{Z_{ni}^2/\nu_{ni}^2,\ 1 \le i \le r_n,\ r_n \ge 1\}$ is uniformly integrable.

This result leads to the following theorem.

24.16 Theorem Under assumptions **24.6**(a)–(d), $\{Z_{ni}\}$ satisfies the Lindeberg condition.

Proof For any i, $\nu_{ni}^2 \le b_nM_{ni}^2 \longrightarrow 0$ as $n \longrightarrow \infty$ by (24.25) and hence, for $\varepsilon > 0$,

$$\max_{1\le i\le r_n}\left\{\frac{E(1_{\{|Z_{ni}|>\varepsilon\}}Z_{ni}^2)}{b_nM_{ni}^2}\right\} \le \max_{1\le i\le r_n}\left\{\frac{E(1_{\{|Z_{ni}/\nu_{ni}|>\varepsilon/\nu_{ni}\}}Z_{ni}^2)}{\nu_{ni}^2}\right\}$$

$$\longrightarrow 0 \text{ as } n \longrightarrow \infty \tag{24.49}$$

by uniform integrability. The conclusion,

$$\sum_{j=1}^{r_n} E(1_{\{|Z_{nj}|>\varepsilon\}}Z_{nj}^2) \le \max_{1\le i\le r_n}\left\{\frac{E(1_{\{|Z_{ni}|>\varepsilon\}}Z_{ni}^2)}{b_nM_{ni}^2}\right\}\sum_{j=1}^{r_n} b_nM_{nj}^2$$

$$\to 0 \text{ as } n \to \infty, \tag{24.50}$$

now follows since the sum of r_n terms on the majorant side is $O(1)$ from (24.27). ■

This theorem leads in turn to two further crucial results. First, by way of **23.16** we know that condition **24.1**(d) is satisfied (and if this holds for Z_{ni} it is certainly true for $\tilde{Z}_{ni}$); and second, note that for any $\varepsilon > 0$

$$\max_{1\le i\le r_n} Z_{ni}^2 \le \varepsilon^2 + \sum_{i=1}^{r_n} 1_{\{|Z_{ni}|>\varepsilon\}}Z_{ni}^2. \tag{24.51}$$

Taking expectations of both sides of this inequality, and then the limit as $n \to \infty$, shows that (24.11) holds, and therefore that $\tilde{T}_{r_n}$ is uniformly integrable (that is, condition **24.1**(a) holds) by **24.2**(i). This leaves two results yet to be proven, $E(\tilde{T}_{r_n}) \to 1$ (corresponding to **24.1**(b) for the truncated array), and **24.1**(c). By the latter result we shall establish parts (ii) and (iii) of **24.2**, and then in view of **24.2**(iii) the proof will be complete.

We tackle **24.1**(c) first. Consider

$$\sum_{i=1}^{r_n} Z_{ni}^2 - 1 = \sum_{i=1}^{r_n}\left(\sum_{t=(i-1)b_n+1}^{ib_n} X_{nt}\right)^2 - 1 = A_n - B_n, \tag{24.52}$$

say, where

$$A_n = \sum_{i=1}^{r_n}(Z_{ni}^2 - E(Z_{ni}^2))$$

$$= \sum_{i=1}^{r_n}\left[\sum_{t=(i-1)b_n+1}^{ib_n}\left((X_{nt}^2 - \sigma_{nt}^2) + 2\sum_{k=1,\, t<ib_n}^{ib_n-t}(X_{nt}X_{n,t+k} - \sigma_{nt,t+k})\right)\right], \tag{24.53}$$

and $B_n = B_n' + B_n''$, where

$$B_n' = 2\sum_{i=1}^{r_n}\left[\sum_{t=(i-1)b_n+1}^{ib_n}\left(\sum_{k=ib_n-t+1}^{n-t}\sigma_{nt,t+k}\right)\right], \tag{24.54}$$

$$B_n'' = \sum_{t=r_nb_n+1}^{n-1}\left(\sigma_{nt}^2 + 2\sum_{k=1}^{n-t}\sigma_{nt,t+k}\right) + \sigma_{nn}^2. \tag{24.55}$$

Here, $\sigma_{nts} = E(X_{nt}X_{ns})$, and recall that $E(S_n^2) = \sum_{t=1}^{n-1}(\sigma_{nt}^2 + 2\sum_{j=t+1}^{n}\sigma_{nt,t+j}) + \sigma_{nn}^2 = 1$. It may be helpful to visualize these expressions as made up of elements from outer product and covariance matrices divided into r_n^2 blocks of dimension $b_n \times b_n$, with a border corresponding to the final $n - r_nb_n$ terms, if any; see Fig. 24.1.

The terms in A_n correspond to the r_n diagonal blocks, and B_n' and B_n'' contain the remaining covariances, those from the off-diagonal and final blocks.

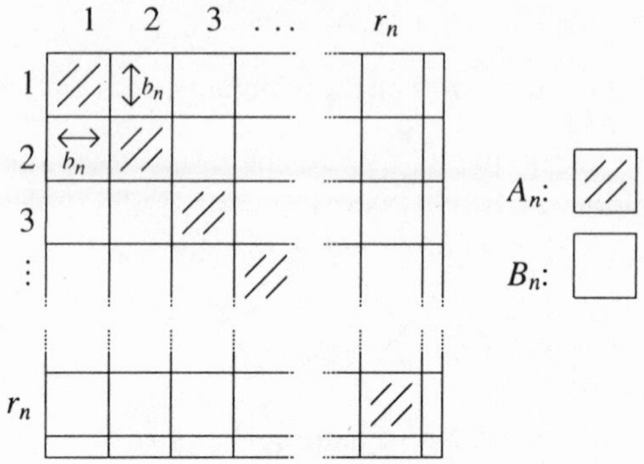

Fig. 24.1

A_n is stochastic and so must be shown to converge in probability, whereas the components of B_n are nonstochastic. The nonstochastic part of the problem is the more straightforward, so we start with this.

24.17 Theorem Under assumptions **24.6**(a)–(d), $B_n \to 0$.

Proof Since $r > 2$, $r/(r-1) < 2$ and conditions **24.6**(b) and (c) imply by **17.7** that

$$|\sigma_{nts}| \le c_{nt}c_{ns}\xi_{|t-s|}, \tag{24.56}$$

where $\{\xi_m\}$ is a constant sequence of size -1. Hence,

$$|B_n'| \le 2\sum_{i=1}^{r_n}\sum_{l=i+1}^{r_n+1}\sum_{j=1}^{b_n}\sum_{k=1}^{b_n}\left|\sigma_{n,(i-1)b_n+j,(l-1)b_n+k}\right|$$

$$\ll \sum_{i=1}^{r_n}\sum_{l=i+1}^{r_n+1}M_{ni}M_{nl}\left(\sum_{j=1}^{b_n}\sum_{k=1}^{b_n}\xi_{|(l-i)b_n+k-j|}\right). \tag{24.57}$$

To determine the order of magnitude of the majorant expression, verify that the terms in the parentheses are $O(b_n^{1-\delta}(l-i)^{-1-\delta})$ for $l = i+1,\ldots,r_n+1$, and some $\delta > 0$. Changing the order of summation and putting $k = l-i$ allows us to write

$$|B_n'| \ll b_n^{1-\delta}\sum_{k=1}^{r_n}\left(\sum_{i=1}^{r_n+1-k}M_{ni}M_{n,i+k}\right)k^{-1-\delta}. \tag{24.58}$$

But for every k in this sum, the Cauchy-Schwartz inequality and (24.27) give

$$\sum_{i=1}^{r_n+1-k}M_{ni}M_{n,i+k} \le \sum_{i=1}^{r_n+1}M_{ni}^2 = O(b_n^{-1}), \tag{24.59}$$

so that (24.58) implies, as required, that

$$|B_n'| = O(b_n^{-\delta}) = O(n^{-\delta(1-\alpha)}). \tag{24.60}$$

To complete the proof we can also show, by a similar kind of argument but applying (24.25), that

$$B_n'' = O(M_{n,r_n+1}^2 b_n) = o(1). \ \blacksquare \tag{24.61}$$

To solve the stochastic part of the problem, decompose the terms $Z_{ni}^2 - E(Z_{ni}^2)$ in (24.53) into individual mixingale components, each indexed by $i = 1,...,r_n$. For a pair of positive integers j and k, let

$$W_{ni}(j,k) = X_{n,(i-1)b_n+j}X_{n,(i-1)b_n+j+k} - \sigma_{n,(i-1)b_n+j,(i-1)b_n+j+k}. \tag{24.62}$$

It is an immediate consequence of **24.9**, specifically of (24.32) and (24.33), that for fixed j and k the triangular array

$$\{W_{ni}(j,k), \mathcal{F}_{n,-\infty}^{ib_n}; 1 \le i \le r_n, n \ge N(j,k)\}, \tag{24.63}$$

where $N(j,k) = \min\{n: r_n \ge 1, b_n \ge j+k\}$, is an L_1-mixingale of size -1, with mixing coefficients $\psi_0 = \xi_0$ and $\psi_p = \xi_{(p-1)b_n+j}$ for $p \ge 1$, and constants

$$a_{ni}(j,k) = c_{n,(i-1)b_n+j}c_{n,(i-1)b_n+j+k}. \tag{24.64}$$

Substituting from (24.62) into (24.53), we have the sum of b_n^2 such mixingales,

$$Z_{ni}^2 - E(Z_{ni}^2) = \sum_{j=1}^{b_n-1}\left(W_{ni}(j,0) + 2\sum_{k=1}^{b_n-j}W_{ni}(j,k)\right) + W_{ni}(b_n,0). \tag{24.65}$$

Although this definition entails considering k of order b_n as $n \to \infty$, note that the inter-block dependence of the summands does not depend on k. The designation of 'mixingale' is convenient here, but it need not be taken more literally than the inequalities (24.32) and (24.33) require. The crucial conclusion is that a weak law of large numbers can be applied to these terms.

24.18 Theorem Under assumptions **24.6**(a)–(d), $A_n \xrightarrow{pr} 0$. □

The object here is to show that the array

$$\{(Z_{ni}^2 - E(Z_{ni}^2)), \mathcal{F}_{n,-\infty}^{ib_n}; 1 \le i \le r_n, r_n \ge 1\} \tag{24.66}$$

is an L_1-mixingale with constants $\{a_{ni}\}$ which satisfy conditions (a), (b), and (c) of **19.11**. The proof could be simplified in the present case by using the fact that Z_{ni} is $\mathcal{F}_{n,-\infty}^{ib_n}$-measurable (by **24.6**(a)) so that the minorant side of (24.68) below actually disappears identically for $p \ge 0$. But since the result could find other applications, we establish the mixingale property formally, without appealing to this assumption.

Proof By multiplying out Z_{ni}^2 and applying **24.9** term by term, we obtain

$$E\left|E(Z_{ni}^2 - E(Z_{ni}^2)|\mathcal{F}_{-\infty}^{(i-p)b_n})\right|$$

$$\leq \sum_{j=1}^{b_n-1}\left(E\left|E(W_{ni}(j,0)|\mathcal{F}_{-\infty}^{(i-p)b_n})\right| + 2\sum_{k=1}^{b_n-j}E\left|E(W_{ni}(j,k)|\mathcal{F}_{-\infty}^{(i-p)b_n})\right|\right)$$

$$+ E\left|E(W_{ni}(b_n,0)|\mathcal{F}_{-\infty}^{(i-p)b_n})\right|$$

$$\ll M_{ni}^2\left(\sum_{j=1}^{b_n-1}(1+2(b_n-j))\xi_{(p-1)b_n+j}+\xi_{pb_n}\right), \tag{24.67}$$

and similarly,

$$E\left|Z_{ni}^2 - E(Z_{ni}^2|\mathcal{F}_{-\infty}^{(i+p)b_n})\right|$$

$$\ll M_{ni}^2\left[\sum_{j=1}^{b_n-1}\left(\xi_{(p+1)b_n-j}+2\sum_{k=1}^{b_n-j}\xi_{(p+1)b_n-j-k}\right)+\xi_{pb_n}\right], \tag{24.68}$$

where $\xi_j = O(j^{-1-\delta})$ for $\delta > 0$. Write, formally, $a_{ni}\psi_p^*$ to denote the larger of the two majorant expressions in (24.67) and (24.68), such that $\psi_p^* \to 0$ and a_{ni} is fixed by setting $\psi_0^* = 1$. Evaluating (24.68) at $p = 1$ and (24.68) at $p = 0$ respectively gives

$$E\left|E(Z_{ni}^2 - E(Z_{ni}^2)|\mathcal{F}_{-\infty}^{(i-1)b_n})\right| \ll M_{ni}^2\left(\sum_{j=1}^{b_n-1}(1+2(b_n-j))j^{-1-\delta}+b_n^{-1-\delta}\right)$$

$$\ll M_{ni}^2 b_n, \tag{24.69}$$

and also, putting $j' = b_n - j$ and $k' = j' - k$,

$$E\left|Z_{ni}^2 - E(Z_{ni}^2|\mathcal{F}_{-\infty}^{ib_n})\right| \ll M_{ni}^2\left[\sum_{j'=1}^{b_n-1}\left(j'^{-1-\delta}+2\sum_{k'=0}^{j'-1}k'^{-1-\delta}\right)+1\right] \tag{24.70}$$

$$\ll M_{ni}^2 b_n.$$

Hence, $a_{ni} = BM_{ni}^2 b_n$ for some finite constant B. Since

$$\sum_{i=1}^{r_n} M_{ni}^4 \leq \max_{1\leq i\leq r_n+1} M_{ni}^2 \sum_{i=1}^{r_n} M_{ni}^2 = o(b_n^{-2}) \tag{24.71}$$

in view of (24.27) and (24.25), these constants satisfy conditions **19.11**(b) and (c). And since $Z_{ni}^2/b_nM_{ni}^2 \leq Z_{ni}^2/v_{ni}^2$ where Z_{ni}^2/v_{ni}^2 is uniformly integrable, they also satisfy condition **19.11**(a). It follows that $A_n \xrightarrow{L_1} 0$, and the proof is complete. ■

This brings us to the final step in the argument, establishing the asymptotic m.d. property of the Bernstein blocks.

24.19 Theorem Under **24.6**(a)–(d), $\lim_{n\to\infty}E(\tilde{T}_{r_n}) = 1$.

Proof Applying (24.17),

$$\widetilde{T}_{r_n} = \prod_{i=1}^{r_n}(1+i\lambda\widetilde{Z}_{ni}) = 1+i\lambda\sum_{i=1}^{r_n}\widetilde{T}_{i-1}\widetilde{Z}_{ni}, \tag{24.72}$$

where $\widetilde{T}_{i-1} = \prod_{j=1}^{i-1}(1+i\lambda\widetilde{Z}_{nj})$ is an $\mathcal{F}_{n,-\infty}^{(i-1)b_n}$-measurable r.v. by **24.6**(a), and hence

$$E(\widetilde{T}_{r_n}) = 1+\mathrm{i}\lambda\sum_{i=1}^{r_n}E(\widetilde{T}_{i-1}\widetilde{Z}_{ni})$$

$$= 1+\mathrm{i}\lambda\sum_{i=1}^{r_n}E(\widetilde{T}_{i-1}E(\widetilde{Z}_{ni}|\mathcal{F}_{n,-\infty}^{(i-1)b_n})). \tag{24.73}$$

By the Cauchy-Schwartz inequality,

$$\sum_{i=1}^{r_n}E|\widetilde{T}_{i-1}E(\widetilde{Z}_{ni}|\mathcal{F}_{n,-\infty}^{(i-1)b_n})| \le \sum_{i=1}^{r_n}\|\widetilde{T}_{i-1}\|_2\|E(\widetilde{Z}_{ni}|\mathcal{F}_{n,-\infty}^{(i-1)b_n})\|_2, \tag{24.74}$$

where $\|\widetilde{T}_{i-1}\|_2$ is uniformly bounded by (24.15), which follows in turn by (24.11), so the result hinges on the rate of approach to zero of $\|E(\widetilde{Z}_{ni}|\mathcal{F}_{n,-\infty}^{(i-1)b_n})\|_2$. This cannot be less than that for Z_{ni}, so consider, more conveniently, the latter case.

$$\|E(Z_{ni}|\mathcal{F}_{n,-\infty}^{(i-1)b_n})\|_2 = \left[E\left(\sum_{t=(i-1)b_n+1}^{ib_n}E(X_{nt}|\mathcal{F}_{n,-\infty}^{(i-1)b_n})\right)^2\right]^{1/2}$$

$$\le \left[\sum_{t=(i-1)b_n+1}^{ib_n}E(E(X_{nt}|\mathcal{F}_{n,-\infty}^{(i-1)b_n}))^2\right.$$

$$\left.+\,2\sum_{t=(i-1)b_n+1}^{ib_n-1}\sum_{k=1}^{ib_n-t}\left|E(E(X_{nt}|\mathcal{F}_{n,-\infty}^{(i-1)b_n})E(X_{nt+k}|\mathcal{F}_{n,-\infty}^{(i-1)b_n}))\right|\right]^{1/2}. \tag{24.75}$$

Applying **24.8**,

$$E(E(X_{nt}|\mathcal{F}_{n,-\infty}^{(i-1)b_n}))^2 \le c_{nt}^2(\zeta_{t-(i-1)b_n})^2 \tag{24.76}$$

and

$$E\left|E(E(X_{nt}|\mathcal{F}_{n,-\infty}^{(i-1)b_n})E(X_{nt+k}|\mathcal{F}_{n,-\infty}^{(i-1)b_n}))\right|$$

$$\le \|E(X_{nt}|\mathcal{F}_{n,-\infty}^{(i-1)b_n})\|_2\|E(X_{nt+k}|\mathcal{F}_{n,-\infty}^{(i-1)b_n})\|_2$$

$$\le c_{nt}\zeta_{t-(i-1)b_n}c_{n,t+k}\zeta_{t-(i-1)b_n+k}, \tag{24.77}$$

where $\zeta_j = O(j^{-1/2-\mu})$ for $\mu > \theta$ for the θ defined in **24.6**(c). Hence,

$$\|E(Z_{ni}|\mathcal{F}_{n,-\infty}^{(i-1)b_n})\|_2 \ll M_{ni}\left(\sum_{j=1}^{b_n}\zeta_j^2+2\sum_{j=1}^{b_n-1}\zeta_j\sum_{k=j+1}^{b_n}\zeta_k\right)^{1/2}, \tag{24.78}$$

where the sum of squares is $O(1)$ and the double sum is $O(b_n^{1-2\mu})$. Applying (24.26), assumption **24.6**(d) implies

$$\sum_{i=1}^{r_n} \left| E(\tilde{T}_{i-1}E(\tilde{Z}_{ni}|\mathcal{F}_{n,-\infty}^{(i-1)b_n})) \right| = \sum_{i=1}^{r_n} M_{ni}O(\max\{b_n^{(1-2\mu)/2},1\})$$
$$= O(\max\{b_n^{\theta-\mu},b_n^{\theta-1/2}\}) = o(1). \qquad (24.79)$$

This ensures that $\sum_{i=1}^{r_n}E(\tilde{T}_{i-1}\tilde{Z}_{ni}) \to 0$ as $n \to \infty$, which is the desired result. ■

Proof of 24.6 We have established that $\sum_{i=1}^{r_n}Z_{ni} = \sum_{t=1}^{r_nb_n}X_{nt} \xrightarrow{D} N(0,1)$. There remains the formality of extending the same conclusion to S_n, but this is easy since

$$|S_n - \sum_{t=1}^{r_nb_n}X_{nt}| = |X_{n,r_nb_n+1} + \ldots + X_{nn}| = O_p(r_n^{-1/2}), \qquad (24.80)$$

and S_n has the same limiting distribution by **22.18**. The proof of **24.6** is therefore complete. ■

It remains just to modify the proof for the martingale difference case, as was promised above.

Proof of 24.14 It is easily seen that **24.16** holds for $r_n = n$ and $b_n = 1$. In **24.17**, $B_n = 0$ identically since $\xi_k = 0$ for $k > 0$ in (24.57). In **24.18** one may put $Z_{ni} = X_{nt}$, and the conditions for **19.10** follow directly from the assumptions. Lastly, **24.19** holds since the sum in (24.79) vanishes identically under the martingale difference assumption. The proof is completed just as for **24.6**. ■

25
Some Extensions

25.1 The CLT with Estimated Normalization

The results of the last two chapters, applied to the case $X_{nt} = X_t/s_n$ where $E(X_t) = 0$ and $s_n^2 = E(\sum_{t=1}^n X_t)^2$, would not be particularly useful if it were necessary to *know* the sequences $\{\sigma_t^2\}$, and $\{\sigma_{t,t-k}\}$ for $k \geq 1$, in order to apply them. Obviously, the relevant normalizing constants must be estimated in practice. Consider the independent case initially, and let $S_n = \sum_{t=1}^n X_t/s_n$ where $s_n^2 = \sum_{t=1}^n \sigma_t^2$. Also let $\hat{s}_n^2 = \sum_{t=1}^n X_t^2$, and we may write

$$\hat{S}_n = \frac{1}{\hat{s}_n}\sum_{t=1}^n X_t = d_n S_n, \tag{25.1}$$

where $d_n = s_n/\hat{s}_n$. If $d_n \xrightarrow{pr} 1$, we could appeal to **22.14** to show that $\hat{S}_n \xrightarrow{D} N(0,1)$ whenever $S_n \xrightarrow{D} N(0,1)$. The interesting question is whether the minimal conditions sufficient for the CLT are also sufficient for the relevant convergence in probability.

If the sequence is stationary as well as independent, existence of the variance σ^2 is sufficient for both the CLT (**23.3**) and for $n^{-1}\sum_{t=1}^n X_t^2 \xrightarrow{pr} \sigma^2$ (applying **23.5** to X_t^2). In the heterogeneous case, we do not have a weak law of large numbers for $\{X_t^2\}$ based solely on the Lindeberg condition. However, the various sufficient conditions for the Lindeberg condition given in Chapter 23, based on uniform integrability, *are* sufficient for a WLLN. Without loss of generality, take the case of possibly trending variances.

25.1 Theorem If $\{X_t\}$ is an independent sequence satisfying the conditions of **23.18**, then

$$\frac{\hat{s}_n^2}{s_n^2} \xrightarrow{pr} 1. \tag{25.2}$$

Proof Consider the sequence $(X_t^2 - \sigma_t^2)/c_t^2$. By assumption this has zero mean, is independent (and hence an m.d.), and uniformly integrable. The conditions of **19.8**, with $p = 1$, $b_t = c_t^2$, and $a_n = s_n^2$, are satisfied since, by (23.57),

$$\sum_{t=1}^n c_t^2 \leq nM_n^2 = O(s_n^2), \tag{25.3}$$

where $M_n = \max_{1\leq t\leq n}\{c_t\}$. Hence

$$E\left|\frac{\sum_{t=1}^n (X_t^2 - \sigma_t^2)}{s_n^2}\right| = E\left|\frac{\sum_{t=1}^n X_t^2}{s_n^2} - 1\right| \to 0, \tag{25.4}$$

which is sufficient for convergence in probability. ■

When the sequence $\{X_t\}$ is a martingale difference, supplementary conditions are needed for $\{X_t^2\}$ to obey a WLLN, but these turn out to be the same as are needed for the martingale CLTs of **24.3** and **24.4**. In fact, condition **24.3**(a) corresponds precisely to the required result. We have, immediately, the following theorem.

25.2 Theorem Let $\{X_t,\mathcal{F}_t\}$ be a m.d., and let the conditions of **24.3** or **24.4** be satisfied; then (25.2) holds. □

Although we have spoken of estimating the variance, there is clearly no necessity for $\{s_n^2/n\}$, or any other sequence apart from $\{d_n\}$, to converge. Example **24.11** is a case in point. In those globally covariance stationary cases (see §13.2) where s_n^2/n converges to a finite positive constant, say $\bar{\sigma}^2$, the 'average variance' of the sequence, we conventionally refer to $\hat{s}_n^2/n$ as a consistent estimator of $\bar{\sigma}^2$. But more generally, the same terminology can always be applied to $\hat{s}_n^2$ with respect to s_n^2, in the sense of (25.2).

Alternative variance estimators can sometimes be defined which exploit the particular structure of the random sequence. In regression analysis, we typically apply the CLT to sequences of the form $X_t = W_tU_t$ where $\{U_t,\mathcal{F}_t\}$ is assumed to be a m.d. with fixed variance σ^2 (the disturbance), and where W_t (a regressor) is $\mathcal{F}_{t-1}$-measurable. In this case, $\{X_t,\mathcal{F}_t\}$ is a m.d. with variances $\sigma_t^2 = \sigma^2E(W_t^2)$, which suggests the estimator $\tilde{s}_n^2 = (n^{-1}\sum_{t=1}^n U_t^2)\sum_{t=1}^n W_t^2$, for s_n^2. This is the usual approach in regression analysis, but of course the method is not robust to the failure of the fixed-variance assumption. By contrast, $\hat{s}_n^2 = \sum_{t=1}^n W_t^2U_t^2$ possesses the property cited in (25.2) under the stated conditions, regardless of the distributions of the sequence. The latter type of estimator is termed heteroscedasticity-consistent.[26]

Now consider the case of general dependence. The complicating factor here is that s_n^2 contains covariances as well as variances, and $\hat{s}_n^2$ is no longer a suitable estimator. A sample analogue of s_n^2 must include terms of the form X_tX_{t+j} for $|j| \geq 1$ as well as for $j = 0$, but the problem is to know how many of these to include. If we include *all* of them, in other words for $j = 1-t,\dots,n-t$, the resulting sum is equal to $(\sum_{t=1}^n X_t)^2$, and the ratio of this quantity to s_n^2 is converging, *not* in probability to 1, but in distribution to $\chi^2(1)$. For consistent estimation we must make use of the knowledge that all but a finite number of the covariances are arbitrarily close to 0, and omit the corresponding sample products from the sum.

Similarly to the m.d. case, the conditions of **24.6** contain the required convergence result. Consider (24.46) and (24.47) where $X_{nt} = X_t/s_n$, but now write

$$Z_{ni}^* = s_nZ_{ni} = \sum_{t=(i-1)b_n+1}^{ib_n} X_t,\ i = 1,\dots,r_n. \tag{25.5}$$

In the proof of the CLT the construction of the Bernstein blocks was purely conceptual, but we might consider the option of actually computing them. The sum of squares of the unweighted blocks, $\hat{s}_{n1}^2 = \sum_{i=1}^{r_n} Z_{ni}^{*2}$, is consistent for s_n^2 in the sense that

$$\frac{\hat{s}_{n1}^2}{s_n^2} = \sum_{i=1}^{r_n} Z_{ni}^2 \xrightarrow{pr} 1, \tag{25.6}$$

according to **24.17** and **24.18**. An important rider to this proposal is that **24.17** and **24.18** were proved using only (24.25) and (24.27), so that, as noted previously, any $\alpha \in (0,1)$ will serve to construct the blocks. In the context of the conditions of **24.12** at least, the only constraint imposed by **24.6**(d) is represented by (24.39), which puts a possible lower bound on α in the case of decreasing variances ($\gamma > 0$), but no upper bound strictly less than 1. It is sufficient for consistency if b_n goes to infinity at a positive rate, and we are not bound to use the α that satisfies the conditions of the CLT to construct the blocks in (25.6).

But although consistent, $\hat{s}_{n1}^2$ is not the obvious choice of estimator. It would be more natural to follow authors such as Newey and West (1987) and Gallant and White (1988), *inter alia*, who consider estimators based on all the cross-products X_tX_{t-k} for $t = k+1,\ldots,n$ and $k = 0,\ldots,b_n$. In terms of the array represention of Fig. 24.1, these are the elements in the diagonal *band* of width $2b_n$, rather than the diagonal blocks only. (In this context, b_n is referred to as the *band width*.) The simplest such estimator is

$$\hat{s}_{n2}^2 = \sum_{t=1}^{n} X_t^2 + 2\sum_{k=1}^{b_n}\sum_{t=k+1}^{n} X_tX_{t-k}. \tag{25.7}$$

25.3 Theorem Under the conditions of **24.6**, applied to X_t/s_n, $\hat{s}_{n2}^2/s_n^2 \xrightarrow{pr} 1$.

Proof Let $X_{nt} = X_t/s_n$ in (24.53), so that $s_n^2 A_n$ denotes the same sum constructed from the X_t in place of the X_{nt}. The difference between A_n and $(\hat{s}_{n2}^2 - E(\hat{s}_{n2}^2))/s_n^2$ is the quantity

$$A_n^* = \frac{1}{s_n^2}\left[2\sum_{i=1}^{r_n-1}\left(\sum_{t=(i-1)b_n+1}^{ib_n}\ \sum_{k=1}^{ib_n-t+1}(X_tX_{t-k} - \sigma_{t,t-k})\right)\right.$$

$$\left. + \sum_{t=r_nb_n+1}^{n}\left((X_t^2 - \sigma_t^2) + 2\sum_{k=1}^{b_n-1}(X_tX_{t-k} - \sigma_{t,t-k})\right)\right] \tag{25.8}$$

The components of this sum correspond to the $r_n - 1$ 'triangles' which separate the diagonal blocks in Fig. 24.1, each containing $\frac{1}{2}b_n(b_n-1)$ terms, plus the terms from the lower-right corner blocks. Reasoning closely analogous to the proof of **24.18** shows that $A_n^* \xrightarrow{L_1} 0$. The sums of the corresponding covariances converge absolutely to 0 by **24.17**, since they are components of B_n' in (24.54), and it follows that

$$\frac{|\hat{s}_{n2}^2 - \hat{s}_{n1}^2|}{s_n^2} \xrightarrow{pr} 0.$$

The theorem therefore follows from **24.18.** ■

Since this estimator uses sample data which are discarded in $\hat{s}_{n1}^2$, there are informal reasons for preferring it in small samples. But there is a problem in that (the chosen notation notwithstanding) $\hat{s}_{n2}^2$ is *not* a square, and not always non-negative except in the limit. This difficulty can be overcome by inserting fixed weights in the sum, as in

$$\hat{s}_{n3}^2 = \sum_{t=1}^{n} X_t^2 + 2\sum_{k=1}^{b_n} w_{nk} \sum_{t=k+1}^{n} X_t X_{t-k}. \tag{25.9}$$

Suppose $w_{nk} \to 1$ as $n \to \infty$ for every $k \le K$, for every fixed $K < \infty$. Then

$$\frac{|\hat{s}_{n2}^2 - \hat{s}_{n3}^2|}{s_n^2} = \frac{2}{s_n^2}\left|\sum_{k=1}^{b_n}(1 - w_{nk})\sum_{t=k+1}^{n} X_t X_{t-k}\right| \xrightarrow{pr} r(K), \tag{25.10}$$

where

$$r(K) = 2\operatorname*{plim}_{n\to\infty}\frac{1}{s_n^2}\left|\sum_{k=K+1}^{b_n}(1 - w_{nk})\sum_{t=k+1}^{n} X_t X_{t-k}\right|. \tag{25.11}$$

Since $r(K)$ can be made as small as desired by taking K large enough, in view of **25.3** and **24.18**, $\hat{s}_{n3}^2$ is consistent when the weights have this property. It remains to see if they can also be chosen in such a way that (25.9) is a sum of squares.

Following Gallant and White (1988), choose $b_n + 1$ real numbers $a_{n1},\dots,a_{n,b_n+1}$, satisfying $\sum_{j=1}^{b_n+1} a_{nj}^2 = 1$, and consider the $n + b_n$ variables

$$\begin{aligned}
Y_{n1} &= a_1 X_1,\\
Y_{n2} &= a_{n1}X_2 + a_{n2}X_1,\\
&\dots\\
Y_{n,b_n+1} &= a_{n1}X_{b_n+1} + \dots + a_{n,b_n+1}X_1,\\
Y_{n,b_n+2} &= a_{n1}X_{b_n+2} + \dots + a_{n,b_n+1}X_2,\\
&\dots\\
Y_{nn} &= a_{n1}X_n + \dots + a_{n,b_n+1}X_{n-b_n},\\
Y_{n,n+1} &= a_{n2}X_n + \dots + a_{nb_n}X_{n-b_n+1},\\
&\dots\\
Y_{n,n+b_n} &= a_{nb_n}X_n.
\end{aligned}$$

Observe that

$$\begin{aligned}
\sum_{t=1}^{n+b_n} Y_{nt}^2 &= \left(\sum_{j=1}^{b_n+1} a_{nj}^2\right)\sum_{t=1}^{n} X_t^2 + 2\left(\sum_{j=2}^{bn+1} a_{nj}a_{n,j-1}\right)\sum_{t=2}^{n} X_t X_{t-1}\\
&\quad + 2\left(\sum_{j=3}^{bn+1} a_{nj}a_{n,j-2}\right)\sum_{t=3}^{n} X_t X_{t-2} + \dots + 2a_{n,b_n+1}a_{n1}\sum_{t=b_n+1}^{n} X_t X_{t-b_n},
\end{aligned} \tag{25.12}$$

which shows that any weights of the form $w_{nk} = \sum_{j=k+1}^{b_n+1} a_{n,j}a_{n,j-k}$, $k = 0,\ldots,b_n$ impose non-negativity, and also give $w_{n0} = 1$. A case that fulfils the consistency requirement is $a_{nj} = (b_n+1)^{-1/2}$, all j, which yields $w_{nk} = 1 - k/(b_n+1)$.

Variance estimators having the general form

$$\sum_{t=1}^{n}\sum_{s=1}^{n} w(|t-s|/b_n)X_tX_s$$

are known as *kernel estimators*. The function $w(x) = 1 - |x|$ for $|x| \le 1$, 0 otherwise, which corresponds to $\hat{s}_{n3}^2$, is the *Bartlett* kernel. The estimator $\hat{s}_{n2}^2$, by contrast, uses the *truncated* kernel, $w(x) = 1_{\{|x|\le 1\}}$. Other possibilities exist; see Andrews (1991) for details.

One other point to note is that much of the literature on covariance matrix estimation relies on L_2-convergence results for the sums and products, and accordingly requires L_r-boundedness of the variables for $r \ge 4$. The present results hold under the milder moment conditions sufficient for the CLT, by using a weak law of large numbers based on **19.11**. See Hansen (1992b) for a comparable approach to the problem.

25.2 The CLT with Random Norming

Here is a problem not unconnected with the last one. We will discuss it in the context of the m.d. case for simplicity, but it clearly exists more generally.

Consider a m.d. sequence $\{X_t\}$ which instead of (25.2) has the property

$$\frac{\sum_{t=1}^{n} X_t^2}{s_n^2} \xrightarrow{pr} \eta^2, \tag{25.13}$$

where η^2 is a random variable. This might arise in the following manner. Let $X_t = W_tU_t$ where $\{U_t,\mathcal{F}_t\}_{-\infty}^{\infty}$ is a m.d. and $\{W_t\}_{-\infty}^{\infty}$ a sequence of r.v.s which are measurable with respect to the remote σ-field $\mathcal{R} = \bigcap_{s=-\infty}^{\infty}\mathcal{F}_s$. The implication is that W_t is 'strongly exogenous' (see Engle *et al.* 1983). with respect to the generation mechanism of U_t. Then

$$E(X_t|\mathcal{F}_{t-1}) = W_tE(U_t|\mathcal{F}_{t-1}) = 0 \text{ a.s.}, \tag{25.14}$$

since $\mathcal{R} \subseteq \mathcal{F}_{t-1}$ for every t, hence X_t is a m.d. Provided the W_t are distributed in such a way that $\sum_{t=1}^{n} W_t^2U_t^2/s_n^2 \xrightarrow{pr} 1$, the analysis can proceed exactly as in §24.2. There is no practical need to draw a distinction between nonstochastic W_t and $\mathcal{R}$-measurable W_t. But this need not be the case, as the following example shows.

25.4 Example Anticipating some distributional results from Part VI, let $W_t = \sum_{s=1}^{t} V_s$ where $\{V_s\}$ is a stationary m.d. sequence with $E(V_s^2) = \tau^2$ for all s. Also assume, for simplicity, that $E(U_t^2) = \sigma^2$, all t. Then, $E(W_t^2) = t\tau^2$ and $s_n^2 = \frac{1}{2}n(n+1)\tau^2\sigma^2$. If we further assume that $\{V_s\}$ satisfies the conditions of **24.3**, it will be shown below (see **27.14**) that

$$\frac{1}{\tau^2 n^2}\sum_{t=1}^{n} W_t^2 \xrightarrow{D} \int_0^1 B(r)^2 dr, \tag{25.15}$$

where $B(r)$ is a Brownian motion process. Under the distribution conditional upon $\mathcal{R}$, we may treat the sequence $\{W_t\}$ as nonstochastic and apply the weak LLN (by an argument paralleling **25.2**) to say that

$$\operatorname*{plim}_{n\to\infty}\frac{\sum_{t=1}^{n}X_t^2}{s_n^2} = 2\operatorname*{plim}_{n\to\infty}\frac{\sum_{t=1}^{n}W_t^2U_t^2}{\tau^2\sigma^2 n(n+1)} = 2\lim_{n\to\infty}\frac{\sum_{t=1}^{n}W_t^2}{\tau^2 n^2} = \eta^2, \tag{25.16}$$

where η^2 merely denotes the limit indicated. Under the joint distribution of $\{U_t\}$ and $\{W_t\}$, $\frac{1}{2}\eta^2$ is a drawing from the limiting distribution specified in (25.15). □

The application of the CLT to $\{X_t\}$ can proceed under the conditional distribution (defined according to **10.30**), replacing each expectation by $E(.|\mathcal{R})$. Let $\sigma_t^2 = E(U_t^2|\mathcal{R})$, defining an $\mathcal{R}$-measurable random sequence, so that

$$E\left(\sum_{t=1}^{n}X_t^2\,\middle|\,\mathcal{R}\right) = \sum_{t=1}^{n}W_t^2\sigma_t^2. \tag{25.17}$$

We can then apply a result for heterogeneously distributed sequences, such as **24.4**, letting $c_t = W_t\sigma_t$. Assuming that $E(X_t^2|\mathcal{F}_{t-1}) = W_t^2\sigma_t^2$, and that condition (24.19) is almost surely satisfied, the conditional CLT takes the form

$$\lim_{n\to\infty} E\left(\exp\left\{\frac{i\lambda}{(\sum_{t=1}^{n}W_t^2\sigma_t^2)^{1/2}}\sum_{t=1}^{n}X_t\right\}\middle|\,\mathcal{R}\right) = e^{-\lambda^2/2}, \text{ a.s.} \tag{25.18}$$

But if we normalize by the *un*conditional variance, the situation is quite different. W_t must be treated as stochastic and $E(X_t^2|\mathcal{F}_{t-1}) \neq E(X_t^2)$, so the conditions of **24.4** are violated. However, if (25.13) holds with η an $\mathcal{R}$-measurable r.v., then according to **22.14**(ii) the conditional distribution has the property

$$\frac{1}{s_n}\sum_{t=1}^{n}X_t\,\middle|\,\mathcal{R} \xrightarrow{D} N(0,\eta^2), \text{ a.s.} \tag{25.19}$$

(see §10.6 for the relevant theory). This result can also be expressed in the form

$$\lim_{n\to\infty} E\left(\exp\left\{\frac{i\lambda}{s_n}\sum_{t=1}^{n}X_t\right\}\middle|\,\mathcal{R}\right) = e^{-\lambda^2\eta^2/2}, \text{ a.s.} \tag{25.20}$$

Hence, the limiting unconditional distribution is given by

$$\lim_{n\to\infty} E\left(\exp\left\{\frac{i\lambda}{s_n}\sum_{t=1}^{n}X_t\right\}\right) = E(e^{-\lambda^2\eta^2/2}). \tag{25.21}$$

This is a novel central limit result, because we have established that $\sum_{t=1}^{n}X_t/s_n$ is not asymptotically Gaussian. The right-hand side of (25.21) is the ch.f. of a *mixed Gaussian* distribution. One may visualize this distribution by noting that drawings can be generated in the following way. First, draw η^2 from the appropriate distribution, for example the functional of Brownian motion defined in (25.15); then draw a standard Gaussian variate and multiply it by η. If X is mixed Gaussian with respect to a marginal c.d.f. $G(\eta)$ (say), and ϕ_η is the Gaussian density with mean 0 and variance η^2, the moments of the distribution are easily computed, and as well as $E(X) = E(X^3) = 0$ we find

$$E(X^2) = \int_0^\infty \int_{-\infty}^\infty x^2 \phi_\eta(x) dx dG(\eta) = \int_0^\infty \eta^2 dG(\eta) = E(\eta^2). \tag{25.22}$$

However, the kurtosis is non-Gaussian, for

$$E(X^4) = \int_0^\infty \int_{-\infty}^\infty x^4 \phi_\eta(x) dx dG(\eta) = \frac{1}{3}\int_0^\infty \eta^4 dG(\eta) = \frac{E(\eta^4)}{3}, \tag{25.23}$$

where the right-hand side is in general different from $\frac{1}{3}E(\eta^2)^2$ (see **9.7**).

25.3 The Multivariate CLT

An array $\{X_{nt}\}$ of p-vectors of random variables is said to satisfy the CLT if the joint distribution of $\mathbf{S}_n = \sum_{t=1}^n X_{nt}$ converges weakly to the multivariate Gaussian. In its multivariate version, the central limit theorem contributes a new and powerful approximation result. Given a vector of stochastic processes exhibiting arbitrary (contemporaneous) dependence among themselves, we can show that there exist different *linear* combinations of the processes which are asymptotically *independent* of one another (uncorrelated Gaussian variables being of course independent). This is a fundamental result in the general theory of asymptotic inference in econometrics.

The main step in the solution to the multivariate problem sometimes goes by the name of the 'Cramér-Wold device'.

25.5 Cramér-Wold theorem A vector random sequence $\{S_n\}_1^\infty$, $S_n \in \mathbb{R}^k$, converges in distribution to a random vector S if and only if $\boldsymbol{\alpha}'S_n \xrightarrow{D} \boldsymbol{\alpha}'S$ for every fixed k-vector $\boldsymbol{\alpha} \neq \mathbf{0}$.

Proof For given $\boldsymbol{\alpha}$ the characteristic function of the scalar $\boldsymbol{\alpha}'S_n$ is $E(\exp\{i\lambda\boldsymbol{\alpha}'S_n\}) = \phi_{n,\alpha}(\lambda)$. By the Lévy continuity theorem (**22.17**), $\boldsymbol{\alpha}'S_n \xrightarrow{D} \boldsymbol{\alpha}'S$ if and only if $\phi_{n,\alpha}(\lambda) \to \phi_\alpha(\lambda)$ and ϕ_α is continuous at $\lambda = 0$. Since $\boldsymbol{\alpha}$ is arbitrary, we can put $\boldsymbol{t} = \lambda\boldsymbol{\alpha}$ and obtain

$$E(\exp\{i\boldsymbol{t}'S_n\}) \to E(\exp\{i\boldsymbol{t}'S\}) = \psi(\boldsymbol{t}), \tag{25.24}$$

(say) where by assumption the convergence is pointwise on $\mathbb{R}^k$. By (11.39), the left-hand side of (25.24) is the ch.f. of S_n, and the right-hand side is the ch.f. of S. The continuity of ψ at the origin is ensured by the continuity of ϕ_α at 0 for all $\boldsymbol{\alpha}$, and it follows that $S_n \xrightarrow{D} S$. ■

Now let $\{X_t\}$ be a sequence of random vectors, and let $\boldsymbol{\Sigma}_n$ be the variance matrix of $\sum_{t=1}^n X_t$. Being symmetric and positive semidefinite by construction, this matrix possesses the factorization

$$\boldsymbol{\Sigma}_n = \boldsymbol{C}_n\boldsymbol{\Lambda}_n\boldsymbol{C}_n' = \boldsymbol{L}_n\boldsymbol{L}_n', \tag{25.25}$$

where $\boldsymbol{L}_n = \boldsymbol{C}_n\boldsymbol{\Lambda}_n^{1/2}$, $\boldsymbol{C}_n$ and $\boldsymbol{\Lambda}_n$ being respectively the eigenvector matrix (satisfying $\boldsymbol{C}_n\boldsymbol{C}_n' = \boldsymbol{C}_n'\boldsymbol{C}_n = \boldsymbol{I}_p$) and the diagonal, non-negative matrix of eigenvalues.

Let $\boldsymbol{X}_{nt} = \boldsymbol{L}_n^-\boldsymbol{X}_t$, where if $\boldsymbol{\Sigma}_n$ has full rank then $\boldsymbol{L}_n^- = \boldsymbol{\Lambda}_n^{-1/2}\boldsymbol{C}_n'$ so that $\boldsymbol{L}_n^-\boldsymbol{\Sigma}_n\boldsymbol{L}_n^{-\prime} = \boldsymbol{I}_p$. However, $\boldsymbol{\Sigma}_n$ need not have full rank for every n. If it is singular with

$$\boldsymbol{\Lambda}_n = \begin{bmatrix} \boldsymbol{\Lambda}_{1n} & \boldsymbol{0} \\ \boldsymbol{0} & \boldsymbol{0} \end{bmatrix},$$

let $\boldsymbol{L}_n^{-\prime} = [\boldsymbol{C}_{n1}\boldsymbol{\Lambda}_{1n}^{-1/2}\colon \boldsymbol{0}]$ where $\boldsymbol{C}_{n1}$ is the appropriate submatrix of $\boldsymbol{C}_n$. In this case, $\boldsymbol{L}_n^-\boldsymbol{\Sigma}_n\boldsymbol{L}_n^{-\prime}$ has either ones or zeros on the diagonal. We do however require $\boldsymbol{\Sigma}_n$ to be asymptotically of full rank, in the sense that $\boldsymbol{L}_n^-\boldsymbol{\Sigma}_n\boldsymbol{L}_n^{-\prime} \to \boldsymbol{I}_p$. If $\boldsymbol{S}_n = \sum_{t=1}^n \boldsymbol{X}_{nt}$, then for any p-vector $\boldsymbol{\alpha}$ with $\boldsymbol{\alpha}'\boldsymbol{\alpha} = 1$, we have $E(\boldsymbol{\alpha}'\boldsymbol{S}_n)^2 \to 1$. If this condition fails, and there exists $\boldsymbol{\alpha} \neq \boldsymbol{0}$ such that $E(\boldsymbol{\alpha}'\boldsymbol{S}_n)^2 \to 0$, the asymptotic distribution of $\boldsymbol{S}_n$ is said to be singular. In this case, some elements of the limiting vector are linear combinations of the remainder. Their distribution is therefore determined, and nothing is lost by dropping these variables from the analysis.

To obtain the multivariate CLT it is necessary to show that the scalar sequences $\{\boldsymbol{\alpha}'\boldsymbol{X}_{nt}\}$ satisfy the ordinary scalar CLT, for any $\boldsymbol{\alpha}$. If sufficient conditions hold for $\boldsymbol{\alpha}'\boldsymbol{S}_n \xrightarrow{D} N(0,1)$, the Cramér-Wold theorem allows us to say that $\boldsymbol{S}_n \xrightarrow{D} \boldsymbol{S}$, and it remains to determine the distribution of $\boldsymbol{S}$. For any $\boldsymbol{\alpha}$, the ch.f. of $\boldsymbol{\alpha}'\boldsymbol{S}$ is

$$\phi(\lambda) = E(\exp\{i\lambda\boldsymbol{\alpha}'\boldsymbol{S}\}) = e^{-\lambda^2/2}. \tag{25.26}$$

But letting $\boldsymbol{t} = \lambda\boldsymbol{\alpha}$ be a vector of length λ, it follows from (11.41) that (25.26) is the ch.f. of a standard multi-Gaussian vector. (Recall that $\boldsymbol{\alpha}'\boldsymbol{\alpha} = 1$.) By the inversion theorem we get the required result that $\boldsymbol{S} \sim N(\boldsymbol{0}, \boldsymbol{I}_p)$. We have therefore proved the following theorem.

25.6 Theorem Let $\{\boldsymbol{X}_t\}$ be a stochastic sequence of p-vectors and let $\boldsymbol{\Sigma}_n = E((\sum_{t=1}^n \boldsymbol{X}_t)(\sum_{t=1}^n \boldsymbol{X}_t)')$. If $\boldsymbol{L}_n^-\boldsymbol{\Sigma}_n\boldsymbol{L}_n^{-\prime} \to \boldsymbol{I}_p$ and $\sum_{t=1}^n \boldsymbol{\alpha}'\boldsymbol{L}_n^-\boldsymbol{X}_t \xrightarrow{D} N(0,1)$ for every $\boldsymbol{\alpha}$ satisfying $\boldsymbol{\alpha}'\boldsymbol{\alpha} = 1$, then

$$\sum_{t=1}^n \boldsymbol{L}_n^-\boldsymbol{X}_t \xrightarrow{D} N(\boldsymbol{0}, \boldsymbol{I}_p). \ \square \tag{25.27}$$

In this result the elements of $\boldsymbol{\Sigma}_n$ need not have the same orders of magnitude in n. The variances can be tending to infinity for some elements of $\boldsymbol{X}_t$, and to zero for others, within the bounds set by the Lindeberg condition. However, in the case when all of the elements of $\boldsymbol{\Sigma}_n$ have the same order of magnitude, say n^δ for some $\delta > 0$ such that $n^{-\delta}\boldsymbol{\Sigma}_n \to \boldsymbol{\Sigma}$, a finite constant matrix, it is easy to manipulate (25.27) into the form

$$n^{-\delta/2}\sum_{t=1}^n \boldsymbol{X}_t \xrightarrow{D} N(\boldsymbol{0}, \boldsymbol{\Sigma}). \tag{25.28}$$

Techniques for estimating the normalization factors generalize naturally from the scalar case discussed in §25.1, just like the CLT itself. Consider the m.d. case in which $\boldsymbol{\Sigma}_n = \sum_{t=1}^n E(\boldsymbol{X}_t\boldsymbol{X}_t')$, and assume this matrix has rank p asymptotically in the sense defined above. Under the assumptions of **25.2**,

$$\frac{\sum_{t=1}^n(\boldsymbol{\alpha}'\boldsymbol{X}_t)^2}{\boldsymbol{\alpha}'\boldsymbol{\Sigma}_n\boldsymbol{\alpha}} = \frac{\boldsymbol{\alpha}'(\sum_{t=1}^n\boldsymbol{X}_t\boldsymbol{X}_t')\boldsymbol{\alpha}}{\boldsymbol{\alpha}'\boldsymbol{\Sigma}_n\boldsymbol{\alpha}} \xrightarrow{pr} 1 \tag{25.29}$$

for any $\boldsymbol{\alpha}$ with $\boldsymbol{\alpha}'\boldsymbol{\alpha} = 1$, where the ratio is always well defined on taking n large enough, by assumption. This suggests that the positive semidefinite matrix $\hat{\boldsymbol{\Sigma}}_n = \sum_{t=1}^n\boldsymbol{X}_t\boldsymbol{X}_t'$ is the natural estimator for $\boldsymbol{\Sigma}_n$.

To be more precise: (25.29) says that $P(|\boldsymbol{\alpha}'\hat{\boldsymbol{\Sigma}}_n\boldsymbol{\alpha}/\boldsymbol{\alpha}'\boldsymbol{\Sigma}_n\boldsymbol{\alpha} - 1|)$ can be made as small as desired for *arbitrary* $\boldsymbol{\alpha} \neq \boldsymbol{0}$ by taking n large enough, since the normalization to unit length cancels in the ratio. This is therefore true in the particular case $\boldsymbol{\alpha}^* = \boldsymbol{L}_n^{-\prime}\boldsymbol{\alpha}$, and since $\boldsymbol{\alpha}_n^{*\prime}\boldsymbol{\Sigma}_n\boldsymbol{\alpha}_n^* = 1$, we are able to conclude that $\boldsymbol{\alpha}'\boldsymbol{L}_n^{-}\hat{\boldsymbol{\Sigma}}_n\boldsymbol{L}_n^{-\prime}\boldsymbol{\alpha} \xrightarrow{pr} 1$. We can further deduce from this fact that $\boldsymbol{L}_n^{-}\hat{\boldsymbol{\Sigma}}_n\boldsymbol{L}_n^{-\prime} \xrightarrow{pr} \boldsymbol{I}_p$. To show this, note that if a matrix $\boldsymbol{B}$ $(p \times p)$ is nonsingular, and $g(\boldsymbol{\alpha}) = \boldsymbol{\alpha}'\boldsymbol{B}\boldsymbol{\alpha}/\boldsymbol{\alpha}'\boldsymbol{\alpha} = 1$ for every $\boldsymbol{\alpha} \neq \boldsymbol{0}$, g has the gradient vector $g'(\boldsymbol{\alpha}) = 2\boldsymbol{B}\boldsymbol{\alpha}/\boldsymbol{\alpha}'\boldsymbol{\alpha} - 2\boldsymbol{\alpha}/\boldsymbol{\alpha}'\boldsymbol{\alpha}$, for any $\boldsymbol{\alpha}$, and the system of equations $\boldsymbol{B}\boldsymbol{\alpha}/\boldsymbol{\alpha}'\boldsymbol{\alpha} - \boldsymbol{\alpha}/\boldsymbol{\alpha}'\boldsymbol{\alpha} = \boldsymbol{0}$ has the unique solution $\boldsymbol{B} = \boldsymbol{I}_p$. If $\hat{\boldsymbol{L}}_n$ is the factorization of $\hat{\boldsymbol{\Sigma}}_n$, since $\boldsymbol{L}_n$ is asymptotically of rank p it follows by **18.10**(ii) that $\hat{\boldsymbol{L}}_n\boldsymbol{L}_n^{-} \xrightarrow{pr} \boldsymbol{I}_p$, and we arrive at the desired conclusion, for comparison with (25.27):

$$\hat{\boldsymbol{L}}_n^{-}\sum_{t=1}^n \boldsymbol{X}_t \xrightarrow{D} N(\boldsymbol{0}, \boldsymbol{I}_p). \tag{25.30}$$

The extension to general dependence is a matter of estimating $\boldsymbol{\Sigma}_n$ by a generalization of the consistent methods discussed in §25.1, either $\hat{\boldsymbol{\Sigma}}_{n1} = \sum_{i=1}^{r_n}\boldsymbol{Z}_{ni}^*\boldsymbol{Z}_{ni}^{*\prime}$ where $\boldsymbol{Z}_{ni}^* = \sum_{t=(i-1)b_n+1}^{ib_n}\boldsymbol{X}_t$, or, letting weights $\{w_{nk}\}$ represent the Bartlett kernel,

$$\hat{\boldsymbol{\Sigma}}_{n3} = \sum_{t=1}^n \boldsymbol{X}_t\boldsymbol{X}_t' + \sum_{k=1}^{b_n} w_{nk}\sum_{t=k+1}^n(\boldsymbol{X}_t\boldsymbol{X}_{t-k}' + \boldsymbol{X}_{t-k}\boldsymbol{X}_t'). \tag{25.31}$$

The latter matrix is assuredly positive definite, since $\boldsymbol{\alpha}'\hat{\boldsymbol{\Sigma}}_{n3}\boldsymbol{\alpha} \geq 0$ with arbitrary $\boldsymbol{\alpha}$ by application of (25.12) with $X_t = \boldsymbol{X}_t\boldsymbol{\alpha}$.

25.4 Error Estimation

There are a number of celebrated theorems in the classical probability literature on the rates at which the deviations of distributions from their weak limits, and also stochastic sequences from their almost sure limits, decline with n. Most are for the independent case, and the extensions to general dependent sequences are not much researched to date. These results will not be treated in detail, but it is useful to know of their existence. For details and proofs the reader is referred to texts such as Chung (1974) and Loève (1977).

If $\{F_n\}$ is a sequence of c.d.f.s and $F_n \Rightarrow \Phi$ (the Gaussian c.d.f.), the Berry-Esséen theorem sets limits on the largest deviation of F_n from Φ. The setting for this result is the integer-moment case of the Liapunov CLT; see (23.37).

25.7 Berry-Esséen theorem Let $\{X_t\}$ be a zero-mean, independent, L_3-bounded random sequence, with variances $\{\sigma_t^2\}$, let $s_n^2 = \sum_{t=1}^n \sigma_t^2$, and let F_n be the c.d.f. of $S_n = \sum_{t=1}^n X_t / s_n$. There exists a constant $C > 0$ such that, for all n,

$$\sup_x |F_n(x) - \Phi(x)| \leq C \sum_{t=1}^n E|X_t|^3 / s_n^3. \quad \square \tag{25.32}$$

The measure of distance between functions F_n and Φ appearing on the left-hand side of (25.32) is the uniform metric (see §5.5). As was noted in §23.1, convergence to the Gaussian limit can be very rapid, with favourable choice of F_n. The Berry-Esséen bounds represent the 'worst case' scenario, the slowest rate of uniform convergence of the c.d.f.s to be expected over all sampling distributions having third absolute moments. For the uniformly L_3-bounded case in which $s_n^2 = O(n)$, inequality (25.32) establishes convergence at the rate $n^{1/2}$.

Another famous set of results on rates of convergence goes under the name of the *law of the iterated logarithm* (LIL). These results yield error bounds for the strong law of large numbers although they tell us something important about the rate of weak convergence as well. The best known is the following.

25.8 Hartman-Wintner theorem If $\{X_t\}$ is i.i.d. with mean μ and variance σ^2, then

$$\limsup_{n\to\infty} \frac{\sum_{t=1}^n X_t - \mu}{\sigma(2n \log\log n)^{1/2}} = 1 \text{ a.s.} \quad \square \tag{25.33}$$

Notice the extraordinary delicacy of this result, being an equality. It is equivalent to the condition that, for any $\varepsilon > 0$, both

$$P\left(\frac{\sum_{t=1}^n X_t - \mu}{\sigma(2n \log\log n)^{1/2}} \geq 1 + \varepsilon, \text{ i.o.}\right) = 0, \tag{25.34}$$

and

$$P\left(\frac{\sum_{t=1}^n X_t - \mu}{\sigma(2n \log\log n)^{1/2}} \geq 1 - \varepsilon, \text{ i.o.}\right) = 1. \tag{25.35}$$

In words, infinitely many of these sequence coordinates will come arbitrarily close to 1, but no more than a finite number will exceed it, almost surely. By symmetry, there is a similar a.s. bound of -1 on the liminf of the sequence.

Under these assumptions, $n^{-1/2}\sum_{t=1}^n (X_t - \mu)/\sigma \xrightarrow{D} N(0,1)$ according to the Lindeberg-Lévy theorem, and so is asymptotically supported on the whole real line. On the other hand, $n^{-1}\sum_{t=1}^n (X_t - \mu)/\sigma \to 0$ a.s. by the law of large numbers. It is clear there is a function of n, lying between 1 and $n^{1/2}$, representing the 'knife-edge' between the degenerate and non-degenerate asymptotic distributions, being the smallest scaling factor which frustrates a.s. convergence on being applied to the sequence of means. The Hartman-Wintner law tells us that the knife-edge is *precisely* $n^{1/2}(2\log\log n)^{-1/2}$.

A feel for the precision involved can be grasped by trying some numbers: $(2\log\log 10^{99})^{1/2} \approx 3.3$! A check with the tabulation of the standard Gaussian probabilities will show that 3.3 is far enough into the tail that the probability of exceeding it is arbitrarily close to zero. What the LIL reveals is that for the scaled partial sums this probability *is* zero for some n not exceeding 10^{99}, although not for yet larger n. Be careful to note how this is true even if the X_t variables have the whole real line as their support.

For nonstationary sequences there is the following version of the LIL.

25.9 Theorem (Chung 1974: th. 7.5.1) Let $\{X_t\}$ be independent and L_3-bounded with variance sequence $\{\sigma_t^2\}$, and let $s_n^2 = \sum_{t=1}^n \sigma_t^2$. Then (25.33) holds if for $\varepsilon > 0$,

$$\sum_{t=1}^n E|X_t|^3 = O(s_n^3/(\log s_n)^{1+\varepsilon}). \ \square$$

Generalizations to martingale differences also exist; see Stout (1974) and Hall and Heyde (1980) *inter alia* for further details.

VI

THE FUNCTIONAL CENTRAL LIMIT THEOREM

26
Weak Convergence in Metric Spaces

26.1 Probability Measures on a Metric Space

In any topological space $\mathbb{S}$, for which open and closed subsets are defined, the Borel field of $\mathbb{S}$ is defined as the smallest σ-field containing the open sets (and hence also the closed sets) of $\mathbb{S}$. In this chapter we are concerned with the properties of measurable spaces $(\mathbb{S},\mathcal{S})$, where $\mathbb{S}$ is a metric space endowed with a metric d, and $\mathcal{S}$ will always be taken to be the Borel field of $\mathbb{S}$.

If a probability measure μ is defined on the elements of $\mathcal{S}$, we obtain a probability space $((\mathbb{S},d),\mathcal{S},\mu)$, and an element $x \in \mathbb{S}$ is referred to as a *random element*. As in the theory of random variables, it is often convenient to specify an underlying probability space $(\Omega,\mathcal{F},P)$ and let $((\mathbb{S},d),\mathcal{S},\mu)$ be a derived space with the property $\mu(A) = P(x^{-1}(A))$ for each $A \in \mathcal{S}$, where

$$x\colon \Omega \mapsto (\mathbb{S},d)$$

is a measurable mapping. We shall often write $\mathbb{S}$ for $(\mathbb{S},d)$ when the choice of metric is understood, but it is important to keep in mind that d matters in this theory, because $\mathcal{S}$ is not invariant to the choice of metric; unless d_1 and d_2 are equivalent metrics, the open sets of $(\mathbb{S},d_1)$ are not the same as those of $(\mathbb{S},d_2)$.

A property of measure spaces that is sometimes useful to assume is *regularity* (yet another usage of an overworked word, not to be confused with regularity of sequences etc.): $(\mathbb{S},\mathcal{S},\mu)$ is called a regular measure space (or μ a regular measure with respect to $(\mathbb{S},\mathcal{S})$) if for each $A \in \mathcal{S}$ and each $\varepsilon > 0$ there exists an open set O_ε and a closed set C_ε such that

$$C_\varepsilon \subseteq A \subseteq O_\varepsilon \tag{26.1}$$

and

$$\mu(O_\varepsilon - C_\varepsilon) < \varepsilon. \tag{26.2}$$

Happily, as the following theorem shows, this condition can be relied upon when $\mathbb{S}$ is a metric space.

26.1 Theorem On a metric space $((\mathbb{S},d),\mathcal{S})$, every measure is regular.

Proof Call a set $A \in \mathcal{S}$ regular if it satisfies (26.1) and (26.2). The first step is to show that any closed set is regular. Let $A_n = \{x\colon d(A,x) < 1/n\}$, $n = 1,2,3,\ldots$ denote a family of open sets. (Think of A with a 'halo' of width $1/n$.) When A is closed we may write $A = \bigcap_{n=1}^{\infty} A_n$, and $A_n \downarrow A$ as $n \to \infty$. By continuity of the measure this means $\mu(A_n - A) \to 0$. For any $\varepsilon > 0$ there therefore exists N such that $\mu(A_N - A) < \varepsilon$. Choosing $O_\varepsilon = A_N$ and $C_\varepsilon = A$ shows that A is regular.

Since $\mathbb{S}$ is both open and closed, it is clearly regular. If a set A is regular, so is its complement, since O_ε^c is closed, C_ε^c is open, $O_\varepsilon^c \subseteq A^c \subseteq C_\varepsilon^c$ and $C_\varepsilon^c - O_\varepsilon^c = O_\varepsilon - C_\varepsilon$. If we can show that the class of regular sets is also closed under count-able unions, we will have shown that every Borel set is regular, which is the required result. Let $A_1, A_2,...$ be regular sets, and define $A = \bigcup_{n=1}^\infty A_n$. Fixing $\varepsilon > 0$, let $O_{n\varepsilon}$ and $C_{n\varepsilon}$ be open and closed sets respectively, satisfying

$$C_{n\varepsilon} \subseteq A_n \subseteq O_{n\varepsilon} \tag{26.3}$$

and

$$\mu(O_{n\varepsilon} - C_{n\varepsilon}) < \varepsilon/2^{n+1}. \tag{26.4}$$

Let $O_\varepsilon = \bigcup_{n=1}^\infty O_{n\varepsilon}$, which is open, and $A \subseteq O_\varepsilon$. Also let $C_\varepsilon = \bigcup_{n=1}^\infty C_{n\varepsilon}$, where the latter set is not necessarily closed, but $C_\varepsilon^k = \bigcup_{n=1}^k C_{n\varepsilon}$ where k is finite *is* closed, and $C_\varepsilon^k \subseteq A$; and since $C_\varepsilon^k \uparrow C_\varepsilon$, continuity of the measure implies that k can be chosen large enough that $\mu(C_\varepsilon - C_\varepsilon^k) < \varepsilon/2$. For such a k,

$$\begin{aligned}\mu(O_\varepsilon - C_\varepsilon^k) &\le \mu(O_\varepsilon - C_\varepsilon) + \mu(C_\varepsilon - C_\varepsilon^k)\\ &\le \sum_{n=1}^\infty \mu(O_{n\varepsilon} - C_{n\varepsilon}) + \mu(C_\varepsilon - C_\varepsilon^k) < \varepsilon.\end{aligned} \tag{26.5}$$

It follows that A is regular, and this completes the proof. ∎

Often the theory of random variables has a straightforward generalization to the case of random elements. Consider the properties of mappings, for example. If $(\mathbb{S},d)$ and $(\mathbb{T},\rho)$ are metric spaces with Borel fields $\mathcal{S}$ and $\mathcal{T}$, and $f: \mathbb{S} \mapsto \mathbb{T}$ is a function, there is a natural extension of **3.32**(i), as follows.

26.2 Theorem If f is continuous, it is Borel-measurable.

Proof Direct froms **5.19** and **3.22**, and the fact that $\mathcal{S}$ and $\mathcal{T}$ contain the open sets of $\mathbb{S}$ and $\mathbb{T}$ respectively. ∎

Let $((\mathbb{S},d),\mathcal{S})$ and $((\mathbb{T},\rho),\mathcal{T})$ be two measurable spaces, and let $h: \mathbb{S} \mapsto \mathbb{T}$ define a measurable mapping, such that $A \in \mathcal{T}$ implies that $h^{-1}(A) \in \mathcal{S}$; then each measure μ on $\mathbb{S}$ has the property that μh^{-1}, defined by

$$\mu h^{-1}(A) = \mu(h^{-1}(A)),\ A \in \mathcal{T}, \tag{26.6}$$

is a measure on $((\mathbb{T},\rho),\mathcal{T})$. This is just an application of **3.21**, which does not use topological properties of the spaces and deals solely with the set mappings involved.

However, the theory also presents some novel difficulties. A fundamental one concerns measurability. It is not always possible to assign probabilities to the Borel sets of a metric space—not, at least, without violating the axiom of choice.

26.3 Example Consider the space $(D_{[0,1]},d_U)$, the case of **5.27** with $a = 0$ and $b = 1$. Recall that each of the random elements f_θ specified by (5.43) are at a mutual distance of 1 from one another. Hence, the spheres $B(f_\theta,\frac{1}{2})$ are all disjoint, and any union of them is an open set (**5.4**). This means that the Borel field $\mathcal{D}_{[0,1]}$ on $(D_{[0,1]},d_U)$ contains all of these sets. Suppose we attempt to construct a probability space on $((D_{[0,1]},d_U),\ \mathcal{D}_{[0,1]})$ which assigns a uniform distribution to the f_θ, such that $\mu(\{f_\theta\colon a < \theta \le b\}) = b-a$ for $0 \le a < b \le 1$. Superficially this appears to be a perfectly reasonable project. The problem is formally identical to that of constructing the uniform distribution on [0,1]. But there is one crucial difference: here, sets of f_θ functions corresponding to *every* subset of the interval are elements of $\mathcal{D}_{[0,1]}$. We know that there are subsets of [0,1] that are not Lebesgue-measurable unless the axiom of choice is violated; see **3.17**. Hence, there is no consistent way of constructing the probability space $((D_{[0,1]},d_U),\mathcal{D}_{[0,1]},\mu)$, where μ assigns the uniform measure to sets of f_θ elements. This is merely a simple case, but any other scheme for assigning probabilities to these events would founder in a similar way. □

There is no reason why we should not assign probabilities consistently to smaller σ-fields which exclude such odd cases, and in the case of $(D_{[0,1]},d_U)$ the so-called *projection σ-field* will serve this purpose (see §28.1 below for details). The point is that with spaces like this we have to move beyond the familiar intuitions of the random variable case to avoid contradictions.

The space $(D_{[0,1]},d_U)$ is of course nonseparable, and nonseparability is the source of the difficulty encountered in the last example. The characteristic of a separable metric space which matters most in the present theory is the following.

26.4 Theorem In a separable metric space, there exists a countable collection $\mathcal{V}$ of open spheres, such that $\sigma(\mathcal{V})$ is the Borel field.

Proof This is direct from **5.6**, $\mathcal{V}$ being any collection of spheres $S(x,r)$ where x ranges over a countable dense subset of $\mathbb{S}$ and r over the positive rationals. ■

The possible failure of the extension of a p.m. to $(\mathbb{S},\mathcal{S})$ is avoided when there is a countable set which functions as a determining class for the space. Measurability difficulties on $\mathbb{R}$ were avoided in Chapter 3 by sticking to the Borel sets (which are generated from countable collections of intervals, you may recall) and this dictum extends to other metric spaces so long as they are separable.

Another situation where separability is a useful property is the construction of product spaces. In §3.4 some aspects of measures on product spaces were discussed, but we can now extend the theory in the light of the additional structure contributed by the product topology. Let $(\mathbb{S},\mathcal{S})$ and $(\mathbb{T},\mathcal{T})$ be a pair of measurable topological spaces, with $\mathcal{S}$ and $\mathcal{T}$ the respective Borel fields. If $\mathcal{R}$ denotes the set of open rectangles of $\mathbb{S}\times\mathbb{T}$, and $\mathcal{S}\otimes\mathcal{T} = \sigma(\mathcal{R})$, we have the following result.

26.5 Theorem If $\mathbb{S}$ and $\mathbb{T}$ are separable spaces, $\mathcal{S}\otimes\mathcal{T}$ is the Borel field of $\mathbb{S}\times\mathbb{T}$ with the product topology.

Proof Under the product topology, $\mathcal{R}$ is a base for the open sets (see §6.5). Since $\mathbb{S}\times\mathbb{T}$ is separable by **6.16**, any open set of $\mathbb{S}\times\mathbb{T}$ can be generated as a countable union of $\mathcal{R}$-sets. It follows that any σ-field containing $\mathcal{R}$ also contains the open sets of $\mathbb{S}\times\mathbb{T}$, and in particular, $\mathcal{S}\otimes\mathcal{T}$ contains the Borel field. Since the sets of $\mathcal{R}$ are open, it is also true that any σ-field containing the open sets of $\mathbb{S}\times\mathbb{T}$ also contains $\mathcal{R}$, and it follows likewise that the Borel field contains $\mathcal{S}\otimes\mathcal{T}$. ■

If either $\mathbb{S}$ or $\mathbb{T}$ are nonseparable, the last result does not generally hold. A counter-example is easily exhibited.

26.6 Example Consider the space $(D_{[0,1]}\times D_{[0,1]},\, \rho_U)$, where ρ_U is the max metric defined by (6.13) with d_U for each of the component metrics. Let E denote the union of the open balls $B((x_\theta,y_\theta),\frac{1}{2})$ over $\theta \in [0,1]$, where x_θ and y_θ are functions of the form f_θ in (5.43). In this metric the sets $B((x_\theta,y_\theta),\frac{1}{2})$ are mutually disjoint rectangles, of which E is the uncountable union; if $\mathcal{R}$ denotes the open rectangles of $(D_{[0,1]}\times D_{[0,1]},\, \rho_U)$, $E \notin \sigma(\mathcal{R})$, even though E is in the Borel field of $D_{[0,1]}\times D_{[0,1]}$, being an open set. □

The importance of this last result is shown by the following case. Given a probability space $(\Omega,\mathcal{F},P)$, let x and y be random elements of derived probability spaces $((\mathbb{S},d),\mathcal{S},\mu_x)$ and $((\mathbb{S},d),\mathcal{S},\mu_y)$. Implicitly, the pair (x,y) can always be thought of as a random element of a product space of which the μ_x and μ_y are the marginal measures. Since x and y are points in the same metric space, for given $\omega \in \Omega$ a distance $d(x(\omega),y(\omega))$ is a well-defined non-negative real number. The question of obvious interest is whether d is also a measurable function on $(\Omega,\mathcal{F})$. This we can answer as follows.

26.7 Theorem If $(\mathbb{S},d)$ is a separable space, $d(x,y)$ is a random variable.

Proof The inverse image of a rectangle $A\times B$ under the mapping

$$(x,y)\colon \Omega \mapsto \mathbb{S}\times\mathbb{S}$$

lies in $\mathcal{F}$, being the intersection of the $\mathcal{F}$-sets $x^{-1}(A)$ and $y^{-1}(B)$. The mapping is therefore $\mathcal{F}/\mathcal{S}\otimes\mathcal{S}$-measurable by **3.22.** But under separability, $\mathcal{S}\otimes\mathcal{S}$ is the Borel field of $\mathbb{S}\times\mathbb{S}$ according to **26.5**. Hence $(x,y)(\omega) = (x(\omega),y(\omega))$ is a $\mathcal{F}$/Borel-measurable random element of $\mathbb{S}\times\mathbb{S}$. If the space $\mathbb{S}\times\mathbb{S}$ is endowed with the product topology, the function

$$d\colon \mathbb{S}\times\mathbb{S} \mapsto \mathbb{R}^+$$

is continuous by construction, and this mapping is also Borel-measurable. The composite mapping

$$(x,y)\circ d\colon \Omega \mapsto \mathbb{R}$$

is therefore $\mathcal{F}/\mathcal{B}$-measurable, and the theorem follows. ■

26.2 Measures and Expectations

As well as taking care to avoid measurability problems, we must learn to do without various analytical tools which proved fundamental in the study of random variables, in particular the c.d.f. and ch.f. as representations of the distribution. These handy constructions are available only for r.v.s. However, if $U_{\mathbb{S}}$ is the set of bounded, uniformly continuous real functions $f\colon \mathbb{S} \mapsto \mathbb{R}$, the expectations

$$E(f) = \int_{\mathbb{S}} f d\mu, \quad f \in U_{\mathbb{S}} \tag{26.7}$$

are always well defined. (From now on, the domain of integration will be understood to be $\mathbb{S}$ unless otherwise specified.)

The theory makes use of this family of expectations to fingerprint a distribution uniquely, a device that works regardless of the nature of the underlying space. While there is no single all-purpose function that will do this job, like $e^{i\lambda X}$ in the case $X \in \mathbb{R}$, the expectations in (26.7) play a role in this theory analogous to that of the ch.f. in the earlier theory.

As a preliminary, we give here a pair of lemmas which establish the unique represention of a measure on $(\mathbb{S},\mathcal{S})$ in terms of expectations of real functions on $\mathbb{S}$. The first establishes the uniqueness of the representation by integrals.

26.8 Lemma If μ and ν are measures on $((\mathbb{S},d),\mathcal{S})$ ($\mathcal{S}$ the Borel field), and

$$\int f d\mu = \int f d\nu, \text{ all } f \in U_{\mathbb{S}}, \tag{26.8}$$

then $\mu = \nu$.

Proof We show that $U_{\mathbb{S}}$ contains an element for which (26.8) directly yields the conclusion. Let $B \in \mathcal{S}$ be closed, and define $B_n = \{x: d(x,B) < 1/n\}$. Think of B_n as B with an open halo of width $1/n$. $B_n \downarrow B$ as $n \to \infty$, B and B_n^c are closed and mutually disjoint, and $\inf_{x\in B_n^c, y\in B} d(x,y) \geq 1/n$ for each n. Let $g_{B_n^c,B} \in U_{\mathbb{S}}$ be a separating function such that $g_{B_n^c,B}(x) = 0$ for $x \in B_n^c$ and 1 for $x \in B$ (see **6.13**). Then

$$\mu(B) \leq \int g_{B_n^c,B} d\mu = \int g_{B_n^c,B} d\nu = \int_{B_n} g_{B_n^c,B} d\nu \leq \nu(B_n), \tag{26.9}$$

where the last inequality is because $g_{B_n^c,B}(x) \leq 1$. Letting $n \to \infty$, we have $\mu(B) \leq \nu(B)$. But μ and ν can be interchanged, so $\mu(B) = \nu(B)$. This holds for all closed sets, which form a determining class for the space, so the theorem follows. ■

Since $U_{\mathbb{S}} \subseteq C_{\mathbb{S}}$, the set of all continuous functions on $\mathbb{S}$, this result remains true if we substitute $C_{\mathbb{S}}$ for $U_{\mathbb{S}}$; the point is that $U_{\mathbb{S}}$ is the *smallest* class of general functions for which it holds, by virtue of the fact that it contains the required separating function for each closed set.

The second result, although intuitively very plausible, is considerably deeper. Given a p.m. μ on a space $\mathbb{S}$, define $\Lambda(f) = \int f d\mu$ for $f \in U_{\mathbb{S}}$. We know that Λ is a functional on $U_{\mathbb{S}}$ with the following properties:

$$f(x) \geq 0, \text{ all } x \in \mathbb{S} \;\Rightarrow\; \Lambda(f) \geq 0 \tag{26.10}$$

$$f(x) = 1, \text{ all } x \in \mathbb{S} \;\Rightarrow\; \Lambda(f) = 1 \tag{26.11}$$

$$\Lambda(af_1 + bf_2) = a\Lambda(f_1) + b\Lambda(f_2), \; f_1, f_2 \in U, \; a,b \in \mathbb{R}, \tag{26.12}$$

where (26.11) holds since $\int d\mu = 1$, and (26.12) is the linearity property of integrals. The following lemma states that on compact spaces the implication also runs the other way.

26.9 Lemma Let $\mathbb{S}$ be a compact metric space, and let $\Lambda(f): U_{\mathbb{S}} \to \mathbb{R}$ define a functional satisfying (26.10)–(26.12). There exists a unique p.m. μ on $(\mathbb{S},\mathcal{S})$ satisfying $\int f d\mu = \Lambda(f)$, each $f \in U_{\mathbb{S}}$. □

In other words, functionals Λ and measures μ are uniquely paired. At a later stage we use this result to establish the existence of a measure (the limit of a sequence) by exhibiting the corresponding Λ functional. We shall not attempt to give a proof of this result here; see Parthasarathy (1967: ch. 2.5) for the details. Note that because $\mathbb{S}$ is compact, $U_{\mathbb{S}}$ and $C_{\mathbb{S}}$ coincide here; see **5.21**.

26.3 Weak Convergence

Consider $\mathbb{M}$, the set of all probability measures on $((\mathbb{S},d),\mathcal{S})$. As a matter of fact, we can extend our results to cover the set of all finite measures, and there are a couple of cases in the sequel where we shall want to apply the results of this chapter to measures μ where $\int d\mu \neq 1$. However, the modifications required for the extension are trivial. It is helpful in the proofs to have an agreed normalization, and $\int d\mu = 1$ is as good as any, so let $\mathbb{M}$ be the p.m.s, while keeping the possibility of generalization in mind.

Weak convergence concerns the properties of sequences in $\mathbb{M}$, and it is mathematically convenient to approach this problem by treating $\mathbb{M}$ as a topological space. The natural means of doing this is to define a collection of real-valued functions on $\mathbb{M}$, and adopt the weak topology that they induce. And in view of (26.7), a natural class to consider are the integrals of bounded, continuous real-valued functions with respect to the elements of $\mathbb{M}$.

For a point $\mu \in \mathbb{M}$, define the base sets

$$V_\mu(k,f_1,\dots,f_k,\varepsilon) = \left\{\nu\colon \nu \in \mathbb{M},\ \left|\int f_i d\nu - \int f_i d\mu\right| < \varepsilon,\ i = 1,\dots,k\right\}, \tag{26.13}$$

where $f_i \in U_{\mathbb{S}}$ for each i, and $\varepsilon > 0$. By ranging over all the possible $f_1,\dots,f_k$ and ε, for each $k \in \mathbb{N}$, (26.13) defines a collection of open neighbourhoods of μ. The base collection $V_\mu(k,f_1,\dots,f_k,\varepsilon)$, $\mu \in \mathbb{M}$, defines the weak topology on $\mathbb{M}$.

The idea is that two measures are close to one another when the expectations of various elements of $U_{\mathbb{S}}$ are close to one another. The more functions this applies to, and the closer they are, the closer are the measures. This is not the consequence of some more fundamental notion of closeness, but is the defining property itself. This simple yet remarkable application illustrates the power of the topological ideas developed in Chapter 6. The weak topology is the basic trick which allows distributions on general metric spaces to be handled by a single theory.

Given a concept of closeness, we have immediately a companion concept of convergence. A sequence of measures $\{\mu_n, n \in \mathbb{N}\}$ is said to converge in the weak topology, or *converge weakly*, to a limit μ, written $\mu_n \Rightarrow \mu$, if, for every neighbourhood V_μ, $\exists\, N$ such that $\mu_n \in V_\mu$ for all $n \geq N$. If x_n is a random element from a probability space $(\mathbb{S},\mathcal{S},\mu_n)$, and $\mu_n \Rightarrow \mu$, we shall say that x_n converges in distribution to x and write $x_n \xrightarrow{D} x$, where x is a random element from $(\mathbb{S},\mathcal{S},\mu)$. Essentially, the same caveats noted in §22.1 apply in the use of this terminology.

The following theorem shows that there are several ways to characterize weak convergence.

26.10 Theorem The following conditions are equivalent to one another:

(a) $\mu_n \Rightarrow \mu$.

(b) $\int f d\mu_n \to \int f d\mu$ for every $f \in U_{\mathbb{S}}$.

(c) $\limsup_n \mu_n(C) \le \mu(C)$ for every closed set $C \in \mathcal{S}$.

(d) $\liminf_n \mu_n(B) \ge \mu(B)$ for every open set $B \in \mathcal{S}$.

(e) $\lim_n \mu_n(A) = \mu(A)$ for every $A \in \mathcal{S}$ for which $\mu(\partial A) = 0$. □

The equivalence of (a) and (b), and of (a) and (e), were proved for the case of measures on the line as **22.8** and **22.1** respectively; in that case weak convergence was identified with the convergence of the sequence of c.d.f.s, but this characterization has no counterpart here. A noteworthy consequence of the theorem is the fact that the sets (26.13) are not the only way to generate the topology of weak convergence. The alternative corresponding to part (e) of the theorem, for example, is the system of neighbourhoods,

$$V'_\mu(k, A_1, \dots, A_k, \varepsilon) = \left\{ \nu \colon \nu \in \mathbb{M}, \ \left| \nu(A_i) - \mu(A_i) \right| < \varepsilon, \ i = 1, \dots, k \right\}, \tag{26.14}$$

where $A_i \in \mathcal{S}$, $i = 1, \dots, k$ and $\mu(\partial A_i) = 0$.

Proof of 26.10 This theorem is proved by showing the circular set of implications, (a) ⇒ (b) ⇒ (c) ⇒ (c),(d) ⇒ (e) ⇒ (a). The first is by definition. To show that (b) ⇒ (c), we can use the device of **26.8**; let B be any closed set in $\mathcal{S}$, and put $B_m = \{x \colon d(x,B) < 1/m\}$, so that B and B_m^c are closed and $\inf_{x \in B_m^c, y \in B} d(x,y) \ge 1/m$. Letting $g_{B_m^c, B} \in U_{\mathbb{S}}$ be the separating function defined above (26.9), we have

$$\limsup_{n\to\infty} \mu_n(B) \le \limsup_{n\to\infty} \int g_{B_m^c, B} d\mu_n = \int g_{B_m^c, B} d\mu = \int_{B_m} g_{B_m^c, B} d\mu \le \mu(B_m), \tag{26.15}$$

where the first equality is by (b). (c) now follows on letting $m \to \infty$.

(c) ⇒ (d) is immediate since every closed set is the complement of an open set relative to $\mathbb{S}$, and $\mu(\mathbb{S}) = 1$.

To show (c) and (d) ⇒ (e): for any $A \in \mathcal{S}$, $A^o \subseteq A \subseteq \bar{A}$, where A^o is open and $\bar{A}$ is closed, and $\partial A = \bar{A} - A^o$. From (c),

$$\limsup_{n\to\infty} \mu_n(A) \le \limsup_{n\to\infty} \mu_n(\bar{A}) \le \mu(\bar{A}) = \mu(A), \tag{26.16}$$

and from (d),

$$\liminf_{n\to\infty} \mu_n(A) \ge \liminf_{n\to\infty} \mu_n(A^o) \ge \mu(A^o) = \mu(A), \tag{26.17}$$

hence $\lim_n \mu_n(A) = \mu(A)$.

The one relatively tricky step is to show (e) ⇒ (a). Let $f \in U_{\mathbb{S}}$, and define (what is easily verified to be) a measure, μ^f, on the real line $(\mathbb{R}, \mathcal{B})$ by

$$\mu^f(B) = \mu(\{x\colon f(x) \in B\}),\ B \in \mathcal{B}. \tag{26.18}$$

f is bounded, so there exists an interval (a,b) such that $a < f(x) < b$, all $x \in \mathbb{S}$. Recall that a distribution on $(\mathbb{R},\mathcal{B})$ has at most a countable number of atoms. Also, a finite interval can be divided into a finite collection of disjoint subintervals of width not exceeding ε, for any $\varepsilon > 0$. Therefore it is possible to choose m points t_j, with $a = t_0 < t_1 < \ldots < t_m = b$, such that $t_j - t_{j-1} < \varepsilon$, and $\mu^f(\{t_j\}) = 0$, for each j. Use these to construct a simple r.v.

$$g_m(x) = \sum_{j=1}^{m} t_{j-1}1_{A_j}(x), \tag{26.19}$$

where $A_j = \{x\colon t_{j-1} \le f(x) \le t_j\}$, and note that $\sup_x|f(x) - g_m(x)| < \varepsilon$. Thus,

$$\left|\int fd\mu_n - \int fd\mu\right| \le \int|f - g_m|d\mu_n + \int|f - g_m|d\mu + \left|\int g_m d\mu_n - \int g_m d\mu\right|$$

$$\le 2\varepsilon + \sum_{j=1}^{m}|t_{j-1}||\mu_n(A_j) - \mu(A_j)|. \tag{26.20}$$

Since $\mu(\partial A_j) = 0$ by the choice of t_j, so that $\lim_n\mu_n(A_j) = \mu(A_j)$, for each j by (e),

$$\limsup_{n\to\infty}\left|\int fd\mu_n - \int fd\mu\right| \le 2\varepsilon. \tag{26.21}$$

Since ε can be chosen arbitrarily small, (a) follows and the proof is complete. ∎

A *convergence-determining class* for $(\mathbb{S},\mathcal{S})$ is a class of sets $\mathcal{U} \subseteq \mathcal{S}$ which satisfy the following condition: if $\mu_n(A) \to \mu(A)$ for every $A \in \mathcal{U}$ with $\mu(\partial A) = 0$, then $\mu_n \Rightarrow \mu$. This notion may be helpful for establishing weak convergence in cases where the conditions of **26.10** are difficult to show directly. The following theorem is just such an example.

26.11 Theorem If $\mathcal{U}$ is a class of sets which is closed under finite intersections, and such that every open set is a finite or countable union of $\mathcal{U}$-sets, then $\mathcal{U}$ is convergence-determining.

Proof We first show that the measures μ_n converge for a finite union of $\mathcal{U}$-sets $A_1,\ldots,A_m$. Applying the inclusion-exclusion formula (3.4),

$$\mu_n\left(\bigcup_{j=1}^{m}A_j\right) = \sum_{k=1}^{2^m-1}\pm\mu_n(C_k), \tag{26.22}$$

where the sets C_k consist of the A_j and all their mutual intersections and hence are in $\mathcal{U}$ whenever the A_j are, and '±' indicates that the sign of the term is given in accordance with (3.4). By hypothesis, therefore,

$$\mu_n\left(\bigcup_{j=1}^{m}A_j\right) \to \mu\left(\bigcup_{j=1}^{m}A_j\right). \tag{26.23}$$

To extend this result to a countable union $B = \bigcup_{j=1}^{\infty} A_j$, note that continuity of μ implies $\mu(\bigcup_{j=1}^{m} A_j) \uparrow \mu(B)$ as $m \to \infty$, so for any $\varepsilon > 0$ a finite m may be chosen large enough that $\mu(B) - \mu(\bigcup_{j=1}^{m} A_j) < \varepsilon$. Then

$$\liminf_{n\to\infty} \mu_n(B) \geq \liminf_{n\to\infty} \mu_n\left(\bigcup_{j=1}^{m} A_j\right) = \mu\left(\bigcup_{j=1}^{m} A_j\right) > \mu(B) - \varepsilon. \tag{26.24}$$

Since ε is arbitrary and (26.24) holds for any open $B \in \mathcal{S}$ by hypothesis on $\mathcal{U}$, condition (d) of **26.10** is satisfied. ■

A convergence-determining class must also be a determining class for the space (see §3.2). But caution is necessary since the converse does not hold, as the following counter-example given by Billingsley (1968) shows.

26.12 Example Consider the family of p.m.s $\{\mu_n\}$ on the half-open unit interval $[0,1)$ with μ_n assigning unit measure to the singleton set $\{1 - 1/n\}$. That is, $\mu_n(\{1 - 1/n\}) = 1$. Evidently, $\{\mu_n\}$ does not have a weak limit. The collection $\mathcal{C}$ of half-open intervals $[a,b)$ for $0 < a < b < 1$ generate the Borel field of $[0,1)$, and so are a determining class. But $\mu_n([a,b)) \to 0$ for every fixed $a > 0$ and $b < 1$, and the p.m. μ for which $\mu(\{0\}) = 1$ has the property that $\mu([a,b)) = 0$ for all $a > 0$. It is therefore valid to write

$$\mu_n(A) \to \mu(A), \text{ all } A \in \mathcal{C}, \tag{26.25}$$

even though $\mu_n \not\Rightarrow \mu$ in this case, so $\mathcal{C}$ is not convergence-determining. □

The last topic we need to consider in this section is the preservation of weak convergence under mappings from one metric space to another. Since $\mu_n \Rightarrow \mu$ means $\int f d\mu_n \to \int f d\mu$ for any $f \in U_{\mathbb{S}}$, it is clear, since $f \circ h \in U_{\mathbb{S}}$ when h is continuous, that $\int f(h(x))d\mu_n(x) \to \int f(h(x))d\mu(x)$. Writing y for $h(x)$, we have the result

$$\int f(y)d\mu_n h^{-1}(y) \to \int f(y)d\mu h^{-1}(y). \tag{26.26}$$

So much is direct, and relatively trivial. But what we can also show, and is often much more useful, is that mappings that are 'almost' continuous have the same property. This is the continuous mapping theorem proper, the desired generalization of **22.11**.

26.13 Continuous mapping theorem Let $h: \mathbb{S} \mapsto \mathbb{T}$ be a measurable function, and let $D_h \subseteq \mathbb{S}$ be the set of discontinuity points of h. If $\mu_n \Rightarrow \mu$ and $\mu(D_h) = 0$, then $\mu_n h^{-1} \Rightarrow \mu h^{-1}$.

Proof Let C be a closed subset of $\mathbb{T}$. Recalling that $(A)^-$ denotes the closure of A,

$$\begin{aligned}\limsup_{n\to\infty} \mu_n h^{-1}(C) &= \limsup_{n\to\infty} \mu_n(h^{-1}(C)) \leq \limsup_{n\to\infty} \mu_n((h^{-1}(C))^-) \\ &\leq \mu((h^{-1}(C))^-) \leq \mu(h^{-1}(C) \cup D_h) \\ &\leq \mu(h^{-1}(C)) + \mu(D_h) = \mu(h^{-1}(C)) = \mu h^{-1}(C),\end{aligned} \tag{26.27}$$

noting for the third inequality that $(h^{-1}(C))^- \subseteq h^{-1}(C) \cup D_h$; i.e., a closure point of $h^{-1}(C)$ is either in $h^{-1}(C)$, or is not a continuity point of h. The second inequality is by **26.10**(c), and the conclusion follows similarly. ∎

26.4 Metrizing the Space of Measures

We can now outline the strategy for determining the weak limit of a sequence of measures $\{\mu_n\}$ on $(\mathbb{S},\mathcal{S})$. The problem falls into two parts. One of these is to determine the limits of the sequences $\{\mu_n(A)\}$ for each $A \in \mathscr{C}$, where $\mathscr{C}$ is a determining class for the space. This part of the programme is specific to the particular space under consideration. The other part, which is quite general, is to verify conditions under which the sequence of measures as a whole has a weak limit. Without this reassurance, the convergence of measures of elements of $\mathscr{C}$ is not generally sufficient to ensure that the extensions to $\mathcal{S}$ also converge. It is this second aspect of the problem that we focus on here.

It is sufficient if every sequence of measures on the space is shown to have a cluster point. If a subsequence converges to a limit, this must agree with the unique ordinary limit we have (by assumption) established for the determining class. Our goal is achieved by finding conditions under which the relevant topological space of measures is sequentially compact (see §6.2). This is similar to what Billingsley (1968) calls 'relative' compactness, and the required results can be derived in his framework. However, we shall follow Prokhorov (1956) and Parthasarathy (1967) in making $\mathbb{M}$ a metric space which will under appropriate circumstances be compact. The following theorem shows that this project is feasible; the basic idea is an application of the embedding theorem (**6.20/6.22**).

26.14 Theorem (Parthasarathy 1967: th. II.6.2) If and only if $(\mathbb{S},d)$ is separable, $\mathbb{M}$ can be metrized as a separable space and embedded in $[0,1]^\infty$.

Proof Assume $(\mathbb{S},d)$ is separable. The first task is to show that $U_\mathbb{S}$ is also separable. According to **6.22**, $\mathbb{S}$ can be metrized as a totally bounded space $(\mathbb{S},d')$ where d' is equivalent to d. Let $\bar{\mathbb{S}}$ denote the completion of $\mathbb{S}$ under d' (including the limits of all Cauchy sequences on $\mathbb{S}$) and then $\bar{\mathbb{S}}$ is a compact space (**5.12**). The space of continuous functions $C_{\bar{\mathbb{S}}}$ is accordingly separable under the uniform metric (**5.26**(ii)).

Now, every continuous function on a compact set is also uniformly continuous (**5.21**), so that $U_{\bar{\mathbb{S}}} = C_{\bar{\mathbb{S}}}$. Moreover, the spaces $C_{\bar{\mathbb{S}}}$ and $U_\mathbb{S}$ are isometric (see §5.5) and if the former is separable so is the latter.

Let $\{g_m, m \in \mathbb{N}\}$ be a dense subset of $U_\mathbb{S}$, and define the mapping $T\colon \mathbb{M} \to \mathbb{R}^\infty$ by

$$T(\mu) = \left(\int g_1 d\mu,\ \int g_2 d\mu, \ldots\right). \tag{26.28}$$

The object is to show that T embeds $\mathbb{M}$ in $\mathbb{R}^\infty$. Suppose $T(\mu) = T(\nu)$, so that $\int g_m d\mu = \int g_m d\nu$ for all m. Since $\{g_m\}$ is dense in $U_\mathbb{S}$, $f \in U_\mathbb{S}$ implies that

$$\left|\int f d\mu - \int g_m d\mu\right| \leq \int |f - g_m| d\mu \leq d_U(f, g_m) < \varepsilon \tag{26.29}$$

for some m, and every $\varepsilon > 0$. (The second inequality is because $\int d\mu = 1$, note.) The same inequalities hold for ν, and hence we may say that $\int f d\mu = \int f d\nu$ for all $f \in U_{\mathbb{S}}$. It follows by **26.8** that $\mu = \nu$, so T is 1-1.

Continuity of T follows from the equivalence of (a) and (b) in **26.10**. To show that T^{-1} is continuous, let $\{\mu_n\}$ be a sequence of measures and assume $T(\mu_n) \to T(\mu)$. For $f \in U_{\mathbb{S}}$ and any $m \geq 1$,

$$\left|\int f d\mu_n - \int f d\mu\right| = \left|\int (f - g_m) d\mu_n + \int (g_m - f) d\mu + \int g_m d\mu_n - \int g_m d\mu\right|$$

$$\leq 2d_U(f, g_m) + \left|\int g_m d\mu_n - \int g_m d\mu\right|. \tag{26.30}$$

Since the second term of the majorant side converges to zero by assumption,

$$\text{limsup}_n \left|\int f d\mu_n - \int f d\mu\right| \leq 2d_U(f, g_m) < 2\varepsilon \tag{26.31}$$

for some m, and $\varepsilon > 0$, by the right-hand inequality of (26.29). Hence $\lim_n |\int f d\mu_n - \int f d\mu| = 0$, and $\mu_n \Rightarrow \mu$ by **26.10**(b).

We have therefore shown that $\mathbb{M}$ is homeomorphic with the set $T(\mathbb{M}) \subseteq \mathbb{R}^\infty$, and $\mathbb{R}^\infty$ is homeomorphic to $[0,1]^\infty$ as noted in **5.22**. The distance d_∞ between the images of points of $\mathbb{M}$ under T defines a metric on $\mathbb{M}$ which induces the weak topology. The space $T(\mathbb{M})$ with the product topology is separable (see **6.16**), so applying **6.9**(i) to T^{-1} yields the result that $\mathbb{M}$ is separable. This completes the sufficiency part of the proof.

The necessity part requires a lemma, which will be needed again later on. Let $p_x \in \mathbb{M}$ be the degenerate p.m. with unit mass at x, that is, $p_x(\{x\}) = 1$ and $p_x(\mathbb{S} - \{x\}) = 0$, and so let $D = \{p_x\colon x \in \mathbb{S}\} \subseteq \mathbb{M}$.

26.15 Lemma The topological spaces $\mathbb{S}$ and D are homeomorphic.

Proof The mapping $p\colon \mathbb{S} \mapsto D$ taking points $x \in \mathbb{S}$ to points $p_x \in D$ is clearly 1-1, onto. For $f \in C_{\mathbb{S}}$, $\int f dp_x = f(x)$, and $x_n \to x$ implies $f(x_n) \to f(x)$ and hence $p_{x_n} \Rightarrow p_x$ by **26.10**, establishing continuity of p. Conversely, suppose $x_n \not\to x$. There is then an open set A containing x, such that for every $N \in \mathbb{N}$, $x_n \in \mathbb{S} - A$ for some $n \geq N$. Let f be a separating function such that $f(x) = 0$, $f(y) = 1$ for $y \in \mathbb{S} - A$, and $0 \leq f \leq 1$. Then $\int f dp_{x_n} = 1$ and $\int f dp_x = 0$, so $p_{x_n} \not\Rightarrow p_x$. This establishes continuity of p^{-1}, and p is a homeomorphism, as required. ■

Proof of 26.14, continued Now suppose $\mathbb{M}$ is a separable metric space. It can be embedded in a subset of $[0,1]^\infty$, and the subsets of $\mathbb{M}$ are homeomorphic to their images in $[0,1]^\infty$ under the embedding, which are separable sets, and hence are themselves separable (again, by **6.16** and **6.9**(i)). Since $D \subseteq \mathbb{M}$, D is separable and hence $\mathbb{S}$ must be separable since it is homeomorphic to D by **26.15**. This proves necessity. ■

The last theorem showed that $\mathbb{M}$ is metrizable, but did not exhibit a specific metric on $\mathbb{M}$. Note that different collections of functions $\{g_m\}$ yield different metrics, given how d_∞ is defined. Another approach to the problem is to construct such a metric directly, and one such was proposed by Prokhorov (1956). For a set $A \in \mathcal{S}$, define the open set $A^\delta = \{x: d(x,A) < \delta\}$, that is, '$A$ with a δ-halo'. The *Prokhorov distance* between measures μ, $\nu \in \mathbb{M}$, is

$$L(\mu,\nu) = \inf\{\delta > 0: \mu(A^\delta) + \delta \geq \nu(A), \text{ all } A \in \mathcal{S}\}. \tag{26.32}$$

Since $\mathcal{S}$ contains complements and $\mu(\mathbb{S}) = \nu(\mathbb{S}) = 1$, it must be the case, unless $\mu = \nu$, that $\mu(A) \geq \nu(A)$ for some sets $A \in \mathcal{S}$, and $\mu(A) < \nu(A)$ for others. The idea of the Prokhorov distance is to focus on the latter cases, and see how much has to be added to both the sets *and* their μ-measures, to reverse all the inequalities. When the measures are close this amount should be small, but you might like to convince yourself that both the adjustments are necessary to get the desired properties. As we show below, L is a metric, and hence is symmetric in μ and ν. The properties are most easily appreciated in the case of measures on the real line, in which case the metric has the representation in terms of the c.d.f.s,

$$L^*(F_1,F_2) = \inf\{\delta>0: F_2(x-\delta)-\delta \leq F_1(x) \leq F_2(x+\delta)+\delta,\ \forall x \in \mathbb{R}\}, \tag{26.33}$$

for c.d.f.s F_1 and F_2. This is also known as *Lévy's metric*.

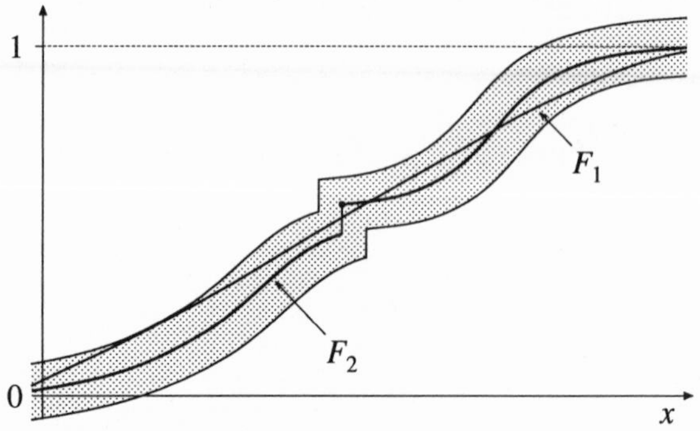

Fig. 26.1

Fig. 26.1 sketches this case, and F_2 has been given a discontinuity, so that the form of the bounding functions $F_2(x+\delta)+\delta$ and $F_2(x-\delta)-\delta$ can be easily discerned. Any c.d.f. lying wholly within the region defined by these extremes, such as the one shown, is within δ of F_2 in the L^* metric.

26.16 Theorem L is a metric.

Proof $L(\mu,\nu) = L(\nu,\mu)$ is not obvious from the definition; but for any $\delta > 0$ consider $B = (A^\delta)^c$. If $x \in A$, then $d(x,y) \geq \delta$ for each $y \in B$, whereas if $x \in B^\delta$, $d(x,y) < \delta$ for some $y \in B$; or in other words, $B^\delta = A^c$. If $L(\mu,\nu) \leq \delta$, then

$$\mu(A^c) + \delta = \mu(B^\delta) + \delta \geq \nu(B). \tag{26.34}$$

Subtracting both sides of (26.34) from 1 gives

$$\mu(A) \leq \nu(B^c) + \delta = \nu(A^\delta) + \delta, \tag{26.35}$$

and hence $L(\nu,\mu) \le \delta$. This means there is no δ for which $L(\mu,\nu) > \delta \ge L(\nu,\mu)$, nor, by symmetry, for which $L(\nu,\mu) > \delta \ge L(\mu,\nu)$, and equality follows.

It is immediate that $L(\mu,\nu) = 0$ if $\mu = \nu$. To show the converse holds, note that if $L(\mu,\nu) = 0$, $\mu(A^{1/n}) + 1/n \ge \nu(A)$ for $A \in \mathcal{S}$, and any $n \in \mathbb{N}$. If A is closed, $A^{1/n} \downarrow A$ as $n \to \infty$. By continuity of μ, $\mu(A) = \lim_n(\mu(A^{1/n}) + 1/n) \ge \nu(A)$, and by symmetry, $\nu(A) = \lim_n(\nu(A^{1/n}) + 1/n) \ge \mu(A)$ likewise. It follows that $\mu(A) = \nu(A)$ for all closed A. Since the closed sets are a determining class, $\mu = \nu$.

Finally, for measures μ, ν, and τ let $L(\mu,\nu) = \delta$ and $L(\nu,\tau) = \eta$. Then for any $A \in \mathcal{S}$,

$$\mu(A) \le \nu(A^\delta) + \delta \le \tau((A^\delta)^\eta) + \delta + \eta \le \tau(A^{\delta+\eta}) + \delta + \eta, \tag{26.36}$$

where the last inequality holds because

$$(A^\delta)^\eta = \{x: d(x,A^\delta) < \eta\} \subseteq \{x: d(x,A) < \delta + \eta)\} = A^{\delta+\eta}, \tag{26.37}$$

the inclusion being valid since d satisfies the triangle inequality. Hence $L(\mu,\tau) \le \delta + \eta = L(\mu,\nu) + L(\nu,\tau)$. ∎

We can also show that L induces the topology of weak convergence.

26.17 Theorem If $\{\mu_n\}$ is a sequence of measures in $\mathbb{M}$, $\mu_n \Rightarrow \mu$ if and only if $L(\mu_n,\mu) \to 0$.

Proof To show 'if', suppose $L(\mu_n,\mu) \to 0$. For each closed set $A \in \mathcal{S}$, $\limsup_n \mu_n(A) \le \mu(A^\delta) + \delta$ for every $\delta > 0$, and hence, letting $\delta \downarrow 0$, $\limsup_n \mu_n(A) \le \mu(A)$ by continuity. Weak convergence follows by (c) of **26.10**. To show 'only if', consider for $A \in \mathcal{S}$ and fixed δ the bounded function

$$f_A(x) = \max\left\{0,\ 1 - \frac{d(x,A)}{\delta}\right\}. \tag{26.38}$$

Note that $f_A(x) = 1$ for $x \in A$, $0 < f_A(x) \le 1$ for $x \in A^\delta$, and $f_A(x) = 0$ for $x \notin A^\delta$. Since

$$|f_A(x) - f_A(y)| \le \frac{|d(x,A) - d(y,A)|}{\delta} \le \frac{d(x,y)}{\delta}, \tag{26.39}$$

independent of A, the family $\{f_A, A \in \mathcal{S}\}$ is uniformly equicontinuous (see §5.5) and so is a subset of $U_{\mathbb{S}}$. If $\mu_n \Rightarrow \mu$, then by **26.10**(b),

$$\Delta_n = \sup_{A \in \mathcal{S}} \left| \int f_A d\mu_n - \int f_A d\mu \right| \to 0. \tag{26.40}$$

Hence, n can be chosen large enough that $\Delta_n \le \delta$, for any $\delta > 0$. For this n or larger,

$$\mu_n(A) \le \int f_A d\mu_n \le \int f_A d\mu + \Delta_n \le \int f_A d\mu + \delta \le \mu(A^\delta) + \delta, \tag{26.41}$$

or, equivalently, $L(\mu_n,\mu) \le \delta$. It follows that $L(\mu_n,\mu) \to 0$. ∎

It is possible to establish the theory of convergence on $\mathbb{M}$ by working explicitly in the metric space $(\mathbb{M},L)$. However, we will follow the approach of Varadarajan (1958), of working in the equivalent space derived in **26.14**. The treatment in this section and the following one draws principally on Parthasarathy (1967). The Prokhorov metric has an application in a different context, in §28.5.

The next theorem leads on from **26.14** by answering the crucial question – when is $\mathbb{M}$ compact?

26.18 Theorem (Parthasarathy 1967: th. II.6.4) $\mathbb{M}$ is compact if and only if $\mathbb{S}$ is compact.

Proof First, let $\mathbb{S}$ be compact, and recall that in this case $C_{\mathbb{S}} = U_{\mathbb{S}}$ (**5.21**), and $C_{\mathbb{S}}$ is separable (**5.26**(ii)). For simplicity of notation write just C for $C_{\mathbb{S}}$, and write 0 for that element of C which takes the value 0 everywhere in $\mathbb{S}$. Let $\bar{S}_C(0,1)$ denote the closed unit sphere around 0 in C, such that $\sup_t|f(t)| \leq 1$ for all $f \in \bar{S}_C(0,1)$, and let $\{g_m,\ m \in \mathbb{N}\}$ be a sequence that is dense in $\bar{S}_C(0,1)$. For this sequence of functions, the map T defined in (26.28) is a homeomorphism taking $\mathbb{M}$ into $T(\mathbb{M})$, a subset of the compact space $[-1,1]^\infty$. This follows by the argument used in **26.14**. It must be shown that $T(\mathbb{M})$ is closed and therefore compact. Let $\{\mu_n\}$ be a sequence of measures in $\mathbb{M}$ such that $T(\mu_n) \to y \in [-1,1]^\infty$. What we have to show to prove sufficiency is that $y \in T(\mathbb{M})$. Since the mapping T^{-1} onto $\mathbb{M}$ is continuous, this would imply (**6.9**(ii)) that $\mathbb{M}$ itself is compact.

Write $\Lambda_n(f) = \int f d\mu_n$, and note that, since $|\int f d\mu_n| \leq \sup_t|f(t)| \leq 1$, this defines a functional

$$\Lambda_n(f)\colon \bar{S}_C(0,1) \mapsto [-1,1]. \tag{26.42}$$

In this notation we have $T(\mu_n) = (\Lambda_n(g_1), \Lambda_n(g_2), \ldots)$. Since $\bar{S}_C(0,1)$ is compact and $\{g_m\}$ is dense in it, we can choose for every $f \in \bar{S}_C(0,1)$ a subsequence $\{g_{m_k},\ k \in \mathbb{N}\}$ converging to f. Then, as in (26.30),

$$|\Lambda_n(f) - \Lambda_{n'}(f)| \leq 2d_U(f,g_{m_k}) + |\Lambda_n(g_{m_k}) - \Lambda_{n'}(g_{m_k})|. \tag{26.43}$$

The second term of the majorant side contains a coordinate of $T(\mu_n) - T(\mu_{n'})$ and converges to 0 as n and $n' \to \infty$ by assumption. Letting $k \to \infty$, we obtain, as in (26.31),

$$\lim_{n,n' \to \infty} |\Lambda_n(f) - \Lambda_{n'}(f)| = 0. \tag{26.44}$$

This says that $\{\Lambda_n\}$ is a Cauchy sequence of real functionals on $[-1,1]$, and so must have a limit Λ; in particular, $y = (\Lambda(g_1), \Lambda(g_2), \ldots)$.

It is easy to verify that each $\Lambda_n(f)$, and hence also $\Lambda(f)$, satisfy conditions (26.10)–(26.12) for $f \in \bar{S}_C(0,1)$. Since for every $f \in C$ there is a constant $c > 0$ such that $cf \in \bar{S}_C(0,1)$, we may further say, by (26.12), that $\Lambda(f) = c\Lambda^*(f/c)$ where $\Lambda^*(.)$ is a functional on C which must also satisfy (26.10)-(26.12). From **26.9**, there exists a unique $\mu \in \mathbb{M}$ such that $\Lambda^*(f) = \int f d\mu$, $f \in C$. Hence, we may write $y = T(\mu)$. It follows that $T(\mathbb{M})$ contains its limit points, and being also bounded is compact; and since T^{-1} is a homeomorphism, $\mathbb{M}$ is also compact. This completes the proof of sufficiency.

To prove necessity, consider $D = \{p_x: x \in \mathbb{S}\} \subseteq \mathbb{M}$, the set shown to be homeomorphic to $\mathbb{S}$ in **26.15**. If D is compact, then so is $\mathbb{S}$. D is totally bounded when $\mathbb{M}$ is compact, so by **5.12** it suffices to show completeness. Every sequence in D is the image of a sequence $\{x_n \in \mathbb{S}\}$, and can be written as $\{p_{x_n}\}$, so suppose $p_{x_n} \Rightarrow q \in \mathbb{M}$. If $x_n \to x \in \mathbb{S}$, then $q = p_x \in D$ by **26.15**, so it suffices to show that $x_n \not\to x$ is impossible.

The possibility that $\{x_n\}$ has two or more distinct cluster points in $\mathbb{S}$ is ruled out by the assumption $p_{x_n} \Rightarrow q$, so $x_n \not\to x$ means that the sequence has no cluster points in $\mathbb{S}$. We assume this, and obtain a contradiction. Let $E = \{x_1, x_2, \ldots\} \subseteq \mathbb{S}$ be the set of the sequence coordinates, and let E_1 be any infinite subset of E. If the sequence has no cluster points, every point $y \in E_1$ is isolated, in that $E_1 \cap S(y,\varepsilon) - \{y\}$ is empty for some $\varepsilon > 0$. Otherwise, there would have to exist a sequence $\{y_n \in E_1\}$ such that $y_n \in S(y, 1/n)$ for every n, and y would be a cluster point of $\{x_n\}$ contrary to assumption. A set containing only isolated points is closed, so E_1 is closed and, by **26.10**(c),

$$q(E_1) \geq \limsup_{n\to\infty} p_{x_n}(E_1) = 1, \tag{26.45}$$

where the equality must obtain since E_1 contains x_n for *some* $n \geq N$, for every $N \in \mathbb{N}$. Since $q \in \mathbb{M}$, this has to mean $q(E_1) = 1$. But clearly we can choose another subset from E, say E_2, such that E_1 and E_2 are disjoint, and the same logic would give $q(E_2) = 1$. This is impossible. The contradiction is shown, concluding the proof. ■

26.5 Tightness and Convergence

In §22.5 we met the idea of a tight probability measure, as one whose mass is concentrated on a compact subset of the sample space. Formally, a measure μ on a space $(\mathbb{S},\mathcal{S})$ is said to be tight if, for every $\varepsilon > 0$, there exists a compact set $K_\varepsilon \in \mathcal{S}$ such that $\mu(K_\varepsilon^c) \leq \varepsilon$. Let $\Pi \subseteq \mathbb{M}$ denote any family of measures. The family Π is said to be *uniformly tight* if $\sup_{\mu\in\Pi}\mu(K_\varepsilon^c) \leq \varepsilon$.

Tightness is a property of general measures, although we shall concentrate here on the case of p.m.s. In the applications below, Π typically represents the sequence of p.m.s associated with a stochastic sequence $\{X_n\}_1^\infty$. If a p.m. μ is tight, then of course $\mu(K_\varepsilon) > 1 - \varepsilon$ for compact K_ε. In §22.5 uniform tightness of a sequence of p.m.s on the line was shown to be a necessary condition for weak convergence of the sequence, and here we shall obtain the same result for any metric space that is separable and complete. The first result needed is the following.

26.19 Theorem (Parthasarathy 1967: th. II.3.2) When $\mathbb{S}$ is separable and complete, every p.m. on the space is tight. □

Notice, this proves the earlier assertion that every measure on $(\mathbb{R},\mathcal{B})$ is tight, given that $\mathbb{R}$ is a separable, complete space. Another lemma is needed for the proof, and also subsequently.

26.20 Lemma Let $\mathbb{S}$ be a complete space, and let

$$K = \bigcap_{n=1}^{\infty}\left(\bigcup_{i=1}^{j_n}\bar{S}_{ni}\right), \tag{26.46}$$

where S_{ni} is a sphere of radius $1/n$ in $\mathbb{S}$, $\bar{S}_{ni}$ is its closure, and j_n is a finite integer for each n. Then K is compact.

Proof Being covered by a finite collection of the $\bar{S}_{ni}$ for each n, K is totally bounded. If $\{x_j, j \in \mathbb{N}\}$ is a Cauchy sequence in K, completeness of $\mathbb{S}$ implies that $x_j \to x \in \mathbb{S}$. For each n, since $K \subseteq \bigcup_{i=1}^{j_n}\bar{S}_{ni}$, infinitely many of the sequence coordinates must lie in $K_n = K \cap \bar{S}_{nk}$ for *some* k, $1 \le k \le j_n$. Since $\bar{S}_{nk}$ has radius $1/n$, taking n to the limit leads to the conclusion that $\bigcap_n K_n = \{x\}$, and hence $x \in K$; K is therefore complete, and the lemma follows by **5.12**. ■

Proof of 26.19 By separability, a covering of $\mathbb{S}$ by $1/n$-balls $S_n = S(x, 1/n)$, $x \in \mathbb{S}$, has a countable subcover, say $\{S_{ni}\ i \in \mathbb{N}\}$, for each $n = 1,2,\ldots$. Fix n. For any $\varepsilon > 0$ there must exist j_n large enough that $\mu(A_n) \ge 1 - \varepsilon/2^n$, where $A_n = \bigcup_{i=1}^{j_n}S_{ni}$; otherwise we would have $\mu(\bigcup_{i=1}^{\infty}S_{ni}) = \mu(\mathbb{S}) < 1 - \varepsilon/2^n$, which is a contradiction since μ is a p.m.

Given ε, choose A_n in this manner for each n and let $K_\varepsilon = \bigcap_{n=1}^{\infty}\bar{A}_n$ where $\bar{A}_n = \bigcup_{i=1}^{j_n}\bar{S}_{ni}$, note. Then K_ε is compact by **26.20**. Further, since

$$K_\varepsilon^c = \left(\bigcap_{n=1}^{\infty}\bar{A}_n\right)^c = \bigcup_{n=1}^{\infty}(\bar{A}_n)^c, \tag{26.47}$$

and noting that $\mu((\bar{A}_n)^c) = 1 - \mu(\bar{A}_n) \le 1 - \mu(A_n) \le \varepsilon/2^n$, we have

$$\mu(K_\varepsilon^c) \le \sum_{n=1}^{\infty}\mu((\bar{A}_n)^c) \le \varepsilon\sum_{n=1}^{\infty}1/2^n = \varepsilon, \tag{26.48}$$

or, in other words, $\mu(K_\varepsilon) > 1 - \varepsilon$. ■

Before moving on, note that the promised proof of **12.6** can be obtained as a corollary of **26.19**.

26.21 Corollary Let $(\mathbb{S},\mathcal{S},\mu)$ be a separable complete probability space. For any $E \in \mathcal{S}$, there is for any $\varepsilon > 0$ a compact subset K of E such that $\mu(E - K) < \varepsilon$.

Proof Let the compact set $\Delta \in \mathcal{S}$ satisfy $\mu(\Delta) > 1 - \varepsilon/2$, as is possible by **26.19**, and let $(\Delta,\mathcal{S}_\Delta,\mu_\Delta)$ denote the trace of $(\mathbb{S},\mathcal{S},\mu)$ on Δ. This is a compact space, such that every set in $\mathcal{S}_\Delta$ is totally bounded. By regularity of the measure (**26.1**) there exists for any $A \in \mathcal{S}_\Delta$ an open set $A' \supseteq A$ such that $\mu_\Delta(A' - A) < \varepsilon/2$. Moving to the complements, A'^c is a closed, and hence compact, set contained in A^c. But $A^c - A'^c = A' - A$, and $\mu(A^c - A'^c) = \mu_\Delta(A^c - A'^c)\mu(\Delta) < \varepsilon/2$.

Now for any set $E \in \mathcal{S}$ let $A = (E \cap \Delta)^c$, and let $K = A'^c$, and this argument shows that there is a compact subset K of $E \cap \Delta$ (and hence of E) such that $\mu((E \cap \Delta) - K) < \varepsilon/2$. Since $\mu(E \cap \Delta^c) \le \mu(\Delta^c) \le \varepsilon/2$, $\mu(E - K) < \varepsilon$, as required. ■

Lemma **12.6** follows from this result on noting that $\mathbb{R}^k$ is a separable complete space.

Theorem **26.19** tells us that on a separable complete space, every measure μ_n of a sequence is tight. It remains to be established whether the same property applies to the weak limit of any such sequence. Here the reader should review examples **22.19** and **22.20** to appreciate how this need not be the case. The next theorem is a partial parallel of **22.22**, although the latter result goes further in giving sufficient conditions for a weak limit to exist. Here we merely establish the possibility of weak convergence, via an application of theorems **5.10** and **5.11**, by showing the link between uniform tightness and compactness.

26.22 Theorem (Parthasarathy 1967: th. II.6.7) Let $(\mathbb{S},d)$ be a separable complete space, and let $\Pi \subseteq \mathbb{M}$ be a family of p.m.s on $(\mathbb{S},\mathcal{S})$. Π is compact if and only if it is uniformly tight.

Proof Since $(\mathbb{S},d)$ is separable, it is homeomorphic to a subset of $[0,1]^\infty$, by **6.22**. Accordingly, there exists a metric d' equivalent to d such that $(\mathbb{S},d')$ is relatively compact. In this metric, let $\hat{\mathbb{S}}$ be a compact space containing $\mathbb{S}$ and let $\hat{\mathcal{S}}$ be the Borel field on $\hat{\mathbb{S}}$. We cannot assume that $\mathbb{S} \in \hat{\mathcal{S}}$, but $\mathcal{S}$, the Borel field of $\mathbb{S}$, is the trace of $\hat{\mathcal{S}}$ on $\mathbb{S}$.

Define a family of measures $\hat{\Pi}$ on $\hat{\mathbb{S}}$ such that, for $\hat{\mu} \in \hat{\Pi}$, $\hat{\mu}(A) = \mu(A \cap \mathbb{S})$, $\mu \in \Pi$, for each $A \in \hat{\mathcal{S}}$. To prove that Π is compact, we show that a sequence of measures $\{\mu_n, n \in \mathbb{N}\}$ from Π has a cluster point in Π. Consider the counterpart sequence $\{\hat{\mu}_n, n \in \mathbb{N}\}$ in $\hat{\Pi}$. Since $\hat{\mathbb{S}}$ is compact, $\hat{\Pi}$ is compact by **26.18**, so this sequence has one or more cluster points in $\hat{\Pi}$. Let ν be such a cluster point. The object is to show that there exists a p.m. $\mu \in \Pi$ such that $\hat{\mu} = \nu$.

Tightness of Π means that for every integer r there is a compact set $K_r \subseteq \mathbb{S}$ such that $\mu(K_r) \geq 1 - 1/r$, for all $\mu \in \Pi$. Being closed in $\hat{\mathbb{S}}$, $K_r \in \hat{\mathcal{S}}$ and $\hat{\mu}(K_r) = \mu(K_r \cap \mathbb{S}) = \mu(K_r)$, all $\mu \in \Pi$. Since K_r is closed we have for some subsequence $\{n_k, k \in \mathbb{N}\}$

$$\nu(K_r) \geq \limsup_{k\to\infty} \hat{\mu}_{n_k}(K_r) \geq 1 - 1/r, \tag{26.49}$$

by **26.10**(c). Since $\bigcup_r K_r \in \hat{\mathcal{S}}$, we have in particular that $\nu(\bigcup_r K_r) = 1$. Now, suppose we let $\nu^*(\mathbb{S})$ denote the outer measure of $\mathbb{S}$ in terms of coverings by $\hat{\mathcal{S}}$-sets. Since $\bigcup_r K_r \subseteq \mathbb{S}$, we must have $\nu^*(\mathbb{S}) \geq \nu^*(\bigcup_r K_r) = \nu(\bigcup_r K_r) = 1$. Applying **3.10**, note that $\mathbb{S}$ is ν-measurable since the inequality in (3.19) becomes

$$\nu^*(B \cap \mathbb{S}) \leq \nu^*(B), \tag{26.50}$$

which holds for all $B \subseteq \hat{\mathbb{S}}$. Since $\mathcal{S}$ is the trace of $\hat{\mathcal{S}}$ on $\mathbb{S}$, all the sets of $\mathcal{S}$ are accordingly ν-measurable and there exists a p.m. $\mu \in \Pi$ such that $\hat{\mu} = \nu$, as required. For any closed subset C of $\mathbb{S}$, there exists a closed $D \subseteq \hat{\mathbb{S}}$ such that $C = D \cap \mathbb{S}$, the assertions $\limsup_k \hat{\mu}_{n_k}(D) \leq \hat{\mu}(D)$ and $\limsup_k \mu_{n_k}(C) \leq \mu(C)$ are equivalent, and hence, by **26.10**, $\mu_{n_k} \Rightarrow \mu$. This means that $\{\mu_n\}$ has a convergent subsequence, proving sufficiency.

Notice that completeness of $\mathbb{S}$ is not needed for this part of the proof.

To prove necessity, assume Π is compact. Letting $\{S_{ni}, i \in \mathbb{N}\}$ be a countable covering of $\mathbb{S}$ by $1/n$-spheres, and $\{j_n, n \in \mathbb{N}\}$ any increasing subsequence of integers, define $\overline{A}_n = \bigcup_{i=1}^{j_n} \overline{S}_{ni}$. We show first that the assumption, $\exists\ \mu \in \Pi$ such that, for $\delta > 0$,

$$\mu(\overline{A}_n) \leq 1 - \delta, \text{ all } n, \tag{26.51}$$

leads to a contradiction, and so has to be false. If (26.51) is true for at least one element of (compact) Π, there is a convergent sequence $\{\mu_k, k \in \mathbb{N}\}$ in Π, with $\mu_k \Rightarrow \mu$, such that it holds for all μ_k. (Even if there is only one such element, we can put $\mu_k = \mu$, all k). Fix m. By **26.10**,

$$\mu(\overline{A}_n) \leq \limsup_{k\to\infty} \mu_k(\overline{A}_n) \leq 1 - \delta. \tag{26.52}$$

Letting $n \to \infty$ yields $\mu(\mathbb{S}) \leq 1 - \delta$, which is a contradiction.

Putting $\delta = \varepsilon/2^n$, we may therefore assert

$$\mu(\overline{A}_n) > 1 - \varepsilon/2^n, \text{ all } n, \text{ all } \mu \in \Pi. \tag{26.53}$$

Letting $K_\varepsilon = \bigcap_{n=1}^{\infty} \overline{A}_n$, this set is compact by **26.20** ($\mathbb{S}$ being complete) and it follows as in (26.48) above that $\mu(K_\varepsilon) > 1 - \varepsilon$. Since μ is an arbitrary element of Π, the family is uniformly tight. ■

We conclude this section with a useful result for measures on product spaces. See §7.4 for a discussion of the marginal measures.

26.23 Theorem *A* p.m. μ *on the space* $(\mathbb{S}\times\mathbb{T}, \mathcal{S}\otimes\mathcal{T})$ *with the product topology is tight iff the marginal p.m.s* μ_x *and* μ_y *are tight.*

Proof For a set $K \in \mathbb{S}\times\mathbb{T}$, let $K_x = \pi_x(K)$ denote the projection of K onto $\mathbb{S}$. Since the projection is continuous (see §6.5), K_x is compact if K is compact (**5.20**). Since

$$\mu_x(K_x) = \mu(K_x\times\mathbb{T}) \geq \mu(K), \tag{26.54}$$

tightness of μ implies tightness of μ_x. Repeating the argument for μ_y proves the necessity. For sufficiency we have to show that there exists a compact set $K \in \mathcal{S}\otimes\mathcal{T}$, having measure exceeding $1 - \varepsilon$. Consider the set $K = A\times B$ where $A \in \mathcal{S}$ and $\mu_x(A) > 1 - \varepsilon/2$, and $B \in \mathcal{T}$ where $\mu_y(B) > 1 - \varepsilon/2$. Note that

$$K^c = (A\times B^c)\cup(A^c\times B)\cup(A^c\times B^c), \tag{26.55}$$

where the sets of the union on the right are disjoint. Thus,

$$\begin{aligned} \mu(K^c) &\leq \mu(A^c\times B) + \mu(A\times B^c) + 2\mu(A^c\times B^c) \\ &= \mu(A^c\times\mathbb{T}) + \mu(\mathbb{S}\times B^c) \\ &= \mu_x(A^c) + \mu_y(B^c) \leq \varepsilon. \end{aligned} \tag{26.56}$$

If A and B are compact they are separable in the relative topologies generated from $\mathbb{S}$ and $\mathbb{T}$ (**5.7**), and hence K is compact by **6.17**. ■

26.6 Skorokhod's Representation

Considering a sequence of random elements, we can now give a generalization of some familiar ideas from the theory of random variables. Recall from **26.7** that separability ensures that the distance functions in the following definitions are r.v.s.

Let $\{x_n\}$ be a sequence of random elements and x a given random element of a separable space $(\mathbb{S},\mathcal{S})$. If

$$d(x_n(\omega),x(\omega)) \to 0 \text{ for } \omega \in C, \text{ with } P(C) = 1, \tag{26.57}$$

we say that x_n converges almost surely to x, and also write $x_n \xrightarrow{as} x$. Also, if

$$P(d(x_n,x) \geq \varepsilon) \to 0, \text{ all } \varepsilon > 0, \tag{26.58}$$

we say that x_n converges in probability to x, and write $x_n \xrightarrow{pr} x$. A.s. convergence is sufficient for convergence in probability, which in turn is sufficient for $x_n \xrightarrow{D} x$. A case subsumed in the above definition is where $x = a$ with probability 1, a being a fixed element of $\mathbb{S}$.

We now have the following result generalizing **22.18**.

26.24 Theorem Given a probability space $(\Omega,\mathcal{F},P)$, let $\{x_n(\omega)\}$ and $\{y_n(\omega)\}$ be random sequences on a separable space $(\mathbb{S},\mathcal{S})$. If $x_n \xrightarrow{D} x$ and $d(x_n,y_n) \xrightarrow{pr} 0$, then $y_n \xrightarrow{D} x$.

Proof Let $A \in \mathcal{S}$ be a closed set, and for $\varepsilon > 0$ put $A_\varepsilon = \{x: d(x,A) \leq \varepsilon\} \in \mathcal{S}$, also a closed set for each ε, and $A_\varepsilon \downarrow A$ as $\varepsilon \downarrow 0$. Since

$$\{\omega: y_n(\omega) \in A\} \subseteq \{\omega: x_n(\omega) \in A_\varepsilon\} \cup \{\omega: d(x_n(\omega),y_n(\omega)) \geq \varepsilon\},$$

we have

$$P(y_n \in A) \leq P(x_n \in A_\varepsilon) + P(d(x_n,y_n) \geq \varepsilon), \tag{26.59}$$

and, letting $n \to \infty$,

$$\limsup_{n\to\infty} P(y_n \in A) \leq \limsup_{n\to\infty} \mu_n(A_\varepsilon) \leq \mu(A_\varepsilon), \tag{26.60}$$

where μ_n is the measure associated with x_n, μ the measure associated with x, and the second inequality of (26.60) is by hypothesis on $\{x_n\}$ and **26.10**(c). Since this inequality holds for every $\varepsilon > 0$, we have

$$\limsup_{n\to\infty} P(y_n \in A) \leq \mu(A), \tag{26.61}$$

by continuity of the measure. This is sufficient for the result by **26.10**. ■

In §22.2, we showed that the weak convergence of a sequence of distributions on the line implies the a.s. convergence of a sequence of random variables. This is the Skorokhod representation of weak convergence. That result was in fact a special case of the final theorem of this chapter.

26.25 Theorem (Skorokhod 1956: 3.1) Let $\{\mu_n\}$ be a sequence of measures on the separable, complete metric space $(\mathbb{S},\mathcal{S})$. There exists a sequence of $\mathcal{B}_{[0,1]}/\mathcal{S}$-measurable functions

$$x_n\colon [0,1] \mapsto \mathbb{S}$$

such that $\mu_n(A) = m(\{\omega: x_n(\omega) \in A\})$ for each $A \in \mathcal{S}$, where m is Lebesgue measure. If $\mu_n \Rightarrow \mu$, there exists a function $x(\omega)$ such that $\mu(A) = m(\{\omega: x(\omega) \in A\})$ for each $A \in \mathcal{S}$, and $d(x_n(\omega),x(\omega)) \to 0$ a.s.$[m]$ as $n \to \infty$.

Proof This is by construction of the functions $x_n(\omega)$. For some $k \in \mathbb{N}$ let $\{x_i^{(k)}, i \in \mathbb{N}\}$ denote a countable collection of points in $\mathbb{S}$ such that, for every $x \in \mathbb{S}$, $d(x,x_i^{(k)}) \le 1/2^{k+1}$ for some i. Such sequences exist for every k by separability. Let $S(x_i^{(k)},r_k)$, for $1/2^{k+1} < r_k < 1/2^k$, denote a system of spheres in $\mathbb{S}$ having the property $\mu(\partial S(x_i^{(k)},r_k)) = 0$ for every i. An r_k satisfying this condition exists, since there can be at most a countable number of points r such that $\mu(\partial S(x_i^{(k)},r)) > 0$ for one or more i; this fact follows from **7.4**.

For given k, the system $\{S(x_i^{(k)},r_k),\ i \in \mathbb{N}\}$ covers $\mathbb{S}$, and accordingly the sets

$$D_i^k = S(x_i^{(k)},r_k) - \bigcup_{j=1}^{i-1} S(x_j^{(k)},r_k),\ i \in \mathbb{N}, \tag{26.62}$$

form a partition of $\mathbb{S}$. By letting each of the k integers $i_1,\dots,i_k$ range independently over $\mathbb{N}$, define the countable collection of sets

$$S_{i_1,\dots,i_k} = D_{i_1}^1 \cap D_{i_2}^2 \cap \dots \cap D_{i_k}^k \in \mathcal{S}. \tag{26.63}$$

Each $S_{i_1,\dots,i_k}$ is a subset of a sphere of radius $r_k < 1/2^k$, and $\mu(\partial S_{i_1,\dots,i_k}) = 0$. By construction, any pair $S_{i_1,\dots,i_k}$ and $S_{i_1',\dots,i_k'}$ are disjoint unless $i_k = i_k'$. Fixing $i_1,\dots,i_{k-1}$ we have

$$\bigcup_{i_k=1}^{\infty} S_{i_1,\dots,i_k} = S_{i_1,\dots,i_{k-1}}, \tag{26.64}$$

and in particular,

$$\bigcup_{i_1=1}^{\infty} S_{i_1} = \mathbb{S}. \tag{26.65}$$

That is to say, for any k the collection $\{S_{i_1,\dots,i_k}\}$ forms a partition of $\mathbb{S}$, which gets finer as k increases. These sets are not all required to be non-empty. For any $n \in \mathbb{N}$ and $k \in \mathbb{N}$, define a partition of $[0,1]$ into intervals $\Delta_{i_1,\dots,i_k}^{(n)}$, where it is understood that $\Delta_{i_1,\dots,i_k}^{(n)}$ lies to the left of $\Delta_{i_1',\dots,i_k'}^{(n)}$ if $i_j = i_j'$ for $j = 1,\dots,r-1$ and $i_r < i_r'$ for some r, and the lengths of the segments equal the probabilities $\mu_n(S_{i_1,\dots,i_k})$.

We are now ready to define a measurable mapping from $[0,1]$ to $\mathbb{S}$. Choose an element $\bar{x}_{i_1,\dots,i_k}$ from each non-empty $S_{i_1,\dots,i_k}$, and for $\omega \in [0,1]$ put

$$x_n^k(\omega) = \bar{x}_{i_1,\dots,i_k} \text{ if } \omega \in \Delta_{i_1,\dots,i_k}^{(n)}. \tag{26.66}$$

Note that by construction $d(x_n^k(\omega),x_n^{k+m}(\omega)) \le 1/2^k$ for $m \ge 1$, and taking $k = 1,2,\dots$ defines a Cauchy sequence in $\mathbb{S}$ which is convergent since $\mathbb{S}$ is a complete space by assumption. Write $x_n(\omega) = \lim_{k\to\infty} x_n^k(\omega)$.

To show that $x_n(\omega)$ is a random element with distribution defined by μ_n, it is sufficient to verify that

$$\mu_n(A) = P(x_n \in A) = m(\{\omega\colon x_n(\omega) \in A\}), \tag{26.67}$$

for, at least, all $A \in \mathcal{S}$ such that $\mu_n(\partial A) = 0$. If we let $A^{(k)}$ denote the union of all $S_{i_1,\ldots,i_k} \subseteq A$ and $A'^{(k)}$ the union of all $S_{i_1,\ldots,i_k} \subseteq A^c$, it is clear that $A^{(k)} \subseteq A \subseteq A'^{(k)}$, and that (26.67) holds in respect of $A^{(k)}$ and $A'^{(k)}$. Let

$$C^{(k)} = \{x\colon d(x,\partial A) \le 1/2^k\}, \tag{26.68}$$

so that $A'^{(k)} - A^{(k)} \subseteq C^{(k)}$. Since $\mu_n(C^{(k)}) \to \mu_n(\partial A) = 0$ as $k \to \infty$, it follows that $\mu_n(A'^{(k)} - A^{(k)}) \to 0$, and hence $\mu_n(A^{(k)}) \to \mu_n(A)$. This proves (26.67).

It remains to show that, if $\mu_n \Rightarrow \mu$, then $x_n \to x$ a.s.$[m]$. Since the length of $\Delta^{(n)}_{i_1,\ldots,i_k}$ equals $\mu_n(S_{i_1,\ldots,i_k})$, we can conclude that the sequence of intervals $\{\Delta^{(n)}_{i_1,\ldots,i_k}\}$ has a limit $\Delta_{i_1,\ldots,i_k}$ as $n \to \infty$. Pick an interior point ω of $\Delta_{i_1,\ldots,i_k}$, and note that x^k meets the condition $x^k(\omega) \in S_{i_1,\ldots,i_k}$, by definition. Then for N large enough we can be sure that, for $n \ge N$, $\omega \in \Delta^{(n)}_{i_1,\ldots,i_k}$ and hence $d(x^k_n(\omega), x^k(\omega)) \le 1/2^{k-1}$. Letting $k \to \infty$, we conclude that $d(x_n(\omega), x(\omega)) \le \varepsilon$ for any $\varepsilon > 0$ whenever n is large enough. We cannot draw this conclusion for the boundary points of the $\Delta_{i_1,\ldots,i_k}$, but these are at most countable even as $k \to \infty$, and have Lebesgue measure 0. This completes the proof. ■

The construction of §22.2 is now revealed as a particularly elegant special case, since the mapping from [0,1] to $\mathbb{S}$ is none other than the inverse of the c.d.f. when $\mathbb{S} = \mathbb{R}$. In his 1956 paper, Skorokhod goes on to use this theorem to prove convergence results in spaces such as $D[0,1]$. We shall not use his approach directly, but this is a useful trick which has a variety of potential applications, just as in the case of $\mathbb{R}$. One of these will be encountered in Chapter 30.

27
Weak Convergence in a Function Space

27.1 Measures on Function Spaces

This chapter is mainly about the space of continuous functions on the unit interval, but an important preliminary is to consider the space $R_{[0,1]}$ of *all* real functions on [0,1]. We shall tend to write just R for this space, for brevity, when the context is clear. In this chapter and the following ones we also tend to use the symbols x,y etc. to denote functions, and t,s etc. to denote their arguments, instead of f,g and x,y respectively as in previous chapters. This is conventional, and reflects the fact that the objects under consideration are usually to be interpreted as empirical processes in the time domain. Thus,

$$x\colon [0,1] \mapsto \mathbb{R}$$

will be the function which assumes the value $x(t)$ at the point t.

In what follows the element x will typically be stochastic, a measurable mapping from a probability space $(\Omega,\mathcal{F},P)$. We may legitimately write

$$x\colon \Omega \mapsto R,$$

assigning $x(\omega)$ as the image of the element ω, but also

$$x\colon \Omega\times[0,1] \mapsto \mathbb{R},$$

where $x(\omega,t)$ denotes the value of x at (ω,t). We may also write $x(t)$ to denote the ordinate at t where dependence on ω is left implicit. The potential ambiguity should be resolved by the context. Sometimes one writes x_t to denote the random ordinate where $x_t(\omega) = x(\omega,t)$, but we avoid this as far as possible, given our use of the subscript notation in the context of a sequence with countable domain.

The notion of evaluating the function at a point is formalized as a projection mapping. The *coordinate projections* are the mappings $\pi_t\colon R_{[0,1]} \to \mathbb{R}$, where $\pi_t(x) = x(t)$. The projections define cylinder sets in R; for example, the set $\pi_t^{-1}(a)$, $a \in \mathbb{R}$, is the collection of all functions on [0,1] which pass through the point of the plane with coordinates (a,t). This sort of thing is familiar from §12.3, and the union or intersection of a collection of k such cylinders with different coordinates is a k-dimensional cylinder; the difference is that the number of coordinates we have to choose from here is uncountable.

Let $\{t_1,\dots,t_k\}$ be any finite collection of points in [0,1], and let

$$\pi_{t_1,\dots,t_k}(x) = (\pi_{t_1}(x),\dots,\pi_{t_k}(x)) \in \mathbb{R}^k \tag{27.1}$$

denote the k-vector of projections from these coordinates. The sets of the collection

$$\mathcal{H} = \{\pi^{-1}_{t_1,\dots,t_k}(B) \subseteq R_{[0,1]}\colon B \in \mathcal{B}^k,\ t_1,\dots,t_k \in [0,1],\ k \in \mathbb{N}\}, \tag{27.2}$$

are called the *finite-dimensional sets* of $R_{[0,1]}$. It is easy to verify that $\mathcal{H}$ is a field. The *projection σ-field* is defined as $\mathcal{P} = \sigma(\mathcal{H})$.

Fig. 27.1 shows a few of the elements of a rather simple $\mathcal{H}$-set, with $k = 1$, and B an interval $[a,b]$ of $\mathbb{R}$. The set $H = \pi^{-1}_{t_1}([a,b]) \in \mathcal{H}$ consists of all those functions that succeed in passing through a hole of width $b-a$ in a barrier erected at the point t_1 of the interval. Similarly, the set of all the functions passing through holes in two such barriers, at t_1 and t_2, is the image under $\pi^{-1}_{t_1,t_2}$ of a rectangle in the plane—and so forth.

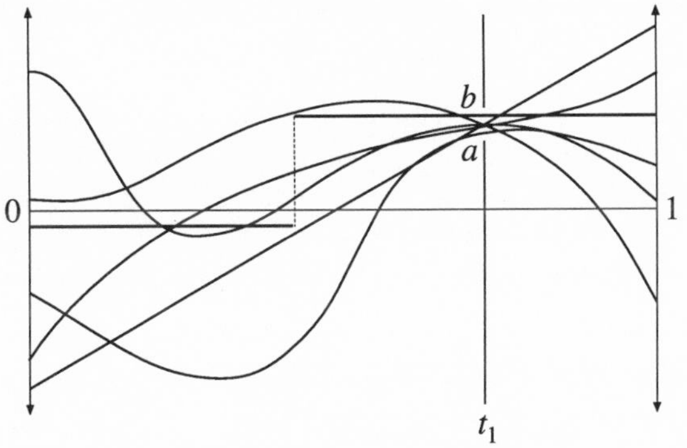

Fig. 27.1

If the domain of the function had been countable, the projection σ-field $\mathcal{P}$ would be effectively the same collection as $\mathcal{B}^\infty$ of **12.3**. But since the domain is uncountable, $\mathcal{P}$ is strictly smaller than the Borel field on R. The sets of example **26.3** are Borel sets but are not in $\mathcal{P}$, since their elements are restricted at uncountably many points of the interval. As that example showed, the Borel sets of R are not generally measurable; but $(R,\mathcal{P})$ *is* a measurable space, as we now show.

Define for $k = 1,2,3,\dots$ the family of finite-dimensional p.m.s $\mu_{t_1,\dots,t_k}$ on $(\mathbb{R}^k,\mathcal{B}^k)$, indexed on the collection of all the k-vectors of indices,

$$\{(t_1,\dots,t_k)\colon t_j \in [0,1],\ j = 1,\dots,k\}.$$

This family will be required to satisfy two *consistency properties*. The first is

$$\mu_{t_1,\dots,t_k}(E) = \mu_{t_1,\dots,t_m}(E\times\mathbb{R}^{m-k}) \tag{27.3}$$

for $E \in \mathcal{B}_k$ and all $m > k > 0$. In other words, a k-dimensional distribution can be obtained from an m-dimensional distribution with $m > k$, by the usual operation of marginalization. This is simply the generalization to arbitrary collections of coordinates of condition (12.7). The second is

$$\mu_{t_1,\dots,t_k} = \mu_{t_{p(1)},\dots,t_{p(k)}}\phi^{-1}, \tag{27.4}$$

where $p(1),\dots,p(k)$ is a permutation of the integers $1,\dots,k$, and $\phi\colon \mathbb{R}^k \mapsto \mathbb{R}^k$

denotes the (measurable) transformation which reorders the elements of a k-vector according to the inverse permutation; that is, $\phi(x_{p(1)},\ldots x_{p(k)}) = x_1,\ldots,x_k$. This condition basically means that re-ordering the vector elements transforms the measure in the way we would expect if the indices were $1,\ldots,k$ instead of $t_1,\ldots,t_k$.

The following extends the consistency theorem, **12.4**.

27.1 Theorem For any family of finite-dimensional p.m.s $\{\mu_{t_1,\ldots,t_k}\}$ satisfying conditions (27.3) and (27.4), there exists a unique p.m. μ on $(R,\mathcal{P})$, such that $\mu_{t_1,\ldots,t_k} = \mu\pi^{-1}_{t_1,\ldots,t_k}$ for each finite collection of indices.

Proof Let T denote the set of countable sequences of real numbers from $[0,1]$; that is, $\tau \in T$ if $\tau = \{s_j \in [0,1],\ j \in \mathbb{N}\}$. Define the projections $\pi_\tau\colon R \mapsto \mathbb{R}^\infty$ by

$$\pi_\tau(x) = (x(s_1),x(s_2),\ldots). \tag{27.5}$$

For any τ, write $\nu^\tau_n = \mu_{s_1,\ldots,s_n}$ for $n = 1,2,\ldots$ Then by **12.4**, which applies thanks to (27.3), there exist p.m.s ν^τ on $(\mathbb{R}^\infty,\mathcal{B}^\infty)$ such that $\nu^\tau_n = \nu^\tau\pi_n^{-1}$, where $\pi_n(y)$ is the projection of the first n coordinates of y, for $y \in \mathbb{R}^\infty$. Consistency requires that $\nu^\tau_n = \nu^{\tau'}_n$ if sequences τ and τ' have their first n coordinates the same. Since evidently $\mathcal{P} \subseteq \{\pi_\tau^{-1}(B)\colon B \in \mathcal{B}^\infty, \tau \in T\}$, we may define a p.m. μ on $(R,\mathcal{P})$ by setting

$$\mu(\pi_\tau^{-1}(B)) = \nu^\tau(B) \tag{27.6}$$

for each $B \in \mathcal{B}^\infty$. No extension is necessary here, since the measure is uniquely defined for each element of $\mathcal{P}$.

It remains to show that the family $\{\mu_{t_1,\ldots,t_k}\}$ corresponds to the finite-dimensional distributions of μ. For any $\mu_{t_1,\ldots,t_k}$ there exists $\tau \in T$ such that $\{t_1,\ldots,t_k\} \subseteq \{s_1,\ldots,s_n\}$, for some n large enough. Construct a mapping $\psi\colon \mathbb{R}^n \mapsto \mathbb{R}^k$, by first applying a permutation p to the indices $s_1,\ldots,s_n$ which sets $x(p(s_i)) = x(t_i)$ for $i = 1,\ldots,k$, and then projecting from $\mathbb{R}^n$ to $\mathbb{R}^k$ by suppressing the indices $s_{p(k+1)},\ldots,s_{p(n)}$. The consistency properties imply that

$$\mu_{t_1,\ldots,t_k} = \mu_{s_1,\ldots,s_n}\psi^{-1} = \nu^\tau_n\psi^{-1} = \nu^\tau(\psi\circ\pi_n)^{-1} = \mu(\psi\circ\pi_n\circ\pi_\tau)^{-1}. \tag{27.7}$$

Since $\psi\circ\pi_n\circ\pi_\tau = \pi_{t_1,\ldots,t_k}$ is a projection, $\mu_{t_1,\ldots,t_k}$ is a finite-dimensional distribution of μ. ∎

If we have a scheme for assigning a joint distribution to any finite collection of coordinate functions $\{x(t_1),\ldots,x(t_k)\}$ with rational coordinates, this can be extended, according to the theorem, to define a unique measure on $(R,\mathcal{P})$. These p.m.s are called the finite-dimensional distributions of the stochastic process x. The sets generated by considering this vector of real r.v.s are elements of $\mathcal{H}$, and hence there is a corollary which exactly parallels **12.5**.

27.2 Corollary $\mathcal{H}$ is a determining class for $(R,\mathcal{P})$. □

27.2 The Space C

Visualize an element of $C_{[0,1]}$, the space of continuous real-valued functions on [0,1], as a curve drawn by the pen of a seismograph or similar instrument, as it traverses a sheet of paper of unit width, making arbitrary movements up and down, but never being lifted from the paper. Since [0,1] is a compact set, the elements of $C_{[0,1]}$ are actually uniformly continuous.

To get an idea why distributions on $C_{[0,1]}$ might be of interest to us, imagine observing a realization of a stochastic sequence $\{S_j(\omega)\}_1^n$, from a probability space $(\Omega,\mathcal{F},P)$, for some finite n. A natural way to study these data is to display them on a page or a computer screen. We would typically construct a graph of S_j against the integer values of j from 1 to n on the abscissa, the discrete points being joined up with ruled lines to produce a 'time plot', the kind of thing shown in Fig. 27.2.

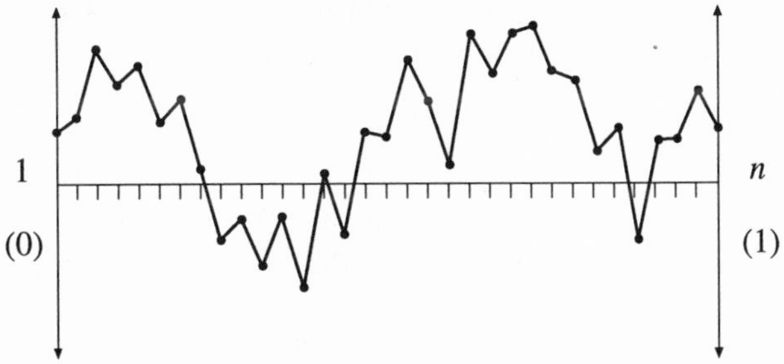

Fig. 27.2

We will then have done rather more than just drawn a picture; by connecting the points we have defined a random continuous function, a random drawing (the word here operates in both its senses!) from the space $C[1,n]$. It is convenient, and there is obviously no loss of generality, if instead of plotting the points at unit intervals we plot them at intervals of $1/(n-1)$; in other words, let the width of the paper or computer screen be set at unity by choice of units of measurement. Also, relocating the origin at 0, we obtain by this means an element of $C_{[0,1]}$, a member of the subclass of *piecewise linear* functions, with formula

$$x(t) = (i-tm)x((i-1)/m) + (1+tm-i)x(i/m) \tag{27.8}$$

for $t \in [(i-1)/m,\ i/m]$, and $i = 1,\dots,m$, $m = n-1$. The points $x(i/m) \in \mathbb{R}$ for $i = 0,\dots,m$ are the $m+1$ *vertices* of the function.

In effect, we have defined a measurable mapping between points of $\mathbb{R}^n$ and elements of $C_{[0,1]}$, and hence a family of distributions on $C_{[0,1]}$ derived from $(\Omega,\mathcal{F},P)$, indexed on n. The specific problem to be studied is the distribution of these graphs as n tends to infinity, under particular assumptions about the sequence $\{S_j\}$. When $\{S_j\}$ is a sequence of scaled partial sums of independent or asymptotically independent random variables, we shall obtain a useful generalization of the central limit theorem.

As in §5.5, we metrize $C_{[0,1]}$ with the uniform metric

$$d_U(x,y) = \sup_t |x(t) - y(t)|. \tag{27.9}$$

Imagine tying two pens to a rod, so that moving the rod up and down as it traverses a sheet of paper draws a band of fixed width. The uniform distance $d_U(x,y)$ between two elements of $C_{[0,1]}$ is the width of the narrowest such band that will contain both curves at all points. We will henceforth tend to write C for $(C_{[0,1]},d_U)$ when the context is clear.

C is a complete space by **5.24**, and, since [0,1] is compact, is also separable by **5.26**(ii). In this case an approximating function for any element of C, fully determined by its values at a finite number of points of the interval (compare **5.25**) is available in the form of a piecewise linear function. A set $\Pi_m = \{t_1,\ldots,t_m\}$ satisfying $0 = t_0 < t_1 < \ldots < t_m = 1$ is called a *partition* of [0,1]. This is a slight abuse of language, an abbreviated way of saying that the collection *defines* such a partition into subintervals, say, $A_i = [t_{i-1},t_i)$ for $i = 1,\ldots,m-1$ together with $A_m = [t_{m-1},1]$. The norm

$$\|\Pi_m\| = \max_{1\le i\le m} \{t_i - t_{i-1}\} \tag{27.10}$$

is called the *fineness* of the partition, and a *refinement* of Π_m is any partition of which Π_m is a proper subset. We could similarly refer to $\min_{1\le i\le m}\{t_i - t_{i-1}\}$ as the *coarseness* of Π_m.

The following approximation lemma specializes **5.25** with the partition $\Pi_{2^n} = \{i/2^n,\ i = 1,\ldots,2^n\}$ for $n \ge 1$ playing the role of the δ-net on the domain, with in this case $\delta < 2/2^n$.

27.3 Theorem Given $x \in C$, let $y_n \in C$ be piecewise linear, having $2^n + 1$ vertices, with

$$\max_{1\le i\le 2^n} \left\{ |x(2^{-n}i) - y_n(2^{-n}i)| \right\} < \tfrac{1}{2}\varepsilon. \tag{27.11}$$

There exists n large enough that $d_U(x,y_n) < \varepsilon$.

Proof Write $A_i = [2^{-n}(i-1),\ 2^{-n}i]$, $i = 1,\ldots,2^n$. (Inclusion of both endpoints is innocuous here.) Applying (27.8) we find that, for $t \in A_i$, $y_n(t) = \lambda y_n(t') + (1-\lambda)y_n(t'')$ where $t' = 2^{-n}(i-1)$, $t'' = 2^{-n}i$, and $\lambda = i - 2^n t$. Noting that

$$\begin{aligned}|x(t) - y_n(t)| \le{}& \lambda|x(t) - x(t')| + (1-\lambda)|x(t) - x(t'')| \\ &+ \lambda|x(t') - y_n(t')| + (1-\lambda)|x(t'') - y_n(t'')|,\end{aligned} \tag{27.12}$$

and that for n large enough, $\sup_{s,t\in A_i}|x(s) - x(t)| < \frac{1}{2}\varepsilon$ by continuity, it follows that for such n,

$$d_U(x,y_n) = \max_{1\le i\le 2^n} \left\{ \sup_{t\in A_i} \left| x(t) - y_n(t) \right| \right\} < \varepsilon. \ \blacksquare \tag{27.13}$$

Note that as $n \to \infty$, $\Pi_{2^n} \to \mathbb{D}$ (the dyadic rationals). There is the following important implication.

27.4 Theorem If $x,y \in C$ and $x(t) = y(t)$ whenever $t \in \mathbb{D}$, then $x = y$.

Proof Let z_n be piecewise linear with $z_n(t) = x(t) = y(t)$ for $t \in \Pi_{2^n}$. By assumption, such a z_n exists for every $n \in \mathbb{N}$. Fix ε, and by taking n large enough that $\max\{d_U(x,z_n), d_U(y,z_n)\} < \frac{1}{2}\varepsilon$, as is possible by **27.3**, we can conclude by the triangle inequality that $d_U(x,y) < \varepsilon$. Since ε is arbitrary it follows that $d_U(x,y) = 0$, and hence $x = y$ since d_U is a metric. ∎

The continuity of certain elements of R, particularly the limits of sequences of functions, is a crucial feature of several of the limit arguments to follow. An important tool is the *modulus of continuity* of a function $x \in R$, the monotone function w_x: $(0,1] \mapsto \mathbb{R}^+$ defined by

$$w_x(\delta) = \sup_{|s-t|<\delta} |x(s) - x(t)|. \tag{27.14}$$

w_x has already been encountered in the more general context of the Arzelà-Ascoli theorem in §5.5. It tells us how rapidly x may change over intervals of width δ. Setting $\delta = 1$, for example, defines the range of x. But in particular, the fact that the x are uniformly continuous functions implies that, for every $x \in C$,

$$w_x(\delta) \downarrow 0 \text{ as } \delta \downarrow 0. \tag{27.15}$$

For fixed δ, we may think of $w_x(\delta) = w(x,\delta)$ as a function on the domain C. Since $|w(x,\delta) - w(y,\delta)| \le 2d_U(x,y)$, $w(x,\delta)$ is continuous on C, and hence a measurable function of x.

The following is the version of the Arzelà-Ascoli theorem relevant to C.

27.5 Theorem A set $A \subset C$ is relatively compact iff

$$\sup_{x\in A} |x(0)| < \infty, \tag{27.16}$$

$$\lim_{\delta\to 0} \sup_{x\in A} w_x(\delta) = 0. \;\square \tag{27.17}$$

These conditions together impose total boundedness and uniform equicontinuity on A. Consider, for some $t \in [0,1]$ and $k \in \mathbb{N}$,

$$|x(t)| \le |x(0)| + \sum_{i=1}^{k} \left| x\left(\frac{i}{k}t\right) - x\left(\frac{i-1}{k}t\right) \right|. \tag{27.18}$$

Equality (27.17) implies that for large enough k, $\sup_{x\in A} w_x(1/k) < \infty$. Therefore (27.16) and (27.17) together imply that

$$\sup_t \sup_{x\in A} |x(t)| < \infty. \tag{27.19}$$

In other words, all the elements of A must be contained in a band of finite width around 0. This theorem is therefore a straightforward corollary of **5.28**.

27.3 Measures on C

We now see how **27.1** specializes when we restrict the class of functions under consideration to the members of C. The open spheres of C are sets with the form

$$S(x,r) = \{y \in C\colon d_U(x,y) < r\} \tag{27.20}$$

for $x \in C$.

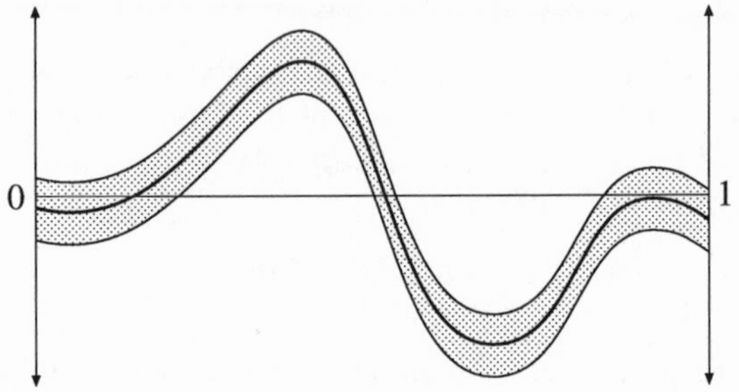

Fig. 27.3

Such sets can be visualized as a bundle of continuous graphs, with radius r and the function x at the core, traversing the unit interval—for example all the functions lying within the shaded band in Fig. 27.3. We shall write $\mathcal{B}_C$ for the Borel field on C, and since (C,d_U) is separable each open set has a countable covering by open spheres and $\mathcal{B}_C$ can be thought of as the σ-field generated by the open spheres of C. Each open sphere can be represented as a countable union of closed spheres,

$$S(x,r) = \bigcup_{n=1}^{\infty}\bar{S}(x,\ r-1/n), \tag{27.21}$$

and hence $\mathcal{B}_C$ is also the σ-field generated from the closed spheres.

Now consider the coordinate projections on C. Happily we know these to be continuous (see **6.15**), and hence the image of an open (closed) finite-dimensional rectangle under the inverse projection mapping is an open (closed) element of $\mathcal{P}$. Letting $\mathcal{H}_C = \{H \cap C\colon H \in \mathcal{H}\}$ with $\mathcal{H}$ defined in (27.2), and so defining $\mathcal{P}_C = \sigma(\mathcal{H}_C)$, we have the following important property:

27.6 Theorem $\mathcal{B}_C = \mathcal{P}_C$.

Proof Let

$$H_k(x,\alpha) = \left\{y \in C\colon \max_{1\le i\le 2^k} |y(2^{-k}i) - x(2^{-k}i)| < \alpha\right\} \in \mathcal{H}_C, \tag{27.22}$$

and so let

$$H(x,\alpha) = \bigcap_{k=1}^{\infty} H_k(x,\alpha)$$

$$= \left\{ y \in C\colon \sup_{t \in \mathbb{D}} |y(t) - x(t)| \le \alpha \right\} \in \mathcal{P}_C, \tag{27.23}$$

where $\mathbb{D}$ denotes the dyadic rationals. Note that we cannot rely on the inequality in (27.22) remaining strict in the limit, but we can say by **27.4** that

$$H(x,\alpha) = \overline{S}(x,\alpha), \tag{27.24}$$

where $\overline{S}$ is the closure of S. Using (27.21), we obtain

$$S(x,r) = \bigcup_{n=1}^{\infty} H(x,\ r - 1/n). \tag{27.25}$$

It follows that the open spheres of C lie in $\mathcal{P}_C$, and so $\mathcal{B}_C \subseteq \mathcal{P}_C$.

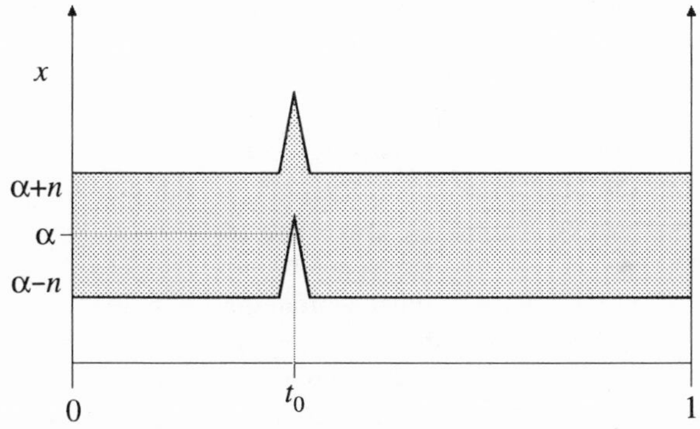

Fig. 27.4

To show $\mathcal{P}_C \subseteq \mathcal{B}_C$ consider, for $\alpha \in \mathbb{R}$ and $t_0 \in [0,1]$, functions $x_n \in C$ defined by the restriction to [0,1] of the functions on $\mathbb{R}$,

$$x_n(t) = \begin{cases} \alpha + n(n+1/n)(t+1/n-t_0), & t_0 - 1/n \le t < t_0 \\ \alpha + n(n+1/n)(t_0+1/n-t), & t_0 \le t < t_0 + 1/n \\ \alpha, & \text{otherwise.} \end{cases} \tag{27.26}$$

Every element y of the set $S(x_n,n) \in \mathcal{B}_C$ has the property $y(t_0) > \alpha$. (This is the shaded region in Fig. 27.4.) Note that

$$G(\alpha,t_0) = \{y \in C\colon \pi_{t_0}(y) > \alpha\} = \bigcup_{n=1}^{\infty} S(x_n,n) \in \mathcal{B}_C. \tag{27.27}$$

Now, $G(\alpha,t_0)$ is an element of the collection $\mathcal{H}_{Ct_0}$ where for general t we define

$$\mathcal{H}_{Ct} = \{\pi_t^{-1}(B),\ B \in \mathcal{B}\}. \tag{27.28}$$

In words, the elements of $\mathcal{H}_{Ct}$ are the sets of continuous functions x having $x(t) \in B$, for each $B \in \mathcal{B}$. In view of parts (ii) and (iii) of **1.2**, and the fact that $\mathcal{B}$ can be generated by the collection of open half-lines (α,∞), it is easy to see that $\mathcal{H}_{Ct}$ is the σ-field generated from the sets of the form $G(\alpha,t)$ for fixed t and $\alpha \in \mathbb{R}$. Moreover, $\mathcal{H}_C$ is the σ-field generated by $\{\mathcal{H}_{Ct}, t \in [0,1]\}$. Since $G(\alpha,t) \in \mathcal{B}_C$ for any α and t by (27.27), it follows that $\mathcal{H}_C \subseteq \mathcal{B}_C$ and hence $\mathcal{P}_C \subseteq \mathcal{B}_C$. ■

It will be noted that the limit $x_\infty(t)$ of (27.26) is not an element of C, taking the value α at all points except t_0, and $+\infty$ at t_0. Of course, $\{x_n\}$ is not a Cauchy sequence. However, the countable union of open spheres in (27.27) is an open set (the inverse projection of the open half line) and omits this point.

$\mathcal{P}_C$ is the projection σ-field on C with respect to arbitrary points of the continuum [0,1], but consider the collection $\mathcal{P}'_C = \{H \cap C: H \in \mathcal{P}'\}$, where $\mathcal{P}'$ is the collection of cylinder sets of $R_{[0,1]}$ having rational coordinates as a base. In other words, the sets of $\mathcal{P}'$ contain functions whose values $x(t)$ are unrestricted except at rational t. Since elements of C which agree on the rational coordinates agree everywhere by **27.4**,

$$\mathcal{P}'_C = \mathcal{P}_C. \tag{27.29}$$

This argument is just an alternative route to the conclusion (from **6.22**) that C is homeomorphic to a subset of $\mathbb{R}^\infty$. However, it is *not* true that $\mathcal{P} = \mathcal{P}'$, because $\mathcal{P}$ is generated from the projections of every point of the continuum [0,1], and arbitrary functions can be distinct in spite of agreeing on rational t.

Evidently $(C,\mathcal{B}_C)$ is a measurable space, and according to **27.2** and **27.6**, $\mathcal{H}_C$ is a determining class for the space. In other words, the finite-dimensional distributions of a space of continuous functions uniquely determine a p.m. on the space. Every p.m. on $R_{[0,1]}$ must satisfy the consistency conditions, but the elements of C have the special property that $x(t_1)$ and $x(t_2)$ are close together whenever t_1 and t_2 are close together, and this puts a further restriction on the class of finite-dimensional distributions which can generate distributions on C. Such distributions must have the property that for any $\varepsilon > 0$, $\exists\, \delta > 0$ such that

$$|t_1 - t_2| < \delta \;\Rightarrow\; \mu(\{x: |x(t_1) - x(t_2)| < \varepsilon\}) = 1. \tag{27.30}$$

The class of p.m.s in $(C,\mathcal{B}_C)$, whose finite-dimensional distributions satisfy this requirement, will be denoted $\mathbb{M}_C$. Note that, thanks to **26.14**, we are able to treat $\mathbb{M}_C$ as a separable metric space. This fact will be most important below.

27.4 Brownian Motion

The original and best-known example of a p.m. on C, whose theory is due to Norbert Wiener (Wiener 1923) is also the one that matters most from our point of view, since in the theory of weak convergence it plays the role of the attractor measure which the Gaussian distribution plays on the line. It is in fact the natural generalization of that distribution to function spaces.

27.7 Definition *Wiener measure* W is the p.m. on $(C,\mathcal{B}_C)$ having these properties:

(a) $W(x(0) = 0) = 1$;

(b) $W(x(t) \leq a) = \dfrac{1}{\sqrt{2\pi t}}\displaystyle\int_{-\infty}^{a} e^{-\xi^2/2t}d\xi,\ 0 < t \leq 1$;

(c) for every partition $\{t_1,\dots,t_k\}$ of $[0,1]$, the increments $x(t_1)-x(t_0)$, $x(t_3)-x(t_2),\dots,x(t_k)-x(t_{k-1})$ are totally independent. □

Parts (a) and (b) of the definition give the marginal distributions of the coordinate functions, while condition (c) fixes their joint distribution. Any finite collection of process coordinates $\{x(t_i),\ i = 1,\dots,k\}$ has the multivariate Gaussian distribution, with $x(t_j) \sim N(0,t_j)$, and $E(x(t_j)x(t_{j'})) = \min\{t_j,t_{j'}\}$. Hence, $x(t_1)-x(t_2) \sim N(0,\ |t_1-t_2|)$, which agrees with the requirements of continuity. This full specification of the finite-dimensional distributions suffices to define a unique measure on $(C,\mathcal{B}_C)$. This does not amount to proving that such a measure exists, but we shall show this below; see **27.15**.

W may equally well be defined on the interval $[0,b)$ for any $b > 0$, including $b = \infty$, but the cases with $b \neq 1$ will not usually concern us here.

A random element distributed according to W is called a Wiener process or a *Brownian motion* process. The latter term refers to the use of this p.m. as a mathematical model of the random movements of pollen grains suspended in water resulting from thermal agitation of the water molecules, first observed by the botanist Robert Brown.[27] In practice, the terms Wiener process and Brownian motion tend to be used synonymously. The symbol W conventionally stands for the p.m., and we also follow convention in using the symbol B to denote a random element from the derived probability space $(C,\mathcal{B}_C,W)$. In terms of the underlying probability space $(\Omega,\mathcal{F},P)$ on which we assume $B\colon \Omega \mapsto C$ to be a $\mathcal{F}/\mathcal{B}_C$-measurable mapping, we have $W(E) = P(B \in E)$ for each set $E \in \mathcal{B}_C$.

The continuous graph of a random element of Brownian motion, $B(\omega)$ for $\omega \in \Omega$, is quite a remarkable object (see Fig. 27.5). It belongs to the class of geometrical forms named *fractals* (Mandelbrot 1983). These are curves possessing the property of *self-similarity*, meaning essentially that their appearance is invariant to scaling operations. It is straightforward to verify from the definition that if B is a Brownian motion so is B^*, where

$$B^*(\omega,t) = k^{-1/2}(B(\omega,s+kt) - B(\omega,s)) \tag{27.31}$$

for any $s \in [0,1)$ and $k \in (0,1-s]$. Varying s and k can be thought of as 'zooming in' on the portion of the process from s to $s+k$.

The key property is the one contained in part (iii) of the definition, that of independent increments. A little thought is required to see what this means. In the definition, the points $t_1,\dots,t_k$ may be arbitrarily close together. Considering a pair of points t and $t+\Delta$, the increment $B(\omega,t+\Delta)-B(\omega,t)$ is Gaussian with variance Δ, and independent of $B(\omega,t)$. Symmetry of the Gaussian density implies that

$$P(\omega\colon (B(\omega,t+\Delta)-B(\omega,t))(B(\omega,t)-B(\omega,t-\Delta)) < 0) = \tfrac{1}{2}$$

for $\Delta \leq t \leq 1-\Delta$ and *every* $\Delta > 0$. This is compatible with continuity, but completely rules out smoothness; in any realization of the process, almost every point of the graph is a corner, and has no tangent. This property is also apparent when we attempt to differentiate $B(\omega)$. Note from the definition that

$$\frac{B(\omega,t+h)-B(\omega,t)}{h} \sim N(0,1/h). \tag{27.32}$$

The sequence of measures defined by letting $h \to 0$ in (27.32) is not uniformly tight, and fails to converge to any limit. To be precise, the probability that the difference quotients in (27.32) fall in any finite interval is zero, another way of saying that the sample path $x(t,\omega)$ is non-differentiable at t, almost surely.

A way to think about Brownian motion which makes its relation to the problem of weak convergence fairly explicit is as the limit of the sequence of partial sums of n independent standard Gaussian r.v.s, scaled by $n^{-1/2}$. Note that

$$\xi_j(\omega) = n^{1/2}(B(\omega,j/n)-B(\omega,(j-1)/n)) \sim N(0,1) \tag{27.33}$$

for $j = 1,\dots,n$ and $B(\omega,j/n) = n^{-1/2}\sum_{i=1}^{j}\xi_i(\omega)$. By taking n large enough, we can express $B(\omega,t)$ in this form for any rational t, and by a.s. continuity of the process we may write

$$B(\omega,t) = \lim_{n\to\infty} n^{-1/2}\sum_{i=1}^{[nt]}\xi_i(\omega) \text{ a.s.} \tag{27.34}$$

for any $t \in [0,1]$, where $[nt]$ denotes the integer part of nt.

Consider the expected sum of the absolute increments contributing to $B(t)$. According to **9.8**, $|\xi_j|$ has mean $(2/\pi)^{1/2}$ and variance $1-2/\pi$, and so by independence of the increments the r.v. $A_n(t) = n^{-1/2}\sum_{i=1}^{[nt]}|\xi_i|$ has mean $[nt](2/n\pi)^{1/2} = m(t,n)$ (say) and variance $1-2/\pi$. Applying Chebyshev's inequality, we have that for $t > 0$,

$$\begin{aligned} P(A_n(t) > \tfrac{1}{2}m(t,n)) &\geq P(|A_n(t)-m(t,n)| \leq \tfrac{1}{2}m(t,n)) \\ &\geq 1 - \frac{4(1-2/\pi)}{m(t,n)^2}. \end{aligned} \tag{27.35}$$

Since $m(t,n) = O(n^{1/2})$, $A_n(t) \to \infty$ a.s.[W] for all $t > 0$. This means that the random element $B(\omega)$ is a function of unbounded variation, almost surely. Since $\lim_{n\to\infty}A_n(t)$ is the total distance supposedly travelled by a Brownian particle as it traverses the interval from 0 to t, and this turns out to be infinite for $t > 0$, Brownian motion cannot be taken as a literal description of such things as particles undergoing thermal agitation. Rather, it provides a simple limiting approximation to actual behaviour when the increments are small.

Standard Brownian motion is merely the leading member of an extensive family of a.s. continuous processes on [0,1] having Gaussian characteristics. For example, if we multiply B by a constant $\sigma > 0$, we obtain what is called a Brownian motion with variance σ^2. Adding the deterministic function μt to the process defines a Brownian motion with *drift* μ. Thus, $X(t) = \sigma B(t) + \mu t$ represents a family of processes having independent increments $X(t)-X(s) \sim N(\mu(t-s), \sigma^2|t-s|)$.

More elaborate generalizations of Brownian motion include the following.

27.8 Example Let $X(t) = B(t^{1+\beta})$ for $-1 < \beta < \infty$. X is a Brownian motion which has been subjected to stretching and squeezing of the time domain. Like B, it is a.s. continuous with independent Gaussian increments. It can be thought of as the limit of a partial sum process whose increments have trending variance. Suppose $\xi_i(\omega) \sim N(0,i^\beta)$, which means the variances are tending to 0 if $\beta < 0$, or to infinity if $\beta > 0$. Then $n^{-1-\beta}E(\sum_{i=1}^{[nt]}\xi_i)^2 \to t^{1+\beta}$, and

$$n^{-(1+\beta)/2}\sum_{i=1}^{[nt]}\xi_i(\omega) \to B(\omega,t^{1+\beta}) \text{ a.s. } \square \tag{27.36}$$

27.9 Example Let $X(t) = \theta(t)B(t)$ where $\theta\colon [0,1] \mapsto \mathbb{R}$ is any continuous deterministic function, and B is a Brownian motion. For $s < t$,

$$X(t)-X(s) = \theta(t)(B(t)-B(s))+(\theta(t)-\theta(s))B(s), \tag{27.37}$$

which means that the increments of this process, while Gaussian, are not independent. It can be thought of as the almost sure limit as $n \to \infty$ of a double partial sum process,

$$n^{-1/2}\sum_{i=1}^{[nt]}\left[\theta(i/n)\xi_i(\omega)+(\theta(i/n)-\theta((i-1)/n))\sum_{j=1}^{i-1}\xi_j(\omega)\right], \tag{27.38}$$

where $\xi_i \sim N(0,1)$. $\square$

27.10 Example Letting B denote standard Brownian motion on $[0,\infty)$, define

$$X(t) = e^{-\beta t}B(e^{2\beta t}) \tag{27.39}$$

for fixed $\beta > 0$. This is a zero-mean Gaussian process, having dependent increments like **27.9**. The remarkable feature of this process is that it is stationary, with $X(t) \sim N(0,1)$ for all $t > 0$, and

$$E(X(t)X(s)) = e^{\beta(2\min\{t,s\}-t-s)} = e^{-\beta|t-s|}. \tag{27.40}$$

This is the *Ornstein-Uhlenbeck process*. $\square$

27.11 Example The *Brownian bridge* is the process $B^o \in C$ where

$$B^o(t) = B(t)-tB(1),\ t \in [0,1]. \tag{27.41}$$

This is a Brownian motion tied down at both ends, and has $E(B^o(t)B^o(s)) = \min\{t,s\}-ts$. A natural way to think about B^o is as the limit of the partial sums of a mean-deviation process, that is

$$B^o(t,\omega) = \lim_{n\to\infty} n^{-1/2}\sum_{i=1}^{[nt]}\left(\xi_i(\omega) - \frac{1}{n}\sum_{j=1}^{n}\xi_j(\omega)\right) \text{ a.s.} \tag{27.42}$$

where $\xi_i(\omega) \sim N(0,1)$. $\square$

We have asserted the existence of Wiener measure, but we have not so far offered a proof. The consistency theorem (**27.1**) establishes the existence of a measure on $(C,\mathcal{B}_C)$ whose finite-dimensional distributions satisfy conditions (a)–(c) of **27.7**, so we might attempt to construct a continuous process having these properties. Consider

$$Y_n(t,\omega) = n^{-1/2}\left(\sum_{i=1}^{[nt]}\xi_i(\omega) + (nt-[nt])\xi_{[nt]+1}(\omega)\right), \tag{27.43}$$

where $\xi_i \sim N(0,1)$ and the set $\{\xi_1,\ldots,\xi_n\}$ are totally independent. For given ω, $Y_n(.,\omega)$ is a piecewise linear function of the type sketched in Fig. 27.2, although with $Y_n(0,\omega) = 0$ (the ξ_i represent the vertical distances from one vertex to the next), and is an element of C. $Y_n(t)$ is Gaussian with mean 0, and

$$\begin{aligned} E(Y_n(t))^2 &= n^{-1}([nt] + (nt-[nt])^2) \\ &= t + n^{-1}([nt] - nt + (nt-[nt])^2) \\ &= t + K(n,t)/n, \end{aligned} \tag{27.44}$$

(say) where $0 < K(n,t) < 2$. Moreover, the Gaussian pair $Y_n(t)$ and $Y_n(t+s+n^{-1}) - Y_n(t+n^{-1})$, $s > 0$, are independent. Extrapolating the same argument to general collections of non-overlapping increments, it becomes clear $Y_n(t) \xrightarrow{D} N(0,t)$, and more generally that if $Y_n \xrightarrow{D} Y$, then Y is a stochastic process whose finite-dimensional distributions match those of W. Fig. 27.5, which plots the partial sums of around 8000 (computer-generated) independent random numbers, shows the typical appearance of a realization of the process approaching the limit.

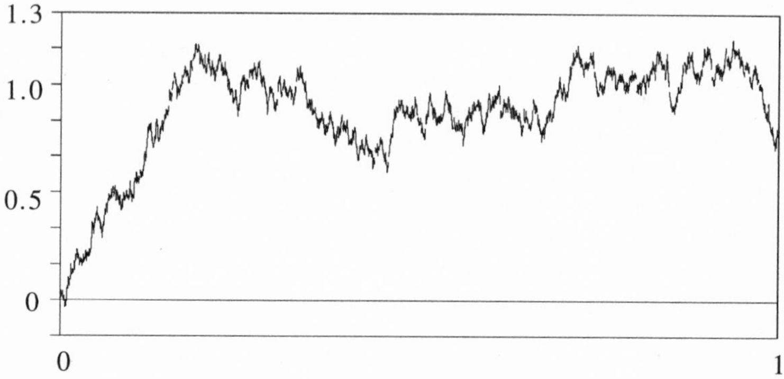

Fig. 27.5

This argument does not show that the measure on $(C,\mathcal{B}_C)$ corresponding to Y actually is W. There are attributes of the sample paths of the process which are not specified by the finite dimensional distributions. According to the continuous mapping theorem, $Y_n \xrightarrow{D} W$ would imply that $h(Y_n) \xrightarrow{D} h(W)$ for any a.s. continuous function h. For example, $\sup_t|Y_n(t)|$ is such a function, and there are no grounds from the arguments considered above for supposing that $\sup_t|Y_n(t)| \xrightarrow{D} \sup_t|W(t)|$.

However, if we are able to show that the sequence of measures corresponding to Y_n converges to a unique limit, this can only be W, since the finite-dimensional cylinder sets of C are a determining class for distributions on $(C,\mathcal{B}_C)$. This is what we were able to conclude from **27.6**, in view of **27.1**. This question is taken up in the next section, and the proof of existence will eventually emerge as a corollary to the main weak convergence result in §27.6.

27.5 Weak Convergence on C

Let $\{\mu_n\}$ be a sequence of probability measures in $\mathbb{M}_C$. For example, consider the distributions associated with a sequence like $\{Y_n,\ n \in \mathbb{N}\}$, whose elements are defined in (27.43). According to **26.22**, the necessary and sufficient condition for the family $\{\mu_n\}$ to be compact, and hence to possess (by **5.10**) a cluster point in $\mathbb{M}_C$, is that it is uniformly tight. Theorem **27.5** provides us with the relevant compactness criteria. The message of the following theorem is that the uniform tightness of measures on C is equivalent to boundedness at the origin and continuity arising with sufficiently high probability, in the limit. Since tightness is the concentration of the mass of the distribution in a compact set, this is just a stochastic version of the Arzelà-Ascoli theorem.

27.12 Theorem (Billingsley 1968: th. 8.2) $\{\mu_n\}$ is uniformly tight iff there exists $N \in \mathbb{N}$ such that, for all $\eta > 0$ and for all $n \geq N$,

(a) there exists $M < \infty$ such that

$$\mu_n(\{x\colon\ |x(0)| > M\}) \leq \eta; \tag{27.45}$$

(b) for each $\varepsilon > 0$, there exists $\delta \in (0,1)$ such that

$$\mu_n(\{x\colon\ w_x(\delta) \geq \varepsilon\}) \leq \eta. \ \square \tag{27.46}$$

Condition (b) is a form of stochastic equicontinuity (compare §21.3). It is easier to appreciate the connection with the notions of equicontinuity defined in §5.5 if we write it in the form $P(w(X_n,\delta) \geq \varepsilon) \leq \eta$, where $\{X_n\}$ is the sequence of stochastic functions on [0,1] having derived measures μ_n. Asymptotic equicontinuity is sufficient in this application, and the conditions need hold only over $n \geq N$, for some finite N. Since C is a separable complete space, each individual member of $\{\mu_n\}$ is tight, and for uniform tightness it suffices to show that the conditions hold 'in the tail'.

Proof of 27.12 To prove the necessity, let $\{\mu_n\}$ be uniformly tight, and for $\eta > 0$ choose a compact set K with $\mu_n(K) > 1 - \eta$. By **27.5**, there exist $M < \infty$ and $\delta \in (0,1)$ such that

$$K \subseteq \{x\colon\ |x(0)| \leq M\} \cap \{x\colon\ w_x(\delta) < \varepsilon\} \tag{27.47}$$

for any $\varepsilon > 0$. Applying the De Morgan law,

$$\eta \geq \mu_n(K^c) \geq \mu_n(\{x\colon\ |x(0)| > M\} \cup \{x\colon\ w_x(\delta) \geq \varepsilon\})$$

$$\geq \max\{\mu_n(\{x\colon |x(0)| > M\}),\ \mu_n(\{x\colon w_x(\delta) \geq \varepsilon\})\}. \tag{27.48}$$

Hence (27.45) and (27.46) hold, for all $n \in \mathbb{N}$.

Write $\mu^*(.)$ as shorthand for $\sup_{n\geq N}\mu_n(.)$. To prove sufficiency, consider for $k = 1,2,...$ the sets

$$A_k = \{x\colon w_x(\delta_k) < 1/k\}, \tag{27.49}$$

where $\{\delta_k\}$ is a sequence chosen so that $\mu^*(A_k) > 1 - \theta/2^{k+1}$, for $\theta > 0$. This is possible by condition (b). Also set $B = \{x\colon |x(0)| \leq M\}$, where M is chosen so that $\mu^*(B) > 1 - \theta/2$, which is possible by condition (a). Then define a closed set $K = (\bigcap_{k=1}^{\infty} A_k \cap B)^-$, and note that conditions (27.16) and (27.17) hold for the case $A = K$. Hence by **27.5**, K is compact. But

$$\mu^*(K^c) \leq \mu^*\left(\bigcup_{k=1}^{\infty} A_k^c \cup B^c\right)$$

$$\leq \sum_{k=1}^{\infty} \mu^*(A_k^c) + \mu^*(B^c)$$

$$\leq 2\theta \sum_{k=1}^{\infty} 1/2^{k+2} + \theta/2 = \theta. \tag{27.50}$$

This last inequality is to be read as $\sup_{n\geq N}\mu_n(K^c) \leq \theta$, or equivalently $\inf_{n\geq N}\mu_n(K) > 1 - \theta$. Since θ is arbitrary, and every individual μ_n is tight by **26.19**, in particular for $1 \leq n < N$, it follows that the sequence $\{\mu_n\}$ is uniformly tight. ■

The following lemma is a companion to the last result, supplying in conjunction with it a relatively primitive sufficient condition for uniform tightness.

27.13 Lemma (adapted from Billingsley 1968: th 8.3) Suppose that, for some $\delta \in (0,1)$,

$$\sup_{0\leq t\leq 1-\delta} \mu_n\left(\left\{x\colon \sup_{t\leq s\leq t+\delta} |x(s) - x(t)| \geq \tfrac{1}{2}\varepsilon\right\}\right) \leq \tfrac{1}{2}\eta\delta. \tag{27.51}$$

Then (27.46) holds.

Proof Fixing δ, consider the partition $\{t_1,...,t_r\}$ of $[0,1]$, for $r = 1+[1/\delta]$, where $t_i = i\delta$ for $i = 1,...,r-1$ and $t_r = 1$. Thus, for $\frac{1}{2} < \delta < 1$ we have $r = 2$ and the partition $\{\delta, 1\}$, for $\frac{1}{3} < \delta \leq \frac{1}{2}$ we have $r = 2$ and the partition $\{\delta, 2\delta, 1\}$, and so on. The width of these intervals is at most δ. A given interval $[t,t']$ with $|t' - t| \leq \delta$ must either lie within an interval of the partition, or at most overlap two adjoining intervals; it cannot span three or more. In the event that $|x(t') - x(t)| \geq \varepsilon$, x must change absolutely by at least $\frac{1}{2}\varepsilon$ in at least one of the interval(s) overlapping $[t,t']$, and the probability of the latter event is at least that of the former. In other words, considering all such intervals,

$$\mu_n(\{x\colon w_x(\delta) \geq \varepsilon\}) \leq \mu_n\left(\bigcup_{i=1}^{r}\left\{x\colon \sup_{s,s' \in [t_{i-1},t_i]} |x(s') - x(s)| \geq \tfrac{1}{2}\varepsilon\right\}\right)$$

$$\leq \sum_{i=1}^{r}\mu_n\left(\left\{x\colon \sup_{s,s' \in [t_{i-1},t_i]} |x(s') - x(s)| \geq \tfrac{1}{2}\varepsilon\right\}\right)$$

$$\leq \tfrac{1}{2}r\eta\delta \leq \eta, \tag{27.52}$$

where the third of these inequalities applies (27.51), and the final one follows because $r\delta \leq 2$. ■

These results provoke a technical query over measurability. In §21.1 we indicated difficulties with standard measure theory in showing that functions such as $\sup_{t \leq s \leq t+\delta}|x(s) - x(t)|$ in (27.51), and $w_x(\delta)$ in (27.46), are random variables. However, it is possible to show that sets such as the one in (27.51) are $\mathcal{F}$-analytic, and hence nearly measurable. In other words, complacency about this issue can be justified. The same qualification can be taken as implicit wherever such sets arise below.

27.6 The Functional Central Limit Theorem

Let $S_{n0} = 0$ and $S_{nj} = \sum_{i=1}^{j} U_{ni}$ for $j = 1,\ldots,n$, where $\{U_{ni}\}$ is a zero-mean stochastic array, normalized so that $E(S_{nn}^2) = 1$. As in the previous applications of array notation, in Part V and elsewhere, the leading example is $U_{ni} = U_i/s_n$, where $\{U_i\}$ is a zero-mean sequence and $s_n^2 = E(\sum_{i=1}^{n} U_i)^2$. Define an element Y_n of $C_{[0,1]}$, somewhat as in (27.43) above, as follows:

$$Y_n(t) = S_{n,[nt]} + (nt - [nt])U_{n,[nt]+1},$$

$$= S_{n,j-1} + (nt - j + 1)U_{nj} \text{ for } (j-1)/n \leq t < j/n,\ j = 1,\ldots,n; \tag{27.53}$$

$$Y_n(1) = S_{nn}. \tag{27.54}$$

This is the type of process sketched in Fig. 27.2. The question of whether the distribution of Y_n possesses a weak limit as $n \to \infty$ is the one we now address.

The interpolation terms in $Y_n(t)$ are necessary to generate a continuous function, but from an algebraic point of view they are a nuisance; dropping them, we obtain

$$X_n(t) = S_{n,[nt]} = S_{n,j-1} \text{ for } (j-1)/n \leq t < j/n,\ j = 1,\ldots,n, \tag{27.55}$$

$$X_n(1) = S_{nn}. \tag{27.56}$$

If conditions of the type discussed in Chapters 23 and 24 are imposed on $\{U_{ni}\}$, $X_n(1) \xrightarrow{D} N(0,1)$ as $n \to \infty$. If for example $U_i \sim \text{i.i.d.}(0,\sigma^2)$, so that $U_{ni} = U_i/s_n$ where $s_n^2 = n\sigma^2$, this is just the Lindeberg-Levy theorem. However, the Lindeberg-Levy theorem yields additional conclusions which are less often remarked; it is easy to verify that, for each distinct pair $t_1,t_2 \in [0,1]$,

$$X_n(t_2) - X_n(t_1) \xrightarrow{D} N(0,\ |t_2 - t_1|). \tag{27.57}$$

Since non-overlapping partial sums of independent variates are independent, we find for example that, for any $0 \le t_1 < t_2 < t_3 \le 1$, $X_n(t_2) - X_n(t_1)$ and $X_n(t_3) - X_n(t_2)$ converge to a pair of independent Gaussian variates with variances $t_2 - t_1$ and $t_3 - t_2$, so that their sum $X_n(t_3) - X_n(t_1)$ is asymptotically Gaussian with variance $t_3 - t_1$, as required. Under our assumptions,

$$|Y_n(t) - X_n(t)| = (nt - [nt])|U_{n,[nt]+1}| \xrightarrow{pr} 0, \tag{27.58}$$

so that $Y_n(t)$ and $X_n(t)$ have the same asymptotic distribution. Since $Y_n(0) = 0$, the finite-dimensional distributions of Y_n converge to those of a Brownian motion process as $n \to \infty$.

As noted in §27.4, this is not a sufficient condition for the convergence of the p.m.s of Y_n to Wiener measure. But with the aid of **27.12** we can prove that $\{Y_n\}$ is uniformly tight, and hence that the sequence has at least one cluster point in $\mathbb{M}_C$. Since all such points must have the finite-dimensional distributions of W, and the finite-dimensional cylinders are a determining class for $(C,\mathcal{B}_C)$, W must be the weak limit of the sequence. This convergence will be expressed either by writing $\mu_n \Rightarrow W$, or, more commonly in what follows, by $Y_n \xrightarrow{D} B$.

This type of result is called a functional central limit theorem (FCLT), although the term *invariance principle* is also used. The original FCLT for i.i.d. increments (the generalization of the Lindeberg-Levy theorem) is known as Donsker's theorem (Donsker 1951). Using the results of previous chapters, in particular **24.3**, we shall generalize the theorem to the case of a heterogeneously distributed martingale difference, although the basic idea is the same.

27.14 Theorem Let Y_n be defined by (27.53) and (27.54), where $\{U_{ni},\mathcal{F}_{ni}\}$ is a martingale difference array with variance array $\{\sigma^2_{ni}\}$, and $\sum_{i=1}^n \sigma^2_{ni} = 1$. If

(a) $\displaystyle\sum_{i=1}^n U^2_{ni} \xrightarrow{pr} 1$,

(b) $\displaystyle\max_{1\le i\le n} |U_{ni}| \xrightarrow{pr} 0$,

(c) $\displaystyle\lim_{n\to\infty} \sum_{i=1}^{[nt]} \sigma^2_{ni} = t$, for all $t \in [0,1]$,

then $Y_n \xrightarrow{D} B$. □

Conditions (a) and (b) reproduce the corresponding conditions of **24.3**, and their role is to establish the finite-dimensional distributions of the process, *via* the conventional CLT. Condition (c) is a global stationarity condition (see §13.2) which has no counterpart in the CLT conditions of Chapter 24. Its effect is to rule out cases such as **24.10** and **24.11**. By simple subtraction, the condition is sufficient for

$$\lim_{n\to\infty} \sum_{i=[nt]+1}^{[ns]} \sigma_{ni}^2 = s - t, \tag{27.59}$$

for $0 \le t < s \le 1$. Clearly, without this restriction condition (27.57) could not hold for any t_1 and t_2.

Proof of 27.14 Conditions **24.3**(a) and **24.3**(b) are satisfied, on writing U_{ni} for X_{nt}. In view of the last remarks, the finite-dimensional distributions of Y_n converge to those of W, and it remains to prove that $\{Y_n\}$ is uniformly tight (i.e., that the sequence of p.m.s of the Y_n is uniformly tight).

Define, for positive integers k and m with $k+m \le n$, $s_{nkm}^2 = \sum_{i=k+1}^{k+m}\sigma_{ni}^2 = E(S_{n,k+m} - S_{nk})^2$, where $S_{n,k+j} - S_{nk} = \sum_{i=k+1}^{k+j} U_{ni}$. The maximal inequality for martingales in **15.14** implies that, for $\lambda > 0$,

$$P\left(\max_{1\le j\le m} |S_{n,k+j} - S_{nk}| > \lambda s_{nkm}\right) \le \frac{E|S_{n,k+m} - S_{nk}|^p}{(\lambda s_{nkm})^p}. \tag{27.60}$$

In particular, set $k = [nt]$ and $m = [n\delta]$ for fixed $\delta \in (0,1)$ and $t \in [0, 1-\delta]$ so that m increases with n, and then we may say that $(S_{n,k+m} - S_{nk})/s_{nkm} \xrightarrow{D} Z \sim N(0,1)$, by **24.3**. For given positive numbers η and ε, choose λ satisfying

$$\lambda > \max\{\varepsilon/8,\ 256E|Z|^3/\eta\varepsilon^2\}, \tag{27.61}$$

and consider the case $\delta = \varepsilon^2/64\lambda^2 < 1$. There must exist $N_0 \ge 1$ for which, with $n \ge N_0$, the Gaussian approximation is sufficiently close that

$$\frac{E|S_{n,k+m} - S_{nk}|^3}{(\lambda s_{nkm})^3} \le \frac{\eta\varepsilon^2}{256\lambda^2} = \tfrac{1}{4}\eta\delta. \tag{27.62}$$

Also observe from (27.59) that $\lim_{n\to\infty} s_{nkm}^2 = \delta$. For the choice of δ indicated there exists $N_1 \ge 1$ such that $\lambda s_{nkm} < \frac{1}{4}\varepsilon$ for $n \ge N_1$, and hence, combining (27.60) with $p = 3$ with (27.62), such that

$$P\left(\max_{1\le j\le m} |S_{n,k+j} - S_{nk}| \ge \tfrac{1}{4}\varepsilon\right) \le \tfrac{1}{4}\eta\delta, \tag{27.63}$$

for $n \ge \max\{N_0, N_1\}$.

Now,

$$Y_n(s) - Y_n(t) = S_{n,[ns]} - S_{n,[nt]} + R_n(s,t) \tag{27.64}$$

for $s > t$, from (27.53) and (27.54), where

$$R_n(s,t) = (ns - [ns])U_{n,[ns]+1} - (nt - [nt])U_{n,[nt]+1}. \tag{27.65}$$

For $t \in [0, 1-\delta]$, there exists $s' \in [t, t+\delta]$ such that

$$|Y_n(s') - Y_n(t)| = \sup_{t\le s\le t+\delta} |Y_n(s) - Y_n(t)|. \tag{27.66}$$

There also exists n large enough (say, $n \ge N_2$) that, for any such t and s', $[nt] \le$

$[ns'] \le [nt] + [n\delta]$ and hence

$$|S_{n,[ns']} - S_{n,[nt]}| \le \max_{1 \le j \le [n\delta]} |S_{n,[nt]+j} - S_{n,[nt]}|. \tag{27.67}$$

It follows (also invoking the triangle inequality) that for $n \ge N_2$,

$$\begin{aligned} |Y_n(s') - Y_n(t)| &= |S_{n,[ns']} - S_{n,[nt]} + R_n(s',t)| \\ &\le \max_{1 \le j \le [n\delta]} |S_{n,[nt]+j} - S_{n,[nt]}| + |R_n(s',t)|. \end{aligned} \tag{27.68}$$

By condition (b) of the theorem, $P(\sup_{s,t}|R_n(s,t)| \ge \frac{1}{4}\varepsilon) \to 0$ as $n \to \infty$, and hence there exists $N_3 \ge 1$ such that, for $n \ge N_3$,

$$P(|R_n(s',t)| \ge \tfrac{1}{4}\varepsilon) \le \tfrac{1}{4}\eta\delta. \tag{27.69}$$

Inequalities (27.69) and (27.63) jointly imply that, for all $t \in [0, 1-\delta]$ and $n \ge N^* = \max\{N_0, N_1, N_2, N_3\}$,

$$\begin{aligned} &P(|Y_n(s') - Y_n(t)| \ge \tfrac{1}{2}\varepsilon) \\ &\quad \le P\left(\max_{1 \le j \le [n\delta]} |S_{n,[nt]+j} - S_{n,[nt]}| + |R_n(s',t)| \ge \tfrac{1}{2}\varepsilon\right) \\ &\quad \le P\left(\left\{\max_{1 \le j [n\delta]} |S_{n,[nt]+j} - S_{n,[nt]}| \ge \tfrac{1}{4}\varepsilon\right\} \cup \left\{|R_n(s',t)| \ge \tfrac{1}{4}\varepsilon\right\}\right) \\ &\quad \le P\left(\max_{1 \le j [n\delta]} |S_{n,[nt]+j} - S_{n,[nt]}| \ge \tfrac{1}{4}\varepsilon\right) + P(|R_n(s',t)| \ge \tfrac{1}{4}\varepsilon) \\ &\quad \le \tfrac{1}{2}\eta\delta. \end{aligned} \tag{27.70}$$

The conclusion may be written as

$$\sup_{0 \le t \le 1-\delta} P\left(\sup_{t \le s \le t+\delta} |Y_n(s) - Y_n(t)| \ge \tfrac{1}{2}\varepsilon\right) \le \tfrac{1}{2}\eta\delta,\ n \ge N^*. \tag{27.71}$$

Note that (27.51) is identical with (27.71) for the case $\mu_n(A) = P(Y_n \in A)$, and that η and ε are arbitrary. Therefore, uniform tightness of the corresponding sequence of measures follows by **27.12** and **27.13**. This completes the proof. ■

We conclude this section with the result promised in §27.4:

27.15 Corollary Wiener measure exists. □

The existence is actually proved in **27.14**, since we derived a unique limiting distribution which satisfied the specifications of **27.7**. The points which are conveniently highlighted by a separate statement are that the tightness argument developed to prove **27.14** holds independently of the existence of W as such, and that the central limit theorem plays no role in the proof of existence.

Proof Consider the process Y_n of (27.41). We shall show that, on putting $U_{ni} = n^{-1/2}\xi_i$, conditions **27.14**(a), (b), and (c) are satisfied. It will follow by the reasoning of **27.12** that the associated sequence of measures is uniformly tight, and possesses a limit. This limit has been shown above by direct calculation to have the finite-dimensional distributions specified by **27.7**, which will conclude the proof.

Condition **27.14**(c) holds by construction. Condition **27.12**(a)) follows from an application of the weak law of large numbers (e.g. Khinchine's theorem), recalling that since ξ_i is Gaussian $\{\xi_i^2\}$ is an independent sequence possessing all its moments. Finally, condition **27.14**(b) holds by **23.16** if the collection $\{\xi_1,\ldots,\xi_n\}$ satisfy the Lindeberg condition, which is obvious given their Gaussianity and **23.10**. ∎

27.7 The Multivariate Case

We would like to extend these results to vector-valued processes, and there is no difficulty in extending the approach of §25.3. Define the space $C_{[0,1]^m}$, which we write as C^m for brevity, as the space of continuous vector functions

$$\boldsymbol{x} = (x_1,\ldots,x_k)'\colon [0,1]^m \mapsto \mathbb{R}^m,$$

where $[0,1]^m$ and $\mathbb{R}^m$ are the Cartesian products of m copies of $[0,1]$ and $\mathbb{R}$ respectively. C^m is itself the product of m copies of C. It can be endowed with a metric such as

$$d_U^m(\boldsymbol{x},\boldsymbol{y}) = \max_{1\le j\le m} \{d_U(x_j,y_j)\}, \tag{27.72}$$

which induces the product topology, and coordinate projections remain continuous. Since C is separable, C^m is also separable by **6.16**, and $\mathcal{B}_C^m = \mathcal{B}_C \otimes \mathcal{B}_C \otimes \ldots \otimes \mathcal{B}_C$ (the σ-field generated by the open rectangles of $[0,1]^m$) is the Borel field of C^m by m-fold iteration of **26.5**. $(C^m, \mathcal{B}_C^m)$ is therefore a measurable space.

Let

$$\mathcal{H}_C^m = \{\pi_{t_1,\ldots,t_k}^{-1}(B) \subseteq C^m\colon B \in \mathcal{B}^{mk},\ t_1,\ldots,t_k \in [0,1],\ k \in \mathbb{N}\}, \tag{27.73}$$

denote the finite-dimensional sets of C^m. Again thanks to the product topology, $\mathcal{H}_C^m$ is the field generated from the sets in the product of m copies of $\mathcal{H}_C$.

27.16 Theorem $\mathcal{H}_C^m$ is a determining class for $(C^m, \mathcal{B}_C^m)$.

Proof An open sphere in $\mathcal{B}_C^m$ is a set

$$\begin{aligned} S(\boldsymbol{x},\alpha) &= \{\boldsymbol{y} \in C^m\colon d_U^m(\boldsymbol{x},\boldsymbol{y}) < \alpha\}, \\ &= \left\{\boldsymbol{y} \in C^m\colon \max_{1\le j\le m} \sup_t |y_j(t) - x_j(t)| < \alpha\right\}. \end{aligned} \tag{27.74}$$

The set

$$H_k(\boldsymbol{x},\alpha) = \left\{\boldsymbol{y} \in C^m\colon \max_{1\le j\le m}\max_{1\le i\le 2^k} |y_j(2^{-k}i) - x_j(2^{-k}i)| < \alpha\right\}, \tag{27.75}$$

is an element $\mathcal{H}_C^m$. It follows by the argument of **27.6** that

$$S(\boldsymbol{x},r) = \bigcup_{n=1}^{\infty}\bigcap_{k=1}^{\infty} H_k(\boldsymbol{x},\, r - 1/n) \in \mathcal{P}_C^m = \sigma(\mathcal{H}_C^m), \tag{27.76}$$

and hence, that $\mathcal{B}_C^m \subseteq \mathcal{P}_C^m$. Since $\mathcal{H}_C^m$ is a field, the result follows by the extension theorem. ■

It is also straightforward to show that $\mathcal{B}_C^m = \mathcal{P}_C^m$, by a similar generalization from **27.6**, but the above is all that is required for the present purpose.

A leading example of a measure on $(C^m,\mathcal{B}_C^m)$ is W^m, the p.m. of m-dimensional standard Brownian motion. A m-vector $\boldsymbol{B}$ distributed according to W^m has as its elements m mutually independent Brownian motions, such that

$$\boldsymbol{B}(t) \sim N(\boldsymbol{0},\, t\boldsymbol{I}_m), \tag{27.77}$$

where $\boldsymbol{I}_m$ is the $m\times m$ identity matrix, and the process has independent increments with

$$E\big((\boldsymbol{B}(s) - \boldsymbol{B}(t))(\boldsymbol{B}(s) - \boldsymbol{B}(t))'\big) = (s-t)\boldsymbol{I}_m \tag{27.78}$$

for $0 \le t < s \le 1$. The following general result can now be proved.

27.17 Theorem Let $\{\boldsymbol{U}_{ni},\mathcal{F}_{ni}\}$ be a m-vector martingale difference array with variance matrix array $\{\boldsymbol{\Sigma}_{ni}\}$, such that $\sum_{i=1}^n \boldsymbol{\Sigma}_{ni} = \boldsymbol{I}_m$. Then let

$$\boldsymbol{Y}_n(t) = \boldsymbol{S}_{n,j-1} + (nt - j + 1)\boldsymbol{U}_{nj} \text{ for } (j-1)/n \le t < j/n, \tag{27.79}$$

for $j = 1,\ldots,n$, and $\boldsymbol{Y}_n(1) = \boldsymbol{S}_{nn}$, where $\boldsymbol{S}_{n0} = \boldsymbol{0}$ and

$$\boldsymbol{S}_{nj} = \sum_{i=1}^{j} \boldsymbol{U}_{ni},\; j = 1,\ldots,n. \tag{27.80}$$

If

(a) $\displaystyle\sum_{i=1}^{n} \boldsymbol{U}_{ni}\boldsymbol{U}_{ni}' \xrightarrow{pr} \boldsymbol{I}_m,$

(b) $\displaystyle\max_{1\le i\le n} \boldsymbol{U}_{ni}'\boldsymbol{U}_{ni} \xrightarrow{pr} 0,$

(c) $\displaystyle\lim_{n\to\infty}\sum_{i=1}^{[nt]} \boldsymbol{\Sigma}_{ni} = t\boldsymbol{I}_m, \text{ for all } t \in [0,1],$

then $\boldsymbol{Y}_n \xrightarrow{D} \boldsymbol{B}$.

Proof Consider for an m-vector $\boldsymbol{\lambda}$ of unit length the scalar process $\boldsymbol{\lambda}'\boldsymbol{Y}_n$, having increments $\boldsymbol{\lambda}'\boldsymbol{U}_{ni}$. By definition, $\{\boldsymbol{\lambda}'\boldsymbol{U}_{ni},\mathcal{F}_{ni}\}$ is a scalar martingale difference array with variance sequence $\boldsymbol{\lambda}'\boldsymbol{\Sigma}_{ni}\boldsymbol{\lambda}$. It is easily verified that all the conditions of **27.14** are satisfied, and so $\boldsymbol{\lambda}'\boldsymbol{Y}_n \xrightarrow{D} B$. This holds for any choice of $\boldsymbol{\lambda}$. In particular, $\boldsymbol{\lambda}'\boldsymbol{Y}_n(t) \xrightarrow{D} N(0,t)$, with similar conclusions regarding all the finite-dimensional distributions of the process.

It follows by the Cramér-Wold theorem that

$$\boldsymbol{Y}_n(t) \xrightarrow{D} N(0, t\boldsymbol{I}_m), \tag{27.81}$$

with similar conclusions regarding all the finite-dimensional distributions of the process; these are identical to the finite-dimensional distributions of W^m. Since $\mathcal{H}_C^m$ is a determining class for $(C^m,\mathcal{B}^m)$, any weak limit of the p.m.s of $\{\boldsymbol{Y}_n\}$ can only be W^m. It remains to show that these p.m.s are uniformly tight. But this is true provided the marginal p.m.s of the process are uniformly tight, by **26.23**. Picking $\boldsymbol{\lambda}$ to be the jth column of $\boldsymbol{I}_m$ for $j = 1,...,m$ and applying the argument of **27.14** shows that this condition holds, and completes the proof. ∎

The arguments of §25.3 can be extended to convert **27.17** into provide an unusually powerful limit result. The conditions of the theorem are easily generalized, by replacing **27.17**(c) by

(c′) $\lim_{n\to\infty} \sum_{i=1}^{[nt]} \boldsymbol{\Sigma}_{ni} = t\boldsymbol{\Sigma}$,

where $\boldsymbol{\Sigma}$ is an arbitrary variance matrix. Defining $\boldsymbol{L}^-$ such that $\boldsymbol{L}^-\boldsymbol{\Sigma}\boldsymbol{L}^{-\prime} = \boldsymbol{I}_m$ as in **25.6**, **27.17** holds for the transformed vector process $\boldsymbol{Z}_n = \boldsymbol{L}^-\boldsymbol{Y}_n$. The limit of the process $\boldsymbol{Y}_n$ itself can then be determined by applying the continuous mapping theorem. This is a linear combination of independent Brownian motions, the finite-dimensional distributions of which are jointly Gaussian by **11.13**. We call it an m-dimensional correlated Brownian motion, having covariance matrix $\boldsymbol{\Sigma}$, and denoted $\boldsymbol{B}(\boldsymbol{\Sigma})$. The result is written in the form

$$\boldsymbol{Y}_n \xrightarrow{D} \boldsymbol{B}(\boldsymbol{\Sigma}). \tag{27.82}$$

An invariance principle can be used in this way to convert propositions about dependence between stochastic processes converging to Brownian motion into more tractable results about correlation in large samples. Given an arbitrarily related set of such processes, there always exist linear combinations of the set which are asymptotically independent of one another.[28]

28
Cadlag Functions

28.1 The Space D

The proof of the FCLT in the last chapter was made more complicated by the presence of terms necessary to ensure that the random functions under consideration lay in the space C. Since these terms were shown to be asymptotically negligible, it might reasonably be asked whether they are needed. Why not, in other words, work directly with X_n of (27.55) and (27.56), instead of Y_n of (27.53) and (27.54)? Fig. 28.1 shows (apart from the omission of the point $X_n(1)$, to be explained below) the graph of the process X_n corresponding to the Y_n sketched in Fig. 27.2. X_n as shown does not lie in $C_{[0,1]}$ but it does lie in $D_{[0,1]}$, the space of cadlag functions on the unit interval (see **5.27**), of which $C_{[0,1]}$ is a subset. Henceforth, we will write D to mean $D_{[0,1]}$ when there is no risk of confusion with other usages.

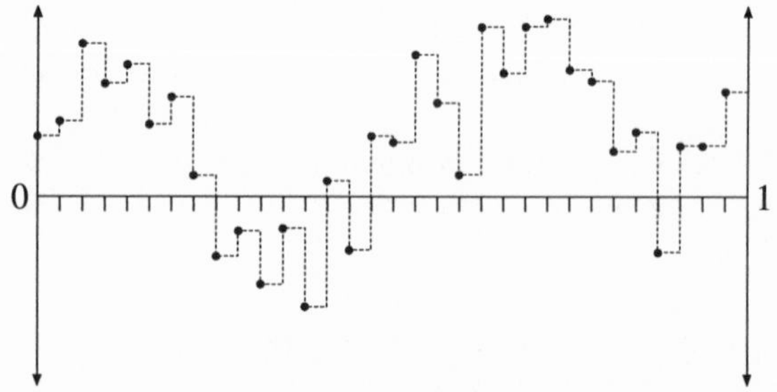

Fig. 28.1

As shown in **26.3**, D is not a separable space under the uniform metric, which means that the convergence theory of Chapter 26 will not apply to (D,d_U). d_U is not the only metric that can be defined on D, and it is worth investigating alternatives because, once the theory can be shown to work on D in the same kind of way that it does on C, a great simplification is achieved.

Abandoning d_U is not the only way of overcoming measurability problems. Another approach is simply to agree to exclude the pathological cases from the field of events under consideration. This can be achieved by working with the σ-field $\mathcal{P}_D$, the restriction to D of the projection σ-field (see §27.1). In contrast with the case of C, $\mathcal{P}_D \subset \mathcal{B}_D$ (compare **27.6**) and all the awkward cases such as uncountable discrete subsets are excluded from $\mathcal{P}_D$, while all the ones likely to arise in our theory (which exclusively concerns convergence to limit points lying in C) are included. Studying measures on the space $((D,d_U),\mathcal{P}_D)$ is an interesting line of attack, proposed originally by Dudley (1966, 1967) and described in detail in the book by Pollard (1984).

While this approach represents a large potential simplification (much of the present chapter could be dispensed with), an early decision has to be made about which line to adopt; there is little overlap between this theory and the methods pioneered by Skorokhod (1956, 1957), Prokhorov (1956), and Billingsley (1968), which involves metrizing D as a separable complete space. Although the technical overheads of the latter approach are greater, it has the advantage that, once the investment is made, the probabilistic environment is familiar; at whatever remove, one is still working in an analogue of Euclidean space for which all sorts of useful topological and metric properties are known to hold. There is scope for debate on the relative merits of the two approaches, but we follow the majority of subsequent authors who take their cue from Billingsley's work.

The possibility of metrizing D as a separable space depends crucially on the fact that in D the permitted departures from continuity are of a relatively limited kind. The only ones possible are jump discontinuities (also called 'discontinuities of the first kind'): points t at which $|x(t)-x(t-)| > 0$. There is no possibility of isolated discontinuity points t at which both $|x(t)-x(t-)|$ and $|x(t)-x(t+)|$ are positive, because that would contradict right-continuity. There is however the possibility that $x(1)$ is isolated; it will be necessary to discard this point, and let $x(1) = x(1-)$. This is a little unfortunate, but since we shall be studying convergence to a limit lying in $C_{[0,1]}$ (e.g., B), it will not change anything material. We adopt the following definition.

28.1 Definition $D_{[0,1]}$ is the space of functions satisfying the following conditions:

(a) $x(t+)$ exists for $t \in [0,1)$;
(b) $x(t-)$ exists for $t \in (0,1]$;
(c) $x(t) = x(t+)$, $t < 1$, and $x(1) = x(1-)$. □

The first theorem shows how, under these conditions, the maximum number of jumps is limited.

28.2 Theorem There exists, for all $x \in D$ and every $\varepsilon > 0$, a finite partition $\{t_1,\dots,t_r\}$ of $[0,1]$ with the property

$$\sup_{s,t\in[t_{i-1},t_i)} |x(t)-x(s)| < \varepsilon \tag{28.1}$$

for each $i = 1,\dots,r$.

Proof This is by showing that $t_r = 1$ for a collection $\{t_1,\dots,t_r\}$ satisfying (28.1), with $t_0 = 0$. For given x and ε let $\tau = \sup\{t_r\}$, the supremum being taken over all these collections. Since $x(t-)$ exists for all $t > 0$, τ belongs to the set; that is, there exists r such that $\tau = t_r$.

Suppose $t_r < 1$, and consider the point $t_r+\delta \le 1$, for some $\delta > 0$. By definition of t_r, $|x(t_r+\delta)-x(t_{r-1})| \ge \varepsilon$. Hence consider the interval $[t_r,t_r+\delta)$. By choice of δ we can ensure by right continuity that $|x(t_r+\delta)-x(t_r)| < \varepsilon$. Hence there exists an $(r+1)$-fold collection satisfying the conditions of the theorem. We must have $\tau \geq t_{r+1} = t_r+\delta$, and the assertion that $t_r = \tau$ is contradicted. It follows that $t_r = 1$. ■

This elementary but slightly startling result shows that the number of jump points at which $|x(t)-x(t-)|$ exceeds any given positive number are at most finite. The number of jumps such that $|x(t)-x(t-)| > 1/n$ is finite for every n, and the entire set of discontinuities is a countable union of finite sets, hence countable. Further, we see that

$$\sup_t |x(t)| < \infty, \tag{28.2}$$

since for any $t \in [0,1]$, $x(t)$ is expressible according to (28.1) as a finite sum of finite increments.

The modulus of continuity $w_x(\delta)$ in (27.14) provides a means of discriminating between functions in $C_{[0,1]}$ and functions outside the space. For just the same reasons, it is helpful to have a means of discriminating between cadlag functions and those with arbitrary discontinuities. For $\delta \in (0,1)$, let Π_δ denote a partition $\{t_1,\ldots,t_r\}$ with $r \leq [1/\delta]$ and $\min_i\{t_i-t_{i-1}\} > \delta$, and then define

$$w_x'(\delta) = \inf_{\Pi_\delta}\left\{\max_{1\leq i\leq r}\left\{\sup_{s,t\in[t_{i-1},t_i)} |x(t)-x(s)|\right\}\right\}. \tag{28.3}$$

Let's attempt to say this in English! $w_x'(\delta)$ is the smallest value, over all partitions of [0,1] coarser than δ, of the largest change in x within an interval of the partition. This notion differs from, and weakens, that of $w_x(\delta)$, in that $w_x'(\delta)$ can be small even if the points t_i are jump points such that $w_x(\delta)$ would be large. For $\delta < \frac{1}{2}$ there is always a partition Π_δ in which $t_i-t_{i-1} < 2\delta$ for some i, so that for any $x \in D$,

$$w_x'(\delta) \leq w_x(2\delta) \tag{28.4}$$

for $\delta < \frac{1}{2}$. So obviously, $\lim_{\delta\to 0} w_x'(\delta) = 0$ for any $x \in C$. On the other hand,

$$\lim_{\delta\to 0} w_x'(\delta) = 0 \tag{28.5}$$

is a property which holds for elements of D, but not for more general functions.

28.3 Theorem If and only if $x \in D$, $\exists\ \delta$ such that $w_x'(\delta) < \varepsilon$, for any $\varepsilon > 0$.

Proof Sufficiency is immediate from **28.2**. Necessity follows from the fact that if $x \notin D$ there is a point other than 1 at which x is not right-continuous; in other words, a point t at which $|x(t)-x(t+)| \geq \varepsilon$ for some $\varepsilon > 0$. Choose arbitrary δ and consider (28.3). If $t \neq t_i$ for any i, then $w_x'(\delta) \geq \varepsilon$ by definition. But even if $t = t_i$ for some i, $t_i \in [t_i,t_{i+1})$ and $|x(t_i)-x(t_i+)| \geq \varepsilon$, and again $w_x'(\delta) \geq \varepsilon$. ■

28.2 Metrizing D

Recall the difficulty presented by the existence of uncountable discrete sets in (D,d_U), such as the sets of functions

$$x_\theta(t) = \begin{cases} 0, & 0 \le t < \theta \\ 1, & \theta \le t \le 1, \end{cases} \tag{28.6}$$

the case of (5.43) with $a = 0$ and $b = 1$. We need a topology in which x_θ and $x_{\theta'}$ are regarded as close when $|\theta - \theta'|$ is small. Skorokhod (1956) devised a metric with this property.

Let Λ denote the collection of all homeomorphisms λ: $[0,1] \mapsto [0,1]$ with $\lambda(0) = 0$ and $\lambda(1) = 1$; think of these as the set of increasing graphs connecting the opposite corners of the unit square (see Fig. 28.2). The Skorokhod J1 metric is defined as

$$d_S(x,y) = \inf_{\lambda \in \Lambda}\left\{\varepsilon > 0\text{: } \sup_t |\lambda(t) - t| \le \varepsilon,\ \sup_t |x(t) - y(\lambda(t))| \le \varepsilon\right\}. \tag{28.7}$$

In his 1956 paper Skorokhod proposes four metrics, denoted J1, J2, M1, and M2. We shall not be concerned with the others, and will refer to d_S as is customary, as 'the' Skorokhod metric.

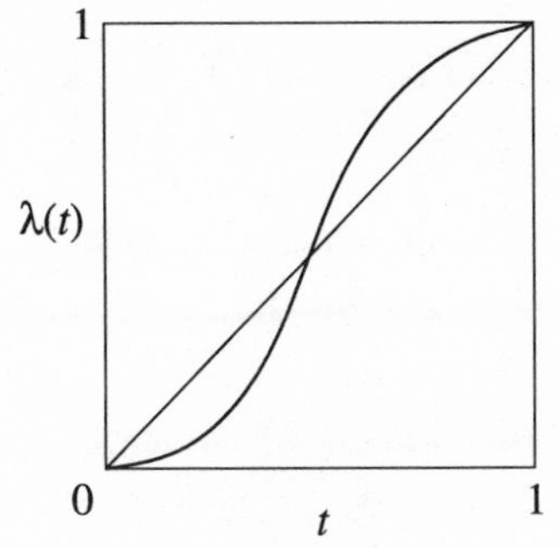

Fig. 28.2

It is easy to verify that d_S is a metric, if you note that $\sup_t|\lambda(t) - t| = \sup_t|t - \lambda^{-1}(t)|$ and $\sup_t|x(t) - y(\lambda(t))| = \sup_t|x(\lambda^{-1}(t)) - y(t)|$, where $\lambda^{-1} \in \Lambda$ if $\lambda \in \Lambda$. While in the uniform metric two functions are close only if their vertical separation is uniformly small, the Skorokhod metric also takes into account the possibility that the *horizontal* separation is small. If x is uniformly close to y except that it jumps slightly before or slightly after y, the functions would be considered close as measured by d_S, if not by d_U.

Consider x_θ in (28.6), and another element $x_{\theta+\delta}$. The uniform distance between these elements is 1, as noted above. To calculate the Skorokhod distance, note that the quantity in braces in (28.7) will be 1 for any λ for which $\lambda(\theta) \ne \theta + \delta$. Confining consideration to the subclass of Λ with $\lambda(\theta) = \theta + \delta$, choose a case where $|\lambda(t) - t| \leq \delta$ (for example, the graph $\{t, \lambda(t)\}$, obtained by joining the three points (0,0), $(\theta,\theta+\delta)$, and (1,1) with straight lines, will fulfil the definition) and hence,

$$d_S(x_\theta, x_{\theta+\delta}) = \delta. \tag{28.8}$$

This distance approaches zero smoothly as $\delta \downarrow 0$, which might conform better to our intuitive idea of 'proximity' than the uniform metric in these circumstances.

28.4 Theorem On C, d_S, and d_U are equivalent metrics.

Proof Obviously $d_S(x,y) \leq d_U(x,y)$, since the latter corresponds to the case where λ is the identity function in (28.7). On the other hand, for any λ,

$$d_U(x,y) \leq \sup_t |x(t) - y(\lambda(t))| + \sup_t |y(\lambda(t)) - y(t)|. \tag{28.9}$$

Suppose y is uniformly continuous. For every $\varepsilon > 0$ there must exist $\delta > 0$ such that, if $d_S(x,y) < \delta$ (and hence $\sup_t|\lambda(t) - t| < \delta$), then $\sup_t|y(\lambda(t)) - y(t)| < \varepsilon$. In other words,

$$d_S(x,y) < \delta \;\Rightarrow\; d_U(x,y) < \delta + \varepsilon. \tag{28.10}$$

The criteria of (5.5) and (5.6) are therefore satisfied. Uniform continuity is equivalent to continuity on [0,1], and so the stated inequalities hold for all $y \in C$. ∎

The following result explains our interest in the Skorokhod metric.

28.5 Theorem (D,d_S) is separable.

Proof As usual, this is shown by exhibiting a countable dense subset. The counterpart in D of the piecewise linear function defined for C is the piecewise constant function (as in Fig. 28.1) defined as

$$y(t) = y(t_i),\; t \in [t_i, t_{i+1})\;\; i = 0,\ldots,m-1, \tag{28.11}$$

where the $y(t_i)$ are specified real numbers. For some $n \in \mathbb{N}$, define the set A_n as the countable collection of the piecewise constant functions of form (28.11), with $t_i = i/2^n$ for $i = 0,\ldots,2^n - 1$, and $y(t_i)$ assuming *rational* values for each i. Letting A denote the limit of the sequence $\{A_n\}$, A is a set of functions taking rational values at a set of points indexed on the dyadic rationals $\mathbb{D}$, and hence is countable by **1.5**.

According to **28.2**, there exists for $x \in D$ a finite partition $\{t_1,\ldots,t_m\}$ of [0,1], such that, for each i,

$$\sup_{s,t \in [t_{i-1},t_i)} |x(s) - x(t)| < \varepsilon.$$

Let y be a piecewise constant function constructed on the same intervals, assuming rational values $y_1,\ldots,y_m$ where y_i differs by no more than ε from a value assumed by x on $[t_i,t_{i+1})$. Then, $d_S(x,y) < 2\varepsilon$. Now, given $n \geq 1$, choose $z \in A_n$ such that $z_j = y_i$ when $j/2^n \in [t_i,t_{i+1})$. Since $\mathbb{D}$ is dense in [0,1], $d_S(y,z) \to 0$ as $n \to \infty$.

Hence, $d_S(x,z) \leq d_S(x,y) + d_S(y,z)$ is tending to a value not exceeding 2ε. Since by taking m large enough ε can be made as small as desired, x is a closure point of A. And since x was arbitrary, we have shown that A is dense in D. ■

Notice how this argument would fail under the uniform metric in the cases where x has discontinuities at one or more of the points t_i. Then, $d_U(y,z)$ will be small only if the two sets of intervals overlap precisely, such that $t_i = j/2^n$ for some j. If t_i were irrational, this would not occur for any finite m, since $j/2^n$ is rational. Under these circumstances x would fail to be a closure point of A. This shows why we need the Skorokhod topology (that is, the topology induced by the Skorokhod metric) to ensure separability.

Working with d_S will none the less complicate matters somewhat. For one thing, d_S does not generate the Tychonoff topology, and the coordinate projections are not in general continuous mappings. The fact that x and y are close in the Skorokhod metric does not imply that $x(t)$ is close to $y(t)$ for every t, the examples of x_θ and $x_{\theta+\delta}$ cited above being a case in point. We must therefore find alternative ways of showing that the projections are measurable.

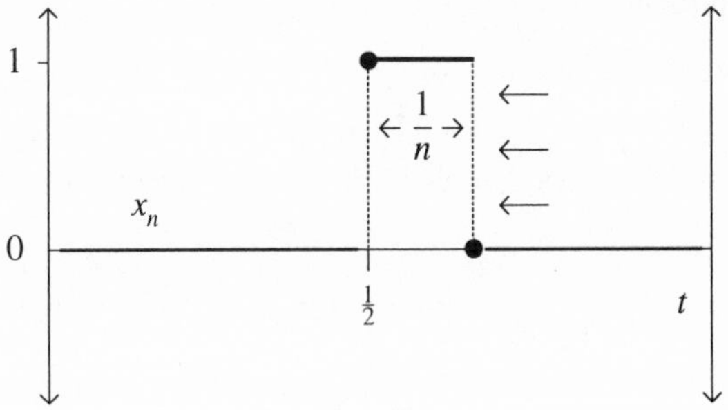

Fig. 28.3

And there is another serious problem: (D,d_S) is not complete. This is easily seen by considering the sequence of elements $\{x_n\}$ where

$$x_n(t) = \begin{cases} 1, & t \in [\frac{1}{2}, \frac{1}{2}+\frac{1}{n}) \\ 0, & \text{otherwise} \end{cases} \tag{28.12}$$

(see Fig. 28.3). The limit of this sequence is a function having an isolated point of discontinuity at $\frac{1}{2}$, and hence is not in D. However, to calculate $d_S(x_n,x_m)$ λ must be chosen so that $\lambda(\frac{1}{2}) = \frac{1}{2}$, and $\lambda(\frac{1}{2}+\frac{1}{n}) = \frac{1}{2}+\frac{1}{m}$; the distance is 1 for any other choice. The piecewise-linear graph with vertices at (0,0), $(\frac{1}{2},\frac{1}{2})$, $(\frac{1}{2}+\frac{1}{n}, \frac{1}{2}+\frac{1}{m})$, and (1,1) fulfils the definition, and satisfies (28.7). It appears that $d_S(x_n,x_m) = |\frac{1}{n}-\frac{1}{m}|$, and so $\{x_n\}$ is a Cauchy sequence.

28.3 Billingsley's Metric

The solution to this problem is to devise a metric that is equivalent to d_S (in the sense of generating the same topology, and hence a separable space) but in which sequences such as the one in (28.12) are not Cauchy sequences. Ingenious alternatives have been suggested by different authors. The following is due to Billingsley (1968), from which source the results of this section and the next are adapted.

Let Λ be the collection of homeomorphisms λ from [0,1] to [0,1] with $\lambda(0) = 0$ and $\lambda(1) = 1$, and satisfying

$$\|\lambda\| = \sup_{t \neq s} \left| \log \frac{\lambda(t) - \lambda(s)}{t - s} \right| < \infty. \tag{28.13}$$

Here, $\|\lambda\|: \Lambda \mapsto \mathbb{R}^+$ is a functional measuring the maximum deviation of the gradient of λ from 1, so that in particular $\|\lambda\| = 0$ for the case $\lambda(t) = t$. The set Λ is like the one defined for the Skorokhod metric with the added proviso that $\|\lambda\|$ be finite; both λ and λ^{-1} must be strictly increasing functions. Then define

$$d_B(x,y) = \inf_{\lambda \in \Lambda} \left\{ \varepsilon > 0: \ \|\lambda\| \leq \varepsilon, \ \sup_t |x(t) - y(\lambda(t))| \leq \varepsilon \right\}. \tag{28.14}$$

We review the essential properties of d_B.

28.6 Theorem d_B is a metric.

Proof $d_B(x,y) = 0$ iff $x = y$ is immediate. $d_B(x,y) = d_B(y,x)$ is also easy once it is noted that $\|\lambda^{-1}\| = \|\lambda\|$. To show the triangle inequality, note that

$$\begin{aligned} \|\lambda_1\| + \|\lambda_2\| &\geq \sup_{t \neq s} \left\{ \left| \log \frac{\lambda_1(t) - \lambda_1(s)}{t - s} \right| + \left| \log \frac{\lambda_2(t) - \lambda_2(s)}{t - s} \right| \right\} \\ &\geq \sup_{t \neq s} \left\{ \left| \log \frac{(\lambda_1(t) - \lambda_1(s))(\lambda_2(t) - \lambda_2(s))}{(t - s)^2} \right| \right\} \\ &\geq \sup_{t \neq s} \left\{ \left| \log \frac{(\lambda_1(t) - \lambda_1(s))(\lambda_2(t') - \lambda_2(s'))}{(t - s)(t' - s')} \right| \right\} \end{aligned} \tag{28.15}$$

for arbitrary t' and s'. On setting $t' = \lambda_1(t)$ and $s' = \lambda_2(s)$, we obtain

$$\|\lambda_1\| + \|\lambda_2\| \geq \|\lambda_1 \circ \lambda_2\|, \tag{28.16}$$

where $\lambda_1 \circ \lambda_2(t) = \lambda_1(\lambda_2(t))$, and $\lambda_1 \circ \lambda_2$ is clearly an element of Λ. Since

$$\sup_t |x(t) - z(\lambda_2(\lambda_1(t)))| \leq \sup_t |x(t) - y(\lambda_1(t))| + \sup_t |y(t) - z(\lambda_2(t))| \tag{28.17}$$

by the ordinary triangle inequality for points of $\mathbb{R}$, the condition $d_S(x,z) \leq d_S(x,y) + d_S(y,z)$ follows from the definition. ∎

Next we explore the relationship between d_S and d_B, and verify that they are equivalent metrics. Inequalities going in both directions can be derived provided the distances are sufficiently small. Given functions x and y for which $d_B(x,y) =$

$\varepsilon \leq \frac{1}{2}$, consider $\lambda \in \Lambda$ satisfying the definition of d_B for this pair, such that, in particular, $\|\lambda\| \leq \varepsilon$. Since $\lambda(0) = 0$, there evidently must exist $t \in (0,1]$ such that $|\log(\lambda(t)/t)| \leq \|\lambda\|$, or

$$e^{-\varepsilon} \leq \frac{\lambda(t)}{t} \leq e^{\varepsilon}. \tag{28.18}$$

Using the series expansion of e^{ε}, we find $e^{\varepsilon} - 1 \leq 2\varepsilon$ for $\varepsilon \leq \frac{1}{2}$, and $e^{-\varepsilon} - 1 \geq -2\varepsilon$ similarly, which implies that

$$-2\varepsilon \leq t(e^{-\varepsilon} - 1) \leq \lambda(t) - t \leq t(e^{\varepsilon} - 1) \leq 2\varepsilon, \tag{28.19}$$

or, $|\lambda(t) - t| \leq 2\varepsilon$. And in view of our assumption about λ, $\sup_t|x(t) - y(\lambda(t))| \leq \varepsilon$ and hence $d_S(x,y)$ cannot exceed 2ε. In other words,

$$d_S(x,y) \leq 2d_B(x,y) \tag{28.20}$$

whenever $d_B(x,y) \leq \frac{1}{2}$.

Now consider a function $\mu \in \Lambda$ which is piecewise-linear with vertices at the points of a partition Π_δ, as defined above (28.3) for a suitable choice of δ to be specified. The slope of μ is equal to $(\mu(t_i) - \mu(t_{i-1}))/(t_i - t_{i-1})$ on the intervals $[t_{i-1},t_i)$, where $t_i - t_{i-1} > \delta$. Notice that, if $\sup_t|\mu(t) - t| \leq \delta^2$,

$$\left|\frac{\mu(t_i) - \mu(t_{i-1})}{t_i - t_{i-1}} - 1\right| \leq \frac{|\mu(t_i) - t_i| + |\mu(t_{i-1}) - t_{i-1}|}{\delta} \leq 2\delta. \tag{28.21}$$

For $|x| \leq \frac{1}{2}$, the series expansion $\log\{1+x\} = x - \frac{1}{2}x^2 + \frac{1}{3}x^3 - \ldots$ implies

$$|\log\{1+x\}| \leq \max\{|x|,\ |x - x^2|\} \leq 2|x|. \tag{28.22}$$

Substituting for x in (28.22) the quantity whose absolute value is the minorant side of (28.21), we must conclude that, if $\sup_t|\mu(t) - t| \leq \delta^2$ for $0 < \delta \leq \frac{1}{4}$, then

$$\|\mu\| \leq 4\delta. \tag{28.23}$$

Now, suppose $d_S(x,y) = \delta^2$, which means there exists $\lambda \in \Lambda$ satisfying $\sup_t|\lambda(t) - t| \leq \delta^2$, and $\sup_t|y(t) - x(\lambda(t))| \leq \delta^2$. Choose μ as the piecewise linear function with $\mu(t_i) = \lambda(t_i)$ for $i = 0,\ldots,r$. The function $\lambda^{-1}\mu$ is 'tied down' to the diagonal at the points of the partition; that is, it is increasing on the intervals $[t_{i-1},t_i)$ with $\lambda^{-1}\mu(t) \in [t_{i-1},t_i)$ if and only if $t \in [t_{i-1},t_i)$. Therefore, choosing Π_δ to correspond to the definition of $w'_x(\delta)$, we can say

$$\begin{aligned}|x(t) - x(\mu(t))| &\leq |x(t) - x(\lambda^{-1}\mu(t))| + |x(\lambda^{-1}\mu(t)) - x(\mu(t))| \\ &\leq w'_x(\delta) + \delta^2.\end{aligned} \tag{28.24}$$

Putting this together with (28.23) gives for $0 < \delta \leq \frac{1}{4}$ the inequality

$$d_B(x,y) \leq \max\{4\delta, w'_x(\delta) + \delta^2\} \leq w'_x(\delta) + 4\delta. \tag{28.25}$$

Since for $x \in D$ we may make $w'_x(\delta)$ arbitrarily small by choice of δ, we have

$$d_B(x,y) \leq 4d_S(x,y)^{1/2} \tag{28.26}$$

whenever $d_S(x,y)$ is sufficiently small. We may conclude as follows.

28.7 Theorem In D, metrics d_B and d_S are equivalent.

Proof Given $\varepsilon > 0$, choose $\delta \leq \frac{1}{4}$, and also small enough that $w'_x(\delta)+4\delta \leq \varepsilon$. Then, for $\eta \leq \min\{\delta^2, \frac{1}{2}\varepsilon\}$,

$$d_B(x,y) < \eta \Rightarrow d_S(x,y) < \varepsilon, \tag{28.27}$$

$$d_S(x,y) < \eta \Rightarrow d_B(x,y) < \varepsilon, \tag{28.28}$$

by (28.20) and (28.25) respectively, The criteria of (5.5) and (5.6) are therefore satisfied. ■

Equivalence means that the two metrics induce the same topology on D (the Skorokhod topology). Given a sequence of elements $\{x_n\}$, $d_B(x_n,x) \to 0$ if and only if $d_S(x_n,x) \to 0$, whenever $x \in D$. But it does *not* imply that $\{x_n\}$ is a Cauchy sequence in (D,d_B) whenever it is a Cauchy sequence in (D,d_S), because the latter space is incomplete and a sequence may have its limit outside the space. It is clear in particular that $d_B(x_n,x) \to 0$ only if $d_S(x_n,x) \to 0$ *and* $\lim_{\delta\to 0}w'_x(\delta) = 0$.

For example, the sequence of functions in (28.12) is not a Cauchy sequence in (D,d_B). To define $d_B(x_n,x_m)$ (for $n \geq 3$, $m \geq 4$) it is necessary to find the element of Λ for which $\lambda(\frac{1}{2}) = \frac{1}{2}$ and $\lambda(\frac{1}{2}+\frac{1}{n}) = \frac{1}{2}+\frac{1}{m}$, and whose gradient deviates as little as possible from 1. This is obviously the same piecewise-linear function, with vertices at the points (0,0), $(\frac{1}{2},\frac{1}{2})$, $(\frac{1}{2}+\frac{1}{n}, \frac{1}{2}+\frac{1}{m})$ and (1,1), as defined for d_S. But the maximum gradient is n/m, corresponding to the segment connecting the second and third vertices. $d_B(x_n,x_m) = \min\{1, |\log(n/m)|\}$, which does not approach zero for large n and m (set $m = 2n$, for example).

28.8 Theorem The space (D,d_B) is complete.

Proof Let $\{y_k, k \in \mathbb{N}\}$ be a Cauchy sequence in (D,d_B) satisfying $d_B(y_k,y_{k+1}) < 1/2^k$, implying the existence of a sequence of functions $\{\mu_k \in \Lambda\}$ with

$$\sup_t |y_k(t) - y_{k+1}(\mu_k(t))| < 1/2^k, \tag{28.29}$$

$$\|\mu_k\| < 1/2^k. \tag{28.30}$$

It follows from (28.20) that $\sup_t|\mu_{k+m}(t) - t| \leq 2/2^{k+m}$ for $m > 0$. Define $\mu_{k,m} = \mu_{k+m}\circ\mu_{k+m-1}\circ\ldots\circ\mu_k$, also an element of Λ for each finite m; the sequence $\{\mu_{k,m}, m = 1,2,\ldots\}$ is a Cauchy sequence in (C,d_U) because

$$\sup_t |\mu_{k,m+1}(t) - \mu_{k,m}(t)| = \sup_s |\mu_{k+m+1}(s) - s| \leq 1/2^{k+m}. \tag{28.31}$$

Since (C,d_U) is complete there exists a limit function $\lambda_k = \lim_{k\to\infty}\mu_{k,m}$. To show that $\lambda_k \in \Lambda$, it is sufficient to show that $\|\lambda_k\| < \infty$. But by (28.16),

$$\|\mu_{k,m}\| \leq \|\mu_k \circ \mu_{k+1} \circ \ldots \circ \mu_{k+m}\| \leq \sum_{j=0}^{m} \|\mu_{k+j}\| < \sum_{j=0}^{m} \frac{1}{2^{k+j}} \leq \frac{1}{2^{k-1}}, \tag{28.32}$$

for any m, so $\|\lambda_k\| \leq 1/2^{k-1}$.

Note that $\lambda_k = \lambda_{k+1} \circ \mu_k$, so that $\lambda_{k+1}^{-1} = \mu_k \circ \lambda_k^{-1}$ and hence, by (28.29),

$$\sup_t |y_k(\lambda_k^{-1}(t)) - y_{k+1}(\lambda_{k+1}^{-1}(t))| = \sup_s |y_k(s) - y_{k+1}(\mu_k(s))| < 1/2^k. \tag{28.33}$$

So consider the sequence $\{y_k \circ \lambda_k^{-1} \in D, k \in \mathbb{N}\}$. According to (28.33) this is actually a Cauchy sequence in (D,d_U). But the latter space is complete; this is easily shown as a corollary of **5.24**, whose proof shows completeness of (C,d_U) without using any of the properties of C, so that it applies without modification to the case of D. Hence $y_k \circ \lambda_k^{-1}$ has a limit $y \in D$. Since this means both that $\sup_t |y_k(t) - y(\lambda_k(t))| = \sup_t |y_k(\lambda_k^{-1}(t)) - y(t)| \to 0$ and that $\|\lambda_k\| = \|\lambda_k^{-1}\| \to 0$, $d_B(y_k,y) \to 0$ and so $\{y_k\}$ has a limit y in (D,d_B).

We began by assuming that $\{y_k\}$ was a Cauchy sequence with $d_B(y_k,y_{k+1}) < 1/2^k$. But this involves no loss of generality because it suffices to show that any Cauchy sequence $\{x_n, n \in \mathbb{N}\}$ contains a convergent subsequence $\{y_k = x_{n_k}, k \in \mathbb{N}\}$. Clearly, a Cauchy sequence cannot have a cluster point which is not a limit point. Every Cauchy sequence contains a subsequence with the required property; if $d_B(x_n,x_{n+1}) < 1/g(n) \to 0$ (say), choosing $n_k \geq g^{-1}(2^k)$ is appropriate. This completes the proof. ■

28.4 Measures on D

We write $\mathcal{B}_D$ for the Borel field on (D,d_B). Henceforth, we will also write just D to denote (D,d_B), and will indicate the metric specifically only if one different from d_B is intended. The basic property we need the measurable space $(D,\mathcal{B}_D)$ to possess is that measures can be fully specified by the finite-dimensional sets. An argument analogous to **27.6** is called for, although some elaboration will be needed. In particular, we have to show, without appealing to continuity of the projections, that the finite-dimensional distributions are well-defined and that there are finite-dimensional sets which constitute a determining class for $(D,\mathcal{B}_D)$.

We start with a lemma. Define the field of finite-dimensional sets of D as $\mathcal{H}_D = \{H \cap D\colon H \in \mathcal{H}\}$, where $\mathcal{H}$ was defined in §27.1.

28.9 Lemma Given $x \in D$, $\alpha > 0$, and any $t_1,\ldots,t_m \in [0,1]$, let

$$H_m(x,\alpha) = \left\{ y \in D\colon \exists\ \lambda \in \Lambda \text{ s.t. } \|\lambda\| < \alpha,\ \max_{1 \leq i \leq m} |y(t_i) - x(\lambda(t_i))| < \alpha \right\}. \tag{28.34}$$

Then $H_m(x,\alpha) \in \mathcal{H}_D$.

Proof Since $H_m(x,\alpha) \subseteq D$, all we have to show according to (27.2) is that $\pi_{t_1,\ldots,t_m}(H_m(x,\alpha)) \in \mathcal{B}^m$. This is the set whose elements are $(y(t_1),\ldots,y(t_m))$ for each $y \in H_m(x,\alpha)$. To identify these, first define the set

$$A_m(x,\alpha) = \{x(\lambda(t_1)),\dots,x(\lambda(t_m)) \colon \lambda \in \Lambda,\ \|\lambda\| < \alpha\} \subseteq \mathbb{R}^m. \tag{28.35}$$

Then it is apparent that

$$\pi_{t_1,\dots,t_m}(H_m(x,\alpha))$$

$$= \left\{b_1,\dots,b_m\colon \max_{1\le i\le m} |a_i - b_i| < \alpha,\ (a_1,\dots,a_m) \in A_m(x,\alpha)\right\} \subseteq \mathbb{R}^m. \tag{28.36}$$

In words, this is the set $A_m(x,\alpha)$ with an open α-halo, and it is an open set. It therefore belongs to $\mathcal{B}^m$. ∎

To compare the present situation with that for C, it may be helpful to look at the case $k = 1$. The one-dimensional projection $\pi_t(H_t(x,\alpha))$, where

$$H_t(x,\alpha) = \{y \in D\colon \exists\ \lambda \in \Lambda \text{ s.t. } \|\lambda\| < \alpha,\ |y(t) - x(\lambda(t))| < \alpha\}, \tag{28.37}$$

is in general different from $S(x(t),\alpha)$, that is, the interval of width 2α centred on $x(t)$. If x is continuous at t the difference between these two sets can be made arbitrarily small by taking α small enough, and at these points the projections are in fact continuous. Since the discontinuity points are at most countable, they can be ignored in specifying finite-dimensional distributions for x, as will be apparent in the next theorem.

However, the point that matters here is that we have the material for the extension of a measure to $(D,\mathcal{B}_D)$ from the finite-dimensional distributions. It is easily verified that $\mathcal{H}_D$, like $\mathcal{H}$, is a field. The final link in the chain is to show that $\mathcal{H}_D$ is a determining class for $(D,\mathcal{B}_D)$.

28.10 Theorem (cf. Billingsley 1968: th. 14.5) $\mathcal{B}_D = \sigma(\mathcal{H}_D)$.

Proof An open sphere in (D,d_B) is a set of the form

$$S(x,\alpha) = \{y \in D\colon d_B(y,x) < \alpha\}$$

$$= \left\{y \in D\colon \exists\ \lambda \in \Lambda \text{ s.t. } \|\lambda\| < \alpha,\ \sup_t |y(t) - x(\lambda(t))| < \alpha\right\} \tag{28.38}$$

for $x \in D$, $\alpha > 0$. Since these sets generate $\mathcal{B}_D$, it will suffice to show they can be constructed by countable unions and complements (and hence also countable intersections) of sets in $\mathcal{H}_D$. Let $H(x,\alpha) = \bigcap_{k=1}^{\infty} H_k(x,\alpha)$, where $H_k(x,\alpha)$ is a set with the form of H_m defined in (28.34), but with $m = 2^k - 1$ and $t_i = i/2^k$, so that the set $\{t_1,\dots,t_{2^k-1}\}$ converges on $\mathbb{D}$ (the dyadic rationals) as $k \to \infty$. Consider $y \in H(x,\alpha)$. Since $y \in H_k(x,\alpha)$ for every k, we may choose a sequence $\{\lambda_k\}$ such that, for each $k \ge 1$,

$$\|\lambda_k\| < \alpha, \tag{28.39}$$

$$\max_{1\le i\le 2^k-1} |y(2^{-k}i) - x(\lambda_k(2^{-k}i))| < \alpha. \tag{28.40}$$

Making use of the fortuitous fact that λ_k has the properties of a c.d.f. on [0,1], Helly's theorem (**22.21**) may be applied to show that there is a subsequence $\{\lambda_{k_n},$

$n \in \mathbb{N}\}$ converging to a limit function λ which is non-decreasing on $[0,1]$ with $\lambda(0) = 0$ and $\lambda(1) = 1$. λ is necessarily in Λ, satisfying

$$\|\lambda\| \leq \alpha \tag{28.41}$$

according to (28.39). And in view of (28.40), and the facts that $\lambda_k(t) \to \lambda(t)$ and x is right-continuous on $[0,1)$, it must also satisfy either $|y(t) - x(\lambda(t))| \leq \alpha$ or $|y(t) - x(\lambda(t)-)| \leq \alpha$ for every $t \in \mathbb{D}$. Since $\mathbb{D}$ is dense in $[0,1]$, this is equivalent to

$$\sup_t |y(t) - x(\lambda(t))| \leq \alpha. \tag{28.42}$$

The limiting inequalities (28.41) or (28.42) cannot be relied on to be strict, but comparing with (28.38) we can conclude that $y \in \bar{S}(x,\alpha)$. This holds for all such y, so that $H(x,\alpha) \subseteq \bar{S}(x,\alpha)$. Put $\alpha = r - 1/n$, and take the countable union to give

$$\bigcup_{n=1}^{\infty} H(x,\, r - 1/n) \subseteq \bigcup_{n=1}^{\infty} \bar{S}(x,\, r - 1/n) = S(x,r). \tag{28.43}$$

It is also evident on comparing (28.34) with (28.38) that $S(x,\alpha) \subseteq H_k(x,\alpha)$ for $\alpha > 0$. Again, put $\alpha = r - 1/n$, and

$$S(x,r) = \bigcup_{n=1}^{\infty} S(x,\, r - 1/n) \subseteq \bigcup_{n=1}^{\infty} H(x,\, r - 1/n). \tag{28.44}$$

It follows that, for any $x \in D$ and $r > 0$, $S(x,r) = \bigcup_{n=1}^{\infty}\bigcap_{k=1}^{\infty} H_k(x,\, r - 1/n)$ where $H_k(x,\, r - 1/n) \in \mathcal{H}_D$. This completes the proof. ■

The defining of measures on $(D,\mathcal{B}_D)$ is now possible by arguments that broadly parallel those for C. The one pitfall we may encounter when assigning measures to finite-dimensional sets is that the coordinate projections of $\mathcal{B}_D$ sets may have no 'natural' interpretation in terms of observed increments of the random process. For example, suppose $X_n \in D$ is the process defined in (27.55) and (27.56), with respect to the underlying space $(\Omega,\mathcal{F},P)$. It is *not* necessarily the case that $\pi_t(X_n(\omega))$ is measurable with respect to $\mathcal{F}_{n,[nt]} = \sigma(U_{ni},\, i \leq [nt])$, as casual intuition might suggest. A $\mathcal{B}_D$-set like $H_t(x,\alpha)$ in (28.37) is the image under the mapping $X_n\colon \Omega \mapsto D$ of a set $E \in \mathcal{F}$; in fact, we could write $E = X_n^{-1}(\pi_t^{-1}(B))$, where $B \in \mathcal{B}$. But E depends on the value that x assumes at $\lambda(t)$, and if $\lambda(t) > t$ then E cannot be in $\mathcal{F}_{n,[nt]}$.

However, this difficulty goes away for processes lying in C almost surely. In view of **28.4**, we may 'embed' $((C,d_U),\mathcal{B}_C)$ in $((D,d_B),\mathcal{B}_D)$ and a p.m. defined on the former space can be extended to the latter, with support in C. In particular, Wiener measure is defined on $(D,\mathcal{B}_D)$ by simply augmenting the conditions in **27.7** with the stipulation that $W(x \in C) = 1$.

28.5 Prokhorov's Metric

The material of this section is not essential to the development since Billingsley's metric is all that we need to work successfully in D. But it is interesting to compare it with the alternative approach due to Prokhorov (1956). We begin with an alternative approach to defining a continuity modulus for cadlag functions. Let

$$\tilde{w}_x(\delta) = \max\left\{ \sup_{t-\delta\le t'\le t\le t''\le t+\delta} (\min\{|x(t')-x(t)|,\ |x(t'')-x(t)|\}),\right.$$
$$\left. \sup_{0\le t<\delta} |x(0)-x(\delta)|,\quad \sup_{1-\delta<t\le 1} |x(\delta)-x(1)| \right\}. \qquad (28.45)$$

Again, it may be helpful to restate this definition in English. The idea is that, for every $t \in [\delta, 1-\delta]$, a pair of adjacent intervals of width δ are constructed around the point, and we determine the maximum change over each of these intervals; the smaller of these two values measures the δ-continuity at point t, and this quantity is supped over the interval. This means that the function can jump discontinuously without affecting $\tilde{w}_x(\delta)$, so long as no two jumps are too close together. The exceptions are the two points 0 and 1, which for $\tilde{w}_x(\delta) \to 0$ must be true continuity points from the right and left respectively.

The following theorem parallels **28.3**.

28.11 Theorem If and only if $x \in D$,

$$\lim_{\delta\to 0} \tilde{w}_x(\delta) = 0. \qquad (28.46)$$

Proof Suppose $x \in D$. By **28.1**(c), the second and third terms under the 'max' in (28.45) definitely go to zero with δ. Hence consider the first term. Let $\{t_k,t'_k,t''_k\}$ denote the sequence of points at which the supremum is attained on setting $\delta = 1/k$ for $k = 1,2,...$ Assume $t_k \to t$. (If need be consider a convergent subsequence.) Then $t'_k \to t$ and $t''_k \to t$. Since $x(t) = x(t+)$, this implies $|x(t_k)-x(t''_k)| \to 0$, which proves sufficiency.

Now suppose $\tilde{w}_x(\delta) \to \tilde{w}_x(0) > 0$. Since

$$\tilde{w}_x(0) = \max\{|x(0)-x(0+)|, |x(1)-x(1-)|, \min\{|x(t)-x(t-)|, |x(t)-x(t+)|\}\},$$

it follows that $x \notin D$, proving necessity. ■

Now define the function

$$\overline{w}_x(z) = \begin{cases} \tilde{w}_x(e^z+), & z < 0, \\ \tilde{w}_x(1), & z \ge 0. \end{cases} \qquad (28.47)$$

This is non-decreasing, right-continuous, bounded below by 0 and above by $\tilde{w}_x(1)$. It therefore defines a finite measure on $\mathbb{R}$, just as a c.d.f. defines a p.m. on $\mathbb{R}$. By defining a family of measures in this way (indexed on x) on a separable space, we can exploit the fact that a space of measures is metrizable. In fact, we can use Lévy's metric L^* defined in (26.33). The Prokhorov metric for D is

$$d_P(x,y) = d_H(\Gamma_x,\Gamma_y) + L^*(\overline{w}_x,\overline{w}_y), \qquad (28.48)$$

where Γ_x and Γ_y are the graphs of x and y and d_H is the Hausdorff metric.

The idea here should be clear. With the first term alone, we should obtain a property similar to that of the Skorokhod metric; if we write $d(x(t),\Gamma_y) = \inf_{t'} d_E(x(t),y(t'))$, then

$$d_H(\Gamma_x,\Gamma_y) = \max\left\{\sup_t d(x(t),\Gamma_y),\ \sup_{t'} d(\Gamma_x,y(t'))\right\}. \tag{28.49}$$

In words, the smallest Euclidean distances between $x(t)$ and a point of y, and $y(t)$ and a point of x, are supped over t. For comparison, the Skorokhod metric minimizes the greater of the horizontal and vertical distances separating points on Γ_x and Γ_y in the plane, subject to the constraints imposed on the choice of λ such as continuity. In cases such as the functions x_θ of (28.6), x_θ and $x_{\theta+\delta}$ are close in (D,d_H) when δ is small. (Think in terms of the distances the graphs would have to be moved to fit over one another.)

The purpose of the second term is to ensure completeness. By **28.11**, $\lim_{z\to-\infty}\overline{w}_x(z) = 0$ if and only if $x \in D$; otherwise this limit will be strictly positive. Unlike the case of (D,d_H), it is not possible to have a Cauchy sequence in (D,d_P) aproaching a point outside the space. It can be shown that d_P is equivalent to d_S, and hence of course also to d_B, and that the space (D,d_P) is complete. The proofs of these propositions can be found in Parthasarathy (1967). For practical purposes, therefore, there is nothing to choose between d_P and d_B.

28.6 Compactness and Tightness in *D*

The remaining task is to characterize the compact sets of D, in parallel with the earlier application of the Arzelà-Ascoli theorem for C.

28.12 Theorem (Billingsley 1968: th. 14.3) A set $A \subset D$ is relatively compact in (D,d_B) if and only if

$$\sup_{x\in A}\sup_t |x(t)| < \infty, \tag{28.50}$$

$$\lim_{\delta\to 0}\sup_{x\in A} w'_x(\delta) = 0. \ \square \tag{28.51}$$

This theorem obviously parallels **27.5** but there are significant differences in the conditions. The modulus of continuity w'_x appears in place of w_x which is a weakening of the previous conditions, but, on the other hand, (28.50) replaces (27.16). Instead of $\sup_t|x(t)|$ we could write $d_B(|x|,0)$, where 0 denotes the element of D which is identically zero everywhere on [0,1]. It is no longer sufficient to bound the elements at one point of the interval to ensure that they are bounded everywhere: the whole element must be bounded.

A feature of the proof that follows, which is basically similar to that of **5.28**, is that we can avoid invoking completeness of the space until, so to speak, the last moment. The sufficiency argument establishing total boundness of A is couched in terms of the more tractable Skorokhod metric, and then we can exploit the equivalence of d_S with a complete metric such as d_B to get the compactness of $\overline{A}$.

The argument for necessity also uses d_S to prove upper semicontinuity of $w'_x(\delta)$, a property that, as we show, implies (28.51) when the space is compact.

Proof of 28.12 Let $\sup_{x\in A}\sup_t|x(t)| = M$. To show sufficiency, fix $\varepsilon > 0$ and choose m as the smallest integer such that both $1/m < \frac{1}{2}\varepsilon$ and $\sup_{x\in A}w'_x(1/m) < \frac{1}{2}\varepsilon$. Such an m exists by (28.51). Construct the finite collection E_m of piecewise *constant* functions, whose values at the discontinuity points $t = j/m$ for $j = 0,\dots,m-1$, are drawn from the set $\{M(2u/v-1),\ u = 0,1,\dots,v\}$ where v is an integer exceeding $2M/\varepsilon$; hence, E_m has $(v+1)^m$ different elements. This set is shown to be an ε-net for A.

Given the definition of m, one can choose for $x \in A$ a partition $\Pi_{1/m} = \{t_1,\dots,t_r\}$, defined as above (28.3), to satisfy

$$\max_{1\le i\le r}\left\{\sup_{s,t\in[t_{i-1},t_i)}|x(t)-x(s)|\right\} < \tfrac{1}{2}\varepsilon. \tag{28.52}$$

For $i = 0,\dots,r-1$ let j_i be the integer such that $j_i/m \le t_i < (j_i+1)/m$, noting that, since the t_i are at a distance more than $1/m$, there is at most one of them in any one of the intervals $[j/m,(j+1)/m)$, $j = 0,\dots,m-1$. Choose a piecewise linear function $\lambda \in \Lambda$ with vertices $\lambda(j_i/m) = t_i$, $i = 0,\dots,r$. Since $|t_i-j_i/m| \le 1/m$, $\max_{0\le i\le r}|\lambda(j_i/m)-j_i/m| \le \frac{1}{2}\varepsilon$, and the linearity of λ between these points means that

$$\sup_t|\lambda(t)-t| \le \tfrac{1}{2}\varepsilon. \tag{28.53}$$

By construction, λ maps points in $[j/m,(j+1)/m)$ into $[t_i,t_{i+1})$ whenever $j_i \le j \le j_{i+1}$, and since x varies by at most $\frac{1}{2}\varepsilon$ over intervals $[t_i,t_{i+1})$, the composite function $x\circ\lambda$ can vary by at most $\frac{1}{2}\varepsilon$ over intervals $[j/m,(j+1)/m)$. An example with $m = 10$ and $r = 4$ is sketched in Fig. 28.4; here, $j_1 = 2$, $j_2 = 4$ and $j_3 = 6$. The points $t_0,\dots,t_4$ must be more than a distance 1/10 apart in this instance. One can therefore choose $y \in E_m$ such that

$$|y(j/m)-x(\lambda(j/m))| < \tfrac{1}{2}\varepsilon,\ j = 0,\dots,m-1. \tag{28.54}$$

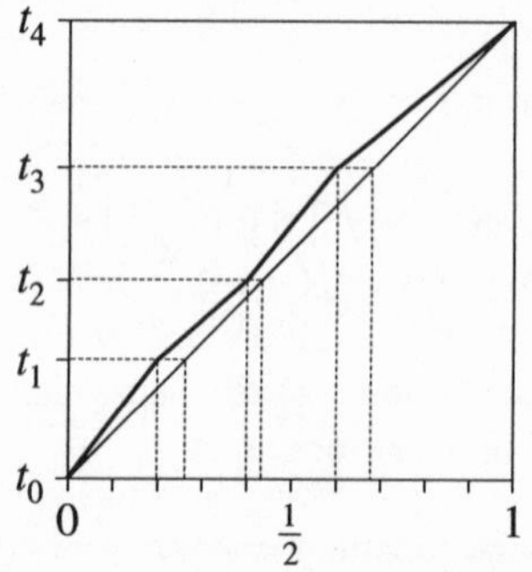

Fig. 28.4

Since $y(t) = y(j/m)$ for $t \in [j/m,(j+1)/m)$, we have by (28.52) and (28.54),

$$\sup_t |y(t) - x(\lambda(t))| \le \max_{0 \le j \le m-1} \left\{ \left| y(j/m) - x(\lambda(j/m)) \right| + \sup_{t \in [j/m,(j+1)/m)} \left| x(\lambda(j/m)) - x(\lambda(t)) \right| \right\}$$
$$< \varepsilon. \tag{28.55}$$

Together, (28.55) and (28.53) imply $d_S(x,y) \le \varepsilon$, showing that E_m is an ε-net for A as required. This proves that A is totally bounded in (D,d_S). But since d_S and d_B are equivalent (**28.7**), A is also totally bounded in (D,d_B); in particular, if E_m is an ε-net for A in (D,d_S), then we can find η such that it is also an η-net for A in (D,d_B) according to (28.27) and (28.28), where η can be set arbitrarily small. Since (D,d_B) is complete, $\bar{A}$ is therefore compact, proving sufficiency.

When A is totally bounded it is bounded, proving the necessity of (28.50). To show the necessity of (28.51), we show that the functions $w'(x,1/m) = w'_x(1/m)$ are upper semicontinuous on (D,d_S) for each m. This means that the sets $B_m = \{x: w'_x(1/m) < \varepsilon\}$ are open in (D,d_S) for each $\varepsilon > 0$. By equivalence of the metrics, they are also open in (D,d_B). In this case, for any such ε, the sets $\{B_m,\ m \in \mathbb{N}\}$ are an open covering for D by **28.3**. Any compact subset of D then has a finite subcovering, or in other words, if $\bar{A}$ is compact there is an m such that $\bar{A} \subseteq B_m$. By definition of B_m, this implies that (28.51) holds.

To show upper semicontinuity, fix $\varepsilon > 0$, $\delta > 0$, and $x \in D$, and choose a partition Π_δ satisfying

$$\max_{1 \le i \le r} \left\{ \sup_{s,t \in [t_{i-1},t_i)} |x(t) - x(s)| \right\} < w'_x(\delta) + \tfrac{1}{2}\varepsilon. \tag{28.56}$$

Also choose $\eta < \frac{1}{4}\varepsilon$, and small enough that

$$\max_{1 \le i \le r} \{t_i - t_{i-1}\} > \delta + 2\eta. \tag{28.57}$$

Our object is to show, after (5.32), that if $y \in D$ and $d_S(x,y) < \eta$ then

$$w'_y(\delta) < w'_x(\delta) + \varepsilon. \tag{28.58}$$

If $d_S(x,y) < \eta$ there is $\lambda \in \Lambda$ such that

$$\sup_t |y(\lambda(t)) - x(t)| < \eta \tag{28.59}$$

and

$$\sup_t |\lambda(t) - t| < \eta. \tag{28.60}$$

Letting $s_i = \lambda(t_i)$, (28.57) and (28.60) and the triangle inequality imply that

$$\max_{1 \le i \le r} \{s_i - s_{i-1}\} > \max_{1 \le i \le r} \{t_i - t_{i-1}\} - 2\eta > \delta. \tag{28.61}$$

If both s and t lie in $[t_{i-1},t_i)$ $\lambda(s)$ and $\lambda(t)$ must both lie in $[s_{i-1},s_i)$. It follows by (28.56), (28.59), and the choice of η that

$$\max_{1\le i\le r}\left\{\sup_{s,t\in[s_{i-1},s_i)}|y(s)-y(t)|\right\} < w'_x(\delta)+\varepsilon. \tag{28.62}$$

In view of (28.61), this shows that (28.58) holds, and since ε and x are arbitrary the proof is complete. ∎

This result is used to characterize uniform tightness of a sequence in D. The next theorem directly parallels **27.12**. We need completeness for this argument to avoid having to prove tightness of every μ_n, so it is necessary to specify an appropriate metric. Without loss of generality, we can cite d_B where required.

28.13 Theorem (Billingsley 1968: th. 15.2) A sequence $\{\mu_n\}$ of p.m.s on $((D,d_B), \mathcal{B}_D)$ is uniformly tight iff there exists $N \in \mathbb{N}$ such that, for all $n \ge N$,

(a) For each $\eta > 0$ there exists M such that

$$\mu_n(\{x: \sup_t |x(t)| > M\}) \le \eta; \tag{28.63}$$

(b) for each $\varepsilon > 0$, $\eta > 0$ there exists $\delta \in (0,1)$ such that

$$\mu_n(\{x: w'_x(\delta) \ge \varepsilon\}) \le \eta. \tag{28.64}$$

Proof Let $\{\mu_n\}$ be uniformly tight, and for $\eta > 0$ choose a compact set K with $\mu_n(K) > 1-\eta$. By **28.12** there exist $M < \infty$ and $\delta \in (0,1)$ such that

$$K \subseteq \{x: \sup_t |x(t)| \le M\} \cap \{x: w'_x(\delta) < \varepsilon\} \tag{28.65}$$

for any $\varepsilon > 0$. Inequalities (28.63) and (28.64) follow for $n \in \mathbb{N}$, proving necessity.

The object is now to find a set satisfying the conditions of **28.12**, whose closure K satisfies $\sup_{n\ge N}\mu_n(K) > 1-\theta$ for some $N \in \mathbb{N}$ and all $\theta > 0$. Because (D,d_B) is a complete separable space, each μ_n is tight (**26.19**) and the above is sufficient for uniform tightness. As in **27.12**, let μ^* stand for $\sup_{n\ge N}\mu_n$. For $\theta > 0$, define

$$A_k = \{x: w'_x(\delta_k) < 1/k\}, \tag{28.66}$$

where $\{\delta_k\}$ is chosen so that $\mu^*(A_k) > 1-\theta/2^{k+1}$, possible by condition (b). Also set $B = \{x: \sup_t|x(t)| \le M\}$ such that $\mu^*(B) > 1-\frac{1}{2}\theta$, possible by condition (a). Let $K = (\bigcap_{k=1}^{\infty}A_k \cap B)^-$, and note that K satisfies the conditions in (28.50) and (28.51), and hence is compact by **28.12**. With these definitions, the argument follows that of **27.12** word for word. ∎

The last result of this chapter concerns an issue of obvious relevance to the functional CLT; how to characterize a sequence in D which is converging to a limit in C. Since in all our applications the weak limit we desire to establish is in C, no other case has to be considered here. The modulus of continuity w_x is the natural medium for expressing this property of a sequence. Essentially, the following theorem amounts to the result that the sufficiency part of **27.12** holds in (D,d_B) just as in (C,d_U).

28.14 Theorem (Billingsley 1968: th. 15.5) Let $\{\mu_n\}$ be a sequence of measures on $((D,d_B),\mathcal{B}_D)$. If there exists $N \in \mathbb{N}$ such that, for $n \geq N$,

(a) for each $\eta > 0$ there is a finite M such that

$$\mu_n(\{x\colon |x(0)| > M\}) \leq \eta; \tag{28.67}$$

(b) for each $\varepsilon > 0$, $\eta > 0$ there is a $\delta \in (0,1)$ such that

$$\mu_n(\{x\colon w_x(\delta) \geq \varepsilon\}) \leq \eta; \tag{28.68}$$

then $\{\mu_n\}$ is uniformly tight, and if μ is any cluster point of the sequence, $\mu(C) = 1$.

Proof By (28.4), if (28.68) holds for a given δ then (28.64) holds for $\delta/2$. Let $k = [1/\delta]+1$ (so that $k\delta > 1$) where $\delta > 0$ is specified by condition (b). Then according to (28.68), $\mu_n(\{x\colon |x(ti/k) - x(t(i-1)/k)| \geq \varepsilon\}) \leq \eta$ for $i = 1,\ldots,k$, and $t \in [0,1]$. We have noted previously that

$$|x(t)| \leq |x(0)| + \sum_{i=1}^{k}\left|x\left(\frac{i}{k}t\right) - x\left(\frac{i-1}{k}t\right)\right|, \tag{28.69}$$

where each of the k intervals indicated has width less than δ. It follows by (28.68) and (28.67) that

$$\mu_n(\{x\colon \sup_t |x(t)| > M+k\varepsilon\}) \leq \mu_n(\{x\colon |x(0)| > M\}) \leq \eta, \tag{28.70}$$

so that (28.63) also holds for finite M. The conditions of **28.13** are therefore satisfied, proving uniform tightness.

Let μ be a cluster point such that $\mu_{n_k} \Rightarrow \mu$ for some subsequence $\{n_k, k \in \mathbb{N}\}$. Defining $A = \{x\colon w_x(\delta) \geq \varepsilon\}$, consider the open set A^o, the interior of A; for example, $x \in A^o$ if $w_x(\delta/2) \geq 2\varepsilon$. Then by (d) of **26.10**, and (28.68),

$$\mu(A^o) \leq \liminf_{k\to\infty} \mu_{n_k}(A^o) \leq \eta. \tag{28.71}$$

Hence $\mu(B) \leq \eta$ for any set $B \subseteq A^o$. Since ε and η are arbitrary here, it is possible to choose a decreasing sequence $\{\delta_j\}$ such that $\mu(B_j) \leq 1/j$, where $B_j = \{x\colon w_x(\delta_j) \geq 1/j\}$. For each $m \geq 1$, $\mu(\bigcap_{j=m}^{\infty} B_j) = 0$, and so, by subadditivity, $\mu(B) = 0$ where $B = \liminf B_j$. But suppose $x \in B^c$, where $B^c = \bigcap_{m=1}^{\infty}\bigcup_{j=m}^{\infty} B_j^c$ is the set

$$\{x\colon w_x(\delta_j) < 1/j,\ \text{some } j \geq m;\ \text{all } m \in \mathbb{N}\}.$$

Since $\{\delta_j\}$ is monotonic, it must be the case that $\lim_{\delta\to 0} w_x(\delta) = 0$ for this x. Hence $B^c \subseteq C$, and since $\mu(B^c) = 1$, $\mu(C) = 1$ follows. ∎

29
FCLTs for Dependent Variables

29.1 The Distribution of Continuous Functions on D

A surprising fact about Wiener measure is that definition **27.7** is actually redundant; if part (b) of that definition is replaced by the specification merely of the first two moments of $x(t)$, Gaussianity of $x(t)$ must follow. This fact leads to a class of functional CLTs of considerably greater power and generality than is possible with the approach of §27.6.

29.1 Theorem (Billingsley 1968: th. 19.1) Let X be a random element of $D_{[0,1]}$ with the following properties:

(a) $E(X(t)) = 0$, $E(X(t)^2) = t$, $0 \le t \le 1$.

(b) $P(X \in C) = 1$.

(c) For any partition $\{t_1,\dots,t_k\}$ of $[0,1]$, the increments $X(t_2) - X(t_1)$, $X(t_3) - X(t_2)$, ..., $X(t_k) - X(t_{k-1})$, are totally independent.

Then $X \sim B$. □

This is a remarkable theorem, in the apparent triviality of the conditions; if an element of D is a.s. continuous, independence of its increments is equivalent to Gaussianity! The essential insight it provides is that continuity of the sample paths is equivalent to the Lindeberg condition being satisfied by the increments.

The virtuosity of Billingsley's proof is also remarkable. The two preliminary lemmas are technical, and in the second case the proof is rather lengthy; the reader might prefer to take this one on trust initially. If $\xi_1,\dots,\xi_m$ is a random sequence, and we define $S_j = \sum_{i=1}^{j}\xi_i$ for $1 \le j \le m$, and $S_0 = 0$, the problem is to bound the probability of $|S_m|$ exceeding a given value. The lemmas are obviously designed to work together to this end.

29.2 Lemma $|S_m| \le 2 \max\limits_{0 \le j \le m} \min\{|S_j|, |S_m - S_j|\} + \max\limits_{0 \le j \le m} |\xi_j|$.

Proof Let $I \subseteq \{0,\dots,m\}$ denote the set of integers k for which $|S_k| \le |S_m - S_k|$. If $S_m = 0$ the lemma holds, and if $S_m \ne 0$ then $m \notin I$. On the other hand, $0 \in I$. It follows that there is a $k \notin I$ such that $k-1 \in I$. For this choice of k,

$$\begin{aligned} |S_m| &\le |S_m - S_k| + |S_k| \\ &\le |S_m - S_k| + |S_{k-1}| + |\xi_k| \\ &\le 2 \max_{0 \le j \le m} \min\{|S_j|, |S_m - S_j|\} + \max_{0 \le j \le m} |\xi_j|. \quad ■ \end{aligned} \tag{29.1}$$

The second lemma is a variation on the maximal inequality for partial sums.

29.3 Lemma (Billingsley 1968: th. 12.1) If

$$E((S_j - S_i)^2(S_k - S_j)^2) \leq \left(\sum_{l=i+1}^{k} b_l\right)^2, \; j = i,\ldots,k, \tag{29.2}$$

for each pair i,k with $0 \leq i \leq k \leq m$, where $\{b_1,\ldots,b_m\}$ is a collection of positive numbers, then $\exists$ $K > 0$ such that, for all $\alpha > 0$ and all m,

$$P\left(\max_{0\leq j\leq m} \min\{|S_j|, |S_m - S_j|\} \geq \alpha\right) \leq \frac{KB^2}{\alpha^4}, \tag{29.3}$$

where $B = \sum_{j=1}^m b_j$.

Proof For $0 \leq i \leq k \leq m$ and $\alpha > 0$, we have

$$\begin{aligned} P(\min\{|S_j - S_i|, |S_k - S_j|\} \geq \alpha) &= P(\{|S_j - S_i| \geq \alpha\} \cap \{|S_k - S_j| \geq \alpha\}) \\ &\leq P(|S_j - S_i||S_k - S_j| \geq \alpha^2) \\ &\leq \frac{1}{\alpha^4}\left(\sum_{l=i+1}^{k} b_l\right)^2, \end{aligned} \tag{29.4}$$

where Chebyshev's inequality and (29.2) give the final inequality. If $m = 1$, the minorant side of (29.3) is zero. If $m = 2$, (29.4) with $i = 0$ and $k = 2$ yields

$$P(\max\{0, \min\{|S_1|, |S_2 - S_1|\}\} \geq \alpha) \leq \frac{(b_1 + b_2)^2}{\alpha^4}, \tag{29.5}$$

so that (29.3) holds for $K = 1$ and hence for any $K \geq 1$.

The proof now proceeds by induction. Assuming there is a K for which (29.3) holds when m is replaced by any integer between 1 and $m - 1$, we show it holds for m itself, with the same K. The basic idea is to split the sum into two parts, each with fewer than m terms, obtain valid inequalities for each part, and combine these. Choose h to be the largest integer such that $\sum_{j=1}^{h-1} b_j \leq B/2$ (the sum is zero if $h = 1$); it is easy to see that $\sum_{j=h+1}^{m} b_j \leq B/2$ also (the sum being zero if $h = m$). First define

$$U_1 = \max_{0\leq j\leq h-1} \min\{|S_j|, |S_{h-1} - S_j|\} \tag{29.6}$$

$$D_1 = \min\{|S_{h-1}|, |S_m - S_{h-1}|\}. \tag{29.7}$$

Evidently,

$$P(U_1 \geq \alpha) \leq \frac{K}{\alpha^4}\left(\sum_{j=1}^{h-1} b_j\right)^2 \leq \frac{KB^2}{4\alpha^4} \tag{29.8}$$

by the induction hypothesis. Also, by (29.4) with $i = 0$ and $k = m$,

$$P(D_1 \geq \alpha) \leq \frac{B^2}{\alpha^4}. \tag{29.9}$$

The object is now to show that

$$\min\{|S_j|, |S_m - S_j|\} \leq U_1 + D_1, \; 0 \leq j \leq h-1. \tag{29.10}$$

If $|S_j| \leq U_1$, (29.10) holds, hence suppose $|S_{h-1} - S_j| \leq U_1$, the only other possibility according to (29.6). If $D_1 = |S_{h-1}|$, then

$$\min\{|S_j|,|S_m - S_j|\} \leq |S_j| \leq |S_{h-1} - S_j| + |S_{h-1}| \leq U_1 + D_1.$$

And if $D_1 = |S_m - S_{h-1}|$ then again,

$$\min\{|S_j|, |S_m - S_j|\} \leq |S_m - S_j| \leq |S_{h-1} - S_j| + |S_m - S_{h-1}| \leq U_1 + D_1.$$

Hence (29.10) holds in all cases. Now, for $0 \leq \mu \leq 1$,

$$\begin{aligned} P(U_1 + D_1 \geq \alpha) &\leq P(\{U_1 \geq \mu\alpha\} \cup \{D_1 \geq (1-\mu)\alpha\}) \\ &\leq P(U_1 \geq \mu\alpha) + P(D_1 \geq (1-\mu)\alpha) \\ &\leq \frac{KB^2}{4\alpha^4\mu^4} + \frac{B^2}{\alpha^4(1-\mu)^4}. \end{aligned} \tag{29.11}$$

Choosing μ to minimize $K/4\mu^4 + 1/(1-\mu)^4$ yields $\mu = (\frac{1}{4}K)^{1/5}/[1 + (\frac{1}{4}K)^{1/5}]$ (use calculus). Back-substituting for μ and simplifying yields, for $K \geq 2[1 - (\frac{1}{2})^{1/5}]^{-5} \approx 55{,}021$,

$$P(U_1 + D_1 \geq \alpha) \leq \frac{B^2[(\frac{1}{4}K)^{1/5} + 1]^5}{\alpha^4} \leq \frac{KB^2}{2\alpha^4}. \tag{29.12}$$

According to (29.10), we have bounded $\min\{|S_j|,|S_m - S_j|\}$ in the range $0 \leq j \leq h-1$. To do the same for the range $h \leq j \leq m$, define

$$U_2 = \max_{h \leq j \leq m} \min\{|S_j - S_h|,|S_m - S_j|\} \tag{29.13}$$

$$D_2 = \min\{|S_h|,|S_m - S_h|\}. \tag{29.14}$$

It can be verified by variants of the previous arguments that

$$\min\{|S_j|, |S_m - S_j|\} \leq U_2 + D_2, \; h \leq j \leq m, \tag{29.15}$$

and also that

$$P(U_2 + D_2 \geq \alpha) \leq \frac{KB^2}{2\alpha^4} \tag{29.16}$$

for the same choice of K. Combining (29.16) with (29.12), we obtain

$$P\left(\max_{0\le j\le m}\min\{|S_j|,|S_m-S_j|\}\ge\alpha\right)\le P(\max\{U_1+D_1,\,U_2+D_2\}\ge\alpha)$$
$$= P(\{U_1+D_1\ge\alpha\}\cup\{U_2+D_2\ge\alpha\})$$
$$\le P(U_1+D_1\ge\alpha)+P(U_2+D_2\ge\alpha)$$
$$\le\frac{KB^2}{\alpha^4}.\ \blacksquare \tag{29.17}$$

Proof of 29.1 Let the characteristic function of $X(t)$ be

$$\phi(t,\lambda)=E(e^{i\lambda X(t)}). \tag{29.18}$$

We can write, by (11.25),

$$e^{iu}=1+iu-\tfrac{1}{2}u^2+r(u), \tag{29.19}$$

where $|r(u)|\le|u|^3$. We shall write either $\Delta_{s,t}$ or $\Delta(s,t)$, as is most convenient, to denote $X(s)-X(t)$ for $0\le t\le s\le 1$. Observe that by conditions (a) and (c) of the theorem, $E(\Delta^2_{t+h,t})=h$. Hence,

$$\begin{aligned}\phi(t+h,\lambda)-\phi(t,\lambda)&=E[\mathrm{e}^{i\lambda X(t)}(e^{i\lambda\Delta_{t+h,t}}-1)]\\&=E[\mathrm{e}^{i\lambda X(t)}(i\lambda\Delta_{t+h,t}-\tfrac{1}{2}\lambda^2\Delta^2_{t+h,t}+r(\lambda\Delta_{t+h,t}))]\\&=\phi(t,\lambda)[-\tfrac{1}{2}\lambda^2h+E(r(\lambda\Delta_{t+h,t}))],\end{aligned} \tag{29.20}$$

where the last equality is because $X(t)$ and $\Delta_{t+h,t}$ are independent by condition (c). Since $E(r(\lambda\Delta_{t+h,t}))\le\lambda^3E|\Delta_{t+h,t}|^3$, it follows that

$$\left|\frac{\phi(t+h,\lambda)-\phi(t,\lambda)}{h}+\tfrac{1}{2}\lambda^2\phi(t,\lambda)\right|\le\frac{\phi(t,\lambda)\lambda^3E|\Delta_{t+h,t}|^3}{h}. \tag{29.21}$$

Now, suppose that

$$\lim_{h\downarrow 0}\frac{1}{h}E|\Delta_{t+h,t}|^3=0. \tag{29.22}$$

It will then follow that, for all $0\le t<1$, ϕ possesses a right-hand derivative,

$$\lim_{h\downarrow 0}\frac{\phi(t+h,\lambda)-\phi(t,\lambda)}{h}=-\tfrac{1}{2}\lambda^2\phi(t,\lambda). \tag{29.23}$$

Further, for $h>0$ and $h\le t\le 1$, (29.21) holds at the point $t-h$, so by considering a path to the limit through such points we may also conclude that

$$\lim_{h\downarrow 0}\frac{\phi(t,\lambda)-\phi(t-h,\lambda)}{h}=-\tfrac{1}{2}\lambda^2\phi(t-,\lambda). \tag{29.24}$$

Since $\phi(t-,\lambda)=\phi(t,\lambda)$ because ϕ is continuous in t, by condition (b) of the theorem, ϕ is differentiable on (0,1) and

$$\frac{\partial\phi}{\partial t} = -\tfrac{1}{2}\lambda^2\phi(t,\lambda). \tag{29.25}$$

This differential equation is well known to have the solution

$$\phi(t,\lambda) = \phi(0,\lambda)e^{-t\lambda^2/2},\ t \geq 0. \tag{29.26}$$

(Verify this by differentiating $\log\phi$ with respect to t.) Since $X(0) = 0$ a.s., $\phi(0,\lambda) = 1$, and applying the inversion theorem we conclude that $X(t) \sim N(0,t)$ for each $t \in (0,1)$. By continuity of ϕ at 1, the result also extends to $t = 1$.

Hence, the task is to prove (29.22). This requires the application of **29.2** and **29.3**. For some finite m let $\xi_j = \Delta(t+hj/m, t+h(j-1)/m)$ for $j = 1,\dots,m$. By assumption, the ξ_j are independent r.v.s with variances of h/m. If $S_j = \sum_{i=1}^{j}\xi_i = \Delta(t+jh/m, t)$, then

$$E((S_j - S_i)^2(S_k - S_j)^2) = (j-i)(k-j)h^2/m^2 \leq h^2. \tag{29.27}$$

By **29.3**, setting $b_j = h/m$, we have

$$P\left(\max_{0\leq j\leq m}\min\left\{\left|\Delta(t+\frac{j}{m}h,\ t)\right|,\left|\Delta(t+h,\ t+\frac{j}{m}h)\right|\right\} \geq \alpha\right) \leq \frac{Kh^2}{\alpha^4}. \tag{29.28}$$

Hence by **29.2**,

$$\begin{aligned}P(|\Delta(t+h,t)| \geq \alpha) &\leq P\left(2\max_{0\leq j\leq m}\min\left\{\left|\Delta(t+\frac{j}{m}h,\ t)\right|,\left|\Delta(t+h,\ t+\frac{j}{m}h)\right|\right\}\right.\\ &\qquad\left. + \max_{0\leq j\leq m}\left|\Delta(t+\frac{j}{m}h,\ t+\frac{j-1}{m}h)\right| \geq \alpha\right)\\ &\leq \frac{K^*h^2}{\alpha^4} + P\left(\max_{0\leq j\leq m}\left|\Delta(t+\frac{j}{m}h,\ t+\frac{j-1}{m}h)\right| \geq \tfrac{1}{2}\alpha\right),\end{aligned} \tag{29.29}$$

where $K^* = 4^4K$. Letting $m \to \infty$, the second term of the majorant member must go to zero, since $X \in C$ with probability 1 by condition (b), so we can say that

$$P(|\Delta_{t+h,t}| \geq \alpha) \leq \frac{K^*h^2}{\alpha^4}. \tag{29.30}$$

We may now use **9.15** to give

$$\begin{aligned}E|\Delta_{t+h,t}|^3 &= \int_0^\varepsilon |\Delta_{t+h,t}|^3 dF + \varepsilon P(|\Delta_{t+h,t}|^3 \geq \varepsilon) + \int_\varepsilon^\infty P(|\Delta_{t+h,t}|^3 > \zeta)d\zeta\\ &\leq \varepsilon + \int_\varepsilon^\infty P(|\Delta_{t+h,t}| \geq \zeta^{1/3})d\zeta\\ &\leq \varepsilon + K^*h^2\int_\varepsilon^\infty \frac{1}{\zeta^{4/3}}\,d\zeta = \varepsilon + \frac{3K^*h^2}{\varepsilon^{1/3}}.\end{aligned} \tag{29.31}$$

Choose $\varepsilon = (K^*)^{3/4}h^{3/2}$ to minimize the last member above, and we obtain

$$E|\Delta_{t+h,t}|^3 \le 4(K^*)^{3/4}h^{3/2}. \tag{29.32}$$

This condition verifies (29.22), and completes the proof. ■

Notice how (29.30) is a substantial strengthening of the Chebyshev inequality, which gives merely $P(|\Delta_{t+h,t}| \ge \alpha) \le h/\alpha^2$. We have not assumed the existence of the third moment at the outset; this emerges (along with the Gaussianity) from the assumption of independent increments of arbitrarily small width, which allows us to take (29.29) to the limit.

29.2 Asymptotic Independence

Let $\{X_n\}_1^\infty$ denote a stochastic sequence in $(D,\mathcal{B}_D)$. We say that X_n has asymptotically independent increments if, for any collection of points $\{s_i,t_i,\ i = 1,\dots,r\}$ such that

$$0 \le s_1 \le t_1 < s_2 \le t_2 < \dots < s_r \le t_r \le 1,$$

and all collections of linear Borel sets $B_1,\dots,B_r \in \mathcal{B}$,

$$P(X_n(t_i) - X_n(s_i) \in B_i,\ i = 1,\dots,r) \to \prod_{i=1}^r P(X_n(t_i) - X_n(s_i) \in B_i) \tag{29.33}$$

as $n \to \infty$. Notice that in this definition, gaps of positive width are allowed to separate the increments, which will be essential to establish asymptotic independence in the partial sums of mixing sequences. The gaps can be arbitrarily small, however, and continuity allows us to ignore them as we see below.

Given this idea, we have the following consequence of **29.1**.

29.4 Theorem Let $\{X_n\}_{n=1}^\infty$ have the following properties:

(a) The increments are asymptotically independent.

(b) For any $\varepsilon > 0$ and $\eta > 0$, $\exists\ \delta \in (0,1)$ s.t. $\limsup_{n\to\infty} P(w(X_n,\delta) \ge \varepsilon) \le \eta$.

(c) $\{X_n(t)^2\}_{n=1}^\infty$ is uniformly integrable for each $t \in [0,1]$.

(d) $E(X_n(t)) \to 0$ and $E(X_n(t)^2) \to t$ as $n \to \infty$, each $t \in [0,1]$.

Then $X_n \xrightarrow{D} B$. □

Be careful to note that $w(.,\delta)$ in (b) is the modulus of continuity of (27.14), *not* w' of (28.3).

Proof Condition (b), and the fact that $E|X_n(0)| \to 0$ by (d), imply by **28.14** that the associated sequence of p.m.s is uniformly tight. Theorem **26.22** then implies that the latter sequence is compact, and so has one or more cluster points. To complete the proof, we show that all such cluster points must have the characteristics of Wiener measure, and hence that the sequence has this p.m. as its unique weak limit.

Consider the properties the limiting p.m. must possess. Writing X for the random element, **28.14** also gives $P(X \in C) = 1$. Uniform integrability of $X_n(t)^2$, and hence of $X_n(t)$, implies that $E(X(t)) = 0$ and $E(X(t)^2) = t$, by **22.16**. By condition (a) we may say that the increments $X(t_1)-X(s_1),\dots,X(t_r)-X(s_r)$ are totally independent according to (29.33). Specifically, consider increments $X(t_i)-X(s_i)$ and $X(t_{i+1})-X(s_{i+1})$ for the case where $s_{i+1} = t_i + 1/m$. By a.s. continuity,

$$\lim_{m\to\infty} \left(X(t_{i+1})-X(t_i+1/m)\right) = X(t_{i+1})-X(t_i) \text{ w.p.1}, \tag{29.34}$$

so that asymptotic independence extends to contiguous increments. All the conditions of **29.1** are therefore satisfied by X, and $X \sim B$. ■

Our aim is now to get a FCLT for partial-sum processes by linking up the asymptotic independence idea with our established characterization of a dependent increment process; that is to say, as a near-epoch dependent function of a mixing process. Making this connection is perhaps the biggest difficulty we still have to surmount. An approach comparable to the 'blocking' argument used in the CLTs of §24.4 is needed; and in the present context we can proceed by mapping an infinite sequence into [0,1] and identifying the increments with asymptotically independent blocks of summands. This is a particularly elegant route to the result. However, an asymptotic martingale difference-type property of the type exploited in **24.6** is not going to work in our present approach to the problem. While the terms of a mixing process (of suitable size) can be 'blocked' so that the blocks are asymptotically independent (more or less by definition of mixing), mixingale theory will not serve here; near-epoch dependent functions can be dealt with only by a direct approximation argument.

What we shall show is that, if the difference between two stochastic processes is $o_p(1)$ and one of them exhibits asymptotic independence, so must the other, in a sense to be defined. Near-epoch dependent functions can be approximated in the required way by their near-epoch conditional expectations, where the latter are functions of mixing variables. This result is established in the following lemma in terms of the independence of a pair of sequences, which in the application will be adjacent increments of a partial sum process.

29.5 Lemma (Wooldridge and White 1986: Lemma A.3) If $\{Y_{jn}\}$ and $\{Z_{jn}\}$ are real stochastic sequences, and

(a) $Y_{jn}-Z_{jn} \xrightarrow{pr} 0$, for $j = 1,2$;
(b) $Y_{jn} \xrightarrow{D} Y_j$ for $j = 1,2$;
(c) for any $A_1, A_2 \in \mathcal{B}$,

$$P(\{Z_{1n} \in A_1\}\cap\{Z_{2n} \in A_2\}) \to P(Z_{1n} \in A_1)P(Z_{2n} \in A_2) \tag{29.35}$$

as $n \to \infty$;

then

$$P(\{Y_{1n} \in B_1\}\cap\{Y_{2n} \in B_2\}) \to P(Y_1 \in B_1)P(Y_2 \in B_2) \tag{29.36}$$

for all Y_j-continuity sets (sets $B_j \in \mathcal{B}$ such that $P(Y_j \in \partial B_j) = 0$) for $j = 1,2$.

Proof Considering (Z_{1n},Z_{2n}) and (Y_{1n},Y_{2n}) as points of $\mathbb{R}^2$ with the Euclidean metric, (a) implies $d_E((Z_{1n},Z_{2n}),(Y_{1n},Y_{2n})) \to 0$, and by an application of **26.24**, (b) implies both $(Z_{1n},Z_{2n}) \xrightarrow{D} (Y_1,Y_2)$, and $j = 1,2$. Write

$$P(\{Z_{1n} \in B_1\} \cap \{Z_{2n} \in B_2\}) = \mu_n(B_1 \times B_2), \tag{29.37}$$

where μ_n is the measure associated with the element (Z_{1n}, Z_{2n}). If μ is the measure associated with (Y_1, Y_2), define the marginal measures μ^j by $\mu^j(B_j) = P(Y_j \in B_j)$; then $\mu^j(\partial B_j) = 0$ for $j = 1,2$ implies $\mu(\partial(B_1 \times B_2)) = 0$, in view of the fact that

$$\partial(B_1 \times B_2) \subseteq (\partial B_1 \times \mathbb{R}) \cup (\mathbb{R} \times \partial B_2). \tag{29.38}$$

Applying (e) of **26.10**, it follows from the weak convergence of the joint distributions that, for all Y_j-continuity sets B_j,

$$\begin{aligned} P(\{Z_{1n} \in B_1\} \cap \{Z_{2n} \in B_2\}) &= \mu_n(B_1 \times B_2) \\ &\to \mu(B_1 \times B_2) \\ &= P(\{Y_1 \in B_1\} \cap \{Y_2 \in B_2\}). \end{aligned} \tag{29.39}$$

And by the weak convergence of both sets of marginal distributions it follows that, for these same B_j,

$$P(Z_{1n} \in B_1)P(Z_{2n} \in B_2) \to P(Y_1 \in B_1)P(Y_2 \in B_2). \tag{29.40}$$

This completes the proof, since the limits of the left-hand sides of (29.39) and (29.40) are the same by condition (c). ∎

29.3 The FCLT for NED Functions of Mixing Processes

From **29.4** to a general invariance principle for dependent sequences is only a short step, even though some of the details in the following version of the result are quite fiddly. This is basically the one given by Wooldridge and White (1988).

29.6 Theorem Let $\{U_{ni}\}$ be a zero-mean stochastic array, $\{c_{ni}\}$ an array of positive constants, and $\{K_n(t), n \in \mathbb{N}\}$ a sequence of integer-valued, right-continuous, increasing functions of t, with $K_n(0) = 0$ for all n, and $K_n(t) - K_n(s) \to \infty$ as $n \to \infty$ if $t > s$. Also define $X_n^K(t) = \sum_{i=1}^{K_n(t)} U_{ni}$. If

(a) $E(U_{ni}) = 0$;

(b) $\sup_{i,n} \|U_{ni}/c_{ni}\|_r < \infty$, for $r > 2$;

(c) U_{ni} is L_2-NED of size $-\gamma$, for $\frac{1}{2} \le \gamma \le 1$, with respect to the constants $\{c_{ni}\}$, on an array $\{V_{ni}\}$ which is α-mixing of size $-r/(r-2)$;

(d) $\sup_{t \in [0,1), \delta \in (0,1-t]} \left\{ \limsup_{n \to \infty} \frac{\nu_n^2(t,\delta)}{\delta} \right\} < \infty$, where $\nu_n^2(t,\delta) = \sum_{i=K_n(t)+1}^{K_n(t+\delta)} c_{ni}^2$;

(e) $\max_{1 \le i \le K_n(1)} c_{ni} = O(K_n(1)^{\gamma-1})$, where γ is defined in (c);

(f) $E(X_n^K(t)^2) \to t$ as $n \to \infty$, for each $t \in [0,1]$;

then $X_n^K \xrightarrow{D} B$. □

Right-continuity of $K_n(t)$ ensures that $\nu_n^2(t,\delta) \to 0$ as $\delta \to 0$, if we agree that a sum is equal to zero whenever the lower limit exceeds the upper.

If γ is set to 1 in condition (c), condition (e) can be omitted. It is important to emphasize that this statement of the assumptions, while technically correct, is somewhat misleading in that condition (c) is not the only constraint on the dependence. In the leading cases discussed below, condition (f) will as a rule imply a L_2-NED size of -1.

Theorem **29.6** is very general, and it may help in getting to grips with it to extract a more basic and easily comprehended set of sufficient conditions. What we might think of as the 'standard' case of the FCLT—that of convergence of a partial sum process to Wiener measure—corresponds to the case $K_n(t) = [nt]$. We will omit the K superscript to denote this case, writing $X_n(t) = \sum_{i=1}^{[nt]} U_{ni}$. The full conditions of the theorem allow different modes of convergence to be defined for various kinds of heterogeneous processes, and these issues are taken up again in §29.4 below. But it might be a good plan to focus initially on the case $X_n(t)$, mentally making the required substitutions of $[nt]$ for $K_n(t)$ in the formulae.

In particular, consider the case $U_{ni} = U_i/s_n$ where

$$s_n^2 = E\left(\sum_{i=1}^{n} U_i\right)^2 = \sum_{i=1}^{n} \sigma_i^2 + 2\sum_{i=1}^{n-1}\sum_{m=1}^{n-i} \sigma_{i,i+m}, \tag{29.41}$$

with $\sigma_i^2 = \mathrm{Var}(U_i)$ and $\sigma_{i,i+m} = \mathrm{Cov}(U_i, U_{i+m})$. Also, require that $\sup_i \|U_i\|_r < \infty$, $r > 2$. Then we may choose $c_{ni} = 1/s_n$, and with $K_n(t) = [nt]$, condition **29.6**(d) reduces to the requirement that $s_n^2/n > 0$, uniformly in n. In this case, **29.6**(e) is satisfied for $\gamma = \frac{1}{2}$. If in addition $s_n^2/n \to \sigma^2 < \infty$, then $\mathrm{E}(X_n(t))^2 = s_{[nt]}^2/s_n^2 \to t$ and **29.6**(f) also holds. These conclusions are summarized in the following corollary.

29.7 Corollary Let the sequence $\{U_i\}$ have mean zero, be uniformly L_r-bounded, and L_2-NED of size $-\frac{1}{2}$ on an α-mixing process of size $-r/(r-2)$, and let $X_n(t) = n^{-1/2}\sum_{i=1}^{[nt]} U_i$. If $n^{-1}(\sum_{i=1}^{n} U_i)^2 \to \sigma^2$, $0 < \sigma^2 < \infty$, then $X_n \xrightarrow{D} \sigma^2 B$. □

Be careful to note that $\sigma^2 = \bar{\sigma}^2 + 2\sum_{m=1}^{\infty}\lambda_m$, where $\bar{\sigma}^2 = \lim_{n\to\infty} n^{-1}\sum_{i=1}^{n}\sigma_i^2$ and $\lambda_m = \lim_{n\to\infty} n^{-1}\sum_{i=1}^{n-m}\sigma_{i,i+m}$. This and *not* $\bar{\sigma}^2$ is the variance of the limiting Brownian motion, notwithstanding the fact that B has independent increments. The condition $s_n^2/n \to \sigma^2$ has two parts. The first is that the limits $\bar{\sigma}^2$ and λ_m for $m = 1,2,3,\ldots$ all exist, which is the condition of global wide-sense stationarity discussed in §13.2. Examples where this condition is violated is provided by **24.10** and **24.11**. The second is that $\sum_{m=1}^{\infty}\lambda_m < \infty$, for which it is sufficient that $\sum_{m=1}^{\infty}|\sigma_{i,i+m}| < \infty$ for each i. According to **17.7** this follows from condition **29.6**(c), with the additional requirement that $\gamma = 1$.

The complications of **29.6** are chiefly to accommodate global nonstationarity. The following is such a case.

29.8 Example Let the sequence $\{U_i\}$ have variances $\sigma_i^2 \sim i^{\beta}$ and (just for simplicity's sake) be serially uncorrelated. Then, $s_n^2 = O(n^{1+\beta})$, and choosing $K_n(t) = [nt^{1/(1+\beta)}]$ will serve to satisfy conditions **29.6**(d) and **29.6**(f). □

It is instructive to compare the conditions of **29.6** with those of **24.6** and **24.7.** Since $X_n^K(1) \xrightarrow{D} B(1) \sim N(0,1)$, the two theorems give alternative sets of conditions for the central limit theorem. Although they are stated in very different terms, conditions **29.6**(d) and (e) clearly have a role analogous to **24.6**(d). While **24.6** required a L_2-NED size of -1, it was pointed out above how the same condition is generally enforced by **29.6**(f). However, **29.6**(f) itself has no counterpart in the CLT conditions. It is not clear how tough this restriction is, given our free choice of K_n, and this is a question we attempt to shed light on in §29.4. What is clear is that the convergence of the partial sum process X_n to B requires stronger conditions than are required just for the convergence of $X_n(1)$ to $B(1)$, which is the CLT.

Proof of 29.6 We will establish that the conditions of **29.4** hold for the sequence $\{X_t^K\}$. Condition **29.4**(d) holds directly, by the present conditions (a) and (f). Conditions (a), (b), and (c) imply by **17.6**(i) that $\{U_{ni},\mathcal{F}_{ni}\}$ is a L_2-mixingale of size $-\frac{1}{2}$ with respect to the scaling constants $\{c_{ni}\}$, where $\mathcal{F}_{ni} = \sigma(V_{i-j},\ j \geq 0)$. In view of the uniform L_r-boundedness with $r > 2$, the array $\{U_{ni}^2/c_{ni}^2\}$ is uniformly integrable. If we let $k = K_n(t)$ and $m = K_n(t+\delta) - K_n(t)$ for $\delta \in [0,1-t)$, it follows by **16.14** (which holds irrespective of shifts in the coordinate index) that the set

$$\left\{\max_{j\leq m}\frac{(S_{n,k+j}-S_{nk})^2}{\nu_n^2(t,\delta)},\ n \geq 1\right\} \tag{29.42}$$

is uniformly integrable, for any t and δ. Further, because of condition (d) we may assume there is a positive constant $M < \infty$ such that for any $t \in [0,1)$ and any $\delta \in (0,\ 1-t])$, there exists $N(t,\delta) \geq 1$ with the property $\nu_n^2(t,\delta)/\delta \leq M$ for $n \geq N(t,\delta)$. Therefore the set

$$\left\{\max_{j\leq m}\frac{(S_{n,k+j}-S_{nk})^2}{\delta},\ n \geq N(t,\delta)\right\} \tag{29.43}$$

is also uniformly integrable. If $N^* = \sup_{t,\delta}N(t,\delta)$, condition (d) implies that N^* is finite.

Taking the case $t = 0$ and hence $k = 0$ and $m = K_n(\delta)$ in (29.43) (but then writing t in place of δ for consistency of notation), we deduce uniform integrability of $\{X_n^K(t)\}_{n=1}^\infty$ for any $t \in (0,1]$ (the summands from 1 to $N(0,t) - 1$ can be included by condition (b)). In other words, condition **29.4**(c) holds for $\{X_n^K\}_{n=1}^\infty$.

Note that $\lambda^2 P(|X| > \lambda) \leq E(X^2 1_{\{|X|>\lambda\}})$ for any square-integrable r.v. X. Therefore, the uniform integrability of (29.43) implies that for any $\delta \in (0,1)$, any $t \leq 1-\delta$, and any $\varepsilon > 0$ and $\eta > 0$, $\exists\ \lambda > 0$ large enough that for $n \geq N^*$,

$$P\left(\max_{1\leq j\leq m}|S_{n,k+j}-S_{nk}| \geq \lambda\sqrt{\delta}\right) \leq \frac{\eta\varepsilon^2}{8\lambda^2}, \tag{29.44}$$

where k amd m are defined as before. The argument now follows similar lines to the proof of **27.14**. For the case $\delta = \varepsilon^2/4\lambda^2$, (29.44) implies

$$\sup_{0\le t\le 1-\delta} P\left(\sup_{t\le s\le t+\delta} |X_n^K(s) - X_n^K(t)| \ge \tfrac{1}{2}\varepsilon \right) \le \tfrac{1}{2}\eta\delta,\ n \ge N^*, \tag{29.45}$$

which is identical to (27.71). Condition **29.4**(b) now follows by **27.13**, as before.

The final step is to show asymptotic independence. Whereas the theorem requires us to show that (29.33) holds for any r, since the argument is based on the mixing property and the linear separation of the increments, it will suffice to show independence for adjacent pairs of increments $(i, i+1)$ having $t_i < s_{i+1}$. The extension to the general case is easy in principle, though tedious to write out. Hence we consider, without loss of generality, the pair of variables

$$Y_{jn} = X_n^K(t_j) - X_n^K(s_j) = \sum_{i=K_n(s_j)+1}^{K_n(t_j)} U_{ni},\ \ j = 1 \text{ and } 2, \tag{29.46}$$

where $0 \le s_1 < t_1 < s_2 < t_2 \le 1$. We cannot show asymptotic independence of Y_{1n} and Y_{2n} directly because the increment process need not be mixing, but there is an approximation argument direct from the NED property. Defining $\mathcal{F}_{n,j}^k = \sigma(V_{nj},\ldots,V_{nk})$, the r.v. $E(Y_{1n}|\mathcal{F}_{n,-\infty}^{K_n(t_1)})$ is $\mathcal{F}_{n,-\infty}^{K_n(t_1)}$-measurable, and similarly $E(Y_{2n}|\mathcal{F}_{n,K_n(s_2)}^{\infty})$ is $\mathcal{F}_{n,K_n(s_2)}^{\infty}$-measurable. By assumption (c),

$$\sup_{A \in \mathcal{F}_{n,-\infty}^{K_n(t_1)},\ B \in \mathcal{F}_{n,K_n(s_2)}^{\infty}} \left|P(A\cap B) - P(A)P(B)\right| = \alpha(K_n(s_2) - K_n(t_1)) \to 0 \text{ as } n \to \infty \tag{29.47}$$

whenever $t_1 < s_2$, where the events A include those of the form $\{E(Y_{1n}|\mathcal{F}_{n,-\infty}^{K_n(t_1)}) \in E\}$ for $E \in \mathcal{B}$, and similarly events B include those of the type $\{E(Y_{2n}|\mathcal{F}_{n,K_n(s_2)}^{\infty}) \in E\}$. These conditional expectations are asymptotically independent r.v.s, and it remains to show that Y_{1n} and Y_{2n} share the same property.

We show that the conditions of **29.5** are satisfied when $Z_{1n} = E(Y_{1n}|\mathcal{F}_{n,-\infty}^{K_n(t_1)})$ and $Z_{2n} = E(Y_{2n}|\mathcal{F}_{n,K_n(s_2)}^{\infty})$. This is sufficient in view of the fact that the Y_j-continuity sets are a convergence-determining class for the sequences $\{Y_{jn}\}$, by **26.10**(e). The argument of the preceding paragraph has already established condition **29.5**(c). To show condition **29.5**(a) we have the inequalities

$$\begin{aligned} E\|Y_{1n} - E(Y_{1n}|\mathcal{F}_{n,-\infty}^{K_n(t_1)})\|_2 &\le \sum_{i=K_n(s_1)+1}^{K_n(t_1)} \|U_{ni} - E(U_{ni}|\mathcal{F}_{n,-\infty}^{K_n(t_1)})\|_2 \\ &\le 2\sum_{i=K_n(s_1)+1}^{K_n(t_1)} \|U_{ni} - E(U_{ni}|\mathcal{F}_{n,2i-K_n(t_1)}^{K_n(t_1)})\|_2 \\ &\le 2\sum_{i=K_n(s_1)+1}^{K_n(t_1)} c_{ni}\nu_{K_n(t_1)-i} \end{aligned}$$

$$\leq 2 \max_{K_n(s_1)<i\leq K_n(t_1)} c_{ni} \sum_{m=0}^{K_n(t_1)-K_n(s_1)-1} \nu_m$$

$$\to 0 \text{ as } n \to \infty, \tag{29.48}$$

where we have applied Minkowski's inequality, **10.28**, and finally assumptions (c) and (e), and **2.27**. This implies that $Y_{1n} - E(Y_{1n}|\mathcal{F}^{K_n(t_1)}_{n,-\infty}) \xrightarrow{pr} 0$. Note that condition (d) implies that $\sup_i c_{ni} \to 0$ as $n \to \infty$, so in the case $\gamma = 1$, (e) can be dispensed with. By the same reasoning, $Y_{2n} - E(Y_{2n}|\mathcal{F}^{\infty}_{n,K_n(s_2)}) \xrightarrow{pr} 0$ also.

Since we have established that conditions **29.4**(b) and **29.4**(d) hold, we know that the sequence of measures associated with $\{X_n^K\}$ is uniformly tight, and so contains at least one convergent subsequence—$\{n_k, k \in \mathbb{N}\}$, say—such that $X^K_{n_k} \xrightarrow{D} X^K$ (say) as $k \to \infty$ where $P(X^K \in C) = 1$. It follows that the continuous mapping theorem applies to the coordinate projections $\pi_t(X^K) = X^K(t)$, and we may assert that $X^K_{n_k}(t) \xrightarrow{D} X^K(t)$. Confining attention to this subsequence, condition **29.5**(b) is satisfied for the case $Y_{n_k,j} = X^K_n(t_j) - X^K_n(s_j)$. All the conditions of **29.5** have now been confirmed, so these increments are asymptotically independent in the sense of (29.36). But since this is true for every convergent subsequence $\{n_k\}$, we can conclude that the weak limit of $\{X_n^K\}$ has asymptotically independent increments whenever it exists. All the conditions of **29.4** are therefore fulfilled by $\{X_n^K\}$, and the proof is complete. ∎

It is possible to relax the moment conditions of this theorem if we substitute a uniform mixing condition for the strong mixing in condition (c).

29.9 Theorem Let $\{U_{ni}\}$, $\{c_{ni}\}$, $\{K_n(t)\}$, and $\{X_n^K\}$ be defined as in **29.6**; assume that conditions **29.6**(a), (d), (e) and (f) hold, but replace conditions **29.6**(b) and (c) by the following:

(b′) $\sup_{i,n}\|U_{ni}/c_{ni}\|_r < \infty$, for $r \geq 2$, and $\{U^2_{ni}/c^2_{ni}\}$ is uniformly integrable;

(c′) U_{ni} is L_2-NED of size $-\gamma$, for $\frac{1}{2} \leq \gamma \leq 1$, with respect to constants $\{c_{ni}\}$, on an array $\{V_{ni}\}$ which is ϕ-mixing of size $-r/2(r-1)$, for $r \geq 2$;

then $X_n^K \xrightarrow{D} B$. □

The uniform integrability stipulation in (b′) is required only for the case $r = 2$, and the difference between this and the α-mixing case is that this value of r is permitted, corresponding to a ϕ-mixing size of -1.

Proof By **17.6**(ii), $\{U_{ni}\}$ is again an L_2-mixingale of size $-\frac{1}{2}$ in this case. The same arguments as before establish that conditions **29.4**(b),(c) and (d) hold; and, since $\alpha(m) \leq \phi(m)$, condition (29.47) remains valid so that asymptotic independence also holds by the same arguments as before. ∎

29.4 Transformed Brownian Motion

To develop a fully general theory of weak convergence of partial sum processes, permitting global heterogeneity of the increments with possibly trending moments, and particularly to accommodate the multivariate case, we shall need to extend the class of limit processes beyond ordinary Brownian motion. The desired generalization has already been introduced as example **27.8**, but now we consider the theory of these processes a little more formally. A *transformed* (or *variance-transformed*) *Brownian motion* B_η will be defined as a stochastic process on [0,1] with finite-dimensional distributions given by

$$B_\eta(t) \sim B(\eta(t)),\ t \in [0,1]. \tag{29.49}$$

where B is a Brownian motion and η is an increasing homeomorphism on [0,1] with $\eta(0) = 0$. The increments of this process, $B_\eta(t) - B_\eta(s)$ for $0 \le t < s \le 1$, are therefore independent and Gaussian with mean 0 and variance $\eta(t) - \eta(s)$. Since $\eta(1)$ must be finite, the condition $\eta(1) = 1$ can be achieved by a trivial normalization.

To appreciate the relevance of these processes, consider, as was done in §27.4 the characterization of B as the limit of a partial-sum process with independent Gaussian summands. Here we let the variance of the terms change with time. Suppose $\xi_i \sim N(0,\sigma_i^2)$, and let $s_n^2 = E(\sum_{i=1}^n \xi_i)^2 = \sum_{i=1}^n \sigma_i^2$. Also suppose the variance sequence $\{\sigma_i^2\}_{i=1}^\infty$ has the property that, for each $t \in [0,1]$,

$$\frac{s_{[nt]}^2}{s_n^2} \to \eta(t) \text{ as } n \to \infty, \tag{29.50}$$

where the limit function η: $[0,1] \mapsto [0,1]$ is continuous and strictly increasing everywhere. In this case, according to the definition of B_η, we have

$$\frac{\sum_{i=1}^{[nt]} \xi_i}{s_n} \xrightarrow{D} B_\eta(t), \tag{29.51}$$

for each $t \in [0,1]$.

What mode of evolution of the variances might satisfy (29.50), and give rise to this limiting result? In what we called, in §13.2, the globally stationary case, where the sequence $\{\sigma_i^2\}_1^\infty$ is Cesàro-summable and the Cesàro limit is strictly positive, it is fairly easy to see that $\eta(t) = t$ is the only possible limit for (29.50). This conclusion extends to any case where the variances are uniformly bounded and the limit exists; however, the fact that uniform boundedness of the variances is not sufficient is illustrated by **24.11**. (Try evaluating the sequence in (29.50) for this case.)

Alternatively, consider the example in **27.8**. It may be surprising to find that (for the case $-1 < \beta < 0$) the partial sums have a well defined limit process even when the Cesàro limit of the variances is 0. However, **27.8** is more general than it may at first appear. Define a continuous function on $[0,\infty)$ by

$$g(\nu) = s_{[\nu]}^2 + (\nu - [\nu])\sigma_{[\nu+1]}^2. \tag{29.52}$$

If s_n^2 satisfies (29.50), g is regularly varying at infinity according to **2.32**. g has right derivative $g'(\nu) = \sigma_{[\nu]+1}^2$ for $\nu \in [[\nu], [\nu]+1)$, such that $g(n+1) =$

$g(n)+g'(n)$ for integer n, and note that by **2.33** (which holds for right derivatives) g' is also regularly varying. The variance process of **27.8** can be generalized at most by the inclusion of a slowly varying component.

This is the situation for the case of unweighted partial sums, as in (29.53), the one that probably has the greatest relevance for applications. But remember there are other ways to define the limit of a partial-sum process, using an array formulation. There need only exist a sequence $\{g_n\}_1^\infty$ of strictly increasing functions on the integers such that $g_n([nt])/g_n(n) \to \eta(t)$, and the partial sums of the array $\{\xi_{ni}\}$, where $\xi_{ni} \sim N(0,\sigma_{ni}^2)$ and

$$\sigma_{ni}^2 = (g_n(i) - g_n(i-1))/g_n(n), \tag{29.53}$$

will converge to B_η. And since such a sequence can always be generated by setting $g_n([nt]) = \eta(t)a_n$, where a_n is any monotone positive real sequence, any desired member of the family B_η can be constructed from Gaussian increments in this manner.

The results obtained in §29.1 and §29.2 are now found to have generalizations from B to the class B_η. For **29.1** we have the following corollary.

29.10 Corollary Let condition **29.1**(a) be replaced by

(a′) $E(X(t)) = 0$, $E(X(t)^2) = \eta(t)$, $0 \le t \le 1$.

Then $X \sim B_\eta$.

Proof Define $X^*(t) = X(\eta^{-1}(t))$ and apply **29.1 to** X^*. $\eta^{-1}(.)$ is continuous, so condition **29.1**(b) continues to hold. Strict monotonicity ensures that if $\{t_1,\dots,t_m\}$ define arbitrary non-overlapping intervals, so also do $\{\eta^{-1}(t_1),\dots,\eta^{-1}(t_m)\}$, so **29.1**(c) continues to hold. ■

Similarly, for **29.4** there is the following corollary.

29.11 Corollary Let the conditions (a), (b), and (c) of **29.4** hold, and instead of condition **29.4**(d) assume

(d′) $E(X_n(t)) \to 0$ and $E(X_n(t)^2) \to \eta(t)$ as $n \to \infty$, each $t \in [0,1]$.

Then $X_n \xrightarrow{D} B_\eta$.

Proof The argument in the proof of **29.4** shows that the conditions of **29.10** hold for X. ■

29.12 Example Let $\{U_i\}_1^n$ denote a sequence satisfying the conditions of **29.7**, with the extra stipulation that the L_2-NED size is -1. Define the cadlag process

$$X_n(t) = \frac{1}{\sigma n^{3/2}} \sum_{j=1}^{[nt]} jU_j. \tag{29.54}$$

This differs from the process $n^{-1/2}\sum_{j=1}^{[nt]} U_j/\sigma$ only by the multiplication of the summands by constant weights j/n, taking values between $1/n$ and 1. The arguments of **29.6** show that conditions **29.4**(a), (b), and (c) are satisfied for this case, and it remains to check **29.11**(d′). We show that

$$E(X_n(t)^2) \to \tfrac{1}{3}t^3. \tag{29.55}$$

Choose a monotone sequence $\{b_n \in \mathbb{N}\}$ such that $b_n \to \infty$ but $b_n/n \to 0$; $b_n = [n^{1/2}]$ will do. Putting $r_n = [nt/b_n]$ for $t \in (0,1]$ and n large enough that $r_n \geq 1$, we have

$$X_n(t) = \frac{1}{\sigma n^{3/2}}\left[\sum_{i=1}^{r_n}\left(\sum_{j=(i-1)b_n+1}^{ib_n} jU_j\right) + \sum_{j=r_nb_n+1}^{[nt]} jU_j\right]. \tag{29.56}$$

The terms in this sum have the decomposition

$$\sum_{j=(i-1)b_n+1}^{ib_n} jU_j = ib_nS_{ni} + b_nS^*_{ni}, \tag{29.57}$$

in which $S_{ni} = \sum_{j=(i-1)b_n+1}^{ib_n} U_j$, and $S^*_{ni} = \sum_{j=(i-1)b_n+1}^{ib_n} a_{nij}U_j$, where $a_{nij} = (ib_n - j)/b_n \in [0,1]$. The assumptions, and **17.7**, imply that $b_n^{-1}E(S_{ni}^2) \to \sigma^2$ for each $i = 1,\dots,r_n$, and that $b_n^{-1}|E(S_{ni}S_{ni'})| = O(|i-i'|^{-1-\delta})$ for $\delta > 0$. Neither $\limsup_n b_n^{-1}E(S_{ni}^{*2})$ nor $\limsup_n b_n^{-1}|E(S_{ni}S^*_{ni})|$ exceed σ^2, whereas $b_n^{-1}|E(S^*_{ni}S^*_{ni'})|$ and $b_n^{-1}E(S_{ni}S^*_{ni'})$ are of $O(|i-i'|^{-1-\delta})$. The same results apply to S_{n,r_n+1} and S^*_{n,r_n+1}, the analogous terms corresponding to the residual sum in (29.56).

Thus, consider $E(X_n(t)^2)$. Multiplying out the square of (29.56) after substituting (29.57), we have three types of summand: those involving squares and products of the S_{ni} ($(r_n+1)^2$ terms); those involving squares and products of the S^*_{ni} ($(r_n+1)^2$ terms); and those involving products of S^*_{ni} with S_{ni} ($2(r_n+1)^2$ terms). The terms of the second type are each of $O(b_n^2n^{-3}) = O(n^{-1}r_n^{-2})$, and this block vanishes asymptotically. The terms in the third block (given $ib_n = O(n)$) are of $O(b_nn^{-2}) = o(r_n^{-2})$, and hence this block also vanishes. This leaves the terms of the first type, and this block has the form

$$\frac{1}{n^3}E\left(\sum_{i=1}^{r_n+1} ib_nS_{ni}\right)^2 = \frac{r_n^3b_n^3}{n^3}\left(\frac{1}{r_n^3}\sum_{i=1}^{r_n+1} i^2\frac{E(S_{ni}^2)}{b_n}\right.$$
$$\left. + \frac{2}{r_n^3}\sum_{i=2}^{r_n+1}\sum_{m=1}^{i-1} i(i-m)\frac{E(S_{ni}S_{n,i-m})}{b_n}\right). \tag{29.58}$$

Noting that $r_nb_n/n \to t$, applying standard summation formulae and taking the limit yields (29.55). Thus, according to **29.11**, $X_n(t) \xrightarrow{D} B_\eta$ where $\eta(t) = \tfrac{1}{3}t^3$. □

There is an intimate connection between the generalization from B to B_η and the style of the result in **29.6**. The latter theorem does *not* establish the convergence of the partial sum sequences $X_n(t) = \sum_{i=1}^{[nt]} U_{ni}$, either to B or to any other limit. In fact there are two distinct possibilities. In the first, $K_n(t)/n$ converges to $\eta^{-1}(t)$ for $t \in [0,1]$, for some η as in (29.49). If this holds, there is no loss of generality in setting $K_n(t) = [n\eta^{-1}(t)]$, and under condition **29.6**(f) this has the implication

$$E(X_n(t)^2) = E(X_n^K(\eta(t))^2) \to \eta(t). \tag{29.59}$$

In other words, $X_n \xrightarrow{D} B_\eta$ by **29.11**. Example **29.8** is a case in point, for which $\eta(t) = t^{1+\beta}$. In these cases the convergence of the process $\{X_n^K\}$ to Brownian motion can be also represented as the convergence of the partial sum process $(X_n\}$ to B_η.

On the other hand, it is possible that no such η exists, and the partial sums have *no* weak limit, as the following case demonstrates.

29.13 Example Let a sequence $\{U_i\}$ have the property

$$U_i = \begin{cases} 0 \text{ a.s.,} & 2^{2k} \le i < 2^{2k+1},\ k = 0,1,2,3,... \\ N(0,\sigma^2), & \text{otherwise.} \end{cases}$$

Thus, $U_1 = 0$, $U_4 = U_5 = U_6 = U_7 = 0$, $U_{16} = U_{17} = ... = U_{31} = 0$, and so forth. Let $U_{ni} = U_i/s_n$ as before, and put $X_n(t) = \sum_{i=1}^{[nt]} U_{ni}$. Then, observe that for $\frac{1}{2} < t \le 1$,

$$X_n(t) = X_n(\tfrac{1}{2}) \text{ with probability } \begin{cases} 1 \text{ when } n = 2^k - 1 \text{ for } k \text{ even,} \\ 0 \text{ when } n = 2^k - 1 \text{ for } k \text{ odd.} \end{cases}$$

Since this 'cycling' in the behaviour of X_n is present however large n is, X_n does not possess a limit in distribution.

However, let $K_n(t)$ be the integer that satisfies

$$\sum_{i=2}^{K_n(t)} 1(2^{2k-1} \le i < 2^{2k},\ k \in \mathbb{N}) = [nt], \tag{29.60}$$

where 1(.) is the indicator function, equal to 1 when i is in the indicated range and 0 otherwise. With this arrangement, n counts the actual number of increments in the sum, while $K_n(1)$ counts the nominal number, including the zeros; $K_{n+1}(1) = K_n(1) + 1$ except when $K_n(1) = 2^{2k}$, in which case $K_{n+1}(1) = 2^{2k+1}$. The conditions of **29.6** are satisfied with $\eta(t) = t$, and $X_n^K \xrightarrow{D} B$. □

Incidentally, since condition **29.6**(f) imposes

$$E(X_n^K(1)^2) = E\left(\sum_{i=1}^{K_n(1)} U_{ni}\right)^2 \to 1, \tag{29.61}$$

one might expect that $K_n(1)/n \to 1$. The last example shows that this is not necessarily the case.

To get multivariate versions of **29.6** and **29.9**, as we undertake in the next section, it will be necessary to restate these theorems in a slightly more general form, following the lines of **29.10** and **29.11**.

29.14 Corollary Let conditions **29.6**(a), (b), (c), (d), and (e) hold, and replace **29.6**(f) by

(f′) $E(X_n^K(t)^2) \to \eta(t)$ as $n \to \infty$, for each $t \in [0,1]$;

then $X_n^K \xrightarrow{D} B_\eta$. The same modification in **29.9** leads to the same result. □

The main practical reason why this extension is needed is because we shall wish to specify K_n in advance, rather than tailor it to a particular process; the same choice will need to work for a range of different processes – to be precise, for every linear combination of a vector of processes, for each of which a compatible η will need to exist. However, the fact that partial sum processes may converge to limits different from simple Brownian motion may be of interest for its own sake, so that **29.14** (with $K_n(t) = [nt]$) becomes the more appropriate form of the FCLT. See Theorem **30.2** below for a case in point.

29.5 The Multivariate Case

To extend the FCLT to vector processes requires an approach similar in principle to that of §27.7. However, the results of this chapter have so far been obtained, unlike those of §27, without explicit derivation of the finite-dimensional distributions. It has not been necessary to use the results of §28.4 at any point. Because we have to rely on the Cramér-Wold device to go from univariate to multivariate limits, it is now necessary to consider the finite dimensional sets of D, and indeed to generalize the results of §28.4. This section draws on Phillips and Durlauf (1986).

We define D^m as the space of m-vectors of cadlag functions, which we endow with the metric

$$d_B^m(x,y) = \max_{1\le j\le m}\{d_B(x_j,y_j)\}, \tag{29.62}$$

where d_B is the Billingsley metric as before. d_B^m induces the product topology, and the separability of (D,d_S) implies both separability of (D^m,d_B^m) and also that $\mathcal{B}_D^m = \mathcal{B}_D\times\mathcal{B}_D\times\ldots\times\mathcal{B}_D$ is the Borel field of (D^m,d_B^m). Also let

$$\mathcal{H}_D^m = \{\pi^{-1}_{t_1,\ldots,t_k}(B) \subseteq D^m\colon B \in \mathcal{B}^{mk},\ t_1,\ldots,t_k \in [0,1],\ k \in \mathbb{N}\} \tag{29.63}$$

be the finite-dimensional sets of D^m, the field generated from the product of m copies of $\mathcal{H}_D$. The following theorem extends **28.10** in a way which closely parallels the extension of **27.6** to **27.16**.

29.15 Theorem $\mathcal{H}_D^m$ is a determining class for $(D^m, \mathcal{B}_D^m)$.

Proof An open sphere in $\mathcal{B}_D^m$ is

$$S(x,\alpha) = \{y \in D^m\colon d_B^m(x,y) < \alpha\}$$

$$= \left\{y\in D^m\colon \exists\ \lambda\in\Lambda \text{ s.t. } \|\lambda\| <\alpha,\ \max_{1\le j\le m}\sup_t|y_j(t)-x_j(\lambda(t))| <\alpha\right\}. \tag{29.64}$$

Define, for $\{t_1\ldots,t_k \in [0,1],\ k \in \mathbb{N}\}$,

$$H_k(x,\alpha) = \left\{ y \in D^m \colon \exists\, \lambda \in \Lambda \text{ s.t. } \|\lambda\| < \alpha, \right.$$

$$\left. \max_{1\le j\le m} \max_{1\le i\le k} |y_j(t_i) - x_j(\lambda(t_i))| < \alpha \right\} \in \mathcal{H}_D^m. \tag{29.65}$$

It follows by direct generalization of the argument of **28.10** that, for any $x \in D^m$ and $r > 0$,

$$S(x,r) = \bigcup_{n=1}^{\infty} \bigcap_{k=1}^{\infty} H_k(x,\, r - 1/n) \in \sigma(\mathcal{H}_D^m). \tag{29.66}$$

Hence, $\mathcal{B}_D^m \subseteq \sigma(\mathcal{H}_D^m)$ as required. ■

The following can be thought of as a generic multivariate convergence theorem, in that the weak limit specified need only be a.s. continuous. It is not necessarily B^m.

29.16 Theorem[29] Let $X_n \in D^m$ be an m-vector of random elements. $X_n \xrightarrow{D} X$, where $P(X \in C^m) = 1$, iff $\lambda' X_n \xrightarrow{D} \lambda' X$ for every fixed λ with $\lambda'\lambda = 1$.

Proof If $x_j \in D$, $j = 1,\ldots,m$, $\sum_{j=1}^m \lambda_j x_j$ possesses a left limit and is continuous on the right, since for $t \in [0,1)$,

$$\lim_{\varepsilon\downarrow 0} \sum_{j=1}^m \lambda_j x_j(t+\varepsilon) = \sum_{j=1}^m \lambda_j \lim_{\varepsilon\downarrow 0} x_j(t+\varepsilon) = \sum_{j=1}^m \lambda_j x_j(t). \tag{29.67}$$

Hence, $x = (x_1,\ldots,x_m)' \in D^m$ implies $\lambda' x \in D$. It follows that $\lambda' X_n$ is a random element of D. It is clear similarly that $x \in C^m$ implies $\lambda' x \in C$, and hence $P(\lambda' X \in C) = 1$.

To prove sufficiency, let μ_n^λ denote the sequence of measures corresponding to $\lambda' X_n$, and assume $\mu_n^\lambda \Rightarrow \mu^\lambda$. Fix $t_1,\ldots,t_k \in [0,1]$, for finite k. Noting that $\pi_{t_1,\ldots,t_k}^{-1}(B) \cap D \in \mathcal{H}_D \subseteq \mathcal{B}_D$ for each $B \in \mathcal{B}^k$ (see **28.10**), the projections are measurable and $\nu_n^\lambda = \mu_n^\lambda \pi_{t_1,\ldots,t_k}^{-1}$ is a measure on $(\mathbb{R}^k, \mathcal{B}^k)$. Although $\pi_{t_1,\ldots,t_k}$ is not continuous (see the discussion in §28.2), the stipulation $\mu^\lambda(C) = 1$ implies that the discontinuity points have μ^λ-measure 0, and hence $\nu_n^\lambda \Rightarrow \nu^\lambda$ by the continuous mapping theorem (**26.13**). Since ν_n^λ is the p.m. of a k-vector of r.v.s, and λ is arbitrary, the Cramér-Wold theorem (**25.5**) implies that $\nu_n \Rightarrow \nu$, where $\nu_n = \mu_n \pi_{t_1,\ldots,t_k}^{-1}$ is the p.m. of an mk-vector, the distribution of $X_n(t_1),\ldots,X_n(t_k)$. Since $t_1,\ldots,t_k$ are arbitrary, the finite dimensional distributions of X_n converge.

To complete the proof of sufficiency, we must show that $\{\mu_n\}$ is uniformly tight. Choose $\lambda = e_j$, the vector with 1 in position j and 0 elsewhere, to show that $X_{nj} \xrightarrow{D} X_j$; this means the marginal p.m.s are uniformly tight, and so $\{\mu_n\}$ is uniformly tight by **26.23**. Then $X_n \xrightarrow{D} X$ by **29.15**.

To show necessity, on the other hand, simply apply the continuous mapping theorem to the continuous functional $h(x) = \lambda' x$. ■

Although this is a general result, note the importance of the requirement $\mu(C) = 1$. It is easy to devise a counter-example where this condition is violated, in which case convergence fails.

29.17 Example Suppose μ is the p.m. on $(D,\mathcal{B}_D)$ which assigns probability 1 to elements x with

$$x(t) = \begin{cases} 0, & t < \frac{1}{2} \\ 1, & t \ge \frac{1}{2} \end{cases}.$$

Also, let μ_n assign probability 1 to elements with

$$x(t) = \begin{cases} 0, & t < \frac{1}{2}+\frac{1}{n} \\ 1, & t \ge \frac{1}{2}+\frac{1}{n} \end{cases}.$$

If $X_{1n} \sim \mu$ all n, and $X_{2n} \sim \mu_n$, then clearly $(X_{1n},X_{2n}) \xrightarrow{D} (X_1,X_2) = (x,x)$ w.p.1. But $X_{2n} - X_{1n}$ is equal w.p.1 to the function in (28.12), which does not converge in (D,d_B). □

Now we are ready to state the main result. Let $\{\boldsymbol{B}_\eta(\boldsymbol{\Omega})\}$ denote the family of $m \times 1$ vector transformed-Brownian motion processes on [0,1], whose members are defined by a vector of homeomorphisms $(\eta^1,\ldots,\eta^p)'$ and a covariance matrix $\boldsymbol{\Omega}$ $(m \times m)$. If $\boldsymbol{X} \sim \boldsymbol{B}_\eta(\boldsymbol{\Omega})$, the finite-dimensional distributions of $\boldsymbol{X}$ are jointly Gaussian with independent increments, zero mean, and

$$E(\boldsymbol{X}(t)\boldsymbol{X}(t)') = \boldsymbol{D}\boldsymbol{H}(t)\boldsymbol{D}',$$

where $\boldsymbol{D}$ $(m \times p)$ has rank p, $\boldsymbol{D}\boldsymbol{D}' = \boldsymbol{\Omega}$ and $\boldsymbol{H}(t) = \text{diag}\{\eta^1(t), \ldots., \eta^p(t)\}$, with $\boldsymbol{H}(1) = \boldsymbol{I}_p$. In other words, the jth element of $\boldsymbol{X}$ may be expressed as a linear combination $\sum_{k=1}^p d_{jk}Z_k$ where $\boldsymbol{Z} = (Z_1,\ldots,Z_p)'$ is a vector of independent processes with $Z_k \sim B_{\eta^k}$. With $p < m$, a singular limit is possible. Note, $\boldsymbol{Z} = (\boldsymbol{D}'\boldsymbol{D})^{-1}\boldsymbol{D}'\boldsymbol{X}$.

29.18 Theorem Let $\{\boldsymbol{U}_{ni}\}$ be an array of zero-mean stochastic m-vectors. For an increasing, integer-valued right-continuous function $K_n(.)$ define $\boldsymbol{X}_n^K = \sum_{i=1}^{K_n(t)}\boldsymbol{U}_{ni}$, and suppose that

(a) For each fixed m-vector $\boldsymbol{\lambda}$ satisfying $\boldsymbol{\lambda}'\boldsymbol{\lambda} = 1$ there exists a scalar array $\{c_{ni}^\lambda\}$ and a homeomorphism η^λ on [0,1] with $\eta^\lambda(0) = 0$ and $\eta^\lambda(1) = 1$, such that the conditions of **29.14** hold for the arrays $\{\boldsymbol{\lambda}'\boldsymbol{U}_{ni}\}$ and $\{c_{ni}^\lambda\}$, with respect to η^λ.

(b) Letting $\boldsymbol{H}(t)$ be defined as above with elements η^j denoting η^λ for the case $\boldsymbol{\lambda} = \boldsymbol{e}_j$ (jth column of the identity matrix), for $j = 1,\ldots,p$,

$$E(\boldsymbol{X}_n^K(t)\boldsymbol{X}_n^K(t)') \to \boldsymbol{D}\boldsymbol{H}(t)\boldsymbol{D}' \text{ as } n \to \infty. \tag{29.68}$$

Then $\boldsymbol{X}_n^K \xrightarrow{D} \boldsymbol{X} \sim \boldsymbol{B}_\eta(\boldsymbol{\Omega})$. □

A point already indicated above is that under these conditions K_n must be the same function for each $\boldsymbol{\lambda}$, and must satisfy condition **29.6**(d) in each case as well as **29.14**(f′). The condition $\eta^\lambda(1) = 1$ can always be achieved by a renormalization, and simply requires that differences in scale of the vector elements be absorbed in the matrix $\boldsymbol{D}$.

Proof Consider first the case $m = p$ and $\boldsymbol{D} = \boldsymbol{I}_m$. Condition (a) is sufficient under **29.14** for $\boldsymbol{\lambda}'\boldsymbol{X}_n^K \xrightarrow{D} B_\eta\lambda$, where this limit is a.s. continuous, for each $\boldsymbol{\lambda}$. The convergence of the joint distribution of $\boldsymbol{X}_n^K$ now follows by **29.16**. The form of the marginal distributions is implied by **29.14**, independence of the vector elements following from condition (b). If $\boldsymbol{D} \neq \boldsymbol{I}_m$, the theorem can be applied to the array $\{(\boldsymbol{D}'\boldsymbol{D})^{-1}\boldsymbol{D}'\boldsymbol{U}_{ni}\}$, for which the limit in (29.68) is $\boldsymbol{H}(t)$ as before. Since linear transformations preserve Gaussianity, the general conclusion follows by the continuous mapping theorem. ■

Theorem **29.18** is a highly general result, and the interest lies in establishing how the conditions might come to be satisfied in practice. While we permit $K_n(.) \neq [nt]$ to allow cases like **29.13**, these are of relatively small importance, and it will simplify the discussion if it is conducted in terms of the case $K_n(t) = [nt]$. The K superscript can then be dropped and $\boldsymbol{X}_n$ becomes the vector of ordinary partial sum processes.

Even then, the result has considerable generality thanks to the array formulation, and its interpretation requires care. We can invoke the decomposition

$$\boldsymbol{\Omega} = \boldsymbol{\Sigma} + \boldsymbol{\Lambda} + \boldsymbol{\Lambda}', \tag{29.69}$$

where

$$\boldsymbol{\Sigma} = \lim_{n\to\infty} \sum_{i=1}^{n} E(\boldsymbol{U}_{ni}\boldsymbol{U}_{ni}'), \tag{29.70}$$

$$\boldsymbol{\Lambda} = \lim_{n\to\infty} \sum_{i=2}^{n} \sum_{m=1}^{i-1} E(\boldsymbol{U}_{n,i-m}\boldsymbol{U}_{ni}'). \tag{29.71}$$

But it should be observed that the conditions of **29.18** do not explicitly impose summability of the covariances. While $\boldsymbol{\Sigma}$ and $\boldsymbol{\Lambda}$ are finite by construction, without summability it would be possible to have $\boldsymbol{\Sigma} = \boldsymbol{0}$. We noted previously that condition **29.6**(f) appeared to impose summability, but it remains a conjecture that the more general **29.14**(f′) must always do the same. This conjecture is supported by the need for a summability condition in **24.6**, whose conclusion must hold whenever **29.14** holds for the partial sums, but is yet to be demonstrated. Replacing **29.14**(f′) with more primitive conditions on the increment processes would be a useful extension of the present results, but would probably be difficult at the present level of generality.

Note that $\boldsymbol{\Omega}$, not $\boldsymbol{\Sigma}$, is the covariance of the process, notwithstanding the fact that $\boldsymbol{B}_\eta(\boldsymbol{\Omega})$ is a process with independent increments. The condition $\boldsymbol{\Omega} = \boldsymbol{I}$, such that the elements of $\boldsymbol{B}_\eta$ are independent, neither implies nor is implied by the contemporaneous uncorrelatedness of the $\boldsymbol{U}_{ni}$. While uncorrelatedness at all lags is sufficient, with $\boldsymbol{\Sigma} = \boldsymbol{I}$ and $\boldsymbol{\Lambda} = \boldsymbol{0}$, it is important to note that when the elements of $\boldsymbol{U}_{ni}$ are related *arbitrarily* (contemporaneously and/or with a lag) there always exists a linear transformation $(\boldsymbol{D}'\boldsymbol{D})^{-1}\boldsymbol{D}'$, under which the elements of the limiting process are independent of one another.

As we did for the scalar case, we review some of the simplest sets of sufficient conditions. Let $\boldsymbol{U}_{ni} = \boldsymbol{S}_n^{-1/2}\boldsymbol{U}_i$ where $\boldsymbol{S}_n = E(\sum_{i=1}^n \boldsymbol{U}_i\boldsymbol{U}_i')$. For this choice, $\boldsymbol{D} = \boldsymbol{I}_m$ is imposed automatically. If $\{\boldsymbol{U}_i\}$ is uniformly L_r-bounded, choose $c_{ni}^{\lambda} = (\boldsymbol{\lambda}'\boldsymbol{S}_n^{-1}\boldsymbol{\lambda})^{1/2}$. Then $\boldsymbol{\lambda}'\boldsymbol{U}_{ni}/c_{ni}^{\lambda}$ is a linear combination of the $\boldsymbol{U}_i$ with weights summing to 1 and $\sup_{i,n}\|\boldsymbol{\lambda}'\boldsymbol{U}_{ni}/c_{ni}^{\lambda}\|_r < \infty$ holds for any $\boldsymbol{\lambda}$, so that conditions (a) and (b) of **29.6** are satisfied. The multivariate analogue of **29.7** is then easily obtained:

29.19 Corollary Let $\{\boldsymbol{U}_i\}$ be a zero-mean, uniformly L_r-bounded m-vector sequence, with each element L_2-NED of size $-\frac{1}{2}$ on an α-mixing process of size $-r/(r-2)$; and assume $n^{-1}\boldsymbol{S}_n \to \boldsymbol{\Omega} < \infty$. If $\boldsymbol{X}_n(t) = n^{-1/2}\sum_{i=1}^{[nt]}\boldsymbol{U}_i$, then $\boldsymbol{X}_n \xrightarrow{D} \boldsymbol{B}(\boldsymbol{\Omega})$. □

Compare this formulation with (27.82), and as with **29.7**, note the important difference from the martingale difference case, with $\boldsymbol{\Omega}$ taking the place of $\boldsymbol{\Sigma}$. It is also worth reiterating how the statement of conditions is potentially misleading, given that the last one is typically hard to fulfil without a NED size of -1.

Somewhat trickier is the case of trending moments, where different elements of the vector may even be subject to different trends. The discussion here will have some close parallels with §24.4. Diagonalize $\boldsymbol{S}_n$ as

$$\boldsymbol{S}_n = \boldsymbol{C}_n\boldsymbol{M}_n\boldsymbol{C}_n', \tag{29.72}$$

where $\boldsymbol{M}_n$ is diagonal of rank m, and $\boldsymbol{C}_n\boldsymbol{C}_n' = \boldsymbol{C}_n'\boldsymbol{C}_n = \boldsymbol{I}_m$. Assume, to fix ideas, that $\boldsymbol{C}_n \to \boldsymbol{C}$, which can be thought of as imposing a form of global stationarity on the cross-correlations. Then $\boldsymbol{S}_n^{-1/2} = \boldsymbol{M}_n^{-1/2}\boldsymbol{C}_n'$ and

$$\begin{aligned} E(\boldsymbol{X}_n(t)\boldsymbol{X}_n(t)') &= \boldsymbol{M}_n^{-1/2}\boldsymbol{C}_n'E\left(\sum_{i=1}^{[nt]}\boldsymbol{U}_i\sum_{i=1}^{[nt]}\boldsymbol{U}_i'\right)\boldsymbol{C}_n\boldsymbol{M}_n^{-1/2} \\ &\approx \boldsymbol{M}_n^{-1/2}\boldsymbol{M}_{[nt]}\boldsymbol{M}_n^{-1/2} \to \boldsymbol{H}(t), \end{aligned} \tag{29.73}$$

where the approximation is got by setting $\boldsymbol{C}_n$ to $\boldsymbol{C}$, and can be made as good as desired by taking n large enough. The status of conditions **29.18**(a) and (b) must be checked by evaluating the elements of $\boldsymbol{H}$ in (29.73). An example is the best way to illustrate the possibilities.

29.20 Example Let $m = 2$, and assume $E(\boldsymbol{U}_i\boldsymbol{U}_{i-m}') = \boldsymbol{0}$ for $m \neq 0$, but let

$$E(\boldsymbol{U}_i\boldsymbol{U}_i') = \boldsymbol{C}\begin{bmatrix} i^{\beta_1} & 0 \\ 0 & i^{\beta_2} \end{bmatrix}\boldsymbol{C}' \tag{29.74}$$

for fixed $\boldsymbol{C}$. Then, $\boldsymbol{M}_n = \text{diag}\{n^{\beta_1+1}, n^{\beta_2+1}\}$ and $\boldsymbol{H}(t) = \text{diag}\{t^{\beta_1+1}, t^{\beta_2+1}\}$. For β_1, $\beta_2 > -1$, t^{β_1+1} and t^{β_2+1} are increasing homeomorphisms on the unit square, and condition **29.18**(b) is satisfied. It remains to check **29.18**(a). Condition **29.14**(f′) holds for the array $\{\boldsymbol{\lambda}'\boldsymbol{U}_{ni}\}$ with respect to

$$\eta^{\lambda}(t) = \lambda_1^2 t^{\beta_1+1} + \lambda_2^2 t^{\beta_2+1}, \tag{29.75}$$

which, since $\lambda_1^2 + \lambda_2^2 = 1$, is an increasing homeomorphism on the unit square with $\eta^\lambda(1) = 1$ and $\eta^\lambda(0) = 0$ whenever $\beta_1, \beta_2 > -1$. Assuming that **29.6**(b) holds for

$$c_{ni}^\lambda = \|\boldsymbol{\lambda}'\boldsymbol{U}_{ni}\|_2 = \left[\lambda_1^2\left(\frac{i^{\beta_1}}{n^{\beta_1+1}}\right) + \lambda_2^2\left(\frac{i^{\beta_2}}{n^{\beta_2+1}}\right)\right]^{1/2}, \tag{29.76}$$

we can check conditions **29.6**(d) and **29.6**(e). The latter holds for $\gamma = \frac{1}{2}$. We also find that

$$\begin{aligned} \frac{\nu_n^2(t,\delta)}{\delta} &= \frac{1}{\delta}\sum_{i=[ns]+1}^{[n(t+\delta)]} (c_{ni}^\lambda)^2 \\ &\approx \frac{\lambda_1^2((t+\delta)^{\beta_1+1} - t^{\beta_1+1}) + \lambda_2^2((t+\delta)^{\beta_2+1} - t^{\beta_2+1})}{\delta} \\ &\to \lambda_1^2(\beta_1+1)t^{\beta_1} + \lambda_2^2(\beta_2+1)t^{\beta_2} < \infty \end{aligned} \tag{29.77}$$

as $\delta \to 0$, where the approximation is as good as desired with large enough n. Condition **29.6**(d) is satisfied, and hence **29.18**(a) holds. This completes the verification of the conditions. □

30

Weak Convergence to Stochastic Integrals

30.1 Weak Limit Results for Random Functionals

The main task of this chapter is to treat an important corollary to the functional central limit theorem: convergence of a particular class of partial sums to a limit distribution which can be identified with a stochastic integral with respect to Brownian motion, or another Gaussian process. But before embarking on this topic, we first review another class of results involving integrals, superficially similar to what follows, but actually different and rather more straightforward. There will, in fact, turn out to be an unexpected correspondence in certain cases between the results obtained by each approach.

For a probability space $(\Omega,\mathcal{F},P)$, we are familiar with the notion of a measurable mapping

$$f\colon \Omega \mapsto C,$$

where C is $C_{[0,1]}$ as usual. We now want to extend measurability to functionals on C, and especially to integrals. Let $F(t) = \int_0^t f ds\colon C \mapsto \mathbb{R}$ denote the ordinary Riemann integral of f over $[0,t]$.

30.1 Theorem If f is $\mathcal{F}/\mathcal{B}_C$-measurable, the composite mapping

$$F(t)\circ f\colon \Omega \mapsto \mathbb{R}$$

is $\mathcal{F}/\mathcal{B}$-measurable for $t \in [0,1]$.

Proof It is sufficient to show that $F(t)$ is continuous on (C,d_U). This follows since, for $G(t) = \int_0^t g ds$, $g \in C$, and $0 \le t \le 1$,

$$|F(t) - G(t)| \le \int_0^t |f-g| ds \le \sup_s |f(s) - g(s)|. \blacksquare \tag{30.1}$$

This shows that $F(t)$ is a random variable for any t. Now, writing

$$F\colon C \mapsto C$$

as the mapping whose range is the set of functions assuming the values $F(t)$ at t, it can further be shown that F is a new random function whose distribution is uniquely found by extension from the finite-dimensional distributions, just as for f. The same reasoning extends to $F^2(t) = \int_0^t F ds$, to F^3, and so on.

Other important examples of measurable functionals under d_U include the extrema, $\sup_t\{f(t)\}$ and $\inf_t\{f(t)\}$. As a simple example of technique, here is an ingenious argument which shows that if B is standard Brownian motion, $\sup_t\{B(t)\}$ has the half-normal distribution (see (8.26)). Consider the partial sum process S_n

$= \sum_{i=1}^n \xi_i$, where the ξ_i are independent binary r.v.s with $P(\xi_i = 1) = P(\xi_i = -1) = \frac{1}{2}$. Straightforward enumeration of the sample space shows that

$$P\left(\max_{1\le i\le n} S_i \ge a_n\right) = 2P(S_n > a_n) + P(S_n = a_n), \tag{30.2}$$

for any $a_n \ge 0$ (see Billingsley 1968: ch. 2.10). Since this holds for any n, on putting $a_n = \sqrt{n}\alpha$ the FCLT implies that the limiting case of (30.2) applies to B, in respect of any constant $\alpha \ge 0$. This also defines the limit in distribution of $\sup_t\{X_n(t)\}$ for *every* process X_n satisfying the conditions of **29.4**. This is a neat demonstration of the method of extending a limit result from a special case to a general case, using an invariance principle.

Limit results for the integrals (i.e, sample means) of partial-sum processes, or continuous functions thereof, are obtained by the straightforward method of teaming a functional central limit theorem with the continuous mapping theorem.

30.2 Theorem Let $S_{n0} = 0$ and $S_{nj} = \sum_{i=1}^j U_{ni}$ for $j = 1,\dots,n-1$. If $X_n(t) = S_{n,[nt]}$, assume that $X_n \xrightarrow{D} B_\eta$ (see **29.11**). For any continuous function $g: \mathbb{R} \mapsto \mathbb{R}$,

$$\frac{1}{n}\sum_{j=0}^{n-1} g(S_{nj}) \xrightarrow{D} \int_0^1 g(B_\eta)dt. \tag{30.3}$$

Proof Formally,

$$g(S_{nj}) = ng(S_{nj})\int_{j/n}^{(j+1)/n} dt = n\int_{j/n}^{(j+1)/n} g(X_n(t))dt. \tag{30.4}$$

Hence,

$$\frac{1}{n}\sum_{j=0}^{n-1} g(S_{nj}) = \sum_{j=0}^{n-1}\int_{j/n}^{(j+1)/n} g(X_n(t))dt = \int_0^1 g(X_n(t))dt. \tag{30.5}$$

Since $\int_0^1 g(x(t))dt$, $x \in C$, is a continuous mapping from C to $\mathbb{R}$, the result follows by the continuous mapping theorem (**26.13**). ∎

Note how $g(S_{nn})$ is omitted from these sums in accordance with the convention that elements of D are right-continuous. Since the limit process is continuous almost surely, its inclusion would change nothing material. These results illustrate the importance of having **29.14** (with $K_n(t) = [nt]$) as an alternative to **29.6** as a representation of the invariance principle. The processes $X_n^K(t)$ are defined in [0,1], and cannot be mapped onto the integers $1,\dots,n$ by setting $t = j/n$. There is no obvious way of defining the sample average of $g(X_n^K)$ in the manner of (30.3), and for this purpose the partial-sum process X_n with limit B_η has no substitute.

The leading cases of $g(.)$ include the identity function, and the square. For the former case, **30.2** should be compared with **29.12**. Observe that $\sum_{j=1}^{n-1} S_{nj} = \sum_{i=1}^{n-1}(n-i)U_{ni}$. If $U_{ni} = n^{-1/2}U_{n-i}/\sigma$, reversing the order of summation in **29.12** shows, in effect, that $n^{-1}\sum_{j=1}^{n-1} S_{nj} \xrightarrow{D} B_\eta(1)$, for the case $\eta(t) = \frac{1}{3}t^3$. In other words, $\int_0^1 Bdt \sim N(0,\frac{1}{3})$.

However, there is no such simple equivalence for the functional $\int_0^1 B^2 dt$, the limit for the case $g(.) = (.)^2$. These limit results do not generally yield closed formulae for the c.d.f., so there are no exact tabulations of the percentage points such as we have for the Gaussian case. Their main practical value is in letting us know that the limits *exist*. Applications in statistical inference usually involve estimating the percentiles of the distributions by Monte Carlo simulation; in other words, tabulating random variates generated as the averages of large but finite samples of g evaluated at a Gaussian drawing, to approximate integrals of $g(B_\eta)$. Knowledge of the weak convergence assures us that such approximations can be made as close as desired by taking n large enough.

Given a basic repertoire of limit results, it is not difficult to find the distributions of other limit processes and random variables in the same manner. To take a simple case, if $\{U_i\}$ is a sequence with constant variance σ^2, and $n^{-1/2}S_{[nt]}/\sigma \xrightarrow{D} B(t)$ where $S_{[nt]} = \sum_{i=1}^{[nt]} U_i$, we can deduce from the continuous mapping theorem that the partial sums of the sample mean deviations converge to the Brownian bridge; i.e.,

$$\frac{1}{\sigma n^{1/2}}\sum_{i=1}^{[nt]}(U_i - \bar{U}_n) \xrightarrow{D} B(t) - tB(1) = B^o(t), \tag{30.6}$$

where $\bar{U}_n = n^{-1}\sum_{i=1}^n U_i$. On the other hand, if we express the partial sum process *itself* in mean deviations, $S_j - \bar{S}_n$ where $\bar{S}_n = n^{-1}\sum_{j=0}^{n-1} S_j$, we find convergence according to

$$\frac{1}{\sigma n^{1/2}}(S_{[nt]} - \bar{S}_n) \xrightarrow{D} B(t) - \int_0^1 Bds. \tag{30.7}$$

The limit process on the right-hand side of (30.7) is the *de-meaned Brownian motion*. One must be careful to distinguish the last two cases. The integral of the latter over [0,1] is identically zero. The mean square of the mean deviations converges similarly, according to

$$\frac{1}{\sigma^2 n^2}\sum_{j=0}^{n-1}(S_j - \bar{S}_n)^2 \xrightarrow{D} \int_0^1 B^2 ds - \left(\int_0^1 Bds\right)^2. \tag{30.8}$$

There is also an easy generalization of these results to vector processes. The following is the vector counterpart of the leading cases of **30.2**, the details of whose proof the reader can readily supply.

30.3 Corollary Let $\{\boldsymbol{U}_{ni}\}$ satisfy the conditions of **29.18**. If $\boldsymbol{S}_{nj} = \sum_{i=1}^{j} \boldsymbol{U}_{ni}$, then

$$\frac{1}{n}\sum_{j=1}^{n-1} \boldsymbol{S}_{nj} \xrightarrow{D} \int_0^1 \boldsymbol{B}_\eta dt, \tag{30.9}$$

$$\frac{1}{n}\sum_{j=1}^{n-1} \boldsymbol{S}_{nj}\boldsymbol{S}'_{nj} \xrightarrow{D} \int_0^1 \boldsymbol{B}_\eta \boldsymbol{B}'_\eta dt. \ \square \tag{30.10}$$

Note in particular that for $\boldsymbol{B}$, the m-dimensional standard Brownian motion, $\int_0^1 \boldsymbol{B}dt \sim N(\boldsymbol{0}, \frac{1}{3}\boldsymbol{I}_m)$.

The same approach of applying the continuous mapping theorem yields an important result involving the product of the partial-sum process with its increment. The limits obtained do not appear at first sight to involve stochastic integrals, although there will turn out to be an intimate connection.

30.4 Theorem Let the assumptions of **30.2** hold, with $\eta(1) = 1$. Then

$$\sum_{j=1}^{n-1} S_{nj}U_{n,j+1} \xrightarrow{D} \tfrac{1}{2}(\chi^2(1) - \bar{\sigma}^2), \tag{30.11}$$

where $\bar{\sigma}^2 = \lim_{n\to\infty} n^{-1}\sum_{i=1}^n \sigma_{ni}^2$.

Proof Letting $S_{nj} = \sum_{i=1}^j U_{ni} = S_{n,j-1} + U_{nj}$, note the identity

$$S_{n,j+1}^2 = S_{nj}^2 + 2S_{nj}U_{n,j+1} + U_{n,j+1}^2. \tag{30.12}$$

Summing from 0 to $n-1$, setting $S_{n0} = 0$, yields

$$S_{nn}^2 = \sum_{j=0}^{n-1}(S_{n,j+1}^2 - S_{nj}^2) = 2\sum_{j=1}^{n-1} S_{nj}U_{n,j+1} + \sum_{j=1}^{n} U_{nj}^2, \tag{30.13}$$

or

$$\sum_{j=1}^{n-1} S_{nj}U_{n,j+1} = \tfrac{1}{2}\left(S_{nn}^2 - \sum_{j=1}^{n} U_{nj}^2\right). \tag{30.14}$$

Under the assumptions, $S_{nn} \xrightarrow{D} B_\eta(1) \sim N(0,1)$ and $\sum_{i=1}^n U_{ni}^2 \xrightarrow{pr} \bar{\sigma}^2$. The result follows on applying the continuous mapping theorem and **22.14**(i). ■

This is an unexpectedly universal result, for it actually does not depend on the FCLT at all for its validity. It is true so long as $\{U_{ni}\}$ satisfies the conditions for a CLT. Since $\bar{\sigma}^2 = 1 - 2\lambda$ where $\lambda = \lim_{n\to\infty}\sum_{i=2}^n\sum_{m=1}^{i-1}E(U_{n,i-m}U_{ni})$, the left-hand side of (30.11) has a mean of zero in the limit if and only if the sequence $\{U_{ni}\}$ is serially uncorrelated.

There is again a generalization to the vector case, although only in a restricted sense. Let $\boldsymbol{S}_{nj} = \sum_{i=1}^j \boldsymbol{U}_{ni}$, and then generalizing (30.12) we have the identity

$$\boldsymbol{S}_{n,j+1}\boldsymbol{S}_{n,j+1}' = \boldsymbol{S}_{nj}\boldsymbol{S}_{nj}' + \boldsymbol{S}_{nj}\boldsymbol{U}_{n,j+1}' + \boldsymbol{U}_{n,j+1}\boldsymbol{S}_{nj}' + \boldsymbol{U}_{n,j+1}\boldsymbol{U}_{n,j+1}'. \tag{30.15}$$

Summing and taking limits in the same manner as before leads to the following result.

30.5 Theorem Let $\{\boldsymbol{U}_{ni}\}$ satisfy the conditions of **29.18**. Then

$$\sum_{j=1}^{n} \boldsymbol{S}_{nj}\boldsymbol{U}_{n,j+1}' + \sum_{j=1}^{n} \boldsymbol{U}_{n,j+1}\boldsymbol{S}_{nj}' \xrightarrow{D} \boldsymbol{B}_\eta(1)\boldsymbol{B}_\eta(1)' - \boldsymbol{\Sigma}$$
$$\sim \boldsymbol{B}(1)\boldsymbol{B}(1)' - \boldsymbol{\Sigma}. \ \square \tag{30.16}$$

Details of the proof are left to the reader. The peculiarity of this result is that it does *not* lead to a limiting distribution for the stochastic matrix $n^{-1}\sum_{j=1}^{n-1}S_{nj}U'_{n,j+1}$. This must be obtained by an entirely different approach, which is explored in §30.4.

30.2 Stochastic Processes in Continuous Time

To understand how stochastic integrals are constructed requires some additional theory for continuous stochastic processes on [0,1]. Much of this material is a natural analogue of the results for random sequences studied in Part III.

A *filtration* is a collection $\{\mathcal{F}(t),\ t \in [0,1]\}$ of σ-subfields of events in a complete probability space $(\Omega,\mathcal{F},P)$ with the property

$$\mathcal{F}(t) \subseteq \mathcal{F}(s) \text{ when } t \le s. \tag{30.17}$$

The filtration $\{\mathcal{F}(t)\}$ is said to be *right-continuous* if

$$\mathcal{F}(t) = \mathcal{F}(t+) = \bigcap_{s>t} \mathcal{F}(s). \tag{30.18}$$

A stochastic process $X = \{X(t),\ t \in [0,1]\}$ is said to be *adapted* to $\{\mathcal{F}(t)\}$ if $X(t)$ is $\mathcal{F}(t)$-measurable for each t (compare §15.1). Note that right-continuity of the filtration is not the same thing as right-continuity of X, but if $X \in D$ (which will be the case in all our examples) adaptation of $X(t)$ to $\mathcal{F}(t)$ implies adaptation to $\mathcal{F}(t+)$ and there is typically no loss of generality in assuming (30.18).

A stronger notion of measurability is needed for defining stochastic integrals of the X process. $\{X(t)\}$ is said to be *progressively measurable* with respect to $\{\mathcal{F}(t)\}$ if the mappings

$$X(.,.)\colon \Omega\times[0,t] \mapsto \mathbb{R}$$

are $\mathcal{F}(t)\otimes\mathcal{B}_{[0,t]}/\mathcal{B}$-measurable, for each $t \in [0,1]$. Every progressively measurable process is adapted (just consider the rectangles $E\times[0,t]$ for $E \in \mathcal{F}(t)$) but the converse is not always true; with arbitrary functions, measurability problems can arise. However, we do have the following result.

30.6 Theorem An adapted cadlag process is progressively measurable.

Proof For an adapted process $X \in D$ and any $t \in (0,1]$, define the simple process on $[0,t]$:

$$X_{(n)}(\omega,s) = X(\omega,\ 2^{-n}k),\ s \in [2^{-n}(k-1),\ 2^{-n}k),\ k = 1,\dots,[2^n t], \tag{30.19}$$

with $X_{(n)}(\omega,t) = X(\omega,t)$. $X_{(n)}$ need not be adapted, but it is a right-continuous function on $\Omega\times[0,t]$. If $E_k^x = \{\omega\colon X(\omega,2^{-n}k) \le x\} \in \mathcal{F}(t)$, then

$$\begin{aligned} A_x &= \{(\omega,s)\colon X_{(n)}(\omega,s) \le x\} \\ &= \left(\bigcup_k [2^{-n}(k-1),\ 2^{-n}k)\times E_k^x\right) \cup \{t\}\times E_{[2^n t]+1}^x \end{aligned} \tag{30.20}$$

is a finite union of measurable rectangles, and so $A_x \in \mathcal{F}(t)\otimes\mathcal{B}_{[0,t]}$. This is true for each $x \in \mathbb{R}$, and hence $X_{(n)}$ is $\mathcal{F}(t)\otimes\mathcal{B}_{[0,t]}/\mathcal{B}$-measurable. Fix ω and s, and note that for each n

$$X_{(n)}(\omega,s) = X(\omega,u), \tag{30.21}$$

where $u > s$, and $u \downarrow s$ as $n \to \infty$. Since $X(\omega,u) \to X(\omega,s)$ by right-continuity, it follows that $X_{(n)}(\omega,s) \to X(\omega,s)$ everywhere on $\Omega\times[0,t]$ and hence X is $\mathcal{F}(t)\otimes\mathcal{B}_{[0,t]}/\mathcal{B}$-measurable (apply **3.26**). This holds for any t, and the theorem follows. ∎

Since we are dealing with time as a continuum, we can think of the moment at which some event in the evolution of X occurs as a real random variable. For example, the first time $X(t)$ exceeds some positive constant M in absolute value is

$$T(\omega) = \inf_{t\in[0,1]} \{t\colon |X(\omega,t)| > M\}. \tag{30.22}$$

$T(\omega)$ is called a *stopping time* of the filtration $\{\mathcal{F}(t),\ t \in [0,1]\}$ if $\{\omega\colon T(\omega) \le t\} \in \mathcal{F}(t)$ (compare §15.2). It is a simple exercise to show that, if X is progressively measurable, so is the stopped process X^T where $X^T(t) = X(t\wedge T)$.

Let $X \in D$, and let $X(t)$ be an $\mathcal{F}(t)$-measurable r.v. for each $t \in [0,1]$. The adapted pair $\{X(t),\mathcal{F}(t)\}$ is said to be a *martingale in continuous time* if

$$\sup_t E|X(t)| < \infty, \tag{30.23}$$

$$E(X(s)|\mathcal{F}(t)) = X(t) \text{ a.s.}[P],\ 0 \le t \le s \le 1. \tag{30.24}$$

It is called a semimartingale (sub- or super-) if (30.23) plus one of the inequalities

$$E(X(s)|\mathcal{F}(t)) \begin{Bmatrix}\ge\\ \le\end{Bmatrix} X(t) \text{ a.s.}[P],\ 0 \le t \le s \le 1 \tag{30.25}$$

hold. One way to generate a continuous-time martingale is by mapping a discrete-time martingale $\{S_j,\mathcal{F}_j\}_1^n$ into [0,1], rather in the manner of (27.55) and (27.56). If we let $X(t) = S_{[nt]+1}$, this is a right-continuous simple function which jumps at the points where $[nt] = nt$. It is $\mathcal{F}(t)$-measurable where $\mathcal{F}(t) = \mathcal{F}_{[nt]+1}$, and the collection $\{\mathcal{F}(t),\ 0 \le t < 1\}$ is right-continuous.

Properties of the martingale can often be generalized from the discrete case. The following result extends the maximal inequalities of **15.14** and **15.15**.

30.7 Theorem Let $\{(X(t),\mathcal{F}(t))\ t \in [0,1]\}$ be a martingale. Then

(i) $P\left(\sup_{s\in[0,t]} |X(s)| > \varepsilon\right) \le \dfrac{E|X(t)|^p}{\varepsilon^p}$, $p \ge 1$, (Kolmogorov inequality).

(ii) $E\left(\sup_{s\in[0,t]} |X(s)|^p\right) \le \left(\dfrac{p}{p-1}\right)^p E|X(t)|^p$, $p > 1$, (Doob inequality).

Proof These inequalities hold if they hold for the supremum over the interval [0,t), noting in (i) that the case $s = t$ is just the Chebyshev inequality. Given a discrete martingale $\{S_k,\mathcal{F}_k\}_{k=1}^m$ with $m = [2^n t]$, define a continuous martingale $X_{(n)}$ on $[0,t]$ as in the previous paragraph, by setting $X_{(n)}(s) = S_{[2^n s]+1}$ for $s \in [0,t)$, with $X_{(n)}(t) = X_{(n)}(t-) = S_{[2^n t]}$. The inequalities hold for $X_{(n)}$ by **15.14** and **15.15**, noting that

$$\sup_{s\in[0,t)} |X_{(n)}(s)|^p = \max_{1\le k\le m} |S_k|^p \tag{30.26}$$

for $p \ge 1$. Now, given an arbitrary continuous martingale $\{X(t), \mathcal{F}(t)\}$, a discrete martingale is defined by setting

$$(S_k,\mathcal{F}_k) = (X(2^{-n}k), \mathcal{F}(2^{-n}k)),\ k = 1,\dots,[2^n t]. \tag{30.27}$$

For this case we have $X_{(n)}(s) = X(u)$ for $u = 2^{-n}([2^n s]+1)$, so that $u \downarrow s$ as $n \to \infty$. Hence $X_{(n)}(s) \to X(s)$ for $s \in [0,t)$, by right continuity. ■

The class of martingale processes we shall be mainly concerned with satisfy two extra conditions: almost sure continuity ($P(X \in C) = 1$), and square integrability. A martingale X is said to be square-integrable if $E(X(t)^2) < \infty$ for each $t \in [0,1]$. For such processes, the inequality

$$E(X(s)^2|\mathcal{F}(t)) = X(t)^2 + E([X(s)-X(t)]^2|\mathcal{F}(t)) \ge X(t)^2 \tag{30.28}$$

holds a.s.$[P]$ for $s \ge t$ in view of (30.24), and it follows that X^2 is a submartingale. The *Doob-Mayer* (DM) *decomposition* of an integrable submartingale, when it exists, is the unique decomposition

$$X(t) = M(t) + A(t), \tag{30.29}$$

where M is a martingale and A an integrable increasing process.

The DM decomposition has been shown to exist, with M uniformly integrable, if the set $\{X(t),\, t \in \mathcal{T}\}$ is uniformly integrable, where $\mathcal{T}$ denotes the set of stopping times of $\{\mathcal{F}(t)\}$ (see e.g. Karatzas and Shreve 1988: th. 4.10). In particular, suppose there exists for a martingale $\{X(t),\mathcal{F}(t)\}$ an increasing, adapted stochastic process $\{\langle X\rangle(t), \mathcal{F}(t)\}$ on $[0,1]$, whose conditionally expected variations match those of X^2 almost surely; that is,

$$E(\langle X\rangle(s)|\mathcal{F}(t)) - \langle X\rangle(t) = E(X(s)^2|\mathcal{F}(t)) - X(t)^2 \text{ a.s.}[P] \tag{30.30}$$

for $s \ge$ t. Rearranging (30.30) gives

$$E(X^2(s) - \langle X\rangle(s)|\mathcal{F}(t)) = X(t)^2 - \langle X\rangle(t), \text{ a.s.}[P], \tag{30.31}$$

which shows that $\{X(t)^2 - \langle X\rangle(t),\ \mathcal{F}(t)\}$ is a martingale, and this process accordingly defines the DM decomposition of X^2. An increasing adapted process $\{\langle X\rangle(t),\mathcal{F}(t)\}$ satisfying (30.30), which is unique a.s. if it exists, is called the *quadratic variation process* of X.

30.8 Example The Brownian motion process B is a square-integrable martingale with respect to the filtration $\mathcal{F}(t) = \sigma(B(s),\ s \le t)$. The martingale property is an obvious consequence of the independence of the increments of B. A special feature of B is that the quadratic variation process is deterministic. Definition

27.7 implies that, for $s \geq t$,

$$E(B(s)^2|\mathcal{F}(t)) - B(t)^2 = E([B(s)-B(t)]^2|\mathcal{F}(t))$$
$$= s-t, \text{ a.s.}[P], \tag{30.32}$$

and rearrangement of the equality shows that $B(t)^2 - t$ is a martingale; that is, $\langle B\rangle(t) = t$. □

Two additional pieces of terminology often arise in this context. A *Markov process* is an adapted process $\{X(t),\mathcal{F}(t)\}$ having the property

$$P(X(t+s) \in A|\mathcal{F}(t)) = P(X(t+s) \in A|\sigma(X(t)) \text{ a.s.}[P] \tag{30.33}$$

for $A \in \mathcal{B}$ and $t, s \geq 0$. This means that all the information capable of predicting the future path of a Markov process is contained in its current realized value. A *diffusion process* is a Markov process having continuous sample paths. The sample paths of a diffusion process must be describable in terms of a stochastic mechanism generating infinitesimal increments, although these need not be independent or identically distributed, nor for that matter Gaussian. A Brownian motion, however, is both a Markov process and a diffusion process. We shall not pursue these generalizations very far, but works such as Cox and Miller (1965) or Karatzas and Shreve (1988) might be consulted for further details.

The family B_η defined in (29.49) are diffusion processes. They are also martingales, and it is easy to verify that in this case $\langle B_\eta\rangle = \eta$. However, a diffusion process need not be a martingale. An example with increments that are Gaussian but not independent is $X(t) = \theta(t)B(t)$ (see **27.9**). Observe that

$$E(X(t+s)-X(t)|\mathcal{F}(t)) = (\theta(t+s)-\theta(t))B(t)$$
$$= \left(\frac{\theta(t+s)}{\theta(t)} - 1\right)X(t) \neq 0, \text{ a.s.}[P]. \tag{30.34}$$

A larger class of diffusion processes is defined by the scheme $X(t) = \theta(t)B_\eta(t)$, for eligible choices of θ and η. The Ornstein-Uhlenbeck process (**27.10**) is another example. However, the class B_η is the only one we shall be concerned with here.

30.3 Stochastic Integrals

In this section we introduce a class of stochastic integrals on [0,1]. Let $\{M(t),\mathcal{F}(t)\}$ denote a martingale having a *deterministic* quadratic variation process $\langle M\rangle$. For a function $f \in D$, satisfying a prescribed set of properties to be detailed below, a stochastic process on [0,1] will be represented by

$$I(\omega,t) = \int_0^t f(\omega,\tau)dM(\omega,\tau), \quad t \in [0,1], \tag{30.35}$$

more compactly written as $I(t) = \int_0^t f dM$. The notation corresponds, for fixed ω, to what we would use for the Riemann-Stieljtes integral of $f(\omega,.)$ over $[0,t]$ with respect to $M(\omega,.)$. However, it is important to appreciate that, for almost every

ω, this Riemann-Stieljtes integral *does not exist*; quite simply, we have not required $M(\omega,.)$ to be of bounded variation, and the example of Brownian motion shows that this requirement could fail for almost all ω. Hence, a different interpretation of the process $I(t)$ is called for.

The results we shall obtain are actually available for a larger class of integrator functions, including martingales whose quadratic variation is a stochastic process. However, it is substantially easier to prove the existence of the integral for the case indicated, and this covers the applications of interest to us.

We assume the existence of a filtration $\{\mathcal{F}(t),\ t \in [0,1]\}$, on a probability space $(\Omega,\mathcal{F},P)$. Let

$$\alpha\colon [0,1] \mapsto \mathbb{R}$$

be a positive, increasing element of D, and let $\alpha(0) = 0$ and $\alpha(1) = 1$, with no loss of generality as it turns out. For any $t \in (0,1]$, the restriction of α to $[0,t]$ induces a finite Lebesgue-Stieltjes measure. That is to say, α is a c.d.f., and the function $\int_B d\alpha(s)$ assigns a measure to each $B \in \mathcal{B}_{[0,t]}$. Accordingly we can define on the product space $(\Omega\times[0,t],\ \mathcal{F}(t)\otimes\mathcal{B}_{[0,t]})$ the product measure μ_α, where

$$\mu_\alpha(A) = \int_\Omega\int_0^t 1_A(\omega,s)d\alpha(s)dP(\omega) = E\left(\int_0^t 1_A(\omega,s)d\alpha(s)\right) \tag{30.36}$$

for each $A \in \mathcal{F}(t)\otimes\mathcal{B}_{[0,t]}$.

Let $\mathbb{L}_\alpha$ denote the class of functions

$$f\colon \Omega \mapsto R[0,1]$$

which are (a) progressively measurable (and hence adapted to $\{\mathcal{F}(t)\}$), and (b) square-integrable with respect to μ_α; that is to say, $\|f\| < \infty$ where

$$\|f\| = E\left(\int_0^1 f^2 d\alpha\right)^{1/2}. \tag{30.37}$$

It is then easy to verify that $\|f-g\|$ is a pseudo-metric on $\mathbb{L}_\alpha$. While $\|f-g\| = 0$ does not guarantee that $f(\omega) = g(\omega)$ for every $\omega \in \Omega$, it does imply that the integrals of f and g with respect to α will be equal almost surely $[P]$. In this case we call functions f and g *equivalent*.

The chief technical result we need is to show that a class of simple functions is dense in $\mathbb{L}_\alpha$. Let $\mathbb{E}_\alpha \subseteq \mathbb{L}_\alpha$ denote the class such that $f(t) = f(t_k)$ for $t \in [t_k,t_{k+1})$, $k = 0,\dots,m-1$ and $f(1) = f(1-)$, where $\{t_1,\dots,t_m\} = \Pi_m$ is a partition of $[0,1]$ for some $m \in \mathbb{N}$.

30.9 Lemma (after Kopp 1984) For each $f\in \mathbb{L}_\alpha$, there exists a sequence $\{f_{(n)} \in \mathbb{E}_\alpha,\ n \in \mathbb{N}\}$ with $\|f_{(n)} - f\| \to 0$ as $n \to \infty$.

Proof Let the domain of f be extended to $\mathbb{R}$ by setting $f(t) = 0$ for $t \notin [0,1]$. By square-integrability, $\int_{-\infty}^{+\infty} f(\omega,t)^2 d\alpha(t) < \infty$ a.s.$[P]$, and

$$\int_{-\infty}^{+\infty}(f(\omega,t\,h) - f(\omega,t))^2 d\alpha(t) \to 0 \text{ a.s.}[P] \text{ as } h \to 0;$$

hence

$$\lim_{h\to 0} E\left(\int_{-\infty}^{+\infty}(f(s+h)-f(s))^2 d\alpha(s)\right) = 0 \tag{30.38}$$

by the bounded convergence theorem. This holds for any sequence of points going to 0, so, given a partition $\Pi_{m(n)}$ such that $\|\Pi_{m(n)}\| \to 0$ as $n \to \infty$, and $t \in [0,1]$, consider the case $h = k_n(t) - t$, where

$$k_n(t) = t_i,\ t \in [t_i,\ t_{i+1}),\ i = 0,\ldots,m-1, \tag{30.39}$$

$$k_n(1) = t_{m-1}. \tag{30.40}$$

Clearly, $k_n(t) \to t$. Hence, (30.38) implies that

$$\begin{aligned}
\int_{-\infty}^{+\infty} E\left(\int_{-1}^{1}(f(s+k_n(t)) - f(s+t))^2 d\alpha(t)\right) d\alpha(s)
&= \int_{-1}^{1} E\left(\int_{-\infty}^{+\infty}(f(s+k_n(t)) - f(s+t))^2 d\alpha(s)\right) d\alpha(t)\\
&= \int_{-1}^{1} E\left(\int_{-\infty}^{+\infty}(f(s+k_n(t)-t) - f(s))^2 d\alpha(s)\right) d\alpha(t)\\
&\to 0 \text{ as } n \to \infty,
\end{aligned} \tag{30.41}$$

where the first equality is an application of Fubini's theorem. Since the inner integral on the left-hand side is non-negative, (30.41) implies

$$\lim_{n\to\infty} E\left(\int_{-1}^{1}(f(s+k_n(t))-f(s+t))^2 d\alpha(t)\right) = 0 \tag{30.42}$$

for almost all $s \in \mathbb{R}$. Fixing $s \in [0,1]$ and making a change of variable from t to $t-s$ gives

$$\lim_{n\to\infty} E\left(\int_{s-1}^{1+s}(f(t+l_n(t))-f(t))^2 d\alpha(t)\right) = 0, \tag{30.43}$$

where $l_n(t) = k_n(t-s)-(t-s)$. Define a function

$$f_{(n)}(t) = \begin{cases} f(t+l_n(t)), & t+l_n(t) \in [0,1] \\ 0 & \text{otherwise,} \end{cases} \tag{30.44}$$

noting that $f_{(n)}(t) = f(t_i+s)$ for $t \in [t_i+s,\ t_{i+1}+s)\cap[0,1]$ and hence $f_{(n)} \in \mathbb{E}_\alpha$. Given (30.43), the proof is completed by noting that $[0,1] \subseteq [s-1,\ 1+s]$, and hence

$$\begin{aligned}
E\left(\int_{0}^{1}(f_{(n)}(t)-f(t))^2 d\alpha(t)\right) &= E\left(\int_{s-1}^{1+s}(f_{(n)}(t)-f(t))^2 d\alpha(t)\right)\\
&\le E\left(\int_{s-1}^{1+s}(f(t+l_n(t))-f(t))^2 d\alpha(t)\right).
\end{aligned} \tag{30.45}$$

The final inequality uses the fact that outside [0,1], $f_{(n)}(t) = f(t) = 0$, whereas $f(t+l_n(t)) \neq 0$ is possible. ■

Be careful to note the role of the assumptions here. We can use Fubini's theorem in (30.41) because the function α is nonstochastic and does not depend on ω, and hence, μ_α is a product measure. Without this property, more roundabout arguments are needed.

The construction of $I(t)$ for martingales with a deterministic quadratic variation process $\langle M\rangle$ proceeds by applying **30.9** for the case $\alpha = \langle M\rangle$. The integral is first defined for simple functions, and then a limit argument will give the extension to $\mathbb{L}_{\langle M\rangle}$. Let $f \in \mathbb{E}_{\langle M\rangle}$ be defined on a partition Π_m, and then, for $t \in [t_{k-1},t_k]$, $k = 1,\dots,m$, and $\omega \in \Omega$, let

$$I(\omega,t) = \sum_{j=0}^{k-1} f(\omega,t_j)\big(M(\omega,t_{j+1}) - M(\omega,t_j)\big) + f(\omega,t_k)\big(M(\omega,t) - M(\omega,t_k)\big)$$

$$= \sum_{j=0}^{k} f(\omega,t_j)\big(M(\omega, t\wedge t_{j+1}) - M(\omega,t_j)\big), \tag{30.46}$$

where $t\wedge t_j$ denotes $\min\{t,t_j\}$. The stochastic process $\{I(\omega,t),\ t \in [0,1]\}$ is an element of D. For $t \in [t_k,t_{k+1})$ and $s \in (t,t_{k+1})$,

$$I(\omega,s) - I(\omega,t) = f(\omega,t_k)(M(\omega,s) - M(\omega,t)),$$

so that right-continuity is shared with the process M. It is easily verified that

$$E(I(s)|\mathcal{F}(t)) = I(t) \text{ a.s.}[P], \text{ for } 0 \le t \le s \le 1. \tag{30.47}$$

Also, applying the orthogonality of the martingale increments, the law of iterated expectations and (30.30),

$$E(I(t)^2) = E\left(\sum_{j=0}^{k-1} f(t_j)^2 E\big((M(t\wedge t_{j+1}) - M(t_j))^2|\mathcal{F}(t_j)\big)\right)$$

$$= E\left(\sum_{j=0}^{k-1} f(t_j)^2\big(\langle M\rangle(t\wedge t_{j+1}) - \langle M\rangle(t_j)\big)\right)$$

$$= E\left(\int_0^t f(\tau)^2 d\langle M\rangle(\tau)\right) = \|1_{[0,t]}f\|^2. \tag{30.48}$$

Since the last member is finite by assumption on $\mathbb{L}_{\langle M\rangle}$, $I_n(t)$ is found to be itself a square-integrable martingale.

We shall now show that (30.46) is an adequate definition of the integral, in the sense that $\mathbb{E}_{\langle M\rangle}$ is dense in $\mathbb{L}_{\langle M\rangle}$; every $f \in \mathbb{L}_{\langle M\rangle}$ is arbitrarily close to an element of $\mathbb{E}_{\langle M\rangle}$. Given $f \in \mathbb{L}_{\langle M\rangle}$, let a sequence of functions $\{f_{(n)} \in \mathbb{E}_{\langle M\rangle}\}$ be defined with respect to partitions $\Pi_{m(n)}$, such that $\|\Pi_{m(n)}\| \to 0$ and $\|f_{(n)} - f\| \to 0$. For example, setting $m(n) = 2^n$ and $t_i = i/2^n$ means that the intervals of the partition are bisected each time n is incremented, and $\Pi_{2^n} \to \mathbb{D}$. For $f_{(n)}$, the construction in (30.44) will serve. Then the integrals of $f_{(n)}$, say $\{I_n(t),\ n \in \mathbb{N}\}$

for fixed t, form a real stochastic sequence, and for any $m > 0$,

$$E(I_{n+m}(t) - I_n(t))^2 = \|(f_{(n+m)} - f_{(n)})1_{[0,t]}\|^2 \to 0 \text{ as } n \to \infty \tag{30.49}$$

for each $t \in [0,1]$. It follows that the sequence $\{I_n(t)\}$ converges in mean square as $f_{(n)}$ approaches f. Moreover, for any n and m the process $\{I_{n+m}(t) - I_n(t),\ t \in [0,1]\}$ is a martingale, and applying the Doob inequality (**30.7**(ii)) we find

$$\begin{aligned} E\left(\sup_{t\in[0,1]} (I_{n+m}(t) - I_n(t))^2\right) &\le 4E(I_{n+m}(1) - I_n(1))^2 \\ &= 4\|f_{(n+m)} - f_{(n)}\|^2 \to 0. \end{aligned} \tag{30.50}$$

The mean square convergence is therefore uniform in t.

However, L_2 convergence implies in view of **18.6** that there exists a subsequence $\{n_i, i \in \mathbb{N}\}$ on which the convergence occurs with probability 1. Since the sequence of partitions $\{\Pi_{m(n)}\}$ specified in the construction of $f_{(n)}$ is required only to converge in the sense $\|\Pi_{m(n)}\| \to 0$ as $n \to \infty$, the sequence $\{\Pi_{m(n_i)}\}$ can be used in the construction with no loss of generality, and so $\lim_{m,n\to\infty} d_U(I_{n+m}, I_n) = 0$, a.s.$[P]$. Since $I_n \in D$ and the space (D,d_U) is complete, a limit function I exists in D, almost surely. If f and g are equivalent in the sense defined following (30.37), then $\int_0^t f dM = \int_0^t g dM$ a.s.$[P]$. Moreover, mean squared convergence implies weak convergence, so that the distribution of $I(t)$ can be characterized as the weak limit of the sequence of distributions of the $I_n(t)$. Note the characteristic property of the integral, applying the limit to (30.48):

$$E(I(t)^2) = E\left(\int_0^t f dM\right)^2 = E\left(\int_0^t f^2 d\langle M\rangle\right). \tag{30.51}$$

For the case $M = B$, Brownian motion, I is commonly known as the *Itô integral.* The so-called fundamental theorem of stochastic calculus, or Itô rule, shows very clearly that these objects are quite different from the Riemann-Stieltjes integrals which they superficially resemble. The best-known version is the following.

30.10 Itô's rule Let $g: \mathbb{R} \mapsto \mathbb{R}$ be twice-continuously differentiable, and let B be a Brownian motion on $[0,1]$. Then

$$g(B(t)) - g(0) = \int_0^t g'(B)dB + \tfrac{1}{2}\int_0^t g''(B)ds, \text{ a.s. } \square \tag{30.52}$$

30.11 Example Let $g(B) = B^2$. Itô's rule yields the result

$$\int_0^t BdB = \tfrac{1}{2}(B(t)^2 - t) \text{ a.s.,} \tag{30.53}$$

which may be compared with the standard Riemann-Stieltjes formula for integration by parts, under which the second right-hand side term in (30.53) is replaced by 0. Since $B(t) \sim N(0,t)$, we obtain from the continuous mapping theorem the result that

$$\int_0^t BdB \sim \frac{t}{2}(\chi^2(1) - 1). \tag{30.54}$$

Put $t = 1$ and compare this with **30.4**. It is apparent (and will be proved rigorously in **30.13** below) that the limit in (30.11) can be expressed as $\int_0^1 BdB + \lambda$ where $\lambda = \frac{1}{2}(1 - \overline{\sigma}^2)$, as before. □

A form of Itô's rule holds for a general class of continuous semi-martingales. The proof of the general result is lengthy (see for example Karatzas and Shreve 1988 or McKean 1969 for details) and we will give the proof just for the case of **30.11**, to avoid complications with the possible unboundedness of g''. However, there is little extra difficulty in extending from ordinary Brownian motion to the class of diffusion processes B_η.

30.12 Theorem $\int_0^t B_\eta dB_\eta = \frac{1}{2}(B_\eta(t)^2 - \eta(t))$, a.s.

Proof Let Π_n denote the partition of $[0,t]$ in which $t_j = tj/n$ for $j = 1,\dots,n$. Use Taylor expansions to second order to obtain the identity

$$B_\eta(t)^2 = \sum_{j=0}^{n-1}(B_\eta(t_{j+1})^2 - B_\eta(t_j)^2)$$

$$= 2\sum_{j=0}^{n-1} B_\eta(t_j)(B_\eta(t_{j+1}) - B_\eta(t_j)) + \sum_{j=0}^{n-1}(B_\eta(t_{j+1}) - B_\eta(t_j))^2. \tag{30.55}$$

We show the L_2 convergence of each of the sums in the right-hand member. $B_\eta \in \mathbb{L}_\eta$, so define $p_n \in \mathbb{E}_\eta$ by

$$p_n(s) = B_\eta(t_j),\ s \in [t_j, t_{j+1}),\ j = 0,\dots,n-1, \tag{30.56}$$

and $p_n(s) = B_\eta(s)$ for $t \le s \le 1$. This is a construction similar to that used in the proof of **30.9**, and $\|p_n - B_\eta\| \to 0$ as $n \to \infty$. We may write

$$\sum_{j=0}^{n-1} B_\eta(t_j)(B_\eta(t_{j+1}) - B_\eta(t_j)) = \sum_{j=0}^{n-1}\int_{t_j}^{t_{j+1}} B_\eta(t_j)dB_\eta(s)$$

$$= \int_0^t p_n(s)dB_\eta(s), \tag{30.57}$$

and it follows that

$$E\left(\sum_{j=0}^{n-1} B_\eta(t_j)(B_\eta(t_{j+1}) - B_\eta(t_j)) - \int_0^t B_\eta dB_\eta\right)^2 = E\left(\int_0^t (p_n - B_\eta)dB_\eta\right)^2$$

$$= \|(p_n - B_\eta)1_{[0,t]}\|^2 \to 0. \tag{30.58}$$

Considering the second sum on the right-hand side of (30.55), we have

$$E\left(\sum_{j=0}^{n-1}(B_\eta(t_{j+1}) - B_\eta(t_j))^2 - \eta(t)\right)^2$$

$$= E\left(\sum_{j=0}^{n-1}[(B_\eta(t_{j+1})-B_\eta(t_j))^2 - (\eta(t_{j+1})-\eta(t_j))]\right)^2$$

$$= \sum_{j=0}^{n-1}E[(B_\eta(t_{j+1})-B_\eta(t_j))^2 - (\eta(t_{j+1})-\eta(t_j))]^2$$

$$= 2\sum_{j=0}^{n-1}(\eta(t_{j+1}) - \eta(t_j))^2$$

$$\leq 2\eta(t) \max_{0\leq j\leq n-1}\{\eta(t_{j+1}) - \eta(t_j)\}$$

$$\leq \to 0 \text{ as } n \to \infty. \tag{30.59}$$

The second equality here is due to the fact that the cross-products disappear in expectation, thanks to the law of iterated expectations and the fact that

$$E[(B(t_{j+1})-B(t_j))^2|\mathcal{F}(t_j)] = \eta(t_{j+1})-\eta(t_j). \tag{30.60}$$

The third equality applies the Gaussianity of the increments, together with **9.7** for the fourth moments, and the inequality uses the continuity of η and the fact that $\|\Pi_n\| \to 0$.

Thus, $B_\eta(t)^2$ can be decomposed as the sum of sequences converging in L_2-norm to, respectively, $2\int_0^t B_\eta dB_\eta$ and $\eta(t)$. However, according to **18.6**, L_2 convergence implies convergence with probability 1 on a subsequence $\{n_k\}$. Since the choice of partitions is arbitrary so long as $\|\Pi_{n_k}\| \to 0$, the theorem follows. ∎

The special step in this result is of course (30.59). In a continuous function of bounded variation, the sum of the squared increments is dominated by the largest increment and so must vanish by continuity, just as happens with $\eta(t)$ in the last line of the expression. It is because it is unbounded a.s. that the same sort of thing does not happen with B_η.

30.4 Convergence to Stochastic Integrals

Let $\{U_{nj}\}$ and $\{W_{nj}\}$ be a pair of stochastic arrays, let $X_n(t) = \sum_{j=1}^{[nt]}U_{nj}$ and $Y_n(t) = \sum_{j=1}^{[nt]}W_{nj}$, and suppose that $(X_n,Y_n) \xrightarrow{D} (B_X,B_Y)$ where B_X and B_Y are a pair of transformed Brownian motions from the class B_η, with quadratic variation processes η^X and η^Y, the latter being homeomorphisms on the unit interval. In what follows it is always possible for fixing ideas to think of B_X and B_Y as simple Brownian motions, having $\eta^X(t) = \eta^Y(t) = t$. However, the extensions required to relax this assumption are fairly trivial. The problem we wish to consider is the convergence of the partial sums

$$G_n = \sum_{j=1}^{n-1}\left(\sum_{i=1}^{j}U_{ni}\right)W_{n,j+1}$$

$$= \sum_{j=1}^{n-1} X_n(j/n)(Y_n((j+1)/n) - Y_n(j/n)). \tag{30.61}$$

This problem differs from those of §30.1 because it cannot be deduced merely from combining the functional CLT with the continuous mapping theorem. None the less, it is possible to show that the convergence holds under the conditions of **29.14**.

The following theorem generalizes one given by Chan and Wei (1988). See *inter alia* Strasser (1986), Phillips (1988), Kurtz and Protter (1991), Hansen (1992c), for alternative approaches to this type of result.

30.13 Theorem Let $\{U_{nj},W_{nj}\}$ be a (2×1) stochastic array satisfying the conditions of **29.18** for the case $K_n(t) = [nt]$. In addition, assume that both U_{nj} and W_{nj} are L_2-NED of size -1 on $\{V_{ni}\}$. Then

$$G_n \xrightarrow{D} \int_0^1 B_X dB_Y + \Lambda_{XY}, \tag{30.62}$$

where, with $\lambda_{njk} = E(U_{nj}W_{nk})$,

$$\Lambda_{XY} = \lim_{n\to\infty} \sum_{i=1}^{n-1}\sum_{m=0}^{i-1} \lambda_{n,i-m,i+1}. \; \square \tag{30.63}$$

An admissable case here is $U_{nj} = W_{nj}$, in which case the relevant joint distribution is singular.

Setting the L_2-NED size at -1 ensures that the covariances are summable in the sense of **17.7**. This strengthening of the conditions of **29.18** is typically only nominal, in the light of the discussions that follow **29.6** and **29.18**. However, be careful to see that summability is not required to ensure that $|\Lambda_{XY}| < \infty$, which holds under the conditions of **29.18** merely by choice of normalization. Its role will become apparent in the course of the proof.

Proof The main ingredient of this proof is the Skorokhod representation theorem, **26.25**, which at crucial steps in the argument allows us to deduce weak convergence from the a.s. convergence of a random sequence, and vice versa. Let (X_n,Y_n) be an element of the separable, complete metric space (D^2,d_B^2) (see §29.5). Since

$$(X_n,Y_n) \xrightarrow{D} (B_X,B_Y) \tag{30.64}$$

by **29.18**, Skorokhod's theorem implies the existence of a sequence $\{(X^n,Y^n)\in D^2, n\in\mathbb{N}\}$ such that (X_n,Y_n) is distributed like (X^n,Y^n), and $d_B^2((X^n,Y^n),(B_X,B_Y)) \xrightarrow{as} 0$. According to Egoroff's theorem (**18.4**) and the equivalence of d_S and d_B in D, (30.64) implies that, for a set $C_\varepsilon \in \mathcal{F}$ with $P(C_\varepsilon) \ge 1-\varepsilon$,

$$\sup_{\omega\in C_\varepsilon} d_S^2((X^n(\omega),Y^n(\omega)),(B_X(\omega),B_Y(\omega))) \to 0 \tag{30.65}$$

for each $\varepsilon > 0$. Since B_X is a.s. continuous, there exists a set E_X with $P(E_X) = 1$ and the following property: if $\omega \in E_X$, then for any $\eta > 0$ there is a constant $\delta > 0$, such that, if $d_S(X^n(\omega),B_X(\omega)) \le \delta$,

$$\sup_t |X^n(\omega,t) - B_X(\omega,t)| \leq \sup_t |X^n(\omega,t) - B_X(\omega,\lambda(t))| + \sup_t |B_X(\omega,t) - B_X(\omega,\lambda(t))|$$
$$\leq \delta + \eta, \tag{30.66}$$

where $\lambda(.))$ is the function from (28.7). The same result holds for Y in respect of a set E_Y with $P(E_Y) = 1$. It follows from (30.65) that, for $\omega \in C^*_\varepsilon = C_\varepsilon \cap E_X \cap E_Y$,

$$d_U^2((X^n(\omega),Y^n(\omega)),\ (B_X(\omega),B_Y(\omega))) = \delta_n \to 0, \tag{30.67}$$

where the equality defines δ_n. Note too that $P(C^*_\varepsilon) = P(C_\varepsilon)$.

For each member of an increasing integer subsequence $\{k_n, n \in \mathbb{N}\}$, choose an ordered subset $\{n_1,n_2,...,n_{k_n}\}$ of the integers $1,...,n$, with $n_{k_n} = n$, such that $\min_{1\leq j\leq k_n}\{n_j - n_{j-1}\} \to \infty$. Use these sets to define partitions of $[0,1]$, $\Pi_n = \{t_1,...,t_{k_n}\}$, where $t_j = n_j/n$. Assume that $\{k_n\}$ is increasing slowly enough that $k_n\delta_n^2 \to 0$ and $k_n/n \to 0$, but note that provided $k_n \uparrow \infty$ it is always possible to have $\|\Pi_n\| \to 0$. For example, choosing $n_j = [nk_j/k_n]$ will satisfy these conditions.

The main steps to be taken are now basically two. Define

$$G^*_n = \sum_{j=1}^{k_n} X_n(t_{j-1})(Y_n(t_j) - Y_n(t_{j-1})), \tag{30.68}$$

and also let G^{*n} represent the same expression except that the Skorokhod variables X^n and Y^n are substituted for X_n and Y_n. In view of **22.18** and the fact that G^{*n} and G^*_n have the same distribution, to establish $G^*_n \xrightarrow{D} \int_0^1 B_X dB_Y$ it will suffice to prove that

$$\left| G^{*n} - \int_0^1 B_X dB_Y \right| \xrightarrow{pr} 0. \tag{30.69}$$

The proof will then be completed, in view of **22.14**(i), by showing

$$G_n - G^*_n \xrightarrow{pr} \Lambda_{XY}. \tag{30.70}$$

The Cauchy-Schwartz inequality and (30.67) give, for each $\omega \in C^*_\varepsilon$,

$$\left(\sum_{j=1}^{k_n}(X^n(\omega,t_{j-1}) - B_X(\omega,t_{j-1}))(Y^n(\omega,t_j) - Y^n(\omega,t_{j-1}))\right)^2$$
$$\leq \sum_{j=1}^{k_n}(X^n(\omega,t_{j-1}) - B_X(\omega,t_{j-1}))^2 \sum_{j=1}^{k_n}(Y^n(\omega,t_j) - Y^n(\omega,t_{j-1}))^2$$
$$\leq k_n\delta_n^2 \sum_{j=1}^{k_n}(Y^n(\omega,t_j) - Y^n(\omega,t_{j-1}))^2. \tag{30.71}$$

Also the assumptions on Y_n, and equivalence of the distributions, imply that

$$E(Y^n(t_j) - Y^n(t_{j-1}))^2 = E\left(\sum_{i=n_{j-1}+1}^{n_j} W_{ni}\right)^2$$

$$\to \eta^Y(t_j) - \eta^Y(t_{j-1}) < \infty, \tag{30.72}$$

and hence from (30.71),

$$E\left(\sum_{j=1}^{k_n} (X^n(t_{j-1}) - B_X(t_{j-1}))(Y^n(t_j) - Y^n(t_{j-1}))1_{C_\varepsilon^*}\right)^2 \to 0. \tag{30.73}$$

Closely similar arguments give

$$E\left(\sum_{j=1}^{k_n} (Y^n(t_j) - B_Y(t_j))(B_X(t_j) - B_X(t_{j-1}))1_{C_\varepsilon^*}\right)^2 \to 0, \tag{30.74}$$

and also

$$E(B_X(1)(Y^n(1) - B_Y(1))1_{C_\varepsilon^*})^2 \le \delta_n^2 \to 0. \tag{30.75}$$

We now use the method of 'summation by parts'; given arbitrary real numbers $\{a_j,b_j,\alpha_j,\beta_j,\ j = 1,\dots,k\}$ with $a_0 = b_0 = \alpha_0 = \beta_0 = 0$, we have the identity

$$\sum_{j=1}^{k} a_{j-1}(b_j - b_{j-1}) - \sum_{j=1}^{k} \alpha_{j-1}(\beta_j - \beta_{j-1})$$

$$= \sum_{j=1}^{k} (a_{j-1} - \alpha_{j-1})(b_j - b_{j-1}) + \alpha_k(b_k - \beta_k) - \sum_{j=1}^{k} (b_j - \beta_j)(\alpha_j - \alpha_{j-1}). \tag{30.76}$$

Put $k = k_n$, $a_j = X^n(\omega,t_j)$, $b_j = Y^n(\omega,t_j)$, $\alpha_j = B_X(\omega,t_j)$, and $\beta_j = B_Y(\omega,t_j)$. Then the left-hand side of (30.76) corresponds to $G^{*n} - P_n$, where

$$P_n = \sum_{j=1}^{k_n} B_X(t_{j-1})(B_Y(t_j) - B_Y(t_{j-1}))$$

$$= \sum_{j=1}^{k_n} \int_{t_j-1}^{t_j} B_X(t_{j-1})dB_Y(t), \tag{30.77}$$

and the squares of the right-hand side terms correspond to the integrands in (30.73), (30.74), and (30.75). Since ε is arbitrary, $P(C_\varepsilon^*)$ can be set arbitrarily close to 1, so that each of these terms vanishes in L_2-norm. We may conclude that $|G^{*n} - P_n| \xrightarrow{L_2} 0$. So, to get (30.69), it suffices to show that $|P_n - \int_0^1 B_X dB_Y| \xrightarrow{L_2} 0$. But

$$E\left(P_n - \int_0^1 B_X dB_Y\right)^2 = E\left(\sum_{j=1}^{k_n} \int_{t_j-1}^{t_j} (B_X(t_{j-1}) - B_X(t))dB_Y(t)\right)^2$$

$$= \sum_{j=1}^{k_n} \int_{t_j-1}^{t_j} (\eta^X(t) - \eta^X(t_{j-1}))d\eta^Y(t)$$

$$\leq \max_{1\leq j\leq k_n} \{\eta^X(t_j) - \eta^X(t_{j-1})\}\eta^Y(1) \to 0 \tag{30.78}$$

where the second equality applies (30.51) and then Fubini's theorem, and the convergence is by continuity of η^X. This completes the proof of (30.69).

To show (30.70), we use the fact that

$$Y_n(t_j) - Y_n(t_{j-1}) = \sum_{i=n_{j-1}}^{n_j-1} (Y_n((i+1)/n) - Y_n(i/n)),$$

and so

$$G_n - G_n^* = \sum_{j=1}^{k_n} \left[\left(\sum_{i=n_{j-1}}^{n_j-1} X_n(i/n)(Y_n((i+1)/n) - Y_n(i/n)) \right) - X_n(t_{j-1})(Y_n(t_j) - Y_n(t_{j-1})) \right]$$

$$= \sum_{j=1}^{k_n} \left(\sum_{i=n_{j-1}}^{n_j-1} (X_n(i/n) - X_n(t_{j-1}))(Y_n((i+1)/n) - Y_n(i/n)) \right)$$

$$= \sum_{j=1}^{k_n} \left(\sum_{i=n_{j-1}}^{n_j-1} \sum_{m=0}^{i-n_{j-1}} U_{n,i-m}W_{n,i+1} \right)$$

$$= \sum_{j=1}^{k_n} \left(\sum_{m=0}^{n_j-n_{j-1}-1} \sum_{i=m+n_{j-1}}^{n_j-1} U_{n,i-m}W_{n,i+1} \right), \tag{30.79}$$

where we have formally set $U_{n0} = 0$. The final equality represents the shift from summing the elements of a triangular array by rows to summing by diagonals, and we use whichever of the two versions of the expression is most convenient. In view of (30.63), $G_n - G_n^* - \Lambda_{XY} = A_n - B_n$, where (summing by diagonals)

$$A_n = \sum_{j=1}^{k_n} \left(\sum_{m=0}^{n_j-n_{j-1}-1} \sum_{i=m+n_{j-1}}^{n_j-1} (U_{n,i-m}W_{n,i+1} - \lambda_{n,i-m,i+1}) \right) \tag{30.80}$$

and (summing by rows)

$$B_n = \sum_{j=1}^{k_n} \left(\sum_{i=n_{j-1}}^{n_j-1} \sum_{m=i-n_{j-1}+1}^{i-1} \lambda_{n,i-m,i+1} \right). \tag{30.81}$$

The problem is to show that both $A_n \xrightarrow{pr} 0$ and $B_n \to 0$.

Choose a finite integer N and break up A_n into $N+1$ additive components $A_{n0},\dots,A_{nN}$, where by taking n large enough that $N \leq \min_{1\leq j\leq k_n}\{n_j - n_{j-1}\}$ we can write

$$A_{nm} = \sum_{j=1}^{k_n} \sum_{i=m+n_{j-1}}^{n_j-1} (U_{n,i-m}W_{n,i+1} - \lambda_{n,i-m,i+1}), \tag{30.82}$$

for $m = 0,\dots,N-1$, and

$$A_{nN} = \sum_{j=1}^{k_n} \left(\sum_{m=N}^{n_j-n_{j-1}-1} \sum_{i=m+n_{j-1}}^{n_j-1} (U_{n,i-m}W_{n,i+1} - \lambda_{n,i-m,i+1}) \right). \tag{30.83}$$

For fixed finite m, the process

$$\{U_{n,i-m}W_{n,i+1} - \lambda_{n,i-m,i+1},\ \sigma(V_{nk},\ k \le i+1)\}$$

is, according to **17.11** and **17.6**, an L_1-mixingale array of size -1 with respect to the constant array $\{4c^U_{n,i-m}c^W_{n,i+1}\}$, where $\{c^U_{ni}\}$ and $\{c^W_{ni}\}$ are the constants specified by **29.18** for $\boldsymbol{\lambda} = (1,0)'$ and $(0,1)'$ respectively. We next show that the conditions of **19.11** are satisfied by these terms, so that

$$A^*_{nm} = \sum_{i=m+1}^{n-1} (U_{n,i-m}W_{n,i+1} - \lambda_{n,i-m,i+1}). \xrightarrow{L_1} 0. \tag{30.84}$$

First, for $r > 2$ in the α-mixing case (**29.6**) or for $r \ge 2$ in the ϕ-mixing case (**29.9**),

$$\begin{aligned} \sup_{i,n} E\left|\frac{U_{n,i-m}W_{n,i+1} - \lambda_{n,i-m,i+1}}{c^U_{n,i-m}c^W_{n,i+1}}\right|^{r/2} &\le 2^{r/2} \sup_{i,n}\left|\frac{U_{n,i-m}W_{n,i+1}}{c^U_{n,i-m}c^W_{n,i+1}}\right|^{r/2} \\ &\le 2^{r/2} \sup_{i,n}\left\|\frac{U_{n,i-m}}{c^U_{n,i-m}}\right\|_r^{r/2}\left\|\frac{W_{n,i+1}}{c^W_{n,i+1}}\right\|_r^{r/2} \\ &< \infty, \end{aligned} \tag{30.85}$$

where the first inequality makes use successively of Loève's c_r inequality and Jensen's inequality, the second one is by the Cauchy-Schwartz inequality, and the finiteness is because the arrays satisfy either **29.6**(b) or **29.9**(b′) by assumption. In the latter case, note that the assumptions include uniform square-integrability. Therefore the array

$$\left\{\frac{U_{n,i-m}W_{n,i+1} - \lambda_{n,i-m,i+1}}{c^U_{n,i-m}c^W_{n,i+1}}\right\}$$

is uniformly integrable in either case, and condition **19.11**(a) is met.

Next, the arrays $\{c^U_{ni}\}$ and $\{c^W_{ni}\}$ satisfy condition **29.6**(d) by assumption, which by the Cauchy-Schwartz inequality implies that

$$\sup_{t\in[0,1),\,\delta\in(0,1-t]}\left\{\limsup_{n\to\infty}\frac{1}{\delta}\sum_{i=[nt]+m+1}^{[n(t+\delta)]-1} c^U_{n,i-m}c^W_{n,i+1}\right\} < \infty. \tag{30.86}$$

Setting $t = 0$ and $\delta = 1$ in (30.86) gives

$$\limsup_{n\to\infty}\sum_{i=m+1}^{n-1} c^U_{n,i-m}c^W_{n,i+1} < \infty, \tag{30.87}$$

which is condition **19.11**(b), whereas setting $\delta = 1/n$ gives

$$\max_{m+1\le i\le n-1}\{c^U_{n,i-m}c^W_{n,i+1}\} = O(1/n), \tag{30.88}$$

and (30.87) and (30.88) together imply

$$\sum_{i=m+1}^{n-1}(c^U_{n,i-m}c^W_{n,i+1})^2 \to 0, \tag{30.89}$$

which is condition **19.11**(c). So $A^*_{nm} \xrightarrow{L_1} 0$ is proved. But for $m \ge 1$, according to (30.82),

$$\begin{aligned} E|A_{nm} - A^*_{nm}| &\le \sum_{j=1}^{k_n}\sum_{i=n_{j-1}}^{m+n_{j-1}-1} E|U_{n,i-m}W_{n,i+1} - \lambda_{n,i-m,i+1}|, \\ &= O(k_n/n), \end{aligned} \tag{30.90}$$

where the order of magnitude is by (30.85) and (30.88), so $A_{nm} \xrightarrow{L_1} 0$ also holds, for each $m = 0,\dots,N-1$. Similarly $E|U_{n,i-m}W_{n,i+1} - \lambda_{n,i-m,i+1}| \le 2|\lambda_{n,i-m,i+1}|$, and applying **17.7** yields

$$\begin{aligned} E|A_{nN}| &= O\left(\sum_{j=1}^{k_n}\sum_{m=N}^{n_j-n_{j-1}-1}\sum_{i=m+n_{j-1}}^{n_j-1} c^U_{n,i-m}c^W_{n,i+1}\zeta_{m+1}\right) \\ &= O(N^{-\delta}) \end{aligned} \tag{30.91}$$

for some $\delta > 0$, where the order of magnitude follows by a combination of (30.87) with the fact that the sequence $\{\zeta_m\}$ is of size -1, according to the mixing and L_2-NED size assumptions. Thus, $\lim_{n\to\infty}E|A_n| \le \lim_{n\to\infty}E|A_{nN}|$, which by taking N large enough can be made as close to 0 as desired. In the same manner, recalling $N \le \min_{1\le j\le k_n}\{n_j - n_{j-1}\}$,

$$|B_n| = O\left(\sum_{j=1}^{k_n}\sum_{i=n_{j-1}}^{n_j-1}\sum_{m=i-n_{j-1}+1}^{i-1} c^U_{n,i-m}c^W_{n,i+1}\zeta_{m+1}\right) = O(N^{-\delta}). \tag{30.92}$$

It follows that $G_n - G^*_n - \Lambda_{XY} \xrightarrow{L_1} 0$, and this completes the proof of (30.70), and of the theorem. ■

Now let $\{U_{ni}\}$ $(m \times 1)$ be a vector array satisfying the conditions of **29.18**, plus the extra condition that the L_2-NED size of the increments is -1 for each element. Since **30.13** holds for each element paired with each element, including itself, the argument may be generalized in the following manner.

30.14 Theorem Let $S_{nj} = \sum_{i=1}^{j} U_{ni}$. Then

$$\sum_{j=1}^{n-1} S_{nj} U_{n,j+1} \xrightarrow{D} \int_0^1 B_\eta dB_\eta' + \Lambda \ (m \times m). \tag{30.93}$$

Proof For arbitrary m-vectors of unit length, λ and μ, the scalar arrays $\{\lambda' S_{nj}\}$ and $\{\mu' U_{n,j+1}\}$ satisfy the conditions of **30.13**. Letting G_n denote the matrix on the left-hand side of (30.93), and G the matrix on the right-hand side, the result $\lambda' G_n \mu \xrightarrow{D} \lambda' G \mu$ is therefore given. A well-known matrix formula (see e.g. Magnus and Neudecker 1988: th. 2.2) yields

$$\lambda' G_n \mu = (\mu' \otimes \lambda') \mathrm{Vec}\, G_n, \tag{30.94}$$

where $\mu' \otimes \lambda'$ is the *Kronecker product* of the vectors, the row vector $(\mu_1\lambda_1, \ldots, \mu_1\lambda_m, \mu_2\lambda_1, \ldots, \ldots, \mu_m\lambda_m)$ $(1 \times m^2)$, and $\mathrm{Vec}\, G_n$ $(m^2 \times 1)$ is the vector consisting of the columns of G_n stacked one above the other. $\mu' \otimes \lambda'$ is of unit length, and applying the Cramér-Wold theorem (**25.5**) in respect of (30.94) implies that $G_n \xrightarrow{D} G$, as asserted in (30.93). ■

This result is to be compared with **30.5**. Between them they provide the intriguing incidental information that

$$\int_0^1 B_\eta dB_\eta' + \int_0^1 dB_\eta B_\eta' \sim B_\eta(1) B_\eta(1)' - \Omega. \tag{30.95}$$

(Note that the stochastic matrix on the right has rank 1.) Of the two, **30.14** is much the stronger result, since it derives from the FCLT and is specific to the pattern of the increment variances.

Between them, **30.3** and **30.14** provide the basic theoretical tools necessary to analyse the linear regression model in variables generated as partial-sum processes (integrated processes). See Phillips and Durlauf (1986), and Park and Phillips (1988, 1989) among many other recent references.

Notes

1. See Billingsley (1979, 1986). The definition of a λ-system is given as **1.25** in Billingsley (1979), and as **1.26** in Billingsley (1986).

2. The 'prime' symbol ′ denotes transposition. $\boldsymbol{f}$ is a column vector, written as a row for convenience.

3. An affine transformation is a linear transformation $\boldsymbol{x} \mapsto \boldsymbol{A}\boldsymbol{x}$ followed by a translation, addition of a constant vector $\boldsymbol{b}$. By an accepted abuse of terminology, such transformations tend to be referred to as 'linear'.

4. That is, $|x + y| \le |x| + |y|$. See §5.1 for more details.

5. The notations $\int f d\mu$, $\int f\mu(d\omega)$, or simply $\int f$ when the relevant measure is understood, are used synonymously by different authors.

6. I thank Elizabeth Boardman for supplying this proof.

7. Elizabeth Boardman also suggested this proof.

8. If there is a subset $N \subset \Omega$ such that either N or N^c is contained in every $\mathcal{F}$-set, the elements of N cease to be distinguishable as different outcomes. An equivalent model of the random experiment is obtained by redefining Ω to have N itself as an element, replacing its individual members.

9. Random variables may also be complex-valued; see §11.2.

10. In statements of general definitions and results we usually consider the case of a one-sided sequence $\{X_t\}_1^\infty$. There is no difficulty in extending the concepts to the case $\{X_t\}_{-\infty}^\infty$, and this is left implicit, except when the mapping from $\mathbb{Z}$ plays a specific role in the argument.

11. We adhere somewhat reluctantly to the convention of defining size as a negative number. The use of terms such as 'large size' to mean a slow (or rapid?) rate of mixing can obviously lead to confusion, and is best avoided.

12. This is a problem of the weak convergence of distributions; see §22.4 for further details.

13. This is similar to an example due to Athreya and Pantula (1986a).

14. In the theory of functions of a complex variable, an analytic function is one possessing finite derivatives everywhere in its domain.

15. I am grateful to Graham Brightwell for this argument.

16. For convergence to fail, the discontinuities of f (which must be Borel measurable) would have to occupy a set of positive Lebesgue measure.

17. Conventionally, and for ease of notation, the symbol $\mathcal{F}_t$ is used here to denote

what has been previously written as $\mathcal{F}_{-\infty}^t$. No confusion need arise, since a σ-subfield bearing a time subscript but no superscript will always be interpreted in this way.

18. Some quoted versions of this result (e.g. Hall and Heyde 1980) are for $p > \frac{1}{2}$, whereas the present version, adapted from Karatzas and Shreve (1988), extends to $0 < p \leq \frac{1}{2}$ as well.

19. The *norm*, or length, of a k-vector $\boldsymbol{X}$ is $\|\boldsymbol{X}\| = (\boldsymbol{X}'\boldsymbol{X})^{1/2}$. To avoid confusion with the L_2 norm of a r.v., the latter is always written with a subscript.

20. The original St Petersburg Paradox, enunciated by Daniel Bernoulli in 1758, considered a game in which the player wins £2^{n-1} if the first head appears on the nth toss for *any* n. The expected winnings in this case are infinite, but the principle involved is the same in either case. See Shafer (1988).

21. See the remarks following **3.18**. It is true that in topological spaces projections are continuous, and hence measurable, under the product topology (see §6.5), but of course, the abstract space $(\Omega,\mathcal{F})$ lacks topological structure and this reasoning does not apply.

22. Since $\boldsymbol{\theta}$ is here a real k-vector it is written in bold face by convention, notwithstanding that θ is used to denote the generic element of (Θ,ρ), in the abstract.

23. This is the basis of a method for generating random numbers having a distribution F. Take a drawing from the uniform distribution on [0,1] (i.e., a random string of digits with a decimal point placed in front) and apply the transformation F^{-1} (or Y) to give a drawing from the desired distribution.

24. λ is used here as the argument of the ch.f. instead of the t used in Chapter 11, to avoid confusion with the time subscript.

25. The symbol i appearing as a factor in these expressions denotes $\sqrt{-1}$. The context distinguishes the use of the same symbol as an array index.

26. In practice, of course, U_t usually has to be estimated by a residual $\hat{U}_t$, depending on consistent estimates of model parameters. In this case, a result such as **21.6** is also required to show convergence.

27. More precisely, of course, W models the projection of the motion of a particle in three-dimensional space onto an axis of the coordinate system.

28. A cautionary note: these combinations cannot be constructed as residuals from least squares regressions. If $\boldsymbol{\Sigma}$ has full rank, the regression of one element of $\boldsymbol{Y}_n$ onto the rest yields coefficients which are asymptotically random. $\boldsymbol{\Sigma}$ must be estimated from the increments using the methods discussed in §25.1.

29. Compare Wooldridge and White (1988: Prop. 4.1). Wooldridge and White's result is incorrect as stated, since they omit the stipulation of almost sure continuity.

References

Amemiya, Takeshi (1985), *Advanced Econometrics*, Basil Blackwell, Oxford.

Andrews, Donald W. K. (1984), 'Non-strong mixing autoregressive processes', *Journal of Applied Probability* 21, 930–4.

—————— (1987a), 'Consistency in nonlinear econometric models: a generic uniform law of large numbers', *Econometrica* 55, 1465–71.

—————— (1988), 'Laws of large numbers for dependent non-identically distributed random variables', *Econometric Theory* 4, 458–67.

—————— (1991), 'Heteroscedasticity and autocorrelation consistent covariance matrix estimation', *Econometrica* 59, 817–58.

—————— (1992), 'Generic uniform convergence', *Econometric Theory* 8, 241–57.

Apostol, Tom M. (1974), *Mathematical Analysis* (2nd edn.) Addison-Wesley, Menlo Park.

Ash, R. (1972), *Real Analysis and Probability*, Academic Press, New York.

Athreya, Krishna B. and Pantula, Sastry G.(1986a), 'Mixing properties of Harris chains and autoregressive processes', *Journal of Applied Probability* 23, 880–92.

—————— —————— (1986b), 'A note on strong mixing of ARMA processes', *Statistics and Probability Letters* 4, 187–90.

Azuma, K. (1967), 'Weighted sums of certain dependent random variables', *Tohoku Mathematical Journal* 19, 357–67.

Barnsley, Michael (1988), *Fractals Everywhere*, Academic Press, Boston.

Bates, Charles and White, Halbert (1985), 'A unified theory of consistent estimation for parametric models', *Econometric Theory* 1, 151–78.

Bernstein, S. (1927), 'Sur l'extension du théorème du calcul des probabilités aux sommes de quantités dependantes', *Mathematische Annalen* 97, 1–59.

Bierens, Herman (1983), 'Uniform consistency of kernel estimators of a regression function under generalized conditions', *Journal of the American Statistical Association* 77, 699–707.

—————— (1989), 'Least squares estimation of linear and nonlinear ARMAX models under data heterogeneity', Working Paper, Department of Econometrics, Free University of Amsterdam.

Billingsley, Patrick (1968), *Convergence of Probability Measures*, John Wiley, New York.

——————— (1979), *Probability and Measure*, John Wiley, New York.

Borowski, E. J. and Borwein, J. M. (1989), *The Collins Reference Dictionary of Mathematics*, Collins, London and Glasgow.

Bradley, Richard C., Bryc, W. and Janson, S. (1987), 'On dominations between measures of dependence', *Journal of Multivariate Analysis* 23, 312–29.

Breiman, Leo (1968), *Probability*, Addison-Wesley, Reading, Mass.

Brown, B. M. (1971), 'Martingale central limit theorems', *Annals of Mathematical Statistics* 42, 59–66.

Burkholder, D. L. (1973), 'Distribution function inequalities for martingales', *Annals of Probability* 1, 19–42.

Chan, N. H. and Wei, C. Z. (1988), 'Limiting distributions of least squares estimates of unstable autoregressive processes', *Annals of Statistics*, 16, 367–401.

Chanda, K. C. (1974), 'Strong mixing properties of linear stochastic processes', *Journal of Applied Probability* 11, 401–8.

Chow, Y. S. (1971), 'On the L_p convergence for $n^{-1/p}S_n$, $0 < p < 2$', *Annals of Mathematical Statistics* 36, 393–4

————— and Teicher, H. (1978), *Probability Theory: Independence, Interchangeability and Martingales*, Springer-Verlag, Berlin.

Chung, Kai Lai (1974), *A Course in Probability Theory* (2nd edn.), Academic Press, Orlando, Fla.

Cox, D. R. and Miller, H. D. (1965), *The Theory of Stochastic Processes*, Methuen, London.

Cramér, Harald (1946), *Mathematical Methods of Statistics*, Princeton University Press, Princeton, NJ.

Davidson, James (1992), 'A central limit theorem for globally nonstationary near-epoch dependent functions of mixing processes', *Econometric Theory*, 8, 313–29.

——————— (1993a) 'An L_1-convergence theorem for heterogeneous mixingale arrays with trending moments', *Statistics and Probability Letters* 16, 301–4

——————— (1993b), 'The central limit theorem for globally nonstationary near-epoch dependent functions of mixing processes: the asymptotically degenerate case', *Econometric Theory* 9, 402–12.

de Jong, R. M. (1992), 'Laws of large numbers for dependent heterogeneous processes', Working Paper, Free University of Amsterdam (forthcoming in *Econometric Theory*, 1995).

——— (1994), 'A strong law for L_2-mixingale sequences', Working Paper, Department of Econometrics, University of Tilburg.

Dellacherie, C. and Meyer, P.-A. (1978), *Probabilities amd Potential*, North-Holland, Amsterdam.

Dhrymes, Phoebus J. (1989) *Topics in Advanced Econometrics*, Springer-Verlag, New York.

Dieudonné, J. (1969), *Foundations of Modern Analysis*, Academic Press, New York and London.

Domowitz, I. and White, H. (1982), 'Misspecified models with dependent observations', *Journal of Econometrics* 20, 35–58

Donsker, M. D. (1951) 'An invariance principle for certain probability limit theorems', *Memoirs of the American Mathematical Society*, 6, 1–12.

Doob, J. L. (1953), *Stochastic Processes*, John Wiley, New York; Chapman & Hall, London.

Dudley, R. M. (1966), 'Weak convergence of probabilities on nonseparable metric spaces and empirical measures on Euclidean spaces', *Illinois Journal of Mathematics* 10, 109–26.

——— (1967), 'Measures on non-separable metric spaces', *Illinois Journal of Mathematics* 11, 109–26.

——— (1989), *Real Analysis and Probability*, Wadsworth and Brooks/Cole, Pacific Grove, Calif.

Dvoretsky, A. (1972), 'Asymptotic normality of sums of dependent random variables', in *Proceedings of the Sixth Berkeley Symposium on Mathematical Statistics and Probability*, ii, University of California Press, Berkeley, Calif., 513–35.

Eberlein, Ernst and Taqqu, Murad S. (eds.) (1986), *Dependence in Probability and Statistics: a Survey of Recent Results*, Birkhauser, Boston.

Engle, R. F., Hendry, D. F. and Richard, J.-F. (1983), 'Exogeneity', *Econometrica* 51, 277–304

Feller, W. (1971), *An Introduction to Probability Theory and its Applications*, ii, John Wiley, New York.

Gallant, A. Ronald (1987), *Nonlinear Statistical Models*, John Wiley, New York.

——— and White, Halbert (1988), *A Unified Theory of Estimation and Inference for Nonlinear Dynamic Models*, Basil Blackwell, Oxford.

Gastwirth, Joseph L. and Rubin, Herman (1975), 'The asymptotic distribution theory of the empiric CDF for mixing stochastic processes', *Annals of Statistics* 3, 809–24.

Gnedenko, B. V. (1967), *The Theory of Probability* (4th edn.), Chelsea Publishing, New York.

Gorodetskii, V. V. (1977), 'On the strong mixing property for linear sequences', *Theory of Probability and its Applications*, 22, 411–13.

Halmos, Paul R. (1956), *Lectures in Ergodic Theory*, Chelsea Publishing, New York

——— (1960), *Naive Set Theory*, Van Nostrand Reinhold, New York.

——— (1974), *Measure Theory*, Springer-Verlag, New York.

Hall, P and Heyde, C. C. (1980), *Martingale Limit Theory and its Application*, Academic Press, New York and London.

Hannan, E. J. (1970), *Multiple Time Series*, John Wiley, New York.

Hansen, L. P. (1982), 'Large sample properties of generalized method of moments estimators', *Econometrica* 50, 1029–54.

Hansen, Bruce E. (1991), 'Strong laws for dependent heterogeneous processes', *Econometric Theory* 7, 213–21.

——— (1992a), 'Errata', *Econometric Theory* 8, 421–2.

——— (1992b), 'Consistent covariance matrix estimation for dependent heterogeneous processes', *Econometrica* 60, 967–72

——— (1992c), 'Convergence to stochastic integrals for dependent heterogeneous processes', *Econometric Theory* 8, 489–500.

Herrndorf, Norbert (1984), 'A functional central limit theorem for weakly dependent sequences of random variables', *Annals of Probability* 12, 141–53.

——— (1985), 'A functional central limit theorem for strongly mixing sequences of random variables', *Wahrscheinlichkeitstheorie verw. Gebeite* 69, 540–50.

Hoadley, Bruce (1971), 'Asymptotic properties of maximum likelihood estimators for the independent not identically distributed case', *Annals of Mathematical Statistics* 42, 1977–91.

Hoeffding, W. (1963), 'Probability inequalities for sums of bounded random variables', *Journal of the American Statistical Association* 58, 13–30.

Ibragimov, I. A. (1962), 'Some limit theorems for stationary processes', *Theory of Probability and its Applications* 7, 349–82.

——— (1965), 'On the spectrum of stationary Gaussian sequences satisfying the strong mixing condition. I: Necessary conditions', *Theory of Probability and its Applications* 10, 85–106.

——— and Linnik, Yu. V. (1971), *Independent and Stationary Sequences of Random Variables*, Wolters-Noordhoff, Groningen.

Iosifescu, M. and Theodorescu, R. (1969), *Random Processes and Learning*, Springer-Verlag, Berlin.

Karatzas, Ioannis and Shreve, Steven E. (1988), *Brownian Motion and Stochastic Calculus*, Springer-Verlag, New York.

Kelley, John L. (1955), *General Topology*, Springer-Verlag, New York.

Kingman, J. F. C. and Taylor, S. J. (1966), *Introduction to Measure and Probability*, Cambridge University Press, London and New York.

Kolmogorov, A. N. (1950), *Foundations of the Theory of Probability*, Chelsea Publishing, New York (published in German as *Grundbegriffe der Wahrscheinlichkeitsrechnung*, Springer-Verlag, Berlin, 1933).

——— and Rozanov, Yu. A. (1960), 'On strong mixing conditions for stationary Gaussian processes', *Theory of Probability and its Applications* 5, 204–8.

Kopp, P. E. (1984), *Martingales and Stochastic Integrals*, Cambridge University Press.

Kurtz, T. G. and Protter, P. (1991), 'Weak limit theorems for stochastic integrals and stochastic differential equations', *Annals of Probability* 19, 1035–70.

Loève, Michel (1977), *Probability Theory*, i (4th edn.), Springer-Verlag, New York.

Lukacs, Eugene (1975), *Stochastic Convergence* (2nd edn.), Academic Press, New York.

Magnus, J. R., and Neudecker, H. (1988), *Marix Differential Calculus with Applications in Statistics and Econometrics*, John Wiley, Chichester.

Mandelbrot, Benoit B. (1983), *The Fractal Geometry of Nature*, W. H. Freeman, New York.

Mann, H. B. and Wald, A. (1943a), 'On the statistical treatment of linear stochastic difference equations', *Econometrica* 11, 173–220.

——— ——— (1943b), 'On stochastic limit and order relationships', *Annals of Mathematical Statistics* 14, 390–402.

McKean, H. P., Jr. (1969), *Stochastic Integrals*, Academic Press, New York.

McLeish, D. L. (1974), 'Dependent central limit theorems and invariance principles', *Annals of Probability* 2,4, 620–8.

——————— (1975a), 'A maximal inequality and dependent strong laws', *Annals of Probability* 3,5, 329–39.

——————— (1975b), 'Invariance principles for dependent variables', *Z. Wahrscheinlichkeitstheorie verw. Gebeite* 32, 165–78.

——————— (1977), 'On the invariance principle for nonstationary mixingales', *Annals of Probability* 5,4, 616–21.

Nagaev, S. V. and Fuk, A. Kh. (1971), 'Probability inequalities for sums of independent random variables', *Theory of Probability and its Applications* 6, 643–60.

Newey, W. K. (1991), 'Uniform convergence in probability and stochastic equicontinuity', *Econometrica* 59, 1161–8.

——————— and West, K. (1987), 'A simple positive definite heteroskedasticity and correlation consistent covariance matrix', *Econometrica* 55, 703–8.

Park, J. Y. and Phillips, P. C. B. (1988), 'Statistical inference in regressions with integrated processes, Part 1', *Econometric Theory* 4, 468–98.

——————— ——————— (1989), 'Statistical inference in regressions with integrated processes, Part 2', *Econometric Theory* 5, 95–132.

Parthasarathy, K. R. (1967), *Probability Measures on Metric Spaces*, Academic Press, New York and London.

Pham, Tuan D. and Tran, Lanh T. (1985), 'Some mixing properties of time series models', *Stochastic Processes and their Applications* 19, 297–303.

Phillips, P. C. B. (1988), 'Weak convergence to the matrix stochastic integral $\int_0^1 BdB'$', *Journal of Multivariate Analysis* 24, 252–64.

——————— and Durlauf, S. N. (1986), 'Multiple time series regression with integrated processes', *Review of Economic Studies* 53, 473–95.

Pollard, David (1984), *Convergence of Stochastic Processes*, Springer-Verlag, New York.

Pötscher, B. M. and Prucha, I. R. (1989), 'A uniform law of large numbers for dependent and heterogeneous data processes', *Econometrica* 57, 675–84.

——————— ——————— (1994), 'Generic uniform convergence and equicontinuity concepts for random functions: an exploration of the basic structure', *Journal of Econometrics* 60, 23–63.

——————— ——————— (1991a), 'Basic structure of the asymptotic theory in dynamic nonlinear econometric models, Part I: Consistency and approximation concepts', *Econometric Reviews* 10, 125–216.

——— ———(1991b), 'Basic structure of the asymptotic theory in dynamic nonlinear econometric models, Part II: Asymptotic normality', *Econometric Reviews* 10, 253–325.

Prokhorov, Yu. V (1956), 'Convergence of random processes and limit theorems in probability theory', *Theory of Probability and its Applications* 1, 157–213.

Rao, C. Radhakrishna (1973), *Linear Statistical Inference and its Applications* (2nd edn.), John Wiley, New York.

Révész, Pál (1968), *The Laws of Large Numbers*, Academic Press, New York.

Rosenblatt, M. (1956), 'A central limit theorem and a strong mixing condition', *Proceedings of the National Academy of Science, USA*, 42, 43–7.

——— (1972), 'Uniform ergodicity and strong mixing', *Z. Wahrscheinlichkeitstheorie verw. Gebeite* 24, 79–84.

——— (1978), 'Dependence and asymptotic independence for random processes', in *Studies in Probability Theory* (ed. M. Rosenblatt), Mathematical Association of America, Washington DC.

Royden, H. L. (1968), *Real Analysis*, Macmillan, New York.

Seneta, E. (1976), *Regularly Varying Functions*, Springer-Verlag, Berlin.

Serfling, R. J. (1968), 'Contributions to central limit theory for dependent variables', *Annals of Mathematical Statistics* 39, 1158–75.

——— (1980), *Approximation Theorems of Mathematical Statistics*, John Wiley, New York.

Shafer, G. (1988), 'The St Petersburg Paradox', in *Encyclopaedia of the Statistical Sciences*, viii (ed. S. Kotz and N. L. Johnson), John Wiley, New York.

Shiryayev, A. N. (1984), *Probability*, Springer-Verlag, New York.

Skorokhod, A. V. (1956), 'Limit theorems for stochastic processes', *Theory of Probability and its Applications* 1, 261–90.

——— (1957), 'Limit theorems for stochastic processes with independent increments', *Theory of Probability and its Applications* 2, 138–71.

Slutsky, E. (1925), 'Über stochastiche Asymptoter und Grenzwerte', *Math. Annalen* 5, 93.

Stinchcombe, M. B. and White, H. (1992), 'Some measurability results for extrema of random functions over random sets', *Review of Economic Studies* 59, 495–514.

Stone, Charles (1963), 'Weak convergence of stochastic processes defined on semi-infinite time intervals', *Proceedings of the American Mathematical Society* 14, 694–6.

Stout, W. F. (1974), *Almost Sure Convergence*, Academic Press, New York.

Strasser, H. (1986), 'Martingale difference arrays and stochastic integrals', *Probability Theory and Related Fields* 72, 83–98.

Varadarajan, V. S. (1958), 'Weak convergence of measures on separable metric spaces', *Sankhya* 19, 15–22.

von Bahr, Bengt, and Esséen, Carl-Gustav (1965), 'Inequalities for the rth absolute moment of a sum of random variables, $1 \leq r \leq 2$', *Annals of Mathematical Statistics* 36, 299–303.

White, Halbert (1984), *Asymptotic Theory for Econometricians*, Academic Press, New York.

——— and Domowitz, I. (1984), 'Nonlinear regression with dependent observations', *Econometrica* 52, 143–62.

Wiener, Norbert (1923), 'Differential space', *Journal of Mathematical Physics* 2, 131–74

Willard, Stephen (1970), *General Topology*, Addison-Wesley, Reading, Mass.

Withers, C. S. (1981a), 'Conditions for linear processes to be strong-mixing', *Z. Wahrscheinlichkeitstheorie verw. Gebeite* 57, 477–80.

——— (1981b), 'Central limit theorems for dependent variables, I', *Z. Wahrscheinlichkeitstheorie verw. Gebeite* 57, 509–34.

Wooldridge, Jeffrey M. and White, Halbert (1986), 'Some invariance principles and central limit theorems for dependent heterogeneous processes', University of California (San Diego) Working Paper.

——— ——— (1988), 'Some invariance principles and central limit theorems for dependent heterogeneous processes', *Econometric Theory* 4, 210–30.

Index